E BIBLICAL

General Editors

ASTRID B. BECK

DAVID NOEL FREEDMAN

Editorial Board

HAROLD W. ATTRIDGE, *History and Literature of Early Christianity*

ADELA YARBRO COLLINS, *New Testament*

JOHN HUEHNERGARD, *Ancient Near Eastern Languages and Literatures*

PETER MACHINIST, *Ancient Near Eastern Languages and Literatures*

JOHN P. MEIER, *New Testament*

SHALOM M. PAUL, *Hebrew Bible*

STANLEY E. PORTER, *New Testament Language and Literature*

JAMES C. VANDERKAM, *History and Literature of Early Judaism*

THE BIBLICAL RESOURCE SERI

Available

Frank Moore Cross, Jr., and David Noel Freedman,
Studies in Ancient Yahwistic Poetry

S. R. Driver, *A Treatise on the Use of the Tenses in Hebrew and Some Other Syntactical Questions*

Joseph A. Fitzmyer, *The Semitic Background of the New Testament*

Birger Gerhardsson, *Memory and Manuscript* and
Tradition and Transmission in Early Christianity

Roland de Vaux, *Ancient Israel: Its Life and Institutions*

THE SEMITIC BACKGROUND OF THE NEW TESTAMENT

Combined Edition of

Essays on the Semitic Background
of the New Testament

and

A Wandering Aramean:
Collected Aramaic Essays

JOSEPH A. FITZMYER, S.J.

WILLIAM B. EERDMANS PUBLISHING COMPANY
GRAND RAPIDS, MICHIGAN / CAMBRIDGE, U.K.

DOVE BOOKSELLERS
LIVONIA, MICHIGAN

First published in two volumes:

Essays on the Semitic Background of the New Testament
© 1971, 1974 Joseph A. Fitzmyer, S.J.
Published by G. Chapman, London, 1971 and
Scholars Press, 1974

A Wandering Aramean: Collected Aramaic Essays
© 1979 Joseph A. Fitzmyer, S.J.
Published by Scholars Press

This combined edition, with new Appendix, published jointly 1997 by
Wm. B. Eerdmans Publishing Company
255 Jefferson Ave. S.E., Grand Rapids, Michigan 49503 /
P.O. Box 163, Cambridge CB3 9PU U.K.
and by
Dove Booksellers
30633 Schoolcraft Road, Suite C, Livonia, Michigan 48150

Printed in the United States of America

02 01 00 99 98 97 5 4 3 2 1

Library of Congress Cataloging-in-Publication Data

Fitzmyer, Joseph A.
[Essays on the Semitic Background of the New Testament]
Essays on the Semitic Background of the New Testament;
A wandering Aramean: collected Aramaic essays / Joseph A. Fitzmyer — Combined ed.
p. cm. — (The biblical resource series)
"This combined edition reprints the text of two works, A wandering Aramean, originally published in 1979 by Scholars Press and Essays on the Semitic background of the New Testament, originally published in 1971 by Geoffrey Chapman Ltd." — T.p. verso.
Includes bibliographical references and indexes.
ISBN 0-8028-4344-1 (pbk.: alk. paper)
1. Bible. N.T. — Criticism, interpretation, etc.
2. Dead Sea scrolls — Relation to the New Testament.
3. Aramaic philology. 4. Aramaic literature — Relation to the New Testament.
5. Bible. N.T. — Language, style.
I. Fitzmyer, Joseph A. Wandering Aramean.
II. Title. III. Title: Wandering Aramean. IV. Series.
225.6′6 — dc21 97-10581
CIP

Contents

PUBLISHER'S NOTE

This combined edition reprints the text of the original two volumes exactly as it originally appeared. Thus the pagination for *A Wandering Aramean* begins again at page 1 midway through this volume.

Preface to the Reprint

When Eerdmans Publishing Company approached me about the possibility of reprinting *Essays on the Semitic Background of the New Testament* and *A Wandering Aramean: Collected Aramaic Essays,* I was only too happy to comply, since these books have been out of print for a few years. *Essays on the Semitic Background of the New Testament* was originally published by G. Chapman of London (1971) and reprinted for U.S.A. readers by Scholars Press (1974). *A Wandering Aramean: Collected Aramaic Essays* was originally published in the SBL Monograph Series (Scholars Press, 1979). The new title, *The Semitic Background of the New Testament,* will mark off this combined reprint of the two books from the original forms. The note with an asterisk at the beginning of the footnotes or endnotes in each book indicates where the essay was published initially.

The essays collected in this volume represent reflections on a variety of New Testament problems that have been illustrated by data from the Semitic world of the eastern Mediterranean. The unity of such a collection is not organic or closely knit, but this disadvantage is offset by the convenience of having a number of studies on an important aspect of New Testament study brought together within the covers of one volume. In the last quarter of a century there has been much interest in the hermeneutical aspects of the New Testament or in its Hellenistic social and anthropological backgrounds, but the Semitic angle of the New Testament writings has not been accorded the same concern. This is sadly so, even though there have been important discoveries in the areas of the Aramaic language and the Dead Sea Scrolls that shed new light on the Semitic background of the New Testament. Some of the essays in this volume seek to interpret the relevance of the Qumran texts to the interpretation of certain New Testament passages.

Others do the same for various Aramaic texts that have come to light in the past twenty-five years.

A further word has to be said about the essays that deal with the Aramaic language and its bearing on the study of the New Testament. Aramaic was long known through its biblical, rabbinic, and Syriac forms, but most of the texts that are known today as Aramaic, dating from the ninth century B.C. down to the second century A.D., have come to light only within the last seventy-five to a hundred years. The number of Aramaic texts found in the famous *Corpus inscriptionum semiticarum* is small indeed, but how that situation has changed in the twentieth century. The important corpora of Aramaic texts from Egypt were published for the first time between 1910 and 1960. Though most of the Qumran Aramaic texts are fragmentary, they are known today to number about 120 and were discovered only between 1947 and 1956. Most of them have been published in scattered, often out-of-the-way places, yet they represent a corpus of precious documents and give us evidence of the kind of Aramaic written (and spoken) by Jews and others in Judea in the time of Jesus and the early Jewish Christians. As a result, one no longer has to have recourse to the Aramaic of the classic targums or the rabbinic writings of later centuries and extrapolate from them questionable interpretations of the New Testament writings. Moreover, even though the vast majority of New Testament books was composed outside of Judea and in the eastern Mediterranean world, the Semitic background of Judea, where the Christian movement began, lurks behind the Greek text of many of them. This is especially true of the four Gospels and Acts, but there are instances where Aramaic influence has been detected in other writings of the Greek New Testament.

For such reasons the issue of the Semitic background of the New Testament has become important, and I have sought to show in the essays collected in this volume the pertinence of the Dead Sea Scrolls and the study of ancient Aramaic texts to the interpretation of the Greek New Testament.

Even though the essays published in these books are somewhat dated, because many of them were first written over twenty-five years ago, I realize that this reprinting is a way of adding further notes or at least some bibliographical references to other studies that have dealt with the topics discussed in the essays. Such notes will be found in the appendix, where they are presented with suitable references to the pages and lines concerned. In general, I think that the theses and interpretations once proposed in these essays are still valid. Some point or other in the interpretation given may have to be modified in the light of new discussions or new data that have come to light, but otherwise they seem to be still worthy of consideration. This is also a reason for making them available in this reprint form.

I am grateful to Dennis Ford, the associate director of Scholars Press of Atlanta, GA, for the permission to allow Eerdmans to produce this reprint, and to Mr. Michael Thomson and Mr. Charles Van Hof and his staff at Eerdmans for their help in the production of this book. I am likewise grateful to the editors of the various periodicals and books in which the essays were originally published for permission to reprint them; those editors and publishers have already been mentioned in the forewords to the earlier books, so there is no need to repeat their names here.

JOSEPH A. FITZMYER, S.J.
Professor Emeritus of Biblical Studies,
The Catholic University of America,
Washington, DC 20064.
Resident at the Jesuit Community,
Georgetown University,
Washington, DC 20057-1200.

Abbreviations

A	Aḥiqar
AAH	F. Rosenthal (ed.), *An Aramaic Handbook* (Porta linguarum orientalium, ns 10; Wiesbaden: Harrassowitz, 1967)
AASOR	*Annual of the American Schools of Oriental Research*
AB	Anchor Bible
ABL	R. F. Harper (ed.), *Assyrian and Babylonian Letters . . .* (Chicago: University of Chicago, 1892-1914)
AC	J. Koopmans, *Aramäische Chrestomathie* (Leiden: Nederlands Instituut voor het Nabije Oosten, 1962)
AcOr	*Acta orientalia*
AD	G. R. Driver, *Aramaic Documents of the Fifth Century B.C. Transcribed and Edited* (Oxford: Clarendon, 1954; repr. Osnabrück: Zeller, 1968; abridged edition: Oxford: Clarendon, 1957; rev. 1965)
ADAJ	*Annual of the Department of Antiquities of Jordan*
AdANdL	*Atti dell'Accademia Nazionale dei Lincei*
AdonL	*Adon Letter* (see *WA*, 242)
AER	*American Ecclesiastical Review*
AfO	*Archiv für Orientforschung*
AG	See BAG
Ag. Ap.	Josephus, *Against Apion*
AGJU	Arbeiten zur Geschichte des antiken Judentums und des Urchristentums
AION	*Annali dell'istituto orientale di Napoli*
AIPHOS	*Annuaire de l'institut philologique et historique orientale et slave*
AJA	*American Journal of Archaeology*
AJBA	*Australian Journal of Biblical Archaeology*
AJSL	*American Journal of Semitic Languages and Literature*
ALBO	Analecta lovaniensia biblica et orientalia

Albright, *AP*	W. F. Albright, *The Archaeology of Palestine* (Harmondsworth: Penguin Books, 1960)
AnalGreg	Analecta gregoriana
AnBib	Analecta biblica
ANEP	J. B. Pritchard (ed.), *The Ancient Near East in Pictures* (Princeton, NJ: Princeton University, 1955)
ANET	J. B. Pritchard (ed.), *Ancient Near Eastern Texts* (rev. ed.; Princeton, NJ: Princeton University, 1955)
ANHW	G. Dalman, *Aramäisches und neuhebräisches Handwörterbuch* (Göttingen: Pfeiffer, 1938)
AnOr	Analecta orientalia (Rome)
ANRW	H. Temporini and W. Haase (eds.), *Aufstieg und Niedergang der römischen Welt* (Berlin/New York: de Gruyter, 1975–)
Ant.	Josephus, *Antiquities*
AOS	American Oriental Series
AP	A. Cowley, *Aramaic Papyri of the Fifth Century* (Oxford: Clarendon, 1923; repr. Osnabrück: Zeller, 1967)
APE	A. Ungnad, *Aramäische Papyri aus Elephantine* (Leipzig: Hinrichs, 1911)
APN	K. L. Tallqvist (ed.), *Assyrian Personal Names* (Helsingfors: Finnish Academy of Sciences, 1914)
APO	E. Sachau, *Aramäische Papyrus und Ostraka aus einer jüdischen Militär-Kolonie zu Elephantine* (Leipzig: Hinrichs, 1911)
APOT	R. H. Charles, *Apocrypha and Pseudepigrapha of the Old Testament* (2 vols.; Oxford: Clarendon, 1913)
ArDial	G. Dalman, *Aramäische Dialektproben* (Darmstadt: Wissenschaftliche Buchgesellschaft, 1960)
ARM	A. Parrot and G. Dossin (eds.), *Archives royales de Mari* (Paris: Imprimerie Nationale, 1950–)
ArOr	*Archiv Orientální*
ASAE	*Annales du service des antiquités de l'Egypte*
ASOR	American School of Oriental Research
AšOst	Aššur Ostracon
ASTI	*Annual of the Swedish Theological Institute*
ATANT	Abhandlungen zur Theologie des Alten und Neuen Testaments
ATD	Das Alte Testament Deutsch
ATR	*Anglican Theological Review*
AUSS	*Andrews University Seminary Studies*
B	*Behistun* (or *Bisitun*) inscription (see *AP*, 248-71)
BA	*Biblical Archaeologist*
BAG	W. Bauer, *A Greek-English Dictionary of the New Testament . . .* (tr.

	W. F. Arndt and W. F. Gingrich; Chicago: University of Chicago, 1957; 2d ed., rev. F. W. Danker, 1979)
BANE	G. E. Wright (ed.), *The Bible and the Ancient Near East: Essays in Honor of William Foxwell Albright* (New York: Doubleday, 1961; repr. Anchor Books; New York: Doubleday, 1965)
BARev	*Biblical Archaeology Review*
BASOR	*Bulletin of the American Schools of Oriental Research*
BASP	*Bulletin of the American Society of Papyrologists*
BBB	Bonner biblische Beiträge
BBR	*Bulletin for Biblical Research*
BC	F. J. Foakes Jackson and K. Lake (eds.), *The Beginnings of Christianity* (5 vols.; London: Macmillan, 1920-33; repr. Grand Rapids: Baker, 1979)
BCCT	J. L. McKenzie (ed.), *The Bible in Current Catholic Thought* (New York: Herder and Herder, 1962)
BDF	F. Blass and A. Debrunner, *A Greek Grammar of the New Testament* (tr. R. W. Funk; Chicago: University of Chicago, 1961)
BeO	*Bibbia e oriente*
BETL	Bibliotheca ephemeridum theologicarum lovaniensium
BFTh	Beiträge zur Förderung christlicher Theologie
Bib	*Biblica*
BibOr	Biblica et orientalia
BIES	*Bulletin of the Israel Exploration Society*
BIFAO	*Bulletin de l'institut français d'archéologie orientale*
BJPES	*Bulletin of the Jewish Palestine Exploration Society*
BIOSCS	*Bulletin of the International Organization for Septuagint and Cognate Studies*
BJRL	*Bulletin of the John Rylands University Library of Manchester*
BK	*Bibel und Kirche*
BKAT	Biblischer Kommentar, Altes Testament (Neukirchen)
BLA	H. Bauer and P. Leander, *Grammatik des Biblisch-Aramäischen* (Halle: Niemeyer, 1927)
B-M	H. Bauer and B. Meissner, "Ein aramäischer Pachtvertrag aus dem 7. Jahre Darius I," *SPAW* 72 (1936) 414-24
BMAP	E. G. Kraeling, *Brooklyn Museum Aramaic Papyri* (New Haven, CT: Yale University, 1953)
BMB	*Bulletin du Musée de Beyrouth*
BNTC	Black's New Testament Commentaries (London)
BO	*Bibliotheca orientalis*
Bodl Aram Inscr	Bodleian Library, Aramaic Inscription(s)
Bowm	R. A. Bowman, "An Aramaic Journal Page," *AJSL* 58 (1941) 302-13

BSOAS	*Bulletin of the School of Oriental and African Studies*
BT	*The Bible Today*
BTS	*Bible et terre sainte*
BVC	*Bible et vie chrétienne*
BWANT	Beiträge zur Wissenschaft vom Alten und Neuen Testament
BZ	*Biblische Zeitschrift*
BZAW	Beihefte zur *ZAW*
BZNW	Beihefte zur *ZNW*
CBQ	*Catholic Biblical Quarterly*
CBQMS	Catholic Biblical Quarterly — Monograph Series
CC (in *ESBNT*)	*Civiltà cattolica*
CC (in *WA*)	*Corpus christianorum* (patristic series)
CCD	Confraternity of Christian Doctrine (Version of the Bible)
ChQR	*Church Quarterly Review*
CIG	*Corpus inscriptionum graecarum*
CII	J.-B. Frey (ed.), *Corpus inscriptionum iudaicarum* (2 vols.; Vatican City: Institute of Christian Archaeology, 1936, 1952)
CIL	*Corpus inscriptionum latinarum*
CIS	*Corpus inscriptionum semiticarum*
CJT	*Canadian Journal of Theology*
Cl-G Ost	Clermont-Ganneau Ostracon
ConNeot	*Coniectanea neotestamentica*
CRAIBL	*Comptes-rendus de l'académie des inscriptions et belles-lettres*
CSCO	Corpus scriptorum christianorum orientalium
CSEL	Corpus scriptorum ecclesiasticorum latinorum
DACL	*Dictionnaire d'archéologie chrétienne et de liturgie* (15 vols.; Paris: Letouzey et Ané, 1907-53)
DBSup	*Dictionnaire de la Bible, Supplément* (so far 12 vols.; Paris: Letouzey & Ané, 1928–) (see *VDBS*)
DISO	C.-F. Jean and J. Hoftijzer (eds.), *Dictionnaire des inscriptions sémitiques de l'ouest* (Leiden: Brill, 1965)
DTC	*Dictionnaire de théologie catholique* (16 vols.; Paris: Letouzey et Ané, 1909-65)
DTT	*Dansk teologisk tidsskrift*
EBib	Etudes bibliques (Paris)
Ephemeris	M. Lidzbarski, *Ephemeris für semitische Epigraphik* (3 vols.; Giessen: Töpelmann, 1900-1915)
ESBNT	J. A. Fitzmyer, *Essays on the Semitic Background of the New Testament* (London: Chapman, 1971; repr. Missoula, MT: Scholars, 1974)
EstBíb	*Estudios bíblicos*
EstEcl	*Estudios eclesiásticos*

ET	See *EvT*
ETL	*Ephemerides theologicae lovanienses*
ETR	*Etudes théologiques et religieuses*
EVO	*Egitto e vicino oriente*
EvT	*Evanglische Theologie*
ExpT	See *ExpTim*
FRLANT	Forschungen zur Religion und Literatur des Alten und Neuen Testaments
Gabba	E. Gabba, *Iscrizioni greche e latine per lo studio della Bibbia* (Turin: Marietti, 1958)
GCS	Griechische christliche Schriftsteller
GJPA	G. Dalman, *Grammatik des jüdisch-palästinischen Aramäisch* (Leipzig: Hinrichs, 1905; repr. Darmstadt: Wissenschaftliche Buchgesellschaft, 1960)
GJV	E. Schürer, *Geschichte des jüdischen Volkes im Zeitalter Jesu Christi* (3 vols.; Leipzig: Hinrichs, 1901-11)
GPL	Z. S. Harris, *A Grammar of the Phoenician Language* (AOS 8; New Haven, CT: American Oriental Society, 1936)
HermWP	Hermopolis West Papyri (see *WA*, 76)
HeyJ	*Heythrop Journal*
HeythJ	See *HeyJ*
HJ	*Hibbert Journal*
HJPAJC	E. Schürer, *History of the Jewish People in the Age of Jesus Christ* (rev. ed.; 3 vols. in 4; Edinburgh: Clark, 1973-87)
HNT	Handbuch zum Neuen Testament (Tübingen)
HSS	Harvard Semitic Series
HTR	*Harvard Theological Review*
HUCA	*Hebrew Union College Annual*
IBS	*Irish Biblical Studies*
ICC	International Critical Commentary (Edinburgh)
IEJ	*Israel Exploration Journal*
IER	*Irish Ecclesiastical Record*
Int	*Interpretation*
IPN	M. Noth, *Israelitische Personennamen* (BWANT 3/10; Stuttgart: Kohlhammer, 1928; repr. Hildesheim: Olms, 1966)
IR	R. Hestrin (ed.), *Inscriptions Reveal* (Jerusalem: Israel Museum, 1973)
ITQ	*Irish Theological Quarterly*
J	P. Joüon, "Notes grammaticales, lexicographiques et philologiques sur les papyrus araméens d'Egypte," *MUSJ* 18 (1934) 1-90
JA	*Journal asiatique*
JANESCU	*Journal of the Ancient Near Eastern Society of Columbia University*

JAOS	*Journal of the American Oriental Society*
JBL	*Journal of Biblical Literature*
JBR	*Journal of Bible and Religion*
JEA	*Journal of Egyptian Archaeology*
JEOL	*Jaarbericht . . . ex oriente lux*
JJS	*Journal of Jewish Studies*
JNES	*Journal of Near Eastern Studies*
JPCI	S. Klein, *Jüdisch-palästinisches corpus inscriptionum* (Vienna/Berlin: Löwit, 1920; repr. Hildesheim: Gerstenberg, 1971)
JPOS	*Journal of the Palestine Oriental Society*
JQR	*Jewish Quarterly Review*
JRAS	*Journal of the Royal Asiatic Society*
JRel	*Journal of Religion*
JRS	*Journal of Roman Studies*
JSJ	*Journal for the Study of Judaism in the Persian, Hellenistic and Roman Periods*
JSNT	*Journal for the Study of the New Testament*
JSNTSup	Supplements to *JSNT*
JSS	*Journal of Semitic Studies*
JTS	*Journal of Theological Studies*
JW	Josephus, *Jewish War*
KAI	H. Donner and W. Röllig, *Kanaanäische und aramäische Inschriften* (3 vols.; Wiesbaden: Harrassowitz, 1962-64)
KB	L. Koehler and W. Baumgartner, *Lexicon in Veteris Testamenti libros* (Leiden: Brill, 1958)
KlT	Kleine Texte
L	P. Leander, "Laut- und Formenlehre des Ägyptisch-Aramäischen," *Göteborgs Högskolas Årsskrift* 34 (1928) 1-135; repr. Hildesheim: Olms, 1966)
LCL	Loeb Classical Library
LXX	Septuagint (Greek translation of the Old Testament)
Mansi	G. D. Mansi, *Sacrorum conciliorum nova et amplissima collectio* (54 vols.; Florence, 1758-98; repr. Paris/Leipzig: Welter, 1903-27)
MDOG	Mitteilungen der deutschen Orient-Gesellschaft
MGWJ	*Monatsschrift für Geschichte und Wissenschaft des Judentums*
MPAIBL	*Mémoires présentés à l'académie des inscriptions et belles-lettres*
MPAT	J. A. Fitzmyer and D. J. Harrington, *Manual of Palestinian Aramaic Texts* (BibOr 34; Rome: Biblical Institute, 1978)
MT	Masoretic Text
MTZ	*Münchener theologische Zeitschrift*
Mur	Murabbaʿat texts (see DJD 2)
MUSJ	*Mélanges de l'Université St.-Joseph*

NEB	New English Bible (Version of the Bible)
NHS	Nag Hammadi Studies
NKGWG	*Nachrichten der königlichen Gesellschaft der Wissenschaften zu Göttingen*
NKZ	*Neue kirchliche Zeitschrift*
NovT	*Novum Testamentum* (Leiden)
NovTSup	Supplements to *NovT*
NSI	G. A. Cooke, *A Text-Book of North-Semitic Inscriptions* (Oxford: Clarendon, 1903)
NT	New Testament
NT	See *NovT*
NTA	*New Testament Abstracts*
NTAbh	Neutestamentliche Abhandlungen
NTB	C. K. Barrett, *The New Testament Background: Selected Documents* (New York: Harper, 1961; rev. ed.; New York: Harper & Row, 1987)
NTD	Das Neue Testament Deutsch
NTS	*New Testament Studies*
NTSup	See NovTSup
NTTS	New Testament Tools and Studies
OGIS	W. Dittenberger, *Orientis graeci inscriptiones selectae* (2 vols.; Leipzig: Hinrichs, 1903-5; repr. Hildesheim: Olms, 1960)
OLZ	*Orientalische Literaturzeitung*
OrAn	*Oriens antiquus*
Ost	Ostracon
OT	Old Testament
OTS	*Oudtestamentische Studiën*
Pad	Padua Aramaic Papyri (see *WA*, 230)
PAM	Palestine Archaeological Museum, Jerusalem
Pan	*Panammu* (see *WA*, 76)
PEFQS	*Palestine Exploration Fund, Quarterly Statement*
PEQ	*Palestine Exploration Quarterly*
PG	J. Migne, *Patrologia graeca*
PJB	*Palästina-Jahrbuch*
PL	J. Migne, *Patrologia latina*
PPG	J. Friedrich, *Phönizisch-punische Grammatik* (AnOr 46; Rome: Biblical Institute, 1970)
PRU	J. Nougayrol, *Le palais royal d'Ugarit III* (Mission de Ras Shamra 6; Paris: Imprimerie Nationale/Geuthner, 1955)
PSB	L. Pirot, *La sainte Bible* (12 vols.; rev. A. Clamer; Paris: Letouzey et Ané, 1935–)
PSBA	*Proceedings of the Society of Biblical Archaeology*
PW	"Pauly-Wissowa": *Paulys Real-Encyclopädie der classischen Alter-*

	tumswissenschaft (neue Bearbeitung, ed. G. Wissowa; Stuttgart: Metzler, 1905-78)
QDAP	*Quarterly of the Department of Antiquities of Palestine*
RA	*Revue d'assyriologie*
RArch	*Revue archéologique*
RB	*Revue biblique*
RBiblt	See *RivB*
RE	See PW
RechBib	Recherches bibliques
REG	*Revue des études grecques*
REJ	*Revue des études juives*
RES	*Répertoire d'épigraphie sémitique*
RevBén	*Revue bénédictine*
RevDTour	*Revue diocésaine de Tournai*
RevEtSém	*Revue des études sémitiques*
RevScRel	*Revue des sciences religieuses*
RGG	K. Galling (ed.), *Die Religion in Geschichte und Gegenwart* (7 vols.; 3d ed.; Tübingen: Mohr [Siebeck], 1957-65)
RHPR	*Revue d'histoire et de philosophie religieuses*
RHR	*Revue de l'histoire des religions*
RivB	*Rivista biblica (italiana)*
RQ	*Revue de Qumran*
RScRel	See *RevScRel*
RSO	*Rivista degli studi orientali*
RSPT	*Revue des sciences philosophiques et théologiques*
RSR	*Recherches de science religieuse*
RTL	*Revue théologique de Louvain*
RTP	*Revue de théologie et de philosophie*
SBAW	*Sitzungsberichte der bayerischen Akademie der Wissenschaften*
SBFLA	*Studii biblici franciscani liber annuus*
SBLDS	Society of Biblical Literature Dissertation Series
SBLMS	Society of Biblical Literature Monograph Series
SBLSBS	Society of Biblical Literature Sources for Biblical Study
SBT	Studies in Biblical Theology
SBU	*Symbolae biblicae upsalienses*
ScEccl	*Sciences ecclésiastiques* (now *Science et Esprit*)
SE I, II, III	F. L. Cross (ed.), *Studia evangelica* (TU 73 [1959], 87 [1964], 88 [1964])
SEÅ	*Svensk exegetisk årsbok*
SEG	*Supplementum epigraphicum graecum*
Sem	*Semitica*
Sf	Sefire Inscription(s) (see *WA,* 76)

Shunnar	Papyrus Letter published by Z. Shunnar (see *WA,* 198)
SMR	*Studia montis regii*
SNTS	Studiorum Novi Testamenti Societas
SNTSMS	SNTS Monograph Series
SPap	*Studia papyrologica*
SPAW	*Sitzungsberichte der preussischen Akademie der Wissenschaften*
SPB	Studia postbiblica (Leiden)
SSS	Semitic Study Series
ST	*Studia theologica*
StCath	*Studia catholica*
STDJ	Studies on the Texts of the Desert of Judah
Str-B	(H. L. Strack and) P. Billerbeck, *Kommentar zum Neuen Testament . . .* (6 vols.; Munich: Beck, 1922-61)
SUNT	Studien zur Umwelt des Neuen Testaments
SZ	*Stimmen der Zeit*
TDNT	G. Kittel and G. Friedrich, *Theological Dictionary of the New Testament* (10 vols.; Grand Rapids: Eerdmans, 1964-76) (English translation of *TWNT*)
TGI	K. Galling (ed.), *Textbuch zur Geschichte Israels* (2d ed.; Tübingen: Mohr [Siebeck], 1968)
TGl	*Theologie und Glaube*
ThStKr	*Theologische Studien und Kritiken*
TLZ	*Theologische Literaturzeitung*
TQ	*Theologische Quartalschrift*
TRu	*Theologische Rundschau*
TS	*Theological Studies*
TTKi	*Tidskrift for teologi og kirke*
TU	Texte und Untersuchungen (Berlin)
TWAT	J. Botterweck and H. Ringgren (eds.), *Theologisches Wörterbuch zum Alten Testament* (so far 8 vols.; Stuttgart: Kohlhammer, 1970–)
TWNT	G. Kittel and G. Friedrich (eds.), *Theologisches Wörterbuch zum Neuen Testament* (10 vols.; Stuttgart: Kohlhammer, 1933-79)
TZ	*Theologische Zeitschrift*
UT	C. H. Gordon, *Ugaritic Textbook* (Rome: Biblical Institute, 1965)
VC	*Vigiliae christianae*
VD	*Verbum domini*
VDBS	F. Vigouroux, *Dictionnaire de la Bible* (5 vols. in 7; Paris: Letouzey et Ané, 1895-1912) (see *DBSup*)
VDI	*Vestnik drevnei istorii*
VerbC	*Verbum caro*
Vg	Vulgate (Jerome's Latin version of the Bible)
VT	*Vetus Testamentum* (Leiden)

VTSup	Supplements to *VT*
WA	J. A. Fitzmyer, *A Wandering Aramean: Collected Aramaic Essays* (SBLMS 25; Missoula, MT: Scholars, 1979)
WO	*Die Welt des Orients*
ZA	*Zeitschrift für Assyriologie*
ZAW	*Zeitschrift für die alttestamentliche Wissenschaft*
ZDMG	*Zeitschrift der deutschen morgenländischen Gesellschaft*
ZDPV	*Zeitschrift des deutschen Palästina-Vereins*
ZKG	*Zeitschrift für Kirchengeschichte*
ZKT	*Zeitschrift für katholische Theologie*
ZNW	*Zeitschrift für die neutestamentliche Wissenschaft*
ZTK	*Zeitschrift für Theologie und Kirche*

Abbreviations of Qumran Texts

CD	Cairo (Genizah text of the) Damascus (Document)
DJD	Discoveries in the Judaean Desert (of Jordan) (so far 19 vols; Oxford: Clarendon, 1955–)
Hev	Naḥal Ḥever Caves
Mur	Murabbaʿat Caves
p	Pesher (Qumran commentary on OT books)
Q	Qumran (caves)
1Q, 2Q, 3Q, etc.	Numbered caves of Qumran area that yielded written material; followed by standard abbreviations of biblical and apocryphal books (e.g., 4QEx^{a}) or by numbers assigned to texts in volumes of the DJD series (e.g., 1Q**19**, 4Q**175**).
1QapGn/Gen	Cave 1, Genesis Apocryphon
1QH	Cave 1, *Hôdāyôt,* Thanksgiving Psalms
1QM	Cave 1, *Milḥāmāh,* War Scroll
1QpHab	Cave 1, Pesher on Habakkuk
1QpMic	Cave 1, Pesher on Micah (= 1Q**14**)
1QpPs	Cave 1, Pesher on the Psalms (= 1Q**16**)
1QpZeph	Cave 1, Pesher on Zephaniah (= 1Q**15**)
1QS	Cave 1, *Serek hay-Yaḥad,* Rule of the Community or Manual of Discipline
1QSa	Appendix A to 1QS, Rule of the Congregation (= 1Q**28a**)
1QSb	Appendix B to 1QS, Blessings (= 1Q**28b**)
4QAhA	Cave 4, Aaron text, copy A (to be published)
4QarP	Cave 4, Aramaic papyrus (to be published)
4QCatena^{a}	Cave 4, Catena of OT passages, copy a (= 4Q**177**)
4QD^{b}	Cave 4, Damascus Document, copy b (to be published)
4QFlor	Cave 4, Florilegium, Eschatological Midrashim (= 4Q**174**)
4QHen^{a}	Cave 4, Enoch text, copy a (published by Milik)

4QHen astr[b]	Cave 4, Enoch astronomical text, copy b (Milik)
4Qḥ'A[c]	Cave 4, *Ḥăzût 'Amram,* Vision of Amram, copy c
4QM[a]	Cave 4, *Milḥāmāh,* War Scroll fragment, copy a, published in *ZAW* 69 (1957) 131-51
4QpHos[a-b]	Cave 4, Pesher on Hosea, copies a and b (= 4Q**166-167**)
4QpIs[a-e]	Cave 4, Pesher on Isaiah, copies a to e (= 4Q**161-165**)
4QpNah	Cave 4, Pesher on Nahum (= 4Q**169**)
4QpPs 37	Cave 4, Pesher on Ps 37 (part of 4QpPs[a] [= 4Q**177**])
4QPatrBless	Cave 4, Patriarchal Blessings (*JBL* 75 [1956] 174-87)
4QS	Cave 4, *Serek hay-Yaḥad,* Rule of the Community or Manual of Discipline, related to 1QS
4QTest	Cave 4, Testimonia (= 4Q**175**)
4QtgJob	Cave 4, Targum of Job
4QtgLev	Cave 4, Targum of Leviticus
11QMelch	Cave 11, Melchizedek fragments (*OTS* 14 [1965] 354-73)
11QPs[a]	Cave 11, Psalms Scroll, copy a (= DJD 4)
11QPs[a] DavComp	Cave 11, prose insertion in 11QPs[a], David's Compositions
11QtgJob	Cave 11, Targum of Job

ESSAYS ON THE SEMITIC BACKGROUND OF THE NEW TESTAMENT

CONTENTS

I

THE USE OF THE OLD TESTAMENT

1

THE USE OF EXPLICIT OLD TESTAMENT QUOTATIONS IN QUMRAN LITERATURE AND IN THE NEW TESTAMENT*

The problem of the use of the Old Testament in the New Testament is a vast one, complicated by side-issues of textual variants and involved in the kindred problem of the relation or harmony of the two Testaments. It is also a problem which has been well worked over by many scholars. Books have been written on the subject, comparing the text of the Old Testament quotations with the existing Greek and Hebrew recensions or comparing the exegetical principles and methods of the New Testament writers with those of the rabbis.[1] In particular, Paul's use of the Old Testament has been the special object of such study. It would seem useless, then, to take up again such a well-worked subject, were it not for the new light which has been shed on the problem by the discovery of the Qumran scrolls. The Jewish roots of the New Testament have always made it *a priori* likely that its use of the Old Testament would resemble that of contemporary Judaism to some extent. Indeed, resemblances with the rabbinical writings have long since been established. Yet one of the main difficulties in this comparative

* Originally published in *NTS* 7 (1960–61) 297–333.

[1] A convenient sketch of previous work, together with references to the pertinent literature, can be found in E.E. Ellis, *Paul's Use of the Old Testament* (Edinburgh, 1957) 1–5. See also J. Bonsirven, *Exégèse rabbinique et exégèse paulinienne* (Bibliothèque de théologie historique; Paris, 1939) 264–5.

study has always been the extent to which one can trust the contemporaneity of the so-called early material incorporated in these writings.[2] Now, however, we have in the Qumran scrolls Jewish writings which antedate for the most part the composition of the New Testament books—or at the latest are in part contemporary with them. Moreover, in many of these scrolls, which are admittedly sectarian writings and perhaps not characteristic of all contemporary Jewish thought, we find the Old Testament used in a manner and with a frequency which rivals that of the New Testament. It is certainly to our advantage, then, to examine this use of the Old Testament in the Qumran literature, in order to see what can be learned from it for the study of the related New Testament problem. For in both cases we are dealing with documents stemming from a group in which a theology built on the Old Testament motivated its way of life. Indeed, it would be difficult to find a more ideal set of documents to illustrate the New Testament use of the Old Testament than the Qumran scrolls, in which we see how contemporary Jews made use of their Scriptures.

Some of the methods of Qumran exegesis have already been studied;[3] a thorough, systematic investigation of all the evidence

[2] See E. E. Ellis, *op. cit.*, 42, 83.

[3] See W. H. Brownlee, 'Biblical Interpretation among the Sectaries of the DSS', *BA* XIV (1951) 54–76; F. F. Bruce, *Biblical Exegesis in the Qumran Texts* (Grand Rapids: Michigan, 1959); M. H. Gottstein, 'Bible Quotations in the Sectarian Dead Sea Scrolls', *VT* III (1953) 79–82; K. Elliger, *Studien zum Habakuk-Kommentar vom Toten Meer* (Beiträge zur historischen Theologie 15; Tübingen, 1953) 118–64; E. Osswald, 'Zur Hermeneutik des Habakuk-Kommentars', *ZAW* LXVIII (1956) 243–56; J. van der Ploeg, 'Bijbeltekst en theologie in de teksten van Qumrân', *Vox theologica* XXVII (1956–57) 33–45; B. J. Roberts, 'The Dead Sea Scrolls and the O.T. Scriptures', *BJRL* XXXVI (1953–54) 75–96; 'Some Observations on the Damascus Documents and the Dead Sea Scrolls', *ibid.*, XXXIV (1951–52) 366–87; J. A. Sanders, 'Habakkuk in Qumran, Paul and the Old Testament', *JRel* XXXVIII (1959) 232–44; G. Vermès, 'Le "Commentaire d'Habacuc" et le Nouveau Testament', *Cahiers Sioniens* V (1951) 337–49; P. Wernberg-Møller, 'Some Reflexions on the Biblical Materials in the Manual of Discipline', *ST* IX (1955) 40–66; C. Roth, 'The Subject Matter of Qumran

is still needed. The present study is limited to one aspect of Qumran exegesis and its bearing on the New Testament. It is hoped that it will be a useful contribution to the whole.

In both the Qumran literature and the New Testament we frequently find what has been called *le style anthologique*, the working of Old Testament expressions and phrases into the very fabric of the composition, in a manner which resembles a *cento*. It is well known that a book like the Apocalypse, which does not contain a single explicit quotation from the Old Testament, abounds none the less in Old Testament allusions. The same is true of the Qumran War Scroll, as clearly appears from the studies of J. Carmignac.[4] Such a *style anthologique* involves an implicit exegesis and is usually due to thorough acquaintance with and a reverent meditation upon the Old Testament. However, in this discussion I am not concerned with this *use* of the Old Testament by way of allusion or verbal echoes or reminiscences, even though it is an important aspect of the whole problem.

Attention will be centred rather on the *explicit quotations* of the Old Testament, such as are found in both the New Testament and in Qumran literature. In doing so, I am also leaving out of consideration the *pesharim* and 4QTestimonia. In an effort to delimit the problem I have deliberately excluded the *pesher*,[5] for it is a unique type of *midrash* having no exact counterpart in the

---

Exegesis', *VT* X (1960) 51–65; J. C. Trever, 'The Qumran Covenanters and Their Use of Scripture', *Personalist* XXXIX (1958) 128–38; G. Vermès, 'A propos des commentaires bibliques découverts à Qumrân', *RHPR* XXXIII (1955) 95–102; M. Black, 'Theological Conceptions in the Dead Sea Scrolls', *SEA* XVIII–XIX (1953–54) 72–97.

[4] 'Les citations de l'Ancien Testament dans "La guerre des fils de lumière contre les fils de ténèbres"', *RB* LXIII (1956) 234–60, 373–90.

[5] I have thus excluded the 1QpHab (M. Burrows, ed., *The Dead Sea Scrolls of St Mark's Monastery*, vol 1 [New Haven, 1950] pl. 55–61), 1QpNah (D. Barthélemy and J. T. Milik, *Qumran Cave I* [DJD 1; Oxford, 1955] 77–80); 1QpPs 57; 1QpPs 58 (*ibid.*, 81–2); 1QpZeph (*ibid.*, 80); 4QpNah (J. M. Allegro, 'Further Light on the History of the Qumran Sect', *JBL* LXXV [1956] 89–93); 4QpPs 37 (*ibid.*, 94–5 and *PEQ* LXXXVI [1954]

New Testament. There is no book or part of a book in the latter which is, strictly speaking, a *pesher*.[6] I am likewise omitting 4QTestimonia since I treat it below.[7]

There is, however, in the Qumran literature a body of isolated explicit quotations of the Old Testament, which are introduced by special formulae and are cited to bolster up or illustrate an argument, to serve as a *point de départ* in a discussion or to act as a sort of proof-text. This conscious and deliberate quotation of the Old Testament in the Qumran literature provides the most apt frame of reference in our comparative study. Hence, though it may appear arbitrary at first to exclude from our consideration the Qumran *pesher*—which is the biblical commentary *par excellence* in the sect—the reason for this exclusion becomes clear upon reflection. The isolated explicit quotations are closer in their use to those found in the New Testament and furnish the more valid type of Old Testament exegesis with which to compare those of the New. To be sure, the exegetical principles underlying the *pesher* and the isolated quotations are often the same, and there will be occasion to point this out; in this way the evidence of the *pesharim* will be used indirectly.

Fortunately, a good group of passages in the Qumran literature can be found, containing explicit quotations. Three of these passages occur in the *Manual of Discipline* (1QS), thirty in the

---

69–75; 4QpHos[a] (*JBL ibid.*, 93); 4QpHos[b] (J. M. Allegro, 'A Recently Discovered Fragment of a Commentary on Hosea from Qumran's Fourth Cave', *JBL* LXXVIII [1959] 142–7); 4QpGn 49 (*JBL* LXXV [1956] 174–6); 4QpIs[a] (*ibid.*, 177–82); 4QpIs[b] ('More Isaiah Commentaries from Qumran's Fourth Cave', *JBL* LXXVII [1958] 215–18); 4QpIs[c] (*ibid.*, 218–20); 4QpIs[d] (*ibid.*, 220–1).

[6] This has been recognized, among others, by W. Baumgartner, *TRu* XIX (1951) 117; F. F. Bruce, *Biblical Exegesis in the Qumran Texts*, 71–2; *NTS* II (1955–56) 181. See further A. G. Wright, 'The Literary Genre Midrash (Part 2)', *CBQ* XXVIII (1966) 417–57, esp. 418–22. Cf. B. Lindars, *New Testament Apologetic* (London: SCM, 1961); N. Perrin, 'Mark xiv. 62: The End Product of a Christian Pesher Tradition', *NTS* XII (1965–66) 150–5.

[7] See pp. 59–89.

Damascus Document (CD), five in the *War Scroll* (1QM), and four in the text labelled provisionally 4Q*Florilegium*.[8] In all, forty-two passages involving forty-four certain explicit Old Testament quotations and two probable ones occur in the published Qumran literature. This is a manageable group with which one can work.

In this treatment of the explicit quotations I shall first of all discuss briefly the introductory formulae and then the classes into which the quotations fall. In doing so, I shall be exposing the exegetical principles and methods at work in the two groups of quotations. I shall concentrate mainly on the new Qumran material, but also show how it illustrates the New Testament usage.

I. THE INTRODUCTORY FORMULAE

The fundamental attitude of both the Qumran sect and the early Christian Church toward the Old Testament is manifested in the introductory formulae used by their writers. While these formulae were often stereotyped in both literatures, they nevertheless indicate the conscious and deliberate appeal made by these writers to the Old Testament as the 'Scriptures'. The motivation and religious presuppositions of the two groups, which were founded on the Old Testament, are often best re-

[8] 4Q Florilegium was published at first only in part; see J. M. Allegro, 'Further Messianic References in Qumran Literature', *JBL* LXXV (1956) 176–7 [= Document II]; 'Fragments of a Qumran Scroll of Eschatological *Midrāšîm*', *JBL* LXXVII (1958) 350–4. See now 4Q*174* (DJD 5, 53–7). That this text is actually 'a more complex type of *pesher*—one that employs additional biblical material [that is, isolated explicit quotations] to expound the biblical passage under consideration', has been shown by one of my students, W. R. Lane, 'A New Commentary Structure in 4Q Florilegium', *JBL* LXXVIII (1959) 343–6. See also the improvements in the understanding of the text suggested by Y. Yadin, 'A Midrash on 2 Sam vii and Ps i–ii (4QFlorilegium)', *IEJ* IX (1959) 95–8. A few further examples of explicit quotations are to be found in the more recently published 11QMelchizedek (see pp. 245–68 below).

vealed by the formulae used to introduce the quotation itself. Quotations so introduced obviously differ from mere allusions, in which it is often difficult to decide to what extent or degree the use of an Old Testament expression was intended by the writer to carry the impression that a reference to it was actually being made. Modern writers are wont to use a phrase or expression from older classical sources, but it is not always with the same degree of deliberate reference. There is no doubt of the reference to the Old Testament, however, when the quotation is explicitly introduced by a formula. I shall list the introductory formulae used in the Qumran literature and indicate those which have counterparts in the New Testament. Certain features will emerge from the classification of them. A purely mechanical division of them is best made according to the verb used: (A) 'to write', (B) 'to say', (C) other formulae.[9]

(A) *Written:* Though we never find in the Qumran literature any expression which corresponds to the noun *hē graphē* (or *hai graphai*) as a designation for the Old Testament, such as we find in the New Testament, there are eight formulae which employ the verb *ktb* of the Old Testament. This, in itself, is not surprising for the same usage is found in the later books of the Old Testament and manifests only the common Jewish regard for their normative Scriptures.

(*a*) *ky' kn ktwb* (1QS 5:15; CD 11:18; 2Q*25* 1:3), 'for it is written', which seems to be the Hebrew equivalent of the New Testament formula, *houtōs gar gegraptai* (Mt 2:5; see also 1 Cor 15:45).

(*b*) *k'šr ktwb* (1QS 8:14; 5:17; CD 7:19; 4QFlor 1:12; 4QpIs[c] 4–7 ii 18; 4QCatena[a] 10–11:1; 4Q*178* 3:2; this is probably the full form of the abbreviation *kk* found in CD 19:1), 'as it was written'. This formula is, of course, found in the Old Testament (1 Kgs 21:11; Dn 9:13, though the more usual form is *kktwb*). Compare the variant, *w'šr ktwb* (4QpIs[e] 1–2:2). A

[9] A sketchy comparison of some of these formulae can be found in E. E. Ellis, *op. cit.*, 48–9; R. H. Charles, *APOT* II, 789.

variety of New Testament formulae corresponds to this one:

kathōs gegraptai (also found in the LXX: 2 Kgs 14:6; Dn 9:13 [Theodotion]): Lk 2:23; Acts 15:15; Rom 1:17; 2:24; 3:10; 4:17; 8:36; 9:33; 11:26; 15:3, 9, 21; 1 Cor 1:31; 2:9; 2 Cor 9:9; 13:15.

kata to gegrammenon (plural is used in Dn 9:13 [LXX]: 2 Cor 4:13.

kathōs estin gegrammenon: Jn 6:31; 12:14.

kathaper gegraptai: Rom 3:4; 9:13; 10:15; 11:8.

hōs gegraptai (used in *2 Esdras* 20:35): Lk 3:4 [see below under (*e*)]; Mk 7:6.

hōsper gegraptai: 1 Cor 10:7.

(*c*) *k'šr ktwb bspr* [*mwšh*] (4QFlor 1:2; cf. 4QpIs[c] 1:4), 'as it was written in the book of Moses'. A fuller form is found in *k'šr ktwb 'lyw bšyry dwyd 'šr 'mr*, 'as it was written concerning him in the hymns of David, who said . . .' (11QMelch 9–10; cf. also 11QMelch 24). Compare the New Testament expression: *kathōs gegraptai en biblō tōn prophētōn* (Acts 7:42; see also Mk 1:2; Lk 2:23; Acts 13:33; 1 Cor 9:9; 14:21); also *estin gegrammenon en tois prophētais* (Jn 6:45).

(*d*) *ky ktwb* (CD 11:20), 'for it was written', the Hebrew equivalent of the New Testament *gegraptai gar* (Mt 4:6, 10; 26:31; Lk 4:10; Acts 1:20; 23:5; Rom 12:19; 14:11; 1 Cor 1:19; 3:19; Gal 3:10; 4:27 [in Gal 4:22 it occurs without an explicit quotation!]). Possibly we should also compare *dioti gegraptai* (1 Pt 1:16) and *hoti gegraptai* (Mk 14:27; Gal 3:13).

(*e*) *'šr ktwb bspr yš'yh hnby' l'ḥryt hymym* (4QFlor 1:15), 'as it was written in the book of Isaiah the prophet for the end of days'. See also 4QFlor 1-3 ii 3 (*bspr dny'l*); 4QCatena[a] 7:3; 4QCatena[b] 1:4. Compare: *hōs gegraptai en biblō logōn Ēsaïou tou prophētou* (Lk 3:4).

(*f*) *whmh 'šr ktwb 'lyhmh bspr yḥzq'l hnby' 'šr* . . . (4QFlor 1:16), 'These are the ones about whom it was written in the book of Ezekiel the prophet, who . . .'. See CD 1:13; 4QCatena[a] 1–4:7;

5–6:11. Compare: *houtos estin peri hou gegraptai* (Mt 11:10; Lk 7:27).

(*g*) *w'yn ktwb ky 'm* . . . (CD 9:5), 'And is it not written that . . .?' Compare: *ouk estin gegrammenon en tō nomō hymōn hoti* . . . (Jn 10:34, quoting Ps 82:6 as the 'Law') or *ou gegraptai hoti* . . . (Mk 11:17).

(*h*) *w'l hnśy' ktwb* (CD 5:1), 'and concerning the prince it was written'. The strict formula here is probably only *ktwb*, and thus corresponds to the use in the New Testament of *gegraptai* alone (Mt 4:4; 21:13; Lk 4:4, 8; 19:46). Cf. 4Q*180* 5–6:2, 5.

(B) *Said:* The Old Testament was not only looked upon as the *written* tradition of Israel both by the Qumran sect and the New Testament writers, but it was also the collection of what had once been 'said'. Just as we find in the New Testament formulae a frequent use of the verb *legein*, so too in the Qumran literature there is a correspondingly frequent use of the verbs *'mr* (16 times), *dbr* (3 times), *hgyd* (3 times). The verb 'say' is thus used more frequently than the verb 'write', as is true of the Mishnaic formulae in contrast to those in Paul's letters, where forms of the verb 'write' are more numerous.[10]

(*a*) *k'šr 'mr* (CD 7:8 [=19:5], 14, 16; 20:16; [13:23], 'as it said', or possibly sometimes 'as he said'; it is often not possible to determine who or what the subject is in these formulae. A similar formula is *k'šr dbr* (CD 19:15). With these should be compared the New Testament expressions *kathōs eirēken* (Heb 4:3), *kata to eirēmenon* (Lk 2:24; Rom 4:18), *kathōs eipen hē graphē* (Jn 7:38); *kathōs legei* (Heb 3:7). See below, p.255.

(*b*) *'šr 'mr* (CD 4:20), 'as it (or he) said'. This formula also occurs in a fuller form, listed below under C (*d*).

(*c*) *w'šr 'mr* (CD 9:2; 16:6), 'and as for what it (or he) said'.

[10] See B. M. Metzger, 'The Formulas Introducing Quotations of Scripture in the N.T. and the Mishnah', *JBL* LXX (1951) 305, and cf. the slightly revised form of this article in Metzger's *Historical and Literary Studies: Pagan, Jewish, and Christian* (NTTS 8; Leiden: Brill, 1968) 52–63; E. E. Ellis, *op. cit.*, 48–9.

This formula is frequently found in the *pesharim* (1QpHab 6:2; 7:3; 9:2–3; 10:1–2; 12:6; 4QFlor 1:7; 4QpIs^a D 5; 4QpIs^a 1:3 [4–5]; 4Q*161* fr. 8–10:6; 4Q*183* 1 ii. 9; 11QMelch [2], [3], [11]). But in the latter case its use is different from that in CD, for a formal commentary is being written in the *pesharim,* and this formula is used to reintroduce a portion of a verse already fully quoted in order to comment upon it.[11] In CD there is no such reintroduction, and the formula acts almost as any other one.

In some cases, however, it is clear that God is the subject of the verb of saying.

(*d*) *'šr 'mr 'l* (*'lyhm*) (CD 6:13; 8:9), 'as for what (or: about whom) God said'. Similarly, . . . *k'šr hgdth lnw m'z l'mwr* (1QM 11:5–6), 'as you spoke to us of old saying . . .', . . .*'l 'šr 'mr lw* (CD 9:7), 'Who said to him . . .'. ⟨*'mr*⟩ *lhm bqdš* (CD 3:7), 'He said to them in Qadesh'. New Testament counterparts of these expressions can be found in the following: *elalēsen de houtōs ho theos* (Acts 7:6); *kathōs eipen ho theos hoti* (2 Cor 6:16); *ho gar theos eipen* (Mt 15:4); *ho theos eipen* (Acts 7:7; see also 7:3). In both bodies of literature we have the same underlying idea of the Old Testament Scriptures as the 'Word of God'.[12] At the same time we find formulae which express the instrumentality of the Old Testament writer: *'šr 'mr byd yḥzq'l* (CD 19:11–12); *k'šr dbr 'l byd yš'yh hnby' bn 'mwṣ l'mwr* (CD 4:13–14); *w'šr d[brt]h byd mwšh l'mwr* (1QM 10:6). The same instrumentality is sometimes noted in the New Testament in such phrases as *elalēsen ho theos dia stomatos tōn hagiōn ap' aiōnos autou prophētōn* (Acts 3:21), or *hōs kai en tō Hōsēe legei* (Rom 9:25).[13]

(*e*) *'šr 'mr yš'yh* (CD 6:7–8), 'as Isaiah said'. Note that the subject of the verb of saying is sometimes the human author of

[11] See M. Burrows, 'The Meaning of *'šr 'mr* in DSH', *VT* II (1952) 255–60. K. Elliger, *op. cit.*, 123–5, calls this expression in the *pesharim* a 'Wiederaufnahmeformel'.

[12] For the same underlying presupposition in the Mishnaic use of the Old Testament, see B. M. Metzger, *op. cit.*, 306.

[13] See also CD 19:7, quoted below in C(*b*.)

the Old Testament composition. Further: *w'šr 'mr mwšh (lyśr'l)* (CD8:14; 19:26–27); *wmwšh 'mr* (CD 5:8); *w'šr hgyd (mwšh) lnw* (1QM 10:1). This type of formula has its counterpart also in the New Testament: *prōtos Mōÿsēs legei* (Rom 10:19; see also Heb 12:21); *Dauid gar legei eis auton* (Acts 2:25; see also 2:34; Rom 11:9); *pros de ton Israēl legei (Ēsaïas)* (Rom 10:22); see further Rom 9:27; 10:16, 20; 15:12; Jn 1:23.[14] Cf. 11QMelch 15: *[']šr 'mr [l'ḥryt hymym byd yš']yh hnby' 'šr 'm[r]*, 'who said concerning the end of days through Isaiah the prophet, who said'.

(*f*) *ky hw' 'šr 'mr* (CD 10:16; 16:15), 'for that is what it (or: he) said'. Cf. 11QMelch 14. This formula has a perfect counterpart in the New Testament expression *houtos gar estin ho rhētheis dia Ēsaïou tou prophētou legontos* (Mt 3:3); *touto estin to eirēmenon dia tou prophētou Iōēl* (Acts 2:16). See also Mt 11:10; Lk 7:27.[15] It should not be confused with a somewhat similar expression, *houtos estin ho Mōÿsēs ho eipas tois huiois Israēl* (Acts 7:37).

(C) *Other formulae.* There are a number of formulae which use neither 'writing' nor 'saying'. In some of these we again find God the subject of the verb.

(*a*) *k'šr hqym 'l lhm byd yḥzq'l hnby' l'mwr* (CD 3:21), As 'God confirmed (it) for them through Ezekiel the prophet, saying . . .'. *wm'z hšm['th mw]'d gbwrt ydkh bktyym l'mwr* (1QM 11:11), 'And of old you caused us to hear the appointed time of the power of your hand against the Kittim, saying . . .'; *wylmdnw m'z ldwrwtynw l'mwr* (1QM 10:2), 'And he taught us of old for our generations, saying . . .'.

[14] For the Mishnaic idea of instrumentality see B. M. Metzger, *op. cit.*, 306.

[15] This formula also occurs in the *pesharim* (see 1QpHab 3:2, 13–14; 5:6). Once again there is a slight difference in the usage; in CD it introduces an Old Testament quotation supporting the injunction which precedes, whereas in 1QpHab it repeats a portion of a longer text which has already been given and partly expounded. See M. Burrows, *op. cit.*, 257. K. Elliger, *op. cit.*, 124, calls this a 'Rückverweisungsformel'. It should be noted, moreover, that the New Testament counterpart is used in the same way as the formula in CD and not as that in the *pesher*.

(*b*) The famous formulae of fulfilment or realization which are frequently found in the New Testament have practically speaking no equivalent in the Qumran literature. This may strike us as strange, since the expression has its roots in the Old Testament itself (1 Kgs 2:27; 2 Chr 36:21) and the Qumran sect did look upon certain events in their history as 'fulfilling', as it were, the utterances of the prophets. While there are no formulae which employ the verb *ml'*, there are two examples of a formula which comes close to the idea, but even these differ from the New Testament formulae in referring to a future event.

bbw' hdbr 'šr ktwb bdbry yš'yh bn 'mwṣ hnby' 'šr 'mr . . . (CD 7: 10–11), 'when the word will come true which is written in the words of the prophet Isaiah, son of Amoz, who said . . .' (Rabin).

bbw' hdbr 'šr ktwb byd zkryh hnby' . . . (CD 19:7), 'when the word will come true which was written by Zechariah the prophet . . .'. Yet even this type of expression finds a very close parallel in the New Testament, without, however, containing the verb *plēroun*. In 1 Cor 15:54 we read: *tote genēsetai ho logos gegrammenos*, 'Then will come true the word which is written . . .'. One other formula should be mentioned here, which does refer to the past, but again lacks the idea of fulfilment. It is *hy' h't 'šr hyh ktwb 'lyh* (CD 1:13), 'this is the time about which it was written'. But this formula in many respects is closer to the *houtos estin* type quoted above.

Probably the real reason for the lack of 'fulfilment' formulae in the Qumran literature is that they are a peculiarly New Testament type. More fundamental still is the difference of outlook which characterizes the two groups. The Qumran theology is still dominated by a forward look, an expectation of what is to come about in the *eschaton*, whereas the Christian theology is more characterized by a backward glance, seeing the culmination of all that preceded in the advent of Christ. As F. F. Bruce expresses it, 'The New Testament interpretation of the Old

Testament is not only eschatological but Christological'.[16] This difference is probably brought out most significantly in the use and non-use of the 'fulfilment' formulae when Scripture is quoted.[17]

(*c*) Just as we find a few explicit quotations of the Old Testament in the New, which are directly intended to be such, but which lack an introductory formula (see Mt 7:23; Lk 8:16; Mk 10:6–8; Rom 10:18; 2 Cor 10:17 [contrast 1 Cor 1:31]; 13:1; Eph 5:31; Gal 3:11 [contrast Rom 1:17]; Heb 10:37–38), so too we find the same phenomenon in CD 6:3, quoting Nm 21:18. These should not be confused with mere allusions, for they are obviously intended to be quotations. Perhaps we should refer to them as 'virtual citations'.[18]

(*d*) The converse of this phenomenon is also found both in the New Testament and in the Qumran literature, that is, the use of the well-known introductory formulae to cite a passage which is not found in the Old Testament (or at least which is not found in any of its known texts or versions). Mt 2:23, 'in fulfilment of the saying of the prophets, "He shall be called a Nazarene"', is a prime example of this phenomenon; see further 1 Cor 2:9; Eph 5:14; Jas 4:5; 2 Pt 2:22; possibly also 1 Tm 5:18. This same phenomenon appears in the CD 9:8–9, *'šr 'mr l' twšy'k ydk lk*, 'As for that which it said, "Your own hand shall not avenge you"'. Likewise CD 16:10, *'šr 'mr [l]'yšh lhny' 't šbw'th*, 'As for that which it said, "It is for her husband to annul her oath"'. Again CD 4:15, *'šr 'mr 'lyhm lwy bn y'qb*, 'concerning which Levi, the son of Jacob spoke'; it is just possibly a reference to a Testament of Levi, though the

[16] *Biblical Exegesis in the Qumran Texts*, 68. The same idea has been stressed by K. Stendahl, 'The Scrolls, and the New Testament: an Introduction and a Perspective', *The Scrolls and the New Testament* (New York, 1957) 17. See further C. F. D. Moule, 'Fulfilment Words in the New Testament: Use and Abuse', *NTS XIV* (1967–68) 293–320.

[17] The same absence of these formulae has been noted in the Mishnah by B. M. Metzger, *op. cit.*, 306–7.

[18] J. Bonsirven (*op. cit.*, 27–8) mentions the occurrence of the same feature in the Tannaitic literature.

text quoted is not found in the Greek *Testaments of the Twelve Patriarchs*.[19] Such a feature, found both in the New Testament and in the Qumran literature, would hardly warrant the conclusion that other works were regarded as 'canonical' than those which subsequently came to be regarded as such in the various canonical lists; it is much more likely that the introductory formulae were at times used loosely also of other literature which served some didactic or ethical purpose.

One last remark concerning the introductory formulae is in order. Many of the features which I have pointed out as emerging from a study of these formulae, for instance, the idea of the Old Testament as the word of God, the instrumentality of the human author, the absence of fulfilment formulae in Qumran literature, are also found in the formulae used to introduce the Old Testament in the Mishnah. Some years ago B. M. Metzger made a comparative study of the formulae in the Mishnah and the New Testament. Many of the points which I have noted can be paralleled in his article. However, the significant difference is the great diversity in the actual formulae. 'By far the majority of quotations in the Mishnah are introduced by the verb *'mr*.'[20] The forms most frequently attested are the participle *'wmr* or the Niphal perfect *n'mr* or *šn'mr* (with some other variations). But there is not one formula involving this verb in his list which corresponds to anything in the list constructed from the Qumran texts. The Mishnah also employs the root *ktb* in both nominal and verbal forms. Yet once again not one of the examples given parallels any of the usages from the Qumran literature. There are, of course, a few formulae found in the New Testament which have closer parallels with the Mishnaic material (such as the use of *hē graphē* for *hktwb*; or *hy'k 'th qwr'* for *pōs anaginōskeis* [Lk 10:26]). But such a comparison as I have made shows that the Hebrew equivalents of

[19] See the notes on these passages in C. Rabin, *The Zadokite Documents: I. The Admonition; II. The Laws* (2nd ed.; Oxford, 1958).

[20] *Op. cit.*, 298. See also J. Bonsirven, *op. cit.*, 29–32.

the New Testament introductory formulae are far more numerous in the Qumran literature than in the Mishnah. Consequently, the comparative study of the Qumran and the New Testament introductory formulae would tend to indicate a closer connection of the New Testament writings with the contemporary Qumran material than with the later Mishnaic.

II. THE CLASSES OF OLD TESTAMENT QUOTATIONS

The next step in this study of the Old Testament quotations used in both literatures is to examine the way in which the writers made use of the quotation. I have tried to determine the extent to which the Qumran author respects the meaning and original sense of the passage which he quotes. It is obviously of importance to know whether the Old Testament text which is quoted is understood according to its original context, or is adapted to a new situation, or is entirely twisted to the purpose of the one quoting. In sifting the forty-two passages, I have found that they fall into four categories. They are the following: (A) the Literal or Historical class, in which the Old Testament is actually quoted in the same sense in which it was intended by the original writers; (B) the class of Modernization, in which the Old Testament text, which originally had a reference to some event in the contemporary scene at the time it was written, nevertheless was vague enough to be applied to some new event in the history of the Qumran sect; (C) the class of Accommodation, in which the Old Testament text was obviously wrested from its original context, modified or deliberately changed by the new writer in order to adapt it to a new situation or purpose; (D) the Eschatological class, in which the Old Testament quotation expressed a promise or threat about something to be accomplished in the *eschaton* and which the Qumran writer cited as something still to be accomplished in the new *eschaton* of which he wrote. In classifying this material I have tried to let the texts speak for themselves, without trying to impose on them any preconceived ideas. I readily admit that in a few instances it is difficult to decide whether a particular text should be in one class or another, since the borderline especially between class B (Modernization) and class C (Accommodation) is at times debatable.

Having discovered these four classes of Old Testament quotations in Qumran literature, I tried to see to what extent they were also verifiable of the New Testament. All four classes can be illustrated by New Testament passages as well. I do not want to imply that these four classes exhaust the grouping of the New Testament quotations. It would lead us too far astray to try to analyse all the New Testament examples in the same way as those of the Qumran literature. This must be left to someone else. However, I have made enough of a check to know that all of the four classes found in the Qumran material can be paralleled as well in the New Testament. There is, moreover, a small group of Old Testament texts which have been used by both the Qumran writers and the authors of the New Testament books. By comparing the way in which the same quotation is treated in both literatures, one can discern still more clearly the similarities and differences which appear in the methods of quotation. Thirty-two of the quotations found in the Qumran texts are not found in the New Testament; in three cases, however, the *Damascus Document* explicitly quotes an Old Testament passage to which a New Testament writer merely alludes (CD 4:12–18, quoting Is 24:17—see Lk 21:35; CD 6:3–11, quoting Is 54:16—see Rom 9:22; CD 19:11–12, quoting Ez 9:4—see Rev 9:4). But five Old Testament quotations are explicitly quoted by both the New Testament and the Qumran literature.[21]

(A) *The Literal or Historical Class*

The first category of Old Testament citations is that in which the Qumran author quotes the Old Testament in the same sense

[21] In one case (Lv 19:18) CD 9:2 quotes the first part of the verse, while the New Testament (Mt 5:43; 19:19; 22:39; Mk 12:31; Lk 10:27; Rom 13:9; Gal 5:14; Jas 2:8) quotes the second half.

in which it was used in the original writing. As will be seen, almost all of the seven examples which are found in this category cite precepts which the Qumran sect still regards as valid. It is not surprising, then, that the same sense of the Old Testament passage would be preserved in such quotations. This use of the Old Testament is found in the following instances:

(1) *k'šr 'mr byn 'yš l'štw wbyn 'b lbnw* (CD 7:8–9, quoting Nm 30:17), 'As it said, "Between a man and his wife and between a father and his son"'. *Context:* An instruction is being given concerning the observance of the Law and in particular the rule of binding oaths formulated in Nm 30. The rules there stated are still in force, apparently in the same sense in which they were originally intended, as far as the sect of Qumran is concerned. The text of CD reads *wbyn 'b lbnw,* whereas the Masoretic text has *lbtw,* which is obviously correct, since there is no mention of a son's vow in Nm 30, nor does the context of CD demand it. Hence, the reading *lbnw* should be regarded as a curious mistake which has crept into the text of CD.[22]

(2) *w'šr 'mr l' tqwm wl' tṭwr 't bny 'mk* (CD 9:2, quoting Lv 19:18). 'And as for what it said, "You shall not take vengeance nor bear a grudge against the sons of your own people"'. *Context:* Among the Laws in the second part of the *Damascus Document* the injunction against vengeance and bearing a grudge from the Holiness Code is cited as still having validity in the community. CD further specifies by concrete examples who such a person would be. There is no perceptible change in the meaning of the text which is cited.

(3) *w'yn ktwb ky 'm nwqm hw' lṣryw wnwṭr hw' l'wybyw* (CD 9:5, quoting Na 1:2), 'Is it not rather written that "He is the one who takes vengeance on his enemies and he bears a grudge against his adversaries"?' *Context:* In support of the prohibition of seeking revenge, which was discussed in (2) above, the *Damascus Document* now cites a verse from the writings of the

[22] See C. Rabin, *op. cit.*, 28.

prophets to confirm the injunction derived from the Law.[23] Nahum was describing God's vengeance and insisted that it was reserved to God and did not belong to man. The words of the prophet are now cited in the same sense.

(4) *l' hqym 't mṣwt 'l 'šr 'mr lw hwkḥ twkyḥ 't r'yk wl' tś' 'lyw ḥṭ'* (CD 9:7–8, quoting Lv 19:17), 'He has not carried out the command of God who said to him, "You must indeed reprove your neighbour and not bear sin because of him"'. *Context:* This passage is related to the two foregoing ones in which a prohibition of revenge is formulated. Again a precept of the Holiness Code in Leviticus is quoted, and is intended in the same sense as the original.[24]

(5) *ky hw' 'šr 'mr šmwr 't ywm hšbt lqdšw* (CD 10:16–17, quoting Dt 5:12), 'For that is what it said, "Be careful to keep the Sabbath day holy"'. *Context:* The regulations for the observance of the Sabbath in the community of Qumran are begun with the prescription that no one is to work on the sixth day from the setting of the sun, for that is what is meant by the precept. CD here quotes the Deuteronomic decalogue in the same sense in which it was originally intended, but adds the further prescription about the determination of the time, 'when the sun's full disc is distant from the gate'.

(6) *w'šr 'mr mwṣ' śptyk tšmwr lhqym* (CD 16:6–7, quoting Dt 23:24), 'And as for what it said, "A spoken promise you must be careful to observe"'. *Context:* This quotation is found in a passage of CD dealing with oaths. Whoever binds himself by an oath to return to the Law of Moses must do so, and the Qumran interpreter adds, 'even under pain of death'. The Deuteronomic precept, obviously still valid for the Qumran

[23] This combining of texts from the Torah and the prophets is well known in the combined quotations in Paul and rabbinical literature; see below, pp. 71–2; E. E. Ellis, *op. cit.*, 49–51. In this passage quoted from Nahum it should be noted that the well-known reverence for the Tetragrammaton, attested elsewhere in Qumran literature, is evidenced here again, for the author has written *hw'* instead of *Yhwh*, found in MT.

[24] CD has a slight variant in reading *r'yk* instead of MT's *'mytk*.

community, is applied here to the case of conversion to the Law.

(7) Possibly we should also list here CD 3:7, quoting Dt 9:23; some hesitation arises because the text of CD appears to be corrupt, and it is difficult to say for sure that an explicit quotation was here intended. It reads *⟨'mr⟩ lhm bqdš 'lw wršw 't ⟨h'rṣ wybḥrw brṣwn⟩ rwḥm wl' šm'w lqwl 'śyhm*, '⟨He said⟩ to them in Qadesh, "Go up and inherit the ⟨land"; but they chose the desire⟩ of their spirit(s) and did not heed the voice of their Maker'.[25] *Context:* A historical survey of the fidelity of the Patriarchs to the commandments of God and of the infidelity of the sons of Jacob who walked in the stubbornness of their hearts, doing as they pleased, is being given in the *Damascus Document.* As a part of the narrative Dt 9:23 is quoted, obviously in its historical sense.

These are the seven cases which have been found to preserve the literal or historical sense of the Old Testament passage, as they were quoted by the Qumran authors. Similar texts can be found in the New Testament. I shall cite but a few examples. Jn 6:31 quotes Ps 78:24 in a sentence which relates the event of the feeding of the forefathers in the desert with manna. 'Our forefathers in the desert had manna to eat: as the Scripture says, "He gave them bread out of heaven to eat!"' The words of the Psalm are quoted in the same sense which they have in the Old Testament. Again in Jn 10:34 Jesus says, 'Is it not declared in your Law, "I said, 'You are gods!'" ?',[26] when he wants to show that he is not guilty of blasphemy in saying that he is God's Son. It is a mere quotation of the words of the Psalm without any change in meaning. Several clear examples of this usage are also found in Stephen's speech in Acts where he is

[25] See C. Rabin, *op. cit.*, 10.

[26] The Fourth Gospel is here quoting Ps 82:6, where *'lhym* has been interpreted by some scholars to mean 'judges'. However, from the fact that it is parallel to *bny 'lywn*, a good case can be made out for the meaning 'gods'. On this text, see below, pp. 261–2; cf. J. A. Emerton, 'Melchizedek and the Gods: Fresh Evidence for the Jewish Background of John X. 34–36', *JTS XVII* (1966) 399–401.

giving a résumé of Israel's history. 'And he [God] said to him [Abraham], "Leave your country and your relatives and come to the country that I will show you"' (Acts 7:3, quoting Gn 12:1). Or again, 'This is what God said, "His descendants will be strangers, living in a foreign land, and they will be enslaved and misused for four hundred years, and I will sentence the nation that has enslaved them, and afterward they will leave that country and worship me on this spot"' (Acts 7:6–7, quoting Gn 15:13–14). The foregoing New Testament examples are mainly historical and resemble that last quotation (see (7) above) cited from CD.[27] There are, however, also examples in the New Testament in which precepts are quoted from the Old Testament as still valid in the same manner as the Qumran quotations. When Jesus quotes Scripture to Satan in the Temptation scenes, he is made to use it in the same sense (see Mt 4:4; Lk 4:4, quoting Dt 8:3; Mt 4:6; Lk 4:10, quoting Ps 91:11; Mt 4:7; Lk 4:12, quoting Dt 6:16; Mt 4:10; Lk 4:8, quoting Dt 6:13). There is here merely a reaffirmation of what was written earlier. Likewise in the Sermon on the Mount Jesus cites a number of Old Testament precepts, implicitly affirming their validity and sometimes specifying them still further in a way which resembles the Qumran specification (see Mt 5:21, 27, 31, 33, 38, 43).[28]

There are, then, clear examples in both bodies of literature of Old Testament quotations used in the literal or historical sense. In this respect we see the same type of use of the Old Testament in the New Testament and in the Qumran literature.

(B) *The Class of Modernized Texts*

In the second class there is a group of quotations in which the words of the Old Testament refer to a specific event in their

[27] See further Acts 7:37, 49–50; Rom 4:3, 18; 9:15–16; 11:3–4; 1 Cor 10:7; Heb 6:13–14; 9:20.

[28] Further examples of precepts quoted in the New Testament are Mt 15:4; 22:24, 37; Mk 7:10; 12:19, 29; Lk 2:24; 10:27; Rom 7:7; 13:9; Gal 5:14; Jas 2:11.

original context, but which are nevertheless vague enough in themselves to be used by the Qumran author of some new event on the contemporary scene. In other words, the same *general* sense of the Old Testament text is preserved, but it is applied to a new subject. Usually it is the new situation which determines the use of the old Testament text; a situation is found in the Old Testament which is analogous to the new one and the two are linked together by the common element in such wise that the old one sheds light and meaning on the new and invests it with a deeper significance. In some quarters the name *typological* is applied to such use of the Old Testament.[29] However, I have preferred to avoid this name because it is not always univocally used. In this class of quotations one normally finds the Old Testament text quoted in the same way it is found in the original context, without modification or deliberate changing of it. A new reference or a new dimension, however, is given to it in the way it is quoted.

The principle at work in such application of an Old Testament text to a new subject or situation is abundantly attested also in the *pesharim*, and in this regard we find an identical use of the Old Testament both in the commentaries of Qumran and in the isolated explicit quotations. Two passages of the *pesher* on Habakkuk explain the principle which underlies this common type of exegesis of the Old Testament.

> God told Habakkuk to write the things which were to come upon the last generation, but the consummation of the period he did not make known to him. And as for what it says, 'That he may run who reads it', this means the Righteous Teacher, to whom God made known all the mysteries of the words of his servants the prophets (1Q Hab 7:1–5).

The second passage reads:

> This means that the last period extends over and above all that the prophets said, for the mysteries of God are marvellous (1QpHab 7:7–8).

In these two comments we find the recognition of a revelation

[29] Cf. E. E. Ellis, *op. cit.*, 126.

made to the prophet Habakkuk for the last generation, but also of the fact that the words in Habakkuk's oracle transcend the immediate reference of his own day and in the light of the charismatic interpretation of the Righteous Teacher they are now referred to a situation in the time of the Qumran sect.[30] An analogous notion is found in the New Testament, in Rom 15:4, 'For everything that was written in earlier times was written for our instruction, so that by being steadfast and through the encouragement the Scriptures give, we might hold our hope fast'. Or again, 'These things happened to them as a warning to others, but they were written down to instruct us, in whose days the ages have reached their climax' (1 Cor 10:11; cf. Rom 4:23–24). In both groups we find the conviction that they were living in the 'end of days' and that the Old Testament writings have a special pertinence in their time.

There are eleven Qumran passages in which cases of the modernization of an Old Testament passage are found.

(8) *hy' h't 'šr hyh ktwb 'lyh kprh swryrh kn srr yśr'l* (CD 1:13–14, quoting Hos 4:16), 'This is the time about which it was written, "Like a wild heifer, so Israel is wild"'.[31] *Context:* The *Damascus Document* is describing the faithless backsliders of the last generation, obviously of its own time, and it applies to them the description of Israel's apostasy taken from the oracle of Hosea. This is a clear case of an Old Testament text being cited in the same general sense in which it was originally uttered, but merely applied to a new situation. The situation of which the Qumran author writes is thus invested with a new meaning by being associated with the apostate Israel of Hosea's day.

(9) *wbkl hšnym h'lh yhyh bly'l mšwlḥ byśr'l k'šr dbr 'l byd yš'yh hnby' bn 'mwṣ l'mr pḥd wpḥt wpḥ 'lyk ywšb h'rṣ* (CD 4:12–18, quoting Is 24:17), 'And during all those years Belial will be let

[30] See also 1QpHab 2:8–10. F. F. Bruce, *op. cit.*, 7–17, has well analysed this exegetical principle.

[31] M. H. Gottstein (*VT* III [1953] 82) has pointed out that the text of CD, reading *kn*, agrees rather with the Targum and the Peshitta than with MT.

loose against Israel, as God spoke through Isaiah the prophet, the son of Amoz, saying, "Terror and pit and snare are upon you, O inhabitant of the earth"'. *Context:* The *Damascus Document* envisages the years before the consummation of the end-time as a period when Belial is let loose upon the earth with three nets to ensnare the house of Israel; they are allegorized as harlotry, wealth and bringing unclean offerings to the sanctuary. The Old Testament text which is cited is taken from Isaiah's vision of the cataclysm in which the world is to be involved on the day of Judgment (Is 24:1–27:13). The words cited, however, are vague enough to be applied by the writer to the evils of his own time. The only real connection between the Isaian text and the interpretation (which is here called *pšrw*) is the mention of three things: 'Terror, pit and snare'; they become the three nets, and so the evil times in which the sect finds itself living take on the character of the Isaian day of judgment.[32]

(10) *wkl 'šr hwb'w bbryt lblty bw' 'l hmqdš lh'yr mzbḥw ḥnm wyhyw msgyry hdlt 'šr 'mr 'l my bkm ysgwr dltw wl' t'yrw mzbḥy ḥnm 'm l' yšmrw l'śwt kprwš htwrh lqṣ hrš'* (CD 6:11–14, quoting Mal 1:10), 'And all who have been brought into the covenant, (agreeing) not to come to the sanctuary to kindle a fire on his altar in vain, shall become those who have closed the portal, as God said, "Who among you will close its portal and not kindle a fire on my altar in vain?"—unless (it be those who) take care to act according to the explanation of the law for the period of wickedness'.[33] *Context:* This passage refers most likely to the community's abstention from participation in the sacrifices of the Jerusalem temple.[34] Those who entered the covenant

[32] See F. F. Bruce, *op. cit.*, 28; B. J. Roberts, *BJRL* XXXIV (1951–52) 371.

[33] There are two variants in the text of Malachi cited in CD: it omits *gm* after *my*, which is found in MT (see also *dioti kai en hymin* of LXX) and it reads *dltw* instead of MT's *dltym*. If the reading in CD should rather be *dlty*, 'my portals' (confusion of *waw* for *yodh* by the medieval scribe), we would have a better parallel with 'my altar' in the second member.

[34] See pp. 466–7 below.

of the community were regarded as fulfilling the task indicated in the words of Malachi: Yahweh's yearning for someone to close the doors of the temple and to prevent polluted sacrifices from being offered to him. The community by its covenant 'has closed the doors' in withdrawing to the desert to study the Law. The text of Malachi is thus modernized in being applied to the sect's withdrawal from the temple.

(11) *spry htwrh hm swkt k'šr 'mr whqymwty hmlk 't swkt dwd hnplt* (CD 7:15–16, quoting Am 9:11), 'The books of the Law are the hut of the king, as it said, "And I shall raise up the fallen hut of David"'.[35] *Context:* This passage forms part of a larger interpretation given to another passage from Am 5:26–27, where we find the word *skwt*, 'Sakkuth', an astral deity worshipped in Israel in the days of Amos. For that idolatry they were exiled 'beyond Damascus'. In this reference to Damascus the sect of Qumran saw some reference to its own history. But just as the MT wrongly vocalized the operative words here as 'Sikkuth', so too the Qumran commentator misunderstood *skwt*. The translation of *skwt mlkkm* (Am 5:26) in the Greek version as *tēn skēnēn tou Moloch* probably gives us the interpretation of this difficult verse which was current when the *Damascus Document* was composed, for it enables us to see how *skwt* could be related to *swkt dwyd* of Am 9:11. God's promise to raise up the fallen hut of David is seen to be verified in the sect's renewed reverence for the Law. The 'hut of David' is allegorized as the books of the Law and the text of Amos is thereby modernized. The promise of ultimate restoration of Israel which is to follow upon the destruction foreseen by the prophet belongs to what is regarded today as an appendix to Amos' prophecy.

(12) *whkwkb hw' dwrš htwrh hb' dmśq k'šr ktwb drk kwkb my'qb wqm šbṭ myśr'l hšbṭ hw' nśy' kl h'dh wb'mdw wqrqr 't kl bny št* (CD 7:18–21, quoting Nm 24:17), 'And the star is the Interpreter of

[35] MT has the imperfect *'qym*, whereas CD has read the perfect with *waw*-conversive. The latter is also found in the other passage in the Qumran literature which quotes this text from Amos (4QFlor 1-3 ii 11-13): see (40) on p. 50 below.

the Law, who came to Damascus, as it was written, "A star comes forth[36] from Jacob and a sceptre rises from Israel". The sceptre is the prince of the whole congregation, and at his rising "he shatters all the sons of Seth".' *Context:* The history of the sect is being interpreted in terms of Old Testament passages. Two personages in the sect are identified as the star and the sceptre mentioned in the oracle of Balaam, which was often regarded as the promise of a messianic figure. The Qumran writer saw the promise fulfilled in two important figures in his community. In the interpretation and application of this verse to the new situation we find the same technique here which is abundantly attested in the *pesher* on Habakkuk, namely, the use of the third personal pronoun as the copula in a phrase of identification.[37] Moreover, one should note the 'atomization' of the text, which is characteristic of the interpretation found in the *pesharim*, for what may have been intended as the promise of *a* messianic figure in the oracle of Balaam has become here the promise of two figures, the star and the sceptre. This oracle of Balaam was obviously a favourite Old Testament text in the Qumran community, for it occurs at least twice elsewhere: 4QTest 9–13[38] and 1QM 11:5–7 (see (30) below). For all this

[36] The perfect of the verbs is used here and it is difficult to say just what nuance of the perfect the sect saw in them. In view of the fact that this oracle is also quoted in 4QTestimonia 9–13 along with other texts which promise the *future* coming of expected figures, it is quite likely that the perfect should be regarded as the so-called prophetic perfect. It should also be noted that one of the members of the verse is omitted ('and he shatters the temples of Moab').

[37] The same device is also found in the New Testament; see, for example, 1 Cor 10:4; 2 Cor 3:17; Gal 3:16. Cf. 1QpHab 12:3, 4, 7, 9; 4QpPs 37 1:5; 2:12; 4QpIs^b 2:10(?).

[38] In 4QTestimonia the interpretation of this verse is contested. The first paragraph (quoting Dt 5:28–29 and 18:18–19 [or better, Ex 20:21; see below, pp. 82–3]) refers to the coming of a prophet like Moses, the second paragraph (quoting Nm 24:15–17) to the coming Davidic Messiah and another figure, probably a priestly 'Interpreter of the Law', and the third paragraph (quoting Dt 33:8–11) to the coming priestly Messiah. In *T. Levi* 18:3 the oracle of Balaam is applied to the Aaronitic Messiah.

text may have meant to early Christianity (see Justin, *Dial.* 106, 3), it is not cited in the New Testament.

(13) *wypr'w byd rmh llkt bdrk rš'ym 'šr 'mr 'l 'lyhm ḥmt tnynym yynm wr'š ptnym 'kzr htnynym hm mlky h'mym [wyy]nm hw' drkyhm wr'š hptnym hw' r'š mlky ywn hb' l'śwt bhm nqmh* (CD 8:9–12, quoting Dt 32:33), 'And they rebelled high-handedly by walking in the way of the wicked; about them God said, "Their wine is the venom of dragons, the pitiless poison of cobras". The dragons are the kings of the nations; and their wine is their ways and the poison of cobras is the chief of the kings of Greece, who has come to wreak vengeance on them.' *Context:* The text describes the community's enemies from whom it has separated itself, for these preferred to follow the stubbornness of their hearts and to walk rebelliously in the way of the wicked. The enemies are described by the use of a part of the Song of Moses, in which Israel's enemies are depicted and compared to Yahweh and his people. The text is thus modernized by being applied to a new enemy of Israel. Once again there are atomized comments on certain words of the verse of Deuteronomy, and there is a play on the words *r'š* meaning 'head, chief' and *r'š* meaning 'poison'. Both of these features are found in the exegesis of 1QpHab.

(14) *w'šr 'mr mšh l' bṣdqtk wbyšr lbbk 'th b' lršt 't hgwym h'lh ky m'hbtw 't 'bwtk wmšmrw 't hšbw'h wkn hmšpṭ lšby yśr'l* (CD 8:14–16, quoting Dt 9:5), 'And as for what Moses said, "It is not because of your righteousness nor because of the uprightness of your heart that you are entering to inherit (the land of) these nations, but rather because he loved your fathers and he has kept the oath". So is the case with those who return in Israel . . . .'[39] *Context:* This passage stresses the idea that those who have joined the community, having turned from the impiety of Israel and forsaken the way of the people, are not to think that they have done this by any merit of their own; it is rather due

[39] The first part of this quotation agrees with MT; the last part, however, is dependent on Dt 7:8, but is not introduced as an explicit quotation.

to God's love of their forefathers and the oath which he swore to them. The words of Moses which are quoted are taken from his second discourse, addressed to Israel when it was about to cross the Jordan. Though the two situations are not parallel, there is a common element which permits the words of Moses to be applied to the new situation. (See the use of the same text in CD 19:26.)

(15) *kk šwmr hbryt whḥsd l'hb⟨yw⟩ wlšmrw mṣwty⟨w⟩ l'lp dwr* (CD 19:1, quoting Dt 7:9), 'As it was written, "(He) keeps the covenant and mercy for ⟨those⟩ who love ⟨him⟩ and for those who keep ⟨his⟩ commandments for a thousand generations"'.[40] *Context:* The passage announces that all those who enter the new covenant and perfect themselves in the observance of the ordinances of the community will find that God is faithful to the covenant and to them for a thousand generations. Once again a part of Moses' second discourse is cited in which the election of Israel and Yahweh's divine favour toward it are made known. The *Damascus Document* modernizes the text in applying it to the new situation of the community.

(16) *hw'h hbyt 'šr [y'śh] l[k b']ḥryt hymym k'šr ktwb bspr [mwšh mqdš 'dwny k]wnnw ydykh Yhwh ymlwk 'wlm w'd hw'h hbyt 'šr lw' ybw' šmh* (4QFlor 1:2–3, quoting Ex 15:17b–18), 'That is the house which [He will make for] you [in the] end of days, as it was written in the book of [Moses, "A sanctuary, O Lord,] your hands have [e]rected, Yahweh will reign for ever and ever". That is the house to which there will not come [. . . .'[41] *Context:* This Old Testament quotation is used within what appears to be the commentary of a *pesher* or *midrash* on 2 Sm 7:10 ff.[42] After the verse from 2 Samuel has been quoted, the

[40] The text of CD is obviously corrupt here, reading *l'hb* and *mṣwtyy*, neither of which makes any sense. I have accordingly corrected them to agree with MT.

[41] The restoration of the lacunae follows that of Y. Yadin, *IEJ* IX (1959) 95–8. The latter part of the comment contains an allusion to Dt 23:3–4 and Ez 44:9.

[42] See above, p. 7, n. 8.

commentary begins and brings in as part of its comment a verse from the national anthem of ancient Israel (sometimes called the Song of Miriam). In the Exodus context Yahweh has brought his people into his inheritance where he will reign forever. 4QFlor now quotes this verse, applying it to the Qumran community, which is the new Israel, the new 'house'. The modernization of the verse of Exodus is presented as intended by God for 'the end of days'. The Qumran sect thought that it was living already in that period; but if that existence should rather be regarded as something still in the future, then possibly this example belongs to the class of eschatological quotations in class D.

(17) *pšr hdb[r 'šr] srw mdrk [h'm] 'šr ktwb bspr yš'yh hnby' l'ḥryt hymym wyhy kḥzqt [hyd wysyrny mlkt bdrk] h'm hzh* (4QFlor 1:14–16, quoting Is 8:11), 'The interpretation of the passage (is about those) who turned away from the path of the people, (about) whom it was written in the Book of Isaiah the prophet for the end of days, And it was "while he grasped me by [the hand that he turned me aside from the path] of this people"'.[43] *Context:* This is the beginning of the commentary on Ps 1:1, 'Happy is the man who walks not in the counsel of the wicked'. As part of the commentary, Is 8:11 is quoted, a verse from the 'Book of Emmanuel', oracles which pertain to the Syro-Ephraimite war and the first Assyrian invasion. According to Isaiah, Yahweh is with his people to turn them aside from the path of the terrifying invaders. 4QFlor quotes the text, which is vague enough to be modernized and applied to the situation in the 'end of days'.

(18) *whmh 'šr ktwb 'lyhmh bspr yḥzq'l hnby' 'šr lw[' yṭm'w 'wd bg]lwlyhmh hmh bny ṣdwq w['n]šy 'ṣ[t]w rw[* . . . (4QFlor 1:16–17, quoting Ez 37:23), 'And they are the ones about whom it was written in the book of Ezekiel the prophet, who "will no [longer

[43] The reconstruction offered here is that of Y. Yadin (*op. cit.*, 96), which is based on MT. It should be noted, however, that the text of 4QFlor, in so far as it is preserved, agrees rather with 1QIs[a], which differs from MT somewhat, *kḥzqt yd ysyrny*.

defile themselves with] their [i]dols". They are the sons of Zadok and the men of His council. . . .'[44] *Context:* The continuation of the commentary on Ps 1:1 identifies those who turned aside from the way of the people, the 'happy ones' of Ps 1:1, as the sons of Zadok, the members of the community. They are the ones about whom Ezekiel wrote. The words of the prophet were part of a promise to unite Israel and Judah again in one kingdom in the days when they will not defile themselves with idols and abominable practices. They are here referred to a new situation which is found in the Qumran community.

There are, then, eleven instances in which the Old Testament texts have been quoted and related by Qumran authors to contemporary events or the situation in which they lived. In most cases the situation itself already existed and it was enhanced with special meaning because of a similarity or an analogy which they saw between it and some Old Testament situation. There is little doubt that they believed that their own history was guided by the hand of God and that these similarities or analogies were somehow intended by him.[45]

The New Testament too has similar groups of texts in which one finds the Old Testament modernized. No less than the

[44] We are again following the reconstruction of the text suggested by Y. Yadin, *ibid.* He has more correctly identified the text of Ezekiel as 37:23 than Allegro, who proposed 44:10.

[45] Modernization of the prophet's text is very frequent in 1QpHab, as might be expected (see 1:5, 6, 7, 8, 9, 10*c–d*, 11, 13*c–d*, 14–15, 16*a–b*, 17; 2:2*d*, 5–6, 8*a*, 12–13, 15, 16, 17). Cf. E. Osswald, *op. cit.*, 247 ff.—I am touching here on an acute modern hermeneutical problem. As far as I am concerned, the interpretation of any Old Testament text should be one that a Jew and a Christian could work out and agree on, from the standpoint of philology, exegesis, and Old Testament biblical theology. I see no reason why a Jewish synthesis of Old Testament theology would be *radically* different from a Christian synthesis. To admit this is not to deny the 'harmony of the Testaments', nor to abandon one's Christian heritage. Nor is it said merely to be irenic. The Christian interpretation of the Old Testament must begin with that which a Jewish interpreter, writing with the empathy of his own heritage and a recognition of the value of modern historical, critical interpretation of the Bible, would set forth. The difference between the Jewish and the Christian interpretation of the Old Testament lies not in the primary literal sense of

Qumran authors, the New Testament writers considered their history to be guided by the hand of God. But for the New Testament authors his word spoken through the prophets and writers of the Old Testament had already seen fulfilment in the new events and situations of the early Christian history. Due to the predominantly backward glance of the New Testament writers, which we have already noted, the number of such modernized texts in the New Testament is considerably greater. While some commentators prefer to regard the fulfilment quotations in the New Testament as literal realizations of prophecy, I believe that most of them belong more properly in this group of modernized texts. For the words cited usually have a specific reference in their Old Testament context. The new reference which they acquire in the New Testament is due to the application of those words to a new situation by the New Testament writer—a God-directed situation, whose meaning for the Christian community is enhanced by the significance of the previous divine intervention. I am not trying to deny that the New Testament writer regarded the new event as a fulfilment of what was uttered of old; he explicitly says so. But what does he mean by it? Cognizance must be taken of the fact that

---

the Old Testament text (arrived at with the same philological, historical, and literary critical means), but in the plus value that the Old Testament takes on when it becomes part of the Christian Bible. One may call this a fuller dimension that the Hebrew Scriptures have because of their relation to the book of the Christian community. This fuller sense is one which a Christian interpreter would not expect a Jewish reader to accept. But it is at the same time one which the Jewish reader, with his keen sense of God's providence, must also learn to live with. If twentieth-century Christians have not worked out for themselves a 'theology of Israel' (how it is that God in his providence has permitted the Jewish people to survive and maintain its corporate religious identity, despite the fact that Christianity's first theologian characterized them as 'a disobedient and contrary people' [RSV, Rom 10:21, adapting Is 65:2]), similarly Jews of the twentieth century have scarcely reckoned sufficiently with the historical dimension of their existence in a culture which has developed largely in a belief that Yahweh, the God of Israel, intervened again in man's history in the person, life, and career of Jesus of Nazareth. This cultural problem underlies the hermeneutical problem briefly sketched above.

the Old Testament passage which he quotes usually has a more immediate, literal reference which cannot be simply ignored.

For instance, when Matthew (4:15–16) cites the words of Isaiah (8:23–9:1): 'Zebulon's land, and Naphtali's land, along the road to the sea, across the Jordan, Galilee of the heathen! The people that were living in darkness have seen a great light, and on those who were living in the land of the shadow of death a light has dawned', he introduces them thus: 'And he left Nazareth and went and settled in Capernaum, by the sea, in the district of Zebulon and Naphtali, in fulfilment of what was said by the prophet Isaiah. . . .' The words quoted from the prophet belong to the Emmanuel oracle and in their original context refer to the liberation to come after the Assyrian conquest. But the great light of which the prophet spoke could also carry a further meaning, which it acquires in the use of it by Matthew, who applies it to the Galilean ministry of Christ.[46]

When Luke (4:16–21) records the episode of Christ's reading from the scroll of Isaiah in the synagogue of Nazareth, he quotes Is 61:1–2. Jesus' commentary on it begins: 'This passage of Scripture has been fulfilled here in your hearing today!' New meaning is given to those words of Isaiah by the event taking place—a new meaning which has little to do with the original context in which the words are understood either of the Servant of Yahweh or of Deutero-Isaiah himself. But they are expressed in a general enough way so that they could be used of the New Testament situation.

Similarly, when Paul writes, 'As God's fellow-worker, I appeal to you, too, not to accept the favour of God and then waste it. For he says, "I have listened to you at a welcome time, and helped you on a day of deliverance!" Now the welcome time has come' (2 Cor 6:1–2, quoting Is 49:8). Paul here quotes the words of Deutero-Isaiah, which refer immediately to the return from exile, but which are general enough to be applied to his

[46] Further examples in Matthew: 8:17; 11:10; 13:35; 15:8; 21:42.

own preaching and apostolic activity among the Corinthians. Further examples of this use of the Old Testament texts in the New Testament could easily be cited; those already mentioned suffice to show the existence of them.[47]

(C) *Accommodated Texts*

Akin to the second class of Old Testament quotations is another group, which has in common with the foregoing the application of the text to a new situation or subject. However, it differs in this that the Old Testament text in this case is usually wrested from its original context or modified somehow to suit the new situation. I have included here the instances in which the Old Testament text appears somewhat confused when compared with the existing Hebrew and Greek recensions, although it is admittedly not easy to determine in each case whether mere textual corruption has occurred or a different recension was used.

Twelve passages are found in the Qumran literature in which accommodations of the Old Testament texts have been made.

(19) *ky' yrḥq mmnw bkwl dbr ky' kn ktwb mkwl dbr šqr trḥq* (1QS 5:15, quoting Ex 23:7), 'But he shall keep far away from him in everything, for so it was written, "From everything deceitful you must withdraw"'. *Context:* The community's rule-book prescribes that the member must avoid all contact with the impure, wicked outsider. As support for this prescription, it cites Ex 13:7, a text which actually has to do with law-suits and social conduct: 'You must not pervert the justice due to your poor in his case. Avoid false charges; do not have innocent and guiltless persons put to death, nor acquit the wicked.' The phrase, 'avoid false charges', contains in Hebrew the word *dbr*, which also has the generic meaning of 'thing', and so the *Manual*

[47] See further Lk 22:37; Jn 12:38; 13:18; 19:24; Acts 3:25; 13:33–34; Rom 9:29; 10:15–16; 15:21; 2 Cor 6:2; Heb 1:5, 8–9, 10–12, 13; 3:7–11; 4:3, 7; 5:6; 8:8–12; 10:16–18.

of Discipline was able to quote the phrase without any regard to its original judicial context and apply it to the question of contact with wicked outsiders. The possibility of so using the text was probably also due to the fact that the Hebrew text cited contains the indefinite pronoun *kwl* (thus agreeing with the Septuagint's *apo pantos rhēmatos adikou* rather than with MT which omits it).[48] We have, then, in this instance a clear case of the accommodation of the Old Testament verse to a new situation, in which the original context is wholly disregarded.

(20) *k'šr ktwb ḥdlw lkm mn h'dm 'šr nšmh b'pw ky' bmh nḥšb hw'h ky' kwl 'šr lw' nḥšbw bbrytw lhbdyl 'wtm w't kwl 'šr lhm* (1QS 5:17–18, quoting Is 2:22), 'As it was written, "Desist from the man whose breath is in his nostrils, for by what can he be reckoned?" For all who are not reckoned in his covenant, they and all they have are to be excluded.' *Context:* This text continues the prohibition of contact with the wicked outsider begun in the previous passage. Here the *Manual of Discipline* quotes a text of Isaiah, actually a gloss, in which the writer counsels the people to cease trusting in the proud man, 'Cease trusting a man in whose nostrils is breath, for of what account is he?' The Qumran author twists the sense of the verb *nḥšb* to carry the meaning of 'being reckoned in the covenant' of the community, and so uses it to support the prohibition of contact with wicked outsiders. The warning of Isaiah has been turned into a sort of precept about an entirely different matter.

(21) *llkt lmdbr lpnwt šm 't drk hw'h' k'šr ktwb bmdbr pnw drk .... yšrw b'rbh mslh l'lwhynw hw'h mdrš htwrh* ['*šr*] *ṣwh byd mwšh l'śwt kkwl hnglh 't b't wk'šr glw hnby'ym brwḥ qwdšw* (1QS 8:13–16, quoting Is 40:3), '... to go into the desert to prepare there the way of Him, as it was written, "In the desert make ready the way of ...., make straight in the wilderness a highway for our God". This is the study of the Law which he commanded through Moses to be done according to all that was revealed from time to time and according to what the prophets revealed

[48] As was pointed out by M. H. Gottstein, *op. cit.*, 79.

through his holy spirit.'[49] *Context:* The *Manual of Discipline* is expressing the desert mystique of the community, which withdrew from the abodes of the men of deceit to go into the wilderness to relive there the experience of their forefathers in the desert. The motivation for this withdrawal is derived from Is 40:3, which is actually part of the Book of the Consolation of Israel. There, according to some interpreters, it is Yahweh who calls to his prophet, but more likely it is the voice of a herald which cries. Yahweh is going to put himself at the head of his people and lead them to freedom from exile across the desert, as he had done at the Exodus from Egypt into the Promised Land. But the Qumran author interprets the verse in a very specific way, disregarding the historical context; the preparation of the way of the Lord in the desert motivated the community's retreat into the wilderness of Qumran to live lives in perfect conformity with the Law and the utterances of the prophets, the study of which was their main occupation. This is an accommodated use of the Isaian verse. The same text is used in the New Testament about John the Baptist by all four evangelists (Mt 3:3; Mk 1:3; Lk 3:4–6; Jn 1:23), in a form which is closer to the Septuagint than to the Hebrew. Here we find an almost identical use of the text, for the apparent reason in citing it is to explain John's presence in the desert of Judah, where he is preaching and baptizing. Admittedly, the abrupt beginning of the Gospel of Mark makes it almost impossible to discern the motive in the use of the Isaian text, but in Matthew and Luke the connection between John and the *phōnē boōntos* is made explicit, 'It was he who was spoken of by the prophet Isaiah, when he said . . .'. The linking of *en tē erēmō* with *phōnē boōntos*, as in the Septuagint, is part of the reason why the verse could be applied to John in the desert. Hence, in both the Qumran and the New Testament contexts the sense of the original has been dis-

[49] Except for the four dots instead of the Tetragrammaton the quotation agrees with the text of the Masoretes. 1QIs[a], however, reads *wyšrw* instead of *yšrw*.

regarded, in that there is no longer a reference to Yahweh at the head of his people returning from exile, and the text is used to explain the presence of the community and of John in the desert.[50]

(22) *wkl kbwd ʾdm lhm hwʾ kʾšr hqym ʾl lhm byd yḥzqʾl hnbyʾ lʾmr hkhnym whlwym wbny ṣdwq ʾšr šmrw ʾt mšmrt mqdšy btʿwt bny yśrʾl mʿly hm ygyšw ly ḥlb wdm* (CD 3:20–4:2, quoting Ez 44:15), 'And all the glory of Adam is theirs, as God swore to them through Ezekiel the prophet, saying, "The priests and the levites and the sons of Zadoq who have kept charge of my sanctuary when the children of Israel went astray from me, they shall bring me fat and blood"'. *Context:* In this passage the *Damascus Document* is explaining that when God pardoned the impiety of Israel and made his covenant with it—that is, established the Zadoqite community at Qumran—he destined it for eternal life and all the glory of Adam. This community was made up of priests, levites and the sons of Zadoq, whose lot it would be to minister to Yahweh in the end of days. As part of this explanation the text of Ezekiel is cited in which the promise is made that Yahweh will be served by 'the levitical priests, sons of Zadoq'. However, in quoting this text of Ezekiel, the *Damascus Document* inserts the conjunction 'and' twice, so that the phrase becomes 'the priests and the levites and the sons of Zadoq', probably with the intention of including in such an expression all the members of the community. There is here an accommodation of the text of Ezekiel, which consists in a deliberate manipulation of the text in order to suit the purpose of the passage in which it is quoted.[51]

(23) Perhaps one of the most striking cases of accommodation which occurs in the Qumran literature is found in the following passage, in which four Old Testament passages are used. It also has a striking parallel in the New Testament. *bwny*

[50] Cf. C. F. D. Moule, *NTS* XIV (1967–68) 294, n. 1, for a rather different interpretation of this use of Isaiah.

[51] See the similar interpretation of F. F. Bruce, *op. cit.*, 31.

hḥwṣ ʾšr hlkw ʾḥry ṣw hṣw hwʾ mṭyp ʾšr ʾmr hṭp yṭypwn hm nytpśym bštym bznwt lqḥt šty nšym bḥyyhm wyswd hbryʾh zkr wnqbh brʾ ʾwtm wbʾy htbh šnym šnym bʾw ʾl htbh wʿl hnśyʾ ktwb lʾ yrbh lw nšym wdwyd lʾ qrʾ bspr htwrh hḥtwm (CD 4:19–5:2, quoting Mi 2:6; Gn 1:27; 7:9; Dt 17:17), 'The builders of the wall—who have walked after Zaw (Zaw is a preacher, as it said, "They must indeed preach")—are those caught in two ways: in harlotry, by marrying two women in their lifetime, whereas the principle of creation is: "Male and female he created them", and "those who entered the ark went into the ark by twos"; and concerning the prince it was written, "Let him not multiply wives unto himself". But David had not read the sealed book of the Law....'

Context: The meaning of the first part of this passage is not clear. The passage itself forms part of the explanation of the three nets of Belial, which was cited earlier (see (9) above), but just who the 'builders of the wall' are is obscure. They are said to have walked after a mysterious *Zaw*, a 'preacher'. He is described in terms of a verse of Micah (2:6). In its original context this verse describes the people's protests against the prophet's threats, which they believe are contrary to the traditional faith in the alliance with Yahweh: *ʾl-tṭpw yṭypwn lʾ-yṭpw lʾlh*, '"Do not keep on harping", they harp; "One should not be harping upon such things"'. Explicitly introduced as a quotation in CD, this becomes *hṭp yṭypwn*, 'They must indeed preach'. If the text is sound, then we have a deliberate manipulation of the prophet's words, first of all by the omission of the negative, and secondly by the complete disregard of the context. But the accommodation of the sense of a text is still more evident in the next two verses from Genesis which are cited to support the prohibition of polygamy (which is the net of 'fornication' let loose by Belial). One does not have here the characteristic introductory formulae, but the intention to quote Scripture is evident from the use of the texts which are cited as the 'principle of creation'. As proof against polygamy CD quotes the description of the creation of man in the image of God from Gn 1:27 (in which passage there is really no reference to monogamous marriage) and the story of the entrance of the animals into Noah's ark *in pairs* from Gn 7:9. This is rounded off by an Old Testament text which forbids the prince a multiplicity of wives, a text which has some pertinence in the context in which it is used. Now there is the almost identical use of the first text from Genesis (1:27) in the New Testament, in this case joined to Gn 2:24 ('That is why a man leaves his father and mother, and clings to his wife, so that they form one flesh'), as the scriptural support for the prohibition of divorce. Indeed, in Mk 10:6 the quotation is introduced by the words, 'From the beginning of creation', which certainly resembles the 'principle of creation' phrase of the *Damascus Document*.[52] In both cases, then, there is a description of man in the image of God ('male and female he created them') cited in support of a notion which actually goes beyond the immediate intention of the verse in Genesis.

(24) *wlwqḥym 'yš 't bt 'ḥyhw w't bt 'ḥwtw wmšh 'mr 'l 'ḥwt 'mk l' tqrb š'r 'mk hy'* (CD 5:7–9, quoting Lv 18:13), 'And they marry each man the daughter of his brother and the daughter of his sister, whereas Moses said, "You shall not approach your mother's sister, she is your mother's kin"'.[53] *Context:* This passage describes the second of the two ways the 'builders of the wall' are caught in the net of harlotry, namely, by marriage between an uncle and his niece. But to prevent such marriages the author of CD invokes a text of Leviticus which actually forbids the marriage of a man with his *aunt*. The marriage of a man with his niece is not explicitly forbidden in the Leviticus passage on forbidden degrees of kinship (18:6 ff.), but the Qumran author extends the legislation by analogy, which we must recognize as a sort of accommodation of the text cited.[54]

[52] Cf. Mt 19:4. See the similar explanation of F. F. Bruce, *op. cit.*, 29. Cf. D. Daube, *The New Testament and Rabbinic Judaism* (Jordan Lectures in Comparative Religion II; London, 1956) 71–85.

[53] The text in CD agrees neither with MT (*'rwt 'ḥwt-'mk l' tglh ky-š'r 'mk hw'*) nor with LXX. Possibly CD has preserved a different Hebrew recension here.

[54] Cf. F. F. Bruce, *op. cit.*, 28 for a similar explanation.

(25) *wyšmyʿm wyḥpwrw ʾt hbʾr bʾr ḥprwh śrym krwh ndyby hʿm bmḥwqq hbʾr hyʾ htwrh wḥwpryh hm šby yśrʾl hywṣʾym mʾrṣ yhwdh wygwrw bʾrṣ dmśq ʾšr qrʾ ʾl ʾt kwlm śrym ky dršwhw wlʾ hwšbh pʾrtm bpy ʾḥd whmḥwqq hwʾ dwrš htwrh ʾšr ʾmr yšʿyh mwṣyʾ kly lmʿśyhw wndyby hʿm hm hbʾym lkrwt ʾt hbʾr bmḥwqqwt ʾšr ḥqq hmḥwqq lhthlk bmh bkl qṣ hršyʿ wzwltm lʾ yśygw ʿd ʿmd ywrh hṣdq bʾḥryt hymym* (CD 6:3–11, quoting Nm 21:18 and Is 54:16), 'And he caused them to listen, and they dug the well, "a well which princes dug, which the nobles of the people sunk with a tool". The well is the Law and those who dug it are the converts of Israel, who went out of the land of Judah and sojourned in the land of Damascus, all of whom God called princes, for they sought him and their glory was not withdrawn (?) on the lips of anyone. And the tool is the Interpreter of the Law, as Isaiah said, "Who bringeth forth a tool for his work". And the nobles of the people are those who have come to dig the well with the tools which the lawgiver set up, to walk according to them in the whole period of wickedness and without which they will not succeed, until there rises one who teaches righteousness in the end of days.' *Context:* In this passage God, remembering the covenant which he had made with the forefathers of Israel, raised up men of understanding from both Aaron and Israel, who dug the well of the Torah. CD applies to the Torah Israel's Song of the Well, found in Nm 21:18, where it refers to a well in the desert provided by Yahweh for his thirsty people. A completely allegorical meaning is given to the well in the CD context, without any reference to the original context of the song.[55] The second text which is quoted comes from Is 54:16, which is part of Deutero-Isaiah's description of the future glory of Jerusalem. Yahweh, consoling Israel in her tribulation from

[55] The meaning of 'staff' which is usually employed for *mḥwqq* in this passage can hardly be correct. Aside from the fact that the digging of a well with a staff is rather peculiar, the rapprochement of the two texts (Nm 21:18 and Is 54:16) here suggests that the author of CD understood *mḥwqq* in the same sense as *kly*, hence our translation 'tool'. In MT *bmšʿntm* may well be a gloss; cf. LXX. It is difficult to say what the connecting link between

outside enemies, makes it known that it is he who has made the smith who produces the tool or weapon suited to its work; hence he shall not permit any weapon forged against Israel to succeed. CD quotes this verse completely out of its context, relating to it the 'tool' of the former quotation from Numbers, for the word *mḥwqq* can have two meanings, 'a tool', as in Nm 21:18, and 'a lawmaker', as in Gn 49:10, which obviously led to its allegorization as the 'Interpreter of the Law'. So he becomes the tool brought forth by Yahweh and suited for *his* work, for a task ordained by Yahweh. The verse of Isaiah thus quoted is used with complete disregard of its original context.

(26) *k'šr 'mr whglyty 't skwt mlkkm w't kywn ṣlmykm m'hly dmśq* (CD 7:14–15, quoting Am 5:26–27), 'As it said, "I shall exile Sikkuth your king and Kiyyun your images from the tents of Damascus"'. *Context:* This is one of four quotations in a passage to which I have referred earlier. In it we are told that when the two houses of Israel, Ephraim and Judah, separated, those who were turned back were put to the sword, but those who remained firm escaped to the land of the north, as it said. . . . CD looks upon a certain event in the history of the community as fulfilling this utterance of Amos. The text of Amos is somewhat different. First of all, it seems evident from what I have said earlier (see (11) above) that the author of CD did not understand what Sakkuth and Kewan were, i.e., astral deities worshipped by idolatrous Israelites. Secondly, the text of Amos has been somewhat telescoped. His words were: 'But you have carried around Sakkuth, your king, and Kewan, your images, the star of your god, which you have made for yourselves, so I will carry you into exile beyond Damascus.' This form of the text, taken from the Masoretic Bible, actually fits the context in

---

the well and the Torah was in the passage. According to W. H. Brownlee (*BA* XIV [1951] 56), the link was the Hebrew radicals *b'r* which could be vocalized as *beʾēr*, 'a well', or as *bēʾēr*, 'he explained', as in Dt 1:5. He also saw a connection between *krwt*, 'to dig', and *krt*, 'to cut; form (a covenant)'. F. F. Bruce (*op. cit.*, 31), on the other hand, saw a connection in the 'obvious appropriateness of pure water as a figure of sound doctrine'.

CD better than the form cited there. For the commentary continues to speak about the 'star', explained in terms of Nm 24:17 (see (12) above), but the 'star' does not appear in the form of the Amos text cited in CD. This may be due, of course, to some corruption in the transmission of the text of CD. At any rate, as B. J. Roberts has already pointed out:

The source is Am 5:26 f., but the context of the original is wholly disregarded, and terms of offensive associations are correlated to personalities with the highest possible prestige. Thus Torah is represented by Sikkuth, a pagan astral deity-king, and—even if this happened through ignorance and the connection with the festival *par excellence* of all Jews was made by false etymology and a change of vocalization—there is still greater incongruity in the subsequent correlation of obnoxious idols with the spurned prophets and their ignored oracles, and again, of an astral deity with the Messianic 'Star of Jacob'. . . . The significance in each instance lies in the 'key-words': they are symbols of historical events, but these are only intimated as fulfilments of the uttered oracle, and do not of themselves offer the means of reconstructing a historical account. Such a reconstruction is rendered still more difficult by the obvious dissociation of the interpretation from the context of the original oracle.[56]

If the text is sound, the use made of the Old Testament quotation can only be classed as one of accommodation. One finds a rather different use of this passage in Acts 7:42–43, where Stephen uses it in his historical résumé of Israel's infidelity, citing it as an example of what happened to Israel because of her idolatry. He thus uses the text in a way which is far more faithful to the original context than does the author of CD.

(27) *'l y'l 'yš lmzbḥ bšbt ky 'm 'wlt hšbt ky kn ktwb mlbd šbtwtykm* (CD 11:17–18, quoting Lv 23:38), 'Let no one offer (anything) on the altar on the Sabbath except the burnt-offering of the Sabbath, for thus it was written, "apart from your Sabbath-offerings"'. *Context:* As part of the regulations made to enforce the Old Testament law of observance of the Sabbath, CD proscribes the offering of anything except the Sabbath holocaust.

[56] *BJRL* XXXIV (1951–52) 373.

However, in its use of Lv 23:38 it completely disregards the sense of the original. The words quoted occur at the end of a list of festivals and their sacrifices; it is stated that the latter are to take place each on its proper day in addition to the Sabbaths of the Lord, the gifts, votive-offerings and voluntary offerings. The words are quoted in CD, however, with a different sense given to *mlbd*, which no longer means 'besides, in addition to', but 'except'. The words are thus wrested from their original context and used to serve the purpose of the author of the *Damascus Document*.

(28) *ky ktwb zbḥ rš'ym tw'bh wtplt ṣdqm kmnḥt rṣwn* (CD 11:20–21, quoting Prv 15:8), 'For it was written, "The sacrifice of the wicked is an abomination but the prayer of the righteous is like a delightful offering"'.[57] The *Damascus Document* here forbids the sending of an offering to the sanctuary through the intermediary of a man afflicted with any uncleanness, thus empowering him to convey uncleanness to the altar. In support of this prohibition Prv 15:8 is cited, but with a change in the meaning of the text. For in its original context it is a proverb referring to moral wickedness in contrast to righteousness; here, however, the question of moral evil is disregarded and the verse is cited to forbid the use of an unclean man as the bearer of a gift to the altar.

(29) *['l] yqdš 'yš 't m'kl p[yhw l']l ky hw' 'šr 'mr 'yš 't r'yhw yṣ[w]dw ḥrm* (CD 16:14–15, quoting Mi 7:2), 'Let no one declare holy to God the food of his mouth, for that is what it said, 'Each traps his neighbour with a vow"'. *Context:* This is a prohibition of the dedication of any food to God so that it might not be used to help one's neighbour. In support of this prohibition, Mi 7:2 is cited, again with complete disregard of the sense of the original context. Micah is describing the moral collapse of Israel: 'The godly has perished from the land, and there is none righteous among men. They all lie in wait for

[57] This agrees with neither MT nor LXX completely; possibly a different recension of the verse is here preserved.

blood; each hunts his brother with a net.' The last part of this verse contains the Hebrew word *ḥrm*, which in Micah means a 'snare, trap', but in CD has been understood in the sense of 'something consecrated, dedicated, removed from profane use'. This play on the word is responsible for the accommodation of the text.

(30) *wlw' kwḥnw w'ṣwm ydynw 'śh ḥyl ky' bkwḥkh wb'wz ḥylkh hgdwl k'*[*šr*] *hgdth lnw m'z l'mwr drk kwkb my'qwb qm šbṭ myśr'l wmḥṣ p'ty mw'b w*qrqr kwl bny šyt wyrd my'qwb wh'byd śryd* [*m*]*'yr whyh 'wyb yršh wyśr'l 'śh ḥyl* (1QM 11:5–7, quoting Nm 24:17–19), 'Nor has our strength or the might of our hands done valiantly, but it is by your strength and the power of your great might, as you declared to us of old, saying, "A star comes forth out of Jacob, a sceptre rises from Israel; and it crushes the fore-heads of Moab and breaks down all the sons of Seth; and it goes down from Jacob to destroy the remnant of the city and the enemy is dispossessed and Israel acts valiantly"'.[58] *Context:* This is part of the discourse of the High Priest before the eschatological battle, when he encourages the troops to fight valiantly. However, they are to remember that any success will not be due to them but to the promise of victory which he finds in the oracle of Balaam. The promise of messianic figures, which is the normal understanding of the verse,[59] is here completely set aside in the new context of encouragement.

The twelve passages from Qumran literature, which have been examined, contain sixteen Old Testament quotations, all of which manifest a loose application of the Old Testament verse to a new situation with either a manipulation of the text itself or a complete disregard for the original context. The accommodation was often made by the adoption of another meaning which the same Hebrew radicals could support, by giving the words an allegorical meaning, by atomizing the sense

[58] See above, p. 26. This text is also cited in (12). For a discussion of the form of the text used here and a comparison with MT and versions, see J. Carmignac, *RB* LXIII (1956) 238.

[59] See pp. 82–4 below.

of the Old Testament expression or by omitting words (for example, negatives).[60]

It has long been recognized that there are Old Testament quotations in the New Testament, which appear to be based on the literal sense of the original text, but which give it an extension of meaning that it did not have in its original context. Such quotations are not always introduced in the New Testament as a sort of proof, but often merely as an illustration—a distinction which we should also admit in certain cases in the Qumran literature. A clear case of the accommodation of a text in the New Testament is furnished by Mt 12:32, where Jesus, speaking to the Sadducees about the resurrection of the dead, is presented as asking them, 'Did you never read what was said to you by God, "I am the God of Abraham, the God of Isaac, and the God of Jacob"? He is not the God of dead men but of living!' To confute the Sadducees, Christ quoted Ex 3:6 (or 15, 16). But in this passage there is certainly no reference at all to the resurrection of the dead; and L. Venard remarks, 'L'idée de la survivance des patriarches . . . dépasse le sens primitif direct de ce passage'.[61] In fact, it is the same type of disregard for the original context which we found so frequently in the Qumran passages listed above.

Paul, writing frequently in the rhetorical style of a preacher, often fails to take into consideration the original context of the Old Testament and twists the quotation which he uses to his own purpose. For instance, in Rom 2:23–24 he says to the Jew, 'Will you boast of the law and yet dishonour God by breaking it? For, as the Scripture says, "The very name of God is abused among the heathen because of you"' (Is 52:5). Paul is here quoting the fuller text of the Septuagint; but in any case the meaning of the original is that at the time of the Babylonian captivity God's name was despised among the Gentiles because

[60] Similar devices have been found also in the *pesher* on Habakkuk; see the list in W. H. Brownlee, *BA* XIV (1951) 60–2.

[61] 'Citations de l'Ancien Testament dans le Nouveau Testament', *VDBS* II, 43.

fortune had turned against the Israelites, and it looked as though Israel's God was impotent to help or rescue them and thus on their account God's name was continually blasphemed. In Paul's context, however, the name of Yahweh is an object of blasphemy among the Gentiles who see that the Jews boast of the Law but do not observe it and hence spurn the will of God. This is obviously a free adaptation of the text of Isaiah, which goes beyond the original sense of it. Paul likewise indulges in a play on words in order to bring in an Old Testament text, when he applies Dt 21:23 to the crucified Christ. 'Christ ransomed us from the Law's curse by taking our curse upon himself (for the Scripture says, "Cursed be anyone who is hung on a tree") in order that the blessing given to Abraham might through Jesus Christ reach the heathen.' The only connection here between the verse of Deuteronomy and the Pauline use of it is the double pun of the Law's curse and the word 'cursed' and the crucifixion of Christ and 'hung on a tree'. The orator Paul is the one who makes the connection by putting them together. Again in Eph 4:8 he atomizes the sense of the text in quoting Ps 68:19, 'So it says, "When he went up on high, he led a host of captives, and gave gifts to mankind". What does "he went up" mean, except that he had first gone down to the under parts of the earth? It is he who went down who has also gone up above all the heavens, to fill the universe.' Here Paul completely disregards the original context of the Psalm in order to retain only the words 'he went up' and 'he gave'.

Further examples could easily be cited to illustrate many of the same devices which are found in the Qumran literature. These can be found in the lists which L. Venard and J. Bonsirven have supplied.[62]

[62] *Ibid.*; J. Bonsirven, *op. cit.*, 320 ff. See especially J. Schmid, 'Die alttestamentlichen Zitate bei Paulus und die Theorie vom sensus plenior', *BZ* III (1959) 161–73, where the instances from Paul's letters which are discussed give numerous examples of this use of Scripture.

(D) *The Eschatological Class of Texts*

The last group of Old Testament quotations may be called eschatological, for they usually express in the Old Testament context a promise or threat about something still to be accomplished in the *eschaton*, which the Qumran writer cites as something still to be accomplished in the new *eschaton* of which he writes. In some ways this group of quotations occupies a middle ground, as it were, between the first group and the other two, for in many cases the Old Testament text is quoted in the sense originally intended, but it is also extended to a new situation which is expected.

There are ten passages in the Qumran literature of this sort.

(31) *bbw' hdbr 'šr ktwb bdbry yšʿyh bn 'mwṣ hnby' 'šr 'mr ybw' ʿlyk wʿl ʿmk wʿl byt 'byk ymym 'šr b'w mywm swr 'prym mʿl yhwdh* (CD 7:10–12, quoting Is 7:17), 'When the utterance will come true which was written in the words of Isaiah the son of Amoz, the prophet, who said, "There will come[63] upon you and upon your people and upon your father's house days such as have ⟨not⟩ come to pass since the day when Ephraim parted from Judah"'. *Context:* The *Damascus Document* here describes what will happen at the time of God's visitation: He will requite those who despise his commandments and ordinances and the words of Isaiah will be fulfilled at that time. These words are part of the Emmanuel Oracle in the book of Isaiah; the prophet's threat of a coming visitation by God is reaffirmed by the Qumran

[63] CD reads *ybw'* whereas MT and 1QIs[a] have *yby' Yhwh*. B. J. Roberts (*BJRL* XXXIV [1951–52] 372) ascribes the change to the unwillingness of the author to attribute these events to God. This is possible, but it is more likely that the medieval copyist confused a *waw* and a *yodh*. The general reluctance of the Qumran scribes to write the tetragrammaton would account for its omission here; in such case *yby'* would be preferable. If we should not restore the negative according to MT, then the translation would run, 'He will bring upon you and upon your people and upon your father's house days such as have come to pass since the day when Ephraim parted from Judah'. However, I prefer to restore it with C. Rabin (*op. cit.*, 28).

author as something to come true in the *eschaton* awaited by them.[64]

(32) *bbw' hdbr 'šr ktwb byd zkryh hnby' ḥrb ʿwry ʿl rwʿy wʿl gbr ʿmyty n'm 'l hk 't hrʿh wtpwṣynh hṣ'n whšybwty ydy ʿl hṣwʿrym whšwmrym 'wtw hm ʿnyy hṣ'n* (CD 19:7–9, quoting Zech 13:7), 'When the utterance will come true which was written by Zechariah the prophet, "Rise, O sword, against my shepherd and against the man, my companion. The oracle of God: Strike the shepherd and you will disperse the flock; and I shall turn my hand against the little ones." Now these who give heed to him are the poor of the flock.' *Context:* This passage occurs in MS. B of the *Damascus Document* and should parallel the previous quotation; however, the text is quite different, even though the context is roughly the same. When God visits the land, those who reject his commandments and statutes will receive the recompense of their wicked deeds and the utterance of Zechariah will come to pass. Just what the context in Zechariah is has been a matter of dispute among scholars, since many believe that it is misplaced. In the words themselves there is clearly a threat uttered; this is repeated by the Qumran author as something to take place at the awaited visitation of God upon the enemies of the sect. 'The poor of the flock' which is to be dispersed is the Qumran community. In a similar manner this text has been used in the New Testament; in Mk 14:27 it refers to the disciples who deserted Jesus as his passion approached. In both cases the text was used of a coming trial.

(33) *k'šr hyh bqṣ pqdt hr'šwn 'šr 'mr byd yḥzq'l lhtwt htyw ʿl mṣḥwt n'nḥym wn'nqym* (CD 19:11–12, quoting Ez 9:4), 'As it was in the time of the first visitation, as he said through Ezekiel, "to set a mark upon the foreheads of those who sigh and groan"'.[65] *Context:* At the time of God's visitation the 'poor of

[64] There is a play on words in the sentence. In Is 7:17 we find the words *mywm swr 'prym mʿl yhwdh*. The word *swr* is first explained by *bhprd*, 'when the two houses separated', and then by *śr*, 'Ephraim became ruler over Israel'. See the note in C. Rabin, *op. cit.*, 28.

[65] The ending of this quotation is somewhat telescoped in CD.

the flock' will be dispersed, but will escape, whereas the others will be handed over to the sword. The sparing of the poor of the flock is likened to what happened at God's first visitation, when those who sighed and groaned at the abominations wrought in the city were signed with a mark and spared from destruction by the sword. This same thing is to take place again in the *eschaton* awaited by the community, to which Ezekiel's words are now applied. Cf. Ap 7:3; 9:4; 14:1.

(34) *hw' hywm 'šr ypqd 'l k'šr dbr hyw śry yhwdh kmśygy gbwl ʿlyhm 'špk km*[*ym*] *ʿbrh* (CD 19:15–16, quoting Hos 5:10), 'That is the day on which God will visit, as it said, "The princes of Judah have become like those who remove the boundary-stones; upon them I shall pour out wrath like [wa]ter"'. (Cf. CD 8:2–3.) *Context:* When God comes in his day of visitation, extinction is threatened for all who will not hold fast to the ordinances. In support of this, CD quotes a part of Hosea's description of the guilt of Judah and Israel and the punishment which awaits them from God's wrath. It is now applied to those who in the community's estimation do not observe his ordinances.

(35) *wbqṣ hhw' yḥrh 'p 'l byśr'l k'šr 'mr 'yn mlk w'yn śr w'yn šwpṭ w*[*'y*]*n mwkyḥ bṣdq* (CD 20:15–17, quoting Hos 3:4), 'And in that time the anger of God will be kindled against Israel, as it said, "There is no king and there is no prince and there is no judge and there is none to reprove in righteousness"'.[66] *Context:* This passage is part of a description of the time which lasted from the 'gathering in' of the Teacher until the annihilation of all the men of war who returned with the 'Man of the Lie', forty years during which God's anger will be enkindled against Israel, with no one to direct men in the way of righteousness. CD compares the situation to that which would exist later in Israel in the days described by the Old Testament writer.

(36) *w'šr hgyd lnw ky' 'th bqrbnw 'l gdwl wnwr' lšwl 't kwl*

[66] The ending of this quotation in CD is different from that of MT. See the note in C. Rabin, *op. cit.*, 40.

'wybynw lp[nyn]w (1QM 10:1–2, quoting Dt 7: 21–22), 'And as (Moses) declared to us that "You are in our midst, a great and awesome God, to despoil all our enemies before us"'. *Context:* This is part of the discourse of the High Priest to be used before the eschatological battle; he quotes the significant words of Moses' second discourse in which he explained to the Israelites the strength and power which Yahweh would give them against their enemies. The *War Scroll* now applies them to the combatants of the coming eschatological war.[67]

(37) *wylmdnw m'z ldwrwtynw l'mwr bqrbkm lmlḥmh w'md hkwhn wdbr 'l h'm l'mwr šm'h yśr'l 'tmh qrbym hywm lmlḥmh 'l 'wybykmh 'l tyr'w w'l yrk lbbkmh w'l tḥ[pzw w']l t'rwṣw mpnyhm ky' 'lwhykm hwlk 'mkm lhlḥm lkm 'm 'wybykm lhwšy' 'tkmh w[š]wṭrynw ydbrw lkwl 'twdy hmlḥmh* (1QM 10:2–5, quoting Dt 20:2–5), 'And he taught us of old for our generations saying, "When you approach the battle, the priest shall stand and address the people saying, 'Hear, O Israel, you are approaching the battle today with your enemies; fear not, let not your heart waver, do not tremble nor stand in dread of them, for your God walks with you to do battle for you against your enemies, to save you'. And our officers shall speak to all those prepared for the battle."' *Context:* This is a continuation of the High Priest's exhortation before the eschatological battle. With a few slight inversions the exhortation which Moses addressed to the Israelites is applied to the new situation which will arise in the end of days. The same quotation is used again in 1QM 15:8–9 in a similar way, but without being introduced as an explicit quotation.

(38) *w'šr d[brt]h byd mwšh l'mwr ky' tbw' mlḥmh b'rṣkmh 'l hṣr hṣwrr 'tkmh whry'wt[mh] bḥṣwṣrwt wnzkrtmh lpny 'lwhykm wnwš'tm m'wybykm* (1QM 10:6–8, quoting Nm 10:9), 'And as you s[pok]e through Moses, saying, "When war comes in your land, against an enemy who oppresses you you

[67] This text is also listed by J. Carmignac (*RB* LXIII [1956] 235) as one of the explicit quotations, even though he admits that 'pour intégrer ce texte dans sa propre phrase il le retouche assez profondément'.

shall sound a war-blast on the trumpets and you will be remembered before your God and saved from your enemies"' *Context:* This is still another part of the High Priest's exhortation addressed to the warriors who are to engage in the eschatological battle. Here he cites the words of Moses who ordered the making of two silver trumpets and gave instructions for their use. In case of an invasion they were to be blown and Yahweh would deliver Israel. These words of Moses are now recalled and applied to the coming war in which evil will be wiped out in the end of days.

(39) *wm'z hšm['th mw]'d gbwrt ydkh bktyym l'mwr wnpl 'šwr bḥrb lw' 'yš wḥrb lw' 'dm tw'klnw* (1QM 11:11—12, quoting Is 31:8), 'Of old you made [known the sea]son of the power of your hand against the Kittim, saying, "And Assyria shall fall by the sword, not of man, and a sword, not of man, shall devour him"'. *Context:* Another part of the High Priest's exhortation cites the promise uttered by Isaiah, that Assyria would fall by Yahweh's might, which he would manifest on behalf of his chosen ones. Assyria here is modernized to refer to the Kittim of Assyria (see 1QM 1:2), the enemy of the new Israel, whose definitive destruction was awaited by the community in God's good time.[68]

(40) *hw'h ṣmḥ dwyd h'wmd 'm dwrš htwrh 'šr* [***] *bṣywn b'ḥryt hymym k'šr ktwb whqymwty 't swkt dwyd hnwplt hy'h swkt dwyd hnwpl[t ']šr y'mwd lhwšy' 't yśr'l* (4QFlor 1–3 ii 11–13, quoting Am 9:11), 'He is the scion of David who rises with the Interpreter of the Law, who [***] in Zion in the end of days, as it was written, "And I shall raise up the fallen hut of David". It is the fallen hut of David which will stand up to save Israel.' *Context:* This passage is part of the *pesher* on the dynastic oracle of 2 Sm 7:11 ff. The 'seed' to be raised up by God in the future is identified as the 'scion of David' and in him the promise of

[68] 'Nous avons ici un bel exemple d'exégèse "extensive", qui dépasse le sens littéral, la ruine d'Assour, pour appliquer ce texte à la ruine définitive de tous les ennemis du peuple juif' (J. Carmignac, *RB* LXIII [1956] 239).

the ultimate restoration of Israel is to be accomplished, by applying to him the words of the oracle of Amos. The Qumran author related the two texts as an expression of his messianic hope, that Yahweh will yet save Israel by raising up the fallen hut of David in the end of days. Both of the Old Testament texts involved here are actually given an eschatological twist. This text of Amos is unique in that it occurs twice in the Qumran literature (see (11) above) and also in the New Testament (Acts 15:16). There is, however, no similarity in the use of this text in the three places. In the *Damascus Document* it occurs in a passage which is not too clear and in which the books of the Law are said to be the 'hut of the king', and this hut is related to the 'fallen hut of David'. In 4QFlor the scion of David is associated with the Interpreter of the Law, but he is to bring about the salvation of Israel. In the New Testament James uses the text in his speech to the assembly in Jerusalem; without any reference to a scion of David he asserts the fulfilment of the verse in the conversion of the Gentiles to the Gospel, 'Symeon has told how God first showed an interest in taking from among the heathen a people to bear his name. And this agrees with the predictions of the prophets which say . . .' (Acts 15:14–15). He has thus extended the sense of the text far beyond its original intention in seeing in the conversion of the Gentiles the fulfilment of the promise to 'possess the remnant of Edom and all the nations over whom my name is called'.

As the texts are used in the Qumran literature, all ten in this class apply Old Testament verses to some eschatological event, either the battle in which the community is to take part, or the day of Yahweh's visitation. The *eschaton* which was often envisaged in the Old Testament text itself has now found a new emphasis in being identified with the *eschaton* of the community.

There are a few examples of the 'eschatological' use of the Old Testament in the New Testament. The number of quotations, however, in this class from the New Testament is considerably less than in the other groups, and the Qumran quotations are proportionally more numerous. This is probably due again to the fact that Christian writers were more often looking back at the central event in which salvation had been accomplished rather than forward to a deliverance by Yahweh, which seems to characterize the Qumran literature.

In Rom 11:26–27 Paul quotes Is 59:20–21 and 27:9 in support of his contention that only partial insensibility has come upon Israel, to last until all the heathen have come in, and then all Israel will be saved, 'just as the Scripture says, "The deliverer will come from Zion, he will drive all ungodliness away from Jacob and this will be my agreement with them, when I take away their sins"'. Paul is looking forward to a point in the Christian *eschaton*, wherein he believes the words of Isaiah will finally find fulfilment. Similarly, in Mt 7:23 Jesus, discussing the division of men which his coming was to effect, announced that not everyone who said to him 'Lord, Lord', would enter the kingdom of heaven, but only those who did the will of his Father. 'Many will say to me *on that day*, "Lord! Lord". Was it not in your name that we prophesied, and by your name that we drove out demons, and by your name that we did many mighty acts? Then I will say to them plainly, "I never knew you! Depart from me, you who do wrong!"' In the last sentence Jesus is quoting Ps 6:9 (without an introductory formula), 'Depart from me all evildoers'. The day to which he refers is the day of eschatological judgment. We likewise find this use of the Old Testament in paraenetic passages. 'Do not take your revenge, dear friends, but leave room for God's anger, for the Scripture says, "Vengeance belongs to me; I will pay them back, says the Lord"'. Here (Rom 12:19) Paul is citing Dt 32:35, referring the words to a future punishment by God of those who seek vengeance. See further Heb 10:30, 37–38; 1 Cor 15:54–55.[69]

[69] Earlier in my discussion I mentioned forty-two passages in the Qumran

CONCLUSION

The foregoing analysis of the isolated explicit quotations of the Old Testament which occur in various Qumran writings reveals four generic uses of those quotations, literal or historical, modernized, accommodated, eschatological. These uses can likewise be illustrated from the many Old Testament quotations which exist in the New Testament.[70] Moreover, the introductory formulae which are found in the Qumran texts appear to be without parallel in the Mishnah, despite the common use of the verbs 'to say' and 'to write', while a great number of the Qumran expressions prove to be the exact Semitic equivalents of the New Testament formulae. There is, further, a variety of minor exegetical devices common to the Qumran texts and the New Testament (which are not without parallels, however, in the rabbinical writings). The conclusion drawn from these details is that the exegetical practice of the New Testament writers is quite similar to that of their Jewish contemporaries, which is best illustrated by the Qumran literature.

We may characterize both the Qumran and the New Testament use of the Old Testament *in general* as a literal exegesis, when this is defined in opposition to the allegorical exegesis of Philo and the Alexandrian school of later times. There are, it is true, some allegorical interpretations in both, but these are not

---

literature which contain Old Testament quotations, but have presented an analysis of only forty of them. In two cases introductory formulae are used, but the quotation introduced is not from the Old Testament, or at least cannot be found in any of the known texts or versions. They are CD 9:8–9 and 16:10.

[70] I have re-examined all the New Testament quotations in the light of the four categories which emerged from my analysis of the Qumran passages. Many of them fall easily into the same categories, as I have tried to indicate above. However, I do not want to give the impression that these four categories exhaust the uses of the Old Testament in the New; there is always the danger in such a comparative study of creating a Procrustean bed. Further analysis of the New Testament passages along lines which I have suggested here may necessitate more categories than the four which emerge from the Qumran material.

characteristic. Nor is it a *strictly literal* exegesis which respects the original meaning and context of the words quoted; however, examples of this do occur occasionally. Normally, it is an exegesis based on the words quoted, even though the relevance of them to their historical setting means very little to the Qumran or New Testament writers. This is often due to the fact that both the Qumran sect and the early Christians believed that they were living in some sense 'in the end of days'. This notion, however, did not have a univocal meaning for the two groups. At Qumran many of the Old Testament texts were applied to events in the recent history of the sect; in this respect there is some similarity to the backward glance of the New Testament writers. But the messianic hope at Qumran shifted the emphasis much more to a *coming fulfilment* of the Old Testament scriptures. Again, common to both was the implicit desire to enhance some recent event in their histories or some idea or person with an Old Testament association, as a result of a certain analogy which they saw between the event and some event in Israel's history.

In the isolated explicit quotations many of the exegetical devices are found to be at work which have been found also in the *pesharim* (for example, the actualization of the text, the atomistic interpretation of it, the use of textual variants, a play on words, a deliberate manipulation of the text to suit the new context better). These devices were not, therefore, exclusive to the *pesher*, which was essentially a sort of midrashic running commentary on a continuous text of a prophet or some other Old Testament writing. The data which we have collected above confirm the criticism which B. Gärtner wrote[71] of K. Stendahl's thesis about the 'formula quotations' in Matthew, which the latter labelled as *pesher*-type quotations.[72] Aside from the diffi-

[71] 'The Habakkuk Commentary (DSH) and the Gospel of Matthew', *ST* VIII (1954) 1–24.

[72] *The School of St Matthew and Its Use of the Old Testament* (Uppsala, 1954; reprinted, Philadelphia, 1968) 200 ff.

culties which that thesis encounters on the textual basis, it is evident that many of the devices which are found in the *pesharim* are not exclusive to them. Moreover, the 'formula quotations' in Matthew are all of the so-called 'fulfilment' type. As I have pointed out earlier, this type of introductory formula is singularly absent from the Qumran texts.[73] So I question the advisability of continuing to speak of *pesher*-type quotations or a *pesher*-type interpretation, unless this is defined more accurately and restricted to definite cases.

There is no evidence at Qumran of a systematic, uniform exegesis of the Old Testament. The same text was not always given the same interpretation (see the variants in CD 7 and 19 and compare the use of Nm 24:17 and Am 9:11 in different contexts). Nor does any pattern appear in the Old Testament quotations in the Qumran texts such as that which C. H. Dodd has detected in the New Testament.[74]

A. von Harnack once maintained that Paul was the originator of typological exegesis. E. E. Ellis[75] has shown, however, that such typological interpretation of the Old Testament existed in pre-Pauline strata of the New Testament. But many of the examples cited in classes B and C above will show that this type of interpretation was also pre-Christian, being practised by contemporary Jews as well, even though we do not find in the Qumran material any Semitic equivalent of the Pauline *typos* or *typikōs*.

The similarities in the exegetical practices of the two groups do not affect anything more than the periphery of their theologies. Both depend on the Old Testament, but both have certain presuppositions in the light of which they read the Old Testament. It is these presuppositions which distinguish the two groups despite the similarities in their exegetical procedures.

[73] In this I disagree with B. Gärtner's remarks (*op. cit.*, 14) about the similarity of these 'fulfilment' quotations to certain Qumran formulae.

[74] *According to the Scriptures: the Sub-Structure of New Testament Theology* (London, 1953).

[75] *Op. cit.*, 129 and 90 ff.

The foregoing study has a certain pertinence also for the question of the *sensus plenior* of Scripture. This is not the place for an extended discussion of this pertinence, but it should be noted at least. Many passages in the Old Testament are claimed to have such a sense because of the subsequent use of them in the New Testament. The interpretation in the latter is often said to be *homogeneous* with the literal sense of the Old Testament. However, J. Schmid has recently shown that this theory does not adequately explain the Pauline use of the Scriptures, since many of his examples can hardly be said to be homogeneous.[76] The evidence which I have amassed in my analysis reveals that many of the Qumran cases of modernized or accommodated interpretations might just as easily be called the *sensus plenior* of the Old Testament passages, because they are derived by the same exegetical methods and devices. Some of them at least are no less homogeneous than those in the New Testament. In both cases there is a similar use of the Old Testament. As a result, one would be is forced to admit that the New Testament interpretations are instances of the *sensus plenior* of the Old Testament and the Qumran interpretations are not, simply because the former are found in inspired texts.[77] Certainly, the extension of the meaning of an Old Testament

[76] *Op. cit.*, 173.

[77] R. E. Brown ('The Sensus Plenior in the Last Ten Years', *CBQ* 25 [1963] 265–85) criticized this position, saying that my view 'is perhaps handicapped by Benoit's theory that SP [= *sensus plenior*] may be uncovered only by the NT'. I would not ascribe it to Benoit's restrictive theory, since I do admit that *genuine* dogmatic tradition or development (in conciliar or papal definitions) can also be a source of learning the *sensus plenior* of an Old Testament passage, and even of a New Testament text. The *dogma* of the Trinity is a good example of the latter. But I cannot understand how Brown can say that 'Qumrân by its relation to Judaism is *part of a stream of divine revelation* [my italics] and so the Qumran exegetes could come to recognize a SP of the OT' (p. 272, n. 55). To accord Qumran literature such a quality is to equate it with the Old Testament, the New Testament, and genuine Christian tradition. As far as I am concerned, the *sensus plenior* of an Old Testament text could be given in a later Old Testament book, or in the New Testament, or in *genuine* Christian dogmatic tradition (such as that mentioned

passage in the New could be the result also of a rhetorical device. The mere occurrence of an Old Testament quotation in the New does not give the Old Testament passage a *sensus plenior,* in particular when the extended sense is a sheer accommodation. I would admit the *sensus plenior* only when some basic homogeneity is detected between the Old Testament meaning and the sense the text acquires by its use in the New Testament. This is demanded by the idea of the unity or harmony of the inspired Testaments. But inspiration does not exclude the possibility of New Testament writers accommodating an Old Testament text, even arbitrarily suiting it to their heterogeneous purpose. Because this does happen at times (e.g. 1 Cor 9:9), a real hermeneutical problem arises.

Finally, to forestall a possible objection, one should remember that the New Testament writers and even the Qumran authors did not read their Scriptures as a modern biblical scholar does. My entire discussion above might imply that I think they did. To modern critical scholarship their way of reading the Old Testament often appears quite arbitrary in that it disregards the sense and context of the original. Yet if we are ever going to discover the sense in which such writers used their Scriptures and the presuppositions which they brought to the reading of them, their quotations of the Old Testament must be analysed somewhat along the lines which I have attempted, that is, of a comparison of the text and context in which they occur with the text and context of the original. The introductory formulae used by the Qumran and New Testament writers reveal a profound reverence for the Old Testament as the word of God; they obviously believed, moreover, that their interpretative use of it was legitimate for the

---

above). The common element here is Spirit-guided inspiration or assistance (*assistentia* in the technical theological sense). I cannot ascribe either of these to Qumran literature, any more than I can to other intertestamental literature or rabbinic writings. It should be obvious that this is a hermeneutical problem that is tied to the Catholic idea of biblical inspiration.

religious purpose of their compositions. Nowhere do they make the claim that they are quoting it according to what we call its strict literal sense; that they do on occasion appears from class A above. But generally their use of the Old Testament was a free, sometimes figurative, extension or accommodation of the words to support a position already taken.[78]

[78] See further S. L. Edgar, 'Respect for Context in Quotations from the Old Testament', *NTS* IX (1962–63) 55–62; J. J. O'Rourke, 'The Fulfilment Texts in Matthew', *CBQ* XXIV (1962) 394–403; 'Explicit Old Testament Citations in "the Gospels"', *SMR* VII (1964) 37–64.

2

'4QTESTIMONIA' AND THE NEW TESTAMENT*

A Hebrew text, discovered in Qumran Cave 4, was published by J. M. Allegro, who gave it the provisional title of '4QTestimonia'.[1] Its contents are described as 'a group of *testimonia* of the type long ago proposed by Burkitt, Rendel Harris and others to have existed in the early Church'.[2] *Testimonia* is the current name for systematic collections of Old Testament passages, often of messianic import, which are thought to have been used by early Christians. This name is derived from a work of Cyprian, *Ad Quirinum*, whose subtitle is *Testimoniorum libri tres*.[3] Cyprian's work, at least in its first two books,[4] is a collection of Old Testament passages, compiled with an apologetic purpose *adversus Iudaeos*. Similar collections were made by other patristic writers as well. But the existence of such collections of *testimonia* in the primitive Church and the relation of them to the formation of the New Testament have often been denied and affirmed during the past sixty years. To some scholars it seems that such collections, which they also call 'florilegia',

* Originally published in *TS* 18 (1957) 513–37.

[1] J. M. Allegro, 'Further Messianic References in Qumran Literature', *JBL* 75 (1956) 182–7, Document IV. See now the definitive edition of this text, 4Q*175*, in J. M. Allegro, *Qumrân Cave 4: I* (*4Q158–4Q186*) (DJD 5; Oxford: Clarendon, 1968) 57–60.

[2] *JBL* 75 (1956) 186. J. T. Milik, DJD 1, 121, has also referred to this text as *testimonia;* see also *RB* 60 (1953) 290.

[3] Edited by G. Hartel, CSEL 3/1 (1868) 33–184.

[4] The third book is generally regarded as a later edition; cf. J. Quasten, *Patrology* 2 (Utrecht and Antwerp, 1953) 363.

'anthologies', or 'a catena of fulfilments of prophecy', must be the basis of some of the Old Testament quotations in the New Testament. Others have denied the existence of such *testimonia*. Consequently, if the provisional title, '4QTestimonia', given to the new Qumran text proves to be correct, then Allegro is right in saying that 'this document will certainly revive interest in the question' of the *testimonia*.[5]

The present article, at any rate, will bear out Allegro's prediction of interest. I propose to give a brief survey of the problem of the *testimonia* in the study of the New Testament and then try to situate the new document in the context of that problem. Our discussion will treat: (1) the hypothesis of the *testimonia* collections, (2) the reaction to the hypothesis, (3) extant *testimonia*, and (4) the significance of '4QTestimonia'.

THE HYPOTHESIS OF THE TESTIMONIA COLLECTIONS

While the majority of the OT quotations in the NT agree substantially with the text of the Septuagint (LXX), as we know it today, there is a good number of quotations that are closer to the Masoretic Hebrew text (MT). Some, however, diverge considerably from both. The Epistle to the Hebrews, for instance, is a striking example of dependence on the LXX, while a certain group of quotations in the Gospel according to Matthew has always been considered outstanding for its departure from this text. The picture presented by the OT quotations in the NT is a complicated one and has evoked study from the early centuries of the Church's existence on. The facile solution, often employed to explain the discrepancies between the quotations and the known Greek or Hebrew texts of the OT, is that of the 'quotation from memory'. Even St Jerome took refuge in this solution: 'In omnibus paene testimoniis quae de Vetere Testamento sumuntur istiusmodi esse errorem, ut aut ordo mutetur aut verba, et interdum sensus quoque ipse diversus sit vel Apostolis vel Evangelistis non ex libro carpentibus

[5] Allegro, *art. cit.*, 186, n. 107.

testimonia, sed memoria credentibus, quae nonnumquam fallitur.'[6] It would be foolish to deny that the NT writers, especially Paul in his letters, quoted the OT at times from memory. But to use this solution everywhere would be a gross oversimplification.

Recourse to the hypothesis of previously compiled collections of OT passages, especially to those which might have depended on different recensions of the OT books, has often been had by scholars in recent times to explain some of the problems that arise from the use of the OT by Paul and Matthew. It is thought that these collections of *testimonia* were composed for various purposes, devotional, liturgical, or apologetic. Providing handy summaries of the main OT passages for the busy missionary or apostolic teacher, they would have dispensed him from consulting the OT itself or from carrying it around with him. To use a phrase of Rendel Harris, they would have been 'a controversialists' *vade mecum*'.[7] It has even been suggested that Paul refers to such collections, when he instructs Timothy to bring along with him 'the cloak that I left with Carpus at Troas, and the books, especially the parchments (*tas membranas*)' (2 Tm 4:13).

The use of such collections of *testimonia* was postulated to explain four problems of OT citations in the NT: (*a*) the attribution of citations to wrong OT authors; (*b*) the 'formula quotations'[8] found in Matthew; (*c*) the divergence of the OT

[6] *Comm. in Michaeam* 2, 5 (*PL* 25, 1255 [ed. 1865]). For ancient discussions of the use of the OT in the NT, see H. Vollmer, *Die alttestamentlichen Citate bei Paulus, textkritisch und biblisch-theologisch gewürdigt nebst einem Anhang über das Verhältnis des Apostels zu Philo* (Freiburg and Leipzig, 1895) 1–6.

[7] Rendel Harris, *Testimonies* 1 (Cambridge, 1916) 55.

[8] This term has been used by Sherman Johnson, 'The Biblical Quotations in Matthew', *HTR* 36 (1943) 135, and adopted by K. Stendahl, *The School of St Matthew and Its Use of the Old Testament* (Uppsala, 1954; reprinted Philadelphia: Fortress, 1968) 45, as the translation of the German 'Reflexionszitate'. Such quotations are introduced by the evangelist himself into his account of an event, which he regards as the fulfilment of a saying of the OT. The German term is actually a better expression than the current English phrase, as it reveals the nature of the quotation.

citations from the LXX and their closer agreement with the Hebrew; (*d*) the composite quotations.

Citations Attributed to Wrong Authors

The chief cases of such ascription are Mk 1:2–3 and Mt 27:9–10.[9] In Mk 1:2–3 we read: 'As is written in the prophet Isaiah: "Here I send my messenger on before you; he will prepare your way. Hark! Someone is shouting in the desert: Get the Lord's way ready, make his paths straight."'[10] Although the second citation in verse 3 is taken from Is 40:3, the first is drawn from Mal 3:1, or possibly from Ex 23:20. Yet both are introduced by the phrase, 'As is written in the prophet Isaiah'. Rendel Harris suggested that this ascription in the earliest of our Synoptic Gospels was due to 'some collection of Testimonies'.[11] If we imagine a collection of prophetic texts strung together, some with and some without their sources indicated, the solution suggested by Harris would not be impossible.[12] Krister Stendahl has pointed out that a stronger argument for such an interpretation is that both the Malachi and Isaiah texts contain the phrase *pinnāh derek*, 'to prepare the way', an expression which occurs only here and in two closely related Isaiah passages, 57:14 and 62:10.[13] Possibly a collection of texts existed that dealt

[9] A third case might be added, Mt 13:35, if the reading in Sinaiticus is adopted, where *Ēsaiou* is added after *dia* in the phrase *dia tou prophētou legontos*. But Isaiah is not quoted; the text comes rather from Ps 78:2. If the name of Isaiah is omitted with most of the other MSS., the sense of the word *prophētou* can be explained with K. Stendahl (*op. cit.*, 117–18) by showing that the quotation comes from a psalm of Asaph, whom early Jewish tradition regarded as a prophet (1 Chr 25:2).

[10] Translations of the NT are taken from E. J. Goodspeed, *The Complete Bible: An American Translation* (Chicago, 1951).

[11] Rendel Harris, *op. cit.*, 49; see also 21–22.

[12] V. Taylor in his commentary, *The Gospel according to St Mark* (London, 1953) 153, admits that 'Mark may have inadvertently introduced it from a collection of Messianic proof-texts', while observing that there are good reasons for the view of Holtzmann, Lagrange, and Rawlinson that the Malachi-Exodus text might be a 'copyist's gloss'.

[13] Stendahl, *op. cit.*, 51.

with 'preparing the way' and in the course of time it was thought that all the passages were from Isaiah.[14]

In Mt 27:9–10 Jeremiah is said to have written, 'They took the thirty silver pieces, the price of the one whose price had been fixed, on whom some of the Israelites had set a price, and gave them for the Potter's Field as the Lord directed me.' But this saying is partly a quotation and partly a paraphrase of Zech 11:13 with a possible allusion to Jer 18:1 (LXX) and Ex 9:12. Once again Rendel Harris suggests that 'Matthew has been using a *Book of Testimonies*, in which the history and tragic end of Judas was explained as a fulfilment of ancient prophecy, and that the mistake . . . either existed in the *Book of Testimonies*, or was accidentally made by the evangelist in using such a book.'[15]

The 'Formula Quotations'

In the Gospel according to Matthew there are ten citations from the OT which form a special group within that Gospel. They occur in various places throughout the work: four in the infancy stories, five in the ministry narratives, and one in the account of the passion.

	Group A		*Group B*
1:22–23	(Is 7:14)	4:15–16	(Is 8:23; 9:1)
2:15	(Hos 11:1)	8:17	(Is 53:4)
2:17–18	(Jer 31:15)	12:17–21	(Is 42:1–4)
2:23	(Is 11:1)	13:35	(Ps 78:2)
27:9	(Zech 11:12–13)	21:4–5	(Zech 9:9; Is 62:11)

The citations of Group A are found in passages that are peculiar to Matthew; those of Group B occur in passages that have Synoptic parallels, but which Matthew has modified to suit the incorporation of the quotation (contrast the Marcan parallels). Now several points are to be noted in connection with these passages of Matthew. First of all, they have a special introductory formula, either *hina* (*hopōs*) *plērōthē to rēthen* or *tote*

[14] See N. J. Hommes, *Het Testimoniaboek* (Amsterdam, 1935) 174 ff., who maintains that such a group of texts did exist under the heading of Isaiah in pre-Christian times.

[15] Rendel Harris, *op. cit.*, 56.

eplērōthē to rēthen tou prophētou legontos, not found with the other OT citations in the first Gospel.[16] Secondly, this type of citation is found in the Synoptic tradition only in Matthew;[17] it is a *Reflexionszitat*, added by the writer and not attributed to another person. Thirdly, the language of these citations is generally judged to be different from the other citations of the OT in Matthew and from those in Mark and Luke. They manifest a much greater similarity to the Hebrew text of the OT than the others, which are more faithful to the LXX.[18] Such peculiarities of this group of citations demand an explanation and that has often been found in the theory of the *testimonia*.[19] It is thought that Matthew drew upon a collection of such texts, since their use admirably suited the purpose he had in writing his Gospel.

Citations that Diverge from the Text of the LXX

This feature of some of the OT citations has already been mentioned, especially in the case of the formula quotations. Such a deviation from the LXX text, however, is found in a number of instances outside of Matthew. According to E. F. Kautzsch,[20] who made a thorough study of the eighty-four Pauline citations and compared them with the LXX (Alexandrinus), thirty-four of them agree with the LXX, while thirty-six depart from it 'leviter'. There are ten passages where the citations 'longius recedunt' from the LXX, 'ita tamen ut dissensus . . . ad liberam allegandi rationem referendus videatur'. In two passages (Rom 12:19; 1 Cor 14:21) the 'quotation' is judged to be quite free,

[16] Chiefly for this reason we have not included in this group the quotation of Mi 5:2, which occurs in Mt 2:6. However, a case might be made out for its inclusion in Group A. Stendahl treats it in his discussion of the formula quotations; cf. *op. cit.*, 99–101.

[17] The quotation of Zech 9:9, employed in Mt 21:5, is also found in Jn 12:15, but this is outside the Synoptic tradition.

[18] See Johnson, *art. cit.*, 152.

[19] See T. Stephenson, 'The Old Testament Quotations Peculiar to Matthew', *JTS* 20 (1918–19) 227–9; L. Vaganay, *Le problème synoptique* (Paris, 1954) 237–40.

[20] E. F. Kautzsch, *De Veteris Testamenti locis a Paulo apostolo allegatis* (Leipzig, 1869) 109.

but is still capable of being recognized as a quotation. Finally, in two other passages Paul cites Job clearly according to the Hebrew text.[21] Kautzsch suggests that Paul only knew Job in the Hebrew and had no acquaintance with the Greek translation of that book. But these differences that exist between the various classes of citations are significant enough to make Vollmer have recourse to 'Citatenkomposition'[22] as well as to different Greek versions (Aquila or Theodotion or Symmachus) to explain the variants. It should be noted, however, that deviation from the text of the LXX, taken by itself, is rarely considered sufficient evidence to postulate the previous existence of a quotation in a collection of *testimonia*. But it is often a confirmation of one of the other reasons for such a postulate.

The Composite Quotations

Perhaps the chief reason for postulating the existence of collections of *testimonia* in the early Church is the phenomenon of composite quotations found in various NT books. We met an example of such a quotation in discussing the text of Malachi that is attributed to Isaiah in Mk 1:2. The term, composite quotation, designates the stringing together of two or more OT quotations which are given more or less completely. It is to be distinguished from a conflated quotation, such as Mt 22:24: 'Master, Moses said, "If a man dies without children, his brother shall marry his widow and raise up a family for him."' Here we have parts of Gn 38:8 and Dt 25:5 fused together. Moreover, a composite quotation is different from allusions to the OT which are strung together. The Apocalypse is generally said to contain not a single OT quotation, yet is replete with OT allusions. The clearest examples of composite quotations are the citations that are strung together without intervening comments or identification of their author(s). Such citations are rare in the Gospels; the following is usually given as an example:

[21] See Stendahl, *op. cit.*, 159, for slightly different figures, but substantial agreement.

[22] Vollmer, *op. cit.*, 48.

'*My house shall be called a house of prayer*, but you make it *a robbers' den*' (Mt 21:13). The italicized words come from Is 56:7 and Jer 7:11; in both cases the text is quite similar to the LXX. See further examples in Mk 10:6–8 (Gn 1:27; 2:24); Mt 19:18–19 (Ex 20:12–16 or Dt 5:16–20 and Lv 19:18).

It is in the Pauline letters that we find the best examples of composite quotations. We shall give but two examples. In the first instance the 'catchword-bond' that unites them is 'heathen' or 'nation'. In the second the unifying element is rather the description of the man who is not upright, with the enumeration of different parts of the body as a secondary element.[23]

Rom 15:9–12
As the Scripture says,
'I will give thanks to you for this among the heathen,
 And sing in honour of your name.' (Ps 17/18:50; cf. 2 Sm 22:50)
And again,
'Rejoice, you heathen, with his people.' (Dt 32:43 LXX)
And again,
'Praise the Lord, all you heathen, (Ps 116/17:1)
 And let all nations sing his praises.'
Again Isaiah says,
'The descendant of Jesse will come, (Is 11:1, 10)
 The one who is to rise to rule the heathen;
  The heathen will set their hopes on him.'

Rom 3:10–18
As the Scripture says,
'There is not a single man who is upright, (Ps 13/14:1–3)
 No one understands, no one searches for God.
All have turned away, they are one and all worthless;
 No one does right, not a single one.'
'Their throats are like open graves, (Ps 5:10)
 They use their tongues to deceive.'
'The venom of asps is behind their lips.' (Ps 139/40:4)
 'And their mouths are full of bitter curses.' (Ps 9B/10:7)

[23] See J. Huby, *Saint Paul, Epître aux Romains* (11th ed.; Paris, 1940) 145, n. 1.

'Their feet are swift when it comes to shedding blood, (Is 59:7–8; cf. Prv 1:16)
Ruin and wretchedness mark their paths,
They do not know the way of peace.'
'There is no reverence for God before their eyes.'[24] (Ps 35/36:2)

Further examples may be found in Rom 9:25–29 (Hos 2:25,1; Is 10:22–23; 1:9); 10:15–21 (Is 52:7; 53:1; Ps 18/19:5; Dt 32:21; Is 65:1–2); 11:8–10 (Dt 29:3 [cf. Is 29:10]; Ps 68/69: 23–24); 11:26 (Is 59:20; 27:9); 11:34–35 (Is 40:13; Jb 41:3); 2 Cor 6:16–18 (Lv 26:12 [cf. Ez 37:27]; Jer 51:45; Is 52:11; Ez 20:34; 2 Sm 7:14).[25]

Composite quotations are also found in the early patristic writers (e.g., Clement of Rome, Barnabas, Justin Martyr) and they obviously served as a basis for the later extended collections of *testimonia* by Tertullian, Cyprian, and Pseudo-Gregory of Nyssa. After studying the composite quotations in the NT and the early Fathers, E. Hatch postulated the existence of collections of such texts. This was the beginning of the *testimonia* hypothesis in 1889, although Hatch did not use this name for

[24] M. Dibelius, 'Zur Formgeschichte des Neuen Testaments ausserhalb der Evangelien', *TRu*, N. F. 3 (1931) 228, finds it hard to believe that Paul himself sought out all these passages from the OT for the purpose of incorporating them in the Epistle to the Romans. He, too, thinks in terms of a pre-existing list of passages that Paul simply made use of here.

[25] It may be debated whether the following passages are really composite quotations, because of the intervening comments: Rom 9:12–13 (Gn 25: 23; Mal 1:2–3); 9:33 (Is 28:16; 8:14); 10:6–8 (Dt 30:12; Ps 106/7:26); 10:11–13 (Is 28:16; Jl 2:32); 12:19–20 (Dt 32:35; Prv 25:21–22); Gal 4: 27–30 (Is 54:1; Gn 21:10–12); 1 Cor 3:19–20 (Jb 5:13; Ps 93/94:11); 2 Cor 9:9–10 (Ps 111/12:9; Is 55:10; Hos 10:12). Composite citations are also found in Heb 1:5 (Ps 2:7; 2 Sm 7:14); 1:7–13 (Dt 32:42 LXX and 4Q Deut; Ps 103/4:4; 44/45:7–8; 101/2:26–28; 109/10:1); 2:12–13 (Ps 21/22: 23; Is 8:17–18); 5:5–6 (Ps 2:7; 109/10:4); 1 Pt 2:6–10 (Is 28:16; Ps 117/18:22; Is 8:14; 43:20–21; Ex 19:6 [cf. 23:22]; Hos 1:6, 9).—L. Cerfaux proposes the extended use of a florilegium in 1 Corinthians; see 'Vestiges d'un florilège dans 1 Cor. 1,18–3.24?', *Revue d'histoire ecclésiastique* 27 (1931) 521–34; *Recueil Cerfaux* 2 (Gembloux, 1954) 319–32.

it.[26] A thorough study of the Pauline composite citations was undertaken by Hans Vollmer, who published his results in 1895.[27] He believed that some combinations of texts were due merely to the juxtaposition of certain key-words ('zufällige Berührung eines Stichwortes').[28] Such a case is found in Rom 11:26, where the *kai hautē* of Is 59:21 brings to mind the *kai touto* of 27:9; such a similarity would be sufficient reason to join these two verses. Likewise in Rom 10:6–8 the *anabēsetai* of Dt 30:12 provides the link with *katabēsetai* of Ps 107:26. But he also found other cases of combined citations that reveal a deliberate process of compilation ('eine planmässige Zusammenstellung').[29] The latter citations reveal a tendency in Paul to cite passages

[26] E. Hatch, *Essays in Biblical Greek* (Oxford, 1889) 203: 'It would be improbable, even if there were no positive evidence on the point, that the Greek-speaking Jews, who were themselves cultured, and who lived in great centres of culture, should not have had a literature of their own. It is no less improbable that such a literature should have consisted only of the Apocalyptic books, and the scanty fragments of other books, which have come down to us. It may naturally be supposed that a race which laid stress on moral progress, whose religious services had variable elements of both prayer and praise, and which was carrying on an active propaganda, would have, among other books, manuals of morals, of devotion, and of controversy. It may also be supposed, if we take into consideration the contemporary habit of making collections of *excerpta*, and the special authority which the Jews attached to their sacred books, that some of these manuals would consist of extracts from the Old Testament. The existence of composite quotations in the New Testament, and in some of the early Fathers suggests the hypothesis that we have in them relics of such manuals.' —Prior to Hatch's study, C. Weizsäcker thought that Paul had composed for himself a sort of 'creed' in the form of citations from the OT which he used in his teaching. He compared the quotations in Rom 1–4 with those in Galatians and showed how they could be separated from their context to give this impression. Similarly the citations in Rom 9–11. 'Dieser Schriftbeweis ist nun ohne Zweifel nicht erst bei Abfassung der Briefe so aufgestellt, sondern der Apostel hat ihn sich überhaupt zurecht gemacht, und nur in diesen Briefen bei gegebenen Anlass verwendet' (*Das apostolische Zeitalter der christlichen Kirche* [Freiburg, 1886] 113–14; 3rd ed. [1902] 110–11).

[27] Vollmer, *op. cit.* (see n. 6 above).

[28] *Ibid.*, 36.

[29] *Ibid.*, 37.

from the three parts of the OT: the Law, the Prophets, and the Writings (or at least from two of them). See the examples cited above from Rom 11:8–10 and 15:9–12.[30]

Whereas E. Hatch had postulated a collection of Greek testimonies, compiled by Hellenistic Jews, Vollmer preferred to think that the compilations had already existed in Hebrew, in which such passages were assembled for dogmatic purposes from the Law, the Prophets, and the Writings. This, he thought, could be established by such a passage as 2 Cor 9:10, where the word 'rain' is the unitive element of the last three quotations (Is 55:10; Dt 28:11–12; Hos 10:12) that are fused together—even though this word does not appear in the parts quoted by Paul. Such a compilation of texts would have been impossible in Greek, since the unitive element is lacking in the third text according to the LXX. Hence, the 'rain' texts must have been collected in Hebrew, and probably in pre-Christian times.[31]

Whenever the *testimonia* hypothesis is discussed, the names of Burkitt and Rendel Harris always come to the fore. Though the idea did not originate with Burkitt, it seems that he was the first to use the name, *testimonia*, to designate the systematic collection of such OT texts.[32] Harris gathered evidence to support the hypothesis both from the NT and from the early Fathers.[33]

[30] This manner of quoting the OT had been pointed out long ago by Surhenus: '*spr hmšyh* sive *biblos katallagēs*, in quo secundum veterum theologorum Hebraeorum formulas allegandi et modos interpretandi conciliantur loca ex Vetere in Novo Testamento allegata' ([Amsterdam, 1713] Book 2, Thesis 11, p. 49). He showed that Paul was following good rabbinical practice in citing the OT in this fashion.

[31] Vollmer, *op. cit.*, 41–2. But the case is weakened by the fact that the words for 'rain' are not the same in all the passages; moreover, in the third instance the verb *ywrh* is used in a figurative sense (and contains a play on its meaning). For further criticism of this example, see O. Michel, *Paulus und seine Bibel* (Gütersloh, 1929) 42–3; Hommes, *op. cit.*, 349.

[32] F. C. Burkitt, *The Gospel History and Its Transmission* (Edinburgh, 1907) 126.

[33] Rendel Harris, *Testimonies*, 2 vols (Cambridge, 1916, 1920). Stendahl, *op. cit.*, 207, has pointed out that most of the patristic material to which

However, Harris went beyond Burkitt in maintaining that the passages all belonged to one Testimony Book. Nor was he content to regard the collections as *testimonia pro Iudaeis*, as E. Hatch had done, but considered them as Christian compilations (therefore, in Greek), *testimonia adversus Iudaeos*. 'If such collections of Testimonies on behalf of the Jews existed in early times, before the diffusion of Christianity, then there must have been, *a fortiori*, similar collections produced in later times, when the Christian religion was being actively pushed by the Church in the Synagogue.'[34] His contention is supported by the existence of such collections *adversus Iudaeos* in the writings of Cyprian, Tertullian, and Pseudo-Gregory of Nyssa.

But Harris went still further with his theory. The various composite quotations and those that are attributed to wrong authors not only belonged to an original Testimony Book, but they were actually part of 'the missing *Dominical Oracles* written by Matthew and commented on by Papias'.[35] Matthew, a member of the apostolic company, who is credited with the composition of *ta kyriaka logia*, is now claimed as the author of the *testimonia*. The five books of Papias' commentary could conceivably refer to this Testimony Book, divided into five parts, just as the first Gospel is. In this way Harris thought that he had found an answer to the oft-repeated question, 'What were the logia on which Papias commented?'

THE REACTION TO THE HYPOTHESIS

It is not surprising that the theory of the *testimonia* in the extreme form presented by Rendel Harris was not accepted by most scholars. While the evidence he had collected might support the contention that collections of *testimonia* did exist in the

---

Harris refers was previously collected by A. von Ungern-Sternberg, *Der traditionelle alttestamentliche Schriftbeweis 'De Christo' und 'De Evangelio' in der alten Kirche bis zur Zeit Eusebs von Caesarea* (Halle a. S., 1913).

[34] Rendel Harris, *op. cit.*, I, 2.

[35] *Ibid.*, 109, 116–17.

early Church and possibly even prior to NT writings, there is certainly no evidence that they formed one book, nor that they had anything to do with the Logia of Papias' statement about Matthew.[36] Consequently, the extreme form of the hypothesis has been generally abandoned, but many scholars admit that *testimonia* collections must have preceded various sections of the NT.[37]

There have been a few scholars, however, in recent times who have questioned both the existence of *testimonia* and the extent to which they were used in the early Church. So far we have seen that the existence of *testimonia* collections was a mere postulate; they are a convenient way of explaining certain puzzling features in the NT. But possibly these features can be explained in another way.

It has often been pointed out that Paul had rabbinical tradition to give him the model for his composite quotations from the Law, the Prophets, and the Writings. This method of 'stringing together' texts like pearls on a thread was known to the rabbinical schools; he who strung the texts together was called *ḥārōzā'* (from *ḥrz*, 'to pierce', 'to bore through' in order

[36] For criticism of Harris' work see A. L. Williams, *Adversus Judaeos* (Cambridge, 1935) 6–10; Hommes, *op. cit.*, 251. ('Papias is de *Deus ex machina* in zijn systeem'); L. Cerfaux, 'Un chapitre du Livre des "Testimonia" (Pap. Ryl. Gr. 460)', in *Recueil Cerfaux* 2, 226, note; Stendahl, *op. cit.*, 209 ff.; P. Feine and J. Behm, *Einleitung in das Neue Testament* (10th ed.; Heidelberg, 1954) 24; J. A. Findlay, 'The First Gospel and the Book of Testimonies', in *Amicitiae corolla: Essays Presented to J. R. Harris*, ed. H. G. Wood (London, 1933) 57–71; Ch. Guignebert, in RHR 81 (1920) 58–69.

[37] See, for instance, W. Sanday and A. C. Headlam, *Commentary on the Epistle to the Romans* (*International Critical Commentary*; Edinburgh, 1908) 264, 282; J. Moffatt, *An Introduction to the Literature of the New Testament* (Edinburgh, 1920) 23–5; M. Simon, *Verus Israel: Etude sur les relations entre chrétiens et juifs dans l'empire romain (135–425)* (*Bibliothèque des Ecoles Françaises d'Athènes et de Rome* 166; Paris, 1948) 186; Vaganay, *op. cit.*, 237–40; H. Lietzmann, *An die Galater* (HNT 10; 2nd ed.; Tübingen, 1923) 33; D. Plooij, 'Studies in the Testimony Book', *Verhandelingen der Koninklijke Akademie van Wetenschappen te Amsterdam* (Literature Section, New Series, Part 32, No. 2; 1932) 5–27.

to put on a string). Such a stringing together of texts was especially common at the beginning of synagogal homilies.[38] Since the Torah was the definitive deposit of God's revelation to Israel, there was no idea of a progressive revelation. Moses had revealed all and no prophet could ever add to the Torah. The Law was only to be explained, and the Prophets and Writings quoted in conjunction with a passage from the Law were intended only to show how Scripture repeated what was already in the Torah. Given such an interpretative method of quoting Scripture in rabbinical circles, Paul's composite quotations might be judged merely to be an imitation of this method. If that is so, then one of the main reasons for postulating the existence of the *testimonia* disappears.

O. Michel, in his painstaking study of the OT in the Pauline letters, uses this argument and goes even further in denying the existence of *testimonia* collections, mainly because 'es fehlt jede Spur spätjüdischer Florilegien. Das bleibt zu beachten.'[39] He remarks:

> There are no traces of pre-Christian *florilegia*, neither of the late Hellenistic Jewish type (Hatch), nor of the late rabbinical sort (Vollmer). Moreover, the hypothesis of R. Harris, that there were early Christian *florilegia*, which would have been composed prior to the writings of the NT, cannot be regarded as probable. Collections of that sort occur first in an early Christian setting; they can be proved to exist with Melito of Sardis and Cyprian. Probably their origin can be traced to an even earlier time; the Epistle of Barnabas perhaps supposes them. But the impression we get is that the Gentile Christian Church compiled these *florilegia* for missionary and polemical purposes.[40]

Others have not been so radical in their denial as Michel. Their criticism of the hypothesis affects rather the way in which the *testimonia* are said to have been used or the extent to which

[38] See A. F. Puukko, 'Paulus und das Judentum', *Studia orientalia* 2 (1928) 62; Michel, *op. cit.* (n. 31 above) 12–13, 83; Hommes, *op. cit.*, 324–54. Cf. n. 30 above.

[39] Michel, *op. cit.*, 43.

[40] *Ibid.*, 52.

they were employed. For example, C. H. Dodd is of the opinion that the theory as proposed by Harris 'outruns the evidence, which is not sufficient to prove so formidable a literary enterprise at so early a date'.[41] Dodd has studied fifteen of the OT passages that occur in the NT, which are cited by two or more writers in prima facie independence of one another (Ps 2:7; 8:4–6; 110:1; 118:22–23; Is 6:9–10; 53:1; 40:3–5; 28:16; Gn 12:3; Jer 31:31–34; Jl 2:28–32; Zech 9:9; Hab 2:3–4; Is 61:1–2; Dt 18:15, 19). An examination of the contexts of these passages shows that they served as units of reference usually wider than the brief form of the words actually quoted. For the context, and not merely the individual verse of the OT that is quoted, has often influenced the vocabulary and the idea of the passage of the NT into which it is incorporated. The fifteen passages and their contexts should be reckoned as wholes or units of reference in the OT for some of the essential articles of the primitive kerygma.[42] Hence it seems that large sections of the OT, especially of Isaiah, Jeremiah, and the Psalms, were

[41] C. H. Dodd, *According to the Scriptures: the Sub-Structure of New Testament Theology* (London, 1952) 26.

[42] Dodd divides the OT citations into four groups to illustrate these themes (see pp. 107–8):

	Primary Sources	Supplementary Sources
Apocalyptic-eschatological Scriptures	Jl 2–3; Zech 9–14; Dn 7	Mal 3:1–6; Dn 12
Scriptures of the New Israel	Hos; Is 6:1–9:7; 11:1–10; 28:16; 40:1–11; Jer 31:10–34	Is 29:9–14; Jer 7:1–15; Heb 1–2
Scriptures of the Servant of the Lord and the Righteous Sufferer	Is 42:1–44:5; 49:1–13; 50:4–11; 52:13–53:12; 61; Ps 69; 22; 31; 38; 88; 34; 118; 41; 42–43; 80	Is 58:6–10
Unclassified Scriptures	Ps 8; 110; 2; Gn 12:3; 22:18; Dt 18:15–19	Ps 132; 16; 2 Sm 7:13–14; Is 55:3; Am 9:11–12

selected as the result of a convention among early Christian evangelists and teachers to support their kerygmatic activities. These sections reveal, then, their method of biblical study. Consequently, particular verses quoted from such OT passages should be regarded 'rather as pointers to the whole context than as constituting testimonies in and for themselves. At the same time detached sentences from other parts of the Old Testament could be adduced to illustrate or elucidate the meaning of the main section under consideration.'[43] The quotations from the OT, then, are not to be accounted for by the postulate of a primitive anthology or isolated proof-texts. 'The composition of "testimony books" was the result, not the presupposition, of the work of early Christian biblical scholars.'[44]

K. Stendahl is in agreement with this last statement of Dodd. His book, *The School of St Matthew and Its Use of the Old Testament*,[45] presents a thorough study of the quotations of the first Gospel. Along with many others, he distinguishes two sorts of quotations in Matthew. He calls one group a 'liturgical' type, because the text of these quotations agrees closely with that of the LXX, the version of the OT which was standard for the liturgy. The other group is a *pesher* type of quotation, which manifests a dependence on a Greek text of the OT, but which also 'presupposes an advanced study of the Scriptures and familiarity with the Hebrew text and with the traditions of interpretation known to us from the Versions'.[46] The latter type is distinguished by the introductory formulas of express fulfilment—the 'formula quotations'. They are called a *pesher* type, because they are considered to be the result of a targumizing procedure, resembling the interpretation of Habakkuk that is found in the Qumran *pesher* on Habakkuk (1QpHab). 'All of Matthew's formula quotations give evidence of features of text

[43] *Ibid.*, 126.

[44] *Loc. cit.*

[45] See n. 8 above.

[46] Stendahl, *op. cit.*, 203.

interpretation of an actualizing nature, often closely associated with the context in the gospel.'[47] Stendahl believes that the Habakkuk text found in 1QpHab never existed as a 'text' outside the commentary. The eschatological conviction of the Qumran sect explains the remarkable freedom they exercised with regard to the text. As the significance of Habakkuk's words became gradually more and more understood through the coming and the instruction of the Teacher of Righteousness, the prophet's message could be made more lucid. Hence the scholarly study, in which the sect engaged,[48] would make it possible, in the light of this greater comprehension of Habakkuk's message, to choose or reject among the various traditions of interpretation they were acquainted with. This study resulted in the adoption of variant readings, or perhaps even in a deliberate change of the text, to suit their theological ideas. Hence the text in the *pesher* would not really represent the text found in a copy of Habakkuk used by them, for instance, for liturgical purposes. Stendahl believes that a similar interpretative or targumizing process was at work on the OT text that is found in the formula quotations of Matthew. The special formulas of introduction would correspond to the Qumran *pesher* formula, *pšrw* '*l*. . . . Consequently, the fact that the text of these quotations differs from the LXX in contrast to the 'liturgical' type of citation is to be explained more by this interpretative process than by appeal to citations from the Hebrew or to derivation from a list of *testimonia*.

Moreover, Stendahl finds that the formula quotations of Matthew show a greater similarity to the LXX than is often claimed—a fact which makes it necessary to correct the prevailing view that they are dependent on the MT. He believes that the formula quotations originated in Greek, the language of the Matthaean Church; he denies, therefore, that the first Gospel

[47] *Ibid.*, 200–1.

[48] For the Qumran sect's study of the Scriptures see 1QS 6:6–7 and the activity of the *dôrēš hattôrāh* in CD 8:6 ff.; 9:8; 4QFlor 2 (Allegro, *art. cit.*, 176).

ever existed as a consistent Aramaic unity. The first Gospel is for him a handbook for teaching, preaching, and church government, into which the formula quotations have been worked, side by side with the other type of quotation. They are the specific product of the School of St Matthew.

In the last chapter of his book Stendahl asks the question, 'Did Matthew make use of Testimonies?' He thinks that a Book of Testimonies might explain (1) the composite quotations, (2) the ascription to wrong authors, and (3) the readings which differ from the editions known to us—especially if these differences remain constant in the testimony tradition. He admits, moreover, that the *testimonia* might fit well into the picture of early Christian preaching. But there are simpler alternatives than the testimony hypothesis to explain the composite quotations. The *midrashim* provide us with an example of a storehouse of quotations brought together by means of association; rabbinical methods account for most of the features Harris wanted to explain by his Book of Testimonies. 'This is not to say that the primitive church did not know and use testimonies, oral or even written, but so far as Matthew is concerned, these testimonies are not responsible for the form of the quotations, least of all for that of the formula quotations.'[49] Thus Stendahl's position comes close to that of Dodd.

ARE THERE ANY EXTANT LISTS OF TESTIMONIA?

When we ask this question, we mean aside from the evidence in the patristic writers such as Cyprian and Pseudo-Gregory of Nyssa. There are two texts that have been considered as *testimonia* that we must now consider. The first is a Greek text published by C. H. Roberts in 1936, bearing the identification P. Ryl. Gk. 460.[50] It is a fragmentary papyrus, which had been

[49] Stendahl, *op. cit.*, 217.

[50] C. H. Roberts, *Two Biblical Papyri in the John Rylands Library, Manchester* (Manchester, 1936) 47–62. 'It is not to be expected that the text of such a manuscript would be of any importance for textual criticism; neither its omissions . . . or additions . . . are of any significance, although a tendency to disagree with Vaticanus (B) may be noticed' (p. 56).

acquired by the John Rylands Library, Manchester, in 1917; its provenance was probably the Fayyûm and it is dated in the fourth century A.D. This fragment of two columns belongs to two other scraps of an Oslo papyrus codex published by G. Rudberg in 1923.[51] When put together, the three pieces contain the following verses of the OT in Greek:

Folio i recto	Is 42:3–4
	66:18–19
Folio i verso	Is 52:15
	53:1–3
Folio ii verso	Is 53:6–7; 11–12
Folio ii recto	An unidentified verse
	Gn 26:13–14
	2 Chr 1:12
	Dt 29:8, 11

Roberts published together with the photograph of the Rylands papyrus the text of both the Rylands and the Oslo fragments. The latter were described by their first editor 'as a *Textbuch für kultische Zweck* [sic], the property of some poor Christian community in Egypt, and the editors of the Oslo papyri write that "Isaiah combined with Genesis suggests that the book was meant for liturgical use"'.[52] But since the verses from Isaiah include parts of the famous Servant passages from chapters 52–3, while all the other extracts in this papyrus, if not 'messianic' in character, can be related to the history of Christ or of Christianity, Roberts suggested that we have a part of a Book of Testimonies in these fragments.

But because the passages from Isaiah found in this text are not among those that appear in Harris' *Testimonies* and because there is no trace of introductory formulas, Roberts did not think that he had found a 'fragment of *the* Testimony Book desider-

[51] G. Rudberg, *Septuaginta-Fragmente unter den Papyri Osloenses* (*Proceedings of the Scientific Society of Kristiania* 1923/2; Kristiania, 1923); later republished by S. Eitrem and L. Amundsen, *Papyri Osloenses* 2 (1931) 10 f.

[52] Roberts, *op. cit.*, 49–50.

ated by Dr Harris'.[53] Rather, it was probably a collection of 'prophetic' passages of the OT, composed for a devotional purpose in the fourth century, when the need for polemics against the Jews would be less than in the second.

While one cannot say with certainty that this papyrus fragment belongs to a list of *testimonia*, it is most probable that it does. I have found no reviewer of Roberts' publication who questions his identification of this text.[54] If one rejects this identification, one may well ask for an alternative satisfactory explanation. The fact that the fragments date from the fourth century A.D. does not exclude the previous existence of such a list, of which this might be a copy.[55] Whether one wishes to ascribe to this collection of texts a merely devotional scope, as does Roberts, or a polemical (anti-Jewish) purpose, as does L. Cerfaux,[56] the fact is that this papyrus bears witness to the existence of such lists at a fairly early date. It lends some sup-

[53] *Ibid.*, 53.

[54] See H. I. Bell, in *JEA* 23 (1937) 138: 'Mr Roberts is almost certainly right in describing it as a portion of a book of "Testimonies". . . . Every one of the extracts contained in them can, without too much forcing, be made to serve as a "testimony".' L. Cerfaux, in *Revue d'histoire ecclésiastique* 33 (1937) 71: 'Il est clair maintenant que nous avons affaire à des *Testimonia*.' E. C. Colwell, in *JRel* 18 (1938) 462: 'The most important of the editor's conclusions is that this papyrus in its disagreements with the testimonies of Cyprian and Gregory of Nyssa shows that there were various testimony books in use in the early Christian centuries.' J. Finegan, *Light from the Ancient Past* (Princeton, 1946) 324. Only H. G. Opitz, in *ZKG* 56 (1937) 436, expressed himself with a bit of caution.

[55] See L. Cerfaux, *Recueil Cerfaux* 2, 225, note 31: 'Notre collection est assez artificielle et tardive. Le texte a été revisé à la bonne tradition des LXX: les variantes ne sont guère que celles des grands onciaux. Néanmoins, il subsiste des indices que l'auteur a travaillé sur des florilèges antérieurs.'

[56] In *Revue d'histoire ecclésiastique* 33 (1937) 71–2: 'M. Roberts estime que son florilège est simplement messianique et qu'il a été formé par un motif de piété. Il paraît cependant assez proche de deux chapitres des *Testimonia* de Cyprien pour que nous lui soupçonnions une parenté plus marquée avec la littérature antijuive. On peut le comparer en effet avec *Test.*, I, 21: *Quod gentes magis in Christum crediturae essent* et avec *Test.*, II, 13: *Quod humilis in primo adventu suo* (*Christus*) *veniret.* Il est construit comme *Test.*, II, 13, com-

port to the hypothesis of the *testimonia*, which cannot be lightly dismissed.

Strangely enough, C. H. Dodd, who devoted a whole book to the OT passages cited in the NT and who more or less rejects the idea of collections of *testimonia* prior to the NT, does not mention this papyrus. Perhaps he does not consider it of any value for the early period. In itself it is not proof for the period in which the NT was formed. Consequently, O. Michel's view would still seem to be valid.

It is at this point that we return to the Qumran fragments published by Allegro. '4QTestimonia' is a fragment that is apparently almost complete in itself, lacking only the lower right-hand corner. 'It is clearly not part of a scroll, for there is none of the close stitching at the left-hand side one associates with a scroll page.'[57] It consists of a single page measuring about 23 cm. high and 14 cm. wide. Its text is a compilation of the following biblical passages: Dt 5:28–29;18: 18–19; Nm 24:15–17; Dt 33: 8–11; and finally a section which 'has no apparent messianic import and is not entirely scriptural'.[58] J. Strugnell, one of the international group of scholars working in Jerusalem on the publication of the Cave 4 documents, has discovered this same passage among other 4Q fragments, to which he has given the provisional title of 4Q Psalms of Joshua. The fragments seem to be part of an apocryphal work used by the Qumran sect and hitherto unknown.

The following is a translation of 4QTestimonia:

And . . . . [=Yahweh] spoke to Moses, saying,

---

mençant par trois longues citations d'Isaïe (la première et la troisième communes avec ce chapitre) et continuant par une seconde série de citations scripturaires. Avec *Test.*, I, 21 il a en commun le deuxième texte d'Isaïe et le début du troisième. La deuxième série de citations du pap., ayant son point de départ en Gen., est très proche de la série correspondante de *Test.*, I, 21; on se base de part et d'autre sur un même principe en recourant aux bénédictions et promesses de l'Ancien Testament.'

[57] Allegro, *art. cit.*, 182.

[58] *Ibid.*, 186.

Dt 5:28 'You (or I) have heard the sound of the words of this people who have spoken to you. They have spoken well everything that they have said. (29) If only this were their determination: to fear me and to keep all my commandments throughout all the days that it might go well with them and with their children forever.'

Dt 18:18 'A prophet like you I shall raise up for them from the midst of their brothers, and I shall put my words in his mouth, and he will tell them all that I command him. (19) Whoever does not listen to my words which the prophet will speak in my name, I shall seek a reckoning from him.'

Nm 24:15 And he uttered his message and said, 'Oracle of Balaam, son of Beor, and oracle of the man whose eye is clear; (16) oracle of one who hears the sayings of El, and who knows the knowledge of Elyon; who sees the vision of Shaddai, (who) falls, yet with opened eye. (17) I see him, but not now; I watch him, but not near. A star shall march forth from Jacob, and a sceptre shall rise from Israel; it shall crush the heads of Moab and destroy all the children of Sheth.'

Dt 33:8 And of Levi he said, 'Give to Levi your Thummim, and your Urim to your loyal bondsman, whom you tested at Massah, and with whom you strove at the waters of Meribah; (9) who said to his father and to his mother, I do (not) know you; and whose brother(s) he did not acknowledge and whose sons he did not recognize. For he kept your word and guarded your covenant; (10) he shall make your judgments clear to Jacob, your Torah to Israel. He (or they) shall set incense before you, and a whole burnt offering on your altar. (11) Bless his might, ... [= O Yahweh], and accept the work of his hands. Smite the loins of his adversaries and those who hate him, that they may never rise (again).'[59]

4QPs Jos At the time when Joshua finished praising and uttering his hymns of thanksgiving, he said, 'Cursed be the

[59] I call attention to the reading, *bl yqwmw*, instead of the MT *mn yqwmwn* in v. 11. At the time of the composition of this list the archaic *mn* (= *man*, the interrogative pronoun) was probably no longer understood and

man who rebuilds this city; with his firstborn may he lay its foundation, and with his lastborn may he set up its gates' (Jos 6:26). Now behold, an accursed man, one belonging to Belial, arises, to be a fowl[er's sn]are to his people and a destruction to all his neighbours. He arose [and made his sons] rulers so that the two of them became vessels of violence. They returned and built (i.e., built again) [this city and es]tablished for it a wall and towers, to provide a refuge for wickedness [. . .] in Israel and a horrible thing in Ephraim, and in Judah [. . . and they] caused pollution in the land, and great contempt among the sons of [Jacob. They shed bl]ood like water on the rampart of the daughter of Zion and within the boundary of Jerusalem.[60]

The 4QTestimonia resemble the Roberts Papyrus in that they are strung together without introductory formulae and intervening comments on the text. In the same article Allegro also published part of another fragment from Qumran Cave 4, which he entitled provisionally '4QFlorilegium'.[61] Only four of the nineteen lines it was said to contain were published in that article. Further fragments of the same text were subsequently published, and the title of this article referred to a 'scroll of eschatological midrāšîm'.[62] Now that the full text of this

---

so was changed to *bl*, just as the archaic *yqwmwn* was changed to *yqwmw*. A less likely possibility, however, is that this fragment preserves for us a reading that is older than that of the MT. For *mn* as *man*, see F. M. Cross and D. N. Freedman, 'The Blessing of Moses', *JBL* 67 (1948) 204; W. F. Albright, 'The Old Testament and Canaanite Language', *CBQ* 7 (1945) 23–4; *id.*, 'A Catalogue of Early Hebrew Lyric Poems', *HUCA* 23/1 (1950–51) 29.

[60] For other translations and further studies of 4QTestimonia, see my bibliography in *CBQ* 30 (1969) 68–70.

[61] Allegro, *art. cit.*, 176–7, Document II.

[62] Allegro, 'Further Light on the History of the Qumran Sect', *JBL* 75 (1956) 95, had previously revealed that 4QFlorilegium also contains a 'comment on Ps 2:1–2'; 'all that remains of the *pešer* itself, apart from the introduction, is: ". . . the chosen ones of Israel in the last days, that is, the time of trial which is com[ing]."' The other fragments were published in 'Fragments of a Qumran Scroll of Eschatological Midrāšîm', *JBL* 77 (1958) 350–4. References to further studies of this text can be found in my bibliography in *CBQ* 30 (1969) 67–8.

Qumran document (4Q*174*) is available,[63] it is apparent how ineptly the original title was chosen. Certainly Allegro's second title, 'eschatological midrash', is better suited to the nature of the text, mainly because of the interwoven commentary on the texts cited (2 Sm 7:10–14 [=1 Chr 17:9–13]; Ex 15:17–18; Am 9:11; Ps 1:1; Is 8:11; Ez 37:23; Ps 2:1). However, in the definitive edition of the text in DJD Allegro continues to label it 'Florilegium', implying that it is somehow related to the anthological literature to which the Testimonia belong. This general relationship can be admitted, but even though 4QFlorilegium is important as a genre that illustrates NT usage of OT citations with interwoven commentary, nevertheless it is not a *testimonia* list as such.

THE SIGNIFICANCE OF THE 4QTESTIMONIA

The first question that must be answered with regard to the 4QTestimonia text is, 'Is it really a collection of *testimonia*?' If a doubt arises about Allegro's identification, it is because of the last section, a *pesher* on Jos 6:26 quoted from the 4Q Psalms of Joshua. Until we see the other fragments of this work, we cannot be sure about its character. Allegro admits that the part here quoted has no messianic import. There is, of course, no reason why all the texts must have it, for we are not sure of the reason why they were so compiled. Hence, the presence of such a text in the list does not prevent it from being a collection of *testimonia*. Yet its presence is peculiar, even though we do admit that its incorporation in such a list can be compared to the NT use of extracanonical works like Enoch (see Jude 14).[64]

Moreover, the first section quoted in this text comes from Dt 5:28–29, which de facto has no more messianic import than the

[63] See 4Q*174* in DJD 5, 53–7.

[64] N. Wieder, 'Notes on the New Documents from the Fourth Cave of Qumran', *JJS* 7 (1956) 75–6, thinks that rabbinical haggadah may help solve the riddle of the relationship between the first three *testimonia* and the final section. The rabbis regarded the story of Hiel (1 Kgs 16:34), to which the last passage refers, as testimony to the truth of the biblical prophecies of Joshua.

4Q Psalms of Joshua. But it is closely joined to Dt 18:18–19 in the first paragraph (note the paragraph dividers on the plate published by Allegro). Mgr P. W. Skehan is quoted as saying that 'the combination of Dt 18:18–19 with Dt 5:28–29 is already found in the Samaritan Pentateuch at Ex 20:21'.[65] This fact likewise explains the first few words of the fragment, *wydbr* : : : : *'l mwšh l'mwr*, 'And (Yahweh) spoke to Moses saying'. They differ from the introductory formula of Dt 5:28, *wy'mr yhwh 'ly*, which Allegro thinks has been changed 'for the purpose of the Testimonia selection'.[66] As a matter of fact, the introductory phrase found in 4QTestimonia is identical with that used in the Samaritan Hebrew Pentateuch at Ex 20:21b; it reads *wydbr yhwh 'l mšh l'mr*.[67] That there is some connection here between this text and the Samaritan Pentateuch is obvious, even though we have not yet discovered just what it is. At any rate, the close joining of the two passages of Deuteronomy in one paragraph shows that they were regarded as a unit, which ends with the promise of a prophet to come.

The promise of a prophet, a successor to Moses, in the first paragraph, followed by the Oracle of Balaam in the second, and the Blessing of Moses (Jacob) accorded to Levi in the third, presents a sequence that can only be described as a collection of *testimonia* used in Qumran theological circles. Nm 24:17 must have enjoyed a certain favour in these circles, for it is quoted once in the War Scroll (1QM 11:6) and once in the Damascus Document (CD 7:18–20).[68] If, then, the identification of this text as a list of *testimonia* compiled in view of Qumran theology is rejected, we have a right to ask for a better explanation of the text.

[65] See R. E. Brown, "The Messianism of Qumrân', *CBQ* 19 (1957) 82. See further P. W. Skehan, *CBQ* 19 (1957), 435–40.

[66] Allegro, *art. cit.* (n. 1 above) 182, note 48.

[67] A. von Gall, *Der hebräische Pentateuch der Samaritaner* (Giessen, 1918) 159. Cf. H. Petermann, *Pentateuchus Samaritanus*, fasc. 2: Exodus (Berlin, 1882) 189: *wmll yhwh 'm mšh lmymr*.

[68] See J. Carmignac, 'Les citations de l'Ancien Testament dans "La guerre des fils de lumière contre les fils de ténèbres"', *RB* 63 (1956) 237–9.

To regard this sequence of texts from the OT as *testimonia* does not ipso facto mean that it is a messianic *testimonia* list, even in the loose sense. It is well known that 1QS 9:11 refers to the 'coming of a prophet and the Messiahs of Aaron and Israel'. The prophet that is meant here is almost certainly the Prophet-like-Moses; the Messiah of Aaron is an expected anointed high-priestly figure; the Messiah of Israel is an expected anointed king, the ideal Davidic heir. To a number of scholars the first three paragraphs of 4QTestimonia refer to Qumran messianic belief: Dt 5:28–29 and 18:18–19 would allude to the Prophet-like-Moses who is awaited; Nm 24:15–17 to the Messiah of Israel; and Dt 33:8–11, the blessing of Levi, to the Messiah of Aaron. This is the view of A. Dupont-Sommer, G. Vermes, T. H. Gaster, and many others.[69] The fact that the two passages derived from Dt 5 and 18 were undoubtedly derived from the Samaritan text tradition, which quotes them together at Ex 20:21b, does not really militate against the reference of these passages to the Qumran belief in the coming prophet. The real difficulty in the list is the reference of Nm 24:15–17 to the kingly Messiah, since the same passage is referred to in CD 7:18–20 and interpreted of *two* figures, not one: the Star is understood to be the Interpreter of the Law (probably a priestly figure), and the Sceptre is the Prince of all the congregation (probably the Davidic Messiah). This means that the first three paragraphs of 4QTestimonia cannot be taken as exact allusions to the three expected figures of 1QS 9:11. It is more complicated than that. But in any case, one cannot deny the *testimonia*-character of the text.

Accepting, then, the identification of this text as most likely a

[69] See, e.g., A. Dupont-Sommer, *Ecrits esséniens découverts près de la Mer Morte* (Paris: Payot, 1959) 328–33; G. Vermes, *The Dead Sea Scrolls in English* (Pelican; Harmondsworth and Baltimore: Penguin, 1965) 247–9; T. H. Gaster, *The Scriptures of the Dead Sea Sect* (London: Secker and Warburg, 1957) 353–9 (who notes on p. 327 that 'the same passages of Scripture are used by the Samaritans as the stock *testimonia* to the coming of the Taheb, or future "Restorer"'[?]).

collection of *testimonia*, one asks what light it sheds on the problem of *testimonia* in NT study. The particular sequence of texts found in 4QTestimonia and in the Roberts Papyrus does not agree with any of the NT or patristic composite citations. In fact, one of the striking features about the whole problem of the *testimonia* is that there are very few composite citations that are repeated in the various NT or patristic writers. Even the sequence of Is 28:16, Ps 117/18:22, Is 8:14 (found in Mt 21:42, Rom 9:33, 1 Pt 2:6–8, and *Ep. Barn.* 6, 2, 4) appears with such differences and omissions that it would be hard to establish that they all came from one collection.[70] Such a fact should not be lost sight of.

On the other hand, we do have in 4QTestimonia a collection of OT passages strung together in a way that resembles the composite citations of the NT. If we are right in thinking that 4QFlorilegium is related to the *testimonia*, then we have a concrete example of how *testimonia* were worked into the text of a sectarian writing. This use of OT citations will illustrate the Pauline usage of OT quotations with intervening comments.[71] If the hypothesis of *testimonia* lists had been excogitated to explain the existence of the Roberts Papyrus and the 4QTestimonia, we might have reason to suspect it. But most of the discussion antedates the publication of these documents, which, in turn, confirm the existence of such collections. One can now point to 4QTestimonia to answer Michel's objection, 'Es fehlt jede Spur spätjüdischer Florilegien'. For this text from the fourth cave at Qumran bears witness to the existence of such a literary procedure in late Judaism. Moreover, both Dodd and Stendahl will have to alter their views slightly. While the collections of *testimonia* that are found in patristic writers might be regarded as the result of early Christian catechetical and mis-

[70] Harris, *op. cit.*, 1, 26–32, makes much of this example. Dodd, *op. cit.*, 26, comments: 'Indeed striking, but it is almost the only one of its kind.' Stendahl, *op. cit.*, 212, thinks that it is rather 'a *verbum Christi*', which served as the 'nucleus for the later formation of the testimony'.

[71] See the texts listed in n. 25 above.

sionary activity, 4QTestimonia shows that the stringing together of OT texts from various books was a pre-Christian literary procedure, which may well have been imitated in the early stage of the formation of the NT. It resembles so strongly the composite citations of the NT writers that it is difficult not to admit that *testimonia* influenced certain parts of the NT.

Even if we have not uncovered in these texts any exact parallel for the sequences of OT passages cited in the NT, it is not without significance that the extant *testimonia*, especially those of Qumran, contain passages which are quoted in the NT —outside of composite quotations. Dt 18:18–19 is used in Acts 3:23; 7:37; 2 Sm 7:11–14 in 2 Cor 6:18; Jn 7:42; Heb 1:5 (in a composite quotation); Am 9:11 in Acts 15:16. Like the early Christian Church, the sect of Qumran had favourite texts of the OT. From what we have already learned about Qumran theology, it is not surprising that many of these texts are the same as those in the NT. Given the use of similar texts and given a similar way of handling OT texts, we must conclude that the 4QTestimonia document is an important discovery for the understanding of the formation of the NT.

Stendahl's study of the quotations in Matthew is a careful comparison of the passages cited with the various Greek and Hebrew texts and versions of the OT. He has convincingly shown that the formula quotations in Mt depend much more on the LXX than was previously thought.[72] On the other hand,

[72] An extensive criticism of Stendahl's book can be found in B. Gärtner, 'The Habakkuk Commentary (DSH) and the Gospel of Matthew', *ST* 8 (1954) 1–24. He questions Stendahl's interpretation of the double readings in the Habakkuk *pesher*, which led him to maintain that the OT text found in 1QpHab was not known outside this commentary. Utilizing a fragment of a Greek translation of Habakkuk, found in the Judean desert and published by D. Barthélemy, 'Redécouverte d'un chaînon manquant de l'histoire de la Septante', *RB* 60 (1953) 18–29, Gärtner has convincingly shown that 'in three passages where DSH [= 1QpHab] offers a reading differing significantly from the MT, the Greek version agrees with DSH.... Similarly on a number of other points it seems to me that the Greek version gives evidence that the sect had its own peculiar tradition of the text of the Minor Prophets' (p. 5).

recently published preliminary reports about the Qumran biblical texts indicate that we shall have to revise some of the notions commonly held about the relation of the LXX to the MT. Fragments from Cave 4 have revealed a Hebrew text of various biblical books that support the readings of the LXX against those of the MT.[73] The text tradition of the LXX must be taken seriously and the differences between it and the MT can no longer be written off merely as 'free' translations or as mistranslations. Theological opinions of the translators influenced their work at times, as is well known, but outside of such areas where this is obvious or proven, the LXX should be regarded as a witness of a different Hebrew recension, when it does not agree completely with the MT. The discrepancy in readings, however, between the LXX and the MT varies in value according to the OT book under discussion.[74]

The Qumran discoveries have brought to light Hebrew recensions, differing from the MT, which were in use in Palestine in the last centuries B.C. and in the first A.D. It is possible that such recensions influenced also the NT.[75] If readings from

---

Consequently, 'one may ask whether the sect in general had knowledge of what we call the MT to the Minor Prophets' (p. 6). If this is so, then there is no basis for Stendahl's contention that the sect deliberately altered the text according to its theological interpretations. Gärtner also criticizes Stendahl's use of the term *pesher* to designate the type of quotation that would have been produced by the school of St Matthew. He shows that the manner of citation in Matthew is quite different from that of the *pesher* on Habakkuk. See the comments of K. Stendahl in the reprint of his book (cf. n. 8 above) pp. i–xiv.

[73] See F. M. Cross, Jr, 'A New Qumrân Biblical Fragment Related to the Original Hebrew Underlying the Septuagint', *BASOR* 132 (1953) 15–26; Moshe Greenberg, 'Stabilization of the Text of the Hebrew Bible, Reviewed in the Light of the Biblical Materials from the Judean Desert', *JAOS* 76 (1956) 157–67. Cf. F. M. Cross, Jr., *IEJ* 16 (1966) 81-95.

[74] See F. M. Cross, Jr, 'The Scrolls and the Old Testament', *Christian Century*, Aug. 10, 1955, 920–1; P. Katz, 'Septuagintal Studies in the Mid-Century', *The Background of the New Testament and Its Eschatology: Studies in Honour of C. H. Dodd* (Cambridge, 1956) 200–8.

[75] A text of Exodus from Qumran Cave 4 (4QEx[a]) reads *ḥmš wšbʿym npš wymt,* thus confirming the LXX version of Ex 1:5, which has *pente kai*

the OT were taken from Hebrew texts of this sort—often betraying a 'Septuagintal tendency'—and were incorporated into lists of *testimonia*, this could explain the different textual tradition that sometimes appears in the quotations in the NT. As for the formula quotations, which as a group are closer to the Hebrew than to the LXX, when compared with the 'liturgical' type of quotations, it may be that the 'Septuagintal tendency' that Stendahl has found in them is due to dependence on a Hebrew text with such a tendency, such as we know existed in Palestine at the beginning of our era. It should be noted that Allegro has emphasized the 'Septuagintal tendency of the text tradition used by the compiler of 4Q[Testimonia]'.[76] But the further publication of the 4Q biblical fragments must be awaited before this aspect of the problem can be pursued.

In conclusion, the text of 4QTestimonia furnishes pre-Christian evidence of a literary process that led to the use of composite quotations in the NT and thus supports the hypothesis of *testimonia*. The discovery of this text thus confirms the opinion of Vollmer that Hebrew collections of OT passages did exist among the Jews before the time of Christ. This discovery, however, does not invalidate the views of C. H. Dodd about the

---

hebdomēkonta eteleutēsan, whereas the MT mentions only 'seventy' persons. Acts 7:14, however, mentions 'seventy-five'; see *RB* 63 (1956) 56. Heb 1:6 quotes Dt 32:43, agreeing with the LXX against the MT; a text from 4Q now confirms the reading in the LXX and Hebrews: *whšthww lw kl 'lhym*; see P. W. Skehan, *BASOR* 136 (1954) 12–15. Allegro, *art. cit.* (supra n. 1) 176, n. 25, seems to think that Am 9:11, which is quoted in 4QFlorilegium and in CD 7:16, is 'in the form offered by . . . Acts 15:16, against MT and LXX'. The MT has *'qym*; 4QFlorilegium and the Damascus Document have *whqymwty*, a waw-conversive perfect instead of the imperfect. This is supposed to reflect a text tradition preserved in Acts by *kai anoikodomēsō*; see C. Rabin, *The Zadokite Documents* (Oxford, 1954) 29, whom Allegro quotes. This interpretation is certainly possible, but there is just a chance that too much is being derived from the form of the waw-conversive perfect. Actually the LXX reads *anastēsō*, a form that is certainly closer in meaning to *qwm*, used by both the MT and the 4QFlorilegium, than is the *anoikodomēsō* of Acts.

[76] Allegro, *art. cit.* (supra n. 1) 186, n. 107. In Dt 18:19 the word *hnby*,

use of OT contexts among early Christian writers and teachers. But it is not possible to regard the use of *testimonia* as the final term of such a development, as Dodd has suggested. Nor does it rule out the activity of a 'School of St Matthew', as postulated by K. Stendahl, but the activity of that school will have to be explained otherwise. While I would not go so far as to say with Allegro that 'this *testimonia* document from Qumran is one of the most important of the works found',[77] it is true that it throws new light on an old problem.[78]

'the prophet', is found in the 4Q text, in the LXX, and in the citation used in Acts 3:23, but it is missing in the MT. In Dt 33:8 the LXX and 4Q Testimonia read, 'Give to Levi', which is not found in the MT.

[77] J. M. Allegro, *The Dead Sea Scrolls* (Harmondsworth, 1956) 139.

[78] See further P. Prigent, 'Les récits évangéliques de la Passion et l'utilisation des "Testimonia"', *RHR* 161 (1962) 130–2; J.-P. Audet, 'L'hypothèse des Testimonia: Remarques autour d'un livre récent', *RB* 70 (1963) 381–405; P. Prigent, *Les Testimonia dans le christianisme primitif: L'épître de Barnabé I–XVI et ses sources* (EBib; Paris: Gabalda, 1961); R. A. Kraft, Review of P. Prigent, *JTS* n.s. 13 (1962) 401–8; 'Barnabas' Isaiah Text and the "Testimony Book" Hypothesis', *JBL* 79 (1960) 336–50; E. D. Freed, *Old Testament Quotations in the Gospel of John* (NTSup 11; Leiden: Brill, 1965) 44–5; M. Treves, 'On the Meaning of the Qumran Testimonia', *RQ* 2 (1960) 569–71.

II

THE SEMITIC BACKGROUND OF VARIOUS GOSPEL PASSAGES

3

THE ARAMAIC QORBĀN INSCRIPTION FROM JEBEL ḪALLET EṬ-ṬÛRI AND MK 7:11/MT 15:5 *

When Jesus was arguing with the Pharisees, he reproached them with nullifying what God had commanded in order to observe their own traditions. As an example he cited the commandments, 'Honour your father and your mother', and 'Whoever abuses his father or mother must be put to death'. In contrast, the Pharisees and scribes were teaching, 'If a man says to his father or mother, "Anything of mine that might have been of use to you is Korban" (that is, a gift), they let him off from doing anything more for his father or mother' (Mk 7:9–13 = Mt 15:3–6). Mark has preserved the Aramaic word in his account, *korban, ho estin dōron, ho ean ex emou ōphelēthēs* (7:11), which he also translated for his Gentile readers, whereas Matthew has simply *dōron ho ean ex emou ōphelēthēs* (15:5). Commentators have been accustomed to explain the word *korban* in Mark by appealing to the Mishnah and to statements in Josephus.

A recently discovered tomb in the area south-east of Jerusalem has yielded an inscribed ossuary-lid that sheds new light on this verse in Mark. The tomb was found at Jebel Ḫallet eṭ-Ṭûri, a spot south of Bîr-'Ayyûb in the extension of the Cedron Valley just before it becomes the Wâdi en-Nâr. It is a Jewish tomb dating from the beginning of the Christian era. The inscription has been published with a photo and facsimile by Fr

* Originally published in *JBL* 78 (1959) 60–5.

Jozef T. Milik in an article entitled 'Trois tombeaux juifs récemment découverts au Sud-Est de Jérusalem'.[1]

According to Milik's description, the inscription consists of two lines scratched with a fairly broad-pointed nail (about 0.2 cm. wide). The characters are firmly made but not deeply incised, with the exception of a few at the beginning. The length of the first line of the inscription is 54 cm. and of the second 38 cm. The letters have an average height of 2.5 cm. It is written on a lid 64.5 cm. long, 19.5 cm. wide and about 3 cm. thick.

The inscription reads as follows (Milik's translation):[2]

kl dy 'nš mthnh bḥlth dh *qrbn 'lh mn dbgwh*	Quiconque réutilisera à son profit cet ossuaire-ci, malédiction (*litt.* offrande) de Dieu de la part de celui qui est dedans!

Milik comments, 'La lecture matérielle et la traduction sont certaines.' Since he was kind enough to show me the ossuary-lid while I was in Jerusalem, I was able to check his reading and

[1] *Studii Biblici Franciscani Liber Annuus* 7 (1956–57) 232–9. The text and Milik's translation can also be found in *RB* 65 (1958) 409.

[2] The script of the inscription is described as close to the Herodian type (related to the Uzziah inscription and 1QIs[b], 1QM, 1QH, 1QapGn), introduced into public use *c.* 30 B.C. Milik dates the inscription on paleographical evidence to the end of the first century B.C. He also calls attention to a few of the grammatical peculiarities of the text: 1) the emphatic state of *hlth* written with *he* instead of *aleph*, a phenomenon which he finds paralleled in the Elephantine papyri, twice in the *Genesis Apocryphon* (see E. Y. Kutscher, 'The Language of the Genesis Apocryphon, a Preliminary Study', *Scripta Hierosolymitana* 4 [1957] 26), and in two unpublished texts from Qumran Cave 4 (very frequently in 4QHen[a] [from the second century B.C.] and by way of exception in 4QHen astr[b] [end of the second-beginning of the first century B.C.]; 2) both *dy* and *d* occurring as the relative pronoun; this feature too is found in 1QapGn (see Kutscher, p. 6 [six instances of *d* against 60–70 of *dy*]; 3) *dh* as the demonstrative adjective feminine instead of *d'*; the latter alone is found in Qumran Aramaic with one doubtful exception (see *RB* 63 [1956] 413); 4) *ḥlth*, 'box, ossuary', is also found in the Phoenician Ešmun'azor inscription (*CIS* 3: 3, 5, 7, 10, 21) and in *Midraš Tanna'im* (ed. D. Z. Hoffmann, 175 f.).

agree that it is certain. It was only subsequently that I developed some doubts about the translation.

To justify his translation, Milik explains that the beginning of the inscription, *kl dy 'nš mthnh*, is syntactically impossible. He supposes that the scribe began with *kl dy*, originally intending to continue with a finite verb (e.g., *ythnh*). This supposition is based on traces of a letter within the *aleph* of *'nš* which Milik considers may well be a *yodh*. The scribe is thought to have corrected himself, recalling a more general formula requiring a participle and *kl 'nš*. Consequently, the first line would more properly be transcribed thus: *kl {dy} 'nš mthnh bḥlth dh*. But such an explanation and his translation do violence to the text, which can be understood more simply on closer examination.

First of all, there is no doubt that there are extra traces within the *aleph*; but they are not of the form of a *yodh* at all. They seem to be nothing more than attempts to write *aleph* correctly and are of the same type as the extra traces within the *lamedh* of *kl*.

Secondly, the elimination of *dy* must be regarded as gratuitous. It is rather to be construed as a compound relative pronoun,[3] having a function both in the main clause and in the subordinate clause. In the main clause *kl dy* obviously acts as the subject of the nominal sentence whose predicate is *qrbn*. In the subordinate clause *dy* serves as the complement (or possibly as the internal object) of *mthnh*. The subject of this participle is the indefinite *'nš*.

Thirdly, Milik's translation disregards or misinterprets the preposition *b* before *ḥlth dh*. Part of this difficulty lies in the sense he gives to the participle, 'réutilisera à son profit'. The root of the verb is *hny*, known in Jewish Aramaic, Syriac, and Modern

[3] This analysis of *dy* as a compound relative is based on the usual interpretation to *kl* as a construct state in this *kl dy* expression. See P. Leander, 'Laut- und Formenlehre des Ägyptisch-Aramäischen', *Göteborgs Högskolas Årsskrift* 34 (1928) #18j; J. A. Fitzmyer, 'The syntax of *kl*, *kl'* in the Aramaic Texts from Egypt and in Biblical Aramaic', *Bib* 38 (1957) 175–6. If one prefers to regard *kl* as the absolute and *dy* as a simple relative, then *dy* alone is the subject of the nominal sentence.

Hebrew and meaning, 'to be pleasing, profitable'. Brockelmann relates it to Arabic *hani'a*, Sabaean *hn'm*, 'lucrum'.[4] In the Ithpeel it means 'to enjoy, to derive profit from, to profit from'. The Ithpeel is found elsewhere with the preposition *b*,[5] which at first sight might seem to confirm Milik's translation of the first line. However, it should be noted that we here find a direct object *dy*, which prevents us from regarding the construction as *hny b*. Hence we must restore to *beth* its basic prepositional force.

Fourthly, the translation of *qrbn* as 'malédiction' is highly questionable. What reason is there for supposing that *qrbn* is used here like the *qwnm* of later rabbinical writings? Moreover, such a translation leaves the syntax of the sentence completely unexplained; the only way it could possibly be saved would be to emend the beginning of the first line thus: *⟨l⟩kl {dy} 'nš mthnh*. . . .

Consequently, the inscription should rather be translated as follows:

> 'All that a man may find-to-his-profit in this ossuary
> (is) an offering to God from him who is within it.'[6]

This translation is confirmed by the Peshitta version of Mt 15:5, which uses precisely the same verb in connection with *qrbn*. It reads as follows:[7] *qurbān(y) meddem dᵉtethᵉnē' men(y)*. It is

[4] *Lexicon Syriacum* (Halle/S., 1928) 178.

[5] J. Levy (*Chaldäisches Wörterbuch über die Targumin* [Leipzig, 1881] lists an example from Ez 16:31 which illustrates this usage: 'Eine Buhlerin *dmthny' b'gr'* die sich Nutzen (od. Vergnügen) verschafft durch den Buhlerlohn oder für Buhlen.'

[6] For similar uses of *kl dy* see Dn 2:38; 6:8; Ezr 7:21, 23, 26; Cowley, *AP* 15:19, 24, 27; 40:3; 49:4; Kraeling, *BMAP* 2:8, 10; 7:22, 31, 35; 1QapGn 22:30. For the indefinite use of *'nš* see *AP* 28:8, 10; *BMAP* 8:5, 8; 1QapGn 21:13. For further uses of the emphatic in *he* see *AP* 14:5 (*'lhth*); 14:4, 6, 9; 6:6 (*mwm'h*); *Aḥiqar* 204 (*'rdh*); *BMAP* 12:9 (*byth* [but not 3:4, where *byth* is followed by *zy* and a proper name; *pace* Kraeling, it is to be interpreted as a prospective suffix followed by *zy* and a proper name similar to *'nny zy 'ḥwhy*, *AP* 30:18–19; 31:18; cf. *byth zy 'sḥwr*, *AP* 15:30]); 1QapGn 22:2 (*'nh*); 7:1 (*'r'ḥ*); 19:18 (*ḥlmh*); 17:16 (*ktrh?*). For further uses of *daleth* see 1QapGn 2:25; 20:10, 27; 21:29; 22:21, 22 (*bis*). The form *bgwh* is also found in Zakir b. 3; Ezr 5:7; 6:2.

[7] P. E. Pusey, G. H. Gwilliam, *Tetraeuangelium sanctum, simplex Syrorum versio* (Oxford, 1901) 94.

to be noted that the syntax of this verse closely parallels the main part of the ossuary inscription. Instead of *kl dy* we have *meddem de*; instead of the generic *'nš mthnh* we have the finite verb with a personal (2 sg.) subject; instead of *bḥlth dh* we have *men(y)*, though the preposition is admittedly different. In both cases the predicate of the sentence is *qrbn*. Whereas the Syriac has *qurbān(y)* 'my offering', the ossuary-lid has preserved a fuller and more formal expression *qrbn 'lh mn dbgwh*. In other words, the use of *qrbn* in the ossuary inscription is identical with that preserved in the Greek of Mark: *korban ho ean ex emou ōphelēthēs*. We have to do with a dedicatory formula in common use among the Jews of the last few centuries B.C. and well into Christian times. Probably it is a vestigial survival of much older mortuary offerings. Whether we classify this formula with other *ndrym*, as does the Mishnah, or speak of it as a *horkos*, as does Josephus, makes little difference as long as we recognize its basic character as an expression that *puts a ban* on something, reserving it for sacred use and withdrawing it from the profane.

Milik has pointed out the pertinence of this inscription to the NT passages in Matthew and Mark. He does not stress, however, the similarity of the two expressions, as his interest lies rather in the evolution of various *qrbn* expressions with their successive changes, which he believes are due to 'scrupule religieux'.[8] According to him the ossuary-lid already manifests the fashion of the first century B.C. in substituting *'lh* for the tetragrammaton of the expression *qrbn Yhwh* found in Nm 9:13; 31:50.[9] Later in the first century A.D. *qrbn* is used alone (as we find it in Mt 15:5 and Mk 7:11). Still later in the second century A.D. we find the palliative *qwnm* being used instead of *qrbn*, 'à cause de sa signification sacrale'.

We should, however, beware of stressing such an evolution merely on the basis of these texts. There is no doubt about the

[8] *Op. cit.*, 238.

[9] To these references of Milik add Nm 9:7.

OT roots of the expression. But in addition to *qrbn Yhwh* from Numbers, we also find another expression in Lv 23:14, *'d hby'km 't qrbn 'lhykm*. This is admittedly not the stereotyped formula *qrbn 'lh* of the ossuary lid, but then neither is *qrbn Yhwh* of Nm 9:7, 13; 31:50. It shows, however, that the combination *qrbn 'lh* did exist earlier. Furthermore, the testimony of Josephus indicates that *qrbn 'lh* was also in use as late as the first century A.D. and that *qrbn* alone was known as an oath-formula in the late fourth century B.C.

All who consecrate themselves in fulfilment of a vow—Nazirites as they are called, people who grow long hair and abstain from wine—these too, when they dedicate their hair and offer it in sacrifice assign their shorn locks to the priests. Again, those who describe themselves as 'Corban' to God—meaning what the Greeks would call 'a gift'—when desirous to be relieved of this obligation must pay down to the priests a fixed sum.[10]

And again,

This [acquaintance of various cities in ancient times with the Jewish nation] is apparent from a passage in the works of Theophrastus[11] on *Laws*, where he says that the laws of the Tyrians prohibit the use of foreign oaths, in enumerating which he includes among others the oath called 'Corban'. Now this oath will be found in no other nation except the Jews and, translated from the Hebrew, one may interpret it as meaning God's gift.[12]

Such evidence seems to preclude any attempt to show that a development in the use of this dedicatory formula existed at an early period. It is more likely that a variety of formulae existed side by side, some expanded and formal like the ossuary in-

[10] *Ant.* 4, 72–3. Important words in Greek are: *kai hoi korban hautous onomasantes tō theō, dōron de touto sēmainei kata Hellēnōn glōttan*. Translation of H. St J. Thackeray, *Josephus* (Loeb Classical Library IV; London, 1930) 511. *tō theō* must be taken with *korban* and therefore reflects *qrbn 'lh*. Cf. H. Grégoire, 'La première mention de *Korbân* ou *Korbanâs* dans l'épigraphie grecque', *Bulletin de l'académie royale de Belgique*, Classe des lettres, 1953, 657–63; H. Hommel, 'Das Wort korban und seine Verwandten', *Philologus* 98 (1954) 132–49.

[11] The pupil of Aristotle, who lived *c.* 372–288 B.C.

[12] *Against Apion* 1, 166–7. *dēloi d', hōs an eipoi tis, ek tēs Hebraiōn methermēneuomenos dialektou dōron theou.* Thackeray's translation, LCL I, 229–31.

scription, others abbreviated like the NT expression or that indicated by Josephus. A similar variety of formulae that existed in the later period, when there admittedly was a semantic development, confirms this—in general at least.

For I do admit that the expressions found in the Mishnah reveal a later stage of development in the use of the *qrbn* formula. There is some indication that the nominal sentence formula (such as we have in Mark/Matthew and in the ossuary inscription) was still in use. In Nedarim 1:4 we find the expression *qrbn š'wkl lk*, 'What I eat of thine be . . . "a Korban"'.[13] But the development is seen, first of all, in the substitution of *qwnm, qwns, qwnḥ* for *qrbn* (Nedarim 1:2). Secondly, there is an obvious development in the meaning of the word in some of the rabbinical formulae; it no longer means merely 'an offering to God', pronounced over some object to remove it from profane use, but acquires the force of an asseverative and even an imprecatory interjection. It is frequently followed by a *š*-clause (a remnant of the old formula) and a conditional clause: *qwnm š'th nhnh ly 'm 'yn 'th b' wnwtn lbny kwr 'ḥd šl ḥytyn wšty ḥbywt šl yyn*, '*Konam* be the benefit thou hast from me if thou come not and give my son a *kor* of wheat and two jars of wine!' (Nedarim 8:7).[14] Or *qwnm šdy š'yny ḥwrš bh l'wlm* (said of a cow, which a neighbour refuses to lend), '*Konam!* if I ever again plough my field with it' (Nedarim 4:6). In my opinion, this usage is definitely a development beyond that which is found in the NT or ossuary expression—at least we have no evidence of this usage at an earlier period.

[13] Translation of H. Danby, *The Mishnah* (London, 1933) 265.

[14] *Ibid.*, 275. It does not seem to be correct to say with Rengstorf (Kittel *TDNT* 3, 865) that 'the sentence [in Mt/Mk] . . . has its literal and real counterpart in the rabbinical expression *qwnm š'th nhnyth ly*', because this is a quotation of only half of the pertinent saying. Aside from this point Rengstorf's treatment of *korban* is very well done. See also Str-B I, 711–17. It is rather characteristic of commentators on Mk 7:11 that they cite only *half* of these rabbinical statements; see e.g., E. Klostermann, *Das Markusevangelium* (HNT III; 4. Aufl.; Tübingen, 1950) 69; V. Taylor, *The Gospel according to St Mark* (London: Macmillan, 1953) 342; M.-J. Lagrange, *Evangile selon Saint Marc* (EBib; Paris, 1929) 185.

Now it is precisely this imprecatory usage that Milik has imposed upon *qrbn* in the translation he has given of the inscription. But since the syntax of the latter reveals the same construction as that found in the NT, I prefer to give it the simple meaning of 'an offering to God' rather than 'a curse of God'. We should not lose sight of the fact that the ossuary inscription has preserved for us the formula complete in itself; it is thus of far greater importance for the interpretation of Mark 7:11 than the somewhat cryptic formulae that we find in the casuistic passages of Nedarim. In it we have a concrete example of how the formula was used. The new inscription does not alter the sense of the word in Matthew or Mark but provides a perfect contemporary parallel.[15]

[15] See further Z. W. Falk, 'Notes and Observations on Talmudic Vows', *HTR* 59 (1966) 309–12; J. Bligh, 'Korban!', *HeythJ* 5 (1964) 192–3; S. Zeitlin, 'Korban', *JQR* 53 (1962) 160–3; 'Korban: A Gift', *JQR* 59 (1968) 135–5. To be noted is the discovery of a stone jar, inscribed with the word *qrbn* and two birds (turtle-doves?), recently found in the excavation of Jerusalem by B. Mazar south of the temple area (see 'The Excavations in the Old City of Jerusalem', *Eretz-Israel* 9: *W. F. Albright Volume* [Jerusalem: Israel Exploration Society, 1969] 168–70 [+pl. 45, #5]. The word designates the vessel as a 'gift', probably for the service of the temple. Since it is an isolated word, it does not add much to the meaning of *qorbān* found in the ossuary inscription. It undoubtedly illustrates the Mishnah, *Maaser Sheni* 4:10. See also G. W. Buchanan, 'Some Vow and Oath Formulas in the New Testament', *HTR* 58 (1965) 319–26. He discusses the *qorbān* formula, but with no reference to this Aramaic inscription. It is mentioned, however, in the inconsequential article of J. D. M. Derrett, '*Korban, ho estin dōron*', *NTS* 16 (1969–70) 364–8. Derrett suggests that the word be vocalized 'properly *ḳārebān*'. But this is impossible!

4

'PEACE UPON EARTH AMONG MEN OF HIS GOOD WILL' (LK 2:14)*

It was Dr Claus-Hunno Hunzinger who first pointed out the pertinence of a Qumran expression to the understanding of the Lucan Christmas greeting: *kai epi gēs eirēnē en anthrōpois eudokias* (2:14).[1] He found the phrase *b^e^nê r^e^ṣônô*, 'sons of his good pleasure', in one of the Qumran Thanksgiving Hymns (1QH 4:32–33). Though it had previously been pointed out, perhaps best by J. Jeremias,[2] that *eudokias* must refer to God and not to man, there was no direct parallel for the expression 'men of God's good pleasure'. Now at last there was found in the Qumran texts a contemporary expression that provided the missing Hebrew equivalent.

Fr Ernst Vogt, S.J., wrote a résumé of Hunzinger's article[3] and stressed especially that *eudokia* and *rāṣôn* express God's will in electing and predestining man rather than his pleasure in man's goodness. The phrase 'sons of his good pleasure' indicates

* Originally published in *TS* 19 (1958) 225–7.

[1] 'Neues Licht auf Lc 2:14 *anthrōpoi eudokias*', *ZNW* 44 (1952–53) 85–90.

[2] '*Anthrōpoi eudokias* (Lc 2:14)', *ZNW* 28 (1929) 13–20.

[3] '"Pax hominibus bonae voluntatis" Lc 2:14', *Bib* 34 (1953) 427–9. An English translation of this article, with some revisions, appears in K. Stendahl (ed.), *The Scrolls and the New Testament* (New York, 1957) 114–17. The author here points out that the phrase occurs again in 1QH 11:9. See also C. H. Hunzinger, 'Ein weiterer Beleg zu Lc 2:14 *anthrōpoi eudokias*', *ZNW* 49 (1958) 129–30. If Allegro's restoration is acceptable, another occurrence of the phrase would be found in 4QpPs^a^ 1–2 ii 24–25 (DJD 5, 44): [*pišrô 'al 'anšê*] *r^e^ṣôn*[*ô*].

in Qumran literature those who are the object of divine predilection. Moreover, since 'men' and 'sons' are frequently interchanged in kindred Qumran expressions, *bᵉnê rᵉṣônô* can easily be the Hebrew equivalent of *anthrōpois eudokias*.

The Qumran expression contains a pronominal suffix which makes it clear that the good will refers to God. But the Greek of Luke's verse merely has *eudokias* without a possessive—a fact which has led to the frequently used but erroneous interpretation 'men of good will' (i.e., who have good will). Both Hunzinger and Vogt have pointed out that *eudokia* without *autou* could pass as the Greek equivalent of *rᵉṣônô*. In Sir 15:15 and 39:18, *rᵉṣônô* is translated merely by *eudokia*.[4]

However, I wish to call attention here to the reading which is found in the Coptic (Sahidic) version. There we read: *awō tirēnē hiǧᵉm pkah hᵉn ᵉnrōme ᵉmpefwōš*, 'And peace upon the earth among men of his will'.[5] The *apparatus criticus* in modern New Testaments and the commentators often cite the Sahidic version in support of the genitive *eudokias*, the reading of the better manuscripts, against the nominative *eudokia*.[6] But they fail to indicate that the Sahidic also includes the personal pronominal prefix, *pef-*. This prefix corresponds, then, to the Hebrew pronominal suffix found on *rᵉṣônô* in the Qumran expression. Such a detail of the Coptic translation should not be lost sight of, as it gives us valuable testimony that *eudokias* was understood in the past as 'of *his* good will'. It thus confirms the interpretation based on the Qumran expression: 'Peace upon earth among men of his good will'.

The expression *bᵉnê rᵉṣônô*, being Hebrew, fits in well with the hypothesis, often used today, that the source of Luke's first two chapters was originally a Hebrew composition.[7] Recently, how-

[4] See N. Walker, 'The Renderings of *Rāṣôn*', JBL 81 (1962) 182–4.

[5] *The Coptic Version of the New Testament in the Southern Dialect, Otherwise Called Sahidic and Theban* (Oxford, 1911) 30–2.

[6] See, e.g., A. Merk, *Novum Testamentum graece et latine* (7th ed.; Rome 1951) 195; K. Aland *et al.*, *The Greek New Testament* (United Bible Societies, 1966) 207.

[7] See P. Winter, 'Some Observations on the Language in the Birth and

ever, the Aramaic equivalent of the Lucan phrase has turned up in a Qumran text being prepared for publication by M. l'Abbé J. Starcky. The latter, with whom I have had occasion to go over the text for the Cave 4 concordance, has graciously permitted me to cite the relevant passage here. The fragmentary manuscript in which the phrase occurs has been tentatively labelled *ḥ^{a}zût ʿAmram* ^{c}, and assigned the siglum 4Q ḥʿA^{c}; it tells of the vision enjoyed by Amram, the father of Aaron, Moses, and Miriam. The pertinent text is found in fragment 9, line 18. Unfortunately, only the beginning of the lines has been preserved in this fragment; what is left seems to be the end of the work. Though Aaron is not named, it seems that he is the subject.

18 *šbyʿy b'nwš rʿwt*[*h wy*]*qrh wyt'm*[*r*

19 *ytbḥr lkhn ʿlmyn* (vacat)

'he will be seventh among men of [his] good will [and ho]nour
and it (he?) will be said . . .
he will be chosen as a priest forever.'

The phrase which interests us is *b'nwš rʿwt*[*h*], 'among men of [his] good will'. The text is unfortunately damaged and the pronominal suffix lost; but it can be supplied on the basis of the one found on the parallel, coordinated noun, [*wy*]*qrh*. The suffix refers most likely to God, as it does in the Hebrew counterpart, *b^{e}nê r^{e}ṣônô*. The most interesting detail in the phrase is the noun *'nwš*, 'men', for it is the exact equivalent of the Lucan[8] expression, *anthrōpois eudokias*. Since *r^{e}ʿû* is the normal Aramaic cognate for the Hebrew *rāṣôn*, we now have both an Aramaic and a Hebrew equivalent for Luke's expression.[9] The occur-

---

Infancy Stories of the Third Gospel', *NTS* 1 (1954–55) 111–21; see also the literature cited there.

[8] Actually *'nwš* is a singular noun, but its collective force is quite frequently found, as here.

[9] This is not the first instance in which a NT expression, previously identified in Qumran Hebrew, has turned up in Aramaic dress as well. In the *Genesis Apocryphon*, published by N. Avigad and Y. Yadin (Jerusalem,

rence of the same phrase in both languages indicates its common and frequent usage and confirms the interpretation that Dr Hunzinger first suggested.[10]

1956), a few words can be read on the left-hand side of column 1, lines 1–4 (see the photo of column 2). The editors say that these words 'are as yet unclear' (p. 16). But in line 2 one can clearly read *'p rz rš'' dy*. The words *rz rš''* are the Aramaic equivalent of the Hebrew *rzy pš'* (1Q27 1:2; 1QH 5:36; 1QH fr 50:5) and of the Greek *mystērion tēs anomias*, 'the mystery of iniquity' (2 Thes 2:7).

[10] See further R. Deichgräber, 'Lc 2:14: *anthrōpoi eudokias*', *ZNW* 51 (1960) 132 [The phrase is also found in the Samaritan Marqa's commentary on the Pentateuch.]; E. F. F. Bishop, 'Men of God's Good Pleasure', *ATR* 48 (1966) 63–9; F. Vattioni, 'Pax hominibus bonae voluntatis', *RBibIt* 7 (1959) 369–70; H. Rusche, '"Et in terra pax hominibus bonae voluntatis"', *Bibel und Leben* 2 (1961) 229–34.

5

THE NAME SIMON*

Speculation about the 'change' in the name of the apostle Peter (cf. Mt 16:18; Jn 1:42) will undoubtedly always be in order. In this respect the recent article of Cecil Roth of Oxford[1] raises an interesting point. He suggests that the apostle's name Peter prevailed in time over Simon because of a current tendency of contemporary Judaism to avoid the use of the name *Simōn* in Greek or *Šim'ôn* in Hebrew. The latter name was 'commonly or even methodically modified or eliminated, for some reason or the other, among the Jews at the beginning of the Christian era. One finds it difficult to avoid the conclusion that the modification of the name of the Apostle by the elimination of "Simon" was connected with this and due to the same cause, whatever that may have been.'[2] Roth offers parallels of persons whose name was Simon, but who were known more usually by a patronymic or a nickname (ben Sira, ben Zoma, ben Azzai, ben Nanos, bar Cochba), and suggests that it was a peculiarly 'patriotic' name, borne by great national and revolutionary leaders such as Simon Maccabee, Simon the High Priest (Sir 50:1–2), Simeon ben Šeṭaḥ (politician-Rabbi of the second century B.C.), Simon the rebel (Josephus, *JW* 2, 4, 2, #57; *Ant.* 17, 10, 6, #273), Simon the son of the founder of the Zealots, Judah the Galilean (Josephus, *Ant.* 20, 5, 2, #102), Simon bar Giora (leader in the First Revolt), Simon bar Cochba (leader

* Originally published in *HTR* 56 (1963) 1–5.

[1] 'Simon-Peter', *HTR* 54 (1961) 91–7.

[2] *Ibid.*, 94.

of the Second Revolt).[3] Roth raises the question: Was the name Simon forbidden by the Romans because of hyper-patriotic associations, or was it possibly regarded as too sacred for normal use by nationalistic Jews? Could possibly a 'proto-Midrashic interpretation' of the Blessing of Jacob in Gn 49:5–7, a 'comminatory' verse, have resulted in an inhibition to use the name, so that the person who bore it came to be referred to only by a patronymic periphrasis ('the son of so-and-so') or a nickname (such as Kaipha = Peter)? His conclusion: 'It seems certain that in the first century and perhaps for some time afterwards the use of the name Simon was deliberately avoided by Jews, whether from symbolic or patriotic or superstitious reasons, or even out of sheer nervousness.'[4]

Such a thesis, however, for all its interesting speculative and suggestive character, has to face a certain *factual* aspect of the problem of the 'change' of the name of the apostle from Simon to Peter. It is an aspect that Roth has for some reason or other been silent about; it certainly will not hurt to recall it here. For it so happens that *Simōn* or *Šmʿwn* is the most frequently attested name for Jews[5] of the period which Roth discusses. Admittedly, we do not have the complete onomasticon of the Jews even of Palestine for the first century B.C. or for the first two centuries A.D. But any number of names of Jews of this period are known to us, and the most significant feature is that the name 'Simon' is one which occurs most frequently in precisely this period, viz. of Roman domination.

Some years ago G. Hölscher pointed out that the name was not in great use among the Jews of an earlier period.[6] The old

[3] See below pp. 305—54.

[4] *Ibid.*, 96–7.

[5] Included are the names of those who were so named as Jews, even though they may have subsequently been converted to Christianity.

[6] 'Zur jüdischen Namenkunde', *Vom Alten Testament: Karl Marti zum siebzigsten Geburtstage gewidmet* (BZAW XLI, Giessen, 1925) 148–57. See also M. Noth, *Die israelitischen Personennamen im Rahmen der gemeinsemitischen Namengebung* (Stuttgart, 1928) 60.

tribal name given to individuals turns up in more or less common usage in the fifth century B.C., being attested in the Aramaic texts from Elephantine, among the Jewish names recorded in the Murašu texts from Nippur, and in the Old Testament (Ezr 10:31). In Hellenistic times *Šmʿwn* became still more common, because it was assimilated to the Greek name *Simōn*.

The names *Šmʿwn* (regarded as the equivalent of the Greek name *Simōn*), *Yhwdh* and *Ywsp* become ever more numerous, and in the time of the Roman Empire these three names belong to the most frequently used Jewish names. Besides them there occur quite often from the Augustan period on the name *Lwy*, and more rarely those of *Bnymyn* and *R'wbn*. Only in Talmudic times are still others of these tribal names attested as the names of individuals.[7]

Further on he adds:

When one surveys the Hebrew masculine names which were in use from early Roman times until about A.D. 200 among the Jews of Palestine, the name *Šmʿwn* (*Simōn*) is by far the most popular.[8]

Hölscher did not document the remarks which he published, and in the absence of the full onomasticon of the Jews of the period we can only appeal to the *known* lists of Jewish names. The most recent treatment of the name *Šmʿwn* has been presented by J. T. Milik in connection with his study of the proper names found on the ossuaries discovered in the tombs of the property of the Franciscan Friars on the slope of the Mount of Olives, called Dominus Flevit. Though he wrote in complete independence of Hölscher, it is interesting to note that his findings confirm those of the latter.

This biblical name (the patriarch, Ezr 10:31 = 1 Esdras 9:32; Sir 51:30) is one of the most frequently used among the Jews, and remained popular in the Greco-Roman period due to its phonetic identity [*sic*] with the Greek name *Simōn* which was equally current among the Greeks. Josephus knows 29 persons with this name, which is always written *Simōn*, except for *Symeōn* the patriarch and the ancestor of Matthatiah; Niese, *Index*, p. 564. In the Jewish community of Egypt *Simōn* (never *Sym*(*e*)*ōn* before the Byzantine period) takes second place only after Sabbathai, being attested some thirty times; Tcherikover, pp. 28 and 232–3. To these should be added the three

[7] *Op. cit.*, 150–1.
[8] *Op. cit.*, 155.

'sages' of the *Letter of Aristeas* (#47, 48, 49). In the New Testament (Bauer, 1367) there are nine examples[9] and thirty-two on the ossuaries: Bene Ḥazir, line 1; Frey #1254, 1317, 1318, 1173 (*Simōnos*, Lydda), 1182 (read *Šm*ʿ[*wn*], Gezer), Bethphage col. 1, line 10; Frey #1350, 1351 and 1352, 1354, 1355 (*Simōnos*, twice), 1194 (er-Ram), 1191 (Michmas), 1292–1297–1299, 1298, 1411, 1384, 1246; *Kedem* II, pp. 24–5, n. 5; p. 31, n. 29; *AJA* 1947, pp. 351 ff., n. 1 and 2; *LA* VII, pp. 232 ff., n. 3 (twice), 4, 6, 10, 12; *PAM* 36. 911 (published by Sukenik in the *Kraus-Festschrift*) and unpublished: *PAM* 32.314 (Ḥizmeh), 42.125 (*Simōnos*) and finally three others described in the archives of the PAM of which two are mentioned below under no. 9.[10]

This gives some indication of the places where the occurrences of the name Simon can be found. Later on Milik gives a table in which he compares the number of occurrences of various Jewish names found in Egypt, Josephus, the Palestinian ossuaries, the New Testament and the new texts from Murabba'ât.[11] A glance at this table reveals that *Simon* or *Symeon* heads the list as the most frequently attested among the following not unusual names of the period in question: Joseph, Salome, Judah, Mary, John, Eleazar, Jesus, Martha, Matthias, Sapphira, Jonathe, Zachary, Azariah, Jairus, Menahem. In each group of texts listed the name most frequently attested is Simon (in some form or other).[12] Finally, Milik notes: 'The frequency of proper names on the ossuaries is, then, practically identical

[9] As a matter of fact, there are nine instances in the New Testament spelled *Simōn*; see W. F. Arndt and F. W. Gingrich, *A Greek-English Lexicon of the New Testament and Other Early Christian Literature* (Chicago, 1957) 758. But to these should be added two instances of *Symeōn* (Lk 2:25, 34 and Acts 13:1, the former referring to the devout old man of Jerusalem, the latter to Simeon Niger, who is perhaps also the Simeon of Acts 15:14. See S. Giet, 'L'assemblée apostolique et le décret de Jérusalem. Qui était Siméon?', *RSR* 39 [1951] 203–20).

[10] B. Bagatti and J. T. Milik, *Gli scavi del 'Dominus Flevit'* (Monte Oliveto—Gerusalemme): Part I, La necropoli del periodo romano (Pubblicazioni dello Studium Biblicum Franciscanum XIII; Jerusalem, 1958) 76–7.

[11] *Ibid.*, 108.

[12] A slight qualification should be made here because in the column in which the instances from Murabba'ât are recorded, the total is given for Simon as '*ca* 14 + 7', i.e. 14 occurrences in Hebrew or Aramaic texts and 7

with that of the New Testament—which is natural because the majority of the graffiti date from the first half of the first century A.D.'[13]

To the foregoing evidence must likewise be added the occurrences of the name in the texts from the cave in the Wâdi Ḫabra (=Naḥal Ḥever), which likewise come from the time of the Second Revolt; so far we have learned the names of two of Bar Cochba's officers: Masabbalah bar Simon (*Mśblh br Šmʿwn*) and Simon bar Judah (*Šmʿwn br Yhwdh*).[14]

In all of the texts from Murabbaʿât or Wâdi Ḫabra it is, moreover, significant that Bar Cochba, who is frequently mentioned, is never referred to merely by his patronymic, ben/bar Kosibah, but always either as *Šmʿwn* or *Šmʿwn bn/br Ksbh* or *Šmʿwn nsy' Yśr'l*.[15]

In view of such evidence it is difficult to agree with Roth's

---

occurrences in Greek texts. While the total is greater for Simon than for any other name, the name Joseph appears more frequently in the Greek texts, 9 times. A further slight modification is in order, for in checking the Hebrew and Aramaic texts of Murabbaʿât I have found 17 instances of persons with the name *Šmʿwn*, apart from the frequent mention of *Šmʿwn bn Kwsbh*, Bar Cochba himself. See P. Benoit, J. T. Milik and R. de Vaux, *Les Grottes de Murabbaʿât* (DJD 2; Oxford, 1961): 9 i 1 (*Šmʿwn br sk.* [ ]); 28 i–ii 9 (*Šmʿwn br Pnḥs*); 29:10 (*Šmʿwn br Šby* and *Šmʿwn br Zkryh*); 29 verso 4 (*Šmʿwn br Šby br H*[ ]—possibly the same person as the first one mentioned in 29:10); 30:9 (*Šmʿwn br Symy*): 31 i 4 (*Šm*[*ʿwn*]); 31 iv 2 ([*Š*]*mʿwn*); 33:2 (*Šmʿwn br Ḥnyn*); 39 iii 1 (*Šmʿwn br M.*[ ]); 41 i–iv 4 (*Šm*[*ʿw*]*n br* [*?*]); 41 i–iv 7 (*Šmʿwn*); 48:1 ([*Šmʿ*]*wn* [*bn?*]); 48:2 (*Šmʿ*[*wn*]); 73:3 ([*Š*]*mʿwn br Yš*[ ]); 74:1 (*Šmʿwn*); 29 verso 6 (*Šmʿwn bn*. . [ ]).

[13] *Gli scavi* . . ., 108.

[14] See Y. Yadin, 'Expedition D', *IEJ* II (1961) 36–52, especially 44–5. Cf. 'New Discoveries in the Judean Desert', *BA* 24 (1961) 48.

[15] Even granting that the tradition preserved by Origen and a number of New Testament MSS. is worthless, that Barabbas' name was really Jesus Barabbas (i.e. *Yšwʿ br 'b'*), is it not somewhat gratuitous to suggest that the first name of the brigand was really Simon? The question of the use of patronymics alone as the identification of Jews is a complicated one and has an old tradition behind it (Barrakkab, Barhadad, Bartholomew, Barsabba [Murabbaʿât 25 i 4]; cf. Acts 1:23; 15:22). See A. Alt, 'Menschen ohne Namen', *ArOr* 18 (1950) 9–24; reprinted in *Kleine Schriften zur Geschichte des Volkes Israel* (München, 1959) 3, 198–213.

conclusion that 'in the first century and perhaps for some time afterwards the use of the name Simon was deliberately avoided by Jews'. It seems rather that since Simon or Simeon was such a commonly used name, the patronymics or nicknames were frequently used as a means of distinguishing those who bore the name of the tribal patriarch of old. Even though we do not have a complete listing of all the names of Jewish males in the Roman period, the evidence which has come to light in the various areas seems all to point in the direction of the great frequency of the name Simon.

The names found on the Palestinian ossuaries and in the texts from Murabba'ât and the Wâdi Ḫabra are obviously not those of 'personalities' or 'well-known persons', aside possibly from the officers of Bar Cochba. The fact that ordinary people used the name Simon in this period argues against its prohibition or the avoidance of it out of any superstitious or patriotic motive. By the same token it seems idle to try to explain the 'change' of the name of the apostle from Simon to Peter as a reflection of this supposedly current tendency.[16]

A FURTHER DISCUSSION*

In his article on the name Simon (*HTR* 56 [1963] 1–5) Father Joseph A. Fitzmyer, S.J., assembles a number of instances to show that this 'is the most frequently used name for Jews of the period . . . of Roman domination'. From this he deduces that my suggestion (*HTR* 54 [1961] 91–7) that its use was deliberately avoided for some reason by Jews at this time (this perhaps explaining the change of the name of the Apostle Simon to Peter) can have no basis.

On the contrary, I am inclined to think that his investigation strongly supports my view; he seems to have misunderstood me, unless the inadequacies of language led me to express myself

[16] See further B. Lifshitz, 'Notes d'épigraphie grecque', *RB* 76 (1969) 92–8, especially 94 (#5, *Simōnos Barsemia*); T. Nöldeke, *Zeitschrift für Assyriologie* 20 (1907) 134.

* Originally published in *HTR* 57 (1964) 60–1.

awkwardly. For what I proposed was not that the name Simon (Simeon) was not applied at this period—i.e., was not given by Jewish parents to their children—but that, when given, there was a tendency for it not to be used, the patronymic, 'the son of . . .' being normally substituted.

Clearly in an official act, or on a tombstone, this would not have been the case. The number of funerary inscriptions recording persons officially named Simon is irrelevant, so long as we do not know how they were actually called at home and in the market-place. The recently discovered documents from the Engedi neighbourhood confirm what we already knew, that the leader of the Second Revolt was Simon; but from the literary sources already available it is certain that colloquially he was known as Bar Kosiba (or Bar Kochba). Similarly, we have positive evidence Simon Bar Giora, the leader of the last desperate resistance in Jerusalem in the siege of 69/70, was normally referred to as Bar Giora, and Rabbi Simeon ben Zoma a generation later as Ben Zoma, and so on. As I say in my article: when in this period a man was generally called by a patronymic of this type, and his *Eigenname* is known, that name in a majority of cases was Simon. The fact that it was so popular, as Father Fitzmyer has shown, may perhaps confirm my suggestion that it had patriotic associations, this being the reason for its avoidance in actual usage.

Cecil Roth

Dr Roth's note makes his position clearer. I shall leave to others the judgment whether I misunderstood what was originally written.

But the problem still remains. How do we know that 'there was a tendency for it (the name Simon) not to be used'? Granted, 'we do not know how they were actually called at home and in the market-place'. So we can only depend on the evidence available, not only in the usual literary sources, but in other material as well, which I tried to present. The name

Simon was omitted in several cases, as Dr Roth pointed out (*HTR* 54 [1961] 91–3). But does such an omission really support his contention of a 'tendency' to avoid the name in actual usage (possibly because it had patriotic associations)? Was the name really 'consistently eliminated' (p. 92)? Indeed, it is not the only name omitted in the list he cites (see his footnote 9). Perhaps the reason why it is the most frequently omitted name there is rather the fact that it was the name most frequently given and used. The use of the patronymic in place of it served as a means of distinguishing the many who bore the name, as has been already suggested (*HTR* 56 [1963] 5; see above, p. 110).

But if the evidence for the 'tendency' is slight, that for the application of it to the problem of Simon-Peter is even more so. Every instance cited by Dr Roth (pp. 91–3) shows that when Simon was omitted, a patronymic was used. If the Apostle Simon were called only Bar Jonah later on in his career, then there might be some parallelism. But after trying to build a case on the evidence of patronymics, how can one suddenly introduce 'or a nickname (such as "Kaipha" = Peter would have been)' (p. 96)?

I suspect that our disagreement is basically one of methodology and that neither of us has the same estimate of the sources used by the other.

6

THE SON OF DAVID TRADITION AND MT 22:41–46 AND PARALLELS*

Any discussion of the development of Tradition in its relation to Scripture should cope with examples of this relation in Scripture itself. The problem of Scripture and Tradition in the Christian Church developed in its own way once the canon of the New Testament was fixed. But there is a relationship between those realities which is manifest in the New Testament itself, particularly as Old Testament traditions are taken up and adapted to the formation of later Scriptures. Even if such New Testament examples are not in every respect comparable to instances of the later development of Christian doctrine, nevertheless they have facets which merit a renewed consideration for the light they shed on the contemporary problem.

One passage which lends itself readily to such a consideration is the debate about the Messiah as the son of David in Mt 22:41–46 and its parallels (Mk 12:35–37a; Lk 20:41–44). The figure of the Davidic Messiah expected in Judaism about the time of Christ was the product of a long tradition. However complicated its previous history was, it receives in the Synoptics a significant interpretation. We turn then to this episode as an example of an evolving tradition rooted in the Old Testament motif of the son of David.

* Originally published in *Concilium* (British Edition) 10/2 (1966) 40–6.

Mt 22:41–46	Mk 12:35–37a	Lk 20:41–44
[41]Now when the Pharisees were gathered together, Jesus asked them a question, [42]saying,	[35]And as Jesus taught in the temple, he said,	[41]But he said to them,
'What do you think of the Messiah? Whose son is he?' They said to him, 'The son of David.'	'How can the scribes say that the Messiah is the son of David?	'How can they say that the Messiah is the son of David?
[43]He said to them, 'How is it then that David, inspired by the Spirit, calls him Lord, saying,	[36]David himself, inspired by the Holy Spirit, declared,	[42]For David himself says in the book of Psalms,
[44]The Lord said to my Lord, Sit at my right hand, till I put your enemies under your feet?	The Lord said to my Lord, Sit at my right hand, till I put your enemies under your feet.	The Lord said to my Lord, Sit at my right hand, [43]till I make your enemies a stool for your feet.
[45]If David thus calls him Lord, how is he his son?' [46]And no one was able to answer him a word, nor from that day did any one dare to ask him any more questions.	[37]David himself calls him Lord; so how is he his son?'	[44]David thus calls him Lord; so how is he his son?'

This pericope forms part of the Synoptic account of the last days of Jesus in Jerusalem. In its earliest form (Mk 12) the passage records a Dominical saying, 'As Jesus taught in the temple, he said. . . .' In Mark there is scarcely any evidence of debate; and the setting is hardly different in Luke. But in Mt 22 the Gospel tradition has clothed the saying with controversy so that it rather resembles an apophthegm.[1] In any setting the substance of the saying is the same: Jesus questions the contemporary tradition about the Messiah as the Son of David, implying that the Davidic Messiah must be understood in some other way. Among others, R. Bultmann believes that the early Church, not Jesus himself, has made this identification of Jesus and the Son of David.[2] But V. Taylor has effectively shown that this saying cannot be wholly due to a community-formula-

[1] R. Bultmann, *The History of the Synoptic Tradition* (New York, 1963) 51, 137, 405 (*Die Geschichte der synoptischen Tradition* [4th ed.: Göttingen: Vandenhoeck and Ruprecht, 1958] 54, 145; Ergänzungsheft [3rd ed.] 22).

[2] R. Bultmann, *Theology of the New Testament* (London, 1956) I, 28. Similarly E. Klostermann, *Das Markusevangelium* (HNT 3; Tübingen, 1950) 129. B. H. Branscomb, *The Gospel of Mark* (Moffatt New Testament Commentary; London, 1937) 222–5.

tion, since the allusive character of the saying, half-concealing and half-revealing the 'messianic secret', is difficult to explain as the doctrinal belief of a community. It stands in contrast to the tone and frankness of such passages as Acts 2:34–36; 5:31; 10:42–43; Rom 1:2–4; etc.[3]

Before asking in what sense the saying is to be understood, we must review the prior tradition about David.

THE DAVIDIC TRADITION IN THE OLD TESTAMENT

Within the Old Testament itself the Davidic tradition apparently grew up independently of Israel's ancient *credo* derived from the early period of its salvation history. Only with the passage of time were the two traditions fused, in fact about the time of the exile and in such writers as Ezekiel, Second Isaiah, Haggai, Zechariah, and Nehemiah. Yahweh's intervention on behalf of David was at that time seen to be a continuation of the salvific deeds recalled in Israel's ancient *credo*.

The earliest tradition about David is embedded in the work of the Deuteronomist and concerns David's role in the story of the Ark of the Covenant (1 Sm 4:1–7, 11; 2 Sm 6:1–15, 17–20a), his accession to the throne (1 Sm 16:1–2; 2 Sm 5:25; 6:16, 20b–23; 9:1–13), his dynasty (2 Sm 7:1–29; 11:2–20, 26; 1 Kgs 1:1–2, 46), and his last words (2 Sm 23:1–7). At this stage David is depicted as the zealous worshipper of Yahweh (2 Sm 6:6–9), 'chosen' by him to rule over all Israel in place of Saul (2 Sm 6:21), and favoured by his word (1 Sm 25:31; 2 Sm 3:9–10; 5:2). David is the obedient servant whose respect for Yahweh is shown in his slaying of the Amalekite who raised his hand against Saul, Yahweh's Anointed. Yet Yahweh has not favoured David for himself alone; David is to rule over Israel and his kingly role affects all Israel. Yahweh's choice of David

[3] *The Gospel According to St Mark* (London, 1953) 493. See also R. P. Gagg, 'Jesus und die Davidssohnfrage: Zur Exegese von Markus 12. 35–37', *TZ* 7 (1951) 18–30; O. Cullmann, *The Christology of the New Testament* (2nd ed.; London, 1963) 132.

is, therefore, an event of corporate salvific significance for the history of Israel.[4]

Two passages in particular stress this aspect of David's role: the Oracle of Nathan (2 Sm 7:14–17) and the 'Last Words of David' (2 Sm 23:1–17). Nathan makes it clear that Yahweh's favour is not limited to David himself: 'When your days are fulfilled and you lie down with your fathers, I will raise up after you your offspring who shall come forth from your body; and I will establish its kingdom. He shall build a house for my name and I will establish his royal throne forever. I will be his father and he shall be my son' (2 Sm 7:12–14). And the significance of this oracle is seen in David's 'last words' in which the psalmist of Israel is hailed as 'the anointed of the God of Jacob' (2 Sm 23:1). David is explicitly called *māšîaḥ*, an anointed agent of Yahweh. The oracle is a 'covenant' made by Yahweh with the Davidic dynasty: 'For Yahweh has made with me an everlasting covenant' (23:5). The Davidic tradition is now framed in convenantal terms and rivals, as it were, the ancient covenant of Sinai. It thus gives Israel's traditions a new centre of gravity.

This basic tradition about David underwent development in the Royal Psalms, in the Prophets, and in post-exilic writings. In the psalms which mention David (Pss 18, 72, 89, 132, 144) his title of 'Anointed' is explicitly repeated (Ps 18:51; 89:39, 52 [cf. v. 20]; 132:10, 17). Ps 132:2 ascribes to him a more prominent role in the building of the temple; he is said to have made a *vow* to build it. Yahweh's promise in the oracle of Nathan becomes a divine *oath* (Ps 132:11; 89:4, 36–37, 50). But above all these Psalms stress the enduring and unshakable character of the Davidic dynasty (Ps 18:51; 89:5, 30, 37; 132:10–12). It will last for ever, and the very cultic hymns of the Psalter attest to its continuance. Ps 2, a royal psalm which does not mention David, promises universal dominion to a Davidic king. The king is Yahweh's 'Anointed', indeed his very son, 'You

[4] See S. Mowinckel, *He That Cometh* (Oxford, 1956). S. Amsler, *David, roi messie* (Cahiers theologiques 49; Neuchâtel, 1963). R. A. Carlson, *David, the Chosen King* (Stockholm, 1964).

are my son, today I have begotten you' (2:7). Another royal psalm, probably composed for the enthronement of some Davidic king, depicts him as one invited by Yahweh to sit at his right hand and to share his exalted, heavenly glory: 'The Lord says to my lord, "Sit at my right hand, till I make your enemies your footstool"' (Ps 110:1). Thus an intimate relationship between Yahweh and the anointed Davidic heir is established.

The continuance of the Davidic dynasty is assured at the time of the Syro-Ephraimite war, as Isaiah announces to Ahaz in a moment of impending doom the birth of a royal heir; 'a child' is to be born who will be a 'wonderful Counsellor, mighty God, everlasting Father, prince of peace', and will sit 'upon the throne of David' (Is 9:6–7). He will be 'a shoot from the stump of Jesse' (11:1). To Hezekiah the prophet eventually announces Yahweh's further message, 'I will defend this city to save it, for my own sake and for the sake of my servant David' (37:35).

As Jeremiah confronted the last of the Davidic kings before Nebuchadnezzar's invasion, he called Israel to a renewed fidelity to its ancient *credo*. But he juxtaposed to this appeal allusions to the Davidic tradition. He announced that the Davidic king Jehoiakim would 'have none (i.e., no heir) to sit upon the throne of David' (Jer 36:30); and yet the same prophet uttered the promise of a 'new covenant' and proclaimed that Israel would 'serve Yahweh their God and David their king, whom I will raise up for them' (30:9).

In Jeremiah's words there is a significant development, for 'David' is now regarded as a future occupant of the throne to be raised up by Yahweh. The ideal king will be a 'David'. 'Days are coming, says the Lord, when I will raise up for David a Righteous Branch; he shall reign as king and deal wisely and shall execute justice and righteousness in the land' (Jer 23:5). Salvation, justice, and righteousness are the qualities linked with the reign of the new son of David. Ezekiel's message is similarly reassuring in the wake of the destruction of Jerusalem:

'They shall be my people and I will be their God; my servant David shall be king over them and they shall all have one shepherd' (Ez 37:23–24).

Significant in this prophetic development of a future sense of 'David' is the complete absence of the title *māšîaḥ*. The word occurs but twice in the Prophets: once applied to Cyrus (Is 45:1), and once to the king or the nation (Hab 3:13). The prophets echo indeed the oracle of Nathan in some sense. But even though David was clearly hailed earlier as Yahweh's 'Anointed', they significantly do not speak of the 'coming of a Messiah'. They only announce the hope of a restored kingdom of David, because Yahweh has promised it.

In post-exilic times the Davidic tradition develops still further. A king no longer rules in Jerusalem, for foreign domination prevents this. Yet the Davidic lineage continues in Zerubbabel, the governor of Judah, who has been 'chosen' by Yahweh (Hag 2:23; see Zech 6:12–14). The significant post-exilic development of the Davidic tradition is seen in the Chronicler's work. Here the portrait of David is not only idealized, but the account of his reign is schematized. Though 1 Chr opens with genealogies beginning with Adam, the real history of Israel starts with the death of Saul and the accession of David (1 Chr 10). The Chronicler aims to depict what the ideal kingdom of Israel under God should be like and idyllically describes the reigns of David and Solomon, not as they were, but as they should have been. David is idealized and becomes the real founder of the temple and its cult. The perpetuity of David's reign is stressed (1 Chr 28:4).

In this connection the Chronicler's modifications of the Oracle of Nathan are significant:

2 Sm 7:12, 16	1 Chr 7:11, 14
I will raise up after you your offspring who shall come forth from your body. . . . Your house and your kingdom shall be made sure before me forever; your throne shall be established forever.	I will raise up after you your offspring, who shall be one of your own sons. . . . I will confirm him in my house and in my kingdom forever, and his throne shall be established forever.

Whereas in 2 Sm 'your offspring' (*zarʿakā*) was used in a collective sense, the Chronicler employs it of a particular descendant in the Davidic line (*'ašer yihyeh mibbānêkā*, lit., 'who shall be from among your sons'). Again, 'I will confirm *him* in *my* house and in *my* kingdom forever', a significant change from the original oracle. The shift makes it clear that a Davidic king to come will be Yahweh's representative in the restored Israelite theocracy. But once again we note the absence of the title *māšîaḥ* for the Davidic king. If David himself is so named in 2 Chr 6:42, this refers to the historic David, not to the ideal, expected Davidic ruler; but the word 'anointed' may here even refer to Solomon.

Finally, only in the second century B.C. apocalypse of Daniel is there explicit mention of an expected 'anointed prince' in Jerusalem: '. . . from the going forth of the word to restore and build Jerusalem to (the coming of) an Anointed One, a Prince, there shall be seven weeks' (Dn 9:25, *'ad māšîaḥ nāgîd*). Who is this anointed prince or 'Messiah'? A Son of David? Probably. Yet this occurrence of the word in Daniel is part of a larger, complex picture of messianic expectations which emerge in the second century B.C.

THE DAVIDIC MESSIAH IN LATER JUDAISM

That Dn 9:25–26 fed the Jewish hopes of a restored kingdom of God under the leadership of an ideal king, even called 'the Messiah', can be seen in the literature of Qumran. 1QS 9:11 clearly alludes to Dn 9:25, 'until the coming of a Prophet and the Messiahs of Aaron and Israel'.[5] Both the Danielic text and the Qumran literature reflect this stage in the development of Jewish beliefs when it is legitimate to speak of the coming of 'a (*or* the) Messiah', or even of 'the Messiahs'. Granted that one should beware of reading into these terms all the connotations of New Testament Christology, it would be hypercritical to insist at this stage that one should simply speak of 'Anointed Ones'.[6] For it is precisely these texts which show that a genuine

[5] For a bibliography on Qumran Messianism, see my article below, p. 130, n. 7.

[6] Cf. J. Carmignac, *Les textes de Qumran* (Paris, 1963) II, 13; L. Silber-

Old Testament theme of an anointed agent of Yahweh had developed into the expectation of a Messiah—and, in the specific case in which we are interested, of a Davidic Messiah. (The expected Prophet and the priestly Messiah, or Messiah of Aaron, do not concern us here.)

In the Qumran literature the Davidic Messiah is called the 'Messiah of Israel' (1QSa 2:14, 20; cf. 1QS 9:11; CD 20:1). In 4QPatrBles 2:4 (a sort of commentary on Gn 49:10) we read of the coming of 'the Messiah of Righteousness, the shoot of David' (*'d bw' mšyḥ hṣdq ṣmḥ dwyd*), for to him and to his seed has been given the royal mandate over his people for everlasting generations.[7] Important too is the interpretation of the Oracle of Nathan in 4QFlor 1:11–13.[8] Having quoted 2 Sm 7:11–14 in abbreviated form, the author comments, 'This is the Shoot of David who is to arise with the Interpreter of the Law who [will arise] in Zi[on in the l]ast days; as it is written, *And I will raise up the booth of David that is fallen.* That is the booth of David which is fall[en and after]wards he will arise to save Israel.' A salvific mission is thus clearly associated with the Davidic Messiah. One could also cite 4QpIs[a] 8–10:11–17, which relates Is 11:1 to the 'Shoot of David', and 4QTest 9–13, which applies part of the oracle of Balaam (Nm 24:15–17) to the Davidic Messiah.[9] See also *Enoch* 48:10; 52:4. Qumran literature thus attests the full flowering of an Old Testament tradition about David. The title *māšîᵃḥ* is given to an ideal son of David, expected in the 'end of days'. Elements of that belief sown like seeds in the Old Testament gradually grew and matured into an extra-biblical tradition intimately associated with the biblical books. So far no text has turned up in the

---

man, 'The Two Messiahs of the Manual of Discipline', *VT* 5 (1955) 77–82; M. Smith, 'What is Implied by the Variety of Messianic Figures?', *JBL* 78 (1959) 66–72.

[7] See J. M. Allegro, *JBL* 75 (1956) 174–5.

[8] See *JBL* 77 (1958) 353; cf. 4Q*174* 1–2 i 11–13 (DJD 5, 53).

[9] See *JBL* 75 (1956) 180–1, 183–4; Cf. DJD 5, 13–14, 58, and see my comments above, p. 84.

Qumran caves giving this future Davidic Messiah the title 'Son of God', although it is possible that one text speaks of God 'begetting the Messiah' (1QSa 2:11–12).[10] Again, no text yet applies to him the words of Ps 2:7 or the words of Ps 110.

Outside of Qumran but still in pre-Christian times the expectation of a son of David as a Messiah is also attested in the (probably Pharisaic) *Psalms of Solomon*: 'Raise up, O Lord, unto them their king, the son of David . . . that he may reign over Israel thy servant. . . . There shall be no unrighteousness in their midst in his days, for all shall be holy and their king the Anointed of the Lord' (17:23, 36; see 18:6, 8).[11] This expectation is echoed in the later rabbinical tradition. Though we can never be sure how early the elements of this rabbinical tradition are, it is at least a legitimate continuation of an understanding of the Davidic tradition well attested among the Jews of Palestine in pre-Christian times.[12]

[10] See D. Barthélemy and J. T. Milik, *Qumran Cave I* (DJD 1) 110, 117. On the problem of the reading see my remarks on p. 153 below. Though no published text from the Qumran caves uses the title 'Son of God' for the Messiah, there are reports that the title does occur in unpublished Qumran Cave 4 material. A. J. B. Higgins (*CJT* 6 [1960] 202, n. 12) writes, 'Prof. D. N. Freedman, however, in a private communication from Jerusalem, kindly informs me that the (Davidic) Messiah is called the Son of God in unpublished Qumran material.' Again, A. D. Nock (*Gnomon* 33 [1961] 584) speaks of unpublished Qumran evidence for 'the use of royal ideology, stating the Messiah's relation to God in terms of sonship'. These rumours refer to an Aramaic text acquired by the Palestine Archaeological Museum in July 1958, which is apparently part of J. T. Milik's Pseudo-Daniel fragments. Aramaic phrases for 'the son of God' and 'the son of the Most High' (cf. Lk 1:32, 35) are found in it (see *TS* 25 [1964] 429). But we shall have to await Milik's publication of *Qumran Cave IV* in the DJD series to get the text and to assess it. It is not yet clear that the title is given to a messianic figure.

[11] In this text we meet for the first time the title, Son of David, used in connection with the expectations of Palestinian Jews. See further E. Lohse, 'Der König aus Davids Geschlecht: Bemerkungen zur messianischen Erwartung der Synagoge', *Abraham unser Vater: Juden und Christen im Gespräch über die Bibel: Festschrift für Otto Michel* (Leiden, 1963) 337–45.

[12] In this regard one could cite the Targum on the Prophets, to Is 11:1; Midrash Ps 18, #36; Ps 21, #1. See further Str-B 4, 452–65.

THE SON OF DAVID QUESTION IN THE SYNOPTICS

Against the background of such a tradition and its development the words of Jesus in Mt 22:41–46 must now be judged. In conversation with the Pharisees Jesus raises a question about the Davidic origin of the Messiah.[13] Having posed it, he raises the problem of Ps 110: How could David, the reputed and inspired author of that Psalm, be the father of the messianic king whom he calls 'lord'? 'The Lord (*Yahweh, Kyrios*) said to my lord (*la'ᵃdōnî, tō kyriō mou* [=the anointed king]), "Sit at my right hand. . . ."'

The explanation of this saying of Jesus is not easy and has taken various forms in the history of its exegesis. We single out three general interpretations. (1) J. Klausner and others have thought that Jesus' argumentation implies that he is calling in question the Davidic origin of the Messiah. 'Jesus had already declared himself Messiah. But the Messiah was to be the *son of David*, whereas Jesus was a Galilean and the son of Joseph the carpenter! How could he be the Messiah? To evade this serious difficulty Jesus must find a passage of Scripture according to which the Messiah need not necessarily be the Son of David; and like an expert Pharisee he finds it.'[14] (2) Many ancient and modern commentators have understood his question to imply that the Messiah is something more than a mere son of David, having a more exalted, transcendent origin than David, seeing that the latter calls him 'lord'. Jesus would insinuate thereby a secret about himself, but no further specification is made in the text.[15] (3) J. Schniewind and others press beyond the second interpretation in specifying that Jesus is in fact referring to the vision of the 'Son of Man' in Dn 7:13. Jesus is indeed the son of

[13] One might be tempted to think that the question arose out of the Essene belief in two Messiahs, one of Aaron, the other of Israel. There is, however, no evidence that such a background to the question was involved here. The problem is wholly concerned with the Davidic Messiah.

[14] *Jesus of Nazareth: His Life, Times and Teaching* (New York, 1926) 320. See also C. G. Montefiore, *The Synoptic Gospels* (London, 1909) I, 290–2.

[15] E.g. V. Taylor, *op. cit.*, 492; A. H. McNeile, *The Gospel According to St Matthew* (London, 1915) 328.

David, but he is more; he is the Son of Man in a unique sense.[16]

Regarding these interpretations several points should be noted. The first explanation is generally abandoned because it is inexplicable how Jesus would have intended to attack a well-founded belief in the Davidic origin of the Messiah (see above for the Old Testament texts). The New Testament gives no evidence of such an intention; indeed, such a denial of the Scriptures would have given his opponents ground for the charge against him (cf. Jn 8:5). Again, it is really farfetched to maintain that Jesus did not know that he was of Davidic lineage.[17] An early level of New Testament tradition attests it (Rom 1:3), and ostensibly without any apologetic intent. It is also echoed in later levels (Mk 10:47–48; Mt 1:1; Lk 3:31; 2 Tm 2:8). Would not Jesus' denial of the Davidic origin of the Messiah have left some other trace in view of the New Testament stress on his role as one who fulfilled the Old Testament?

The real choice lies today between the second and the third explanations. Here I think a distinction must be made. For it is not unlikely that the evangelists, especially Matthew with his secondary additions to the episode, was implying something like the third explanation in recording it.[18] But the question is legitimately asked whether Jesus himself in the original *Sitz im Leben* of the incident implied all that the early Church understood by it in the light of its Easter and Pentecostal faith.

It is not impossible that the Synoptic accounts of this episode represent only a torso of the full account. Since the rest of the dialogue resembles similar altercations with Pharisees (cf. Mk 2:9, 17–19; 3:4), it may be that it was they who asked the first

[16] *Das Evangelium nach Markus* (10th ed.; Göttingen, 1963) 164–5. Cf. P. Bonnard, *L'évangile selon saint Matthieu* (Commentaire du Nouveau Testament; Neuchâtel, 1963) 330–1.

[17] See W. Michaelis, 'Die Davidssohnschaft Jesu als historisches und kerygmatisches Problem', *Der historische Jesus und der kerygmatische Christus* (ed. H. Ristow and K. Matthaie; 2nd edition; Berlin, 1961) 317–30, especially 321–4.

[18] *Ibid.*, 318–19; cf. B.M.F. van Iersel, *'Der Sohn' in den synoptischen Jesusworten* (NTSup 3; Leiden, 1964) 171–3.

question, something like, 'You too teach, don't you, that the Messiah is David's son?' And rather than answer it with 'yes' or 'no', Jesus posed a counter-question (cf. Mt 22:17). Jesus' answer then would have had the form of a scribal debate, aimed more at meeting the Pharisees on the level of haggadic scriptural interpretation than of suggesting that he was personally of some other than Davidic origin.[19] The question is one of emphasis, for the latter aspect cannot be fully excluded.

The background of such debate has been plausibly suggested by D. Daube, who has noted in Mt 22 four types of exegetical questions often grouped also in rabbinical tradition.[20] There is the Pharisees' question about tribute to Caesar (15–22), the Sadducees' question about levirate marriage and the resurrection (23–33), the Pharisees' question about the great commandment of the Law (34–40), and finally the Pharisees' question about the Messiah, son of David (41–46). These questions correspond respectively to the rabbinical grouping of four questions concerning *hokmāh* ('wisdom', i.e., halakic interpretation of legal texts), *bōrût* ('vulgarity', i.e., questions designed to ridicule a belief), *derek 'ereṣ* ('the way of the land', i.e., the principle of moral conduct), and *haggādāh* ('legend', i.e., the interpretation of biblical passages with apparent contradictions). In this case, Jesus would be propounding a *haggādāh* question arising from the contradiction of the Messiah as David's son and David's lord. It implies that both ideas are correct: the Messiah is David's son (in his earthly appearance), but also David's Lord.[21] We cannot be certain about this because the passage is so cryptic. It is not impossible that he also implied in his answer[22]

[19] Cf. R. P. Gagg, *op. cit.*, 24–9. I would not necessarily agree with all the individual details of this article.

[20] *The New Testament and Rabbinic Judaism* (London, 1956) 158–63. In quoting Daube, I do not mean to imply that he equates this four-question structure with Jesus' ministry itself; it may be due to the evangelists, as he suggests.

[21] See J. Jeremias, *Jesus' Promise to the Nations* (SBT 24; London, 1958) 53.

[22] See O. Cullman, *op. cit.*, 132–3.

that the Messiah was therefore less involved politically than the common belief depicted him to be.

At any rate, a more developed stage of the Son of David tradition developed with the writing of the Synoptic Gospels. As the evangelists incorporated this episode into their Gospels, it was almost certainly with a view to exploiting the nuances of the title *kyrios* and applying to Jesus the Messiah the words of Ps 110:1. By that time *kyrios*, used of Jesus, carried with it the clear suggestion that he was somehow on a par with Yahweh of the Old Testament. The use, moreover, of Ps 110:1 elsewhere in the New Testament clearly emphasizes Jesus' exaltation to Lordship and heavenly glory (see Mk 16:19; 1 Cor 15:25; Eph 1:20; Col 3:1; Heb 8:1; 10:12, 13; 12:2), and at times stands in contrast to his Davidic relationship (Acts 2:29–35; 13:23–39; Heb 1:3–13).[23]

In this regard three things should be noted: (1) It is highly questionable that the Davidic Messiah was given the title of Son of Man in pre-Christian times.[24] It is unlikely therefore that Jesus himself was referring to a well-known identification of the Messiah in his cryptic question. (2) The disciples, as depicted in the earliest Gospel strata, apparently did not make this equation during the earthly ministry of Jesus.[25] (3) Even though Ps 110 has no clear reference to the Son of Man or, most likely, even to the ideal and expected Davidic Messiah, these links are plausibly traced to Jesus himself. The allusion to Ps 110 in the trial scene (Mt 26:64 par.) suggests this and undoubtedly should be regarded as the springboard for the further development of the Son of David tradition in the Synoptics.[26] The term of this development, climaxing in Jesus' glorious exaltation and divine sonship, receives explicit formulation in *Ep. Barnabae* 12, 10,

[23] See E. Lövestamm, 'Die Davidssohnfrage', *SEA* 27 (1962) 72–82.

[24] See H. H. Rowley, 'The Suffering Servant and the Davidic Messiah', *The Servant of the Lord and other Essays on the Old Testament* (3rd ed.; Oxford, 1965) 82–4.

[25] *Ibid.*, 84

[26] See, however, N. Perrin, 'Mark XIV. 62: The End Product of a Christian Pesher Tradition', *NTS* 12 (1965–66) 150–5.

when Ps 110:1 is quoted in support of the belief that Jesus was 'not the son of a man, but the son of God'.

Thus the Davidic Messiah is a prime example of a biblical motif which developed in a tradition, even extrabiblically attested, but which was never completely divorced from its biblical roots. It grew and evolved beyond the limits of the Old Testament assertions and received a strong further impetus in Jesus' debate with the Pharisees over the Davidic origin of the Messiah.[27]

[27] See further A. Suhl, 'Der Davidssohn in Matthäus-Evangelium', *ZNW* 59 (1968) 57–81; E. Lohse, *'Huios David'*, *TWNT* 8, 482–92.

7

THE ARAMAIC 'ELECT OF GOD' TEXT FROM QUMRAN CAVE 4*

A few years ago there was on display in the U.S.A. a group of Dead Sea Scrolls, lent by the Department of Antiquities of the Hashemite Kingdom of Jordan to the Smithsonian Institution of Washington, D.C. Under the direction of Dr Gus Van Beek, the curator of the section for Old World Archaeology, the Smithsonian Institution handsomely mounted the fourteen texts and other materials from the excavated Qumran caves and the community centre of Khirbet Qumran. The exhibit was sent round the country for display in various museums.[1]

The most important text in the exhibit was undoubtedly the Psalms Scroll from Qumran Cave 11, published by Dr J. A. Sanders, of Union Theological Seminary.[2] However, another piece in the exhibit is of no little interest to students both of the New Testament and of Jewish Messianism in the last two cen-

* Originally published in *CBQ* 27 (1965) 348–72.

[1] Its itinerary: Washington, D.C. (Smithsonian Institution), Feb. 28–Mar. 21, 1965; Philadelphia, Pa. (University of Pennsylvania Museum), Apr. 3–25; Berkeley, Cal. (Lowie Museum, University), May 8–30; Los Angeles, Cal. (Claremont Graduate School), June 12–July 8; Omaha, Nebr. (Joslyn Art Museum), July 17–Aug. 8; Baltimore, Md. (Walters Art Gallery), Aug. 21–Sept. 19; Ottawa, Ont. (National Museum of Canada); London, Engl. (British Museum); Jordan.

[2] *Psalms Scroll of Qumran Cave 11* (DJD 4; Oxford: Clarendon Press, 1965). Other publications: J. A. Sanders, 'The Scroll of Psalms (11QPss) from Cave 11: A Preliminary Report', *BASOR* 165 (1962) 11–15; 'Ps 151 in 11QPss', *ZAW* 75 (1963) 73–86; 'Two Non-Canonical Psalms in 11QPs[a]', *ZAW* 76 (1964) 57–75. P. W. Skehan, 'The Apocryphal Psalm 151', *CBQ*

turies B.C. and the first century A.D., because it mentions an 'Elect of God'. It is to a reconsideration of this text that we turn our attention.

The text was published by M. l'abbé Jean Starcky in a collection of recondite essays commemorating the fiftieth anniversary of the school of Ancient Oriental Languages of the Institut Catholique de Paris. It was labelled by him as 'an Aramaic Messianic Text from Qumran Cave 4' and given the siglum 4QMess ar.[3] But the title is a 'come-on' which excites our curiosity, as did the titles of some earlier articles on Qumran texts. For the text is unfortunately very poorly preserved and has been deteriorating still more in the Palestine Archaeological Museum since its arrival there in 1952. One enigmatic phrase in it should have been reason enough for the early publication of the text, since it bears on the question of God's begetting of

---

25 (1963) 407–9; 'A Broken Acrostic and Psalm 9', *CBQ* 27 (1965) 1–5. W. H. Brownlee, 'The 11Q Counterpart to Ps 151, 1–5', *RQ* 4 (1963) 379–87. J. Carmignac, 'La forme poétique du Ps 151 de la grotte 11', *RQ* 4 (1963) 371–8. I. Rabinowitz, 'The Alleged Orphism of 11QPss 18.3–12', *ZAW* (1964) 193–200. A. Dupont-Sommer, 'Notes qoumraniennes', *Semitica* 15 (1965) 71–8. J. Strugnell, 'More Psalms of "David"', *CBQ* 27 (1965) 207–16. M. Delcor, 'Zum Psalter von Qumran', *BZ* 10 (1966) 15–29. J. A. Sanders, 'Variorum in the Psalms Scroll (11QPs[a])', *HTR* 59 (1966) 83–94. J. Strugnell, 'Notes on the Text and Transmission of the Apocryphal Psalms 151, 154 (=Syr. II) and 155 (=Syr. III)', *HTR* 59 (1966) 257–81. Y. Yadin, 'Another Fragment (E) of the Psalms Scroll from Qumran Cave 11 (11QPs[a])', *Textus* 5 (1966) 1–10. J. A. Sanders, *The Dead Sea Psalms Scroll* (Ithaca, N.Y.: Cornell Univ. Press, 1967). R. Polzin, 'Notes on the Dating of the Non-Massoretic Psalms of 11QPs[a]', *HTR* 60 (1967) 468–76. R. Meyer, 'Die Septuaginta-Fassung von Psalm 151:1–5 als Ergebnis einer dogmatischen Korrektur', *Das ferne und nahe Wort* (ed. F. Maass; *BZAW* 105; Berlin: Töpelmann, 1967) 164–72. A. Hurvitz, 'The Language and Date of Psalm 151 from Qumran', *Sepher Sukenik: Eretz Israel* 8 (Jerusalem: Israel Exploration Society, 1967) 82–7. M. Delcor, 'L'hymne à Sion du rouleau des Psaumes de la grotte 11 de Qumrân (11QPs[a])', *RQ* 6 (1967–68) 71–88. D. Lührmann, 'Ein Weisheitspsalm aus Qumran (11QPs[a] XVIII)', *ZAW* 80 (1968) 87–8.

[3] 'Un texte messianique araméen de la grotte 4 de Qumrân', *Ecole des langues orientales anciennes de l'Institut Catholque de Paris: Mémorial du cinquantenaire 1914–1964* (Travaux de l'Institut Catholique de Paris 10; Paris: Bloud et Gay, 1964) 51–66.

the Messiah.[4] Because this Aramaic text clearly bears the phrase *bḥyr 'lh'* in a context that has something to do with birth, one can understand how Starcky would be led to describe it as 'de caractère à la fois astrologique et messianique'.[5] But the question arises whether it really has anything to do with a Messiah or with an astrological horoscope.

Moreover, it will be recalled that *ho eklektos tou theou*, the exact Greek translation of the Aramaic *bḥyr 'lh'*, is applied to Jesus in some MSS. of Jn 1:34, 'I myself have seen it and have borne witness that this is God's Chosen One'. Though the best MSS. read *ho huios tou theou*, the reading *ho eklektos tou theou* has been preferred by the *NEB*, *La Bible de Jérusalem*, A. Loisy, A. von Harnack, R. Schnackenburg, and R. E. Brown.[6] A few verses later Jesus is given the title *Messias* by Andrew (1:41). The collocation of these titles, 'Elect of God' and 'Messiah', might suggest that the former was an exclusive title for the latter, and that therefore the mention of the Elect of God in this text refers to one of the Messiahs expected at Qumran. An inferior reading in Lk 23:35 has the phrase, 'the Messiah, the Elect of God' (Peshitta, Syr^{sin}, C*) instead of the more usual wording, 'God's Messiah, the Elect One'. However, it is so weakly attested that it scarcely merits the textual critic's attention.

I. QUMRAN MESSIANISM

But this text is important not only because it supplies an extra-biblical attestation of the individual use of the title 'Elect of

[4] See 1QSa 2:11–12 (DJD 1, 110), and further comments below (see p. 153).

[5] *Op. cit.*, 51.

[6] The reading *ho huios tou theou* is found in P^{66}, P^{75}, S^{c}, B, c, f, l, q, vg, whereas *ho eklektos tou theou* is read in Sinaiticus (prima manus), P^{5} (probably), a few MSS. of the *Vetus latina* (e, ff^{2}), the Curetonian and Sinaitic Syriac versions, and is supported by Ambrose. The modern editors who prefer to read *ho eklektos* do so in the conviction that it is more probable that this reading was changed to *ho huios* than vice versa. Moreover, *ho eklektos* is more in harmony with what seems to have been the early Gospel tradition about the heavenly voice at Jesus' baptism (cf. Mk 1:11; Mt 3:17, which echoes Is 42:1). Cf. Lk 23:35; 9:35.

God', thus illustrating Jn 1:34, but also because it has been related to the larger question of Qumran messianism. J. Starcky discussed the relevance of the text to this larger question in an important article published under the title, 'The Four Stages of Messianism at Qumran'.[7] It is well for us to give a brief summary of his position in this article first, because it will serve as a background to our discussion. This article is, indeed, a significant contribution to the study of Qumran messianism, even if some details in his reconstruction are open to question.

The four separate stages which Starcky distinguished in the messianism of Qumran correspond in general to those periods which have been distinguished by the archaeologists and palaeographers who have worked on the Qumran material. Starcky speaks of the Maccabean period (equalling the archaeological phase Ia), the Hasmonean period (equalling the archaeological phase Ibα), the period of Pompey and Caesar (equalling the archaeological phase Ibβ), and finally the Herodian period (equalling the archaeological phase II).

[7] 'Les quatres étapes du messianisme à Qumran', *RB* 70 (1963) 481–505. Beware of the résumé in *NTA* 8 (1963–64) 430 (#1185). Older discussions of Qumran messianism can be found in the following: G. R. Beasley Murray, 'The Two Messiahs in the Testaments of the Twelve Patriarchs', *JTS* 48 (1947) 1–12. M. Black, 'The Messiah of the Testament of Levi XVIII', *ExpT* 60 (1948–49) 321–2; 61 (1949–50) 157–8. R. E. Brown, 'The Messianism of Qumran', *CBQ* 19 (1957) 53–82; 'The Teacher of Righteousness and the Messiah(s)', *The Scrolls and Christianity* (ed. M. Black; SPCK Theological Collections 11; London, 1969) 37–44, 109–12. M. Burrows, 'The Messiahs of Aaron and Israel (DSD IX, 11)', *ATR* 34 (1952) 202–6; J. S. Croatto, 'De messianismo qumranico', *VD* 35 (1957) 279–86; 344–60. E. L. Ehrlich, 'Ein Beitrag zur Messiaslehre der Qumransekte', *ZAW* 58 (1956) 234–43. J. Gnilka, 'Die Erwartung des messianischen Hohenpriesters in den Schriften von Qumran und im Neuen Testament', *RQ* 2 (1959–60) 395–426. R. Gordis, 'The "Begotten" Messiah in the Qumran Scrolls', *VT* 7 (1957) 191–4. A. J. B. Higgins, 'The Priestly Messiah', *NTS* 13 (1966–67) 211–39. K. G. Kuhn, 'Die beiden Messias Aarons und Israels', *NTS* 1 (1954–55) 168–79; translated and adapted in K. Stendahl, *The Scrolls and the New Testament* (New York: Harper, 1957) 54–64; 'Die beiden Messias in den Qumrantexten und die Messiasvorstellung in der rabbinischen Literatur', *ZAW* 70 (1958) 200–8. W. S. LaSor, '"The Messiahs of Aaron and

Starcky discusses the various Qumran texts which come from these periods and traces the development of the messianic expectations of the Qumran sect through them.

In the Maccabean period the Righteous Teacher arose, and his reform-activity got under way in the time of Jonathan who became High Priest *c.* 152 B.C. Starcky follows J. T. Milik and G. Vermes in identifying the persecuting Wicked Priest of the *Pesharim* on *Habakkuk* and *Ps 37* with Jonathan. The Righteous Teacher, whose reform-activity began after the sect's first twenty years of amorphous existence, is regarded as the author of the *Thanksgiving Psalms* and of the *Manual of Discipline*. But the oldest copy of the latter, as yet unpublished, is 4QS^{e} which dates from the end of the second century B.C. This copy of the *Manual of Discipline* lacks the long paragraph which runs from 1QS 8:15b to 9:11 (from *l'śwt* to *wyśr'l*).[8] Hence the oldest copy of the *Manual of Discipline* never had the passage mentioning the advent of a Prophet and the Messiahs of Aaron and Israel—i.e., it lacked the crucial sentence, 'They shall swerve

---

Israel"', *VT* 6 (1956) 425–49; 'The Messianic Idea in Qumran', *Studies Presented to A. A. Neuman* (Leiden: Brill, 1962) 343–64. R. B. Laurin, 'The Problem of the Two Messiahs in the Qumran Scrolls', *RQ* 4 (1963) 39–52. J. Liver, 'The Doctrine of the Two Messiahs in Sectarian Literature in the Time of the Second Commonwealth', *HTR* 52 (1959) 149–85. K. Schubert, 'Der alttestamentliche Hintergrund der Vorstellung von den beiden Messiassen im Schrifttum von Chirbet Qumran', *Judaica* 12 (1956) 24–8; 'Die Messiaslehre in den Texten von Chirbet Qumran', *BZ* 1 (1957) 177–97; 'Zwei Messiasse aus dem Regelbuch von Chirbet Qumran', *Judaica* 11 (1955) 216–35. L. H. Silberman, 'The Two "Messiahs" of the Manual of Discipline', *VT* 5 (1955) 77–82. K. Smyth, 'The Dead Sea Scrolls and the Messiah', *Studies* 45 (1956) 1–14. L. Stefaniak, 'Messianische oder eschatologische Erwartungen in der Qumransekte?', *Festschrift J. Schmid* (Regensburg: Pustet, 1962) 294–302. N. Wieder, 'The Doctrine of the Two Messiahs among the Karaites', *JJS* 6 (1955) 14–25. A. S. van der Woude, *Die messianischen Vorstellungen der Gemeinde von Qumran* (Studia semitica neerlandica 3; Assen: van Gorcum, 1957); 'Le Maître de Justice et les deux messies de la communauté de Qumran', *La secte de Qumran et les origines chrétiennes* (RechBib 4; Bruges: Desclée de Brouwer, 1959) 121–34.

[8] See J. T. Milik, *RB* 67 (1960) 413: 'Dans S^{e}, sur la ligne correspondante, *byd Mšḥ* est suivi immédiatement par IX 12ss.'

from no counsel of the Law to walk in all the stubbornness of their hearts, but shall be guided by the primitive precepts by which the men of the community were first instructed, until there will come a prophet and the Messiahs of Aaron and Israel.' Furthermore, though in the *Thanksgiving Psalms* the term *nēṣer* occurs, 'a shoot, sprout' (1QH 6:15; 7:19; 8:6, 8, 10), it does not refer to the 'scion of David', but to the Qumran community, regarded as a 'plantation'. It alludes not to Is 11:1, but to Is 60:21. The Righteous Teacher has gathered up a shoot from the dried-up trunk of Israel and transplanted it to the desert to bring forth a plantation, the community of the true Israel. Again, the reference in 1QH 3:9–10 to the 'Wonderful Counsellor' of Is 9:5 refers not to an individual, but in some way to the Qumran community (to the *'ṣt hyḥd* of 1QS). The upshot of all this is that in the texts which come from the early period, when the Righteous Teacher was still active, we find no titles used of himself; there is no evidence that he considered himself a 'messiah', nor did he even await one. The Righteous Teacher was a leader in the line of the prophets like Moses or a reformer like Ezra, but not a Messiah, 'car il n'attendait pas de Messie' (p. 487). In other words, in the earliest Qumran texts one is hard put to discern any sort of messianic expectation.

This expectation, however, is detected in the second or Hasmonean period, when either toward the end of the reign of John Hyrcanus or the beginning of that of Alexander Jannaeus a new generation of Essenes emerges. This new generation was undoubtedly influenced by the entrance into the community of persecuted Pharisees. Toward the end of the second century B.C. a Pharisaic influence had previously been noted.[9] From this period come the copy of the *Manual of Discipline* from Cave 1 (1QS, dated palaeographically to the beginning of the first century B.C.), the appendices to it (1 QSa, 1QSb) and the *4QTestimonia*. Starcky attributes to the scribe who composed

[9] See J. T. Milik, *Ten Years of Discovery in the Wilderness of Judaea* (SBT 26; London: SCM, 1959) 87–93.

the *Testimonia* those additions which were made to the original text of the *Manual of Discipline*.

Now it is significant that in these texts of the second period we find the full-blown Messianic expectations which we have come to identify with the Essenes of Qumran: the advent of a Prophet and of the Messiahs of Aaron and Israel (cf. 1QS 9:11). *4QTestimonia* (in which OT texts are quoted in a *catena*: Dt 5:28–29 and 18:18–19; Nm 24:15–17; and Dt 33:8–11) refers to the prophet, a political Messiah, and a priestly Messiah.[10] In 1QSa 2:11–12, 14, 20 the Messiah of Israel and a Priest are mentioned, and in 1QSb there is a blessing for the High Priest (1:21–3:21) which precedes that of the Prince of the Congregation (5:20–29). Under Pharisaic influence the early views of the priestly nucleus of the community were modified and the expectation of a Messiah grew. To this same period Starcky relates the basic form of the *Testaments of the Twelve Patriarchs* with its frequent mention of the Messiahs of Levi (priestly) and of Judah (Davidic). In fact, he thinks that both *Jubilees* and the *Testaments of the Twelve Patriarchs* (in its original form composed by a Pharisaic author) prepared the way for the author of 1QSa to add the paragraph in 1QS 8:15–9:11. Starcky further relates to this period a text as yet unpublished: 4QAhA, which he claims has to do with 'a suffering Messiah in a perspective opened by the Servant Songs' (p. 492). He claims that this text depicts the Messiah of Aaron as the Servant of Yahweh.

From the Pompeian period (63–37 B.C.) Starcky maintains that we have the messianic references found in the *Damascus Document*. This text alludes to Pompey in mentioning 'the head of the kings of Yawan who comes to wreak his vengeance on them' (CD 8:11–12=19:24–25). But in the oldest copy of the *Damascus Document* which is the unpublished 4QD^b dated palaeographically to 75–50 B.C., there is reference to a flight of the Essenes to Damascus camps. Also in this text we see the two Messiahs become *one*: 'the Messiah of Aaron and Israel' (CD

[10] On this text and its messianic references, see my remarks above, pp. 83–4.

19:10–11; 20:1; 12:23; 14:19). In the passage of 4QD[b] which corresponds to CD 14:19 the singular of 'Messiah' is found (*'d ʿmwd mšyḥ 'hrwn wyśr'l*), which shows that it is not due to a medieval copyist, as was at times suspected. This Messiah arises from both Aaron and Israel, which would mean that at least his father would be an Aaronid, and his expiation for the iniquity of the community would imply a *priestly* role. Yet he will also be the Messiah of Israel, a royal Messiah; he is now regarded as the 'Prince of the *Whole* Congregation' (CD 7:20). The two Messiahs merge into a priestly figure.

But the 'Interpreter of the Law' (CD 7:18) is identified by Starcky with the eschatological Prophet (1QS 9:11), who is now none other than the Righteous Teacher, believed to return at the end of time with the Messiah of Aaron and Israel: '. . . to walk according to them in the whole period of wickedness and without them they shall achieve nothing, until he comes who shall teach uprightness at the end of days' (*ʿd ʿmd ywrh hṣdq b'ḥryt hymym*, CD 6:10–11). Starcky finds a further reference to this eschatological Prophet in a tiny unpublished papyrus fragment (4QarP), one line of which begins *lkn 'šlḥ l'lyh qd*[*m*], 'I shall send you Elijah befo[re] . . .', an obvious allusion to Mal 3:23. The preceding line of this fragment reads *tmyny lbḥyr wh'* [ ], 'the eighth as an Elect One; and behold [ ]'. Starcky sees in this 'eighth' a reference to David, who was the eighth son of Jesse and chosen as king (1 Sm 16:10–13). And so for this period Starcky concludes, 'After the taking of Jerusalem in 63, the Essenes awaited only one Messiah and his precursor' (p. 498). To this same period Starcky would also relate the *Psalms of Solomon*, which mention the 'Anointed of the Lord' (17:23–24, 36; 18:6, 8).

Finally, in the fourth or Herodian period (roughly from 4 B.C. to A.D. 68), when the Essenes returned to the mother-house at Qumran to rebuild it after the earthquake of 31 B.C., there developed among them an anti-Roman or Zealot tendency. To this period belongs the *Rule of the War* in which the primary role is played by the High Priest. The 'Prince of the Whole Congregation' is mentioned only in the inscription to be put on his shield (5:1). It was a troubled period, marked by the oppression of Roman procurators; and then it was that older documents, the *Manual of Discipline*, the *Thanksgiving Psalms*, and the *Damascus Document*, were recopied. In the *Rule of the War* there is once again the duality of Messiahs, *byd mšyḥykh ḥwzy t'wdwt*, 'through your Messiahs, the seers of things ordained' (1QM 11:7–8). This, however, seems to be an archaic survival or at most a parallel development to what otherwise appears at this time. In this period too belongs the mention of the 'Messiah of Uprightness, the scion of David' (4QPatrBles 1:3–4), of the 'Scion of David who will rise with the Interpreter of the Law' (4QFlor 1:11), and of the 'scion of David, who will arise in the end of days' (4QpIs^{a} D 1). To this same period Starcky would assign the Parables of the book of *Enoch*, which conflate the titles 'Son of Man', 'the Elect One', 'the Anointed', and the 'Just One', applying them all to one person. Starcky attributes this section of *Enoch* to non-Essene Ḥasidim of the pre-Christian period. Finally, to this Herodian period Starcky also assigns the recently published text which mentions explicitly 'the Elect of God'.

Starcky concludes: 'The evolution which we believe we have detected among the Essenes agrees with what we know of the history of the sect and of Judaism in the last two centuries B.C.: an eclipse of messianism in the Hellenistic era; its reawakening in the time of the Hasmonean kings, with a duplication in terms of a temporal and sacerdotal Messiah; then the absorption of the messianic prerogatives by the future High Priest at the beginning of the Roman period; and finally the renewal of the traditional conception of the Son of David at the very moment when Jesus was going to realize this expectation' (p. 504).

Starcky's reconstruction of the messianism of Qumran has much to commend it. It has been recognized for some time now that some Qumran texts mention no Messiah, some mention a Messiah from Aaron and Israel, and some mention Messiahs from Aaron and Israel. The only way in which this fluctuation of material can be coped with is to line up the Qumran texts in as definite a chronological order as possible. This Starcky has done. He has coped with the fact that a number of these texts have undergone subsequent reduction and editing, and has tried to evaluate the different forms of the texts. (By way of a momentary digression, we might point out the pertinence of such a mode of ancient composition that is well attested in the Qumran literature to the problem of how three different Synoptic accounts of the same Gospel tradition could come into being. Ancient authors did expand existing compositions by adding further material.)

Our criticism of Starcky's reconstruction concerns a number of minor points. First of all, in both of his articles he fails to treat distinctly titles which may represent different trends and beliefs in Judaism. When he finds, for instance, the title 'Elect of God', he immediately concludes that it refers to the Messiah and then cites Is 42:1 (a passage from the Servant Songs).[11] In this he betrays his Christian outlook, and is not disciplined enough in his interpretation of pre-Christian Jewish material. It is not *per se* evident that the title 'Elect of God' was messianic in Qumran circles. It is true that the titles 'Son of Man', 'Elect One' (but not 'the Elect of God'), 'Anointed' and 'Just One' are conflated and applied indiscriminately to one figure in the Parables of *Enoch*. But the date of this section in *Enoch* is quite disputed, and should it be due to a Jew or a Jewish Christian in the first or second century A.D., as Milik would have it,[12] then the first attestation of the conflated titles applied

[11] See J. Starcky, 'Un texte messianique . . .', p. 59: '. . . il s'agit de l'élu de Dieu, c'est-à-dire du Messie (*Is.*, 42:1 et 61, 1).'

[12] Cf. J. T. Milik, *Ten Years*, 33. For a fuller discussion of the problem see P. Grelot, 'Le Messie dans les apocryphes de l'Ancien Testament: Etat de la question', *La venue du Messie: Messianisme et eschatologie* (RechBib 6; Bruges: Desclée de Brouwer, 1962) 19–50, esp. 42–50.

to one person would be in the NT itself.[13] But the 'Elect of God' is a distinct title attested in the NT (Jn 1:34) and in Qumran writings (1QpHab 10:13 and 4QMess ar), which is not found otherwise in the OT nor in Intertestamental Literature, even though it may have its roots in the OT and a congener in 'the Elect One' of *Enoch*.

In a similar way, Starcky's remarks about the cryptic fragment (4QarP) which mentions the sending of Elijah before . . . (?) are tantalizing. If what he says is true, then this tiny fragment preserves the earlier hint of a late Jewish belief in Elijah as the precursor of the Messiah. Starcky identifies him with the 'eschatological Prophet' and in the same context speaks of the Essenes of the Pompeian period expecting 'un seul Messie et son précurseur' (p. 498). But is it really so? Form-critical studies on the Baptist accounts in the Synoptics have shown that John the Baptist expected Jesus to be Elijah and that it was Jesus himself who corrected this notion and taught the people that John was Elijah redivivus (Mt 11:3–14). Then because John was the precursor of Jesus, who was the Messiah, the belief apparently grew that Elijah was the precursor of the Messiah—but it grew up in Christian circles and cannot be traced certainly to any writer earlier than Justin Martyr.[14] Whatever the significance of this tiny papyrus scrap is, it should be thoroughly assessed and not too quickly related to the idea of a 'precursor' of the Messiah.[15]

Secondly, the title 'Messiah' must be used with care, as a number of writers have stressed since the discovery of the Dead Sea Scrolls, and not immediately be associated with Jesus of Nazareth, as Starcky is inclined to do (p. 504). It is a specific

[13] See my comments below, pp. 138, 252-4.

[14] See J. A. T. Robinson, 'Elijah, John and Jesus: An Essay in Detection', *NTS* 4 (1957–58) 263–81; reprinted in *Twelve New Testament Studies* (SBT 34; London: SCM, 1962) 28–52, esp. 37. Cf. J. Jeremias, 'Ēl(e)ias', *TDNT* 2, 928–44. A. J. B. Higgins, 'Jewish Messianic Belief in Justin Martyr's *Dialogue with Trypho*', *NT* 9 (1967) 298–305.

[15] Concerning the 'eighth' mentioned in this fragment, see footnote 31 (below, p. 159).

term which has well-known OT roots. Used of prophets (possibly Ps 105:15; 1 Chr 16:22; Is 61:1), priests (Lv 4:3, 5, 16; Ex 29:7, 29; 30:30; Nm 35:25), and kings (1 Kgs 1:34; 1 Sm 24:7, 11; 26:9, 11; 2 Sm 23:1), it designated in common an anointed agent, sent by God to overcome opposition to him and eventually to secure his reign among men. Only in two places in the OT do we read of promises to raise up an Anointed One or a Priest with him for this purpose (1 Sm 2:35; Dn 9:25–26). And yet this sort of text fed the messianic expectations of some Jews in late Judaism, so that the Messiah came to be related with the 'end of days'. The Qumran texts in some cases openly allude to Dn 9:25 (*'d mšyḥ ngyd*); cf. 1QS 9:11. In my opinion, both the text in Daniel and the Qumran texts manifest a stage in the development of Jewish beliefs when it is thoroughly legitimate to speak of the coming of 'a/the Messiah' or even of 'the Messiahs'. Granted that one should not read into these terms all the connotations of NT Christology, and an effort should be made not to conflate the title 'Messiah' with other so-called messianic titles, nevertheless it is a hypercritical tendency that leads some to say that we should speak of 'Anointed Ones', or of 'Consacrés', or even of messiahs (with a small *m*) in the Qumran texts.[16] For it is precisely these texts which show that the genuine OT theme of an Anointed One had definitely developed into the expectation of a Messiah (or Messiahs). One should not water down the Qumran expressions lest their import in recording phrases which reflect genuine messianic hopes among Jews of the NT period be obscured. After all, the texts do use the word *māšîªḥ* as a substantive, and not just as an adjective, and in an individual, not a collective sense.

Thirdly, and more importantly, as R. E. Brown has pointed out,[17] Starcky has dated the *Damascus Document* too late in

[16] See, for instance, J. Carmignac, *Les textes de Qumran* (Paris: Letouzey et Ané) 2 (1963) 13; L. H. Silberman, 'The Two "Messiahs" of the Manual of Discipline', *VT* 5 (1955) 77–82; M. Smith, 'What is Implied by the Variety of Messianic Figures?', *JBL* 78 (1959) 66–72.

[17] 'J. Starcky's Theory of Qumran Messianic Development', *CBQ* 28 (1966) 51–7.

ascribing it to the third or Pompeian period. Milik dates his oldest copy of it (4QD[b]) to 75–50 B.C., and this is scarcely the original autograph. Again, Starcky has misinterpreted the phrase, 'the head of the kings of Yawan' (CD 8:11) as a reference to Pompey, whereas the Romans are usually referred to in Qumran literature as the Kittim. 'Yawan' means Greece, and the phrase almost certainly refers to the Seleucid kings and Alexander. Furthermore, the reference to 'forty years' in CD 20:13–15 argues for a date for CD shortly prior to 100 B.C. This would put the composition of CD in the second or Hasmonean period. If so, it would come from roughly the same period as 1QS. This text clearly speaks of two Messiahs (1QS 9:11). As far as Brown is concerned, the messianic texts in CD do not unequivocally speak of only one Messiah. Grammatically, 'a Messiah of Aaron and Israel' (CD 12:23–13:1; 14:19; 19:10–11) and 'a Messiah from Aaron and from Israel' (CD 20:1) could mean a Messiah from Aaron and a Messiah from Israel. This is supported by the interpretation given to Nm 24:17 in CD 7:18–20, which calls for two figures: the Star as the Interpreter of the Law, and the Sceptre as the Prince of the whole Congregation. Starcky understood the former to be the eschatological Prophet (of 1QS 9:11), but Brown more rightly identifies him as a priestly figure (cf. *T. Levi* 18:3). The other figure is the Davidic Messiah. This is confirmed by 4QFlor 1–3 i 11 (DJD 5, 54). Consequently, Brown insists that 'from the Hasmonean period on there was at Qumran an expectation of two Messiahs, a special king and a special priest, anointed (and hence messiahs) as kings and priests would be. . . . But we do not think there is sufficient evidence that during one period, the Pompeian period, this expectation was narrowed down to one figure who would be both prince and priest' (pp. 56–7). Brown prefers to speak of a revival of hope in the Davidic Messiah in the Herodian period, and agrees with Starcky that belief in him became stronger in this period because of the Roman occupation. It is a question of emphasis.

Lastly, we come to Starcky's interpretation of the 'Elect of God' text itself.

II. THE TEXT OF 4Q MESS AR

The reader is referred to Starcky's publication for the physical description and the dimensions of the text. Starcky relates the script of the roughly ten fragments which make up the text to F. M. Cross' class of the 'round semiformal' type of Herodian script,[18] which would yield a rough dating of 30 B.C. to A.D. 20. But he even entertains the possibility of extending it to the First Revolt (A.D. 70) and actually prefers a date in the first century A.D. J. Carmignac, who has also studied this new Aramaic text, points out that it was most likely copied by the same scribe who copied the Hebrew texts of the Pesher on Ps 37, the Pesher on Isaiah a, and the Pesher on Hosea b (now relabelled 4QpHos[a] —see 4Q*166* in DJD 5, 31–2).[19]

My transcription of the text follows in the main that of Starcky's publication. I have checked his transcription against the photo accompanying his article and the clearer ones which accompany the original text in the Smithsonian exhibit (PAM 43,590 and 43,591). Any variant readings of my own will be noted in the commentary. In Starcky's article a note at the bottom of the photo labelled 'Fragment i, I' indicates that a small fragment on the lower left does not really belong to the text. It does not appear in the photo on the left, where the two otherwise overlap.

One might also question whether the fragment which bears

[18] 'The Development of the Jewish Scripts', *BANE* 138, 173–4.

[19] See 'Les horoscopes de Qumran', *RQ* 18 (1965) 199–217, esp. 207–10. Confusion is the only word for the way in which J. M. Allegro has published at different times various parts of the same text. E.g., 4QpPs37 col. i (last 11 lines) and col ii were published in 'A Newly Discovered Fragment of a Commentary on Psalm XXXVII from Qumrân', *PEQ* 86 (1954) 69–75. Then fragments of col. iii appeared in 'Further Light on the History of the Qumran Sect', *JBL* 75 (1956) 94 (+pl. 3), together with further lines of col. i (*ibid.*, 9, pl. 4). Then in his book, *The People of the Dead Sea Scrolls* (Garden City, N.Y., 1958) pl. 48, he presents a photo of col. i–ii which is almost unreadable. Cf. H. Stegemann, *RQ* 14 (1964) 235–70.

the end of ll. 1–2 in Col. II is correctly placed. The last words make little sense as they now stand, and though the space between the lines agrees with that to which it is attached, the 'join' is not a perfect one. Though I was able to get very close to the plate containing the text both in Washington and in Philadelphia, I did not arrive at any certain judgment about this problem. Though we must reckon with the possibility that the edge of the fragment has deteriorated a bit or shrunk, yet the judgment will rest with those who can examine the 'join' again at first hand. Having raised the question of the correctness of this 'join', I shall otherwise go along with Starcky's restoration.[20]

Col. I

1. *dy yd' trtyn '*[ ] *kmh* [ ]*w šwmh šb*[*q*] *mn* [ ]
2. *ś'rh*[*w*]*ṭlwpḥyn 'l* [ ]
3. *wšwmn zw'yrn 'l yrkth* [*btr trt*]*yn šnyn dn mn dn yd'* . . *lyh*
4. *b'lymwth lhwh klhwn* [*k'n*]*wš dy l' yd' md'*[*m 'd*] *'dn dy*
5. [*y*]*nd' tltt spry'* [ ]
6. [*b'*]*dyn y'rm wyd' św*[*kl'*]*šn ḥzwn lm'th lh 'l 'rkwbt*[*h*]
7. *wb'bwhy wb'*[*b*]*htwhy* . . [ ]*ḥyn wzqynh 'mh lh*[*ww*]*n mlkh w'rmwm*[*h*]
8. [*w*]*yd' rzy 'nš' wḥwkmth lkwl 'mmy' thk wyd' rzy kwl ḥyy'*
9. [*wk*]*wl ḥšbwnyhwn 'lwhy yswpw wmsrt kwl ḥyy' śgy' thw'*
10. [*ḥ*]*šbwnwhy bdy bḥyr 'lh' hw' mwldh wrwḥ nšmwhy*
11. [*ḥ*]*šbwnwhy lhwwn l'lmyn* [ ]
12. [ ]*' dy l*[ ]. . [ ]*lyn*
13. [ ]*t ḥšb*[*wn*
14. [ ]*b*
15. [ ]*why*
16. [ ].
17. [ ].*š*

[20] Many of the letters of this fragmentary text are restored; the reader should consult Starcky's edition, where some are marked with a dot (indicating a probable reading) and others with a small circle (indicating a possible reading).

Col. II

1. .[ ] *dy m*[ ] *npl lqdmyn bny šḥwh* [
2. [ ]. .*t' b'yš ṭlwpḥ' l*. .[
3. [ ]. . . .[
4. [ ]*m'th*[
5. [ ]*bś*[*r'*
6. *mw*[ ]*h* [
7. *wrwḥ nš*[*mwhy ḥšbwnwhy lhwwn*]
8. *l'lmyn* [
9. . . . .[
10.
11.
12. *wmdynn* . .[
13. *wyḥrbwn t*.[ ].*m*[ ] *wbmln ytbyn dy l*.[
14. *myn yswpwn t*.[ ]*mn* [ ]*bbn yḥrbn kwl 'ln yhk*[*wn*]
15. *yt*.[
16. [ ]. .[ ]. *wkl*[*h*]*n ytbnwn k'yryn 'wbdh*
17. *ḥlp qlh* [ ]*yswdh 'lwhy ysdwn ḥṭ'h wḥwbth*
18. [ ]. .[ ]*ḥdwh*[*y*]. *qdyš w'yry*[*n*]*m'mr*
19. [']*mrw 'lwhy* [ ]
20. [ ]. . .[ ].*b my*[ ]*pwn*
21. [ ].*zh*

There is one further fragment (no. 3) on which Starcky reads .]*mglyn*[.

III. TRANSLATION[21]

Col. I: [1]two . . . of the hand. [ ] [ ] it lef[t] a mark from [like] [2]barley [and] lentils on [ ][3] and tiny marks on his thigh [. After tw]o years he knows this from that. . . . [4]In his youth he will become like [like a ma]n who does not know anyth[ing, until] the time when [5]he shall become skilled in the three books. [6][Th]en he will become wise and will be endowed with disc[retion] . . . visions to

[21] Restorations are indicated by square brackets [ ]; parentheses ( ) indicate words added for the sake of a smoother translation.

come to him upon [his] knees. [7]And with his father and with his forefa[th]ers . . . [ ] life and old age; (and) with him there will be counsel and prudence [8][and] he will know the secrets of man. And his wisdom will go forth to all the peoples, and he will know the secrets of all living things. [9][Al]l their calculations against him will come to naught, although the opposition of all living beings will be great.[10] [But] his [cal]culations [will succeed] because he is the Elect of God. His birth and the (very) spirit of his breath [11][ ] his [cal]culations will exist forever. [ ] [12][ ] [13][ ] calcu[lation]

Col. II: [1][ ] which. [ ] fell to the east. Children of perdition(?) [ ] [2][ ] . . . (was) evil. The lentil(?) . . . [ ] [3][ ] [4][ ] to come [ ] [5][ ] fle[sh] [6][ ] [7]and the spirit of [his] breath [his calculations will exist] [8]forever [ ] [9][ ] [10-11][ ] [12]and cities . . . [ ] [13]and they will lay waste . . . [ ] . . . [ ] and with dwelling which . . . [ ] [14]waters will cease . . . [ ] from [ ] . . . will devastate (the) gates(?). All these will co[me] [15][ ] [16][ ]. and all of [th]em [and] upon it they will base its foundation. Its sin and its guilt [18][ ] . . . [in] hi[s] breast [ ]. a Holy One and Watcher[s] a saying [19][ ]. they have [sp]oken against him.

[20][ ] [21][ ]

IV. COMMENTARY

The preserved text introduces us to a description of a newborn child, as it were, *in medias res.* In the lines best preserved a description is given of the qualities of this child: of his health and his growth, of his intelligence and his wisdom, of his long life and his old age. His favoured position and the success of his plans seem to be ascribed to the fact that he is an 'Elect of God'. Since the first lines of what is called Col. I are not really the beginning of the text, it is impossible to say for certain to whom all this is ascribed. But it is to be noted that there is no mention in the text of an Anointed One, a Messiah; nor is it even certain that the phrase 'Elect of God' is to be understood in a messianic sense.

Col. I

The first three lines of Col. I seem to describe certain physical characteristics of the child.

1. *dy yd' trtyn:* 'Two ? of the hand.' In the context *trtyn* could refer to the fem. pl. *śwmn*, 'marks', a word now lost, but which would have been at the end of the preceding column. Starcky reads *dy yd' trtyn '[w]kmh*, 'de la main (au nombre de) deux; *noire* (est une marque et . . .]'. The text is so broken, however, that the last word, while not impossible, is highly questionable. The letters *kmh* could be the interrogative 'how' (cf. 1QapGn 20:2).

śwmh šb[q] mn [ ]: 'It left a mark from [ ].' The only word which is certain here is *śwmh*, 'a mark'. Quite unlikely is the form suggested by Starcky for the end of this line, *šm[q]mq*, 'red, reddish'. With what would it agree? The syntax of *šmqmq š'rth* is almost impossible, unless one supposes that the latter word is masc. despite its fem. form. J. Carmignac (*op. cit.*, 210) has also questioned whether the traces of the letters correspond to *šmqmq*; he prefers to read *(w)śwmqyn š'ry'*, ('et) roux (seront) les cheveux'. This makes more sense, but no justification is given for the form *śwmqyn*; the adjective is normally written either *śamôq* or *śimmûq*: cf. 1QapGn 21:17 (*ym' śmwq'*, 'the Red Sea'), 18 bis. Cf. G. Dalman, *Aramäisch-Neuhebräisches Handwörlerbuch* (Göttingen: E. Pfeiffer, 1938) 293. There is the further problem of the reading of *š'yr'*; see below. The reading *šb[q] mn* does not help much in the context, but at least it deserves some consideration. If it has any point, then Carmignac's suggested comparison of the child with David, as the 'rejeton de David', has little basis. The word *śwm'* also occurs as *swm'* in later Aramaic, whereas in Hebrew the form is *šwmh.* It is difficult to be certain therefore of the exact form of the initial sibilant.

2. *ś'rh [w]ṭlwpḥyn:* 'Barley and lentils.' Just what such a phrase is doing in a description of the bodily features of a new-born babe is a good question. Starcky read the beginning of this line thus: *š'rt[h w]ṭlwpḥyn 'l* [. . . .], taking *š'rt[h]* with the end of the preceding line. Aside from the fact that *ś'r'*, 'hair', is normally masc. in Aramaic (cf. 1QapGn 20:3), the collocation of the consonants *ś'r* (whatever the ending is!) with *ṭlwpḥyn* would seem more naturally to suggest 'barley'. Hence we take *ś'rh* as fem. sg. absol. in a collective sense. For the collocation *ṭlpḥn* with *ś'rn,* see *AP* 2: 4, 5; 3: 5, 6. Most likely the mention of 'barley and lentils' here is part of a comparison; the marks on the body of the infant resemble barley and lentils. The reference is probably to moles; this meaning is attested for *šwmh* in rabbinical literature.

3. *wświmn zw'yrn 'l yrkth:* 'And tiny marks on his thigh.' The form *zw'yrn* is fem. pl. absol. of the *qutail* (diminutive) type, 'very little'.

[*btr trt*]*yn šnyn dn mn dn yd'* . . . .: 'After two years he knows this from that.' The restoration of the lacuna is conjectural, being suggested only by the context of growth. It is complicated by the reading of the last word. At the end of the line Starcky read *wd'h tlyh,* and he understood *šnyn* earlier in the line to mean 'teeth'. He translated the line thus, '[bien rang]ées sont les dents les unes par rapport aux autres, et (sa) science sera élevée'. Whatever one thinks of *šnyn* as 'teeth' (a possibility scarcely to be excluded), the translation of *wd'h tlyh* is impossible. Starcky had to insert *sa* ('his') in parentheses.

J. Carmignac (*op. cit.,* 211) correctly realized that the first of these two words should be read as *yd'*; but his reading *yd'* [*hp*]*lyh* is likewise improbable. He translates the phrase: 'il saura parler distinctement'. He adds the justification that 'after having spoken of teeth, it is normal enough for one to think of mentioning the distinctness of diction'. Carmignac explains *hplyh* as the causative of *ply*, 'parler distinctement'. This meaning is attested for Hebrew, but we fail to find this causative usage in Aramaic. There is the further problem of the causative in *h-* in Qumran Aramaic, which is otherwise unattested. Moreover, the use of the infinitive as a complement without *l* should be justified from more contemporary texts than the Palestinian Talmud.

The phrase seems to indicate a growth in the child's knowledge, in particular his power to distinguish and discern. If it refers to this, perhaps the length of time of 'two years' will be questioned, as such a length might imply something other than the infant's great powers of intellect, which the context would seem to suggest. But the fragmentary context hinders further conjecture.

4. *bʿlymwth lhwh . . .:* 'In his youth he will become. . . .' As the third word Starcky read *klṭyš*, 'like (something) sharpened', and referred it to the child's acuity of intellect. *lṭyš* would then be pass. ptc. of *lṭš*, 'polish, sharpen'. J. Carmignac questions this reading and prefers *klyyš*, 'like a lion'. But is such an orthography (a doubled y) ever found in Qumran Aramaic? Hebrew knows the form *layiš*, 'lion'. When the word turns up in Late Aramaic (especially in the Targums; cf. Ez 19:2), it becomes *lêtā* (with *t*, not *š*); cf. Arabic *laythu*^{n}. Once again, this undermines Carmignac's speculation which compares the new-born child with a lion, as in Gn 49:9. The allusion to 1 Sm 17:34–36 is too far-fetched to be treated seriously.

[kʾn]wš dy lʾ ydʿ mdʿ[m ʿd]ʿdn dy [y]ndʿ tltt spryʾ: 'Like a man who does not know anything, until the time when he shall become skilled in the Three Books.' The source of the child's extraordinary knowledge and wisdom is thus indicated. There is no problem with the reading of *[kʾn]wš dy lʾ ydʿ*. Starcky preferred to read *mdʿ[n]*, a Palmyrene form which means the same as *mdʿ[m]*, because he thinks that the space is too small for *m*. Cf. *CIS* 2.3912, i, 5 and 3959 for the form. Our reading of the end of line 4 is based on a phrase in the Aramaic description of the

New Jerusalem published by M. Baillet; see 2Q*24* 4:19 (*'d 'dn dy*, followed by a verb). J. Carmignac was independently tempted to read this, but believes that the PAM 43,591 photograph reveals the last letter to be *zayin*, not *yodh*. I am not as confident about this as he is, and prefer to read *dy*. At the end of line 4 Starcky read *md'*[*n*] *mn 'dn rz* [*m*]*nd' tltt spry'*, translating, 'rien du temps du secret de la science des trois livres'. J. Carmignac, however, prefers to read *dy l' yd' md'* '[*d*] *'dn rz* [*m*]*nd'* . . ., translating, 'qui n'a pas la connaissance, j[usqu'] au temps du secret de [la con]naissance des trois livres'. Theoretically, either of these restorations and interpretations is possible, but the piling up of so many construct states is improbable. Nor is it likely that both *md'* and *mnd'* would be used within the same phrase. In my interpretation . . . rst *yd'* is participial and the form *ynd'* is imperfect (cf. Dn 2:9, 30; 4:14; 1QapGn 2:20).

Starcky understood the reference to the Three Books as an allusion to the mystery involved in the manifestation of the Elect of God. He accordingly suggested that the books were of eschatological, and perhaps even of astrological, character. He rightly rejected the identification of them with the three parts of the OT, the *Tôrah*, *N^ebî'îm*, and *K^etûbîm* (see Sirach, Prologue 1). J. Carmignac, however, believes that the *spr hhgy* (=*sēper ha-h^ogî*, 'the book of Meditation') is one of them (see 1QSa 1:7; CD 10:6; 13:2), and asks whether the *Manual of Discipline* and the *Damascus Document* might not constitute the other two. This would be a plausible suggestion, if we were sure that this text were actually a sectarian document, i.e., one composed in the interests of the theology of the Qumran sect. But since Essene tenets are notoriously absent from certain Qumran texts and these could be of extraneous authorship, one always remains uncertain in this matter. For instance very little Essene theology is found in the *Genesis Apocryphon*.

The Three Books are probably apocalyptic, and not specific, real books; rather they allude to such writings as the 'books of the living' (*Enoch* 47:3), the book of man's deeds (Ps 56:9; Dn

7:10; *Enoch* 90:17) and the 'heavenly tablets' (*Jubilees* 30:22; *Enoch* 81:1–2) to which the Intertestamental Literature often makes reference. See R. H. Charles, *APOT* 2,216. Note too that the phrase *yd' spr* is found in Is 29:11–12 in a context dealing with heavenly revelation contained in a sealed scroll. In any case, the Three Books (specific since *spry'* is emphatic) are at least holy and heavenly (see *Enoch* 103:2; 108:3–7). These are the source of the newborn child's knowledge, wisdom, and acquaintance with the secrets of men and of all living things.

6. [*b'*]*dyn y'rm wyd' św*[*kl'*]: 'Then he will become wise and will be endowed with discretion.' Though *w'dyn* is found in Ezr 5:5, the more normal compound form of *'dyn* at this period is *b'dyn* (see Dn 2:14, 35, 46; etc.; 1QapGn 1:3, 13, 19; 20:21; 22: 2, 18). Carmignac rest ... ⌊*w*]*b'dyn*, but gives no parallels for it. Our restoration *yd' św*[*kl'*], lit., 'he will know discretion', is based on 2 Chr 2:11 (*yôdēa' śēkel ûbînāh*). Since the full writing of a short *u* in a closed syllable is well attested in Qumran texts, whereas it is apparently avoided for a short *i*, the form *śuklā* is preferred to the other possibility, *śiklā*. The phrase expresses the child's growth in wisdom and spiritual qualities. Cf. Lk 2:47, 52; Prv 8:12.

[ ]*šn ḥzwn*: Or perhaps *ḥzyn*. In the first case the word would be 'visions' (fem. pl. absol. of *ḥzwh*); in the second, the masc. pl. ptc. 'seeing'. But how does either fit in with the following words?

lm'th lh 'l 'rkwbt[*h*]: 'To come to him upon his knees.' The only problem in this phrase is to decide whether *lh* should be understood as a sort of ethical dative, or as a directional dative, indicating the term of the coming. Starcky understood it as ethical, 'pour aller sur ses genoux'. Cf. 1QapGn 20:2, 6, 34; 21:6 (?), 8, 17, 19. J. Carmignac, however, translates 'verront [=(seront) voyantes] venir à lui sur les genoux', taking *lh* as directional (cf. Dn 3:2). He gives no justification for the reading *'rkwbh*, nor any indication of his understanding of the last word in the line. Does the phrase denote reverence or adoration?

7. *wb'bwhy wb'*[*b*]*htwhy:* 'And with his father and with his forefathers'; or 'among' (them). The first part of this line suggests that the child will enjoy an abundant life and an old age similar to that of his forebears. Our reading follows that of Starcky, which is better than that suggested by Carmignac: *wb'byy' wb*[ ]*htwhy*, 'pendant la croissance, pendant ses [ ]'. He compares the beginning of line 4 with the beginning of this line, believing that he can discern an enumeration of four stages of life after youth: 'Et pendant la croissance et pendant ses [ ] et (pendant) [ ] et (pendant la) vieillesse'. But the lacunae and the words added in parentheses reveal the improbability of this reading. It might be more plausible, if one could read 'pendant *sa* croissance', (parallel with *b'lymwth*); but this would force us back to Starcky's reading, which Carmignac rejects. For the form *'bhtwhy* Starcky refers to G. Dalman, *Grammatik*, 198, 1. 24.

[ ] *ḥyn wzqynh:* 'Life and old age.' Perhaps the lacuna should be filled with some word denoting length of life, *'rykyn* or *'rk* (cst. st.); cf. *CIS* 1.135 (*'rk ḥym*). The form *zqynh* does not seem to be attested elsewhere. Following *ḥyn* (an absol.), it is probably an absol. sg. fem., meaning 'old age'. In form it is a *qatîl-at* type, resembling *'ᵃbîdah*, 'work'. See H. Bauer and P. Leander, *Grammatik des Biblisch-Aramäischen* (Halle/S.: M. Niemeyer, 1927) #51j". One would have expected *dqynh* in this phase of Aramaic, but the form of this root with the archaic *z* persists even later.

'mh lh[*ww*]*n mlk' w'rmwm*[*h*]*:* 'With him there will be counsel and prudence', i.e., *milkāh wa'armûmāh.* The form of the last word is otherwise unattested, but is seemingly related to later *'armûmît*, as Starcky suggested. J. Carmignac (*op. cit.*, 214) believes that the description of the child's spiritual qualities is inspired by Is 11:2. There is not, however, a single quality in Is 11:2 which is mentioned here in an Aramaic equivalent. Though the later Targum Ps-Jonathan does use the word *mylk* for Hebrew *'ēṣāh*, 'counsel', there is no certain indication that

the author is suggesting that the new-born child is the scion of David.

8. [*w*]*yd*ʿ *rzy* ʾ*nš*ʾ: 'And he will know the secrets of man.' If Starcky's reading of the first word is correct, it must be the impf. Peal of *yd*ʿ in its assimilated form (*yidda*ʿ). With it one should compare the restored form in line 5. The phrase seems to be parallel to the end of this line, *wyd*ʿ *rzy kwl ḥyy*ʾ. It is not easy to determine the meaning of the 'secrets of man'. The phrase could be contrasted with the 'secrets of God' (1QpHab 7:8; 1QS 3:23; 1QM 3:9). Possibly one should relate to it the expression in *Enoch* 38:3, 'the secrets of the righteous'; see also 58:5. Recall 1QH 1:29, where *rzyhm* seem to refer to the secret thoughts of man. Cf. 1 Cor 2:11; Rev 2:23. Such knowledge of the secrets of man is due to the new-born child's wisdom, of which there is mention in the next part of the line.

wḥwkmth lkwl ʿ*mmy*ʾ *thk*: 'And his wisdom will go (forth) to all the peoples.' The phrase immediately makes one think of the wisdom of Solomon, to which both Starcky and Carmignac refer (see 1 Kgs 10:2; 5:9–14). Starcky wonders whether there is not also a reference to the Servant of Yahweh who is made a 'light to the nations' (Is 42:1–6; 49:6). In my opinion there is not the slightest trace of this motif here. Starcky continues, 'Quoi qu'il en soit, Salomon est le type du roi-messie (1 Chr., 17, 10–14).' Is he? Cf. E. Lohse, '*Solomōn*', *TWNT* 7, 459–65. We cannot deny that the description of this child—whoever he be—echoes the OT story of Solomon. But this does not immediately suggest the child's messianic character.

*wyd*ʿ *rzy kwl ḥyy*ʾ: 'And he will know the secrets of all living things' (or 'beings'). This may again reflect the OT account of Solomon's knowledge of trees, beasts, birds, reptiles, and fish (1 Kgs 5:13 [Engl. 4:33]). Cf. Wis 7:20.

9. [*wk*]*wl ḥšbwnyhwn* ʿ*lwhy yswpw*: 'All their calculations against him will come to naught' or 'all their plots against him will cease.' Starcky reads *yswpw*[*n*]; but although the photos reveal a tear in the skin, there is no certainty that the form was

yswpwn. It is apparently the short impf. *yswpw*. The form which Starcky read is the more normal form, but *yswpw* must remain in this case a sort of *lectio difficilior*. In any case, the latter form, read also by Carmignac, is not to be regarded as a Hebraism. If the context were better preserved, perhaps we would understand the precise modal usage of the short impf. At any rate, one should note within two lines the use of *rāz* and *ḥešbôn* and recall a similar collocation of these words in 1QH 1:29. Though the word *ḥšbwn* had originally a mathematical or commercial connotation ('reckoning, calculation'), in this context it apparently refers to plots or machinations. Is it a reference to astronomical calculations? Starcky thinks so. Cf. Dn 4:30 for the idiom *swp ʿl*.

wmsrt kwl ḥyy' śgy' thw': 'Although (lit., "and") the opposition of all living beings will be great.' This phrase explains the 'calculations' of the preceding. The problematic word is *msrt*, which Starcky translates 'et *la corruption* de tous les vivants deviendra grande', deriving *msrt* from *sry*, 'be corrupt'. This would refer to the growing corruption of mankind, an apocalyptic theme. Starcky prefers this meaning to another which he had proposed in *RB* 70 (1963) 502, 'le châtiment', from *ysr*. There is another possibility, a form derived from *srr*, 'be rebellious'. In form it could be like *mᵉgillat* from *gll*. The form *śgy'* is fem. sg. absol., with a final *aleph* instead of *he*.

bdy bḥyr 'lh' hw': 'Because he is the Elect of God.' This is the reason for the success of the new-born child's future plans. Starcky writes, 'il s'agit de l'élu de Dieu, c'est-à-dire du Messie (Is., 42, 1 et 61, 1)'. But this identification is not at all certain. True, the word *bᵉḥîrî*, 'my Elect One, my Chosen One', does occur in Is 42:1; yet it is used of the Servant of Yahweh, who is not without further ado a Messiah. In Is 61:1 an anointed messenger is mentioned, but he is not called an 'Elect of God'.

The title 'Elect of God' is not an OT phrase. The closest one comes to it is *bᵉḥîr YHWH* which stands in apposition to *bᵉgibʿat Šā'ûl* in 2 Sm 21:6. But the translation of this phrase is not without its problems, because the text seems to be corrupt. As it stands, it would mean, 'on the hill of Saul, the chosen one of Yahweh'. But modern editors emend the text, appealing to the LXX, 'on Gibeon, the mountain of Yahweh'.[22] The OT *roots* of the title 'Elect of God' are probably to be found rather in the pronominal usage of the singular *bḥyr*, used of Moses (Ps 106: 23; *Môšeh beḥîrî*), of David (Ps 89:4: *kārattî berît libeḥîrî, nišbaʿtî leDāwîd ʿabdî*), and of the Servant of Yahweh (Is 42:1: *hen ʿabdî ʾetmok-bô, beḥîrî rāṣetāh napšî*); and in a collective sense also of Israel (Is 43:20; 45:4).[23]

Outside of this Aramaic text the title occurs once in the plural in a Qumran Hebrew text (1QpHab 10:13: *ʾšr gdpw wyḥrpw bḥyry ʾl*, 'who insulted and outraged the Elect of God'). There it is applied to the Qumran community as such.[24]

The title, however, is not found elsewhere in Intertestamental Literature. In the book of *Enoch* a character is referred to as the 'Elect One' in the Parables (section II, cc. 37–71; e.g. 40:5; 45:3–4; 49:2, 4; 51:3, 5; 52:6, 9; 61:5, 8, 10; 62:1). From *Enoch* 45:3, 4; 55:4 it is clear that this term has developed from a passage like Is 42:1, for we read of 'my Elect One'. From such passages as *Enoch* 48:10; 52:4; 62:1, 5, it is apparent that the title 'the Elect One' was used interchangeably with 'Son of Man' and 'his Anointed'. These passages suggest that 'the Elect One' was a title given to someone regarded as a Messiah. R. H. Charles is certainly of this opinion.[25] But there is a problem connected with these references to which I have already

[22] The LXX actually reads *kai exēliasōmen autous tō kyriō en Gabaōn Saoul ekletous kyriou*, 'and we shall hang them up to the Lord in Gibeon of Saul (as) chosen ones of the Lord'. The LXX takes *eklektous* with *autous*, revealing an underlying *bḥyry Yhwh*, which may be due to a dittography. As the MT stands, *bḥyr Yhwh* must refer to Saul.

[23] The plural usage can also be found: Ps 65:9, 15, 22; Ps 105:6, 43; 106:5; 1 Chr 16:13; Sir 46:1. These refer either to Israel or to Yahweh's faithful ones in Israel.

[24] Cf. 1QpHab 9:12, where *bḥyrw* is used of the Righteous Teacher; and 5:4 where *bḥyrw* = *bḥyryw*.

[25] See *APOT* 2, 184–5.

alluded: the fact that the 'Elect One' is found only in that part of *Enoch* which is as yet unattested at Qumran. Indeed, J. T. Milik is of the opinion that section II, 'The Parables' (or 'Similitudes'), is 'probably to be considered the work of a Jew or a Jewish Christian of the first or second century A.D., who re-utilized the various early Enoch writings to gain acceptance for his own work and gave the whole composition its present form'.[26] But in any case the formula is not quite the same as that found in this Aramaic text, and we should therefore not conclude too hastily to the messianic character of the latter.

mwldh wrwḥ nšmwhy [ ]: 'His birth and the (very) spirit of his breath. . . .' Supply something like 'are blessed' or 'are from God'. The latter suggestion is not impossible in the light of 1Q*28a*2:11 (*'m ywlyd* [*'l*]*'*[*t*] *hmšyḥ*, 'if [or 'when'] God begets the Messiah'),[27] for it is clear that the idea of the divine begetting of an Anointed One is not an impossible notion for an Essene in the 1st century A.D. The phrase *rwḥ nšmwhy* creates little difficulty; its redundancy is derived from OT parallels

[26] *Ten Years of Discovery in the Wilderness of Judaea* (SBT 26; London: SCM, 1959) 33. See further J. Albertson, 'An Application of Mathematical Probability to Manuscript Discoveries', *JBL* 78 (1959) 133–41; H. E. Robbins, 'Comments on a Paper by James Albertson', *JBL* 78 (1959) 347–50; P. Grelot, *op. cit.*, 42–50.

[27] This is the reading of D. Barthélemy in DJD 1,110. Since the text is not perfectly preserved, there was some hesitation at first about the reading of *ywlyd*. In fact, Barthélemy translated it as if it were *ywlyk* (following a suggestion of J. T. Milik). However, further investigation of the skin of the text convinced others that *ywlyd* is the correct reading. Cf. F. M. Cross, Jr., *The Ancient Library of Qumran* (Anchor A 272; Garden City: Doubleday, 1961) 88, n. 67 (which now differs from his main text on p. 67); J. M. Allegro, *JBL* 75 (1956) 177, n. 28; J. Starcky, *op. cit.*, 61, n. 1. See further M. Smith, '"God's Begetting the Messiah" in 1QSa', *NTS* 5 (1958–59) 218–24; R. Gordis, 'The "Begotten Messiah" in the Qumran Scrolls', *VT* 7 (1957) 191–4. O. Michel and O. Betz, 'Von Gott gezeugt', *Judentum, Urchristentum, Kirche: Festschrift für Joachim Jeremias* (BZNW 26; Berlin: Töpelmann, 1960) 3–23; 'Nocheinmal: "Von Gott gezeugt"', *NTS* 9 (1962–63) 129–30; E. Lohse, *'Huios'*, *TWNT* 8, 361–3. Cf. the confident remarks of T. H. Gaster, *The Scriptures of the Dead Sea Sect* (London: Secker and Warburg, 1957) 39, n. 13.

such as Gn 7:22 (*nišmat rûaḥ ḥayyîm*) and Jb 34:14, where the breath of man is regarded as derived from God. Cf. Is 11:4 (*rûaḥ śepātāyw*); 1Q28b 5:24. On the absence of *waw* before *mwldh*, cf. 1QapGn 20:3, 4, 5.

The crucial word in this broken phrase is *mwldh*. At first sight one would be tempted to read the line thus: *bdy bḥyr 'lh' hw' mwldh*, 'because the Elect of God is his begotten one'. The word *mwldh* would then be the pass. ptc. Aphel of *yld*. But even though *mwld* is found in Mishnaic Hebrew in the sense of 'issue, descendant' (= *môlēd*; cf. M. Jastrow, *Dictionary*, 742), apparently also in 1Q27 1 i 5 (*mwldy 'wlh*, 'descendants of iniquity'), and looks like the masc. form of the OT *môledet* (Lv 18:9; Gn 48:6), it is unattested in Aramaic. We know of no instances of the pass. ptc. Aphel in Qumran Aramaic. Again, the suffix on *mwldh*, referring to God, would be strange. J. Carmignac (*op. cit.*, 215) also wants to exclude this meaning, because it seems to contradict the context, presenting as begotten of God a person who is '[like a ma]n who does not know anything'.

At any rate, it seems preferable with Starcky, Dupont-Sommer (*RB* 71 [1964] 298–9) and Carmignac to take *mwldh* as meaning 'his birth'. It is a *maqtal* form of the root *yld*, and the noun in this sense is well attested both in Hebrew (cf. 1QH 3:11; 12:8; 4Qastr 2:8 [*JJS* 9 (1964) 291–4]) and in Aramaic. Carmignac, however, reads *bdy bḥyr 'lh' hw' mwldh*, translating, 'parceque sa naissance est choisie de Dieu'. He begins a new sentence with what follows, 'le vent de son souffle . . .'. He rejects Starcky's interpretation, which we follow, because *mwld*, 'birth' (even in the astrological sense of 'thème de géniture') can scarcely be coordinated with 'the spirit of his breath' to form together the subject of the following sentence. Moreover he thinks that although *bḥyr* is used as a noun in Hebrew and can be applied to an individual (4QpIs[d] 1:3, *'dt bḥyrw*; 1QpHab 9:12; 4QpPs37 1:5; 2:5) or to the collectivity of the Qumran community (*passim*), and even to celestial beings (1QM 12:5), it is and remains a ptc. in Aramaic. He appeals to 1QapGn 22:6 (*gbryn bḥyryn lqrb*, 'men chosen [i.e. suited] for war'). It is certainly used there in its participial sense. But one cannot escape the fact that the normal understanding of *bḥyr 'lh'* is 'Elect of God', a construct chain which means indeed 'chosen by God'. Cf. the OT phrase *beᵉrûk Yhwh* (Gn 24:31; 26:29). Given the immediately preceding context which refers to a person, the most natural explanation is to regard this title as applied to the person. After all, the expression does occur elsewhere in Qumran literature, even though in Hebrew and used in the plural of members of the Qumran community (see 1QpHab 10:13 [*bḥyry 'l*]).[28]

There is the further question whether *mwldh* is used in an astrological sense. Granted that the Hebrew counterpart *hmwld* does occur in 4Qastr in a sense that may be such, it is still not certain that this meaning is intended *here*.[29] It seems rather that the author is giving reasons why the 'plans' of the new-born child will prosper (?); among them is the fact that he is the 'Elect of God' and his birth and the (very) spirit of his breath are under divine influence. The fact that both coordinated nouns (*mwldh wrwḥ nšmwhy*) end in pronominal suffixes suggests that they *are* to be taken together.

11. *[ḥ]šbwnwhy lhwwn lʿlmyn:* 'His calculations will exist forever.' Or it is possible that some predicate adjective preceded this phrase. On *lʿlmyn*, see below 2:8 and 1Q*23* 20:3; also Dn 2:4; 3:9; 5:10; 6:7, 22, 27.

[28] See the text of 4QarP above (p. 134), where *lbḥyr* is hardly used in a participial sense. Perhaps the expression *bḥyry šmym*, applied to celestial beings in 1QM 12:5, should also be considered, for the last word (*šmym*) may simply be a surrogate for 'God'. The plural use of *bḥyr 'l* supplies the Palestinian Semitic background for the NT phrase *eklektoi* (*tou*) *theou* which is used of Christians in Rom 8:33; Col 3:12; Ti 1:1. This plural, however, has little to do with the specific use of *bḥyr 'lh* for an individual—which is our real problem in this Aramaic text.

[29] See J. M. Allegro, 'An Astrological Cryptic Document from Qumran', *JSS* 9 (1964) 291–4.

Col. II

1. *npl lqdmyn:* 'Fell to the east.' Starcky translates this phrase thus: 'tomba aux temps anciens', and alludes to the fall of the angels (Gn 6:1–4). The broken context makes it almost impossible to be sure; but the absol. state would seem to call for 'east' rather than 'former times'.

bny šḥwh: 'Children of perdition', lit., 'of (the) pit'. We are not sure that the fragment bearing these words is rightly placed. The phrase makes no sense here. Starcky compares the Hebrew *bny hšḥt* (CD 6:15; 13:14) and *'nšy hšḥt* or *šḥt* (1QS 9:16, 22). Aramaic *šaḥwâ* is apparently the equivalent of Hebrew *šaḥat*.

7. *wrwḥ nš[mwhy]:* The traces of the letters here suit the phrase which is found in 1:10. Starcky, however, reads *wrwḥ bśr*['], 'et l'esprit de la chair', comparing 1QH 13:13; 17:25.

8. *lʿlmyn:* Starcky excludes this reading, which alone is acceptable in my opinion. He reads *lʿlywn*, but senses the difficulty, noting that it occurs only with *'l* preceding it (1QapGn 12:17; 20:12, 16; 21:2, 20; 22:15, 116bis.-21). See above 1:11.

13. *wyḥrbwn:* 'And they will lay waste', apparently 3 pl. masc. impf. Aphel of *ḥrb*. Starcky translates 'et seront détruits'.

wbmln ytbyn: Starcky reads *wbmln ytbn*, and translates only: 'et par des paroles . . .'. The phrase is too damaged for any plausible interpretation.

14. *myn yswpwn:* 'Waters will cease', i.e., 3 pl. masc. impf. Peal of *swp* (cf. 1:9). Starcky, however, translates, 'les eaux augmenteront', regarding the root as *ysp*, and comparing *yswpwn* with *ykwlwn* of 1QapGn 20:19. He appeals to the explanation of E. Y. Kutscher (*Scripta hierosolymitana* 4 [1958] 13). The latter regards *ykwlwn* as 'entirely "un-Aramaic" (=*yklwn*). It looks like a Hebrew pausal verb form.' *yswpwn*, however, may only represent the full writing of an otherwise reduced vowel (=*yikkᵘlûn*); cf. 1QS 1:16 *yʿbwrw*, 4:4 *yʿrwkw*, 5:17 *ysqwdw*; see J. T. Milik, *RB* 67 (1960) 41. In my opinion *yswpwn* is the ordinary form of the impf. of *swp*. Cf. Ap 21:1;

4Ezr 6:24; *Assump. Mos.* 10:6; *Pss Sol.* 17:21; *T. Levi* 4:1. The cessation of flood-waters is an apocalyptic motif.

bbn yḥrbwn: This reading is far from certain; Starcky read *bmn* instead of our *bbn*.

16. *wkl[h]n ytbnwn kʿyryn:* 'And all of them will be as intelligent as Watchers.' Starcky links the last word in the line with this phrase, translating, 'et tous ceux-là comprendront, comme les Veilleurs, son oeuvre'. He thus makes *ʿwbdh* the direct object of the reflexive *ytbnwn*, which, while not impossible, may not be necessary. For 'the Watchers', cf. 2:18; Dn 4:10, 14, 20; 1QapGn 2:1, 16; CD 2:18; *Jub* 4:15; *T. Reuben* 5:6–7; *T. Naphtali* 3:5; *Enoch* 12:2–3; 20:1; 39:12–13. They represent a class of angelic beings, sometimes identified with archangels, sometimes with the fallen angels. See R. H. Charles, *The Book of Enoch or 1 Enoch* (Oxford: Clarendon, 1912) 6.

ʿwbdh ḥlp qlh: 'His deed instead of his voice. . . .' Perhaps this refers to the exemplary conduct of the new-born child. His action is to be contrasted with his words.

17. *yswdh ʿlwhy ysdwn:* 'And upon it they will base its foundation.' Starcky read *yswrh ʿlwhy ysrwn*, 'ils lui infligeront son châtiment'; but J. Carmignac has also independently recognized that *yswdh* must be read here (*op. cit.*, 216).

18. *qdyš wʿyryn*: 'A Holy One and Watchers.' See above 2:16. Note the compound occurrence also in Dn 4:10, 14, 20.

V. CONCLUDING GENERAL REMARKS

The text which J. Starcky has published certainly presents a fragmentary portion of a prediction or pronouncement about a new-born child. Comparing it with other horoscopic material still to be published, Starcky calls this text 'astrologique'. However, we find in it no reference to stars or to signs of the Zodiac which might suggest its horoscopic nature. That it has parallels in Graeco-Roman physiognomic literature is likely, and perhaps this would be a truer designation of its literary form. For the text describes the temperament and character of the child from its outward appearance. The text is of interest in that its predictions of the qualities of the child provide an extra-biblical parallel for the utterances of the old man Simeon in the Lucan Infancy Narrative, 'This child is marked for the rise and the fall of many in Israel, to be a symbol that men will reject, and thus the thoughts of many minds will be laid bare' (2:34–35).

But we find even greater difficulty in Starcky's designation of this text as messianic. Granted that the idea of God's begetting the Messiah is not impossible for the Qumran community (see 1QSa 2:11–12), nevertheless one must ask whether the title, 'Elect of God', immediately refers to a Messiah. Starcky thinks so. But since this title is never found in the OT, and one can only appeal to the pronominal expression, 'my Chosen One', one must face the fact that the latter is used not only of David (Ps 89:4), of the Servant of Yahweh (Is 42:1), but even of Moses (Ps 106:23). In the NT it is applied to Jesus (Jn 1:34), who happens to be the 'Messiah'. But this represents the usual NT piling up of titles with which we are all familiar.

Given such hesitation about the messianic character of this fragmentary text, I would like to make a different proposal. In the Intertestamental Literature there is a certain fascination with the birth of Noah. His birth is quasi-miraculous, his radiance fills the whole house with light like the sun; he stands in the hands of the midwife, and speaks with the Lord of uprightness. The fascination with his birth is in part due to the late Jewish speculation about the so-called 'Fallen Angels' of Gn 6:1–4, for the Noah story begins in Genesis immediately after this enigmatic passage. Elaborate descriptions of the character of Noah were composed. We should recall the 'Noah Apocalypse' in *Enoch* 106–8, *Jub* 4–10; the fragmentary text in the *Genesis Apocryphon*, col. 2; 1Q*19* fr. 3; and Josephus, *Antiquities* 1, 3, 1–9, #72–108. Another text from Cave 4, as yet unpublished, also deals with the wondrous birth of Noah, and even gives the baby's weight.[30]

Given such material, the question arises whether we are not really dealing with another text belonging to the Noah literature of late Judaism. There is certainly no phrase in the two fragmentary columns which cannot be understood of Noah. Wis 10:4 implies that Noah was saved from the deluge because of his wisdom: 'When the earth was deluged because of him, Wisdom again saved the upright man, steering him with a cheap piece of wood.' Noah's wisdom would be hailed in col. 1, line 8 of this Aramaic text. Nowhere else, however, in this Intertestamental Literature is Noah referred to as the 'Elect of God'. The closest one comes to any title of this sort is found in Josephus, who, speaking in general of the patriarchs and their long lives, gives as the reason for it: 'in the first place, they were beloved of God (*theophileis*)' (*Ant.* 1, 3, 9, #106). If Josephus could say of Noah that he was *theophilēs*, then the author of this Aramaic text could conceivably call him the 'Elect of God'. Much of the vocabulary of this text can also be found in *Enoch* 106–8, 'secrets', 'books', 'sin', 'destruction', 'waters', etc. The mention of the child who would enjoy long life and old age after the fashion of his father (Lamech, who lived 777 years according to Gn 5:31 [MT]) and his forefathers takes on meaning, if it refers to Noah. Cf. Josephus, *Ant* 1, 3, 7, #98, *gēras kai biou mēkos homoion tois tachion eperchomenōn*. Again, the mention of the 'Holy One and Watchers' (2:18, 16) recalls the occurrences of these figures in col. 2 of the *Genesis Apocryphon* which deals with the birth of Noah. They are otherwise unknown in any passage of Intertestamental Literature dealing with a Messiah.[31]

The upshot of all this is to question Starcky's identification of this text as messianic, and to suggest that its pertinence to other

[30] See J. T. Milik, *Ten Years*, 35.

[31] Is it not possible too that the 'eighth' who is an 'Elect', according to the papyrus fragment 4QarP, is a reference to Noah? See 2 Pt 2:5, 'except for Noah, the preacher of uprightness, the eighth'.

literature concerned with the birth of Noah be given some consideration. If it is not messianic, then it can scarcely be used to fill out the picture of Qumran messianic expectations in the Herodian period.[32]

[32] See also I. D. Amusin, '"Izvrannik Voga" b Kumranskich tekstach', *VDI* 1 (92, 1966) 73–9.

8

THE STORY OF THE DISHONEST MANAGER (LK 16:1–13)*

There are few passages in the Synoptic Gospels more puzzling than the well-known story about the Dishonest Manager (or Unjust Steward). Summer after summer Christians used to hear it read as the climactic Scripture message in the liturgy of the eighth Sunday after Pentecost (Lk 16:1–9), and usually came away wondering what it was all about. Commentators have often discussed its meaning, and what some have proposed has not always been enlightening. Preachers have isolated sentences of it for sermons on extraneous topics, often without attempting to analyse the story itself. Over thirty years ago the noted French exegete, Père M.-J. Lagrange, O.P., wrote of it: 'I admit that it is not easy to preach on this subject, because many people imagine that only an edifying story can be told in church.' Whether a clear and definitive explanation of this story will ever be arrived at is hard to say. But there is a growing consensus of opinion about various features of it which will always have to be respected. It is my purpose to try to distil this consensus from some recent studies of the story, and to support an interpretation which, I believe, sheds most light on this puzzling episode.

An initial difficulty—which must be recognized—was caused by the liturgical isolation of this story from its Gospel context. Such a difficulty is associated with many of the Gospel episodes taken over into the liturgy, where they acquire a certain setting

* Originally published in *TS* 25 (1964) 23–42.

not native to them. The proper understanding of the story will only be had when it is considered in its own Gospel setting. Secondly, an added difficulty is often encountered with Gospel passages used in the liturgy, because past practice has often been cavalier in abridging episodes and suppressing important verses. A classic example of this was found in the no longer used Last Gospel of the Roman Mass, where only the first fourteen verses of the prologue of John's Gospel were read and the important ending in vv. 15–18 was omitted. Liturgical usage also abridged the story of the Dishonest Manager, using only vv. 1–9, although the account itself is actually four verses longer. But since the Lucan story is made up of a parable and a multiple conclusion, the result of the abridgment was the adoption of only the parable and *a part* of the conclusion. The relation of the conclusion to the parable itself created a major difficulty in the understanding of the Lucan story as a whole. The liturgical abridgment eliminated some of this difficulty, but enough of the Lucan conclusion remained to complicate the task of anyone who would preach a homily on the story.

THE GENERAL LUCAN CONTEXT

The story of the Dishonest Manager forms part of the Lucan narrative of Jesus' journey to Jerusalem (9:51–19:27). It is found in the specifically Lucan 'travel account', that extended insertion of additional material (Lk 9:51–18:14) which the Evangelist had made into what he had otherwise taken over from Mark. This artificial, literary report of what Jesus said and did on his way to Jerusalem from Galilee comes from two different sources of Gospel traditions: Q (the source for those episodes common to him and to Matthew) and a private source (peculiar to Luke alone).[1] The story of the Dishonest Manager

[1] This analysis of the story of the Dishonest Manager is based on a modified form of the Two-Source theory of the Synoptic problem, similar to that proposed by J. Levie, J. Schmid, A. Wikenhauser, etc. For further details concerning it, the Q-material common to Mt and Lk, the latter's 'travel account', the literary tendencies of the individual Evangelists, see A.

belongs to the latter, being found only in Luke. It is an isolated account of a parable uttered by Jesus which Luke has made part of his 'travel account'.

In the immediate context of chapter 16 there are two stories about riches, separated by sayings of Jesus derived from various contexts. Vv. 1–13 relate the story of the Dishonest Manager, told to the disciples; vv. 19–31 tell the story of Dives[2] and Lazarus. Both of these stories are parables about riches, a subject of no little importance in the third Gospel.[3] But the two stories are separated by isolated logia (or sayings) on Pharisaic hypocrisy (16:14–15), on John the Baptist (16:16), on the Law (16:17), and on divorce (16:18).[4] A similar combination of two

---

Wikenhauser, *New Testament Introduction* (New York, 1958) 209–53; A. Robert and A. Feuillet, *Introduction à la Bible* 2 (Paris, 1959) 233–95; A. H. McNeile, *An Introduction to the Study of the New Testament* (2nd ed.; Oxford, 1953) 59–91; P. Feine–J. Behm, *Einleitung in das Neue Testament* (12th ed., by W. G. Kümmel; Heidelberg, 1963) 11–44.

[2] Since the recent publication of the oldest Greek text (P^{75}) of Luke's Gospel in *Papyrus XIV–XV: Evangiles de Luc et Jean: Tome I, XIV: Luc chap.* 3–24*; Tome II, XV: Jean chap.* 1–15 (ed. V. Martin and R. Kasser; Cologny-Genève, 1961), should we continue to call the rich man by the usual Latin appellative, Dives? His name appears in this 2nd–3rd century Greek text as *Neuēs*. This puzzling name seems to be a scribal abbreviation of *Nineuēs*, the rich man's name recorded in the ancient Coptic (Sahidic) translations of Lk, i.e., 'Nineveh'. See my article, 'Papyrus Bodmer XIV: Some Features of Our Oldest Text of Luke', *CBQ* 24 (1962) 170–9; cf. H. Cadbury, 'A Proper Name for Dives', *JBL* 81 (1962) 399–402.

[3] See X. Léon-Dufour, in Robert-Feuillet, *op. cit.*, 251; J. Dupont, *Les béatitudes* (Bruges, 1958) 52, 212–17, 320–5.

[4] Though the story of the Dishonest Manager is addressed to the disciples, the following saying is uttered in the hearing of the Pharisees; they have listened to 'all this' (*tauta panta*). The latter expression might seem at first to refer to the preceding story (16:1–13); and as used by the Evangelist in his account, it does. But one must not insist on such connections between episodes when it is a question of their setting in the life of Jesus itself. For this reason the attempt of R. Pautrel to interpret the parable together with vv. 14–15 is misleading and has found little support; see '"Aeterna tabernacula" (Luc, XVI, 9)', *RSR* 30 (1940) 307–27.—Moreover, vv. 16–18 represent the combination of three isolated sayings. The first of them (16:16) is a key verse in Luke's theology, expressing the significance of John the Baptist (see H. Conzelmann, *The Theology of St Luke* [tr. G. Buswell; New York, 1961] 22 ff.; W. Wink, *John the Baptist in the Gospel Tradition* [SNTS

parables separated by independent sayings is found in Lk 12:13–37 (the parable of the Rich Fool, 12:13–21; logia, 12:22–34; the parable on watchfulness, 12:35–37). There is another connection between the two parables in chapter 16 and chapter 12. The parable of the Rich Fool teaches the folly of the pursuit of riches and of the belief that one is secure in the possession of wealth. The story of the Dishonest Manager admonishes Christians about the prudent use of riches (the parable) and the danger of slavish servitude to them (the conclusion). The first of the immediately following independent logia (16:14–15) characterizes the money-loving (*philargyroi*) Pharisees as men enmeshed in such servitude and unable to judge by any other standard than that which is an abomination in the sight of God. And shortly thereafter the story of Dives and Lazarus follows. There is, further, an extrinsic connection of this teaching on riches in chapter 16 with the foregoing parable of the Prodigal Son (15:11–32), which deals with the improper use of wealth. In its Lucan context, therefore, the story of the Dishonest Manager forms part of a group of instructions on the use of wealth.

THE GOSPEL STORY ITSELF

1 Jesus said to the disciples: 'There was a certain rich man who had a manager, and he heard complaints that this man was squandering his property. 2 So he called him and said: "What's this I hear about you? Prepare for me an account of your management; you can't be manager around here any longer." 3 Then the manager said to himself: "What am I going to do? My master is taking my job as manager away from me. I am not strong enough to dig; I'm ashamed to beg.—4 Ah, I know what I'll do, so that when I lose this job, I'll be welcome in people's homes." 5 He summoned his master's debtors one by one. He said to the first of them: "How much do you owe my master?" "One hundred jugs of olive oil," was the answer. 6 He said to the man: "Here, take your note; sit down and,

---

Monographs 7; Cambridge, 1968] 51-7). It really has, however, nothing to do with vv. 14–15 or vv. 17, 18. All three verses (16–18) have counterparts, if not strict parallels, in Mt in different contexts (Mt 11:12–13; 5:18; 5:32).

hurry, write one for fifty." 7 Then he said to another debtor: "How much do you owe?" He answered: "A hundred bushels of wheat." Again he said: "Here, take your note and write one for eighty." 8a And the master approved of that dishonest manager because he had acted prudently.'

8b For the children of this world are more prudent in dealing with their own generation than the children of light are. 9 I tell you, make friends with the wealth of dishonesty, so that when it gives out,[5] you will be welcomed into everlasting tents.

10 The man who is trustworthy in little things is also trustworthy in what is big; and the man who is dishonest in little things is also dishonest in what is big. 11 If, then, you are not trustworthy when handling the wealth of dishonesty who will trust you with the wealth that is real? 12 And if you are not trustworthy when handling what belongs to another, who will give you what is your own?[6]

13 No servant can serve two masters; either he will hate the one and love the other, or he will be devoted to the one and despise the other. You cannot serve both God and wealth.

THE LUCAN CONCLUSION TO THE PARABLE

In analysing the story of the Dishonest Manager, the reader must learn to look at it as a parable to which several concluding verses of diverse origin have been added by the Evangelist. This analysis represents the consensus of opinion among Protestant and Catholic scholars who have studied the story on Form Critical methods. Though it is a matter of debate among them just where the parable ends, no one denies the obvious conflated nature of the story as a whole and the traces of the compilatory process that produced it.

Where does the parable end? According to R. Bultmann, W. Grundmann, J. Jeremias, A. R. C. Leaney, H. Preisker, W.

[5] The preferred reading of the Hesychian recension is *eklipē* (3 sg.), 'it gives out', referring to *mamōnas*. The inferior reading of the Koine tradition is *eklipēte* (2 pl.), 'you give out' (=die), and is the source of the Latin *cum defeceritis*.

[6] 'Your own' (*hymeteron*) is the reading of Sinaiticus, P[75], Alexandrinus, Codex Bezae, Koridethi, the Latin and Syriac versions; it is preferred by Aland, Merk and Bover. But Nestle and Kilpatrick read 'our own' (*hēmeteron*), the *lectio difficilior*, which is however less well attested (Vaticanus, Origen).

Michaelis, etc., it consists only of vv. 1–7. In v. 8 *ho kyrios* ('the master') is interpreted as Jesus and vv. 8–13 are further commentary put on his lips. Others would include v. 8 in the parable (so D. Buzy, J. M. Creed, A. Descamps, J. Dupont, A. Loisy, L. Marchal, T. W. Manson, K. H. Rengstorf, J. Schmid, etc.). In this interpretation *ho kyrios* is usually said to be the master of the parable itself (and different explanations are proposed). Still other commentators would include even v. 9 in the parable (so D. R. Fletcher, P. Gaechter, J. Knabenbauer, M.-J. Lagrange, W. Manson, A. Rücker, and most of the older Catholic commentators—many of the latter did so because they felt bound by the liturgical form of the story and were generally reluctant to adopt Form Critical methods of analysis). This last view has so many problems connected with it that it is generally abandoned today.

In my opinion 16:1–8a constitute the parable proper, and vv. 8b–13 represent the added Lucan multiple conclusion. In including the first part of v. 8 in the parable, we are following the view of B. Weiss, F. Tillmann, B. T. D. Smith, W. O. E. Oesterley, L. M. Friedel, J. Volckaert, P. Samain, etc. The main reason for doing so is that without v. 8a the parable has no real ending. From the beginning the reaction of the master to the manager's conduct is expected; it is finally given in v. 8a: 'and the master approved of that dishonest manager because he had acted prudently.'[7] In this view *ho kyrios* is the same as the master in vv. 3, 5.[8] It also is the most natural reading of the first

[7] This division has been well worked out by F. Tillmann, 'Zum Gleichnis vom ungerechten Verwalter. Lk 16, 1–9', *BZ* 9 (1911) 171–84, esp. 177 ff.

[8] J. Jeremias (*The Parables of Jesus* [tr. S. H. Hooke; London, 1958] 33) argues that the absolute use of *ho kyrios* refers in some instances in Luke's Gospel to God, but in all others (18 times in all) to Jesus. Consequently, Jeremias along with many others (J. M. Creed, E. Klostermann, W. Grundmann, K. H. Rengstorf, J. Schmid, etc.) understand 'the master' in v. 8a as Jesus. In this they appeal to the sense of v. 8b, which almost certainly reflects a statement of Jesus and seems out of place in the mouth of the master of the parable. These writers also appeal to Lk 18:6, where an observation of *ho kyrios* is recorded, who cannot be anyone else but Jesus. And in 18:8

part of the verse. To interpret 'the master' as a reference to Jesus is unexpected, and it is really read back into the first part of the verse only by reflection on its second part and the change of subject in v. 9. The change of subject, however, in v. 9 seems precisely to lend support to the view that 'the master' in v. 8a refers to the one in the parable. It is clear that the 'I' of v. 9 ('I tell you') can refer only to Jesus. So the first part of v. 8 is still part of the parable.

Moreover, v. 8b is not part of the original parable at all. J. Jeremias has pointed out how out of place it is on the lips of the master of the parable.[9] It actually reads like a generalizing commentary on the parable: 'the children of this world are more prudent in dealing with their own generation than the children of light are.' While the Palestinian origin of this part of the verse finds support in interesting Essene parallels,[10] the

---

there follows a similar introduction of a saying by *legō hymin* (see 16:9).—However, the situation in chap. 16 is not the same as that in chap. 18. There is an earlier mention of *kyrios* in 16:3, 5, whereas there is nothing similar in Lk 18. Moreover, in Lk 12:42, although the first instance of the absolute use of *ho kyrios* refers to Jesus, the second one is generic and does not refer to him at all, as is commonly recognized by commentators. The attempt to distinguish two different meanings for 'the master' in 16:8a is artificial. A. Descamps ('La composition littéraire de Luc XVI 9–13', *NovT* 1 [1956] 47–53) would have us believe that in Luke's source *ho kyrios* referred to Jesus, but in Luke's Gospel he has been identified with the master of the parable. No reasons, however, have been proposed for this distinction. For a more recent attempt to explain *ho kyrios* as referring to Jesus, see I. H. Marshall, 'Luke xvi. 8—Who Commended the Unjust Steward?' *JTS* 19 (1968) 617–19; H. Drexler, 'Miszellen: zu Lukas 16:1–7', *ZNW* 58 (1967) 286–8. (On p. 288, n. 8, the author calls my attempt to interpret the manager's action after he has been reported to the master in a more favourable light than it is usually understood 'aussichtslos'. But he does not bother to justify this estimate of it.)

[9] *The Parables of Jesus*, 33.

[10] 'The children of this world' (*hoi huioi tou aiōnos toutou*) may be a reflection of the Qumran expression *kl bny tbl* (CD 20:34). More pertinent is the expression 'children of light' (*tous huious tou phōtos*), which was found only in Jn 12:36; 1 Thes 5:5; Eph 5:8 until the Qumran scrolls were discovered. It is now seen to be a favourite Essene designation for their community of the New Covenant. See 1QS 1:9; 2:16; 3:13, 24, 25; 1QM 1:1, 3, 9, 11, 13.

saying preserved here represents an independent logion of Jesus which has been joined to the parable (either by Luke or his source). For it follows strangely on v. 8a, and indeed on the whole preceding parable.

When the Lucan conclusion to the parable is studied, the traces of its compilation in the Greek text are not hard to find. Let us work backwards, beginning with v. 13. First of all, though Lk 16:1–12 is without any real Synoptic parallel, 16:13 is paralleled in Mt 6:24, where the context is that of the Sermon on the Mount and entirely unrelated to such a parable as this one. This verse alone, then, in the whole story of the Dishonest Manager is derived from the Q-material, and has been added to the otherwise peculiarly Lucan material.[11] Secondly, vv. 10–12 form a unit describing the trustworthy (*pistos*) servant and comparing him with one who is not. The adjective *pistos* is the catchword bond linking the three verses.[12] The subject of these

---

The peculiar dualistic character of the expression is well known. It is not found either in the OT or in rabbinical literature. While the contrast of light and darkness is almost a natural figure for good and evil, and is found in the OT, the division of all humanity into two groups so designated is unknown outside of the Qumran literature and the NT. This is one of the reasons for maintaining that the expression is not just part of the general Palestinian intellectual climate of the first century A.D. See H. Braun, 'Qumran und das Neue Testament', *TRu* 28 (1962) 186–7; P. Benoit, 'Qumrân et le Nouveau Testament', *NTS* 7 (1960–61) 276–96, esp. 289–90.

[11] Note too the change of vocabulary. The parable itself concerns a 'manager' (*oikonomos*), but the conclusion mentions a 'servant' (*oiketēs*). This points to a different original context for 16:13, preserved neither in Lk nor in Mt. It is not at all certain that Lk has borrowed the saying from the Matthean tradition, as A. Descamps (*op. cit.*, p. 52) would have it. Another indication of its isolated character is given by the fact that it is used in the Coptic *Gospel according to Thomas* (ed. A. Guillaumont, H.-Ch. Puech, G. Quispel, W. Till, Y. 'Abd-al-Masiḥ; New York, 1959) Log. 47: 'Jesus said: It is impossible for a man to mount two horses and to stretch two bows, and it is impossible for a servant to serve two masters, otherwise he will honour the one and offend the other.'—Cf. J. Dupont, *Les béatitudes*, 107–13.

[12] The adjective *pistos* echoes the fuller expression in Lk 12:42, *ho pistos oikonomos ho phronimos*, 'the faithful, prudent manager'. It is in such an expression that one finds the link between the two characteristics of the ser-

verses is responsibility in handling wealth (or lack of it). It has only an extrinsic connection with the parable of the Dishonest Manager, the point of which is rather another characteristic of that man. This unit of three verses, then, records an instruction on responsibility, which is really extraneous to the parable, but which draws out of it some further implications. When the verses are scrutinized more closely, v. 10 is seen to be a development of Lk 19:17, or at least a reflection of it. This verse occurs in the parable of the Minas: 'Congratulations! You are a good slave! Because you were trustworthy in a small matter, you shall have authority over ten cities.'[13] The verse is more at home in that parable. Lk 16:10 reflects, therefore, a genuine tradition, but it has been attached to a different story of a manager; here it has become the basis of a developed unit of three verses.[14] Thirdly, the joining of the vv. 10–13 to v. 9 is due to another catchword bond, *mamōnas* ('wealth').[15] Three sayings,

---

vants in the parable (prudence) and the conclusion (trustworthiness). Cf. 1 Cor 4:2.

[13] Lk 19:17 is actually Q-material, having a parallel in Mt 20:21, 23. This fact may point to a different original context.

[14] Bp A. Descamps, the rector of the Catholic University of Louvain, has suggested (*op. cit.*, pp. 49–52) that vv. 9–12 are a secondary Lucan construction. V. 9 would have been composed by Luke with vocabulary drawn from the parable proper (16:1–8) and from the isolated saying of 16:13; v. 10 would have been composed on the basis of Lk 12:42 and 19:11–27; and so on. While such an analysis is not absolutely incorrect, it encounters several telling difficulties, not the least being that vv. 10–12 seem to have been composed in Aramaic because of the play on *mamōnas* and *pistos* (see note 15 below). In this respect the critique of J. Dupont (*Les béatitudes*, pp. 109–10) is to be noted. None of the reasons brought forth by Descamps are sufficient to exclude the less radical possibility that vv. 10–12 represent genuine sayings of Jesus derived from another context.

[15] *Mamōnas* is the Greek form of the Hebrew *māmôn* or Aramaic *māmônā*. Though unknown in OT Hebrew, the word has turned up in the Qumran literature (1QS 6:2; 1Q*27* 1 ii 5; CD 14:20 [in the last two instances it occurs only in very fragmentary contexts]). There is, however, another Qumran expression, which does not use *māmôn*, but *hôn ḥāmās*, 'the wealth of violence' (1QS 10:19), which is close in sense to the Lucan 'wealth of dishonesty' (16:9).—The etymology of *māmôn* is uncertain, but it is commonly

dealing with mammon (16:9, 11, 13) and the responsibility or slavish involvement that it entails, are joined together as a multiple conclusion to the parable.[16] (The connection of v. 8a with 8b has always been problematic, and has been discussed above.)

For these reasons—all of which match the general patterns of the recording of Jesus' parables in the Synoptic tradition[17]—the unity of the story of the Dishonest Manager should not be stressed.

THE MEANING OF THE PARABLE ITSELF

As A. Descamps notes, there is nothing against the attribution of the parable to Jesus himself.[18] Like many of the other parables used in the Gospels, its historical basis in the life of Jesus himself offers no difficulty. One may wonder why it should be called a parable, since it lacks the usual introduction which states the comparison. But this is not the only parable of this sort; at the end of the chapter the story of Dives and Lazarus is similar, but

---

explained as derived from the root *'mn* ('to be firm'; causative: 'to trust in, believe'). *Māmôn* (<*ma'môn*) would, therefore, designate that in which one puts one's trust. If this is correct—and vv. 10–12 seem to suggest that it is—the play on the words *mamōnas* and *pistos* is obvious. See F. Hauck, '*Mamōnas*', *TDNT* 4, 389–90; J. Dupont, *Les béatitudes*, 109–10; A. M. Honeyman, 'The Etymology of Mammon', *Archivum linguisticum* 4/1 (Glasgow, 1952) 60–5.—Commentators have often related Luke's phrase to the rabbinical expression *māmôn dišqar*, 'wealth of deceit'. But this expression has a far more pejorative sense than Luke's, suggesting ill-gotten gains or wealth that has been amassed at the expense of justice. In Luke's usage, however, the word designates the tendency that wealth has to make men dishonest. Distracting men from the service and devotion of God, it enslaves them in a pursuit of itself and ends in making them dishonest.

[16] The reasons given by A. Descamps (*op. cit.*, 49–50) for the Lucan construction of 16:9 are not impossible; they are better than his analysis of vv. 10–12.

[17] See J. Jeremias, *The Parables of Jesus*, 20–88; C. H. Dodd, *The Parables of the Kingdom* (rev. ed.; New York, 1961) 1–20; R. E. Brown, *The Parables of the Gospels* (Paulist Press Doctrinal Pamphlet; New York, 1963).

[18] *Op. cit.*, 48.

only in the Codex Bezae is the latter explicitly called a parable (*eipen de kai heteran parabolēn*, 'and he proposed another parable').

In trying to determine the main message of the parable (16:1–8a), certain crucial questions have to be answered. Four of them may be singled out: (1) In what way was the manager dishonest? (2) What was the Palestinian economic situation behind the parable? (3) Why does the master praise the manager's actions? (4) What is the point of the comparison in the parable?

(1) In what way was the manager dishonest? This may seem like a simple question, but in many ways it is fundamental to the understanding of the whole parable (and the subsequent conclusion). From the outset of the parable the manager is accused[19] of having squandered his master's property. We are not told in what way he did this, and it is really immaterial. The manager neither subsequently denies the accusation, nor tries to defend himself, nor even attempts to beg off (as the slave does in Mt 18:26). So a reason is already found in the accusation why he could be called 'the dishonest manager' (*ton oikonomon tēs adikias*, 16:8).

But is not this last description of him due rather to his conduct subsequent to the accusation and the master's decision to call for an inventory? After all, this description does not occur until v. 8a, and might seem to suggest this. The answer to this question depends on whether the manager's subsequent conduct was wrong or not. A very common interpretation of the parable so understands it: he summoned the debtors and suggested to them to falsify their receipts or notes. This was a further dishonest act. Such an interpretation, however, has always encountered the difficulty of explaining how the master (either the master of the parable or Jesus) could commend such

[19] The verb *dieblēthē* could mean 'was calumniated, was accused falsely' (as in *4 Mc* 4:1; Josephus, *Ant.* 7, 11, 3 §267) of having squandered the property. But this meaning does not suit the context. The manager does not try to defend himself, and his subsequent conduct would be illogical if he had not been guilty.

a corrupt manager and hold him up for instruction and example to Christians. In this interpretation, according to which the subsequent conduct of the manager is also flagrantly dishonest (though the text does not say so), the description of him in v. 8a is then said to be merited on two counts: (1) for squandering his master's property; (2) for involvement in graft.

In such an interpretation of the parable, commentators customarily point out that the master commends the manager for his 'prudence', not for his dishonesty. This 'prudence' is then explained as astuteness or cleverness in dealing with his fellow men. So it is not the manager's corruption which is made the object of the application, but only general prudence (if the parable is understood as ending with v. 7) or prudence in the use of money (if v. 8 or v. 9 is included). Or, as J. Jeremias, who limits the parable to vv. 1–7, explains it, the parable describes a criminal threatened with exposure who adopts unscrupulous but resolute measures to ensure his future security. The clever, resolute behaviour of the man threatened with catastrophe becomes an example for Jesus' listeners. Christians too must be aware that they face the crisis of the *eschaton.*[20]

Yet all of this interpretation *presupposes* that the manager's subsequent conduct was dishonest and corrupt. But there is not a detail in the parable text itself which imposes such an interpretation or clearly intimates that the manager was further involved in crooked knavery. It is, to say the least, strange that the only reaction of the master to the subsequent actions of his manager is one of praise for his prudence.[21] Again, there is an

[20] *The Parables of Jesus*, 34.

[21] H. Preisker ('Lukas 16, 1–7', *TLZ* 74 [1949] 85–92) believes that the sense of the adverb *phronimōs* (16:8a) is different from that found elsewhere in the Synoptics (except Mt 14:16b). Elsewhere the adjective *phronimos* describes the person who has grasped the eschatological condition of man (Mt 7:24; 24:45; 25:2, 4, 8, 9; Lk 12:42). But J. Jeremias (*The Parables of Jesus*, 34) has more correctly noted that the adverb is used precisely in this eschatological sense in the parable. The manager stands for the Christian confronted with the crisis that the kingdom brings in the lives of men. In

interesting parallel in the parable of the Dishonest Judge (Lk 18:2–8), who 'neither feared God nor respected men'. The judge in this parable merits a description very similar to that of the dishonest manager, *ho kritēs tēs adikias* ('the dishonest judge', 18:6). This description, moreover, is given to him only at the end of the parable, even though from the outset of it he is said to be unscrupulous—again we are not told precisely in what way. He finally yields to the pestering widow to be rid of her; but no further dishonest conduct is ascribed to him. In fact, the parable was told to teach Christians to 'pray always and not give up' (18:1, probably a secondary application). The similarity with the parable of the Dishonest Manager is striking. Nothing in the latter, subsequent to the reproach of the master, is clearly branded as knavery.

(2) What is the Palestinian economic situation reflected in the parable? According to the usual interpretations, the manager who handled the estate of the rich man had charge not only of his household but also of his financial affairs. In various transactions conducted by him (renting of farms to tenants, loans against a harvest, etc.) the neighbours contracted debts with the master of the estate. The manager kept the accounts of such transactions, and the master who lived perhaps in another part of the country presumably checked up on the manager from time to time. Otherwise he was trusted. He was empowered to handle debts and see to their reduction. In the parable the manager's squandering of the property had been reported and an account was demanded. Realizing that his situation was desperate, he summoned the debtors and in a last act of knavery had them change the amounts on the receipts in order to ingratiate himself with them against the time when his job would be taken away from him. This was a form of graft. One

---

the Lucan conclusion of v. 8b (of distinct origin) the comparative *phronimōteroi* has a little broader meaning because of the reference to the dealings with one's own generation. But even so, the implied contrast is still between those dealings and the reaction to the kingdom.

must presume that this was eventually brought to the master's attention. His only recorded reaction is one of admiration and praise for the manager's astuteness.

However, if there is nothing in the text that clearly labels the manager's subsequent conduct as dishonest, then possibly some other economic situation is reflected in the parable. Another situation has, in fact, been suggested by a number of writers in this century, though it has not been widely adopted. M. D. Gibson was apparently the first to propose it in 1903 on the basis of modern Near Eastern customs.[22] Her suggestion was subsequently supported by others.[23] But none of these writers was able to adduce much evidence for it from antiquity, their parallels being drawn from modern Near and Far Eastern practices. However, a recent writer has amassed an impressive array of data from rabbinical writings and Jewish law to suggest that the practice was known in antiquity too. He is J. Duncan M. Derrett, a reader in Oriental Laws in the University of London.[24]

[22] 'On the Parable of the Unjust Steward', *ExpT* 14 (1902–3) 334.

[23] W. D. Miller, 'The Unjust Steward', *ExpT* 15 (1903–4) 332–4; E. Hampden-Cook, 'The Unjust Steward', *ibid.* 16 (1904–5) 44; P. Gaechter, 'The Parable of the Dishonest Steward after Oriental Conceptions', *CBQ* 12 (1950) 121–31; C. B. Firth, 'The Parable of the Unrighteous Steward (Luke xvi. 1–9)', *ExpT* 63 (1951–52) 93–5; J. Volckaert, 'The Parable of the Clever Steward', *Clergy Monthly* 17 (1953) 332–41; G. Gander, 'Le procédé de l'économe infidèle décrit Luc 16:5–7, est-il répréhensible ou louable?' *VerbC* 7 (1953) 128–41. See also G. Chastand, *Etudes sociales sur les paraboles évangéliques* (Toulouse, 1925) 68–75.—Though the same basic interpretation is common to all these writers, there are variations in details.

[24] 'Fresh Light on St Luke xvi. I. The Parable of the Unjust Steward', *NTS* 7 (1960–61) 198–219; 'II. Dives and Lazarus and the Preceding Sayings', *ibid.*, 364–80. Derrett's competence in the field of Oriental law may be presumed; his explanation of the legal and economic background of the parable seems well enough supported. However, his flight from conclusions generally admitted today about the composition of the Gospels and the recording of Jesus' parables is another matter.; few will follow him in his views on this subject. The same can be said of the general explanation which he proposes for the parable. I have tried to sift from his discussion what seems valid for the understanding of the story as a whole.

Derrett explains the parable as reflecting the Palestinian laws and customs of agency and usury. A duly appointed manager acted as the agent for his master and was legally empowered to act in his name. His job was fiduciary. But 'there was no agency for wrongdoing'. A criminal act on the part of the manager did not necessarily involve the master; and if the latter ordered a criminal act, which the manager carried out, the manager had to bear the responsibility for it and could not take refuge in superior authority. The agent could involve the master in transactions with third parties (e.g., tenant farmers, borrowers, etc.). But custom permitted him to make a profit for himself, which may not have been precisely authorized by the master. Though he was not remunerated by his master, he was normally compensated for his expenses. In many cases he was a household slave, a *ben bayit* ('a son of the house', one born in the familia). Incompetence, misuse of discretion, negligence, and downright swindling were grounds for reprehension by the master and even for the unilateral dismissal of the agent. But he could not be sued in court as a debtor. The agent, however, could release debts owed to his master, and the latter was expected to ratify and abide by such acts.

In the parable the manager was such an agent. Reported as dishonest in his management of the property, he was upbraided by the master and was going to be dismissed. The master demanded that he draw up an inventory of the estate and an account of his handling of it, so that it could be made over to another manager. His social equals, other managers, would not welcome him, once dismissed; and since he could not face the prospect of hard labour or begging, the crisis forced him to build up good will with the general public (the debtors included). In his management of the estate, he had indulged in the commonly practised usury of the time. He lent his master's goods or land to fellow Jews at an interest apparently customary to the practice of his day, even though unauthorized to do so by his master. This was his profit. Such a practice, however, was a violation of the Torah and especially of the Pharisaic, rabbinical interpretation of it (see Dt 15:7–8; 23:20–21; Ex 22:24; Lv 25:36–37). However, as far as the courts were concerned, there were ways of getting around the law. Rabbinical casuistry discussed the legality of contracts for loans and the way in which they were recorded. For instance, if a receipt or note read, 'I will pay Reuben 1 denarius on the 1st of Nisan; and if I do not, then I will pay $\frac{1}{4}$ denarius annually in addition', this was declared to be usury, and the sum could be recovered in the courts by the debtor. However, if the receipt merely said, 'I owe Reuben 10 kor of wheat', this was declared not to be usury in the strict sense (and hence not recoverable), even though the borrower had not actually received the equivalent of 10 kor of wheat. He may have received only 5 or 8, but was constrained by the prevailing customs to write a larger sum on the note, and the difference represented the commission for the agent.[25]

When the parable is read in the light of such an economic background, it is understood in a quite different way. The manager, in the interests of ingratiating himself with others than his master, now that his job is virtually lost, has summoned the debtors and ordered them to write new notes or bonds which represent the real amounts owed to the master.[26] He returns the old ones, gets new ones, and prepares his ac-

[25] While the rabbinical writings know of this custom of usury and discuss various aspects of it, the question inevitably arises about the antiquity of this material. Does it really reflect a situation in Palestine in the time of Christ? There are certain indications that it does. Josephus, for instance, records that when Herod Agrippa I was almost bankrupt (*c.* A.D. 33–34), he borrowed money through an agent Marsyas from a Near Eastern banker, who forced Marsyas to sign a bond for 20,000 Attic drachmae, though he received 2500 drachmae less (*Ant.* 18, 6, 3, §157). Perhaps one could also appeal to the Murabba'ât texts (18 r 4 [DJD 2, 101]; 114 [DJD 2, 240–1]).

[26] Note that Luke's text does not speak of falsifying the text or even of changing it. Nor do we find the technical expression for cancelling a debt, used in the Pap. Flor. I. 61, 65 [A.D. 85]: *ekeleuse to cheirographon chiasthēnai*, 'he ordered the receipt crossed out' (i.e., marked with a *chi*). All that Luke's text says is that the debtor is to write fifty or eighty, presumably a new *cheirographon* (although the newness of it is not essential to this interpretation).

count for the master. The manager has, therefore, merely foregone his own profit or commission on the transactions. In this case his subsequent conduct is hardly dishonest, since he is renouncing what in fact was usury.

(3) Why does the master approve of the manager's actions? The master may well have been ignorant of the precise usurious nature of the original transactions; but it is to be presumed that he was aware of the custom of managers. Since 'there was no agency for wrongdoing', and usury was a violation of the Mosaic legislation, the master could hardly have authorized it. There was the duty of releasing the debts of distressed fellow Jews. While the master might have tried to claim the usurious gains from the debtors, since the receipts were written to include them, there was nothing to prevent him from releasing them from what they did not really owe him in terms of the main transaction. If, therefore, his manager reduced the debts by eliminating the usurious gain without the knowledge of the master, he would have been expected to approve and ratify such an act subsequently. This was apparently what he did in effect, when 'he approved of the dishonest manager'. The master was not cheated of anything that was really his. He commends the prudence of the manager in foregoing his profits to win favour with the debtors and others in view of the impending dismissal. While the verb *epēnesen* directly expresses praise for the manager's prudence, it may also reflect the official act of approval or ratification of the reduction of the debts and the elimination of the usury.

(4) What is the point of comparison in the parable? The conclusion in v. 8a states the important element of the parable: 'The master approved of that dishonest manager because he had acted prudently.' His prudence in the face of the crisis that was before him is commended; it is not just prudence in general, but rather his prudent use of material wealth with respect to it. He used his wealth (the profits that were coming to him) to ensure his future in view of the crisis. In this interpretation the

full eschatological nuance of the adverb *phronimōs* is thus brought out, for the Christian situation is one dominated by a need for decisive action. The dishonest manager has become the model for Christians, who are expected to grasp the dramatic situation of the kingdom and the crisis that it brings into the lives of men. It is a situation which calls for a prudent use of one's material wealth. In this there is a connection between this parable and those of the Rich Fool and Dives and Lazarus.

Is there even a slight allegorization of the parable? Modern students of the parables, who have followed A. Jülicher, A. T. Cadoux, C. H. Dodd, and J. Jeremias, tend to restrict the meaning of the Gospel parables to *one* point. Such a position was a reaction against the hyperallegorization of the parables practised in the interpretation of them for centuries. More recent writers, however, have questioned—and rightly so—the 'strait jacket' exegesis of the parables which has since developed.[27] In some cases there may have been at least a second point of comparison, or even more. Can or should this be admitted for the parable of the Dishonest Manager?

A. Descamps speaks of the slight allegorization of the images in the parable. 'Jesus could scarcely utter this parable without making perceptible a slight allegorical nuance in the images—such as that of the master demanding an account from his manager (God calling man to judgment), of the haste with which the manager sets to work (the urgency of the present situation for the disciple). . . .'[28] Such a restricted use of allegory can be admitted, but any further allegorization of it would have to be carefully scrutinized and would have to remain within known Gospel modes of thought and expression. Above all, the tendency to anachronism would be inadmissible.

[27] See P. Benoit, *RB* 55 (1948) 598; R. E. Brown, 'Parable and Allegory Reconsidered', *NovT* 5 (1962) 36–45 (reprinted in *New Testament Essays* [Milwaukee, 1965; London 1966] 254–64); and more recently D. O. Via, Jr., *The Parables: Their Literary and Existential Dimension* (Philadelphia, 1967) 13-17, 155-62.

[28] *Op. cit.*, 48–9.

THE MEANING OF THE LUCAN MULTIPLE CONCLUSION TO THE PARABLE

The Lucan conclusion, which begins with v. 8b and ends with v. 13, should be understood as three further lessons which are drawn from the parable. In a sense, they are inspired allegorizations of the parable, exploiting its various aspects. However, since the material is more than likely derived from other contexts, as already pointed out, the conclusion is much rather the result of conflation than mere allegorization. C. H. Dodd is undoubtedly right when he looks on these verses as 'notes for three separate sermons on the parable as text'.[29] In other words, Luke records three different ways in which the early Church moralized the parable. The first sermon is outlined in vv. 8b–9, where a further eschatological lesson on prudence is drawn from the parable. In the parable itself the dishonest manager by his prudence was the model for Christians facing the crisis which the coming of the kingdom has brought into their lives. The first conclusion rather equates the manager with the children of this world. Both of them are more prudent than the children of light; i.e., the manager and the children of this world manifest a prudence in their dealings with one another which is greater than that manifested by the children of light.[30] The second sermon is found in vv. 10–12, drawing a lesson of responsible management of what is entrusted to one. The eschatological nuance disappears in this application; the emphasis is shifted rather to day-by-day responsibility and fidelity. There are three points: the contrast of responsibility in the little and big things of life; the contrast of responsibility in handling the wealth of dishonesty[31] and real wealth; the

[29] *Parables of the Kingdom*, 17.

[30] Some might prefer to distinguish v. 8b and v. 9 into two distinct applications. This is possible, since v. 8b and v. 9 are distinct in origin. However, they do have a common eschatological reference and both seem to concentrate on the need of prudent, decisive action in 'the children of light'.

[31] See note 15 above (pp. 169-70).

contrast of responsibility in handling the goods of another and one's own. Finally, the last sermon, which really has nothing to to with the parable, sums up a general attitude toward wealth (or mammon). If a man allows himself to get involved in the pursuit of it and reduces himself thereby to a slavish servitude, he cannot serve God. Mammon becomes almost a god itself.

When the story of the Dishonest Manager is analysed along lines such as these, it is seen to have a certain intelligibility. The analysis is complicated, because of the conflation present in the story. But this interpretation has the advantage of reckoning with the separate elements of it and of interpreting them in their own right. At the same time, there is seen to be a unity in it all, which was what the inspired Evangelist was striving for in uniting the disparate elements in his 'travel account'. When the story is analysed in this fasion, there is no need to invoke irony as the key to the interpretation of the passage. This has often been suggested[32] but has never been very convincing.

HOMILETIC CONSIDERATIONS

The preacher who would present the Gospel of the Dishonest Manager would do well in his homily to recall the general Lucan context of the passage (that this is but one of the Lucan stories inculcating a Christian attitude towards riches). Secondly, he would do well to explain to the congregation the distinction between the parable itself (16:1–8a) and the multiple conclusion (16:8b–13), with its further lessons which the inspired Evangelist draws from the parable. Thirdly, a brief exposé of the Palestinian economic situation

[32] See J. F. McFadyen, 'The Parable of the Unjust Steward', *ExpT* 37 (1925–26) 535–9; R. Pautrel, '"Aeterna tabernacula" (Luc, XVI, 9)', *RSR* 30 (1940) 307–27; J. A. A. Davidson, 'A "Conjecture" about the Parable of the Unjust Steward (Luke xvi, 1–9)', *ExpT* 66 (1954–55) 31; H. Clavier, 'L'ironie dans l'enseignement de Jésus', *NovT* 1 (1956) 3–20, esp. 16–17; G. Paul, 'The Unjust Steward and the Interpretation of Lk 16, 9', *Theology* 61 (1958) 189–93; D. R. Fletcher, 'The Riddle of the Unjust Steward: Is Irony the Key?', *JBL* 82 (1963) 15–30.

reflected in the parable would clear up most of the obscure phrases in the story. This would enable the preacher to drive home the main point of the parable (as explained above). Finally, a brief explanation of any of the added applications would be in order. It should be obvious that a homily based on this Gospel pericope is going to be mainly informative and expository; the moralizing tendency of the preacher would have to be curtailed in this case.

To bring this long discussion to a close, we can recapitulate the essentials by presenting the Gospel text in the following form.

The Parable Proper

1 *Jesus said to the disciples: 'There was a certain rich man* (the owner of an estate) *who had a manager* (a servant empowered to handle the household and financial affairs of the estate; he could contract loans in the name of the master, had to keep the accounts, and could even liquidate debts), *and he heard complaints* (literally, "he [the manager] was accused", but we are not told by whom; it need not have been by the debtors) *that this man was squandering his property* (through negligence, swindling, incompetent use of discretion, etc.). 2 *So he called him and said: "What's this I hear about you? Prepare for me an account of your management* (i.e., give me an inventory and prepare an account of the debtors and what they owe me; the purpose of this account is to prepare for the transfer of management to a new man); *you can't be manager around here any longer* (the master has decided to dismiss the servant)." 3 *Then the manager said to himself* (soliloquy): "*What am I going to do? My master is taking my job as manager away from me. I am not strong enough to dig* (as a servant trained to a 'white-collar' job, he knows that he cannot endure the life of a labourer accustomed to hard, physical labour); *I'm ashamed to beg.*—4 *Ah, I know what I'll do, so that when I lose this job, I'll be welcome in people's homes*' (literally, 'I have known [an aorist expressing decision] what I shall do, that when I am removed from management they will receive me into their houses.' The third plural verb is indefinite, since no persons have yet been mentioned to whom it might refer. It is a Semitic way of paraphrasing the passive.—His decision is to take means to secure his future.). 5 *He summoned his master's debtors one by one* (i.e., those with whom he had transacted various "deals"). *He said to the first of them: "How much do you owe my master?"* (It should

not be presumed that he does not know how much was owed. His question is part of the dramatic presentation of the story.) "*One hundred jugs of olive oil*" (literally, 'one hundred baths of olive oil'. Since the Hebrew measure 'bath' equals between eight and nine gallons, this really represents an amount closer to a thousand gallons), *was the answer.* 6 *He said to the man: "Here, take your note* (literally, 'receive your written statement', the IOU or *cheirographon* ['bond'] originally written by the debtor expressing what he owed to the master), *sit down, and, hurry, write* (one for) *fifty* (i.e., write a new IOU for the real amount of the debt owed to the master, now minus the interest originally demanded by the manager. Fifty baths of oil are the manager's commission. The exorbitant rate [100%] should not be pressed too literally, for high figures are characteristic of Jesus' parables.[33] The rate is exorbitant to drive home the real point in the parable; no one is expected to take the figures seriously.). 7 *Then he said to another debtor: "How much do you owe?" He answered: "A hundred bushels of wheat"* (literally, 'a hundred kor of wheat', which is a considerable sum, since the Hebrew kor equals roughly ten to twelve bushels in our metric system. Again, a more realistic modern equivalent would be a thousand bushels of wheat, cut down to eight hundred.). *Again he said: 'Here, take your note and write* (one for) *eighty* (The manager gives up his claim to twenty-five per cent commission). 8 *And the master approved of that dishonest manager* (Since the dishonesty is to be understood as the squandering of the master's estate, reported in v. 2, this description of the manager is not to be regarded as derived from his conduct subsequent to the master's calling him to task. The master's approval or praise commends the manager for having made prudent use of the resources that were his in the situation. There is also the nuance that he gave his approval to the reduction of the debts.), *because he had acted prudently* (i.e., he had sized up the urgency of the situation, and in this he becomes the model for Christians, who should face up to their eschatological situation).

The Lucan Conclusion

8b *For* (The Greek conjunction *hoti* ['because'] introduces a further lesson drawn from the parable; it is a redactional suture joining to the parable itself a Lucan reflection, based on the words of Jesus.) *the children of this world* (See note 10. The children of this world are contrasted with the children of light [=Christian disciples]. The manager is now equated with them. Their shrewdness in their

[33] See J. Jeremias, *The Parables of Jesus*, 22.

dealings with one another becomes an example of the shrewdness which should characterize the Christian disciples in their endeavours to enter the kingdom.) *are more prudent* (The nuance of prudence in the face of the eschatological situation is not completely lost here, for this is the frame of reference for the Christians' activity. But they are compared to the children of this world in their dealings with their own generation. In this conclusion, therefore, the word *phronimos* takes on a further nuance.) *in dealing with their own generation than the children of light are.* 9 *I* (Jesus, the Master) *tell you, make friends with the wealth of dishonesty* (i.e., use prudently the wealth that you have to insure your status when the eschaton arrives. It does not mean that Christians are to make use of ill-gotten gain; the expression is pejorative and expresses only the tendency of wealth as such. It tends to lead man to dishonesty.), *so that when it gives out* (i.e., when the crisis has come), *you will be welcomed into everlasting tents* (i.e., probably into heaven. The expression 'everlasting tents' is not found in the OT, nor in rabbinical writings, but appears first outside of Luke in 2 Esdras 2:11 [3rd c. A.D.].[34] The saying seems to be inculcating a prudent use of wealth in view of one's future—eschatological—status. The expressions seem to be modelled on v. 4 of the parable.). 10 *The man who is trustworthy in little things is also trustworthy in what is big* (Note that this second application has switched from the eschatological situation of the manager and his prudence in face of the crisis to the day-by-day fidelity in responsible positions. This and the next two verses comment not on the subsequent conduct of the manager, for which he was praised as prudent, but rather on the idea of what was expected of him by his own master, when he first gave him the job.). 11 *If, then, you are not trustworthy when handling the wealth of dishonesty, who will trust you with the wealth that is real* (The contrast is between that which is material wealth and that which is spiritual.)? 12 *And if you are not trustworthy when handling what belongs to another, who will give you what is your own* (Material wealth is treated as something that does not belong to man; his real wealth is something that is truly part of himself. If he is not trustworthy in handling the former, how can he trust himself in the disposition of the latter?)?

13 *No servant* (the Greek word here is *oiketēs*, a more general expression than *oikonomos*, 'manager') *can serve two masters; either he will hate the one and love the other, or he will be devoted to the one and despise the*

[34] For an entirely different interpretation of this phrase, see R. Pautrel, *op. cit.*, 319 ff.

other (The third application made on the parable. It is only loosely connected with it, and really is linked more closely to the preceding vv. 10–12. Devotion to wealth is not compatible with devotion to God; that is why wealth is called the mammon of dishonesty [16:9].). *You cannot serve both God and wealth.*

At the beginning of this article I mentioned a growing consensus of exegetical opinion about this Gospel story. I hope that I have made it clear that this is a consensus about the composite nature of it. Unfortunately, the same consensus is not found about the interpretation of it. The understanding of the parable which I have presented, however, has the advantage of giving an intelligible and coherent meaning to the whole. It is not, moreover, without some foundation.

In the new arrangement of Scripture readings for a three-year liturgical cycle of Sundays, it was wise to adopt the whole story of the Dishonest Manager (16:1–13) and not just the old liturgical form of it. In no case should it have been simply omitted—just because it is difficult to explain or preach about. With the adoption of the full text, the multiple Lucan conclusion is in the liturgy with its perennially valid message for the edification and instruction of God's People in this twentieth century.[35]

[35] The new Gospel for the 25th Sunday of the Year, year C, is Lk 16:1–13; the shorter form is Lk 16:10–13. The Gospel for Friday of the 31st week, years 1 and 2, is Lk 16:1–8.

III

PAULINE PASSAGES

9

A FEATURE OF QUMRAN ANGELOLOGY AND THE ANGELS OF 1 COR 11:10*

The Qumran texts have brought to light a feature of Jewish thought about angels which helps us to interpret the meaning of the phrase *dia tous angelous*, 'on account of the angels', in 1 Cor 11:10. This phrase has been the subject of many interpretations from the time of Tertullian on. The evidence from Qumran, however, does not just add another interpretation to the many that have already been given; rather it adds a detail to one interpretation already rather common, thus supporting it and rendering the other interpretations less probable. It is my purpose in this study to indicate the bearing of the new evidence from Qumran on this Pauline expression.

In 1 Cor 11:3–16, Paul is dealing with an abusive practice that had arisen in the Church of Corinth. It had been reported to him that women were praying and 'prophesying' in the liturgical gatherings with heads uncovered. It has been asserted that Greek women were accustomed to wear a veil on the streets and often even at home, if they were married, but usually removed it in religious assemblies.[1] This custom is supposed to have been imitated by the Christian women of Corinth in their

* Originally published in *NTS* 4 (1957–58) 48–58. The postscript of 1966 was originally prepared for the reprint of this article in *Paul and Qumran* (ed. J. Murphy-O'Connor; London: Chapman, 1968) 31–47.

[1] E. B. Allo, *Saint Paul, Première Épître aux Corinthiens*, Paris (1956) 258; see also 263. The chief source of evidence for Greek women taking part in a religious ceremony with uncovered head is the Andania Mysteries in-

religious assemblies. Though it is not certain just how the abuse arose, we are certain from the way Paul speaks about it that he looked upon it as such, especially because it was contrary to the custom of other Christian communities. In this regard the Church of Corinth was not in conformity with the *paradosis*, 'tradition', which Paul had passed on to them (v. 2).[2] So he writes to correct the abuse.

Four reasons may be distinguished in the course of Paul's remarks why a woman should veil her head in assemblies of public prayer. (1) Theologically, the order of creation found in the Genesis story shows that woman is subordinated to man; she is destined to be his companion, helper and mother.[3] Hence she should manifest that subordination by wearing a veil. (2) Philosophically (or sociologically), natural decency would seem to demand it. (3) As a matter of ecclesiastical discipline, the 'churches of God' recognize no other practice in worship. (4) 'On account of the angels' (v. 10). The last reason causes a

---

scription. See W. Dittenberger, *Sylloge Inscriptionum Graecarum* (Leipzig) vol. II (1917) no. 736, 4. Also important is the *Lycosurae lex sacra* (*ibid.* III [1920] no. 999). For the bearing of these inscriptions (and others) on 1 Cor 11:10, see S. Lösch, 'Christliche Frauen in Corinth (1 Kor 11, 2–16). Ein neuer Lösungsversuch', *TQ* 127 (1947) 230–51. Though many details about the wearing of the veil in antiquity, both by Jewish and Greek women, have been preserved for us, none of them bears directly on the problem of the Church in Corinth. We do not know the exact nature nor the origin of the abuse that Paul was trying to handle. Was it a reaction against a custom that he was trying to introduce? G. Delling, *Paulus' Stellung zur Frau und Ehe* (Stuttgart, 1931) 98, seems to think so; likewise A. Schlatter, *Die korinthische Theologie* (Beiträge zur Förderung christlicher Theologie 18/2; Gütersloh, 1914) 23, 54. On the use of the veil in antiquity see R. de Vaux, 'Sur le voile des femmes dans l'Orient ancien', *RB* 44 (1936) 397–412; A. Jeremias, *Der Schleier von Sumer bis heute* (Der Alte Orient 31/1–2; Leipzig, 1931).

[2] S. Lösch (*op. cit.*, 225–30) rightly rejects the idea that there was a movement in Corinth in favour of the emancipation of women, which Paul was trying to combat.

[3] Paul is obviously speaking in vv. 3–9 of the order of creation; cf. 1 Tm 2:13. Further on, however, in v. 11 he introduces another point of view, namely, *en kyriō* 'in the Lord'. Under this aspect Paul says, in Gal. 3:28, *ouk eni arsen kai thēlu*, 'there is neither male nor female'.

difficulty, because it is abruptly added to a verse which is the conclusion of the theological reason set forth in vv. 3–9. As several commentators have remarked, it is a surprise to find it there.[4] Moreover, it is added without any explanation, and all the attempts that have been made to integrate it with the preceding argument have not succeeded. Hence it is best to regard it as a subsidiary reason stated succinctly.

Because the context of this verse will be necessary for the interpretation, I shall give the translation of the entire passage. Goodspeed's translation,[5] which is being used, is a good example of the way modern translators have wrestled with v. 10.

I appreciate your always remembering me, and your standing by the things I passed on to you, just as you received them. But I want you to understand that Christ is the head of every man, while a woman's head is her husband, and Christ's head is God. Any man who offers prayer or explains the will of God with anything on his head disgraces his head, and any woman who offers prayer or explains the will of God bareheaded disgraces her head, for it is just as though she had her head shaved. For if a woman will not wear a veil, let her cut off her hair too. But if it is a disgrace for a woman to have her hair cut off or her head shaved, let her wear a veil. For a man ought not to wear anything on his head, for he is the image of God and reflects his glory; while woman is the reflection of man's glory. For man was not made from woman, but woman from man, and man was not created for woman, but woman was for man. That is why she ought to wear upon her head something to symbolize her subjection, on account of the angels, if nobody else. But in union with the Lord, woman is not independent of man nor man of woman. For just as woman was made from man, man is born of woman, and it all really comes from God. Judge for yourselves. Is it proper for a woman to offer prayer to God with nothing on her head? Does not nature itself teach you that for a man to wear his hair long is degrading, but a woman's long hair is her pride? For her hair is given

[4] So P. Bachmann, *Der erste Brief des Paulus an die Korinther* (4. Aufl.; Leipzig, 1936) 356; J. Sickenberger, *Die Briefe des hl. Paulus an die Korinther und Römer* (Bonner Bibel 6; Bonn, 1932) 51; J. Héring, *La première épitre de Saint Paul aux Corinthiens* (Neuchâtel, 1949) 94.

[5] In J. M. P. Smith (ed.), *The Complete Bible, an American Translation* (Chicago, 1951) New Testament section, 162.

her as a covering. But if anyone is disposed to be contentious about it, I for my part recognize no other practice in worship than this, and neither do the churches of God.

The Greek text of v. 10 reads as follows: *dia touto opheilei hē gynē exousian echein epi tēs kephalēs dia tous angelous.*

The words *dia touto*, 'that is why', indicate the conclusion to the preceding theological argument. Because of them the unexpected addition of *dia tous angelous*, 'on account of the angels', has made some commentators think that this phrase was a gloss.[6] But Robertson and Plummer have pointed out that it cannot be dismissed so lightly: 'Marcion had the words, and the evidence for them is overwhelming. An interpolator would have made his meaning clearer.'[7] Nor is it possible to admit any of the many purely conjectural and often far-fetched emendations, such as *dia to euangelion*, 'on account of the gospel'; *dia tas agelas*, 'on account of the crowds'; *dia tous agelaious*, 'on account of the men who crowded in'; *dia tous andras*, 'on account of the vulgar' or 'gazing men'; *dia tous engelastas*, 'on account of the mockers'; *dia tous ochlous*, 'on account of the mobs'; *dia tēs angelias*, 'throughout [the whole of] her [divine] message'.[8] Consequently, one must try to understand the words as they stand.

V. 10 contains another difficult expression that has tormented interpreters and no satisfying solution has really been found for it—the word *exousian*. Since this is actually the keyword in the verse, I shall indicate briefly the main attempts to interpret it, as its meaning affects the phrase *dia tous angelous*. Four interpretations are currently proposed and unfortunately no new light from Qumran has been shed on this problem.

In itself *exousia* means 'power, authority, right to do some-

[6] C. Holsten, *Das Evangelium des Paulus* (Berlin, 1880) 472–4, eliminates the whole verse. J. M. S. Baljon, *Novum Testamentum Graece* (Groningen, 1898) 525; A. Jirku, 'Die "Macht" auf dem Haupte (1 Kor 11:10)', *NKZ* 32 (1921) 711, consider *dia tous angelous* a gloss.

[7] *First Epistle of St Paul to the Corinthians* (ICC; Edinburgh, 1911) 233.

[8] See R. Perdelwitz, 'Die *Exousia* auf dem Haupt der Frau', *ThStKr* 86 (1913) 611–13; A. P. Stanley, *Epistles of St Paul to the Corinthians* (3rd ed.; London, 1865) 186.

thing; ability; dominion'.[9] But what is its meaning when Paul says, 'That is why the woman should have *exousian* upon her head'?

(1) Most commentators understand *exousia* today in a figurative sense as a *symbol of the power* to which the woman is subjected (by metonymy). Theophylact expressed it thus: *to tou exousiazesthai symbolon*, 'the symbol of being dominated'.[10] It must be admitted that this sense of the word fits the context well, but the chief difficulty with this interpretation is a philological one, since it attributes to *exousia* a passive sense, which is otherwise unknown. Apropos of this interpretation W. M. Ramsay has remarked: '. . . a preposterous idea which a Greek scholar would laugh at anywhere except in the New Testament, where (as they seem to think) Greek words may mean anything that commentators choose'.[11] *Exousia* should indicate a power that the woman possesses or exercises (cf. Rev 11:6; 14:8; 20:6), not one to which she is subjected or subordinated.[12] One may

[9] See W. Bauer, *Griechisch-Deutsches Wörterbuch zu den Schriften des Neuen Testaments* (4. Aufl.; Berlin, 1952) 502; Liddell-Scott-Jones, *A Greek-English Lexicon* (9th ed.; Oxford, 1925–40) vol. I, 599; C. Spicq, 'Encore la "Puissance sur la tête" (1 Cor 11:10)', *RB* 68 (1939) 557–62. Fr Spicq has studied the uses of *exousia* especially in Ben Sira and the Greek papyri and has shown that the word was used specifically of the authority of a husband over his wife or of a father over his children.

[10] *Expos. in Ep. I ad Cor.* (*PG* 124, 697C); the symbolical meaning has been proposed by Theodoret (*PG* 82, 312D); Chrysostom (*PG* 61, 218); A. Lemonnyer, *Épîtres de saint Paul, première partie* (Paris, 1908) 145; R. Cornely, *Commentarius in S. Pauli apostoli epistolas, II: Prior epistola ad Corinthios* (Paris, 1909) 319; P. Bachmann, *op. cit.*, 356; Str-B 3, 436; J. Huby, *Saint Paul, Première épître aux Corinthens* (Paris, 1946) 248–9; C. Spicq, *op. cit.*, 558; J. Kürzinger, *Die Briefe des Apostels Paulus, die Briefe an die Korinther und Galater* (Würzburg, 1954) 28; *et al.*

[11] *The Cities of St Paul. Their Influence on his Life and Thought* (London, 1907) 203.

[12] This is the weak point, in my opinion, in Spicq's study of *exousia* (see above in n. 9). Granted that metonymy is a legitimate way to interpret the word, and granted that *exousia* does mean in the papyri and Ben Sira the authority of the husband over his wife or of the father over his children, the fact remains that *echein exousian* in the New Testament is used in an *active* sense of a power which one exercises. Even in the examples from the papyri

rightly ask why St Paul says 'power' (or 'authority'), if he really means 'subjection'. Then, too, the shift from an abstract idea like power to the specific meaning of an article of feminine attire is not an easy one to explain, even by metonymy.[13] Wendland asks what evidence there is for the veil as a sign of subordination to a man.[14] Consequently, if this interpretation of *exousia* is to be retained, one must say that Paul has created the figurative meaning to suit his context.

(2) Because of this philological difficulty, some commentators have preferred to interpret *exousia* rather as a symbol of the power, the honour and the dignity of the woman. 'The woman who has a veil on her head wears authority on her head: that is what the Greek text says.'[15] The woman who veils her head exercises control over it and does not expose it to indignity; if she unveils it, everyone has control over it and she loses her dignity.[16] Such an interpretation has the advantage of giving to *exousia* an active meaning, but it seriously forces the context, since Paul is not speaking of the dignity of woman nor of her dignified actions. The context treats rather of woman's subordination to man according to the Genesis account of creation.[17]

---

which Spicq cites the word *exousian* seems to me to have this meaning; thus *didonai exousian* means to transfer the authority to another so that he can exercise it.

[13] Allo (*op. cit.*, 266–7) cites the use of a similar expression in Diodorus Siculus (I, 47, 5), who reports that the statue of an ancient Egyptian goddess bears *treis basileias epi tēs kephalēs*, that is, three diadems, signs of a triple royalty. But there is an important difference to be noted: 'here it is question of the power of its wearer and not of the power of someone else' (J. Héring, *op. cit.*, 95); see also J. Weiss, *Der erste Korintherbrief* (Göttingen, 1910) 274.

[14] *Die Briefe an die Korinther* (Das Neue Testament Deutsch 7; Göttingen, 1954) 83.

[15] W. M. Ramsay, *op. cit.*, 203. E. B. Allo, *op. cit.*, 267, combines this interpretation with the first one: Paul is stressing not only the subordination of the woman, but also strives to bring out her dignity. See Delling, *op. cit.*, 99, n. 4.

[16] Robertson and Plummer, *op. cit.*, 232.

[17] J. Huby, *op. cit.*, 248.

(3) A fairly common interpretation of *exousia* today explains the word in the sense of a *magical power* that the veiled woman possesses to ward off the attacks of evil spirits. Since woman is the secondary product of creation, she requires this additional force 'as the weaker sex' against the fallen angels.[18] She needs this magic force, which is the veil, especially in times of prayer and ecstasy, when the angels draw near, for her natural frailty is not sufficient to protect her. The advantage of this interpretation is that it preserves the active meaning of *exousia* and provides a closer connection with what precedes for the phrase *dia tous angelous*. But the major difficulty with this opinion is the lack of evidence showing that a woman's veil was ever thought of as having such a function in antiquity. J. Héring believes that M. Dibelius proved this very point. Yet H. Lietzmann, whose commentary made this interpretation popular, admits the difficulty: 'Freilich ist bisher die Vorstellung von einer apotropäischen Wirkung des Schleiers nicht nachgewiesen.'[19]

(4) In 1920 G. Kittel proposed a new interpretation of *exousia* which has been adopted in some quarters. He pointed out that an Aramaic word, *šlṭwnyh*, meaning a 'veil' or an 'ornament of the head', occurs in the Jerusalem Talmud.[20] It is given there as the equivalent of the Hebrew *šbys* of Is 3:18. Now the root of this word is *šlṭ*, and is identical with the com-

[18] Thus O. Everling, *Die paulinische Angelologie und Dämonologie* (Göttingen, 1888) 37; M. Dibelius, *Die Geisterwelt im Glauben des Paulus* (Göttingen, 1909) 13–23; J. Weiss, *op. cit.*, 274; J. Lietzmann, *An die Korinther I–II* (4. Aufl.; Tübingen, 1949) 55; R. Reitzenstein, *Poimandres* (Leipzig, 1904) 230, n. 1; J. Héring, *op. cit.*, 90, 94–5; E. Fehrle, *Die kultische Keuschheit im Altertum* (Religionsgeschichtliche Versuche und Vorarbeiten 6; Giessen, 1910) 39; *et al.*

[19] *Op. cit.*, 55. W. G. Kümmel's added note on p. 184 is scarcely pertinent.

[20] *Sabbath* 6:8b, commenting on Is 3:18: *hšbysym: šlṭwnyh kmh d't 'mr šbys šl sbkh.* 'Was die *šebisim* anlangt, so sind damit gemeint die *šalṭonayya*, wie du sagst: der *šabis* des Kopfnetzes.' ('Die "Macht" auf dem Haupt (1 Kor 11:10)', *Rabbinica* (Arbeiten zur Vorgeschichte des Christentums 1/3; Leipzig, 1920) 20. Though this opinion is usually ascribed to G. Kittel, he was actually anticipated by J. Herklotz, 'Zu 1 Kor 11:10', *BZ* 10 (1912) 154. See Levy, *Wörterbuch über die Talmudim und Midraschim*, IV, 562a.

mon Aramaic verb meaning 'to have power, dominion over'. Hence, either by a mistranslation or by a popular etymology, the Greek *exousia* was taken as the equivalent of the Aramaic *šlṭwnyh*. The proponents of this explanation of *exousia* point out that an ancient variant reading in 1 Cor 11:10 is *kalymma*, 'a veil',[21] found in Irenaeus (*PG* 7, 524B), which is supported by *velamen* of Jerome (*PL* 25, 439A) and a codex of the Vulgate. Origen (*PG* 13, 119B) combined the two readings, *velamen et potestatem*. Though we cannot rule out the possibility that the reading *kalymma* or *velamen* is an interpretation of the text or an attempt to eliminate a difficulty of the original text,[22] nevertheless it does show that the word was understood in antiquity in the sense of 'a veil'. This interpretation has been adopted by W. Foerster and M. Ginsburger and seems to underlie the translation given in RSV.[23] The main difficulty with this meaning of *exousia* is that the Greeks of Corinth would never have understood what Paul meant by it.[24] I must admit that this is a real difficulty, but the presupposition on the part of those who propose it usually is that the Church of Corinth was wholly, or almost wholly, Greek. It is, however, beyond doubt that there were *Jewish* elements in the Corinthian community who would have understood the word *exousia* in the sense of *šlṭwnyh*.[25] Consequently, until a better suggestion is made for the sense of *exousia* I prefer to go along with Kittel.

Having given a survey of the main interpretations of *exousia*

[21] Treated as a variant by Nestle, Merk. But is it certain that the text of Irenaeus offers nothing more than a paraphrase of our verse?

[22] See J. Héring, *op. cit.*, 95.

[23] Foerster proposes it only as a conjecture in *TDNT* 2, 574; Ginsburger's discussion ('La "gloire" et l'"autorité" de la femme dans 1 Cor 11:1–10', *RHPR* 12 [1932] 248) was apparently written independently of Kittel's study. G. Delling (*op. cit.*, 105, n. 68) regards this interpretation as 'die annehmbarste Lösung'.

[24] Thus Str-B 3, 437; Allo, *op. cit.*, 264.

[25] According to Acts 18:1–5 Paul on his first arrival in Corinth was given hospitality by 'a Jew named Aquila, a native of Pontus, who had recently come from Italy with his wife Priscilla. . . . Every Sabbath he would preach

we can turn to the phrase *dia tous angelous*. The figurative meanings that have been given to the phrase can be dismissed immediately, as it is obvious that they are 'last-resort' solutions. For instance, Ephraem thought that *angelous* meant *sacerdotes*,[26] while Ambroisiaster commented: *angelos episcopos dicit, sicut in Apocalypsi Ioannis.*[27] But though the word *angelos* is found in the New Testament in the sense of a human messenger (Lk 7:24; 9:52; Jas 2:25), it is never used thus by Paul.

Likewise to be rejected is the interpretation, 'in imitation of the angels', or 'because the angels do so'. Support for this opinion has been sought in Is 6:2, where the angels covered their faces and loins with their wings in the presence of the Lord. So a woman in prayer should cover her head. Just as the angels, who are subordinate to God, veil themselves in his presence, so should woman 'as a subordinate being'[28] follow their example. But one may ask, with J. Huby, why this imitation of the attitude of the angels during divine worship should be prescribed for women only.[29] Moreover, what evidence is there for understanding *dia* in this sense?

---

in the synagogue, and try to convince both Jews and Greeks.' When he turned in anger from the Jews to preach to the heathen, 'he moved to the house of a worshipper of God named Titus Justus, which was next door to the synagogue. But Crispus, the leader of the synagogue, believed in the Lord and so did all his household. . . .' See Allo, *op. cit.*, 12–13; J. Holzner, *Paulus* (Freiburg im B., 1937) 206.

[26] *Commentarii in Epistulas D. Pauli, nunc primum ex Armenio in Latinum sermonem translati* (Venice, 1893) 70. This was likewise the opinion of Pelagius (*PL* 30, 781B) and of Primasius of Hadrumetum (*PL* 118, 532D).

[27] *PL* 17, 253. Similarly D. Bornhäuser, '"Um der Engel willen", 1 Kor 11:10', *NKZ* 41 (1930) 475–88; P. Rose, 'Power on the Head', *ExpT* 23 (1911–12) 183–4.

[28] W. Meyer, *I. Korinther 11–16 Leib Christi* (Zurich, 1945) 26. Similarly K. Roesch, '"Um der Engel willen" (1 Kor 11:10)', *TGl* 24 (1932) 363–5; Robertson and Plummer, *op. cit.*, 233–4 (as a suggestion 'worth considering'); J. Mezzacasa, 'Propter angelos (1 Cor 11:10)', *VD* 11 (1931) 29–42; S. Lösch (*op. cit.*, 255, n. 80) labels K. Roesch's *exposé* as 'die einzig richtige, von den Kirchenvätern übereinstimmend vertretene Deutung'.

[29] *Op. cit.*, 251.

In mentioning above the third interpretation of *exousia* I indicated a meaning of *angelous* that is fairly common among that group of commentators, namely, *fallen angels*. As far as I know, Tertullian was the first to suggest this meaning for *angelous* in this passage. In *De virginibus velandis* 7, he says, *propter angelos, scilicet quos legimus a deo et caelo excidisse ob concupiscentiam feminarum.*[30] Tertullian's suggestion has been illustrated by reference to Gn 6:2, 'the sons of the gods (*b^e^nê 'e^lôhîm*) noticed that the daughters of men were attractive; so they married those whom they liked best'. Lietzmann adds that this passage in Genesis often excited the fantasy of later Jewish writers, for whom bad angels preying on weak, defenceless women were a literary commonplace.[31] He refers, in particular, to the *Testament of Reuben* 5, where women are warned *hina mē kosmōntai tas kephalas kai tas opseis autōn* because the women before the Flood bewitched the angels in that way.[32] But J. Héring thinks that, since it is not certain that the Corinthians were *au courant* with such Jewish beliefs, it is preferable to suppose with M. Dibelius an allusion to Hellenistic ideas, according to which a woman in a state of ecstasy (as in sleep) was by her weakness particularly exposed to the attacks of certain spirits.[33] Hence *exousia* gives her a magic protection against such attacks.

Against this opinion one may point out that the *weakness* of woman is a notion that the interpreters have introduced. Paul speaks of woman's subordination to man; he says nothing of her weakness. Hence a woman's need of an added protection intro-

[30] *PL* 2, 947A; cf. *Contra Marcionem* 5, 8 (CSEL 47, 597); *De cultu feminarum* 2, 10 (CSEL 70, 88).

[31] *Op. cit.*, 55. He refers to W. Bousset, *Die Religion des Judentums im neutestamentlichen Zeitalter* (Berlin, 1906) 382. See also L. Jung, *Fallen Angels in Jewish, Christian and Mohammedan Literature* (Philadelphia, 1926) 97 ff.; W. Weber, 'Die paulinische Vorschrift über die Kopfbedeckung der Christen', *Zeitschrift für wissenschaftliche Theologie* 46 (1903) 487–99. See n. 18 above for others who hold this opinion.

[32] Compare *Enoch* 6 (Charles, *APOT* 2, 191); 19:1 (2,200); *Jub* 4:22 (2, 19); *Apoc. Bar.* 56:12 (2,513); *Tb* 6:14; 8:3.

[33] *Op. cit.*, 94; cf. M. Dibelius, *Die Geisterwelt*, 18 ff.

duces into the context a consideration that is quite foreign to Paul's argumentation. But the most decisive reason against this interpretation is that *angeloi*, used with the article, never designates bad or fallen angels in the Pauline writings.[34] Moreover, sensuality is never attributed to any of the good angels in any of the Christian or Jewish writings of the period.[35] One of the other problems that is met in interpreting this verse is visualizing just what kind of veil Paul has in mind. It is far from certain that he means a veil that covers the face after the fashion of the oriental women in modern times (at least until fairly recently); he speaks of a covering for the head. If it is merely a head-covering, is that sufficient protection against the fallen angels? Consequently, I believe that this opinion must be abandoned, especially since the new evidence from Qumran rules it out.

The most common opinion has always regarded *angelous* as meaning good angels. Theodoret specified this view, by understanding the word of guardian angels.[36] J. Moffatt expands this notion: 'Paul has in mind the midrash on Gn 1:26 f., which made good angels not only mediators of the Law (Gal 3:19), but guardians of the created order. Indeed, according to one ancient midrash, reflected in Philo, when God said, "Let us make man", he was addressing the angels.'[37] Consequently, a woman should wear a veil on her head out of respect for the angels who are guardians of the order of creation (to which Paul alludes in vv. 8–9).

But Moffatt adds another function of the angels, which some commentators either give as the only one, or join, as he does, to

[34] Compare 1 Cor 13:1; Mt 13:49; 25:31; Lk 16:22; Heb 1:4, 5. See Bachmann, *op. cit.*, 357; and p. 203 below.

[35] See Allo, *op. cit.*, 266. J. Héring (*op. cit.*, 95) thinks that he can weaken this point made by Allo by pointing out that the angels of Gn 6 were also good, 'before permitting themselves to be seduced'. This is hardly *ad rem.*

[36] *PG* 82, 312D-313A. So too E. Zolli, *Christus* (Rome, 1946) 88; Str-B 3, 437; Kittel, *op. cit.*, 26, regards the angels rather as guardians of the woman's chastity.

[37] *The First Epistle of Paul to the Corinthians* (London, 1947) 152. See also L. Brun, '"Um der Engel willen" 1 Kor 11:10', *ZNW* 14 (1913) 298–308.

their task as guardians of the created order. This second function is their assistance at gatherings of public worship.[38] I would separate this function from the former for two reasons. First, it is supported elsewhere in the Old and New Testament. In Ps 137 (138):1 we read *enantion angelōn psalō soi* (LXX). In Rev 8:3 an angel is the mediator of the prayers of the saints.[39] Secondly, two passages in the Qumran literature so far published mention the presence of angels in sacred gatherings.

In column 7 of the *War Scroll* the physical requirement of those who would take part in God's war, an eschatological war, are set forth.

No one who is lame or blind or crippled or who has a permanent blemish in his flesh, nor any person afflicted with a disease in his flesh—none of these shall go with them to war. All of them are to be men who volunteer for battle, perfect both in spirit and in body and prepared for the day of vengeance. Nor shall any man go down with them who is not yet cleansed from his bodily discharge on the day of battle, for holy angels accompany their armies (1QM 7:4–6).[40]

The Hebrew of the last clause reads as follows: *ky' ml'ky qwdš 'm ṣb'wtm yḥd*. The same reason is given in the so-called Rule of the Congregation for the exclusion of similar cases of physical unfitness from assemblies of the 'congregation'.

Nor shall anyone who is afflicted by any form of human uncleanness whatsoever be admitted into the assembly of God (*bqhl 'lh*); nor shall anyone who becomes afflicted in this way be allowed to retain his place in the midst of the congregation. No one who is afflicted with a bodily defect or injured in feet or hands, or who is lame or blind or deaf or dumb, or who has a visible blemish in his body, or who is an old man, tottering and unable to stand firm in the midst of the congregation of the men of renown, for holy angels are (present) in their [congre]gation. If anyone of these persons has something to say

[38] See G. Kurze, *Der Engels- und Teufelsglaube des Apostels Paulus* (Freiburg im B., 1915) 12.

[39] See further Tb 12:12; 1 Cor 4:9; Eph 3:10; 1 Tm 5:21; Heb 1:14 for functions of the angels that are similar.

[40] *'Ôṣar hammegillôt haggenûzôt* (Jerusalem, 1954) Milḥemet . . . lûaḥ 22.

to the holy council, let an oral deposition be taken from him; but let him not enter, for he is contaminated (1QSa 2:3–11).[41]

The Hebrew for the clause we are interested in is *ky' ml'ky qwdš* [*b'd*]*tm*.

In these two passages every sort of bodily defect, affliction or discharge was considered a thing unworthy of the sight of the angels, who were believed to be present at the gathering of the army for the eschatological war and at the meeting of the congregation or the assembly of God. The volunteer for the holy war had to be perfect not only in spirit but also in body. One gathers from the expression *lr'wt 'ynym* (1QSa 2:7) that bodily defects offend the sight of the angels who are present.

It is interesting to note in this connection that similar bodily defects excluded descendants of Aaron from service in the temple, according to Lv 21:17–23.

'Say to Aaron, "None of your descendants, from generation to generation, who has a defect, may draw near to offer his God's food; for no one who has a defect may come near, no one who is blind, or lame, or has any perforations, or has a limb too long; no one who has a fractured foot, or a fractured hand, or is a hunchback, or has a cataract, or a defect of eyesight, or scurvy, or scabs, or crushed testicles—no one of the descendants of Aaron, the priest, who has a defect, may come near to offer the Lord's sacrifices; since he has a defect, he may not come near to offer his God's food. He may eat his God's food, some of the most sacred as well as the sacred; only he must not approach the veil nor come near the altar, because he has a defect in him, lest he profane my sanctuaries." '

There is no mention of angels in this passage of Leviticus, but it is clear that a bodily defect was considered in ancient Judaism as a source of irreverence toward that which was *qōdeš*, even independently of any moral culpability. In the two passages from the Qumran literature the angels are specified as *ml'ky qwdš*, and the exclusion of bodily defects from their sight is put on the same basis of reverence. From this notion one may interpret the meaning of *dia tous angelous* in 1 Cor.

[41] D. Barthélemy, J. T. Milik, *Qumrân Cave I*, DJD 1, 110.

The context shows that it is a question of a sacred assembly, for men and women are praying and 'prophesying'.[42] In v. 16 Paul refers to the 'custom' which is current in the 'Church of God' (the resemblance of this last expression to *qhl 'lh* in 1QSa 2:4 should be noted).[43] In such an assembly, Paul says, the woman is to wear upon her head a veil *dia tous angelous*. We are invited by the evidence from Qumran to understand that the unveiled head of a woman is like a bodily defect which should be excluded from such an assembly, 'because holy angels are present in their congregation'.

Furthermore, the Pauline context supports such an interpretation. 'Any woman who prays or "prophesies" with uncovered head disgraces her head, for it is just as though she had her head shaved. For if a woman will not wear a veil, let her cut off her hair too. But if it is a disgrace for a woman to have her hair cut off or her head shaved, let her wear a veil' (v. 6). 'Does not nature itself teach you that . . . a woman's long hair is her pride? For her hair is given her as a covering' (vv. 14–15). In Paul's view there is no difference between the unveiled head of a woman and the shaven head of a woman; and the latter is an unnatural condition. This is not much different from saying that the unveiled head of a woman is like a bodily defect. Hence *dia tous angelous* should be understood in the sense of 'out of reverence for the angels', who are present in such sacred gatherings and who should not look on such a condition.

Though this evidence from Qumran has not solved the problem of *exousia*, it has, I believe, made the interpretation of *dia tous angelous* as 'fallen angels' far less plausible, and consequently the interpretation of *exousia* as a magical power loses much of its force.

One last remark. It may be asked whether it is valid to cite evidence from the Qumran texts to interpret a passage in the

[42] This is the common interpretation of the situation in this passage; see Allo's remarks (*op. cit.*, 257) against Bachmann's understanding of the context.

[43] On *qhl* and *ekklēsia* see Kittel's *TDNT* 3, 524–6.

epistles to the Corinthians. These letters have always been looked upon as the special preserve of those who would point out 'Hellenisms' in Paul's thought or language. Influence from the Greek world on the Apostle's writings cannot be denied, given his background as a Jew of the Diaspora and his vocation as the missionary to the Gentiles. It is to be expected that the Epistles to the Corinthians will continue to be better understood as our knowledge of their Hellenistic background increases. But Paul was a Jew and his chief education was rabbinical, based on a thorough study of the Old Testament and saturated with the ideas of contemporaneous Judaism. Hence it is not surprising that some of the background should appear even in the most Greek of his letters.[44]

No one knows *how* the theological ideas of the Qumran sect influenced Paul. That they *did* so is beyond doubt. J. Coppens, in an early article on the relation of the Qumran scrolls to the New Testament, stated that the influence of the sect was more apparent in the later writings of Paul than in the 'great epistles'.[45] As the Qumran texts continue to be published, one sees this influence appearing abundantly throughout Paul's letters. Consequently, if my suggestion that *dia tous angelous* of 1 Cor 11:10 is to be explained in terms of Qumran angelology were an isolated case of such influence in the Epistles to the Corinthians, I might suspect its validity. But a glance at the list of rapprochements between Qumran and the New Testament writings recently published by R. E. Murphy[46] will show that it is not alone. And that list is far from complete, as its author admits. Consequently, one should not be surprised to find a

[44] In the same vein writes S. Lyonnet ('L'étude du milieu littéraire et l'exégèse du Nouveau Testament', *Bib* 37 [1956] 1–3), apropos of the results of J. Dupont's researches into Pauline gnosis.

[45] 'Les documents du Désert de Juda et les origines du Christianisme', *ALBO* ser. 2, no. 41 (1953) 26.

[46] 'The Dead Sea Scrolls and New Testament Comparisons', *CBQ* 18 (1956) 263–72.

detail of Qumran angelology shedding light on a passage of the Pauline Letters which is otherwise heavily 'Hellenistic'.

Postscript (1957)

After my arrival in Jerusalem I found that there were two other passages in the Qumran Cave 4 material that supported the interpretation set forth in this article. One is in an unpublished fragment of the Damascus Document (provisional abbreviation $4QD^b$). A translation of it appears in J. T. Milik, *Ten Years of Discovery in the Wilderness of Judea*, London, 1959, 114: 'Fools, madmen (*mšwgʿ*), simpletons and imbeciles (*mšwgh*), the blind, the maimed (*ḥgr*), the lame, the deaf, and minors, none of these may enter the midst of the community, for the holy angels [are in the midst of it].' The second passage was pointed out to me by Dr Claus-Hunno Hunzinger, who has found it in a Cave 4 fragment of the *Milḥamah*, which he is preparing for publication ($4QM^a$). Enough of the context has been preserved to show that bodily defects were to be excluded from the presence of the angels. In the immediately preceding lacuna reference was most probably made to a nocturnal pollution. The text reads: [*ly*]*lh hh'wh l*[*w' yṣ*]*' 'tmh l*[*mlḥ*]*mh ky' ml'ky qwdš bmʿrkwtmh* ('for the holy angels are among their battle-lines'). In all of these passages the force of *ky'* should not be overlooked; it gives the reason for the exclusion of the defects in the camps, the battle-lines and the assemblies. It parallels the Pauline use of *dia*.

Postscript (1966)

The interpretation of 1 Cor 11:10 which I have proposed in the above article finds support in the independent study of H. J. Cadbury, 'A Qumran Parallel to Paul', *HTR* 51 (1958) 1–2. It has been favourably adopted by K. H. Schelkle, *Die Gemeinde von Qumran und die Kirche des Neuen Testaments* (Patmos: Düsseldorf, 1960) 82.

Criticism of my interpretation can be found in J. Héring, *The*

First Epistle of Saint Paul to the Corinthians (tr. A. W. Heathcote and P. J. Allcock; London: Epworth, 1962) 108; H. Braun, 'Qumran und das Neue Testament: Ein Bericht über 10 Jahre Forschung (1950–59)', *TRu* 29/3 (1963) 213–14; J. C. Hurd, Jr., *The Origin of 1 Corinthians* (New York: Seabury, 1965) 184, n. 4.

Both Braun and Hurd have noted my omission of a reference to Col 2:18 in the discussion of the Pauline use of *hoi angeloi*. It should certainly have been included in footnote 34. But I am not sure that they are right in saying that the omitted reference militates against my thesis at that point. Is it certain that the angels mentioned in Col 2:18 are 'fallen' or 'bad' angels? It seems to me that the argument in Colossians (whether this is genuinely Pauline or not) does not depend on whether the angels are good or bad. The 'worship of angels' (Col 2:18) is apparently to be understood in terms of the other references to spirits in that letter, i.e. to those beings, good or bad, whom certain Christians in the Colossian church were venerating and whose cult was jeopardizing the cosmic role of Christ. The author's opposition to this cult is just as intelligible if the angels be good or bad.

Braun further criticizes the interpretation of both Cadbury and myself, maintaining that its main point is forced, viz. that the uncovered or shorn head of a woman is comparable to a bodily defect. I probably would never have made such a comparison personally, nor have I found any ancient data to support it. But it should not be overlooked that it is Paul who (at least implicitly) suggests this comparison. He equates the unveiled head of a woman with the shaven or shorn head (1 Cor 11:5–6); again it is Paul who regards such a condition as disgraceful (*aischron*). Is his attitude toward the uncovered head of the woman so radically different from that of the Qumran author who would exclude bodily defects from the sight of the angels?

Lastly, Braun asserts that 'the magically protective effect of a headcovering *is* attested in b. Shabbat 156b' (p. 214 [his italics]). He refers to W. G. Kümmel's revision of Lietzmann's commentary on 1 Cor (HNT 9 [1949] 184). When, however, one checks this reference, one sees how far-fetched the parallel is, as far as the Pauline passage is concerned. I shall quote Kümmel's note in Braun's own language: 'In einer späten talmudischen Erzählung (*Schabbat* 156b, s. W. Foerster, *ZNW* 30 (1931) 185 f.) wird ein Rabbi zum Dieb, als ihm das Kopftuch vom Haupt gleitet: da ist das Kopftuch deutlich ein magischer Schutz gegen den "bösen Trieb" (die Stelle kann unmöglich auf die Kopfbedeckung als "Unterordnung unter Gott" gedeutet werden, so W. Foerster, *TWNT*, vol. II, p.571, Anm. 72). Damit ist, wenn nicht die apotropäische, so doch die magisch beschützende Wirkung einer Kopfbedeckung deutlich belegt.'—But is the head-covering which protected the rabbi against his 'evil impulse' to steal really a parallel to Paul's 'veil' on a woman's head in a sacred assembly? Is the 'evil impulse' (*yṣryh*) comparable to a bad angel? Finally, is this 'late Talmudic narrative' of the Babylonian tractate *Shabbat* (156b; ed. Goldschmidt, 1. 717) a tale that might have been known to Paul? After all, it is told of R. Naḥman bar Isaac who belonged to the fourth generation of Babylonian Amoraim and died *c.* A.D. 356 (see H. L. Strack, *Introduction to the Talmud and Midrash* [Philadelphia: Jewish Publication Society of America, 1931] 130). In short, none of the above mentioned points of criticism seems to be serious enough to invalidate the interpretation.

Hurd speaks of the Qumran parallels as being 'rather distant'. I am fully aware of this difficulty and know no more to say about it than what has already been said on pp. 200–2 above. But until a better solution to this *crux interpretum* comes along, the Qumran parallel seems to shed most light on the problem. For a recent discussion of the passage which makes no reference to Qumran or my interpretation, see M. D. Hooker, 'Authority on Her Head: An Examination of 1 Cor 11:10', *NTS* 10 (1964) 410–16.

10

QUMRAN AND THE INTERPOLATED PARAGRAPH IN 2 COR 6:14–7:1*

That there are contacts between the literature of the Qumran Essene sect and the Pauline corpus is no longer a question of doubt. One may discuss, of course, whether the contacts are direct or indirect, but the general fact is admitted today.[1] There is one passage, however, in the Pauline corpus which has not received the detailed attention it deserves in view of the large number of contacts which it contains and the bearing which they have on its nature. This is the puzzling passage in the Second Epistle to the Corinthians 6:14–7:1.

The problem presented by this passage is perhaps best summed up by a quotation from a commentary written in 1915, well before the discovery of the Qumran texts. At that time A. Plummer wrote, 'This strongly worded admonition to make no compromise with heathenism comes in so abruptly here that a

* Originally published in *CBQ* 23 (1961) 271–80.

[1] To admit this is not to subscribe to a form of pan-Qumranism. The word 'contact', however, is deliberately chosen here, and not 'parallel'. Parallels in literature are legion, and there is undoubtedly truth in the remarks of S. Sandmel, 'Parallelomania', *JBL* 81 (1962) 1–13. Again, one often sees quoted E. R. Goodenough's famous dictum about literary parallels: a parallel by definition consists of straight lines in the same plane which never meet, however far produced in any direction. But the definition is derived from mathematics and applied to literature. To repeat the dictum as if it closes the discussion or absolves one from investigating the literary relationship of authors is only a form of obscurantism—something little better than parallelomania or pan-Qumranism. Moreover, it enables one to avoid asking the question when a *literary* parallel might cease to be such and actually prove to be a 'contact'.

number of critics suppose that it is a fragment of another letter and some maintain that the fragment is not by St Paul.'[2] Three main reasons are given for this critical view. First, the paragraph radically interrupts the chain of thought between 6:13 and 7:2. In the preceding context (6:1–13) Paul is making an eloquent plea for his reconciliation with the Corinthian community, appealing to his own past experience and his efforts expended on their behalf. In the immediately preceding verses (11–13) he pleads, 'I have kept nothing back from you, men of Corinth; I have opened my heart to you (*hē kardia hēmōn peplatyntai*). It is not that I am cramping you, it is your own affections. To pay me back, I tell you, my children, you must open your hearts too (*platynthēte kai hymeis*).' Then comes the puzzling paragraph about avoiding relations with unbelievers (6:14–7:1). Finally, Paul resumes his pleas for open-hearted reconciliation in 7:2 with *chōrēsate hēmas*, 'Make room for me in your hearts. I have not wronged or harmed or got the better of anybody.' And the plea continues for two more verses. The second reason is that the passage has a self-contained, independent character, forming a unit intelligible in itself, like a short homily. It is devoid of any concrete details which would suggest that it was dealing with a specifically Corinthian problem. Thirdly, it has been denied Pauline authorship, because six of the key-words in the passage are not found elsewhere in the New Testament, and some of them are *hapax legomena* in the whole Greek Bible. These are *heterozygeō*, *metochē*, *symphōnēsis*, *synkatathesis*, *Beliar*, *molysmos*.[3] These three reasons, together with

[2] *A Critical and Exegetical Commentary on the Second Epistle of St Paul to the Corinthians* (New York: Scribner, 1915) 204. The critics are divided: (a) some regard the passage as a non-Pauline interpolation; (b) others think that it is Pauline, but belongs to some lost letter of the Apostle (perhaps that referred to in 1 Cor 5:9); (c) still others maintain that it is Pauline, but is merely misplaced within 2 Cor, e.g., that it should follow 2 Cor 6:2. A good summary of critical opinion on this question can be found in E.-B. Allo, *Saint Paul: Seconde Épître aux Corinthiens* (EBib; Paris: Gabalda, 1937) 189–93.

[3] Some critics add to this list the rare words *emperipatēsō* and *eisdexomai*,

a few subsidiary considerations, have been well presented in a careful scrutiny of the usual attempts to defend the authenticity of the passage[4] and its nexus in the letter by the Dutch Catholic scholar W. Grossouw.[5] Without appealing to the Qumran contacts, he concluded to the non-Pauline character of the passage.

It was apparently K. G. Kuhn who first noted the relationship between this paragraph and the Qumran writings and pointed out in a footnote that this passage, more than any other text in Paul's letters, contains 'des affinités de terminologie frappantes avec les textes des Esséniens'.[6] He concluded that 'Paul is perhaps citing here precisely an Essene text.' However, the evidence of these Qumran contacts has not been examined in detail. This I propose to do and to attempt to come to some conclusion about the bearing of them on the nature of this passage in 2 Cor.

First of all, I cite the passage (2 Cor 6:14–7:1) for the convenience of the reader.

Do not be misyoked with unbelievers. What partnership can uprightness have with iniquity? Or what fellowship can light have with darkness? What harmony can there be between Christ and Beliar? Or what part can a believer have with an unbeliever? What agree-

---

which never appear otherwise in the New Testament, and *pantokratōr* which otherwise occurs only in the Apocalypse. But these three words are found here in citations from the Old Testament and may not be used with the same validity as criteria.

[4] Attempts to explain the nexus between the preceding context and the paragraph either by internal analysis of them or by an appeal to Pauline anacolutha (which are claimed to be more numerous in 2 Cor than in other Pauline letters) have been more marked by rhetoric than success. See A. Plummer, *op. cit.*, 205; E.-B. Allo, *op. cit.*, 185–6; C. Spicq, *Épîtres aux Corinthiens* (La Sainte Bible [de Pirot-Clamer] 11/2; Paris: Letouzey et Ané, 1948) 348; A. Menzies, *The Second Epistle of the Apostle Paul to the Corinthians* (London: Macmillan, 1912) 50. (The latter is a good example of the forced attempt to explain the nexus by an analysis of the preceding context and the passage itself.)

[5] 'Over de echtheid van 2 Cor 6:14–7:1', *StudCath* 26 (1951) 203–6.

[6] *RB* 61 (1954) 203, n. 1; see also *ET* 11 (1951) 74; F.-M. Braun, 'L'arrière-fond judaïque du quatrième évangile et la communauté de l'Alliance', *RB* 62 (1955) 33–4.

ment has the temple of God with idols? For we are the temple of the living God; as God has said,
'I shall dwell among them and move about among them,
and I shall be their God and they will be my people.'
(Lv 26:12; Ez 37:27)
Therefore, 'come forth from them, (Is 52:11)
and separate from them, says the Lord,
and touch nothing that is unclean';
then 'I shall welcome you.' (Ez 20:34)
And 'I shall become a father to you, (2 Sm 7:14)
and you will be my sons and daughters,
says the Lord Almighty.'
Since we have such promises, dear friends, let us purify ourselves from all that can taint body and spirit, and let us perfect our holiness in the fear of God.

The elements in this passage which suggest Qumran contacts or the reworking of Qumran ideas are the following: (*a*) the triple dualism of uprightness and iniquity, light and darkness, Christ and Beliar (together with the underlying notion of the 'lot'); (*b*) the opposition to idols; (*c*) the concept of the temple of God; (*d*) the separation from impurity; (*e*) the concatenation of Old Testament texts. Each of these elements is known to have a significant Qumran background which is the basis of our discussion.

(*a*) *The triple dualism*. The purpose of the contrast brought out by the triple dualistic expressions is to divide mankind into two classes, those who follow Christ and those who do not. A similar division of mankind, by now well known, is expressed in many ways in the Qumran literature, but most significantly by the expressions 'sons of light' and 'sons of darkness'. Though the expression 'sons of light' does not occur here, Paul does employ the Greek equivalent of it elsewhere.[7] But the contrast of

[7] The expression 'sons of darkness' does not appear in the New Testament, but 'sons of light' occurs in 1 Thes 5:5 and Eph 5:8 (and outside the Pauline corpus in Jn 12:36 and Lk 16:8). Moreover, the fuller context of 1 Thes 5:4–8 and Eph 5:8–13 exploits the contrast of light and darkness in ways reminiscent of several Qumran passages. See also Rom 13:12–13.

light and darkness in *tís koinōnia phōti pros skotos*[8] in a context of mixing believers with unbelievers is merely another way of saying 'sons of light' and 'sons of darkness'. Pertinent to our discussion here is the well-known passage of the *Manual of Discipline*, 'to love all the sons of light, each according to his lot in God's counsel, and to hate all the sons of darkness, each according to his guilt in God's vengeance' (1QS 1:9–11). Again, 'may he be cut out of the midst of the sons of light because he swerved from following God for the sake of his idols and of that which casts him into iniquity' (1QS 2:16–17).[9] See further 1QS 3:3, 13, 19–20, 24–25; 1QM 1:1, 3, 9, 11, 13; 13: 5–6, 9, 15–16; 1QH 12:6; 4QFlor 1:9. While the opposition of light and darkness is not only a natural one, and one found as a symbolic representation of the forces of good and evil in many literatures, among which we may mention the Old Testament itself (Is 45:7; Mi 7:8; Jb 29:3), it is to be noted that the figure is found neither in the Old Testament nor in Rabbinical literature as a means of expressing two great classes of mankind.[10] In this Corinthian passage mankind is divided according to light and darkness just like the 'sons of light' and the 'sons of darkness' in the Qumran literature.

Several nouns occur in this passage as expressions for the general idea of association with one or other of these classes of mankind: *metochē*, *koinōnia*, *symphōnēsis*, *meris*. It is especially the last one which indirectly suggests that the Qumran notion of

[8] The expression *koinōnia pros* is peculiar; it is found also in Sir 13:2 where it can be explained as reflecting the Hebrew original *ytḥbr 'l* (the preposition *'el*). H. Windisch (*Der zweite Korintherbrief* [Meyer-Kommentar 6; 9th ed.; Göttingen: Vandenhoeck und Ruprecht, 1924]) also suggests a Semitism as the reason for it. If it really is such, then this point of syntax would be an additional support to our thesis.

[9] Note also the proximity of two other ideas in this text which are found in the Corinthian passage under discussion, 'idols' and 'iniquity'.

[10] G. Graystone ('The Dead Sea Scrolls and the New Testament', *ITQ* 23 [1956] 33; *The Dead Sea Scrolls and the Originality of Christ* [New York: Sheed and Ward, 1956] 71–2) tried to minimize the importance of the Qumran phrase 'sons of light' by maintaining that even if it did not occur

'lot' likewise underlies this passage. This will be clarified by referring to a passage in Col 1:12, another Pauline verse which has likewise been shown to have been influenced by Qumran ideas: *eis tēn merida tou klērou tōn hagiōn en tō phōti*, 'to share the lot of the saints in light'. Here we find the noun *meris* explicitly associated with *klēros* in a context of light, and perhaps because of this association K. G. Kuhn was inclined to equate *meris* in 2 Cor 6:15 with the Hebrew word used at Qumran for 'lot', viz. *gôrāl*.[11] However, it is significant that *meris* in the Septuagint never translates *gôrāl*, whereas *klēros* quite frequently does.[12] However, even in the Septuagint these words are related, as passages like Dt 10:9; Jer 13:25 and Wis 2:9 show. When we recall that the members of the Essene community regarded themselves not only as the 'sons of light', but also as the 'lot of light' (*gôral 'ôr*; see 1QM 13:9, 5–6; CD 13:12;[13] 4QIs[d] 13:12) and the 'lot of God' (*gôral 'El*; see 1QS 2:2; 1QM 1:5, 15; 13:5; 15:1; 17:7), it is difficult to escape the

---

in the Old Testament, it is almost a natural Hebraism, using the frequent 'sons of. . . .'. A natural Hebrew idiom, indeed, but the significant fact remains that the expression had not been found outside of the New Testament before the discovery of the Qumran Scrolls. It is, moreover, paralleled only there. See further my remarks above, pp. 167-8, n. 10.

[11] *RB* 61 (1954) 203, n. 2.

[12] Cf. E. Hatch and H. A. Redpath, *A Concordance to the Septuagint and the Other Greek Versions of the Old Testament (Including the Apocryphal Books)* (Graz: Akademische Druck- und Verlagsanstalt, 1954) 2, 911 (*meris*), 770 (*klēros*). O. Procksch has maintained that *klēros* is the usual rendering of the Hebrew *naḥ^a^lāh*, 'inheritance', in the Old Testament (see the article '*klēros*' in Kittel, *TWNT* 1, 108). As a matter of fact, it occurs 48 times as the equivalent of *naḥ^a^lāh* over against 62 times as the translation of *gôrāl*. The Pauline usage may well reflect the meaning 'inheritance' at times, but when the Colossian passage is compared with such a Qumran passage as 1QS 11:7–8, 'To those whom God has chosen . . ., he has given a share in the lot of the saints (*wynḥylm bgwrl qdwšym*)', the later Qumran nuance of *gôrāl* as 'lot' or 'party' seems to be more appropriate in the Colossian passage.

[13] In the light of the other passages where this expression occurs it seems preferable to read *h'*[*wr*] here instead of C. Rabin's *h'*[*mt*]; see *The Zadokite Documents* (Oxford: Clarendon, 1954) 67.

conclusion that this notion underlies the division of mankind described in this passage in Corinthians.

The dominantly ethical character of the cosmic dualism of Qumran[14] is manifest in the contrast of uprightness and iniquity which is often associated with that of light and darkness. This we find also in the 2 Cor passage, where the two pairs are juxtaposed. It is interesting to compare with this the following Qumran texts: 'All iniquity and [wick]edness you will destroy forever and your uprightness will be manifested to the sight of all whom you have made' (1QH 14:16). Again, 'Then iniquity shall depart before uprightness, as darkness departs before the light' (1Q27 1 i 5–6). Here the two pairs are linked. See further CD 20:20–21.

The last couple in the Pauline text is Christ and Beliar. Christ, of course, does not appear in the Qumran texts, and his appearance in the 2 Cor passage is clear proof of the Christian *reworking* of the Qumran material. But Belial frequently is opposed to God as the leader of the hostile lot.[15] At the end of the eschatological war described in the *War Scroll* the priests, levites and all the elders of the community 'shall bless in their places the God of Israel and all his faithful works and the indignation which he has directed against Belial and all the spirits of his lot. And they shall answer and say, "Blessed be the God of Israel . . ., but cursed be Belial with his hostile purpose . . .!"' (1QM 13:1–4). Here we find Belial set over against the God of Israel, just as he is pitted against Christ in the Corinthian text. Belial, as a demon or personified force, occurs further in 1QS 1:18, 24; 2:19, 5 ('all the men of Belial's lot'); 10:21 (?); 1QM 1:1, 5, 13; 4:2; 11:8; 13:[2], 4, 11; 14:9; 15:3; 18:1, 3; 1QH 6:21;

[14] See G. Mensching, 'Dualismus. I. Religionsgeschichtlich', *RGG*³ 2 (1958) 272–4; G. Gloege, 'Dualismus. II. Theologisch', *ibid.*, 274–6.

[15] Beliar, the New Testament form of the name, is merely the result of a late dissimilation of the liquid consonants and is actually identical with the name Belial. The name can now be safely interpreted as the name of a demon opposed to God on the basis of the Qumran parallels and the suggestion of some commentators that it refers to Anti-Christ (e.g., H. Lietz-

1Q40 9:3 (?); 4QFlor 1:8 bis, 9; 2:2; 4QTest 23 (?); 4QM[a] 6.[16] The Hebrew word *b^e^lîya'al* occurs in the Old Testament as a common noun, meaning 'worthlessness, evil, perversion', as it does often also in the Qumran *Hôdāyôt*. There is, further, the expression, *'yš bly'l* or *bny bly'l*, 'an evil man', 'evil men'. This is undoubtedly the root of the Qumran expression, but Belial as the proper name of a demon is otherwise unknown in the Old Testament.[17] Before the discovery of the Qumran texts this usage was known only in this unique New Testament passage and in several Jewish intertestamental compositions, such as *Jubilees* (1:20; 15:33 [?]), the *Testaments of the Twelve Patriarchs* (Reuben 4:11; 6:3 [?]; Simeon 5:3 [explicit contrast of God and Beliar]; Levi 19:1 [where light and darkness are coupled with the Lord and Beliar]; Dn 1:7 [?]; 4:7; 5:1; Naphtali 2:6; 3:1), the *Ascension of Isaiah* (3:11) and the *Damascus Document* (4:13, 15; 5:18; 8:2; 12:2 [?]; 19:14). But several of these works were favourites with the Essenes of Qumran, often copied by them, if not actually composed by them.[18] It is,

---

mann, *An die Korinther, I–II* [Handbuch zum Neuen Testament 9; 4th ed.; Tübingen: Mohr, 1949] 129) can be dismissed. See further W. Foerster, '*Beliar*', *TDNT* 1,607.

[16] Cf. H. W. Huppenbauer, 'Belial in den Qumrantexten', *TZ* 15 (1959) 81–9.

[17] C. Spicq (*op. cit.*, 348) considers it possible that this meaning may occur in 2 Sm 22:5 and Ps 18:5, 'comme Dieu de la mort et du monde souterrain'. Similarly W. Foerster, *op. cit.* This is, however, most unlikely since the word *bly'l* in each case stands in parallelism with *mawet* ('death') and *š^e'ôl* ('Hades'), which supports the abstract meaning given by the dictionaries, 'rivers of destruction'. However, cf. P. Joüon, '*b^elîya'al* Bélial', *Bib* 5 (1924) 178–83.

[18] Five fragmentary MSS. of *Jubilees* have come to light in Qumran Cave IV alone. The same cave has yielded an Aramaic text of the *Testament of Levi* and a Hebrew text of the *Testament of Naphtali*. Even though the latter two are not exactly the same as the Greek version known to us in the *Testaments of the Twelve Patriarchs*, they probably served as the sources of the latter (see J. T. Milik, *Ten Years of Discovery in the Wilderness of Judaea* [SBT 26; London: SCM, 1959] 34–5). Moreover, the *Damascus Document* has turned up in eight fragmentary copies from Cave 4 and one from Cave 6 (see *RB* 63 [1956] 55, 60–1, 407, n. 1; 62 [1955] 398–406).

therefore, significant that the unique occurrence of Beliar in the New Testament should be in this otherwise puzzling paragraph which manifests so many contacts with the Qumran literature. Considering the triple contrast of light and darkness, uprightness and iniquity, Christ and Beliar, it is difficult to deny the reworking of Qumran expressions and ideas.[19]

(*b*) *Opposition to idols*. Following the triple dualistic contrast is the question, 'What agreement has the temple of God with idols?' This question reflects the same attitude found in the Qumran text already cited, 'May he be cut off from the midst of the sons of light because he has swerved from following God for the sake of his idols and of that which casts him into iniquity' (1QS 2:16–17). We do not find here the explicit contrast of idols with the temple of God in the Qumran text, but both elements are frequent in this literature, opposition to idols and the temple of God. This suggests a common conceptual background; see further 1QS 2:11, 17; 4:5; 1QH 4:19; CD 20:9; *T. Reuben* 4:6.

(*c*) *The temple of God*. The contrast of idols with the temple of God leads to the assertion, 'For we are the temple of the living God.' This assertion introduces an idea into the sixth

[19] Another possible contact which may strengthen the evidence thus far adduced is found in the use of *heterozygeō*. This verb obviously reflects the prohibition of Dt 22:10, forbidding a man to plough with an ox and an ass yoked together (see also Lv 19:19). The commentators usually refer to these passages to illustrate the incongruity of the association stressed here. It is, moreover, an Old Testament figure to speak of yoking in the sense of believing a teaching, following a doctrine (see Ps 106:28; Nm 25:3). Hence, the basic idea used here is an Old Testament derivative. But it should be noted that the same nuance occurs also in the Qumran *Hôdāyôt*. If it is correct that the person speaking in the first singular is the Righteous Teacher, the founder of the Qumran movement, as many maintain, then he refers to his followers as 'all those who are yoked to my counsel' (*kwl nṣmdy swdy*, 1QH 5:24), and as 'those who are yoked to my testimony' (*nṣmdy t'wdty*, 1QH 6:19). This is obviously a use of 'yoking' in the sense of following a doctrine.

chapter of 2 Cor which is otherwise quite foreign to it. The 'we' must be understood of the believers, the followers of Christ, the men of his lot. As a community they constitute the temple of God. The same theme can be found also in genuine Pauline passages like 1 Cor 3:16–17 and Eph 2:21–22.[20] But the idea of the community as the 'holy of holies' is a notion cherished by the Qumran Essenes. 'At that time the men of the community shall be set apart as a sanctuary for Aaron (*byt qwdš l'hrwn*), being united as the Holy of Holies, and those who walk in perfection as a house of community for Israel (*wbyt yḥd lyśr'l*, 1QS 9:5–7).[21] Again, 'when all these things shall come to pass in Israel, the council of the community shall be established in truth as an eternal planting, a sanctuary (*byt qwdš*) for Israel and a foundation of the Holy of Holies (*wswd qwdš qwdšym*) for Aaron' (1QS 8:4–6; see further 5:6; 8:8–9; 11:8 [*wswd mbnyt qwdš*]; 4QFlor 1:6 [*lbnwt lw' mqdš 'dm lhywt mqṭyrym bw' lw' lpnyw m'śy twrh*]).

[20] The whole context here forbids us to think of the 'temple of God' in terms of the individual Christian, like the figure employed in 1 Cor 6:19 (*pace* H. Lietzmann, *op. cit.*, 129). K. G. Kuhn (*RB* 61 [1954] 203, n. 2) has indicated that the theme of the human body as the temple of God has parallels rather in the Hellenistic world, especially in Philo, whereas the theme of the community-temple has previously lacked parallels in the literature prior to or contemporary with the New Testament. See the bibliographical references cited by him; but also K. Prümm, *Diakonia Pneumatos, der zweite Korintherbrief als Zugang zur apostolischen Botschaft, Auslegung und Theologie* (Rome: Herder) II/1 (1960) 361–4; G. W. MacRae, 'Building the House of the Lord', *AER* 140 (1959) 361–76; J. Pfammatter, *Die Kirche als Bau* (AnalGreg 110; Rome: Gregorian University, 1960). B. Gärtner, *The Temple and the Community in Qumran and the New Testament: A Comparative Study in the Temple Symbolism of the Qumran Texts and the New Testament* (SNTS Monograph Series, 1; Cambridge: University Press, 1965).

[21] 'Holy of Holies' is an expression used for objects consecrated to Yahweh, especially to his service in the temple of Jerusalem or in the desert Tent. For a discussion of its various uses, see S. R. Driver, *The Book of Daniel* (Cambridge Bible for Schools and Colleges; Cambridge: University Press, 1901) 137. When all the evidence is reviewed, it is seen to be an expression reserved either for the temple or some part of it, and often for the inner-

(*d*) *Separation from all impurity*. It would be surprising in a text which already reveals so many contacts with the Qumran literature, if we did not find some reference to its ideas on purity and defilement. Avoidance of ritual defilement was a major preoccupation of the Essenes and affected many aspects of their way of life. They were expected to 'make a distinction between the clean and the unclean' (CD 6:17), 'not to let their property be mixed with the property of men of deceit who have not purified their conduct by separating from iniquity and by walking with perfect conduct' (1QS 9:8–9). Again, 'let him not come to the water to share in the purification of holy men—for they will not be cleansed, unless they have turned from their wickedness—for he is impure among all those who transgress his word' (1QS 5:13–14). The abhorrence of all unclean idols (*glwly ndh*, 1QS 4:5) was prescribed. Moreover, the regulations for ritual purity among the Essenes were numerous (see 1QS 4:10; CD 7:3; 9:21; 10:10 ff.; 11:19 ff.; 12:19; 1QM 13:5). In the light of such prescriptions the counsel in 2 Cor, to 'cleanse ourselves from everything that can taint body and spirit' in an effort toward perfect holiness, takes on new meaning. It resembles strongly the general Qumran proscription of all contact with outsiders.

(*e*) *Concatenation of Old Testament texts*. The last point of contact to be noted in this passage is the series of Old Testament quotations strung together in the manner of *Testimonia*. We have, first of all, a conflated quotation of Lv 26:12 and Ez 37:27, then an inverted quotation of Is 52:11, followed by part of Ez 20:34 and finally 2 Sm 7:14. The unifying thread running through all the citations is the theme of God's chosen people, 'God's lot', to use the Qumran expression. Collections of Old Testament texts grouped about a certain theme occur elsewhere in Paul's letters and the question has often been

---

most sanctuary. It is therefore a most apt expression for the idea of an object (or a community) withdrawn from profane use and dedicated to God.

raised whether Paul constructed them himself or made use of already existing *testimonia.* The main argument for denying that Paul made use of previously existing *testimonia* has been that there was no evidence for the existence of such lists prior to the patristic writers. But we now have a *testimonia* document from Qumran Cave 4, which groups various texts from the Old Testament.[22] I have discussed the pertinence of this document for the New Testament elsewhere in detail.[23] We need note here only that the early appearance of such a literary form at Qumran does not prove that Paul used already existing *testimonia*; but the likelihood is increased now that a pre-Christian example of it has turned up. Once again the discovery of such a form precisely at Qumran yields another point of contact between it and the 2 Cor passage.[24] Finally, it should be noted that the introductory formula, *kathōs eipen ho theos hoti* . . ., which occurs only here in the New Testament, has its Qumran counterpart in CD 6:13; 8:9 (*'šr 'mr 'l*),[25] but is found neither in the Old Testament nor the Mishnah.

Having examined the five points of contact between this passage and the Qumran literature, we may conclude. Not all the points in this comparison are of equal importance or value, but the cumulative effect of so many of them within such a short passage is the telling factor. We are faced with a paragraph in

[22] See J. M. Allegro, 'Further Messianic References in Qumrân Literature', *JBL* 75 (1956) 182–7, Document IV.

[23] '"4QTestimonia" and the New Testament', pp.59–89 above.

[24] One of the Old Testament passages cited here, 2 Sm 7:14, is used in a Qumran text which at first sight seemed to be related to the *testimonia* form, a text provisionally labelled '4QFlorilegium'. However, further investigation of the text has shown that 'florilegium' is a misnomer for the *genre* employed there, for it is actually 'a more complex type of *pesher*—one that employs additional biblical material [i.e., isolated explicit quotations from other Old Testament books] to expound the biblical passage under consideration' (W. R. Lane, 'A New Commentary Structure in 4Q Florilegium', *JBL* 78 [1959] 343–6). See further pp. 7, 81–2 above.

[25] See my article, 'The Use of Explicit Old Testament Quotations in Qumran Literature and in the New Testament', pp. 3–58 above.

which Qumran ideas and expressions have been reworked in a Christian cast of thought. Some of the contacts can be shown to exist also in genuinely Pauline passages, e.g., the temple of God, the idea of the 'lot', the *testimonia*-form. But when the total Qumran influence is considered along with the other reasons (the interrupted sequence of the surrounding context, the self-contained unit and the strange vocabulary), the evidence seems to total up to the admission of a Christian reworking of an Essene paragraph which has been introduced into the Pauline letter. The problem of how it got there remains unsolved, for 'there is no evidence in MS., or version, or quotation, that any copy of the Epistle ever lacked this passage'.[26] At any rate, this solution seems preferable to those which are content with merely writing the passage off as a digression or just another case of Pauline anacoluthon due to his practice of dictation. It certainly is not a case of anacoluthon, for the grammar is intact. To label the passage as a digression or as a Pauline 'quotation' of an Essene paragraph (as did K. G. Kuhn) is no solution, for the problem still remains, why did he digress *here* with a heavily Qumran passage? Hence, I believe that it is preferable to regard the passage as a non-Pauline interpolation.[27]

[26] A. Plummer, *op. cit.*, 205

[27] See further J. Gnilka, '2 Cor 6:14–7:1 in the Light of the Qumran Texts and the Testaments of the Twelve Patriarchs', *Paul and Qumran: Studies in New Testament Exegesis* (ed. J. Murphy-O'Connor; London: Chapman, 1968) 48–68.

IV

THE EPISTLE TO THE HEBREWS

11

'NOW THIS MELCHIZEDEK . . .' (HEB 7:1)*

To show the superiority of Christ's priesthood over that of Aaron and the levites, the author of the epistle to the Hebrews introduces a comparison between Jesus and Melchizedek. The comparison is briefly stated in Heb 5:6–10 for the first time, but at the end of the following hortatory section the author returns to the Melchizedek theme and affirms that Christian hope is like an anchor firmly rooted in the heavenly sanctuary where Christ has gone on ahead of us, 'forever a high priest according to the order of Melchizedek' (6:20). There follows in chapter 7 an extended discussion of Christ and Melchizedek, which C. Spicq has called the 'culminating point of the epistle's argument'.[1] Whether this view of chapter 7 is correct or not, much has been written on Melchizedek and his relation to Heb. It is our purpose here to sift from the recent studies those elements which seem pertinent to his appearance in Heb and relate to them some new data bearing on the Melchizedek tradition which have come to light in the Qumran literature and in the newly discovered Vatican codex of the Palestinian Targum Neofiti I.

Before turning to the new data, I must stress with several modern writers[2] that the detailed comparison of Christ and

* Originally published in *CBQ* 25 (1963) 305–21.

[1] *L'épître aux Hébreux* (EBib; 3d ed., Paris) 2,203.

[2] See R. Bloch, 'Midrash', *VDBS* 5, 1279; H. Rusche, 'Die Gestalt des Melchisedek', *MTZ* 6 (1955) 230–52. This is certainly a more valid analysis

Melchizedek in Heb 7 is an excellent example of a midrash on Gn 14:18–20. Introducing his implicit quotation of Gn by *houtos gar ho Melchisedek*, the author of Heb first gives a brief résumé in vv. 1–2 and afterwards takes up various elements of it for comment. Thus in this section of Heb are verified the five characteristics of midrash, pointed out by R. Bloch,[3] viz., its *point de départ* in an OT passage (Gn 14:18–20 implicitly quoted), its homiletic character (here for apologetic purposes), its attentive analysis of the text (the interpretation of the names and explanation of the blessing and tithes), its adaptation of the OT text to a present situation (the priesthood of Christ), and its haggadic character (an elaborative exposé in which the interest is centred on the biblical account rather than on the historical figure as such). Even in its outward form this section bears resemblance to a classic midrash in *Genesis Rabbah* 43:6.[4] Moreover, the manner in which Heb introduces into the midrash on Gn 14 phrases from Ps 110 (see Heb 7:11, 15, 17, 21, 28) is strikingly similar to the technique of the so-called 4QFlorilegium,[5] a Qumran text which bears the name *midrāš* as part of an opening formula.[6] The latter text is really a commentary on 2 Sm 7:10–14, followed by one on Ps 1:1 and Ps 2:1; but into the commentary on these passages other OT passages have been introduced (Ex 15:17–18 and Am 9:11 into the part on 2 Sm; Is 8:11 and Ez 37:23 into that on Ps

---

of Heb 7 than Spicq's view that the entire chapter 7 is nothing more than an exegesis of Ps 110:4 (*op. cit.*, 205).

[3] *Op. cit.*, 1265–7.

[4] See H. Freedman, *Genesis* (Midrash Rabbah 1; London, 1951) I, 355 ff. A. G. Wright, 'The Literary Genre Midrash (Part Two)', *CBQ* 28(1966) 437, classes this passage among 'small midrashic units' in the New Testament, which are built on implicit citations of the Old Testament.

[5] See J. M. Allegro, 'Fragments of a Qumran Scroll of Eschatological *Midrāšîm*', *JBL* 77 (1958) 350–4. Cf. my comments on this text above, pp. 7, 81–2.

[6] *Ibid.*, 353 (I, 14). Cf. W. R. Lane, 'A New Commentary Structure in 4Q Florilegium', *JBL* 78 (1959) 343–6; Y. Yadin, 'A Midrash on 2 Sam. vii and Ps. i–ii (4Q Florilegium)', *IEJ* 9 (1959) 95–8.

1:1). The only difference is that the OT texts are here introduced by explicit formulae, whereas they are not in Heb.[7] But the midrashic technique is basically the same. Further, Helga Rusche has recently shown that the treatment of Melchizedek in Heb is not characterized by the extreme allegorical speculations found in Philo, Josephus, several Gnostic writers and the Rabbis.[8] The theological conception used is related much more to controllable Jewish apocalyptic writers with their expectations of a messianic priesthood rooted in Gn 14. Since the two intertestamental writings in which she finds the relevant material are *Jubilees* and the *Testaments of the Twelve Patriarchs*—texts with known connections with the Qumran literature—another point of comparative interest is thus established between Qumran and Heb.[9]

Ps 110:4

Before we take up the use of Gn 14 in Heb, a few preliminary remarks are in order about the author's use of Ps 110. Heb first cites it in 1:13 and uses it again in 5:5–10, to set up the comparison of Jesus and Aaron. The role of high priest was not usurped in either case, but bestowed by divine appointment. This idea forms part of the development of Heb at this point, where Jesus is shown to have all the qualities of the 'perfected' (or 'qualified') high priest. In proof, the author cites Ps 2:7, 'You are my son; this day I have begotten you', and joins to it Ps 110:4, 'The Lord has sworn and will not go back on his

[7] See my essay, 'The Use of Explicit Old Testament Quotations in Qumran Literature and in the New Testament', pp. 3–58 above.

[8] *Op. cit.*, 238–44.

[9] Y. Yadin, 'The Dead Sea Scrolls and the Epistle to the Hebrews', *Aspects of the Dead Sea Scrolls* (Scripta hierosolymitana 4; Jerusalem, 1958) 36–55; C. Spicq, 'L'épître aux Hébreux, Apollos, Jean-Baptiste, les Hellénistes et Qumran', *RQ* 1 (1958–59) 365–90; H. Kosmala, *Hebräer—Essener—Christen. Studien zur Vorgeschichte der frühchristlichen Verkündigung* (SPB 1; Leiden, 1959). F. F. Bruce, '"To the Hebrews" or "To the Essenes"?', *NTS* 9 (1962–63) 217–32; J. Coppens, 'Les affinités qumrâniennes de l'Epître aux Hébreux', *NRT* 84 (1962) 128–41, 257–82 (=ALBO 4/1).

word: "You are a priest forever according to the order of Melchizedek".' As Dom J. Dupont, and more recently a young Swedish scholar, E. Lövestam, have pointed out,[10] all the clear instances of the use of Ps 2:7 in the NT relate it to the Resurrection. As of the time of his resurrection Christ became a 'son of God' in a special sense (in the understanding of the early kerygma reflected here)—God's son endowed with universal and everlasting *royal dominion* (cf. Rom 1:4).[11] To this notion derived from Ps 2:7, Heb now links another from Ps 110:4: God's appointment of the risen royal Son as the possessor of the eternal *priesthood* of Melchizedek.

Though the messianic character of Ps 110 is debated among OT commentators,[12] there is rather general agreement that it is at least a royal psalm, one in which some Davidic king is addressed as the hero[13] and associated with the past as the successor of Melchizedek. Like Ps 2, it echoes the dynastic covenant established in the oracle of Nathan (2 Sm 7:8–16). But the psalmist thinks of the reigning Israelite king, 'not . . . as a simple historical figure, but as a religious figure who incorporates in himself the kingdom of Israel and its hope for a future in which the kingship of Yahweh will become universally effective. In this sense the Ps is messianic since it repeats the

[10] J. Dupont, 'Filius meus es tu', *RSR* 35 (1948) 522–43; E. Lövestam, *Son and Saviour: a Study of Acts 13,32–37* (*ConNeot* 18; Lund, 1961) 15–37; E. Käsemann, *Das wandernde Gottesvolk* (FRLANT 37, Göttingen, 1939) 58–9; R. H. Fuller, *The Mission and Achievement of Jesus* (SBT 12; London, 1954) 87.

[11] See E. Lövestam, *op. cit.*, 37.

[12] See the summary by J. L. McKenzie, 'Royal Messianism', *CBQ* 19 (1957) 25–52, esp. 34–6 (reprinted in *Myths and Realities* [Milwaukee-London, 1963] 203–31).

[13] The opinion of H. H. Rowley, 'Melchizedek and Zadok (Gen 14 and Ps 110)', *Festschrift für Alfred Bertholet* (Tübingen, 1950) 461–72, according to which David addresses Zadok in v. 4, does not seem to have convinced many; see V. Hamp, 'Melchisedech als Typus', *Pro Mundi Vita: Festschrift zum eucharistischen Weltkongress 1960* (München, 1960) 16–17; J. W. Bowker, 'Psalm CX', *VT* 17 (1967) 31–41; H. H. Rowley, 'Melchizedek and David', *VT* 17 (1967) 485.

messianic outlook of the dynasty of David.'[14] It has been maintained that v. 4, in which the Israelite monarch is presented as a king-priest, is a gloss, because it is unique in the OT. However, the excision of it has to be based on something more than a hunch, and the otherwise early date of the Ps points to its composition in the time of David or Solomon,[15] when the connection of the Davidic dynasty with the city of Melchizedek was still fresh and when many of the inhabitants were not Israelites. Ps 110:4 thus presents the king as the heir of Melchizedek, succeeding him as a priest forever.[16]

In Heb 5 the author applies this verse of Ps 110 to Jesus, undoubtedly understanding it as messianic (although he does not expressly state this link).[17] Having first introduced Ps 2:7 to establish the risen Jesus as the possessor of *regal* inheritance, he adds Ps 110:4 to present this Kingly Son of God as one appointed also to an *eternal priesthood.*

Whatever the puzzling Hebrew phrase *'al dibrātî Malkî-ṣedeq* means, no one has ever suggested that it be understood in terms of hereditary succession. Hence the priesthood of the king is due to something else. The commonly accepted interpretation of the form *'al dibrātî* is that it is an alternative, per-

[14] J. L. McKenzie, *op. cit.*, 35–6. H.-J. Kraus, *Psalmen* (BKAT 15/10; Neukirchen, 1959) 763–4; V. Hamp, *op. cit.*, 18.

[15] Since Gunkel the early date of the Ps in the time of David or Solomon has been widely admitted; see H.-J. Kraus, *op. cit.*, 755; E. R. Hardy, 'The Date of Psalm 110', *JBL* 64 (1945) 385–90; H. G. Jefferson, 'Is Ps 110 Canaanite?', *JBL* 73 (1954) 152–6; H. Schmid. 'Jahwe und die Kulttraditionen von Jerusalem', *ZAW* 67 (1955) 175, n. 42. See further W. E. Brooks, 'The Perpetuity of Christ's Sacrifice in the Epistle to the Hebrews', *JBL* 89 (1970) 205–14.

[16] A. Caquot, 'Remarques sur Psaume CX', *Semitica* 6 (1956) 33–52, rightly stresses the emphasis in the Psalm on the eternal aspect; cf. R. Tournay, 'Le Psaume CX', *RB* 67 (1960) 5–41, esp. 19, n. 2.

[17] It is apparently part of the author's own theology to apply Ps 110:4 to Christ as the messianic priest. No rabbi is attested as having applied Ps 110:4 to the Messiah before the second half of the 3d cent. A.D. See C. Spicq, *op. cit.*, 204, n. 4.

haps older, form of the construct *'al dibrat*.[18] Elsewhere in the OT this phrase means 'for the sake of' (Eccl 3:18; 8:2; 7:14). This causal meaning, however, though defended here by a few scholars,[19] scarcely suits the context of the Ps, and has been avoided both by ancient versions and many modern commentators in favour of a modal sense.[20] The LXX rendered it *kata tēn taxin Melchisedek*, and was followed by Heb 5:6; 6:20; 7:11, 17 and the Vg, *secundum ordinem Melchisedech*. But the Greek word *taxis* is of little help, for neither its basic meaning, 'arrangement, fixed order, succession', nor its Hellenistic meaning, 'office, post' of a priest, nor even the meaning 'character, quality' (apparently used in 2 Mc 9:18), has won any general adherence of scholarly opinion. And yet, there is little doubt of its meaning in Heb, for in 7:15—a verse often strangely omitted in many discussions of the meaning of the Greek or Hebrew phrase—it has been paraphrased by the author, *kata tēn homoiotēta Melchisedek*, 'according to the likeness of Melchizedek'.[21] Does the Peshitta reflect this in Ps 110:4 or preserve its own ancient interpretation: *badmûteh d^{e}Melkîz^{e}deq*, 'in the

[18] P. Joüon (*Grammaire de l'hébreu biblique* [2d ed.; Rome, 1947] #93l-m) and G. Beer-R. Meyer (*Hebräische Grammatik* [Sammlung Göschen Berlin, I, 1952] #45d) explain the final *yodh* as *ḥireq compaginis*; but Gesenius-Kautzsch-Cowley (Hebrew Grammar [Oxford, 1946] #90k-l), H. Bauer-P. Leander (*Historische Grammatik der hebräischen Sprache des Alten Testaments* [Halle a. S., 1918] #65j–k) more correctly explain it as an obsolete case-ending. Cf. H.-J. Kraus, *op. cit.*, 753.—Despite a superficial resemblance to (and perhaps a common origin with) the Aramaic *'l dbr* (Cowley, *AP* 6,6 [in a context of swearing]; *BMAP* 4,13) and *'l dbrt dy* (Dn 2:30; 4:14), the phrase in the Ps seems to be different.

[19] Cf. among others Koehler-Baumgartner, *Lexicon in Veteris Testamenti libros* (Leiden; 1958) 202; V. Hamp, *op. cit.*, 18; J. M. P. Smith (*American Translation* [Chicago, 1951] 561): 'A Melchizedek, because of me.' See also B. D. Eerdmans, *The Hebrew Book of Psalms* (Leiden, 1947) 499: 'For the sake of Melchizedek' (explained as 'for the memory of').—Still less convincing are the attempts of A. Caquot (*op. cit.*, 44), 'Tu es prêtre pour toujours. (Il l'a juré) à propos de Melchisedeq'; and of R. Tournay (*op. cit.*, 19, n. 2), 'sur ma parole (jurée)'.

[20] H.-J. Kraus, *op. cit.*, 752; CCD 3,287; Gesenius-Buhl, 155.

[21] It has been noted independently by R. Tournay, *op. cit.*, 19, n. 2.

likeness of Melchizedek'? Heb 7:15 is so obviously an allusion to Ps 110:4 that Nestle prints it in boldface except for *homoiotēta*. It is this notion of 'likeness' which is exploited in the midrashic commentary, even though the text of Heb may not really solve the problem of *'al dibrātî* or *kata tēn taxin*. In reality, *kata tēn homoiotēta* may be no more than a paraphrase of the preposition *kata* alone.

GN 14:18-20

We turn now to the midrash of Heb 7. But it will be well to juxtapose first of all the pertinent verses of Gn as they appear in the MT, the *Genesis Apocryphon*[22] and the *Targum Neofiti I*.[23] Various features of these comparative texts will enter into our discussion of the development in Heb.

MT	1*QapGn*	*Neofiti I*
[17]The king of Sodom went out to meet him, after his return from killing Chedorlaomer and the kings who were with him,	[12]The king of Sodom heard that Abram had brought back all the captives [13]and all the booty, and he went up to meet him. He came to Salem, that is Jerusalem, and Abram was	The king of Sodom went out to meet him after he returned from killing Chedorloamer and the kings who were with him in the plain of Phordesaya,[24] that is the King's Plain. . . .[25] And
to the Valley of Shaveh, that is the King's Valley.	camped in the Valley of [14]Shaveh (that is, the King's Valley, in the	the upright king, the king of Jerusalem, that is the great Shem,

[22] N. Avigad and Y. Yadin, *A Genesis Apocryphon: A Scroll from the Wilderness of Judaea* (Jerusalem, 1956). See also my *The Genesis Apocryphon of Qumran Cave I: A Commentary* (Biblica et Orientalia, 18; Rome: Pontifical Biblical Institute, 1966: 2nd revised edition, 1971).

[23] See A. Díez Macho, 'Una copia de todo el Targum jerosolimitano en la Vaticana', *EstBib* 16 (1956) 446–7; 'Una copia completa del Targum palestinense al Pentateuco en la Biblioteca Vaticana', *Sefarad* 17 (1957) 119–21; P. Boccaccio, 'Integer textus Targum hierosolymitani primum inventus in codice Vaticano', *Bib* 38 (1957) 237–9.—The text given here is taken from a microfilm supplied by the Vatican Library. The text is now available with a Spanish, French, and English translation in A. Díez Macho, *Neophyti I: Targum palestinense . . . Tomo 1: Genesis* (Madrid: Consejo superior de investigaciones científicas, 1969).

[24] See J. T. Milik, '"Saint-Thomas de Phordêsa"', *Bib* 42 (1961) 77–84.

[25] In the text of *Neofiti I* the beginning of each verse is indicated by two or three words of the Hebrew, set off in quotation marks and followed by *sōph pāsûq*. Thereafter follows the Aramaic version of the complete verse. See next note. Dots in the translation represent the omission of the Hebrew words.

[18]And Melchizedek, the king of Salem, brought out bread and wine; and he was a priest of the Most High God; and he blessed him, saying, [19]'Blessed be Abram by the Most High God, the creator of the heavens and the earth! [20]And blessed be the Most High God, who has delivered your enemies into your hand!' And he gave him a tenth of everything. [21]And the king of Sodom said to Abram, 'Give me the men, but the goods take for yourself.' [22]But Abram said to the king of Sodom, 'I raise my hand to Yahweh, the Most High God, the creator of the heavens and the earth, [23]that I shall not take so much as a thread or a sandal-strap from anything that is yours, lest you say, [24]"I have enriched Abram".'

(Gn 14:17–24)

Valley of Beth Kerem). And Melchizedek, the king of Salem, brought out [15]food and drink for Abram and all the men who were with him. And he was a priest of the Most High God. And he blessed [16]Abram and said, 'Blessed be Abram by the Most High God, lord of the heavens and the earth! And blessed be the Most High God, [17]who has delivered your enemies into your hand!' And he gave him a tenth of all the flocks of the king of Elam and his confederates. [18]Then the king of Sodom drew near and said to Abram, 'My lord Abram, [19]give me the men that are mine from the captives who are with you, whom you have rescued from the king of Elam, and [20]all the flocks (are) left for you.' Then Abram said to the king of Sodom, 'I raise [21]my hand this day to the Most High God, the lord of the heavens and the earth, [22]that I shall not take so much as a thread or a sandal-strap from anything that is yours, lest you say, 'From my flocks comes all the wealth of [23]Abram. . . ."'

(22:12–23)

brought out bread and wine; and he was a priest serving in the great priesthood before the Most High God. . . . And he blessed him saying, 'Blessed is Abram before the Most High God, who by his word created the heavens and the earth. . . . And blessed is the Most High God (who) has broken your enemies before you.' And he gave him a tenth of everything. . . . And the king of Sodom said to Abram, 'Give me the men, but the money take for yourself.' . . . And Abram said to the king of Sodom, 'Behold, I raise my hand in oath before Yahweh, the Most High God, who by his word created the heavens and the earth . . . that I shall not take so much as a thread or a shoe-lace from all that is yours, lest you become proud and say, "I have enriched Abram".'[26]

(fol. 23 v., ll. 14 ff.)

[26] *Neofiti I*, f. 23v., line 14 ff.: "*wyṣ' mlk*" : *wnpq mlk' dsdwn* {*lq*} *lqdmwtyh mn btr dy ḥzr mn dqṭl yt kdr l'm*(*r*) *wyt mlkyy'; dhwn 'myh bmyšr prdsy' hy' mšrh dmlk'*: "*wmlky ṣdq mlk šlm*" : *wmlk' ṣdq mlk' dyrwšlm hw' šm rwbh*—f. 24r, l. 1 ff.: *'pq lḥm wḥmr whw' hwh khn mšmš bkhnt*(*t*) *rbth qdm 'lh' 'l'h*: "*wybrkhw wy'mr*" : *wbryk ytyh w'mr bryk hw' 'brm qdm 'lh' 'yl'h dbmymryh qnh šmy' w'r'*: "*brwk 'l 'lywn*" : *wbryk hw' 'lh' 'ly' dy tbr b'ly dbbk qdmk wyhb lh ḥd mn 'šrh mn klh*: "*wy'mr mlk sdwm*" : *w'mr mlk' dsd*(*m*) *l'brm hb ly npšt' wmmwnh sb lk*: "*wy'mr 'brm*" : *w'mr 'brm lmlk' dsdm h' zqp*{*y*} *ydy bšbw'h qdm yyyy 'lh' 'ly' dbmmryh qnh šmy' w'r'*: "*'m mḥwṭ*" : *'m mn ḥwṭ rṣw'h dmsn 'n 'sb mn kl mh dy lk dl' tyhwwy mtg'y wtymr 'n' 'tryt yt 'brm.*

THE NAME MELCHIZEDEK

'First of all, his name is interpreted as the king of uprightness' (Heb 7:2). The author's minute, attentive, midrashic analysis of the OT text centres first on the name of Melchizedek, in a way which was apparently traditional among the Jews of his time. But in fact this analysis contributes little to the development of the argument in Heb. In the light of the modern study of Northwest Semitic personal names, *Malkî-ṣedeq* must have meant originally either '(the god) Ṣedeq is my king', or 'My king is upright'. The first element *malkî-* (with *yodh*) was suffixal, meaning 'my king', like *Malkî-'ēl* ('El is my king' [Gn 46:17]), *Malkî-yāh* or *Malkî-yāhû* ('Yahweh is my king' [Ezr 10:31; Jer 38:6]), and a host of names with similar suffixal elements like *'ābî* ('my father'), *'āḥî* ('my brother'), *'ēlî* ('my god'), *'ammî* ('my kinsman'), *zimrî* ('my protection'), etc.[27] As for the second element *ṣdq*, it was most likely the name of a god,

[27] Compare *'Abî-'ēl* (1 Sm 9:1),*'Abî-yāh* (1 Sm 8:2), *'Abî-yāhû* (2 Chr 13:20), *Abi-dDagan* (*ARM* 2,83.21), *Abi-milki* (*EA* 148,2), *Ilima-abi* (*BASOR* 95 [1944] 22), *Ili-milku* (*EA* 151,45), *'Ĕlî-melek* (Ru 1:2), *'Ĕlî-'ēl* (1 Chr 11:46), *'Elî-yāh* (2 Kgs 1:3), *Ili-Eraḫ* (*ARM* 1,63.6), *Aḫi-milku* (KB 2,148), *'Aḥî-melek* (1 Sm 21:2), *'Ammî-'ēl* (Nm 13:12), *'Ammî-šadday* (Nm 1:12), *Zimrî-dDagan* (*ARM* 1,85.11). See C.-F. Jean, 'Les noms propres de personnes dans les lettres de Mari', *Studia Mariana* (Leiden, 1950) 63–98.—M. Noth (*Die israelitischen Personennamen im Rahmen der gemeinsemitischen Namengebung* [Stuttgart, 1928] 24–5) rejects the explanation that the *yodh* is a suffix, as maintained by Delitzsch, Bauer-Leander, T. Bauer, *et al.*, and sees in it 'nur einen Rest alter Kasusendungen'. In the light of the foregoing material this is most unlikely. All the examples which he offers can be explained otherwise quite easily. Moreover, he is responsible for another analysis of *Malkîṣedeq* often quoted today (p. 161, n. 4), '(the god) Milk is upright'. This is due to his desire to interpret all instances of *mlk* in Canaanite names as a theophoric element. But just as he was forced to admit *ṣdq* as a divine name (in South Arabic *ṣdqḏkr*, *ṣdqyd'*, *ṣdqyp'*; cf. also Chagar Bazar *Ṣidqi-epuḫ*, Mari *Ṣidqu-la-nasi*, Ugaritic *Ṣdq'il*) as well as an epithet, 'upright' (in names like *ṣdqyh*, *yhwṣdq*; cf. Aleppo seal, *Aḫi-ṣaduq*), so too *mlk* in personal names can be either a theophoric element or a simple epithet (as in the examples cited above). Cf. also *Malkî-ram* (1 Chr 3:18), *Malkî-šûa'* (1 Sm 14:49). See W. F. Albright, *JBL* 69 (1950) 389; *AASOR* 6 (1926) 63; contrast W. W. Baudissin, *Kyrios* (Giessen, 1929) 3, 44–51 (*Malkî-ṣedeq* = '(mein) Malk ist gerecht' [?]).

Ṣedeq, a form of the name which Philo Byblius gives in a Phoenician pantheon as *Sydyk*[28] and which Damascius writes as *Sadykos*.[29] However, it is not possible to exclude the meaning of *ṣdq* as an adjective, 'upright'.[30] At any rate, *Malkî-ṣedeq* is related to the name of the Jerusalem king in the time of Joshua, *'Adōnî-ṣedeq* ('Ṣedeq is my lord', or possibly 'My lord is upright' [Jos 10:1, 3]), and to the Amorite name of the Babylonian king, *Ammi-ṣaduqa* (16th cent. B.C.).

Neither of these possible meanings of the name of Melchizedek was preserved, however, in first-century Jewish tradition. Both Philo and Josephus record the popular etymology of their day, *basileus dikaios*.[31] This is reflected in later Targums,[32]

[28] Eusebius, *Praep. evang.* 1, 10, 13–14, 25; GCS 43/1, 46, 48 (ed. K. Mras, 1954): MS. variants: *Sydek* and *Sedek*. See further R. A. Rosenberg, 'The God Ṣedeq', *HUCA* 36 (1965) 161–77; M. C. Astour, 'Some New Divine Names from Ugarit', *JAOS* 86 (1966) 277–84, especially 282–3.

[29] Photius, *Bibl.*, cod. 242, p. 573 H (cited by W. W. Baudissin, *op. cit.*, 3, 411–12).—This form of the name is close to that in *Ammi-ṣaduqa*, *Aḫi-ṣaduq* and the OT name, *Ṣadoq* (which should probably be *Ṣaddûq* [2 Sm 8:17]).

[30] Cf. *Yehôṣādāq* (Hag 1:1), *Yôṣādāq* (Ezr 3:2); perhaps the *a–u* vowels are indicative of an adjectival form in *Ammi-ṣaduqa* and *Aḫi-ṣaduq*. Cf. the Phoenician inscription of Yeḥawmilk: *k mlk ṣdq h'*, 'for he is a loyal king' (line 9).

[31] Josephus, *Ant.* 1, 10, 2, #180; *JW* 6, 10, 1, #438; Philo, *De legum allegoria* 3, 79.

[32] *Neofiti I:* 'And the upright king, the king of Jerusalem, the great Shem, brought out' (*wmlk' ṣdq mlk' dyrwšlm hw' šm rwbh 'pq*); *Fragmententargum:* 'And Melchizedek, the king of Jerusalem, that is the great Shem' (*wmlky ṣdq mlk' dyrwšlm dhw' šm rb'*); *Ps.-Jonathan:* 'And the upright king, that is Shem, the son of Noah, the king of Jerusalem, went out . . .' (*wmlk' ṣdyq' hw' šm br nḥ mlk' dyrwšlym npq*); *Onqelos:* 'And Melchizedek, the king of Jerusalem, brought out . . .' (*wmlky ṣdq mlk' dyrwšlm 'pyq*).—By equating Melchizedek with Shem, the rabbinical tradition thus incorporated him into the Israelite nation and provided him with a genealogy; see Gn 10:1; 11:10–26. C. Spicq (*op. cit.*, 205) further points out that the haggadah identified Melchizedek with Shem, the eldest son of Noah, because from Adam to Levi the cult was supposed to have been cared for by the first-born. See also H. W. Hertzberg, 'Die Melkiṣedeq-Traditionen', *JPOS* 8 (1928) 170; J. J. Petuchowski, 'The Controversial Figure of Melchizedek', *HUCA* 28 (1957) 127–36.—The meaning 'upright king' is used by H. E. del

and underlies the phrase used in Heb itself, *basileus dikaiosynēs*, 'king of uprightness'. Some authors[33] try to defend the translation in Heb as the original one (invoking *ḥireq compaginis*), but unconvincingly. It is to be noted that in the *Genesis Apocryphon* the name is still written as one word, and may reflect a period before the popular etymology set in with the consequent tendency to write the name as two words *Malkî-ṣedeq*. The form preserved in *Neofiti I* is problematical and probably reflects an even later stage of the popular etymology; *mlk' ṣdq* may be a mistake for *mlky ṣdq*, but it may also be an attempt to write *mlk' ṣdyq'* of the tradition in Pseudo-Jonathan. At any rate, there can be no doubt that the explanation of the name used in Heb is one which was in accord with the current popular etymology and in the long run better suited to the purpose of the author of Heb.

THE KING OF 'SALEM'

The analysis of the text of Gn is continued, 'He is also the king of Salem, that is the king of peace' (7:2), according to the usual translation. *Basileus salēm* is once again the use of a contemporary, popular etymology known to us from Philo, *basilea tēs eirēnēs*.[34] However, in this case the meaning is interesting, because the sense of the Hebrew text of Gn itself is not without its problems. Is the expression *melek šālēm* topographical or not? This question has not always been answered in the affirmative. Most recently W. F. Albright has explained the verse with the aid of an haplography which results in an interesting interpretation. He would read, *ū-Malkî-ṣédeq mélek šelôm⟨ōh⟩ hôṣî' léḥem wa-yáyin*, 'And Melchizedek, a king allied to him, brought

---

Medico ('Melchisedech', *ZAW* 69 [1957] 160–70) to eliminate the proper name (Melchizedek) from the text of both Gn and Ps 110, since 'upright king' and 'peaceful king' are epithets of the king of Sodom mentioned in the previous verse of Gn. The explanation is more ingenious than convincing.

[33] C. Spicq, *op. cit.*, 182 ('roi de justice'); similarly P. Joüon, *Grammaire*, #93m; Gesenius-Kautzsch-Cowley, *Hebrew Grammar*, #90*l* ('king of righteousness') ; *et al.*

[34] *De legum allegoria* 3,79.

out bread and wine.'[35] The word *šlm* is explained by him as produced by 'the simplest possible haplography', due to the following *hôṣî'*; he compares such expressions as *'îš šᵉlômî* (Ps 41:10), *'anšê šᵉlômᵉkā* parallel to *'anšê bᵉrîtᵉkā* (Ob 7), etc. The phrase, *melek šᵉlôm⟨ōh⟩*, would then mean 'a king of his alliance' (his 'peace', literally). Along with H. Gunkel and others Albright believes that Gn 14:18–20 had originally nothing to say about Jerusalem—the identification of Salem with it would seem to be a later tradition, reflected in Ps 76:2 ('In Salem is his abode, his dwelling is in Zion'). When it arose is not certain at all, but it was current in the first century A.D., as is evident not only from Josephus, who stated, 'Solyma was in fact the place afterwards called Hierosolyma',[36] but also from the *Genesis Apocryphon* (22:13): Abram 'came to Salem, that is Jerusalem'.[37] The *Targum Neofiti I* agrees with the previously known Targums in reading *mlk' dyrwšlm*, 'king of Jerusalem'. Now given such a long-standing interpretation of *šlm* of Gn 14 as Jerusalem, it is noteworthy that Heb merely transcribes *šālēm* into Greek as *salēm* and interprets it like Philo as *basileus eirēnēs*. Whether Albright's interpretation, eliminating the topographical name, will rally scholarly opinion to it or not, it at least provides an understandable background for the interpretation common to both Philo and Heb. It is also to be noted that the Alexandrian background of Philo and Heb may well account for the interpretation common to them over against that found in Josephus, the *Genesis Apocryphon* and the Targums, which may reflect rather a Palestinian interpretation of *mlk šlm*.

However, in the long run it must be admitted that the ex-

[35] 'Abram the Hebrew: A New Archaeological Interpretation', *BASOR* 163 (1961) 52.

[36] *Ant.* 1,10,2, # 180 (*tēn mentoi Solyma hysteron ekalesan Hierosolyma*); *JW* 6,10,1, # 438.

[37] See *CBQ* 22 (1960) 281; cf. P. Winter, 'Note on Salem-Jerusalem', *NT* 2 (1957) 151-2. This identification gives the lie to the statements of H. E. del Medico (*op. cit.*, 163), who neglects the Jewish tradition on Ps

planation of the names of Melchizedek and of Salem does not really advance the main argument of the midrash. But just as in the later midrashim, even the minor elements of the OT text are exploited to suggest that Christ, the new high priest, *kata tēn taxin Melchizedek*, brings the messianic blessings of uprightness and peace. This seems to be the reason for the adoption of the current popular etymologies. Through Christ come the messianic blessings of 'uprightness' (see Is 9:5–6; 32:1; Jer 23:5–6; Dn 9:24; Mal 3:20 ; Acts 3:14; 1 Cor 4:30) and of 'peace' (Is 9:5; 32:17; Zech 9:9–10; Eph 2:14). As king and priest forever he establishes the new order of hope (Heb 6:15–20), and in him the fruits of the traditional priestly blessing (Nm 6:23–26) take on a new nuance.

MELCHIZEDEK'S LACK OF GENEALOGY

The first of the three main points of the Melchizedek theme used in the midrash of Heb to show the superiority of Jesus' priesthood over that of Aaron is the lack of genealogy: like Melchizedek Jesus too is *agenealogētos*. What ultimately underlies the lack of Melchizedek's genealogy in Gn is that he appears in the original story—in the source which has found its way into Gn 14—as a Canaanite priest-king. His name is of traceable Canaanite origin; if Albright's interpretation of Gn 14:18 be correct, he would be a vassal Canaanite king bound by treaty to Abram; otherwise he would be the king of a Canaanite town of Salem. He is further described as a priest of El 'Elyon (*wᵉhû' kôhēn lᵉ'ēl 'elyôn*). As this phrase stands in the MT (and in the final redaction of Gn), it certainly refers to the service of Yahweh. Indeed, a few verses later (14:22) Abram swears with uplifted hand by 'Yahweh El 'Elyon'. But it has long been suspected that *Yhwh* in 14:22 is a later gloss, since it does not appear in the LXX nor in the Peshitta, and is now found to be lacking in the Aramaic translation of this verse in the *Genesis*

76:2 and rejects Josephus' statements as interpolations of a later date, because 'the identification of Salem with Jerusalem was not followed in the first centuries of our era'.

Apocryphon (22:21).[38] If this be so, then Melchizedek's service of El 'Elyon in 14:18 likewise suggests his Canaanite background. For El is the name of a well-known henotheistic Canaanite deity of the second millennium B.C. Despite the fact the *El* and *'Elyān* later appear on an 8th century Aramaic inscription from Sefire, apparently as the names of a pair of Canaanite gods (Sf I A 11),[39] *'elyôn* eventually became an epithet of the supreme God, the creator of the heavens and the earth, the lord of the gods and the universe. God Most High eventually revealed himself and his personal name, Yahweh, to the patriarchs of his chosen people Israel.[40] But as in the case of other OT passages which reflect a strong Canaanite background (Nm 24:16; Is 14:14; cf. Dn 3:26), it is not unlikely that El 'Elyon in Gn 14:18 was understood as not yet identified as Yahweh; rather it is the name of the Canaanite deity whom the king Melchizedek served as priest.

This question is involved in that of the character of vv. 18–20 in Gn 14. They interrupt the story of the meeting of Abram with the king of Sodom, and though it is now generally recognized that there is no solid reason to reject them as a 'later addition',[41] nevertheless they probably are part of an independent poetic saga, as old as the rest of Gn 14, but incorporated in the story of Abram's meeting with Sodom's king. It

[38] See *CBQ* 22 (1960) 291. O. Eissfeldt, 'El and Yahweh', *JSS* 1 (1956) 29, n. 1, remarks: 'That *yhwh* . . . is secondary may be taken as certain.'

[39] See A. Dupont-Sommer and J. Starcky, 'Les inscriptions araméennes de Sfiré (Stèles I et II)', *Mémoires présentés à l'Académie des Inscriptions et Belles-Lettres* 15 (1958) 193–351, esp. 17, 34; cf. J. A. Fitzmyer, *The Aramaic Inscriptions of Sefîre* (Biblica et orientalia 19; Rome: Pontifical Biblical Institute, 1967) 37–8.

[40] On the relation of El and 'Elyon consult the excellent survey of the question by R. Lack, 'Les origines de *'Elyon*, le Très-Haut, dans la tradition cultuelle d'Israël', *CBQ* 24 (1962) 44–64.

[41] See F. M. Th. Böhl, 'Die Könige von Genesis 14', *ZAW* 36 (1916) 72–3; H. Gunkel, *Genesis* (HKAT 1/1; Göttingen, 1922) 284–5; B. Vawter, *A Path Through Genesis* (New York, 1956) 132; J. Chaine, *Le livre de la Genèse* (Lectio divina 3; Paris, 1949) 202–3.—The recent attempt of G. R. Castellino, 'Il sacrificio di Melchisedec', *Eucaristia* (ed. A. Piolanti; Rome, 1957)

has been proposed that the hero of these verses (or of the whole saga) was Melchizedek, and that it was a *hieros logos* of the Jerusalem sanctuary with the aetiological purpose of showing Abram paying tithes to the Jerusalem priest-king.[42] It is rather more likely that the saga told of the co-operation of Melchizedek, an allied king, who went forth to refresh Abram and his troops, to bless him and give 'him a tithe of everything' (i.e., pay him tribute). Such a hypothesis accounts at least for the choppy character of the three verses and their relation to the whole.

With the insertion of the Melchizedek verses in Gn 14 and the identification of El 'Elyon as Yahweh, Melchizedek was adopted into Israelite tradition. By the time of the establishment of the Maccabean royal priesthood Melchizedek's designation becomes the official title of the Hasmonean dynasty.[43] Josephus, who calls Melchizedek *Chananaiōn dynastēs* ('a lord of the Canaanites'), mentions that he was the first to officiate as the priest of God,[44] and according to Philo God made him 'both king of peace, for that is the meaning of "Salem", and his own priest (*hierea heautou*)'.[45] This Jewish adoption of Melchizedek underlies the treatment of him in Heb, for the author knows that Melchizedek does not share a common ancestry with Abram (7:6).

But the rootless character of the vv. 18–20, to which we have referred, is precisely what provides the author of Heb with a starting-point for his comparison. In good rabbinical fashion

---

12, to defend the unity of Gn 14 amounts to no more than an assertion that it is unified.

[42] See W. F. Albright, *AASOR* 6 (1926) 63; H. W. Hertzberg, *op. cit.*, 169–79; H. Haag, *Bibellexikon* (Zürich, 1951) 1101–2.

[43] See 1 Mc 14:41; cf. Josephus, *Ant.* 16, 6, 2, #162; *Assumptio Mos.* 6:1; *Jub* 32:1; *T. Levi* 8:14–15.

[44] *JW* 6, 10, 1, #438; *Ant.* 1, 10, 2, #181.

[45] *De legum allegoria* 3, 79. See note 32 above for the rabbinical mode of adoption.

the argument is based on the very silence of the OT account; the principle is, as Strack-Billerbeck pointed out long ago, 'quod non in thora, non in mundo'.[46] More recently V. Hamp has labelled it *typologia e silentio*.[47] Because these verses are an insertion in the Abram story, there is no mention of Melchizedek's origins or destiny. The omission of such details led to the formulation of the legend (in a four-lined poetic composition) that he was

> *apatōr, amētōr, agenealogētos,*
> *mēte archēn hēmerōn mēte zōēs telos echōn,*
> *aphōmoiōmenos de tō huiō tou theou,*
> *menei hiereus eis to diēnekes.*[48]

It is an elaboration of the very silence of Gn.

But the point of the comparison is that Melchizedek, who appears in the OT with the title *kôhēn*, 'priest', lacks the all-important priestly genealogy. This situation undoubtedly caused speculation in Jewish circles, because the legitimacy of the priestly family depended on its genealogy,[49] on its ability to trace its descent from Levi via Aaron and Zadok. Aaron was the first high priest appointed by Moses at God's command (Ez 28:1 ff.; Lv 8:2 ff.), and was the model of all Jewish priests of the levitical line. But Aaron's ancestry is given in the OT; he

[46] Str-B 3, 694.

[47] *Op. cit.*, 9.

[48] The possibility that Heb 7:3 depends on an older tradition about Melchizedek is not unlikely. However, that it actually goes back to the middle of the second millennium B. C. and is reflected in the Amarna letters of Abdu-Heba of Urusalim (*EA* 287, 25; 'Behold this land of Jerusalem: (It was) not my father (and) not my mother (who gave (it) to me, (but) the arm of the mighty king (which) gave (it) to me' [*ANET* 488]) is rather unlikely.—One may wonder, however, whether the last two lines would antedate Christian times; or, if so, whether 'son of God' in such a case would mean anything more than 'angel', as in Gn 6:2.

[49] See Ez 40:46; 43:19; 44:15; Ezr 2:61–63; Neh 7:63–65; Philo, *Spec. leg.* 1,110 (cf. Lv 21:7–14); Josephus, *Contra Ap.* 1–7, #31–6; *Ant.* 11, 3, 10, #71; Mishnah, *Middoth* 5, 4; *Kiddushin* 4, 4; Tosephta, *Sanhedrin* 7, 1. Cf. M. D. Johnson, *The Purpose of the Biblical Genealogies* (SNTS Monograph 8; Cambridge: University Press, 1969) 79–80.

was descended from Levi, the son of Jacob the patriarch, via Kohath and Amram (Ex 6:16–19). His birth is mentioned explicitly in Ex 6:20 and his death in Nm 20:24–28. Hence he was scarcely *apatōr*, *amētōr*, *agenealogētos*; nor could he be said to be without an end to his life. Nothing similar is stated, however, of Melchizedek, the priest of God Most High. And yet in him the author of Heb finds the *type* of Jesus, the 'perfected' Son. The word *typos* is not used, but rather an equivalent expression, by which Jesus is not compared to Melchizedek, but Melchizedek to the 'Son of God' (*aphōmoiōmenos de tō huiō tou theou*)—a form of comparison which resembles the Pauline typology of Adam and Christ in Rom 5:14. In this regard, O. Michel has noted that Melchizedek 'has no independent meaning for salvation, but is only a pointer referring to the Son set up by God himself'.[50]

At this point the midrash introduces an element from Ps 110 to complete the comparison, and to emphasize the superiority of Christ. Nothing in Gn indicates that Melchizedek will 'remain a priest forever'. This element is derived from the divine promise made under oath to the Israelite king that he will be a priest *l*e*ʿôlām*. This was, if you will, a midrashic element already introduced into Ps 110. Now with the aid of Ps 110:4 Heb emphasizes that Jesus knows 'no end to his days', but only a 'life that cannot end' (7:15) and a priesthood that is 'untransferable' (7:24).[51] Thus it is that Melchizedek who has not received his priesthood *via generationis carnalis* nor transmitted it to others by the same means—because the Gn story knows no genealogy of him—is the type of Jesus the Son and high priest forever. Precisely in that respect in which his priesthood is farthest removed from the Aaronitic type, viz. the lack of hereditary human descent or genealogy, either antecedent or subsequent, is Melchizedek the prefigured Jesus.[52] We may

[50] *TDNT* 4, 570.

[51] The meaning of *aparabatos* is problematical; see AG 80.—C. Spicq (*op. cit.*, 197) defends the sense used here on the basis of both etymology and context.

[52] Melchizedek is used as the type of Jesus because he is 'a priest forever',

wonder at this point whether the author of Heb ever knew the Lucan and Matthaean genealogies of Jesus. But he does know that 'our Lord sprang from the tribe of Judah' (7:14) according to the flesh—and that is why he hastens to answer this objection with the comment, 'with reference to which (tribe) Moses said nothing at all about priests'. But the similarity with Melchizedek is found precisely in this, that he possesses 'a life which cannot end' (*zōē akatalytos*). Thus has the author of Heb established his basic comparison of Jesus with Melchizedek.

THE TITHES

Two further elements in the Gn story are now pursued, to illustrate the superiority of Christ's priesthood over that of Aaron. The first is tithes. Gn 14:20 relates that after Melchizedek blessed Abram, 'he paid him a tithe of everything'. Who paid whom? The text puzzled Jerome who saw that either interpretation was possible.

(Melchisedech) decimas praedae atque uictoriae acceperit ab eo (Abraham) siue—quoniam habetur ambiguum—ipse dederit ei decimas substantiae suae et auitam largitatem ostenderit in nepotem.[53] utrumque enim intellegi potest et iuxta hebraicum et iuxta septuaginta interpretes, quod et ipse acceperit decimas spoliarum et Abrahae dederit decimas substantiae suae.[54]

Modern commentators also raise the question,[55] for no subject

---

according to Ps 110:4. It should be recalled here, however, that in the fragment of Qumran Cave 4, to which I referred above on p. 103, the Aramaic phrase is found, *ytbḥr lkhn ʿlmyn*, 'he will be chosen as a priest forever' (literally, as a priest of [the] ages). It is part of a text that Starcky labels provisionally 'the Vision of Amram' (4QḥʿA^c 9:19). If it refers to Aaron, as Starcky thinks, then the permanence of his priesthood, which would be of interest to the Essene community, would be stressed. This perdurance of the Aaronid priesthood would then conflict with the argument of the author of Hebrews. Unfortunately, we shall have to await the full publication of this fragmentary text in order to be more definite about the meaning of the phrase and the person to whom it refers.

[53] Jerome followed the rabbinical identification of Melchizedek with Shem; see note 32 above and *Ep.* 73 (*Ad Evangelum*) #5 (CSEL 55, 18–19).

[54] *Ep.* 73, # 6 (CSEL 55, 20).

[55] See F. M. Th. Böhl, *op. cit.*, 72–3, whom we are following in part here.

is expressed in the MT or LXX and the subject of the preceding verb is not Abram but Melchizedek. Once again, the answer is probably to be sought in the fact that vv. 18–20 are an insertion, and that it was originally Melchizedek who as a vassal, an 'allied king', paid tithes to Abram. However, in Heb 7:2 there is no doubt about the subject of the sentence, because in his summary of Gn the author has inserted the name *Abraam*.[56] This is the contemporary understanding of the Gn text, as can be seen from the *Genesis Apocryphon* (22:17: 'And he gave him a tithe of all the goods of the king of Elam and his companions'—which can only refer to Abram), and from Josephus ('Abram then offered him the tithe of the spoil, and he accepted the gift').[57] From this contemporary interpretation of the Gn text Heb draws the conclusion of the superiority of Melchizedek's priesthood over that of Levi: Levi the otherwise privileged collector of tithes according to Mosaic legislation (Dt 10:8–9; 12:2) actually paid tithes to Melchizedek through Abram, 'for Levi was still in the loins of his father Abraham, when Melchizedek met the latter' (7:10). Though descended from the same patriarch Abraham, the levitical priests were permitted even as mortal men to tithe their own brothers. But the patriarch himself paid tithes not to a kinsman, but to a

---

Also G. Wuttke, *Melchisedech der Priesterkönig von Salem; eine Studie zur Geschichte der Exegese* (BZNW 5; Giessen, 1927) 20–1; H. Haag, *Bibellexikon*, 1101–2 ('Ob Abraham dem M. "den Zehnten von allem" gab oder umgekehrt, ist umstritten. Im heutigen Zusammenhang hat Abraham kaum etwas zu verzehnten, weil er ausdrücklich auf die Kriegsbeute verzichtet [14,23]'). See further R. H. Smith, 'Abram and Melchizedek', *ZAW* 77 (1965) 129-53.

[56] The boldface printing of *Abraam* (Heb 7:2) as part of the OT quotation in E. Nestle, *Novum Testamentum graece*, ed. 24 (1960), in the British and Foreign Bible Society's text, *Hē Kainē Diathēkē*, ed. 2 (1958), and in K. Aland *et al.*, *The Greek New Testament* (United Bible Societies, 1966) 758, is misleading at this point. Cf. A. Merk, *Novum Testamentum graece et latine* (9th ed.; Rome, 1964) 720.

[57] *Ant.* 1, 10, 2, #181.—The defective text of *Jub* 13, 25–6 has at least enough preserved to show that it too understood Gn 14:18–19 in the same way; see R. H. Charles, *APOT* 2, 33.

foreign king, who was a priest without ancestry, 'of whom it is testified that he lives' (7:9). This shows 'how great' Melchizedek was.

MELCHIZEDEK'S BLESSING

Lastly, Jesus' superiority over the Aaronitic line is shown by the fact that in Gn Melchizedek, the priest of El 'Elyon, blessed Abram. 'As is quite obvious, it is the inferior who is blessed by the superior' (Heb 7:7). Heb makes use of another current interpretation of Gn, when it links the phrase, 'And he was a priest of the Most High God', with the following verse, 'And he blessed him, saying. . . .' To the author of Heb the priestly act was the *blessing*;[58] no mention is made of the bringing out of bread and wine, much less of any sacrifice. An analogous understanding of Gn is seen in the *Genesis Apocryphon*, where the Aramaic version of Gn reads: 'And Melchizedek, the king of Salem, brought out food and drink for Abram and for all the men who were with him; and he was the priest of the Most High God, and he blessed Abram, saying . . .' (22:14–15). The addition to the text, 'for Abram and for all the men who were with him', as well as the translation of the Hebrew *leḥem wa-yayin* ('bread and wine') by the Aramaic *mēʾkal ū-mištêh* ('food and drink'),[59] show that the following phrase, 'and he was the priest of the Most High God', was scarcely intended as ex-

[58] See A. Vaccari, '"Melchisedec, rex Salem, proferens panem et vinum" (Gen. 14:18)', *VD* 18 (1938) 210–11; V. Hamp, *op. cit.*, 12–13.—Some authors have tried to maintain that though the utterance of a blessing in the OT is not exclusive to priests (see Gn 48:9; 49:28; Ru 2:4; Ps 128:5–6), it is normally uttered by them (Dt 10:8; 18:5; 21:5 [H. Gunkel, *op. cit.*, 286: 'Segnen ist Priesterrecht']). This argument lacks its force, however, precisely because it is not an exclusive prerogative.—The article of J. E. Coleran, 'The Sacrifice of Melchisedech', *TS* 1 (1940) 27–36, shows that no argument can be built up one way or the other from the use of the Hebrew expression *wᵉhûʾ*, for in Gn itself it is found several times to refer both to what follows and to what precedes (more frequently, however, to what precedes).

[59] In contrast to the later Targums, which translate it *lḥm̊ wḥmr̊* (Neofiti I and Ps.-Jonathan), *lḥym wḥmr* (Onqelos), *mzwn wḥmr* (Fragmententargum).

planatory of what preceded. Josephus' understanding of the Gn text is no different.[60]

Thus, when the author of Heb set out to show the superiority of Jesus' priesthood over that of Aaron, he illustrated it from three elements in Gn alone: the lack of genealogy, the reception of tithes, and the blessing bestowed. It has often been noted that the author of Heb seems to be unaware of any sacrificial character of the Gn phrase, 'brought out bread and wine'.[61] In a composition that is otherwise so closely bound up with the notion of sacrifice, it is difficult to understand how he would have omitted it, if it were so understood in his day. It is significant that neither Josephus nor the *Genesis Apocryphon* so understands it. But it is well known that some of the Fathers understood these words in Gn in terms of the sacrifice of Melchizedek.[62] Their exegesis of the text, however, manifests the same midrashic, haggadic development as that of the author of Heb; it lacks only the charism of inspiration. However, it should be admitted with V. Hamp that even if the verb *hôṣî'* ('brought

[60] *Ant.* 1, 10, 2, #181: 'Melchizedek hospitably entertained Abraham's army, providing abundantly for all their needs, and in the course of the feast he began to extol Abraham and to bless God for having delivered his enemies into his hand.'

[61] Admittedly in this part of Heb the author is stressing the eternal character and superiority of Christ's priesthood and is not yet concerned (as in ch. 8–10) with his priestly *activity*. But he does draw two arguments from *actions* of Melchizedek (blessing and reception of tithes) to serve his purpose; if there were any special 'sacrificial' connotation to the bringing out of bread and wine, would he not have used this too?—Catholic exegetes admit frankly today that the verb *hôṣî'* is in no way sacrificial. See V. Hamp, *op. cit.*, 12; H. Rusche, *op. cit.*, 232; J. Chaine, *op. cit.*, 207, n. 89. Nor is there in the text any indication that the sacred author considered the bringing out of bread and wine to be 'un'azione sacra', nor that they were to be consumed 'in un'atmosfera religioso-sacrale di sacrificio'—*pace* G. R. Castellino, *op. cit.*, 16.

[62] But as P. Samain has pointed out, 'la tradition patristique n'établit pas qu'il y eut oblation' ('Melchisédech a-t-il offert un sacrifice, figure de l'Eucharistie?', *RevDTour* 1 [1946] 38–41). The usual patristic fluctuation of interpretation is noted in this question too. Tertullian (*Adv. Iud.* 3; CSEL 70, 258) makes no mention of sacrifice; nor do J. Firmicus Maternus (*De*

forth') can in no wise be forced into a sacrificial expression, nevertheless the bringing out of 'bread and wine' by the priest Melchizedek does prefigure the loving care of the high priest Christ who provides food to still the spiritual hunger of his chosen warriors in their earthly campaign. In this sense Gn 14:18 can be said to prefigure the Eucharist.[63]

There can be little doubt that the 'rootless character' of vv. 18–20 in Gn 14 is responsible for the legends which grew up about Melchizedek. We noted that this started in the OT itself (in Ps 110); it is continued in the *Genesis Apocryphon*, Philo, Josephus and the Targums (which all manifest the Jewish adoption of him). Heb and later patristic writings carry on the adoption, until he becomes in the canon of the Mass of the Roman rite *summus sacerdos tuus Melchisedech*.[64] And the adoption

---

errore prof. rel. 18, 3; ed. K. Ziegler [1953] 62); Ambrosiaster (*Lib. quaest. vet. et novi test.* 109, 18; CSEL 50, 266); Justin (*Dial. c. Tryph.* 33; *PG* 6,545); Theophilus of Antioch (*Ad Autolycum* 2, 31; *PG* 6, 1104). Among these Ambrosiaster mentions the bread and wine as a type of the Eucharistic food offered to Christians by Christ; similarly Clement of Alexandria (*Strom.* 4, 161, 31; GCS 15,319), Epiphanius (*Pan.* 55, 6, 3–4; GCS 31, 331), Chrysostom (*In. Gen. hom.* 35, 5; *PG* 53, 328; *In Ps* 109, 8; *PG* 55, 276), Jerome (*Tract. in libr. Ps.* 109, 4; *CC* 78, 225). The sacrificial note was introduced especially in the West by Cyprian (*Ep.* 63, 4; CSEL 3/2, 703–4) and repeated by many thereafter. It is significant to note in Jerome's case that whereas he often speaks of the sacrificial aspect of Melchizedek's offering (*Comm. in ev. Matt.* 4, 26; *PL* 26, 202–3; *Hebr. quaest. in Gen.* 14, 18; *CC* 72, 19; *Ep.* 73, 3; *CSEL* 55, 16), nevertheless when he explains 'ipsa hebraica verba' (*Ep.* 73, 5), he makes no mention of sacrifice and even goes so far as to say, 'nec esse mirum, si Melchisedech uictori Abraham obuiam processerit et in refectionem tam ipsius quam propugnatorum eius panem uinumque protulerit et benedixerit ei' (*Ep.* 73, 6).—See G. Bardy, 'Melchisédech dans la tradition patristique', *RB* 35 (1926) 496–509; 36 (1927) 25–45; G. Wuttke, *op. cit.*, 43–59; H. Rusche, *op. cit.*, 246–50; R. Galdos, 'Melquisedec en la patrística', *EstEc* 19 (1945) 221–46; P. F. Cremin, 'According to the Order of Melchisedech: the Patristic Interpretation and its Value', *IER* 54 (1929) 385–91.

[63] *Op. cit.*, 14–15—The Council of Trent did not define that Melchizedek offered a sacrifice; see P. Samain, *op. cit.*, 41.

[64] See R. Le Déaut, 'Le titre de *Summus Sacerdos* donné à Melchisédech est-il d'origine juive?', *RSR* 50 (1962) 222–9.

of Melchizedek is not at an end, for in his little book on the *Holy Pagans of the Old Testament* J. Daniélou makes him out to be 'the High Priest of the cosmic religion'.[65]

[65] Tr. F. Faber; Baltimore, 1957, 104.

12

FURTHER LIGHT ON MELCHIZEDEK FROM QUMRAN CAVE 11*

A. S. van der Woude published a group of thirteen small fragments discovered in 1956 in Qumran Cave 11.[1] The title of his article attracts attention immediately, 'Melchizedek as a Heavenly Redemption-Figure in the Newly Discovered Eschatological Midrashim from Qumran Cave 11'.[1] Unfortunately, the state of preservation of these fragments is such that their interpretation will remain problematical; but they do contain a number of interesting phrases revealing new facets of the Melchizedek legend in Palestinian Judaism of the first century A.D., and these will affect in turn our understanding of the OT figure and the interpretation of certain NT passages.

The thirteen fragments furnish the better part of one column of the scroll or text to which they originally belonged; there are also a few isolated words at the beginning of the lines of a second column, but the context is broken and the rest of the lines lost so that they are of little interest to us here. We reproduce the text of Col. I, as it has been published by van der Woude. His reading of the text is in general accurate; occasionally there is room for a slightly different interpretation. He dates the text to the Herodian period, according to the cate-

* Originally published in *JBL* 86 (1967) 25–41.

[1] 'Melchisedek als himmlische Erlösergestalt in den neugefundenen eschatologischen Midraschim aus Qumran Höhle XI', *OTS* 14 (1965) 354–73.

gories established by F. M. Cross, Jr., and prefers a date in 'the first half of the first Christian century'.[2]

11QMelch offers another fragmentary example of a composition which comments on isolated OT texts taken from their original context and strung together with some theological intention. The editor of this text has compared it with that published by J. M. Allegro and often referred to as 4QFlorilegium.[3] In 11QMelch the sectarian comments on the OT passages are introduced by the word *pšr* (lines 4, 12, 17),[4] but they are really quite similar to those introduced by *mdrš* in 4QFlorilegium.[5] In the latter text the biblical verses quoted are drawn from 2 Sm 7:10b–11a; Ex 15:17–18; 2 Sm 7:11b–12; Am 9:11; Ps 1:1; Is 8:11; Ez 37:23; Ps 2:1.[6] We have a similar line-up of OT quotations in the text now under discussion: Lv 25:13; Dt 15:2; Is 61:1; Lv 25:10; Pss 82:1; 7:8—9; 82:2; Is 52:7; Lv 25:9. Although *pšr* has come to mean in modern parlance a special Essene type of commentary on a continuous text of some prophet or psalm, it is apparent that the word must have been used among the Essenes themselves

[2] *Ibid.*, 357.

[3] 'Fragments of a Qumran Scroll of Eschatological *Midrāšîm*', *JBL* 77 (1958) 350–4; see also 'Further Messianic References in Qumran Literature', *ibid.*, 75 (1956) 174–87, esp. 176–7.

[4] For discussions of the meaning of *pšr* and *mdrš*, see J. van der Ploeg, 'Le rouleau d'Habacuc de la grotte de 'Ain Fešḫa', *BO* 8 (1951) 2; 'Les manuscrits du Désert de Juda: Livres récents', *ibid.*, 16 (1959) 163; K. Stendahl, *The School of St Matthew and Its use of the Old Testament*, 200 ff.; J. A. Fitzmyer, 'The Use of Explicit Old Testament Quotations in Qumran Literature and in the New Testament', pp. 3–58 above, esp. p. 55; A. G. Wright, *CBQ* 28 (1966) 116–18, 418–22.

[5] See 11QMelch 14. For other Qumran texts of midrashic character see the remarks of J. T. Milik in 'Le travail d'édition des fragments manuscrits de Qumrân', *RB* 73 (1956) 61. Cf. also W. R. Lane, 'A New Commentary Structure in 4QFlorilegium', *JBL* 78 (1959) 343–6; Y. Yadin, 'A Midrash on 2 Sam VII and Ps I–II (4QFlorilegium)', *IEJ* 9 (1959) 95–8.

[6] In 4QFlor the main comments are made on 2 Sm 7 and on Pss 1–2; the others are introduced to illustrate the development of the midrashic comments. The correlation of Ps 2 and 2 Sm 7 in the one text is noteworthy, but unfortunately the text is very fragmentary and it only excites our curiosity.

as almost synonymous with *mdrš*. Perhaps we should regard the *pšr* as a special Essene type of *mdrš*. At any rate, van der Woude is correct in identifying 11QMelch as another example of an 'eschatological midrash' already found in the Qumran documents. As in the case of 4QFlor, an interpretation of the OT verses is given *l'ḥryt hymym*, 'for the end of days' (see lines 4, [15]; cf. line 20); compare 4QFlor 1:2, 12, 15, 19. Also to be noted is the similarity of phraseology in the comments of 4QFlor and 11QMelch; although different OT texts are commented upon, yet the mode of commenting is very similar. Several phrases recur: 'Belial', 'those who turn away from walking in the way of the people', etc.

THE TEXT[7]

1. [ ].........*yk* .....[
2. [ ]..[*w'*]*šr 'mr bšnt hyw*[*bl hzw't tšwbw 'yš 'l 'ḥwztw*
3. [*w'šr 'mr šmw*]*ṭ kwl b'l mšh yd 'šr yšh* [*br'hw lw' ygwś 't r'hw w't 'ḥyw ky' qr'*] *šmṭh*
4. [*l'l pšrw l'ḥ*]*ryt hymym 'l hšbwyym 'šr* [ ]*'sr*
5. ....*mh* ....*y h*.... *wmnḥlt mlky ṣdq k*[ ]....*hmh b*...[*mlky ṣ*]*dq 'šr*
6. *yšybmh 'lyhmh wqr' lhmh drr l'zwb l*[*h*]*mh* [*wlkpr*] *'l 'wwnwtyhmh w*....... [ ] .. [ ]*dbr hzh*
7. *bšnt hywbl h'ḥ*[*r*]*wn 'm*[*r*] *š*[ ]. *bly*[ ] *wy*[*wm* (?) *hkpw*]*rym h*[*w'*]*h* [ ] ..... [*yw*]*bl h*[*'*]*śyry*
8. *lkpr bw 'l kwl bny* [*'wr w*]*'nš*[*y g*]*wrl ml*[*ky*] *ṣdq*[ ]*m 'ly*[*hm*]*h ht*[ ] *lg*[ ]*wtmh ky'*
9. *hw'h ḥqq šnt hrṣwn lmlky ṣ*[*dq*]*l* .. [ ] *wqdwšy 'l lmm*[*š*]*lt mšpṭ k'šr ktwb*
10. *'lyw bšyry dwyd 'šr 'mr 'lwhym* [*n*]*ṣb b'*[*dt 'l*] *bqwrb 'lwhym yšpwṭ w'lyw 'm*[*r '*]*lyh*
11. *lmrwm šwbh 'l ydyn 'mym w'šr '*[*mr 'd mty t*]*špwṭw 'wwl wpny rš'*[*y*]*m tś*[*'w s*]*lh*

[7] The reader is referred to the *editio princeps* for indications of the certainty or probability of the reading of various letters.

12. *pšrw ʿl blyʿl wʿl rw[ḥ]y gwrlw ʾš[r]..m bsp[ ] .. wqyʾl .* [

13. *wmlky ṣdq yqwm nq[m]t mš[p]ṭy ʾ[l myd b]lyʿl wmyd kwl [rwḥy gwrl]w*

14. *wbʿzrw kwl ʾly [ʿwlmym h]wʾh ʾ[šr ʾmr k]wl bny ḥ[y]l whp*[ ]

15. *hzwʾt hwʾh ywm h[hrgh ʾ]šr ʾmr [lʾḥryt hymym byd yšʿ]yh hnbyʾ ʾšr ʾm[r mh] nʾww*

16. *ʿl hrym rgl[y] mbś[r m]šmyʿ šlwm mb[śr ṭwb mšmyʿ yšwʿ]h ʾwmr lṣywn [mlk] ʾlwhyk*

17. *pšrw hhr[ym]tbyʾw[ty]hmh ʾ[ ]tp[ ]lkwl .* [

18. *whmbśr hw[ʾh m]šwḥ hrw[ḥ] ʾšr ʾmr dn[yʾl mbśr]*

19. *ṭwb mšmy[ʿ yšwʿh] hwʾh hk[tw]b ʿlyw ʾšr [ʾmr*

20. *lnḥ[m ?].....[ ]l [y]śkylmh bkwl qṣy ḥ[rwn*

21. [ ]*ʾmt l .*[ ]...[

22. [ ]...[

23. [ ]*.h srh mblyʿl wt .*[ ]..[

24. [ ]*bmšpṭ[y] ʾl kʾšr ktwb ʿlyw [ʾwmr lṣy]wn mlk ʾlwhyk [ṣy]wn h[yʾh*

25. [ ]... *mqym[y] hbryt hsrym mlkt [bd]rk hʿm wʾl[w]hyk hwʾh*[

26. [ ]..........*d blyʿl wʾšr ʾmr whʿbrtmh šwp[r trwʿh] bḥ[wdš] h[šbyʿy*

Written vertically in the right-hand margin, beginning about line 11: *bmwšh kyʾ*

TRANSLATION[8]

1. [ ].......... your .....[ ]
2. [ ].. [and wh]at he said, '*In this year of ju*[*bilee each of you will return to his possession*'] (Lv 25:13)
3. [and what he said,] '*Let every creditor* [*re*]*mit the due that he claims* [*from his neighbour; let him*

[8] Italics in the translation indicate the parts of OT verses which are quoted in the Hebrew text of the Qumran document.

not dun his neighbour or his brother for there is proclaimed] *a remission* (Dt 15:2)

4. [of God.' Its meaning for the en]d of days concerns *those taken captive* whom [he] imprisoned (Is 61:1)
5. ... MH .... Y H .... and from the heritage of Melchizedek K[ ] ...... their BW .. [Melchized]ek who
6. will restore them to them, and he will *proclaim release* to them, to set them (?) free [and to atone] for their iniquities and ...... [ ] .. [ ] this word. (Lv 25:10)
7. In the year of the la[st] jubilee he sai[d] S[ ]. BLY. [ ] and [tha]t is the d[ay of Atone]ment [ ] ..... the [t]enth [ju]bilee
8. to atone in it for all sons of [light and] men [of the l]ot of Mel[chi]zedek [ ]M upon [th]em HT [ ] LG [ ] WTMH for
9. he has decreed a year of good favour for Melchize[dek] L .. [ ] and the holy ones of God for a re[ig]n of judgment. As it is written
10. about it in the songs of David, who said, '*'Elohim has* [*ta*]*ken his stand in the as*[*sembly of 'El*], *in the midst of gods* [*'lwhym*) *he gives judgment*'. And about it he sa[id, '*A*-] *bove it* (Ps 82:1) (Ps 7:8–9)
11. *take your throne in the heights; let God* (*'l*) *judge* (the) *peoples*.' And he s[aid, '*How long*] *shall you judge unjustly and li*[*ft up*] *the face of* (the) *wic*[*ke*]*d*'? [Se]lah. (Ps 82:2)
12. Its interpretation concerns Belial and concerns the spir[it]s of his lot whi[ch] .. M

in the boo[k of] .. WQY'L .. [ ]

13. And Melchizedek shall exact the ven[ge]ance of the jud[g]ments of God ('[*l*]) [from the hand of Be]lial and from the hand(s) of all [the spirits of] his [lot].

14. And all the [eternal] gods (*'ly*) are for his help. [T]his is wh[at he said, A]ll the sons of mi[gh]t (?) and the P[ ]

15. this. This is the day of the [(about) wh]ich he said [for the end of days through Isai]ah the prophet who sai[d, *'How*] *beautiful* (Is 52:7)

16. *upon the mountains are the feet* [*of*] *the heral*[*d proclaiming peace; the herald of good, proclaiming salvat*]*ion,* (and) *saying to Zion, "Your God* [*is king*]*."'*

17. Its interpretation: The mounta[ins] their pro[du]ce ' [ ] TP [ ] for all. [ ]

18. and the herald i[s the on[e an]ointed with the Spir[it] (about) whom Dan[iel] spoke, [the herald of]

19. good, proclaimin[g salvation.] This is what is wr[itt]en about him, what [he said

20. to conso[le?] .. .. [ ] L [will in]struct them about all the periods of wra[th]

21. [ ] truth for . [ ]

22. [ ]

23. [ ]. H she turned from Belial and she .[ ]

24. [ ] with the judgment[s of] God (*'l*), as it is written concerning him, [*'Saying to Zi*]*on, "Your 'Elohim is king."'* (Now) Zi]on i[s

25. [ ] . . . the establisher[s of] the covenant

are those who turn away from walking [in the p[ath of the people. And (as for) your 'Elohim (*'l*[*w*]*hyk*), he (is) [ ]

26. [ ] .... L ..... D Belial, and what he said, *'And you shall sound the horn* [*loud*] *in the* [*seventh*] *mo*[*nth*] (Lv 25:9)

COMMENTARY

The thread which apparently runs through the whole text and ties together its various elements is Lv 25. Parts of three verses of that chapter are quoted: v. 9 in line 26, v. 10 in line 6, and v. 13 in line 2. The fragmentary text begins *in medias res* with a reference to a jubilee year; it is part of a quotation of Lv 25:13, the first part of the thread running through the text. Into this context of a jubilee year and the regulations prescribed for it in Lv 25 the figure of Melchizedek is introduced. He is apparently being given a special role in the execution of divine judgment which is related to a jubilee year. In the course of the midrashic development the year of jubilee mentioned first in line 2 becomes 'the last jubilee' (line 7) or 'the tenth jubilee' (line 7, at the end). In other words, it seems to refer to the end of the 490 years, or 'the seventy weeks of years' of Dn 9:24–27. It is called the year of 'release' (*šmṭh*) proclaimed for the Lord (lines 3–4) and of 'liberation' (*drr*), such as was announced to the captives of Is 61:1. It is a year which involves atonement for iniquity, and the Day of Atonement is somehow related to it; unfortunately, line 7, where the latter seems to be mentioned, is very fragmentary. It is impossible to specify the relation further.

The characteristics of this year of 'release' and 'liberation' are 'peace, welfare (literally, good), and salvation' (see lines 16, 19). These are ensured because of a judgment in which a figure is involved who is either Melchizedek himself, or someone who enjoys 'the heritage of Melchizedek' (lines 5–6). Even though Melchizedek's name must be partly restored in lines 5, 8, and 9, it is nevertheless read with certainty in line 13. So there is little doubt that he is somewhow connected with the year of jubilee with which the text deals. Not only is 'a year of good favour' (*šᵉnat rāṣôn*, cf. Is 61:2) decreed by God in his regard, but Pss 82 and 7 are quoted in reference to him (lines 10–11). These quotations imply that he is somehow God's agent for the execution of divine judgment on man in this year of jubilee. Depending on how strictly and literally these OT quotations are to be applied to him, Melchizedek seems to enjoy a status among or even above such heavenly beings as 'the holy ones of God' (*qᵉdōšê 'El*). The application of Ps 82:1 to him in line 10 is problematical; van der Woude is of the opinion that *'lwhym* in line 10 refers directly to Melchizedek, who thereby is made to take his stand in the assembly of *'El* and in the midst of *'lwhym* he gives judgment.[9] When Ps 7:8–9 is applied to him, it emerges that Melchizedek is somehow exalted even above the *ʿᵃdat 'El*; and when Ps 82:2 is referred to Belial and the spirits of his lot (line 12), we learn that Melchizedek will exact the vengeance of divine judgment from them, being aided in this by 'all the [eternal] *'ēlîm*', i.e., by the angelic spirits of heaven.

The day of judgment to be executed by Melchizedek (or whoever shares his heritage) is apparently further identified with the salvation proclaimed by the herald of Is 52:7 (see lines 15–16). It is not surprising that the year of jubilee, the 'year of good favour', the 'releases', and the 'liberation' are somehow identified in this text with 'salvation', even the salvation of Is 52:7. But what is striking is that the *mᵉbaśśer*, or 'herald', of the Isaian text is said to be 'anointed with the Spirit'. In line 18 van der Woude restored the article before [*m*]*šyḥ*, thus identifying the 'herald' explicitly with 'the Messiah'. His reading was subsequently challenged by Y. Yadin (see commentary below), who proposed the reading *mšwḥ hrw*[*ḥ*], 'anointed with the Spirit'. This, of course, eliminates the reference to a single Messiah (cf. 4QPatrBless 3). But Yadin's reading is, nevertheless, interesting in that it makes of the

[9] *Op. cit.*, 364.

herald of Is 52:7 a messianic figure, i.e., one anointed. This reading is probably a further allusion to Is 61:1, a passage to which we have already referred in the general comments above (p. 246). The connection of these Isaian passages with Dn 9 receives a further support, if my restoration of the end of line 18 is correct, 'and the herald is the one anointed with the Spirit (about) whom Daniel said . . .'. I proposed to read *Danîyel* and referred it to the *māšîaḥ nāgîd* of Dn 9:25. This identification of the herald with the Anointed One of Dn 9, though not certain, is in reality not so striking as the mention of the *mᵉbaśśer* or 'herald of good tidings', as someone anointed, or as a messianic figure. It is known that the 'herald' of Is 52:7 became a figure expected in the beliefs of Palestinian Judaism. He was in fact identified with the Anointed King or King Messiah by R. Jose the Galilean (*c.* A.D. 110), according to *Derekh 'Ereṣ Zuṭa.*[10]

What is to be noted above all in this text, therefore, are the associations which are made with Melchizedek. He is associated with the deliverance of divine judgment, with a day of atonement, with a year of jubilee, and with a role that exalts him high above the assembly of heavenly beings. Such associations make the comparison in Hebrews between Jesus the high priest and Melchizedek all the more intelligible. The tradition is not the same; but what we have in 11QMelch at least furnishes a new light on the comparison. It reveals an almost contemporary Jewish understanding of Melchizedek, which is not without its pertinence for the midrash on him which is incorporated into Heb 7.[11] Whether Melchizedek is the same as the 'herald'

[10] See also *Pesiqta* 51a, 20. Cf. G. Friedrich, *euangelizomai, TDNT* 2, 716–17; Str-B 3, 9–10.

[11] For a fuller discussion of this subject, see my article, '"Now this Melchizedek . . ." (Heb 7:1)', pp. 221–43 above. J. F. X. Sheehan, 'Melchisedech in Christian Consciousness', *ScEccl* 18 (1966) 127–38, takes me to task for my interpretation of the Melchizedek midrash in Heb 7. He attempts to set forth 'the cumulative thrust of the dogmatic, patristic, and even linguistic evidence in favour of the "classical" or "traditional" notions of the role of the bread and the wine in the Melchisedech episode' (p. 128). By so doing, he hopes to show that Melchizedek is still 'among the most

in this text is difficult to say because of the fragmentary state of the document. If he were, then the identification of these various titles with him would be still more interesting, in that they would illustrate in a Jewish text the conflation of expected figures similar to that found in the NT when the many titles, derived from independent OT themes, are applied to Jesus.[12] The fragmentary state of the text, however, prevents us from saying whether this midrash has any connection with either Gn 14:18–20 or Ps 110, the two places in the OT where Melchizedek is explicitly mentioned. What is preserved is a midrashic development which is independent of the classic OT loci. And this is, in my opinion, the reason for saying that the tradition found here is not the same as that in Hebrews, even though it does shed some light on the more general development. J. A. Sanders has suggested to me that possibly the thought-development of Ps 110 underlies the midrash in this text. Possibly there is an echo of Ps 110:6 in line 11, but then this is a quotation of Ps 7:8–9 (the verb *yādîn* occurs in both places). But beyond this extremely superficial echo the influence of Ps 110 on what is preserved of the midrash in this fragmentary text is almost nil.

Did the author of this text consider Melchizedek to be the

---

beloved of the Old Testament pre-figures of the Eucharistic sacrifice' (p. 127). I am particularly unimpressed by what he calls the 'linguistic' evidence; the use of the copula *w-*, followed by a pronoun, can indeed have subordinate meaning (e.g., 'since'), but does it always have it? This explanation is not acceptable in Gn 14:18 without further ado. Nor has he asked himself whether what he calls 'the cumulative thrust of the dogmatic' and 'patristic . . . evidence' is not really an accommodation of the OT text by a later tradition. For an independent confirmation of my views on the subject, one can consult I. Hunt, 'Recent Melkizedek Study', *BCCT* 21–33. See also F. Moriarty, 'Abel, Melchizedek, Abraham', *The Way* 5 (1965) 95–104, esp. 102.

[12] There is a similar conflation of the Son of Man, Messiah, and Elect One in *Enoch* (e.g., see chapters 48–52). But it is not easy to show the conflation of other titles and the application of them to one person in earlier or contemporary Jewish writings. This, then, is an important aspect of 11QMelch.

archangel Michael? Van der Woude inclines to think that he did, because Melchizedek is called *'lwhym* and is exalted above the heavenly court in lines 10–11. He mentions that Jewish tradition regarded Melchizedek as 'high priest' and that Michael is called the heavenly high priest in the Babylonian Talmud (*Ḥagigah* 12b). The medieval writing *Yalkut ḥadaš* (fol. 115, col. 3, n. 19) makes the identification explicit: *myk'l nqr' mlky ṣdq . . . kwhn 'l 'lywn šhw khn šl m'lh.* This identification is, then, clear in later Jewish tradition; but is it in the mind of the author of this text? Is it an early tradition which he might be reflecting? It is impossible to answer these questions in my opinion. If the interpretation of van der Woude be correct, then this is the earliest attestation of this identification. But it is complicated by the fact that the author of the text seems to refer to Melchizedek as *'Elôhîm* (see lines 10 and possibly 25). This is the suggestion of van der Woude himself and it seems correct. See below for the details. This is the basis for his opinion too that Melchizedek is presented in this text as a heavenly redemption-figure.

The following remarks on various phrases will help to give a more detailed interpretation of the text in support of the general commentary supplied above.

2. *[w']šr 'mr:* 'And what he said', i.e. God. This formula commonly introduces an OT quotation, not only in this text (see lines [3], 10, 11, [14], 15 *bis*, 18, 19, 26), but also in other Qumran literature (cf. my article, 'The Use of Explicit Old Testament Quotations in Qumran literature and in the New Testament', pp. 3–58 above). Van der Woude (*op. cit.*, 360–1) has shown that in the Qumran texts there is really no parallel to the NT and rabbinical instances in which the subject of *'mr* could be understood as 'Scripture' or 'a Scripture passage'. In Qumran literature the sense is rather that of a personal subject, either expressed (Levi, CD 4:15; Moses, CD 8:14; 19:26; Isaiah, CD 6:8; Jeremiah, CD 8:20; or God, either with or

without an intermediary, CD 6:13; 8:9; 19:22: 9:7; 4QFlor 1:7; CD 3:19–20; 19:11; 4:14) or understood, as in this case. Van der Woude translates the expression, however, in the present, 'und das, was Er sagt'. The form *'mr* could indeed be the participle, *'ômēr*; and given the fluctuation in the NT between *legei* and *eipen* (see Heb 1:5–13; cf. G. Kittel, *TDNT* 4, 105–6), one might be inclined to say that either participle or perfect were possible. Indeed, both are used in rabbinical writings. However, the perfect is to be preferred in my opinion because of the tendency to *plena scriptio* in the Qumran writings; we would expect *'wmr* here, if the author meant the participle.

bšnt hyw[bl hzw't]: 'In this year of jubilee.' The OT text quoted is probably Lv 25:13, since Lv 25 is further quoted in lines 6 and 26. Theoretically, Lv 27:24 is also possible. The references to *ywbl*, *šmṭh*, and *drwr* in the context of the returning exiles of the Babylonian captivity are better understood in the quotation of Lv 25. This year of jubilee is further identified in line 9 as a year of good favour (*šnt hrṣwn*) decreed by God for Melchizedek and 'the year of the last jubilee' (*šnt hywbl h'ḥrwn*) in line 7, 'the tenth jubilee'. It is not easy to determine the sense in which Lv 25:13 is used here because of the fragmentary state of the text. Van der Woude may be right in thinking of an eschatological possession of the holy land by the returning captives. At least this would be the sense of line 4. Cf. 1QM 2:6 (*bmw'd šnt hšmṭh*), 2:8 (*wbšny hšmṭym*).

3. [*šmw*]*ṭ kwl b'l mšh yd:* 'Let every creditor remit.' The author of the text now associates Dt 15:2 with the year of jubilee. The text agrees with the MT except for *yd*, which is read instead of the latter's *ydw*. Dt 15:2 is immediately concerned with the Sabbatical year, but van der Woude has pointed out the relation of the two verses to each other which is suggested by the LXX, in which *bšnt hywbl* of Lv 25:13 is rendered by *en tō etei tēs apheseōs* and the same word *aphesis* is used in Dt 15:2 for *wzh dbr hšmṭh*. The use of *aphesis* for both *ywbl* and *šmṭh* forms the link between the two.

4. [*l'l*]: 'Of God', or more literally, 'for God'. The MT has at this point *lYhwh*, but given the Qumran reluctance to write the tetragrammaton (see my *The Genesis Apocryphon of Qumran Cave I: A Commentary* [Rome, 1966] 159), van der Woude's restoration is most plausible. Compare the same substitution of *'l* for *Yhwh* in the quotation of Ps 7:9 in line 11 below. It is interesting to note that Dt 15:2 is also used in 1Q*22* ('Dires de Moïse') 3:4–6, where it is joined to phrases taken from Lv 25. At the end, instead of *lYhwh*, we find the restoration *l*[*'*]*l*[*why 'lwhyk*]*m*, an extended paraphrase demanded by the space. In this text God is called *'l*, and apparently not *'lwhym*; see below on line 10.

[*pšrw l'ḥ*]*ryt hymym*: 'Its meaning for the end of days', i.e., its eschatological meaning. The form *pšrw* is also found in lines 12, 17. But the restoration follows the phrase found in 4QpIs[b] 2:1; 4QpIs[c] 10 (*JBL* 77 [1958] 215, 219); 1QpHab 2:5 (with deleted *aleph*).

'l hšbwyym 'šr: 'Concerns those taken captive whom. . . .' The immediate allusion here is undoubtedly to Is 61:1 (*lqr' lšbwym drwr*), the text to which further reference is made in the following lines. For the *plena scriptio*, see 1QIs[a] 49:26. A return to the holy land formed part of the salvific hope of contemporary Judaism; and van der Woude is more inclined to apply the words here to all the diaspora rather than to the Qumran community. Once again it is the fragmentary state of the text which hinders any certain judgment, but there must be some reference to the Qumran community in these words, given their esoteric way of interpreting Scripture in terms of their own community. The use of the preposition *'l* here sheds light on the Greek *eis* used in Eph 5:32. The Isaian passage is quoted in Lk 4:18–19.

5. *wmnḥlt mlky ṣdq*: 'And from the heritage of Melchizedek.' Unfortunately, the fragmentary state of the text once again hinders any real comprehension of this phrase. Van der Woude appeals to Dt 32:8 apropos of the noun *nḥlt*, 'when the Most High gave to the nations their inheritance'. But this seems

scarcely *ad rem* to me. Rather, *nḥlt* more likely refers to the priestly 'inheritance' of the levites, *kî k*^{e}*hunnat Yahweh naḥ*^{a}*lātô* (Jos 18:7). We should recall that Melchizedek is called *kôhēn* in Gn 14:18 (see my remarks on pp. 233–8 above). It may be that the priests of the Qumran community are thus envisaged; and perhaps an ideal one, possessing the 'heritage of Melchizedek' and thus possessing no land of his own, is here regarded as the person to proclaim the year of jubilee and release to the 'captives', to those who are to return to their own possessions.

The end of this line presents a problem, because it is impossible to say whether the name *mlky ṣ*]*dq* is the *nomen rectum* of a construct chain whose *nomen regens* would be the antecedent of the relative pronoun or is itself the antecedent. The latter seems more plausible in the entire context of the document, but then one may ask who it is that enjoys the 'heritage of Melchizedek'. Note the writing of the name in two words; contrast 1QapGn 22:14. See further pp. 229-31 above.

6. *yšybmh 'lyhmh:* 'Will restore them to them.' The prepositional phrase must refer to the captives mentioned in line 4. But who is the subject and what is the direct object? In the opinion of van der Woude the rest of the line alludes to Is 61:1 and so the subject should likely be the Anointed One of line 18. This may be a little far-fetched, in that the Anointed One is not yet named.

wqr' lhmh drr: 'And he will proclaim release to them.' This phrase could be an allusion to Is 61:1 (so van der Woude) or to Jer 34:8 (which is closer in verbal form; cf. 34:15, 17), or to Lv 25:10 (*ûq*^{e}*ra'tem d*^{e}*rōr*). The occurrence of *d*^{e}*rōr* in both Lv 25 and Is 61 is undoubtedly the reason for relating the texts in this midrash. Cf. Lk 4:18, where Jesus appears as the anointed instrument of Yahweh, performing that which the expected figure in this text is to perform.

l^{c}*zwb l*[*h*]*mh:* 'To set them free.' This is the restoration suggested by van der Woude, who also mentions another possibility, *l*^{c}*zwr*, 'to help'. Is *lhmh* to be taken as the direct object here? D. R. Hillers has pointed out to me two possible parallels of this phrase: CD 5:6 (*wy'zbm lw 'l*) and Sir 3:13 (*'zwb lw*). Possibly, then, we should rather translate the phrase, 'to show forebearance to them'.

[*wlkpr*] *'l 'wwnwtyhmh:* 'To atone for their iniquities.' For the idiom, see line 8 and CD 4:9–10 (where God is the subject); 1QS 11:14 (with *b'd* instead of *'l*); 1QS 3:6 (*ykwprw kwl 'wwnwtw*); see also 1Q22 3:7, where the phrase is also partially restored. Underlying the words is undoubtedly the biblical expression found in Dn 9:24 (*lᵉkappēr 'āwōn*), a passage which has otherwise influenced this midrash.

[ ]*dbr hzh:* 'This word', before which we should probably restore the article *h-*. But cf. Dt 15:2 (*wzh dbr hšmṭh*).

7. *bšnt hywbl h'ḥ*[*r*]*wn:* 'In the year of the last jubilee', i.e., the end of the 490 years, or the tenth jubilee (according to the end of this line).

bly[ ]*:* Van der Woude rules out the possibility of reading here *'blym*, 'mourners' (Is 61:2). One might also think of Belial, but how would it fit into the context?

wy[*wm hkpw*]*rym h*[*w'*]*h:* 'That is the Day of Atonement.' Van der Woude does not translate this phrase, nor does he try to explain it. Recall also the mention of 'the Day of Atonement' in 1Q34bis 2+1:6 (see Milik's note in DJD 1, 153), and in 1QpHab 11:7. Perhaps my suggestion is completely out of place here, and is too much influenced by the Epistle to the Hebrews in which both Melchizedek and the Day of Atonement play a significant role. The restoration, indeed, is not certain, but is possible and does not lack some plausibility, given the mention of the Day of Atonement in Lv 25:9. See also line 26 below, and compare the related text of 1Q22 3:9–12.

[*hyw*]*bl h*[*'*]*śyry:* 'The tenth jubilee.' This phrase is most likely an explanation of the 'last jubilee' mentioned at the beginning of this line. It seems to be an obvious reference to Dn 9:24–27, which alludes to Jer 25:11 and 29:10. Cf. 2 Chr 36:20–21. The plausibility of this interpretation is enhanced by *T.*

Levi 17:2 ff.: 'In each jubilee there shall be a priesthood. In the first jubilee the first who is anointed to the priesthood shall be great and shall speak to God as to a father. . . .' But in the succeeding six jubilees the priesthood deteriorates and becomes progressively corrupt. Finally, after the seventh jubilee, 'then shall the Lord raise up a new priest' (18:2). This reference to the *Testament of Levi* supplies some background which makes the 'tenth jubilee' a little more intelligible in terms of Melchizedek's priestly role. And yet, it must be emphasized that Melchizedek does not appear in *T. Levi* 17–18, where this development is found. Be this as it may, it is important not to stress this too much nor to judge the situation too much from the standpoint of the author of the Epistle to the Hebrews, where Melchizedek is set in contrast to the levitical priesthood.

8. *lkpr bw ʿl kwl bny* [*ʾwr*]: 'To atone in it for all (the) sons of light.' The prepositional phrase *bw* ('in it') refers to the tenth jubilee, which seems to be the time of salvation and atonement, or possibly to the Day of Atonement during it. Parallel expressions can be found in 1QS 5:6 (*lkpr lkwl hmtndbym*); 1QM 2:5 (*lkpr bʿd kwl ʿdtw*); cf. *Jub* 34:18; 1Q*22* 3:9–12.

[*w*]*ʾnš*[*y g*]*wrl ml*[*ky*] *ṣdq*: 'And men of the lot of Melchizedek.' This phrase seems to be the counterpart of Belial and 'the spirits of his lot' (line 12). If the reading *ml*[*ky*] *ṣdq* is correct here, then it is quite interesting, because it would be a parallel to *ʾnšy gwrl ʾl* (1QS 2:2; 1QM 13:5; 17:7), in which Melchizedek's name is substituted for that of God. However, van der Woude indicates that the reading is not entirely certain, even though he prefers it to the other possibility *ʾl* [*h*]*ṣdq*, a phrase which is not without some parallelism in 1QM 18:8; 1QH fr 7:8.

9. *hwʾh ḥqq šnt hrṣwn lmlky ṣ*[*dq w*]*l* . . .: 'He has decreed a year of good favour for Melchizedek and for. . . .' The first word *hwʾh* may be simply a pronoun, being used as an emphatic expression of the subject, but it may also be a surrogate for Yahweh (as in 1QS 8:13). The verb *ḥqq* probably refers to the

divine determination of historical periods (compare 1QpHab 7:13; 1QS 10:1). The phrase *šnt hrṣwn*, lit. 'the year of good favour', meaning a year in which God manifests his good will and predilection toward men. It is an echo of Is 61:2 (*liqrō' šenat rāṣôn laYhwh*); cf. 1QH 15:15 (*mw'd rṣwn*) and Lk 4:18.

wqdwšy 'l: 'The holy ones of God', i.e., the angels; cf. CD 20:8 (*kl wqdšy 'lywn*). Reference seems to be made to these beings in the verses of the Psalms which are quoted in the following lines; cf. C. H. W. Brekelmans, *OTS* 14 (1965) 305–29.

lmmšlt mšpṭ: 'For a reign of judgment.' This is apparently the purpose of Melchizedek's exaltation and of the divine decree concerning him; it is the opposite of *mmšlt 'wlh* (1QS 4:19).

k'šr ktwb 'lyw: 'As it is written about it', or possibly 'about him'. In the first instance the preposition *'lyw* would refer to the judgment; in the second, to Melchizedek. Van der Woude prefers the latter, but P. W. Skehan has suggested to me the former possibility. The introductory formula has not previously been found as such in Qumran literature; it resembles a number of others, however. See pp. 8–10 above. The closest parallel seems to be CD 1:13 (*hy' h't 'šr hyh ktwb 'lyh. . .*).

10. *bšyry dwyd:* 'In the songs of David.' Note that the psalm is referred to here as *šîr*, and not as *tehillāh*; for the distinction see 11QPs[a] DavComp 4–5, 9 (DJD 4, 92); cf. 2 Sm 22:1 (=Ps 18:1).

'lwhym [n]ṣb b'[dt 'l], bqwrb 'lwhym yšpwṭ: These words are taken from Ps 82:1, which the RSV translates as follows: 'God has taken his place in the divine council. In the midst of the gods he holds judgment.' However, in the context of this Qumran document one has to modify the translation slightly, because the author obviously understands *b'dt 'l* as 'in the assembly of 'El (*or* God)', whereas the word *'lwhym* must refer to others than God. For this reason I have translated it, ''Elohim has taken his stand in the assembly of El, in the midst of gods he gives judgment.' The word *'Elohim* in the first instance ap-

parently refers to Melchizedek, who is to execute divine judgment in the year of good favour decreed for him. 'The midst of the gods' must then designate an angelic court, above which Melchizedek is exalted. This is the same interpretation as that of van der Woude, who thinks that Melchizedek is presented here as an exalted heavenly being, presiding over the angels who are his helpers and in whose midst he delivers judgment. For the form *qwrb* instead of *qereb*, a not infrequent *qutl* type found in the Qumran texts, see the remarks of M. H. Goshen-Gottstein, 'Linguistic Structure and Tradition in the Qumran Documents', *Scripta hierosolymitana* 4 (1958) 101–37, esp. 126–7.

w'lyw 'mr. 'And about it he (i.e., God) said.' A second quotation from the Psalms is thus introduced and applied to the judgment to be given by Melchizedek.

11. [']*lyh lmrwm šwbh, 'l ydyn 'mym:* 'Take your throne above it in the heights; let God ('El) judge (the) peoples.' Ps 7:8–9 is quoted in the same form as the MT, except that *'l* is substituted for *Yhwh*; see note on line 4 above. *'lyh* in Ps 7 refers to *'dt l'mym*, 'an assembly of peoples', but in this midrash it refers rather to the *'dt 'l* of Ps 82:1, the only feminine expression in the context. The phrase *lmrwm* refers to the heights of heaven, where 'El dwells, and is another indication of the exaltation of Melchizedek. The problematic word in this verse is *šwbh*, which has the same consonantal spelling as the MT. At first sight, it would seem to be a form of *šwb*, 'return' and possibly the author of the midrash so understood it. However, it makes little sense in the context, and possibly we should rather read *šybh* and understand it as a form of *yšb*, 'sit'. This certainly yields a far better sense; see H.-J. Kraus, *Psalmen* (BKAT XV/1; Neukirchen, 1960) 1, 54; M. J. Dahood, *Psalms I* (AB) 44.

w'šr '[*mr*]*:* See note on line 2.

[*'d mty t*]*špwṭw 'wwl wpny rš'*[*y*]*m tś*[*'w*]*:* 'How long shall you judge unjustly and lift up the face of (the) wicked?' This is a quotation from Ps 82:2; its form corresponds to the MT save for the *plena scriptio* of *tšpwṭw* and *'wwl*. Its collocation with the other two psalm verses just quoted might suggest that it refers to Melchizedek, as they do; but it would then imply that he is being rebuked by the words of the psalm which preserves a divine rebuke of unjust judges. This would be a little strange in the context. However, the explanation which is given immediately after the quotation shows that the words are not addressed to Melchizedek, but to Belial and the spirits of his lot, who are to be judged by Melchizedek.

[*s*]*lh:* 'Selah.' This word is found here, just as in the MT. It is also found in 11QPs[a] 25:12 (DJD 4, 46; =Ps 143:6). For a discussion of its meaning, see H.-J. Kraus, *Psalmen*, 1, xxv–xxvi.

bmwšh ky': 'In Moses, that . . .', i.e., in the Torah, or possibly in the Scriptures. These words are written vertically in the margin, beginning between lines 11 and 12. Perhaps they belong in line 10 after *wʿlyw 'm*[*r*] and before the quotation of Ps 82:2. A. S. van der Woude thinks that these words belonged to a preceding column; they are, however, written very close to the beginning of this one. For a parallel to 'in Moses', see 2 Cor 3:15; cf. Jn 10:34 (where Ps 81:6 is quoted as 'the Law'); Jn 15:25 (Ps 24:19 so quoted).

12. *pšrw ʿl blyʿl wʿl rw*[*ḥ*]*y gwrlw:* 'Its interpretation concerns Belial and concerns the spirits of his lot.' The words of Ps 82:2 are thus applied to Belial in a very vague way. Belial is well known in Qumran literature as the chief spirit of evil, 'the angel of hostility' (1QM 13:11), 'the prince of the dominion of evil' (1QM 17:5). Those identified as belonging to his lot are usually called *kwl 'nšy gwrlw* (1QM 4:2; cf. 1QS 2:4–5; CD 12:2). But in 1QM 13:2, 4, 11 we find *rwḥy gwrlw*, who are 'angels of destruction'. The same phrase is plausibly restored in line 13 below. Cf. 2 Cor 6:15; see pp. 209–13 above.

bsp[*r*] . . . *wqy'l:* Unintelligible.

13. *wmlky ṣdq yqwm nq*[*m*]*t mšpṭy* [*'l*]*:* 'And Melchizedek shall exact the vengeance of the judgments of God (*or* 'El).' Melchizedek now clearly appears in his role as an instrument of the execution of divine judgment. His role is described and related

to the *yôm nāqām lē'lôhênû* (Is 61:2), 'the day of vengeance for our God'. For 'the judgments of God', see line 24.

[*myd b*]*ly'l wmyd kwl* [*rwḥy gwrl*]*w*: 'From the hand of Belial and from the hand(s) of all the spirits of his lot.' See note on line 12 above; cf. 1QS 4:18.

14. *wb'zrw kwl 'ly* ['*wlmym*]: 'And all the eternal gods are for his help.' This is van der Woude's restoration. It is not, however, certain and presents a difficulty. He restores it on the basis of an expression which J. Strugnell says occurs in Qumran literature (see VTSup 7 [1959] 331). What is strange here is that the angels who are to be Melchizedek's helpers are called *'ly*, whereas in the rest of the text *'l* is used for God and *'lwhym* for angels (or Melchizedek). *b'zrw*: b+infinitive construct with the suffix, 'for helping him'.

[*h*]*w'h 'šr 'mr*: 'This is what he said.' A similar expression is found in CD 10:16; 16:15; 1QpHab 3:2, 13–14; cf. p. 12 above.

[*k*]*wl bny ḥ*[*y*]*l whp*[ ]: 'All the sons of might (?) and the P[ ].' The expression *bny ḥyl* is found in the OT (2 Sm 2:7; 13:28; 17:10; etc.), and the introductory phrase which precedes should make this part of a quotation; but I have been unable to find any passage which is suited to this context.

15. *hw'h ywm h*[*hrgh*]: This is van der Woude's restoration, based on 1QH 15:17, where the word is also restored (cf. Jer 12:3). He translates it, 'das ist der Tag der Schlachtung', explaining it as the day of eschatological judgment. While not impossible, it does not seem to fit very well into the context which follows (with its quotation from Isaiah).

[']*šr 'mr* [*l'ḥryt hymym byd yš'*]*yh hnby' 'šr 'm*[*r*]: '(About) which he said for the end of days through Isaiah the prophet, who said. . . .' This full formula occurs here for the first time in Qumran texts; it should be compared with 4QFlor 1:15; CD 4:14; 19:10–11; 3:21.

[*mh*] *n'ww 'l hrym rgl*[*y*] *mbś*[*r*] . . .: 'How beautiful upon the mountains are the feet of the herald', etc. The text is the same

as the MT of Is 52:7, except for the form *hrym* (without the article) and the *plena scriptio* of *'wmr*. Note, however, that *hhrym* occurs in line 17. There is, of course, the earlier passage of Na 2:1 which is echoed. 1QH 18:14 also alludes to Is 52:7.

16. *[m]šmy' šlwm:* 'Proclaiming peace.' Is this possibly the reason why this quotation of Is 52:7 is introduced into this midrash, because it contains a reference to *šlwm*, 'peace', and could be exploiting the pun on the 'king of Salem'? Cf. Heb 7:2; see pp. 231–3 above. It may be, though, that this observation is too much influenced by the Epistle to the Hebrews and the association did not really enter into the mind of the author of this text.

[mlk] 'lwhyk: 'Your God is king', or more literally, 'has reigned'.

17. *pšrw:* 'Its interpretation.' See note on line 4.

hhr[ym]: 'The mountains', here with the article. This suggests that the form in line 16 is a scribal error.

tby'w[ty]hmh: 'Their produce.' The third letter is clearly a *yodh* and not the expected *waw*.

18. *whmbśr hw]'h [m]šwḥ hrw[ḥ] 'šr 'mr dn[y'l] . . .:* 'And the herald is the one anointed with the Spirit (about) whom Daniel said. . . .' Van der Woude first read *whmbśr hw['h hmšyḥ hw'[h]*, 'and the herald is that Anointed One'. However, Y. Yadin ('A Note on Melchizedek and Qumran', *IEJ* 15 [1965] 152–4) called his reading of this line in question and proposed to read rather *[m]šwḥ hrw[ḥ]*, which is certainly better. It has been accepted by M. de Jonge and A. S. van der Woude in *NTS* 12 (1965–66) 301–2. This corrected reading makes an allusion to Is 61:1 rather clear. Given other references in this text to Dn 9:24–27, it is not impossible that the *dn*[ ] should be filled out as we have restored it here; it would thus contain a reference to the *māšîaḥ nāgîd* of Dn 9:25. In fact, even though van der Woude reads only a *daleth* before the lacuna, there is in my opinion also the trace of a *nun* after it. If this reading should prove acceptable, then one might have to reconsider van der

Woude's suggestion that the Anointed One mentioned here was more of a prophetic figure than a political ruler (p. 367). On the other hand, if Melchizedek himself is to be identified with the 'herald' who is also 'the Messiah', then one might hesitate. Melchizedek would be thought of more readily in terms of a priestly Messiah—he was in Gn 14 both priest and king.

What is above all striking here is the mention of the *mᵉbaśśer* of Is 52:7 as one anointed. See the general remarks above, at the beginning of the commentary. Van der Woude restored the article before [*m*]*šyḥ*, but it is almost certainly not to be read thus. The singular reference to 'the Messiah' is thus eliminated. But one should note the joining of the allusion to Is 61:1 with that of Is 52:7—a significant joining of the two Isaian motifs that is paralleled in the New Testament.

19. *hw'h hk*[*tw*]*b ʿlyw 'šr* [*'mr*]: 'That is what is written about him, what he said. . . .' See note on line 9; cf. 4QFlor 1:16.

20. *lnḥm . . .* [*y*]*śkylmh bkwl qṣy ḥ*[*rwn*]: 'to console (?) . . . will instruct them about all the periods of wrath.' Cf. Is 61:2. *qṣy ḥrwn*: See 1QH fr. 1:5; 4QpHos[b] 1:12.

23. *srh mblyʿl wt.* [ ]: 'She turned from Belial and she . . . .' The feminine forms here probably refer to Zion.

24. *bmšpṭy 'l*: 'With the judgments of God (*or* El).' See line 13.

k'šr ktwb ʿlyw: See note on line 9.

[*ṣy*]*wn h*[*y'h . . .*]: '(Now) Zion is. . . .' Perhaps some phrase like 'the abode of' should be restored in the lacuna, because Zion is actually being interpreted in terms of the upright ones in the community who have made the covenant with Yahweh.

25. *mqym*[*y*] *hbryt*: 'The establishers of the covenant.' The phrase *lhqm hbryt* can be found in different forms in 1QS 5:21; 8:10; 1QSb 5:23; 1QM 13:7; CD 3:13; 4:9. Cf. Gn 17:19. The phrase designates obviously members of the Qumran community.

hsrym mlkt [*bd*]*rk hʿm*: 'Those who turn away from walking in the path of the people.' The same phrase is found in 4QFlor 1:14 (see *JBL* 77 [1958] 353; but also Y. Yadin, *IEJ* [1959]

95); 1QSa 1:2–3; CD 8:16; 19:29. The phrase is derived from Is 8:11 (see LXX).

w'l[w]hyk hw'h [ ]: 'And (as for) your 'Elohim, he is. . . .' Van der Woude may well be right to suggest this phrase from Is 52 was explained in terms of Melchizedek; see line 10.

26. *blyʿl:* See note on line 12 above.

w'šr 'mr: See note on line 2 above.

whʿbrtmh šwp[r trwʿh] bḥ[wdš] h[šbyʿy]: 'And you shall sound the horn loud in the seventh month. . . .' This is a quotation from Lv 25:9, in form identical with the MT, except for the 2nd pl. (*hʿbrtmh*) instead of the 2nd sg.; cf. LXX. Van der Woude thinks the quotation would refer to the sounding of the last trumpet on Judgment Day (cf. 1 Thes 4:16); but this seems a little far-fetched to me. Once again, it is the fragmentary state of the text which hinders any certain interpretation.

These remarks scarcely exhaust all the aspects of this interesting, though fragmentary, new text. Perhaps they will stimulate still further discussion of it. Even though it is not possible to say that the presentation of Melchizedek which is found in it directly influenced the midrash on him in Heb 7 (because the latter is developed almost exclusively in terms of the classic OT loci, Gn 14 and Ps 110), nevertheless its exaltation of Melchizedek and its view of him as a heavenly redemption-figure make it understandable how the author of the epistle to the Hebrews could argue for the superiority of Christ the high priest over the levitical priesthood by appeal to such a figure. The exalted status of Melchizedek which is presented in this text gives another aspect to the Christology of the epistle in which Jesus is depicted as a priest *kata tēn taxin Melchisedek.*[13]

[13] See further M. de Jonge and A. S. van der Woude, '11Q Melchizedek and the New Testament', *NTS* 12 (1965–66) 301–26; J. A. Emerton, 'Melchizedek and the Gods: Fresh evidence for the Jewish Background of John X. 34–6', *JTS* 17 (1966) 399–401; R. Meyer, 'Melchisedek von Jerusalem und Moresedek von Qumran', *VTSup* 15 (1966) 228–39; D. Flusser, 'Melchizedek and the Son of Man', *Christian News from Israel* 17 (1966) 228–39; M. P. Miller, 'The Function of Isa 61:1–2 in 11Q Melchizedek', *JBL* 88 (1969) 467–9.

V

EARLY CHRISTIANITY

13

JEWISH CHRISTIANITY IN ACTS IN THE LIGHT OF THE QUMRAN SCROLLS*

It is by now a well-worn platitude to say that the Qumran Scrolls have shed new light on Christian origins. Yet in a volume dealing with studies in Luke–Acts and dedicated to Prof. Paul Schubert, who has shown a long and sustained interest in such studies, there is room for a reassessment of the relationship between Qumran and the early church. The Qumran texts have brought to light many new details of Palestinian Judaism in the period in which Christianity emerged. They have been studied in detail by many scholars and from different points of view. It is not out of place, then, to review here the significance of these new finds for first-century Jewish Christianity as it is depicted in the Acts of the Apostles.

The Qumran literature comes from a group of Jews whose principal community centre existed on the northwest shore of the Dead Sea roughly between 150 B.C. and A.D. 70. These dates are supported by both archaeological and paleographical evidence.[1] The sect, whose beliefs and way of life are made known

* Originally published in *Studies in Luke-Acts: Essays Presented in Honor of Paul Schubert* (ed. L. E. Keck and J. L. Martyn; London: SPCK, 1966) 233–57.

[1] See R. de Vaux, *L'archéologie et les manuscrits de la Mer Morte* (Schweich Lectures, 1959; London, 1961). J. T. Milik, *Ten Years of Discovery in the Wilderness of Judaea* (SBT XXVI; Naperville, 1959) 133–6. F. M. Cross, Jr., *The Ancient Library of Qumran and Modern Biblical Studies* (Anchor, rev. ed.; Garden City, 1961) 117–27. N. Avigad, 'The Palaeography of the Dead Sea Scrolls and Related Documents', *Scripta hierosolymitana* IV (1958) 56–87.

to us in this literature, is revealed to be a community that is wholly Jewish, dedicated to the study and observance of the Torah, yet living a communal, religious, and ascetic mode of life for a considerable period before the emergence of Christianity. The data from these scrolls have made the majority of the scholars who have studied them identify the Qumran sect with the Essenes, even though some of the new material is not always perfectly reconcilable with what was previously known about the Essenes from the classical sources of Philo, Josephus, Pliny the Elder, Hippolytus, and Dio Chrysostom.[2] For my part, this identification is acceptable, and I shall not be concerned with any further attempt to establish it. I do admit, however, especially with J. T. Milik, traces of a Pharisaic influence on the group.[3] But there seems to be little reason to connect them in any way with the Sadducees,[4] the Zealots,[5] or the Ebionites.[6] It is also necessary to distinguish at times between the Essenes

[2] Philo, *Quod omnis probus liber sit* 72–91; *Apologia pro Iudaeis* 11, 1–18 (cf. Eusebius, *Praeparatio evangelica* 8, 11, 1–18); *De vita contemplativa* 1–90. Josephus, *Jewish War* 1, 3, #78–80; 2, 7, #111–13; 2, 8, #119–61; 2, 20, #566–8; *Antiquities* 13, 59, #171–2; 18, 1, 5, #18–22. C. Plinius Secundus (the Elder), *Naturalis historia* 5, 17, 4. Dio Chrysostom, 3, 1–4. Hippolytus, *Refutatio omnium haeresium* 9, 18–28. See A. Adam, *Antike Berichte über die Essener* (Kleine Texte 182; Berlin, 1961).

[3] *Ten Years*, 87–93. A. Dupont-Sommer (*The Essene Writings from Qumran* [tr. G. Vermes; Oxford, 1961] 145, 408) likewise admits such Pharisaic influence on the Qumran sect, although he rightly rejects the thesis of C. Rabin (*Qumran Studies* [Oxford, 1957]) that the sect was in fact Pharisaic.

[4] Despite the frequent use of the term 'sons of Zadok' to designate the members of the Qumran sect (1QS 5:2, 9; 1QSa 1:2, 24; 2:2; etc.). See R. North, 'The Qumran "Saducees"', *CBQ* XVII (1955) 44–68; J. Trinquet, *VT* I (1951) 287–92.

[5] Thus C. Roth, *The Historical Background of the Dead Sea Scrolls* (Oxford, 1958); 'New Light on the Dead Sea Scrolls', *Commentary* XXXVII/6 (June, 1964) 27–32.

[6] So J. L. Teicher in a series of articles in *JJS* II (1951) 67–99; III (1952) 53–5, 87–8, 111–18, 128–32, 139–50; IV (1953) 1–13, 49–58, 93–103, 139–53; V (1954) 38, 93–9; etc. Cf. M. A. Chevallier, *L'esprit et le messie dans le Bas-Judaïsme et le Nouveau Testament* (Paris, 1958) 136–43. This view is without foundation since it utterly neglects archaeological evidence and misinterprets most of the Qumran texts that it uses. See below, pp. 435–80; *TS* XX (1959) 451–5.

of Qumran—of the 'motherhouse', as it were—and those of the 'camps' in the land of Damascus. For in some details the Essene mode of life differed in these two situations.

The other term of our comparison is Jewish Christianity, precisely as it is presented in the Acts of the Apostles. The influence of the Essenes on the Christian church has been detected in other writings, and a consideration of these would give a more complete picture. But we are interested only in trying to assess the extent to which the picture of Jewish Christianity as it is painted in Acts has been illumined by what we know of the Qumran sect and its literature.

If a plausible case has been made for some contact between John the Baptist and the Qumran sect,[7] the extent to which similar contact can be shown between Jesus of Nazareth and this group is far less definable. With the data available at present it is almost impossible to determine it. But in any case it is widely admitted that some influence was exerted by the Qumran Essenes on the early church, at least as it is depicted in the writings of Paul, Matthew, and John.[8] One may debate whether this contact is direct or indirect, and whether it was exerted on the early Palestinian Church or only the New Testament authors. But the data in the Qumran texts provide at least an intelligible Palestinian matrix for many of the practices and tenets of the early church. Our discussion then is an attempt to assess the areas of influence and contact between the Essenes and the Jewish Christian church in Acts.

JEWISH CHRISTIANITY IN ACTS

Before attempting to compare the pertinent material, let us summarize briefly the picture of the Jewish Christian church in

[7] See J. A. T. Robinson, 'The Baptism of John and the Qumran Community', *HTR* L (1957) 175–91; reprinted: *Twelve New Testament Studies* (SBT XXXIV; Naperville, 1962) 11–27. W. H. Brownlee, 'John the Baptist in the Light of Ancient Scrolls', *Int* IX (1955) 71–90.

[8] See P. Benoit, 'Qumran and the New Testament', *Paul and Qumran* (ed. J. Murphy-O'Connor; London, 1968) 1–30.

Acts. When we open the book of Acts, we are immediately introduced to a group of disciples of Jesus of Nazareth who are at least vaguely aware of their identity as a group. They may be addressed simply as 'men of Galilee' (1:11), but they are also 'chosen apostles' (1:2). Scarcely any indication is given of their previous backgrounds, but they seem to have been part of the *'am hā-'āreṣ*. This is at least suggested by the conduct of Peter and John (8:14–25; 9:43; 11:2–3) who were not concerned with Pharisaic prescriptions and distinctions. Some of the eleven bear Greek names, and yet they are Palestinian Jews who have banded together, united by a belief in Jesus, 'a man certified by God with mighty works and wonders' (2:22), whom 'God raised' from the dead (2:32). These disciples are his 'witnesses' (1:8), and under the inspiration of God's Spirit they proclaim him and his message to 'all the house of Israel': God has made this Jesus 'both Lord and Messiah' (2:36). Such a christological belief sets them apart from the rest of the 'house of Israel' and makes them conscious of their Jewish *Christian* character.

But from the very beginning of the story in Acts this Christian group is marked as *Jewish* in its origins and background. Before the event of Pentecost they are depicted as men looking to this Lord and Messiah as the one who would 'restore the kingdom of Israel' (1:6). The 'men of Galilee' go up to the temple daily (2:46; 3:1, 11); they celebrate the festival of Weeks (2:1); they observe the Sabbath (1:12). One of their leaders, James, lends his support to the Jerusalem temple for a considerable time (21:8–26). The God whom they continue to worship is 'the God of Abraham, and of Isaac, and of Jacob, the God of our fathers' (3:13). In time 'a great number of the priests embraced the faith' (6:7), obviously a reference to members of Jewish priestly families. A nucleus of twelve—a number inspired by the twelve tribes of Israel—symbolizes the fact that the group is the New Israel.

These Jewish Christians carry their belief in Jesus of Nazareth as the Lord and Messiah from Jerusalem to Judea, Samaria, and Galilee (1:4, 8; 8:1; 9:31; cf. Lk 24:47). Gradually their numbers increase; the initial 120 members of the Pentecostal assembly in Jerusalem become three thousand (2:41), then five thousand (4:4). The number steadily grows (6:7), until a summary acknowledges, just before the message spreads to Gentile areas, that the 'church throughout all Judea, Galilee and Samaria enjoyed peace and was being built up' (9:31). During all this growth the Christian group is marked off from the Jewish people as such. 'None of the rest of the people dared to join them, but they held them in great esteem' (5:13). While one cannot apodictically exclude from the Palestinian church at this time converts from paganism, the picture in Acts 1–9 is certainly that of a predominantly Jewish Christian church.

Acts vaguely suggests that the Christian group looked on itself as the New Israel; this seems at least implied in the disciples' question about the restoration of the kingdom to Israel (1:6) and in the need felt to reconstitute the twelve (1:15–26). The corporate character of the Jewish Christians is formulated for the first time in the word *koinōnia* (2:42).[9] It is noteworthy that before the account mentions Saul and his career, there is scarcely any attempt to depict the community as *ekklēsia*. The sole exception to this is the summary statement at the end of the story of Ananias and Sapphira (5:11).[10] Once the career of Saul is begun, however, then the Christian community is referred to as *ekklēsia* (8:1, 3; 9:31; 11:22 ['the church in Jerusalem'], 26;

[9] The meaning of *koinōnia* in this text is debated. That it refers to the specific act of a contribution during a liturgical service is not very convincing but has been proposed by J. Jeremias (*Jesus als Weltvollender, BFTh* XXXIII 4 [Gütersloh, 1930] 78; cf. E. Haenchen, *Die Apostelgeschichte* [12th ed.; Göttingen, 1959] 153). The communal sharing of goods, property, and food was an important part of *koinōnia*, as 2:44–46 seems to make clear. But what the word immediately indicates is the corporate character of the Christian group, as it expressed itself in various ways (spiritual, material, and liturgical). See Ph.-H. Menoud, *La vie de l'Église naissante* (Cahiers théologiques XXXI; Neuchâtel, 1952) 22–34.

[10] The use of the word here reflects a later awareness on the part of the author, since it forms part of a 'summary'. See H. J. Cadbury, *BC* V, 402.

12:1, 5; 13:1; etc.). Moreover, in none of his statements in Acts about his early persecution of the young church does Paul speak of *ekklēsia*. The persecuted 'Jesus' is identified in 9:2–5 with 'some belonging to the Way'; in 22:4 he says, 'I persecuted this Way to the death'; and in 26:9, 15 'Jesus' is identified with 'many of the saints'. By the same token, it is only with the beginning of the story of Saul that we meet the expression, 'the Way' (9:2; cf. 19:9, 23; 22:4; 24:14, 22), as a designation of the Christian movement. Finally, we eventually see 'the Way' referred to as a 'sect' (*hairesis*, 24:14).[11] These details seem to indicate the rather nebulous awareness which the early Jewish Christian church had at first of its corporate character.

On the other hand, it is an awareness that grows as the account in Acts advances. Even though the account was written at a later date and from a standpoint which was considerably developed, nevertheless these expressions seem to reflect an early Jewish Christian community gradually becoming consciously structured in its corporate entity. The awareness of itself as *ekklēsia* comes with persecution and missionary effort, both of which are interrelated in the account in Acts.

Though indications are given of a small nucleus in the early community which has authority and shapes the group, nevertheless they are not such as to reveal the community as a well-defined organization. There are the 'chosen apostles' (1:2), the small band of the 'eleven' (1:26; 2:14) or the 'twelve' (6:2), which plays the important role of 'witnesses to his resurrection'. It is the 'teaching of the apostles' (2:42) which shapes the community. Singled out as exercising authority, however, are Peter (1:15; 2:14; 15:7) and James. The latter is recognized by

[11] Josephus never mentions the Christian movement as a *hairesis* among the Jews. But Acts three times (24:14; 24:5; 28:22) calls it such, using the very word that Josephus employs for the Pharisees, Sadducees, and Essenes (*Ant.* 13, 5, 9, #171; see also 20, 9, 1, #199; *Vita* 2, #10, 12; cf. Acts 15:5; 5:17; 26:5). This use of *hairesis* for Christianity records the impression that it made on contemporary Palestinian Jews. It was regarded as another 'sect' springing from the bosom of Judaism, espousing what was central to it (reverence of Yahweh, the Torah, and the temple).

Peter (12:17) and greeted officially by Paul (21:18); he also settles a disputed question for the local churches (15:13). But there is also mention of 'the apostles and the elders' (15:2, 4, 6, 22, 23; 16:4; cf. 21:18), whose advice and decision are sought. Eventually the community appoints seven 'assistants' to care for its dole.

The picture of the life of the early Jewish Christian community is painted in idyllic colours. It is a fervent community, practising a communal form of life; it is devoted 'to the teaching of the apostles, to a community-spirit, to the breaking of bread, and to prayers' (2:42). 'All who believed shared everything in common; they would sell their property and belongings and divide all according to each one's need' (2:44; cf. 2:46). 'One heart and soul animated the company of those who believed, and no one would say that he possessed anything of his own' (4:32).

The first suggestion of some diversity in the Palestinian church is met in 6:1, where the 'Hellenists' murmured against the 'Hebrews' because their widows were neglected in the daily distribution. *Hellēnistai* is the name for certain members of the Christian community. But 9:29 suggests that the name had already been in use among Palestinian Jews and was merely taken over by Christians to designate converts from such a distinctive group.[12] Its meaning among the Jews is a matter of debate. Since the time of John Chrysostom the 'Hellenists' have been understood as 'Greek-speaking Jews'.[13] Their presence in the Palestinian church would be understandable in the light of Acts 2:5, 9–10. They had come from the diaspora and had taken up residence in Jerusalem. This meaning, however,

[12] C. F. D. Moule, whose opinion I otherwise prefer (see 'Once More, Who Were the Hellenists?' *ExpT* LXX [1958–59] 100–2), considers the Hellenists of Acts 9:29 to be Christians. This is difficult to understand in the context. They are preferably to be regarded as Jews (so E. Haenchen, *Die Apostelgeschichte*, 280; M. Simon, *St Stephen and the Hellenists in the Primitive Church* [New York, 1958] 14–15).

[13] *Homily* 14 (in Acts 6:1); *PG* 60, 113; *Homily* 21 (in Acts 9:29); *PG* 60, 164.

has been questioned because Paul was such a diaspora Jew and calls himself *Hebraios* (Phil. 3:5; 2 Cor. 11:22); apparently he did not regard himself as a 'Hellenist'. Some years ago H. J. Cadbury argued that *Hellēnistēs* meant no more than *Hellēn* since it was a derivative of *hellēnizō*, which means 'to live as a Greek' not 'to speak Greek'. For him 'Hellenist' was a title for Gentile members of the Palestinian church.[14] His explanation, however, has not been widely accepted; many commentators still prefer Chrysostom's explanation, especially since the context of Acts 6 seems to demand that the 'Hellenists' were Jewish Christians of some sort. This is likewise the view of C. F. D. Moule, who recently made the attractive suggestion that *Hellēnistai* meant 'Jews who spoke *only* Greek', while *Hebraioi* means 'Jews who, while able to speak Greek, knew a Semitic language *also*'.[15] This explanation seems suitable. But it should also be recalled that such a linguistic difference would also bring with it a difference in outlook and attitude. More than likely the influence of Hellenism would be greater among the 'Hellenists' than among the 'Hebrews'. But in either case it is a question of degree, since this explanation allows the Hellenists to be Jews, as the context apparently demands.[16]

That the Hellenists were Jews of some sort is likewise recognized by O. Cullmann, who has tried to identify them in some vague way with the Qumran sectarians.[17] If this identification were correct, then the Hellenists would belong to the original Palestinian church from the beginning and would have had nothing to do with the diaspora. As Jews who differed from official Judaism and displayed more or less esoteric tendencies and an opposition to the Jerusalem temple, they would have

[14] *BC* V, 59–74; IV, 64.

[15] 'Once More, Who Were the Hellenists?', 100.

[16] Cf. M. Simon, *St Stephen*, 34–5. It is perhaps too strong a judgment to regard them as 'paganizing' Jews, as Simon suggests.

[17] 'The Significance of the Qumran Texts for Research into the Beginnings of Christianity', *JBL* LXXIV (1955) 213–26; reprinted: K. Stendahl (ed.), *The Scrolls and the New Testament* (New York, 1957) 18–32.

been called 'Hellenists' by the rest. From such a background would have come the 'Hellenist' converts of Acts 6:1, and with them Paul disputes in 9:29. But this specific identification of the Hellenists as Jews of Essene background (or of a kind of Judaism close to it) introduces an improbability into the discussion. It is difficult to see how such strict-living Essenes, rigorously observant of the Torah and cultivating a rather exclusive way of life, even hostile to the temporizing and levitically 'unclean' priesthood of Jerusalem, could give to others the impression that they were *hellēnizontes*, 'living like Greeks'. Not even their attitude toward the temple, supposing that it agreed with Stephen's, would imply their adoption of Hellenizing ways, which had become such an abomination to observant Jews since the time of Antiochus IV Epiphanes (cf. 2 Mc 4:13–17). And their connection with Pythagoreans is more alleged than substantiated. So we see no reason to identify the Hellenists of Acts specifically with converts from Essenism or a form of Judaism close to it.

At any rate, the distinction of Hellenists and Hebrews does not introduce into the Palestinian church a non-Jewish element. This does not mean, however, that there was not a variety of Jewish converts. For there were in the early Christian community converts from the priestly families (6:7) and 'believers who belonged to the party of the Pharisees' (15:5). The latter are depicted as Christians who insisted on the strict observance of the Mosaic law. And yet, they can hardly be identified simply with the 'Hebrews'. This latter group must have included also converts from the *'Am hā-'āreṣ*, from the Essenes and from the Samaritans, even though none of the last three groups are mentioned as such in Acts. Possibly some Essenes were included among the priests of 6:7, but one could never restrict this notice to them alone.

The persecution which raged against the early church in Palestine was an important factor in the spread of the gospel among the Gentiles. Yet when Saul made his way to Damascus, it was to the synagogues of that town that he was heading, presumably in pursuit of Jewish Christians (9:2). And even as the missionary effort among the Gentiles got under way, the church in Jerusalem remained notably Jewish. James, the 'brother of the Lord', became its leader; and though he is not called a bishop, his place of prominence there, his stability in one area, and his administrative decision for nearby local churches give him marks that resemble those of the residential bishop of later times. Be this as it may, his prominence reflects at least the predominance of Jewish Christians in the Palestinian church. Jewish practices were still admitted as part of the Christian way of life in Jerusalem as late as *c.* A.D. 58, when Paul after a long apostolate among the Gentiles went through the rite of the Nazirite at James' request (21:23–26).

These would seem to be the main features of the picture of the early Jewish Christian church which is painted in Acts. We want to see how our understanding of such a picture has been affected by the Qumran literature. This entails a consideration of the main points of contact detected between Acts and the Scrolls.[18]

But before we look at the details it would be well to recall that the comparison of the early Jewish Christian church with the Essene communities brings out fundamental differences far more than resemblances. These differences emerge when one considers the character and the goal of the two groups. Even if we admit the difference of Qumran Essenism from that of the 'camps' of Damascus, there is still a vast difference between the Essene movement and that of early Christianity. The difference is more manifest when the Jewish Christians are compared with

[18] Most of the data for this study were amassed when H. Braun's second article ('Qumran und das Neue Testament: Ein Bericht über 10 Jahre Forschung, 1950–59', *TRu* XXIX [1963] 142–76) arrived. My task has been considerably lightened by this invaluable survey. Since Braun's article takes up and discusses many of the small suggestions that have been made apropos of one verse or another, I shall not repeat them here. I concentrate on the major issues on which a judgment can be based.

the Qumran Essenes. The discipline there laid stress on celibacy, obligatory communal ownership of property, common meals, regulated prayer, study and esoteric interpretation of the Torah, probation for candidates, fines and a form of excommunication, and a structured organization in which monarchic and democratic elements were admitted. Such a strictly organized community the early Jewish Christian church never was. Nor did it have the exclusive character of the Essene movement; it did not retire to the desert or to the 'camps'. It adopted an attitude toward the law of Moses that would have been wholly inadmissible among the Essenes. It also had a backward look in that it regarded Jesus of Nazareth as the Messiah who had already come, whereas the Essene movement still shared the hope of the coming of, not *a* Messiah, but a prophet and two Messiahs.

And yet with such fundamental differences between the two groups there are a number of points of contact and influence which must be recognized. To such points we now turn our attention.

QUMRAN PARALLELS

1. Our discussion begins with those designations of the Essene and the Jewish Christian groups which are common to both Acts and the literature of the Scrolls.

The first designation is the absolute use of 'the Way' referring to the mode of life lived in these communities. *hē hodos* is found only in Acts (9:2; 19:9, 23; 22:4; 24:14, 22) among the New Testament writings; it succinctly describes the form of Christianity practised in Jerusalem and Palestine. E. Haenchen in his monumental commentary on Acts wrote, 'We do not know where the absolute use of *hodos* for Christianity comes from.'[19] He compares *tēn hodon tou kyriou* (18:25) and *tēn hodon tou theou* (18:26), but though these expressions fill out the meaning of 'the Way', they do not explain the origin of its absolute use.

[19] *Die Apostelgeschichte*, 268, n. 3. See also the comments of K. Lake and H. J. Cadbury, *BC* IV, 100; V, 391–2.

Acts 24:14 implies that 'the Way' was a term which the Christian community used of itself in contrast to the term *hairesis*, undoubtedly used of it by outsiders who associated it with other movements among the Jews. Haenchen rightly states that the rabbinical parallels listed in Strack-Billerbeck's *Kommentar* (2,690) are scarcely to the point.

However, the same absolute use of 'the Way' occurs in the Qumran writings to designate the mode of life of the Essenes.[20] The following passages best illustrate the use of it. 'Those who have chosen the Way' (1QS 9:17–18, *lbwḥry drk*); 'these are they who turn aside from the Way' (CD 1:13, *hm sry drk*; cf. CD 2:6; 1QS 10:21). 'These are the regulations of the Way for the master' (1QS 9:21, *'lh tkwny hdrk lmśkyl*). (See further 1QS 4:22; 8:10, 18, 21; 9:5, 9; 11:11; 1QM 14:7; 1QH 1:36; 1QSa 1:28.) At Qumran 'the Way' referred above all to a strict observance of the Mosaic law, especially as this was interpreted in the community. This is made clear in 1QS 8:12–15: 'When these become members of the Community in Israel according to these rules, they will separate from the gathering of the men of iniquity to go to the desert to prepare the Way of HIM, as it is written, "In the desert prepare the way of . . . ., make straight in the wilderness a highway for our God" (Is 40:3). This is the study of the Law [which] he ordered to be done through Moses' (cf. 1QS 9:19). The absolute use of 'the Way' among the Essenes may well go back to this passage in Isaiah. It should be noted too that there is a Qumran counterpart for the fuller expressions used in Acts; compare 'the way of the Lord' (18:25) and 'the way of God' (18:26) with *drk hw'h'* (1QS 8:13) and *drk 'l* (CD 20:18). While it might theoretically be possible that both groups (Christian and Essene) derived the

[20] For previous discussions see W. K. M. Grossouw, 'The Dead Sea Scrolls and the New Testament: A Preliminary Survey', *StCath* XXVII (1952) 1–8, esp. 5–6. F. Nötscher, *Gotteswege und Menschenwege in der Bibel und Qumran*, BBB XV (Bonn, 1958) 76–96, 100–1. V. McCasland, '"The Way"', *JBL* LXXVII (1958) 222–30.

use of 'the Way' from Is 40, nevertheless the close similarity of usage suggests in this case Essene influence.

There is, however, an important difference to be noted. Among the Essenes the expression 'the Way' has a dualistic connotation, for it is to be related to the doctrine of the Two Spirits (1QS 3:18 ff.), which are given to men and according to which all are to 'walk'. 'These are their ways in the world: To illumine the heart of man and to make plain before him all the ways of uprightness ⟨and⟩ truth' (1QS 4:2). The word *drk* is not used here absolutely; but it is impossible to divorce the absolute use of it entirely from reference to the 'ways' of these spirits. Such a dualistic connotation, however, is absent from Acts.

Another designation for the Qumran community with a possible bearing on the early Jewish Christian church in Acts is *yḥd*. According to Acts 2:42 the early Christians devoted themselves to *koinōnia*. This included the communal ownership of goods (4:32b–35; 6:1), the common 'breaking of bread' (2:42; 20:7), communal meals (2:46), and their contributions for the relief of the needy (11:29). But the word *koinōnia* probably denoted something more than such details: the communal spirit of co-operation and fellowship existing among the early Christians. Acts 4:32a is probably a description of it: 'The community of believers was of one heart and mind' (*kardia kai psychē mia*).

Even though the precise meaning of *koinōnia* is a matter of debate,[21] the term *yḥd* in Qumran literature sheds some light on it, in providing an intelligible Palestinian background for interpreting it. It is indeed impossible to establish any direct borrowing of the term. But to prescind for the moment from specific Qumran parallels for the elements of the life designated by *koinōnia*—parallels which are not perfect in all details—the sum total of them as expressed by *yḥd* should be included in any discussion of the meaning of *koinōnia*. For in the Qumran writings the word *yḥd* often designates the 'community' as such

[21] See note 9 above.

(1QS 1:1, 16; 5:1, 2, 16; 6:21; 7:20; etc. 1QSa 1:26, 27; 4QPatrBless 5; etc.). In this usage it certainly is more specific than *koinōnia.*[22] The latter may sum up the corporate spirit of the Christian group, but is not used as a name for it. But in the Qumran writings there is also a wider sense of *yḥd*. 'This is the rule for the men of the Community (*'nšy hyḥd*) who devote themselves to turning from all evil and to adhering to all that he has commanded according to his good pleasure: to separate from the congregation of the men of iniquity, to form a communal spirit with respect to the Law and to wealth' (*lhywt lyḥd*). In the first case *yḥd* seems to be the name for the group, 'community', whereas in the second instance it designates rather a common participation in the study and observance of the Torah and in the use of wealth. See also 1QS 6:7 ('The Many shall watch in common', *hrbym yšqwdn byḥd*).[23] Thus even though the word *yḥd* often is the designation for a far more structured community than *koinōnia* is, there is a nuance in the Qumran use of the word that sheds light on the Christian *koinōnia.*

2. The mention of *koinōnia* brings up the question of the community of goods in the early church and in the Essene sect. From Acts we learn of a communal ownership of property among the early Jewish Christians; see 2:44–45; 4:32–35. Selling what they owned, they contributed the proceeds to a common fund, administered at first by the apostles, but later by seven assistants. From it distribution was made, even daily (6:1), to all the faithful according to their needs. The main

[22] S. Talmon ('The Sectarian *yḥd*—A Biblical Noun', *VT* III [1953] 132–40) cites a few places in the Old Testament where *yḥd* may even have the meaning, 'congregation, community' (Dt 33:5; Ez 4:3; 1 Chr 12:18; Ps 2:2). Though the first instance is plausible, the others scarcely are.

[23] Recall that Philo (*Quod omnis probus liber sit,* 84 and 91) speaks of the Essene way of life as an 'indescribable communal life' (*tēn pantos logou kreittona koinōnian*), using of it the very word *koinōnia*. See also no. 85; *Apologia pro Iudaeis* 11, 10–13. Josephus, however, uses *to koinōnikon,* and this in a more restricted sense, as he refers it to the common sharing of possessions (*JW* 2. 8, 3, #122).

elements in this feature of common life were the surrender of private property, the deposit of it with the leaders of the community, punishment for deception, and a care of the needy from the common fund. When one reads Acts 2:44–45; 4:32–35, one gets the impression that the communal ownership was obligatory. However, 4:36–5:11 suggests that it was voluntary. 'Poverty . . . [as] a religious ideal' is the term that O. Cullmann uses to describe the situation.[24] This interpretation seems to be based on 4:32b: 'None of them ever claimed anything as his own.' The motivation for this communal ownership is never described as a fulfilment of the injunctions of Jesus recorded in Mk 10:21; Mt 19:21; Lk 18:22. It seems rather to be an ideal motivated by simplicity, detachment, and charitable sharing which springs from their corporate identity as the Jewish Christian community. As a mode of life common to all Christians it eventually disappears.

But an analogous situation was found among the Essenes of Qumran. They too seem to have practised a form of communal ownership of property though it is not in all respects identical to that of the early church. According to the *Manual of Discipline*, anyone who would enter the 'community' had to reckon with the surrender of his wealth. 'All those who dedicate themselves freely to his truth shall bring all their knowledge, their ability, and their wealth into God's Community in order to purify their knowledge in the truth of God's precepts and to determine exactly their abilities according to the perfection of his ways and their wealth according to his righteous counsel' (1QS 1:11–13; cf. CD 13:11). Explicit mention is made of the property of the whole assembly or of 'the Many' (*hwn hrbym*, 1QS 6:17). Before the probation is over, the candidate's belongings are not to be mingled with those of the community nor spent for common purposes.[25] The mingling of his property

[24] *The Scrolls and the New Testament*, 21.

[25] The meaning of *'rb* in the Qumran writings has been questioned. In my opinion, the word as used in 1QS 6:17, 22 describes the 'mingling' of the

with that of the community occurs only at the end of his second year of probation, when he becomes a full-fledged member (1QS 6:21–23). Deceit in the declaration or deposit of property results in exclusion from the 'Purity' (or sacred meal) of the community for one year, and a reduction of the food allowance by one quarter (1QS 6:24–25; cf. CD 14:20–21).[26] Fraud (or neglect) in the use of common property was punished with the obligation of restitution through one's labour and/or a fine (1QS 7:6). The emphasis on common ownership of property was such among the Essenes of Qumran that the group was characterized by its communal spirit with respect to the law and to wealth (*lhywt lyḥd btwrh wbhwn*, 1QS 5:2).[27]

But while entrance into the Qumran community was voluntary, the surrender of one's property and earnings (*'t hwnw w't ml'ktw*, 1QS 6:19) was not. The surrender was obligatory and detailed. In this the Qumran practice differs considerably from the early Christian communal ownership described in

individual's property with that of the group and does correspond to Josephus' expression (*anamemigmenōn*, *JW* 2, 8, 3, #122). The evidence of Josephus should not be written off too quickly in this regard; cf. C. Rabin, *Qumran Studies*, 22–36. His reasons are not very convincing. See also M. Black, *The Scrolls and Christian Origins* (New York, 1961) 32–9.

[26] The text of CD is at this point fragmentary. Since it also mentions a different fine ('six days'), we might ask whether this passage is really parallel to that in 1QS 6:24–25.

[27] See also CD 13:14; 14:12–16. The regulations regarding communal ownership were not the same in the 'camps' of Damascus as at Qumran itself. However, there has been a tendency to exaggerate the difference. Some of the passages which have been interpreted in terms of private ownership do not clearly state this. CD 14:12–16, for instance, does not necessarily mean that the wages are private. The *śkr* could well refer to the income of the 'work' of the members of the 'camp'; the income of two days would be put aside for the care of orphans, the poor, and the elderly. The passage seems to deal with the *community's* care of such persons, a corporate duty (*srk hrbym*). Likewise, in CD 13:14 the prohibition of trade or traffic with outsiders on an individual basis in any other manner than for cash is understandable in the context of communal ownership. If a member of the 'camps' sold to an outsider or worked for him, his recompense was to be cash, lest he bring into the community unclean produce or products. It does not necessarily mean that the cash was his own.

Acts 4:36–5:11, which is voluntary. If the passages in Acts 2:44–45; 4:32–35 are to be understood in a more obligatory sense, then they are closer to the Qumran practice. At any rate, there is in both groups a willingness to surrender property and earnings as a feature of common life. In the Essene community, however, this is but an element in a closely organized and structured community; since the early church is not depicted in Acts as so highly organized, the surrender of common property was of a looser sort.

As for the motivation of such a way of life, the Qumran literature itself is less explicit than the ancient sources about the Essenes. 1QS 9:22 expresses a certain contempt for riches and a salary: wealth and earnings are to be left to the men of perdition. But Josephus (*JW* 2, 8, 2, #122) explicitly calls the Essenes 'despisers of wealth' (*kataphronētai de ploutou*). And Philo too emphasizes their detachment.[28] In this respect we detect little difference between the Essenes and the early Jewish Christians.[29] Although the ultimate motivation for this poverty might be Old Testament passages such as Prv 30:8–9; 14:20–21; etc., nevertheless this does not account for the communal aspect of it practised in the two groups. The analogy existing between the early Jewish Christians and the Qumran community is such that one should reckon with an imitation of Qumran practices among the former, even if it is clear that modifications were introduced. In this respect we cannot agree with the radical rejection of any Qumran influence on the early Jewish Christians, such as has been proposed by H. H. Rowley, G. Graystone, and N. Adler.[30]

One last observation in this matter. Though there is provision

[28] *Quod omnis probus liber sit* 85–6; *Apologia pro Iudaeis* 11, 11.

[29] According to S. E. Johnson, 'The emphasis is upon communal life and not on poverty as such' (*The Scrolls and the New Testament*, 133).

[30] H. H. Rowley, *The Dead Sea Scrolls and the New Testament* (London, 1957) 13. G. Graystone, *The Dead Sea Scrolls and the Originality of Christ* (New York, 1955) 33–5. N. Adler, 'Die Bedeutung der Qumran-Texte für die neutestamentliche Wissenschaft', *MTZ* VI (1955) 286–301, esp. 299.

for the needy among the Jewish Christians of Acts (2:45; 4:34–35; 6:1), it is striking that the term *hoi ptōchoi* is never used there. Paul uses it in Rom 15:26; Gal 2:10, and one has been inclined to regard the term as a designation for the Jerusalem church. Indeed, it has often been suggested that it is the equivalent of *h'bywnym*. The latter, drawn from the Old Testament (Ex 23:11; Est 9:22; Ps 132:15), seems to have been a rare, non-technical designation for the Qumran sect in use among the Essenes themselves (see 1QpHab 12:3, 6, 10; 4QpPss[a] 1–2 ii 9; 1, 3–4 iii 10 [*'dt h'bywnym*]; 1QM 11:9, 13; 13:14).[31]

3. Another area of contact between the early Jewish Christian church and the Essenes of Qumran which must be discussed is the organizational structure of the two groups. I have already tried to indicate the vagueness of detail that characterizes the description of the community of Christians in Acts. This vagueness must prevent us from being too absolute in any judgment about the similarity of it with the Qumran community, which was certainly much more structured than the Jewish Christian congregation.

Like the early Christians, the Essenes of Qumran considered themselves to be the Israel of the end of days. They patterned their way of life on the Israel of the desert wanderings. The original nucleus of the community seems to have been priestly, and this accounts for the title 'sons of Zadok' often applied to it. But apart from the priests there were also levites and laymen (1QS 2:19–21; cf. 1:18, 21; 2:1, 11). The latter were divided into tribes and groups called 'thousands, hundreds, fifties, and tens' (1QS 2:21; cf. 1QM 4:1–5, 16–17; 1QSa 1:14, 29–2:1; CD 13:1–2). This division is derived from Ex 18:21, 25 (cf.

[31] See L. E. Keck, 'The Poor among the Saints in the New Testament', *ZNW* LVI (1965) 100–29; 'The Poor among the Saints in Jewish Christianity and Qumran', *ZNW* LVII (1966) 54–78. My earlier remarks on this subject (*TS* XVI [1955] 344, n. 22) need some qualification (see below, pp. 438–41, 476–7). I would, however, still reject the suggestion that these 'poor' might be the Ebionites, or simply became the Ebionites later on.

Nm 31:48, 54); it probably designates various groups within the community with diverse status or functions. One may legitimately ask whether there were literally groups of 'thousands' at Qumran. The priestly element in the community was often called 'sons of Aaron', and the title probably included the levites too. But the non-priests were designated as 'Israel'. In the Damascene camps there were also proselytes (CD 14:3).

Both Aaron and Israel were accustomed to meet in a full assembly (*mwšb hrbym*) where they had fixed places and where they in common settled issues of a juridical and executive nature. Some writers have mentioned that there was also in the Qumran community a small 'council' (1QS 8:1, *'ṣt hyḥd*), entrusted with the study of legal matters.[32] The existence of a nucleus of fifteen members is certain, but just what its function was is not clear at all. This will be discussed further below. Finally, in addition to the full assembly authority was vested in various 'overseers' or 'superintendents'. At Qumran itself there was a '(lay)man appointed at the head of the Many' (*h'yš hpqyd brw'š hrbym*, 1QS 6:14) and a lay 'overseer of the Many' (*h'yš hmbqr 'l hrbym*, 1QS 6:11); the latter is probably the same as the 'overseer of the work of the Many' (*h'yš hmbqr 'l ml'kt hrbym*, 1QS 6:20). The first was apparently a sort of superior, and the second a sort of bursar. In the Essene 'camps' of Damascus there was a 'priest appointed over the Many' (*hkwhn 'šr ypqd* ⟨*br*⟩*'š hrbym*, CD 14:6–7; also mentioned in 4QD) and a lay 'overseer for all the camps' (*hmbqr 'šr lkl hmḥnwt*, CD 14:8–11), as well as a lay 'camp overseer' (*hmbqr lmḥnh*, CD 13:7–19). The latter was entrusted with teaching, reprehension, admission of candidates, and the administration of the property of the community in the camp (CD 13:7–19). He was assisted by a group of ten judges (CD 10:4–7). Even though it is not possi-

[32] E.g., J. T. Milik (*Ten Years*, 100); F. M. Cross, Jr. (*Ancient Library of Qumran*, 231); B. Reicke, 'The Constitution of the Primitive Church in the Light of Jewish Documents', *TZ* X (1954) 95–113, reprinted in *The Scrolls and the New Testament*, 151–2.

ble to give in full detail the functions of these different authorities, this brief sketch does make it plain that the Essene communities (either at Qumran or in the Damascene camps) had a structure that was much more organized than anything which emerges from the account in Acts about the early Jewish Christian church.

And yet there are certain elements in common which call for comment. First of all, the absolute use of *to plēthos* to designate the full congregation of the Jerusalem converts. It is commonplace to point out that there are two uses of *to plēthos* in Acts:[33] (a) 'crowd, large number of persons' (so 2:6; etc.); (b) 'the full assembly, congregation'. The latter meaning is found in Acts 6:5; cf. 6:2; 4:32. It refers to the full body of Jerusalem disciples. In a more restricted sense it is used in 15:12 of the body of the apostles and elders. Again, with the spread of Christianity it is applied to the community at Antioch (15:30).[34] Since both meanings are well attested in classical and Hellenistic Greek, it may seem that these have been simply used in the account of Acts. However, given the wide use of *rb*, *rwb* and *hrbym* in the Essene literature there is a likelihood that the designation of the Jewish Christian community as *to plēthos* was an imitation of current terminology. For in the Qumran writings the Essene assembly was often called *hrbym*, 'the Many'. Though pioneer translators sometimes sought to render it as 'the Great Ones', or 'the Masters', the commonly accepted explanation today refers it to the democratic assembly of the Essenes as they met in a session (*mwšb*) to decide common matters (see 1QS 6:1, 7–9, 11–18, 21, 25; 7:16; 8:19, 26; CD 13:7; 14:7, 12; 15:8). The Greek phrase, however, is hardly the literal translation of *hrbym*.[35] It may reflect the Hebrew *rb* or *rwb* (1QS 5:2, 9, 22;

[33] See K. Lake and H. J. Cadbury, *BC* IV, 47–8.

[34] In Acts 19:9 the meaning of *to plēthos* is disputed. E. Haenchen (*Die Apostelgeschichte*, 188, n. 1) maintains that it refers to the Jewish Christian community, while K. Lake and H. J. Cadbury (*BC* IV, 48) refer it to the 'congregation of the Jews'.

[35] *Pace* J. M. Allegro (*The Dead Sea Scrolls* [Pelican ed., Baltimore, 1957]

6:19). But it is to be noted that *rb* and *rwb* seem to designate rather the Essene assembly considered as distinct from the priests, whereas *hrbym* would include them.[36] For this distinction there is no equivalent in the early Christian church; it is a precision which has not been taken over. But this does not seem to invalidate the suggestion that the Essene use of *rb*, *rwb* and *hrbym* underlies in some way the early Christian use of *to plēthos* for the full congregation of disciples.

Secondly, several writers have discussed the possibility of Essene influence in the role of the twelve in the early Jewish Christian church. In Acts 'the twelve' are mentioned indeed, but rarely (explicitly only in 6:2; but cf. 1:15–26; 2:14). They have been compared to 1QS 8:1: 'In the council (?) of the Community [when there are? *or* there shall be?] twelve men and three priests, perfect in all that is revealed in the Law'. It has been suggested that the mention of 'twelve men' is 'an analogue to the college of the twelve apostles of Jesus', since it is 'not clear from the text whether the three priests are inside or outside the circle of twelve. Perhaps the inclusion of the three priests is to be preferred, because it enables one to see in the expression "priest" an especial mark of honour and to avoid the rather improbable result that the other twelve were laymen.'[37] But just why it is not clear that the twelve are distinct from the three is never explained; any normal reading of the line would suggest that the text mentions 15 persons. This number is confirmed, in fact, by a text from Cave 4 which is unfortunately as yet unpublished.[38] Consequently, there is little

---

144), *hrbym* would correspond more exactly to the Pauline use of *hoi polloi* (Rom 5:15, 19) or of *hoi pleiones* (2 Cor 2:6; cf. 1 Cor 9:19). Josephus uses *hoi pleistoi* (*Ant.* 18. 1, 5, #22) and *hoi pleiones* (*JW* 2, 8, 9, #146) of the Essene community as a whole.

[36] See H. Huppenbauer, '*rb, rwb, rbym* in der Sektenregel (1QS)', *TZ* XIII (1957) 136–7.

[37] See B. Reicke, 'The Constitution', *The Scrolls and the New Testament*, 151.

[38] See J. T. Milik, *VD* XXXV (1957) 73; *Ten Years*, 96; *RB* LXIV (1957) 589. See also A. Dupont-Sommer, *Essene Writings*, 90, n. 4. Curiously enough, Milik speaks later on (*Ten Years*, 143) of the early church and the Essenes

reason to think that the apostolic twelve in the early Christian church was modelled on the 'twelve men' mentioned in this one place in the *Manual of Discipline*. J. T. Milik and others have related the three priests mentioned there to the three priestly families descended from Levi through his sons Gershon, Kohath, and Merari (Gn 46:11).[39] In both Essene and Christian circles the number twelve is more plausibly explained as a derivative of the twelve tribes of Israel. The element that is common to the use of this number in both circles is its appearance in an eschatological context. Jesus' saying about the twelve thrones has to do with eschatological judgment (Mt 19:28; Lk 22:30), and the division of the Sons of Light in the eschatological war is according to twelve tribes (1QM 3:13–14; 5:1–2). The real problem in Acts—why the twelve disappear as an authoritative and administrative group within a relatively short time after the need was felt to reconstitute it by the election of Matthias—unfortunately receives no illumination from the Qumran material.

Thirdly, the organization of the Essene camps in the land of Damascus was somewhat different. Here a body of ten judges functions, 'four from the tribe of Levi and Aaron, and six from Israel' (CD 10:4). Again, they represent the priest and non-priest members, but the number twelve is not operative here. It is rather ten, the number otherwise used for small groups or 'cells' within the Essene community which gathered for various purposes (cf. 1QS 6:6; 1QSa 2:22; Josephus, *JW* 2. 8, 9, #146). But this does not seem to have any significance for the Jewish Christian church of Acts.[40]

---

as both holding the 'eschatological concept of the true Israel ruled by twelve leaders'.

[39] The connection between the 'three priests' and the 'pillars' of Gal 2:9 or the mention of Peter, James, and John (Mt 17:1) must be admitted to be extremely tenuous.

[40] Gathering in groups of ten was a principle also recognized in the Pharisaic-Rabbinical tradition; cf. Mishnah, *Megillah* 4:3. But it is debatable whether the idea of a group of ten, of whom one was a priest, had

Fourthly, another feature of organization that has often been discussed is the relation of the *episkopos* in the early church to the Essene *mbqr*. Since both words etymologically mean 'overseer', 'superintendent', the Essene institution has often been considered as a likely model for the early Christian episcopate.[41] As far as the early Jewish Christian church is concerned, the relation seems to be negligible, for the Greek word occurs in Acts only in 20:28, in Paul's discourse to the elders (*presbyteroi*, 20:17) of Ephesus summoned to Miletus. He bids them, 'Keep watch then over yourselves and over all the flock of which the holy Spirit has made you overseers' (*episkopous*). The assimilation of the 'overseer' to a shepherd is used in the instructions for the 'Camp Overseer' in CD 13:7–9: 'He shall bring back all those who have strayed, as a shepherd his flock' (cf. Ez 34:12–16; Nm 27:16; 1 Pt 2:25; 5:2). This would seem to make plausible the suggestion that the *episkopos* was somehow an

---

anything to do with the 120 present in the first Jewish Christian assembly in Acts (1:15): 'ten members to each Apostle' (so J. T. Milik, *Ten Years*, 101; cf. *BC* IV, 12). The problem is that the apostles are not considered to be *hiereis* in Acts. See H. Braun, 'Qumran und das Neue Testament', 147.

[41] Josephus speaks of the Essene *epimelētai* (*JW* 2. 8, 6, # 134; 2. 8, 3, #123); this seems to be his equivalent for the Hebrew *mbqr* or *pqyd*. This Greek word is not used in the New Testament nor in the LXX. Although *episkopos* is used in extrabiblical Greek for a civic, financial, and religious 'overseer', it is also found in the LXX (Nm 4:16; 31:14; Jgs 9:28; 2 Kgs 11:15, 18; etc.). In most cases it translates some form of the root *pqd*, as does the verb *episkopein*. Only rarely does the latter translate the Hebrew *bqr* (Lv 13:36; 2 Esdras 4:15, 19; 5:17; 6:1; 7:14; Ps 26/27:4; Ez 34:11, 12). For further discussions of this problem see J. Jeremias, *Jerusalem zur Zeit Jesu* (Göttingen: 2nd ed.; 1958) II, 1, 132-3; K. G. Goetz, 'Ist der *mbqr* der Genizafragmente wirklich das Vorbild des christlichen Episkopats?', *ZNW* XXX (1931) 89–93; H. W. Beyer, *episkopos*, *TDNT* II, 614–16; B. Reicke, 'The Jewish "Damascus Documents" and the New Testament', *SBU* VI (1946) 16; W. Nauck, 'Probleme des frühchristlichen Amtsverständnisses (I Peter 5:2–3)', *ZNW* XLVIII (1957) 200–20; A. Adam, 'Die Entstehung des Bischofsamtes', *Wort und Dienst* NF V (1957) 103–13; W. Eiss, 'Das Amt des Gemeindeleiters bei den Essenern und der christlichen Episkopat', *WO* II (1959) 514–19; F. Nötscher, 'Vorchristliche Typen urchristlicher Ämter: Episkopos und Mebaqqer', *Die Kirche und ihre Ämter und Stände* (Festgabe J. Kardinal Frings; Köln, 1960) 315–38.

imitation of the Essene *mbqr*.[42] But the leaders of the Jewish Christian church in Palestine are never called *episkopoi* in Acts. And even if we find the apostles performing a role there that resembles a function of an Essene overseer as the Christians who have sold their property come and deposit the proceeds of it at the feet of the apostles (4:35, 37; 5:2; cf. CD 14:13 and possibly also 1QS 6:19–20), there is no trace of the use of such a title in the early Jewish Christian church. Nor does the passage in Acts 1:17–25 really contradict this impression. For although the word *episkopē* does occur in 1:20 in connection with the office that Matthias was elected to fill, it is actually part of an Old Testament quotation, Ps 109:8: *ten episkopēn autou labetō heteros*. In the context *episkopē* is related to both *apostolē* and *diakonia* (1:17, 25). Its sense is obviously generic, and it can in no way be used to show that the 'apostolate' was already an 'episcopate'. Even James who begins to rule the Jerusalem church in a manner that resembles the residential bishop of later date is never called *episkopos*. Indeed, his position of prominence seems to be due to the fact that he is 'a brother of the Lord'. In the New Testament the *episkopoi* emerge in churches of Hellenistic background (see Acts 20:28; Phil 1:1; 1 Tm 3:2; Ti 1:7), as groups of 'guardians' or 'overseers'. It is the Ephesian 'elders' who are called thus by Paul in Acts 20:28. They seem to have been set up by travelling apostles (like Paul) or by apostolic 'delegates' (like Timothy at Ephesus or Titus on Crete) to govern local churches, but it is only gradually that their monarchical function emerges. Granting then the common etymological meaning of *episkopos* and *mbqr*, and certain similar functions, it is nevertheless difficult to set up any direct connection between the Essene 'overseer' and the institution of the early Jewish Christian church in Palestine.[43]

[42] Cf. J. Dupont, *Le discours de Milet: Testament pastoral de saint Paul* (*Acts* 20:18–36) (Paris, 1962) 149, n. 1. This is not the place for a more detailed comparison, but CD 13:5–13 would lend itself to further discussion in this matter of the Christian 'overseer'.

[43] I do not exclude the possibility of Essene influence on the early

Fifthly, the early Christian church gave a special function to 'elders' in addition to the apostles. The *presbyteroi* occur in Acts 11:30; 15:2, 4, 6, 22, 23; 16:4; 21:18. These 'elders' were, however, a natural borrowing from the existing Jewish institution mentioned in Acts itself (4:5, 8, 23; 6:12; 23:14; 24:1; 25:15) and can in no way be traced to the Essene community specifically. The Essenes had such 'elders' too. In the ranks of the Qumran community the priests take precedence over the elders, as they meet in full assembly (1QS 6:8). They take their place along with the priests and the levites in pronouncing blessings and curses after the defeat of the enemy in the eschatological war (1QM 13:1). In general, respect for them is inculcated (CD 9:4). But there is nothing to indicate that the elders of the Christian community were in any way a derivative of the Essene institution. Both communities derived the institution rather from Old Testament tradition, as Acts 2:17 and *Damascus Document* 5:4 would suggest.

Finally, by way of contrast it is remarkable how frequently one reads of the role of the 'priests' and the 'Levites' in the Essene communities (e.g., 1QS 1:18, 21; 2:1, 11, 19; 1QM 7:15; 13:1; 15:4; CD 3:21; etc.) and how silent Acts is about such groups in the early Christian church. 'Priests' and 'levites' are mentioned in Acts only as indications of the former Jewish status of converts (6:7; 4:36). This remarkable difference between the two groups stems from their basic attitude toward the temple in Jerusalem. In both we find a kindred idea that the Jerusalem temple and its sacrificial cultus have been replaced by a community of the faithful.[44] But in the case of the Qumran Essenes this replacement was temporary; the Qumran com-

---

church in non-Palestinian areas. If, as seems likely, some Essene influence reached Damascus in the 'camps' and even further into the hinterlands of Asia Minor (see P. Benoit, *NTS* VII [1961] 287), then possibly the connection of the Essene *mbqr* with the Christian *episkopos* should be sought in such areas.

[44] See B. Gärtner, *The Temple and the Community in Qumran and the New Testament* (SNTS Monograph series, I; Cambridge, 1965) 99–101.

munity is the 'sanctuary for Aaron, . . . the Holy of Holies' (1QS 9:5–7; cf. 8:4–6; 5:6; 11:8; 4QFlor 1:6), but only because it has considered the Jerusalem temple defiled by the worldly, temporizing priests who serve it, and hence unfit for the sacrifice to God according to the prescriptions of Mosaic law.[45] Once God's victory is won, then the pure levitical service of God will be resumed. In the early church, however, the temple and its sacrifices soon cease to have significance for Christians. Even though we read of the apostles 'attending the temple together' (2:46) and 'going up to the temple at the hour of prayer, the ninth hour' (3:1), yet it is not long before the opposition to the temple develops. Stephen's speech reflects this and is the beginning of the development within the early Jerusalem community (cf. Acts 6:14) that culminates in the temple symbolism found in the writings of Paul, 1 Peter, and Hebrews. This temple symbolism is certainly similar to that of the Essene community, but there is a difference, too. This is found chiefly in the preservation within their community of the divisions of priests and levites who by their strict living were preparing themselves for the pure service of God in the ideal eschatological temple. As we have already remarked, there were undoubtedly some Essenes among the priests converted to Christianity (Acts 6:7), and they were most likely the bridge of contact between the two communities. However, it is important to note that they are never found continuing their function as priests even in some new way (such as blessing the bread and wine at the Christian communal meal instead of sacrificing, as did happen in the Essene community, 1QSa 2:18–19).

Such are the observations which seem pertinent to the discussion of influence of the Essene community on the structure and organization of the early Jewish Christian church.

4. When Matthias was elected to replace Judas in the num-

[45] See 1QpHab 9:4–7; 10:9–13; 11:4–12; 4QpIs^b 2:7, 10; 4QpIs^c 10–11; CD 11:17–20; 4QpNah.

ber of the twelve, it is noteworthy that the other eleven are not said to have laid hands on him or 'ordained' him, as is the case with the seven in Acts 6:6. Rather, once the requirements (2:21–22) are met, the commission is given to Matthias by the 'Lord' himself (2:24) through the casting of the lot. The use of this means of determining the will of God is known from the Old Testament: the lot determined priestly functions in the temple (1 Chr 24:5; 26:13–14; Neh 10:34; etc.) and service in the army (Jgs 20:9). It is also known to have been used in rabbinical circles. It is not surprising then that the lot was also in use in the Essene community, given its place in the general Jewish cultural heritage. But several expressions in the Matthias passage are better understood against the specific background of the Essene usage. In the Qumran community the lot was used in some way to determine the candidate's admission into the community and also his rank in it. Using an expression drawn from Nm 33:54 or Jos 16:1, the *Manual of Discipline* (6:16) prescribes apropos of the candidate's admission that the lot be used: *k'šr yṣ' hgwrl 'l 'ṣt hrbym.* At subsequent periods in the candidate's probation further determination is made, and finally, 'if it be his lot to enter the Community then he shall be inscribed in the order of his rank among his brethren' (1QS 6:22, *'m yṣ' lw hgwrl lqrbw lyḥd yktwbhw bsrk tkwnw btwk 'ḥyw*). One's rank in the community was determined by lot, too: 'No man shall move down from his place nor move up from his allotted position' (1QS 2:23, *wlw' yrwm mmqwm gwrlw*). (See also 1QS 1:10; 9:7; CD 13:12; 20:4.) There are elements in this Essene practice which shed light on the details of the election of Matthias. For instance, Judas is said by his vocation as an apostle to 'have obtained the lot of this ministry' (Acts 1:17, *elachen ton klēron tēs diakonias tautēs*). Then, the Christian community prayed that God would indicate who was to take over *ton topon tēs diakonias tautēs* (1:25), an expression which finds its counterpart in *mqwm gwrlw* (1QS 2:23). Though these resemblances are *in se* superficial, taken in conjunction with the use of the lot to designate a man for a specific rank within the community, they do make the story of the election of Matthias a little more intelligible.[46] We would not be able to conclude, however, that the practice was due to imitation of an Essene custom.

5. The communal meal of the early Jewish Christian church (2:46) has often been compared to the religious common meal of the Essenes described in 1QS 6:4–5; 1QSa 2:11–22.[47] The brief notice of the Christian meal in Acts, however, contains so little detail that one cannot really make a valid comparison in this case. Previous discussions of the relationship of the Essene repast to the Christian Eucharist or the Last Supper have exploited the Gospel and Pauline material, as they must; but this is outside our perspective. Even though one were to admit that the Jerusalem church was the source of the tradition about the Last Supper in Matthew and Mark, there is little reason to bring it into this discussion. The only element which should be noted is that the account of the common meal in Acts is framed merely in terms of 'breaking bread', and there is no mention of 'wine', the other element in the Essene meal. Though one may be inclined to admit that the meal was eaten in anticipation of the messianic banquet in the Essene community (1QSa 2:14–20), this note is not found in the account in Acts.

6. The last topic to which we shall turn our attention is the interpretation of the Old Testament found in Acts and in the Essene literature. For despite the difference in the messianic views of the two communities, which we have already noted and which certainly coloured their interpretation of the Old Testa-

[46] Cf. W. Nauck, 'Probleme des frühchristlichen Amtsverständnisses', 209–14. E. Stauffer, 'Jüdisches Erbe im urchristlichen Kirchenrecht', *TLZ* LXXVII (1952) 203–4.

[47] E.g., F. M. Cross, Jr., *Ancient Library*, 235–7. M. Black, *The Scrolls and Christian Origins*, 102–15. K. G. Kuhn, 'The Lord's Supper and the Communal Meal at Qumran', *The Scrolls and the New Testament*, 65–93. J. van der Ploeg, 'The Meals of the Essenes', *JSS* II (1957) 163–75. E. F. Sutcliffe, 'Sacred Meals at Qumran?', *HeythJ* I (1960) 48–65. J. Gnilka, 'Das Gemeinschaftsmahl der Essener', *BZ* V (1961) 39–55.

ment, there is a remarkable similarity in other respects which shows the early Jewish Christian community to be very close to the Essenes. For the Christians of Acts the Messiah has come (2:36), but another definitive coming of his is still awaited (1:11; 3:21). This expectation manifests a similarity with the Essene expectation of a prophet and two Anointed Ones (1QS 9:11), who are in some way related to the day of God's visitation of his people (1QS 3:18). There is the common conviction that they are living in the 'end of days' (1QpHab 2:5; 9:6; 1QSa 1:1; 4QpIs^a A:8; 4QFlor 1:2, 12, 15, 19; CD 4:4; 6:11; etc.; cf. Acts 2:17: *en tais eschatais hēmerais*).[48] This conviction enables both groups to refer sayings of the Old Testament prophets and writings to events or tenets in their own history or beliefs. Especially pertinent is 1QpHab 7:1–5: 'God told Habakkuk to write the things which were to come upon the last generation, but the consummation of the period he did not make known to him. And as for what it says, "That he may run who reads it", this means the Righteous Teacher, to whom God made known all the mysteries of the words of his servants the prophets' (see also 1QpHab 7:7–8). This attitude underlies the constant actualization or modernization of the Old Testament texts being used either in the *peshārîm* or in isolated quotations in other writings. See CD 1:13 ('This is the time about which it was written', introducing Hos 4:16); 10:16; 16:15 ('For that is what it [*or:* he] said'); 1QM 10:1; 11:11. It is this same attitude that underlies the use of the Old Testament in Peter's speech on Pentecost, as the prophet Joel is quoted (cf. Acts 3:24).

The introductory formulas often reveal this attitude more than anything else. I have elsewhere[49] studied the similarity of these Essene formulas and their New Testament counterparts

[48] The phrase is derived from Is 2:2; cf. Mi 4:1; Dn 2:28. There is, however, a textual difficulty here: Vaticanus reads simply *meta tauta*; I have used what seems to be the better reading, based on Sinaiticus, Alexandrinus, and the Codex Bezae.

[49] 'The Use of Explicit Old Testament Quotations in Qumran Literature and in the New Testament', pp. 3–58 above, esp. pp. 7-16.

in detail. I shall give here only the list of those passages which occur in Acts and are pertinent to this discussion.

Acts		*Qumran Literature*
1:20	'for it is written'	CD 11:20
2:16	'this is what was said through the prophet Joel'	CD 10:16; 16:15
2:25	'for David says'	CD 6:7–8 (cf. 6:13)
2:34	'he says'	CD 4:20 (?)
3:21	'God spoke through the mouth of his holy prophets of old'	CD 4:13–14
3:25	'saying to Abraham'	?
4:11	'this is the . . .'	1QpHab 12:3; 4QpIs[b] 2:10
4:25	'spoke through the mouth of David his servant'	CD 4:13–14
7:6	'So God said'	CD 6:13; 8:9
7:7	'God said'	CD 6:13; 8:9
7:42	'As it is written in the book of the prophets'	4QFlor 1:2
7:48	'as the prophet says'	CD 6:7–8 (?)
13:33	'as it is written in the second psalm'	4QFlor 1:2; 11QMelch 9–10
13:33	'and in another place he says'	?
13:40	'Beware then lest what was said by the prophets come true [of you]'	?
15:15	'as it is written'	1QS 8:14; 5:17; CD 7:19; 4QFlor 1:2

28:25	'The holy Spirit has well said through Isaiah the prophet'	CD 4:13–14 ('God said . . .')

Two observations are pertinent. First, the Hebrew equivalents of the introductory formulas in the New Testament are found in greater abundance in the Qumran literature than in the early rabbinical compositions (such as the Mishnah).[50] Even if the formulas used show an affinity to those of the Essene writers, we cannot establish a definite borrowing of the Qumran literary practice by the early Christians. Secondly, it is not insignificant that the majority of explicit quotations introduced by such formulas in Acts are found in the early chapters which deal specifically with the early Jewish Christian church. A glance at the above list shows this. Several reasons, of course, can be suggested for the difference (e.g., that the latter part of Acts deals with Paul, his missions, his evangelization of the Greek world, etc.). But they should not be pressed to the extent of excluding all influence of Palestinian methods of Old Testament exegesis which the data would seem to suggest.

CONCLUSION

The features of Essene tenets and practices which we have surveyed have often shed important light on passages of Acts that describe the early Jewish Christian church. They at least provide concrete and tangible evidence for a Palestinian matrix of the early church as it is described in Acts. The evidence varies, since it is possible at times to think in terms of a direct contact or a direct imitation of Essene usage (as in the case of 'the Way'), while at other times the evidence is not so strong. Certainly, one cannot prove from such points of contact that the early Jewish Christian church developed out of an exclusively Essene framework. The most that one can say is that the early Jewish Christian church was not without some influence from the Essenes.

[50] See pp. 15–16 above.

It is not unlikely, as we have mentioned above, that among the 'great number of priests' (Acts 6:7) who were converted some were Essene and provided the source of Essene influence.

In my opinion, the influence of Qumran literature on Acts is not as marked as it is in other New Testament writings (e.g., John, Paul, Matthew, Hebrews). The parallels that do exist, striking though they may be, are not numerous. In an early article on the subject, S. E. Johnson wrote, 'It also appears that he [the author of Luke–Acts] is in closer touch with the Jewish sectarian background of Christianity than any other New Testament author.'[51] Now that much more of the Essene literature has been published and more of its contacts with the New Testament have been studied, we can see that this judgment would have to be modified, if Johnson meant by 'Jewish sectarian background' specifically the Essene background of the Qumran sect.

It has not been my express intention in this article to use Qumran material to support the historical character of Luke's account of the early Jewish Christian church in Acts. W. C. van Unnik has called Luke–Acts 'a storm centre in contemporary scholarship', and no little part of the reason why it has become such is precisely the need to distinguish the Lucan theologoumena in Acts from what might possibly be the historical data that it also contains. The effort to do this is not slight and it has created the storm. Perhaps a by-product of the above discussion of the light shed on the early Jewish Christian church by the discovery of the Qumran scrolls might be a contribution toward a better assessment of what is historical and what is Lucan theology. For it is obvious that Luke's picture of the early Jewish Christian community has been painted with a certain amount of hindsight, and there is need to read between the lines in seeking to understand it. However, since I am—for obvious reasons—not all that exercised over the so-called early

[51] 'The Dead Sea Manual of Discipline and the Jerusalem Church of Acts', *The Scrolls and the New Testament*, 129.

Catholicism of Luke, I may be permitted to cast some of his data in a different light. I admitted above (see p. 277) that the picture he has painted of the early Church was drawn at times in idyllic colours; but I sought to outline it with a minimum of Lucan theologoumena. Sometimes it is easy to spot the latter, especially when one can compare the Lucan presentation with other New Testament data (e.g., Pauline letters). But when such comparable material within the New Testament is lacking, the judgment about Luke's presentation of the early Church is reduced to speculation or subjective impressions, unless one has the advantage of outside controls, such as material from the Qumran scrolls. To use the latter is not easy. I have sought to make certain comparisons. Some of them bear on the problem of the historicity of the Lucan account; others shed light on Lucan theologoumena (e.g., Luke's use of the Old Testament and his introductory formulas). The material that is presented above must be assessed for what it is worth, and with reference to the double aspect of the problem.

14

THE BAR COCHBA PERIOD*

The number of historical documents pertaining to the second century A.D. in Palestine has always been small. It is consequently of interest to learn of new discoveries of original texts which come from that century and shed light on an otherwise obscure movement in the history of that part of the world. Though this movement has little direct bearing on Christianity, it is an important episode in the history of the Jewish people, for it is in effect the aftermath of the fateful destruction of Jerusalem by the Romans in A.D. 70 and the beginning of their long separation from the Holy City. That movement is the Second Jewish Revolt, which began under Bar Cochba in A.D. 132 and lasted until about 135, when the last remnants of the rebels were wiped out and the emperor Hadrian forbade the Jews to set foot in Jerusalem or even approach it within a certain radius.

In Josephus' writings we have a fairly lengthy and reasonably reliable account of the First Jewish Revolt, which began in A.D. 66 and ended with the destruction of the city of Jerusalem and of the temple of Yahweh in 70.[1] But the details of the Second Revolt under Bar Cochba, which apparently rivalled the first in scope and duration, have been only very briefly recorded by contemporary writers. Hence any new information, no matter how meagre, helps to fill out the picture.

* Originally published in *The Bible in Current Catholic Thought: Gruenthaner Memorial Volume* (ed. J. L. McKenzie; New York: Herder and Herder, 1962) 133–68.

[1] See *Jewish War* 2, 271 ff. to the end of Book 7; *Life* 17–410.

THE NEW FINDS

The new material has so far been published only in part and for some of it we must rely on preliminary reports. It comes from the caves in at least three different wâdies which empty into the west side of the Dead Sea. The first place which yielded written documents pertaining to the period of the Second Revolt was a pair of caves in the Wadi Murabba'ât, discovered sometime during 1951. Murabba'ât is part of the long wâdi which begins to the east of Bethlehem under the name Wâdi Ta'âmireh and ends at the Dead Sea under the name Wâdi Darajeh. The site of the caves in this Jordanian torrent-bed is about a two-hour walk westward in from the Dead Sea, being situated some fifteen miles, as the crow flies, to the south-east of Jerusalem and some eleven miles south of Qumran Cave I. The caves open southward and are found about halfway up the north side of the gorge, which is some 600 ft deep.

News of the discovery of written material in the Murabba'ât caves arrived in Jerusalem in October 1951, and an archaeological expedition was mounted to explore and excavate four caves in that wâdi from 21 January to 21 March, 1952. Two of them were of little importance and yielded no written material; but the other two gave definite evidence of a prolonged occupation in the Roman period, in addition to artifacts of the Chalcolithic, Iron II and Arab periods.[2] From the Iron II period of occupation of one of the caves came the earliest Palestinian papyrus (*Mur* 17)[3] to be found to date, a palimpsest

[2] Details are derived from the full report and publication of the documents of the Murabba'ât caves, which are now available in P. Benoit, J. T. Milik and R. de Vaux, *Les Grottes de Murabba'ât* (Discoveries in the Judaean Desert 2; two parts, Texte, Planches; Oxford: Clarendon, 1961). Hereafter the siglum DJD will refer to this series. See further R. de Vaux, 'Les grottes de Murabba'ât et leurs documents', *RB* 60 (1953) 245–67; G. Lankester Harding, 'Khirbet Qumran and Wady Murabba'ât: Fresh Light on the Dead Sea Scrolls and New Manuscript Discoveries in Jordan', *PEQ* 84 (1952) 104–9 (+five plates); H. Seyrig and J. T. Milik, 'Trésor monétaire de Murabba'ât', *Revue numismatique*, sér. VI, vol. 1 (1958) 11–26.

[3] In accord with the system of abbreviation explained in *Qumrân Cave 1* (DJD 1; Oxford: Clarendon, 1955) 46–8, the siglum *Mur* (=Murabba'ât)

dating from the eighth century, which is bound to arouse palaeographic interest.[4] From the Roman period came documents written in Hebrew, Aramaic, and Greek, which gave evidence of a trilingualism in Palestine, which was already known in the time of Herod and is now confirmed anew.[5] Some of the documents of this Roman period belong to the first century B.C.; a few are dated in the first century A.D. (to the time just prior to the First Revolt—one even in the second year of Nero [*Mur* 18]).[6] But the most important ones are derived from the time of the Second Revolt or the decades immediately preceding it (in the latter case, though the documents were written earlier, they were probably carried to the caves by the refugees who fled there toward the end of the revolt). Later on, in 1955, six Bedouin shepherds found, in a hole not far from the Murabba'ât caves, an important fragmentary scroll of the OT Minor Prophets in Hebrew, which had been buried with a refugee who had fled to the wâdi during the revolt and died there.[7]

---

is used to indicate the texts of DJD 2. The system is also explained in *The Catholic Encyclopedia*, Supplement II, section 9, s.v. 'Dead Sea Scrolls', #VII (where M should be changed to Mur); and in *Evangelisches Kirchenlexikon* 3 (1958) 421.

[4] See F. M. Cross, Jr., *The Ancient Library of Qumran and Modern Biblical Studies* (Garden City, N.Y.: Doubleday, 1958) 14, n. 22.

[5] Cf. DJD 2, 69; M. Smith, 'Aramaic Studies and the Study of the New Testament', *JBR* 26 (1958) 304–13. It is not certain that Bar Cochba himself wrote in all three languages, but they were at least being used by those under him. See Y. Yadin, 'Expedition D.', *Yedî'ôt ha-ḥebrāh la-ḥaqîrat 'ereṣ yiśrā'ēl we-'attîqôtêhā* (=*BIES*) 25 (1961) 63; *IEJ* 11 (1961) 50. Among the Wâdi Ḥabra texts are three letters addressed to his officers, Yehonatan and Masabbalah, one in each language (Papyrus 3, 4, 12). Yadin thinks that the Aramaic of these texts is to be identified with the Aramaic of the Targum Onqelos; this identification, however, must await further study. See my article, 'The Languages of Palestine in the First Century A.D.', *CBQ* 32 (1970) 501-31.

[6] His name is spelled *nrwn qsr*, just as it has often been suggested apropos of Ap 13:18 (=666!). See D. R. Hillers, 'Revelation 13:18 and a Scroll from Murabba'at', *BASOR* 170 (1963) 65.

[7] See DJD 2, 8, 50, 181.

About the same time as the discovery and excavation of the Murabba'ât caves (1951–52) the Bedouins found further materials related to the Second Revolt in other caves whose location was for a long time kept secret. The reluctance of the finders to reveal the name of the area was suspected by the archaeologists and scholars in Jordan to have been related to the fact that the site was across the border in Israel. The texts found in this 'unknown site' were offered for sale in Jerusalem during July and August 1952.[8] They included Hebrew biblical fragments (Gn, Nm, Dt, Ps 7:14–31, 22), a complete phylactery, a fragmentary text of the OT Minor Prophets in Greek,[9] a letter written to Bar Cochba in Hebrew, two Aramaic contracts dated in the 'third year of the liberation of Israel, in the name of Simon ben Kosibah', two Greek and two Aramaic documents dated according to the system used in the Roman Province of Arabia (erected on the ruins of the Nabataean kingdom of Petra in A.D. 106), and finally some Nabataean papyri.[10] 'The group is to be dated toward the end of the first

[8] J. T. Milik, *Ten Years of Discovery in the Wilderness of Judaea* (SBT 26; London: SCM, 1959) 16.

[9] Partially published by D. Barthélemy, 'Redécouverte d'un chaînon manquant de l'histoire de la Septante', *RB* 60 (1953) 18–29; see further his *Les devanciers d'Aquila: Première publication intégrale du texte des fragments du Dodécaprophéton* (VTSup 10; Leiden: Brill, 1963). The parts preserved belong to Micah, Jonah, Nahum, Habakkuk, Zephaniah, Zechariah; they date from the end of the first century A.D. and are important evidence for the study of the Greek translation of the OT. See further E. Vogt, 'Fragmenta prophetarum minorum deserti Iuda', *Bib* 34 (1953) 423–6; P. Kahle, 'Die im August 1952 entdeckte Lederrolle mit dem griechischen Text der kleinen Propheten und das Problem der Septuaginta', *TLZ* 79 (1954) 81–94. Further fragments of the same text were subsequently published by B. Lifshitz, 'The Greek Documents from the Cave of Horror', *IEJ* 12 (1962) 201–14. They include fragments from Hosea, Amos, Joel, Jonah, Nahum, and Zechariah.

[10] One of the Nabataean papyri has been published by J. Starcky, 'Un contrat nabatéen sur papyrus', *RB* 61 (1954) 161–81; see further J. J. Rabinowitz, 'A Clue to the Nabatean Contract from the Dead Sea Region', *BASOR* 139 (1955) 11–14. J. T. Milik has also published a few of the documents from this site: 'Un contrat juif de l'an 134 après J.-C.', *RB* 61 (1954)

and the beginning of the second century A.D.; the *terminus ad quem* is the Second Jewish Revolt, for it was then that these documents were hidden in their caves.'[11] It is now known that the site of the discovery was a cave (or caves) in the Wâdi Seiyâl (or Naḥal Ṣe'ᵉlîm), which is in Israel between Masada and 'En-gedi. The site was explored between 24 January and 2 February 1960 by Israeli archaeologists, who found evidence of fairly recent Bedouin clandestine digging on the spot.[12] The archaeologists also found further material in the Wâdi Seiyâl caves: 'traces of Chalcolithic occupation at some sites and in many caves, two Iron Age and four Roman fortresses in the region, and a group of caves inhabited during the Bar-Kokhba revolt. The most important finds were an arsenal of arrows, including the iron arrow-heads as well as the shafts of wood and cane, coins from the time of Trajan until Severus Alexander, and some fragments of scrolls, including two parchments of a

---

182–90; 'Deux documents inédits du Désert de Juda', *Bib* 38 (1957) 245–68 (II. Acte de vente d'un terrain, 255–64; III. Acte de vente d'une maison, daté de 134 ap. J.-C., 264–8 [a restudy of the text published in *RB* 61 (1954) 182–90]). See further J. T. Milik, 'Note additionnelle sur le contrat juif de l'an 134 après J.-C.', *RB* 62 (1955) 253–4; J. J. Rabinowitz, 'Some Notes on an Aramaic Contract from the Dead Sea Region', *BASOR* 136 (1954) 15–16; S. Abramson and H. L. Ginsberg, 'On the Aramaic Deed of Sale of the Third Year of the Second Jewish Revolt', *BASOR* 136 (1954) 17–19.

[11] J. T. Milik, *Ten Years*, 16. For further details about the contents of this find see J. T. Milik, 'Le travail d'édition des manuscrits du Désert de Juda', VTSup 4 (1957) [Volume du Congrès; Strasbourg: 1956]) 17–26. See further *Bib* 34 (1953) 419.

[12] Y. Yadin, 'New Discoveries in the Judean Desert', *BA* 24 (1961) 34, has recently confirmed the location which was rumoured several years ago in Jerusalem: '. . . according to a reliable report that reached us several months ago, [the documents were] found by Bedouin in a cave of Nahal Tse'elim, north of Massada, i.e.—in Israel territory. . . . the team did indeed find traces of Bedouin search parties in some of the caves.' Likewise, 'Les repaires de Bar Kokhéba', *BTS* 33 (1960) 6. However, some of the texts mentioned above as coming from the 'unknown site' have been identified as coming from the so-called Cave of Horror in the Wâdi Ḫabra (e.g., the fragmentary text of the Minor Prophets in Greek, the siglum for which is 8HevXIIgr. See B. Lifshitz, *IEJ* 12 (1962) 201, n. 1. See further Y. Yadin, 'Expédition D—The Cave of the Letters', *IEJ* 12 (1962) 227–57, esp. 228–9.

phylactery containing parts of Exod. xiii, 1–16, and fragments of Hebrew, Aramaic and Greek papyri.'[13]

Further material pertaining to the Bar Cochba period has come from a third spot. In 1953 and again in April 1955 Y. Aharoni, an Israeli archaeologist, conducted some explorations in the Wâdi Ḫabra (or Naḥal Ḥever in Israel), some six kilometres, as the crow flies, slightly SW of 'En-gedi. Lacking proper equipment, he was not able to do a thorough job at that time, but he discovered that at least one cave was related to the Bar Cochba revolt. In its vicinity were found traces of two Roman camps, strategically built on the two sides of the steep cliffs forming the wâdi and so placed as to keep watch on the cave-mouth visible below them.[14] During a two-week campaign, from 23 March to 5 April 1960, a team of scholars of the Israel Exploration Society (J. Aviram, N. Avigad, Y. Aharoni, P. Bar-Adon and Y. Yadin) explored the desert area about 'En-gedi.[15] In the three-chambered Naḥal Ḥever cave they uncovered in the inmost chamber a burial niche containing a collection of baskets overflowing with skulls and also several layers of large mats covering human bones. A second spot in the cave yielded a basket of nineteen metal objects: twelve bronze jugs of varying sizes, three incense shovels, two large platters, a

[13] J. Aviram, 'Judean Desert', *IEJ* 10 (1960) 125. See also M. Cassuto Salzmann, 'Ricerche in Israele', *BeO* 3 (1961) 24; Y. Aharoni, 'Les nouvelles découvertes de la Mer Morte', *BTS* 29 (1960) 12–13; 'Expedition B', *BIES* 25 (1961) 19–33; *IEJ* 11 (1961) 11–24.—For the text of the phylactery see P. Wernberg-Møller, 'The Exodus Fragment from Massada', *VT* 10 (1960) 229–30; F. Vattioni, 'Ritrovati altri manoscritti sulla riva israeliana del Mar Morto', *RBibIt* 8 (1960) 71–2; 'Il frammento dell' Esodo scoperto a Massada', *ibid.*, 180.

[14] Y. Aharoni, 'Hever Valley (Wadi Habra)', *IEJ* 4 (1954) 126–7; 5 (1955) 272–3; also M. Cassuto Salzmann, *BeO* 3 (1961) 23–5.

[15] See J. Aviram, 'The Judean Desert Expeditions', *BIES* 25 (1961) 5–12; N. Avigad, 'Expedition A.', *ibid.*, 13–18; Y. Aharoni, 'Expedition B.', *ibid.*, 19–33; P. Bar-Adon, 'Expedition C.', *ibid.*, 34–48; Y. Yadin, 'Expedition D.', *ibid.*, 49–64; B. Lifshitz, 'The Greek Documents from Nahal Seelim and Nahal Mishmar', *ibid.*, 65–73. (All are in Modern Hebrew.) See *IEJ* 11 (1961) 3–62.

patera and a key. Most of the objects were clearly identified as Roman and cultic. At a third spot there was discovered a 4×5 cm. fragment of animal hide on which a few words of Ps 15 and the beginning of Ps 16 were written (dated by Y. Yadin to the second half of the first century A.D.). But the most important find in this cave came from still another spot; it was a goat-skin water-bottle stuffed with bundles of coloured raw wool, skeins of wool, beads, and a package which contained a batch of papyri bound together with four pieces of a wooden slat. 'After having been opened, the papyri were read by Yadin and found to contain fifteen letters from the leader of the Revolt, Bar-Kochba, written in Hebrew, Aramaic and Greek.'[16] According to another report four of the letters were written in Hebrew, two in Greek and the rest in Aramaic; they were letters written by Bar Cochba to officers stationed at the oasis of 'En-gedi.[17]

Finally, during the spring of 1961, when the Israeli archaeologists returned to the wâdi, a sensational discovery was made 'in the same cave where the "archives" of the second century Jewish leader Simon Bar-Kochba were found in April, 1960'.[18] The number of papyrus documents discovered there in 'a long, reed-like sheath' was first announced as seventy.[19] But subsequent reports have reduced the number to five documents found in a leather pouch and thirty-six in a water-skin; they too are letters of Bar-Cochba, deeds and contracts of the same

[16] J. Aviram, *IEJ* 10 (1960) 125–6; see further R. North, 'Report from Palestine', *CBQ* 22 (1960) 317.

[17] *BeO* 3 (1961) 25. Y. Yadin (*BA* 24 [1961] 48; *Bible et Terre Sainte* 34 [1961] 14) now specifies that one of the Greek letters 'is apparently not from Bar Kochba'. In fact, in his fuller report (*BIES* 25 [1961] 49–64) he lists eight papyrus letters as Aramaic (Pap. 1, 2, 4, 8, 10, 11, 14, 15), two as Greek (Pap. 3, 6), three as certainly Hebrew (Pap. 5, 7, 12) and two as probably Hebrew (Pap. 9, 13). B. Lifshitz subsequently published the two Greek letters in 'Papyrus grecs du désert de Juda', *Aegyptus* 42 (1962) 240–56 (+2 plates).

[18] Reuter's dispatch from Tel Aviv, dated 18 March; *Washington Post*, 19 March 1961, p. A3.

[19] *Ibid.*

period.[20] But most of this material is as yet unpublished and we are dependent so far only on preliminary reports.[21]

So much for the new finds which have provided the material which sheds new light on the Bar Cochba period. We turn now to an attempt to relate the new material, in so far as it is known, to what was previously known.

BAR COCHBA'S NAME

One of the most interesting features of the new data supplied by the texts found in the caves of the Wâdies Murabba'ât and Ḫabra is the spelling of the name of the leader of the Second Revolt. In English the most commonly used form is Bar Cochba (less frequently spelled Kochba, Kokhba or Cocheba). This name has clung to him in history mainly due to its use by ancient Christian authors who wrote it in Greek or Latin as *Chochebas* or *Chōchebas*.[22] Bar Cochba means 'the son of the star'. In the light of the new data this form is almost certainly to be regarded as a nickname, or at least as a name derived from a word-play on his real name. His full name is given as

[20] Y. Yadin, 'The Secret in the Cliffs: the Discovery of the Bar Kochba Letters', *Atlantic Monthly* 208/5 (Nov. 1961) 129–35. However, in a recent public lecture Yadin reported the number as 47 papyrus letters, contracts, deeds and 1 biblical fragment on skin. See further Y. Yadin, 'Expedition D—The Cave of the Letters', *IEJ* 12 (1962) 227–57, for a fuller description of the cave, its objects and documents (the archive of Babatha, Nabataean documents, Aramaic and Hebrew texts from the time of Bar Cochba).

[21] See Y. Yadin, 'The Nabatean Kingdom, Provincia Arabia, Petra and En-Geddi in the Documents from Naḥal Ḥever', *JEOL* 17 (1963) 227–41; H. J. Polotsky, 'The Greek Papyri from the Cave of the Letters', *IEJ* 12 (1962) 258–62; 'Three Greek Documents from the Family Archive of Babatha', *E. L. Sukenik Memorial Volume (1889–1953)* (Eretz-Israel 8; Jerusalem: Israel Exploration Society, 1967) 46–51 [in Hebrew; English summary, p. 69*].

[22] Justin Martyr wrote *Chochebas* (*Apol.* 1, 31; *PG* 6, 376); likewise Orosius (7, 31; CSEL 5, 468), Jerome's translation of Eusebius' *Chronicon* (283 F; GCS 47, 201). But Eusebius (*Eccl. Hist.* 4, 6, 2; 4, 8, 4; GCS 9, 306 and 316) has *Chōchebas*. This form of the name is also found in a few Rabbinical texts: *Seder 'Olam Rabbah* 30 (ed. R. Ratner, p. 146; one MS. has *br kkb'*); *Šilšelet haqqabbala* of R. Gedalya ben Yahya 40 (*br kwkb'*). See S. Yeivin, *Milḥemet bar Kôkbâ* (2nd ed.; Jerusalem: Mosad Bialik, 1953) 145, 233–4.

Simon ben/bar Kosibah in the new texts: *šmʿwn bn kwsbh* (*Mur* 43:1), *šmʿwn br kwsbh* (*Hev* 1, 3, 11) sometimes spelled *kwsbʾ* (*Mur* 24 B 3, C 3, 30, E 2, G 3, *Hev* 2, 12), *kwśbh* (*Hev* 14) or *kśbh* (*Hev* 8). The Greek form of the name occurs in *Hev* 6 as *Simōn Chōsiba*, giving us precious evidence of the pronunciation of the name.[23] His real name was, then, Simon the son of Kosibah—the latter is apparently the name of his father, and not of the locality from which he comes.[24]

However, in Rabbinical writings his name is often given as *bn* or *br kwzybʾ* (or *kwzbʾ*), 'the son of the lie',[25] a word-play involving the shift of the radicals *ksb* to *kzb*, the root meaning 'to

[23] See Y. Yadin, *BIES* 25 (1961) 54 ff.; *BA* 24 (1961) 48. The siglum *Hev* will hereafter refer to the texts of the Wâdi Ḫabra as they are cited in the *BIES* article of Yadin. An English translation of this article has appeared too: 'Expedition D', *IEJ* 11 (1961) 36–52. See further E. Y. Kutscher, 'The Languages of the Hebrew and Aramaic Letters of Bar Cochba and His Contemporaries', *Leshonenu* 25 (1961) 117–33; 26 (1962) 7–23. The Greek text of *Hev* 6 has been published by B. Lifshitz, *Aegyptus* 42 (1962) 248–52. It reads: '[A]nnanos to brother Jonathe, greetings! Since Simon (ben) Chosiba (*Simōn Chōsiba*) has again written to send [. . . for] the needs of our brothers [. . .], now sen[d] these things im[mediately i]n security. [Anna]nos. Farewell, brother!'

[24] It has been suggested that *bn* or *br kwzybʾ* in the Rabbinical writings may mean 'the man of Kozeba', a town or locality mentioned in 1 Chr 4:22 (*kôzēbāʾ*). But this suggestion can now be disregarded since the name is given in the new documents with a *samekh* or *śin* instead of a *zayin*. J. T. Milik (*RB* 60 [1953] 279–89) discussed the problem of the *bn X* names, whether they are always patronymics or could be designations of quality. However, in DJD 2, 126 he recognizes *bn kwsbh* as a patronymic, even though the etymology of *kwsbh* is quite obscure. This seems to be the better solution, until more evidence is forthcoming. Y. Yadin (*BIES* 25 [1961] 64) apparently also inclines toward the view that *bar Kôkᵉbā* and *bar Kôzibā* are nicknames. Cf. F. Nötscher, 'Bar Kochba, Ben Kosba: der Sternsohn, der Prächtige', *VT* 11 (1961) 449–51. For another discussion of the name, see now B. Lifshitz, *Aegyptus* 42 (1962) 240–56.

[25] Bab. Talmud, *Sanhedrin* XI, 1, 2; fol. 93b (ed. Goldschmidt, 7, 400); Jer. Talmud, *Taʿanith* 4, 68; *Echa Rabbah* 80, 2, 5 (ed. S. Buber, p. 158): 'Do not read *kôkāb*, 'star', but *kôzēb*, "liar".'—J. T. Milik (*RB* 60 [1953] 277–8: DJD 2, 126) suggests that of the two forms of the name attested in the Rabbinical writings, *kwzbʾ* and *kwzybʾ*, the defective form was the more original, since the dissyllabic form **Kosba* becomes **Kozba* ('*s* s'assimilant à la sonore suivante'). The form with *z* would be a phonetic shift introduced

lie'. Though the interpretation is questioned at times,[26] it still seems best to regard the Rabbinical *Kôzibā* form of his name as due either to the Rabbis who did not approve of his anti-Roman uprising or to those who later reflected ironically on its ill-fated outcome. To them he was the 'son of the lie'. The other form of the name, *Kôk'bā*, is likewise due to a word-play attributed to his contemporary, the great Rabbi Aqiba, who did approve of his movement. In fact, he regarded him as a messiah, and applied to him the oracle of Balaam, 'A star shall advance from Jacob' (Nm 24:17).[27] The patronymic *bar Kôsibāh* was changed to the Aramaic *bar kôk'bā*, 'the son of the

---

into the writing, especially by those who only heard the name and related it to an otherwise known root. However, the trisyllabic form of the name is preserved in Greek, *Chōsiba*. When this is considered together with the Rabbinical *plena scriptio, kwzyb'*, it appears that the more original form was *Kôsibah*. Hence, it is better to retain the suggestion that both *kwkb'* and *kwzb'* are the result of a play on the original name.

[26] E. Schürer (*Geschichte des jüdischen Volkes im Zeitalter Jesu Christi* [5th ed.; Leipzig: J. C. Hinrichs, 1920] 1, 683; [Engl. tr. of 2nd ed. by J. MacPherson; Edinburgh: T. and T. Clark, 1905: 1/2, 298]) maintains that it was 'not until a comparatively late period, and only by a few individual writers, in view of his miserable collapse, [that] it was taken to mean liar or deceiver'. Footnote 100 (Engl. 84): 'Since Barcosiba or Bencosiba is the prevailing form, even in the mouths of such as esteemed him highly, like Akiba, it cannot have had a disrespectful meaning.' It should be recalled, however, that Schürer's transliteration of the name with an *s* does not represent the real spelling of the name now known to us from the new finds, but is the frequently used German equivalent of Semitic *z* in the Rabbinical form of the name *kwzyb'*. What Schürer says might be accepted as correct, if we could be sure that R. Aqiba had not in fact used the correct form *kwsbh* (with a *samekh*), which was later normalized in the Rabbinical tradition to agree with the other form *kwzyb'*, precisely because of the ill-fated outcome of the revolt.

[27] Jer. Talmud, *Ta'anith* 4, 68d: 'R. Simon ben Yohai said, "R. Aqiba, my teacher, expounded the passage: 'There shall go forth a star (*kwkb*) out of Jacob' (Nm 24:17), as follows: 'There goes *kwzb'* out from Jacob.' When R. Aqiba saw Barcoziba, he said, 'This is the king Messiah.' Then R. Yoḥanan ben Torta said to him, 'Aqiba, the grass will grow out of your jaw-bone, and the Son of David will not yet have come.'"' Similarly the Midrash *Echa Rabbah* (2, 2, 4, ed. S. Buber, p. 101; tr. by J. Rabinowitz, in *Midrash Rabbah* [London: Soncino, 1951] 157).—Eusebius (*Eccl. Hist.* 4,

star', whence comes our English form Bar Cochba, the name which has persisted for him in our history books.

Coins minted during the first year of the Second Revolt bear the name with a title, 'Simon, Prince of Israel' (*šmʿwn nśyʾ yśrʾl*),[28] and the fuller form of the name and title is now attested in the new documents as 'Simon ben Kosibah, Prince of Israel' (*šmʿwn bn kwsbʾ nsyʾ yśrʾl* [*Mur* 24 B 2–3] or 'Simon bar Kosibah, the prince over Israel' (*šmʿwn br kwsbh hnsyʾ ʿl yśrʾl* [*Hev* 1]). The title, 'Prince of Israel', designates the supreme rank which Bar Cochba held during the period of his leadership of the revolt. There was, however, apparently also a priestly co-leader, for other coins of the same period mention Eleazar, the Priest (*ʾlʿzr hkwhn*).[29]

It is not unlikely that both the title, Prince of Israel, and the appellation, 'the son of the star', are due to the messianic character of the uprising. Thanks to the discovery of the Qumran texts, where we find a developed but complex messianic expectation formulated, it is easy for us to understand how Bar Cochba's movement could have been hailed as the event which was to free Jerusalem and redeem Israel. In the

---

6, 2; GCS 9, 306) is also aware that *Barchōchebas* is related to *kwkb*, 'star', when he says that he was 'a man who was murderous and a bandit, but relied on his name, as if dealing with slaves, and claimed to be a luminary who had come down to them from heaven and was magically enlightening those who were in misery'. This pejorative view of the leader of the Second Revolt agrees with that of other early Christian writers; see footnote 117.

[28] It is now universally admitted that these Simon coins date from the Bar Cochba period; see A. Reifenberg, *Ancient Jewish Coins* (2nd ed.; Jerusalem: Rubin Mass, 1947) 33–4, 64 (#190, 192, 193, 199); likewise DJD 2, 46. Some of the coins with the name *šmʿwn* bear a star, which may refer to Aqiba's appellation of the leader as a messiah (see A. Reifenberg, *op. cit.*, 60 [#164, 167]). Cf. C. Roth, 'Star and Anchor; Coin Symbolism and the End of Days', *ʾEreṣ Yiśrāʾēl* 6 (1960) 13*–15*.

[29] Perhaps this is R. Eleazar ben Azariah, the president of the Beth-Din in the place of Gamaliel II; see A. Reifenberg, *Ancient Jewish Coins*², 34 and 61 (#169, 170), 63 (#189, 189a), 64 (#196), 65 (#203); DJD 2, 47.—Y. Yadin (*BIES* 25 [1961] 59; *IEJ* 11 [1961] 46) mentions that *Hev* 11, a letter written by Simon bar Kosibah to two of his officers at ʿEn-gedi,

messianic expectations of the Qumran sect the Oracle of Balaam played an important role. It is used in the third paragraph of the *Testimonia* text from Cave 4, in 1QM 11:5–7, in CD 7:18–20. In the latter text it refers to the Davidic Messiah and to the Interpreter of the Law (probably a priestly figure), whereas its use in the *T. Levi* (18:3) is applied rather to the Aaronitic Messiah and in *T. Judah* 24:1 it is used of the Kingly Messiah.[30] Even granting that such messianic expectations might have been rather 'sectarian', and not necessarily characteristic of all contemporary Judaism, nevertheless they provide a background against which it is easy to understand how the uprising of the Jews in the second century after the horrible destruction of their 'holy city' and the temple of Yahweh in A.D. 70 could take on the colours and hues of a messianic movement. Simon ben Kosibah, as the leader of that Second Revolt, was the 'Messiah', the 'son of *the star*'. His revolt was dedicated to the 'Liberation of Jerusalem', and the 'Redemption of Israel', as the coins of his time attest.[31] We know nothing about his antecedents, and cannot even conjecture how he came to be the leader of the revolt. But at any rate he became for the Jews the 'Prince of Israel', the *nāśî'*, the name reminiscent of the OT eschatological leader of the people spoken of by the prophet Ezekiel, who was to be descended from David (see Ez 34:24; 37:25; 44:3).

---

contains a reference to a certain Baṭniyah bar Misah, who is called 'our master' (*rbnw*). It is not yet determined who he is, nor what relationship he had to the rebel leader. See further 'Les lettres de Bar Kokhéba', *BTS* 34 (1961) 15.

[30] See J. M. Allegro, 'Further Messianic References in Qumran Literature', *JBL* 75 (1956) 182–7, Document IV. Cf. ' "4QTestimonia" and the New Testament', pp. 58–89 above; 'The Use of Explicit Old Testament Quotations in Qumran Literature and in the New Testament', pp. 3–58 above. Likewise L. E. Toombs, 'Barcosiba and Qumran', *NTS* 4 (1957) 65–71.

[31] See A. Reifenberg, *Ancient Jewish Coins*², 60–6.

THE CAUSES OF THE SECOND REVOLT

The causes of the Second Jewish Revolt have always been a subject of great debate among the historians of second-century Palestine. How grateful we would be, then, if the new documents were to shed some light on this subject. However, the reports about the new discoveries and texts shed no new light on this area of our study and we are in no better position than previously. We present here a brief résumé only of what seems to be the state of the question regarding the sources today.

Ancient authorities assign various causes to the Second Revolt, most of which are not contradictory, but the problem is how to assess them. Modern historians do not always agree. E. Schürer has, however, effectively disposed of one claim that has often been put forward, that the revolt was due to the permission given by Hadrian to the Jews to rebuild the temple of Yahweh, but which was subsequently revoked by him.[32] There is really no foundation for the claim. The two reasons, however, which are seriously considered today as having played a major role in causing the Jews to revolt are those which come to us from Dio Cassius in his *Roman History* and from the *Life of Hadrian*, wrongly attributed to Aelius Spartianus.

The first reason which we shall discuss is that given by Dio Cassius, *viz.* that the Emperor Hadrian, who was visiting the Near East, attempted to rebuild the city of Jerusalem as an important centre of his empire and to erect on the site of the temple of Yahweh a shrine to the Roman god Jupiter Capitolinus. Dio Cassius' text follows:

> At Jerusalem he [Hadrian] founded a city in place of the one which had been razed to the ground, naming it Aelia Capitolina, and on the site of the temple of the god he raised a new temple to Jupiter. This brought on a war of no slight importance nor of brief duration, for the Jews deemed it intolerable that foreign races should be settled in their city and foreign religious rites planted there. So long, indeed, as Hadrian was close by in Egypt and again in Syria, they remained

[32] *GJV* 1, 671, 3 (Engl. tr. 289–91); similarly H. Strathmann, 'Der Kampf um Beth-Ter', *PJB* 23 (1927) 103–5.

quiet, save in so far as they purposely made of poor quality such weapons as they were called upon to furnish, in order that theRomans might reject them and they themselves might thus have the use of them; but when he went farther away, they openly revolted.[33]

This reason, as given by Dio Cassius, seems to fill out with details what the biographer of Hadrian very succinctly said of him in the following words: 'sacra Romana diligentissime curavit, peregrina contempsit; pontificis maximi officium peregit'.[34] In other words, it was completely in character with Hadrian to attempt to rebuild Jerusalem after the fashion of Hellenistic cities and try to establish there the culture of the Greeks which he admired so much.

One of the problems connected with this cause for the Second Revolt is precisely the time when Hadrian began to build Aelia Capitolina. Dio Cassius' report seems to indicate that it was actually begun before the Revolt. Since this point enters into our later discussions of the dates of the revolt, it is important that we review here the reasons for thinking that Dio Cassius is correct.

The reign of Hadrian was marked by long journeys to the various parts of his empire. In the year A.D. 128 he undertook his second protracted visit to the Near East. While the data about his movements, his visits to various colonies, cities and countries, and his inspections of Roman legions and garrisons are relatively abundant, they are not sufficient to establish with certainty their detailed chronological order. But it seems that he was at Antioch in Syria in autumn A.D. 129, and from there made his way to Beirut in Phoenicia, via Palmyra and Damas-

[33] *Roman History* 69, 12, 1–2 (tr. by E. Cary, Loeb Classical Library, vol. 8, 449).

[34] *Vita Hadriani* 22, 10; in the *Scriptores historiae augustae* (tr. by D. Magie, Loeb Classical Library, vol. 1, 68–9). In connection with these testimonies it is customary for historians to discuss the *Epistle of Barnabas* (16, 4), but the value of this text, which is corrupt in a crucial spot, is quite debatable. See E. Schürer, *GJV* 1, 672 (Engl. tr. 290); H. Strathmann, *PJB* 23 (1927) 104; H. Bietenhard, 'Die Freiheitskriege der Juden unter den Kaisern Trajan und Hadrian und der messianische Tempelbau', *Jud* 4 (1948) 95–100.

cus. From Beirut he went to the province of Arabia, the former kingdom of the Nabataeans, and from Petra he came back to Jerash, where he apparently spent the winter of A.D. 129–30.[35] From Jerash he must have made his way to Judaea, for coins have been found commemorating his *parousia* or arrival there: *adventui Aug*(*usti*) *Iudaeae*.[36] He seems to have visited Eleutheropolis, Tiberias, Caesarea Maritima and Gaza.[37] In many of these places he was hailed as *restitutor*, *oikistēs*, *ktistēs*, *euergetēs*, which titles are generally attributed to his policy of setting the Roman garrisons to work in building Hellenistic-style cities in these areas.[38] While there is no direct evidence of Hadrian's visit to Jerusalem, it is quite likely that he visited the town, given its importance in the history of Palestine, its fairly recent destruction by Roman troops, and the fact that a garrison of the *Legio X Fretensis* was still stationed there. En route to Gaza and subsequently to Egypt, where he spent the winter of A.D. 130, he must have passed through Jerusalem. It is likely that he

[35] The inscription on the triumphal arch at Jerash, which was erected on the occasion of Hadrian's visit there, is dated to the fourteenth *tribunicia potestas* and the 192nd year of the era of Jerash (= the Pompeian era), i.e. 1 October 129–30. See W. F. Stinespring, 'The Inscription of the Triumphal Arch at Jerash', *BASOR* 56 (1934) 15–16; C. H. Kraeling (ed.), *Gerasa: City of the Decapolis* (New Haven: American Schools of Oriental Research, 1938) 401–2; C. C. McCown, 'New Historical Items from Jerash Inscriptions', *JPOS* 16 (1936) 69–78, esp. 75–6; M. I. Rostovtzeff, *CRAIBL* 1934, 267.—On the journeys of Hadrian in general see J. Dürr, *Die Reisen des Kaisars Hadrian* (Vienna: G. Gerold, 1881); B. W. Henderson, *The Life and Principate of the Emperor Hadrian A.D. 76–138* (London: Methuen, 1923) 128 ff.; B. d'Orgeval, *L'empereur Hadrien: oeuvre législative et administrative* (Paris: Ed. Domat Montchrestien, 1950) 25 ff.; W. F. Stinespring, 'Hadrian in Palestine, 129/130 A.D.', *JAOS* 59 (1939) 360–5.

[36] See H. Mattingly and E. A. Sydenham, *The Imperial Roman Coinage; Vol. II Vespasian to Hadrian* (London: Spink, 1926) 454 (#890–4); M. Bernhart, *Handbuch zur Münzkunde der römischen Kaiserzeit* (Halle a.d.S.: A. Riechmann, 1926), Textband, 103, n. 1; H. St J. Hart, 'Judaea and Rome: the Official Commentary', *JTS* n.s. 3 (1952) 172–98 (esp. pl. V, #1–4).

[37] See F.-M. Abel, *Histoire de la Palestine depuis la conquête d'Alexandre jusqu'à l'invasion arabe* (EBib; Paris: Gabalda) vol. 2 (1952) 74, 79 ff.

[38] See R. MacMullen, 'Roman Imperial Building in the Provinces', *Harvard Studies in Classical Philology* 64 (1959) 207–35.

ordered the rebuilding of the city as the *colonia Aelia Capitolina* at this time. At any rate, Hadrian was in Egypt by November A.D. 130, for he saluted the colossal statue of Memnon at Thebes on the 21st of that month.[39] Apparently he returned to Syria in the spring of A.D. 131 and then proceeded to visit the regions of Pontus and the Black Sea.[40] He passed the winter of 131–2 at Athens. The withdrawal to these more distant places is probably what Dio Cassius has in mind, when he refers to the outbreak of the Second Revolt.

A different reason, however, is given by the *Life of Hadrian* for the revolt, one which has nothing to do with the attempt to rebuild Jerusalem as a Hellenistic city. The biographer of Hadrian records it thus: 'moverunt ea tempestate et Iudaei bellum, quod vetabantur mutilare genitalia.'[41] The emperor Domitian had earlier forbidden castration. Dio Cassius records, 'He forbade that any person in the Roman Empire should thereafter be castrated.'[42] This prohibition was repeated by the Emperor Nerva.[43] But when Hadrian came along, he interpreted the prohibition in such wise that it included circumcision.[44] The rescript which he issued apropos of it probably does not date from the beginning of his reign; it belongs more likely to the period just before the Second Revolt, and for that reason it is given by the *Life* as a cause of the revolt.[45] Hadrian

[39] Cf. *CIG* 4737.

[40] See Arrian, *Periplus ponti Euxini* 1, 1 (ed. R. Hercher, 1885, p. 86).

[41] *Vita Hadriani* 14, 2.

[42] *Rom. Hist.* 67, 2, 3. See also Suetonius, *Domitian* 7, 1: 'Castrari mares vetuit'; Eusebius, *Chronicon* 272F (GCS 47, 190): 'Domitianus eunuchos fieri prohibuit'. H. Hitzig, 'Castratio', *PW* 3/2 (1889) 1772–3; B. d'Orgeval, *L'empereur Hadrien*, 324.

[43] Dio Cassius, *Rom Hist.* 68, 2, 4.

[44] See Ulpian, *Digesta* 48, 8, 4: 'Divus Hadrianus rescripsit: constitutum quidem est, ne spadones fierent, eos autem, qui hoc crimine arguerentur, Corneliae legis poena teneri. . . .' The *lex Cornelia de sicariis et veneficis* punished murder with death. This was applied to the physician who performed the castration; the eunuch was punished with exile and loss of property.

[45] This is accepted as a cause of the revolt by E. Schürer, *GJV*; M. Noth, *The History of Israel* (2nd English ed.; New York: Harper, 1960) 451–2;

made both castration and circumcision a crime punishable by death, by subsuming it under the existing *lex Cornelia de sicariis et veneficis*. Such a law naturally touched a major tenet of the religion of the Jews and it is not improbable that it contributed to their rebellion against Roman domination.

The widening of the prohibition of castration to include circumcision, however, was not specifically directed against the Jews. There is no evidence that Hadrian so intended it. On the contrary, when under Antoninus Pius permission was given to the Jews to circumcise their children again, the prohibition still was in effect for the non-Jewish peoples.[46] Consequently, it appears that the prohibition of circumcision was a general one, but affected an important Jewish religious rite—a rite for which the Jews were as prompt to rebel as for the building of a shrine of Jupiter on the site of Yahweh's temple in Jerusalem.

The prevailing opinion among modern historians of the period is to accept both the cause given by Dio Cassius and that supplied by the *Life of Hadrian*, since they are not conflicting reasons and both may have been the prime factors in the uprising. Whether there were other subordinate reasons we do not know for certain.[47]

H. Hitzig, 'Circumcisio', *PW* 3/2 (1899) 2570–1. But it is questioned by H. Bietenhard, *Jud* 4 (1948) 92–4.

[46] See Modestinus, *Digesta* 48, 8, 11: 'Circumcidere Iudaeis filios suos tantum rescripto divi Pii permittitur; in non eiusdem religionis qui hoc fecerit, castrantis poena irrogatur.' See E. Schürer, *GJV* 1, 677; E. M. Smallwood, 'The Legislation of Hadrian and Antoninus Pius against Circumcision', *Latomus* 18 (1959) 334–47.

[47] S. Perowne (*Hadrian* [London: Hodder and Stoughton, 1960] 149–50) summarizes thus the grievances which the Jews could have had against Hadrian by the year 130: 'First, he had declared himself the successor to Antiochus Epiphanes. He had finished Antiochus' own temple in Athens. Secondly, like Antiochus, he had adopted, or allowed others to adopt in addressing him, the style of god, of Zeus Olympios. Thirdly, he had permitted this style to appear on coins which circulated among Jewish communities. Fourthly, he had prohibited circumcision, which for the Jews was the very seal of their being and faith. Fifthly, he was on his way to patronize and caress the Greeks of Alexandria, who had shewn themselves the most

It should be noted, however, that Pausanias and Chrysostom were content to ascribe the Second Revolt merely to the general disobedience and the revolutionary tendency of the Jews, who were hankering after the restoration of their ancient political state.[48] But this is a description rather of the general background of the period under Roman domination, especially since the destruction of Jerusalem in A.D. 70. After Titus left the town in ruins and a garrison of the *Legio X Fretensis* was stationed there to maintain Roman military control, the lot of the Jews in the empire was not easy. Under Vespasian the procuratorial province of Judaea was administered as an imperial province with the official name *Iudaea*. It was not a part of the *provincia Syriae*, but depended directly on the emperor and thus had the appearance of independence, at least of the neighbouring Roman administration in Syria. *Iudaea* was governed by a *legatus* who resided at Caesarea Maritima. Roman colonists were settled in Flavia Neapolis (modern Nablus) and 800 veterans were given property in Emmaus. In Jerusalem itself some of the old inhabitants, both Jews and the Christians, who had returned from Pella, lived side by side with the Romans. In fact, in recent times it has become clear that more Jews actually lived in Jerusalem between the two revolts than we normally imagine, as ossuaries and other burials of the period attest. Vespasian had claimed the whole of the land of Judaea as his private property and tenant-farmers worked the land for him. The Jewish community, accustomed to pay a didrachm or half-shekel as a tax for the temple of Yahweh, now had to contribute the same to the *fiscus iudaicus* which eventually bene-

---

ardent enemies of the Jews. Sixthly, he had gone out of his way to honour the very man who had captured Jerusalem, almost two centuries before, and had violated the Holy of Holies [i.e., Pompey]. Seventhly, and finally, he had given orders for the obliteration of Jerusalem, for the construction on the site of a Roman colony, called by his own name, and containing, on the very site of the ancient Temple, a shrine where he himself should be venerated.'

[48] Pausanias, *Periegesis* 1, 5, 5; Chrysostom, *Adv. Judaeos* 5, 11; *PG* 48, 900.

fited the Roman temple of Jupiter Capitolinus. The temple cult was no more and with it passed away the influence of the Jerusalem Sanhedrin headed by the high priest. Religious emphasis among the Jews shifted to certain forms of synagogue worship and to the study of the Torah to ensure its careful observance (especially according to the traditions of the Pharisees and the Rabbis). The council of 72 Elders (or Rabbis) in Jamnia (Yabneh), under the leadership of R. Joḥanan ben Zakkai and later under R. Gamaliel II, took over the rule of the Jewish community in Palestine. It enjoyed a certain autonomy even though the land was still dominated by the Romans, who normally did not interfere with the workings of the council. It is often said to have fixed the calendar and the canon of the Scriptures[49] and functioned as a court of law. But both in Palestine and in the diaspora there was always the yearning for the 'restoration of Israel', a yearning fed by the recollection of what had taken place after the destruction of Jerusalem in 586 B.C. When Trajan (A.D. 98–117) was occupied with the threat of the Parthians, revolts of the Jews occurred in Cyrene, Egypt, Cyprus and in Mesopotamia (toward the end of his reign, *c.* 115–16).[50] These revolts were in part fired by the messianic expectations current among the Jews of the time. The general who finally put down the Mesopotamian revolt was the Romanized Moor, Lusius Quietus, who was subsequently rewarded with the governorship of Palestine.[51] We know little

[49] But cf. J. P. Lewis, 'What Do We Mean by Jabneh?', *JBR* 32 (1964) 125–32.

[50] See Dio Cassius, *Rom. Hist.* 68, 32, 1–3 (which ascribes much bloodshed and gruesome atrocities to the Jews in Cyrene, Egypt and Cyprus). Similarly Eusebius, *Eccl. Hist.* 4, 2, 1–5 (who mentions the revolts in Alexandria, the rest of Egypt, Cyrene and Mesopotamia in the 18th regnal year of Trajan). Cf. V. A. Tcherikover and A. Fuks, *Corpus papyrorum iudaicarum* (Cambridge, Mass: Harvard Univ. Press) vol. 1 (1957) 85–93; H. Bietenhard, *Jud* 4 (1948) 66–7.

[51] Dio Cassius, *Rom. Hist.* 68, 32, 5; Eusebius, *Chronicon* in Armenian translation by J. Karst, GCS 20, 219.—The *Seder 'Olam Rabbah* 30 (ed. B. Ratner, 146) speaks of a 'war of Quietus', but historians are reluctant to

about the conditions of Palestine between the two revolts, but the fact that Lusius Quietus was sent there as governor would indicate that elements of unrest were present there too. It is to this general background of unrest among the Jews, both in the diaspora and in the motherland, that the statements of Pausanias and Chrysostom are best related. Given such hopes of a liberating messiah to come and such hankering after the freedom of old, the two causes of the Second Revolt as stated by Dio Cassius and the *Life of Hadrian* become readily intelligible.

THE DATES OF THE REVOLT

The dates normally given for the Second Revolt are A.D. 132–5. The beginning of the revolt is usually reckoned according to the notice of Dio Cassius, that the Jews 'openly revolted', when Hadrian withdrew from their vicinity to more distant regions, as we have seen. These dates have been preferred by modern historians to those supplied by Epiphanius and the *Chronicon Paschale*. The former gives the forty-seventh year after the destruction of Jerusalem as the date of Hadrian's visit to Jerusalem and the building of Aelia Capitolina, which occasioned the revolt.[52] This, however, cannot be correct, for it would equal A.D. 117, the very year of Hadrian's accession to the imperial throne. The *Chronicon Paschale* also gives a misleading date, in associating the building of Aelia Capitolina with the third year of the 224th Olympiad, in the consulship of Aelius Hadrianus Augustus and Rusticius.[53] This would be the year A.D. 119. Although we cannot date precisely the year in which Hadrian began the

---

take this expression in a strict sense; moreover, the text may not be sound. See H. Bietenhard, *Jud* 4 (1948) 70–7.

[52] Epiphanius, *De mensuris et ponderibus* 14; *PG* 43, 259–61.

[53] *PG* 92, 613; ed. Dindorf, I, 474. For a modern, but isolated, attempt to defend these dates see W. D. Gray, 'The Founding of Aelia Capitolina and the Chronology of the Jewish War under Hadrian', *AJSL* 39 (1922–23) 248–56. See also M. Auerbach, *Zur politischen Geschichte der Juden unter Kaiser Hadrian* (Berlin, 1924) 325.

rebuilding of Jerusalem, it seems to have been before the Second Revolt, and most probably in the year A.D. 130. Dio Cassius' report implies that some time passed before the Jews openly rebelled. Hence the year is usually given as A.D. 132.

New light has been shed on the question by the dates given in one of the documents from a Murabba'ât cave. *Mur* 24 is an abstract of title-deeds written on a papyrus by a deputy of Bar Cochba, in whose name various farm-lands were rented out in return for crops to be paid into the 'treasury' of the Prince of Israel. It belongs to a *genre* called in Greek *diastrōma* and already known from the papyri found at Oxyrhynchus in Egypt.[54] In each case a record is made of the date, the competent authority, the names of the lessees, the fact of the rental, the duration of it, and the terms (stating the exact amount of wheat which is to be paid yearly to the 'treasury'); finally the signatures are appended. In *Mur* 24 there are eleven fragmentary texts of this sort, the wording of which offers at times slight variants. The item of interest to our discussion here is found in texts B and E of this document; it is the synchronism of dates which is given. We supply the text of one of the deeds in order to comment on it and explain the synchronism.[55]

Mur 24 *E* (*DJD* 2, 131)

[*bʿśryn lš*]*bṭ šnt št*[*ym*] *lg'lt*[56]	[The 20th of She]bat, the 2nd year of the Redemption of

[54] Oxy P 274 (dated A.D. 89–97); see B. P. Grenfell and A. S. Hunt, *The Oxyrhynchus Papyri, Edited with Translations and Notes* (London: Egypt Exploration Fund, 1899) 2, 259–62.

[55] The lacunae in the text are restored with certainty due to the very similar wording of these parts in the other fragmentary texts, which fortunately do not have the lacunae always in the identical spot.

[56] *lg'lt yśr'l:* Milik rightly understands this expression as a synonym for *lḥrwt yrwšlm*, adducing as evidence the interchange of these expressions in different dates or years on coins (see A. Reifenberg, *Ancient Jewish Coins*², 60 [#163, *lg'lt yśr'l*, 170–2, 189–95]) and in the new documents (*Mur* 23 and 24). There is no reason to regard *lg'lt yśr'l* as the more messianic title given

[y]śr'l ʿl yd šmʿwn bn k[ws]b' nsy'	[I]srael by Simon ben K[osi]bah, the Prince of
[yś]r'l bmḥnh šywšb bhrwdys[57]	[Is]rael, in the camp which is situated at Herodium.
[y]hwdh bn rb' 'mr lhll bn grys[58]	[Ye]hudah ben Rabba' declared to Hillel ben Garis:
'ny mrṣwny [ḥ]krt[59] *hmk*[60] *hywm 't*	'I, of my own free will, have [ren]ted from you today
hʿpr[61] *šhw' š ly bḥ<k>rty bʿyr*	the farm-land, which is mine by my tenancy in 'Ir-

---

to the revolt and *lḥrwt yrwšlm* as the more political one, as suggested by B. Kanael, 'The Historical Background of the Coins "Year Four . . . of the Redemption of Zion"', *BASOR* 129 (1953) 20. For two hybrid coins in A. Reifenberg, *Ancient Jewish Coins*^{2}, #171–2, bear on the obverse *šnt 'ḥt lg'lt yśr* ('year one of the Redemption of Isr<ael>') and on the reverse *š b lḥr yśr'l* ('yr 2 of the Freed<om> of Israel').

[57] *bmḥnh šywšb bhrwdys:* Milik's translation links these words with the preceding *nsy' yśr'l*, 'Prince d'Israël en campagne, qui réside à Hérodium'. He interprets the expression to mean that Bar Cochba had his headquarters at Herodium. However, Y. Yadin ('Were the Headquarters of Bar Cochba at Herodium?', *Hā-'Āreṣ*, 10 March 1961, 10; see also *IEJ* 11 [1961] 51) has shown that the Hebrew need not mean that; the sense is rather that the contract was made in the camp at Herodium. This interpretation is confirmed by other documents found in the Wâdi Ḫabra cave in 1960, which make it unlikely that the headquarters of Bar Cochba were on Herodium. See further discussion below, pp. 335–7. Cf. *Mur* 18:2, where the place in which the text is written seems to be named; likewise *Mur* 19:1, 12; 115:2.

[58] *hll bn grys:* The same individual is mentioned in other deeds (*Mur* 24 B 6, C 5, [F 4–5], [H 3], J 3), and is probably the administrator in charge of the lands in the village of 'Ir-Naḥaš, near Eleutheropolis, the modern Deir Naḫḫas, about a mile and a half ENE of Beit Jibrin.

[59] *ḥkrt:* The verb *ḥkr* means to 'contract, farm', especially to 'give or take in rent on a fixed rental payable in kind' (Jastrow, 463). The details of the text bear out this meaning.

[60] *hmk:* Defective spelling of the Mishnaic Hebrew *hymk* (*hêm^{e}kā*), an alternate form of *mmk*, 'from you'. See M. H. Segal, *A Grammar of Mishnaic Hebrew* (Oxford: Clarendon, 1958) 144.

[61] *hʿpr:* Normally this word means 'loose earth' (whence a number of

nḥš šḥkrt mšm'wn nsy' yśr'l	Naḥaš (and) which I have rented from Simon, the Prince of Israel.
t[62] *'pr hlz ḥkrty hmk mn hywm*	This land I have rented from you from today
'd swp 'rb hšmṭh šhm šnym	until the end of the eve of Remission, which is (in) complete years,
šlmwt šny [m]ksh[63] *ḥmš t ḥkyr*	[fi]scal years, five. (This is) the rent
[*š'h*]' *mwdd*[64] *lk b*[*hr*]*wdys ḥnṭyn*	[which I sha]ll pay to you at [Her]odium: wheat
[*ypwt wnqywt*] *šlw*[*št kwr*]*yn wltk*	[of good quality and pure], thr[ee ko]rs and a letek,
[*m'srt m'srt*] *t 'lh*	[tithed . . . having tithed] these
[*šth' šwql 'l gg h'wṣr*][65] *w*[*q*]*ym*	[which you will pay into the treasury]. (This document is) valid,

figurative meanings are derived); but here it equals 'a piece of farmland'.

[62] *t:* This form, which is found often in these documents (*Mur* 22 i 2; 24 A 8, B 18, C 16, D 11, E 8, 10, 13; 36 i–ii 3; 43 3, 5; 44 6, 7, 8, 9; 46 3, 5), is related by Milik to the Punic *t*, a form of the *signum accusativi* (See Z. Harris, *A Grammar of the Phoenician Language* [American Oriental Series 8; New Haven: American Oriental Society, 1936] 76; J. Friedrich, *Phönizisch-Punische Grammatik* [Analecta Orientalia 32; Rome: Pontifical Biblical Institute, 1951] #255).

[63] *šny mksh:* Lit. 'years of the toll', from the root *mks*, 'to pay a toll on' (Jastrow, 783). See now the important study of J. R. Donahue, 'Tax Collectors and Sinners', CBQ 33 (1971).

[64] *šh' mwdd:* The relative pronoun *š* precedes the 1st sg. impf. qal of *hyh* in an apocopated form; see M. H. Segal, *op. cit.*, 95. The 2 sg. is restored in 1:14. The rood *mdd*, 'to measure', is often used for measuring off a tithe; compare *šql* in 1:14.

[65] *'l gg h'wṣr:* Lit. 'on the roof of the treasury'. Milik explains the expression by the shape of public granaries in the ancient East, especially in Egypt, which were great round silos with an opening on top through which the grain was poured. *ANEP* #90.

15 [*ʿly lʿmt kkh*[66]]	[therefore, against me].'
[*yhwdh bn rbʾ ʿl npšh ktb*]	[Yehudah ben Rabba', for himself. There wrote (this)]
[*plwny bn ʾlmwny mn mʾmrh*[67]]	[at his dictation X ben Z].

There are several important items in this text which shed new light on the affairs of second-century Palestine. For the moment we are only interested in those which help to fix the date of the Second Revolt more precisely. These are, first of all, the date of the document itself, 'the 20th of Shebat, the 2nd year of the Redemption of Israel'; secondly, the reference to the 'end of the eve of Remission', and lastly the indication that the contract would last up to that time, a period of 'five complete years'. The 'remission' (*šᵉmiṭṭāh*) referred to is the observance of the regulation of Ex 23:10–11, according to which the land is to lie fallow every seventh year.[68] The contract is thus made to be valid up to the end of the sixth year of the current seven-year or Sabbatical cycle. Until that time there are five complete years, i.e. years when the rental on the harvest derived from the land must be paid. This means, therefore, that the 20th of Shebat of the second year of the Redemption of Israel falls in the second year of the Sabbatical cycle. Since Shebat corresponds roughly to January–February, the 20th of this month would equal the early part of February in our calendar.

Now Rabbinical tradition has recorded that the temple was destroyed by Titus during *môṣāʾê šᵉbîʿît*,[69] which means the year

[66] *lʿmt kkh:* Lit. 'in accordance with thus'; =*ʿl kk* of the OT.

[67] *mn mʾmrh:* 'At his dictation', the form of the suffix being an Aramaism, as in *npšh* (1:16). Milik understood this expression to refer to a command given by Bar Cochba to a deputy; but Y. Yadin (*IEJ* 12 [1962] 253–4), on the basis of similar texts in newer documents, has shown that the concluding formula records the name of the town clerk who acted as scribe.

[68] It may also refer to Dt 15:1 ff., which ordains that every seventh year a creditor's claims are to be remitted; *šmṭh*, the noun, is found explicitly in this connection. Cf. *Mur* 18:7.

[69] *Seder ʿOlam Rabbah* 30 (ed. B. Ratner, 147); cf. Bab. Talmud, *ʿArakhin*

after the Sabbath-year. Hence, the year itself was A.D. 68–9, beginning with the month of Tišri.[70] The subsequent Sabbath-years fell on 75–6, 82–3, 89–90, 96–7, 103–4, 110–11, 117–18, 124–5, 131–2.[71] The year 132–3 was, then, the first year of the new cycle and 133–4 its second year. Therefore, the document was written at the beginning of February of the year 134. This date is indicated as corresponding with the second year of the 'Redemption of Israel'. We have unfortunately no certitude as to what month was used as the beginning of the year in this reckoning. Milik has suggested Tišri.[72] In that case, there would

---

11b (ed. Soncino Press, 33, 65); *Ta'anith* 29a (ed. Goldschmidt, 3, 520). Milik (DJD 2, 125) says that Josephus mentions this year as a Sabbath year, but gives no references.

[70] Mishnah, *Roš haššanah* 1, 1; 'There are four "New Year" days: on the 1st of Nisan is the New Year for kings and feasts; on the 1st of Elul is the New Year for the Tithe of Cattle . . .; on the 1st of Tishri is the New Year for [the reckoning of] the years [of foreign kings], of the Years of Release and Jubilee years, for the planting [of trees] and for vegetables; and the 1st of Shebat is the New Year for [fruit-] trees . . .' (tr. H. Danby, *The Mishnah* [London: Oxford, 1954] 188). Josephus (*Ant.* 1, #81) also mentions an autumn New Year for 'selling, buying and other ordinary affairs' (i.e. the making and dating of contracts). Cf. J. Jeremias, *ZNW* 27 (1928) 98.

[71] Milik (DJD 2, 125) says: 'L'année sabbatique la plus proche de la fin de la Révolte, 135 ap J.-C. (date assurée par les sources romaines), est donc 130/1 et la deuxième année du cycle suivant correspond à 132/3.'–The same miscalculation has been noted by S. Zeitlin, 'The Fiction of the Bar Kokba Letters', *JQR* 51 (1960–61) 265–74, esp. 267. See also M. R. Lehmann, *RQ* 4 (1963–64) 56 for further arguments that corroborate my dating. Cf. also L. Kadman, *The Coins of Aelia Capitolina* (Corpus Nummorum Palaestinensium 1; Jerusalem: Universitas, 1956) 17, who shows that a Bar Cochba coin overstruck on a coin from Gaza with the double date of the third year of the visit of Hadrian and the 192nd year of the Era of Gaza (=A.D. 131–2) gives this year as the *terminus post quem* for the outbreak of the revolt. See further E. Koffmahn, 'Zur Datierung der aramäisch/hebräischen Verkunden von Murabba'at', *WZKM* 59-60 (1963-64) 119-36.

[72] Milik is, however, aware of a complication here, when he writes,' On se rappellera cependant que le Nouvel An d'automne ne valait que pour la datation des contrats. Il reste à étudier si cette ère telle qu'elle est attestée par les monnaies ne doit pas plutôt commencer au 1er Nisan, et s'il s'agit du 1er Nisan de 131 ou de 132' (DJD 2, 67); cf. *BTS* 33 (1960) 16. The year is

be a perfect agreement of the beginning of the Sabbatical cycle with that of the new era of the Redemption of Israel. In such a case, the revolt began on, or at least was officially reckoned from, 1 Tišri A.D. 132. This reckoning, however, does not agree with that proposed by Milik, viz. 1 Tišri A.D. 131, for he maintains that we must correct the normally accepted date. I have, however, used the same presuppositions as he has in my reckoning, and it seems to me that his calculation is off by one year. Reckoning the Sabbath-years from 68–9 one does not arrive at 130–1.

Rabbinical tradition has preserved the notice that Bar Cochba's revolt lasted for three and a half years (*mlkwt bn kwzyb' šlš šnym wmḥṣh*).[73] This has often been suspected, because the same tradition ascribes three and a half years to Vespasian's and Titus' siege of Jerusalem, and also because it is reminiscent of the apocalyptic passages in Dn 7:25 and 9:27, which are thought to have been operative in the creation of this tradition. However, one of the new texts from Murabba'ât is dated in the 'third year of the freedom of Jerusalem' (*Mur* 25 i 1) and two Aramaic contracts from the cave in the Wâdi Seiyâl are reported to be dated in the 'third year of the liberation of Israel' (see above). Finally, and best of all, there is *Mur* 30:8, which contains the date the '21st of Tišri of the fourth year of the Redemption of Israel'. This puts an end to a puzzling problem about the duration of the revolt as posed by the coins of the period. Coins had been found dated *šnt 'ḥt lg'lt yśr'l* ('the first year of the Redemption of Israel') or *š b lḥr yśr'l* ('the second year of the Freedom of Israel').[74] But none were dated after that

certainly A.D. 132, but no evidence so far has settled the month, Nisan or Tišri.

[73] *Seder 'Olam Rabbah* 30 (ed. B. Ratner, 146); cf. Jerome, *Comm. in Danielem* 9; *PL* 25, 577–8. The Midrash, *Echa Rabbah* 2, 2, 4 (ed. S. Buber, 101), attributes three and a half years to the siege of Beth-Ter alone; this is impossible.

[74] A. Reifenberg, *Ancient Jewish Coins*², #189, 197; see also p. 35.

year. Reifenberg's solution was to maintain that those which simply bore *lḥrwt yrwšlm* without a date were minted in the third year of the revolt, but after Jerusalem had again fallen into the hands of the Romans. It is now certain that the revolt lasted into the beginning of the fourth year at least, and so the Rabbinical tradition about three and a half years is not far off.

However, according to our calculation the 21st of Tišri of the fourth year of the Redemption of Israel would equal October A.D. 135 (according to Milik it is the year 134). Eusebius (*Eccl. Hist.* 4, 6, 3) mentions that the war 'reached its height in the eighteenth year of the reign of Hadrian in Beththera, which was a strong citadel not very far from Jerusalem; the siege lasted a long time before the rebels were driven to final destruction by famine and thirst'. The eighteenth regnal year of Hadrian is normally reckoned as 11 August 134–5.[75] If our reckoning of the beginning of the era of the 'Redemption of Israel' is correct, and *Mur* 30 is to be dated to the 21st of Tišri A.D. 135, then Eusebius' statement just quoted must be taken more seriously and exactly than it normally is. For it is usual to regard it as meaning that the revolt came to an end in Hadrian's eighteenth year.[76] However, what Eusebius actually says is that the war came to a head or a climax in Hadrian's eighteenth year (*akmasantos de tou polemou etous oktōkaidekatou tēs hēgemonias kata Bēththēra . . . tēs te exōthen poliorkias chroniou genomenēs*) and that the siege lasted a long time. The Armenian text of Eusebius' *Chronicon*, moreover, lists that the Jewish war came to an end in Hadrian's *nineteenth* year.[77]

Further corroboration of this is derived from another source. As a result of the final defeat of the Jewish rebels and the con-

[75] See *Vita Hadriani* 4, 7, where it is recorded that Hadrian's regnal year is to be reckoned from 11 August.

[76] So E. Schürer, *GJV* 1, 695 (Engl. tr. 310) and many others.

[77] Karst's German translation for the 19th year (GCS 20, 221): 'Der jüdische Krieg, der im Palästinerlande war, endigte, indem übel hergenommen die Juden kaum der Vernichtung entgingen.' Cf. H. Strathmann, *PJB* 23 (1927) 100, 111 n. 2.

clusion of the 'Jewish war' Hadrian was acclaimed *imperator* for the second time. For a long time the title *Imp. II* was not found with certainty in any inscription before A.D. 136. But it is now known that the second acclamation occurred toward the end of Hadrian's nineteenth *tribunicia potestas*.[78] The twentieth began on 10 December A.D. 135, and the earliest occurrence of *Imp. II* is thus dated before that, between April and December 135. But if the revolt had already begun its fourth year by the 21st of Tišri (=October) 135, it is hardly likely that Hadrian's troops had as yet put an end to it. So his second acclamation as *imperator* must have occurred between October and 10 December A.D. 135. This still leaves open the question whether the year is to be reckoned from 1 Nisan of 1 Tišri. But it confirms the data advanced above for the termination of the revolt in the year A.D. 135.

Rabbinical tradition has, however, recorded that Beth-Ter

[78] The evidence is complicated. Several inscriptions are known from the year A.D. 134–5 without any mention of Hadrian's second acclamation. The latest of these are *CIL* 3, #XXXV (dated 15 Sept. 134; cf. *CIL* 16, #79); *CIL* 16, #82 (dated 14 Apr. 135). Earlier ones of the same year are: *CIL* 3, #XXXIV; 6, #973; 9, #4359; 10, #7855. On the other hand, it is clearly found in several inscriptions dated to the *trib. pot.* XX (i.e. after 10 December 135): *CIL* 6, #976, 975; *Papyri Osloenses* (ed. S. Eitrem and L. Amundsen) 3, #78 (dated before 31 May 136); R. Cagnat, *Inscriptiones graecae ad res romanas pertinentes*, 3, #896; and probably also in *CIL* 14, #4235 (where [*trib. pot. X*]*X* is restored and the date is 14, 19, 24 or 29 Dec. 135). This would give a date between April and 10 December 135. However, the second acclamation occurs in an inscription which is dated in the *trib. pot. XVIII*, hence before 10 December 135. See *CIG* 12 *Suppl.* (1939), #239; W. Peek, *Archaiologikē Ephēmeris* 1931, 113, #9; C. Seltman, 'Appendix', *Hesperia* 17 (1958) 85; F. M. Heichelheim, 'New Light on the End of Bar Kokba's War', *JQR* 34 (1943–44) 61–3. It may also occur in an undated fragmentary inscription whose restoration is not certain (*CIL* 2, #478); see also *CIL* 6, #974. Since the date of the '21st of Tišri of the fourth year of the Redemption of Israel' is found in *Mur* 30:8, the interval in which the second acclamation took place thus becomes October to 10 December 135. However, it should be noted that there are a few inscriptions of the year 136 which do not mention *Imp. II* (*CIL* 14, #2088; 3, #749), and that S. Perowne (*Hadrian*, 165) reckons the fall of Beth-Ter in A.D. 136. Cf. B. W. Henderson, *Life and Principate*, 218, n. 4.

fell on the 9th of Ab (July). But this date probably represents a conflation of the celebration of three fast-days rather than the recollection of an actual historical date: one fast-day commemorated the three great Jewish defeats. As the Mishnah puts it, 'Five things befell our fathers on the 17th of Tammuz and five on the 9th of Ab. . . . On the 9th of Ab it was decreed against our fathers that they should not enter into the Land [of Israel; Nm 14:29 ff.], and the Temple was destroyed the first and the second time, and Beth-Tor [=Beth-Ter] was captured and the City was ploughed up.'[79]

THE PERIOD OF THE REVOLT ITSELF

The information about the course of the revolt is meagre indeed. From what there is it seems that Jerusalem was wrested once again from the control of the Romans. This is certainly implied in the coins which were minted with the inscription *lḥrwt yrwšlm*, 'Of the Liberation of Jerusalem'. It is not improbable that the cult of Yahweh on the site of the old temple was resumed, and that this was commemorated by the coins struck with the title *'lʿzr hkwhn*, 'Eleazar, the Priest'. That an attempt was made by the Jews to rebuild the temple itself at this time would not surprise us, although there is no definite information regarding this point.[80]

[79] *Ta'anith* 4, 6 (tr. H. Danby, 200). Josephus (*JW* 6, #250) also knows of the tradition which assigns the double destruction of Jerusalem to the same day of the month: 'But now in the revolution of the years had arrived the fated day, the tenth of the month Lous, the day on which of old it had been burnt by the king of Babylon.' H. St J. Thackeray's comment: 'This is in accordance with Jer. lii. 12 f., where the burning of the temple by Nebuzaradan, captain of Nebuchadrezzar's guard, is stated to have occurred on the 10th day of the 5th month (Heb. Ab=Lous in the Syrian calendar). In 2 Kings xxv. 8, on the other hand, the day is given as the 7th of Ab; while, in Jewish tradition, the anniversary of the double burning has always been kept on the 9th Ab. A fictitious symmetry between corresponding events in the two sieges has probably been at work' (Loeb Classical Library, 3, 448–9).

[80] See S. Yeivin, *Milḥemet Bar Kôkbâ*, 78 f. Possibly the obscure reference in the *Epistle of Barnabas* (16, 1–7) should be considered in this connection; see note 34 above and H. Bietenhard, *Jud* 4 (1948) 95 ff.

Did Bar Cochba attempt to reinforce Jerusalem at this time? The archaeologists who have studied the problem of the 'Third Wall' of Jerusalem of which Josephus speaks (*JW* 5, #147) have not always been of one mind regarding it. The line of an ancient wall which has been traced roughly from the old Russian colony, past the front of the American Consulate, to the American School of Oriental Research, was regarded by E. Robinson and more recently by E. L. Sukenik and L. A. Mayer as the third north wall of the city of which Josephus speaks.[81] However, H. Vincent maintained still more recently that the Third Wall built in the time of Herod Agrippa I coincided roughly with the line of the present-day north wall of the Old City. Vincent's view has been supported by British excavations at the Damascus Gate.[82] For him the ancient wall which lies considerably to the north of it is nothing more than remnants of the rampart set up as an outer defence of the city under Bar Cochba. It is the 'wall of Bar Cochba'. But W. F. Albright is inclined to follow the view of Sukenik and Mayer. This is a knotty problem in which the experts do not agree themselves; it must await further excavation and investigation for a solution. But it deserves mention here for the possible connection it may have with the Second Revolt.

It is difficult to understand how Dio Cassius (*Rom. Hist.* 69, 13, 1) could write, 'At first the Romans took no account of

[81] *The Third Wall of Jerusalem: An Account of Excavations* (Jerusalem: Hebrew University Press, 1930). Albright, *AP* 158, favours this view. He reaffirms it in *BASOR* 183 (1966) 26, n. 21. Cf. W. Ross, 'The Four North Walls of Jerusalem', *PEQ* 1942, 69–81.

[82] H. Vincent and M.-A. Stève, *Jérusalem de l'Ancien Testament: Recherches d'archéologie et d'histoire* (Paris: Gabalda, 1954) vol. 1, 146–74. For more recent discussions of this problem, see K. M. Kenyon, 'Excavations in Jerusalem, 1965', *PEQ* 98 (1966) 73–88; *Jerusalem: Excavating 3000 Years of History* (New York: McGraw-Hill, 1967) 162 and plate 86; E. W. Hamrick, 'New Excavations at Sukenik's Third Wall', *BASOR* 183 (1966) 19–26; 'Further Notes on the "Third Wall"', *BASOR* 192 (1968) 21–5; R. P. S. Hubbard, 'The Topography of Ancient Jerusalem', *PEQ* 98 (1966) 130–54; M. Avi-Yonah, 'The Third and Second Walls of Jerusalem', *IEJ* 18 (1968) 98–125.

them [the Jewish insurgents]. Soon, however, all Judaea had been stirred up, and the Jews everywhere were showing signs of disturbance, were gathering together, and giving evidence of great hostility to the Romans, partly by secret and partly by overt acts.' This statement, however, is a brief summary of the whole revolt, and perhaps the liberation of Jerusalem itself was at first regarded as a minor, local skirmish by the Romans. Yet it was a local skirmish which apparently spread rapidly to all parts of Judaea.

Once Jerusalem had been liberated and Israel redeemed, the Prince of Israel had to organize the land for the continuation of the revolt. The administrative machinery and the division of the land into toparchies which had been set up by the Romans were apparently retained by Bar Cochba. He controlled the land of Judaea, especially the fertile Shephelah, and from the new documents we learn additional names of villages and districts under his control. In addition to Jerusalem, which name is probably to be read in *Mur* 29:9, 11; 30:8 (see DJD 2, 205), the following places came under his administration directly or indirectly: Herodium (*Mur* 24 B4, C4, E3, 14), Teqoa' (*Mur* 47:6; *Hev* 1 and 14), 'En-gedi (*Mur* 46:4; *Hev* 12), Qiryat 'Arabayah (*Hev* 15), 'Ir-Naḥaš (*Mur* 24 B8, C7–8, E6–7), Beth Mašiko (*Mur* 42:1, 4), *Mᵉṣad Ḥᵃsîdîn* (identified by Milik with Khirbet Qumran, *Mur* 45:6) and Kᵉpar Biš, Kᵉpar Šaḥalîm, Kᵉpar Dikrîn (the three villages mentioned in Rabbinical writings as destroyed by the Romans [*Echa Rabbah* 53b; *Ta'anith* 4, 69a; *Gittin* 4, 6, 3]). Y. Yadin conjectures that Bar Cochba also controlled Masada at this time.[83] To this list must be added the place of his last stand, Beth-Ter (Eusebius, *Eccl. Hist.* 4, 6, 3).

Herodium is mentioned as the centre of a toparchy in *Mur* 115:2, 21, a Greek document of remarriage dated A.D. 124. In the time of Bar Cochba it probably continued to be the centre of the toparchy, for we learn that a camp was situated there

[83] *BIES* 25 (1961) 63. But cf. his book, *Masada: Herod's Fortress and the Zealots' Last Stand* (London: Weidenfeld and Nicolson, 1966) 207.

(*Mur* 24, E3). Indeed, Milik has suggested on the basis of the phrase, *šmʿwn bn kwsbʾ nsyʾ yśrʾl bmḥnh šywšb bhrwdys*, that Bar Cochba as the warlike Messiah had made his headquarters at Herodium, and that it was from there that he withdrew to Beth-Ter as the Romans closed in about him. As I indicated in note 57, the Hebrew need not be so interpreted. Moreover, new information from the Wâdi Ḫabra texts suggests that it is quite unlikely that his headquarters were there. In *Hev* 12, as Y. Yadin has pointed out,[84] Bar Cochba writes to two of his officers at ʿEn-gedi:

mšmʿwn br kwsbʾ lʾnšy ʿyngdy	From Simon bar Kosibaʾ to the men of ʿEn-gedi,
lmsblʾ [w]lyhw[n]tn b[r] bʿyn šlwm bṭwb	to Masabbalaʾ [and] to Yehonatan ba[r] Baʿyan, greetings! In ease
ʾtn ywšbyn ʾklyn wš[w]tyn mn nksy byt	you are living, eating and dr[i]nking off the goods of the house
yśrʾl wlʾ dʾgyn lʾḥykn lkwl dbr	of Israel, and you care not a whit for your brothers. . . .

This rebuke is addressed to Masabbalah and Yehonatan at ʿEn-gedi. This fact must be coupled with a bit of information found in another papyrus, *Hev* 15, which reads as follows:

šmʿwn lyhwdh br mnšh lqryt ʿrbyh šlḥt lk try ḥmryn dy tšlḥ
ʿmhn (*tr!*) *gbryn lwt yhwntn br bʿyn wlwt msblh dy yʿmrn*
wyšlḥn lmḥnyh lwtk llbyn wʾtrgyn wʾt šlḥ ʾḥrnyn mlwtk
wymṭwn lk hdsyn wʿrbyn wtqn ythn wšlḥ ythn lmḥnyh
. . . . . *hwʾ šlm*

Simon to Yehudah bar Menasseh at Qiryat ʿArabayah. I have sent to you two asses, with which you will send

[84] *HāʾĀreṣ* (10 March 1961) 10; see also *BIES* 25 (1961) *passim.* See now E. M. Laperrousaz, 'L'Hérodium, quartier général de Bar Kokhba?', *Syria* 41 (1964) 347–58.

2. (two?) men to Yehonatan bar Ba'yan and to Masabbalah that they may gather and
3. send to the camp, toward you, palm-branches and citrons. And you send other men from your own quarters
4. and let them bring to you myrtle and willow twigs. Prepare them and send them to the camp.
5. . . . Farewell.

From this letter it is obvious that Bar Cochba is sending the two asses to 'Engedi via Qiryat 'Arabayah. There is no spot between Herodium and 'En-gedi which can be identified with this name. Yadin, following Mazar, had identified Qiryat 'Arabayah with *Birat 'Areva' d^{e}Bêt-leḥem*, mentioned in the Midrashim in connection with the birthplace of the Messiah, the modern village of 'Arṭas, near the pools of Solomon. If this identification is correct, the route which the asses are to take to go to 'En-gedi leads in the opposite direction. In another text (*Hev* 1) Bar Cochba orders the same Masabbalah and Yehonatan bar Ba'yah (*sic*) to punish the men of Teqoa' (*kwl gbr tqw'y*), who were spending time repairing their houses. Teqoa' apparently pertained to the jurisdiction of the officers stationed at 'En-gedi. Consequently, it would be strange, if Bar Cochba's own headquarters were at Herodium, that he would give such orders to the officers of 'En-gedi, given the relative proximity of Teqoa' to Herodium itself. It is better, then, to regard Herodium merely as one of the camps under Bar Cochba's control, the administrative centre of a toparchy as in the days of Roman domination. His headquarters are better sought either in Jerusalem or in Beth-Ter. Sending the letter to Yehudah bar Menasseh from one of these spots with the instruction that he should send men on to 'En-gedi is certainly more logical. The note was probably delivered to Yehonatan and Masabbalah, who kept it in their archives and carried it with the other missives of their chief to the cave in the Wâdi Ḫabra, when they fled there before the advancing Roman soldiers.

'En-gedi thus emerges as a source of supplies for the rebel chief. The oasis there was cut off from the rest of Judaea by the desert and was rich in produce. There was also a small port there for commercial traffic by boat on the Dead Sea. From the rebuke addressed by Bar Cochba to Yehonatan and Masabbalah it would appear that it was something of a sinecure for them, when their lot was compared to that of their 'brothers'.

Besides the military, priestly and intellectual leaders of the period of the Second Revolt, Simon ben Kosibah, Eleazar (ben Azariah?), and the Rabbi Aqiba, we now know of many other Jews who were engaged in the uprising, thanks to the new documents. Their names are preserved on the skin and papyrus documents which they carried with them to the caves of refuge. There is no need to retail them all here, but the more important ones are the names of the officers under Bar Cochba. In addition to Yehonatan bar Ba'yah (or Ba'yan) and Masabbalah bar Šim'ôn[85] there were Yešua' ben Galgulah, who is addressed as *rwš hmḥnyh* (*Mur* 42, 2), and, if Y. Yadin's conjecture is correct,[86] Šim'ôn bar Mattatyah, who is stationed at Masada. Just where Yešua' ben Galgulah had his camp is not certain. The administrators (*hprnsyn*) of the village of Beth-Mašiko address him as *rwš hmḥnyh*, when they write explaining the sale of a cow

[85] In a Greek letter (*Hev* 3) they are addressed as *Iōnathē kai Masabala*. Y. Yadin, *BIES* 25 (1961) 57, suggests the vocalization *Masabbalah* on the basis of Josephus (*JW* 5, #532), which has *masbalos* and *masambalos*. The text of *Hev* 3 has been published by B. Lifshitz, *Aegyptus* 42 (1962) 240–8. It was sent by a certain *Soumaios*, whom the editor takes to be Simon ben Kosibah himself, to *Iōnathē Baianou kai Masabala*. As in the Aramaic letter (*Hev* 15) quoted above, he instructs them to send *s[te]leou[s] kai kitria*, 'twigs(?) and citrons' for the 'Citron-celebration of the Jews' (*⟨e⟩is [k]itreiabolēn Ioudaiōn*), i.e., for Succoth or Tabernacles. The most interesting feature in it, however, if the *Soumaios* is really Bar Cochba, is his reason for writing in Greek: 'No[w] (this) has been written in Greek because the [de]sire has not be[en] found to w[ri]te in "Hebrew"' (*egraphē d[e] helēnisti dia t[o ho]rman mē eurēth[ē]nai hebraesti g[ra]psasthai*). Either Bar Cochba, the Jewish leader of the Second Revolt, or someone very close to him, prefers to communicate with his lieutenants in Greek rather than in 'Hebrew' (=Aramaic?)! See further my article in *CBQ* 32 (1970) 513–15.

[86] *BIES* 25 (1961) 63, apropos of a Wâdi Seiyâl text not yet published; see VTSup 4 (1957) 21.

by an inhabitant of their village to a certain Joseph ben Aristion (*Mur* 42), but no indication is given where that camp is situated. However, two other letters are addressed to him by Bar Cochba himself.

Mur 43

mšmʿwn bn kwsbh lyšʿ	From Simon ben Kosibah
bn glglh wlʾnšy hkrk[87]	to Yešuaʿ ben Galgulah and to the men of the fort,
šlwm mʿyd ʾny ʿly t šmym	greetings! I call the heavens to witness against me that
yps[*d*] *mn hgllʾym šhṣlkm*	(if) any of the Galileans who are with you is mistreated,
kl ʾdm šʾny ntn t kblym	I shall put irons
brglkm kmh šʿst[*y*]	on your feet, as I have done
lbn ʿplwl	to ben ʿAphlul.
[*š*]*mʿwn b*[*n kwsbh*] *ʿl* [*npšh*][88]	Simon b[en Kosibah], for [himself].

[87] The reading of this word is doubtful. Milik at first read *wlʾnšy ḥbrk*, 'aux hommes de ta compagnie' (*RB* 60 [1953] 277), a reading which was accepted by F. M. Cross, Jr., *RB* 63 (1956) 47: 'La première lettre du mot est sûrement ḥeth'. This reading was judged 'graphically impossible' by H. L. Ginsberg, *BASOR* 131 (1953) 25, who read instead *wlʾnšy hkrk*, 'and to the men of the fort'. Milik now reads (DJD 2, 160) the first letter as a *he* and the second as a *beth*, and understands the word as a name of a village mentioned by Jerome as *Caphar Barucha* and by Epiphanius as *Kapar Baricha*, situated about 3 mi. east of Hebron. According to this latest suggestion of Milik, *Yešuaʿ* would be the commander of a camp at *Kᵉpar ha-Baruk*. But since the construction is peculiar (with an article and without *kᵉpar*), and the reading is not at all certain, it seems preferable not to introduce a proper name here. So we retain Ginsberg's suggestion, *hkrk*, 'the fort'.

[88] This restoration, if correct, would mean that Bar Cochba himself has written the letter, and it would be a precious autograph. The phrase *ʿl npšh* is certainly found elsewhere in the new texts (normally in contracts, *Mur* 18:9; 19:26; 21:21, 23; 24 C 19, D 20; 27:6; 28:11, 12; 29 verso 3 [where it is parallel to the Greek *cheiri heautou*]; 36:6; but also in a letter, *Mur* 42:10). However, Y. Yadin, *BIES* 25 (1961) 58; *IEJ* 11 (1961) 45; *BTS* 43 (1961) 16, suggests that since at least one Bar Cochba letter (*Hev* 8) was signed *šmʿwn br yhwdh* (a secretary?), it might also be the case here. Possibly we should read the *ʿl* [*mʾmrh*], as in *Mur* 24 C 20 (where Milik has written

The second letter (*Mur* 44) reads as follows:[89]

mšmʿwn lyšwʿ bn glgwlh [	From Simon to Yešuaʿ ben Galgulah [the head of the camp]
šlwm štšlḥ tbw ḥmšt[	greetings! You should send and bring five [
kwryn ḥ[*ṭy*]*n* [ ].*š lbyty* [	kors of wheat [ ] . . . to my house [
ʾṣlk bdʿt wttqn lhn [	near you with knowledge (?); and you should prepare for them [
mqwm pnwy yhw bw ʾṣlk [	a free (?) place. Let them be in it near you [observe]
t šbt ḥzw ʾm yḥpṣw lbw [	the Sabbath. See (to it) that they be pleased at heart [
whtḥzq wḥzq t mqwm [	Take courage and fortify [that] place [
hwʾ šlwm wpqdty t my [	Farewell! And I have ordered the . . [
šytn lk tḥṭyn šlh ʾḥr [	who will give you his wheat, other [
hšbt yṭlwn	the Sabbath they will take up

[*mn*] but admits in the note that *ʿl* is also possible).

[89] My translation is different from that of Milik, who believes that the text of this letter is intact. However, the grammatical difficulties which his translation encounters (e.g., the continual shift in person and number) make it unlikely that his interpretation is correct. There is not one line which joins necessarily with the beginning of the next, and the photo suggests that possibly we do not have the full width of the original papyrus letter. Hence I have tried to translate the lines only in the most obvious way and leave the rest blank except for line 1, where the restored title is derived from *Mur* 42:2. Milik's translation of *tšbt* (line 6) as 'pendant le sabbat' is almost certainly wrong; the sign of the accusative *t* suggests that some verb is missing in the preceding line.

In general, the new texts from the caves of Murabba'ât, Ḫabra, and Seiyâl reveal Bar Cochba as an administrator, giving orders to subordinates and settling problems which have arisen in the land under his control. Like the Roman Emperor before him, he is the proprietor of the land. Farms are rented out in his name and a yearly rent has to be paid in kind into his granaries.[90] This appears from the *diastrōmata* in *Mur* 24, where the land is rented from Simon the Prince of Israel (*mšm'wn nsy' yśr'l,* E 7). The deputy, Hillel ben Garis, acts as an administrator of the lands of *'Ir-Naḥaš* on his command ([*mn*/*'l*] *m'mrh,* C 20). The Wâdi Ḫabra texts are reported to contain similar details about the leasing of government-owned lands to a four-man syndicate which, in turn, subleased the plots among themselves. Amid the details which concern him Bar Cochba shows himself respecting the traditional Jewish feasts. In *Mur* 44 he is apparently ordering Yešua' ben Galgulah to provide hospitality for a caravan transporting grain over the Sabbath. He orders that Eleazar bar Ḥittah be sent to him 'immediately before the Sabbath' (*Hev* 8). He provides that the palm-branches and citrons be brought for the celebration of the feast of Succoth in one of the camps, and orders Yehuda bar Menasseh to make similar provision where he is (*Hev* 15). In other letters he orders the arrest of a certain Yešua' bar Tadmorayah (whose sword must be taken from him), confiscates wheat, seizes property, and even gives instructions about the harvesting of ripe and unripe grain. It is an abundance of such details which come to light in the new documents, which also reveal that the simple people in Palestine were leading fairly normal lives despite the revolt. They still exchanged property, married, and made their contracts of various sorts.

The list of the few names of villages which were controlled by Bar Cochba given above scarcely exhausts the places which

[90] See further S. Appelbaum, 'The Agrarian Question and the Revolt of Bar Kokhba', *E. L. Sukenik Memorial Volume* (Eretz-Israel 8; Jerusalem: Israel Exploration Society, 1967) 283–7 (in modern Hebrew with an English summary, p. 77*).

were under his authority. Dio Cassius (*Rom. Hist.* 69, 14, 1) mentions that the Romans finally captured 'fifty of their most important outposts and nine hundred and eighty-five of their most famous villages were razed to the ground'. Where Dio Cassius got such figures, we do not know, but they do give some indication of the extent of the control over the land which Bar Cochba must have had.

All of these details confirm the data given in Dio Cassius about the mode of warfare which was practised by the rebels. 'They did not dare try conclusions with the Romans in the open field, but they occupied the advantageous positions in the country and strengthened them with mines and walls, in order that they might have places of refuge whenever they should be hard pressed, and might meet together unobserved under ground.'[91] It was probably a guerrilla-type warfare, well organized on a village and toparchy basis, and resembling that of the Maccabees, especially in the early days of their struggle.

At first sight it might seem that the caves in the Wâdies Murabba'ât, Seiyâl and Ḫabra were actually the outposts (*phrouria*), of which Dio Cassius speaks (*Rom. Hist.* 69, 14, 1). The evidence found in them, however, indicates rather that they were used as places of refuge, like the *anaphygai* also mentioned by him (69, 12, 3). For it appears that Yešua' ben Galgulah fled from his camp to the cave in the Wâdi Murabba'ât, taking with him various household objects, family archives, the letters from his chief, Bar Cochba, and perhaps also his family.[92] Similarly, Yehonatan and Masabbalah fled from their camp at 'En-gedi to the cave in the Wâdi Ḫabra with a whole collection of letters from their chief.

Among the documents taken by the refugees to the caves were biblical scrolls and texts. From the Murabba'ât caves have come fragments of Gn, Ex, Nm (*Mur* 1), Dt (*Mur* 2), Is (*Mur* 3) and the large fragmentary scroll of the Minor Prophets (*Mur*

[91] *Rom. Hist.* 69, 12, 3.
[92] For the artifacts found in the Murabba'ât caves, see DJD 2, 29–48.

88). The latter was found in a hole near the caves, in which a refugee had been buried. Milik mentions that this is the oldest concrete example of a tomb-genizah, of which the Rabbinical writers speak.[93] The text of this scroll is fragmentary in many places, but a substantial portion of ten of the twelve books is preserved (Jl 2:20, 26–4:16; Am 1:5–2:1; 7:3–8:7; 8:11–9:15; Ob 1–21; Jon 1:1–4:11; Mi 1:1–7:20; Na 1:1–3:19; Hab 1:1–2:11; 2:18–3:19; Zeph 1:1; 1:11–3:6; 3:8–20; Hag 1:1–2:10; 2:12–23; Zech 1:1–4). Further, there is a phylactery (*Mur* 4), and possibly a Mezuzah (*Mur* 5). We have mentioned the biblical texts from the other areas earlier in our discussion. In all these biblical documents the remarkable aspect is the close agreement of their text with the *textus receptus* of later centuries. Milik lists for the text of the Minor Prophets (*Mur* 88) only 59 variants, the majority of which are simply cases of *scriptio plena* for *defectiva* or vice versa (about 30) and additions written above the line possibly by the copyist himself (about 8). Many of the others are quite insignificant (prepositional exchanges like *beth* for *kaph*, *'el* for *'al*, etc.).[94] When these texts are compared with the biblical texts from the Qumran caves, where a number of texts manifest different recensions, it looks very much as though we have in the Murabba'ât scrolls the stabilization of the text effected by the academy at Jamnia. Indeed, they apparently determined not only what books belonged to the Palestinian canon of the OT, but also what recension was to be copied in the future, with what spelling and in what script. The script of the Murabba'ât biblical texts bears a very strong resemblance to the script employed by the scribes in the medieval manuscripts. For this reason the biblical texts from the Bar Cochba period are important for the data which they supply for the study of the transmission of the OT.

In the new material which has been published so far there are

[93] DJD 2, 181; see Bab. Talmud, *Megillah*, fol. 26b.

[94] See DJD 2, 183–4, 205. Milik had previously pointed out that the only significant variant in the whole scroll was Hab 3:10: *zrmw mym 'bwt* (as in Ps 77:18) instead of the MT *zrm mym 'br* (VTSup 4 [1957] 20).

strikingly few references to the enemy Romans. The letter of the administrators of Bet-Mašiko to Yešua' ben Galgulah explains that they do not come up with Joseph ben Aristion, who has bought the cow, to give evidence of the purchase, because 'the Gentiles are drawing near to us' (*hgyym qrbym 'lnw*), *Mur* 42:5. Milik has reported that a short letter from the Wâdi Seiyâl addressed to Bar Cochba by Šim'ôn ben Mattatyah mentions *hg'ym* who have moved their camp (*qṣryhm*).[95] But the only explicit reference to the Romans found so far is in *Hev* 11, an Aramaic letter which mentions *rhwmyh* (i.e., *Rhômāyēh*).[96] Perhaps the texts found this year will supply further information about the Romans, who were systematically advancing through the country and wiping out the pockets of resistance, thus driving the refugees to the caves.

THE END OF THE REVOLT AND THE LAST STAND AT BETH-TER

Just where the emperor Hadrian was all during the Second Revolt is not clear. After leaving Palestine and Syria in A.D. 131, he went to Pontus and the Black Sea area and from there to Athens for the winter. On 5 May A.D. 134 he was once again in Rome.[97] By this time the revolt was well under way. He must have returned to Judaea afterwards, to judge by a remark of Dio Cassius about the outcome of the war, which I shall quote later.

The initial lack of concern on the part of the Romans about the Jewish uprising stemmed from the attitude of the Roman governor of Judaea, a certain Tineius Rufus (Eusebius, *Eccl. Hist.* 4, 6, 1). He undoubtedly underestimated the movement and soon it grew to proportions which were beyond his control. Dio Cassius (*Rom. Hist.* 69, 13, 1) mentions that 'all Judaea had been stirred up'. This is to be understood not in the restricted

[95] *Ibid.*, 21.

[96] *BIES* 25 (1961) 60; *IEJ* 11 (1961) 45. On p. 56 Yadin mentions that *hgw'yn* also occurs in one of his Hebrew documents.

[97] *CIG* 3, 5906, which is dated *pro g' Nōnōn Maiōn apo Rōmēs*; the year is given as *dēmarchikēs exousias to iē'*, *hypatos to g'*. See F.-M. Abel, *Histoire*, 2, 93.

sense of Judaea (as opposed to Samaria and Galilee), but in the sense of the Roman province, which included those areas as well. We have already seen the solicitude of Bar Cochba for the Galileans, who apparently had joined his ranks. Dio Cassius (*ibid.*) further adds that 'many outside nations, too, were joining them through eagerness for gain'. The result was that the rebels were getting the better of the Roman garrisons and aid had to be given to the governor. Leaving his own province in the charge of Caius Severus, the legate of the *Legio IV Scythica*, Publicius Marcellus, the governor of Syria, came to the aid of Tineius Rufus, as a Greek inscription attests,[98] probably with the *Legio III Gallica*. Eusebius (*Eccl. Hist.* 4, 6, 1) records that military aid was sent by the Emperor. E. Schürer[99] has made a catalogue of the Roman legions which took part in the Judaean war, using the various direct and indirect references to it found in inscriptions. The following groups of Roman soldiers were engaged at some time or other in putting down the rebellion: *Legio X Fretensis* and *Legio VI Ferrata* (both resident in Judaea),[100] *Legio III Cyrenaica* (brought in from the province of Arabia), *Legio III Gallica* (probably brought by the Governor of Syria), *Legio XXII Deiotariana* (brought in from Egypt), *cohors IV Lingonum*, *cohors I Thracum*; besides several detachments of *Legio I Italica*, *Legio V Macedonica*, *Legio X Gemina* and *Legio XI Claudia*.[101]

[98] *CIG* 3, 4033–4: *hēnika Poublikios Markellos dia tēn kinēsin tēn Ioudaikēn metebebēkei apo Syrias.*

[99] *GJV* 1, 687–9, n. 116 (Engl. tr. 303, n. 96). See further F.-M. Abel, *Histoire*, 2, 92.

[100] See B. Lifshitz, 'Sur la date du transfert de la legio VI Ferrata en Palestine', *Latomus* 19 (1960) 109–11. The transfer took place before the war began, possibly as early as A.D. 130.

[101] An epitaph of a Roman soldier, found at Beisân (ancient Scythopolis), shows clearly that the *Legio XI Claudia* was in Palestine at this time and engaged in operations in the north as well as at Beth-Ter. See M. Avi-Yonah, 'Greek and Latin Inscriptions from Jerusalem and Beisan', *QDAP* 8 (1939) 57–9. This inscription shows that in fact *Legio XI Claudia* was present during the Roman counter-offensive, and that the inscription at the spring in the village of Bittîr also dates from this period: CENTVR. VEXILL. LEG. V. MAC. ET. XI. CL (*CIL* 3/14, 155; cf. *ZDPV* 29 [1906]

Apparently the *classis syriaca* was also somehow involved in the war.

But this was not enough. Finally 'Hadrian sent against them his best generals. First of these was Julius Severus, who was dispatched from Britain, where he was governor,[102] against the Jews' (Dio Cassius, *Rom. Hist.* 69, 13, 2). Although Eusebius gives the impression that Tineius Rufus was always in charge of the operations against the Jewish rebels (*Eccl. Hist.* 4, 6, 1), it was actually Sextus Julius Severus who had the supreme command in the last period and who finally succeeded in putting an end to the rebellion.

Severus did not venture to attack his opponents in the open at any one point, in view of their numbers and their desperation; but by intercepting small groups, thanks to the number of his soldiers and his under-officers, and by depriving them of food and shutting them up, he was able, rather slowly, to be sure, but with comparatively little danger, to crush, exhaust and exterminate them. Very few of them in fact survived. Fifty of their most important outposts and nine hundred and eighty-five of their most famous villages were razed to the ground. Five hundred and eighty thousand men were slain in the various raids and battles, and the number of those that perished by famine, disease and fire was past finding out. Thus nearly the whole of Judaea was made desolate, a result of which the people had had forewarning before the war. For the tomb of Solomon, which the Jews regard as an object of veneration, fell to pieces of itself and collapsed, and many wolves and hyenas rushed howling into their cities' (Dio Cassius, *Rom. Hist.* 69, 13, 3–14, 2 tr. E. Cary).

Not only the Roman sources mention the great number of Jews who perished in this war, but also the Rabbinical and

---

55, n. 1). See further J. Meyshan (Mestschanski), 'The Legion Which Reconquered Jerusalem in the War of Bar Kochba (A.D. 132–135)', *PEQ* 90 (1958) 19–25.

[102] This is confirmed by his *cursus honorum* given in a Latin inscription (*CIL* 3, 2830): *leg(ato) pr(o) pr(aetore) imp(eratoris) Traiani Hadriani Aug(usti) provinciae Daciae, co(n)s(uli) leg(ato) pr(o) pr(aetore) Moesiae inferioris, leg(ato) pr(o) pr(aetore) provinciae Britanniae, leg(ato) pr(o) pr(aetore) provinciae Iudeae, leg(ato) pr(o) pr(aetore) provinciae Suriae.*

Christian writings. The former abound in many legendary and imaginative details, but there can be little doubt about the correctness of the substantial account.[103] Eusebius reports (*Eccl. Hist.* 4, 6, 1): 'He [Rufus] destroyed in heaps thousands of men, women and children, and, under the law of war, enslaved their land.' The slow process of searching out the rebels, of starving them and of killing them off, recorded by Dio Cassius, is now confirmed by the discoveries in the caves of Murabba'ât, Seiyâl and Ḫabra, to which the Jews fled. The burial niche in the Wâdi Ḫabra cave, with its 'collection of baskets overflowing with skulls' and 'layer upon layer of large mats covering human bones',[104] gives eloquent testimony to the Roman mop-up operations. Whole families must have taken refuge in the caves at the advance of the Roman troops; there they died of hunger and thirst.[105] In the case of the Wâdi Ḫabra cave two Roman camps were built in a strategic position atop the cliffs of the gorge so as to keep watch on the opening of the cave, lest the refugees try to escape.[106]

To judge from the Rabbinical writings the greatest opposition to the Romans occurred in Judaea in the region called *har hammelek*, 'The Royal Mountain'.[107] The same sources relate that during the revolt R. Aqiba had preached that salvation

[103] Cf. E. Schürer, *GJV* 1, 694; Engl. tr. 311.

[104] *BA* 24 (1961) 39–40; cf. *IEJ* 4 (1954) 126–7; 5 (1955) 272–3.

[105] This is the conclusion too of the archaeologists who explored the various caves; see Y. Aharoni, *IEJ* 4 (1954) 127; 5 (1955) 272–3; Y. Yadin, *BIES* 25 (1961) 51; R. de Vaux, DJD 2, 48.

[106] 'These camps resemble those found around Masada. They are built with a wall of rough stones *ca.* 1 m. thick, except on the side which touches the cliff. The gates are protected by *claviculi* which, unlike those found in the camps around Masada, turn outwards. Inside the camps were traces of various square and round constructions. These camps seem to have had no other strategic or military purpose than to keep watch on the cave-mouths visible directly below them in the cliff side, at present very difficult of access' (*IEJ* 4 [1954] 126–7).

[107] See J. T. Milik (DJD 2, 126) for an attempt to identify the town and the region connected with this name in the Rabbinical literature. It is apparently the area about Eleutheropolis (Beth Gubrin).

would come to the Jews from Judah and Benjamin, while the other tribes would be the objects of divine rejection.[108] The great Rabbi's preaching fired them to an almost fanatical enthusiasm for wiping out the Romans. It will be remembered that Dio Cassius recorded the caution of the Roman general, Sextus Julius Severus, who was aware of the 'desperation' of the Jews (*Rom Hist.* 69, 13, 3). With craft they managed to annihilate a phalanx of the *Legio XXII Deiotariana.*[109] But in the end the *har hammelek* was devastated, Jerusalem fell to the Romans and the last stand was made at Beth-Ter.

Most of the sources are silent about the recapture of Jerusalem by the Romans, and consequently we do not know exactly when it occurred. Possibly it happened during the second year of the revolt or a little after it, and that is why no coins were issued in the third or the fourth year of the Liberation of Jerusalem. Neither Dio Cassius nor Eusebius mentions the Roman recapture of the town. However, a vague reference to it may be found in the contemporary writer, Appian, who lived both at Alexandria and at Rome in the time of Hadrian, and who wrote: 'Jerusalem, the greatest city, which Ptolemy I, king of Egypt, had destroyed [?], and when it was repopulated again Vespasian razed, and Hadrian again in my own day (did the same). . . .'[110] Was it at the fall of Jerusalem that Hadrian returned to the Near East? Both Appian and the Mishnah (*Ta'anith* 4, 6: the fall of Beth-Ter and the ploughing up of the

[108] See L. Ginzberg, *The Legends of the Jews* (Philadelphia: Jewish Publication Society of America, 1928) 6, 408.

[109] Julius Africanus ascribes it to the Pharisees who served the Romans poisoned wine. See A. von Harnack, 'Medizinisches aus der ältesten Kirchengeschichte', *TU* 8/4 (Leipzig: J. C. Hinrichs, 1892) 44; cf. J.-R. Viellefond, *Jules Africain: Fragments des Cestes* (Paris, 1932) 15.—Y. Yadin (*BA* 24 [1961] 42) suggests that the 19 metal vessels which were found in a basket in the Wâdi Ḥabra cave and which are clearly Roman objects were actually booty taken by Bar Cochba's fighters from the Romans and carried off with them to the refuge-cave. Cf. *BIES* 25 (1961) 52–3.

[110] *De bello syr.* 50 (= *Roman History* 11, 8, 50; ed. H. White, Loeb Classical Library, 2, 199).

City on the 9th of Ab) refer to a destruction of the city under Hadrian. This must refer to what had been built anew since the days of Titus and perhaps under Bar Cochba himself; but it was a destruction in view of the building of Aelia Capitolina.

According to Eusebius (*Eccl. Hist.* 4, 6, 3), the war reached its height at Beth-Ter, a strong citadel not very far from Jerusalem.[111] There the siege lasted a long time before the rebels were driven to final destruction by famine and thirst and 'the instigator of their madness paid the penalty he deserved'. Beth-Ter is identified today with *Khirbet el-Yehûd* ('the ruin of the Jews'), a site on a hill-top about 400 metres WNW of the modern village of *Bittîr*. It overlooks from the south the Wâdi el-Gharbi, through which the railroad makes its way from Jerusalem to Jaffa. The modern village of Bittîr has preserved the ancient name of the place where Bar Cochba made his last stand; it is situated some six and a half miles WSW of Jerusalem.

According to F.-M. Abel, the space within the roughly ellipse-shaped fortified enclosure, which crowns the summit of the hill and of which there are still some traces here and there, scarcely measures 300 × 150 metres.[112] Hadrian had apparently had a road built from Jerusalem to Eleutheropolis in A.D. 130, which made its way through the valley at the foot of the hill itself. The eighth milestone is found in the valley below the ruins and is dated to the year 130. In order to take the citadel, the Roman general had to lay siege to the area. Traces of the

[111] The spelling of the name of this place varies in the sources. The Greek MSS. of Eusebius have *Bēththēra*, *Biththēra*; Latin texts have *Bether* (Jerome, *In Zach.* 8, 9; *PL* 25, 1574), *Bethera*; Rabbinical sources also vary: *byttr*, *bytr*, *btr*. We have followed E. Schürer in regarding *byttr* as the most probably correct form. It is probably the same place as *Baithēr*, a town in Judah in the vicinity of Bethlehem, mentioned in Codex Alexandrinus at Jos 15:59. The word occurs in a phrase not found in the MT, and the Codex Vaticanus of the LXX reads *Thethēr*.—W. D. Carroll, 'Bittîr and its Archaeological Remains', *AASOR* 5 (1923–24) 78, tries unconvincingly to derive the form from *bêt-har* (*bêttar*), 'in view of the mountainous location of the place', and with reference to Ct 2:17.

[112] Abel, *Histoire*, 2, 94.

Roman *circumvallatio* are still visible today to the north and the west of the ruins. They permit one to reconstruct a wall of about 3800 metres, doubled in some places, and fitted with a watch-tower. The size of the *circumvallatio* and its position suggest a rather lengthy siege, thus confirming the suggestion made by Eusebius. Detachments of the *Legio V Macedonica* and the *Legio XI Claudia* left their names on the road to the spring; they seem to have been at least part of the Roman troops which were engaged in this final stage of the war.[113]

There is little information about the siege itself and the conquest of Beth-Ter in the sources. Of all the Rabbinical legends related to this struggle few are regarded as trustworthy by modern historians. E. Schürer and F.-M. Abel retain only one as having some credibility: that before Beth-Ter fell, Bar Cochba himself killed his uncle, the Rabbi Eleazar of Modin, a pious old man who apparently wanted to come to terms with the Romans.[114] There is no reason to doubt the substantial historicity of the accounts about the massacre of the Jews when the citadel was finally taken.

Dio Cassius (*Rom. Hist.* 69, 14, 3) records at the end of his account: 'Many Romans, moreover, perished in this war. Therefore Hadrian in writing to the senate did not employ the opening phrase commonly affected by the emperors, "If you and your children are in health, it is well; I and the legions are in health."' The losses on both sides were apparently heavy, and for that reason the Emperor despite the successful outcome of the war for Rome did not feel that he could send back the usual report to the senate in Rome. This notice found in Dio Cassius suggests, therefore, that in the final stages of the war

[113] On Beth-Ter see A. Alt, 'Die Ausflüge', *PJB* 23 (1927) 9–29 (12–15: 'Reste der römischen Zirkumvallation um Beth-Ter'); A. Schulten, 'Anhang: Beth-Ter', *ZDPV* 56 (1933) 180–4; W. D. Carroll, *AASOR* 5 (1924) 77–103; A. Dowling, 'Interesting Coins of Pella and Bittîr', *PEFQS* 38 (1907) 295–7; H. Strathmann, *PJB* 23 (1927) 114–18; E. Zickermann, 'Chirbet el-jehud (bettir)', *ZDPV* 29 (1906) 51–72.

[114] Jer. Talmud, *Ta'anith* 4, 68d–69a; Midrash, *Echa Rabbah* 2, 2, 4. Cf. *GJV* 1, 695 (Engl. tr. 311); Abel, *Histoire,* 2, 95.

Hadrian was once again in Judaea. At any rate, as a result of the victory over the Jews Hadrian was soon acclaimed *imperator* for the second time, and soon thereafter the title appears on his inscriptions. Within a short time he contracted an illness which was to prove fatal.

Sextus Julius Severus was rewarded by the Senate for his victory over the Jews,[115] and subsequently became the governor of the province of Syria. Apparently Tineius Rufus resumed the control of Judaea, for he is remembered in Jewish tradition as the tyrant and to him is attributed the death of the great Rabbi Aqiba.[116] Once Beth-Ter had fallen, many Jewish captives were sold into slavery by the Romans in markets set up at Mamre ('in tabernaculo Abrahae', Jerome, *In Zach.* 11, 4; *PL* 25, 1573; 'in mercato Terebinthi', Jerome, *In. Jer.* 6, 18, 6; CSEL 59, 390) and at Gaza (later called 'Hadrian's Market'); others were carried off to Egypt.

AELIA CAPITOLINA

The fate of the Jews was sealed. Not only were they defeated and massacred or enslaved, but an imperial edict added the crowning ignominy: they were forbidden access to their 'Holy City'—an edict which had its consequences until the Six-Day War in 1967. Eusebius in his *Ecclesiastical History* recorded:

Hadrian then commanded that by a legal decree and ordinances the whole nation should be absolutely prevented from entering from thenceforth even the district around Jerusalem, so that not even from a distance could it see its ancestral home. Ariston of Pella tells the story. Thus when the city came to be bereft of the nation of the Jews, and its ancient inhabitants had completely perished, it was colonized by foreigners, and the Roman city which afterwards arose changed its name, and in honour of the reigning emperor Aelius Hadrian was called Aelia. The church, too, in it was composed of

[115] *CIL* 3, 2830: 'Huic [senatus, a]uctore [imp(eratore) Tra]iano Hadriano Aug(usto) ornamenta triumphalia decrevit ob res in [Ju]dea prospere gestas. [d(ecurionum)] d(ecreto).'

[116] Cf. P. Benoit, 'Rabbi Aqiba ben Joseph sage et héros du Judaïsme', *RB* 54 (1947) 54–89, esp. 87–9.

Gentiles, and after the Jewish bishops the first who was appointed to minister to those there was Marcus (4, 6, 3–4).[117]

The Bordeaux Pilgrim at the beginning of the fourth century knows of the custom of the Jews who were then permitted to come once a year (probably on the 9th of Ab) to the area of the old temple, not far from Hadrian's statue, to anoint the stones, to rend their garments and to weep in mourning over the fate of Jerusalem.[118] But it was no longer the same old city.

Hadrian built *colonia Aelia capitolina* on the site of the former Jerusalem. The *cardo maximus* of the new city led from north to south, roughly along the route of the present-day *Sûq* in the Old City, beginning at the Damascus Gate (or Bâb el-'Amûd, 'the gate of the Pillar', the name derived from the column which was erected at the north end of the *cardo maximus*, as can be seen on the Madaba Map)[119] and ending at the south wall. The *decumanus* coincided roughly with the *tarîq bâb Sitti Maryam* and led to the triple arch in the east wall of the city, which is called today the *Ecce Homo* Arch.[120] Thus it was that the old temple

[117] Cf. Justin Martyr, *Apol.* 1, 47, 6.—During all this period we hear very little about the Christians in Palestine and any part which they may have had in the revolt. Justin Martyr (*Apol.* 1, 31, 6) records: 'In the recent Jewish war, Bar Kocheba, the leader of the Jewish uprising, ordered that only the Christians should be subjected to dreadful torments, unless they renounced and blasphemed Jesus Christ' (tr. *Fathers of the Church* 6, 67; he is also quoted by Eusebius, *Eccl. Hist.* 4, 8, 4). P. Orosius (*Hist. adv. paganos* 7, 13; CSEL 5, 468): '. . . ultusque est [Hadrianus] Christianos, quos illi [Iudaei] Cocheba duce, cur sibi aduersum Romanos non adsentarentur, excruciabant; praecepitque, ne cui Iudaeo introeundi Hierosolymam esset licentia, Christianis tantum ciuitate permissa; quam ipse in optimum statum murorum exstructione reparauit et Aeliam uocari de praenomine suo praecepit.' Eusebius' *Chronicon* (in Jerome's translation, 283F; GCS 47, 201): 'Chochebas, dux Iudaicae factionis, nolentes sibi XPianos aduersum Romanum militem ferre subsidium omnimodis cruciatibus necat.'

[118] *Itinerarium Burdigalense* 591; CSEL 39, 22.

[119] M. Avi-Yonah, *The Madaba Mosaic Map with Introduction and Commentary* (Jerusalem: Israel Exploration Society, 1954) 52.

[120] See H. Vincent and F.-M. Abel, *Jérusalem: Recherches de topographie, d'archéologie et d'histoire. Tome second: Jérusalem nouvelle* (Paris: Gabalda, 1914) 29: The *Ecce Homo* Arch is judged by Vincent to be 'un débris de la porte orientale d'Aelia Capitolina'.

area was completely excluded from the new Roman colony.

The *Chronicon Paschale* for the year A.D. 119 (miscalculated; see above) records the following details in Hadrian's new city:

> He destroyed the temple of the Jews in Jerusalem and built there two public baths (*ta dyo dēmosia*), the theatre, the *capitolium* (*to trikamaron*), the four-porticoed nymphaeum (*tetranymphon*), and the circus (or amphitheatre, *dōdekapylon*), which was previously called the 'Steps' (*Anabathmoi*), and the Square (*tēn Kodran*). He divided the city into seven districts (*amphoda*), and set his own deputies up as district-rulers; to each of them he assigned a district. To this day each district goes by the name of its district-ruler. He gave his own name to the city, calling it Aelia.[121]

Not far from the intersection of the *cardo maximus* and the *decumanus maximus*, which was situated roughly at the Seventh Station of the *Via dolorosa*, the agora of Aelia was constructed. The remains of the gate of Ephraim were incorporated into its approach, and some remnants of its colonnade can still be seen today in the Russian hospice. At the edge of this forum the temple of Jupiter Capitolinus was erected, the *capitolium* or *Trikamaron* (so named because of its triple-vaulted cella).

On the old temple area was constructed the Square, the *Kodra*, a sanctuary sacred to Zeus and the area where the cult of Hadrian himself was carried out.

The Romans were once again in control of the city and the land. The garrison of the *Legio X Fretensis* took up its quarters anew on the upper hill of the city in the vicinity of the towers which remained from the old palace of Herod (near the Jaffa Gate). Over the gate leading to Bethlehem a dedication to the founder of the colony was inscribed together with the emblem of the Roman legion, a wild boar. Beginning with Eusebius, this figure has often been interpreted as a mockery intended to prevent the Jewish nation from attempting to enter the city which once belonged to it: 'in fronte eius portae, qua Bethleem

[121] *PG* 92, 613. My interpretation of the expressions follows that of H. Vincent, *Jérusalem nouvelle*, 6–18.

egredimur, sus scalptus in marmore significans Romanae potestati subiacere Iudaeos'.[122]

But Roman contingents were scattered throughout the land as well. The new discoveries in the caves of the Wâdi Murabba'ât show that the Romans settled down there as well, perhaps to prevent survivors of the revolt, who had not been sold into slavery, from taking further refuge there. In the Murabba'ât caves were found two coins with the counter-minting of the *Legio X Fretensis*, a contract dated as late as A.D. 171 (?), and a Greek fragment mentioning the Emperor Commodus (180–192). It seems as though Roman soldiers stayed on in this area until the end of the second century.[123]

The defeat of the Jews in the Second Revolt sealed the fate which was to exclude them from the city and the temple area which for so many years had been the rallying point of the nation. After the destruction of Jerusalem in A.D. 70 the hope lived on that it would be rebuilt and restored to the nation. This hope began to see realization in the appearance of the messianic figure of Bar Cochba—but only to be disappointed. He was the last political leader whom the Jews had, until the foundation of the State of Israel in 1948.

That hope of a return to Jerusalem and of a restoration of the Temple is echoed in the fourteenth and seventeenth blessings of the *Š^{e}mônēh 'Eśrēh*:

And to Jerusalem, your city, return in mercy and dwell in it, as you have said; rebuild it soon in our days as an everlasting building; and speedily set up therein the throne of David.

Accept, O Lord our God, your people Israel, and receive in love and favour both the fire-offerings of Israel and their prayer; and may the service of your people Israel be ever acceptable to you. Let our eyes see your return to Zion in mercy.

[122] *Chronicon* 283 F (in Jerome's translation: GCS 47, 201).
[123] See DJD 2, 48.

15

THE OXYRHYNCHUS LOGOI OF JESUS AND THE COPTIC GOSPEL ACCORDING TO THOMAS*

In 1897 Bernard P. Grenfell and Arthur S. Hunt published a papyrus fragment, which had been found during the previous winter in an ancient dump of the hamlet of Behnesa on the edge of the Western Desert about 120 miles south of Cairo, where Oxyrhynchus, the capital of the Oxyrhynchite nome of ancient Egypt, stood in Roman times. This fragment, written on both sides in Greek uncials, contained a collection of eight 'Sayings of Our Lord', some being only partially preserved.[1] It is the remains of a literary work, not just a few notes or jottings, as is shown by the use of 'Jesus says' to introduce the sayings and the absence of any abbreviations except those normally found in biblical manuscripts. The verso of the fragment, written on the vertical fibres of the papyrus, appears to have preceded the recto, strangely enough; it bears the number 11 on its top margin, presumably a page number, which indicates that the fragment was part of a papyrus codex and not of a scroll.[2] Found together with other texts of the first three centuries A.D.,

* Originally published in *TS* 20 (1959) 505–60.

[1] *Logia Iēsou, Sayings of Our Lord from an Early Greek Papyrus* (London, 1897). [Hereafter GH, *Logia*.]

[2] We may ask what the preceding ten pages in the codex contained. The Coptic version preserved in the *Gospel according to Thomas* shows that the first Greek saying is equal to the twenty-seventh Coptic saying. The length of the twenty-six preceding sayings is not such as would take up ten pages of the

the fragment was dated by the first editors *c.* A.D. 150–300, 'probably written not much later than the year 200'.[3] This fragment is known today as Oxy P (=Oxyrhynchus Papyrus) 1.[4]

In 1904 the same editors, Grenfell and Hunt, published two other Oxyrhynchus fragments, one containing 'New Sayings of Jesus', the other a 'Fragment of a Lost Gospel'. The fragment of the New Sayings 'consists of forty-two incomplete lines on the back of a survey-list of various pieces of land', and has been dated 'to the middle or end of the third century; a later date than A.D. 300 is most unlikely'.[5] It must have been the beginning of a collection of sayings, for it contains a prologue and five sayings of Jesus, some again being only partially preserved. It is known today as Oxy P 654.[6]

The 'Fragment of a Lost Gospel' was made up actually of eight small scraps of a papyrus scroll, a well-written specimen dated not later than A.D. 250. In it we have four sayings of Jesus partially preserved. Though it was entitled by the first editors 'Fragment of a Lost Gospel', because it contained a question asked by disciples and thus gave some context to the saying, a feature that is absent in the other two fragments, it has long been obvious that it belongs in general to the same

---

codex, since we can now judge the length of the page—each page must have had about 38 lines. In all probability some other treatise preceded this Greek one, just as a number of treatises are found in the same codex in the Coptic version. There is, of course, no guarantee that the *Apocryphon of John* (*kata Iōhannēn apokryphon*), which precedes the *Gospel according to Thomas* in the Coptic codex, also preceded it in the Greek.

[3] GH, *Logia*, 6.

[4] Numbered thus in Bernard P. Grenfell and Arthur S. Hunt, *The Oxyrhynchus Papyri, Edited with Translations and Notes* (London, Part 1 [1891]) 1–3.

[5] *New Sayings of Jesus and Fragment of a Lost Gospel* (London, 1904) 9. [Hereafter GH, *New Sayings.*] Oxy P 657 (*Oxyrhynchus Papyri*, Part 4, 36 ff.) offers another example of a sacred text written on the back of a used papyrus; it contains fragments of the Epistle to the Hebrews, which had been copied on the back of a text of an *Epitome* of Livy (=Oxy P. 668).

[6] Numbered thus in *Oxyrhynchus Papyri*, Part 4 (1904) 1–22.

genre as the other two fragments. It contains the introductory phrase, 'Jesus says', and manifests the same sort of relation to the canonical Gospels that they do.[7] It is generally referred to today as Oxy P 655.[8]

After their discovery and first publication these fragments—or more precisely, the first two of them, Oxy P 1 and 654—were the subject of much discussion. The question of their identity, of their authenticity, and of the restoration of their partially preserved texts were the causes of many articles and small books. Only recently we have seen the publication of a work by J. Jeremias, *Unknown Sayings of Jesus*,[9] which treats these fragments in the larger context of the Agrapha (sayings attributed to Jesus, but not found in the canonical Gospels), no matter where preserved. Scholars like Batiffol, Deissmann, von Harnack, Klostermann, Lagrange, Preuschen, Reitzenstein, Sanday, C. Taylor, Wilamowitz-Moellendorff, and Zahn have worked over these texts and have tried to restore and interpret them. It seemed, indeed, that all that could be said about them had been said.[10]

But the whole subject has been reopened by the discovery in 1945 or 1946 of Coptic codices of ancient Chenoboskion near the modern village of Nag'- Ḥammâdi, some sixty miles north of Luxor in Upper Egypt. Chenoboskion (literally, 'a place for

[7] The relation of Oxy P 655 to the other two fragments has often been denied; see, e.g., the discussion in H. G. Evelyn White, *The Sayings of Jesus from Oxyrhynchus, Edited with Introduction, Critical Apparatus and Commentary* (Cambridge, 1920) xlix.–lii. [Hereafter: Evelyn White.]

[8] Numbered thus in *Oxyrhynchus Papyri*, Part 4 (1904) 22–8.

[9] Translated by R. H. Fuller (New York, 1957). [Hereafter: *Unknown Sayings*.]

[10] The bibliography of the Oxyrhynchus Sayings of Jesus is quite vast. While much of it is old and no longer pertinent, it contains at times observations which are still valuable in the light of the new Coptic material. I have decided, therefore, to offer as complete a listing of it as possible. It will be found at the end of this article. Unfortunately, it is not exhaustive, because I came across a number of titles with incomplete references and was not in a position to check them, as they were unavailable in the libraries to which I had access.

raising geese') is said to have been the place where Pachomius, the father of Christian Egyptian cenobitism, after release from involuntary service in the Roman army, was converted and baptized *c.* A.D. 320 and became the disciple of the hermit Palaemon, before founding his cenobitic monastery at Tabennisi on the right bank of the Nile. From a big jar found in the cemetery near Chenoboskion came thirteen codices, containing forty-four Coptic treatises, almost all of them Gnostic writings.[11]

One of these forty-four treatises is the *Gospel according to Thomas, peuaggelion pkata Thōmas.* It was published in 1956 as part of the first volume in the series, *Coptic Gnostic Papyri in the Coptic Museum at Old Cairo.*[12] It was written on ten leaves or twenty pages of a papyrus codex in the Sahidic dialect of Coptic, mixed with some Akhmimic or Sub-Akhmimic forms. Save for a few lacunae which are easily filled out the entire

[11] See J. Doresse, *Les livres secrets des Gnostiques d'Egypte* 1 : *Introduction aux écrits gnostiques coptes découverts à Khenoboskion* (Paris, 1958) 133–280. A convenient summary of the discovery, contents of the codices, and importance of the find can be found in E. Meyerovitch, 'The Gnostic Manuscripts of Upper Egypt', *Diogènes* [Engl. ed.] §25 (1959) 84–117. Pp. 115–17 contain a good bibliography of articles relating to the Coptic material. Cf. now J. M. Robinson, 'The Coptic Gnostic Library Today', *NTS* 14 (1967–68) 356–401. (This is an important article for sorting out the relation of the various Coptic tractates to the codices and for threading one's way through the maze of often confusing references to this literature. It also lists the main publications of the Coptic tractates. It has, however, little to do with the Oxyrhynchus papyri and their relation to the *Gospel according to Thomas.*) See also S. Giversen, 'Nag Hammadi Bibliography 1948–63', *ST* 17 (1963) 138–87; J. Simon, 'Bibliographie Copte', *Orientalia* 28 (1959) 93*–4*; 29 (1960) 48*–50*; 30 (1961) 64*–7*; 31 (1962) 53*–6*; 32 (1963) 116*–19*; 33 (1964) 126*–8*; 34 (1965) 219*–22*; 35 (1966) 142*–5*; 36 (1967) 162*–5*; M. Krause, 'Der Stand der Veröffentlichung der Nag Hammadi Texte', *The Origins of Gnosticism* (Studies in the History of Religions 12; Leiden: Brill, 1967) 61–89; R. Haardt, 'Zwanzig Jahre Erforschung der koptisch-gnostischen Schriften von Nag Hammadi', *Theologie und Philosophie* 42 (1967) 390–401; K. Rudolph, 'Gnosis und Gnostizismus, ein Forschungsbericht', *TRu* 34 (1969) 121–75, 181–231. These bibliographical articles deal with the whole area of the Nag' Hammâdi texts; a specific bibliography for the more important studies of the *Gospel according to Thomas* will be found at the end of this article (see pp. 426–33 below).

[12] Published by Pahor Labib (Cairo, 1956). The *Gospel according to Thomas*

text is well preserved. Palaeographically, the document has been variously dated by Coptic specialists: H.-Ch. Puech thinks that it comes 'du milieu ou de la première moitié du IIIe siècle';[13] G. Garitte says that it 'peut dater du IIIe ou du IVe siècle';[14] but J. Leipoldt dates it 'um 500',[15] while J. Doresse gives 'du milieu du IVe siècle'.[16] A date *c.* 400 is probably the safest for the copying of this text;[17] the date of composition is, of course, undoubtedly much earlier.

The *Gospel according to Thomas* is not a gospel in the sense of the canonical Matthew, Mark, Luke, or John, which contain a record of the words and deeds of Jesus, nor even in the sense of some of the apocryphal Gospels, which relate fantastic stories about the Holy Family in imitation of the canonical Gospels. The *Gospel according to Thomas* relates no episodes of the life of Christ and, in general, lacks all narrative and personal information about him. Even the instances in which the disciples or some others question Jesus cannot rightly be described as narrative, as they normally do no more than pose the question. After a prologue of four and a half lines, which itself contains a saying, this Gospel has preserved for us 114 sayings of Jesus, most of them simply introduced by the formula, 'Jesus said', *peže Iēsous*. The prologue, indeed, indicates the nature of the

---

is found on plates 80–99 with the title given at the end of the work as a sort of *explicit*. This edition contains only photographs of the papyrus pages; there is neither a modern Coptic transcription, a translation, nor a commentary. In addition to the *Gospel according to Thomas*, the volume contains part of the *Gospel of Truth* (pl. 1–46), the *Apocryphon of John* (pl. 47–80), the *Gospel according to Philip* (pl. 99–134), the *Hypostasis of the Archons* (pl. 134–45) and a Sethian Apocalypse (pl. 145–58).

[13] 'Un logion de Jésus sur bandelette funéraire', *RHR* 147 (1955) 127.

[14] 'Le premier volume de l'édition photographique des manuscrits gnostiques coptes et l'Evangile de Thomas', *Mus* 70 (1957) 61.

[15] 'Ein neues Evangelium? Das koptische Thomasevangelium übersetzt und besprochen', *TLZ* 83 (1958) 481.

[16] *Les livres secrets des Gnostiques d'Egypte* 2: *L'Evangile selon Thomas ou les paroles secrètes de Jésus* (Paris, 1959) 23. [Hereafter: Doresse, *Thomas*.]

[17] So W. C. Till, 'New Sayings of Jesus in the Recently Discovered Coptic "Gospel of Thomas"', *BJRL* 41 (1958–59) 451.

work as a collection of sayings. These sayings sometimes resemble maxims or proverbs, sometimes parables, but sometimes answer a question put by a disciple and thus form part of a conversation. They are strung together without any apparent logical order; once in a while catchword bonds (*Stichwortverbindungen*) can be the reason for joining two sayings. The collection of sayings is actually an artificial grouping of *dicta Iesu*, cast in a homogeneous format, which are most likely derived from various sources. Prof. Oscar Cullmann, in various lectures on the *Gospel according to Thomas*,[18] divided the sayings into four groups: (1) those which are word-for-word identical with certain sayings in the canonical Gospels; (2) those which are paraphrases or independent variants of canonical sayings; (3) those which reproduce sayings of Jesus which are not found in the NT, but are extant in patristic writings; (4) those which were previously unknown—a good half of the Gospel—and bear a very definite syncretistic, Gnostic stamp. As it stands, there is no doubt that the *Gospel according to Thomas* is an apocryphal work. I shall have more to say about this Gospel and the ancient witnesses to it toward the end of the article.

But now a word about the possible authenticity of these sayings, as this question will come up in the treatment of the individual texts. When one asks how authentic these Coptic sayings are, it should be clear that the answer will not be simple, given the complex nature of the sayings. As for the first group, they should be accorded the same authenticity as those of the NT. It is obviously quite possible that they have been merely lifted from the canonical Gospels; but we cannot exclude the possibility that the *Gospel according to Thomas* is tributary to an independent tradition, derived from one of the various oral or written forms that led to the formation of our canonical

[18] 'The Gospel of Thomas and the Problem of the Age of the Tradition Contained Therein', *Interpretation* 16 (1962) 418–38, especially 425; cf. *TLZ* 85 (1960) 321–34; *Protestantesimo* 15 (1960) 145–52.—I have some hesitation about the number of sayings that can really be classified in the first group; R. North (*CBQ* 24 [1962] 164) lists some twenty-five of them.

Gospels. In the case of the second and third groups we have to reckon seriously with the possibility of a different collection of sayings, i.e., different from those known to us in Mt, Mk, Lk, Jn, but that may have coexisted with them. The variants in the sayings that are found in the Synoptics themselves show us how the same saying has at times undergone modification in the refractory process of oral transmission or of editorial redaction. One must also reckon with the known creative additions and adaptations of sayings of Jesus that are recorded in the canonical Gospels. The same processes might well account for the variants that are found in the Coptic sayings, which we have called 'paraphrases'. Moreover, just as there are sayings of Jesus recorded in the NT outside of the Gospels (e.g. 1 Thes 4:15 ff.; Acts 20:35; 1 Cor 11:24; Ap 16:15), so those in the patristic writers cannot be rejected as unauthentic simply on the grounds that they do not occur in the Gospels. The fourth group of Coptic sayings, however, is so obviously Gnostic in character that we should be inclined to regard them rather as the product of the same type of imagination that produced many of the apocryphal Gospels. In fact, G. Quispel believes that they are derived from the apocryphal *Gospel of the Egyptians*.[19] Scholars will probably be divided as to the category in which some of the sayings are best classified; however, the classification used above is fairly objective, since in the first three groups the criterion is an outside control. In the second group one might dispute whether a given saying is a paraphrase or an entirely different saying. But in every case it will be necessary to judge each saying individually, a task of evaluation that will take a long time.[20]

It was, of course, a pleasant surprise to find that the Oxyrhynchus *logoi* of Jesus have turned up in the collection of the

[19] 'The Gospel of Thomas and the New Testament', *VC* 11 (1957) 189.

[20] See now the highly interesting and important discussion of H. Koester, '*Gnōmai diaphoroi:* The Origin and Nature of Diversification in the History of Early Christianity', *HTR* 58 (1965) 279–318.

Coptic sayings as part of the *Gospel according to Thomas*. When Oxy P 654 was first published, containing the name of Thomas, the editors discussed the possibility of a connection between the fragment and the *Gospel according to Thomas*, only to reject it.[21] In 1952 H.-Ch. Puech discovered the relation between the Oxyrhynchus papyri and the Coptic *Gospel according to Thomas*.[22] Thanks to the recovery of this Gospel, it is now certain that the three Oxyrhynchus fragments (1, 654, 655) are all parts of the same work;[23] they represent three different copies of the Greek text made at different times and give evidence of a fairly frequent copying of it in the third century A.D. On the basis of the Coptic version[24] we can now reconstruct many of the fragmentary lines of the Greek fragments with certainty—unfortunately, however, not all of them, for there are slight variants in the two recensions that still cause problems of interpretation. Oxy P 654=the prologue and the first six sayings of the Coptic Gospel; Oxy P 1=Coptic sayings 26, 27, 28, 29, 30, with the end of 77, 31, 32, 33; Oxy P 655=Coptic sayings 36, 37, 38, 39. (My numbering of the Coptic sayings is now following that which is commonly used [see note 27 below]; my numbering of the Greek sayings in Oxy P 654 has been made to conform to that numbering too.)

[21] GH, *New Sayings*, 30–2.

[22] 'Un logion de Jésus sur bandelette funéraire', *Bulletin de la société Ernest Renan*, n.s. 3 (1954) 126–9; see n. 13 above. Cf. Doresse, *Thomas*, 16, 21.

[23] Previously held by V. Bartlet, but generally rejected (see White, xlix.).

[24] The original form of this article regarded the Coptic version of the *Gospel according to Thomas* as an adapted translation of the Greek sayings in the Oxyrhynchus papyri. This view was challenged by no less an authority than G. Garitte, who thinks rather that the Oxyrhynchus *Logoi* are translated from a Coptic form of the Gospel (see 'Les "logoi" d'Oxyrhynque et l'apocryphe copte dit "Evangile de Thomas"', *Mus* 73 [1960] 151–72). Garitte's view was challenged by A. Guillaumont, 'Les *Logia* d'Oxyrhynchos sont-ils traduits du Copte?', *ibid.*, 325–33, to which Garitte replied, 'Les "logoi" d'Oxyrhynque sont traduits du Copte', *ibid.*, 335–49. Garitte was supported by H. Quecke, 'Het Evangelie volgens Thomas: Inleiding en commentaar', *Streven* 13 (1960) 452–3, and by P. Devos, *Analecta bollandiana* 78 (1960) 446–7. This question is far from resolved and many scholars still regard the Coptic text as an adapted translation from a Greek original. See

The first full translation of the *Gospel according to Thomas* to appear was that by J. Leipoldt in German.[25] The sayings in which we are interested in this paper were also translated into Latin by G. Garitte.[26] The translations of the Coptic sayings that we are using in this paper were worked out independently of these two translations and subsequently compared with them and others. A deluxe edition of the Gospel with better photographs of the papyrus pages, a Coptic transcription, a translation into French, English, and German, and commentary has been promised.[27]

It is my purpose in this essay to restudy the Greek fragments of Oxyrhynchus in the light of the Coptic translation. I have mentioned above the vast literature that was produced on the subject of these fragments. Many of the attempts to interpret and restore the fragments are now seen to have been in vain. However, many comments of former scholars are still valid and it is my aim to sift the existing publications for those which are still pertinent in the light of the new reconstruction that I propose for these texts. If my attempt to restore the Greek text seems bold or rash to anyone, let him recall the galaxy of names that attempted to do the same without any extrinsic guide or control. My restored text will be translated and commented

---

E. Haenchen, 'Literatur zum Thomasevangelium', *TRu* 27 (1961–62) 157–60 ('sein [Garitte's] Beweis hält nicht stand', p. 160); O. Cullmann, *Interpretation* 16 (1962) 421–2; J.-B. Bauer in *Geheime Worte Jesu: Das Thomas-evangelium* (ed. R. M. Grant and D. N. Freedman; Frankfurt, 1960) 188–90. Cf. R. Kasser, *L'évangile selon Thomas: Présentation et commentaire théologique* (Neuchâtel: Delachaux et Niestlé, 1961) and H. Quecke, RechBib 6 (1962) 220–2. Whatever the answer to it is, the reconstruction of the Greek text of the Oxyrhynchus papyri must at present be made with the Coptic text in mind.

[25] See n. 15 above.

[26] See n. 14 above.

[27] An extract of this edition is available in A. Guillaumont, H.-Ch. Puech, G. Quispel, W. Till, and Y. 'Abd-al-Masīḥ, *The Gospel according to Thomas: Coptic Text Established and Translated* (Leiden: Brill; New York: Harper, 1959). I am following the numbering of sayings in this edition. See also J. Leipoldt, *Das Evangelium nach Thomas koptisch und deutsch* (TU 101; Berlin:

upon, and finally I shall conclude with some general remarks on the relation of the Greek fragments to the Coptic text.[28]

Oxy P 654

I begin the discussion of the Greek texts with Oxy P 654, for it contains the prologue which corresponds to that of the Coptic text. It is a long, narrow fragment ($9\frac{5}{8}'' \times 3\frac{1}{16}''$), containing 42 lines of which only the beginnings are preserved. In cases where the reconstruction of the line is certain due to the Coptic version, we are able to ascertain the normal number of letters on a line. For instance, line 4 contained 30 letters (16 restored); line 20 contained 28 (13 restored); line 25 contained 33 letters (15 restored); line 30 contained 29 letters (12 restored). This gives us a fairly certain norm to guide us in restoring other lines. I shall present first the unreconstructed text of Grenfell and Hunt,[29] then an English translation of the corresponding Coptic

---

Akademie-V., 1967); for other translations, see J. M. Robinson, *art. cit.* (n. 11 above) 388–9.

[28] The following are the articles that have appeared, dealing with the Oxyrhynchus *logoi* and the Coptic text: H.-Ch. Puech, 'Une collection de paroles de Jésus récemment retrouvée: l'évangile selon Thomas', *CRAIBL* 1957, 146–66. A. Guillaumont, 'Sémitismes dans les logia de Jésus retrouvés à Nag-Hamâdi', *JA* 246 (1958) 113–23. R. McL. Wilson, 'The Coptic "Gospel of Thomas"', *NTS* 5 (1958–59) 273–6. R. Kasser, 'Les manuscrits de Nag' Hammâdi: Faits, documents, problèmes', *RTP* 9 (1959) 357–70. O. Hofius, 'Das koptische Thomasevangelium und die Oxyrhynchus-Papyri Nr. 1, 654 und 655', *ET* 20 (1960) 21–42, 182–92. A. Rüstow, '*Entos hymōn estin:* Zur Deutung von Lukas 17, 20–21', *ZNW* 51 (1960) 197–224. J.-B. Bauer, 'Arbeitsaufgaben am koptischen Thomasevangelium', *VC* 15 (1961) 1–7. R. A. Kraft, Oxyrhynchus Papyrus 655 Reconsidered', *HTR* 54 (1961) 253–62. Guillaumont, A., '*Nēsteuein ton kosmon* (P. Oxy. 1, verso 1. 5–6)', *BIFAO* 61 (1962) 15–23. A. F. Walls, '"Stone" and "Wood" in Oxyrhynchus Papyrus I', *VC* 16 (1962) 71–6. W. Schrage, 'Evangelienzitate in den Oxyrhynchus-Logien und im koptischen Thomas-Evangelium', *Apophoreta* (Fest. E. Haenchen; BZNW 30; Berlin: Töpelmann, 1964) 251–68. A. Baker, '"Fasting to the World"', *JBL* 84 (1965) 291–4. T. F. Glasson, 'The Gospel of Thomas, Saying 3, and Deuteronomy xxx. 11–14', *ExpT* 78 (1966–67) 151–2. M. Marcovich, 'Textual Criticism on the *Gospel of Thomas*', *JTS* n.s. 20 (1969) 53–74. F. Altheim and R. Stiehl, *Die Araber in der alten Welt* (Berlin: De Gruyter) 5/2 (1969) 368–92. C. H. Roberts, 'The Gospel of Thomas: Logion 30A', *JTS* 21 (1970) 91–2.

[29] I give the text as it appeared in the preliminary editions (GH, *New*

saying, the full Greek text of the Oxyrhynchus saying (restored), a translation of the Greek, and finally comments on each saying.

In this revision of the essay I have changed the reconstruction of the Greek text only in a few instances. Part of the reason for the few changes is the use of my reconstruction in K. Aland, *Synopsis quattuor evangeliorum: Locis parallelis evangeliorum apocryphorum et patrum adhibitis* (Stuttgart: Württembergische Bibelanstalt, 1964) pp. 584–5 *et passim*. But the real reason is that I have not always been convinced that other attempts to reconstruct it are better than my own. Where changes have been made, I have acknowledged my dependence on others.

PROLOGUE AND FIRST SAYING

ΟΙ ΤΟΙΟΙ ΟΙ ΛΟΓΟΙ ΟΙ [
ΛΗΣΕΝ ΙΗΣ Ο ΖΩΝ Κ[
ΚΑΙ ΘΩΜΑ ΚΑΙ ΕΙΠΕΝ [
ΑΝ ΤΩΝ ΛΟΓΩΝ ΤΟΥΤ[
ΟΥ ΜΗ ΓΕΥΣΗΤΑΙ [

The prologue and first saying of the Coptic Gospel read as follows: 'These are the secret words which the living Jesus spoke, and Didymus Judas Thomas wrote them down. And he said, "Whoever discovers the interpretation (*hermēneia*)[30] of these words will not taste death!"' (Plate 80, lines 10–14).[31]

Sayings, 11 and 40; GH, *Logia*, 8) rather than that of the *editio princeps* (*Oxyrhynchus Papyri*, Part 1, p. 3; Part 4, pp. 3 and 23) because the preliminary editions present more objective readings of the fragments, not encumbered with the hypotheses that developed out of the preliminary publications. Any changes that the first editors subsequently made in the *editio princeps* will be noted.

[30] The form of the Greek word found in parentheses in the English translation of the Coptic version is an exact transliteration of the form used by the Coptic. I add this form to the translation, for it will often shed light on the Greek text—as in this very case.

[31] References to plates and lines are made according to the edition of P. Labib (see n. 12 above). I add these references, because they are the only sure way that now exists of referring to the Coptic Gospel. The various scholars who have so far discussed or translated the Gospel have divided the text up according to the sayings it contains. Some number 113, some 114, some 118.

On the basis of this Coptic version we may now restore the Greek text as follows:[32]

Οὗτοι οἱ {οι} λόγοι οἱ [ἀπόκρυφοι οὓς ἐλά]
λησεν Ἰη(σοῦ)ς ὁ ζῶν κ[αὶ ἔγραψεν Ἰούδας ὁ]
καὶ Θωμᾶ<ς> καὶ εἶπεν [ὅστις ἂν τὴν ἑρμηνεί]
αν τῶν λόγων τούτ[ων εὑρίσκῃ, θανάτου]
οὐ μὴ γεύσηται.

'These are the [secret] words [which] the living Jesus [sp]oke, an[d Judas who] (is) also (called) Thomas [wrote (them) down]. And he said, ["Whoever finds the interpre]tation of th[ese] words, will not taste [death!"]'

Comments

1. It is generally admitted that the first line contains 'obviously an uncorrected mistake' (Evelyn White, p. xxiii). The *editio princeps* reads {*hoi*} *toioi hoi logoi*; the editors insist that the second letter can only be an iota and try to explain *toios* as the equivalent of *toiosde* (*Oxyrhynchus Papyri*, Part 4, p. 4). However, many subsequent commentators such as Swete, Heinrici, Taylor, Wilamowitz-Moellendorff, and Evelyn White were not convinced by this questionable Greek construction and read the first line as I have given it, deleting the dittographical article before the noun. Cf. Bar 1:1, *houtoi hoi logoi tou bibliou hous egrapsen Barouch*; Lk 24:44.

logoi: The use of this word to designate the 'sayings' of Jesus in these fragments should be noted. Nowhere do we find *logia* used of these sayings; Grenfell and Hunt were, therefore, not accurate in entitling the preliminary publication of Oxy P 1 *Logia Iēsou*, which did not, of course, become apparent until the discovery of Oxy P 654. From the time of Herodotus on *logion* meant 'oracle', 'a saying derived from a deity'. In the LXX it denotes the 'word of God', having lost the Greek nuance of

[32] I am following the system of the Greek papyrologists in the use of square brackets [ ] to denote the restoration of lacunae, parentheses or round brackets ( ) to denote the resolution of abbreviations, angular brackets ⟨ ⟩ to denote my editorial additions, and braces {} to denote my editorial deletions.

'oracle' and acquired that of OT revelation. In this sense we find it in Acts 7:38; Rom 3:2; 1 Pt 4:11; Heb 5:12 (see G. Kittel, *TDNT* 4, 137–41). In A. Resch's collection of Agrapha (TU 30 [1906]) we find the word used only twice, and in each case it refers to the OT. See further J. Donovan, *The Logia in Ancient and Recent Literature* (Cambridge, 1927). The use of *logoi* here for the sayings of Jesus can be compared to Mt 15:12 and especially to Acts 20:35, *mnēmoneuein te tōn logōn tou Kyriou Iēsou hoti autos eipen*. See also Clement of Rome, *Ad Cor.* 13:1; 46:7 (ed. K. Bihlmeyer, pp. 42, 60) for the use of this word to designate the sayings of Jesus. Now that we know that the Greek fragments belong to a text of the *Gospel according to Thomas*, there is no longer room for the speculation that possibly they contain part of the *Logia* on which Papias wrote his commentary or of the *Logia* that Matthew collected (Eusebius, *Hist. Eccl.* 3, 39, 1 and 16). Consequently, it is better not to refer to the sayings either in the Oxyrhynchus fragments or in the Coptic *Gospel According to Thomas* (where the word used is *šaǧe*, 'word, saying') as *logia*, *pace* R. North (*CBQ* 24 [1962] 164, etc.). See further J. M. Robinson, '*Logoi sophōn:* Zur Gattung der Spruchquelle Q', *Zeit und Geschichte: Dankesgabe an Rudolf Bultmann zum 80. Geburtstag* (ed. E. Dinkler; Tübingen: Mohr, 1964) 77–96, esp. 79–84.

apokryphoi: Of all the adjectives previously suggested by the critics to modify 'sayings' only that of T. Zahn (*NKZ* 16 [1905] 178) has proved to be correct, as the Coptic *ᵉnšaǧe ethêp* shows, although it was not, ironically enough, acceptable to most scholars. The exact expression is to be found, moreover, in Hippolytus' *Elenchus* 7, 20 (GCS 26, 195): *basileidēs toinun kai Isidōros, . . . phēsin eirēkenai Matthian autois logous apokryphous, hous ēkouse para tou sōtēros kat' idian didachtheis*. Moreover, we find the same adjective used of both *logos* and *logia* in a text that is possibly related to this Gospel, viz., *Acta Thomae* 39 (ed. M. Bonnet, p. 156): *ho didymos tou Christou, ho apostolos tou hypsistou kai symmystēs tou logou tou Christou apokryphou, ho dechomenos autou ta apokrypha logia*. The same expression, *ᵉnšaǧe ethēp*, is found at the beginning of another Chenoboskion treatise ascribed to Thomas, the *Book of Thomas*. According to H.-Ch. Puech ('Les nouveaux écrits gnostiques découverts en Haute-Egypte: premier inventaire et essai d'identification', *Coptic Studies in Honor of Walter Ewing Crum* [=Second Bulletin of the Byzantine Institute; Boston, 1950] 105), this book begins, 'Paroles secrètes dites par le Sauveur à Jude et Thomas (*sic*) et consignées par Matthias'. Elsewhere Puech reveals the full title, *Book of Thomas the Athlete Written for the Perfect* (*CRAIBL* 1957, p. 149). We may ask in what sense the sayings of Jesus in this collection are to be regarded as 'secret' (for it is obvious that *apokryphos* does not have the later pejorative meaning of 'apocryphal' here), when many of the sayings contain words which Jesus pronounced openly and publicly. The 'hidden' character is rather to be found in the manner of interpretation which is found in this collection. The quotation from Hippolytus above tells us of 'hidden words' that Matthias had learned from the Saviour in private. This reveals a tradition which undoubtedly is to be traced to Mt 13:10–11, where Christ himself distinguished between the comprehension of the disciples and that of the crowd. The thirteenth Coptic saying illustrates this idea, moreover, when Jesus takes Thomas aside to tell him three words which he is not allowed to repeat to the other disciples. In this very saying we learn that eternal life is promised to him who succeeds in discovering the real meaning of the sayings in the collection. This probably refers to the different application or interpretation which is given to even the canonical sayings that are set in a different context. Such shifts in meaning were undoubtedly part of the esoteric interpretation which is intended by 'hidden' or 'secret'. J.-B. Bauer prefers to restore *kekrymmenoi* (*VC* 15 [1961] 5–7).

2. *ho zōn:* Former commentators often asked whether this adjective was to be referred to Christ's preresurrectional or postresurrectional existence. Leipoldt (col. 481) points out that

the Coptic *etonh* scarcely means, 'while he was living', and should probably be referred to the Risen Christ. But we need not deduce from this that the words recorded in this collection are postresurrectional sayings. There is nothing in the Coptic or Greek versions that supports this; on the contrary, a number of the sayings imply the preresurrectional phase.

[*Ioudas ho*] *kai Thōma*⟨*s*⟩ : The form *THŌMA* creates a problem. Most former commentators interpreted it as a dative in an expression like *kai ophtheis tois deka kai Thōma* (so, e.g., Evelyn White, p. 1). However, it is now clear from the Coptic that Thomas is the alleged compiler of the sayings and the subject of the sentence. At the end of line 2 we must certainly supply *k*[*ai egrapsen*. . . . This is confirmed by the title of the Gospel that is found at the end (Pl. 99): *peuaggelion pkata Thomas*. What, then, is the form of Thomas' name? In Jn 11:16; 20:24 we find Thomas referred to as *ho legomenos Didymos*, as generally in the Western tradition. Such a full form of the name is impossible here. In Jn 14:22 we read of a certain 'Judas, not the Iscariot', which the Curetonian Syriac version gives as 'Judas Thomas', a form which occurs elsewhere in Syriac writings. K. Lake (*HibbJ* 3 [1904–5] 339) suggested that this name be read here (in the dative). In fact, in the *Acta Thomae* we frequently find him referred to as *Ioudas ho kai Thōmas* (§11 [ed. M. Bonnet in R. A. Lipsius, *Acta apostolorum apocrypha* [Leipzig, 1903] p. 116]; also §20 [p. 130], §21 [p. 133] *et passim*). For the form of the name, cf. Acts 13:9, *Saulos ho kai Paulos*, and Blass-Debrunner, *Grammatik des neutestamentlichen Griechisch* (9th ed.; Göttingen, 1954) §268, 1. The real name of the Apostle was 'Judas the Twin'. *Didymos* is the Greek translation of the Hebrew *Teʾôm* or the Aramaic *Teʾômâ*. In Syriac "twin" is *tâʾmâ*, which shows that the Aramaic form of the proper name is actually influenced by the Hebrew in preserving the *ô*. The Greek form *Thōmas* is actually a genuine Greek name which has been substituted for a similarly sounding Semitic name, like *Simōn* for *Šimeʿôn*; cf. Blass-Debrunner §53, 2d. The author of *Acta Thomae* regards Thomas as the twin of our Lord and in the course of the writing they are mistaken for each other. In line 3 we must accordingly read *Thōma⟨s⟩*, since the nominative case is required.[33] M. Marcovich now points out (*JTS* 20 [1969] 53) that the omission of the final *s* on *Thōma* is common enough in the nominative; see E. Mayser, *Grammatik der griechischen Papyri aus der Ptolomäerzeit*, 1. 205.

3. *hermēnei*]*an:* The Coptic has preserved the Greek word for us, which makes the restoration certain.

4. *heuriskē:* Hofius' form *heurēsē* is surely wrong; one might possibly read *heurē*. Marcovich (*JTS* 20 [1969] 53) offers another possibility, *hostis . . . heurēsei*, but he wrongly judges that my *hostis an* is too long.

thanatou: The restoration of former commentators, suggested by Jn 8:52, is now certain. The compiler has modified the Johannine statement slightly in order to suit his prologue. The NT expression always lacks the article, whether used for physical or spiritual death; see Mt 16:28; Mk 9:1; Lk 9:27; Heb 2:9. Here, as in John, the idea of spiritual death is almost certainly intended. There is no apparent reason why this saying could not be authentic, if 'he said' refers to Jesus. E. Jacquier (*RB* 15 [1918] 114) regarded it as authentic. The only hesitation comes from the fact that the apodosis of our saying reflects a Jewish rephrasing of Jesus' statement, rather than the actual way it is recorded in John.

SECOND SAYING

ΜΗ ΠΑΥΣΑΣΘΩ Ο ΖΗ[
ΕΥΡΗ ΚΑΙ ΟΤΑΝ ΕΥΡΗ [
ΒΗΘΕΙΣ ΒΑΣΙΛΕΥΣΗ ΚΑ[
9 ΗΣΕΤΑΙ

The second Coptic saying: 'Jesus said, "Let him who seeks not give up seeking until he finds, and when (*hotan*) he finds, he

[33] I cannot agree with the translation of the Oxyrhynchus prologue as it is given by J. Doresse, *Thomas*, p. 89, which reads thus: 'Voici les paroles [cachées que] Jésus le Vivant a dites e[t qu'a transcrites Didyme Jude] et

will be bewildered; and if he is bewildered, he will marvel and he will become king over all"' (80:14–19).

In this case the Coptic version only helps in part, for it does not completely correspond to the Greek. The latter is shorter than the Coptic and contains a different ending. Since a form of the saying is preserved in Clement of Alexandria, former editors succeeded in restoring it quite well. We add nothing new to the restoration of this saying. The following form is derived from Evelyn White (p. 5):

[λέγει Ἰη(σοῦ)ς·]
μὴ παυσάσθω ὁ ζη[τῶν τοῦ ζητεῖν ἕως ἂν]
εὕρῃ, καὶ ὅταν εὕρῃ, [θαμβηθήσεται καὶ θαμ]
βηθεὶς βασιλεύσῃ κα[ὶ βασιλεύσας ἀναπα]
ήσεται.

'[Jesus says,] "Let him who see[ks] not cease [seeking until] he finds and when he finds, [he will be astounded, and] having been [astoun]ded, he will reign an[d having reigned], he will re[st]."'

Comments

5. After the last word of the first saying there is a *coronis*, a sign used to separate the sayings in this fragment. We may confidently restore in the lacuna at the end of the line *legei Iē(sou)s*, since this is the usual formula of introduction (see lines 9, 27, 36; Oxy P 1:4, 11, [23], 30, 36, 41). It should be noted that whereas the Coptic has the past tense in the introductory formula, *peže*, the Greek uses the present. The past would be more obvious, and the problem is to explain why the Greek version has the present tense. The use of the present tense is quite common in Mt, Mk, and Jn, less so in Lk; in the NT it has

Thomas'. From this it seems that Didyme Jude is not Thomas; moreover, there is no room to restore Didymus. The second relative pronoun which Doresse has introduced into his translation, obviously for the sake of smoothness, does not occur in the Coptic and I have not restored it in the Greek. My reconstruction was made independently of that proposed by H.-Ch. Puech (*Comptes rendus de l'Académie des Inscriptions et Belles-Lettres*, 1957, p. 153), with which it agrees substantially.

a historical sense normally. We find the exact expression in Jn 13:31. But this combination of the present *legei* and *Iēsous* without the article is otherwise unknown. Harnack (*Expositor*, ser. 5, vol. 6 [1897] 403, n. 2) took the use of the present with Jesus, instead of 'the Lord', as a sign of great antiquity, and he contrasted it with the use of *Kyrios* in the *Gospel according to the Egyptians*. Evelyn White (p. lxxv) believes that the anarthrous use of *Iēsous* is a mark of Johannine influence in the collection. Burney suggested (in W. Lock and W. Sanday, *Two Lectures on the 'Sayings of Jesus'* [Oxford, 1897] 47–8) that the formula is possibly a translation 'from a Neo-Hebrew or Aramaic original'. He cites as parallels *Pirqê 'Abôt* 1, 4, 5, 12. But it was often taken with Lock (*op. cit.*, 18) in a 'mystical' sense, meaning simply, 'This is a saying of Jesus'; 'this was said by Jesus in his lifetime and is still the utterance of him who is still a living Master' (see Evelyn White, pp. lxxiii–lxxvi). But since we also find the present used of the disciples (see Oxy P 654:32–33; 655: 17), the 'mystical' sense must yield to the historical present, confirmed by the Coptic past.

6. *ho zētōn:* The saying is probably related to Mt 7:8, 'the one who searches finds'. But it is obviously a development of it.

tou zētein: This restoration (of Heinrici, *Theologische Studien und Kritiken* 78 [1905] 188–210) does not correspond exactly to the Coptic *efšine*, which is rather the 3 sg. m. pres. circumstantial, 'While he is seeking'. Something is needed to fill out the line, and since the circumstantial notion is already expressed in the participle, the infinitive is best retained.

7. [*thambēthēsetai*]*:* At this point the Greek text is shorter than the Coptic. But we are aided in the interpretation of the Greek by several passages from Clement of Alexandria. In *Stromata* 2, 9, 45 (GCS 15, 137) we find a text which is quite close to this fragment, but it is cited as derived from the *Gospel according to the Hebrews: kan tō kath' Hebraious euaggeliō ho thaumasas basileusei gegraptai kai ho basileusas anapaēsetai*. Again in *Stromata* 5, 14, 96 (GCS 15, 389) the saying is found in still fuller form: *ou pausetai*

ho zētōn heōs an heurē; heurōn de thambēthēsetai; thambētheis de basileusei; basileusas de epanapaēsetai. (Cf. M. R. James, *The Apocryphal New Testament, Being the Apocryphal Gospels, Acts, Epistles and Apocalypses* [Oxford, 1953] 2; Resch, *Agrapha*, 70–1; 215–16.) Is it possible that the *Gospel according to Thomas* has also quoted from the *Gospel according to the Hebrews*? In the present state of our knowledge it is impossible to answer this question. We may also ask in what sense the verb *thambēthēsetai* is to be understood. The context in which the saying is quoted in Clement of Alexandria is one in which he is trying to show that the beginning of philosophy is wonder. But this is hardly the meaning in the collection of sayings that we have here. Harnack interpreted it rather in the sense of joyful surprise, comparing the parable of the hidden treasure in Mt 13:24; cf. Evelyn White, p. 6; H. B. Swete, *ExpT* 15 (1903–4) 491.

8. *basileusē:* A misspelling for *basileusei*; at the period when the papyrus was written, *ē*, *ei*, *i*, *y* were all pronounced alike in Egyptian Greek. See further Oxy P 1:13 *sarkei* for *sarki* (in fact, '*sarkei* has been corrected by the original hand from *sarki*'; GH, *Logia*, p. 12); 1:16 *deipsōnta* for *dipsōnta*; 1:35 *geinōskontas* for *ginōskontas*; in 1:22 an epsilon has been inserted above the line in the word *ptōchian*; Oxy P 655:14 *heilikian* for *hēlikian*; 655:16 *hymein* for *hymein;* 655:19 *hēmein* for *hēmin*; Oxy P 654:10 reads *hēmas*, which should probably be *hymas;* 655:20 *esei* (a form acceptable even in earlier Greek for *esē*). Cf. E. Mayser, *Grammatik*, §11, 13, 15.

anapaēsetai: A vulgar form of *anapausetai*; cf. Ap 14:13; Clem. Alex., *Stromata* 2, 9, 45. The Coptic seems to have read here *ana panta*; or is this possibly a deliberate change of meaning that has been introduced?

Though J. H. Ropes (*Die Sprüche Jesu, die in den kanonischen Evangelien nicht überliefert sind* [TU 14/2; Leipzig, 1896] 128) believes that the saying is authentic, Resch (*Agrapha*, 215) called it apocryphal, and Jacquier (*art. cit.*, 101) labelled it doubtfully authentic.

THIRD SAYING

ΛΕΓΕΙ Ι[
ΟΙ ΕΛΚΟΝΤΕΣ ΗΜΑΣ [
Η ΒΑΣΙΛΕΙΑ ΕΝ ΟΥΡΑ[
ΤΑ ΠΕΤΕΙΝΑ ΤΟΥ ΟΥΡ[
ΤΙ ΥΠΟ ΤΗΝ ΓΗΝ ΕΣΤ[
ΟΙ ΙΧΘΥΕΣ ΤΗΣ ΘΑΛΑ[
ΤΕΣ ΥΜΑΣ ΚΑΙ Η ΒΑΣ[
ΕΝΤΟΣ ΥΜΩΝ [.]ΣΤΙ [
ΓΝΩ ΤΑΥΤΗΝ ΕΥΡΗ[
ΕΑΥΤΟΥΣ ΓΝΩΣΕΣΘΑΙ [
ΥΜΕΙΣ
ΕΣΤΕ ΤΟΥ ΠΑΤΡΟΣ ΤΟΥ Τ[
ΓΝΩΣΘΕ ΕΑΥΤΟΥΣ ΕΝ[
ΚΑΙ ΥΜΕΙΣ ΕΣΤΕ ΗΠΤΟ[

'Though no restoration of ll. 9–14 can hope to be very convincing, we think that a fairly good case can be made out in favour of our general interpretation' (GH, *New Sayings*, 16). As it turns out, neither the restoration of Grenfell and Hunt nor that of any of the subsequent commentators was correct. The difficulty lay in the fact that only the beginning of the lines of the Greek saying has been preserved and there was formerly no outside control or guide. Now, however, we have grounds for a fairly convincing restoration in the Coptic translation. The latter shows that we are dealing here with one long saying, not two, as was suggested by P. Parker (*ATR* 22 [1940] 196).[34] The third Coptic saying reads as follows: 'Jesus said, "If those who draw you on say to you, 'Behold, the kingdom is in the heaven', then the birds of the heaven shall be (there) before you. If they say to you, 'It is in the sea (*thalassa*)', then the fishes will be (there) before you. But (*alla*) the kingdom is within you and outside of you. When (*hotan*) you know yourselves, then (*tote*) they will know you (*or*: you will be known) and you will realize that you are the sons of the living Father. But if you do not know yourselves, then you are in poverty and you are poverty"' (80:19–27; 81:1–4).

[34] J. Doresse (*Thomas*, 89–90) likewise breaks up the second saying into two, without, however, giving any justifying reason.

Guided by this Coptic version, which is not in all respects identical, we may suggest the following restoration of the Greek text:

λέγει Ἰ[η(σοῦ)ς· ἐὰν]
οἱ ἕλκοντες ἡμᾶς [εἴπωσιν ὑμῖν· ἰδοὺ]
ἡ βασιλεία ἐν οὐρα[νῷ, ὑμᾶς φθήσεται]
τὰ πετεινὰ τοῦ οὐρ[ανοῦ· ἐὰν δ' εἴπωσιν ὅ]
τι ὑπὸ τὴν γῆν ἐστ[ιν, εἰσελεύσονται]
οἱ ἰχθύες τῆς θαλά[σσης φθάσαν]
τες ὑμᾶς καὶ ἡ βασ[ιλεία τοῦ θεοῦ]
ἐντὸς ὑμῶν [ἐ]στι [κἀκτός. ὃς ἂν ἑαυτὸν]
γνῷ, ταύτην εὑρή[σει καὶ ὅτε ὑμεῖς]
ἑαυτοὺς γνώσεσθαι, [εἰδήσετε ὅτι υἱοί]
ἐστε ὑμεῖς τοῦ πατρὸς τοῦ ζ[ῶντος· εἰ δὲ μὴ]
γνώσ<εσ>θε ἑαυτούς, ἐν [τῇ πτωχείᾳ ἐστὲ]
καὶ ὑμεῖς ἐστε ἡ πτω[χεία]

'Je[sus] says, ["If] those who draw you on [say to you, 'Behold,] the kingdom (is) in the heav[en',] the birds of the hea[ven will be (there) before you. But if they say th]at it is under the earth, the fishes of the se[a will enter before you]. And the king[dom of God] is within you [and outside (of you). Whoever] knows [himself,] will fin[d] it [and when you] know yourselves, [you will realize that] you are [sons] of the li[ving] Father. [But if you will not] know yourselves, [you are] in [poverty] and you are pov[erty.]"'

Comments

9. *I*[*ē*(*sou*)*s*]: Thanks to the Coptic version, we can now eliminate the often proposed restoration of J[udas], 'not the Iscariot'.

10. *hoi helkontes:* We have translated the Coptic above in function of the Greek participle; but it is just possible that the Coptic *netsōk hēttēut*ᵉ*n* means 'those who go before you' (see W. E. Crum, *A Coptic Dictionary* [Oxford, 1939] 327a). But in neither case is the sense clear. Who are those who 'draw you on' or 'go before you'? It is now impossible to explain this word by appealing to Jn 6:44 or 12:32, as was done by the first editors

and many commentators since then. They appear to be opponents of Jesus, whose teachings he is refuting by reducing them to absurdity before he affirms that the kingdom is within and without.

hēmas: My translation corrects this word to *hymas*, which is demanded by the context, as many former editors saw, and also by the Coptic translation. On the interchange of eta and upsilon, see the note on line 8 above.

11. *hē basileia:* The absolute use of this word (without 'of God' or 'of heaven') can be paralleled by Mt 13:38; 24:14; 4:23; 8:12; Acts 20:25.

oura[nō: Restored in the singular because of the article with the word in the following line. Hofius' reconstruction of this line is a trifle too long.

13. *eiseleusontai . . . phthasan]tes hymas:* I am not happy about this reconstruction, because it does not exactly reflect the Coptic, but something similar is needed to fill up the space. For the use of the circumstantial participle of *phthanō* with a finite verb, cf. H. W. Smyth, *Greek Grammar* (Cambridge, 1956) §2062a; R. Kühner and B. Gerth, *Ausführliche Grammatik der griechischen Sprache*, Part 2, 4th ed. (Hanover, 1955) §482, Anm. 14.

15. *kai:* This conjunction is peculiar here, for we would expect an adversative, which is precisely what we have in the Coptic (*alla*, 'but').

hē bas[ileia tou theou]: It would also be possible to restore *tōn ouranōn*. Support for this restoration is had in a passage of Hippolytus, *Elenchus* 5, 7 (GCS 26, 83): *peri tēn . . . physin, hēnper phēsi ⟨tēn⟩ entos anthrōpou basileian ouranōn zētoumenēn, peri hēs diarrēdēn en tō kata Thōman epigraphomenō euangeliō paradidoasi. . . .* The Coptic version which we now have makes it all the more likely that the *Gospel according to Thomas* to which Hippolytus here refers is not the *Infancy Gospel of Thomas the Israelite*, but the one represented by the Oxyrhynchus fragments and the Coptic text. However, I have preferred to restore *tou theou*, because this saying is obviously a development of Lk 17:21, *idou gar hē basileia tou theou entos hymōn estin.* Moreover, in Oxy P 1:7–8 we find the expression *tēn basileian tou theou*, which is rendered in the Coptic (86:18–19) simply by *tmᵉntero*, 'the kingdom' (absolutely), just as we find it here. For the possible use of Dt 30:11–14 in this part of the saying, see T. F. Glasson, *ExpTim* 78 (1966–67) 151–2.

16. [*kaktos*]*:* This restoration is taken from the Coptic *sᵉmpetᵉn bal*, 'Outside'. The exact meaning of the kingdom being 'within you and without' is puzzling. L. Cerfaux and G. Garitte have devoted a study to the parables of the kingdom in this Coptic Gospel, but no attempt has been made by them to explain the sense of this phrase. See 'Les paraboles du royaume dans L'"Evangile de Thomas"', *Mus* 70 (1957) 307–27. See now A. Rüstow, '*Entos hymōn estin*', *ZNW* 51 (1960) 197–224; R. Sneed, '"The Kingdom of God is Within You" (Lk 17, 21)', *CBQ* 24 (1962) 363–82.

hos an heauton] *gnō:* There is a lack of correspondence here between the Greek and the Coptic, for the verb is 3 sg. 2 aor. subj., demanding a 3 sg. subject. We have simply adopted the restoration of this line given by former editors (see Evelyn White, pp. 8–9), which cannot be improved on.

17. *tautēn:* This pronoun must refer to the kingdom, as it is the only feminine in the preceding context. In Clement of Alexandria (*Paidagogos* 3, 1) we find the idea of the knowledge of oneself leading to a knowledge of God developed.

18. *heautous:* For the use of this pronoun as a reflexive with a verb in the 2 pl., see below l. 20 and Blass-Debrunner, §64, 1; Kühner-Gerth, §455, 7.

gnōsesthai: A misspelling for *gnōsesthe*; the diphthong *ai* was pronounced like epsilon, as in Modern Greek, at the time of the writing of this fragment. See further Oxy P 654:37 *-eitai* for *-eite*; Oxy P 1:5–6 *nēsteusētai* for *nēsteusēte*; 1:7 *heurētai* for *heurēte*. For the converse change see below line 23, *eperōtēse* for *eperōtēsai*. Cf. E. Mayser, *op. cit.*, §14.

eidēsete: Or possibly *eisesthe.*

19. *hymeis:* A correction written above the line.

z[ōntos]: GH, *New Sayings,* 11, read T[before the break in the papyrus, admitting that a pi is also possible (17). However, the traces of this letter are quite faint and can also be read as a zeta, which would agree with the Coptic *etonh,* 'who is living'. Cf. Jn 6:57 *ho zōn patēr,* and l. 2 of the prologue above. See also Rom 9:26 (=Hos 2:1).

20. *gnōsthe:* This form looks like a 2 pl. 2 aor. subj. midd. of *ginōskō.* But why should it be middle followed by a reflexive pronoun? Former commentators emended it to *gnōs⟨es⟩the,* a future middle form which would go well with the reflexive pronoun object, and which parallels *gnōsesthai* of 1:18.

en [tē ptōcheia este]: The association of poverty with a lack of knowledge reminds us of the explanations offered by some of the patristic writers why the Ebionites had a name apparently derived from *'ebyôn,* 'poor'. Cf. p. 438 below; 'Ebionites', *Dictionnaire de spiritualité* 4 (fasc. 25, 1958) 33.

21. *hē ptō[cheia:* GH, *New Sayings,* 11, read an omicron before the break in the papyrus. This must be read as an omega, as W. Schubart (*ZNW* 20 [1921] 222) previously suggested, but he restored the word *ptō[sis].* The Coptic version makes our restoration certain. The word itself occurs in Oxy P 1:22.

To what extent this long saying is authentic is difficult to determine.

FOURTH SAYING

ΟΥΚ ΑΠΟΚΝΗΣΕΙ ΑΝΘ[
ΡΩΝ ΕΠΕΡΩΤΗΣΕ ΠΑ[
ΡΩΝ ΠΕΡΙ ΤΟΥ ΤΟΠΟΥ ΤΗ[
   ΟΤΙ
ΣΕΤΕ ΠΟΛΛΟΙ ΕΣΟΝΤΑΙ Π[
ΟΙ ΕΣΧΑΤΟΙ ΠΡΩΤΟΙ ΚΑΙ [
ΣΙΝ

While former commentators succeeded in restoring the second part of this saying, their efforts were not so successful in the first part, as now appears from the Coptic version. The fourth Coptic saying: 'Jesus said, "The man old in his days will not hesitate[35] to ask a little child of seven days about the place (*topos*) of life, and he will live. For many (that are) first will be last and they will be(come) only one"' (81:4–10). The Greek text, which varies slightly, can be restored with great probability except for the last line.

[λέγει Ἰ(ησοῦ)ς·]
οὐκ ἀποκνήσει ἄνθ[ρωπος πλήρης ἡμε]
ρῶν ἐπερωτῆσε πα[ιδίον ἑπτὰ ἡμε]
ρῶν περὶ τοῦ τόπου τῆ[ς ζωῆς καὶ ζή]
σετε ὅτι πολλοὶ ἔσονται π[ρῶτοι ἔσχατοι καὶ]
οἱ ἔσχατοι πρῶτοι καὶ [ζωὴν αἰώνιον ἕξου]
σιν.

'[Jesus says,] "A ma[n full of d]ays will not hesitate to ask a ch[ild of seven da]ys about the place of [life and he will live.] For many (that are) fi[rst] will be [last and] the last will be first and they [will have eternal life]."'

Comments

22. *anthrōpos:* Of all the previous restorations of this line only C. Taylor's came close to the Coptic, *anthrōpos plērēs hēmerōn.* In fact, it is still acceptable. Also possible is *palaios hēmerōn*; so Hofius, appealing to Dn 7:9, 13, 22. This saying is to be compared with a similar one preserved in *A Manichaean Psalm-book*, published by C. R. C. Allberry (Manichaean Manuscripts in the Chester Beatty Collection, vol. 2 [Stuttgart, 1938] 192): 'The grey-haired old men, the little children instruct them. They that are six years old instruct them that are sixty years old.' Though there are differences of detail, the general idea is the same. Possibly the Psalm-book has borrowed from this passage.

23. *eperōtēse:* Misspelling for *eperōtēsai*; see note on line 18.

pa[idion hepta hēme]rōn: The passage quoted above (see note

[35] For some unknown reason J. Doresse (*Thomas*, 90) translates the future (*fnaǧnau*) as a jussive. Likewise, one wonders whence comes the expression 'il apparaîtra que' before 'many (that are) first will be last'.

on line 15) from Hippolytus (*Elenchus* 5, 7), quoting the *Gospel according to Thomas*, has a further expression that is interesting for this passage: *eme ho zētōn heurēsei en paidiois apo etōn hepta*. The idea of an old man being instructed by a small child was apparently a favourite with the Gnostics; see J. Doresse, *Thomas*, 126 ff.

24. *peri tou topou tē[s zōēs:* Cf. the Coptic saying §25 (Pl. 86, lines 4–5), in which the disciples ask, 'Show us the place (*topos*) in which you are, since (*epei*) there is need (*anankē*) for us to seek after it.' The answer given is not exactly *ad rem*, but the question shows that the idea of a 'place' of life or of the presence of Jesus concerned those who used this Gospel. According to J. Doresse (*Thomas*, 120), the same expression occurs in another Chenoboskion text, *The Dialogue of the Saviour* (MS. 1, p. 132?): 'Matthew says, "Lord, I wish [to question you] about the place of life."'

zēsete: This is Hofius' suggestion, which is surely better than my original one. It is a variant of *zēsetai* (see comment on line 18).

25. *hoti:* Inserted above the line.

polloi esontai . . .: Quoted *ad litteram* from Mk 10:31, whereas Mt 19:30 omits *hoi* before the second *eschatoi*. The form in Lk 13:30 is slightly different (Huck-Lietzmann, *Synopse*, p. 147). Cf. also Mt 20:16. Evelyn White (p. 16) has a remark that is worth quoting here. 'The Saying—however we restore it—is a remarkable instance of that salient characteristic of the Oxyrhynchus collection as a whole—the mixture of elements at once parallel to and divergent from the Synoptics. For while the first part of the Saying has nothing exactly similar in the Synoptics, it nevertheless seems related to a clearly marked group of episodes in the Gospels. On the other hand the second part of the Saying corresponds exactly with the Synoptic version. . . . The Synoptics and the Saying are indeed so close that it is incredible that the two are independent, and the evidence

. . . goes to show that it is the writer of the Sayings who is the borrower.'

26. *kai [zōēn aiōnion hexou]sin:* I am at a loss to restore the end of this saying properly according to the version in the Coptic. Is it possible that the Coptic has changed the text here or that it is based on a different Greek recension? Evelyn White (p. 15) restored [*zōēn klēronomēsou*]*sin*, but this yields thirty-four letters to the line. GH (*New Sayings*, 18) suggested, 'shall have eternal life'; cf. Jn 3:16, 36; 5:24. I prefer the latter, being one letter shorter. Lagrange's suggestion (*ibid.*) [*monoi zōēn hexou*]*sin* is also possible. See now M. Marcovich, *JTS* 20 (1969) 60–1.

FIFTH SAYING

ΛΕΓΕΙ ΙΗΣ .[
ΘΕΝ ΤΗΣ ΟΨΕΩΣ ΣΟΥ ΚΑΙ [
ΑΠΟ ΣΟΥ ΑΠΟΚΑΛΥΦΗΣΕΤ[
ΤΙΝ ΚΡΥΠΤΟΝ Ο ΟΥ ΦΑΝΕ[
ΚΑΙ ΘΕΘΑΜΜΕΝΟΝ Ο Ο[

Except for the end of the first line, this saying was correctly restored by the first editors and subsequent commentators. The Coptic version now supplies the end of that line. The fifth Coptic saying: 'Jesus said, "Know what is before your face, and that which is hidden from you will be revealed to you. For (*gar*) there is nothing hidden which will not be revealed"' (81:10–14). The Greek text may now be restored as follows:

λέγει Ἰη(σοῦ)ς· γ[νῶθι τὸ ὂν ἔμπροσ]
θεν τῆς ὄψεως σοῦ, καὶ [τὸ κεκαλυμμένον]
ἀπό σου ἀποκαλυφ<θ>ήσετ[αί σοι· οὐ γάρ ἐσ]
τιν κρυπτὸν ὃ οὐ φανε[ρὸν γενήσεται]
καὶ θεθαμμένον ὃ ο[ὐκ ἐγερθήσεται].

'Jesus says, 'K[now what is be]fore your face, and [that which is hidden] from you will be reveal[ed to you. For there i]s nothing hidden which will not [be made] mani[fest] and (nothing) buried which will not [be raised up.]"'

Comments

27. *g[nōthi to on empros]then:* Thanks to the Coptic we can now eliminate the restoration of former commentators, 'Everything that is not before . . .', and restore an imperative. H.-Ch. Puech (*RHR* 147 [1955] 128) wonders whether we should not read a masculine *ton emprosthen*, in which case our Lord would be referring to himself. The Coptic *pet^{e}mp^{e}mto ^{e}mpekho ebol* can be translated either as 'what is' or 'who is'. If the neuter is read, we may compare Clement of Alexandria, *Stromata* 2, 9, 45: *thaumason ta paronta.*

28. [*to kekalymmenon*]*:* This part of the saying is variously preserved in the Synoptic tradition, with Luke giving us two versions of it. See Mk 4:22—Lk 8:17 and Mt 10:26—Lk 12:2 (Huck-Lietzmann, *Synopse*, p. 74). 'In the first of these groups, where Luke is clearly dependent upon Mark, the Saying occurs in a series of disconnected logia and is therefore without context; but in the second we find it in the Charge to the Twelve (*Matth.* x 5 ff.), or to the Seventy (*Luke* x 1 ff.), though the third evangelist defers some of the most characteristic matter—including the parallel to the present Saying—to chapter xii. Our authorities for the Saying in its two-fold form are, then, Mark (for Group I) and Q (for Group II). . . . Grenfell and Hunt consider it to agree with Matthew and Luke (Group II) in general arrangement, but with Mark in the language of the first clause of the second half. . . . Now the first clause of the second half of Saying IV coincides word for word with the Lucan parallel in Group I, and it therefore seems likely that Mark should be left out of the matter altogether. . . . It may, then, be claimed that the Saying is dependent partly upon the Q tradition, and partly upon the Lucan version of Mark's tradition' (Evelyn White, p. 18). Actually, the saying which is preserved in the Oxyrhynchus fragment and in the Coptic version is not exactly identical with any of the canonical forms of the saying; the greatest similarity is found in the third member of the saying with the beginning of Lk 8:17, while the second

member best resembles Mt 10:26, but the canonical version is in the negative, whereas the saying here is positive. The first and fourth members of the saying are not found in the canonical Gospels at all. H.-Ch. Puech (*art. cit.*, 128) has discovered this same saying also in the Manichaean *Kephalaia* 65 (Manichäische Handschriften der Staatlichen Museen Berlin, 1 [Stuttgart, 1940] 163): 'Know that which is before your face and what is hidden from you will be revealed to you.' He believes there is a deliberate suppression of reference to the resurrection here, evidence of a Gnostic theologoumenon.

29. *apokalyph⟨th⟩ēset[ai:* Corrected from the papyrus' *apokalyphēsetai.*

31. *thethammenon:* To be read as *tethammenon.* See next note. *ho ouk egerthēsetai:* Restoration of GH (*New Sayings*, 18). Cf. their note: 'Instead of "shall be raised" a more general expression such as "shall be made known" can be supplied; but this detracts from the picturesqueness of what is in any case a striking variation of a well-known saying.' The restoration has been confirmed by an inscription on a shroud found in the hamlet of Behnesa and bought in 1953. It is dated palaeographically to the fifth or sixth century A.D. and reads:

legei Iēsous: ouk estin tethamme
non ho ouk egerthēsetai.

'Jesus says, "There is nothing buried which will not be raised up."'

See H.-Ch. Puech, *art. cit.*, 127–8. We have then in the Greek a longer version than the Synoptic accounts or the Coptic traditions. Is it possible to say which was prior, the longer or the shorter? R. Bultmann (*Die Geschichte der synoptischen Tradition* [Göttingen, 1958] 95) and J. Jeremias (*Unknown Sayings*, 16) regard the saying as a secondary expansion of the canonical saying. I believe that this is the correct interpretation, certainly preferable to that suggested by Puech (*art. cit.*, 128–9), according to which the longer text would have been uttered by the Risen Christ and the whole saying would refer to his person (masculine *ton emprosthen*). He is inclined to regard the short version as 'propre au témoignages coptes . . . transmise par des documents émanant de gnostiques et de manichéens, c'est-à-dire de gens qui s'accordent à rejeter toute conception matérielle de la résurrection'. But the short version is also found in the canonical Gospels. The part of the saying that offers a paraphrase of the canonical saying should be regarded with the same authenticity; as for the last member, it is probably a literary embellishment of the canonical saying.

SIXTH SAYING

[..]ΕΤΑΖΟΥΣΙΝ ΑΥΤΟΝ Ο[
[..]ΓΟΥΣΙΝ ΠΩΣ ΝΗΣΤΕΥ[
[.....]ΜΕΘΑ ΚΑΙ ΠΩΣ [
[.....]ΑΙ ΤΙ ΠΑΡΑΤΗΡΗΣ[
[....]Ν ΛΕΓΕΙ $\overline{\text{ΙΗΣ}}$[
[......]ΕΙΤΑΙ ΜΗ ΠΟΙΕΙΤ[
[....]ΗΣ ΑΛΗΘΕΙΑΣ ΑΝ[
[.........]Ν Α[.]ΟΚΕΚΡ[
[.........]ΚΑΡΙ[..] ΕΣΤΙΝ [
[............]Ω ΕΣΤ[
[..............]ΙΝ[
. . . .

Though Grenfell and Hunt (*New Sayings*, 19) admitted that this saying was 'broken beyond hope of recovery', some commentators succeeded in correctly restoring some of the lines. Due to the Coptic version we can advance the restoration still farther; however, once again we are faced with two slightly different recensions. The sixth Coptic saying runs as follows: 'His disciples (*mathētēs*) asked him; they said to him, "Do you wish that we fast (*nēsteue*) ? And in what way shall we pray, shall we give alms (*eleēmosynē*), and what shall we observe (*paratērei*) in eating?" Jesus said, "Do not lie, and what you hate do not do, for all will be revealed before heaven. For (*gar*) there is nothing hidden which will not be revealed, and nothing concealed that will remain without disclosure"' (81:13–14). From this Coptic version it is clear that the disciples were wondering to what extent they, as followers of Jesus, were to retain Jewish practices as the external observances of their religion. Jesus' answer insists rather on the internal aspects of religion. With this to guide us, we may now restore the Greek text thus:

[ἐξ]ετάζουσιν αὐτὸν ο[ἱ μαθηταὶ αὐτοῦ καὶ]
[λέ]γουσιν· πῶς νηστεύ[σομεν, καὶ πῶς προσ]
[ευξό]μεθα καὶ πῶς [ἐλεημοσύνην ποιή]
[σομεν, κ]αὶ τί παρατηρήσ[ομεν ὅταν δειπ]
[νῶμε]ν; λέγει Ἰη(σοῦ)ς· [μὴ ψεύδεσθε καὶ ὅ]
[τι μισ]εῖται μὴ ποιεῖ[τε· πάντα γὰρ ἔστ]
[αι πλήρ]ης ἀληθείας ἀν[τὶ τοῦ οὐρανοῦ· οὐ]
[δὲν γάρ ἐστι]ν ἀ[π]οκεκρ[υμμένον ὃ οὐ φανε]
[ρὸν ἔσται· μα]κάρι[ός] ἐστιν [ὃ ταῦτα μὴ ποιῶν].
[πάντα γὰρ ἐν φανερ]ῷ ἔστ[αι παρὰ τῷ πατρὶ ὅς]
[ἐν τῷ οὐρανῷ ἐστ]ιν. [

'[His disciples] ask him [and s]ay, "How [shall we] fast, [and how shall] we [pray] and how [shall we give alms, a]nd what shall [we] observe [when we sup?"] Jesus says, "[Do not lie and what] you [hate] do not do. [For all things will be full of (?)] truth bef[ore heaven. For there is nothing] hidden [which will not be (made) known. Ha]ppy is [he who does not do these things. For all] will be mani[fest before the Father who] is [in heaven.]"'

Comments

32. *exetazousin:* See Jn 21:12 for the use of this verb in disciples' questions. The question resembles in some ways that of the rich young man (Mt 19:16–22; Lk 18:18–22). It gives a bit of context to the saying, and in this respect resembles Oxy P 655:17 ff. Such an introduction we find in the following Coptic sayings: 12, 19, 21, 24, 37, 43, 51, 52, 53, 99, 113. In three cases the subject is simply 'they' (presumably 'the disciples'): 91, 100, 104. Elsewhere we find Mary speaking (21), Salome (61), a woman of the crowd (79), Simon Peter (13, 114), and Thomas (13).

33. *pōs:* It is clear that the Greek text has a slightly different

recension, for this occurrence of *pōs* does not correspond to the Coptic. We restore the future of the verb to make it similar to the construction of the rest of the Greek saying. The first three subjects about which the disciples inquire, viz., fasting, prayer, and almsgiving, are treated in Mt 6:2–4, 5–15, 16–18, but in reverse order.

34. *eleēmosynēn:* The singular of this noun occurs in Mt 6:2–4, and because the questions asked seem in some way related to this passage (see previous note), we have restored the singular. However, the plural is also possible, as can be seen from Acts 9:36; 10:2; 24:17.

35. *hotan deipnōmen:* This expression is not certain, but I am trying to render the Coptic *ena*^{e}*r paratêrei eou* ^{e}*nči* [for ^{e}*nčin*?] *ouôm*, 'we shall observe what in eating?' The reconstruction is at best a conjecture. Hofius suggests rather [*peri tōn brōmatōn*, 'beim Essen'. Is this really better? Marcovich has accepted it.

36. *pseudesthe:* The aorist subjunctive would also be possible, but I have preferred the present imperative because another occurs in the following line. Cf. H. W. Smyth, *Greek Grammar*, §1800, 1840; Blass-Debrunner, §364, 3.

37. *mis*]*eitai:* A misspelling for *miseite*; see note on line 18. Despite the appeal to a misspelling, the reconstruction can be regarded as certain because of the Coptic version. It should be noted that Jesus does not answer the questions put by the disciples but insists on other things—a fact that former commentators were not able to ascertain.

How are we to restore the end of l. 37 and the beginning of l. 38? The last two letters before the break in l. 38 suggest the original of the Coptic ^{e}*mp*^{e}*mto ebol* ^{e}*ntpe*, 'before heaven'. We have, accordingly, restored *an*[*ti tou ouranou*]. There is nothing in the Coptic that corresponds exactly to]*ēs alētheias*, which reminds us of Jn 1:14 but has an entirely different meaning, of course. The restoration here is highly questionable; Hofius' is no better. But cf. M. Marcovich, *JTS* 20 (1969) 65–6.

39. *apokekrymmenon:* See the preceding saying, ll. 28–30.

40. *makarios estin:* Is this part of the same saying? If so, then we have a different ending in the Greek that is not found in the Coptic. J. Doresse (*Thomas*, p. 91) treats this as part of a distinct saying. He has in his favour the fact that *makarios* is preserved in the Coptic of the following saying. But it would then seem that we must either shorten our restoration of l. 39 and the beginning of l. 40 or suppose that the usual introduction, 'Jesus says', has been omitted. Neither seems possible. Moreover, the letters that remain on the following lines do not seem to agree with any possible reconstruction of the Greek of the following Coptic saying. For an attempt to reconstruct it as a separate saying, see M. Marcovich, *JTS* 20 (1969) 66–7.

40. *tauta:* Refers to lying and doing what one abominates. However, the restoration of this and the next two lines is sheer conjecture on my part.

While certain elements of this saying are derived from the canonical Gospels and to that extent can be regarded as authentic sayings of Jesus, the saying as a whole is most likely the work of later compilers.

Oxy P 1

Fragment 1 measures $3\frac{3}{4}'' \times 5\frac{3}{4}''$ and represents the top part of a page from a papyrus codex. The top right-hand corner of the verso contains IA, the number 11, written in a later hand. 'As it was usual to foliate the right-hand pages of a book, the position of the numeral here is one good reason for supposing the leaf to have been so placed that the *verso* side came uppermost' (GH, *Logia*, 6). While most subsequent commentators accepted this decision of the first editors that the verso of the fragment preceded the recto, P. Batiffol questioned it.[36] That Grenfell and Hunt were correct is now shown by the order of the sayings preserved in the Coptic Gospel. Those on the verso precede those on the recto. Though the fragment has not been broken

[36] 'Les Logia du papyrus de Behnesa', *RB* 6 (1897) 502. A. Ehrhard (*Die altchristliche Literatur und ihre Erforschung von 1884–1900* [Freiburg i. B., 1900] 124) agreed with Batiffol. Also C. Bruston, *Les paroles de Jésus* (Paris, 1898).

vertically down the centre like Oxy P 654, the letters at the beginning of the lines have at times been so effaced that problems of restoration arise (especially at the beginning of the recto). However, since many of the lines are read with complete certainty, we can easily ascertain the number of letters on the normal line; line 1 has 17, line 6 has 16, line 20 has 19, line 29 has 17, line 36 has 18. A line-filler, shaped like a 7, is found at the end of three lines: 3 (with 13 letters), 17 (with 15 letters), 18 (with 14 letters). 21 lines are preserved on both the verso and the recto. As we shall see below, the verso must have contained at least 16 more lines. Consequently, we have only a little more than half of the papyrus page.

The eight sayings of Oxy P 1 correspond to the Coptic sayings 26, 27, 28, 29, 30 with the end of 77, 31, 32, 33. We shall number them here as sayings 7–14.

SEVENTH SAYING

ΚΑΙ ΤΟΤΕ ΔΙΑΒΛΕΨΕΙΣ
ΕΚΒΑΛΕΙΝ ΤΟ ΚΑΡΦΟΣ
ΤΟ ΕΝ ΤΩ ΟΦΘΑΛΜΩ
4 ΤΟΥ ΑΔΕΛΦΟΥ ΣΟΥ

We have unfortunately only the end of the Greek saying, but it is enough to show that it corresponds to the twenty-sixth Coptic saying of the *Gospel according to Thomas*, which reads as follows: 'Jesus said, "The splinter which is in your brother's eye you see, but (*de*) the beam which is in your own eye you do not see. When (*hotan*) you cast the beam out of your own eye,[37] then (*tote*) you will see clearly in order to cast the splinter out of your brother's eye"' (86:12–17).

Before we proceed to the restoration of this saying in its entirety, a preliminary problem must be discussed, which is raised by the first Greek word that is preserved in this fragment. The conjunction *kai* does not correspond to anything in the Coptic, where the adverb *tote* introduces the main clause. But

[37] Not 'la poutre qui est dans ton oeil' (J. Doresse, *Thomas*, 96).

it does correspond exactly to the canonical versions of Mt 7:5 and Lk 6:42, both of which do not have a subordinate temporal clause preceding but an imperative. Consequently, the clause immediately preceding the preserved part must be reconstructed according to the text of the canonical Gospels.

i [λέγει Ἰ(ησοῦ)ς·]
ii [βλέπεις τὸ κάρφος τὸ ἐν]
iii [τῷ ὀφθαλμῷ τοῦ ἀδελ]
iv [φοῦ σου, τὴν δὲ δόκον]
v [τὴν ἐν τῷ ἰδίῳ ὀφθαλμῷ]
vi [οὐ κατανοεῖς· ὑποκρι]
vii [τά, ἔκβαλε τὴν δόκον]
viii [ἐκ τοῦ ὀφθαλμοῦ σου]
1 καὶ τότε διαβλέψεις
2 ἐκβαλεῖν τὸ κάρφος
3 τὸ ἐν τῷ ὀφθαλμῷ
4 τοῦ ἀδελφοῦ σου.

['Jesus says, "You see the splinter in your brother's eye, but the beam in your own eye you do not see. Hypocrite, cast the beam out of your eye,] and then you will see in order to cast out the splinter which (is) in your brother's eye."'

Comments

Our restoration follows the wording of the Coptic version, except for the lines vi–vii, which we have discussed above. The vocabulary is Lucan, since the preserved part of the saying seems to be closer to Lk 6:42 than to Mt 7:5, as will be seen below.

2. *ekbalein:* GH (*Logia*, 10) noted that the preserved part of the saying 'agrees exactly with the wording of' Lk 6:42. However, a glance at a modern critical text of the NT reveals that the infinitive is found at the end of the verse. A. von Harnack (*Expositor*, ser. 5, vol. 6 [1897] 322) explained the discrepancy, noting that 'recent editors, following their preference for B [Vaticanus], have put *ekbalein* at the end, whereas all other Uncials, and also the Coptic version, show the word where we find it in the Papyrus'. This being so, the relation of the saying

to the Lucan version is clear. The close dependence of this saying on the canonical text assures it the same authenticity that the latter enjoys.

EIGHTH SAYING

ΛΕΓΕΙ
5 Ι̅Σ̅ ΕΑΝ ΜΗ ΝΗΣΤΕΥΣΗ
ΤΑΙ ΤΟΝ ΚΟΣΜΟΝ ΟΥ ΜΗ
ΕΥΡΗΤΑΙ ΤΗΝ ΒΑΣΙΛΕΙ
ΑΝ ΤΟΥ Θ̅Υ̅ ΚΑΙ ΕΑΝ ΜΗ
ΣΑΒΒΑΤΙΣΗΤΕ ΤΟ ΣΑΒ̅
10 ΒΑΤΟΝ ΟΥΚ ΟΨΕΣΘΕ ΤΟ̅
Π̅Ρ̅Α

While the Coptic is an almost exact reproduction of the Oxyrhynchus saying, it does not have the introductory *peğe IC* ('Jesus said') at the beginning. G. Garitte (*Mus* 70 [1957] 70) treats this saying as a continuation of the former, whereas J. Leipoldt (col. 486) and J. Doresse (*Thomas*, 96) separate them, following the Greek division. The twenty-seventh Coptic saying runs thus: '⟨Jesus said,⟩ "If you do not fast (*nēsteue*) to the world (*kosmos*), you will not find the kingdom; if you do not make the sabbath a (real) sabbath, you will not see the Father"' (86:17–20).

λέγει
5 Ἰ(ησοῦ)ς· ἐὰν μὴ νηστεύση
ται τὸν κόσμον, οὐ μὴ
εὕρηται τὴν βασιλεί
αν τοῦ θ(εο)ῦ· καὶ ἐὰν μὴ
σαββατίσητε τὸ σάβ
10 βατον, οὐκ ὄψεσθε τὸ(ν)
π(ατέ)ρα.

'Jesus says, "If you do not fast (to) the world, you will not find the kingdom of God; and if you do not make the sabbath a (real) sabbath, you will not see the Father."'

Comments

5. *nēsteusētai:* Misspelling for *nēsteusēte*; see note above on Oxy P 654:18.

ton kosmon: The accusative case here is strange, and former commentators made all sorts of suggestions regarding the interpretation of it. Comparing Clement of Alexandria's expression, *makarioi . . . hoi tou kosmou nēsteuontes* (*Stromata* 3, 15, 99), some regarded it 'as a clerical error for *tou kosmou*'! (e.g., C. Taylor, *The Oxyrhynchus Logia and the Apocryphal Gospels* [Oxford, 1899] 11–13). Others tried to make an accusative of time out of it.[38] However, the sense of the expression is now clear to us from the Coptic, which preserves for us the two Greek words, *nēsteue* and *kosmos* (possibly because the expression was strange to the Coptic translators too!), and adds the preposition *e*, 'to', before the latter word. Hence, the sense is 'to fast to the world'. Since we have no reason to consider the Greek defective, we must regard the accusative as one of respect. 'Fasting to the world' must mean a withdrawal from a worldly or secular outlook; it is an abstention from the world that involves becoming a 'solitary' (*monachos*). See now A. Guillaumont (*BIFAO* 61 [1962] 15–23); A. Baker, *JBL* 84 (1965) 291–4. Both writers have shown that in Syriac there are two forms of an expression which has the same basic meaning, 'abstaining from the world': *ṣūm min ʿālᵉmā* and *ṣūm lᵉʿālᵉmā*. The latter may underlie both the Greek *nēsteuein kosmon* (where the *l* would have been understood as the sign of the accusative) and the Coptic *nēsteue epkosmos* (where the *e* would have been written as the equivalent of the preposition *l*, in the dative).

[38] So Batiffol (*art. cit.*, 505), citing with approval the explanation of Herz (*Guardian*, 28 July 1897) that the Greek is an excessively literal (mis)translation of the Hebrew *'m l' tṣwmw lʿwlm*, which actually meant, 'si vous ne jeûnez toujours . . .'. The most far-fetched explanation was that of P. Cersoy (*RB* 7 [1898] 415–16), who suggested that the Greek translator of this originally Aramaic saying confused *ṣwm* ('a fast') with *ʿlm* ('world') and that we should therefore read here *tēn nēsteian*, a cognate accusative, parallel to the one we have in the second part.

7. *heurētai:* Misspelling for *heurēte*; see note above on Oxy P 654:18. Note that whereas the Greek has 'the kingdom of God', the Coptic simply has *tm^{e}ntero*, 'the kingdom'. See note on Oxy P 654:15.

8. *kai:* 'The use of this conjunction as a short formula of citation, meaning, "And *he saith*," is well established' (C. Taylor, *op. cit.,* 8). Cf. Heb 1:10; *Pirqê 'Abôt* 2, 5; Oxy P 1:15.

9. *sabbatisēte to sabbaton:* Being a construction with a cognate accusative (lit., 'to sabbatize the sabbath'), it explains the peculiar Coptic construction, where the repeated word is really superfluous, *etet^{e}nt^{e}meire ^{e}mpsambaton ^{e}ensabbaton.* (The dissimilation of *bb* to *mb* in the first occurrence of the word in Coptic, but not in the second, should be noted.) The Greek expression occurs in the LXX at Lv 23:32; 2 Chr 36:21. C. Taylor (*op. cit.*, pp. 14–15) showed that it does not simply mean 'to observe the (weekly) sabbath'. In Lv 23:32 it refers to the Day of Atonement, which is to be kept as a real sabbath. Hence, it is likely that we should understand the expression in this saying in a metaphorical sense or a spiritual sense. Cf. Heb 4:9 and Justin (*Dial. w. Trypho* 12, 3; *PG* 6, 500), who uses *sabbatizein* in the sense of a spiritual sabbath opposed to the formal Jewish observance; for him it consisted in abstention from sin. Cf. Resch, *Agrapha*, §74, p. 99.

10. *opsesthe ton patera:* Cf. Jn 6:46; 14:7–9 for the exact expression. Similar expressions: 'to see God' (Mt 5:8; Jn 1:18; 1 Jn 4:20; 3 Jn 11); 'to see the Lord' (Jn 21:18; 1 Cor 9:1; Heb 12:14). For the future indicative interchanging with the aorist subjunctive, see Blass-Debrunner, §365, 3.

I see no reason why this saying could not be an authentic one. E. Jacquier (*art. cit.*, p. 110) regarded it as 'probablement authentique'. But U. Holzmeister (*ZKT* 38 [1914] 118, n. 1) labelled it 'unecht'.

NINTH SAYING

ΛΕΓΕΙ $\overline{\text{ΙΣ}}$ Ε[Σ]ΤΗΝ
ΕΝ ΜΕΣΩ ΤΟΥ ΚΟΣΜΟΥ

ΚΑΙ ΕΝ ΣΑΡΚΕΙ ΩΦΘΗΝ
ΑΥΤΟΙΣ ΚΑΙ ΕΥΡΟΝ ΠΑΝ
ΤΑΣ ΜΕΘΥΟΝΤΑΣ ΚΑΙ
ΟΥΔΕΝΑ ΕΥΡΟΝ ΔΕΙΨΩ
ΤΑ ΕΝ ΑΥΤΟΙΣ ΚΑΙ ΠΟ
ΝΕΙ Η ΨΥΧΗ ΜΟΥ ΕΠΙ
ΤΟΙΣ ΥΙΟΙΣ ΤΩΝ ΑΝΩΝ
ΟΤΙ ΤΥΦΛΟΙ ΕΙΣΙΝ ΤΗ ΚΑΡ
ΔΙΑ ΑΥΤΩ[Ν] ΚΑΙ .. ΒΛΕΙΣ[39]
. . . .

Whereas the Coptic version of this saying has preserved it for us in its entirety, the Oxyrhynchus fragment has only the first half of it. The twenty-eighth Coptic saying reads thus: 'Jesus said, "I stood in the midst of the world (*kosmos*) and I revealed myself to them in flesh (*sarx*). I found them all drunken; I did not find any of them thirsty. My soul (*psychē*) was pained for the sons of men, for they are blind in their heart and do not see that they came into the world (*kosmos*) empty. They seek further to come out of the world (*kosmos*) empty. But (*plēn*) now they are drunk.[40] When (*hotan*) they set aside their wine, then (*tote*) they will do penance (*metanoei*)"' (86:20–31).

[39] But the *editio princeps* (*Oxyrhynchus Papyri*, Part 1, p. 3) reads:

ΚΑΙ ΟΥ ΒΛΕ
ΠΟΥΣΙΝ

[40] In my opinion neither J. Doresse nor G. Garitte has translated the end of this saying correctly. The Coptic reads: *plēn tenou setohe. hotan eušanneh pouērp tote sena^{e}rmetanoei*. J. Doresse (*Thomas*, 97) translates, 'Qu'il vienne cependant quelqu'un qui les redresse. Alors, quand ils auront cuvé leur vin, ils se repentiront'. G. Garitte (*Mus* 70 [1957] 71): 'ceterum (*plēn*) nunc . . .; quando impleverint cor suum, tum paenitentiam agent (*metanoein*).' The crucial form is *setohe* (3 pl. pres. ind. of *tihe*, 'to be drunk'; cf. Crum, *Coptic Dictionary*, 456b, *tohe* for *tahe*). My interpretation agrees with that of Leipoldt (col. 486). A little higher up, my interpretation differs from that of Doresse and Garitte again, in taking *ğe ^{e}ntauei* . . . (l. 27) as the object clause of *senau* and not as a subordinate clause parallel to *ğe h^{e}nb^{e}lle* . . . (again in agreement with Leipoldt). Doresse (*Thomas*, 97) has omitted the Oxyrhynchus parallel to this 28th Coptic saying.

It should be noted how closely the Coptic translates the Greek in this saying, where we have the Greek text. For instance, in 86:22 the Coptic reads *h*^{e}*nsarx*, where we might have expected the definite article; but it is the exact equivalent of the Greek. Likewise 86:23–24 reads *laau* ^{e}*nhêtou*, 'none among them', a literal rendering of *oudena . . . en autois*. Though we cannot generalize from this instance, it should nevertheless be borne in mind when a decision is to be made about the relation of the Coptic version to the Greek text in the Oxyrhynchus papyri.

λέγει Ἰ(ησοῦ)ς· ἔ[σ]την
ἐν μέσῳ τοῦ κόσμου
καὶ ἐν σαρκεὶ ὤφθην
αὐτοῖς καὶ εὗρον πάν
τας μεθύοντας καὶ
οὐδένα εὗρον δειψῶ(ν)
τα ἐν αὐτοῖς καὶ πο
νεῖ ἡ ψυχή μου ἐπὶ
τοῖς υἱοῖς τῶν ἀν(θρώπ)ων
ὅτι τυφλοί εἰσιν τῇ καρ
δίᾳ αὐτῶ[ν] καὶ [οὐ] βλέπ
[ουσιν ὅτι ἥκουσιν εἰς]
[τὸν κόσμον κενοί· ζη]
[τοῦσι δὲ πάλιν ἐξελ]
[θεῖν ἐκ τοῦ κόσμου κε]
[νοί. πλὴν νῦν μεθύου]
[σιν· ὅταν ἀποθῶνται]
[τὸν οἶνον αὐτῶν, τότε]
[μετανοήσουσιν.

'Jesus says, "I s[t]ood in the midst of the world and I appeared to them in flesh and I found them all drunken and I did not find one among them thirsting, and my soul is pained for the sons of men, for they are blind in their heart and do [not] se[e that they have come into the world empty. They seek further to go out of the world empty. But now they are drunk. When they put away their wine, then they will do penance]."'

Comments

As Garitte has already pointed out (*Mus* 70 [1959] 70, n. 5), the Coptic version makes impossible the attempt of some former commentators to join the end of the preserved part of the verso with the first line of the recto. Grenfell and Hunt (*Oxyrhynchus Papyri*, Part 1, p. 1) themselves protested against the 'current view that there is *a priori* probability in favour of only one line being lost at the bottom of the *verso*. The lacuna may have extended to five or even ten lines.' Garitte's conclusion: 'Si le texte grec était aussi long que le copte, la lacune doit être environ 17 lignes.' My own restoration of this and the following Greek saying yields sixteen lines (numbered with Roman numerals). The Coptic version, moreover, shows the unity of this saying, which was contested by P. Batiffol, who wanted to make two sayings out of it, mainly on the basis of the change of tense in the verbs (*RB* 6 [1897] 306–7).

The reader is referred to the treatment of this saying by J. Jeremias (*Unknown Sayings of Jesus*, 69–74), many of whose remarks are still valid.

11. *estēn . . . en sarkei ōphthēn:* Jesus here speaks as a 'Divine Being'; '. . . in these words we must recognize a backward glance upon His work on the part of the still living not the risen Christ' (A. von Harnack, *Expositor*, ser. 5, vol. 6 [1897] 330). The reason for this is the shift in tense from the past (in lines 11, 13, 14, 16) to the present (in lines 17, 20, 21). Evelyn White (p. xxxvi) thought that the whole saying betrays 'incipient rather than fully developed Johannism'. See the references below for verbal parallels to Johannine writing. The whole tone of the first part of the saying should, moreover, be compared with Mt 23:37, 'O Jerusalem, Jerusalem! . . . How often I have longed to gather your children around me, as a hen gathers her brood under her wings, but you refused!' Cf. Lk 13:34.

12. *en mesō tou kosmou:* Cf. Jn 1:9, 10; 3:17; 6:14; 11:27;

12:46; 16:28; 18:37. This use of *kosmos* is distinctively Johannine.

13. *en sarkei ōphthēn:* Cf. 1 Tm 3:16; Jn 1:14; 1 Jn 4:2–3.

15. *methyontas:* This notion has Pauline affinities, cf. 1 Thes 5:7–8. The figurative use of 'sobriety' recurs in 2 Tm 4:5; 1 Pt 1:13; 4:7; 5:8 (J. Jeremias, *Unknown Sayings*, 71).

16. *deipsōnta:* Some former commentators thought that Encratite influence was to be seen in the use of this word. However, it can more easily be explained as Johannine; cf. Jn 4:13–14; 6:35; 7:37, but also Mt 5:6. For the form see note above on Oxy P 654:8.

17. *ponei:* This phrase is certainly dependent on Is 53:11, *bouletai kyrios aphelein apo tou ponou tēs psychēs autou*, as has been generally recognized. Harnack also quoted Mt 26:38; Mk 14:34; Jn 12:27 for canonical statements about Jesus' troubled soul. The tone of the second part of this saying is closely related to that of the Synoptics. See J. Jeremias (*Unknown Sayings*, 71) for the Semitisms in this part of the saying. The Coptic version shows that we are dealing with one long saying here; it is not to be divided into two sayings at this point, as A. de Santos Otero has done (*Los Evangelios apócrifos*, 95–6).

20. *typhloi eisin tē kardia:* Evelyn White (p. 34) cites a parallel expression from the Greek *Gospel according to Thomas* (A viii; ed. Tischendorf): *nyn karpophoreitōsan ta sa, kai blepetōsan hoi typhloi tē kardia.* For the idea of spiritual blindness see Ps 68/69:24; Jn 9:39; Ap 3:17; Mt 15:14.

iv. *kenoi:* Cf. 1 Cor 15:58.

Though there is no direct parallel to this saying in the canonical Gospels there is nothing in it that prevents it from being regarded at least as substantially authentic. Cf. E. Jacquier, *RB* 15 (1918) 111.

TENTH SAYING

E

Recto 22 [....]..[.T]ΗΝ ΠΤΩΧΙᾹ

The twenty-ninth Coptic saying reads as follows: 'Jesus said, "If the flesh (*sarx*) has come to be because of the spirit (*pneuma*), it is a marvel. But (*de*) if the spirit (*pneuma*) (has come to be) because of the body (*sōma*), it is a marvel of marvel(s).[41] But (*alla*) I marvel [. . . *sein?*][42] at this: how this (?) great wealth dwells in this poverty"' (86:31–5; 87:1–2).

Though we have no guarantee that the Coptic version is an exact reproduction of the Greek, one may suggest a tentative restoration somewhat as follows:

viii [*λέγει*]
ix [᾿Ι(*ησοῦ*)*ς*· *εἰ ἐγένετο ἡ σὰρξ*]
x [*ἕνεκεν τοῦ πνεύμα*]
xi [*τος, θαῦμά ἐστιν*· *εἰ δὲ*]
xii [*τὸ πνεῦμα ἕνεκεν τοῦ*]
xiii [*σώματος, θαῦμά ἐστι*]
xiv [*τῶν θαυμάτων*· *ἀλλὰ θαυ*]
xv [*μάζω ἐπὶ τούτῳ ὅτι ὁ*]
xvi [*τοσοῦτος πλοῦτος ἐνοι*]
22 [*κεῖ ταύ*]*τη*[*ν τ*]*ὴν πτωχεία*(*ν*).

Comments

xv. *epi toutō:* Cf. Acts 3:12.

xvi. *ho tosoutos ploutos:* See Ap 18:17.

22. *ptōcheia*(*n*)*:* The epsilon is inserted above the line; see note on Oxy P 654:8. The accusative can be used with the verb *enoikeō*; see Liddell-Scott-Jones, *s.v.*; E. Mayser, *Grammatik* 1/3 (1936) 219. There is no canonical saying that contains *ptōcheia*, nor any that resembles the full saying preserved in the Coptic.

ELEVENTH SAYING

[ΛΕΓ]ΕΙ [ΙΣ ΟΠ]ΟΥ ΕΑΝ ΩΣΙΝ

[41] Reading *oušpēre ᵉnšpēre pe* on Pl. 86, lines 33–4.

[42] On line 35 a word has been added that does not begin at the beginning of the line and does not otherwise seem to fit into the sentence, unless it is an adjective or adverb. Unfortunately, the first two or three letters of it have been lost; what remains of the end of it seems to be *sein*. My restoration disregards it.

[....]Ε[...]..ΘΕΟΙ ΚΑΙ[43]
[..]ΣΟ.Ε[..] ΕΣΤΙΝ ΜΟΝΟΣ
[..]ΤΩ ΕΓΩ ΕΙΜΙ ΜΕΤ ΑΥ
Τ[ΟΥ] ΕΓΕΙ[Ρ]ΟΝ ΤΟΝ ΛΙΘΟ̅
ΚΑΚΕΙ ΕΥΡΗΣΕΙΣ ΜΕ
ΣΧΙΣΟΝ ΤΟ ΞΥΛΟΝ ΚΑΓΩ
ΕΚΕΙ ΕΙΜΙ

It is this saying more than all the others that shows that the Coptic version is not a direct translation of the Greek, for we have here a bipartite saying, whereas the Coptic has preserved the two parts separately—the first part here in its proper place and order, but the second part as the conclusion of a longer, later saying. The text of the thirtieth Coptic saying: 'Jesus said, "In the place where there are three gods, they are gods. In the place where there are two or one, I am with him"' (87:2–5). And the text of the seventy-seventh Coptic saying: 'Jesus said, "I am the light which is over all of them. I am the All; the All has gone forth from me and the All has attained to me. Split wood, I am there; take up the stone, and you will find me there"' (94:22–28).

The first part of the Greek saying does not correspond exactly to the thirtieth Coptic saying, and so our restoration cannot be certain in this case. But taking a lead from the Coptic we may restore it thus:

[λέγ]ει [ʼΙ(ησοῦ)ς· ὅ]που ἐὰν ὦσιν
[γʹ θε]ο[ί,] ε[ἰσὶ]ν θεοί· καὶ
[ὅ]π[ου] ε[ἷς] ἐστιν μόνος
[αὐ]τῷ, ἐγώ εἰμι μετʼ αὐ
τ[οῦ]. ἔγει[ρ]ον τὸν λίθο(ν)
κἀκεῖ εὑρήσεις με,
σχίσον τὸ ξύλον, κἀγὼ
ἐκεῖ εἰμι.

[43] The *editio princeps* (*Oxyrhynchus Papyri*, Part 1, p. 3) gives the following reading, obviously dependent on restorations suggested by scholars:

[Β ΟΥΚ] Ε[ΙΣΙ]Ν ΑΘΕΟΙ ΚΑΙ
[Ο]ΠΟΥ Ε[ΙΣ] ΕΣΤΙΝ ΜΟΝΟΣ
[ΛΕ]ΓΩ ΕΓΩ....

'[Jesus sa]ys, "[Wh]ere there are [three g]o[ds, they ar]e gods. And where one is all alone to himself, I am with him. Take up the stone and there you will find me; split the wood and I am there."'

Comments

23. *hopou:* 'Immediately before *ou* there is part of a stroke which may very well be the end of the crossbar of *p*' (GH, *Logia*, 13). This reading is now confirmed by the Coptic.

24. [*g' the*]*o*[*i,*] *e*[*isi*]*n theoi:* Blass' brilliant restoration, followed by most commentators (see Evelyn White, p. 35), [*b',* *ouk*] *e*[*isi*]*n atheoi*, was certainly a step in the right direction. Objection cannot be made to the use of a cipher in a literary text, even side by side with a number written out, for several cases of this have been found, especially in the papyri; see Evelyn White, p. 36. The Coptic would suggest that we must read *three* instead of *two*. This, of course, yields a sentence in Greek that is as mysterious as the Coptic version. A. Guillaumont (*JA* 246 [1958] 114–16) suggests that a Semitic meaning underlies the use of *theoi* here, in that it reflects the use of Hebrew *ʾelōhîm*, such as one finds in Ps 82:1 and in the rabbinical interpretation of these (angelic) 'judges' in *Pirqê ʾAbot* 3:7. On the other hand, M. Marcovich (*JTS* 20 [1969] 68) cites the suggestion that in the Coptic text the first mention of 'gods' may be dittographical, so that one should understand the text, 'Where they are three, they are gods'. In such case, one would restore *treis* at the beginning of line 24. This is an intriguing possibility; but it is hard to accept the idea of a dittography of this sort (with words intervening). Nor is it a case of horizontal or vertical dittography.

25. *heis estin monos:* The Greek does not correspond to the Coptic here, so we cannot force it. Who is intended here? A god or a man? The first sentence would suggest that a god is meant, but then we have an obvious problem on our hands: how is the speaker to be with him? In this second sentence we find the word 'god' neither in the Greek nor in the Coptic, and there is,

moreover, an obvious reference to Mt 18:20. For these reasons I prefer to think that the sentence refers to a man. A parallel to this saying is found in Ephraem's *Evangelii concordantis expositio* 14, 24 (*CSCO* 145, 144): 'Ubi unus erit, ibi sum et ego.' But see the full context and the discussion in A. Resch, *Agrapha*, §175, p. 201. See further *Pirqê 'Abôt* 3, 2; Str-B 1, 794.

26. *autō:* I prefer this reading, since Grenfell and Hunt (*Logia*, p. 9) first read a 't' after the lacuna. The verb *legō*, which is read by most commentators, disturbs the sense. C. Clemen (*Die christliche Welt*, 29 July 1897, p. 704, n. 4) compared *autō* to the Hebrew *l^ebaddô*. C. H. Roberts ('The Gospel of Thomas: Logion 30^A', *JTS* 21 [1970] 91–2), having re-examined the papyrus itself, admits that the first letter after the lacuna can only be *g*, *t*, or (less probably) *p*. Rejecting my au]*tō* as 'linguistically weak', he prefers to remain with GH's *legō*.

27. *egeiron:* R. Reitzenstein (*ZNW* 6 [1905] 203) pointed out the occurrence of a part of this saying in a gloss of the *Etymologicum Gudianum*. Note that the order of the two members of this second part of the saying is reversed in the Coptic. See further A. F. Walls, *VC* 16 (1962) 71–6.

29. *kagō ekei eimi:* In what sense is this second part of the saying to be understood? It has often been interpreted in a pantheistic sense, or more precisely in a 'panchristic' sense, asserting the ubiquity of Jesus in the world. Cf. Eph 4:6. J. Jeremias (*Unknown Sayings*, 96, n. 2) gives a convenient list of those who so explained it. He rejects this interpretation and prefers that first suggested by H. Lisco and adopted by A. von Harnack, H. B. Swete, and Evelyn White. According to this interpretation, two pictorial illustrations are given to explain *how* Jesus is present to the individual—two kinds of strenuous work, lifting stones and splitting wood. The combination of these two types of work was probably suggested by Eccl 10:9, 'He who quarries stones may be hurt by them, while he who splits logs is endangered by them.' In contrast to the pessimism

of the Preacher, Jesus promises his abiding presence even in the most strenuous type of work.

Now the Coptic version definitely supports the 'panchristic' interpretation, if we take into consideration the full context of the Coptic saying. However, this may be a clear case in which the Coptic offers us a different redaction, for the second part of the Greek saying is separated from the first in the Coptic version, as we have already noted. Consequently, the interpretation offered by J. Jeremias may still be valid for the earlier (or at least different) Greek recension. He is, moreover, inclined to regard the second part of the Greek saying as authentic. E. Jacquier (*RB* 15 [1918] 112) called it 'douteuse'.

TWELFTH SAYING

ΛΕΓΕΙ ΙΣ ΟΥ
Κ ΕΣΤΙΝ ΔΕΚΤΟΣ ΠΡΟ
ΦΗΤΗΣ ΕΝ ΤΗ ΠΡΙΔΙ ΑΥ
Τ[Ο]Υ ΟΥΔΕ ΙΑΤΡΟΣ ΠΟΙΕΙ
ΘΕΡΑΠΕΙΑΣ ΕΙΣ ΤΟΥΣ
ΓΕΙΝΩΣΚΟΝΤΑΣ ΑΥΤΟ

This saying is exactly preserved in the Coptic version of the thirty-first saying. 'Jesus said, "No prophet (*prophētēs*) is accepted in his town; a physician does not heal (*therapeue*) those who know him"'(87:5–7). There is no need to repeat the Greek text in this case. It is translated as follows: 'Jesus says, "A prophet is not acceptable in his own homeland, nor does a physician work cures on those who know him."'

Comments

Parallels to the first part of this saying are to be found in Mt 13:57; Mk 6:4; Lk 4:24; Jn 4:44 (Huck-Lietzmann, *Synopse*, p. 18). But in no case is the wording identical. The closest parallel is offered by Lk, *oudeis prophētēs dektos estin en tē patridi autou*; but the longer forms of Mt and Mk begin in a way that is more similar to this fragment, *ouk estin prophētēs atimos ei mē en tē patridi autou kai en syggeneusin autou kai en tē oikia autou* (Mk 6:4).

Jn 4:44 echoes the Mt-Mk tradition. Luke's editorial handling of this saying in connection with one about a physician (4:23) makes us think that this saying is closer to his tradition than to the other Synoptics. See Evelyn White's comment on p. 42.

33. *poiei therapeias:* This phrase was considered to be an Aramaism by P. Cersoy (*RB* 7 [1898] 417–18); C. Taylor (*The Oxyrhynchus Logia and the Apocryphal Gospels*, 57) has pointed out that the same expression occurs in the *Protevangelium Jacobi* 20:2. Actually it reads *tas therapeias mou epeteloun* (ed. E. Amann, p. 256).

35. *geinōskontas:* For *ginōskontas*; see note on Oxy P 654:8.

The first part of this saying should be considered as authentic as the canonical parallels. The second may be authentic, or may be merely a saying constructed as an answer to the retort, 'Physician, heal thyself'.

THIRTEENTH SAYING

ΛΕΓΕΙ Ι̅Σ̅ ΠΟΛΙΣ ΟΙΚΟΔΟ
ΜΗΜΕΝΗ ΕΠ ΑΚΡΟΝ
[Ο]ΡΟΥΣ ΥΨΗΛΟΥΣ ΚΑΙ ΕΣ
ΤΗΡΙΓΜΕΝΗ ΟΥΤΕ ΠΕ
[Σ]ΕΙΝ ΔΥΝΑΤΑΙ ΟΥΤΕ ΚΡΥ
[Β]ΗΝΑΙ

Once again we have an almost exact correspondnece between the Greek and Coptic saying; the latter (the thirty-second) reads: 'Jesus said, "A city (*polis*) which is built upon a high mountain (and) is fortified cannot fall nor (*oude*) can it hide"' (87:7–10). Since the Greek text is almost perfectly preserved, there is no need to repeat it; it is translated as follows: 'Jesus says, "A city built upon the top of a high mountain and made fast can neither fall nor be hidden."'

Comments

The slight differences in the two versions may simply be translation peculiarities; the Coptic lacks the copula corresponding to *kai*, and repeats the verb 'to be able'. The whole saying is related to Mt 5:14, *ou dynatai polis krybēnai epanō orous keimenē.*

36. *oikodomēmenē:* To be corrected to *ōkodomēmenē*. GH (*Logia*, 15) pointed out that this participle is supported by a variant for Matthew's *keimenē* in the Syriac versions and in Tatian's *Diatessaron* 8, 41. W. Lock (*Two Lectures*, 13 and 26) found support for it also in a Latin version used by Hilary; A. Harnack in the Pseudo-Clementine *Hom.* 3, 67, 1 (GCS 42, 81).

37. *ep' akron orous hypsēlou:* Evelyn White (p. 44) thinks that this variant for Matthew's *epanō* is due to the influence of Is 2:2, *ep' akrou tōn oreōn*, or even of Is 28:4.

38. *hypsēlous:* An error by homoeoteleuton for *hypsēlou;* 'the scribe certainly wrote *hypsēlous*, but he appears to have partially rubbed out the *s*' (GH, *Logia*, 15).

There is no reason why the saying could not be regarded as authentic; but it is more likely a secondary expansion of Mt 5:14. I find it hard to see any connection between this saying and Mt 7:24–25, which has been suggested by various commentators.

FOURTEENTH SAYING

41 ΛΕΓΕΙ ΙΣ ΑΚΟΥΕΙΣ
[.]ΙΣΤΟΕ..ΤΙΟΝ ΣΟΥ ΤΟ[44]

This saying has been fully preserved for us in the thirty-third Coptic saying: 'Jesus said, "What you will hear in your ear (and) in[45] the other ear, preach upon your roof-tops. For (*gar*) no one lights a lamp and places it under a measuring-basket, nor (*oude*) does he put it in a hidden place; but (*alla*) he is wont to place it on a lampstand (*lychnia*) so that everyone who comes in and goes out may see its light"' (87:10–18). Only the beginning of the Greek text is preserved, and it corresponds more

[44] The *editio princeps* (*ibid.*, p. 3) gives the following reading and restoration:

42 [Ε]ΙΣ ΤΟ ΕΝ ΩΤΙΟΝ ΣΟΥ ΤΟ
[ΔΕ ΕΤΕΡΟΝ ΣΥΝΕΚΛΕΙΣΑΣ]

[45] I am indebted to G. W. MacRae, S.J., for the interpretation of this line.

or less to the Coptic; the initial pronoun is missing. We may restore it as follows:

41 *λέγει Ἰ(ησοῦ)ς· <δ> ἀκούεις*
[ε]ἰς τὸ ἓν ὠτίον σου, το[ῦ]
[το κήρυξον ἐπὶ τῶν]
[δωμάτων

'Jesus says, "What you hear in your one ear, preach that upon your roof-tops. . . ."'

Comments

41. *akoueis:* The present tense, whereas the Coptic has the future. Following the latter, we have also supplied a relative pronoun object to this verb. The Coptic version also supports the reading of line 42, which was generally adopted by the former commentators and the *editio princeps.*

The first part of the saying is an expanded version of Mt 10: 27 (cf. Lk 12:13).

The second part of the saying, which is preserved only in the Coptic version, is related to Mt 5:15; Lk 11:33; and to Mk 4: 21; Lk 8:16. See further M. Marcovich, *JTS* 20 (1969) 54–5.

Oxy P 655

The last group of Oxyrhynchus sayings of Jesus is found in the so-called Fragment of a Lost Gospel, Papyrus 655, the largest piece of which measures $3\frac{1}{4}'' \times 3\frac{1}{4}''$ and comprises the middle part of two narrow columns. It contains parts of at least four sayings[46] which correspond to the thirty-sixth to thirty-ninth Coptic sayings of the *Gospel according to Thomas*. We shall refer

[46] Fragment d of this text is very small and contains part of several words on five lines:

]TIN
]ΩΤΕΙΝΩ
]ΟΣΜΩ
]Η
]ΣΤΙΝ
].

Fragment e may be part of d, although this is unlikely (see below); it has only two letters on it:]*KO*[. I made no attempt to deal with these fragments

to them as sayings 15–18. Some of the lines of col. I are completely preserved so that it is possible to determine the normal number of letters on a line: it varies between 12 letters in line 23 and 16 letters in lines 13, 18, 22.

FIFTEENTH SAYING

[...]ΠΟ ΠΡΩΙ Ε[.....
[....]Ε ΑΦ ΕΣΠ[.....
[....]ΡΩΙ ΜΗΤΕ [...
[......]ΜΩΝ ΤΙ ΦΑ[
[.......] ΤΗ ΣΤ[.
[.......] ΤΙ ΕΝΔΥ[.
[..]ΣΘΕ [...]ΛΩ ΚΡΕΙ[.
[...]ΕΣ .[...] ΤΩΝ [..
ΝΩΝ ΑΤΙ[...]ΥΞΑ[.
ΝΕΙ ΟΥΔΕ Ν[..]ΕΙ .[.

---

in the original article. Subsequently, R. Kasser ('Les manuscrits de Nag' Hammâdi: Faits, documents, problèmes', *RTP* 9 [1959] 357–70) established the connection of frag. d with Coptic saying 24. R. A. Kraft (*HTR* 54 [1961] 261–2) sought to relate frag. e to the bottom of frag d. This attempt is, however, questionable, because though both fragments d and e come from the bottom of a column, as the lower straight margin indicates; the letters *KO* on frag. e are more or less on a line with *TIN* of the first line of frag. d. Consequently, frag. e scarcely represents the beginning of lines of the same column as frag. d. Moreover, the Greek text reconstructed by Kraft is scarcely better than Kasser's, which I follow below. Kraft's third line, though closer to the Coptic version, is too cryptic in Greek: the force of the parataxis comes through in the Coptic, but it is unfortunately lost in his form of the Greek text. The Coptic version of saying 24b runs: 'He said to them, "Whoever has ears let him hear. Within a man of light there is light and he lights the whole world (*kosmos*). When he does not shine, there is darkness."' The Greek saying can be reconstructed as follows:

[εἰ φῶς ἐσ]τιν
[ἐν ἀνθρώπῳ φ]ωτεινῷ,
[ἐν ὅλῳ τῷ κ]όσμῳ
[φωτίζει, εἰ δὲ μ]ή,
[σκοτεινός ἐ]στιν.

Its translation: 'If light is in a man of light, it shines in all the world; but if it is not, (then) it (the world) is in darkness.'—It is clear that this fragment d belonged to an earlier column in Oxy P 655.

ΕΝ ΕΧΟΝΤ[...]ΝΔ[.
ΜΑ ΤΙ ΕΝ[....] ΚΑΙ
ΥΜΕΙΣ ΤΙΣ ΑΝ ΠΡΟΣΘΗ
ΕΠΙ ΤΗΝ ΕΙΛΙΚΙΑΝ
ΥΜΩΝ ΑΥΤΟ[..]ΩΣΕΙ
ΥΜΕΙΝ ΤΟ ΕΝΔΥΜΑ Υ
ΜΩΝ

The thirty-sixth Coptic saying, which corresponds to this Oxyrhynchus fragmentary text, is much shorter than the Greek. It may represent a different Greek recension of the Gospel or a deliberate shortening of the text in the Coptic. At any rate, we can only use the Coptic as a control for the restoration of the first few lines of the Greek text. The Coptic version runs as follows: 'Jesus said, "Do not be solicitous from morning till evening and from evening till morning about what you are going to put on"' (87:24–7). Even this part of this saying does not correspond exactly to the beginning of the Greek text. We may restore it as follows:

[λέγει Ἰ(ησοῦ)ς· μὴ μεριμνᾶ]
[τε ἀ]πὸ πρωὶ ἕ[ως ὀψὲ]
[μήτ]ε ἀφ' ἑσπ[έρας]
[ἕως π]ρωὶ μήτε [τῇ]
[τροφῇ ὑ]μῶν τί φά
[γητε μήτε] τῇ στ[ο]
[λῇ ὑμῶν] τί ἐνδύ
[ση]σθε. [πολ]λῷ κρεί[σ]
[σον]ές ἐ[στε] τῶν [κρί]
νων ἅτι[να α]ὐξά
νει οὐδὲ ν[ήθ]ει μ[ηδ]
ὲν ἔχοντ[α ἔ]νδ[υ]
μα. τί ἐν[δεῖτε] καὶ
ὑμεῖς; τίς ἂν προσθ<εί>η
ἐπὶ τὴν εἱλικίαν
ὑμῶν; αὐτὸ[ς δ]ώσει
ὑμεῖν τὸ ἔνδυμα ὑ
μῶν.

'[Jesus says, "Be not solicitous f]rom morning un[til evening, nor] from eve[ning until mo]rning either [for y]our [sustenance], what [you will] eat, [or] for [your] clo[thing], what you [will] put on. [You] are worth [far] more than [the lili]es whi[ch g]row but do not s[pi]n, a[nd] have n[o] clo[th]ing. And you, what do [you lack?] Who of you can add to his stature? *He* will [g]ive you your clothing.'"

Comments

This saying is related to the canonical words recorded by Mt 6:25–32 and Lk 12:22–30, but we have either a different tradition preserved in this fragment or else a deliberate condensation. Lines 7–13 of the fragment can be compared with Mt 6:28 (=Lk 12:27); lines 13–16 with Mt 6:27 (=Lk 12: 25). Cf. also *Acta Thomae* 36 (ed. Bonnet, p. 153). There is no reason why this form of the saying should not be given the same degree of authenticity that is accorded the canonical versions. E. Jacquier (*RB* 15 [1918] 116) regarded it as authentic, but J. Jeremias (*Unknown Sayings*, 86) would consider only the last three lines as authentic. He rejects the rest because he makes of this and the following saying but one unit. Since the following saying is marked with Gnostic ideas on sexual asceticism, it is not to be regarded as authentic (*ibid.*, 17). However, I do not believe that these two sayings should be treated as one. The change of subject in line 17 is the beginning of a new saying, as is now evident from several similar cases in the Coptic version. See note on Oxy P 654:32. This saying deals only with excessive solicitude for food and clothing and the correct dependence that the Christian should have on the Father.

i. This first line can now be restored confidently, thanks to the canonical version (Mt 6:28) and the Coptic, which supplies the negative form of the saying.

4. *trophē:* Suggested by Mt 6:25.

5. *stolē:* The first editors admitted that this word was not the happiest of restorations but nothing else seems to fit and no one else, as far as I can ascertain, has come up with a better solution. R. A. Kraft (*HTR* 54 [1961] 254) would rather read *tei st*[*o*]*lei*, maintaining that 'the difference between EI and H is

very difficult to detect in P. Ox. 655, since the vertical stroke of the E has very little curvature' (p. 258, n. 6). If this is a correct observation, it would involve a simple orthographic variant.

9. *hati[na a]uxanei:* For a different attempt to interpret these words, see R. A. Kraft, *HTR* 54 (1961) 258–9. Though his appeal to a form of the verb *xainein* (instead of *auxanein*) is attractive, it is based on dubious evidence (variants in the New Testament text tradition). Until more light is shed on this textual problem, I prefer to remain with my original reconstruction.

10. GH (*New Sayings*, p. 41) did not attempt to restore the end of this line nor the lacuna in line 12. In the *editio princeps* (*Oxyrhynchus Papyri*, Part 4, p. 25) they discuss the lacunae without bringing anything new to the problem, except the possibility of reading *en[deite]* in line 12. T. Zahn (*NKZ* 16 [1905] 97, n. 1) suggested the reading *[mēd]en echont[a e]nd[y]ma. ti en[dysesth]e kai hymeis.* But the verb *endysesthe* is too long for the lacuna, as is evident from a glance at Plate 2. Hence I suggest a combination of the first part suggested by Zahn with the verb *endeite* in line 12.

13. The corrected optative form was suggested by the first editors.

14. *heilikian:* A misspelling for *hēlikian*; see note on Oxy P 654:8. I have translated the word as 'stature', but it is also quite likely that the meaning 'age, length of life'—which is the more normal meaning of the word—should be used both here and in Mt 6:27 and Lk 12:25. See AG 345.

15. *autos:* This can only refer to the Father, as in Mt 6:26. Zahn refers also to 1 Cor 15:37–38.

16. *hymein:* For *hymin*; see note on Oxy P 654:8.

SIXTEENTH SAYING

ΛΕΓΟΥΣΙΝ ΑΥ
ΤΩ ΟΙ ΜΑΘΗΤΑΙ ΑΥΤΟΥ
ΠΟΤΕ ΗΜΕΙΝ ΕΜΦΑ
ΝΗΣ ΕΣΕΙ ΚΑΙ ΠΟΤΕ

ΣΕ ΟΨΟΜΕΘΑ ΛΕΓΕΙ
ΟΤΑΝ ΕΚΔΥΣΗΣΘΕ ΚΑΙ
ΜΗ ΑΙΣΧΥΝΘΗΤΕ
....
29 Θ[

The thirty-seventh Coptic saying is an almost exact reproduction of the Greek text, in so far as the latter is preserved. 'His disciples said, "On what day will you reveal yourself to us and on what day shall we see you?" Jesus said, "When (*hotan*) you take off your clothes (and) are not ashamed,[47] and take your tunics and lay them under your feet like little children and tread upon them, then (*tote*) [you will become] sons of the Living One and you will not fear"' (87:27–34; 88:1–2). Whereas the Coptic has omitted the translation of *autō* (line 17) and *autou* (line 18), it has added *Iēsous*, which is absent in the Greek. The first part of the saying is perfectly preserved in the Greek and needs no restoration; my attempt to complete it is, of course, based on the supposition that the Coptic and Greek corresponded substantially in the second part.

λέγουσιν αὐ
τῷ οἱ μαθηταὶ αὐτοῦ·
πότε ἡμεῖν ἐμφα
νὴς ἔσει καὶ πότε
σε ὀψόμεθα; λέγει·
ὅταν ἐκδύσησθε καὶ
μὴ αἰσχύνθητε
i [*καὶ λάβητε τοὺς χι*]
ii [*τῶνας ὑμῶν καὶ θῆτε*]
iii [*αὐτοὺς ὑπὸ τοὺς πό*]
iv [*δας ὑμῶν ὡς τὰ παι*]
v [*δία καὶ πατήσητε*]
vi [*αὐτούς, τότε τὸν υἱ*]
vii [*ὸν τοῦ ζῶντος ὄψεσ*]
viii *θ*[*ε οὐδὲ φοβηθήσεσθε*]

[47] The Coptic *etetenšakektēuten ehēu empetenšipe*, 'when you take off your clothes (and) are not ashamed', has been mistranslated both by Leipoldt (col. 486: 'Wenn (*hotan*) ihr eure Scham auszieht') and by Garitte (*art. cit.*, 71: 'Quando (*hotan*) despoliabitis vos a pudore vestro et (au)feretis vesti-

'His disciples say to him, "When will you be revealed to us and when shall we see you?" He says, "When you take off your clothes and are not ashamed, and take your tunics and put them under your feet like little children and tread upon them, then you will see the Son of the Living One and you will not fear."'

Comments

19. *pote . . .:* This question recalls that put in the mouth of 'Judas, not the Iscariot' (most likely Judas Thomas, the alleged compiler of this Gospel), by the writer of the fourth canonical Gospel, 'Master, how does it happen that you are going to show yourself to us and not to the world?' (Jn 14:22).

hēmein: For *hēmin*; see note on Oxy P 654:8.

v. *patēsēte:* Clement of Alexandria (*Stromata* 3, 13, 92; GCS 15, 238) has preserved a quotation from the *Gospel according to the Egyptians*, which has a very similar statement ascribed to Jesus, 'To Salome's question, when the things about which he was speaking will be known, the Lord said, "When you tread upon the garment of shame, and when the two become one and the male (will be) with the female, neither male nor female."' See the discussion in Resch, *Agrapha*, pp. 252–4. Cf. H. C. Kee, '"Becoming a Child" in the Gospel of Thomas', *JBL* 82 (1963) 307–14, esp. 309–11; J. Z. Smith, 'The Garments of Shame', *History of Religions* 5 (1965–66) 217–38.

In this saying, at least as it is preserved for us in the Coptic version, we find the characteristic Gnostic ideas about sexual asceticism that were current in the second and third centuries A.D. These ideas force us to classify this saying in the category of J. Jeremias' 'tendentious inventions'.

SEVENTEENTH SAYING

30 ΛΕ[

Ο[

---

menta vestra et ponetis . . .'). On *kōk ahēu* see W. Till, *Koptische Grammatik* (Leipzig, 1955) §277.

ΤΑ[
ΓΥ[
ΚΑ[
Ν . [
ΚΑ[
ΗΜ[
ΣΙ[
[
[

Because of the fragmentary nature of this part of the fragment, no attempt was made in the past by commentators to restore these lines.[48] The lines that follow (41–6) correspond to the thirty-ninth Coptic saying; hence these lines (beginning at least with line 30) must correspond to the thirty-eighth. Is it possible to restore the Greek text on the basis of this Coptic saying? I have tried various possibilities, but none of them was so obvious as to be convincing, given the present reading of the fragment. Several points, however, should be noted. First of all, at least two blank lines are needed for the restoration of the following saying; these should normally be lines 39–40. But line 37 seems to contain the beginning of the word *hēmerai*, which corresponds to the Coptic. But then there is not room enough to complete the end of this saying in Greek with the present disposition of lines. However, if the fragment (c) is correctly spaced on the plate (and there is no reason to question the spacing of the editors), then at least *three* blank lines must be left between fragment (c) and (b). Secondly, in line 33 the second letter is far from certainly an upsilon; in fact, we may have there no more than one letter, gamma. The same is true of the second letter in line 38; in this case, there is a trace of a letter, but it could be almost anything.

The thirty-eighth Coptic saying: 'Jesus said, "Often have you desired (*epithymei*) to hear these words which I am saying to you, and you have no other from whom to hear them. There will be

[48] T. Zahn (*NKZ* 16 [1905] 99, n. 2) suggested the following possibilities: line 30 *le*[*gousin autō*]; 31 *ho*[*i mathētai autou*]; 33 *gy*[*nē* or *gy*[*mnos*; 35 *hēm*[*eis*.

days, when you will seek me (and) you will not find me''' (88: 2–7).

This saying is related to one that is preserved for us in Irenaeus, *Adv. haer.* 1, 20, 2, *pollakis epethymēsa⟨n⟩ akousai hena tōn logōn toutōn kai ouk eschon ton erounta.* See also Epiphanius, *Pan.* 34, 18, 13 (GCS 31, 34). Resch (*Agrapha*, §139, p. 179) thinks that it is an extracanonical parallel to Lk 10:24 and Mt 13:17. If we use these various leads, we arrive at a Greek form of the saying that is possible, but which is not altogether satisfying when an attempt is made to fit it to the letters that remain on the fragment.

30 λέ[γει Ἰ(ησοῦ)ς· π]
ο[λλάκις ἐπεθυμήσα]
τα[ι ἀκοῦσαι τοὺς λό]
γ[ους οὓς ὑμῖν λέγω]
κα[ὶ οὐκ ἔχετε τὸ]
35 ν [ἐροῦντα ὑμῖν]
κα[ὶ ἐλεύσονται]
ἡμ[έραι ὅτε ζητή]
38 σε[τέ με καὶ οὐχ εὑ]
i [ρήσετέ με.

Comments

I admit that my restoration is quite questionable in many places, but I propose it in the hope that someone will be fortunate enough to see more clearly and make the proper adjustments.

30. The breaking up of *pollakis*, as I have restored the text, is most improbable.

31. The ending *ai* on *epethymēsatai* instead of *epethymēsate* can be paralleled in these papyrus fragments; see note on Oxy P 654:18.

34. The breaking up of *ton* is proposed as a parallel to that of *ouk* in Oxy P 1:30–31 and 655:45–46.

36. *eleusontai hēmerai:* Cf. Mt 9:15. Cyprian, *Testimoniorum libri tres ad Quirinum* 3, 29 (CSEL 3, 143).

37. *zētēsete me:* Cf. Jn 7:34, 36.

EIGHTEENTH SAYING

[
[
ΕΛ[
ΤΗΣ [
ΚΡΥΨ[
ΕΙΣΗΛ[
ΕΙΣΕΡ[
ΚΑΝ[
ΔΕ ΓΕΙ[
ΜΟΙΩ[
ΚΕΡΑΙ[
ΡΑ[
....

As can be seen, lines 41–50 contain but a few letters (a maximum of five) at the beginning of the lines. V. Bartlet succeeded in identifying lines 41–6 as a variant of Lk 11:52, *ouai hymin tois nomikois, hoti ērate tēn kleida tēs gnōseōs; autoi ouk eisēlthate kai tous eiserchomenous ekōlysate* (GH, *New Sayings*, 44). C. Taylor (*op. cit.*, 23) subsequently identified lines 47–50 as related to Mt 10:16, *ginesthe oun phronimoi hōs hoi opheis kai akeraioi hōs hai peristerai.* They were both on the right track, as the Coptic version now shows, but we can still improve on their restoration. The thirty-ninth Coptic saying reads thus: 'Jesus said, "The Pharisees and the scribes have received the keys of knowledge (*gnōsis*); they have hidden them and have not (*oute*) entered, and those who wished to enter they have not permitted. But (*de*) you, become wise (*phronimos*) as the serpents and guileless (*akeraios*) as the doves"' (88:7–13). We may now restore the Greek text as follows:

i [λέγει]
[᾿Ι(ησοῦ)ς· οἱ Φαρισαῖοι καὶ]
[οἱ γραμματεῖς ἀπ]
ἔλ[αβον τὰς κλεῖδας]
τῆς [γνώσεως καὶ ἀπέ]
κρυψ[αν αὐτάς· οὔτε]
εἰσῆλ[θον οὔτε τοὺς]

εἰσερ[χομένους ἀφῆ]
καν [εἰσελθεῖν. ὑμεῖς]
δὲ γεί[νεσθε φρόνι]
μοι ὡ[ς οἱ ὄφεις καί ἀ]
κέραι[οι ὡς αἱ περιστε]
ρα[ί.

'Jesus says, "The Pharisees and the scribes have received the keys of knowledge and have hidden them; neither have they entered nor permitted those who would enter. But you become wise as the serpents and guileless as the doves."'

Comments

The Coptic now agrees with the Greek in every instance except in lines 44–5, where we had to restore the participle as in Lk 11:52, instead of the clause, 'those who wished to enter'.

40. *apelabon:* Having thus restored the text on the basis of the Coptic version, I read in G. Quispel's article (*VC* 11 [1957] 202, n. 17) that I had been anticipated by J. H. A. Michelsen, who suggested long ago reading *el*[*abon*], referring to Pseudo-Clementine *Hom.* 18, 15.

42. *gnōseōs:* Cf. Pseudo-Clementine *Hom.* 18, 16, 2 (GCS 42, 248): *apekrypton tēn gnōsin tēs basileias kai oute autoi eisēlthan oute tois boulomenois eiselthein pareschon.* This form is actually quite close to the Coptic.

apekrypsan: The Codex Bezae on Lk 11:52 reads a form of this verb instead of *ērate.* For a previous reconstruction that is close to my own, see A. de Santos Otero, *Los Evangelios apócrifos*, 83.

44. *eisēlthon:* Or *eisēlthan.*

45. *eiser*[*chomenous*]*:* I now prefer to follow Michelsen, Hofius, and Kraft in the reconstruction of this line.

47. *geinesthe:* For *ginesthe*; see note on Oxy P 654:8.

While E. Jacquier (*RB* 15 [1918] 117) was inclined to regard this saying as authentic, it is much more likely that in its present form it is a conflation of two canonical sayings.

Concluding Remarks

From the foregoing detailed comparison of the Greek sayings of Jesus preserved in the three Oxyrhynchus fragments with the Coptic Gospel it should be evident that we are dealing with two different copies of the *Gospel according to Thomas*. There can no longer be any doubt about the fact that the Oxyrhynchus fragments 1, 654, 655 are part of the *Gospel according to Thomas*. This conclusion is imposed on us by the prologue which introduces the fragments and, even more so, by the almost identical order of sayings within the fragments and the Coptic version. The identification of these fragments with the *Gospel according to Thomas* eliminates all the previous speculation about their relationship to the *logia* that Matthew collected, or to the *logia* on which Papias commented; nor are they part of the *Gospel according to the Egyptians* (so Harnack), nor of the *Gospel according to the Hebrews* (so Batiffol, Grenfell and Hunt, and the majority of critics after them), nor of the *Gospel of the Ebionites* (so Zahn)—not to mention the fantastic opinion of H. A. Redpath, that they are 'a fragment of perhaps some apocryphal gospel claiming to give a sort of *procès verbal* of the indictment or evidence used at the trial of Christ'.[49] The fact that in one or two instances this collection preserves a saying that is also found in one or other of these Gospels does not weaken in the least the identification which is now established. All that can be said on this score is that these other Gospels have preserved the same saying. In fact, given the peculiar character of the *Gospel according to Thomas* as a collection of Jesus' sayings, we would naturally expect some of the Agrapha preserved in other writings to turn up here.[50] Moreover, there are many more Coptic sayings which can be paralleled elsewhere than the few

[49] *Expositor*, ser. 5, vol. 6 (1897) 228.

[50] Apparently those entrusted with the official edition of the *Gospel according to Thomas* are convinced that the principal sources of the sayings are, beside the canonical Gospels, the *Gospels according to the Egyptians* and *according to the Hebrews*. So W. C. Till (*BJRL* 41 [1958–59] 451); H.-Ch. Puech (*CRAIBL*, 1957, p. 160); G. Quispel (*VC* 11 [1957] 194). Should

from the Oxyrhynchus papyri which we happen to have studied in this article.

While in most cases we found an almost word-for-word identity between the Greek and the Coptic versions, there are some differences which force us to conclude that we are not dealing with the same recension of the *Gospel according to Thomas* in the two languages. Allowance must be made, of course, for translation differences, which do not really prove a difference of recension. But there are variants, e.g., shorter and longer versions, or a change in order, which clearly point to a difference in recension. Though it is possible that another Greek recension existed, of which the Coptic is a faithful rendering, it is much more likely that the Coptic version is an adapted translation—most likely with adaptations made to suit some of the theologoumena of the Gnostics who used or translated the Gospel.

This difference of recension, however, is not such as to hinder us from using the Coptic as a guide for the restoration of the lacunae in the Greek text.[51] In some instances we had to depart from the Coptic version since the extant Greek words would not permit a literal translation back into Greek. Nevertheless, the Coptic recension supplies the tenor of the saying and enables us to correct many of the former restorations which were quite acceptable previously because of the lack of an extrinsic guide such as we now have in the Coptic.

---

not the similar positions taken by scholars in the past about the relation of the Oxyrhynchus fragments to these Gospels teach us to be more cautious? After all, what we know of these two Gospels is nothing more than a series of quotations preserved in various patristic writers. To postulate such a collection as the source of the complete Gospel which we now have is to go beyond the evidence. It may be that the *Gospel according to Thomas* is the source of the quotations found in those Gospels, or again maybe all three depend on a common source.

[51] The closeness of the relationship of the Greek and Coptic recensions can be seen from the following list, which attempts to sum up the degree of correspondence which exists between the various sayings. Sayings 10, 14, and 17 are so fragmentary that no judgment can be based on them. But Sayings 8, 12, and 13 are not fragmentary, and of these 12 is identical with

The Gospel to which these Oxyrhynchus fragments belong is not the *Infancy Gospel according to Thomas the Israelite Philosopher.*[52] It is rather another *Gospel according to Thomas*, which was well known in antiquity. I have cited above a passage from Hippolytus, who *c.* A.D. 230 tells us that the Naassenes, a Gnostic sect of the third century, used *to kata Thōman epigraphomenon euangelion.*[53] Likewise Origen mentioned a short time later a heterodox Gospel, *to kata Thōman euangelion*, which existed in his day together with a *Gospel according to Matthias.*[54] Eusebius probably echoed his information, when he spoke of *Thōma euaggelion* as one of those 'revered by the heretics under the name of the Apostles'. Jerome too derived from Origen his

---

the Coptic and the other two are almost identical, having slight variants which we may ascribe to translation and not to a different recension. In the case of the fragmentary sayings we must distinguish between (*a*) those which are split vertically down the centre (Prologue, Sayings 1–6 on Oxy P 654, 11 on Oxy P 1, 18 on Oxy P 655) and (*b*) those which lack a beginning or end, but have the remaining lines well preserved (Sayings 7, 9, and 16). In group *b* we have once again an almost identical correspondence in which the slight variants are most probably due to the translation and not to a difference in recension. In group *a* Saying 2 is shorter than the Coptic, Sayings 5, 6, 11 (=Coptic Sayings 30 and part of 77), 15 contain a longer and different ending, thus giving evidence of a different recension; possibly Saying 4 also belongs here. But the other sayings in this group (Prologue, 3, 18) manifest in their preserved parts an almost identical correspondence with the Coptic again. Hence the number of cases in which we find an exact or almost exact correspondence with the Coptic justifies our using the Coptic as a guide to the restoration of the Greek text, even though we do admit recensional differences, which we have carefully noted at the proper places.

52 See M. R. James, *The Apocryphal New Testament*, 49–70. Anyone who compares the text of the Coptic *Gospel according to Thomas* with this Infancy Gospel will see that it is of an entirely different genre and a completely independent composition. At the time of Cullmann's lectures in the United States on the *Gospel according to Thomas* some Catholic newspapers quoted 'a leading Vatican Biblical expert', Mgr Garofalo, to this effect: the document on which Cullmann had lectured was 'only a new edition of a well-known apocryphal "Gospel of St Thomas" dating from the second century and recounting miracles performed by the Christ Child' (Baltimore *Catholic Review*, 3 April 1959, p. 4). This is not correct.

53 *Elenchus* 5, 7, 20; GCS 26, 83.

54 *Hom in Luc.* 1; GCS 49, 5.

knowledge of the existence of the Gospel (*evangelium, quod appellatur secundum Thomam*, transl. of Origen's *Hom. in Luc.* 1; *PL* 26, 233; GCS 49, 5; *evangelium iuxta Thomam, Comment. in Mt.*, Prol.; *PL* 26, 17).[55] But the testimony of Cyril of Jerusalem causes a problem, for he attributes the Gospel not to the Naassenes, as did Hippolytus, but to the Manicheans: *egrapsan kai Manichaioi kata Thōman euangelion.*[56] And in another place he says, 'Let no one read the *Gospel according to Thomas*, for it is not by one of the twelve apostles, but by one of the three wicked disciples of Manes.'[57] Patristic scholars have debated whether this *Gospel according to Thomas*, attributed by Hippolytus to the Naassenes and by Cyril to the Manicheans, is one and the same. J. Quasten suggested that the Manichean Gospel was 'merely a redaction, a working over of the Gnostic *Evangelium Thomae*'.[58] The heavily Gnostic character of many of the sayings in the Coptic Gospel has already led to the conclusion that the latter is most likely the Manichean version of which Cyril speaks. The deliberate change of ending in the fourth saying, which is paralleled in the Manichean *Kephalaia*, is certainly evidence in this direction, as H.-Ch. Puech has already pointed out.[59] Unfortunately, though it is clear that the Greek text in the Oxyrhynchus papyri represents a different recension, we are not in possession of any evidence to say that this represents the *Gospel according to Thomas* which Hippolytus ascribed to the Naassenes.

Though I have remarked above that this Coptic Gospel is

[55] See further Eusebius (*Hist. eccl.*, TU 5/2 [Leipzig 1889] 169); Ambrose (*Expos. ev. Luc.* 1, 2; CSEL 32, 11); Bede (*In Lucae ev. expositio* 1, prol.; *PL* 92, 307C); Peter of Sicily (*Hist. Manich.* 16; *PG* 104, 1265C); Ps.-Photius (C. *Manich.* 1, 14; *PG* 102, 41B); Ps.-Leontius of Byzantium (*De sectis* 3, 2; *PG* 86/1, 1213C); Timothy of Constantinople (*De recept. haeret.*; *PG* 86/1, 21C); Second Council of Nicaea (787), act. 6, 5 (Mansi 13, 293B); Gelasian Decree (TU 38/4 [Leipzig, 1912] 11, 295–6).

[56] *Catecheses* 4, 36; *PG* 33, 500B.

[57] *Catecheses* 6, 31; *PG* 33, 593A.

[58] *Patrology* 1 (Westminster, 1950) 123.

[59] '. . . il est aujourd'hui évident que l'*Evangile de Thomas* dont les anciens témoignages signalent la présence parmi les Ecritures manichéennes ne fait qu'un avec notre nouvel inédit' (*CRAIBL*, 1957, p. 153).

in no way a 'Gospel' in the sense of the canonical Matthew, Mark, Luke, and John, it is nevertheless significant that it is entitled *peuangelion*. Modern New Testament scholars are wont to define a gospel-form in function of the canonical writings, a composition including the words and deeds of Jesus. Yet the ancient compiler of this collection of sayings apparently had no qualms about calling it a 'Gospel'. May it not be possible that in a collection of sayings such as we have in the *Gospel according to Thomas*, an original idea of a Gospel as the 'good news' is preserved? We recall here Papias' statement about Matthew's collection of the *logia* and the postulated source of the Synoptics, Q. I suggest, therefore, that this fact be kept in mind when discussions are engaged in concerning the nature of this gospel-form, for the ancients obviously could also call a collection of sayings a 'Gospel', even if it did lack a Passion Narrative.[60]

I do not intend to enter into a discussion here of the relation of the sayings of the Coptic Gospel to the Synoptics or to John. This relation exists, but it can only be studied in the light of all of the sayings preserved, and we have been dealing in this paper only with the parallels to the Oxyrhynchus sayings. Moreover, such a study will require a long time yet, for each of the 114 sayings must be studied individually.

Undoubtedly the *Gospel according to Thomas* is one of the most important of the Chenoboskion texts, because it will shed new light on the Gospel tradition of the early Church. While it can and will be studied for the interest it might have as a Manichean Gnostic document, bringing new information to the history of that sect, it has a value which transcends this aspect, which it shares with the other Gnostic texts, in that it also has relevance for the New Testament. It is an apocryphal Gospel, and in no way can it enter the canon as 'the Fifth Gospel'.[61]

[60] *Pace* A. M. Farrer, 'On Dispensing with Q', *Studies in the Gospels: Essays in Memory of R. H. Lightfoot* (ed. D. E. Nineham; Oxford: Blackwell, 1957) 60.

[61] News about this Coptic Gospel stirred up the usual journalistic sensa-

Bibliography of the Oxyrhynchus Sayings

Anonymous, 'Extra-canonical Scriptures', *Academy* 52 (1897) 83; 'Further Research on the Logia', *The Independent*, 2 Sept. 1897, p. 13; Notice of GH, *Logia*, in *Critical Review of Theological and Philosophical Literature* 7 (1897) 485–6; Notice of GH, *New Sayings*, *ibid.*, 14 (1904) 467–8; Notice of GH, *Logia*, in *ChQR* 45 (1897) 215–20; 'The New Sayings of Jesus', *ibid.*, 58 (1904) 422–32; 'The New Logia', *The Independent*, 22 July 1897, p. 12; 'The Sayings of Christ', *ibid.*, 19 Aug 1897, pp. 8–9; 'The "Sayings of Jesus"', *Spectator* 79 (1897) 75–6; 'The Danger of False "Sayings of Christ"', *ibid.*, 107–8; 'What are the New Logia?', *Speaker*, 17 July 1897, pp. 64–5; Abbott, E. A., 'The Logia of Behnesa or the New "Sayings of Jesus"', *AJT* 2 (1898) 1–27; Andrews, H. T., 'Logia', *Encyclopaedia Britannica*, 11th ed., 16 (1911) 878–9; **B**acon, B. W., 'The New Sayings of Jesus', *The Independent*, 22 July 1897, pp. 14–15; Badham, F. P., 'The New Logia', *Athenaeum* 3641 (7 Aug. 1897) 192–3; Bardenhewer, O., *Geschichte der altkirchlichen Litteratur* (Freiburg i. B.; vol. 1 [2nd ed.; 1913]) 511–12, 539–42; Bartlet, V., 'The New Logia', *Athenaeum* 3639 (23 July 1897) 129; 'The Oxyrhynchus "Sayings of Jesus"', *Contemporary Review* 87 (Jan.–June 1905) 116–25; 'The Oxyrhynchus "Sayings of Jesus" in a New Light', *Expositor*, ser. 8, vol. 23 (1922) 136–59; Review of C. Taylor, *The Oxyrhynchus Sayings of Jesus Found in 1903 . . .*, *Review of Theology and Philosophy* 1 (1905) 11–18; Review of Evelyn White, *JTS* 23 (1921–22) 293–300; Batiffol, P., 'Les logia du papyrus de Behnesa', *RB* 6 (1897) 501–15; 'Nouveaux fragments évangéliques de Behnesa', *ibid.*, n.s. 1 (1904) 481–93; Bauer, W., *Das Leben Jesu im Zeitalter der neutestamentlichen Apokryphen* (Tübingen, 1909); Berlin, M., 'The Logia', *JQR* 10 (1897–98)

---

tionalism. Unfortunately, it is not the first time that journalists announced to the world the discovery of a 'Fifth Gospel'. See F.-M. Braun, 'A propos d'un "Cinquième Evangile"', *VieInt* 34 (1935) 220–4. At that time it was a question of some *Fragments of an Unknown Gospel*, published by H. I. Bell and T. C. Skeat (London, 1935).

190; Besson, E., *Les logia agrapha: Paroles du Christ qui ne se trouvent pas dans les évangiles canoniques* (Bihorel-lez-Rouen, 1923); Blass, F., 'Das neue Logia-Fragment von Oxyrhynchus', *Evangelische Kirchenzeitung* 1897, pp. 498–500; Bonaccorsi, G., *I vangeli apocrifi, testo greco-latino e traduzione italiana* (Florence, 1948); **Buonaiuti, E.,** *Detti extracanonici di Gesù* (Scrittori cristiani antichi 11; Rome, 1925); Bruston, C., *Fragments d'un ancien recueil de paroles de Jésus* (Paris, 1905); *Les paroles de Jésus récemment découvertes en Egypte, et remarques sur le texte du fragment de L'Evangile de Pierre* (Paris, 1898); Cabrol, F., 'Agrapha', *DACL* 1 (1907) 979–84; Causse, A., *Les nouveaux logia de Jésus* (Paris, 1898); Cersoy, P., 'Quelques remarques sur les logia de Benhesa [*sic*]', *RB* 7 (1898) 415–20; 'Un mot sur la deuxième sentence du papyrus découvert en 1897 à Behnesa', *L'Université Catholique*, n.s. 28 (1898) 150–3; Chiappelli, A., 'Le nuove Parole di Gesù scoperte in un papiro egizio', *Nuova Antologia*, ser. 4, vol. 71 (1897) 524–34; Christie, F. A., Review of GH, *Logia*, in *The New World* 6 (1897) 576–9; Clemen, C., 'Neugefundene Jesusworte?', *Die christliche Welt*, 29 July 1897, 702–5; Cobern, C. M., 'The Oldest Leaf of the New Testament', *Biblia* 10 (1897–98) 255–7; 'The Recently Discovered "Sayings of Christ" and the Oldest Leaf of the New Testament', *Homiletic Review*, 34 (1897) 505–10; Cotton, J. S., 'Greek Papyri from Egypt', *Biblia* 10 (1897–98) 153–9; 'Latest Views of the Logia', *ibid.*, 315–18; 'The Logia Not Pantheistic', *ibid.*, 213–14; Couard, L., *Altchristliche Sagen über das Leben Jesu und der Apostel* (Gütersloh, 1908); Cross, J. A., 'The Sayings of Jesus', *Expositor*, ser. 5, vol. 6 (1897) 257–67; Davidson, T., Review of GH, *Logia*, in *International Journal of Ethics* 8 (1897–98) 106–10; Deissmann, A., 'On the Text of the Second Logia Fragment from Oxyrhynchus', *Light from the Ancient East* (tr. by L. R. N. Strachan; London, 1910) App. 2, pp. 436–40 [first published in *Beilage zur Allgemeinen Zeitung* (Munich) no. 162, 18 July 1904, pp. 116 ff.]; Dietrich, E. L., *Ausserbiblische Worte Jesu: Grundtext und Übertragung* (Wiesbaden, 1950); Donovan, J., *The Logia in Ancient and Recent Literature*

(Cambridge, 1924); Dräseke, J., Review of GH, *Logia*, in *Wochenschrift für klassische Philologie* 14 (1897) 1171–4; D. R. J., 'Sentences de Jésus', *RevBén* 15 (1897) 433–9; Dunkerley, R., 'The Oxyrhynchus Gospel Fragments', *HTR* 23 (1930) 19–37; *The Unwritten Gospel, Ana and Agrapha of Jesus* (London, 1925); Durand, A., 'Bulletin d'archéologie biblique (part VI)', *Etudes* 72 (1897) 416–20; E. D. V., 'Recent Articles on the Logia', *Biblical World* 10 (1897) 304–8; Ehrhard, A., *Die altchristliche Literatur und ihre Erforschung von 1884–1900* 1 (Strassburger theologische Studien, erster Supplementband; Freiburg i. B., 1900) 124 ff.; Eisler, R., *Iēsous basileus ou basileusas* 2 (Heidelberg, 1930) 218–25; Esser, G., 'Die neu aufgefundenen Sprüche Jesu', *Katholik* 78 (1898) 137–51; Fisher, F. H., 'The New Logia of Jesus', *ExpT* 9 (1897–98) 140–3; Fonseca, L. G. da, 'Agrapha', *VD* 2 (1922) 300–9; Gebhardt, O. von, Review of GH, *Logia*, in *Deutsche Literaturzeitung* 18 (1897) 1281–3; Gomez, J. J., *Loguia o dichos del Señor extraevangélicos: Estudio bíblico-histórico* (Murcia, 1935); Griffinhoofe, C. G., *The Unwritten Sayings of Christ: Words of Our Lord Not Recorded in the Four Gospels, Including Those Recently Discovered* (Cambridge, 1903); Harnack, A., *Über die jüngst entdeckten Sprüche Jesu* (Leipzig and Tübingen, 1897)[translated in *Expositor*, ser. 5, vol. 6 (1897) 321–40; 401–16]; 'Über einige Worte Jesu, die nicht in den kanonischen Evangelien stehen, nebst einem Anhang über die ursprüngliche Gestalt des Vater-Unsers', *Sitzungsberichte der königlichen preussischen Akademie der Wissenschaften* (1904) pp. 170–208; Harris, J. R., 'The "Logia" and the Gospels', *Contemporary Review* 72 (July–Dec., 1897) 341–8; Heinrici, G., 'Die neuen Herrensprüche', *Theologische Studien und Kritiken* 78 (1905) 188–210; Review of GH, *Logia*, in *TLZ* 22 (1897) 449–55; Review of Harnack, *Über die . . .*, in *ibid.*, 455–7; Review of GH, *New Sayings*, *ibid.*, 29 (1904) 428–31; Hennecke, E., 'Agrapha', *Realencyklopädie für protestantische Theologie und Kirche* 23 (3rd ed.; 1913) 16–25; *Neutestamentliche Apokryphen* (2nd ed.; Tübingen, 1924) pp. 35–7,

49–54, 56–8; Hilgenfeld, A., 'Neue Logia Jesu', *Zeitschrift für wissenschaftliche Theologie* 47 (n.s. 12, 1903–04) 414–18; 'Neue gnostische Logia Jesu', *ibid.*, 567–73; 'Die neuesten Logia-Funde von Oxyrhynchus', *ibid.*, 48 (n.s. 13, 1904–5) 343–53; Holtzmann, H., 'Literatur zum Neuen Testament: IV. Evangelienfrage', *Theologischer Jahresbericht* 17 (1897) 115–18; 18 (1898) 148–50; 'Neue Sprüche Jesu', *Protestantisches Monatsheft* 1 (1897) 385–92; Holtzmeister, U., 'Unbeachtete patristische Agrapha', *ZKT* 38 (1914) 113–43; 39 (1915) 98–118; Horder, W. G., *Newly Found Words of Jesus* (London, 1904); **J**acobs, J., 'The New "Logia"', *JQR* 10 (1897–98) 185–90; Jacobus, M. W., 'The Newly Discovered "Sayings of Jesus"', *Hartford Seminary Record* 8 (1897) 5–17; Jacquier, E., 'Les sentences de Jésus récemment découvertes', *L'université catholique* n.s. 27 (1897) 542–72; 'Les sentences du Seigneur extracanoniques (les Agrapha)', *RB* 15 (1918) 93–135; James, M. R., *The Apocryphal New Testament, Being the Apocryphal Gospels, Acts, Epistles and Apocalypses* (Oxford, 1953); 'The New Sayings of Christ', *Contemporary Review* 72 (July–Dec., 1897) 153–60; Jenkinson, J. H., *The Unwritten Sayings of the Lord* (London, 1925); Jeremias, J., *Unknown Sayings of Jesus* (tr. by R. H. Fuller; New York, 1957); Johnson, S. E., 'Stray Pieces of Early Christian Writing', *JNES* 5 (1946) 40–54; Jülicher, A., Review of GH, *Logia*, and Harnack, *Über die*, . . ., in *Göttingsche gelehrte Anzeigen* 159 (1897) 921–9; **K**lostermann, E., *Apocrypha II: Evangelien* (Kleine Texte 8; 3rd ed.; Berlin, 1929); *Apocrypha III: Agrapha, Slavische Josephusstücke, Oxyrhynchus-Fragment 1911* (Kleine Texte 11; 2nd ed.; Bonn, 1911); 'Zu den Agrapha', *ZNW* 6 (1905) 104–6; Krüger, G., Review of GH, *Logia*, and Harnack, *Über die* . . ., in *Literarisches Centralblatt*, 14 Aug. 1897, 1025–8; **L**agrange, M.-J., 'Une des paroles attribuées à Jésus', *RB* 30 (1921) 233–7; 'La seconde parole d'Oxyrhynque', *ibid.*, 31 (1922) 427–33; Lake, K., 'The New Sayings of Jesus and the Synoptic Problem', *HibbJ* 3 (1904–05) 332–41; Lataix, J., 'Une nouvelle série d'*Agrapha*', *Revue d'histoire et de littérature religieuses*

2 (1897) 433–8; Lock, W., 'The New Sayings of Jesus', *ChQR* 58 (1904) 422–32; Lock, W., and W. Sanday, *Two Lectures on the 'Sayings of Jesus' Recently Discovered at Oxyrhynchus* (Oxford, 1897); **M**cGiffert, A. C., 'The New-found Collection of Logia', *The Independent*, 26 Aug. 1897, pp. 8–9; Maas, A. J., 'Agrapha', *Catholic Encyclopedia* 1 (1907) 202–3; 'The Newly discovered "Sayings of Jesus"', *American Catholic Quarterly Review* 30 (1905) 253–67; Mangenot, E., 'Agrapha', *DTC* 1 (1903) 625–7; Michelsen, J. H. A., 'Nieuwontdekte fragmenten', *Teyler's Theologisch Tijdschrift* 3 (1905) 153 ff.; 'Uittreksels uit het Evangelie volgens Thomas', *ibid.* 7 (1909) 214–33; **N**icolassen, G. F., 'The Logia of Jesus', *Presbyterian Quarterly* (1898) 93–7; Nightingale, R. C., 'Sayings of Our Lord', *Sunday Magazine* (1897) 649–50; Noguer, N., 'Los dichos de Jesús llamados "Logia" y "Agrapha"', *Razón y fe* 51 (1918) 19–29; 204–26; **O**sborn, G., 'Note on P. Oxy 655', *JTS* 32 (1930–31) 179; **P**arker, P., 'The "Second" Saying from Oxyrhynchus', *ATR* 22 (1940) 195–8; Petrie, W. M. Flinders, 'The Harvest from Egypt', *Leisure Hour* (1897) 698–701; Pick, B., *Paralipomena: Remains of Gospels and Sayings of Christ* (Chicago, 1908); *The Extra-canonical Life of Christ* (New York, 1903); Preuschen, E., *Antilegomena: Die Rest der ausserkanonischen Evangelien und urchristlichen Überlieferungen* (2nd ed.; Giessen, 1905); *Zur Vorgeschichte des Evangelienkanons Programm* (Darmstadt, 1905); Purves, G. T., Review of GH, *Logia*, in *Presbyterian and Reformed Review* 9 (1897) 801–2; **R**auschen, G., *Monumenta minora saeculi secundi* (Florilegium patristicum 3; 2nd ed.; Bonn, 1914); Rawsley, H. D., *Sayings of Jesus: Six Village Sermons on the Papyrus Fragment* (London, 1897); Redpath, H. A., 'The So-called Logia and Their Relation to the Canonical Scriptures', *Expositor*, ser. 5, vol. 6 (1897) 224–30; Reitzenstein, R., 'Ein Zitat aus den *Logia Iēsou*', *ZNW* 6 (1905) 203; *Poimandres* (Leipzig, 1904) 239–42; Review of Evelyn White, in *Göttingsche gelehrte Anzeigen* 183 (1921) 165–74; Resch, A., *Agrapha: aussercanonische Evangelienfragmente gesammelt und untersucht* (TU 5/4;

Leipzig, 1889; 2nd ed.: 1906 [TU 15]); Réville, J., Review of GH, *Logia*, and Harnack, *Über die . . .*, in *Revue de l'histoire des religions* 36 (1897) 420–6; Rhyn, C. H. van, 'Nieuwe "worden van Jezus"', *Theologisch Studiën* 15 (1897) 403–13; Robertson, A. T., *The Christ of the Logia* (New York, 1924); Robertson, J. A., *Sayings of Jesus of Nazareth* (London, 1920); Robinson, J. A., 'Note by Professor Robinson', *Expositor* ser. 6, vol. 6 (1897) 417–21; Romeo, A., 'Agraphon', *Enciclopedia Cattolica* 1 (1948) 568–70; Ropes, J. H., 'Agrapha', *Hastings' Dictionary of the Bible* (New York, 1904) extra vol., 343–52; *Die Sprüche Jesu, die in den kanonischen Evangelien nicht überliefert sind: Eine kritische Bearbeitung des von D. Alfred Resch gesammelten Materials* (TU 14/2; Leipzig, 1896); 'What May We Expect from Christian Discoveries?', *Congregationalist*, 19 Aug. 1897, pp. 253–4; **S**antos Otero, A. de, *Los evangelios apócrifos* (Biblioteca de autores cristianos 148; Madrid, 1956) pp. 92–101; 81–3; Scholz, A. von, 'Zu den Logia Jesu', *TQ* 82 (1900) 1–22; Schubart, W., 'Das zweite Logion Oxyrhynchus Pap. IV 654', *ZNW* 20 (1921) 215–23; Selbie, J. A., '"The Logia"', *ExpT* 9 (1897–98) 548–9; 'The Oxyrhynchus Fragment', *ibid.*, 221; 'The Recently Discovered Logia', *ibid.*, 68–9; Semeria, G., *Le parole di Gesù recentemente scoperte e l'ultima fase della critica evangelica* (Genoa, 1898); Shahan, T. J., 'The Agrapha or "Unwritten Sayings" of our Lord', *AER* 25 (1901) 458–73; S. M., Review of GH, *Logia*, in *Biblical World* 10 (1897) 151–5; Swete, H. B., 'The New Oxyrhynchus Sayings, a Tentative Interpretation', *ExpT* 15 (1903–04) 488–95; 'The Oxyrhynchus Fragment', *ibid.*, 8 (1896–97) 544–50; *Zwei neue Evangelienfragmente* (Kleine Texte 31; 2nd ed.; Berlin, 1924); **T**aylor, C., *The Oxyrhynchus Logia and the Apocryphal Gospels* (Oxford, 1899); 'The Oxyrhynchus and Other Agrapha', *JTS* 7 (1905–06) 546–62; *The Oxyrhynchus Sayings of Jesus Found in* 1903 *with the Sayings called 'Logia' Found in* 1897 (Oxford, 1905); Thayer, J. H., 'The New "Sayings of Christ"', *The Independent*, 12 Aug. 1897, p. 16; Trabaud, H., 'Les nouvelles paroles de Jésus', *RTP* 31 (1898)

79–84; **U**ckeley, A., *Worte Jesu, die nicht in der Bibel stehen* (Biblische Zeit- und Streitfragen 7/3; Berlin, 1911); **V**aganay, L., 'Agrapha', *VDBS* 1 (1928) 159–98; Votaw, C. W., 'The Newly Discovered "Sayings of Jesus"', *Biblical World* 24 (1904) 261–77; 'The Oxyrhynchus Sayings of Jesus in Relation to the Gospel-making Movement of the First and Second Centuries', *JBL* 24 (1905) 79–90; **W**arschauer, J., *Jesus Saith: Studies in Some 'New Sayings' of Christ* (London, 1905); Weiss, J., 'Neue Logia', *TRu* 1 (1898) 227–36; Wessely, C., 'Les plus anciens monuments du christianisme écrits sur papyrus', *Patrologia orientalis* 4 (1908) 95 [1] 210 [116]; Wendland, P., *Die urchristlichen Literaturformen* (HNT herausg. von H. Lietzmann 1/3; Tübingen, 1912) 231 ff.; Evelyn White, H. G., 'The Fourth Oxyrhynchus Saying', *JTS* 14 (1912–13) 400–3; 'The Introduction to the Oxyrhynchus Sayings', *ibid.*, 13 (1911–12) 74–6; 'The Second Oxyrhynchus Saying', *ibid.*, 16 (1914–15) 246–50; *The Sayings of Jesus from Oxyrhynchus Edited with Introduction, Critical Apparatus and Commentary* (Cambridge, 1920); Wilamowitz-Moellendorff, U. von, 'Oxyrhynchus Papyri IV', *Göttingsche gelehrte Anzeigen* 166 (1904) 663–4; Wilkinson, J. H., *Four Lectures on the Early History of the Gospels* (London, 1898); Workman, W. P., 'Sayings of Jesus: A New Suggestion', *ExpT* 17 (1905–06) 191; Wright, G. F., 'The New "Sayings of Jesus"', *Bibliotheca sacra* 54 (1897) 759–70; **Z**ahn, T., 'Die jüngst gefundenen "Aussprüche Jesu"', *Theologisches Litteraturblatt* 18 (1897) 417–20; 425–31 [translated in *Lutheran Church Review* 17 (1898) 168–83]; 'Neue Funde aus der alten Kirche', *NKZ* 16 (1905) 94–105, 165–78.

ADDITIONAL BIBLIOGRAPHY 1969

Garitte, G., 'Le premier volume de l'édition photographique des manuscrits gnostiques coptes et "l'Evangile de Thomas"', *Mus* 70 (1957) 59–73. Quispel, G., 'The Gospel of Thomas and the New Testament', *VC* 11 (1957) 189–207. Cerfaux, L., and G. Garitte, 'Les paraboles du royaume dans l'"Evangile de

Thomas"', *Mus* 70, 307–27. Gershenson, D., and G. Quispel, 'Meristae', *VC* 12 (1958) 19–26. Quispel, G., 'L'Evangile selon Thomas et les Clémentines', *VC* 12 (1958) 181–96; 'Het Luikse "Leven van Jezus" en het jodenchristelijke "Evangelie der Hebreën"', *De nieuwe Taalgids* 51 (1958) 241–9; 'Neugefundene Worte Jesu', *Universitas* 13 (1958) 359–66. Leipoldt, J., 'Ein neues Evangelium? Das koptische Thomas-evangelium, übersetzt und besprochen', *TLZ* 83 (1958) 481–96. Prigent, P., 'Ce que l'oeil n'a pas vu, I Cor 2, 9: Histoire et préhistoire d'une citation', *TZ* 14 (1958) 416–29. Doresse, J., *Les livres secrets des gnostiques d'Egypte* (Paris: Plon, 1958). Quispel, G., 'Some Remarks on the Gospel of Thomas', *NTS* 5 (1958–59) 276–90. Wilson, R. McL., 'The Gospel of Thomas', *ExpT* 70 (1958–59) 324–5. Till, W. C., 'New Sayings of Jesus in the Recently Discovered Coptic "Gospel of Thomas"', *BJRL* 41 (1958–59) 446–58. Säve-Söderbergh, T., 'Thomasevangeliet', *SBU* 16 (1959) 28–49. Prigent, P., 'L'évangile selon Thomas: Etat de la question', *RHPR* 39 (1959) 39–45. Daniélou, J., 'Un recueil inédit de paroles de Jésus?', *Etudes* 302 (1959) 38–49. Quispel, G., 'L'évangile selon Thomas et le Diatessaron', *VC* 13 (1959) 87–117. Grant, R. M., 'Notes on the Gospel of Thomas', *VC* 13 (1959) 170–80. Collins, J. J., 'A Fifth Gospel?', *America* 101 (1959) 365–7. Bauer, J.-B., 'De agraphis genuinis evangelii secundum Thomam coptici', *VD* 37 (1959) 129–46. Puech, H.-Ch., 'Das Thomas-Evangelium', *Neutestamentliche Apokryphen in deutscher Übersetzung* (3rd ed.; ed. E. Hennecke and W. Schneemelcher; Tübingen: Mohr) 1 (1959) 199–223. Guillaumont, A., *et al.*, *The Gospel according to Thomas: Coptic Text Established and Translated* (New York: Harper; Leiden: Brill, 1959). Giversen, S., *Thomas Evangeliet: Indledning, oversaettelse og kommentarer* (Copenhagen: Gad, 1959). Doresse, J., *L'évangile selon Thomas ou les paroles secrètes de Jésus* (Les livres secrets des Gnostiques d'Egypte 2; Paris: Plon, 1959). Bauer, J.-B., 'Das Jesuswort "Wer mir nahe ist"', *TZ* 15 (1959) 446–50. Piper, O. A., 'The Gospel of Thomas', *PSB* 53 (1959–60)

18–24. Bartsch, H.-W., 'Das Thomas-Evangelium und die synoptischen Evangelien: Zu G. Quispels Bermerkungen zum Thomas-Evangelium', *NTS* 6 (1959–60) 249–61. McArthur, H. K., 'The Dependence of the Gospel of Thomas on the Synoptics', *ExpT* 7 (1959–60) 286–7. Quecke, H., 'Het Evangelie volgens Thomas: Inleiding en commentaar', *Streven* 13 (1959–60) 402–24. Unnik, W. C. van, *Evangelien aus dem Nilsand* (Frankfurt: Scheffler, 1960); *Newly Discovered Gnostic Writings: A Preliminary Survey of the Nag-Hammadi Find* (SBT 30; London: SCM, 1960). Wilson, R. McL., *Studies in the Gospel of Thomas* (London: Mowbray, 1960). Grant, R. M., 'Two Gnostic Gospels', *JBL* 79 (1960) 1–11. Nagel, W., 'Neuer Wein in alten Schläuchen (Mt 9, 17)', *VC* 14 (1960) 1–8. Roques, R., 'Gnosticisme et christianisme: L'évangile selon Thomas', *Irénikon* 33 (1960) 29–40. Smyth, K., 'Gnosticism in the *Gospel according to Thomas*', *HJ* 1 (1960) 189–98. Schäfer, K. T., 'Das neuentdeckte Thomasevangelium', *Bibel und Leben*, 1 (1960) 62–74; MacRae, G. W., 'The Gospel of Thomas—Logia Jesou', *CBQ* 22 (1960) 56–71. Piper, O. A., 'A New Gospel?', *Christian Century* 77 (1960) 96–9. Beare, F. W., 'The Gospel according to Thomas: A Gnostic Manual', *CJT* 9 (1960) 102–12. Cullmann, O., 'L'evangelo di Tommaso', *Protestantesimo* 15 (1960) 145–52. Roques, R., 'L'"évangile selon Thomas": Son édition critique et son identification', *RHR* 157 (1960) 187–218. Rüstow, A., '*Entos hymōn estin:* Zur Deutung von Lukas 17, 20–1', *ZNW* 51 (1960) 197–224. Wilson, R. McL., '"Thomas" and the Growth of the Gospels', *HTR* 53 (1960) 231–50. Schoedel, W. R., 'Naassene Themes in the Coptic Gospel of Thomas', *VC* 14 (1960) 225–34. Schippers, R., and T. Baarda, *Het Evangelie van Thomas: Apocriefe woorden van Jezus* (Boeketreeks 14; Kampen, 1960). McArthur, H. K., 'The Gospel according to Thomas', *New Testament Sidelights: Essays in Honor of A. C. Purdy* (ed. H. K. McArthur; Hartford: Seminary Foundation Press, 1960) 43–77. Munck, J., 'Bemerkungen zum koptischen Thomasevangelium', *ST* 14 (1960) 130–47. Regemorter, B. van, 'La reliure des manuscrits gnostiques découverts à Nag Hamadi', *Scriptorium* 14 (1960) 225–34. Quispel, G., 'L'évangile selon Thomas et le "texte occidental" du Nouveau Testament', *VC* 14 (1960) 204–15. Higgins, A. J. B., 'Non-Gnostic Sayings in the Gospel of Thomas', *NT* 4 (1960) 292–306. Cullmann, O., 'Das Thomasevangelium und die Frage nach dem Alter der in ihm enthaltenen Tradition', *TLZ* 85 (1960) 321–34. Giversen, S., 'Questions and Answers in the Gospel according to Thomas of pl. 81, 14–18 and pl. 83, 14–27', *AcOr* 25 (1960) 332–8. Schäfer, K. T., 'Der Primat Petri und das Thomas-Evangelium', *Die Kirche und ihre Ämter und Stände* (Festgabe J. Kard. Frings; ed. W. Corsten, *et al.*; Cologne: J. P. Bachem, 1960) 353–63. Harl, M., 'A propos de Logia de Jésus: Le sens du mot *monachos*', *REG* 73 (1960) 464–74. Rosa, G. de, 'Un quinto vangelo? Il "Vangelo secondo Tommaso"', *CC* 111/1 (1960) 496–512. Michaelis, W., *Das Thomas-Evangelium* (Calwer Hefte, 34; Stuttgart: Calwer, 1960). Leipoldt, J., and H.-M. Schenke, *Koptisch-gnostische Schriften aus den Papyrus-Codices von Nag-Hamadi* (Theologische Forschung 20; Hamburg-Bersgtedt: H. Reich, 1960) 7–30. Hunzinger, C.-H., 'Unbekannte Gleichnisse Jesu aus dem Thomas-Evangelium', *Judentum, Urchristentum, Kirche* (Fest. J. Jeremias; BZNW 26; Berlin: Töpelmann, 1960) 209–20; 'Aussersynoptisches Traditionsgut im Thomas-Evangelium', *TLZ* 85 (1960) 843–6. Krogmann, W., 'Helian, Tatian und Thomasevangelium', *ZNW* 51 (1960) 255–68. Kuhn, K. H., 'Some Observations on the Coptic Gospel according to Thomas', *Mus* 73 (1960) 317–23. Leipoldt, J., 'Bemerkungen zur Übersetzung des Thomasevangeliums', *TLZ* 85 (1960) 795–8. Grant, R. M., and D. N. Freedman, *The Secret Sayings of Jesus* (London: Collins; Garden City: Doubleday, 1960). Gärtner, B., *Ett nytt evangelium? Thomasevangeliets hemliga Jesusord* (Stockholm, 1960). Doresse, J., *Il vangelo secondo Tommaso: Versione dal copto e commento* (Milan, 1960); 'Le problème des "Paroles secrètes de Jésus" (L'Evangile de Thomas)', *La table ronde* 154 (Oct. 1960) 120–8.

Zandee, J., *Een geheim evangelie* (AO-reeks 807; Amsterdam, 1960). Cullmann, O., 'Das Thomasevangelium und seine Bedeutung für die Erforschung der kanonischen Evangelium', *Universitas* 15 (1960) 865–74. Montefiore, H. W., 'A Comparison of the Parables of the Gospel according to Thomas and of the Synoptic Gospels', *NTS* 7 (1960–61) 220–48. Walls, A. F., 'The References to Apostles in the Gospel of Thomas', *NTS* 7 (1960–61) 266–70. Wilson, R. McL., 'Thomas and the Synoptic Gospels', *ExpT* 72 (1960–61) 36–9. Masing, U., and K. Rätsep, 'Barlaam and Joasaphat and the Acts of Thomas, the Psalms of Thomas and the Gospel of Thomas', *Communio viatorum* 4/1 (1961) 29–36. Schierse, F. J., 'Nag-Hamadi und das Neue Testament', *SZ* 168 (1961) 47–62. Schippers, R., 'Het evangelie van Thomas een onafhankelijke traditie? Antwoord aan professor Quispel', *Gereformeerd theologisch tijdschrift* 61 (1961) 46–54. Cornelis, E. M. J. M., 'Quelques éléments pour une comparaison entre l'Evangile de Thomas et la notice d'Hippolyte sur les Naassènes', *VC* 15 (1961) 83–104. Bauer, J. B., 'Das milde Joch und die Ruhe, Matth. 11, 28–30', *TZ* 17 (1961) 99–106. Klijn, A. F. J., 'Das Thomasevangelium und das alt-syrische Christentum', *VC* 15 (1961) 146–59. Quecke, H., 'Das Evangelium nach Thomas', *Theologisches Jahrbuch* (ed. A. Dänhart; Leipzig, 1961) 226–36. Kasser, R., *'L'évangile selon Thomas: Présentation et commentaire théologique* (Neuchâtel: Delachaux et Niestlé, 1961). Haenchen, E., *Die Botschaft des Thomas-Evangeliums* (Theologische Bibliothek Töpelmann 6; Berlin: Töpelmann, 1961); 'Literatur zum Thomasevangelium', *TRu* 27 (1961) 147–78, 306–38. Gärtner, B., *The Theology of the Gospel according to Thomas* (tr. E. J. Sharpe; New York: Harper, 1961). Grobel, K., 'How Gnostic is the Gospel of Thomas?', *NTS* 8 (1961–62) 367–73. Reichelt, J., 'Das "Evangelium" nach Thomas', *Im Lande der Bibel* 8 (1962) 9–14. North, R., 'Chenoboskion and Q', *CBQ* 24 (1962) 154–70. Klijn, A. F. J., 'The "Single One" in the Gospel of Thomas', *JBL* 81 (1962) 271–8. Cullmann, O., 'The Gospel of Thomas and the Problem of the

Age of the Tradition Contained Therein: A Survey', *Int* 16 (1962) 418–38. Turner, H. E. W., and H. Montefiore, *Thomas and the Evangelists* (SBT 35; London: SCM, 1962). Quispel, G., 'Das Thomasevangelium und das Alte Testament', *Neotestamentica et patristica* (Fest. O. Cullmann; NovTSup 6; Leiden: Brill, 1962) 243–8. Quecke, H., 'L'Evangile de Thomas: Etat des recherches', *La venue du Messie* (RechBib 6; Bruges: Desclée de Brouwer, 1962) 217–41. R. E. Brown, 'The Gospel of Thomas and St John's Gospel', *NTS* 9 (1962–63) 155–77. Saunders, E. W., 'A Trio of Thomas Logia', *BibRes* 8 (1963) 43–59. Houghton, H. P., 'The Coptic Gospel of Thomas', *Aegyptus* 43 (1963) 107–40. Schneemelcher, W., and J. Jeremias, 'Sayings-Collections on Papyrus', *New Testament Apocrypha* (ed. R. Hennecke and W. Schneemelcher; tr. R. McL. Wilson; London: Lutterworth) 1 (1963) 97–113. Strobel, A., 'Textgeschichtliches zum Thomas-Logion 86 (Mt 8, 20; Luk 9, 58)', *VC* 17 (1963) 211–24. Schürmann, H., 'Das Thomasevangelium und das lukanische Sondergut', *BZ* 7 (1963) 236–60. Kee, H. C., '"Becoming a Child" in the Gospel of Thomas', *JBL* 82 (1963) 307–14. Garitte, G., 'Le nouvel évangile copte de Thomas', *L'Académie royale de Belgique*, Classe des lettres, Bulletin, ser. 5, tome 50/1–2 (Bruxelles: Palais des Académies, 1964) 33–54. Krogmann, W., 'Heiland und Thomasevangelium', *VC* 18 (1964) 65–73. Baker, A., 'Pseudo-Macarius and the Gospel of Thomas', *ibid.*, 215–25. Quispel, G., 'The Syrian Thomas and the Syrian Macarius', *ibid.*, 226–35. Haelst, J. van, 'A propos du catalogue raisonné des papyrus littéraires chrétiens d'Egypte, grecs et latins', *Actes du Xe congrès international des papyrologues . . . 1961* (ed. J. Wolski; Wroclaw: Polish Academy of Sciences, 1964) 215–25. Bauer, J.-B., 'The Synoptic Tradition in the Gospel of Thomas', *SE* 3 (TU 88; Berlin: Akademie-V., 1964) 314–17. Stead, G. C., 'Some Reflections on the Gospel of Thomas', *ibid.*, 390–402. Wilson, R. McL., 'The Gospel of Thomas', *ibid.*, 447–59. Vielhauer, P., '*Anapausis:* Zum gnostischen Hintergrund des Thomasevangeliums', *Apophoreta*

(Fest. E. Haenchen; BZNW 30; Berlin: Töpelmann, 1964) 281–99. Schrage, W., *Das Verhältnis des Thomas-Evangeliums zur synoptischen Tradition und zu den koptischen Evangeliensübersetzungen: Zugleich ein Beitrag zur gnostischen Synoptikerdeutung* (BZNW 29; Berlin: Töpelmann, 1964). Durso, M. H., 'The Gospel according to Thomas', *BT* 16 (Feb. 1965) 1067–74. Quispel, G., 'L'évangile selon Thomas et les origines de l'ascèse chrétienne', *Aspects du Judéo-Christianisme: Colloque de Strasbourg, 23–25 avril* 1964 (Paris: Presses universitaires de France, 1965) 35–52. Mees, M., 'Einige Überlegungen zum Thomasevangelium', *Vetera christianorum* 2 (1965) 151–65. Kosnetter, J., 'Das Thomasevangelium und die Synoptiker', *Wissenschaft im Dienste des Glaubens* (Fest. H. Peichl; ed. J. Kisser; Wien: Selbstverlag der Wiener katholischen Akademie, 1965) 29–49. Koester, H., '*Gnōmai diaphoroi:* The Origin and Nature of Diversification in the History of Early Christianity', *HTR* 58 (1965) 279–318. Janssens, Y., 'Deux "évangiles" gnostiques', *Byzantion* 35 (1965) 449–54. Baker, A., 'The *Gospel of Thomas* and the Diatessaron', *JTS* 16 (1965) 449–54. Smith, J. Z., 'The Garments of Shame', *History of Religions* 5 (1965–66) 217–38. Baker, A., 'The "Gospel of Thomas" and the Syriac "Liber graduum"', *NTS* 12 (1965–66) 49–55. Quispel, G., '"The Gospel of Thomas" and the "Gospel of the Hebrews"', *ibid.*, 371–82; 'Das Lied von der Perle', *Eranos-Jahrbuch 1965* 34 (Zurich, 1966) 9–32. Ménard, J.-E., 'L'Evangile selon Thomas et le Nouveau Testament', *Studia montis regii* 9 (1966) 147–53. Schmidt, K. O., *Die geheimen Herren-Worte des Thomas-Evangeliums: Weisweisungen Christi zur Selbstvollendung* (Pfullingen: Baum-V., 1966). Frend, W. H. C., 'The Gospel of Thomas: Is Rehabilitation Possible?', *JTS* 18 (1967) 13–26. Miller, B. F., 'A Study of the Theme of "Kingdom": The Gospel according to Thomas, Logion 18', *NT* 9 (1967) 52–60. Helmbold, A. K., *The Nag Hammadi Gnostic Texts and the Bible* (Baker Studies in Bibl. Archaeology; Grand Rapids: Baker, 1967) 55–63. Schoedel, W., 'The Gospel in the New Gospels', *Dialog* 6 (1957) 115–22. Karavidopoulos, I. D.,

To gnōstikon kata Thōman euangelion (Saloniki, 1967). Leipoldt, J., *Das Evangelium nach Thomas koptisch und deutsch* (TU 101; Berlin: Akademie-V., 1967). Quispel, G., *Makarius, das Thomasevangelium und das Lied von der Perle* (NT Sup 15; Leiden: Brill 1967). Rengstorf, K. H., 'Urchristliches Kerygma und "gnostische" Interpretation in einigen Sprüchen des Thomasevangeliums', *The Origins of Gnosticism* (Studies in the History of Religions 12; Leiden: Brill, 1967) 563–74. Säve-Söderbergh, T., 'Gnostic and Canonical Gospel Traditions (With Special Reference to the Gospel of Thomas)', *ibid.*, 552–62. Ménard, J.-E., 'Le milieu syriaque de l'*Evangile selon Thomas* et de l'*Evangile selon Philippe*', *RevScRel* 42 (1968) 261–6. Summers, R., *The Secret Sayings of the Living Jesus: Studies in the Coptic Gospel According to Thomas* (Waco, Tex.: Word Books, 1968). Kim, Y. O., 'The Gospel of Thomas and the Historical Jesus', *Northeast Asia Journal of Theology* 2 (1969) 17–30.

16

THE QUMRAN SCROLLS, THE EBIONITES AND THEIR LITERATURE*

The importance of the Dead Sea Scrolls for both Old and New Testament study has been increasingly recognized, as these texts are published and studied. Though it will be many years before their exact value can be fully assessed, constant efforts are being made by scholars to interpret these documents. It is not surprising that some interpretations find almost immediate acceptance in scholarly circles, while others are rejected or subjected to long debate. For it is only by a gradual sifting process that the value and importance of these texts can be ascertained.

Shortly after the publication of three of the Qumran scrolls by the American Schools of Oriental Research, J. L. Teicher of Cambridge wrote an article in the *Journal of Jewish Studies*, in which he maintained that the Qumran sect, in whose midst these scrolls originated, was Ebionite.[1] This interpretation has not been accepted by most scholars, who prefer to regard the group who lived at Qumran as Essenes (or at least as a branch of the Essenes). Nevertheless, the fact was recognized that Teicher had indicated a source from which further information might be drawn.[2] Teicher continued to write a series of articles

* Originally published in *TS* 16 (1955) 335–72.

[1] 'The Dead Sea Scrolls—Documents of the Jewish Christian Sect of Ebionites', *JJS* 2 (1951) 67–99.

[2] A. Dupont-Sommer, *Nouveaux aperçus sur les manuscrits de la Mer Morte* (Paris: Maisonneuve, 1953) 205. W. F. Albright, 'Chronology of the Dead Sea Scrolls', Postscript to W. H. Brownlee's translation of the Dead Sea Manual of Discipline, *BASOR Suppl. Stud.* 10–12 (1951) 58, n. 3.

on the Ebionite sect of Qumran and the early Church.[3] Subsequently, however, Oscar Cullmann published an article in *Neutestamentliche Studien für Rudolf Bultmann*,[4] claiming that the remnants of the Essenes went over to the Ebionite group after the destruction of Jerusalem in A.D. 70. Another recent article, by Hans Joachim Schoeps, puts forth the theory that the Qumran sect, the Essenes of Philo and Josephus, the Ossaeans of Epiphanius, the disciples of John the Baptist, and the Ebionites (the latter as the descendants of the Jerusalem *Urgemeinde*) all became representatives of an apocalyptic-gnostic Judaism.[5] This brief survey of opinions suffices to show that the connection between the sect of Qumran and the Ebionites has been discussed in scholarly circles and that the question merits some attention. The present article intends to review the evidence for this connection and to sift the valid from the invalid claims that have been made. A *mise au point* is obviously needed, to see whether the parallels in tenets and practices of both groups are such as to warrant the assertion that the Qumran sect was Ebionite or passed over into Ebionism or even influenced the latter group.

The matter will be discussed under three main headings: the identification of the Ebionites; their literature; the comparison of Ebionites and the Qumran sect.

The sources of information regarding the Qumran sect are mainly the Dead Sea Scrolls, as published by the American Schools and the Hebrew University, as well as the Damascus

[3] Cf. *JJS* 2 (1950–51) 115–43; 3 (1952) 53–5; 111–18; 128–32; 139–50; 4 (1953) 1–13; 49–58; 93–103; 139–53; 5 (1954) 38; 93–9; *ZRGG* 3 (1951) 193–209; *VT* 5 (1955) 189–98.—Teicher has been followed by M.-A. Chevallier, *L'esprit et le messie dans le bas-judaïsme et le Nouveau Testament* (Etudes d'histoire et de philosophie religieuses 49; Paris: Presses universitaires de France, 1958) 115. See my review in *TS* 20 (1959) 451–5.

[4] 'Die neuentdeckten Qumrantexte und das Judenchristentum der Pseudoklementinen', BZNW 21 (1954) 35–51.

[5] 'Das gnostische Judentum in den Dead Sea Scrolls', *ZRGG* 6 (1954) 1–4 [hereafter referred to as Schoeps 2]; 'Ebionite Christianity', *JTS* 4 (1953) 219–24.

Document. The latter is generally recognized today as a work of this group, even though it was not found at Qumran originally. Any information that is drawn from other sources (e.g., Philo or Josephus) is valid only in so far as the identification of the Qumran sect as Essene is correct.

THE EBIONITES

Relatively little is known about the Ebionites. Most of the data concerning them has been preserved in patristic literature, and it is not easy to interpret. Scraps of information are found in Justin, Irenaeus, Tertullian, Origen, Hippolytus, Eusebius, and Jerome, while Epiphanius devotes a full chapter to them in his *Panarion*. Literary borrowing took place in some cases, so that it is not always easy to tell when the patristic writer is supplying data gathered from independent sources. In the preface of his *Theologie und Geschichte des Judenchristentums*, H. J. Schoeps claims to set a new landmark for scholarly research in the study of the Ebionites by being the first to take into account Rabbinic literature and the translation of the Old Testament by Symmachus, the Ebionite. The data from Symmachus are quite fragmentary and do not really concern us here.[6] The interpretation of the material in the Rabbinic sources is so intimately connected with the question of the identity of the *Mînîm*[7] that anything which might be gathered from such a discussion would remain quite problematical. Consequently, in

[6] The questions and problems connected with Symmachus and his translation of the Old Testament are so numerous that it is too hazardous to try to draw any definite conclusions from this source. Important as is the study made by Schoeps, one may still ask whether he has really proved his point; cf. the reviews of his books by R. Bultmann in *Gnomon* 26 (1954) 180, by G. Bornkamm in *ZKG* 64 (1952–53) 197, and by G. Mercati in *Biblica* 32 (1951) 329–35.

[7] Cf. H. J. Schoeps, *Theologie und Geschichte des Judenchristentums* (Tübingen: Mohr, 1949) 21–5 [hereafter referred to as Schoeps 1]. Also J. Thomas, *Le mouvement baptiste en Palestine et Syrie* (*150 v. J.-C.—300 apr. J.-C.*) (Gembloux: Duculot, 1935) 161–2. This author identifies the *Mînîm* with Ebionites and the *Nazōraioi*. But Ralph Marcus, 'Pharisees, Essenes and Gnostics', *JBL* 73

a discussion of the relationship between the sect of Qumran and the Ebionites, I prefer not to use these sources for information regarding the latter.

The English name, Ebionite, is derived from the Latin *Ebionitae*, found in Jerome (*Ep* 112, 13) and in the Latin translation of some of Origen's works of which the Greek originals are now lost (*Hom. in Luc.* 17; *Hom. in Gen.* 3, 5). Another Latin form is *Ebionaei*, found in Irenaeus (*Adv. haer* 1, 26, 2; 5, 1, 3), which is the transliteration of the Greek *Ebiōnaioi* (*Adv. haer.* 3, 21, 1; cf. Origen, *Contra Cels.* 2, 1; 5, 61, 65; *De Princ.* 4, 22; Eusebius, *Hist. Eccl.* 3, 27). This seems to be, in turn, a transliteration of the Aramaic *'ebyônāyê'*, derived from the Hebrew *'ebyônîm*, meaning 'the poor'. Another Greek form, *Ebiōnoi*, is found in Irenaeus (*Adv. haer.* 4, 33, 4), but this looks like a copyist's misspelling.

As the name of a sect, this word appears for the first time in Irenaeus (*Adv. haer.* 1, 26, 2 Latin: *Ebionaei*; 3, 21, 1 Greek: *Ebiōnaioi*). He offers no explanation of its meaning or origin, but several were given in antiquity. They were called Ebionites: (*a*) because of the poverty of their intelligence (Origen, *De princ.* 4, 22; *Hom. in Gen.* 3, 5; Eusebius, *Hist. Eccl.* 3, 27; Epiphanius, *Pan.* 30, 17); (*b*) because of the poverty of the law which they followed (Origen, *Contra Cels.* 2, 1); (*c*) because of the poverty of the opinions they had of Christ (Eusebius, *Hist. eccl.* 3, 27); (*d*) because they were 'poor in understanding, hope, and deeds' (Epiphanius, *Pan.* 30, 17). These are obviously

---

(1954) 159 remarks: '. . . it has become clearer in recent years that while the term *Minim* in the Rabbinic and patristic literature of the third century and afterwards may refer to Jewish Christians, in Tannaitic writings it chiefly designates Jewish Gnostics.' Prof. Marcus quotes L. Ginzberg: 'I may state with certainty that only in a very few places does Minim refer to Judeo-Christians, while in most cases it describes Jewish Gnostics' (*ibid.*, n. 4). Cf. also Bultmann, *op. cit.*, 179; and G. Bornkamm (*op. cit.*, 197) who speaks of the 'nur hypothetisch verwendbaren rabbinischen Zeugnisse über das Judenchristentum'.

pejorative afterthoughts, which scarcely give us a clue to the origin of the term.

Epiphanius (*Pan.* 30, 1; 30, 17; etc.) derived the name from a founder, named Ebion. Tertullian (*De praescrip.* 33; *De carne Christi* 14, 18) speaks of a man named Ebion. This notion, however, is associated with the ancient belief that the unorthodox teaching or opinion was named after those who started it (see Justin, *Dial. cum Tryph.* 35, 4). Despite this tradition, which also ascribes to Ebion certain fragments in the work *Doctrina patrum de incarnatione Verbi*, modern scholars are inclined to look on Ebion merely as an eponymous hero, a personification of the sect itself.[8] There is really no evidence that such a person ever existed, though some scholars in modern times have repeated the ancient allegation found in Tertullian, Jerome, and Epiphanius.[9]

We know from the New Testament that certain early Christians were referred to as 'the poor' (Rom 15:26; Gal 2:10). This undoubtedly refers to the poor members of the community at Jerusalem. But it is often thought that the name *Ebiōnaioi* grew out of a practice of referring to the early Jewish Christians in Jerusalem as the poor, especially after the destruction of the city in A.D. 70. At some time during the first two centuries (it is impossible to be more precise) this designation would have been restricted to Jewish Christians who lived in

[8] Cf. J. Thomas, *op. cit.*, 160; Schoeps 1, 9. The latter maintains that this idea of Ebion as a founder is due to Hippolytus, but he gives no references for this statement (cf. p. 9, n. 2). This is but one example of the carelessness that is found in this book amid an otherwise mammoth display of erudition, which makes it necessary to use Schoeps' work only with the greatest caution. Cf. Bornkamm's review, p. 196: 'leider in Zitaten und Literaturangaben fehlerreich'. Similarly Bultmann, *op. cit.*, 189. In the light of such criticism it is quite surprising to read the highly laudatory review of Schoeps' books written by P. Benoit, O.P., in *RB* 57 (1950) 604–9: 'un magistral exposé'; 'd'une richesse peu ordinaire'; '. . . par le soin scrupuleux qu'il met à prouver scientifiquement tout ce qu'il avance . . .'.

[9] See A. Hilgenfeld, *Die Ketzergeschichte des Urchristentums* (Leipzig, 1884) 423–36.

Palestine and Syria, and who continued to observe the Mosaic Law.

The Ebionites were, then, a Jewish-Christian group, first mentioned by Irenaeus *ca.* A.D. 175, which flourished during the second, third, and early fourth centuries (at least). In the New Testament there is mention of Jewish Christians, who believed in Christ but also observed the Mosaic Law (Acts 15:1 ff.; 21:21; Gal 2). This was the community at Jerusalem, headed by James, the 'brother of the Lord'. Remnants of this group after the destruction of Jerusalem may have developed into the Ebionite sect, acquiring heterodox notions in time from other sources, such as Cerinthus and the Elchesaites. Eusebius (*Hist. eccl.* 3, 5) tells us:

> The people of the church in Jerusalem were commanded by an oracle given by revelation before the war to those in the city who were worthy of it to depart and dwell in one of the cities of Perea which they called Pella. To it those who believed in Christ migrated from Jerusalem, that when holy men had altogether deserted the royal capital of the Jews and the whole land of Judaea, the judgement of God might at last overtake them for all their crimes against the Christ and his Apostles.[10]

It is important to note here that Eusebius does not call these emigrants by the name of Ebionites, nor have we any reason to assume that he was speaking of them specifically. They were merely some of the Christians of the original community of Jerusalem. Justin distinguished two sorts of Jewish Christians, those who observe the Mosaic Law but do not require its observance of all others, and those who maintain that this observance is necessary for salvation. Justin would communicate with the former, but not with the latter (*Dial. cum Tryph.* 47; 48). Schoeps equates the Ebionites with the more intransigent group.[11] By the time of Irenaeus there was definitely a sect named *Ebiōnaioi*, who were considered heretical by him and

[10] Kirsopp Lake's translation in the Loeb Classical Library, *Eusebius* 1, 201.

[11] Schoeps 1, 8.

were listed among the Gnostics (*Adv. haer.* 1, 26, 2). He mentions specifically that they rejected the virgin birth of Christ (5, 1, 3; 3, 21, 1) and denied the Incarnation (4, 33, 4).[12]

Tertullian adds no new details, except to speak of *Ebion*, not of the *Ebionaei*. One phrase of his, however, is interesting, for he mentions that Ebion was influenced by Cerinthus, 'non in omni parte consentiens' (*Adv. omn. haer.* 3.)[13] It is often admitted that the christological tenets of the Ebionites came from this Cerinthian influence. Hippolytus (*Philosoph.* 7, 34; 10, 22) adds a few details to our knowledge, but they are not important here (see Chart 1).

CHART 1

TENETS AND PRACTICES OF THE EBIONITES AND NAZORAIOI ACCORDING TO THE FATHERS

The Ebionites

a) they depend on Cerinthus and Carpocrates (Iren, Tertull, Hipp)
b) they believe in one God, the creator of the world (Iren, Tert, Hipp)
c) they use the gospel of Matthew only (Iren, Tert [?], Epiph)
d) they reject Paul as an apostate from the law (Iren, Orig, Epiph)
e) they interpret the prophets *curiosius* (Iren)
f) they practise circumcision (Iren, Orig, Epiph)
g) they observe the Sabbath (Euseb, Epiph)
h) they live according to the Jewish way of life, according to the Law (Iren, Tert, Hipp, Orig, Euseb, Epiph)

[12] It is important to remember that the type of patristic writing in which the Ebionites are usually mentioned is heresiography. They were classed as christological heretics; such a classification, though important to the theologian, leaves us, however, with a paucity of details for our comparison with the Qumran sect.

[13] Perhaps it would be better to describe this work as Pseudo-Tertullian; it is generally held today that cc. 46–53 of the *De praescriptione* are actually a digest of Hippolytus' lost *Syntagma*; cf. J. Quasten, *Patrology* 2 (Westminster, Md.: Newman, 1953) 169–70.

i) they face Jerusalem when they pray (Iren)
j) they hold the observance of the Mosaic Law as necessary for salvation (Hipp, Euseb)
k) they reject the virgin birth of Christ (Iren, Tert, Orig, Euseb, Epiph)
l) they hold Christ to be a mere man (Iren, Tert, Hipp, Euseb, Epiph)
m) they maintain Jesus had to merit his title, Christ, by fulfilling the Law (Hipp, Epiph)
n) they reject virginity and continence (Epiph)
o) they use purificatory baths (Epiph)
p) they use remedial baths (Epiph)
q) they admit baptism (Epiph)
r) they celebrate the mysteries with unleavened bread and mere water (Epiph)
s) they hold that Christ came to abrogate sacrifice in the temple (Epiph)
t) they believe that God set the devil and Christ to rule over this world and the world to come respectively (Epiph)
u) they give up all goods and possessions (Epiph)
v) they permit divorce (Epiph)
w) they admit Abraham, Isaac, Jacob, Moses, Aaron, Joshua, but none of the prophets (David, Solomon, Isaiah, Jeremiah, Daniel, Ezekiel, Elijah, Elisha) (Epiph)
x) they claim that Christ alone is the *prophētēs . . . tēs alētheias* (Epiph)
y) they use the book, *Periodoi Petrou dia Klēmentos* (Epiph)
z) they abstain from meat like Peter (Epiph)

The Nazōraioi

a) they believe in one God, Creator of the world (Epiph)
b) they use the Gospel of Matthew only (Euseb, Epiph)
c) they reject Paul as an apostate from the Law (Orig, Euseb)
d) they practise circumcision (Epiph)

e) they observe the Sabbath (Euseb, Epiph [Euseb says they observed Sunday too])
f) they follow the Jewish way of life according to the Law (Euseb, Epiph)
g) they do not reject the virgin birth of Christ (Orig, Euseb, Jerome; Epiph is not sure about this)
h) they deny Jesus' preexistence as God (Euseb)
i) they call Jesus the Son of God (Epiph, Jerome)
j) they believe in the resurrection of the dead (Epiph)

It is Origen who first distinguishes for us two kinds of Ebionites: those who admit the virgin birth of Christ, and those who reject it (*Contra Cels.* 5, 61). Both groups, however, reject the epistles of Paul (5, 65). Eusebius (*Hist. eccl.* 3, 27) has likewise recorded the fact of two groups of Ebionites:

But others the wicked demon, when he could not alienate them from God's plan in Christ, made his own, when he found them by a different snare. The first Christians gave these the suitable name of Ebionites because they had poor and mean opinions concerning Christ. They held him to be a plain and ordinary man who had achieved righteousness merely by the progress of his character and had been born naturally from Mary and her husband. They insisted on the complete observation of the Law, and did not think that they would be saved by faith in Christ alone and by a life in accordance with it. But there were others besides these who have the same name. These escaped the absurd folly of the first mentioned, and did not deny that the Lord was born of a Virgin and the Holy Spirit, but nevertheless agreed with them in not confessing his pre-existence as God, being the Logos and Wisdom. Thus they shared in the impiety of the former class, especially in that they were equally zealous to insist on the literal observance of the Law. They thought that the letters of the Apostle ought to be wholly rejected and called him an apostate from the Law. They used only the Gospel called according to the Hebrews and made little account of the rest. Like the former they used to observe the sabbath and the rest of the Jewish ceremonial, but on Sundays celebrated rites like ours in commemoration of the Saviour's resurrection. Wherefore from these practices they have obtained their name, for the name of Ebionites indicates the poverty of their intelligence, for this name means 'poor' in Hebrew.[14]

Epiphanius, who of all the patristic writers gives most space to the Ebionites, supplies names for the two groups. The more orthodox group, which probably admits the virgin birth of Christ (*Pan.* 29), is called *Nazōraioi*; the more heterodox group is labelled *Ebiōnaioi* (*Pan.* 30). The identification of the Nazoraioi as an orthodox group of Jewish Christians, related somehow to the Ebionites, is admitted by many scholars; but the identification has problems connected with it that we cannot discuss here.[15] It is complicated by the fact that Jerome equates *Ebionitae*, *Nazaraei*, and *Minaei*.[16] At any rate, we are sure that there was a definite group of christological heretics in the early centuries of the Church who were called Ebionites.

Among the details supplied by Epiphanius, mention is made of the influence of the Elchesaites on the Ebionites (*Pan.* 30, 17). He goes to the trouble of indicating that this influence affected the followers of Ebion, not Ebion himself. Elchesai was a heretical leader who preached (*ca.* A.D. 100) a doctrine of baptism unto the remission of sins which was heavily infected with Gnostic ideas (so, at least, it is usually judged). Schoeps,[17] following C. Schmidt and others, maintains that Epiphanius has confused the Ebionites with the Elchesaites, so that his

[14] Kirsopp Lake's translation, *op. cit.*, 261–3.

[15] Cf. J. Thomas, *op. cit.*, 156–70, for a detailed discussion and references to the literature on the subject. Schoeps (1, 8 ff.) likewise discusses the problem briefly.

[16] Cf. *Ep.* 112, 13 (*PL* 22, 924): 'Quid dicam de Ebionitis, qui Christianos esse se simulant? Usque hodie per totas Orientis synagogas inter Iudaeos haeresis est, quae dicitur Minaeorum, et a Pharisaeis nunc usque damnatur: quos vulgo Nazaraeos nuncupant, qui credunt in Christum Filium Dei, natum de virgine Maria, et eum dicunt esse, qui sub Pontio Pilato passus est, et resurrexit, in quem et nos credimus: sed dum volunt et Iudaei esse et Christiani, nec Iudaei sunt nec Christiani.'

[17] 1, 11; Schoeps is continually stressing throughout his book that the Ebionites were not Gnostics. He finds it convenient for his thesis to attribute all Gnostic elements that might be found in the Ebionite tenets to the Elchesaites. This may well be true, but it does not follow that Epiphanius

account of the Ebionites can be accepted only when there is outside control. It is true that Epiphanius adds details about the Ebionites not found elsewhere in patristic writings. If we glance at Chart 1, we will see that the items listed under *n–z* come from Epiphanius alone. Among these we find mention of dualism, various types of baths, peculiar ideas about the prophets, Christ—all of which have been associated with Jewish-Christian Gnosticism. Has Epiphanius confused the Ebionites with the Elchesaites? We just do not know. It is just as reasonable to admit the explanation given by J. Thomas,[18] that the Ebionites were influenced by three groups: the Essenes, the early Christians, the Elchesaites.

Before terminating this section on the identification of the Ebionites, I shall mention briefly the opinion of J. L. Teicher regarding the Qumran sect, which he maintains is Ebionite. One might be surprised that I am bringing up this point now. The reason is that, since Teicher does not depend upon a discussion of the Pseudo-Clementines for his 'proof' that the sect is Ebionite,[19] his view can be best set forth here.

From the description thus far given of the Ebionites, one might well wonder if there is any connection between them and the sect of Qumran. Certainly the climate of opinion in which the latter group lived was that of the Old Testament, as is evident to all who are acquainted with the Qumran literature.[20] The early Christian Church and certain New Testament writings,

---

has confused the Elchesaites and the Ebionites. Later Ebionites may well have been Gnostics, precisely because of the Elchesaite influence. Does not this seem to be indicated by the fact that Epiphanius notes a distinction between Ebion and later Ebionites?

[18] *Op. cit.*, 171–83; cf. Bultmann, *op. cit.*, 185.

[19] In his first article on the Ebionites and the Dead Sea Scrolls (cf. note 1 above) Teicher gives one reference to two places in the Pseudo-Clementines; cf. p. 98, n. 4. This is supposed to support his contention that Paul is the adversary referred to in the *pesher* on Habakkuk and in the Pseudo-Clementines.

[20] Cf. Karl Georg Kuhn, 'Die in Palästina gefundenen hebräischen Texte und das Neue Testament', *ZThK* 47 (1950) 207.

on the other hand, are definitely the framework and background of the Ebionite way of life, even though they have retained the observance of the Mosaic Law. This we know from patristic information and from the Pseudo-Clementine writings. Yet for Prof. Teicher the Qumran sect is Ebionite, Christ is the Teacher of Righteousness, and Paul is the 'Man of Lies'. The Ebionites, being Christians, were affected by Diocletian's edict of persecution, and so, rather than hand over their sacred books according to the royal decree, they hid them in the caves of Qumran. The Qumran sect is Ebionite because they are mentioned in the *pesher* on Habakkuk as *'ebyônîm* (12:3, 6); and Qumran is 'in the vicinity' of the spot in Transjordan where the Ebionites lived. Efforts were made to point out the weaknesses in the arguments of Prof. Teicher,[21] but he wrote on undaunted.[22]

The most serious difficulty, of course, with Teicher's opinion is that of chronology. The latest possible date for the deposit of the manuscripts is the destruction of Qumran in A.D. 68. Though the first explicit mention of the Ebionites dates from

[21] Cf., for instance, G. Vermès, 'Le "Commentaire d'Habacuc" et le Nouveau Testament', *Cahiers Sioniens* 5 (1951) 337–49; K. Elliger, *Studien zum Habakkuk-Kommentar* (Tübingen: Mohr) 244; H. J. Schoeps, 'Der Habakuk-Kommentar von 'Ain-Feshkha—ein Dokument der hasmonäischen Spätzeit', *ZAW* 63 (1951) 249–50. Also by Schoeps, 'Handelt es sich wirklich um ebionitische Dokumente?', *ZRGG* 3 (1951) 322. [Hereafter Schoeps 3.]

[22] Cf. n. 3 above for references to his articles. Just a few points will be mentioned here. For the identification of Jesus as the True Teacher and Paul as the 'Man of Lies' Teicher is relying on the article of G. Margoliouth, 'The Sadducean Christians of Damascus', *Athenaeum* 4335 (Nov. 26, 1910) 657–9, where the identification is merely asserted. Prof. Teicher does little more when he says, 'The "True Teacher" is, in fact, Jesus. He is addressed as such in Mark 12.14, "Master (Teacher) we know that thou art true."' This is the only evidence given that the *môreh haṣṣedeq* of the Qumran literature is Jesus. Another point is the problem of the Jewish Christians mentioned by Eusebius (*Hist. eccl.* 3, 5; quoted above). All we know is that they were early Christians from Jerusalem, most likely Jewish. Pella, the place to which they went according to Eusebius, is about 50–60 miles away from Qumran, as the crow flies, and on the other side of the Jordan—hardly 'in

Irenaeus (*ca.* A.D. 175), and though it is quite probable that they existed as a sect much earlier, there is simply no evidence for their existence in the first century A.D., either before or after the destruction of Jerusalem.[23] Consequently, the simple identification of the Qumran sect and the Ebionites is untenable.

EBIONITE LITERATURE

By Ebionite literature I mean here material embedded in the Pseudo-Clementine *Homilies* and *Recognitions*, often called merely the *Pseudoclementines* (PsC).[24] Various spurious works circulated in antiquity under the name of Clement of Rome, and among these was the romantic novel which exists today under the title

---

the vicinity of the 'Ain Feshkha cave' (*JJS* 2:93). Another gratuitous statement is the assertion that the Ebionites are mentioned by name in the *pesher* on Habakkuk (12:3, 6). K. Elliger (*op. cit.*, p. 244) has pointed out that the article would be necessary before *'ebyônîm* for this word to be capable of meaning 'the Ebionites'. The word has indeed turned up with the article in the *pesher* on the Psalms from Qumran Cave 4, where the words *'bywnym* and *'dt h'bywnym* are found. Cf. J. M. Allegro, 'A Newly Discovered Fragment of a Commentary on Psalm XXXVII from Qumrân', *PEQ* 86 (1954) 69–75; see now 4QPss[a] (=4Q*171*) 1–2 ii 9; 1, 3–4 iii 10 (DJD 5, 43–4). This still does not prove that *'ebyônîm* means 'Ebionites', for the word is obviously used in all places in the sense found so often in the Old Testament, God's poor. 1QpHab 12:10 can easily be translated 'who robbed the possessions of the poor'; meaning 'what little they had'. The parallelism between the 'poor' and the 'simple' in 1QpHab 12:3–4 cannot be disregarded. For other passages in the Qumran literature where *'bywnym* means the 'poor', cf. 1QM 11:9, 13; 13:12–14 ('a virtual self-designation of the [Qumran] group as "the poor"'—so L. E. Keck, *ZNW* 57 [1966] 71).

[23] Cf. A. Dupont-Sommer, *The Jewish Sect of Qumran and the Essenes* (London: Valentine Mitchell, 1954) 158: 'The excavations of Khirbet Qumrân, by establishing that the manuscripts were conveyed to their hiding-place about A.D. 66–70, show that Dr Teicher's dates are too late, and accordingly suffice to undermine the whole of his theory.' Cf. G. Vermès, *Les Manuscrits du Désert de Juda* (2nd ed.; Paris: Desclée, 1954) 36; Schoeps 2, 1. These authors' remarks are all based on the report of R. de Vaux, 'Fouille au Khirbet Qumrân', *RB* 60 (1953) 94; *CRAIBL*, 1953, p. 317; see now his *L'archéologie et les manuscrits de la Mer Morte* (Schweich Lectures, 1959; London: British Academy, 1961) and his answer to Teicher in 'Archaeology and the Dead Sea Scrolls', *Antiquity* 37 (1963) 126–7 (cf. pp. 25–30).

[24] For the purpose of this essay we do not have to consider the transla-

of *Homilies and Recognitions*. The PsC contain five documents: (*a*) the *Epistle of Peter to James*, instructing the latter that the accompanying writings are not to be entrusted to any but the initiated; (*b*) *Diamartyria* or *Contestatio*, the 'oath' to be taken by the initiated concerning these writings; (*c*) *Epistle of Clement to James*, telling of Peter's martyrdom, Clement's ordination, Peter's instruction to Clement his successor, and Peter's order to write down an epitome of his sermons in the various cities that it might be sent to James, the bishop of Jerusalem; this serves as an introduction to the *Homilies*, for Clement says that he is sending *Klēmentos tōn Petrou epidēmiōn kērygmatōn epitōme*; (*d*) *Homiliai*, 20 books of the 'Homilies'; (*e*) *Anagnorismoi*, 10 books of the 'Recognitions.'[25]

The *Homilies* (hereafter, *Hom*) and the *Recognitions* (hereafter, *Rec*) are two forms of a novel about the fate of the various members of the noble family of Clement of Rome. Clement himself is portrayed as a searcher for truth, going about to the various schools of philosophy for a solution of his doubts concerning the origin of the world, the immortality of the soul, etc. At length he hears that the Son of God has appeared in distant Judea. After a long journey, which takes him to Egypt and Palestine, he meets Peter in Caesarea, is instructed in the doctrine of the True Prophet, and becomes a Christian. He is invited by Peter to accompany him on his missionary journeys in pursuit of Simon Magus. Curious circumstances had brought about the break-up of Clement's family: his mother and two brothers leave Rome because of a warning his mother receives in a dream, and sail for Athens; but they are shipwrecked and separated. Finally, father, mother, and the three sons set out to

---

tion of the Old Testament by Symmachus, nor the *Gospel according to the Hebrews*, which are generally judged to be Ebionite compositions. The latter is 'some sort of reworking and extension of the Hebrew original of the canonical Gospel of Matthew' (J. Quasten, *op. cit.*, 1, 112). Cf. the remarks of Bornkamm, *op. cit.*, 197.

[25] The *Hom* are extant today in Greek; the text has recently been edited by Bernhard Rehm, *Die Pseudoklementinen: I, Homilien*, in the series, *Die*

find each other, and the successive recognitions of the members of the family, aided by the efforts of Peter, give the title of 'Recognitions' to one of the versions of this novel. The greater part of the novel is given over, however, to the sermons of Peter and his debates with Simon Magus. This is responsible for the title of the other extant version, 'Homilies'. Actually there is as much homiletic material in the *Recognitions* as there is recognition in the *Homilies*. Long passages parallel each other, sometimes with word-for-word identity.

Popular in the last century as the basis of the Tübingen-School theory of opposition between the Petrine and Pauline churches of early Christianity,[26] the PsC were first subjected to critical study by Adolf Hilgenfeld, a disciple of that same school, toward the end of the nineteenth century. Since the beginning of this century numerous scholars have worked over them; among these are especially Waitz, Heintze, Carl Schmidt, Cullmann, Thomas, Rehm, and Schoeps.[27] Waitz was the first

---

griechischen christlichen Schriftsteller der ersten Jahrhunderte 42 (Berlin: Akademie-Verlag, 1953). The *Rec* are extant only in a Latin translation (or, according to many scholars, a Latin adaptation) by Rufinus (*c.* A.D. 405). A new edition has been promised for the Berlin *Corpus*. For the time being we must use the text found in Migne, *PL* 1, 1158–1474. There is also a Syriac MS., dated A.D. 411, which contains the text of *Hom* 10–14 and *Rec* 1–4; cf. W. Frankenberg, *Die syrischen Clementinen mit griechischem Paralleltext* (Leipzig: Hinrichs, 1937; TU 48/3). A few other fragments also are extant; cf. J. Quasten, *op. cit.*, 1, 61. An English translation (which must now be checked against the new critical edition of the *Hom*) can be found in A. Roberts and Donaldson, *Ante-Nicene Christian Library* (Edinburgh: T. and T. Clark) 3 (Recognitions, 1875) 17 (Homilies, 1870).

26 In the PsC Paul is alluded to, frequently under the designation of *inimicus homo* or *ho echthros anthrōpos*, being depicted as the adversary of James, the Bishop of Jerusalem. Though Peter is identified with the camp of James, we do not find Paul pictured as the enemy of Peter; the latter role is played by Simon Magus throughout. But the critics of the last century found no difficulty in asserting that the figure of Simon Magus was really a literary mask for the real opponent, Paul; cf. J. Chapman, 'On the Date of the Clementines', *ZNW* 9 (1908) 150–1.

27 The chief works are: Hans Waitz, *Die Pseudoklementinen, Homilien und Rekognitionen, eine quellenkritische Untersuchung* (Leipzig: Hinrichs, 1904; TU

to subject the PsC to a searching literary analysis and to uncover the *Grundschrift* (hereafter, *G*). *G* was thought to have been a novel, composed of material that dates back to subapostolic times, in which Peter was the dominant figure. Though *G* is now lost, fragments of it are thought to be extant in the PsC, well reworked by different redactors.

G is considered to be a compilation, composed of fragments of five works: (*a*) the *Kērygmata Petrou*, sermons of Peter on his missionary journeys, digested by Clement; (*b*) the story of the wondrous deeds of Simon Magus and of his debates with Peter; (*c*) Appion-dialogues in *Hom* 4–6 and *Rec* 10: Clement argues with Appion against the latter's pagan ideas about fate, astrology, polytheism; cf. Eusebius, *Hist. eccl.*, 3, 38, 5; (*d*) the Graeco-Oriental Recognition-novel, about the members of the family of Clement of Rome; (*e*) Bardesanes' *Book of the Laws of the Lands*.[28]

The compilatory character of *G* is responsible for the impression of the reader that the *Hom* and *Rec* are quite a hodgepodge. Waitz maintained a date in the early third century for the composition of *G*; with slight variations this has been more or less generally admitted.[29] Practically all scholars admit today the existence of *G* and its compilatory character. The relationship of *G*, however, to the later reworkings, whether *Hom* and *Rec* represent independent versions of *G* or depend one on the other, is a question that has been hotly debated; it does not

---

25/4); Carl Schmidt, *Studien zu den Pseudoklementinen* (Leipzig: Hinrichs, 1929; TU 46/1); Oscar Cullmann, *Le problème littéraire et historique du roman pseudo-clémentin: Etude sur le rapport entre le Gnosticisme et le Judéo-Christianisme* (Paris: F. Alcan, 1930); J. Thomas, *op. cit.*, 174 ff.; Bernhard Rehm, 'Zur Entstehung der pseudoclementinischen Schriften', *ZNW* 37 (1938) 77–184; H. J. Schoeps 1, 37–61 *et passim.* An extensive bibliography is to be found in the last cited work; cf. also J. Quasten, *op. cit.*, 1, 62–3. See further H. J. Schoeps, 'Die Pseudoklementinen und das Urchristentum', *ZRGG* 10 (1958) 3–15.

[28] The inclusion of this last section is rather doubtful; cf. J. Quasten, *op. cit.*, 1, 263.

[29] C. Schoeps 1, 38.

concern us here. A Syriac version of *Hom* 10–14 and of *Rec* 1–4 is extant in a manuscript dated A.D. 411. Its text of *Hom* is slightly different at times from the Greek, and Schoeps is of the opinion that it represents an earlier form of the novel.[30]

It has been quite generally held that the PsC are Ebionite in origin; however, not all scholars agree. Evidence for the Ebionite origin comes from Epiphanius (*Pan.* 30, 15), who tells us that they used the *Periodoi Petrou dia Klēmentos*. This is the name by which *G* apparently went in antiquity.[31] Schoeps, following other scholars, maintains that the *Kērygmata Petrou* (hereafter, *KP*) were definitely the Ebionite writing among the sources of *G*, having been written by an Ebionite of the second century who led the defence of his co-religionists against the attacks of the Marcionite Gnosis.[32] The extent of the original *KP* was first determined by Waitz on the basis of the summary given in the third book of *Rec*, chap. 75. Clement mentions here that he has already sent to James a book of Peter's sermons, the contents of which he proceeds to summarize, dividing them into ten *tomoi*. Using this as a starting point, Waitz indicated the passages of the PsC that originally belonged to the *KP* section of *G*. This reconstruction of *KP* was checked by subsequent studies, accepted by many, expanded in slight details by still others, and enjoys a certain vogue today. However, as early as 1908 Dom John Chapman questioned the analysis.[33] In 1932 Ed. Schwartz and M. Goguel rejected it.[34] Schoeps is of the opinion that their arguments were answered by Waitz and others 'gebührend'.[35]

[30] *Ibid.*, 40.

[31] Cf. Origen, *Comm. in Gen.* according to *Philocalia* 23 (*PG* 12, 85); *Opus imperf. ad Matt.*, ser. 77; perhaps also Epiphanius, *Pan.* 30, 15; Jerome, *Comm. in Gal.* 1, 18; *Adv. Iovin.* 1, 14.

[32] Schoeps 1, 313; '. . . ein rein ebionitisches Werk aus der Zeit des antignostischen Kampfes . . .' (p. 58).

[33] *Op. cit.*, 147 ff.

[34] 'Unzeitgemässe Beobachtungen zu den Clementinen', *ZNW* 31 (1932) 151–99.

[35] Schoeps 1, 44.

However, Bernard Rehm, a student of Schwartz and editor of the latest critical edition of the *Hom*, has proposed an entirely different analysis of the redactions. While admitting an original G, he believes that the recognitive section was the nucleus (therefore not *KP*) about which the four other sections clustered. *G* was reworked in an early form of *Hom*, which was suspect in the Church at large, but found reception among the heretic Ebionites. An attempt to make the novel orthodox resulted in an early redaction of *Rec*. This analysis of Rehm cannot be lightly dismissed—and so the question arises whether there really were any *KP* at all. Bultmann, in his review of Schoeps' *Theologie*, states this question quite frankly and in the end admits his extreme scepticism, as do others, about the whole literary analysis of the sources of PsC.[36]

We have gone into details here merely to show how uncertain the reconstruction, extent, and original character of *KP* really are. Who is right, Schoeps and those he follows, or Rehm? Schoeps would have us believe that the *KP* were originally Ebionite, reworked later by Christians of different hues. Rehm proposes that the original *G* was Christian, later contaminated by Ebionite notions. It is obvious that the answer to this problem, if it can ever be found, will radically determine one's use of the *KP* in a comparison of Ebionite and Qumran tenets and practices. Cullmann has made such a comparison, utilizing the Qumran material that had been previously published, and the *KP*, apparently according to his own reconstruction of the document, as if this were a *chose acquise*. Nowhere in the article does he mention the analysis of Rehm, not even the summary given in the *Einleitung* of the latter's critical edition.

[36] *Op. cit.*, 181. Cf. Bornkamm, *op. cit.*, 197–8; J. Quasten, *op. cit.*, 1, 61–2. For Rehm's views see the introduction to his critical edition, *Die Pseudoklementinen*, cited above, pp. vii–ix; and especially his article, quoted in n. 27 above. Cf. E. Molland, 'La circoncision, le baptême et l'autorité du décret apostolique (Actes XV, 28 sq.) dans les milieux judéochrétiens des Pseudo-Clementines', *ST* 9 (1955) 1–8; G. Strecker, *Das Judenchristentum in den Pseudoklementinen* (TU 70; Berlin: Akademie-Verlag, 1958) 1–34.

In the following section of this paper I am going to compare the Ebionites and the sect of Qumran. For the sake of this comparison I shall accept the list of passages of the PsC which are judged by Schoeps as belonging to *KP*. His list represents the latest investigation and the widest range of passages that could pertain to the original *KP*.[37] The validity of such a list, of course, depends on how the previous questions are resolved. In all references to the PsC I shall indicate, in parentheses, whether or not the passage belongs to *KP*, according to this list (see Chart 2).

CHART 2

KĒRYGMATA PETROU

(found in the following passages of the PsC, according to the studies of Waitz, as modified by subsequent scholars, Bousset, Cullmann; the references in parentheses indicate the additions of Schoeps, *Theologie*, pp. 45-53)

Hom	*Rec*
1:18–20	1:15–17, 22–4, 32–44, 46–71, 74 (omit 23; add 27–31, 45)
2:6–12, 14–18, 33–4; 38–40, 43–52 (omit 6–12, 14–15, 34; add 41, 42)	2:20–48, 55, 62–5 (omit 55, 62–5; add 66–7)
3:17–28, 33–8, 43–56 (add 2–10; 39–42)	3:2–10, 12–30, 52–61 (add 33–8)
8:2–20 (add 21–3; omit 2–3)	4:2–20 (add 1, 21, 25–6)
9:1–23	5:34–5
11:16, 19–33 (add 35)	6:4–14
15:5–11	
16:5–14, 16 (add 15, 21)	
17:3, 6–19 (add 4–5)	
18:6–10; 19–22	
19:1–23	
20:1–10	

[37] Cf. Schoeps 1, 50–3. This list incorporates passages ascribed to *KP* by Waitz, Bousset, Cullmann, and Schoeps. Cf. Schoeps 1, 38 for a descrip-

COMPARISON OF THE EBIONITES AND THE SECT OF QUMRAN

I shall discuss in detail various points of similarity and dissimilarity that exist between the Ebionites and the Qumran sect, to see whether there is any basis for the assertion that the latter was or became Ebionite. It will be evident that I am not trying to trace the history of each idea or practice that I take up; nor am I trying to list all the possible sources from which either group may have derived its tenets and customs. I am concerned merely with the influence of Qumran on the Ebionites.

At the outset it should be noted that the PsC do not depict the Ebionites as living a communal existence, as does the Manual of Discipline with respect to the Qumran sect. There is nothing 'monastic'[38] about the group described in PsC. Hence the comparison will not be based on rules, ways of acting, punishments, etc., such as are found in 1QS.[39] But there are many other points that can well be compared.

Dualism

This term is used normally of those opposites which have been found in Gnostic literature, the Johannine and Pauline writings, Greek philosophy, and other writings. It should be obvious that the principle of contradiction, being a basic metaphysical principle, could be made the support for many sets of opposites which are not specifically 'dualistic'. Such notions as the levitical contrast of clean-unclean, God's creation of the heaven and the earth, the tree of the knowledge of good and evil, could be forced into a system of dualism. But we must be more specific; we must beware of trying to interpret every set of opposites as

---

tion of his 'orthodox' position in this matter. It is to be noted that Bornkamm (pp. 197–8) criticizes Schoeps for expanding the list of the other scholars 'ohne nähere Begründung'.

38 Cf. Cullmann, 'Die neuentdeckten Qumrantexte und das Judenchristentum der Pseudoklementinen' [see n. 4] p. 42; unless otherwise noted, henceforth all references to Cullmann will be to this article.

39 Millar Burrows, *The Dead Sea Scrolls of St Mark's Monastery* (New Haven: American Schools of Oriental Research) 1 (The Isaiah Manuscript and the Habakkuk Commentary, 1950); 2, fasc. 2 (The Manual of Discipline, 1951).

dualistic (in the sense usually intended by those who treat this question).

We can summarize the dualism of 1QS as follows: the members are to do good and avoid evil (1:4–5), to turn to the truth and away from perversity (6:15; cf. 1:5–6; 1:15–17; 5:1). This simple contrast of good-evil, truth-perversity soon appears more complex; for the members are to love the sons of light and hate the sons of darkness (1:10), to bless the men of God's lot and curse the men of Belial's lot (2:2, 5). These two groups of men are divided according to the divine appointment of two spirits (truth and perversity) which are to guide men until the period of visitation (3:17–19). These spirits are the 'prince of light' and the 'angel of darkness' (3:20–21). Truth is derived from the spring of light and perversity from the fountain of darkness (3:19–23). The angel of truth is on the side of the God of Israel (3:24), whose enemy is Belial (1:21–23; 7:1–3). For God loves the spirit of truth and hates the spirit of perversity (4:1). These two spirits are the source of all good and evil works of man in this world (3:26; 4:2 ff.). God has set them up to reign in equal parts with eternal, mutual enmity until the time of his visitation (4:17–19). Then God will destroy the spirit of perversity and the Truth will prevail (4:19). The spirits of truth and perversity both strive within the heart of man (4:23.)

Dualism is found as well in the War Scroll (1QM), but the system does not appear to be as developed as that in 1QS. This is slightly surprising, because 1QM is a manual for the conduct of God's war, in which the sons of light are to battle against the sons of darkness. The opposition of light and darkness is frequent enough; likewise that of God's lot and Belial's lot. But we find little mention of the opposition between truth and perversity. Columns 1 and 13 in particular contain dualistic concepts. A war is to be waged against the 'sons of darkness' (1:1, 7, 10, 16; 13:16; 14:17) by the 'sons of light' (1:1, 3, 9, 11, 13), against the 'lot of darkness' (1:1, 5, 11; 13:5) by the 'lot of light' (13:5, 9) or 'God's lot' (1:5; 13:6, 12; 15:1). We read of the 'army of Belial' (1:13; 11:8; 15:2–3; 18:3), the 'lot of Belial' (1:5; 4:2; 13:2, 4, 12; 14:10); the 'prince of light' (13:10), 'spirits of truth' (13:10); 'prince of the dominion of impiety' (17:5–6). It is God's war (11:1) that the sons of light are waging. The period of darkness reigns now, but in God's time the sons of light will prevail (1:8). For God has determined of old the day for the war to wipe out the sons of darkness (1:10).

In the Thanksgiving Psalms (1QH) we read that both the just man and the evil man proceed from God the Creator (4:38).

It is noteworthy that this dualism is lacking in 1QpHab and CD. As in the passage in 1QS 3:6, the contrast between clean and unclean might possibly be considered a manifestation of dualism (CD 6:17; 11:19–20; 12:20). But this is obviously an opposition known from the Levitical laws of the Bible.[40]

In the PsC there is also a dualism which can be compared with that of Qumran. God, the sole Creator of all, has differentiated all principles into pairs of opposites from the beginning—heaven, earth; day, night; light, fire; sun, moon; life, death (*Hom* 2:15 *KP*). This is the system that is known as the syzygies or combinations, according to which all things come in pairs (*Hom* 2:15, 33 *KP*). The smaller precedes the larger, the female the male, the inferior the superior, and evil precedes good (*Rec* 3:59 *KP*). Outside the passages thought to belong to the original *KP* we also find a dualism, the doctrine of the 'two paths', presided over by Belief and Unbelief (*Hom* 7:6–7).

Another way of expressing this dualism is the contrast of two kingdoms. 'The prophet of truth who appeared [on earth] taught us that the Maker and God of all gave two kingdoms to two, good and evil: granting to the evil the sovereignty over the present world along with the law, so that he [it] should have the right to punish those who act unjustly; but to the good He gave the eternal age to come. But He made each man free with

[40] Charles, *APOT* (Oxford: Clarendon Press, 1913) 2, 184, compares CD 6:17 with Ez 22:26.

the power to give himself up to whatsoever he prefers, either to the present evil or to the future good' (*Hom* 15:7 *KP*; 8:55 not *KP*). Elsewhere we learn that Christ is the ruler of the future ages as the King of righteousness, whereas the Tempter is the ruler of the present; that is why he tempted Christ saying, 'All the kingdoms of the present world are subject to me' (*Hom* 8:21 *KP* [according to Schoeps]). Truth and error are contrasted in *Rec* 6:4 *KP*. We will recall that Epiphanius recorded this opposition or dualism (*Pan.* 30, 16).

From the summaries given above it should be obvious that there is a definite similarity in the dualisms of Qumran and of the PsC. Cullmann has pointed out that in both cases there is a subordination of the dualistic system to Jewish monotheistic ideas. God set up the kings of the two domains in the PsC just as he set up the spirits of truth and perversity of 1QS.[41] Both Karl Georg Kuhn[42] and A. Dupont-Sommer[43] have related this Qumran dualism to Iranian sources. The latter maintains that precisely this subordination of the two spirits to the supreme God is found in the Iranian source.[44]

There seems, however, to be some difference of opinion among scholars about this Iranian influence. Quite recently H. Michaud has suggested an even more specific source of the Qumran dualism, i.e., Zervanism. Zervanism was a particular branch of Zoroastrianism, in which the protagonist, Ahura Mazda, and the antagonist in the dualistic system are both born of a superior deity, *Zurvan* or *chronos*, time. It dates from the time of the Achaemenian empire and was regarded as

[41] *Op. cit.*, 38–9.

[42] 'Die Sektenschrift und die iranische Religion', *ZThK* 49 (1952) 296–316.

[43] *Nouveaux aperçus sur les manuscrits de la Mer Morte* (Paris: Maisonneuve, 1953) 157–72.

[44] 'Ce qui frappe dans l'instruction du *Manuel*, c'est que les deux Esprits, comme dans les Gâthâ, restent subordonnés à Dieu: l'Esprit du bien n'est pas confondu avec Dieu, tandis qu'il est identifié avec Ahoura Mazda dans les speculations ultérieures du Mazdéisme' (p. 170). Cf. Engl. tr., p. 128.

heretical only in the time of the Sassanids. Michaud is of the opinion that the author of the Qumran theological system either knew the Zervanite myth of creation or was influenced by a system of thought that has been infected with it.[45] The possibility of such Iranian influence cannot be disregarded, but the full implication of this influence has not yet been explored. There is certainly no obstacle, theologically speaking, which would prevent such a dualism subordinated to a Supreme Being from being adopted either into the Jewish or Jewish-Christian way of thinking.

Cullmann has, however, pointed out a difference between the Qumran dualism and that of the PsC, i.e., that the opposition—light-darkness, truth-perversity—in 1QS is never brought into line with the opposition—male-female, light-fire—as it is in the PsC.[46] This is true, but it seems that the difference is much more fundamental. Kuhn has already described the Qumran dualism as ethical and eschatological, akin to the Iranian source.[47] This is true, for no pair of Qumran opposites can be found which is not to be understood in an ethical sense.[48] Light

[45] Kuhn (*op. cit.*, 311–12) asserts that the subordination to God in the Qumran literature is a feature not found in the Iranian source. That an Iranian source had influenced as well the PsC seems indicated by the interest shown in these writings in Nimrod-Zoroaster. Cullmann (*op. cit.*, 38, n. 14) pointed out the passages, *Hom* 9:4; *Rec* 1:30; to these we may add *Rec* 4:27–29 (all *KP*). For the ideas of Michaud, cf. 'Un mythe zervanite dans un des manuscrits de Qumrân', *VT* 5 (1955) 137–47. See further D. Winston, 'The Iranian Component in the Bible, Apocrypha, and Qumran: A Review of the Evidence', *History of Religions* 5 (1965–66) 183–216. H.-J. Schoeps, 'Iranisches in den Pseudoklementinen', *ZNW* 51 (1960) 1–10. R. G. Jones, 'The Manual of Discipline (1QS), Persian Religion and the Old Testament', *The Teacher's Yoke: Studies in Memory of Henry Trantham* (ed. E. J. Vardaman and J. L. Garrett, Jr.; Waco, Texas: Baylor University Press, 1964) 94–108. R. N. Frye, 'Zurvanism Again', *HTR* 52 (1959) 63–73.

[46] *Ibid.*, 39.

[47] *Op. cit.*, 305.

[48] This I maintain against W. Baumgartner, 'Die Bedeutung der Höhlenfunde aus Palästina für die Theologie', *Schweizerische theologische Umschau* 24 (1954) 62, who thinks that the opposition between the sons of light and the

and darkness are only symbols for the other pair, truth and perversity, good and evil, God and Belial. But in the PsC the dualism is definitely physical. *All* principles have been divided into opposites (*Hom* 2:15 *KP*); the *syzygies* dominate everything (*Hom* 2:15–16, 33; *Rec* 3:59 *KP*): heaven, earth; day, night; light, fire; sun, moon—as well as good, evil. The opposition in the ethical sphere is expressed in the PsC in terms of two kingdoms, two paths, two beings, whereas in 1QS it is a question of two spirits. This, of course, may be a mere manner of expression. But the dualism of Qumran, though similar in its general conception to that of the Ebionites, is of a simpler type. An ethical dualism, like that of Qumran, could have developed—especially under other influences—into a dualism that was both physical and ethical, like that of the PsC.

Before leaving this question of dualism, I must say a word about its possible Gnostic character. In the first article that Kuhn wrote on the ideas of the Qumran sect, he labelled its dualism as 'Gnostic'.[49] Later, in discussing its connection with Iranian religion, he showed how the ideas of 1QS confirmed the thesis once put forth by Bousset-Gressmann that the Jewish apocalyptic ideas of the last centuries B.C. had been affected by Persian thought. He emphasized the fact that the ethical character of the Qumran dualism definitely connected it with Old Iranian ideas and clearly separated it from Gnosticism.[50] Schoeps constantly rejected throughout his book the idea that the Ebionites were Gnostics.[51] He accused Epiphanius of confusing them with the Elchesaites, and of erroneously ascribing to them the Gnostic ideas of the latter. For him the PsC dualism

---

sons of darkness is physical. What the basis of this physical interpretation is, Baumgartner does not tell us.

[49] 'Die in Palästina gefundenen hebräischen Texte und das Neue Testament', *ZThK* 57 (1950) 210: 'eine palästinische-jüdische Sektenfrömmigkeit gnostischer Struktur'; p. 207: 'die dualistischgnostische Denkstruktur'.

[50] 'Die Sektenschrift und die iranische Religion', *op. cit.*, 315.

[51] Cf. Schoeps I, 305–6: '*In Wirklichkeit sind die Ebioniten niemals Gnostiker gewesen, sondern im Gegenteil ihre allerschärfsten Gegner*' [emphasis supplied by Schoeps]. Cf. Bultmann's review, p. 188.

is nothing but a development of a trend, which has 'a legitimate Jewish root . . . for the *zûgôt*-principle is very ancient [*uralt*] in Judaism'.[52] Yet in an article written in 1954 Schoeps apparently abandoned this fundamental position; for he claims that he has finally realized that the Gnostic syzygy-system of Book 6 of *KP* is derived from the 1QS teaching of the two spirits.[53] This is a complete *volte-face*, the denial of a main contention in his book. Though the Qumran dualism could be the source of the Ebionite dualism of the PsC, we still have no real evidence for labelling either of them as Gnostic. It is to be hoped that the publication of the Gnostic Codices of Chenoboskion will shed light on the dualism of the PsC and give us a better understanding of early Gnositicism. But there is certainly no reason to call the Qumran dualism Gnostic.[54]

Teacher of Righteousness

The *môrēh haṣṣedeq* of 1QpHab (1:13; 2:2; 5:10; 7:4; 8:3; 9:9), of CD 1:11; 6:11; 20:1, 14, 28, 32), of 4QpPss[a] (1, 3–4 iii 15, 19; 3–10 iv 27), and of 4QpPss[b] (1:4; 2:2) has certain characteristics which resemble those of the *prophētēs alētheias* or *ho alēthēs prophētēs* of *KP* (*Hom* 1:18–19; 2:6 and *passim*). The latter is sometimes called merely 'the Prophet' (*Hom* 2:6) or 'the Teacher' (*Hom* 11:20, 28). This last description is also found for the Teacher of Righteousness in CD 20:28. But it should be

[52] *Ibid.*, 161. To be fair, we must indicate that he does admit in a footnote the possibility of the Persian source. The proof advanced for the *uralt* Jewish root is Rabbinic literature, whose antiquity is very hard to determine.

[53] 'Die Lehre [von den beiden Geistern] ist vielmehr Eigenbau, beste 'Ain-Feshkha Theologie. Jetzt weiss ich es endlich, *woher* die ebionitischen *Kerygmata Petrou* (K.P.), deren sechstes Buch die hochgnostische Syzygienlehre von den Gegensatzpaaren behandelt, ihre Lehre von den beiden Geistern bezogen haben' (Schoeps 2, 2).

[54] Cf. Heinrich Schlier, 'Das Denken der frühchristlichen Gnosis', *Neutestamentliche Studien für R. Bultmann*, *op. cit.*, 67–82, for an example of how different early Christian Gnosticism was from Qumran ideas. Bo Reicke has also recently pointed out another difference in that the God of Qumran is a *personal* God; see 'Traces cf Gnosticism in the Dead Sea Scrolls?', *NTS* 1 (1954) 140.

noted immediately that, whereas the identity of the Teacher of Righteousness in the Qumran documents is unknown, there can be no doubt that Jesus is the True Prophet of the PsC (cf. Epiphanius, *Pan.* 30, 18; *Hom* 3:52–56 *KP*).

The function of the Teacher of Righteousness is to lead men in the way of God's heart (CD 1:11); his words come from the mouth of God (1QpHab 2:2), for God has revealed to him all the mysteries of the words of his servants the prophets (7:4). The men of the community are to listen to him (CD 9:28, 32), and God will deliver from the house of condemnation all those who suffer for him and show their fidelity to him (1QpHab 2:7–8). He also seems to have been a priest (1QpHab 2:7),[55] 'persecuted' by the 'Man of the Lie', who rejected the Law (5:10; 11:5; CD 20:32). According to CD 6:11, someone is expected 'at the end of the days' and the phrase *ywrh hṣdq* plays on his name. Is it a reference to the Teacher of Righteousness? CD 19:35–20:1 seems to distinguish him from the Messiah expected 'from Aaron and from Israel'.[56]

[55] This is now confirmed by 4QpPss[a] 1,3–4 iii 15–16, where we read (2:15) *pšrw ʿl hkwhn mwrh h[ṣdq]*, 'its interpretation concerns the priest, the Teacher of [Righteousness whom] God has [or]dered to arise and [whom] he has established in order to build for him the congregation [of the Poor]' (see also 4QpPss[a] 1–2 ii 18; DJD 5, 44). J. L. Teicher denies, of course, that the Teacher of Righteousness was a priest; cf. *JJS* 3 (1952) 54; 5 (1954) 96: 'But he [the Teacher of Righteousness] was a teacher, not a sacrificing priest, and the term 'priest' applied to him in the Fragments is merely a metaphor.' 'The term *kohen* (priest) is thus equivalent to the term *doresh hatorah* (he who searches the scripture).' That the *dôreš hattôrāh*, 'the Interpreter of the Law', was a priestly figure in the Qumran literature is easily admitted. However, this does not mean that the Teacher of Righteousness was not a *kôhēn* ('priest') in the ordinary sense, i.e., a member of a priestly family closely related to the cultic service of the Jerusalem temple. He may have broken with the Jerusalem priests because of their laxity and corruption. But he is still regarded as *kôhēn*, and any attempt to water down the meaning of this term must offer some proof for the contention. On the other hand, CD 7:18 seems to think of an 'Interpreter of the Law' yet to come, a figure who seems to be distinct from the Teacher of Righteousness.

[56] See now R. E. Brown, 'The Teacher of Righteousness and the Messiah(s)', *The Scrolls and Christianity* (ed. M. Black; London: SPCK, 1969) 37–44, 109–12.

The function of the True Prophet in *KP* is similar to that of the Teacher of Righteousness at least in that he too is looked upon as the leader of the group, and the helper of mankind which is enshrouded in darkness and ignorance, communicating to it knowledge.[57] 'He alone is able to enlighten the souls of men, so that with our own eyes we may be able to see the way of eternal salvation' (*Hom* 1:19 *KP*; cf. *Rec* 1:15–16 *KP*). 'This is peculiar to the Prophet, to reveal the truth, even as it is peculiar to the sun to bring the day' (*Hom* 2:6 *KP*).

In this connection Cullmann speaks of an *Erlösergestalt* found in both sets of documents, whose specific role is to reveal the truth.[58] One may question whether the Teacher of Righteousness is aptly described as an *Erlösergestalt*. 1QpHab 8:2–3 is apparently the only passage (doubtful at that) that would lend itself to such an interpretation. For, though 'deliverance from the house of condemnation (*or* judgment)' might conceivably be understood in the sense of redemption, yet this may refer as well to some contemporary political situation, described by this vague expression, as do others in 1QpHab. As for the PsC, the True Prophet could be called an *Erlöser*; but Bultmann is undoubtedly right in stressing that the Pseudoclementine Christology is anything but soteriological in the Pauline sense, adopted by the early Church.[59]

As a revealer of truth, then, the Teacher of Righteousness and the True Prophet can be favourably compared, for their functions are definitely similar.[60] Nothing, however, warrants more than a possible connection between these two figures, when we are trying to trace the influence of Qumran on the Ebionites.

[57] K. Elliger, *op. cit.*, 285, and J. L. Teicher, *JJS* 2 (1951) 97, points out that the words *ṣdq* and *'mt* are really synonymous, so that we could well speak of the 'Teacher of Truth' or the 'True Teacher'. The other expression, however, has become customary already, so that it is retained here.

[58] *Op. cit.*, 39.

[59] *Op. cit.*, 183–6.

[60] Cullmann (*op. cit.*, 40) points out a dissimilarity in that the Teacher of

The Man of the Lie

The antagonist of the Teacher of Righteousness is described as the 'Man of the Lie' (cf. 1QpHab 2:1–2; 5:11; CD 20:15) or the 'Preacher of the Lie' (1QpHab 10:9; CD 8:13): *'îš hakkāzāb*; *maṭṭîp hakkāzāb*. In the PsC, however, the antagonist of Christ, the True Prophet, is Satan, the prince of evil (*Hom* 8:21 *KP*). Peter, too, has an adversary throughout, Simon Magus. But there is an unnamed figure referred to as *inimicus homo*, *ho echthros anthrōpos*, *planos tis* (*Rec* 1:70, 71, 73; *Hom* 2:17; 11:35; *Ep. Petri* 2, 3), who is identified as the Apostle Paul on the basis of *Rec* 1:71, alluding to Acts 22:5. But it should be noted that he is definitely considered to be the adversary of James, the bishop of Jerusalem. It is, therefore, a gratuitous assertion to equate the *inimicus homo* of PsC with the *'îš hakkāzāb*, and to maintain on this basis that Paul is the antagonist referred to in the Qumran literature. Both the Qumran scrolls and the PsC speak of a figure who is an adversary, but the differing details prevent any further identification.[61]

Attitude toward the Old Testament

Under this heading we will discuss the attitude of both groups toward the prophets, the Pentateuch, the sacrifice of the Temple, and the priesthood.

a) *The prophets*. The Qumran sect not only held to the strict observance of the Torah, but also regarded the prophets of the Old Testament with great esteem. This is evident not only from statements of 1QS (1:3; 8:16), 4QpHos[a] (2:5), CD (7:17), 1QpHab (2:9), but also from the way they quote the prophets

---

Righteousness is a priest, whereas the True Prophet is not. See footnote 55 and compare 1QpHab 2:7 with 7:4. As for the PsC, the situation is not clear. From the general context we would not expect the True Prophet to be a priest, and *Rec* 1:46–48 (*KP*) are certainly difficult to understand if he were not one.

[61] Cullmann (*op. cit.*, 40) speaks of a *Lügenprophet* in 1QpHab 7:9. I can find no such character in 1QpHab, unless that is the translation he is using for *mṭyp hkzb* in 10:9.

(CD 7:10; 9:5) and from the writings they composed to interpret the biblical prophets (e.g., the *pesharim*, 1QpHab, 1QpMic, 1QpZeph, 3QpIs, 4QpIs^{a-e}, 4QpHos^{a-b}, 4QpNah, 4QpMic, 4QpZeph, 5QpMal.[62]

As for the Ebionites, Irenaeus tells us that they had developed their own way of expounding the prophets, 'quae autem sunt prophetica curiosius exponere nituntur' (*Adv. haer.* 1, 26, 2). What does *curiosius* mean? It has been explained (Schoeps 1, 159) in terms of the information supplied by the *Panarion* of Epiphanius (30, 17), where we learn that the Ebionites admitted Abraham, Isaac, Jacob, Moses, Aaron, and Joshua, but rejected all the prophets, David, Solomon, Isaiah, Jeremiah, Daniel, Ezekiel, Elijah, and Elisha together with their oracles.

This explanation, however, is not certain. *Curiosius* is the Latin translation of a lost Greek word. Since we have no reason to assume that it is not an accurate translation, we may legitimately ask what Irenaeus, writing *ca.* 175, could have meant by it. Epiphanius' statement about the rejection of the prophets remains, of course, a possible interpretation, but it represents more likely the attitude of a later stage of Ebionism. Between Irenaeus and Epiphanius (310–403), the Ebionites could have been subjected to other influences (Samaritan, for instance) with regard to the prophets. Certainly there is no foundation for the opinion of J. Thomas[63] that *curiosius* shows that some Ebionites were Gnostics. *Curiosus* means 'bestowing care or pains upon a thing, applying one's self assiduously', as well as 'curious, inquisitive'.[64] It is just as likely that the Ebionites of Irenaeus' time had something like *pesharim*, and that *curiosius* is his way of describing this detailed, careful exegesis of the prophets.

[62] See J. Milik, 'Fragments d'un Midrasch de Michée dans les manuscrits de Qumran', *RB* 59 (1952) 412–18; DJD 1, 77–80; 3, 95–6, 180; 5, 11–42.

[63] *Op. cit.*, 169.

[64] *Harper's Latin Dictionary* (N.Y.: American Book Co., 1907) 502; cf. also *Thesaurus linguae latinae* 4, 1493.

In the PsC Jesus is the only true prophet. Owing to their peculiar Christology, the Holy Spirit, who was believed to be in Christ, was also present in Adam, so that he too is called the 'only true prophet'. 'The only true prophet gave names to each animal' (*Hom* 3:21 *KP*). Moreover, 'the true prophet appeared to Moses' in Egypt (*Rec* 1:34 *KP*). This probably refers, not to Christ as such, but to the spirit which made him the True Prophet. 'Know then that Christ, who was from the beginning, and always, was ever present with the pious, though secretly, through all their generations; especially with those who waited for him to whom he frequently appeared' (*Rec* 1:52 *KP*). This attitude toward Christ is responsible for the Ebionite rejection of the prophets of the Old Testament.[65] But an even stranger reason is found in the view of the Old Testament prophets as representatives of female prophecy, having been born of women. The True Prophet, being the Son of *Man* represents male prophecy, and so is accepted on the principle of the syzygies (*Hom* 3:22–23).

There are a few references to the Old Testament prophets in the PsC.[66] But it is hard to deduce anything from these, because they may have passed into Ebionite literature via works that were more acceptable to them. One clear case is found in *Rec* 1:37, where Hos 6:6 is cited: 'For I delight in piety, not sacrifice.' This text of Hosea, however, is used by Matthew (9:13; 12:7).

The attitude of the Qumran sect toward the Old Testament prophets, then, is entirely different from that of the Ebionites, at least as they are known to us from Epiphanius and the PsC. Consequently, we cannot look to the tenets of Qumran as a source for the Ebionite attitude.

b) The 'false pericopes'. Epiphanius (*Pan.* 30, 18) tells us that the Ebionites did not accept the whole Pentateuch, but rejected certain passages of it (*oute gar dechontai tēn Pentateuchon Mōÿseōs*

[65] *Rec* 1:59; 68–69 *KP*.

[66] Cf. Schoeps 1, 160.

holēn, alla tina rēmata apoballousin). The PsC, too, know of falsehoods that have been added to the Law of Moses. 'The Scriptures have had joined to them many falsehoods against God' (*Hom* 2:38 *KP*). By labelling certain passages of the Pentateuch as false chapters, the Ebionites managed to eliminate those that seemed in conflict with their beliefs about God. Peter cites as examples the following: 'Neither was Adam a transgressor, who was fashioned by the hands of God; nor was Noah drunken, who was found righteous above all the world; nor did Abraham live with three wives at once, who, on account of his sobriety, was thought worthy of a numerous posterity; nor did Jacob associate with four—of whom two were sisters—who was the father of the twelve tribes, and who intimated the coming of the presence of our Master; nor was Moses a murderer, nor did he learn to judge from an idolatrous priest . . .' (*Hom* 2:52 *KP*).

There is not the slightest trace of such an attitude in the writings of the sect of Qumran.[67]

c) *Sacrifice*. Though there was formerly some hesitation about the attitude of the Qumran sect with regard to sacrifice, it seems clear from the War-Scroll that they did not reject it. In 1QM 2:5–6 we read: 'These shall be posted at the burnt-offerings and the sacrifices, to prepare an offering of incense, agreeable to the good pleasure of God, to make atonement on behalf of all his community, to burn flesh continually before him on the table of glory.' According to J. Baumgarten, 'We do not find in DSD [=1QS] any law concerning animal sacrifice. There are only figurative references to sacrificial offerings.'[68] But 'DSH and CDC [=1QS and CD] tell us of a sect which looked with disfavor upon the priests of the Temple of Jerusalem. They

[67] Cf. G. Vermès, *op. cit.*, 109–12. Bultmann (*op. cit.*, 187) maintains that this rejection of the false pericopes by the Ebionites presupposes a Gnostic rejection of the Old Testament, and is merely another example of the compromise made by the Ebionites between Gnosticism and Jewish-Christian tradition. The theory of the false pericopes represents a 'mysterion' transmitted by Peter to the Ebionite community. This is sheer speculation.

[68] 'Sacrifice and Worship among the Jewish Sectarians of the Dead Sea (Qumran) Scrolls', *HTR* 46 (1953) 149.

accused them of violating the sanctity of the Temple and the Holy City by failure to observe the laws of ritual purity and appropriating sacred property. The sectarians, who were themselves identified with the Zadokite priestly tradition, held that it was preferable, under such conditions, not to bring sacrifices to the altar. Consequently they entered a covenant to avoid the Sanctuary. In support of their position, they turned to Prophetic denunciations of sinful offerings. The Halakah of CDC, however, preserved several laws relating to the Temple and the sacrifices.'[69] This supports Josephus' testimony about the Essenes, who 'do not offer sacrifices, because they profess to have more pure lustrations' (*Ant.* 18, 1, 5).

But the Ebionites did reject sacrifice without a doubt. 'It is Jesus who has put out, by the grace of baptism, that fire which the priest kindled for sins' (*Rec* 1:48 *KP*; cf. also 1:36, 37, 39, 55, 62; *Hom* 3:45 all *KP*). Peter even preaches that the destruction of the Temple is due to the continuance of sacrifice at a time when it had been officially abolished (*Rec* 1:64 *KP*). This evidence from PsC agrees with the testimony of Epiphanius (*Pan* 30,16).

The radical difference of outlook here between the two sects prevents us from saying that the Ebionite attitude developed out of that of Qumran.[70]

d) *Priesthood.* The priesthood was a recognized group in the Qumran sect. Baumgarten has given a good summary of their attitude, as it is known from the scrolls published by the American Schools:

[69] *Ibid.*, 153–4. Cf. also p. 155 for a discussion of the following text of Josephus. See, however, J. Strugnell, *JBL* 77 (1958) 113–15.

[70] Bultmann (*op. cit.*, 187) would derive the Ebionite outlook from the attitude found in the primitive community of the Christian Church itself, not as dependent on passages in Mk 12:33, Mt 9:13; 12:7, but rather as coming from the attitude of the Jews among whom Christ lived. Jesus was not the opponent of the priests, as the prophets of the Old Law had been, but of the Scribes. As far as Jewish piety was concerned, the Synagogue had pressed the cult of the temple into the background, and so sacrifice had lost its meaning for early Christianity. In an article on 'L'opposition contre le

To the priests, DSD assigns an exalted position within the community. As in CDC, the sect is conceived as joining Aaron and Israel (DSD 5:6), but while the Israelite sectaries formed a 'holy house' (*bêt qōdeš*), the priests were to be established as a 'most holy institution' (*sôd qōdeš qodāšîm*) [1QS 8:5–6; cf. 8:8–9; 9:6]. Legal decisions were made 'according to the sons of Zadok, the priests who keep the Covenant, and according to the majority of the men of the community' [1QS 5:2–3; 5:9,21–22;6:19;8:9]. DSD 9:7 provides that 'only the sons of Aaron shall have authority in matters of law and property'. In the council of the community there were twelve lay men and three priests (DSD 8:1). A priest was required to be present in every place where ten men formed a unit of the community. At the sessions of the sectarians, the priests were given preference in seating and procedure. A priest invoked the blessing over the bread and wine before communal meals (DSD 6:5–6). The priests also played a significant role in the annual covenant ceremony, which was one of the important institutions of the sect.[71]

In 1QM we learn that there are priests (7:10–15; 8:2–7, 13–14), but also 'leaders of the priests' (2:1), a 'chief priest' (2:1; 15:4; 16:13; 18:5),[72] and 'the priest appointed for the time of vengeance according to the vote of his brethren' (15, 6). The robes of the priests in battle are described (7:9–11), and the role the priests are to perform in the course of the battle is detailed (7:12–18). They are to blow the trumpets (7:15), encourage the soldiers (7:12), bless God and curse Belial (13:1–6).[73]

Temple de Jérusalem, motif commun de la théologie johannique et du monde ambiant', *NTS* 5 (1958–59) 157–73, O. Cullmann writes, '. . . nous constatons que les Pseudo-Clémentines qui adoptent en partie jusque dans leur moindres détails les idées et les usages de Qumran vont sur cette question du Temple et des sacrifices beaucoup plus loin que la secte de Qumran et se rapprochent, sur ce point, de l'attitude d'Etienne. Les Pseudo-Clémentines doivent être citées dans ce contexte du judaïsme ésoterique dont nous nous occupons . . . et encore leur radicalisme [i.e., des Pseudo-Clémentines] n'est-il qu'un développement naturel, pour ainsi dire, de l'attitude qumranienne à l'égard du Temple et de son culte' (p. 166).

71 *Op. cit.*, 152; cf. G. Vermès, *op. cit.*, 78.

72 Cf. H. L. Ginsberg, 'The Hebrew University Scrolls from the Sectarian Cache', *BASOR* 112 (1948) 20–1.

73 This brief description shows that the function of the priest or *kôhēn* can

Such passages leave no doubt as to the status of the priests in the sect of Qumran. Levites, too, are often mentioned as a specific class. This is in sharp contrast to the attitude of the Ebionites as manifested by PsC. Their rejection of the priesthood logically follows the substitution of baptism for sacrifice. The priesthood had its function and meaning in history in the days when God *permitted* sacrifice, but that time has passed (*Rec* 1:48 KP). Cullmann looks upon this attitude as an extension of the attitude of the Qumran sect, adopted with reference to the official priesthood in the Temple.[74] 1 QpHab 8:8 ff. speaks of a 'wicked priest', who rebelled against the statutes of God, and 9:4 ff. of the 'priests of Jerusalem', who gather wealth and loot. Consequently, Cullmann may well be right in relating the Ebionite rejection of the priesthood to such a movement in Palestine as the Qumran disapproval of the official priesthood in Jerusalem.

The general conclusion to be drawn from the treatment of the attitudes of these two sects with regard to the Old Testament and its institutions is that they differ considerably. It is only in the last point that there is a possible kinship of ideas. For the rest the difference is radical.

Baths and Baptism

Several passages in the Qumran literature have been interpreted as referring to the bathing practices of the sect. Cullmann[75] cites 1QS 3:4, 9; 5:13–14. It will be profitable to examine these and other texts.

---

hardly be that as described by Teicher in his later article in *JJS* 5 (1954) 96; see footnote 55 above. According to 1QM 7:11 at the end of the description of the robes of the priests in battle it is prescribed that this battledress shall not be worn in the sanctuary. This same word, *miqdāš*, is used in 1QM 2:3 in a context where *'ôlôt* and *zebāḥîm* are also mentioned; so there is no reason to maintain that the priests of Qumran had nothing to do with sacrifice. One should also recall in this connection the possibility of sacrifice at Qumran itself; see R. de Vaux, *L'archéologie et les manuscrits de la Mer Morte* (London, 1961) 10–11.

[74] *Op. cit.*, 41.

[75] *Ibid.*, 44. Are we sure that 1QS 6:13 ff. refer to baths? M. H. Gottstein

He cannot be justified while he conceals his stubbornness of heart
And with darkened mind looks upon ways of light.
While in iniquity, he cannot be reckoned perfect.
He cannot purify himself by atonement,
Nor cleanse himself with water-for-impurity,
Nor sanctify himself with seas or rivers
Nor cleanse himself with any water for washing!
Unclean! Unclean! shall he be as long as he rejects God's laws
So as not to be instructed by the Community of his counsel
(1QS 3:3–6)

It is most probable that we have here a veiled reference to some bathing practice of the Qumran sect, to a purificatory bath perhaps. But it is remotely possible that this is a rhetorical way of stressing the uncleanness and guilt of the man who rejects God's laws. The same could be said of 1QS 3:9. But 1QS 4:20–21 is more explicit: 'Then God will purge with his truth all the deeds of man, and will refine for himself the frame of man by rooting out every spirit of falsehood from the bounds of his flesh, to cleanse him with a holy spirit from all wicked practices, sprinkling upon him a spirit of truth like water-for-impurity against all untrue abominations. . . .' However, the passage in 1QS 5:13 alludes to some bathing practice: 'He [the perverse one] may not enter into water to [be permitted to] touch the Purity of the holy men, for they will not be cleansed unless they have turned from their wickedness. . . .' Two passages in CD 10:11–12; 11:22) seem to be a mere repetition of the Levitical purity laws prescribed in Lv 11:40; 15:10. There is also one passage in 1QM 14:2–3 which may or may not refer to a purificatory bath. 'After they have gone up from among the slain to return to the camp, they will intone the hymn of Return. In

---

has gone to an opposite extreme in maintaining that the Qumran sect was not a baptist sect, whereas the Essenes are known to have been definitely such; cf. 'Anti-Essene traits in the DSS', *VT* 4 (1954) 141–7. Even Schoeps, who thinks that the identification of the 'Sadoqiten von 'Ain Feshkha' with the Essenes of Philo and Josephus is highly problematical, admits that Gottstein has gone too far (cf. Schoeps 2, 4); cf. R. North, S.J., 'The Qumrân "Sadducees"', *CBQ* 17 (1955) 44–68.

the morning they will wash their garments and cleanse themselves of the blood of the sinners' corpses.'

Perhaps no special meaning would be attached to references such as these, were it not for the fact that we know from other sources that the Essenes were a baptist sect (Josephus, *JW* 2, 129–32). Baumgarten has emphasized the adherence to stringent laws of purity and purification among the Essenes of Qumran.[76] Contact with a member of lower grade necessitates a purification (Josephus, *op. cit.* 2, 8; 2, 10). Excavations at Khirbet Qumran uncovered seven large cisterns, the nature of which was not at first definitely established. They have been considered as the bathing places of the Qumran sect; A. Dupont-Sommer called them 'swimming-pools' in the Postscript (dated 10 February 1954) to the English translation of his *Nouveaux aperçus sur les manuscrits de la Mer Morte.*[77] Partially roofed-over cisterns, fitted with steps by which one could descend to reach the water-level, are not unknown in Roman Palestine.[78] These cisterns were not baptisteries of any sort. However, there were also uncovered in the excavations at Khirbet Qumran at least two small baths, which undoubtedly did serve as places for ritual washings (see R. de Vaux, *L'archéologie*, pp. 98–9).

The conclusion, then, regarding the sect of Qumran is that it was baptist. Against the background of a general baptist movement, which is known to have existed in Palestine and

[76] *Op. cit.*, 155.

[77] The English title is *The Jewish Sect of Qumrân and the Essenes* (London: Valentine Mitchell, 1954) 167–8; Cullmann (*op. cit.*, 44) referred to these same excavated reservoirs or cisterns as proof that 'das Kloster von Qumrân ein wirkliches Taufzentrum war'.

[78] A stepped reservoir was found at Gezer; cf. R. A. S. Macalister, *Excavation of Gezer* (London: John Murray, 1912) 1, 274–6; 3, pl. LIV. Cf. also F. J. Bliss and R. A. S. Macalister, *Excavations in Palestine during the years 1898–1900* (London: Pal. Expl. Fund, 1902) 21. Mention is made here of a 'vaulted cistern' at Tell Zakarîyā. 'Similar stepped cisterns were excavated by me at Jerusalem' (p. 21). 'It is quite possible that we have here an ancient cistern vaulted over during the brief Roman occupation' (*ibid.*). See further, R. North, 'The Qumran Reservoirs', *BCCT* 100–32.

Syria between 150 B.C. and A.D. 300, the conclusion is even more plausible.[79]

There is a great deal of evidence for the bathing practices of the Ebionites both in Epiphanius (*Pan.* 30, 21) and the PsC. However, the one big difference in this regard is that they admitted Christian baptism as well. 'This is the service he [God] has appointed: to worship him only, and trust only in the Prophet of Truth, and to be baptized for the remission of sins, and thus by this pure baptism to be born again unto God by saving water . . .' (*Hom* 7:8 not *KP*; cf. *Rec* 1:39 *KP*). 'Unless a man be baptized in water, in the name of the threefold blessedness, as the true Prophet taught, he can neither receive the remission of sins nor enter into the Kingdom of heaven' (*Rec* 1:69 *KP*; cf. *Hom* 11:27 *KP*). This baptism is necessary before Peter and his followers will partake of food with a man (*Hom* 1:22 not *KP*; cf. 13:4–5 not *KP*).

But in addition to baptism, which is definitely considered an initiation-rite to be conferred only once in the PsC, there are other baths of a purificatory ritualistic character that remind one of the Essene practices mentioned above. These take place before meals and before prayer (*Hom* 8:2; 9:23 *KP*; 10:1 not *KP*; etc.). 'Peter rose early and went into the garden, where there was a great water-reservoir (*hydrochoeion*),[80] into which a full stream of water constantly flowed. There having bathed, and then having prayed, he sat down' (*Hom* 10:1 not *KP*; cf. 10:26 not *KP*: Peter bathes with others before a common meal; 11:1 not *KP*: Peter bathes before prayer; *Rec* 4:3 *KP*: Peter bathes in the sea before eating). Washing with water was prescribed after sexual intercourse (*Hom* 11:30, 33 *KP*). These baths are highly recommended by Peter in his preaching (*Hom*

[79] Cf. J. Thomas, *Le mouvement baptiste*, already referred to.

[80] The Syriac MS., containing parts of the *Hom* and *Rec*, unfortunately has a paraphrase for the Greek word, *hydrochoeion*, so that we are not given any clue to the Semitic word in question; e.g., *Hom* 10:1 reads *'tr dmy' sgy" 'myn'yt rdyn hww*.

11:28 ff.; *Rec* 6:11 *KP*).[81] Such baths could well have been received into the Ebionite group from the Qumran sect; but, in view of the fact of a general baptist movement in Palestine and Syria at that time, we cannot restrict the source of this practice to Qumran alone.

As a matter of fact, there seems to be evidence of other influence. Epiphanius mentions the Elchesaites as the source of some of the baths in vogue among the Ebionites. 'Whenever any one of them is sick or bitten by a snake, he goes down into the water. There he makes use of all the invocations which Helxai composed, calling upon the heavens and the earth, salt and water, winds and the angels of justice (as they say), likewise bread and oil; then he says, 'Come to my aid, and free me from this pain''' (*Pan.* 30, 17). The similarity that exists between this practice and the 'oath' to be taken by the neophyte before he is entrusted with the sacred books and traditions of the Ebionites, described in *Diam.* 2, support this contention of other than Essene influence on the Ebionites. There is certainly nothing like this oath, taken by a stream of water with an invocation of elements, in the Qumran literature. J. Thomas maintains that they were influenced by the Christian Church, the Essenes, and the Elchesaites.[82]

Communal Meal

In 1QS 6:2 we learn about the Qumran sect that 'they shall eat communally'. 'When they arrange the table to eat or [arrange] the wine to drink, the priest shall first stretch out his hand to invoke a blessing with the first of the bread and/or

[81] The question of baths in the PsC is one that is involved in the discussion of sources. Most of the cases cited above of Peter's bath before meals and prayer are found in non-*KP* passages; the scene is Tripoli. Cullmann maintains that these passages represent later Ebionite practices (*op. cit.*, 45). It is precisely because of the bathing practices that J. Thomas decided to revise the usual theory of PsC sources and present his own (cf. *op. cit.*, 175). This cannot be discussed at length here. But it indicates once again the tenuous character of this entire comparison.

[82] *Ibid.*, 181.

wine' (6:4–6). 'He [the neophyte] shall not touch the drink of the Many until his completion of a second year among the men of the Community' (6:20; cf. 7:20). The room in which this communal meal was most likely taken has been found at Khirbet Qumran.[83] In the 'Two Column' Document (=1QSa) we hear of a Messiah of Israel sharing in the banquet of the sect, but he remains subordinate to the priest, whom Abbé Milik has identified as the Messiah of Aaron.[84]

As for the Ebionites of the PsC, I have already mentioned that they did not eat with the non-baptized (*Hom* 1:22; 3:4, 9; *Rec* 2:71 not *KP*). But they too had a communal meal. References to it are vague at times, but there seem to have been fixed places at table ('unusquisque ex more recognoscens proprii ordinis locum', *Rec* 4:37 not *KP*). Though the expression used to indicate the meal is often merely 'to partake of food' (*sitiōn metalabein, Hom* 8:2 *KP*; *trophēs metalabein,* 10:26 not *KP*; *cibum sumere, Rec* 4:37; 5:36 not *KP*), we meet on occasion a peculiar expression, *halōn metalabein,* 'to partake of salt' (*Hom* 4:6; 11:34; 19:25 not *KP*) or *meta tēn halōn koinōnian* (*Hom* 14:8 not *KP*; cf. *Ep. Clem.* 9, 1). Salt and bread are mentioned together in *Diam.* 4:3, and we even find the verb, *synalizesthai* (*Hom* 13:4 not *KP*).[85]

There is another set of expressions, which indicate that the Ebionites of the PsC celebrated the Eucharist. These are *klasas eucharistian* (*Hom* 11:36 not *KP*); *eucharistiam fragens cum eis* (*Rec* 6:15 not *KP*); *ton arton ep' eucharistia klasas kai epitheis halas* (*Hom* 14:1 not *KP*). Connection with the Christian Eucharist seems clear from the following passage: 'For I showed them that

[83] Cf. R. de Vaux, 'La seconde saison de fouilles à Khirbet Qumrân', *CRAIBL*, 1953, 310–11.

[84] 'Une lettre de Siméon bar Kokheba', *RB* 60 (1953) 291.

[85] This verb occurs in Acts 1:4, where it is variously interpreted; cf. W. Bauer, *Wörterbuch zum Neuen Testament* (4th ed.; Berlin, A. Töpelmann, 1952) col. 1425. Philo (*Vita Contemp.* 4, 9) mentions the use of salt at the meals of the Therapeutae, who have been generally considered as related to the Essenes.

in no way else could they be saved, unless through the grace of the Holy Spirit they hastened to be washed with the baptism of the threefold invocation, and received the eucharist of Christ the Lord . . .' (*Rec* 1:63 *KP*). Whether these were two separate types of communal meals is hard to say. The mention of bread and salt in *Hom* 14:1 recalls the passage in *Diam.* 4, 3, where there is no mention of the Eucharist. The question is further complicated by the fact that Epiphanius (*Pan.* 30, 16) mentions that the Ebionites celebrated the mysteries with unleavened bread and water.

The main fact, however, is certain, that a communal meal was found in both the Qumran sect and the Ebionites of the PsC. Whereas bread and wine figure in the former, bread, salt, and water (?) are found associated with the latter. In both cases the meal was only for the initiated. Neither similarities nor dissimilarities in this case should be overlooked in drawing conclusions.

Sacred Books

Mention of an enigmatic book of *H^{o}gî* is found in CD 10:6; 13:2; 1QSa 1:7; and possibly in CD14:8, 'the book of Meditation', which is understood differently by various scholars. Dupont-Sommer thinks that this might refer to 1QS itself.[86] Others think that it refers to the Hebrew Scriptures. This is by no means certain, and we have no indication that the Qumran sect treated this book as secret. On the other hand, Josephus speaks of 'the books of the sect' which each member swears to preserve (*JW* 2, 8, 8 #142). The Manual of Discipline prescribes the concealment of 'the teaching of the Law' (1QS 9:17), but it is not easy to equate this with the preservation of secret books.

In the PsC the sermons of Peter were treated as secret writings, which were to be entrusted only to the initiated; cf. *Ep. Petr.* 1, 2; 3, 1; *Diam.* 1–3. It is in connection with these books that the period of probation is mentioned, which lasts for six

[86] *Nouveaux aperçus*, 88–9; cf. Vermès, *op. cit.*, 176.

years (*Diam.* 1, 2; 2, 2). This is the only connection in which a probation is mentioned, whereas in the Qumran sect an elaborate process of initiation is found. It has nothing to do with the receiving of sacred books, but leads up to the acceptance as a full member of the Community.

Consequently, both on the score of sacred books and the probation or initiation connected with them, there is much more dissimilarity than similarity between the Qumran sect and the Ebionites of the PsC.

Community of Goods

Even though details may not be very clear, it is quite certain that the sect of Qumran practised some sort of communal poverty. 'All who dedicate themselves to his Truth shall bring all their mind and their strength and their property into the Community of God . . . to direct all their property according to his righteous counsels' (1QS 1:11–13; cf. 5:2). After a year's probation the novice's property will be handed over to the Custodian of Property of the Many (6:20), but it will not be pooled with the rest until the second year of probation is completed (6:22). 'If there be found among them a man who lies in the matter of wealth, and it become known, they shall exclude him from the Purity of the Many for one year, and he shall be fined one-fourth of his food-allowance' (6:25). No one may share in the property of those that transgress the laws of the community (7:25; 8:23; 9:22). The priests (sons of Aaron) will regulate the property (9:8) (see further, pp. 284–8 above).

Epiphanius (*Pan.* 30, 17) tells us that the Ebionites practised poverty, selling their goods as was the custom in the days of the Apostles. In the PsC poverty is praised and possessions are regarded as sinful (*Hom* 15:7 *KP*). 'To all of us possessions are sins' (*Hom* 15:9 *KP*). Yet, as Cullmann has pointed out,[87] the fact is that we find no practice of poverty in the PsC and do not see the members pooling their wealth as does the sect of Qum-

[87] *Op. cit.*, 47.

ran; it is thus an ideal rather than established practice. As previously mentioned, the Ebionites did not live a communal life (though they might have come together at times for communal meals). And though they might praise poverty, they could still judge as follows: 'One is not unquestionably righteous because he happens to be poor' (*Hom* 15:10 *KP*). This may be a bit surprising, in view of the fact that the group was known as Ebionite, a name which has often been explained in connection with the Hebrew word for 'the poor', as already discussed. Of course, Epiphanius' testimony stands as evidence to the contrary, but even here it is just possible that he or his sources have reasoned from the name to the practice, especially when the example of the Apostles could be cited in favour of early Church practices.[88]

At any rate, this is another significant difference between the sect of Qumran and the Ebionites, at least as they are known from the PsC.

CONCLUSION

To sum up, then, we can say that whereas there are many similarities between the sect of Qumran and the Ebionites, there are also striking dissimilarities. The Qumran dualism resembles the Ebionite in that it is subordinated to Jewish monotheism and both are ethical. But the Qumran dualism is ethical alone, whereas the Ebionite is also physical; the Qumran dualism is simpler (being a contrast merely of light-darkness, truth-perversity, good-evil, and two spirits), but the Ebionite is much more complex. In both groups we find two main figures: the Teacher of Righteousness and the Man of the Lie, the Prophet of Truth and the *inimicus homo*. In the Qumran literature they are protagonist and antagonist. The Ebionite Prophet of Truth has a role similar to that of the Teacher of Righteousness, whereas the *inimicus homo* can be compared with the Man of the Lie only in that he is an adversary. However,

[88] See further L. E. Keck, *ZNW* 57 (1966) 55–66.

we find a radical difference of outlook when we consider the attitude of the two groups toward the Old Testament and its institutions. Qumran esteems the Torah, the Prophets, the priests, and sacrifice (when their own rigid ideas of purity are observed by the priests during sacrifice). But the Ebionites reject the 'false pericopes' of the Pentateuch, reject the prophets of the Old Testament, reject priesthood, and claim that baptism has replaced sacrificial cult. Whereas the Ebionites admitted Christian baptism and had purificatory baths of different sorts, we find at Qumran only simple purificatory baths. Though both had some sort of a communal meal, bread and wine were used at Qumran, while the Ebionites used bread, salt, and water (?), and celebrated the Christian Eucharist. Some sort of sacred book (*H^{o}gî*) was used at Qumran, but we are not sure that it was a secret writing, so that it can scarcely be compared with the Sermons of Peter, which were to be entrusted only to the initiated among the Ebionites, who had passed a long probation. Whereas communal poverty was definitely practised at Qumran, there is no evidence of its practice in the PsC, where it is, however, praised. Epiphanius tells us, however, that the Ebionites did practise poverty.

From the preceding survey of the main points,[89] which have served as the basis of our comparison between the sect of Qumran and the Ebionites, several conclusions can be drawn. First, as already stated above, there is no real evidence for the identification of the sect of Qumran as Ebionite. This opinion is

[89] One main point has been purposely omitted; this is the question of 'knowledge' in the Qumran and Ebionite sects. To treat this point adequately would demand a separate paper in itself. From the standpoint of Qumran, we already have a good treatment of the question in the scrolls previously published, written by W. D. Davies, '"Knowledge" in the Dead Sea Scrolls and Matthew 11:25–30', *HTR* 46 (1953) 113–39. See esp. 129 ff., where he rejects the identification of Qumran 'knowledge' with any of three ways of understanding 'gnosticism' or 'gnosis'. Strangely enough, Cullmann has not considered this point. Cf. W. Baumgartner, *op. cit.*, 62, where the Qumran emphasis on wisdom and intelligence is labelled 'gnostic'. Cf. also Bo Reicke, *op. cit.*, 137–41.

contrary to that of J. L. Teicher of Cambridge, but finds itself in good company.[90] Secondly, it does not seem possible to admit that the Essenes of Qumran became the Ebionites. Cullmann's conclusion is: 'die Reste der Essener vom Toten Meer im Judenchristentum aufgingen.'[91] Such an opinion demands that the strict-living Qumran sect, adhering rigorously to the Torah, the teaching of the prophets, and their own ascetical rules of communal life, abandoned their main tenets and practices and became Christians. We have no evidence for this. As should be obvious to anyone reading this essay, I have utilized much of the material Cullmann has brought together in his enlightening article. Many of the similarities and dissimilarities here pointed out were indicated previously by him. Consequently, one is surprised to read at the end of his article that one group passed over into the other. It seems that the most we can say is that the sect of Qumran influenced the Ebionites in many ways; Essene tenets and practices were undoubtedly adopted or adapted into the Ebionite way of life. To try to state more than this is to overstep the limits set by the evidence we have at our disposal.[92]

In my discussion of dualism I rejected the idea that either the Qumran or the Pseudoclementine dualism was Gnostic. I

[90] Cullmann, *op. cit.*, 35; A. Dupont-Sommer, *Nouveaux aperçus*, 201–6; K. Elliger, *op. cit.*, 242–5; Schoeps 3, 322–8.

[91] *Op. cit.*, 50.

[92] It seems, too, that Cullmann has overemphasized the importance of the destruction of Jerusalem to the Ebionites of the PsC and to the sect of Qumran.—When this essay was reprinted in a slightly abridged form in K. Stendahl, *The Scrolls and the New Testament* (New York: Harper, 1957) 208–31, 291–8, it found itself in company with an article by O. Cullmann, 'The Significance of the Qumran Texts for Research into the Beginnings of Christianity', pp. 18–32, 251–2. Cullmann had the opportunity of including a note (on p. 252) in which he maintains that I have misunderstood his intention: 'I naturally do not mean that "the Essenes of Qumran became the Ebionites." What I say, however, is that after the dispersion of the community during the war of A.D. 70 the remnants of the sect were absorbed into the Jewish-Christian groups of the East Jordan district, which degenerated more and more into a Jewish sect, and were open to all kinds of

do not intend to claim that there is no Gnosticism at all in the PsC. It is, moreover, quite conceivable that many of the ideas of the Qumran writings would easily lend themselves to Gnostic adaptation. To admit this is not at all the same as to speak of a 'gnostisches Judentum' at Qumran, as Schoeps has done.

This discussion has tried to furnish a *mise au point* in the problem of the relationship between Qumran and the Ebionites. It is obvious that the last word has not yet been said.[93]

---

syncretistic influence.' I shall leave to others the judgment about whether I have misunderstood his intention. He has not always written so clearly as in the above-quoted note. For instance, in his article, 'Ebioniten' (*Die Religion in Geschichte und Gegenwart* [3rd ed.; Tübingen: Mohr], vol. 2 [1958], col. 298), he writes, 'Möglicherweise sind Reste der Qumransekte nach der Katastrophe von 70 nChr in den ebionitischen Gruppen des Ostjordanlandes aufgegangen.'

[93] See further my article, 'Ebionites', *Dictionnaire de Spiritualité* 4/25 (1958) cols. 32–40. F. Paschke, *Die beiden griechischen Klementinen-Epitomen und ihre Anhänge* (TU 90; Berlin: Akademie-V., 1966).

INDEX OF MODERN AUTHORS

INDEX OF SUBJECTS

INDEX OF SCRIPTURAL REFERENCES

APOCRYPHA (DEUTEROCANONICAL BOOKS)

INDEX OF PSEUDEPIGRAPHAL REFERENCES

TESTAMENT OF THE TWELVE PATRIARCHS

INDEX OF DEAD SEA SCROLLS REFERENCES

A WANDERING ARAMEAN

CONTENTS

Chapter 1

The Study of the Aramaic Background of the New Testament*

The discussion of Jesus and the beginnings of Christology sooner or later always comes to grips with the so-called Aramaic substratum of his sayings in the NT. This is not to deny that the person of the historical Jesus of Nazareth is in reality much more significant for those beginnings. What he was and what he did must in the long run be considered more important for the christology of the NT and of the Christian church than merely what he said. But, unfortunately, in the writings of the NT, we have no pipeline to the person or the deeds of the historical Jesus that can be separated from what the early Christian community recounted of him, of his sayings, and of the movement that he began. His sayings, of course, form an important *part* of the written heritage of the early Christian community, which is in its own way part of the norm of Christian belief in every century. Hence the sayings of Jesus bear directly on the question of the beginnings of christological faith.

Because Jesus of Nazareth has normally been regarded as the founder of Christianity and because he was a Palestinian Jew of what we call today the first century, students of the NT have always looked to first-century Palestinian customs and phenomena for an intelligible background of the traditions that have come down to us about him and his early disciples. But the writings of that early phase of Christianity and the sayings of Jesus preserved in them are couched in Greek, in effect, in a translation. Even if we make allowances for sayings that were put on his lips by evangelists or by the tradition before them, we still have to cope with the degree to which the Greek saying might reflect an Aramaic saying that he might have uttered. In effect, the question of the origins of christology cannot dispense with the Aramaic problem—unless, of course, one's hermeneutical approach to the New Testament is dominated by a philosophy in which such a question is *belanglos*.

Claims are sometimes made for the authenticity of Jesus' sayings, based on the Aramaic substratum that is said to shine through the Greek in which they are preserved.[1] Such claims are at least insinuated on all sorts of Aramaic evidence; and anyone who tries to cope with the matter today realizes how complex it is. My purpose is to sort out here a number of generic aspects of the problem of the Aramaic substratum of the sayings of Jesus in the NT and to set forth a programmatic approach to each one on the basis of the new Aramaic evidence that has come to light from the contemporary period. Unravelling the complex strands is not easy, and my remarks in this essay may at times seem rather general; but I shall try to introduce specific examples.

Eight aspects of the problem can be isolated at present, and their diversity calls for a variety of treatment, and hence of methodology. The eight aspects are these: (1) the question of Aramaic as a language of Jesus, or more broadly, as a language in use in first-century Palestine; (2) the question of Aramaic words, names, phrases preserved in NT writings, Josephus, the Mishnaic tradition, etc.; (3) the question of Aramaisms in NT Greek, usually of a lexical or a syntactic nature (this is the question of Aramaic interference); (4) the question of mistranslations; (5) the question of Aramaic literary forms in prose and poetry; (6) the question of Aramaic and variant readings in the NT text tradition; (7) the question of Jewish literary traditions that are found in the NT and in known Aramaic literature of various periods; and (8) the question of Aramaic epistolography. One or other issue may be lacking in this line-up, but the bulk of the problem is made up of these eight aspects.

Before the discussion of these aspects three preliminary remarks are in order about the history of the inquiry into the Aramaic problem, the diversity of the NT writings, and the appeal that is often made to so-called Semitisms.

First, the study of the Aramaic background of the NT has been complicated by the history of the inquiry into it and by the way that history has developed from the time that scholars began to be interested in it. But we have come to a point where a radical break must be made with some of the methods of investigation that have been used and where a more rigorous critique and sorting out of evidence must be undertaken.

It is impossible to survey here all the phases of the inquiry into the Aramaic substratum of the NT and the contributions of all who took part in them. The early phases of the inquiry have been set forth in Arnold Meyer's monograph, *Jesu Muttersprache.*[2] From it I shall cull only a few items that will serve to illustrate my first remark. Though certain patristic writers, such as Eusebius, Epiphanius, Jerome, and Julius Africanus,[3] were, in general, aware of Aramaisms in NT Greek, the history of the inquiry into the Aramaic substratum began only with the Renaissance and the Humanists' return *ad fontes.* The inquiry was thus remotely associated with the study of the Greek text of the NT, and even more closely with the emergence of Syriac literature and of Syriac translations of the Bible in the West.[4] In yet another way, the name of Nicholas of Lyra came to the fore when he began to interest himself in rabbinic lore and its possible relation to the NT.[5] At that time, what we call Aramaisms today were often labelled Syriacisms. In 1555 Johann Albrecht von Widmanstadt translated the Syriac NT and entitled it, *Liber sacrosancti Evangelii de Iesu Christo Domino & Deo nostro—lingua syra Jesu Christi vernacula divino ipsius ore consecrata et a Joanne evangelista hebraica dicta.*[6] From this translation and its title stems the long and well-known tradition of claims that Syriac was the mother-tongue of Jesus. Between 1609 and 1639 the two Buxtorfs (père et fils) published their Chaldaic Lexicon.[7] But it remained for Joseph Justus Scaliger to distinguish Syriac from what he called Chaldaic; he regarded the language of the non-Hebrew chapters of Daniel and Ezra as "Babylonian Chaldee," whereas "Jewish Chaldee" became his name for the Aramaic of the targums. Together, all of these constituted for him "Aramaic."[8] Again, little do we realize today how much Brian Walton's London Polyglot Bible of 1657 contributed to the sorting out of the languages, as he published the OT in the original Hebrew and, besides the usual versions (Latin and Greek), added also the Syriac version and the targums of Onqelos, Jonathan, and the so-called Fragmentary Targum.[9] Walton looked on the language of Onqelos and Jonathan as the Jerusalem dialect of Jesus' day. This historical litany of the names of scholars who contributed to the inquiry into the Aramaic problem could be easily prolonged, especially with those of the last century and of the beginning of this.

However, I have sketched the beginnings of the inquiry merely to indicate the piece-meal fashion in which it was often carried out in the past. This is not meant as a criticism of the scholars who wrestled with one or other aspect of the problem, as they related words or phrases in the New Testament to resemblances in the Syriac Bible, in the "Chaldee" of Daniel or Ezra, or in the various targums that had come to light. Their piece-meal work was determined by what little was known about Aramaic and its various phases at that time. Moreover, most of their knowledge of Aramaic was derived from texts that came into existence after the beginning of the Christian movement and the composition of the Greek NT itself. As is well known, the dates for the translation of the Bible into Syriac and for the composition of the traditional, non-Qumran targums are disputed; but in the form in which we have them today they all postdate the Greek NT, and the evidence derived from them for illustration of the NT poses a real problem.

The recovery of earlier Aramaic from extrabiblical sources has been largely an achievement of this century; and when it comes to Palestinian Aramaic of the first century it is almost a matter of discoveries of the last two decades.[10] As a result, the older material that has been written on the problem of Aramaic and the NT can only be used today *with great caution.* It is part of the material to which the aforementioned rigorous critique must now be applied.

It is, moreover, not simply a question of sorting out Aramaic into various phases or periods[11] or of scrutinizing with rigor the claims made for the dates of various Aramaic texts.[12] This brief and very incomplete sketch of the beginnings of the inquiry into the Aramaic problem has been made for another purpose. For one notes in the course of the history of the inquiry a tendency to compile what had been said earlier by others without a sufficiently critical examination of the evidence or material itself. When Matthew Black first wrote his *Aramaic Approach to the Gospels and Acts,*[13] he criticized indeed Wellhausen, Nestle, Dalman, Torrey and others for their almost exclusive dependence on the late targums, Onqelos for the Pentateuch and Jonathan for the Prophets. He preferred to use instead the so-called Palestinian targums (e.g., the Cairo Genizah texts, alleged to be of earlier vintage), Christian Palestinian Aramaic texts, and the Samaritan targum. Black's attitude was certainly correct, and his work remains the first real attempt to be critical in the matter. But one must note that his own discussion of individual texts depends largely on what others have said.[14] All too frequently he cites would-be Aramaic expressions, culling them from others without sufficient scrutiny so that his book, especially in its third edition, remains a compilation of proposals about Aramaisms in the Gospels and Acts that are good, bad, and indifferent, When he seems to be critical of some proposal or other, it is often not easy to know just where he stands.

The history of the inquiry into the Aramaic background of the NT has thus brought with it a certain determinism which reveals a strange reluctance to sort out what is really valid from claims made in the past. When this is coupled with a reluctance to cope with newer aspects of the problem, then the call for a break with methods of the past can legitimately be raised.

My second preliminary remark concerns the diversity of books in the NT and the difficulty that this diversity causes for the inquiry. How few Aramaisms are claimed for the writings of Paul, despite the fact that he called himself Ἑβραῖος (Phil 3:5; 2 Cor 11:22)[15] and that he it is who has preserved two of the Aramaic expressions normally attributed to Jesus and the early Palestinian Christian church (respectively), *ἀββά* (Gal 4:6; Rom 8:15) and *μαραναθά* (1 Cor 16:22). Most discussions of the Aramaic problem have been limited to the Gospels and Acts, but even there the problem differs, depending on the gospel, whether it is a Synoptic or John; and each of them has problems that are not the same as the Aramaic substratum of Acts, if it exists at all. The idea of Aramaic sources of Acts, once put forth by C. C. Torrey, now seems to be wholly discredited.

But this question of the diversity of the NT books and the varied approach to a possible Aramaic substratum is compounded by the problem of just how many of the Greek NT writings were actually composed in Palestine itself. The vast majority of the Pauline and Deuteropauline literature seems to have been composed elsewhere: 1-2 Thessalonians probably in Corinth; Galatians, Philippians, 1 Corinthians probably in Ephesus; 2 Corinthians probably in Macedonia (in part at least); Philemon, Colossians, Ephesians, possibly in Rome.[16] Only if one were to consider seriously the Caesarean origin of some of the Pauline Captivity Letters would there be a Palestinian origin for them. As for the Gospels, again even though one might agree that they reached their final stage of redaction in places other than Palestine (Mark possibly in Italy; Luke possibly in Greece; Matthew possibly in Syria; John possibly in Ephesus), there is nevertheless a certain proneness to reckon with an underlying tradition that may ultimately have been Palestinian. While the same is possibly to be admitted for the Acts of the Apostles, the extent to which any of the other NT writings comes from a Palestinian locality is indefinite and can be debated. In a highly interesting discussion, entitled *Do You Know Greek?,* J. N. Sevenster raised the question about "How much Greek could the first Jewish Christians have known?"[17] He raised this question specifically about such NT writings as 1 Peter and James and gathered all sorts of material that not only bear indirectly on the attribution of these NT writings to the persons whose names they bear, but even more importantly on the question of the knowledge and use of Greek in Palestine by Jews of the first century.

Today we hear much about the Hellenistic background of the NT writings. The work on the *Corpus hellenisticum* is doing much to elucidate that background with detailed, critical studies that are badly needed. But however important the need is to pursue the study of that background, the need to reckon seriously with the Aramaic background has also to be stressed—and precisely because of the diversity of the books in the NT.

The third preliminary remark concerns so-called Semitisms and the Semitic background of the NT. There are obviously times when one can legitimately discuss matters that are best grouped as pertaining to the Semitic background of the NT.[18] But the word "Semitism" can be abused and can turn out to be a weasel-word. It is obviously legitimate to use it in a generic sense to refer to Jewish or OT traditions or to expressions which are clearly different from classical or Hellenistic Greek, but which are common to both Aramaic and Hebrew. Thus, e.g., a superfluous retrospective personal pronoun turns up in a Greek relative clause which could reflect either a Hebrew or an Aramaic retrospective pronominal suffix in a relative clause, since in both Hebrew and Aramaic the relative pronoun is indeclinable: *ἀλλ᾿ εὐθὺς ἀκούουσα γυνὴ περὶ αὐτοῦ, ἧς εἶχεν τὸ θυγάτριον αὐτῆς πνεῦμα ἀκάθαρτον, ἐλθοῦσα προσέπεσεν πρὸς τοὺς πόδας αὐτοῦ,* "But immediately a woman, whose little daughter was possessed by an unclean spirit, heard of him, and came and fell down at his feet" (Mark 7:25[*RSV*]).[19] But the way in which claims are sometimes made for the Aramaic substratum of the sayings of Jesus, when the evidence is merely "Semitic" in general, or, worse still, derived from some other Semitic language, e.g., Hebrew, should no longer be countenanced.[20] In other words, the discussion of the Aramaic background of the NT should be limited to *Aramaic* evidence, and to Aramaic evidence of the period contemporary with or slightly prior to the composition of the Greek New Testament writings themselves. The ideal period would be from the first century and the beginning of the second up until the revolt of Simon ben Kosiba (132-35). Of course, one can more easily grant the evidence from a still earlier period of Palestinian Aramaic (e.g., from Ezra or Daniel) than from a later period (e.g., from the traditional, non-Qumran targums and rabbinic writings). But in any case it must be Aramaic evidence. So much for the preliminary remarks, which have been judged necessary in a discussion of methodology such as this. We can now turn to the various aspects of the Aramaic problem outlined earlier.

I. *Aramaic as a Language of Jesus*

First of all, concerning Aramaic as a language of Jesus, or more broadly, as a language of first-century Palestine, I need not repeat here the details that I amassed in my presidential address before the Catholic Biblical Association of America in 1970, "The Languages of Palestine in the First Century A.D."[21] I shall rather single out a few elements that call for some further comment and that bear precisely on the question of methodology.

From at least the eighth century B.C. Aramaic had become a *lingua franca* in the ancient Near East; and contrary to the impression that one gets from the ordinary Hebrew Bible, in which (according to Kittel's edition[22]) the Aramaic portions occupy a maximum of 22 pages and a few stray verses in Genesis (31:47) and Jeremiah (10:11)[23] out of a total of 1434 pages, Aramaic was not the less important of the two languages. Hebrew, which as the שפת כנען (Isa 19:18) or even as יהודית (Isa 36:11, 13), was apparently the more indigenous of the two in Palestine. Indeed, it seems never to have disappeared completely in the first millennium B.C. or even in the early centuries of the Christian era, despite the affirmations about its dying out in the postexilic period that are legion in the history of this inquiry.[24] Small pockets of the population (grouped geographically or sociologically?) in that period apparently continued to use a form of the language, often called today "Postbiblical Hebrew," which was related to the Hebrew in Qoheleth, Canticles, and Lamentations, and which eventually developed into what is now called Mishnaic Hebrew. Evidence of such Hebrew is now found in Qumran texts, graffiti, and epitaphs of the early Roman period in Palestine, the Copper Roll, and in the letters and contracts of the caves of Murabbaᶜat, Ḫabra, and Seiyal. But the evidence is not abundant and comes from restricted areas; it has been suggested that it should be ascribed to small groups who deliberately sought to revive the use of Hebrew at the time of the Maccabean movement or similar national reforms.

As for the use of Aramaic in Palestine, it is now attested from the middle of the ninth century B.C. onward.[25] The earliest text is a short inscription on a jar from ᶜEin Gev, dated to the middle of the ninth century by B. Mazar; and likewise from that century comes an inscribed bowl from Tell Dan, published by N. Avigad.[26] From these (currently) earliest attestations of the language right down to roughly A.D. 500 one can trace a line of evidence showing a continuous use of Aramaic in Palestine, which includes the numerous fragments from the Qumran caves,[27] and not a few from various synagogue inscriptions dating from the third to the sixth centuries.[28]

Moreover, the invasion of Aramaisms, Aramaic vocabulary, and Aramaic syntax into the Hebrew of the later books of the Bible and into Post-Biblical Hebrew suggests its predominant use.[29] This is detected in certain Qumran texts, which have been composed in Post-Biblical Hebrew, but which manifest no small amount of Aramaic influence (e.g., 4QTestimonia).[30] There is, moreover, the evidence of the Aramaic form of Tobit, extant now in four fragmentary copies from Qumran Cave IV, which when compared with the one Hebrew copy reveals not only that the Aramaic is the more original, but that the Hebrew version is no little Aramaized. The texts of Tobit still await publication, but Milik has revealed some information on them.[31] Furthermore, the existence of Aramaic targums in written form from Qumran (4QtgJob, 11QtgJob, 4QtgLev) indicates that the practice of translating the Hebrew Scriptures into Aramaic was well under way, and presumably for the usually stated reason, because the original Hebrew text read in the synagogues was no longer so readily and widely understood.[32] (This evidence from pre-Christian times does not, however, permit one to attribute the traditional, non-Qumran targums to this period—or to think that there was only one Palestinian targum). Lastly, the use of Aramaic on tombstones and ossuaries of the first century in and around Jerusalem clearly shows that the language was in popular use, not to mention an Aramaic I.O.U. dated to the second year of Nero Caesar, A.D. 56 (Mur 18).

Such an attestation of the use of Aramaic in Palestine does not, of course, deny the use of Greek there in the first century B.C. or A.D. This is too well attested to deny it, as I have indicated elsewhere.[33]

As a result of the survey of the current evidence for the use of such languages in Palestine in the first century, one can cautiously conclude that "the most commonly used language of Palestine in the first century A.D. was Aramaic, but that many Palestinian Jews, not only those in Hellenistic towns, but farmers and craftsmen of less obviously Hellenistic areas used Greek, at least as a second language," and that "pockets of Palestinian Jews also used Hebrew, even though its use was not widespread."[34] As for the language that Jesus would have used, the evidence seems to point mainly to Aramaic. There is little cogency in the thesis of Harris Birkeland and others who maintain that it was normally Hebrew (which Birkeland regarded as the language of the common people).[35] Presumably, Jesus used Hebrew on occasion. If one could give historical credence to the details of Jesus' visit to Nazareth as depicted in Luke 4:16-20, one would have to conclude that he read Isaiah in the original; but that is a big "if," in view of the Lucan redaction of the passage. That Hebrew was the Semitic language that he regularly used is not yet sufficiently substantiated, despite the attempts of I. Rabinowitz, J. Cantineau, and others to support the thesis of Birkeland in one way or another.[36] S. Segert and others have tellingly criticized the Birkeland thesis.[37] For this reason the consensus of opinion at the moment seems to support Aramaic as the language most commonly used by Jesus and his immediate disciples in Palestine.

But the use of Aramaic in first-century Palestine and by Jesus or his disciples raises a further question. How much of the extant Aramaic language can be considered valid for comparison, when one is studying the substratum of the Greek sayings attributed to Jesus in the NT? Some years ago I proposed a fivefold division of the phases of the Aramaic language,[38] and it has found acceptance with a number of scholars (E. Y. Kutscher,[39] H. L. Ginsberg,[40] E. Vogt,[41] and others). Since the composition of NT writings, and indeed the utterances of Jesus himself, fit into the phase of Middle Aramaic chronologically, it is methodologically correct to look to Aramaic of this phase for the best evidence of the Aramaic substratum. I still think that "Qumran Aramaic, either slightly prior to the NT period or contemporary with at least part of it—and other first-century Aramaic, such as tomb and ossuary inscriptions—must be the latest Aramaic that should be used for philological comparisons of the Aramaic substratum of the Gospels and Acts."[42] J. C. Greenfield has recently stressed the same idea: "Properly speaking, this [Qumran Aramaic] is the only literary Aramaic that we have that is contemporaneous with the Gospels and Acts and theoretically it is with the Aramaic of the Qumran finds that one should begin the examination of a possible *Aramaic approach.*"[43]

However, it has been contended that "if an Aramaic sayings source was written in A.D. 50, it would be closer to rabbinical material of A.D. 150 than to a Qumran document of 100 B.C. In the absence of evidence to the contrary one would suppose that different groups spoke and wrote different dialects; this is normal."[44] Why would it be closer to "rabbinical material of A.D. 150"? This is merely asserted without any evidence. It is conceivable that the content of the sayings may be closer to rabbinical utterances, but it is not evident that the form of the language and the expressions would be such. Moreover, what is this rabbinic *Aramaic* "material of A.D. 150" to which reference is being made? In the absence of clear examples of it, I prefer to stand by the contention set forth above.

As for the supposition that "different groups spoke and wrote different dialects," since "this is normal," something more than mere assertion is needed. Was the Aramaic used in the Qumran group so different from the language spoken or used in the rest of the small country of Palestine? S. Segert, who has been studying various linguistic aspects of Qumran Aramaic texts, has shown that some of them vary slightly and that we should have to allow for earlier and later texts within the phase of Middle Aramaic. I should also admit slight differences between Qumran and Murabbaᶜat texts; but that these differences really constitute a variety of dialects would have to be debated.[45] Segert has noted that Aramaic was not used for the Qumran rule-books, halakah, and pesher interpretations of the OT Prophets and Psalms, or for other sectarian literature; for these Post-Biblical Hebrew was rather employed.[46] By and large, this is correct. In the case of the Aramaic Genesis Apocryphon of Qumran Cave I and of the Targum of Job from Qumran Cave XI, there is not the slightest hint of Essene authorship,[47] so that the content of these scrolls even supports Segert's contention that they were literary productions introduced into the community from outside, composed elsewhere in Palestine, and were representative of Aramaic used on a larger scale than in the small esoteric community of Qumran. While Segert's view has much to commend it, I am not wholly convinced that the Aramaic composition betrays extra-Qumran provenience in all cases, or that Aramaic was not used in the community itself. Recently, J. T. Milik published some fragments from Qumran Cave IV, entitled the Visions of ᶜAmran,[48] and in them one now finds the typically Qumran dualistic vocabulary of the sectarian literature and theology turning up in Aramaic dress: not only the new counterpart of מלכיצדק called מלכירשע, but the contrast of נהורא, "light," and חשוכא, "darkness," and the classic designation of the members of the community, "all the sons of light," [כול בני נהו]רא (partly, but certainly, restored in the context). Consequently, it seems that one cannot exclude the composition of works in Aramaic from the Qumran community. But the similarity in language between these texts and others without the distinctive Essene traits suggests that the language in writings of possibly diverse provenience was not really that much different. So in the long run the bulk of Aramaic texts from Qumran remains the best available material for the study of the Aramaic substratum sayings of Jesus in the Greek NT.

I remain very skeptical about the alleged differences between the literary and spoken forms of Aramaic of this period. While every one knows that the distinction is valid and that it is precisely the spoken form of a language that eventually invades the literary and brings about the development of one dialect or phase of it from another, it is another thing to document this distinction and make it the basis of synchronic datings. A. Díez Macho has tried to insist on this distinction in his effort to maintain a first-century (or even earlier) dating of the Aramaic of the so-called Palestinian targums (e.g., of the Cairo Genizah, or of Neofiti I).[49] But until we get real evidence about the form of the spoken Aramaic of the first century—which is presently more postulated than attested—this mode of argument is wistful. This is especially true since the best instances of the language, which one normally finds in the traditional, non-Qumran targums, are found on the inscriptions from synagogues of the third to the sixth centuries.

As a result, correct methodology would seem to call for the comparison of the sayings of Jesus with Aramaic of the contemporary phase, the Middle Period, in preference to that of the later phases, such as is found in the various classic targumim, Syriac writings, Christian Palestinian Aramaic lectionaries, and so-called Palestinian Jewish Aramaic in general.

There is, however, another angle to this question, which must be considered for a moment. Jesus' words are recorded *in Greek* in the NT. Is it possible that he uttered some of them in Greek? This question has been raised in recent times.[50] It has also been asked in what language Jesus would have conversed with Pilate, and Greek is the likely answer; but I am extremely skeptical about the sayings-tradition in the NT being rooted, even in part, in Greek sayings of Jesus himself.

If one considers the sayings-tradition to be rooted in Aramaic sayings, there is a reason for it—and we shall be coming to that shortly. But a *caveat* must be introduced at this point, which affects the whole question of the origin of the sayings-tradition. It is introduced because it bears directly on the problem of the sayings of Jesus in the NT and their roots in either Aramaic or Greek words on the lips of the historical Jesus. The *caveat* is derived ultimately from other aspects of modern Gospel study, for no discussion of the Aramaic problem of the Gospels can prescind from the issues raised by Synoptic source criticism, form criticism, and redaction criticism. Consequently, in treating of the Aramaic background of the NT, and especially of the sayings of Jesus within it, one has to reckon with (*a*) the well-known refractory process of underlying oral tradition; (*b*) the coloring of the tradition by a later faith-experience of the early Christians; (*c*) likely additions to the traditional collections of sayings, made perhaps in a spirit of a genuine extension of his words or an adaptive reinterpretation of them to new situations; (*d*) words actually put on his lips by early Christians (e.g., in the Johannine discourses); and (*e*) the language of the given evangelist. When due regard is had for these legitimate factors, then the real discussion about the Aramaic substratum of the sayings of Jesus can be undertaken. This *caveat* forms a digression; but it has to be introduced because of the obvious tendency in the question raised about whether Jesus might have uttered some of his sayings in Greek. The possibility of it is always there, but when other factors are taken into consideration, it seems rather unlikely.

II. *Aramaic Names, Words, and Phrases Preserved in the New Testament*

No little part of the evidence for the conclusion that Jesus' words were by and large uttered originally in Aramaic and for the Aramaic substratum of various parts of the New Testament is found in the existence of Aramaic words, names, and phrases in the Greek text itself. Puzzling indeed is the complete loss of Aramaic source material of early Palestinian Christianity; and it is just as puzzling as the lack of reference to Jesus, his disciples, or anything Christian—so far at least—in the documents from Qumran. The tour de force of C. C. Torrey, who tried to translate the Gospels back into Aramaic and to maintain that they were all originally written in Aramaic has convinced no one.[51] It is in reality no proof of the Aramaic substratum itself. Moreover, the Aramaic background to the sayings of Jesus has often been argued on the testimony of Papias' statement about the First Gospel: Ματθαῖος *μὲν οὖν* Ἑβραΐδι *διαλέκτῳ τὰ λόγια συνετάξατο, ἡρμήνευσεν δ' αὐτὰ ὡς ἦν δυνατὸς ἕκαστος*, "Now Matthew compiled the sayings in a

'Hebrew' dialect, but each person translated (interpreted?) them as best he could" (Eusebius, *Hist. eccl.* 3.39.16). Even granting for the moment that Ἑβραΐδι διαλέκτῳ most likely means "in the Aramaic language,"[52] the collection of logia so written remains an unknown quantity, and the relation of it to the sayings of Jesus in our Greek First Gospel is highly debatable. As a result, Papias' testimony is little more than a red herring drawn across the path of the modern discussion of the Aramaic substratum of the sayings of Jesus.

The classic discussions of the Aramaic words, names, and phrases preserved in the New Testament—by such scholars as G. Dalman, E. Kautzsch, A. Meyer, J. Koopmans, J. Jeremias, and others[53] —need to be updated. What is needed, first of all, is a *complete* catalogue of such items; many of the usual lists merely repeat what was collected earlier, and some items have never been introduced (e.g., ἄλφα, ἰῶτα, μνᾶ). Once the list is fully compiled, it will have to be evaluated in the light of the Palestinian Aramaic now known to come from the contemporary period and rigorously distinguished from the material of later targumic or midrashic sources.

Two examples may be cited, for which contemporary evidence can be used in different senses. The Greek word κορβᾶν is still explained by M. Black as "a form of solemn prohibition found . . . in the Talmud" (with support drawn from J. Lightfoot's *Horae hebraicae* and J. Levy's references to *Nedarim* 3:2).[54] But the overtones of the talmudic usage have always embarrassed the NT commentator who appealed to them to illustrate the Marcan usage, κορβᾶν, ὅ ἐστιν δῶρον, ὃ ἐὰν ἐξ ἐμου ὠφεληθῇς, "any support you might have had from me is *korban*" (i.e., a gift [made to God]), Mark 7:11. And the cryptic Matthean formula (15:5), δῶρον ὅ ἐὰν ἐξ ἐμου ὠφεληθῇς, has even less of the overtones. (Indeed, it might be queried whether we would ever have understood the meaning of the Greek text of Matthew, if we did not know of the earlier Marcan form of the episode with its preserved Aramaic word.) The use of the word קרבן on two Palestinian Aramaic inscriptions of the first-century reveals its dedicatory sense, with the connotation of tabu, that is better suited to illustrate the Marcan and Matthean usage of the words κορβᾶν and δῶρον. One instance of it comes from a Palestinian ossuary published by J. T. Milik some years ago, which reads, כל די אנש מתהנה בחלתה דה קרבן אלה מן דבגוה "All that a man may find to his profit in this ossuary (is) an offering to God from him who is within it."[55] No one will miss the pertinence of the phrase קרבן אלה to the Marcan word, κορβᾶν.[56] The other instance is found on a stone jar discovered by B. Mazar in the excavation of Jerusalem south of the Temple area, which again indicates the dedicatory sense of the word.[57] Such evidence, in fact, renders unnecessary the references to later Jewish material from sources such as the Talmud.

On the other hand, the alleged Aramaic background for μαμωνᾶ may have to be questioned. Such a background has been illustrated by appeals to the Babylonian Talmud (*Berakoth* 61b), to a Palestinian targum of Gen 34:23

(Kahle's Cairo Genizah text, C—which he dates between 700–900), and to passages in the Palestinian Talmud.[58] But can one pass over the occurrence of the word in the Hebrew text of Sir 31:8 and in Qumran Hebrew (ממון, 1QS 6:2; 1Q27 a ii 5; and even CD 14:20) or over Augustine's testimony to the word as current in the Punic of his day (ממן, *De serm. Dom.*, 2/14.47; *Sermo* 113, ch. 2), or over the un-Aramaic ending *-ôn* that the Greek reflects?[59] Here is an instance where we may have to cease appealing to Aramaic for the explanation of the Greek *μαμωνᾶ* and resort merely to a common Semitic background of the word.

With regard to the forms of some proper names in the NT that have often been puzzling, W. F. Albright was long of the opinion that some of them reflect Aramaic forms, which are preserved in various Syriac versions of the NT. Perhaps a fresh investigation of some of the Syriac variants will shed fresh light on names that still puzzle us. Albright himself made some brief suggestions about them in the Anchor Bible commentary on *Matthew,*[60] but even he did no more than open an area of investigation. The point here is that though the Syriac tradition is obviously secondary and derivative from the Greek, it is not impossible that, in the choice of Syriac forms of names, especially geographical names, that tradition may be closer to some of the native Palestinian names that have become Grecized in the NT text tradition. Personally, I have not yet had the time to investigate this aspect of the problem, but it needs attention.

III. *Aramaisms in New Testament Greek*

Beyond the preservation of Aramaic names, words, and phrases in the NT there is the question of Aramaisms in the Greek text, i.e., Aramaic interference in the lexicon or syntax of the Greek, when Greek words or phrases are used with nuances that reflect Aramaic usage. Again, what is needed, first of all, is a comprehensive listing of these items, and comparison with genuine Aramaic evidence. Several recent works have discussed aspects of this problem, but not from the viewpoint that interests us now. For instance, K. Beyer devoted a volume to *Semitische Syntax im Neuen Testament,*[61] but for all its excellence it does not always specify sufficiently the Semitic data involved. From a different standpoint, D. Hill's monograph, *Greek Words and Hebrew Meanings: Studies in the Semantics of Soteriological Terms,*[62] adopted a clearly theological approach to the words so that the philological approach that the Aramaic problem demands is still wanting.

As an example of a Greek word with an Aramaic nuance, I may be permitted to cite here a form that is now familiar. In Luke 6:7 the evangelist records that the scribes and Pharisees kept watching Jesus to see whether *ἐν τῷ σαββάτῳ θεραπεύει, ἵνα εὕρωσιν κατηγορεῖν αὐτοῦ,* "he would heal on the Sabbath so that they might find an accusation against him" (*RSV*). The use of *εὕρωσιν* with a dependent complementary infinitive (*κατηγορεῖν*) is peculiar. Bauer-Arndt-Gingrich have cited a supposed parallel from an Egyptian papyrus in a Parisian collection, dated 153 B.C., *μὴ εὕρῃ τι κατά σου* ⟨*ε*⟩*ἰπεῖν*, "lest he find anything to say against you."[63] But the parallel is not perfect, because *εὕρῃ* has the object *τι* expressed in the papyrus and the infinitive (*εἰπεῖν*) is epexegetic, not complementary. A propos of this construction in another Lucan passage (13:24), M. Black wrote, "There is no instance hitherto adduced of this verb (*ʾaškaḥ*) in the sense 'to be able' for Palestinian Aramaic; it means 'to find' only; it is in Syriac that it has the two senses 'to find' and 'to be able.'"[64] Though Black is reluctant to call it therefore a Syriacism, he concludes that "our knowledge of Palestinian Aramaic is still far from complete." That conclusion will probably always remain true; but for this specific case the verb אשכח in the sense of "be able" is clearly attested in Palestinian Aramaic, in 1QapGen 21:13: God promises Abram, "I shall make your descendants as numerous as the dust of the earth which no man can number" (די לא ישכח כול בר אנוש למִמניה).[65] And another example of it seems to be present in Milik's recently published "Book of the Giants" section of Enoch.[66] This makes it plausible that *εὕρωσιν* with its dependent complementary infinitive in Luke 6:7 means simply, "so that they might be able to accuse him." The verb *εὕρωσιν* would reflect Aramaic interference, and the Greek verb *εὑρίσκειν* would have been made to carry the Aramaic nuance of "be able."

Another instance of a Greek phrase that is often said to carry an Aramaic nuance is *ὁ υἱὸς τοῦ ἀνθρώπου* or *υἱὸς ἀνθρώπου* (John 5:27; Rev 1:13; 14:14), being said to reflect בר נשא or בר נש by a literal translation or a mistranslation. In this matter I cannot go into great detail here and must reserve for elsewhere a fuller discussion of this issue.[67] I shall confine myself here to three comments. First, we have in such a view of the matter a good example of the uncritical repetition of phrases from the days of Dalman et al. and of the determinism in the inquiry into the Aramaic problem of which I spoke earlier. This concerns the linguistic feature that is involved in the spelling of the word for "man," *ʾĕnāš* (or in the Hebraized form *ʾĕnōš*), which never seems to occur in any pre-Christian texts or in any Palestinian Aramaic texts of the first century or of the early second century without the initial consonant *ʾaleph*.[68] This fact is now recognized by J. Jeremias.[69] Consequently, the form בר נשא or בר נש immediately reveals its late provenience, and one should therefore be wary of citing texts in which this form of the expression occurs as if they were contemporary with the NT material. Secondly, the form בר אנש or בר אנוש designates the individual belonging to the collectivity (mankind), so that it can mean generically "a human being" (so in 11QtgJob 26:3 [in parallelism with גבר], or some word for "man"; cf. the Hebrew text), or more indefinitely "someone" (or with the negative לא, "no one"; so in 1QapGen 21:13). This generic or indefinite sense, which was once thought to be unattested or unusual in Aramaic,[70] is now clearly in evidence. But what is significant for the first century is that the phrase is still to be found in any of the three following senses: (*a*) as a form of address directed to some person, like the Hebrew בן אדם used of the prophet Ezekiel—and this despite the multiple occurrences of it in that biblical book; (*b*) as a title for an expected or apocalyptic figure—and herein one notes that the Greek phrase applied to Jesus as a title in various senses has no precise Aramaic counterpart; and (*c*) as a surrogate or a circumlocution for "I."[71] The phrase *ὁ υἱὸς τοῦ ἀνθρώπου,* used of Jesus in the NT, is almost certainly intended in each case as a title, and thus we are still looking for the link between the corporate sense given to the phrase in Dan 7:13 and 18 and the NT titular sense. A further question is raised whether Jesus himself might have used בר אנש in the generic or indefinite sense referred to above and whether this might have given rise to a later titular interpretation within the Christian community; but to go into this question here would take us too far astray, important though it is. Thirdly, if J. T. Milik is correct about the form of the Book of Enoch in Palestine of the first century B.C., when the five parts of it were the Book of the Heavenly Luminaries, the Book of the Watchers, the Book of the Giants, the Book of Dreams, and the Letter of Enoch,[72] then we can no longer look to the second part of Enoch, as we now know it in the Ethiopic translation, the so-called Similitudes, for the titular use of "Son of Man." For Milik, the "Similitudes" never formed part of the pre-Christian Book of Enoch; it was substituted for the Book of the Giants in Christian times.[73]

In much of this discussion the evidence from the Aramaic texts of the first century is negative and amounts at most to an argument from silence—or at least it may seem so. But it is enough to warn us in using Aramaic material of a later date too facilely in constructing arguments about the first-century material.

IV. *Mistranslations*

The question of Aramaic interference in the Greek of the NT is related to another problem, on which I can only comment briefly, viz., that of the mistranslation of an Aramaic source. The number of alleged mistranslations is almost legion, and some rigorous assessment has to be found to cope with them. Again, the criteria used must be contemporaneous.

For example, in Matt 7:6 the *RSV* reads, "Do not give dogs what is holy; and do not throw your pearls before swine, lest they trample them under foot and turn to attack you." The parallelism of *τὸ ἅγιον* and *τοὺς μαργαρίτας ὑμῶν* is striking, and from at least 1700 it seems to have been suggested that *τὸ ἅγιον* is a mistranslation of the Aramaic קדשא. It would have been understood as *qudšāʾ*, an abstraction, "what is holy," instead of *qĕdāšāʾ*, "ring." Without going into all the other less plausible suggestions that have been made for alleged mistranslations of the Aramaic in other words of the verse,[74] one can now cite the passage in 11QtgJob 38:8, where the Aramaic word for "ring" has turned up precisely in the form that makes the suggestion plausible: ויהבו לה גבר אמרה חדה וגבר קדש חד די דהב, "and they gave him (Job), each one a lamb and a ring of gold." No matter what one will say about the plausibility of the suggestion in this case, the Aramaic evidence for the parallelism will no longer have to be sought in late Syriac or other texts. Moreover, the parallelism of the "ring" and the "pearls" in a proverbial saying not unlike the Aramaic Wisdom-aphorisms of Aḥiqar now becomes plausible because of a closely contemporary Palestinian Aramaic text.

In discussing this question some years ago, R. M. Grant maintained that the view that some parts of the NT were originally composed in Aramaic, not in Greek, while interesting, could "never be convincing."[75] He claimed that one had to show that the existing Greek is bad Greek, a feature which might not appear in the work of a "really good translator," that the alleged bad Greek could not be accepted as Hellenistic Greek of the time, that the existing Greek did not make sense, and lastly that the passage if retranslated into Aramaic does make sense. He emphasized the difficulty of this process and concluded, "Moreover, experts in Aramaic have a tendency to disagree as to what the original was."[76] Most of what Grant maintained is, in my opinion, correct; for the problem of mistranslation has to be rigorously scrutinized in terms of the items which he has mentioned. But his last comment about the disagreement of Aramaists represents an excuse to flee from a problem. Will Aramaists—or any other group of human beings—ever be unanimous? Perhaps, however, a more rigorous methodology and approach will eliminate some of the disagreement. Moreover, the hypothesis of mistranslations, which has to be seriously entertained because of the possibility of different vocalizations of one consonantal Aramaic text, should not, however, be confused with the question whether parts of the NT were originally composed in Aramaic (Torrey's *tour de force*). This Grant seems to have done.

V. *Aramaic Literary Forms in Prose and Poetry*

The fifth question concerns Aramaic literary forms in prose and poetry. The question may seem idle until one recalls the famous debate between E. J. Goodspeed and A. T. Olmstead, "Could an Aramaic Gospel Be Written?"—i.e., in first-century Palestine. Goodspeed thought that it would have been impossible because there was no "creative Aramaic literary writing" attested in that period.[77] He was thinking of the lacuna that existed between the final redaction of the Book of Daniel and the beginning of the so-called rabbinic Aramaic writings, the *Mĕgillat Taᶜănīt,* "Scroll of Fasting," which may be dated somewhere between A.D. 66 and 100.[78] This lacuna has since been filled somewhat by the Qumran Aramaic texts, and though they are not abundant, they are extensive enough to show that Aramaic literary compositions were in fact produced. Unfortunately, because of the fragmentary state of so many of the texts we are not able to discern the degree of inventiveness or creativity that was at work in such compositions. Was some new or characteristically Aramaic literary form produced? We know of only the targum as specifically Aramaic, but that is a translation process. Using other considerations, M. Smith has argued for Palestinian "romantic narrative literature about biblical heroes" composed prior to 70, i.e., works in Aramaic produced in Greco-Roman literary forms.[79]

Much more crucial in the discussion of the Aramaic substratum of the sayings of Jesus is the question of Aramaic poetry. Claims have been made for the "formal elements of Aramaic poetry in non-dominical sayings or speeches and in the Gospel dialogue as well as in the sayings of Jesus."[80] M. Black has discussed this aspect of the sayings and dialogue in Part III of his *Aramaic Approach to the Gospels and Acts*.[81] This is one of the areas where the evidence has not been restricted to Aramaic, and refuge has been taken in "Semitic poetic form." Black's discussion builds on C. F. Burney's *Poetry of Our Lord*,[82] and in it he treats of such things as "the formal element of Semitic poetry in the Gospels," i.e., "alliteration, assonance, and paronomasia." He began his chapter with a reference to Burney, who, he said, "has shown that the sayings of Jesus are cast in the form of Semitic poetry, with such characteristic features as parallelism of lines and clauses, rhythmic structure, and possibly even rhyme."[83] Without questioning the validity of such elements as specifically Aramaic, Black proceeded to adduce further instances of them in the non-dominical sayings or in the dialogue of the Gospels (in such passages as the sayings of the Baptist, the sources of the Fourth Gospel, the Lucan hymns, the Beatitudes, and various other dialogues). The subtle shifting back and forth between the adjectives "Aramaic" and "Semitic" in his discussion is revealing, for the question arises whether such formal rhetorical elements as parallelism, rhythm, rhyme, alliteration, assonance, and paronomasia are really the specific elements of *Aramaic* poetry. Such things may not be the usual features of classic Greek poetry and were studied more in connection with rhetoric in classical antiquity than with poetry, and one wonders to what extent Hellenistic poetic forms may not be operative here.[84]

No little part of the hesitation that one has in this question is the scarcity of what may be called Aramaic poetry, which should logically serve as a basis for comparison. As far as I can see, it is quite limited: (1) the Carpentras stele (KAI § 269), a four-line Egyptian Aramaic funerary stele, usually regarded as rhythmic in form and dated to the fourth century B.C.;[85] (2) several passages in the Book of Daniel (2:20-23; 3:31-33; 4:7-13, 31-32; 6:26-28; 7:9-10, 13-14, 23-27);[86]; (3) Tobit 8:5-6, 15-17; 13:1-8, which at present are accessible only in the Greek or Latin forms of the book, but some of which are preserved in the as yet unpublished texts of Qumran Cave IV;[87] (4) 11QtgJob, which may be regarded as poetry *in* Aramaic—but is it really Aramaic poetry?[88] (5) some of the proverbs of *Aḥiqar;*[89] (6) possibly part of the description of Sarai's beauty in the *Genesis Apocryphon* (1QapGen 20:2-7), if M. Black's view be accepted,[90] for some of it is written in parallelism, although it is scarcely well balanced; and finally (7) possibly 4QpsDan^c, the so-called Son of God text in Milik's lot, which is composed in a series of paratactic clauses that manifest a certain rhythm.[91] In all of this material, meagre as it is, one has to ask, What are the features of such poetic writing? That question is not easily answered at present. How does it differ from Hebrew poetry? Should it? In this instance the evidence is not such as to present a clear answer, but one should at least pose the question about the evidence for the nature of Aramaic poetry. I am not calling in question the existence of the rhythmic sayings attributed to Jesus in the Greek gospels or even their poetic character. The question is merely whether these elements necessarily indicate an *Aramaic* substratum. I am, moreover, aware of the thrust of the argument, that such formal elements are detected when one retrojects the Greek sayings back into Aramaic and that they are often not detected in the Greek itself. But I am not too sure that the presence of such elements, when thus detected, can be made to bear the weight of the argument that is often constructed upon them.

VI. *Aramaic and Variant Readings in the New Testament Text-Tradition*

This aspect of the Aramaic problem can only be mentioned briefly here, because I have never been able to go deeply into it; and yet it is an area that differs considerably from the others and merits further investigation. Some studies have been devoted to it by others,[92] and one crucial question always seems to emerge in them: Suppose a variant reading—say in Codex Bezae—manifests an Aramaism, whereas other Greek MSS have none of this, does that mean that Codex Bezae has preserved for us an earlier, or even more original, form of the saying or narrative? It has been debated whether the so-called Aramaisms in the Codex Bezae are dependent on some Syriac version.[93] But has the view that the Greek tradition of that MS, which is several centuries younger than the oldest Greek texts on parchment or papyrus, has been somewhat Syriacized been completely ruled out of court? The source of the alleged Aramaic material in Codex Bezae has not been convincingly ferreted out, and since we know so little about the provenience of that NT MS, distinctive and important though it be, one should be reluctant to regard its readings as more primitive simply because they seem to be more Aramaized.

VII. *Jewish Literary Traditions Found in the New Testament and in Known Aramaic Literature*

Another aspect of the Aramaic problem is the question of Jewish literary traditions that are found in the NT and in known Aramaic literature. Here it is not so much a question of Aramaic words or Aramaic interference as of motifs, modes of interpretation of the OT, or additions made to OT passages because of some halakic or haggadic process. A great amount of work has been done in this area in recent years by scholars such P. Grelot, M.-E. Boismard, M. McNamara, R. Le Déaut, B. Malina, et al.,[94] who have turned up paraphrases of OT texts in the targums or other literature that have distinctive motifs, themes, expansions, or expressions that resemble certain NT passages. They seem to suggest that the NT writers were often dependent on a targumic tradition rather than on the OT itself, in either the Hebrew or Greek form. In this matter the question is the extent to which the NT writers are dependent on such targumic traditions; it is, moreover, aggravated by the problematic dates assigned to much of the targumic material and by the multiplicity of so-called Palestinian targums that have come to light.

P. Kahle was apparently responsible for inaugurating a way of speaking about the Palestinian targums, giving one the impression that "the Palestinian targum" had been recovered, i.e., that the multiple copies that have turned up were all copies of *one* Palestinian targum. This mode of reference, "the Palestinian targum," turns up constantly in the writings of some of the scholars just mentioned. Indeed, on one occasion M. McNamara even went so far as to say, "The text of the PT as Paul found it was very apt for the doctrine Paul expresses in Rm 10,6-8."[95] This is obviously an exaggeration. Such targums may indeed preserve a literary tradition that Paul knew or used; but it has to be shown by outside control of some sort (e.g., from Philo or Josephus or some other contemporary source) that the Jewish literary tradition was actually known in the first century. The mere fact that the same tradition appears in Paul and in a non-Qumran, classical targum does not immediately mean that Paul's use of it is derived from such a source, i.e., explicitly or directly from a Palestinian targum.

There is a further aspect of this problem that needs more extensive investigation: What constitutes a "Palestinian" targum? Normally, the adjective "Palestinian" has been applied to Pseudo-Jonathan on the Pentateuch or the Fragmententargum in contrast to Targum Onqelos, which, whether it originated there or was merely given its final form there, at least has been recognized to have some historical connection with Jewish Babylonia. Its official character and its more or less word-for-word version of the Hebrew Pentateuch makes it stand out from Pseudo-Jonathan and the Fragmententargum, which are characterized by paraphrases of the Hebrew text in varying lengths, by significant additions, etc. When P. Kahle discovered the Cairo Genizah targumic texts,[96] they were seen to resemble Pseudo-Jonathan and the Fragmententargum more than Onqelos, and because of their paraphrastic character were labelled "Palestinian." But the language in these Cairo Genizah targumic texts is at times rather peculiar, if they are judged by what we know of first-century Palestinian Aramaic. In some instances at least the language is closer to Syriac or Eastern Aramaic than to Palestinian material.[97] The problem can only be broached here and a fuller investigation of it must really await the publication of critical editions of the so-called Palestinian targums and more extensive studies of the language used in them.

VIII. *Aramaic Epistolography*

In the study of NT epistles a considerable amount of work has been done on the comparison of them with extant extra-biblical letters of various sorts. The studies of A. Deissmann, L. Champion, J. -A. Eschlimann, F. X. J. Exler, E. Fascher, O. Roller, H. Koskenniemi, W. G. Doty, L. Stirewalt, J. L. White, C.-H. Kim, and others have contributed much to the understanding of the Greek letters of the NT.[98] But it has been felt that just as the Hellenistic background of other NT problems does not represent the sole influence on them, so too perhaps one should look into the Semitic background, and specifically the Aramaic background, of NT epistolography. At a consultation on letter-writing in the ancient Near East, held at the 1973 annual meeting of the Society of Biblical Literature in Chicago, I was asked to present a survey of Aramaic epistolography, the text of which appears elsewhere in this volume.[99] There one will find a list of Aramaic letters on skin, papyrus, and ostraca, a brief sketch of the contents, types, and provenience of such letters, as well as of details in the letters such as the names for the Aramaic letter, its *praescriptio,* initial greeting, secondary greetings, concluding formulas, dates, scribes or secretaries, and the exterior addresses.

Several factors lie behind the concern to look into Aramaic epistolography in the study of NT letters. First of all, the fact that Paul who labels himself a "Hebrew" and who preserves two Aramaic words in his letters, writes in Greek. Yet one wonders to what extent Aramaic epistolographic customs have influenced his writing. Is it possible that some distinctively Pauline epistolographic features are derived from Aramaic letter-writing habits? This would only be able to be established if Aramaic epistolography were studied more than it has been. Secondly, if the Caesarean hypothesis of the origin of the Captivity Letters in the Pauline corpus were to prove acceptable,[100] would there be any elements in them that might be related to Palestinian Aramaic letter-writing habits? Though I am personally skeptical about this origin of these letters, this aspect of that hypothesis might deserve some further investigation. Thirdly, we have already referred to J. N. Sevenster's thesis about Greek in Palestine and its relation to the epistles of James and 1 Peter.[101] The further implications of that thesis with regard to epistolography may need some exploration. Finally, among others M. Black has called attention to the Aramaic background of the initial greeting in 1 Pet 1:2, *χάρις ὑμῖν καὶ εἰρήνη πληθυνθείη*, and compares it with Dan 3:31, שלמכון ישגא.[102] He also wonders whether Aramaic was not the recognized medium of communication with the Diaspora in the first century.[103] Finally, I may mention in passing two letters coming from Palestine of the time of the Bar Cochba revolt, which deal with the same matter, one in Aramaic and the other in Greek. They deal with the requisitioning of materials for the celebration of Succoth,[104] and the similarity of subject-matter and vocabulary, despite the difference of the languages, cannot be missed. Coming from the same situation and revealing an identical concern about religious matters, they illustrate the use of the two languages in epistolary correspondence that makes Aramaic epistolography of some importance for the study of Greek letters from the eastern Mediterranean area.

Even if the study of Aramaic epistolography would have little direct bearing on NT letters, there is still the likelihood that the study of it would shed some comparative light on them, since it represents a form of ancient letter-writing from the eastern Mediterranean area.

Conclusion

An attempt has been made here to gather together some thoughts on the problems involved in the study of the Aramaic substratum of the NT. In some instances the remarks go beyond the question of the Aramaic substratum of the sayings of Jesus, which is the specific topic. But this specific question is part of the larger one that needs new attention. Each aspect of the larger problem discussed above usually bears in some way on the specific question.

Moreover, the remarks have been at times deliberately generic. I am all too aware of the fact that they have not always been supported specifically with as much evidence as they should have. But that is owing in part at least to the limitations of time and space. My intention has been to outline and delimit areas and aspects of the generic problem in view of further research. The paper is programmatic. It has been made such because of the evidence that has become available for the study of Palestinian Aramaic in the first centuries B.C. and A.D. in the last few decades, which is now forcing us to reopen many questions and approach them anew. This has called for the methodological considerations set forth above. I am not persuaded that all of these considerations are of equal value or have been refined as they should be or that they are as definitive as they may appear. But an attempt has at least been made to formulate them.

There are those who will read the above pages and think that I am trying to "gerrymander" the study of the NT. This would obviously be a delusion, if it were so. The study of the Aramaic problem will never dominate NT studies, but it will remain a facet of that study and will continue to intrigue students as long as new Aramaic texts from the contemporary period continue to come to light. Fortunately, it is an aspect or a facet of that study that exposes itself to outside control and that can reflect new gains. Because it reflects such material, it is not *immediately* caught up into the dialectic and hermeneutical cycle of interpretation born of a certain philosophy. The latter have given rise to an introspective hermeneutic—even a certain "hypochondria" or a morbid worry about the state of NT (or biblical) theology. Who knows but that a little more attention paid to the positive aspects of NT study (such as its Aramaic substratum) will enable one to break into the cycle with new evidence.[105]

NOTES TO CHAPTER 1

*A slightly revised form of a lecture delivered at the *Journées bibliques* de Louvain in 1973 and published as "Methodology in the Study of the Aramaic Substratum of Jesus' Sayings in the New Testament," *Jésus aux origines de la christologie* (ed. J. Dupont; BETL 40; Gembloux: Duculot, 1975) 73-102.

[1]See, e.g., B. Fletcher, *The Aramaic Sayings of Jesus* (London: Hodder & Stoughton, 1967).

[2]Subtitle: *Das galiläische Aramäisch in seiner Bedeutung für die Erklärung der Reden Jesu und der Evangelien überhaupt* (Freiburg im B. / Leipzig: Mohr, 1896) 1-35.

[3]Eusebius, *Demonstratio evangelica* 3.4.44 (*GCS*, 23. 119); 3.7.10 (*GCS*, 23. 142); Epiphanius, *Panarion* 69.68 (*GCS*, 37. 216); John Chrysostom, *In Matthaeum homilia 88* (*PG*, 58. 776); Jerome, *Comm. in Danielem* 1.2.4 (*CC* ser. lat., 75A. 785); 2.7.28 (*CC* ser. lat., 75A. 850).

[4]See A. Meyer, *Jesu Muttersprache,* 9.

[5]Ibid., 10.

[6]Vienna: M. Cymbermannus (Zimmermann), 1555. Cf. W. Strothmann, *Die Anfänge der syrischen Studien in Europa* (Göttinger Orientforschung, 1 / 1; Wiesbaden: Harrassowitz, 1971).

[7]J. Buxtorf, *Lexicon chaldaicum talmudicum et rabbinicum* . . . (Basel: L. König, 1640).

[8]See Meyer, *Jesu Muttersprache,* 12.

[9]*Sacrae Scripturae Biblia polyglotta* . . . (6 vols.; London: Thomas Roycroft, 1657).

[10]For a list of Palestinian Aramaic texts and in particular of Qumran Aramaic texts (both published and otherwise known to exist), see pp. 99–102 below.

[11]See p. 57–84 below.

[12]The dating of ancient Aramaic texts is always a problem. But it should be noted that in some cases texts have come to light that are dated (e.g., Mur 18, dated to the second year of Nero, A.D. 55 / 56; or Mur 19, dated to A.D. 111[?]) and in others archaeological evidence of a different sort bears on the issue of dating. For example, the kind of Aramaic that turns up on inscriptions from synagogues dated archaeologically from the third to the sixth centuries, A.D. This sort of evidence is precious, indeed, and not easy to use, but it cannot be disregarded.

[13]Oxford: Clarendon, 1946. (The second edition appeared in 1954; the third in 1967.)

[14]For instance, in chap. 4 of the third edition.

[15]The meaning of ἑβραῖος is, of course, debated. It may also be questioned whether Paul (Phil 3:5; 2 Cor 11:22) uses it precisely in the same sense as it is used in Acts 6:1. But in any case the most plausible solution to the problem seems to be that proposed by C. F. D. Moule, "Once More, Who Were the Hellenists?" *ExpTim* 60 (1958-59) 100-2: the "Hellenists" were "Jews who spoke *only* Greek," whereas "Hebrews" were "Jews who, while able to speak Greek, knew a Semitic language *also.*" For discussions of Aramaisms in Pauline writings, see W. C. van Unnik, "Aramaeismen bij Paulus," *Vox theologica* 14 (1943) 117-26; tr. into English, "Aramaisms in Paul," *Sparsa collecta: The Collected Essays of W. C. van Unnik: Part One, Evangelia, Paulina, Acta* (NovTSup 29; Leiden: Brill, 1973) 129-43; W. F. Albright and C. S. Mann, "Two Texts in I Corinthians," *NTS* 16 (1969-70) 271-76; P. Grelot, "Deux notes critiques sur Philippiens 2,6-11," *Bib* 54 (1973) 169-86.

[16]I am assuming proveniences for these books that are often proposed; if they are not correct or if others are preferred, there is little likelihood of their Palestinian provenience in any case.

[17]This is actually the subtitle of the book (NovTSup 19; Leiden: Brill, 1968).

[18]I am aware that I have used the adjective this way myself, in the title of the first book of my collected essays, *Essays on the Semitic Background of the New Testament* (London: Chapman, 1971; reprinted as paperback, Missoula: Scholars Press, 1974).

[19]See further Luke 3:16; Apoc 3:8; 7:29; 13:8; 20:8; 12:6 (ἐκεῖ, an adverb used similarly); Mark 13:16. See BDF §297, 466; M. Zerwick, *Biblical Greek* (Rome: Biblical Institute, 1963) §201-3.

[20]See further *CBQ* 30 (1968) 422.

[21]See pp. 38–43 below.

[22]*Biblia hebraica* (10th ed.; Stuttgart: Privileg. Würtembergische Bibelanstalt, 1951).

[23]And possibly Prov 30:1, if the suggestion of C. C. Torrey were to prove to be right (see "Proverbs, Chapter 30," *JBL* 73 [1954] 93-96).

[24]See, for example, the opinions of A. Dupont-Sommer and of F. Altheim and R. Stiehl quoted below on p. 55 n. 99.

[25]See p. 99–102 below.

[26]B. Mazar et al., "^{c}Ein Gev: Excavations in 1961," *IEJ* 14 (1964) 1-49, esp. pp. 27-29 (+ pl. 13B); N. Avigad, "כתובת ארמית על קערה מתל דן [An Aramaic Inscription on the Tell Dan Bowl]," *Yediot* 30 (1966) 209-12; "An Inscribed Bowl from Dan," *PEQ* 100 (1968) 42-44 (+ pl. XVIII).

[27]For a list of the Qumran texts published so far, see pp. 101–2 below; also *The Genesis Apocryphon of Qumran Cave 1: A Commentary* (BibOr 18A; 2d ed.; Rome: Biblical Institute, 1971) 20 n. 55; 28 n. 67.

[28]For a collection of these inscriptions, see the appendix in J. A. Fitzmyer and D. J. Harrington, *A Manual of Palestinian Aramaic Texts (200 B.C. to A.D. 200)* (BibOr 34; Rome: Biblical Institute, 1978) 151–303 see also p. 54 below.

[29]Cf. M. Wagner, *Die lexikalischen und grammatikalischen Aramaismen im alttestamentlichen Hebräisch* (BZAW 96; Berlin: de Gruyter, 1966); E. F. Kautzsch, *Die Aramaismen im Alten Testament* (Halle a.S.: M. Niemeyer, 1902); A. Hurvitz, "The Chronological Significance of 'Aramaisms' in Biblical Hebrew," *IEJ* 18 (1968) 234-40.

[30]Or 4Q*175* (DJD, 5. 57-60). See also S. Segert, "Aramäische Studien: II. Zur Verbreitung des Aramäischen in Palästina zur Zeit Jesu," *ArOr* 25 (1967) 21-27, esp. pp. 34-35. Further bibliography on this text can be found in my article, "A Bibliographical Aid to the Study of the Qumran Cave IV Texts 158-186," *CBQ* 31 (1969) 59-71, esp. pp. 68-70.

[31]See his article, "La patrie de Tobie," *RB* 73 (1966) 522-30, especially the list of passages in Tobit identified in the four Aramaic texts and the one Hebrew copy (p. 522 n. 3); see also his *Ten Years of Discovery in the Wilderness of Judaea* (SBT 26; Naperville, IL: Allenson, 1959) 31, 139.

[32]The targums from Qumran Cave IV are now published; see J. T. Milik, DJD, 6.86–90; R. Le Déaut, *Introduction à la littérature targumique* (Rome: Biblical Institute, 1966) 64-68. For 11QtgJob, see J. P. M. van der Ploeg and A. S. van der Woude, *Le targum de Job de la grotte XI de Qumrân* (Koninklijke nederlandse Akademie van Wetenschappen; Leiden: Brill, 1971); also pp. 161–82 below for bibliography and comments on this targum.

[33]See p. 32–38 below.

[34]See p. 46 below.

[35]*The Language of Jesus* (Avhandlinger utgitt av det Norske Videnskaps-Akademi i Oslo, II. Hist.-Filos. Kl., 1954/1; Oslo: J. Dybwad, 1954) 1-40, esp. p. 16.

[36]E.g., I. Rabinowitz, "Be Opened = Ἐφφαθά (Mark 7,34): Did Jesus Speak Hebrew?" *ZNW* 53 (1962) 229-38; J. Cantineau, "Quelle langue parlait le peuple en Palestine au 1er siècle de notre ère," *Sem* 5 (1955) 99-101; W. Chomsky, "What Was the Jewish Vernacular during the Second Commonwealth?" *JQR* 42 (1951-52) 193-212; S. Aalen, Review of H. Birkeland, *The Language of Jesus, TTKi* 26 (1955) 45-61; R. Meyer, Review of the same, *OLZ* 52 (1957) 47-50; J. M. Grintz, "Hebrew as the Spoken and Written Language in the Last Days of the Second Temple," *JBL* 79 (1960) 32-47; J. A. Emerton, "Did Jesus Speak Hebrew?" *JTS* 12 (1961) 189-202; "*Maranatha* and *Ephphatha*," *JTS* 18 (1967) 427-31; M. Black, "Ἐφφαθά (Mk. 7.34), [τὰ] πάσχα (Mt. 26.18W), [τὰ] σάββατα (passim), [τὰ] δίδραχμα (Mt. 17.24bis)," *Mélanges bibliques en hommage au R. P. Béda Rigaux* (eds. A. Descamps et A. de Halleux; Gembloux: Duculot, 1970) 57-62; S. Morag, "Ἐφφαθά (Mark vii. 34): Certainly Hebrew, not Aramaic?" *JSS* 17 (1972) 198-202; J. Barr, "Which Language Did Jesus Speak—Some Remarks of a Semitist," *BJRL* 52 (1970) 9-29; J. A. Emerton, "The Problem of Vernacular Hebrew in the First Century A.D. and the Language of Jesus," *JTS* 24 (1973) 1-23; P. Lapide, "Insights from Qumran into the Languages of Jesus," *RQ* 8 (1972-76) 483-501.

[37]S. Segert, "Zur Orthographie und Sprache der aramäischen Texte von Wadi Murrabba^{c}at," *ArOr* 31 (1963) 122-37; A. Díez Macho, "La lengua hablada por Jesucristo," *OrAn* 2 (1963) 95-132, esp. pp. 113-14, 122-23; W. Eiss, *EvT* 16 (1956) 170-81; J. A. Emerton, *JTS* 12 (1961) 189-202.

[38]In my commentary on the *Genesis Apocryphon of Qumran Cave 1* (1st ed., 1966) 19-20; for a slight modification of it, see the 2d ed., pp. 22-23. For an explanation of the divison, see pp. 57–84 below.

[39]In his article, "Aramaic" (*Current Trends in Linguistics 6: Linguistics in South West Asia and North Africa* [The Hague: Mouton, 1971] 347-412), Kutscher presents abundant evidence in support of the divisions of Old and Official Aramaic. Unfortunately, he died before he was able to complete his discussion of the later phases. But he did adopt in principle the division of the phases, as I had proposed them (see pp. 347-48); and coming from an authority in the Semitic languages such as this, it is a welcome recognition.

[40]Private communication.

[41]See *Lexicon linguae aramaicae Veteris Testamenti documentis antiquis illustratum* (Rome: Biblical Institute, 1971) 6*-8*.

[42]See *CBQ* 30 (1968) 420.

[43]In his review of M. Black, *An Aramaic Approach to the Gospels and Acts* (3d ed.; Oxford: Clarendon, 1967), *JNES* 31 (1972) 58-61, esp. p. 60.

[44]M. Smith, in his review of the same edition of Black's book, *JBL* 90 (1971) 247. Smith's comment has been quoted with approval by G. Vermes, *Jesus the Jew: A Historian's Reading of the Gospels* [London: Collins, 1973] 190. He thinks that "the illogicality" of my thesis has been exposed by Smith's "critical acumen." But has it? And is it really illogical? This is a Vermes flight to *obscurum per obscurius*. The problems which this "historian's reading of the Gospels" raises will have to be dealt with elsewhere; they are legion. Meanwhile, see the review of L. E. Keck, *JBL* 95 (1976) 508-9.

[45]"Sprachliche Bemerkungen zu einigen aramäischen Texten von Qumran," *ArOr* 33 (1965) 190-206; and his article cited in n. 37 above.

[46]*ArOr* 33 (1965) 205.

[47]See my commentary on *The Genesis Apocryphon of Qumran Cave I* (2d ed., 1971) 11-14, where I have become a little more open to the Essene composition of 1QapGen in view of the observation made by R. de Vaux; but even that is an extrinsic argument. The Essene composition of 11QtgJob has been proposed by E. W. Tuinstra, *Hermeneutische Aspecten van de Targum van Job uit Grot XI van Qumrân* (Dissertation, Rijksuniversiteit te Groningen, 1970), but the arguments proposed are singularly unconvincing; see below. pp. 166–67.

[48]"4Q Visions de ᶜAmram et une citation d'Origène," *RB* 79 (1972) 77-97.

[49]*El Targum: Introducción a las traducciones aramaicas de la Biblia* (Barcelona: Consejo superior de investigaciones científicas, 1972), esp. pp. 46-54.

[50]See further below, p. 37.

[51]See "The Translations Made from the Original Aramaic Gospels," *Studies in the History of Religions Presented to Crawford Howell Toy* (New York: Macmillan, 1912) 269-317; *The Four Gospels* (New York: Harper, 1933); "The Aramaic Gospels," *Christian Century* 51 (1934) 1338-40; *Our Translated Gospels* (New York: Harper, 1936); *Documents of the Primitive Church* (New York: Harper, 1941).

[52]This meaning is, of course, not certain, but it still remains the best interpretation. See W. Gutbrod, *TDNT* 3 (1965) 374, 388; see below pp. 45–46.

[53]E.g., G. Dalman, *The Words of Jesus Considered in the Light of Post-Biblical Jewish Writings and the Aramaic Language* (tr. D. M. Kay; Edinburgh: Clark, 1902); E. Kautzsch, *Grammatik des Biblisch-aramäischen, mit einer kritischen Erörterung der aramäischen Wörter im Neuen Testament* (Leipzig: F. C. W. Vogel, 1884) 4-21; A. Meyer, *Jesu Muttersprache* (n. 2 above), 47-53; J. Koopmans, *Aramäische Chrestomathie: Ausgewählte Texte (Inschriften, Ostraka und Papyri) bis zum 3. Jahrhundert n. Chr. für das Studium der aramäischen Sprache gesammelt* (Leiden: Nederlands Instituut vor het Nabije Oosten, 1962) §68, pp. 209-12; J. Jeremias, *New Testament Theology: The Proclamation of Jesus* (New York: Scribner, 1971) passim; S. Segert, *Altaramäische Grammatik mit Bibliographie, Chrestomathie und Glossar* (Leipzig: VEB Berlag Enzyklopädie, 1975) 519. Cf. A. Neubauer, "On the Dialects Spoken in

Palestine in the Time of Christ," *Studia biblica: Essays in Biblical Archaeology and Criticism* (Oxford: Clarendon, 1885) 39-74, esp. pp. 55-57, 62.

[54]*Aramaic Approach* (3d ed.), 139.

[55]"Trois tombeaux juifs récemment découverts au Sud-Est de Jérusalem," *SBFLA* 7 (1956-57), esp. pp. 232-39.

[56]I have tried to bring this out in my discussion of the inscription, "The Aramaic Qorban Inscription from Jebel Ḫallet eṭ-Ṭûri and Mark 7 11 / Matt 15 5," *JBL* 78 (1959) 60-65; reprinted with slight revisions in *ESBNT*, 93-101. A query was recently posed about this inscription: Why could not קרבן אלה in this text mean "a qorban, a curse" (from him who is within it)? Then it would be closer to the rabbinic use of קרבן. My interpretation of the phrase was based rather on קרבן יהוה (Num 9:13; 31:50), "an offering to Yahweh," with the divine name changed to Aramaic אלה, hence "an offering to God." However, the question is really whether אלה, which is a good biblical Hebrew word for "curse" (see Gen 24:41; Deut 29:19), is also known in Aramaic. As far as I can see, the only place where it might possibly occur is in the *Panammu* inscription from Zenjirli (line 2). Here A. Dupont-Sommer (*An Aramaic Handbook* [ed. F. Rosenthal; Porta linguarum orientalium, ns 10; Wiesbaden: Harrassowitz, 1967], I/1.7) reads אלה hesitatingly. J. C. L. Gibson (*Textbook of Syrian Semitic Inscriptions, Volume 2: Aramaic Inscriptions Including Inscriptions in the Dialect of Zenjirli* [Oxford: Clarendon, 1975] 78) reads it unhesitatingly, rejecting the meaning "conspiracy" (p. 82) that is sometimes given to it. However, H. Donner and W. Röllig, *KAI* §215:2, read אזה as a fem. rel. pronoun. Given this state of affairs, I am reluctant to consider אלה here as meaning "curse." See, however, the remarks of J. C. Greenfield in a review of my *ESBNT, JNES* 35 (1976) 59-61.

[57]"The Excavations in the Old City of Jerusalem," *W. F. Albright Volume* (Eretz-Israel, 9; Jerusalem: Israel Exploration Society, 1969) 168-70 (+ pl. 45, 5).

[58]See M. Black, *Aramaic Approach* (3d ed.), 139-40.

[59]The vocalization of the word is problematic. The Greek suggests the vocalization *māmôn*, and this would be a better Hebrew form (with the lengthened pretonic vowel) than an Aramaic form, despite the Aramaic-like ending on the word (*-a*). I have partially discussed the meaning and form of the word elsewhere (see "The Story of the Dishonest Manager [Lk 16:1-13]," *TS* 25 '1964] 23-41, esp. p. 30; reprinted, *ESBNT*, 161-84, esp. pp. 169-70). The English spelling "mammon" (with two m's) is said to be derived from Latin usage (although the Vulgate has *mamona* in Luke 16:9 [see R. Weber, *Biblia sacra iuxta Vulgatam versionem* (Stuttgart: Württembergische Bibelanstalt, 1969), 2. 1640], where no variant spelling is given). However, in the *Compact Edition of the Oxford English Dictionary* (London / New York: Oxford University, 1971), 1. 1709, the Vulgate spelling is listed as *mam(m)ona*]). The form with two m's would better reflect the Semitic spelling *mammōnā* (< *maʾmôn*). But the English spelling is still problematic.

[60]W. F. Albright and C. S. Mann, *Matthew: Introduction, Translation, and Notes* (AB 26; Garden City: Doubleday, 1971) clxviii-clxxii.

[61]*Band I, Satzlehre Teil 1* (2d ed.; SUNT 1; Göttingen: Vandenhoeck & Ruprecht, 1968).

[62]SNTSMS 5; Cambridge: Cambridge University, 1967.

[63]BAG, 325b.

[64]*Aramaic Approach* (3d ed.), 133.

[65]See my commentary (2d ed., 1971), 150-51.

[66]See "Turfan et Qumran: Livre des Géants juif et manichéen," *Tradition und Glaube: Das frühe Christentum in seiner Umwelt: Festgabe für Karl Georg Kuhn zum 65. Geburtstag* (eds. G. Jeremias et al.; Göttingen: Vandenhoeck & Ruprecht, 1971) 117-27, esp. p. 122: 4QEnGiants[b] 1 ii 13, which Milik reads as follows: [. . . השכחו גבריא לחויא להן[ון]/[חלמא] [ ], and translates: "Les géants cherchaient (quelqu'un) qui pût leur expliquer [le songe]," and so they sought out Enoch, "the distinguished scribe" (לספר פרשא). But does השכח ever have the meaning "chercher"? It seems to me rather that one should restore the first lacuna, in part at least, with כדי לא, and then translate: "[since] the giants were [not] able to explain [the dream] for them[selves], . . ." But any certainty in this matter will have to await further discussion of this text. Meanwhile, one can consult *The Books of Enoch* (see p. 112 below, n. 72), 305. In any case,

another clear example of the verb has appeared in 4QEn^a 1 ii 8: [ולמ]דרך על עפרה ו[ע]ל [כפ]יה לא תשכחון מן / [חמתה], "and you are not able [to tr]ead on the dust or o[n] the [ro]cks because of / [the heat]." See *The Books of Enoch*, 146-47. But שכח in the sense of "to find" is also found: 4QEn^c 4:50; 4QEnGiants^c 2:5. Cf. M. Black, "The Fragments of the Aramaic Enoch from Qumran," *La littérature juive entre Tenach et Mischna: Quelques problèmes* (RechBib 9; Leiden: Brill, 1974) 15-28.

[67]See G. Vermes, "The Use of בר נשא / בר נש in Jewish Aramaic," in M. Black, *Aramaic Approach* (3d ed.), 310-28; but cf. my discussion on pp. 143–60 below.

[68]See p. 149 below.

[69]*New Testament Theology*, 260-62 (see n. 53 above).

[70]E.g., see P. Benoit, "La divinité de Jésus," *Exégèse et théologie* (Paris: Cerf, 1961), 1. 134 ("insolite en araméen").

[71]G. Vermes ("The Use," 320) has, in particular, argued strongly for the circumlocutional meaning, even going so far as to say that it "means 'I'" (p. 323). See further *Jesus the Jew*, pp. 188-91. However, J. Jeremias (*New Testament Theology*, 261 n. 1) has also raised his voice against this interpretation and against Vermes' use of the evidence.

[72]See "Problèmes de la littérature hénochique à la lumière des fragments de Qumrân," *HTR* 64 (1971) 333-78, esp. p. 334.

[73]Ibid., 373-78.

[74]E.g., M. Black, *Aramaic Approach* (3d ed.), 200-202.

[75]*A Historical Introduction to the New Testament* (New York: Harper & Row, 1963) 41.

[76]Ibid.

[77]*New Chapters in New Testament Study* (New York: Macmillan, 1937) 127-68, esp. pp. 165-66; A. T. Olmstead, "Could an Aramaic Gospel Be Written?" *JNES* 1 (1942) 41-75; E. J. Goodspeed, "The Possible Aramaic Gospel," ibid., 315-40, esp. p. 328.

[78]For this text, see *MPAT*, 184–87; also my commentary on *The Genesis Apocryphon* (2d ed., 1971), 21 n. 57.

[79]"Aramaic Studies and the Study of the New Testament," *JBR* 26 (1958) 304-13.

[80]*Aramaic Approach* (3d ed.), 184.

[81]Ibid., 143-85.

[82]Oxford: Clarendon, 1925.

[83]*Aramaic Approach* (3d ed.), 143.

[84]I hesitatingly mention this aspect of the problem because I have not yet had the time to investigate it; but it is a legitimate question that must be asked.

[85]See, e.g., [J. J.] Barthélemy, "Explication d'un bas-relief égyptien, et de l'inscription phénicienne [sic] qui l'accompagne," *Mémoires de littérature tirêz des regîtres de l'Académie royale des inscriptions et belles lettres* 32 (1768) 725-38; M. Lanci, *Osservazioni sul basso-rilievo fenico-egizio che si conserva in Carpentrasso* (Rome: F. Bourlié, 1825); A. Merx, "Bemerkungen zur bis jetzt bekannten aramäischen Inschriften," *ZDMG* 22 (1868) 674-99, esp. pp. 697-99; J. Derenbourg, "Notes épigraphiques: V. L'inscription dite de Carpentras," *JA* 6 / 11 (1868) 277-87; [J.] Lauth, "Aegyptisch-aramäische Inschriften," *SBAW* 1878 / 2, pp. 97-149, esp. pp. 115-31; C. Clermont-Ganneau, "Origine perse des monuments araméens d'Egypte," *RArch* ns 37 (1879) 21-39, esp. pp. 31-33; K. Schlottmann, "Metrum und Reim auf einer ägyptisch-aramäischen Inschrift," *ZDMG* 32 (1878) 187-97; P. de Lagarde, "Zur Erklärung der aramäischen Inschrift von Carpentras," *NKGWG* 1878, pp. 357-72; E. Ledrain, "Mots égyptiens contenus dans quelques stèles araméennes d'Egypte," *RA* 1 (1884) 18-23, esp. pp. 18-21; S. R. Driver, *Notes on the Hebrew Text and the Topography of the Books of Samuel* (Oxford: Clarendon, 1913) xii-xv; C. C. Torrey, "A Specimen of Old Aramaic Verse," *JAOS* 46 (1926) 241-47; P. Grelot, "Sur la stèle de Carpentras," *Sem* 17 (1967) 73-75; B. Couroyer, "A propos de la stèle de Carpentras," *Sem* 20 (1970) 17-21 (with a postscript by P. Grelot, pp. 21-22).

[86]See W. S. Towner, "The Poetic Passages of Daniel 1-6," *CBQ* 31 (1969) 317-26.

[87]See J. T. Milik, "La patrie de Tobie," *RB* 73 (1966) 522-30, esp. p. 522 n. 3.

[88]See note 32 above.

[89]The litterature on this text is vast and will have to be sought elsewhere; for a recent discussion of the proverbs, see P. Grelot, "Les proverbes d'Ahiqar," *RB* 68 (19 61) 178-94; *Documents araméens d'Egypte* (Litteratures anciennes du Proche-Orient; Paris: Cerf, 1972) 425-52.

[90]*Aramaic Approach* (3d ed.), 41.

[91]See pp. 90–94 below.

[92]E.g., M. Black, *Aramaic Approach* (3d ed.), 244-71, 277-80, 303-4; M.-E. Boismard, "Importance de la critique textuelle pour établir l'origine araméenne du quatrième évangile," *L'évangile de Jean: Etudes et problèmes* (RechBib 3; Bruges: Desclée de Brouwer, 1958) 41-57.

[93]See, e.g., F. H. Chase, *The Old Syriac Element in the Text of Codex Bezae* (London: Macmillan, 1893). This question, however, is far from simple; cf. E. Ferguson, "Qumran and Codex 'D,'" *RQ* 8 (1972-76) 75-80; S. P. Brock, Review of J. D. Yoder, *Concordance to the Distinctive Greek Text of Codex Bezae* (NTTS 2; Leiden: Brill, 1961), *TLZ* 88 (1963) 351-52, esp. col. 352.

[94]E.g., "'De son ventre couleront des fleuves d'eau'—La citation scripturaire de Jean, vii, 38," *RB* 66 (1959) 369-74; "A propos de Jean vii, 38," *RB* 67 (1960) 224-25; M.-E. Boismard, "Les citations targumiques dans le quatrième évangile," *RB* 66 (1959) 374-78; M. McNamara, *The New Testament and the Palestinian Targum to the Pentateuch* (AnBib 27; Rome: Biblical Institute, 1966); *Targum and Testament: Aramaic Paraphrases of the Hebrew Bible: A Light on the New Testament* (Grand Rapids: Eerdmans, 1972); R. Le Déaut, *La nuit pascale* (AnBib 22; Rome: Biblical Institute, 1963); *Liturgie juive et Nouveau Testament* (Rome: Biblical Institute, 1965); B. J. Malina, *The Palestinian Manna Tradition: The Manna Tradition in the Palestinian Targums and Its Relationship to the New Testament Writings* (AGJU 7; Leiden: Brill, 1968). See further P. Nickels, *Targum and New Testament: A Bibliography together with a New Testament Index* (Rome: Biblical Institute, 1967).

[95]*The New Testament and the Palestinian Targum to the Pentateuch,* 77. McNamara (*Targum and Testament,* 14-15) tries to brush aside my criticism of this usage: "Every student of this material is, of course, acutely conscious of the complexity to which Fitzmyer refers." But if so, then why is it better "to abide by the traditional name 'Palestinian Targum'"? One suspects that this is being done because it is more convenient in view of the thesis being propounded. Keep it vague, and no one will question the weakness in the thesis itself!

[96]See *Masoreten des Westens* (Stuttgart: Kohlhammer, 1930; reprinted, Hildesheim: Olms, 1967), 2. 1-62.

[97]See especially Cairo Genizah Text C. This whole area needs further scrutiny.

[98]See, e.g., A. Deissmann, "Prolegomena to the Biblical Letters and Epistles," *Bible Studies: Contributions Chiefly from Papyri and Inscriptions to the History of the Language, the Literature, and the Religion of Hellenistic Judaism and Primitive Christianity* (tr. A. Grieve; Edinburgh: Clark, 1901) 3-59; L. Champion, *Benedictions and Doxologies in the Epistles of Paul* (Oxford: Privately printed Heidelberg dissertation, 1935); J.-A. Eschlimann, "La rédaction des épîtres pauliniennes d'après une comparaison avec les lettres profanes de son temps," *RB* 53 (1946) 185-96; F. X. J. Exler, *The Form of the Ancient Greek Letter: A Study in Greek Epistolography* (Washington: Catholic University, 1923); E. Fascher, "Briefliteratur, urchristliche, formgeschichtlich," *RGG*³ 1 (1957) 1412-15; O. Roller, *Das Formular der paulinischen Briefen: Ein Beitrag zur Lehre vom antiken Briefe* (BWANT 58; Stuttgart: Kohlhammer, 1933); H. Koskenniemi, *Studien zur Idee und Phraseologie des griechischen Briefes bis 400 n. Chr.* (Suomalaisen Tiedeakatemian Toimituksia: Annales academiae scientiarum fennicae, ser. B, tom. 102/2; Helsinki: Suomalaisen Tiedeakatemia, 1956); W. G. Doty, *Letters in Primitive Christianity* (Guides to Biblical Scholarship, NT series; Philadelphia: Fortress, 1973); J. L. White, *The Form and Function of the Body of the Greek Letter: A Study of the Letter-Body in the Non-Literary Papyri and in Paul the Apostle* (SBLDS 2; Missoula: Scholars Press, 1972); *The Form and Structure of the Official Petition: A Study in Greek Epistolography* (SBLDS 5; Missoula: Society of Biblical Literature, 1972); C.-H. Kim, *Form and*

Structure of the Familiar Greek Letter of Recommendation (SBLDS 4; Missoula: Society of Biblical Literature, 1972).

[99]See p. 183–204 below.

[100]See p. 200 n. 7 below.

[101]See p. 5 above.

[102]*Aramaic Approach* (3d ed.), 300.

[103]Ibid., n. 2.

[104]See pp. 35–36 below.

[105]See further my review of M. Black, *Aramaic Approach* (3d ed.), *CBQ* 30 (1968) 417–28.

Chapter 2

The Languages of Palestine in the First Century A.D.*

With the deportation of Palestinian Jews to Babylonia in the early sixth century B.C. there began a gradual but distinctive shift in the language-habits of the people of Palestine. What had been known as *śĕpat Kĕnaᶜan,* "the language of Canaan" (Isa 19:18) or *Yĕhûdît*, "the language of Judah" (2 Kgs 18:26, 28; Isa 36:11, 13), or what is often called today classical Hebrew of the pre-exilic period, gave way at first to a more Aramaicized form of the language.[1] Though the two languages, Hebrew and Aramaic, had co-existed for several centuries in the Near East before this, Aramaic became the more important of the two, serving as the *lingua franca* during the latter part of the Neo-Assyrian empire and during the Persian period. Hebrew is usually regarded today as the more important of the two languages, because it is the tongue of the bulk of the OT. And yet, historically it was restricted to a small area on the south-eastern coast of the Mediterranean, whereas Official or Imperial Aramaic was used across a major portion of the Near Eastern world, from Egypt to Asia Minor to Pakistan. Indeed, it gradually supplanted Hebrew in most of Palestine itself as the common tongue.[2]

With the conquest of the East by Alexander a new linguistic influence was felt in Palestine. Even prior to the golden age of Greece, its culture had been influencing the eastern Mediterranean world, and Palestine was affected. But the extent to which the Greek language was advancing into the area at an early period is not easy to say. The evidence for the use of Greek in Palestine prior to the third century B.C. is very sparse indeed, the oldest extant Greek inscription dating from only 277 B.C.[3]

Hebrew did not wholly disappear from Palestine, either when Aramaic had become the more common language or when Palestinian Jews gradually began to use Greek. The composition of Daniel and of Ben Sira is an indication of the continued use of it.[4] Though these compositions may point to a learned and literary use of the language, it would be oversimplified to regard it as only that. There were areas or pockets in Palestine, and perhaps even strata of society, where Hebrew continued as a spoken language too. It is often thought that an effort was made to resurrect it (if that is the proper term) at the time of the Maccabean revolt and that the use of Hebrew became a token of one's loyalty to the national effort.[5] If the origins of the Qumran Essene community are rightly related to the aftermath of that revolt, this may explain why the majority of the Qumran texts discovered to date were written in Hebrew and composed at a time when most Palestinian Jews were thought to be speaking Aramaic. These texts, of course, do not tell us how much Hebrew was *spoken* among the Essenes, because they bear witness only to what is called a "neo-classical Hebrew," a form of the language that may be only literary. Since, however, the majority of the sectarian literature was composed in Hebrew, this seems to mean that it was being spoken. But in any case, the use of Hebrew for such compositions did not exclude the use of Aramaic; the latter is also found in the Qumran fragments, but not to the same extent as the Hebrew. A few fragments of an Old Greek translation of the OT were also found in Qumran Cave IV; they suggest that at least some of the community were reading Greek, and possibly speaking it.[6] The relative paucity of the Greek texts in comparison with the Hebrew and Aramaic is noteworthy.

With the advent of the Romans in 63 B.C. and the conquest of Pompey, Latin too was introduced into the area. Again, the evidence for its early use is exceedingly sparse.[7] Yet it must be considered among the languages of Palestine at the beginning of the Christian era.

This very brief historical sketch provides the background for the use of four languages in Palestine about the time when Christianity emerged. The complex linguistic picture that they created is not easy to draw. Yet that complexity bears on a number of problems in the interpretation of the NT and of intertestamental writings. It bears too on the use and interpretation of the targums. My topic is one that has been discussed many times over during the last century and the opinions expressed have often been in favor of one language over another; the topic is vast and my treatment here can only hope to survey it without going into great detail.

In speaking of first-century Palestine, I would like to include the first part of the second century too, up to the time of the Second Revolt against Rome (A.D. 132-135), since this marks a logical cut-off point in the history of Palestine and is often regarded as the end of the NT era. The sources that I shall be using in this discussion will be both literary and epigraphic.

I. *Latin*

I shall begin with the latest language to appear on the scene and work back to the oldest. The evidence of Latin in first-century Palestine indicates that it was used mainly by the Romans who occupied the land and for more or less official purposes. Thus there are dedicatory inscriptions on buildings and aqueducts, funerary inscriptions on tombstones of Roman legionnaires who died in Palestine, milestones on Roman roads with Latin inscriptions,[8] and the ubiquitous Roman terra-cotta tiles stamped with various abbreviations of the Tenth Legion, the *Legio decima fretensis* (LX, LXF, LXFRE, LEXFR, LCXF, LEG X F).[9]

Two of the most interesting Latin inscriptions have only recently come to light and both of them are from Caesarea Maritima, the town rebuilt by Herod the Great between 22 and 9 B.C. in honor of Augustus, which eventually became the seat of the Roman governor. Tacitus called it *caput Iudaeae* (*Hist.* 2.78.10). One of the inscriptions comes from the architrave of a building in Caesarea and partly preserves the name of the Roman colony established by the emperor Vespasian. It reads:[10]

[COLONIAE] PRIMAE FL(aviae) AVG(vstae) [Caesareae?]
[CLEO]PATRA MATER EIVS HOC F(ieri) I(vssit)

The other is the now famous fragment of a dedicatory inscription on a building, the Tiberieum, that Pontius Pilate erected in honor of the emperor Tiberius It reads:[11]

[TI(berio) CAES(are) AVG(vsto) V CO(n)]S(vle) TIBERIEVM
[PO]NTIVS PILATVS
[PRAEF]ECTVS IVDA[EA]E
[ ] ´[ ]

This inscription thus attests the official use of Latin in Palestine, prior to A.D. 36, the year of Pilate's recall to Rome. It also records the historical presence of Pilate in Judea, a fact scarcely doubted,[12] but never before attested epigraphically. Finally, it confirms the suggestion made by Roman historians that Pilate's official title was not *procurator,*[13] but rather *praefectus.*[14]

Such Latin inscriptions as these illustrate the information supplied by Josephus who tells us that prohibitions forbidding non-Jews to enter the inner courts of the Jerusalem temple were erected along the stone balustrades surrounding them, "some in Greek, and some in Latin characters" (*αἱ μὲν ἑλληνικοῖς, αἱ δὲ ῥωμαϊκοῖς γράμμασιν*).[15] Though exemplars of this warning have been found in Greek,[16] none has yet turned up in Latin. Such a prohibition carrying the death penalty would understandably be erected in Greek and Latin to warn foreign visitors little acquainted with the Semitic languages. But one cannot restrict the understanding of them to foreigners alone. Josephus also mentions decrees of Caesar concerning the Jews which were formulated in Latin as well as in Greek.[17]

All of this makes intelligible the action of Pilate recorded in the Fourth Gospel,[18] writing the official title on Jesus' cross *ῥωμαϊστί,* "in Latin," as well as *ἑβραϊστί* and *ἑλληνιστί* (John 19:20).

This evidence points to an official use of Latin in Palestine by Romans which might have been expected. From the period between the two revolts there are four (or five) fragmentary papyrus Latin texts which were found in the caves of Murabbaᶜat. Though they are so fragmentary that one cannot be certain about their contents, yet one of them (Mur 158) seems to have been an official, archival copy of a document belonging to the Roman invaders.[19] Part of a Roman name is preserved on it, *C. Iulius R*[ ].

There are also a few funerary inscriptions, one of them marking the burial of a Roman soldier of the Tenth Legion, Lucius Magniu[s] Felix.[20] From the same period come other Latin inscriptions too, e.g., one belonging to a monument, possibly an altar, dedicated to Jupiter Sarapis and found in Jerusalem itself. It is dated to A.D. 116, and invokes Jupiter for the health and victory of the emperor Trajan.[21]

Such evidence is precious, indeed, because it is not abundant. It says, however, little about the amount of Latin that might have been spoken in Palestine by the indigenous population, despite the long time since the Roman occupation began in 63 B.C.[22] But one reason for this is that Greek was still a common means of communication not only between Romans in the provinces, but also between the capital and the provinces. Greek was still more or less the *lingua franca* in the Near East.

II. *Greek*

Greek culture had been increasingly affecting the Jews of Palestine for some time prior to the conquest of Alexander.[23] The influence of this culture continued after his conquest, especially with the Hellenizing efforts of the Lagide and Seleucid kings, and even with the Herods. Greek cities were founded in Palestine and older towns were transformed into *poleis.* Alexander himself ordered the reconstruction of Gaza. The names of some towns of the Decapolis, Pella and Dion, reveal the early Macedonian influence. Under Lagide domination Acco became Ptolemais and Rabbat-Ammon became Philadelphia, another town of the Decapolis. Philoteria was established under the same influence on the western shore of Lake Gennesareth, and Joppa was hellenized. Ancient Beth-shan was conquered by Antiochus III the Great in 218 B.C. and became Scythopolis. The Hellenization continued under Herod the Great, who transformed the ancient town of Strato's Tower into Caesarea Maritima, Samaria into Sebaste, and established a number of other towns and fortresses throughout the country on Greek models (Antipatris, Phasaelis, Antonia at Jerusalem, etc.). Nor did his heirs desist from such activity, because to them is ascribed the founding of such places as Caesarea Philippi, Tiberias, Bethsaida Julias. In all some thirty towns of the area have been counted that were either Greek foundations or transformed *poleis.*[24] These Hellenistic cities dotted the countryside of Palestine for several centuries prior to the first Christian century and were clearly centers from which the Greek language spread to less formally Hellenistic towns, such as Jerusalem, Jericho, or Nazareth. As in the case of the Roman occupiers of the land, the new language was undoubtedly used at first in official texts, decrees, and inscriptions, and from such use it spread to the indigenous population.

However, it is not possible to document the use of Greek in Palestine prior to Alexander or to indicate what influence it might have had then. The earliest Greek text found there is apparently the bilingual Edomite-Greek ostracon dated in the sixth year of Ptolemy II Philadelphus (277 B.C.), discovered in the spring of 1971 at Khirbet el-Kom, along with other ostraca (see n. 3 above). Prior to this discovery the earliest known inscription was that erected by Anaxikles, a priest of the royal cult of Ptolemy IV Philopator, who was installed at Joppa shortly after the Egyptian victory over Antiochus III at Raphia in 217 B.C. It gives clear evidence of the use of the language by foreigners, but says little about the use of it by the indigenous population.

When the Hellenization of Palestine under Antiochus IV Epiphanes began, his efforts were aided by the Jews themselves, as both 1 Maccabees and Josephus make clear.[25] There seems to be little doubt that the use of the Greek language was part of this assistance.[26] Antiochus' reign, however, lasted only a little over a decade, and in its aftermath, the Maccabean revolt, the book of Daniel was reduced to its final form. In the Aramaic stories that form part of that book one finds the first clear instance of Greek invading a Palestinian Aramaic text. In Dan 3:5 the names of three of the musical instruments, "the lyre, the harp, and the bagpipe" (*RSV*—קיתרוס < Gk. *κίθαρις,* פסנתרין < *ψαλτήριον;* סומפניה < *συμφωνία*), are all given in slightly Aramaicized forms of clearly Greek names.[27] Further evidence of Greek influence is seen also in the linguistic problem of the book as a whole; in its protocanonical form it is composed in two languages, Hebrew and Aramaic, but in its deuterocanonical form Greek appears. This influence is further seen in other apocryphal and deuterocanonical compositions in Greek by Jews, such as 1 Esdras, 2 Maccabees, and the additions to Esther (to mention only those writings that are probably of Palestinian origin).

Though the names of a host of Hellenistic Jewish litterateurs who wrote in Greek are known,[28] and some fragments of their writings are preserved in patristic authors such as Clement of Alexandria,[29] or Eusebius of Caesarea,[30] there are only a few whose writings are related to first-century Palestine. The most important of these are Justus of Tiberias and Flavius Josephus, both of whom wrote mainly historical works. The first was the bitter opponent of Josephus in the First Revolt against Rome, a man of Hellenistic education and noted for his eloquence, the author of *Ἱστορία ἡ τοῦ Ἰουδαϊκοῦ πολέμου τοῦ κατὰ Οὐεσπασιάνου.*[31]

Josephus tells us something about his own knowledge of Greek and about his use of it to compose his works. At the end of the *Antiquities,* he says of himself:

> My compatriots admit that in our Jewish learning (*παρ' ἡμῖν παιδείαν*) I far excel them. But I labored hard to steep myself in Greek prose [and poetic learning], after having gained a knowledge of Greek grammar; but the constant use of my native tongue (*πάτριος . . . συνήθεια*) hindered my achieving precision in pronunciation. For our people do not welcome those who have mastered the speech of many nations or adorn

> their style with smoothness of diction, because they consider that such skill is not only common to ordinary freemen but that even slaves acquire it, if they so choose. Rather, they give credit for wisdom to those who acquire an exact knowledge of the Law and can interpret the Holy Scriptures. Consequently, though many have laboriously undertaken this study, scarcely two or three have succeeded (in it) and reaped the fruit of their labors.[32]

Several points should be noted in Josephus' statement. First, his record of a popular boastful attitude that the learning of Greek would be an ordinary achievement for many Palestinians, even for freemen and slaves, if they wanted to do so. The attitude is at least condescending. Secondly, such learning was not so much esteemed as knowledge of the Mosaic Law and the interpretation of Scripture. Thirdly, Josephus testifies about the efforts that he personally made to acquire a good command of Greek. Fourthly, he also gives the impression that few Palestinian Jews of his day could speak Greek well.

From other places in his writings we know that he acted as an interpreter for Titus, speaking "in his native tongue" to the populace toward the end of the war.[33] Titus himself had addressed the Jews of Palestine in Greek, but preferred to have Josephus parley with them *hebraïzōn.* This may suggest that Palestinian Jews did not understand Greek very well, and bear out the comment of Josephus himself cited above. However, J. N. Sevenster has plausibly noted that we do not know how well Titus himself could speak Greek.[34] Hence Josephus' task as interpreter does not necessarily mean that little Greek was actually understood.

Again Josephus informs us that he composed his *Jewish War* originally "in his native tongue" (τῇ πατρίῳ [γλώσσῃ]), destining it for Parthians, Babylonians, the tribes of Arabia, Jews beyond the Euphrates and in Adiabene.[35] This destination almost certainly implies that it was originally written in the *lingua franca*, Aramaic.[36] Josephus subsequently translated this composition into Greek (ἕλλαδι γλώσσῃ μεταβαλών),[37] to provide subjects of the Roman empire with his version of the Palestinian revolt. What a problem this was for him he reveals in the *Antiquities,* where he still looks on Greek as "foreign and unfamiliar."[38] And yet, despite this attitude, the end-product of his efforts has been hailed as "an excellent specimen of the Atticistic Greek of the first century."[39]

But the real difficulty in this testimony of Josephus is that his Greek writings were composed in Rome, not in Palestine; and he frankly admits that he composed the Greek version of the *Jewish War* in the leisure that Rome afforded, "making use of some assistants for the sake of the Greek" (χρησάμενός τισι πρὸς τὴν ἑλληνίδα φωνὴν συνέργοις).[40] Presumably, other Jewish authors in Palestine who might have wanted to write in Greek could have found there comparable assistants. This may seem to have been essential for literary composition, but it says little about the degree of communication between Palestinian Jews in Greek.

If Josephus' testimony leaves the picture of Greek in first-century Palestine unclear, there are many other considerations that persuade us that Greek was widely used at this time and not only in the clearly Hellenized towns, but in many others as well. Indeed, there are some indications that Palestinian Jews in some areas may have used nothing else but Greek. Reasons for considering the matter in this way may now be briefly set forth.

There is first the epigraphic material. Several famous Greek inscriptions are extant from this period. There is the Greek inscription forbidding non-Jews to enter the inner courts of the Jerusalem temple,[41] the Jerusalem synagogue inscription which commemorates its building by Theodotos Vettenos, a priest and leader of the synagogue,[42] the hymn inscribed in the necropolis of Marisa,[43] the edict of Augustus (or some first-century Roman emperor) found at Nazareth concerning the violation of tombs,[44] the Capernaum dedicatory inscription,[45] and the numberless ossuary inscriptions, some written in Greek alone, others in Greek and Hebrew (or Aramaic) from the vicinity of Jerusalem.[46] In several cases the Greek inscriptions on these ossuaries have outnumbered those in Aramaic or Hebrew,[47] and it is unlikely that the language chosen for most of these crudely incised identifications was merely the *lingua franca* of the day. Rather, they bear witness to the widespread and living use of Greek among first-century Palestinian Jews, as does the adoption of Greek and Roman names by many of them in this period. H. J. Leon is undoubtedly right when he writes that such "sepulchral inscriptions . . . best indicate the language of the common people."[48] For they reveal that Greek was not confined merely to official inscriptions. The real question, however, is how widespread it was among the common people.

Information concerning Palestine during the period between the two revolts against Rome has always been sparse, and information about the use of Greek at that time is no exception. Recently, however, some new material has come to light in the Greek papyri from the Murabbaᶜat caves and in copies of Greek letters from the Bar Cochba revolt.

From the Murabbaᶜat caves have come examples of grain transactions (Mur 89-107), IOU's (Mur 114), contracts of marriage and remarriage among Jews (Mur 115-16), fragments of philosophical and literary texts (Mur 108-12), even texts written in a Greek shorthand (Mur 164).[49] The letters from a cave in the Wadi Ḫabra indicate that Greek was also used in a less official kind of writing. From the period just before the Second Revolt there is a batch of letters which are communications between Bar Cochba and his lieutenants, and surprisingly enough written even in Greek.[50]

One letter, in particular, merits some attention because of the special bearing it has on the topic under discussion. It comes from the so-called Cave of Letters in the Wadi Ḫabra and was discovered in 1960. It is written in the name of one *Soumaios*. The editor of the letter, B. Lifshitz, thinks that this is a Greek form of the name of *Šimĕᶜōn ben Kōsibāh,* the real name of Bar

Cochba. If it is not Bar Cochba himself, then it is someone very closely associated with him, who writes to the same two lieutenants to whom Bar Cochba wrote in other letters—and, indeed, about the same matter. Soumaios requests of Jonathan bar Baᶜyan and Masabbala that they send wooden-beams (?) and citrons (the *ᵓetrōgîm*) for the celebration of Succoth or Tabernacles. The text reads:

Σου[μαῖ]ος Ἰωναθῆι	Sou[mai]os to Jonathe,
Βαϊανοῦ καὶ Μα-	(son of) Baianos, and Ma-
[σ]άβαλα χαίρειν.	[s]abbala, greetings!
Ἐ[π]ηδὴ ἔπεμσα πρὸς	S[i]nce I have sent to
ὑμᾶς Ἀ[γ]ρίππαν σπου-	you A[g]rippa, make
δ[άσα]τε πέμσε μοι	h[ast]e to send me
σ[τε]λεοὺ[ς] καὶ κίτρια	b[e]am[s] and citrons.
α[ὐτὰ] δ' ἀνασθήσεται	And furnish th[em]
ἰς [χ]ιτρειαβολὴν Ἰου-	for the [C]itron-celebration of the
δαίων καὶ μὴ ἄλως	Jews; and do not do
ποιήσηται. Ἐγράφη	otherwise. No[w] (this) has been writ-
δ[ὲ] Ἐληνιστὶ διὰ	ten in Greek because
τ[ὸ ὁρ]μὰν μὴ εὑρη-	a [des]ire has not be[en]
θ[ῆ]ναι Ἑβραεστὶ	found to w[ri]te in Hebrew. De[s]patch
γ[ρά]ψασθαι. Αὐτὸν	him quickly
ἀπ[ο]λῦσαι τάχιον	fo[r t]he feast,
δι[ὰ τ]ην Ἑορτὴν	an[d do no]t
κα[ὶ μ]ὴ ἄλλως ποιή-	do otherwise.
ση[τα]ι.	
Σουμαῖος	Soumaios.
ἔρρωσο	Farewell.[51]

Two things are of importance in this letter. First, Bar Cochba's solicitude to have provisions for the celebration of Succoth is again attested; a similar request for citrons and willow-branches is found in one of his Aramaic letters.[52] Secondly, at a time when the nationalist fever of the Jews must have been running high the leader of the revolt—or someone close to him, if Soumaios is not Šimĕᶜōn bar Kōsibāh—frankly prefers to write in Greek, or at least has to write in Greek. He does not find the ὅρμα, "impulse, desire," to compose the letter ἑβραϊστί. The cursive handwriting is not elegant and the spelling leaves much to be desired; if a scribe were employed for the writing of it, then he was not very well trained. In any case, this Palestinian Greek is not much worse than other examples of Greek in the provinces that have been found elsewhere.

A NT problem that bears on this discussion may be introduced at this point. It is the names for Jerusalem Christians recorded in Acts 6:1, the Ἑλληνισταί and the Ἑβραῖοι. I have discussed this matter more fully elsewhere,[53] adopting the interesting suggestion of C. F. D. Moule,[54] which seems to cope best with the data available and seems to be far more plausible than other attempts to explain these names.[55] Moule proposes that these names designate two groups of Palestinian *Jewish* Christians in Jerusalem. The Ἑλληνισταί were not simply Gentile converts who spoke Greek, while the Ἑβραῖοι were Jewish converts who spoke Hebrew (or possibly Aramaic). The Greek-speaking Paul of Tarsus stoutly maintained that he was Ἑβραῖος ἐξ Ἑβραίων (Phil 3:5). Rather, Ἑλληνισταί undoubtedly denotes Jerusalem Jews or Jewish Christians who habitually spoke Greek only (and for that reason were more affected by Hellenistic culture), while the Ἑβραῖοι were those who also spoke a Semitic language. In any case, it can scarcely be maintained that ἑλληνίζειν did not mean "to speak Greek" at all. Moule's distinction fits in very well with the widespread use of Greek in first-century Palestine. It raises a further problem of the determination of what Semitic language would have been commonly used along with it by the Ἑβραῖοι.

Before we approach that problem, however, two final remarks about the use of Greek in first-century Palestine are in order. The first concerns Jesus' use of Greek. This question has been raised from time to time for a variety of reasons, and obviously little can be asserted about it.[56] "Galilee of the Gentiles" (Matt 4:15) has often been said to have been an area of Palestine where the population was more bilingual than in the south, e.g., at Jerusalem. Hence it is argued: Coming from an area such as this, Jesus would have shared this double linguistic heritage. While it must be admitted that there were undoubtedly areas where less Greek was used than others, nevertheless the widespread attestation of Greek material in Palestine would indicate that "Galilee of the Gentiles" did not have a monopoly on it. The general evidence that we have been considering would suggest the likelihood that Jesus did speak Greek. Further, his conversations with Roman officials—Pilate or the centurion, and perhaps even that reflected in John 12—would point in this direction. This question, however, is related to the others about the Semitic language that he used, and I shall return to it later. However, what evidence there is that he used Greek yields at most a probability; if it be used to insist that we might even have in the Gospels some of the *ipsissima verba Iesu graeca,* actually uttered by him as he addressed his bilingual Galilean compatriots,[57] then the evidence is being pressed beyond legitimate bounds.

The other remark concerns the researches and studies of such scholars as S. Krauss, M. Schwabe, S. Liebermann, B. Lifshitz et al., who have done yeoman service in ferreting out the evidence for the Hellenization of Palestinian Jews. In particular, the two books of S. Liebermann, *Greek in Jewish Palestine* and *Hellenism in Jewish Palestine,*[58] are outstanding in this regard; but their subtitles reveal that they are largely based on materials of a much later date than the first century—on the Mishnah, the Talmud, and other rabbinical writings. J. N. Sevenster has frankly stated the difficulty in using this material as an indication of the first-century situation.[59] Moreover, Liebermann has been criticized for neglecting the inscriptional material from the cemetery of Beth-Sheᶜarim,[60] and for not using the older Greek materials from Joppa, Capernaum, etc., that have been known for a long time. The materials which these scholars have amassed make it abundantly clear that the Palestinian Jews *of the third and fourth centuries A.D.* were quite hellenized and used Greek widely. This is the sort of situation that the numerous hebraized and aramaicized Greek words that appear in rabbinical literature also suggest.[61] From 200 on it is clear that not only Hellenism but even the Greek language used by the Jews had made heavy inroads into the Aramaic being spoken; it is the same sort of influence that one detects in the Aramaic being spoken in the territory of Palestine's neighbor to the north, in Syriac. This is, by contrast, the advantage of J. N. Sevenster's recent book, *Do You Know Greek?* For he has sought to sift data from literary and epigraphic sources and presents an intriguing thesis on the wide use of Greek in first-century Palestine both among Jews and Christians. Unfortunately, the reader is distracted at times by lengthy discussions of texts from periods prior and posterior to this century.[62]

III. *Aramaic*

If asked what was the language commonly spoken in Palestine in the time of Jesus of Nazareth, most people with some acquaintance of that era and area would almost spontaneously answer Aramaic. To my way of thinking, this is still the correct answer for the *most commonly* used language, but the defense of this thesis must reckon with the growing mass of evidence that both Greek and Hebrew were being used as well. I would, however, hesitate to say with M. Smith that "at least as much Greek as Aramaic was spoken in Palestine."[63] In any case, the evidence for the use of Aramaic has also been growing in recent years.

Evidence for the use of Aramaic toward the end of the first millennium B.C. has never been abundant. A scholar such as W. F. Albright was led by this situation to think that its use was actually on the wane, especially during the Seleucid period. He writes:

> There are no Aramaic literary works extant from the period between the third or second century B.C. and the second or third A.D., a period of over three hundred years. There can be little doubt that there was a real eclipse of Aramaic during the period of the Seleucid Empire (312 B.C. to the early first century B.C.), since scarcely a single Aramaic inscription from this period has been discovered, except in Transjordan and the adjacent parts of Arabia, which were relatively freer from Greek influence than Western Palestine and Syria proper. After this epigraphic hiatus, Palmyrene inscriptions began to appear in the second half of the first century B.C.; recent excavations have brought to light an inscription dating from the year 44 B.C. Inscriptions in Jewish Aramaic first appeared about the middle of the first century B.C., and became more abundant during the reign of Herod the Great, just before the Christian era. . . . They thus help to clarify the actual Aramaic of Jewish Palestine in the time of Jesus and the Apostles. If the Megillat Taᶜanith, or 'Scroll of Fastings,' a list of official Jewish fasts with accompanying historical notations, really precedes the year A.D. 70, as held by some scholars, it belongs to our period, but it is safer to date it in the second century A.D., in accordance with its present chronological content.[64]

Between the final redaction of Daniel (ca. 165 B.C.), in which roughly six chapters are written in Aramaic, and the first of the rabbinical writings, *Mĕgillat Taᶜănît*,[65] dating from the end of the first Christian century, there had never been much evidence of the use of Aramaic in Palestine prior to the discovery of the Qumran scrolls and fragments. Before 1947 numberless ossuary and sepulchral inscriptions had been coming to light.[66] But they were scarcely evidence of what E. J. Goodspeed has called "creative Aramaic literary writing."[67] Except for a few with extended texts, they consist for the most part of proper names, written in the cursive Hebrew-Aramaic script of the time. Indeed, it is often hard to tell whether their inscribers spoke Hebrew or Aramaic. The most important of the extended texts are the Uzziah plaque, commemorating the first-century transfer of the alleged bones of the famous eighth-century king of Judah,[68] an ossuary lid with a *qorban* inscription that illustrates the use of this Aramaic word in Mark 7:11,[69] and a Kidron Valley dipinto.[70] There was also the evidence of Aramaic words preserved in the Greek Gospels and Josephus' writings, as well as the Aramaisms in the syntax of the NT in general.[71] This was more or less the extent of the evidence up to 1947.

Since the discovery of the Qumran material it is now evident that literature was indeed being composed in Aramaic in the last century B.C. and in the first century A.D. The number of extant Aramaic texts of a literary nature is not small, even though the fragments of them found in the various Qumran caves may be. Only a few of these texts have been published so far: the *Genesis Apocryphon,*[72] *the Prayer of Nabonidus, the Description of the New Jerusalem,* the *Elect of God* text; parts of such texts as the *Testament of Levi, Enoch, Pseudo-Daniel,* a *Targum of Job,* and a number of untitled texts to which a number has merely been assigned. Reports have been made on still other Aramaic texts from Caves IV and XI, such as several copies of Tobit, of targums of Job and Leviticus, of a text mentioning "the Son of God" and "the Son of the Most High" in phrases remarkably close to Luke 1:32, 35.[73] All of this points to an extensive Aramaic literary activity and an Aramaic literature, at least used by the Essenes, if not composed by them.

Objection might be made at this point that this evidence points only to a literary use of Aramaic and that it really says little about the current spoken form of the language. True, but then one must beware of exaggerating theoretically the difference between the literary and spoken forms of the language. Contemporary with the Qumran evidence are the ossuary and sepulchral inscriptions already mentioned, many more of which have been coming to light in recent years.[74] Again, an Aramaic IOU, dated in the second year of Nero (i.e., 55-56), came to light in one of the Murabbaᶜat caves, and a letter on an ostracon from Masada.[75] And from a slightly later period comes a batch of legal documents, composed in Aramaic as well as in Greek and Hebrew, from caves in the wadies Murabbaᶜat, Ḫabra, and Seiyâl.[76] Many of these still await publication.

One of them, which has already been published by H. J. Polotsky,[77] merits some attention here because of its unique bilingual character. Discovered in 1961 in the so-called Cave of Letters of the Wadi Ḫabra, it belongs to the family archives of Babatha, daughter of Simeon, who at one time lived in a small Nabatean town called Maḥoz ᶜEglatain (or in Greek, *Maōza*), which since A.D. 106 had become part of *provincia Arabia.* The main part of the text, which is a copy of a receipt given by Babatha to a Jewish guardian of her orphan son, is written in Greek. It is dated to 19 August 132 and acknowledges the payment of six denarii for the boy's food and clothing. The ten lines of Greek text of the receipt are followed by three in Aramaic that summarize the Greek statement. This Aramaic summary, however, is immediately followed by four lines of Greek, written by the same scribe who composed the main text; they give an almost literal translation of the Aramaic and are explicitly introduced by the word *ἑρμενίας,* "translation." The text ends with *Γέρμαν[ος] ᾿Ιούδ[ο]υ ἔγραψα*, "I, Germanus, (son) of Judah, have written (this)." Though this receipt was found in the southern part of Palestine, it was actually written in Nabatean country, to the southeast of the Dead Sea. From the same place comes yet another Greek document, a *Doppelurkunde,* with the Greek text written twice, but with the *scriptura exterior* endorsed by two men who write, one in Aramaic, the other in Nabatean.[78] It is dated to 12 Oct. 125. Apparently there are other examples of bilingual or trilingual texts still to be published by Yadin or Polotsky.[79] Here we have in official documents the simultaneous use of Greek, Aramaic, and Nabatean; the problem is to say to what extent this might represent language habits in southern Palestine of roughly the same period.

Given this simultaneous use, the real question is to what extent Greek would be affecting the Aramaic and vice versa. In the case of the receipt from the Babatha archive, the main text written in Greek, with an Aramaic abstract itself rendered again in a Greek translation, obviously attests to the importance of Greek in the area where such documents were composed. The woman was Jewish, and it is scarcely credible that she would have legal and financial documents drawn up for her in a language that she did not understand or read. But the text raises the question to what extent Greek vocabulary and idiom were invading Aramaic. We know that the converse took place. Aramaic certainly affected the Greek used by Jews. The Aramaic words in the Gospels and Josephus, and the Aramaisms in their Greek syntax reveal this. A small Greek fragment from Murabbaᶜat, containing a broken list of proper names, gives one of them as ᾿Ιώσηπος *ἀσωφήρ* Κητα[ ], "Josephus, the scribe, *Keta* [ ]." Here a Hebrew title, *has-sōphēr,* has simply been transcribed.[80] Even though this is evidence for Hebrew affecting Greek, it serves as an illustration of the sort of data we should expect in Aramaic texts of the period: Greek words transcribed into Aramaic, such as we have in the names of the musical instruments in Dan 3:5.

However, this sort of evidence is surprisingly lacking in the first-century Aramaic texts that are extant. This phenomenon is still to be discovered in Qumran Aramaic texts or in the Aramaic IOU of 55/56 (Mur 18). In all of the Aramaic texts of slightly later date from the caves of the wadies Murabbaᶜat and Ḫabra that have either been published so far or reported on with partial publication of texts, I have found to date only four isolated words and one formula that are clearly due to Greek. These are:

כנמסא,	"according to the Law" (Mur 21:11 [a marriage contract with the date missing; Milik would not exclude a first century date])	*νόμος*
באספליא,	"in security" (5/6Ḥev 1 ar:2 [an Aramaic letter of Bar Cochba])	*ἀσφάλεια*
רהומיה,	"Romans" (5/6Ḥev 6 ar:2 [another letter of Bar Cochba])	*Ῥωμαῖοι*
אפ[טרפא],	"guardian" (5/6Ḥev 27:12 [receipt of payment from Babatha archive, dated 19 August 132; Polotsky's restoration is certain, because *ἐπίτροπος* occurs in the Greek version, line 16]).[81]	*ἐπίτροπος*

A date formula in an Aramaic text was taken over from Greek usage:

על הפטות ליקים קטילים סורס תנינותא ומרקס
אורלים אנתונינס שנת תלת לאוטוקרטור קסר טרינס
הדרינס סבסטס ועל מנין הפרכיה דא בעשרין וארבעה
בתמוז שנת עשר וחמש

"in the consulship of Lucius Catilius Severus for the second time and Marcus Aurelius Antoninus, in the third year of Imperator Caesar Traianus Hadrianus Augustus and according to the era of this province, on the 24th of Tammuz, year 15" (= 13 July 120).[82] The date is given by the consulship, by Hadrian's regnal year, and by the era of *provincia Arabia.* Aside from the proper names, the clear Grecisms are על הפטות for *ἐπὶ ὑπάτων*, לאוטוקרטור for *αὐτοκράτωρ* ("emperor"), קסר for Καῖσαρ, סבסטס for *σέβαστος*, ועל מנין הפרכיה דא for *κατὰ τὸν τῆς νέας ἐπαρχίας* Ἀραβίας *ἄριθμον*.[83] This is a clear example of Greek affecting Aramaic; it is a stereotyped legal formula that was undoubtedly often used and perhaps required in official documents of that province. Again, it is not easy to say to what extent this clear Greek influence was also found in first-century Palestine itself.

In sum, there is precious little evidence for the influence of Greek on Palestinian Aramaic, and none of it certainly from the first century. This is indeed surprising and may be a sheer coincidence; it is purely "negative evidence"[84] at this time. It is an argument from silence that could be proved wrong tomorrow—by the discovery of first-century Palestinian Aramaic texts with abundant examples of borrowed Grecisms. But at the moment we have to await such a discovery.

The reason for making something of all this is the contention of M. Black, A. Díez Macho, and others that the language of the Palestinian targum(s) is that of the first century, and indeed represents spoken Aramaic of that time in contrast to the literary Aramaic of Qumran. Black's main argument for the thesis that "the language of the Palestinian Targum is . . . first-century Aramaic" is this: "The large number of borrowings in it from Greek point to a period for its composition when Palestinian Aramaic was spoken in a hellenistic environment."[85] But, as we have already seen, the Hellenization of Palestine stretched over a long period, from at least the time of Antiochus IV Epiphanes (if not much earlier) well into the first half of the first Christian millennium. And yet what evidence there is for Greek words borrowed into Palestinian Aramaic is very sparse indeed up to A.D. 200. There comes a time, however, *after that* when it is surprisingly abundant, as epigraphic material and the researches of S. Krauss, S. Liebermann, et al. have shown time and again.[86] The same heavy influence of Greek is paralleled in classical Syriac too—a form of Aramaic that emerges toward the beginning of the third century C.E. The fact, then, that the Aramaic of the Palestinian targums contains a "large number of borrowings in it from Greek" could point theoretically to any period from the third century B.C. (at least) to A.D. 500 (at least). But when we look for the first-century evidence, it is certainly negative.

There is no doubt that targums were beginning to be written down in first-century Palestine, as the discovery of fragments of a targum on Job from Qumran caves IV and XI and a targum on Leviticus from Qumran Cave IV illustrate. Until these are fully published and the relation of them to the previously known and existing targums can be assessed, we cannot without further ado assume a genetic relationship between them or believe that they manifest the same degree of Greek influence as the other targums. J. van der Ploeg has already indicated in a preliminary report that 11QtgJob is unrelated to the later, little-known targum on Job, the origin of which is quite obscure.[87] As for 4QtgLev, which is the sole fragment of a targum on the Pentateuch, Milik has already revealed some differences in it.[88] In my opinion, the evidence from the borrowing of Greek words in the Palestinian targums argues for a date after A.D. 200—a date that could be supported by a number of other orthographic, lexical, and grammatical considerations which are absent from Biblical, Qumran, and similar Aramaic texts, but that begin to appear in Murabbaᶜat and Ḫabra texts and become abundant in the targums, in Syriac, and in dated Aramaic inscriptions from Palestinian synagogues from the third to the sixth centuries.[89] A handy catalogue of such synagogues has now been made available by S. J. Saller.[90]

In speaking of the influence of another language on first-century Aramaic we must not restrict our remarks to Greek alone. For the influence of Hebrew on it is also evident. This issue is more difficult to assess because the languages are so closely related. But a number of Hebraisms are clearly evident in the literary Aramaic of the *Genesis Apocryphon*,[91] and in the less literary writings from Murabbaᶜat and Ḫabra. There are masculine plural absolute endings in *-îm* instead of *-în*, the occasional use of the prepositive article (הנסי, 5/6Ḥev 1 ar:1[92]), the conjunction אם, "if," instead of הן or אן, the apocopated form of the imperfect of the verb "to be," יהי; etc. This Hebraized Aramaic is, of course, not surprising; nor is it confined to the first-century evidence, since it is already found in Ezra and Daniel.[93]

Two last remarks concerning the Aramaic of first-century Palestine. The first deals with the Nabatean dialect; so far I have left it out of consideration for the most part. It is a dialect of Aramaic, which betrays Arabic influence. There is no doubt that it was being used in Petra and in the Nabatean country to the south of Palestine. Was it also being used in the southern part of Palestine as well? In the Daroma? In Idumea? We do not know for certain, and the possibility cannot be excluded. The fragments and documents written in Nabatean and recovered from the Cave of Letters in Wadi Ḫabra were obviously brought there by refugees who hid in the caves of the area. They were written, as we have already indicated, for the most part in Maḥoz ᶜEglatain, a town or village in Nabatea. Yet they speak of relations with En-Gedi and persons who lived on the western shore of the Dead Sea. When these texts are finally published, perhaps it will be possible to establish more definitely the use of this special dialect of Aramaic in first-century southern Palestine as well.

The other remark concerns the name for Aramaic. It is well known that the Aramaic portion of Daniel begins with the adverb *ᵓărāmît* (Dan 2:4b). This gloss, which at some point in the transmission of the book crept into the text itself, reflects the ancient name of the language attested in the OT and in Elephantine papyrus texts.[94] Greek writers of a later period refer to the language as *συριστί* or *συριακή*.[95] When, however, Greek writers of the first century refer to the native Semitic language of Palestine, they use *ἑβραϊστί*, *ἑβραῒς διάλεκτος*, or *ἑβραΐζων*. As far as I can see, no one has yet found the adverb *aramaïsti*.[96] The adverb *ἑβραϊστί* (and its related expressions) seems to mean "in Hebrew," and it has often been argued that it means this and nothing more.[97] As is well known, it is used at times with words and expressions that are clearly Aramaic. Thus in John 19:13, *ἑβραϊστὶ δὲ Γαββαθᾶ* is given as an explanation of the Lithostrotos, and *γαββαθᾶ* is a Grecized form of the Aramaic word *gabbĕtā*, "raised place."[98] This long-standing, thorny question is still debated; and unfortunately, the Greek letter of Bar Cochba (?) cited earlier does not shed a ray of light on the meaning of *ἑβραϊστί*. We know that the author preferred to write "in Greek" than in it; but both Aramaic and Hebrew letters belong to the same cache of documents and the question still remains unresolved about the precise meaning of *ἑβραϊστί*. In any case, this problem forms a fitting transition to the consideration of the fourth language of first-century Palestine, viz., Hebrew.

IV. *Hebrew*

Hebrew probably was the oldest language still spoken in first-century Palestine. We may speculate about the language that was spoken by the "wandering Aramean" (Deut 26:5) who returned from Egypt at the time of the conquest of Palestine. Was it Old Aramaic of the form known in the early inscriptions from northern Syria? Or had this semi-nomadic people already adopted the *śĕpat Kĕnaᶜan* of the inhabitants who preceded them? The likelihood is that the "nomad" was still speaking the tongue of his forebears (Aḫlamē). In any case, the earliest epigraphic material points heavily in the direction of Hebrew, as a Canaanite dialect, dominating the land. It was never completely supplanted by Aramaic after the exile, when the latter became more commonly used because of its international prominence. It is, however, often asserted that Aramaic was the only Semitic language in use in Palestine at the time of Jesus and the Apostles.[99] But there are clear indications, both epigraphic and literary, that Hebrew continued in use in certain social strata of the people and perhaps also in certain geographical areas. The evidence, however, is not as abundant as it is for Aramaic.

It is true that the number of Qumran texts written in Hebrew far outnumber those in Aramaic, and these bear witness to a lively literary productivity in the language. It is not great literature, no more than the Aramaic literature of the time; even the War Scroll and the Thanksgiving Psalms are scarcely exceptions to this, though they are the most literary pieces in the Qumran scrolls. However, much of this Qumran Hebrew composition dates from the last two centuries B.C. But the *pĕšārîm*, which exist in only one copy of each *pēšer* and were written for the most part in the late Herodian script, may be regarded as first-century compositions.[100] They are literary compositions, reflecting on earlier stages of the sect's history and interpreting the biblical books in the light of that history and of the sect's beliefs. Along with the rest of Qumran Hebrew, the language of these texts represents a slight development beyond that of the late books of the OT. It has been called a "neo-classical Hebrew," lacking in spontaneity and contaminated by the contemporary colloquial dialect.[101]

The evidence for colloquial Hebrew is not abundant. What is surprising is that there is scarcely a Hebrew inscription from Palestine in the first century outside of the Qumran material—the inscription of the *Bĕnê Ḥēzîr* tomb being almost the sole exception.[102] There are, of course, ossuaries with Semitic names that could have been inscribed by Hebrew-speaking Jews as well as by Aramaic-speaking Jews. The use of *ben* instead of *bar* in the patronymics is no sure indication of a Hebrew proper name, even though it is often used to distinguish Hebrew from Aramaic inscriptions on the ossuaries. This is a recognized convenience and no more. The proper name with *ben* or *bar* could have been used properly in its own language milieu or could easily have been borrowed into the other because of the close relationship of the two; it is even conceivable that the stereotyped character of the *ben or bar* might have been the unique borrowed element.[103] Texts from Murabba^cat illustrate this.[104] *Bar* is found in Semitic names in a text written in Hebrew, and *ben* in a text written in Aramaic. The only noteworthy thing in the Murabbaᶜat texts is that *bar* is more frequent in Hebrew texts than *ben* is in Aramaic texts. The evidence, however, is so slight that one could scarcely conclude that this argues for Aramaic as the more common language.

The Copper Roll from Qumran Cave III, which almost certainly had nothing to do with the Essenes themselves, is "the oldest known text to be written in Mishnaic Hebrew,"[105] or perhaps more accurately, in Proto-Mishnaic Hebrew. Texts from the Murabbaᶜat and Ḫabra caves, which consist of letters as well as quasi-official documents, are written in practically the same form of Hebrew. Mishnaic Hebrew, reflecting a still further development of the language, is usually regarded as a literary dialect. But it is now seen to have been a development of the colloquial Hebrew of the first century. All of this points to a clear use of Hebrew in Palestine of that time, but it is really not sufficient to say with J. T. Milik that it proves "beyond reasonable doubt that Mishnaic was the normal language of the Judaean population in the Roman period,"[106] unless one is willing to specify what part of the Roman period is meant. For that must be reckoned as lasting from the Pompeian conquest of Palestine (63 B.C.) until at least the time of Constantine (early fourth century), if not later. While it seems apparent that certain pockets, or perhaps strata, of the population in the early Roman period were using Hebrew and that this language became enshrined in the Mishnah in a still more developed form, as of its codification ca. 200, I find it difficult to think of Hebrew as "the normal language of the Judaean population" in the *whole* Roman period. If it were, one would expect more evidence of it to turn up—especially in the first century and in more widespread locales.

This leads us naturally to the issue raised by H. Birkeland some years ago that Hebrew was actually the language of Jesus, because it had still "remained the language of the common people."[107] Little can actually be said about Jesus' use of Hebrew. That Hebrew was being used in first-century Palestine is beyond doubt, as we have been saying; but this fact is scarcely sufficient evidence for maintaining that Jesus therefore made use of it. We would have to look for further indications of this fact. If Luke 4:16-30 records a historical visit of Jesus to Nazareth with all its details, it might suggest that Jesus opened the scroll to Isaiah 61, found his place there, and read from it, presumably in Hebrew. The Lucan text completely prescinds from any use of a targum. Literalists among commentators on Acts 26:14 have also sought to insist that the risen Jesus, appearing to Paul on the road to Damascus and speaking τῇ ἑβραΐδι διαλέκτῳ, actually spoke in real Hebrew, not Aramaic. A similar suggestion is made that the *logia* that Matthew put together, according to Papias' statement in Eusebius (*HE* 3.39.16), were actually Hebrew, not

Aramaic. And the appeal is made to the extensive literature in Hebrew from Qumran as an indication of the possibility of writing a Hebrew gospel. There is certainly some plausibility in such suggestions; but do they really exceed the bounds of speculation?

Just as we mentioned the influence of other languages on the Greek and Aramaic spoken in Palestine, so too one can detect foreign influence on the non-literary Hebrew of this period. Phoenician or Punic influence has been claimed for the use of *t* as the sign of the accusative (instead of the older, Biblical *ʾet*); Aramaic influence for the frequent use of *-în* instead of *-îm* as the absolute masc. plur. ending (5/6 Ḥev hebr 1:3, 4; 2:1),[108] of the 3d plur. masc. suffix in *-hn* instead of *-hm* (Mur 44:4; 45:7), of the 3d sing. masc. suffix in *-h* instead of *-w* (Mur 44:9; 42:8, 9 [*ktbh*, "wrote it"]). Aramaic influence is clear in the Hebrew text of 4QTestimonia.[109] Is it, again, sheer coincidence that the only Greek word that I have been able to detect in this non-literary Hebrew is הפרנסים, a form that some have explained as derived from Greek πρόνοος? An Aramaic lexical expression may be found in Mur 46:7: בשל ש, possibly reflecting the Aramaic בדיל די.[110] In this case, the evidence is truly negative, because there is so little to go on.

By way of conclusion, I should maintain that the most commonly used language of Palestine in the first century A.D. was Aramaic, but that many Palestinian Jews, not only those in Hellenistic towns, but farmers and craftsmen of less obviously Hellenized areas used Greek, at least as a second language. The data collected from Greek inscriptions and literary sources indicate that Greek was widely used. In fact, there is indication, despite Josephus' testimony, that some Palestinians spoke only Greek, the Ἑλληνισταί. But pockets of Palestinian Jews also used Hebrew, even though its use was not widespread. The emergence of the targums supports this. The real problem is the influence of these languages on one another. Grecized Aramaic is still to be attested in the first century. It begins to be attested in the early second century and becomes abundant in the third and fourth centuries. Is it legitimate to appeal to this evidence to postulate the same situation earlier? Latin was really a negligible factor in the language-situation of first-century Palestine, since it was confined for the most part to the Roman occupiers. If Aramaic did go into an eclipse in the Seleucid period, as some maintain, it did not remain there. The first-century evidence points, indeed, to its use as the most common language in Palestine.

NOTES TO CHAPTER 2

*Originally published as the presidential address of the Catholic Biblical Association (21 August 1970) in the *CBQ* 32 (1970) 501-31.

[1]Evidence of this can be found in the Aramaisms in Biblical Hebrew. See p. 22 above, n. 29. See also A. Kropat, *Die Syntax des Autors der Chronik verglichen mit der seiner Quellen* (BZAW 16; Berlin: Töpelmann, 1906); J. Courtenay James, *The Language of Palestine and Adjacent Regions* (Edinburgh: Clark, 1920) [to be used with caution].

[2]Neh 8:8 may be hinting at this situation. The interpretation of the participle מפרש is quite disputed. Does it mean "clearly" (*RSV*)? Or "with interpretation" (*RSV* margin)? Cf. Ezra 4:18, where it occurs in a context suggesting translation; but also Ezra 4:7, which uses מתרגם explicitly for this idea. For a recent discussion of the verse and its meaning, see R. Le Déaut, *Introduction à la littérature targumique* (p. 22 above, n. 32), 29.

[3]See B. Lifshitz, "Beiträge zur palästinischen Epigraphik," *ZDPV* 78 (1962) 64-88, esp. pp. 82-84 (+ pl. 10), for the Raphia inscription of 217 B.C. For an earlier bilingual inscription (Greek and Edomite) on an ostracon, dating from 277 B.C., see the dissertation of L. T. Geraty, *Third Century B.C. Ostraca from Khirbet el-Kom* (dissertation summary in *HTR* 65 [1972] 595-96); also his article, "The Khirbet el-Kom Bilingual Ostracon," *BASOR* 220 (1975) 55-61.

[4]This evidence depends on the usual interpretation of Sir 50:27, that "Yeshua ben Eleazar ben Sira," of Jerusalem composed his book in Palestine ca. 180 B.C. and that the Book of Daniel took its final protocanonical form there within a short time after the Maccabean revolt, ca. 165 B.C. Parts of Daniel, however, especially the Aramaic stories about the hero at the Persian court, may well be older, as some scholars have argued. For an important discussion of this view, see K. A. Kitchen, "The Aramaic of Daniel," *Notes on Some Problems in the Book of Daniel* (London: Tyndale, 1965) 31-79. If this is so, it makes little difference to the issue being discussed here.

[5]See J. T. Milik, *Ten Years* (p. 22 above, n. 31), 130.

[6]See P. W. Skehan, "The Qumran Manuscripts and Textual Criticism," *Volume du congrès, Strasbourg 1956* (VTSup 4; Leiden: Brill, 1957) 148-60, esp. pp. 155-57 (4QLXX Num [3:40-42; 4:6-9]; 4QLXX Lev^{a} [26:2-16]). See also the Greek papyrus fragments discovered in Qumran Cave VII, where apparently nothing but Greek texts was found (M. Baillet et al., *Les 'Petites Grottes' de Qumran* [DJD 3; Oxford: Clarendon, 1962] 142-47). They have been dated by C. H. Roberts to ca. 100-50 B.C. 7Q*1* is a fragment of Exod 28:4-7; 7Q*2* is a fragment of the Letter of Jeremy (vv. 43-44). For an attempt to interpret the Greek texts of Qumran Cave VII as Christian, see the writings of J. O'Callaghan cited in my book, *The Dead Sea Scrolls: Major Publications and Tools for Study* (SBLSBS 8; Missoula: Scholars Press, 1975) 119-23. P. W. Skehan informs me that there are also three pieces of non-biblical Greek texts in Cave IV; they are as yet unpublished but are apparently of literary and liturgical character. For the view that the Aramaic texts of Qumran are of non-Essene origin, see pp. 8–9 above.

[7]The earliest Latin texts from Palestine that I have been able to uncover are all dated to the first century A.D. L. Kadman (*The Coins of Caesarea Maritima* [Jerusalem: Schocken, 1957]) lists no coins from Caesarea with Latin inscriptions before the time of Domitian.

[8]M. Avi-Yonah, "The Development of the Roman Road System in Palestine," *IEJ* 1 (1950-51) 54-60. Some of the milestones were erected in both Latin and Greek; see B. Lifshitz, *Latomus* 19 (1960) 111 (+ pl. IV). Cf. *Année épigraphique* 1925, §95; 1927, §151; 1948, §142.

[9]The Tenth Legion was transferred from northern Syria to Palestine (Ptolemais) by Nero, who put it under the command of Vespasian. See D. Barag, "Brick Stamp-Impressions of the *Legio X Fretensis*," *E. L. Sukenik Memorial Volume (1899-1953)* (Eretz-Israel, 8; Jerusalem: Israel Exploration Society, 1967) 168-82 [Hebrew; English summary, p. 73*]. This article has an ample bibliography on the subject. See further N. Avigad, "Excavations in the Jewish Quarter of the Old City of Jerusalem, 1969/70 (Preliminary Report)," *IEJ* 20 (1970) 1-8, esp. p. 3; B. Mazar, *The Excavations in the Old City of Jerusalem near the Temple Mount: Preliminary Report of the Second and Third Seasons 1969-1970* (Jerusalem: Institute of Archaeology, Hebrew University, 1971) 5 (fig. 6); "Excavations near the Temple Mount," *Qadmoniot* 5 (1972) 74-90, esp. p. 83 (an

inscription mentioning LEG X FR and Lucius Flavius Silva, governor of Judea, A.D. 73-79/80); J. Olami and J. Ringel, "New Inscriptions of the Tenth Legion Fretensis from the High Level Aqueduct of Caesarea," *IEJ* 25 (1975) 148-50; cf. *Qadmoniot* 7 (1974) 44-46; G. B. Sarfatti, "A Fragmentary Roman Inscription in the Turkish Wall of Jerusalem," *IEJ* 25 (1975) 151. Cf. D. Bahat, "A Roof Tile of the Legio VI Ferrata and Pottery Vessels from Ḥorvat Ḥazon," *IEJ* 24 (1974) 160-69. See also *IR* §217.

[10]A. Negev, "Caesarea Maritima," *Christian News from Israel* 11/4 (1960) 17-22; "New Inscriptions from the High Level Aqueduct of Caesarea," *Yediot* 30 (1966) 135-41 [Hebrew]; B. Lifshitz, "Inscriptions latines de Césarée (Caesarea Palestinae)," *Latomus* 22 (1963) 783-84; *Année épigraphique* 1964, §188; cf. K. Zangmeister, "Inschrift der vespasianischen Colonie Caesarea in Palästina," *ZDPV* 13 (1890) 25-30; A. Negev, "Inscriptions hébraïques, grecques et latines de Césarée Maritime," *RB* 78 (1971) 247-63 (+ pls. I-IX); J. Ringel, "Deux nouvelles inscriptions de l'aquéduc de Césarée Maritime," *RB* 81 (1974) 597-600. Cf. M. Gichon and B. H. Isaac, "A Flavian Inscription from Jerusalem," *IEJ* 24 (1974) 117-23.

[11]This fragmentary inscription was found in the northern part of the orchestra of the Roman theatre of Caesarea. In the fourth century the stone was used as part of a small stairway which was then being constructed; the stairway was obviously more important than the memory of the man mentioned on the stone. See A. Frova, "L'iscrizione di Ponzio Pilato a Cesarea," *Rendiconti dell'istituto lombardo, Accademia di scienze e lettere,* cl. di lettere, 95 (1961) 419-34; "Quattro campagne di scavo della missione archeologica milanese a Caesarea Maritima (Israele) 1959-1962," *Atti del convegno La Lombardia e l'Oriente* (Milan: 1963) 175. Also J. Vardaman, "A New Inscription Which Mentions Pilate as 'Prefect,'" *JBL* 81 (1962) 70-71; B. Lifshitz, *Latomus* 22 (1963) 783; J. H. Gauze, *Ecclesia* 174 (1963) 137; A. Calderini, "L'inscription de Ponce Pilate à Césarée," *BTS* 57 (1963) 8-19; A. Degrassi, "Sull'iscrizione di Ponzio Pilato," *ANL Rendiconti,* cl. di sc. morali, 8/19 (1964), fasc. 3-4, 59-65; E. Stauffer, "Die Pilatusinschrift von Caesarea," *Erlangen Universitätsreden* 12 (1965) [Erlangen: Palm und Enke, 1966]; L. A. Yelnitzky, "The Caesarea Inscription of Pontius Pilate and Its Historical Significance," *Vestnik drevnei istorii* 3 (93, 1965) 142-46 [Russian]; C. Brusa Gerra, "Le iscrizioni," *Scavi di Caesarea Maritima* (Milan: Istituto lombardo, 1965) 217-20; A. N. Sherwin-White, Review of A. Frova, "L'iscrizione . . . ," *JRS* 54 (1964) 258-59. H. Volkmann, *Gymnasium* 75 (1968) 124-35; E. Weber, "Zur Inschrift des Pontius Pilatus," *Bonner Jahrbücher* 171 (1971) 194-200; E. Schürer, *HJPAJC* (rev. ed., 1973), 1. 357-59. Cf. L. I. Levine, *Roman Caesarea: An Archaeological-Topographical Study* (Qedem, 2; Jerusalem: Hebrew University, 1975) 19-21.

Various attempts have been made to restore line 1: (a) Frova: [CAESARIEN]S(ibus)—Pilate would have dedicated the Tiberieum to the citizens of Caesarea; (b) Lifshitz: [TIB(erio) CAES(are) AVG(vsto) V? CON]S(vle)—the date of the inscription in Tiberius' fifth(?) consulate; (c) Degrassi: [DIS AVGVSTI]S—Pilate dedicates the building to Augustus and Livia, who were considered *theoi sebastoi* in the east.

The name *Tiberieum* is not attested elsewhere, but it is similar to *Hadrianeum* (*RB* 4 [1895] 75-76), *Kaisareion,* and *Agrippeion* (Josephus, *JW* 1.21.1 §402). The accent in the fourth line was probably over an E (possibly [D]É[DICAVIT] or [D]É[DIT] or [F]É[CIT].

[12]Josephus mentions him (*Ant.* 18.2.2 §35; 18.3.1-3 §55-64; 18.4.1-2 §87-89; 18.6.5 §177), as does also Philo (*Embassy to Gaius* 38, §299-305). Cf. Mark 15:1-44; Matt 27:2-65; Luke 3:1; 13:1; 23:1-52; John 18:29-38; 19:1-38; Acts 3:13; 4:27; 13:28; 1 Tim 6:13. Cf. F. Morison [= A. H. Ross], *And Pilate Said—A New Study of the Roman Procurator* (New York: Scribner, 1940); Paul L. Maier, *Pontius Pilate* (Garden City, NY: Doubleday, 1968).

[13]As Tacitus entitled him proleptically (*Annales* 15.44.2); cf. Tertullian, *Apologeticum* 21:18, "Pontio Pilato Syriam tunc ex parte romana procuranti" (*CSEL* 69.57); Philo, *Embassy to Gaius* 38 §299, Πιλᾶτος ἦν τῶν ὑπάρχων ἐπίτροπος ἀποδεδειγμένος τῆς Ἰουδαίας. Philo's text may well reflect the shift in title that apparently took place about the time of the emperor Claudius (ca. A.D. 46). Latin *praefectus* was usually rendered in Greek as ἔπαρχος, and *procurator* as ἐπίτροπος.

[14]See O. Hirschfeld, *Die kaiserlichen Verwaltungsbeamten bis auf Diocletian* (2d ed.; Berlin: Wiedman, 1905) 382-83; A. N. Sherwin-White, "Procurator Augusti," *Paper of the British School at Rome* 15 (1939) 11-26; *Society and Roman Law in the New Testament* (Sarum Lectures, 1960-61; Oxford: Clarendon, 1963) 6, 12; A. H. M. Jones, "Procurators and Prefects in the Early Principate," *Studies in Roman Government and Law* (Oxford: Blackwell 1960), 115-25; E. Schürer, *A History of the Jewish People in the Time of Jesus Christ* (6 vols.; Edinburgh: T. and T. Clark) 1 / 2 (1905) 45; rev. ed. (1973), 1. 357-59; H. G. Pflaum, *Les procurateurs équestres sous le haut-empire romain* (Paris: Maisonneuve, 1950) 23-25.

[15]"Proceeding across this [open court] towards the second court of the temple, one found it surrounded by a stone balustrade, three cubits high and of exquisite workmanship; in this at regular intervals stood slabs giving warning, some in Greek, others in Latin characters, of the law of purification, to wit that no foreigner was permitted to enter the holy place" (*JW* 5.5.2 §193-94). Cf. *Ant.* 15.11.5 §417; Philo, *Embassy to Gaius,* 31 §212; Acts 21:26-30.

[16]See p. 35.

[17]*Ant.* 14.10.2 §191.

[18]A similar notice is also found in some MSS of Luke 23:38 (S*,C,A,D,W, the Koine tradition, etc.); but it is undoubtedly due to scribal harmonization.

[19]See P. Benoit, J. T. Milik, R. de Vaux, *Les grottes de Murabbaᶜât* (DJD 2; Oxford: Clarendon, 1961) 270-74 (Mur 158-63).

[20]*CIL,* 3. 14155:3; Thomsen §178 (cf. G. Jeffery, *PEFQS* 29 [1898] 35).

[21]*CIL,* 2. 13587; Thomsen §1 (cf. F. J. Bliss, *PEFQS* 26 [1895] 25). For other Latin inscriptions of this period, see Thomsen §92, 237; *Année épigraphique* 1927, §151; Z. Vilnay, *PEFQS* 1928, 45-47 (cf. D. Barag, *IEJ* 14 [1964] 250-52), 108-9; A. Negev, *IEJ* 14 (1964) 237-49, esp. pp. 244-48; Y. Yadin, *IEJ* 15 (1965) 1-120, esp. p. 110.

[22]See T. Frankfort, "Présence de Rome en Israël," *Latomus* 19 (1960) 708-23.

[23]D. Auscher, "Les relations entre la Grèce et la Palestine avant la conquête d'Alexandre," *VT* 17 (1967) 8-30. Auscher's evidence consists of three things: (a) the remains of Greek pottery in Palestine; (b) Greek coins and Palestinian imitations of them; (c) the problematic Proto-Ionic pillar capitals. Cf. K. A. Kitchen, "The Aramaic of Daniel" (n. 4 above), 44-50. Kitchen amasses all sorts of evidence for Greek influence in the Near East from the eighth century on: Greek pottery in many places, Greek mercenaries, Greek papyri in fourth-century Egypt, etc. But his evidence is drawn from all over the Near East, and his argumentation about the two or three Greek words in Elephantine Aramaic papyri says nothing about the influence of Greek on Palestinian Aramaic. Cf. W. F. Albright, *The Archaeology of Palestine* (Pelican A199; rev. ed.; Baltimore: Penguin, 1960) 143-44; *From the Stone Age to Christianity* (Baltimore: Johns Hopkins, 1946) 256-61. Clear evidence of Greek (and Roman) arts and mythology in first-century Palestine can now be found in artifacts from the Cave of Letters of Wadi Ḫabra; see Y. Yadin, "Expedition D," *IEJ* 11 (1961) 49-64, esp. p. 52.

See now the monumental treatment of this subject by M. Hengel, *Judaism and Hellenism: Studies in Their Encounter in Palestine during the Early Hellenistic Period* (Philadelphia: Fortress, 1974).

[24]See V. Tcherikover, *Hellenistic Civilization and the Jews* (Philadelphia: Jewish Publication Society of America, 1959) 90-116. Cf. the Ḥepṣiba Slab of 195 B.C. (*IR* §214).

[25]1 Macc 1:11-15; Josephus, *Ant.* 12.5.1 §240 (*τὴν ἑλληνικὴν πολιτείαν ἔχειν*, "adopt the Greek way of life" [R. Marcus, *LCL*, 7. 123]). This Jewish support scarcely substantiates the thesis once proposed by I. Voss that Greek became the only language spoken in Palestine since Alexander.

[26]For further Greek epigraphic material from Palestine in the last two centuries B.C., see the graffiti from Marisa (*SEG*, 8. §247-51; E. Oren, *Archaeology* 18 [1965] 218-24); a dedication to Serapis and Isis from Samaria, probably dating from the end of the third century B.C. (*SEG*, 8. §95); a sepulchral poem from Gaza of the third century B.C. (*SEG*, 8. §269); a Gazara (Gezer) graffito, dated ca. 142 B.C. and bearing on 1 Macc 13:43, 48 (*CII* §1184; Gabba §9); the dedication

to Zeus Soter from Ptolemais, ca. 130-29 B.C. (*SEG*, 19. §904; 20. §413); an inscribed handle of the same period from Joppa (*SEG*, 18. §627; cf. *SEG*, 9. §252-60 [Marisa]); an execration from Marisa, dated before 128 B.C. (*SEG*, 8. §246; Gabba §10); the dedication to Herod the Great on a statue from Bashan, dated ca. 23 B.C. (*OGIS* §415; Gabba §12); the second-century list of priests of the temple of Zeus Olympios at Samaria (*SEG*, 8. §96); a second-century inscription about Antiochus VII Sidetes from Acre (Y. H. Landau, *IEJ* 11 [1961] 118-26; J. Schwartz, *IEJ* 12 [1962] 135-36); the votive offering on an altar to Syrian gods, Hadad and Atargatis, from Ptolemais, probably from the second century B.C. (*SEG*, 18. §622). Y. H. Landau ("A Greek Inscription Found Near Hefzibah," *IEJ* 16 [1966] 54-70) has published an unusual inscription recording orders issued by Antiochus III and his eldest son, the junior king Antiochus, for the benefit of Ptolemaios, the military governor (*στρατηγός*) and high priest (*ἀρχιερεύς*) of Coele-Syria and Phoenicia, along with the memoranda sent by Ptolemaios to the king. The documents come from the time of the Fifth Syrian War, begun by Antiochus III in 202-201, and are variously dated between 202 and 195 B.C. Part of the orders include the royal instruction to record them on stone stelae or white tablets in the villages. The foregoing list scarcely pretends to be exhaustive for this period. See further, Y. Meshorer, "A Stone Weight from the Reign of Herod," *IEJ* 20 (1970) 97-98 (with a Greek inscription dated to the 32d year of Herod, 9 B.C.); K. Treu, "Die Bedeutung des Griechischen für die Juden im römischen Reich," *Kairos* 15 (1973) 124-44.

[27]Part of the evidence that these words are foreign in the Aramaic text is the lack of the distinctive Aramaic ending on them in contrast to the names of other instruments in the same verse. These are the only words of certain Greek origin in Daniel; it is significant that they are the names of musical instruments and were probably borrowed with the importation of the instruments themselves. Since they are isolated instances and technical words, it is difficult to say to what extent they are a gauge of the influence of Greek on the Palestinian Semitic languages. See T. C. Mitchell and R. Joyce, "The Musical Instruments in Nebuchadrezzar's Orchestra," *Notes on Some Problems in the Book of Daniel* (London: Tyndale, 1965) 19–27. Cf. E. M. Yamauchi, "The Greek Words in Daniel in the Light of Greek Influence in the Near East," *New Perspectives on the Old Testament* (ed. J. B. Payne; Waco, TX: Word Books, 1970) 170-200. Other words, which were once thought to be Greek derivatives (e.g., *pitgām* in Dan 3:16, allegedly from either *ἐπίταγμα* or *φθέγμα*), are more correctly recognized today as of Persian origin. See S. Telegdi, "Essai sur la phonétique des emprunts iraniens en araméen talmudique," *JA* 226 (1935) 177-256, esp. p. 253; H. H. Schaeder, *Iranische Beiträge* (Schriften der Königsberger gelehrten Gesellschaft, Geisteswiss. Kl., 6/5; Halle a.S.: M. Niemeyer, 1930) 199-296; reprinted, Darmstadt: Wissenschaftliche Buchgesellschaft, 1972) 272.

[28]A convenient list of them can be found in C. Colpe, "Jüdisch-hellenistische Literatur," *Der kleine Pauly: Lexikon der Antike* (Stuttgart: A. Drückenmüller) 2 (1967) 1507-12; cf. E. J. Goodspeed, *JNES* 1 (1942) 315-28.

[29]*Stromata* 1. 21-23 §141-55 (*GCS*, 15. 87-98).

[30]*Praeparatio evangelica* 9. 22-28 (*GCS*, 43/1. 512-27).

[31]Most of what we know about him comes from the not unbiassed account in Josephus (*Life* §34-41, 65, 88, 175-78, 186, 279, 336-40, 355-60, 390-93, 410). Josephus severely criticized his ability as an historian (§336, 357-58), but openly admitted his good Greek training. Cf. Eusebius, *History of the Church* 3.10.8 (*GCS*, 9/1. 226); F. Jacoby, *PW* 10/2 (1919) 1341-46; S. Krauss, "Justus of Tiberias," *Jewish Encyclopedia* 7 (1904) 398-99; C. Mueller, *Fragmenta historicorum graecorum* (Paris: Didot, 1848-74), 3. 523.

[32]*Ant.* 20.12.1 §263-65. The interpretation of these words of Josephus is notoriously difficult, and the manuscript tradition in this passage is not firm. For a recent discussion of the problems involved in an interpretation largely identical with mine, see J. N. Sevenster, *Do You Know Greek? How Much Greek Could the First Jewish Christians Have Known?* (NovTSup 19; Leiden: Brill, 1968) 65-71.

[33]*τῇ πατρίῳ γλώσσῃ* (*JW* 5.9.2 §361). Cf. 6.2.1 §96; 6.2.5 §129; 6.6.2 §327.

[34]*Do You Know Greek?*, 63-65. Sevenster compares the emperor Claudius' excellent command of Greek with the halting use of it by the emperor Augustus, who was, nevertheless,

greatly interested in it and intensely applied himself to the study of it (see Suetonius, *Vita Claudii* §42; *Vita Augusti* §89).

[35]*JW* 1.1,2 §6.

[36]This is also the opinion of F. Büchsel, "Die griechische Sprache der Juden in der Zeit der Septuaginta und des Neuen Testaments," *ZAW* 60 (1944) 132-49, esp. p. 140. But H. Birkeland (*The Language of Jesus* [p. 22 above, n. 5], 13–14) contests this view: "That Josephus should name Aramaic 'the ancestral language,' when he knows the difference between this language and Hebrew, cannot seriously be maintained." He insists that Josephus was using the common language of Palestine, which was Hebrew.

[37]*JW* 1.1,1 §3.

[38]*Ant.* 1.1.2 §7 (*εἰς ἀλλοδάπην ἡμῖν καὶ ξένην διαλέκτου συνήθειαν*).

[39]H. S. J. Thackeray, *Josephus, the Man and the Historian* (New York: Jewish Institute of Religion, 1929) 104.

[40]*Ag. Ap.* 1.9 §50.

[41]Two exemplars of this inscription have been found; the better preserved is in the Istanbul Museum, the other in the Palestine Archaeological Museum, Jerusalem. See *OGIS*, 2. §598; *SEG*, 8. §169; 20. §477; Thomsen, *ZDPV* 44 (1921) 7-8; *TGI* §52; Gabba §24; Barrett, *NTB* §47. Two modern falsified reproductions of it have also been reported; see W. R. Taylor, *JPOS* 13 [1933] 137-39. See note 15 above for Josephus' description of such inscriptions.

[42]See R. Weill, *REJ* 71 (1920) 30-34; Thomsen, 261; *SEG*, 8. §170; 20. §478; *Année épigraphique* 1922, §117; *CII*, 2. §1404; Gabba §23; *TGI* §54; Barrett, *NTB* §50.

[43]*SEG*, 8. §244; cf. H. W. Garrod, "Locrica," *Classical Review* 37 (1923) 161-62; H. Lamer, "Der Kalypso-Graffito in Marissa (Palästina)," *ZDPV* 54 (1931) 59-67.

[44]This inscription begins *διάταγμα* Καίσαρος; but it is neither certainly attributed to Augustus nor certainly of Nazareth provenience. See F. Cumont, "Un rescrit impérial sur la violation de sépulture," *Revue historique* 163 (1930) 241-66; cf. S. Lösch, *Diatagma Kaisaros: Die Inschrift von Nazareth und das Neue Testament* (Freiburg im B.: Herder, 1936); S. Riccobono, *Fontes iuris romani antejustiniani, pars prima: Leges* (Florence: Barbera, 1941) 414-16; J. Schmitt, *DBSup* 6 (1960) 333-63.

[45]See G. Orfali, "Une nouvelle inscription grecque découverte à Capharnaüm," *JPOS* 6 (1926) 159-63; cf. *SEG*, 8. §4; 17. §774.

[46]What is badly needed is a systematic collection of the Greek, Aramaic, and Hebrew inscriptions on ossuaries from Jerusalem and elsewhere. It is impossible at the moment to give any sort of comprehensive view of this topic. Many of the Aramaic inscriptions can now be found in *MPAT*; see p. 22 above, n. 28. Some examples of Greek inscriptions from Jerusalem can be found in *CII* 2; Thomsen §190-97, 199, 201-5; *SEG*, 8. §179-86, 197, 201, 208-9, 221, 224; 6. §849; 17. §784; 19. §922; 20. §483-92.

[47]M. Smith ("Aramaic Studies and the Study of the New Testament," *JBR* 26 [1958] 310) says, "Of the 168 published in Frey's *Corpus inscriptionum iudaicarum*, 5 are illegible, 32 are in Hebrew or Aramaic or both, 17 are in a Semitic language and Greek, but 114 are in Greek only." But are they all of the first century?

[48]*The Jews of Ancient Rome* (Philadelphia: Jewish Publication Society of America, 1960) 75.

[49]See P. Benoit et al., *Les grottes de Murabbaᶜât* [n. 19 above], 212-33, 243-56, 234-40, 275-79.

[50]B. Lifshitz, "Papyrus grecs du désert de Juda," *Aegyptus* 42 (1962) 240-56 (+ 2 pls.). The first text is apparently the one that Y. Yadin refers to as Ḥev 3 (see *IEJ* 11 [1961] 42-43; *BIES* 25 [1961] 57). Cf. Y. Yadin, "New Discoveries in the Judean Desert," *BA* 24 (1961) 34-50; "More on the Letters of Bar Kochba," ibid., 96-95.

[51]Lifshitz takes *Σουμαῖος* as a Greek transcription of *Šamay* or *Šemaᶜ*, which he regards as a hypocoristicon of *Šimᶜôn*. In the second papyrus letter that Lifshitz publishes in the same article, the name is written in Greek as *Σίμων*, with *Χώσιβα* clearly written above it (between the lines). For a discussion of the name of Bar Cochba, see my article, "The Bar Cochba Period," *The Bible in Current Catholic Thought* [ed. J. L. McKenzie; New York: Herder and Herder, 1962], 133-68, esp. pp. 138-41. Cf. the revised form in *ESBNT*, 305-54, esp. pp. 312-16.

The spelling of certain words in this document is defective: thus Ἐπηδὴ = ἐπειδὴ; ἔπεμσα = ἔπεμψα; πέμσε = πεμψαι; ἀνασθήσεται = ἀναστήσετε; ἰς = εἰς; ἄλως = ἄλλως; ποιήσηται = ποιήσητε; Ἑλην
ιστὶ = Ἑλληνιστὶ; Ἑβραεστὶ = Ἑβραϊστὶ. The meaning of στελεούς is not clear; does it refer to "beams" that might be used for huts, or to the "branches" (*lûlāb*)?

The real problem in this letter is the restoration of the word [ ]μαν in line 13, and even the reading of it. Though I originally went along with Lifshitz's reading of [ὁρ]μὰν, I have never been satisfied with it, because it looks like a Doric form of the accusative singular of the feminine noun, which should otherwise be ὁρμήν at this period in Palestine. The same difficulty has been noted by G. Howard and J. C. Shelton ("The Bar-Kokhba Letters and Palestinian Greek," *IEJ* 23 [1973] 101-2), who suggest as "the most obvious possibility" for restoring the lacuna [Ἑρ]μαν, comparing Rom 16:14. But they do not tell us how to construe the rest of the Greek with such a restoration (does the preceding neuter article remain?). Y. Yadin (*Bar-Kokhba: The Rediscovery of the Legendary Hero of the Second Jewish Revolt against Rome* [London: Weinfeld and Nicholson, 1971] 130-31) gives an abbreviated translation of the letter, especially of this crucial part: "'the letter is written in Greek as we have no one who knows Hebrew [or Aramaic].'" Yadin supplies a good photo of the text, but he does not tell us how he reads the text's Greek writing; and it is not possible to puzzle out what in the text could be understood as "no one" in his translation. As a result, I leave the translation and interpretation of the text stand according to the original Lifshitz interpretation until further light is shed on it by someone.

As for the four elements required for Succoth, one should consult Lev 23:40 and Josephus, *Ant.* 3.10.3 §245.

[52]See Y. Yadin, "*Mḥnh* D," *BIES* 25 (1960) 49-64, esp. pp. 60-61; also my article, "The Bar Cochba Period," 155–56; *ESBNT*, 336–37; cf. *MPAT* §60.

[53]"Jewish Christianity in Acts in Light of the Qumran Scrolls," *Studies in Luke-Acts: Essays . . . in Honor of Paul Schubert* (eds. L. E. Keck and J. L. Martyn; Nashville: Abingdon, 1966) 233-57, esp. pp. 237-38; *ESBNT*, 271-303.

[54]"Once More, Who Were the Hellenists?" *ExpTim* 70 (1958-59) 100-102; see also J. N. Sevenster, *Do You Know Greek?* 37; W. G. Kümmel, *RGG*³ 6 (1962) 1189.

[55]Compare the opinion of C. S. Mann (Appendix VI in J. Munck, *The Acts of the Apostles* [AB 31; Garden City: Doubleday, 1967] 301-4); he believes that Ἑβραῖοι refers to Samaritans or Samaritan Christians! Older discussions can be found in H. J. Cadbury, "The Hellenists," *The Beginnings of Christianity* (London: Macmillan), 5 (1933) 59-74; H. Windisch, *"Hellēn," TDNT* 2 (1964) 504-15, esp. pp. 511-12. Note the use of Josephus' ἑβραΐζων, meaning "speaking in 'Hebrew'" (*JW* 6.2.1 §96).

[56]For some literature on the subject, see A. Roberts, *Greek the Language of Christ and His Apostles* (London: Longmans, Green, 1888); S. Greijdanus, *Het gebruik van het Grieksch door den Heere en zijne apostelen in Palestine* (Kampen: Kok, 1932); S. M. Patterson, "What Language Did Jesus Speak?" *Classical Outlook* 23 (1946) 65-67; L. Rood, "Heeft Jezus Grieks gesproken?" *Streven* 2 (1949) 1026-35; A. W. Argyle, "Did Jesus Speak Greek?" *ExpTim* 67 (1955-56) 92-93; J. K. Russel (same title), ibid., 246; H. M. Draper (same title), ibid., 317; A. W. Argyle (same title), ibid., 383; R. M. Wilson (same title), *ExpTim* 68 (1956-57) 121-22; R. O. P. Taylor, "Did Jesus Speak Aramaic?" *ExpTim* 56 (1944-45) 95-97; *The Groundwork of the Gospels* (Oxford: Blackwell, 1946) 91-105.

For some older discussions, see also D. Diodati, *De Christo graece loquente exercitatio* (Naples, 1767; reissued, ed. by O. T. Dobbin; London: J. Gladding, 1843); A. Paulus, *Verosimilia de Judaeis palaestinensibus, Jesu atque etiam Apostolis non aramaea dialecto sola, sed graeca quoque aramaizante locutis* (Jena, 1803 [*non vidi*]).

[57]Cf. A. W. Argyle, *ExpTim* 67 (1955-56) 93: "The importance of establishing that Jesus and His disciples sometimes spoke Greek cannot be overestimated. It means that in some cases we may have direct access to the original utterances of our Lord and not only to a translation of them." See also his articles, "'Hypocrites and the Aramaic Theory,' *ExpTim* 75 (1963-64) 113-14; "Greek among the Jews of Palestine in New Testament Times," *NTS* 20 (1973-74) 87-89.

[58]*Greek in Jewish Palestine: Studies in the Life and Manners of Jewish Palestine in the II-IV Centuries C.E.* (2d ed.; New York: P. Feldheim, 1965); *Hellenism in Jewish Palestine: Studies in the Literary Transmission, Beliefs and Manners of Palestine in the I Century B.C.E.—IV Century C.E.* (New York: Jewish Theological Seminary of America, 1950). Though the latter does go back to an earlier date, it is largely devoted to a broader topic than the first book and the issue being treated here.

[59]*Do You Know Greek?*, 38-44.

[60]See G. Alon, *Kirjath Sepher* 20 (1943-44) 76-95; B. Lifshitz, *Aegyptus* 42 (1962) 254-56; "L'hellénisation des Juifs de Palestine: A propos des inscriptions de Besara (Beth-Shearim)," *RB* 72 (1965) 520-38; *"Yĕwānît wîwānût bên Yĕhûdê ʾereṣ-Yiśrāʾēl," Eshkoloth* 5 (1966-67) 20-28.

For the important Greek material coming from Beth-Sheᶜarim, see M. Schwabe and B. Lifshitz, *Beth Sheᶜarim: Volume Two: The Greek Inscriptions* (Jerusalem: Israel Exploration Society, 1967). These inscriptions date from the first quarter of the third century A.D., when R. Judah the Prince was buried there. To be buried in the vicinity of this Jewish leader and compiler of the Mishnah was regarded as a privilege and a sizeable necropolis developed there up until A.D. 352, when the city was destroyed by the army of Gallus. These dates are also confirmed by coins found there. See further B. Lifshitz, "Beiträge zur palästinischen Epigraphik," *ZDPV* 78 (1962) 64-88; 82 (1966) 57-63; "Les inscriptions grecques de Beth Sheᶜarim (Besara)," *IEJ* 17 (1967) 194.

For a similar important group of sepulchral inscriptions dated merely to "the Roman period," see B. Lifshitz's articles on the necropolis of Caesarea Maritima: "La nécropole juive de Césarée," *RB* 71 (1964) 384-87; "Inscriptions de Césarée en Palestine," *RB* 72 (1965) 98-107; "Notes d'épigraphie palestinienne," *RB* 73 (1966) 248-57; "Inscriptions de Césarée," *RB* 74 (1967) 50-59.

[61]See the old, but still useful list in S. Krauss, *Griechische und lateinische Lehnwörter im Talmud, Midrasch und Targum* (Berlin: S. Calvary, 1899-1900).

[62]Cf. M. Smith, "Palestinian Judaism in the First Century," *Israel: Its Role in Civilization* (ed. M. Davis; New York: Jewish Theological Seminary of America, 1956) 67-81 (much of the material used as evidence in this article is not derived from the first century).

[63]"Aramaic Studies and the Study of the New Testament," *JBR* 26 (1958) 304-13, esp. p. 310.

[64]*The Archaeology of Palestine* (5th ed.; Pelican A199; Baltimore: Penguin, 1960) 201-2. See also V. Tcherikover, *Corpus papyrorum judaicarum* (Cambridge: Harvard, 1957), 1. 30.

[65]For literature on this text, see my commentary on the *Genesis Apocryphon* (2d ed., 1971), 21 n. 57; also *MPAT* § 150.

[66]For an attempt to gather the Aramaic ossuary inscriptions from Palestine, see *MPAT* § 69-148 (and the literature cited there).

[67]Goodspeed's skepticism about the "possibility of an Aramaic Gospel" was first expressed in his *New Chapters in New Testament Study* (New York: Macmillan, 1937) 127-68, esp. pp. 165-66. A. T. Olmstead sought to answer Goodspeed in an article, "Could an Aramaic Gospel be Written?" *JNES* 1 (1942) 41-75. Goodspeed replied in another, "The Possible Aramaic Gospel," ibid., 315-40 (his words quoted in the text are taken from p. 328 of this reply). The heat of the debate between Olmstead and Goodspeed produced more rhetoric than clarity; some of the new factors that I have been trying to draw together here would change a number of contentions of both of these writers. The limited topic of my discussion does not bear exactly on the point at issue between them.

[68]See E. L. Sukenik, *"Ṣiyyûn ᶜUzziyāhû melek Yĕhûdāh," Tarbiz* 2 (1930-31) 288-92; W. F. Albright, "The Discovery of an Aramaic Inscription Relating to King Uzziah," *BASOR* 44 (1931) 8-10; J. N. Epstein, *"LĕṢiyyûn ᶜUzziyāhû," Tarbiz* 2 (1930-31) 293-94; J. M. van der Ploeg, *JEOL* 11 (1949) pl. XVIII, fg. 29; *TGI* §55.

[69]See pp. 11, 24 above, nn. 55–57. Cf. J. Bligh, "'Qorban,'" *HeyJ* 5 (1964) 192–93; S. Zeitlin, "Korban," *JQR* 53 (1962) 160-63; "Korban: A Gift," *JQR* 59 (1968) 133-35; Z. W. Falk, "Notes and Observations on Talmudic Vows," *HTR* 59 (1966) 309-12.

[70]See E. L. Sukenik, "A Jewish Tomb in the Kidon Valey[sic]," *Tarbiz* 6 (1934-35) 190-96; for the literature on this inscription, see *MPAT* §71.

[71]See p. 23 above, n. 53.

[72]N. Avigad and Y. Yadin, *A Genesis Apocryphon: A Scroll from the Wilderness of Judaea* (Jerusalem: Magnes, 1956); see my commentary on it (2d ed., 1971). The other Qumran Aramaic texts are listed on pp. 101–2 below.

[73]On this text, see pp. 90–94 below.

[74]These too have been gathered together with those referred to in n. 66 above in *MPAT*, §69–148 (see the literature cited there).

[75]See Mur 18 (DJD, 2. 100-104); also Y. Yadin, "The Excavation of Masada—1963/64: Preliminary Report," *IEJ* 15 (1965) 1-120, esp. p. 111.

[76]See Mur 8, 19, 20, 21, 23, 25, 26, 27, 28, 31, 32, 33, 34, 35, 72. Cf. S. Segert, "Zur Orthographie und Sprache der aramäischen Texte von W. Murabbaᶜat (Auf Grund von DJD II)," *ArOr* 31 (1963) 122-37. The material from Wadi Ḫabra is still to be published; for preliminary reports and partial publication of it, see Y. Yadin, "Expedition D," *IEJ* 11 (1961) 36-52; *BIES* 25 (1961) 49-64; "Expedition D—The Cave of Letters," *IEJ* 12 (1962) 227-57. Cf. E. Y. Kutscher, "The Language of the Hebrew and Aramaic Letters of Bar Cochba and His Contemporaries," *Lĕšonénu* 25 (1961) 117-33; 26 (1962) 7-23. From this cave (official siglum 5/6Ḥev) came the Nabatean contract published by J. Starcky, "Un contrat nabatéen sur papyrus," *RB* 61 (1954) 161-81. Yadin (*IEJ* 12 [1962] 229) reveals that he recovered the *scriptura interior* of this "tied deed" and thus established the provenience of the contract. It is also likely that two other Aramaic documents published by J. T. Milik come from the same cave ("Un contrat juif de l'an 134 après J.-C.," *RB* 61 [1954] 182-90; "Deux documents inédits du désert de Juda," *Bib* 38 [1957] 245-68, esp. pp. 255-64). Cf. E. Koffmahn, *Die Doppelurkunden aus der Wüste Juda* (STDJ 5; Leiden: Brill, 1968). See *MPAT*, §38–64.

[77]"Three Greek Documents from the Family Archive of Babatha," *E. L. Sukenik Memorial Volume*, 46-51, esp. p. 50 (document 27); cf. "The Greek Papyri from the Cave of the Letters," *IEJ* 12 (1962) 258-62.

[78]See H. J. Polotsky, "Three Greek Documents," 46-49.

[79]See Y. Yadin, *IEJ* 12 (1962) 246.

[80]Mur 103a 1 (DJD, 2. 232).

[81]See DJD, 2. 115; *Lĕšonénu* 25 (1961) 119, 126; *E. L. Sukenik Memorial Volume*, 50.

[82]See Y. Yadin, *IEJ* 12 (1962) 242; cf. his article, "The Nabatean Kingdom, Provincia Arabia, Petra and En-Geddi in the Documents from Nahal Hever," *JEOL* 17 (1963) 227-41, esp. pp. 232-33.

[83]The last Greek formula is taken from the receipt in the Babatha archive, document 27 (see note 77 above), lines 2-3.

[84]To borrow a phrase from K. A. Kitchen, used in his critique of H. H. Rowley's studies of the Aramaic of Daniel (see note 4 above).

[85]*Aramaic Approach* (p. 23 above, n. 43), 22.

[86]See nn. 58 and 61 above. On early Syriac inscriptions, see p. 71 below.

[87]"Le targum de Job de la grotte 11 de Qumran [11QtgJob]: Première communication," *Mededelingen der koninklijke Nederlandse Akademie van Wetenschappen*, Afd. Letterkunde, n.r. 25/9 (Amsterdam: Noord-Hollandsche Uitgevers M., 1962) 543-57, esp. 552. The full text of the Qumran targum of Job has been published; see J. P. M. van der Ploeg and A. S. van der Woude (avec la collaboration de B. Jongeling), *Le targum de Job de la grotte XI de Qumrân* (Koninklijke nederlandse Akademie van Wetenschappen; Leiden: Brill, 1971). For a comparison of it with the earlier-known targum of Job, see pp. 167–74 below.

[88]*Ten Years* (p. 22 above, n. 31), 31. See further p. 22 above, n. 32.

[89]E.g., the inscriptions from the ᶜAin-Dûq synagogue (see E. L. Sukenik, *Ancient Synagogues in Palestine and Greece* [Schweich Lectures, 1930; London: British Academy, 1934] 73-74 [I], 75-76 [II], 76 [III]), the ᶜAlma synagogue (R. Hestrin, "A New Aramaic Inscription from ᶜAlma," *L. M. Rabinowitz Fund for the Exploration of Ancient Synagogues, Bulletin* 3 [1960] 65-67), the Beth Alpha synagogue (E. L. Sukenik, *The Ancient Synagogue of Beth Alpha* [Jerusalem: University Press, 1932] 43-46), the Beth Gubrin synagogue (E. L. Sukenik, "A Synagogue

Inscription from Beit Jibrin," *JPOS* 10 [1930] 76-78), the Capernaum synagogue (G. Orfali, "Deux inscriptions de Capharnaüm," *Antonianum* 1 [1926] 401-12), the Chorazin synagogue (J. Ory, "An Inscription Newly Found in the Synagogue of Kerazah," *PEFQS* 1927, 51-52), the Fiq synagogue (S. A. Cook, "Hebrew Inscription at Fik," *PEFQS* 1903, 185-86; cf. p. 274), the Gaza synagogue (D. J. Saul, "Von el-ᶜAkabe über Gaza nach Jerusalem," *Mitteilungen des deutschen Palästina-Vereins* 7 [1901] 9-14, esp. 12-13), the Gischala synagogue (G. Dalman, "Die Zeltreise," *PJB* 10 [1914] 47-48), the Hammath-by-Gadara synagogue (E. L. Sukenik, *The Ancient Synagogue of El Hammeh* (Hammath-by-Gadara) [Jerusalem: R. Mass, 1935]), the Hamat-Tiberias synagogue (M. Dothan, "The Aramaic Inscription from the Synagogue of Severus at Hamat-Tiberias," *E. L. Sukenik Memorial Volume,* pp. 183-85), the ᶜIsfiyah synagogue (M. Avi-Yonah, "A Sixth Century Synagogue at ᶜ(Isfiyā," *QDAP* 3 [1933] 119-31), the Khirbet Kanef synagogue (G. Dalman, "Inschriften aus Palästina," *ZDPV* 37 [1914] 138), the Jerash synagogue (J. W. Crowfoot and R. W. Hamilton, "The Discovery of a Synagogue at Jerash," *PEFQS* 1929, 211-19, esp. 218; see E. L. Sukenik, "Note on the Aramaic Inscription at the Synagogue of Gerasa," *PEFQS* 1930, 48-49), the Kafr Birᶜim school inscription (*JPCI* §9), the Kafr Kenna synagogue (C. Clermont-Ganneau, "Mosaïque à inscription hébraïque de Kefr Kenna," *CRAIBL* 1900, pp. 555-57), the Umm el-ᶜAmed synagogue (N. Avigad, "An Aramaic Inscription from the Ancient Synagogue of Umm el-ᶜAmed," *BIES* 19 (1956-57) 183-87. S. Segert once reported (*ArOr* 33 [1965] 196 n. 12) that E. Y. Kutscher was preparing a "zusammenfassende Ausgabe dieser Texte." Since, however, death has taken Kutscher away, one may have to be content with the collection that D. J. Harrington and I have made in *MPAT,* App., § A1-A156.

[90]*A Revised Catalogue of the Ancient Synagogues of the Holy Land* (Publications of the Studium Biblicum Franciscanum, collectio minor, 6; Jerusalem: Franciscan Press, 1969). Cf. B. Lifshitz, *Donateurs et fondateurs dans les synagogues juives: Répertoires des dédicaces grecques relatives à la construction et à la réfection des synagogues* (Cahiers de la RB, 7; Paris: Gabalda, 1967).

[91]See my commentary (2d ed., 1971), 25-26. Cf. E. Y. Kutscher, *Or* 39 (1970) 178-83.

[92]This is an instance of the prepositive article and may have to be discounted, because it is the title of Bar Cochba. It may be part of a stereotyped way of referring to him, even if one spoke or wrote in Aramaic. However, there is another instance of it on a Jerusalem ossuary, *Yhwdh br ˀlᶜzr hswpr* (see *MPAT,* §99). Compare the Greek fragment mentioned above, p. 40.

[93]Cf. F. Rosenthal, *A Grammar of Biblical Aramaic* (Porta linguarum orientalium, ns 5; Wiesbaden: Harrassowitz, 1961), §187; H. Bauer and P. Leander, *Grammatik des Biblisch-Aramäischen* (Halle: Niemeyer, 1927), §1 t-v (p. 10). This reference to Daniel (and even to Ezra) should not be misunderstood. It may seem that such "Hebraisms" were already a living part of Aramaic of an earlier day. This is undoubtedly true; but it does not make them indigenous in Aramaic. They were originally Hebraisms, and they persisted in the language because of the more or less simultaneous use of the languages throughout a long period. Cf. S. Segert, "Sprachliche Bemerkungen zu einigen aramäischen Texten von Qumran," *ArOr* 33 (1965) 190-206.

[94]2 Kgs 18:26; Isa 36:11; Ezra 4:7—cf. Cowley, *AP* 28:4, 6.

[95]Cf. the LXX passages corresponding to the OT passages in the preceding note; also Job 42:17b (συριακῇ) and the *Letter of Aristeas* §11. This Greek name may be reflected in the Hebrew (contemptuous ?) name for Aramaic, לשון סורסי (*b. Soṭah* 49b; *b. B. Qam.* 82b, 83a).

[96]However, χαλδαϊστί is added in the LXX of Dan 2:26, corresponding to nothing in the MT.

[97]As it certainly does in the Greek prologue of Ben Sira. This exclusive meaning has been argued for it by H. Birkeland, "The Language of Jesus" (p. 22 above, n. 35), 12–16.

[98]See further G. Dalman, *The Words of Jesus* (p. 23 above, n. 53).

[99]E.g., A. Dupont-Sommer, *Les araméens* [L'orient ancien illustré, 4; Paris: Maisonneuve, 1949] 99 ("L'araméen continua longtemps à se parler et à s'écrire en Palestine. A l'époque du Christ, il était la seule langue courante pour la masse du peuple; c'est l'araméen que parlaient Jésus et les Apôtres"). F. Altheim and R. Stiehl, "Jesus der Galiläer," *Die Araber in der alten Welt* (Berlin: de Gruyter) 3 (1966) 92 ("Das Hebräische war als lebende Sprache seit dem Beginn der hellenistischen Zeit ausgestorben und in Palästina durch Aramäische ersetzt worden.")

[100]See J. T. Milik, *Ten Years* (p. 22 above, n. 31), 41.

[101]Ibid., 130.

[102]See N. Avigad, *Ancient Monuments in the Kidron Valley* (Jerusalem: Bialik, 1954) 59-66. Also the Bethphage ossuary lid may be considered here (R. Dussaud, "Comptes d'ouvriers d'une entreprise funéraire juive," *Syria* 4 [1923] 241-49).

[103]As בר in the Phoenician inscription of Kilamuwa I (*KAI* §24).

[104]For instance, Mur 22:1-9 i 3, 4, 11-12; 29:1, 2, 10, 11-12; 30:1, 4, 6, 9, 10, 11, 17, 26, 32; 36:1, 2, 8; 42:12; 46:10. These examples are scarcely exhaustive.

[105]J. T. Milik, *Ten Years* (p. 22 above, n. 31), 130. Here Milik dates the text to "the middle of the first century A.D."; but in the official publication of this text (DJD, 3. 217) he says, "le document se situe par conséquent au premier siècle de notre ère ou au début du siècle suivant, entre 30 et 130 après J.-C. en chiffres ronds, avec préférence pour la second moitié de cette période." He also cites the date proposed by W. F. Albright, "between cir. 70 and cir. 135 A.D." S. Segert (*ArOr* 33 [1965] 190-206, esp. p. 191) thinks that 3Q*15* was written in Hebrew by a Jew who otherwise spoke Aramaic; but he does not specify how this is revealed in this text.

[106]*Ten Years*, 130.

[107]"The Language of Jesus" (p. 22 above, n. 35), 16. For further negative reactions to Birkeland's thesis, see p. 22 above, n. 37.

[108]M. H. Segal (*A Grammar of Mishnaic Hebrew* [Oxford: Clarendon, 1927] §281, p. 126) is often cited in opposition to this claim: "The termination *-în* [in Mishnaic Hebrew] is not an Aramaism," but rather "a purely Hebraic phenomenon." Yet the fact that "*-n* is common to nearly all Semitic languages" or is "the only one found on the Mešaᶜ stone" or that it occurs "as early as the Song of Deborah" still does not rule out the influence of a dominant language of the area (such as Aramaic was) on Hebrew (or Moabite).

[109]See the analysis of this text by S. Segert, *ArOr* 25 (1967) 34-35. Aramaic orthographic practice seems to be the best explanation of such further forms as [*kwḥ*] *gbwrʾ*[ ] in 6Q9 45:2 and of [ ]*ʾḥt ᶜśrʾ*[ ] in 6Q9 1:1.

[110]See J. T. Milik, DJD, 2. 166.

Chapter 3

The Phases of the Aramaic Language*

In 1966, as part of a discussion of the language of the *Genesis Apocryphon* from Qumran Cave I, I proposed a five-fold division of the Aramaic language. It was no more than a footnote in the introduction to a commentary on that Qumran scroll.[1] The reasons for the phases and for the proposed division of Aramaic were not explained. This I should like to attempt here, as a background for further discussion of the Aramaic substratum of the NT. One reason for this latter-day explanation is that my proposed phases of Aramaic have been adopted in some quarters and criticized in others. Perhaps the attempt to explain the division will meet some of the objections and also provide the opportunity to utilize further data and some of the material that others have brought to light in support of the division.

Why propose a reclassification of the phases of Aramaic? The answer to such a question is complex. First of all, there was no generally accepted division of the phases of the language. Second, some of the divisions being used were clearly inadequate, because much of the evidence that has come to light in the last two or three decades has called for a reassessment of categories that have become obsolete. Third, there is still no little disagreement about some of the phases, and an attempt is needed to discuss them. It is undoubtedly a pipe-dream to think that there will ever be a universally-accepted view of this matter—any more than of other matters. Yet the *student* who begins to interest him / herself in Aramaic is immediately confronted with scholarly opinions which use labels for phases of the language which are nominally the same, but differ widely in extension. Thus, one is consequently confronted with the task of trying to discover what a given writer means by "Old Aramaic," "Middle Aramaic," and so on. And many of these labels come from a period of the study of Aramaic that is *passé*. Hence it might be well, first of all, to survey various attempts to divide up the Aramaic language and comment on their adequacy or inadequacy. Then, we shall propose the five phases again—this time a little more fully. And finally, the reasons for the division of the phases and their related problems will be discussed.

I. *Earlier Attempts to Divide the Aramaic Language*

In his monumental survey of Aramaic research in 1939,[2] F. Rosenthal included under "Altaramäisch" not only the 9th/8th century inscriptions from North Syria, but Reichsaramäisch, Pahlevi ideograms, Nabatean, and Palmyrene. All of this he distinguished from "Jungaramäisch," by which he meant Jewish Palestinian Aramaic, Samaritan Aramaic, Christian Palestinian Aramaic, and Modern Syrian Aramaic—as well as from "Ostaramäisch," by which he meant Syriac, Babylonian Talmudic Aramaic, Mandaic, and Modern East Aramaic. Thus he began with a chronological division (Altaramäisch—Jungaramäisch) but shifted to a geographical one (Ostaramäisch); and the rationale for the division of the phases is thus not consistent. Moreover, the grouping together of the early inscriptions with such dialects as Nabatean and Palmyrene—to mention only the most obviously disparate elements—as "Altaramäisch" raises all sorts of questions today. But the categories that Rosenthal used were adequate to the survey that he was making; he was not really discussing the specific problem to which this paper addresses itself. Rosenthal was followed, in part at least, by E. G. Kraeling (in his lengthy introducion to the *Brooklyn Museum Aramaic Papyri*),[3] E. Y. Kutscher (in an early article),[4] A. F. Johns,[5] and most recently by S. Segert.[6]

But even earlier than Rosenthal the term "Altaramäisch" had been given a broad range of meaning by G. Bergsträsser in his *Einführung in die semitischen Sprachen*,[7] where he distinguished in it three dialects: Biblical Aramaic (the oldest), Syriac, and Mandaic. He used "Old Aramaic" in a *wide* sense to include forms of the language in pre-Christian centuries (as the aforementioned divisions reveal), but also in a *narrow* sense to include inscriptions and papyri down to about 400 B.C. In his wide sense "Old Aramaic" was obviously being used in contradistinction to present-day, living forms of the language.[8] The inadequacy, however, of such terminology was and is apparent.

In 1948, R. A. Bowman restricted the term "Old Aramaic" to the early inscriptions of North Syria.[9] This was apparently not original with him, but it was indicative of the growing awareness of the need to set apart the phase of the language found in these inscriptions, as more and more of them were gradually coming to light. This restricted sense of "Old Aramaic" has been used by others, such as F. M. Cross and D. N. Freedman,[10] W. Baumgartner,[11] S. Moscati,[12] S. Segert,[13] K. A. Kitchen,[14] K. Beyer,[15] R. Degen,[16] although the number of texts included in this phase varies with the writer. The purpose of the restricting the sense of "Old Aramaic" was to set it off from a vast body of Aramaic texts that emerge from the seventh century B.C. and onwards, representing a form of the language that seems to have been standardized and from which, in fact, we get most of our impressions of what might be called "normal" Aramaic and by which we tend to judge the earlier inscriptions of the "Old Aramaic" period.

The name "Reichsaramäisch" for these texts of the seventh century onward was first coined by an Iranian scholar, Josef Markwart in 1927. He used this label in a footnote to a discussion of a matter quite unrelated; but it was quickly picked up and its use became widespread—and, in fact, is still widely used—despite its inadequacies. It is sometimes translated into English as "Imperial Aramaic," and the empire that Markwart had in mind when he wrote his footnote was Persia: "So nenne ich die aramäische Kanzleisprache der Achaimeniden, in welcher die Mehrzahl, wenn nicht alle, aramäischen Inschriften und sämtliche Papyri der Achaimenidenzeit, sowie die Stücke in den Büchern ᶜEsra und Daniel abgefasst sind."[17] Markwart's label was derived from the period in which this sort of "chancery" Aramaic was widely used; it had the advantage of being a chronological designation. But it seemed to suggest that the use of this sort of Aramaic began in the Persian period, whereas it was obviously in use already in the time of the Neo-Assyrian empire. It was H. L. Ginsberg who pointed out the use of it in pre-Persian times, calling attention to the *rab-šāqeh* episode in 2 Kgs 18:26-28 and Isa 36:11–13 and to the language in the Aššur Ostracon (*KAI* 233), dated ca. 660–50 B.C.[18] As a result, Ginsberg suggested the use of the name "Official Aramaic" for this phase of the language. Later on, E. G. Kraeling, thinking that Ginsberg's view might be somewhat entangled in hypotheses, suggested that it might be better to "speak of 'standard Aramaic.'"[19] One reason to support Kraeling's opinion is the fact that the same form of the language is now found in ostraca from Egypt which record everyday messages between persons who were almost certainly not officials or persons in chancery work. In any case, the names "Imperial Aramaic" or "Official Aramaic" are quite commonly used for this phase of the language today.

The extent of "Imperial Aramaic" or "Official Aramaic" is, however, the problem that is of concern today. For it is differently proposed by various scholars; it is often not demarcated from what seems to be a phase of the language that follows it, in which there is a seemingly direct linear development of it, but also a number of side, local dialects. Even F. Rosenthal, who grouped Reichsaramäisch, Nabatean, and Palmyrene under "Old Aramaic," sensed the need to set off from Reichsaramäisch both Nabatean and Palmyrene.[20] However, W. Baumgartner considered Reichsaramäisch to include not only the Pahlevi ideograms, the Aramaic texts from Egypt,[21] the Arsames correspondence,[22] and Biblical Aramaic, but also Nabatean and Palmyrene. From this huge group of texts Baumgartner distinguished what he called "real local dialects," i.e., Jewish Aramaic, including that of the Babylonian Talmud, the targums, Samaritan texts, and even Christian Palestinian Aramaic.[23] All of these in turn were distinguished by him from Modern Syriac.[24]

To add to the confusion, E. Y. Kutscher seems at one time to have listed under Reichsaramäisch such disparate types as Biblical Aramaic, Targumic Aramaic, and later Western Aramaic (i.e., Galilean, Samaritan, and Christian

Palestinian Aramaic).[25] As one reads on in that early article of Kutscher, one perceives that for him all of this was to be understood in addition to Egyptian Aramaic, the Arsames correspondence, Nabatean, and Palmyrene. All was to be grouped together as Reichsaramäisch and distinguished from "Middle Aramaic," which began for him "about 500 C.E."[26] Somehow, in between this Reichsaramäisch and this Middle Aramaic Kutscher sought to find room for Qumran Aramaic, especially that of the *Genesis Apocryphon.* Admittedly, Kutscher had not proposed these classifications in a well thought out scheme of the phases of the Aramaic language; that was not the purpose of his article. The grouping of texts under Reichsaramäisch according to Kutscher, that we have given above, has been garnered from his valuable article on "The Language of the Genesis Apocryphon," the purpose of which was to situate the Aramaic of that text among the known dialects of the language. It is a basic study that excels in comparative material. As far as I know, no one has contested his fundamental work on the grammar of 1QapGen or his judgment about the kind of Aramaic that it contains, or his dating of it to the first century B.C. or A.D.[27] Though his classification of the phases of the Aramaic language in that article did not invalidate the basic thrust and purpose of the article, it is, nevertheless, problematic. Fortunately, one can use his data and consider their relative value, without always identifying the forms as he did.

Because of problems of this sort which the earlier use of labels for phases of the Aramaic language caused—and still others could be mentioned—I sought to introduce *a purely chronological division* into the discussion of the phases of the Aramaic language. The dominant view of dividing the language would be chronological, i.e., by centuries, even though the labels might not always be immediately indicative of chronology. Within such categories or phases one could allow for local or geographical subdivisions into further dialectal differences (e.g., into eastern and western Aramaic), when necessary. The names that I have used are not ideal, I realize, since that of the second phase is not expressive of time, being still tied to the groping, traditional way of looking at that phase. But it is retained in view of the popularity of the label, and it is done with the conviction that it would be hard to start a new name in this phase. Below, I shall propose an alternative name, but also the problems that attend it.

II. *The Five Phases of Aramaic*

The reclassification of the known phases of the Aramaic language is proposed as follows:

(1) *Old Aramaic,* from roughly 925 B.C. to 700 B.C. This phase is represented by inscriptions on stone and other materials, written in the borrowed Phoenician alphabet[28] and preserving the earliest known forms of the language that we have come to recognize as Aramaic. The evidence for this phase comes not only from Northern Syria and Upper Mesopotamia, as was

known for a long time, but also from Northern Palestine. Included in this phase of the language are the Tell Halaf inscription, the Bir Hadad inscriptions, the ᶜEin Gev jar inscription, the Tell Dan Bowl, the Hazaᵓel Ivory inlay, the Ördek Burnu inscription, the Hamath graffiti, the Zakir inscription, Hadad, Panammu, the Sefire inscriptions, eight Bar Rākib inscriptions, the Hazor sherd, the Calah ostracon, the Nērab inscriptions, and possibly the Luristan Bronzes I-II and the Nineveh Lion Weights.[29] These texts all represent an archaic form of the language, and though two of them have peculiarities that set them apart within this group (i.e., the Hadad and Panammu inscriptions from ancient Yaᵓdi),[30] the general character of the group is sufficiently homogeneous to be recognized as representatives of "Old Aramaic."[31]

(2) *Official Aramaic,* from roughly 700 B.C. to 200 B.C.[32] The Aramaic of this phase, also called Reichsaramäisch, Imperial, or Standard Aramaic, is a form of the language which was not only relatively standardized, but also widespread. "Standardized" may, indeed, be too strong a word for the language of this phase and may seem to fail to reckon with minor local differences that too appear from time to time. But it is used to stress the otherwise striking homogeneity of the language at this period despite the vast range of geographical areas in which it has been found to have been in use. Moreover, it is this form of the language that we normally use to judge whether that of other phases is really related to it or not. In this phase Aramaic is attested in Egypt (chiefly in Upper Egypt at Elephantine and Aswan, but also in Lower Egypt at Saqqarah and Hermopolis West),[33] in Arabia and Palestine, in Syria and in scattered areas of Asia Minor, in Assyria and Babylonia, in Armenia, and in the ancient Indus Valley (what is now Afghanistan and Pakistan). The vast corpus of Official Aramaic texts knows of letters written on papyrus and skin, contracts or deeds of various legal proceedings, literary texts, graffiti, ostraca messages, wooden labels, clay tablets, etc., all of which present a fairly homogeneous form of the language. Local differences have been detected at times, and some have sought to distinguish between eastern and western forms of Official Aramaic.[34] But this is a debatable matter;[35] and if it is valid, it is not simply to be equated with the similar distinction made at a later phase of the language. In any case, to Official Aramaic certainly belongs the Aramaic of Ezra (minus the Masoretic encrustations),[36] and undoubtedly also the Aramaic of Daniel (at the very end of this phase).

(3) *Middle Aramaic*, from roughly 200 B.C. to A.D. 200. Here one notes the development of Official Aramaic and the emergence of "real local dialects."[37] To this phase belong the dialects of (a) *Palestine and Arabia*: Nabatean, Qumran, Murabbaᵓat, that of the inscriptions on Palestinian ossuaries and tombstones, of the Aramaic words preserved in the Greek texts of Josephus and the NT, and some of the texts of early Palestinian rabbinic literature (without their obvious later encrustations); (b) *Syria and*

Mesopotamia: those of Palmyra, Edessa, and Hatra, and perhaps also the beginnings of early Babylonian rabbinic literature.

(4) *Late Aramaic*, roughly A.D. 200 to 700. These Aramaic texts of various areas and dialects have further peculiarities that distance them even more from Official Aramaic than those in the Middle phase. They fall into two large geographic subdivisions: (a) *Western:* the dialects of Jewish Palestinian Aramaic,[38] Samaritan Aramaic, and Christian Syro-Palestinian Aramaic; (b) *Eastern:* the dialects of Syriac (further distinguished into a western [Jacobite] form and an eastern [Nestorian] form), Babylonian Talmudic Aramaic, and Mandaic.

The closing limit of this phase of the language is not easily set. 700 is taken merely as a round number close to the Muhammadan Conquest and the consequent spread of Arabic which put an end to the active use of Aramaic in many areas of the Near East.[39] But it is obvious that neither Aramaic nor Syriac died out at this time. There are, indeed, all sorts of reasons for extending the lower limit of the phase to the end of the 11th century (i.e., to the end of the Gaonic period in Palestine and Babylonia) and even to the end of the 13th century among Syriac writers (Bar Hebraeus, or Abu ᵓl-Faraj Gregory [1226-86], and his contemporaries). The extent of the areas in which Aramaic or Syriac was still spoken was greatly reduced; and the position that it assumed vis-à-vis Arabic even in those areas is problematic. Was it being used only in closed circles (domestic, scholastic, synagogal)? In any case, it is obvious that the language did not die out completely, as the following fifth phase shows, even though it is not easy to trace the line of connection between the Late and the Modern phases.

What is striking in the Late phase of Aramaic is not only the elements that set off its various local dialects (such as imperfects in *neqtol* or *liqtul*, the waning of the absolute and construct states of the noun, the piling up of pronominal forms, the widespread use of the possessive pronoun *dīl-*, etc.), but also the mounting influx of Greek words and constructions into almost all dialects of the language. Though the Hellenization of the eastern Mediterranean areas, such as Palestine and Syria, began much earlier,[40] the sparse incidence of Greek words in Aramaic texts of the Middle phase stands in contrast to that of this phase.

(5) *Modern Aramaic,* still spoken in various areas of northern Syria, Iran, Iraq and related regions. It is found in the West in isolated villages of the Anti-Lebanon region, north of Damascus (Maᶜlūla, Jubbᶜadîn, Baḫᶜa); in the East it is found in several areas (Ṭūr ᶜAbdîn, between the Lakes Urmia and Van [in Kurdistan and Azerbaijan], and north of Mossul [Iraq]).[41] The language spoken in these regions is a remnant of Aramaic or Syriac, heavily influenced, however, by other modern local languages such as Arabic, Kurdish, or Turkish.

In a sense, the reclassification of the phases of the Aramaic language that I have been proposing is nothing more than the distillation of views of scholars that have been emerging with the gradual increase of the documentation of the Aramaic language in the last two or three decades. The major divisions of "Old Aramaic" and "Official Aramaic" were already in use. What I have called "Late Aramaic" was likewise admitted by many scholars before me, even though they did not use this name. The major difference, then, lies in the recognition of the "Middle Aramaic" phase between that of "Official" and "Late" Aramaic. Given the nature of the dialects found in that phase—Palestinian, Nabatean, Edessene, Palmyrene, and Hatran, all of which coexisted more or less simultaneously—I thought that it was necessary to recognize them as a development of "Official Aramaic," but not yet the same as "Late Aramaic."

III. *Reasons for the Phases and Related Problems*

As a result of the discoveries of the last fifty to seventy-five years, we realize that the starting-point for the discussion of the phases of the Aramaic language is the relation of it to the Northwest branch of the Semitic languages. It emerges in history as a language only several centuries after the earliest attestation of the Arameans as a people, and its character is discerned in any given phase from a comparison with other phases of the language and with cognate Northwest Semitic languages.

The Arameans appear explicitly for the first time in the records of the fourth regnal year of the Assyrian king Tiglath-Pileser I (1115-1076 B.C.).[42] As far as we can judge today, the Arameans spoke a language that was apparently derived ultimately from a common Northwest Semitic stock, but that developed separately from cognate Canaanite dialects.[43] The first emergence of the language in the Old Aramaic inscriptions reveals it to be written in the alphabet of the Phoenicians.[44] Though it eventually developed on its own specific forms of some of the letters,[45] it is to be noted that the Arameans adopted the Phoenician alphabet and suited it to their distinctively Aramaic sounds.[46] Whereas Phoenician had already lost some of the original Proto-Semitic sounds by several consonantal shifts (e.g., *ḏ* had already become *z*, *ṯ̣* had already become *ṣ*, as had *ḏ̣*, *ṯ* had already become *š*—so that there were no consonants in the Phoenician alphabet to represent the Proto-Semitic sounds, *ḏ*, *ṯ*, *ḏ̣*, *ṯ̣*), Aramaic still retained the original Proto-Semitic sounds. Hence some adjustment had to be made in the use of the 22 characters of the Phoenician alphabet. Hence Aramaic *ḏ* was written, not with *d*, but with *z*; Aramaic *ṯ* was written, not with *t*, but with *š*; Aramaic *ḏ̣* was written with *q*;[47] and Aramaic *ṯ̣* was written with *ṣ*. This is the question of the treatment of the sibilants and the interdentals in Old Aramaic,[48] which is one of the characteristics of this phase.

A further characteristic of this phase of the Aramaic language is concerned with the orthography. Phoenician itself had not developed a system of writing vocalic sounds, and the diphthongs were usually contracted and represented as zero in the writing. But at an early stage the Arameans developed a system of using certain consonants to represent vocalic sounds. At first this system was confined to final long vowels: *y* was used to write long *i*, *w* to write long *u*, and *h* to write long *a*. Moreover, the diphthongs *ay* and *aw* were normally uncontracted in Aramaic, and these sounds, whether final or medial, were represented respectively as *y* or *w*, but the occasional contraction of *-ay* to *-ê* in a final position was also written with *h*. The thesis of F. M. Cross and D. N. Freedman that it was from the use of *w, y, h* as final vowel letters that the medial vowel letters were developed in Aramaic (and then spread to other Northwest Semitic languages) is still valid,[49] even though these authors had glossed over some problematic instances in their original dissertation and would now have to admit more exceptions to the occurrence of medial long vowels being written with *w* or *y*, given the further publication of Old Aramaic texts since the dissertation was written.[50] A further detail in their thesis is that *aleph* in these Old Aramaic texts was still treated as a consonant, and was not a vowel-letter. This thesis was proposed as a hypothesis; but, as far as I can see, the evidence that they amassed has been supported by subsequent texts that were published (e.g., Sefire II and III, and the more adequate publication of Sefire I by A. Dupont-Sommer and J. Starcky[51]).

An extensive critique of the thesis of Cross and Freedman has been written by D. W. Goodwin, *Text-Restoration Methods in Contemporary U.S.A. Biblical Scholarship*.[52] But it not only indulges in uncalled-for and arrogant criticism but is fundamentally misconceived; Cross and Freedman were easily able to defend their position and answer the criticism.[53] In spite of the heat engendered, there was, alas, no light. A more serious criticism of their thesis was attempted by L. A. Bange, *A Study of the Use of Vowel-Letters in Alphabetic Consonantal Writing (Inauguraldissertation 1961-62 an der Universität Oxford)*.[54] It was written almost ten years prior to its publication, contains some interesting minor corrections, but in the long run scarcely overthrows the basic thesis of Cross and Freedman.

Their treatment of the vowel-letters was first criticized by G. Garbini,[55] and a number of his points have been repeated by others, so that it merits a reconsideration. Most of his arguments, however, are based on a faulty explanation of the words that he uses as examples of forms with vowel-letters; only one of them, a proper name—which is readily arguable—might be a valid criticism.[56] In a later publication, Garbini returned to the attack and accused Cross and Freedman (and myself) of arguing in a vicious circle and without any real proof in two respects: (a) in treating final *aleph* as a consonant, not a vowel-letter; and (b) in treating most instances of medial *yodh* and *waw* as diphthongal.[57] To many readers it looks as though Cross and Freedman just asserted, for instance, that final *aleph* was consonantal and then proceeded to cite examples of it. But Garbini and their other critics fail to recognize that the hypothesis that Cross and Freedman sought to test by their examples had its starting-point, not in the Aramaic evidence alone, but in Phoenician (and a number of other Canaanite texts), in which in the early contemporary period the writing was wholly consonantal.[58] In agreement with the Phoenician consonantal *aleph,* the Arameans, it was argued, used it likewise—even as a marker of a final *a*-vowel in certain cases; and there is no instance in the Old Aramaic texts, which Cross and Freedman treated or which have subsequently been published,[59] that militates against this thesis. In the case of medial *waw* and *yodh,* their starting-point again was the normal Phoenician zero-writing of the diphthongs, but also the evidence of comparative Northwest Semitic grammar (and other comparative Semitic grammar) which would call for diphthongal usage. Thus, the Cross and Freedman thesis is not dependent on a vicious circle; the only problem with it originally was their reluctance to admit the inceptive use of medial vowel-letters in some Old Aramaic texts, for which the evidence is now clear. But this use is scarcely as abundant or widespread as the evidence in favor of their original position. In a sense, the evidence, such as it is, merely confirms the basic thrust of their original contention.

Criticism of Cross and Freedman's treatment of the Old Aramaic consonantal *aleph* has also been voiced by M. Tsevat[60] and S. Segert,[61] but their affirmation that Cross and Freedman have merely affirmed the consonantal character of *aleph* with no proof is really met only with a parallel affirmation of it as a vowel-letter. No real example of the latter is given that cannot be contested. In support of the Cross and Freedman thesis, one should perhaps recall that the prefixed negative *lā-* is never written in these texts with an *aleph;*[62] it is difficult to explain such a form if *aleph* were a real vowel-letter in this phase, especially in the light of the subsequent development in Aramaic, where it is almost always written separately and with final *aleph,* which has by this time become a vowel-letter (as far as we can judge—at least there is no reason in Official Aramaic texts to treat it any differently than it is in Biblical Aramaic). Moreover, the feminine demonstrative pronoun may seem to be a problem at first sight, in that it is written זא (Sf I A 35, [36], 37, [42]; III 9). But this form is attested in Phoenician both for the masculine[63] and for the feminine demonstrative.[64] This Phoenician evidence argues for the consonantal character of the *aleph (zaʾ);*[65] and the Phoenician origin of the borrowed alphabet would argue in favor of the same character for the *aleph* in such a form in Aramaic.

Besides the foregoing characteristics of Aramaic in this early phase (the widespread preservation of the Proto-Semitic phonemes,[66] and the development of orthographic habits from the initial Phoenician starting-point), one should also consider the following elements that are more or less distinctive of this phase of the language: (a) *morphological:* the use of *ʾnh,* "I," in contrast to *ʾnk* in Phoenician, Ugaritic, and the Zenjirli inscriptions (Hadad 1, Panammu 1); the Peal infinitive without preformative *m-* (e.g., Sf I B 32); Peal passive forms in *yuqtal;*[67] and the prefixed negative *lā-;* the 3d sg. masc. suffix on plural nouns in *-wh;* (b) *syntactic:* the use of the intensifying infinitive, resembling the infinitive absolute in Hebrew (Sf I B 30[?]; II C 8; III 2, 6, 12, 13, 18; Nerab 2:6); the use of the *waw*-consecutive (Zakir a 11). Finally, one should consider here the emergence of the post-positive article, a characteristic of this phase of Aramaic that is now clear (since it appears abundantly in the Sefire inscriptions); it is not as rare as it once seemed. It persists in later phases of the language, of course; but the real problem is to explain its origin. In this I again go along with the highly plausible suggestion made by Cross and Freedman, that it represents the addition of the deictic particle *haʾ* (often translated "lo, behold") to the noun for emphasis.[68] The problem is to explain why it appears in the postpositive position in this language alone of the Northwest Semitic tongues.

Two problems are related to the attempt to describe the character of Old Aramaic. The first is the number of texts that should be attributed to it; or, perhaps a better way of putting it, the lower limit of the phase. I have suggested 700 B.C. as a cut-off, in dependence on other writers who have proposed this date, which should obviously be understood broadly. Cross and Freedman limited their discussion to the inscriptions from Tell Halaf, Bir-Hadad, Zakir, Sujin (as Sefire I was then called), and Bar-Rakib.[69] They treated the Hadad and Panammu inscriptions from Zenjirli in an appendix, regarding them as Aramaic "with occasional Canaanite borrowing," but in reality a sort of "archaizing Aramaic." [70] S. Segert would prefer to put the lower limit of the phase at 612 B.C.[71] More recently R. Degen, in an excellently conceived and executed comprehensive treatment of some Old Aramaic texts, limited them to Zakir, Bir-Hadad, Hama graffiti, Bar-Rākib I-III, Bar-Rākib fr. I, Sefire I-III, Luristan I, and ʿEn-Gev Bowl, which he assigned to the tenth-eighth centuries B.C.[72] His study excels in that it is conducted on an admirable syntactic approach, which has enabled him to resolve some of the outstanding problems of phonology and morphology; and his categorization of the texts is significant. He writes, further, that "the monuments from the seventh century on agree with the texts from the fifth century B.C. in phonology, morphology, and syntax. . . . From the seventh century on begins the dissolution of the set word-order, and there begins to appear multiple word-positions that are well-known in later dialects." [73] I agree fully with the first sentence quoted here; and am inclined to go along with the basic thrust of the second.

But I find it difficult to agree with him when he omits certain inscriptions from this Old Aramaic phase; one wonders whether a new Procrustean bed has not been constructed.[74] To cite but one problematic example: I am not happy about the exclusion of the Nērab inscriptions from the phase of Old Aramaic.[75] This is not said because of the supposed presence of Akkadian (or Canaanite?) *š*- at the beginning of these inscriptions, a phenomenon that S. Kaufman has recently disposed of in an obviously enlightened solution.[76] Yet these inscriptions belong to the phase of Old Aramaic because of certain forms that are found in them (*nṣr,* "guard, preserve" [Nērab 1:12-13], instead of *nṭr;* the 3d sg. masc. suffix in *-wh* [*qdmwh,* Nērab 2:2 (cf. *ᵓlwh,* Sf III 8)]; the prefixed negative *l-* (Nērab 2:4, 6, 8) and of the syntactic feature of the intensifying infinitive (*hwm* [Nērab 2:6]). One would have to wait to see what elements in these inscriptions Degen would consider different in syntax from the Old Aramaic word order, before one could agree with the exclusion of them from this phase. These inscriptions are often dated ca. 700 B.C., and they may represent borderline cases.[77] But they contain enough characteristics of the Old Aramaic phase to keep them there. And the same would have to be said about some of the other inscriptions mentioned above in part II.

A second problem of a different sort has been raised by G. Garbini and R. Degen. In my commentary on the Sefire inscriptions I considered the Aramaic of this phase to be "definitely under Canaanite influence."[78] In this judgment I was concurring with that of C. Brockelmann, W. F. Albright, Cross and Freedman, et al.[79] Degen has objected to this characterization of Old Aramaic and called in question its so-called Canaanitisms.[80] Garbini has not spared his scorn of it, when he writes, "'cananeismi' cari agli studiosi ancora legati alla tradizione ottocentesca."[81] Concerning the Canaanitisms, Degen writes:

> Phenomena so described and originally isolated have subsequently often been found in later discovered inscriptions; the correctness of the original name has not yet been demonstrated. In my opinion, they must be regarded as genuine components of Old Aramaic as long as their dependence on "Canaanite" cannot be proven. Since this proof is lacking, one can only say that the phenomenon in question is attested in several of the Semitic languages.[82]

In a footnote Degen discusses the instances of the imperfect with *waw*-consecutive in the Zakir inscription (a 11, [12], 15), which is otherwise attested only in Hebrew, Moabite, and probably in the Aḥiram inscription in Phoenician.[83] This is the only item that Degen discusses at any length, and most of the data used by him taken from South Arabic are irrelevant.

However, when one considers some of the orthographic, morphological, and syntactic elements that I have discussed above as characteristics of Old Aramaic, one would have to consider some sort of Canaanite influence. As for the *waw*-consecutive, it is at home in the three above-mentioned Northwest Semitic languages; it is not found in any of the later phases of Aramaic. Many features of Old Aramaic are found in later phases of the languages, and these may not count as "characteristics" of the Old Aramaic phase. The characteristics are not overly abundant, but they are in the Old phase and do mark it off from what follows. The *yuqtal*-forms, the Peal infinitives without preformative *m-,* the use of the infinitive to intensify a finite verb, the use of the *waw*-consecutive are phenomena that I would consider Canaanite. These phenomena are not known in the later phases of the language and therefore they are not "genuine components" of the language.[84] Moreover, the mere fact that an alleged Canaanitism does turn up at a later stage of the language does not show that it is a "genuine component," because it still has to be shown that it is a *native* element. The element might have been borrowed at any early period and might have persisted in isolated forms in the language or in isolated areas. This is the explanation that I prefer to give for the instances of the Peal infinitive without preformative *m-*, which is found in inscriptions of this period,[85] and even for the stereotyped לאמר which is found in Official Aramaic texts, not only in the early Aššur Ostracon, but in Elephantine texts as well.[86] Merely to point to the occurrence of infinitives without *mem* in a later phase does not prove that it is genuinely Aramaic, since that obscures the question of origin.

It may be that the term Canaanitism should be dropped and an attempt made to specify the Canaanite dialect which is involved. If this is all that Degen means, then I should agree. E. Y. Kutscher used to like to speak of "languages in contact,"[87] and in such a sense the source of the Canaanite interference in this phase of Aramaic should have to be made more specific.

A slightly different attitude toward the problem has been adopted by G. Garbini. He quotes approvingly S. Moscati's view of the "non-existence of the Aramaic-Canaanite subdivision in the 2d millennium B.C."[88] Moreover, he refuses to admit that the known first millennium Northwest Semitic languages can be reduced to the Canaanite-Aramaic "binomial." This is partly because he refuses to see Ugaritic as Canaanite and partly because he prefers to treat so-called Yaᵓudic as distinct from Aramaic — if I understand him correctly.[89] He lays great stress on Amorite as the background of an Aramaic-Arabic branch and as having great influence on Canaanite, "Yaᵓudic," and Ugaritic. The whole is a process of Amoritization *(amorreizazione).* The following chart gives a quick view of his theory:[90]

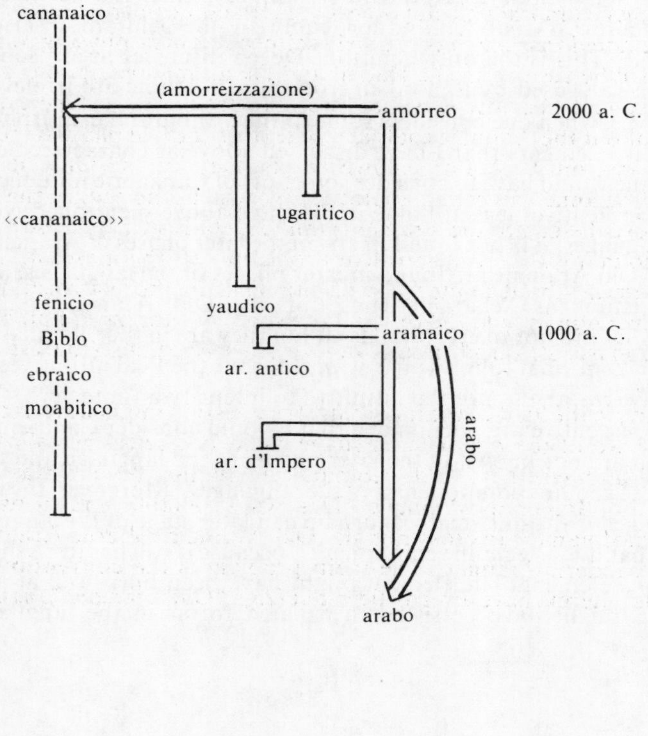

The upshot is that those components of Old Aramaic that are often regarded as (ottocentesque) Canaanitisms really become Amoriticisms, and a direct line of descent from Old Aramaic to Official Aramaic is denied.

Now it may be that the usual division of the Northwest Semitic languages into two branches, Canaanite and Aramaic,[91] is in need of revision and more account should be taken of the Amorite culture and language in Palestine and Syria of the second millennium. However, the evidence for a sweeping revision of the relationships between the Northwest Semitic languages, such as Garbini proposes, is simply non-existent. It is all too speculative. What little we know about the Amorite language is almost wholly confined to proper names,[92] and to use such material to construct a more elaborate explanation of the relation of Northwest Semitic languages in this early period is asking for too much.

The thesis that Garbini is proposing is speculative and far less well-founded than the Cross and Freedman thesis that he otherwise criticizes. Garbini may be right in rejecting the idea of Old Aramaic as a "Mischsprache,"[93] or as "una lingua ibrida, mosaico di elementi cananaici et aramaici," a description that he attributes to me,[94] though I have never so expressed it; nor would I. One has to insist, with him, that Old Aramaic has a well-defined physiognomy; but that does not prevent it from being "under Canaanite influence," especially when one realizes that part of that well-defined physiognomy is a stock of material common to Old Aramaic and Official Aramaic and of other elements that I have tried to isolate above as "characteristics" of Old Aramaic (some of which are legitimate Aramaic developments from Phoenician; others are Canaanite borrowings). However, it has to be noted that much of the well-defined Aramaic physiognomy of Old Aramaic will be verified in the Hadad and Panammu inscriptions of Zenjirli as well, despite the peculiarities that these inscriptions have. Operative in any judgment about the Aramaic character of texts in the Old phase is the use—at least subconscious—of data known to characterize the Official Aramaic texts; they become the prime analogate by which one judges that the Old Aramaic texts belong to the Aramaic family. Details such as these are part of that physiognomy: the post-positive article in *-aʾ*, the masc. pl. emphatic ending in *-ayyāʾ*, the absolute masc. pl. ending in *-īn*, the relative *zy*, the 1st sg. personal pronoun in *ʾnh*, the *br* form of "son," the absence of niphal forms, the 3d sg. masc. sf. on pl. nouns in *-wh* (> *-why*),[95] etc. (the list could be prolonged).

Finally, in the light of the foregoing, the question might be raised whether the first phase of the Aramaic language could not better be called "Proto-Aramaic," and whether "Old Aramaic" might not be a better label for "Official" or "Imperial" Aramaic. This would enable one to use strictly chronological names: Proto-Aramaic, Old Aramaic, Middle Aramaic, Late Aramaic, Modern Aramaic. The main problem is the conventional use to which certain terms have already been put (e.g., "Old Aramaic"), as explained above. There is the further difficulty that "Proto-Aramaic" has already been used to designate a form of the language that some scholars think they can detect in the second millennium B.C.[96] In the light of these difficulties, I think that it is better to stick with the ones proposed above.

So much for the discussion of the Old Aramaic phase and its problems. We now pass to the phase of Official Aramaic.

The first problem that confronts one in the discussion of Official Aramaic texts is whether they may be clearly divided into Eastern and Western dialects. This distinction is well known in the phase that I call Late Aramaic; and J. C. Greenfield has tried to show the evidence for it even in the phase of Old Aramaic.[97] E. Y. Kutscher presents a strong case for the distinction in the phase of Official Aramaic.[98] But he never finished his discussion of it, and hence I hesitate to be too critical of it. On the one hand, his evidence for Eastern Aramaic in this phase depends on the provenience or supposed provenience of certain documents (e.g., the Aššur Ostracon, the Behistun inscription are undoubtedly of historical eastern provenience). But even Kutscher eventually sensed the difficulty that one faces about the origin of Aḥiqar (East? West?); and the "eastern" character of the letter of the Elephantine Jews (*AP* 30) is an issue that must be further investigated, since it is far from clear. On the other hand, Kutscher eventually admitted that he had not taken into consideration a major bulk of this Official Aramaic material. What he did do[99] has to be taken seriously; but that has not closed the matter, and the eight characteristics of so-called eastern Official Aramaic isolated by him need rigorous scrutiny. Judged against the whole corpus of Official Aramaic texts, they evoke no little hesitation. Kutscher had relied on the work of Y. Muffs[100] in part, and appealed to the "difference between deeds, in which the wording does not change too easily, and administrative documents that try to keep as close as possible to the Eastern *OfA* [= Official Aramaic]."[101] This may be, but Kutscher has not presented the evidence that bears him out. Moreover, when at the end of his discussion of Official Aramaic distinctions he says that "it is impossible to deal here with the language of the letters of Cowley and of the ostraca,"[102] then he is saying that the last word in the matter has not yet been spoken. Because of this and because of several hesitations about a number of the eight criteria that Kutscher has proposed, I hesitate to use the distinction of eastern and western Official Aramaic.

I recognize with H. L. Ginsberg that "official Aramaic was never absolutely uniform except in intention."[103] But I have a problem with the rest of his judgment, that ". . . in the course of time, especially after the destruction of the Achaemenian empire, [it] became more and more colored by the spoken languages of the writers." *In se,* I fully agree with what is said here, but it is the coloring of Official Aramaic after the Achaemenian empire that leads me to conclude that a new phase of the language has to be reckoned with, viz., the Middle Aramaic phase. Ginsberg's presupposition, when he wrote that statement, was that Official Aramaic persisted as such, and in this I hesitate. I am not trying to maintain that Official Aramaic was monolithic; I recognize that the division of it into eastern and western is debatable, but it needs more evidence and a better sifting of the data for support.

A more crucial problem is the lower limit of Official Aramaic, or the existence of the phase of Middle Aramaic. Kutscher eventually accepted the phase in the sense in which I had proposed it.[104] I have adopted the suggestion of S. Segert that the cut-off date should be 200 B.C. rather than 300 B.C.[105] The main reason for the distinction of Middle Aramaic from Official Aramaic is the coexistence of a number of local dialects: Palestinian Aramaic (from Jerusalem, Qumran, Murabbaᶜat, Seiyal, etc.),[106] Nabatean, Palmyrene, Hatran, and the early Syriac material. Of these forms of Aramaic the closest to Official Aramaic seems to be that represented in Palestine, and I tend to regard this as the direct lineal descent, with the others as manifestations of local dialects or side developments. I should be ready to consider the distinction between eastern and western forms of the language in this phase; but this has not yet been worked out in detail.

Special note, however, has to be made here of the long neglected early Syriac inscriptions, texts from Edessa, Dura Europos, and their environs. They date from the first to the third centuries in the Christian era, but are almost exclusively written by non-Christians and certainly antedate the rise of Christian Syriac literature. They are important because of certain orthographic, phonetic, and morphological peculiarities which relate them to the Middle phase of Aramaic (because of what K. Beyer has called the *Einschlag* of Official Aramaic still present in them[107]) and set them off from classical Syriac of the Late phase. For instance, the preformative of the 3d masc. sg. and pl. of the imperfect is still *y-* in most instances (and not yet *n-*); the *śīn* of earlier Aramaic, which becomes *samekh* in later Syriac, is represented in these texts by *šīn*; short *o* and *u* are still written defectively (in contrast to the usual full writing of later Syriac).[108]

When one takes cognizance of this early Syriac material along with the growing corpus of Palestinian Aramaic, which must be recognized as existing more or less at the same time as Nabatean, Palmyrene, and Hatran Aramaic, then there is real reason to speak of Aramaic of the Middle phase.

Why make the lower limit of this period A.D. 200? This is a somewhat arbitrary date, adopted mainly because of the beginning of the rabbinic literary tradition that coincides with the codification of the Mishnah by R. Judah the Prince. Moreover, it is not far removed from the beginning of the classical Syriac literary period. With further study and the further acquisition of Aramaic texts, it may be possible to specify the limit better. I have toyed with the date of the Bar Cochba revolt (A.D. 135), but that would cut out later Palmyrene material.

There are, however, some scholars who think that the Aramaic of the last two centuries B.C. and of the first two centuries A.D. should be considered part of Official or Imperial Aramaic. For example, P. Grelot, in his review of the first edition of my commentary on the *Genesis Apocryphon,* wrote that "there are hardly any differences between this language [i.e., that of 1QapGen] and those of Daniel, of the fragments of Enoch (4Q), of the Prayer of Nabonidus, of the Testament of Levi (4Q). The differences of orthography can be explained by the fact that the copy would have been *dictated,* and not read by the scribe from another manuscript. It is a question in all these cases of a literary Aramaic which was able to impose itself on a more developed spoken language, already oriented toward the peculiar forms attested in the Palestinian targum."[109] Similarly, A. Díez Macho writes that "the targum of Job of Qumran Cave XI (11QtgJob) was written in the literary Aramaic called 'imperial' or, with the German designation, 'Reichsaramäisch.'"[110] Or again, "all the Aramaic writings of Qumran or Murabba^{c}at have been written in this type of Aramaic. It is a question of the Aramaic which followed that called 'Old Aramaic,' of which Rainer Degen recently published an excellent grammar. . . . Klaus Beyer, who is preparing a grammar of Imperial Aramaic, situates it between the 5th century B.C. and the 4th century A.D., but warns that since the second century B.C. this Aramaic bears the impress of spoken local dialects."[111]

Aside from the fact that the last half of Díez Macho's last statement merely points up in its own way the very distinction that I have been trying to make, it is obvious that he and Grelot are thinking only of a lineal connection between Official Aramaic, Qumran Aramaic, and the Aramaic of *the* (so-called) Palestinian Targum. The statement attributed to Beyer at least allows for the other dialects that constitute part of the evidence for the Middle phase.

At issue here are several things that often enter the discussion: (1) whether one can speak of the form*s* of Aramaic that are attested between 200 B.C. and A.D. 200 as the same as those which preceded them (from 700–200 B.C.)—all of them, not just Qumram Aramaic; (2) whether the forms of Aramaic that develop after A.D. 200 must not be reckoned as a still further development (with its clear distinction into Eastern and Western Aramaic); and (3) whether the distinction between literary and spoken Aramaic, that has recently been introduced into parts of the discussion, is a tolerable way of clinging to the label of "Official" or "Imperial" Aramaic for all of this. The latter distinction is invoked to establish a synchronic explanation for various forms of so-called Official Aramaic: Qumran Aramaic as "literary" Aramaic, that of the Palestinian targums as "spoken" Aramaic, all of which allegedly comes from the same chronological period.

Involved in this view of Official Aramaic is the claim that is made by Díez Macho and his followers for early dating of the Palestinian targums, and especially of that of Tg. Neofiti 1.[112] I have already set forth my hesitations about the list of arguments presented by Díez Macho for an early dating in the introduction to the volume on Genesis in that targum.[113] More recently, he has returned to the question of the language that is found in that targum, in an article entitled, "Le targum palestinien," in which he seems to follow the opinion of K. Beyer already quoted that Official Aramaic stretched from the fifth century B.C. to the fourth century A.D. and brands my presentation of the phases of Aramaic as "une présentation diachronique simpliste qui ne semble pas tenir suffisament compte des arguments favorisant la solution synchronique du problème. . . . On n'envisage pas sérieusement que l'araméen de Qumrân et celui du TargP soient contemporain, le premier littéraire, le second parlé, populaire."[114] This is Díez Macho's main contention (and is shared by P. Grelot, by implication at least), that the classic (non-Qumran) targums of Palestine date from the first century (or earlier) and have been composed in *spoken* Aramaic, which is somewhat different from the literary Aramaic of the Qumran material. This, of course, allows Díez Macho to claim an early date for the Targum Neofiti 1, which he is publishing, and which he would like to see utilized for all sorts of reasons in NT study.

But before such a distinction, which lays claims to a "synchronic" approach to the matter and, therefore, is not "simplistic," can be admitted, there are a number of factors to be considered: (1) Palestinian Aramaic in the Roman period is not represented solely by the literary texts of Qumran; there are inscriptions on tombstones and ossuaries, letters of Bar Cochba and his colleagues, legal and commercial contracts or deeds, etc.[115] Most of these texts have come to light in the last 25-50 years and they force us to raise the question about what we know of a distinction between literary and spoken Aramaic of this period. (2) How can one draw a distinction between common, spoken, or popular Aramaic and literary Aramaic in an historic period? We all recognize that there is a difference between the spoken and literary form of the language, and that the development of a language begins in the mouths of those who speak it and only after a certain amount of time does it invade the written language itself. It is the spoken form of a language that is alive and developing, and it manifests itself gradually in writing despite the weight of the literary tradition. But when one is dealing with ancient written texts, especially of limited number, and of (in some cases) uncertain provenience, it is a moot question whether one can say that one text is written in a literary form of the language and that another is composed in the spoken or popular form—unless, of course, one has some independent, extrinsic evidence of such a distinction. How do we know what the spoken form of Aramaic was like in first-century Palestine? There is no reason to deny that the targums came into existence as orally translated forms of the Scriptures being read in Hebrew in the synagogues. We may even like to assume that the meturgeman turned the sacred Hebrew text into the currently spoken form of Aramaic so that it would fully correspond to the very purpose of a targum. Moreover, from references in rabbinic literature we know that *written* targums were at one point prohibited. And who has not heard by now of the immuring of a copy of the written targum of Job under R. Gamaliel I during some construction on the site of the Jerusalem temple?[116] But do such reasons (speculative assumptions and unrelated historical data) amount to proof that the Aramaic text in any of the classic non-Qumran targums of Palestinian provenience (Pseudo-Jonathan, the Fragmentary Targum, Neofiti 1—or even Onqelos) preserves a popular, spoken form of Aramaic in contrast to the literary Aramaic of the Qumran texts? Moreover, we must not forget that the targumim are a form of literature, an Aramaic creation. The presumption would be that they are just as much a form of literary Aramaic as that of the Qumran texts. For a synchronic approach to this matter to be valid, one would have to show that the Aramaic of the so-called Palestinian targums is, in fact, contemporary with that of the Qumran literature. In the case of the latter there is archaeological evidence for dating it prior to A.D. 70. The only reasons that are ever given for the first-century dating of the so-called Palestinian targums are philological, based on the assumption that we can identify their language with the spoken, popular form of first-century Palestinian Aramaic. The loud and constant assertion of this thesis evokes only an equally vociferous counter-assertion. (3) It is well known that the Aramaic in the classic, non-Qumran targums abounds in Greek words that have been transliterated and/or slightly Aramaized. This, however, is not necessarily a sign of antiquity or of first-century Palestinian provenience; Greek words in such texts do not necessarily mean that the texts themselves date from the beginning of Hellenization in Palestine.[117] Rather, the closest parallels to the sort of Aramaic in which the non-Qumran targums are written are found in the inscriptions from synagogues and tombs of the Byzantine period in Palestine (roughly from the third to the sixth centuries),[118] and often enough in the literary texts of rabbinical literature and classical Syriac.[119]

But E. Y. Kutscher and J. C. Greenfield have insisted that common or popular Aramaic has been used in *Genesis Rabbah*.[120] This I would not contest. But that writing comes clearly from a period later than the Middle phase of Aramaic; it is usually ascribed (at the earliest) to the first generation of the Palestinian Amoraim.[121]

The debate over the phase of Middle Aramaic will continue until more reliable criteria for dating some of the texts emerge. The biggest problem is the dating of the non-Qumran targums. As far as I am concerned, until proof emerges to establish an earlier date, they are to be reckoned as part of the literature of the Late Aramaic phase, when due allowance is made for their obviously later encrustations at times.

These are the main issues that confront one who is concerned about the phases of the Aramaic language today. Further discussion will obviously clarify a number of the points that I have raised above.

NOTES TO CHAPTER 3

*This essay appears here for the first time; it is a revision of one of the Speaker's Lectures, delivered at Oxford University in May 1974.

[1] *The Genesis Apocryphon of Qumran Cave I: A Commentary* (BibOr 18; Rome: Biblical Institute, 1966) 19–20 n. 60. The second edition (see p. 22 above, n. 27) appeared in 1971, with a slight modification of the phases that will be mentioned below. See also "Ancient Aramaic Language," *New Catholic Encyclopedia* (New York: McGraw-Hill, 1967), 1. 736-37.

[2] *Die aramaistische Forschung seit Theodor Nöldeke's Veroffentlichungen* (Leiden: Brill, 1939; reprinted, 1964) vii-ix, 1, and passim.

[3] *The Brooklyn Museum Aramaic Papyri: New Documents of the Fifth Century B.C. from the Jewish Colony at Elephantine* (New Haven: Yale University, 1953; reprinted, New York: Arno, 1969) 4-7.

[4] "The Language of the Genesis Apocryphon: A Preliminary Study," *Aspects of the Dead Sea Scrolls* (Scripta hierosolymitana, 4; Jerusalem: Magnes, 1958) 1-35, esp. pp. 1-3. Cf. "Aramaic," *Encyclopaedia judaica* (Jerusalem: Keter; New York: Macmillan, 1971), 3. 259-87.

[5] *A Short Grammar of Biblical Aramaic* (Berrien Springs, MI: Andrews University, 1966) 2.

[6] *Altaramäische Grammatik* (p. 23 above, n. 53), 5: "Der so aufgefasste Bereich des Altaramäischen entspricht grundsätzlich der Terminologie von Franz Rosenthal und anderen Semitisten (Nabatäisch und Palmyrenisch sind jedoch nicht einbezogen[!]), während sich die unter demselben Titel (nach Abschluss des vorliegenden Werkes) 1970 erschienene 'Altaramäische Grammatik' von Reinhold [*sic*] Degen nur auf die Texte aus der älteren Periode, d.h. aus 9.-7. Jh. v. u. Z., beschränkt, die in der vorliegenden Grammatik als 'früharamäisch' bezeichnet werden." To be fair to Segert, one has to know that his manuscript was already composed and lay with the publisher in East Germany for many years. It is a wonder that it finally appeared at all; and for that we are grateful to him. The advantage of it is that it stresses the homogeneity of the language in what I should call the "Old Aramaic," "Official Aramaic," and "Middle Aramaic" phases (from the latter phase he includes even Qumran Aramaic texts under "Altaramäisch"). He marks the differences of the dialects, indeed (using sigla such as AA [Altaramäisch], BA [Biblisch-Aramäisch], FA [Früharamäisch], Ja [Jaʾudisch], Q [Qumran-Aramäisch], RA [Reichsaramäisch]); but it is difficult to acquire a good view in this grammar of the nature of any of these dialects. Moreover, see n. 13 below.

[7] (Munich: M. Hueber, 1928) 59-80. "Neuaramäisch" includes for him the dialects of Maʿlula and Urmia (pp. 80-95).

[8] This is similarly used by P. Grelot, *RB* 80 (1973) 144.

[9] "Arameans, Aramaic, and the Bible," *JNES* 7 (1948) 65-90, esp. p. 71.

[10] *Early Hebrew Orthography: A Study of the Epigraphic Evidence* (AOS 36; New Haven: American Oriental Society, 1952) 21 n. 1 ("from the tenth to the seventh centuries B.C."). See also F. M. Cross, Jr., "Semitische Epigraphik," *RGG*[3] (ed. K. Galling; Tübingen: Mohr [Siebeck]) 2 (1958) 523-26, esp. col. 523 ("Altaramäisch, 10-8. Jh. v. Chr.").

[11] L. Koehler and W. Baumgartner, *Lexicon in Veteris Testamenti libros* (Leiden: Brill, 1958) xix.

[12] *An Introduction to the Comparative Grammar of the Semitic Languages* (Porta linguarum orientalium, ns 6; Wiesbaden: Harrassowitz, 1964) 11.

[13] "Zur Schrift und Orthographie der altaramäischen Stelen von Sfire," *ArOr* 32 (1964) 110-26, esp. pp. 115-18; see also his review of J. J. Koopmans, *Aramäische Chrestomathie*, ibid., 454; "Aramäische Studien: III. Zum Problem der altaramäischen Dialekte," ibid., 26 (1958) 564.

[14] "The Aramaic of Daniel," *Notes on Some Problems in the Book of Daniel* (London: Tyndale, 1965) 50.

[15] "Der reichsaramäische Einschlag in der ältesten syrischen Literatur," *ZDMG* 116 (1966) 242-54, esp. p. 247 n. 10.

[16] *Altaramäische Grammatik der Inschriften des 10.-8. Jh. v. Chr.* (Abhandlungen für die Kunde des Morgenlandes, 38/3; Wiesbaden: Deutsche morgenländische Gesellschaft, 1969) 1-3.

[17]"Np. *adīna* 'Freitag,'" *Ungarische Jahrbücher* 7 (1927) 89-121, esp. p. 91 n. 1.

[18]"Aramaic Dialect Problems," *AJSL* 50 (1933-34) 1-9; 52 (1935-36) 95-103. E. Y. Kutscher ("New Aramaic Texts," *JAOS* 74 [1954] 233-48, esp. p. 246) and R. A. Bowman ("Arameans, Aramaic, and the Bible," *JNES* 7 [1948] 65-90, esp. p. 76) have further cited the Sheikh Fadl Tomb Inscriptions from a site near Oxyrhynchus in Egypt, which they date to 663 B.C. and take as an indication of the use of this sort of Aramaic in Egypt in the 7th century B.C. However, J. Naveh (*The Development of the Aramaic Script* [Proceedings of the Israel Academy of Sciences and Humanities, 5/1; Jerusalem: Israel Academy, 1970] 41), after a fresh study of the original photographs, has concluded that paleographically "the inscriptions are from approximately the second quarter of the fifth century B.C.E."

[19]*BMAP*, 6 n. 11.

[20]*Die aramaistische Forschung,* 92.

[21]KB, xxxvi-xli. By "Aramaic texts from Egypt," we mean those published by A. H. Sayce and A. E. Cowley, *Aramaic Papyri Discovered at Assuan* (London: A. Moring, 1906); E. Sachau. *Aramäische Papyrus und Ostraka aus einer jüdischen Militär-Kolonie zu Elephantine. Altorientalische Sprachdenkmäler des 5. Jahrhunderts vor Chr.* (Leipzig: Hinrichs, 1911); N. Aimé-Giron, *Textes araméens d'Egypte* (Cairo: Institut français d'archéologie orientale, 1931); "Adversaria semitica," *BIFAO* 38 (1939) 1-63; E. G. Kraeling, *BMAP* (n. 3 above); G. R. Driver, *Aramaic Documents of the Fifth Century B.C.: Transcribed and Edited* (Oxford: Clarendon, 1954; reprinted, Osnabrück: Zeller, 1968); an abridged and revised edition of the same title was subsequently issued [without plates] (Oxford: Clarendon, 1957; further revised [with pages of additions and corrections], 1965); E. Bresciani and M. Kamil, "Le lettere aramaiche di Hermopoli," *Atti della Accademia Nazionale dei Lincei,* Memorie, Classe di scienze morali. . . , 8/12, fasc. 5 (Rome: Accademia Nazionale dei Lincei, 1966) 357-428 (+ pls. I-X). The foregoing list gives the main collections of so-called Egyptian Aramaic texts; many further texts were published singly in various periodicals. Convenient handbook-collections of these texts can be found in the following: A. Cowley, *Aramaic Papyri of the Fifth Century B.C.: Edited with Translation and Notes* (Oxford: Clarendon, 1923; reprinted, Osnabrück: Zeller, 1967); A. Ungnad, *Aramäische Papyrus aus Elephantine: Kleine Ausgabe unter Zugrundelegung von Eduard Sachau's Erstausgabe* (Leipzig: Hinrichs, 1911); B. Porten and J. C. Greenfield, *Jews of Elephantine and Arameans of Syene: Aramaic Texts with Translation* (Jerusalem: Hebrew University, 1974).

[22]This is a commonly used title for the texts published by G. R. Driver (see the preceding note).

[23]KB, xl.

[24]Ibid., xli. Or better, "Modern Aramaic." See n. 41 below.

[25]"Language" (n. 4 above), 1. At least so I read his first paragraph, which is scarcely clear, in the light of what follows in the rest of the article.

[26]Ibid., 3. In a later article ("Aramaic," *Current Trends in Linguistics: 6. Linguistics in South West Asia and North Africa* [The Hague: Mouton, 1971] 347-412, esp. p. 347) he speaks of Rosenthal's division as "the accepted division" (Old Aramaic, Middle Aramaic, Late Aramaic), but then he abandons it in favor of mine.

[27]Now that the Targum of Job from Qumran Cave XI is published and the language of it has been examined, it seems that the *Genesis Apocryphon* represents a stage of Middle Aramaic that is later than that of the targum (see further p. 164 below); hence we may have to date the *Genesis Apocryphon* more specifically to the first century A.D. (without, however, being apodictic about it).

[28]On this problem, see further p. 63 below.

[29]Most of these texts can be found in *KAI* (§201 [Bir Hadad], §202 [Zakir], §203-13 [Hamath graffiti], §214 [Hadad], §215 [Panammu], §216-21 [Bar-Rākib inscriptions], §222-24 [Sefire inscriptions; see further my commentary, *The Aramaic Inscriptions of Sefire* (BibOr 19; Rome: Biblical Institute, 1967)], 225-26 [Nērab], 231 (Tell Halaf), 232 (Hazaᵓel). See further J. C. L. Gibson, *Textbook of Syrian Semitic Inscriptions: Volume II, Aramaic Inscriptions* (p. 24 above, n. 56).

[30]The language of these two inscriptions should not be called "Yaʾudic" (see my commentary on *The Aramaic Inscriptions of Sefîre* [BibOr 19; Rome: Biblical Institute, 1967] 62-63). The peculiarities in them are not sufficient to merit the designation of a "Sondersprache," as J. Friedrich once sought to characterize it (see "Skizze der Sprache von Jaʾudi im nördlichen Syrien (8. Jhd. v. Chr.)," *Phönizisch-punische Grammatik* [AnOr 32; Rome: Biblical Institute, 1951] 153-62; "Zur Stellung des Jaudischen innerhalb der nordwestsemitischen Sprachgeschichte," *Studies in Honor of Benno Landsberger* [Chicago: University of Chicago, 1965] 425-29). See G. Garbini, "Studi aramaici—1-2," *AION* 29 (1969) 1-15, esp. pp. 1-8; "L'Aramaico antico," *Atti della Accademia Nazionale dei Lincei,* Memorie, Classe di scienze morali. . . , 8/7, fasc. 5; Rome: Accademia Nazionale dei Lincei, 1956) 242-43.

R. Degen (*Altaramäische Grammatik* [n. 16 above], 2 n. 17) recognizes that Friedrich's work is "weitgehend überholt," but he still persists in regarding these inscriptions as representatives of a "Sondersprache" and promises a new grammatical treatment of them. To be noted, however, is that Friedrich's *Skizze* has not been included in the new edition of his Phoenician grammar, published in collaboration with W. Röllig, *Phönizisch-punische Grammatik* (AnOr 46; Rome: Biblical Institute, 1970).

J. C. Greenfield ("קווים דיאלקטיים בארמית הקדומה [Dialect Traits in Early Aramaic]," *Lěšonénu* 32 [1967-68] 359-68) came closer to the truth of the matter in seeing these inscriptions as fundamentally part of "Old Aramaic." A refutation of Friedrich is included in E. Y. Kutscher's article, "Aramaic," *Current Trends* (n. 26 above) 350-51; cf. H. L. Ginsberg, "The Classification of North-West Semitic Languages," *Akten des XXIV. internationalen Orientalisten-Kongresses* (Wiesbaden: Harrassowitz, 1959) 256-57; H. Tadmor, "Azriyau of Yaudi," *Studies in the Bible* (ed. C. Rabin; Scripta hierosolymitana, 8; Jerusalem: Magnes, 1961) 232-71.

[31]For the texts of Palestinian provenience, see the list given on p. 99–100 below. I have not included here the following inscriptions, which may be Ammonite written in Old Aramaic script (at least they are so judged by F. M. Cross): Amman Citadel Inscription (see S. H. Horn, "The Ammān Citadel Inscription," *BASOR* 193 [1969] 2-13; F. M. Cross, "Epigraphic Notes on the Ammān Citadel Inscription," ibid., 13-19); Deir ᶜAlla Inscription (see H. J. Franken, "Texts from the Persian Period from Tell Deir ᶜAlla," *VT* 17 [1967] 479-81; this text was originally wrongly dated. See further J. Naveh, "The Date of the Deir *ᶜAllā Inscription in Aramaic Script," IEJ* 17 [1967] 256-58; F. M. Cross, "Epigraphic Notes," 14 n. 2; "Ammonite Ostraca from Heshbon: Heshbon Ostraca IV-VIII," *AUSS* 13 [1975] 1-20, esp. pp. 11-12). See now J. Hoftijzer and G. van der Kooij, *Aramaic Texts from Deir ᶜAlla* (Documenta et monumenta orientis antiqui, 19; Leiden: Brill, 1976); and my review, *CBQ* 40 (1978) 93-95. If one were not to agree with Cross and were to regard these as Aramaic, then they would have to be included in the above list.

[32]Originally, I set the lower limit as 300 B.C. (see *The Genesis Apocryphon of Qumran Cave I* [1966], 19 n. 60), taking 300 B.C. as a round number shortly after the time of the conquest of the East by Alexander the Great. The waning of Aramaic as a *lingua franca* and the rise of Greek in its place in the eastern Mediterranean world was the main reason for that cut-off point. However, further consideration of a number of texts and of the problem of the Aramaic of Daniel have moved me to set the lower limit at about 200 B.C. But even that should not be pressed too rigidly.

[33]For the texts from Hermopolis West, see those published by E. Bresciani and M. Kamil in n. 21 above. A number of texts have also been found at Saqqarah (e.g., the letter of King Adon to an Egyptian Pharaoh, see pp. 231–42 below), but they have not yet been published. See the preliminary reports on these discoveries in the following articles: J. Leclant, "Fouilles et travaux en Egypte et au Soudan," *Orientalia* 37 (1968) 103 (mentions 51 Aramaic papyri); 38 (1969) 254 (mentions 83 Aramaic papyri); 42 (1973) 400 (". . . plus de 230 fragments de papyri démotiques, grecs et même araméens").

[34]E.g., E. Y. Kutscher, "Aramaic," *Current Trends* (n. 26 above), 361-62; J. C. Greenfield ("Standard Literary Aramaic," *Actes du premier congrès international de linguistique sémitique et chamito-sémitique Paris 16-19 juillet 1969* (The Hague: Mouton, 1974) 280-89.

[35]E.g., A. F. Johns, *Short Grammar* (n. 5 above), 2. He speaks against the division at this early stage.

[36]By "Masoretic encrustations" I mean chiefly the vocalization of Biblical Aramaic in the different later traditions (Tiberian, Palestinian, or Babylonian). At times, especially in the Tiberian system, certain forms have been Hebraized; others have been vocalized according to a pronunciation that was characteristic of later periods (and is attested in Jewish Palestinian Aramaic or in Syriac). The distinctions between *Qĕrê* and *Kĕtîb* is often an example of this (e.g., the Masoretic pronunciation of the 2d sg. masc. pronominal suffix on *plural* nouns as *-āk*, in contrast to the *Kĕtîb* which preserves the *y* [= older *ayk*]; the segholate forms of nouns [like *melek*, instead of *mĕlēk*]; or the occurrence of lengthened vowels in open pretonic syllables [e.g., ʾ*ābî*, instead of ʾ*ăbî*]. See further H. H. Powell, *The Supposed Hebraisms in the Grammar of the Biblical Aramaic* (University of California Publications, Semitic Philology, 1; Berkeley: University of California, 1906; F. R. Blake, *A Resurvey of Hebrew Tenses with an Appendix, Hebrew Influence on Biblical Aramaic* (Rome: Biblical Institute, 1951) 81-96.

[37]To use the phrase of W. Baumgartner quoted above, p. 59 (see n. 23).

[38]I retain this name for such Aramaic at this period, along with F. Rosenthal (*A Grammar of Biblical Aramaic* [Porta linguarum orientalium, ns 5; Wiesbaden: Harrassowitz, 1961] 5). Others, e.g., E. Y. Kutscher ("Aramaic," *Encyclopaedia judaica*, 3. 270), have objected to the use of this name, preferring to speak of "Galilean Aramaic." The extent to which this is a better designation is quite debatable.

I would include under this heading not only the so-called Palestinian targums and the usual literary texts of the late Tannaʾitic and Amoriac periods, but also the inscriptions from numerous synagogues of Palestine (for a list of which, see *MPAT*, App. A1–A56.

[39]See T. Nöldeke, *Compendious Syriac Grammar* (tr. J. A. Crichton; London: Williams & Norgate, 1904) xxxiii.

[40]See further p. 32 above.

[41]In general, see F. Rosenthal, *Die aramaistische Forschung* (note 2 above), 104-5, 160-72, 255-69; H. Fleisch, *Introduction à l'étude des langues sémitiques: Eléments de bibliographie* (Paris: Maisonneuve, 1947) 84-87; J. Friedrich, "Das Neusyrische als Typus einer entarteten semitischen Sprache," *AION* 4 (1962) 95-106; H. Polotsky, "Studies in Modern Syriac," *JSS* 6 (1961) 1-60. On *Maᶜlūla:* G. Bergsträsser, *Glossar des neuaramäischen Dialekts von Maᶜlūla* (Abhandlungen für die Kunde des Morgenlandes, 14/4; Leipzig: Brockhaus, 1921); *Neuaramäische Märchen und andere Texte aus Maᶜlūla* (Abhandlungen für die Kunde des Morgenlandes, 13/2; Leipzig: Brockhaus, 1915); "Neue Texte im neuaramäischen Dialekt von Maᶜlula," *ZA* 32 (1919) 150-70; C. Correll, "Ein Vorschlag zur Erklärung der Negation *ču (ću)* in den neuwestaramäischen Dialekten des Antilibanon," *ZDMG* 124 (1974) 271-85; E. Littmann,"Der neuaramäische Dialekt von Maᶜlūla," *OLZ* 29 (1926) 803-9; H. Müller, "Maᶜlūla vor hundert Jahren: Reisebriefe von Albert Socin aus dem Jahre 1869," *ZDPV* 85 (1969) 1-23; T. Nöldeke, "Beiträge zur Kenntniss der aramäischen Dialecte," *ZDMG* 21 (1867) 183-200; "Texte im aramäischen Dialekt von Maᶜlula," *ZA* 31 (1917-18) 203-30. A. Spitaler, *Grammatik des neuaramäischen Dialekts von Maᶜlūla (Antilibanon)* (Abhandlungen für die Kunde des Morgenlandes, 23/1; Leipzig: Brockhaus, 1938); reprinted, 1966; F. Rosenthal, "Spitalers Grammatik des neuaramäischen Dialekts von Maᶜlula," *Or* 8 (1939) 346-60; A. Spitaler, "Neue Materialen zum aramäischen Dialekt von Maᶜlula," *ZDMG* 107 (1957) 299-339. On *Jubbᶜadîn*: V. Cantarino, *Der neuaramäische Dialekt von Ğubb Adin (Texte und Übersetzung)* (Chapel Hill, NC: Curriculum in Linguistics of North Carolina, 1961); S. Reich, *Etudes sur les villages araméens de l'Anti-Liban* (Documents d'études orientales, 7; Damascus: Institut français de Damas, 1937). On *Baḫᶜa:* C. Correll, *Materialien zur Kenntnis des neuaramäischen Dialekts von Baḫᶜa* (Munich: University Dissertation, 1969).

On *Tur ᶜAbdin:* H. Anschütz, "Zur Gegenwartslage der syrischen Christen im Tur ᶜAbdin, in Hakkarigebiet und im Iran," *ZDMG* 118 suppl. 1/2 (1969) 483-510; O. Jastrow, *Laut- und Formenlehre des neuaramäischen Dialektes von Mīḏin im Ṭūr ᶜAbdīn* (Bamberg: R. Rodenbusch, 1966; 2d ed.; Bamberg: Bamberger Fotodruck, 1970); H. Ritter, *Ṭūrōyo: Die Volkssprache der syrischen Christen des Ṭūr-ᶜAbdīn* (Orient-Institut der DMG, Beirut; 2 vols.; Wiesbaden: F. Steiner, 1967-69). A. Siegel, *Laut - und Formenlehre des neuaramäischen Dialekts des Tûr Abdîn* (Hanover: Lefaire, 1923). On *Urmia:* A. J. MacLean, *A Dictionary of the Dialects of Vernacular Syriac, as Spoken by the Eastern Syrians of Kurdistan, North-West Persia, and the Plain of Moṣul* (Oxford: Clarendon, 1901; reprinted, Amsterdam, 1971); *Grammar of the Dialects of Vernacular Syriac as Spoken by the Eastern Syrians of Kurdistanc, North-West Persia, and the Plain of Mosul— With Notices of the Vernacular of the Jews of Azerbaijan and of Zakhu near Mosul* (Cambridge: University Press, 1895); R. Macuch and E.Panoussi, *Neusyrische Chrestomathie* (Porta linguarum orientalium, ns 13; Wiesbaden: Harrassowitz, 1974); A. Merx, *Neusyrisches Lesebuch: Texte im Dialekte von Urmia* (Breslau/Tübingen, 1873); T. Nöldeke, *Grammatik der neusyrischen Sprache am Urmia-See und in Kurdistan* (Leipzig: T. O. Weigel, 1868); R. Hetzron, "The Morphology of the Verb in Modern Syriac (Christian Colloquial of Urmi)," *JAOS* 89 (1969) 112-27. On *Salamas:* J. Rhétoré, *Grammaire de la langue soureth ou chaldéen vulgaire selon le dialecte de la plaine de Mossoul et des pays adjacents* (Mosul: Dominican Press, 1912); R. Duval, *Les dialectes néo-araméens de Salamas: Textes sur l'état de la Perse et contes populaires publiés avec une traduction française* (Paris, 1883). On *Thumic:* H. Jacobi, *Grammatik des thumischen Neuaramäisch (Nordostsyrien)* (Abhandlungen für die Kunde des Morgenlandes, 40/3; Wiesbaden: DMG [F. Steiner], 1973). On *Zakho:* Y. Sabar, "The Hebrew Elements in the Neo-Aramaic Dialect of Zakho in Kurdistan," *Lĕšonénu* 38 (1974) 206-19; J. B. Segal, "Neo-Aramaic Proverbs of the Jews of Zakho," *JNES* 14 (1955) 251-70. On *Azerbaijan:* I. Garbell, *The Jewish Neo-Aramaic Dialect of Persian Azerbaijan: Linguistic Analysis and Folkloristic Texts* (The Hague: Mouton, 1965); E. Cerulli and F. A. Pennacchietti, *Testi neo-aramaici dell'Iran settentrionale* (Pubblicazioni del seminario di semitistica, ricerche 8; Naples: Istituto orientale di Napoli, 1971).

[42]See O. Schroeder, *Keilschrifttexte aus Assur historischen Inhalts* (Wissenschaftliche Veröffentlichungen der deutschen Orient-Gesellschaft, 37; Berlin/Leipzig: Deutsche Orient-Gesellschaft, 1922) §63. Cf. D. D. Luckenbill, *Ancient Records of Assyria and Babylonia* (Chicago: University of Chicago, 1926), 1. §286–87; J. B. Pritchard, *ANET*, 275. Here they are listed specifically as Arameans; even earlier they were probably included in the *Aḫlame.* See E. Fohrer, "Aramau," *Reallexikon für Assyriologie* 1 (1928) 130-39; R. T. O'Callaghan, *Aram Naharaim: A Contribution to the History of Upper Mesopotamia in the Second Millennium B.C.* (AnOr 26; Rome: Biblical Institute, 1948) 93-118; A. Dupont-Sommer, *Les Araméens* (L'orient ancien illustré; Paris: Maisonneuve, 1949) 15–19.

[43]See W. F. Albright, "Recent Progress in North-Canaanite Research," *BASOR* 70 (1938) 18-24, esp. p. 21.

[44]This is a widely-held opinion about the origin of the alphabet; if it is not correct, its origin would have to be sought in some Semitic people in an area adjacent to Phoenicia (see T. O. Lambdin, "Alphabet," *IDB*, 1. 89; cf. K. Beyer, "Die Problematik der semitischen Konsonantenschrift," *Ruperto-Carola* 42 (1967) 12-17). In any case, the immediate source of the alphabet used by the Arameans was that of the Phoenicians. The Aramean role in the spread of the alphabet may have been as important as that of the Phoenicians, since at the time that it was adopted by the Greeks, it was adopted with signs already being used for vocalic sounds. Indeed, S. Segert ("Altaramäische Schrift und Anfänge des griechischen Alphabets," *Klio* 41 [1963] 38-57) has argued: "Da eine direkte Bezeichnung von Vokalen bei den Phönikern nicht in Gebrauch war, ergibt sich die Schlussfolgerung, dass die Griechen die Vokalbuchstaben und die Buchstaben überhaupt von der Aramäern übernommen haben" (pp. 48-49). The names of most of the letters of the alphabet, however, seem to have been derived from Phoenician (because of their vocalization [e.g., ἰῶτα ‹ *yod*] in Greek form). Whether the Greek names with the ending *-a* (such as *alpha, bēta, delta, zēta, ēta, thēta, iōta, kappa, lambda, sigma*) could be regarded as Aramaized forms of the Phoenician names might be debated. A case might be made out for *alpha, bēta*, and possibly for *kappa* (with the doubled *p*). But here one has to be cautious, because of an inner-Greek development: the adding of an *a*-sound to foreign words taken over that end in a consonant other than *n, r,* and *s.* See E. Schwyzer, *Griechische Grammatik* (Handbuch der Altertumswissenschaft, 2/1/1; 2d ed.; Munich: Beck, 1953), 1. 140. Cf. T. Nöldeke, "Die semitischen Buchstabennamen," *Beiträge zur semitischen Sprachwissenschaft* (Strassburg: Trübner, 1904)

124-36; S. Segert, "Aramäische Studien: IV. Die Rolle der Aramäer bei der Vermittlung des westsemitischen Alphabets an die Griechen," *ArOr* 26 (1958) 572-78. C. H. Gordon ("The Greek Unilinguals from Parisos and Dreros and Their Bearing on Eteocretan and Minoan," *Πεπραγμένα τοῦ γ́ διεθνοῦς* Κ*ρητηλογικοῦ συνεδρίου* [Athens, 1973], 1. 97-103, esp. p. 102) lists the following letters as borrowed from "a people using the Aramaic forms with the postpositive article *ā*": *alpha, bēta, gamma, delta, ēta, zēta, thēta, iōta, kappa, lambda,* the old letter *koppa*, and perhaps *sigma.* Cf. J. Naveh, "Some Semitic Epigraphical Considerations on the Antiquity of the Greek Alphabet," *AJA* 77 (1973) 1-8.

[45]See J. Naveh, *The Development of the Aramaic Script* (n. 18 above). Cf. G. R. Driver, *Semitic Writing from Pictograph to Alphabet* (Schweich Lectures, 1944; London: British Academy, 1948) 119-23; F. M. Cross, Jr., "The Development of the Jewish Scripts," *The Bible and the Ancient Near East: Essays in Honor of William Foxwell Albright* (ed. G. E. Wright; Anchor Books; Garden City: Doubleday, 1965) 170-264; N. Avigad, "The Palaeography of the Dead Sea Scrolls and Related Documents," *Aspects of the Dead Sea Scrolls* (Scripta hiersolymitana, 4; Jerusalem: Magnes, 1958) 56-87.

[46]E.g., the voiced dental sibilant *(z)* was used to write the voiced dental spirant *(ḏ)*; the unvoiced dental sibilant *(š)* was used to write the unvoiced dental spirant *(ṯ)*.

[47]How this sound was originally pronounced in Proto-Semitic is quite debatable. It is usually said to represent *ḍ*, but its Ugaritic counterpart(s) create(s) a problem. It is not easy to say why the Aramaic sound would have been represented in the script by a Phoenician *q*.

[48]See further my commentary on the Sefire Inscriptions (n. 29 above), 149-50; S. Moscati, *An Introduction to the Comparative Grammar of the Semitic Languages: Phonology and Morphology* (Porta linguarum orientalium, ns 6; Wiesbaden: Harrassowitz, 1964) §8.18.

[49]*Early Hebrew Orthography* (n. 10 above).

[50]Cross and Freedman failed to treat certain forms (*mlkh* in Hamath Graffito 1; *šwr*ᵓ in Zakir a 17) and wrongly analyzed other forms (*lḥzy* in Sujin Aa 13 [read now *lḥzyh*, a Pael infinitive, Sf I 13]; *klmh*, Sujin Ab 7 [understand it now as *kl mh*, Sf I A 26]). They were embarrassed by *tgltplysr* (Bar-Rakib 3, 6) for *Tukulti-apilešarra.* But such defects are now seen as minor; some of them indicate the *inceptive* use of vowel letters in a medial position—the adjustment that has to be made to their otherwise acceptable basic thesis.

[51]"Une inscription araméenne inédite de Sfiré," *BMB* 13 (1956, appeared in early 1958) 23-41; "Les inscriptions araméennes de Sfiré (Stèles I et II)," *MPAIBL* 15 (1960, appeared in 1958) 197-351 (+ 29 pls.). For the evidence that bears out the Cross and Freedman thesis, see my commentary on these inscriptions (n. 29 above), 139-49.

[52](Pubblicazioni del seminario di semitistica, Ricerche 5; Naples: Istituto orientale di Napoli, 1969).

[53]"Some Observations on Early Hebrew," *Bib* 53 (1972) 413-20.

[54](Munich: UNI-Druck, 1971). Cf. K. Beyer, *BZ* 18 (1974) 139-40.

[55]"L'aramaico antico" (n. 30 above), 245-47.

[56]Garbini states (p. 247): "Nelle iscrizioni di Suğīn l'enfatico appare generalmente in ה- al maschile e in א- al feminile: ארבה (A b,8), ארקה (A b,9), רחבה (A a,10), שעותה (A b,16)." But every instance cited here is questionable, if not wrong: ארבה almost certainly represents ᵓ*arbêh* (< ᵓ*arbay*; cf. Hebr. ᵓ*arbēh*; Ugar. *irby*; Akkad. *arbū*); ארקה is a suffixal form on a fem. noun, "its land" (= ᵓ*arqah*); שעותה is non-existent; read שעותא (just what one would expect!); and רחבה is undoubtedly a proper name, about which little can be said. Similarly, מלכה in Hamath Graffito 1 is not certainly the emphatic state in ה, but the suffixal form, "his king" *(malkēh)*.

[57]"Studi aramaici—1-2," *AION* 29 (1969) 1-15, esp. pp. 8-15.

[58]See *PPG*^{2} §67; Z. S. Harris, *A Grammar of the Phoenician Language* (AOS 8; New Haven: American Oriental Society, 1936) 11-19.

[59]See n. 51 above. Cf. F. Rosenthal, *Die aramaistische Forschung* (n. 2 above), 22.

[60]"A Chapter on Old West Semitic Orthography," *The Joshua Bloch Memorial Volume: Studies in Booklore and History* (eds. A. Berger et al.; New York: New York Public Library, 1960) 82-91.

[61]"Aramäische Studien: III. Zum Problem der altaramäischen Dialekte," *ArOr* 26 (1958) 561-72. See also his *Altaramäische Grammatik* (p. 23 above, n. 53), §2.4.1-7 (pp. 62-65), which does not really cope with the problem.

[62]M. Tsevat ("A Chapter," 85) claims that לא "occurs in the Sujin Stele (Ab 9)," but his claim was based on the older publication of Ronzevalle that is now obsolete; cf. Sf I A 28. Moreover, what bearing does its occurrence in the Lachish letters have on this Aramaic problem? E. Y. Kutscher ("Aramaic," *Current Trends* [p. 23 above, n. 39] 373) quotes Tsevat approvingly; but he never checked out the Sefire inscription itself! What he says there contradicts what he says on p. 354 about "the (originally) consonantal character of the [']." The example of *nbʾ*, "Nabu" begs the question; why should it not be *nābūʾ*, like *hʾ = hūʾ* (Sf I B 24) or *hʾ = hīʾ* (Sf I A 37)? In all these cases, the only real explanation is the persistence of the consonantal writing of *aleph* as a consonant. Both of the latter forms are identical with their Phoenician counterparts; see *PPG*² §110.

[63]In a 9th century Cyprus Tomb inscription, לקבר זא (*KAI* §30:2).

[64]In the Yehawmilk inscription 6, 12, 14 (*KAI* §10:6, 12, 14). See further *PPG*² §113, 115.

[65]Could not one also appeal to the historical spelling preserved in Hebrew זאת, where the fem. *-t* has been added to the original form of the demonstrative (possibly after the quiescence of the *aleph*)?

[66]There is, to be sure, evidence of some of the phonetic shifts that characterize the later phases of the language (e.g., *yrt* [Sf I C 24]; possibly *btn* [Sf I A 32]; see further my commentary, p. 150); but this is so sporadic and debatable that it perhaps should not even be considered.

[67]Ibid., 156.

[68]*Early Hebrew Orthography* (n. 10 above), 33 n. 53.

[69]Ibid., 21-34.

[70]Ibid., 64.

[71]See his review of the first edition of my commentary on the *Genesis Apocryphon*, *JSS* 13 (1968) 281-82.

[72]*Altaramäische Grammatik* (n. 16 above), 4-5.

[73]Ibid., 2.

[74]G. Garbini expresses this wonder a little more strongly in his review of Degen's grammar, *AION* ns 20 (1970) 275-77, esp. pp. 275-76.

[75]Degen is not alone in this separation of the Nērab inscriptions from Old Aramaic; cf. J. J. Koopmans, *Aramäische Chrestomathie* (p. 23 above, n. 53), v; F. M. Cross and D. N. Freedman, *Early Hebrew Orthography* (n. 10 above); G. Garbini, "L'aramaico antico" (n. 30 above); J. C. L. Gibson, *Textbook of Syrian Semitic Inscriptions* (p. 24 above, n. 56), 93-98 (he also includes Bar-Rākib 1-3 under "Imperial or Official Aramaic"!). But A. Dupont-Sommer has included the Nērab inscriptions in his treatment of "Ancient Aramaic Monumental Inscriptions" in *An Aramaic Handbook* (ed. F. Rosenthal; Porta linguarum orientalium, ns 10; Wiesbaden: Harrassowitz, 1967), I/1, 1-9; this section precedes that on "Aramaic Texts from Achaemenid Times."

[76]"'Siʾgabbar, Priest of Sahr in Nerab,'" *JAOS* 90 (1970) 270-71. Cf. E. Y. Kutscher, "Aramaic," *Current Trends* (p. 23 above, n. 39), 353.

[77]Approximate dates are the only ones ever given for these inscriptions: "7. Jh. v. Chr." (*KAI*, 3. §274); "probably vii cent. B.C." (G. A. Cooke, *NSI*, 186, 189); "aus dem 7. Jahrh. v. Chr." (J. J. Koopmans, *AC*, 92).

[78]*Aramaic Inscriptions of Sefire*, 140.

[79]C. Brockelmann, "Das Aramäische, einschliesslich des Syrischen," *Handbuch der Orientalistik: III. Semitistik* (Leiden: Brill, 1954) 135-62, esp. p. 136; W. F. Albright, *Syria, the Philistines and Phoenicia* (Cambridge Ancient History, rev. ed., I-II/51; Cambridge: Cambridge University, 1966), 47; F. M. Cross and D. N. Freedman, *Early Hebrew Orthography*, 64; R. Stiehl, "Kanaanäisch und Aramäisch," *Die Araber in der alten Welt: I. Bis zum Beginn der Kaiserzeit* (Berlin: de Gruyter, 1964) 213-36, esp. p. 219 n. 21. I should not go so far as to say with R. A. Bowman that "the so-called 'Old Aramaic' of the region . . . is almost completely

Canaanite rather than Aramaic. . . ." (*JNES* 7 [1948] 71). Bowman includes the Kilamuwa inscription, which is completely Phoenician save for the word בר, "son."

[80]*Altaramäische Grammatik,* 1-3.

[81]"Studi aramaici—1-2," *AION* 29 (1969) 1-15, esp. p. 3.

[82]*Altaramäische Grammatik,* 2-3.

[83]See Aḥiram 2 (*KAI* §1:2); cf. W. F. Albright, "The Phoenician Inscriptions of the Tenth Century B.C. from Byblus," *JAOS* 67 (1947) 153-60, esp. p. 156 n. 24. (R. Degen [*Altaramäische Grammatik,* 3 n. 20, citing J. Friedrich, *PPG* §266] is apparently not convinced of this example.) An example of an imperfect with *waw* occurs in 1QapGen 20:26; but there is here no real consecution, since the form really expresses contemporaneity: "What have you done to me because of Sarai, in telling me . . ." (תאמר); cf. 2:12; 19:19; Dan 4:31.

[84]The intensifying infinitive occurs in Sf II C 8; III 2, 6, 12, 13, 18; I B 30[?] and in Nērab 2:6. It is unknown in Official Aramaic and Middle Aramaic; yet it is frequent in Hebrew, Phoenician (*PPG*² §267), and Ugaritic (*UT* §9.27). It begins to turn up again in Late Aramaic texts (e.g., in Tg. Onqelos, Tg. Neofiti I [Exod 19:13], and in Syriac). G. Dalman (*GJPA*, 280) is almost certainly correct when he says, "ohne Zweifel infolge des Einflusses der hebräischen Vorlage," with reference to the targums. For its use in Syriac, see T. Nöldeke, *Compendious Syriac Grammar* (n. 39 above), §295-96. Its appearance in Syriac is undoubtedly owing to biblical influence (through the Peshitta or other Old Syriac versions); in neither of these instances in Late Aramaic is it possible to establish a connection with the Old Aramaic usage.

[85]E.g., Sf I B 32; III 12, 13; Hadad 10, 23, 13, 14, 34. Cf. Ezra 5:3, 13 (*lbn*ʾ).

[86]See *KAI* §233:8; cf. *AP* 2:3; 5:3, 12; 6:4; 8:3; 9:3; 10:3 and passim.

[87]"New Aramaic Texts," *JAOS* 74 (1954) 233-48; he borrowed the phrase from U. Weinreich (Publications of the Linguistic Circle of New York, 1; New York: International Linguistic Association, 1953). For a related problem involving "Canaanite," see J. C. Greenfield, "Amurrite, Ugaritic and Canaanite," *Proceedings of the International Conference on Semitic Studies, Jerusalem, 1965* (Leiden: Brill, 1969) 1-10. As I am using "Canaanite," I mean it as a tag to bind "Amurrite, Ugaritic and Canaanite into a group" (to paraphrase Greenfield, p. 2).

[88]"Studi aramaici—1-2," *AION* 29 (1969) 5; cf. S. Moscati, "Il semitico di nord-ovest," *Studi orientalistici in onore di Giorgio Levi della Vida* (Roma: Istituto per l'Oriente, 1956), 2. 202-21; "Sulla posizione linguistica del semitico nord-occidentale," *RSO* 31 (1956) 229-34.

[89]*AION* 29 (1969) 5.

[90]Ibid., 7.

[91]As is proposed by many writers; see, e.g., A. F. Johns, *A Short Grammar of Biblical Aramaic* (n. 5 above), 1.

[92]See H. B. Huffmon, *Amorite Personal Names in the Mari Texts: A Structural and Lexical Study* (Baltimore: Johns Hopkins, 1965). Cf. I. J. Gelb, "La lingua degli Amoriti," *Atti dell'Accademia Nazionale dei Lincei,* Rendiconti, 8/13 (1958) 143-64; A. Caquot, "Remarques sur la langue et le panthéon des Amorites de Mari," *Les annales archéologiques de Syrie* 1 (1951) 206-25. See further the bibliography presented by G. Garbini, "Semitico nord-occidentale e aramaico," *Linguistica presente e futuro* (ed. G. Levi della Vida; Studi semitici, 4; Roma: Centro di studi semitici, 1961) 59-90, esp. pp. 64-65 n. 15.

[93]"L'aramaico antico" (see n. 30 above), 241.

[94]*AION* 29 (1969) 4. A language can have its own definite character or physiognomy and still be under the influence of another; compare the Gallicisms in English.

[95]The Old Aramaic ending *-wh* is puzzling and is obviously related to the later ending *-why* of Official Aramaic (as well as to *-ôhī* of Biblical Aramaic and *-awhī* [better, *-aw(hy)*] of Syriac). E. Y. Kutscher ("Aramaic," *Current Trends,* 350) took an easy way out, when he wrote: "The defective spelling of the personal suffix in the 3rd person masculine singular of a masculine plural noun, e.g., *mlkwh* 'his kings', which in Elephantine *(E)* is generally spelt *mlkwhy* (=[*mal*k*o:hi:] in Biblical Aramaic [BA]), does not indicate that there was no vowel after the [h]. The suffix had a final vowel in Proto-Semitic (PS). Of course, it might have disappeared in *OA*. But then, how are we to account for its (re)appearance, e.g., in *OfA* (*E* and *BA*)?" Kutscher was obviously striving

for exactness, and his last two sentences are a commentary on the preceding ones. It is clear that Old Aramaic מלכוה and Official Aramaic מלכוהי must be traced back to an original form like **malkay-hū*; with the loss of intervocalic *he*, the form became **malkayū*, and eventually **malkaw*. Since this was soon to be contracted to *malkô*, the real sign of the 3d sg. masc. suffix was obscured and the suffix *-hū* was again, secondarily, added. But how was it added? The Old Aramaic evidence would suggest that consonantal *he* was added—perhaps on an analogy with ה of the singular מלכה, "his king." In Official Aramaic the added *-hū* became הי- (= *hī*, generally regarded as a dissimilation of *-hū*, perhaps on the analogy of such verbal forms as נקטלנהי [*A* 61]). In any case, to invoke a "defective spelling" in Old Aramaic for this sole case of final *ī* is problematic, in view of all the other evidence pointing to the full writing of final *ī* with *yodh*. See my commentary on the Sefire Inscriptions, p. 142. Note too that the ending וה- is occasionally found in Official Aramaic texts (e.g., *BMAP* 3:4, where Kraeling's note suggests reading אגרוה[י], following Rosenthal and Albright). It may be a scribal error; but it may also be a case of an archaizing historical spelling. Cf. *BMAP* 6:9, הח[ו]מוה. See further Cross and Freedman's attempt to vocalize the Old Aramaic form, *Early Hebrew Orthography* (n. 10 above), 68-69.

96See D. O. Edzard, "Mari und Aramäer," *ZA* 56 (1964) 142-49.

97"Standard Literary Aramaic" (n. 34 above); "Dialect Traits in Early Aramaic" (n. 30 above).

98"Aramaic," *Current Trends* (see p. 23 above, n. 39), 361–66.

99Ibid.

100*Studies in the Aramaic Legal Papyri from Elephantine* (Studia et documenta ad iura orientis antiqui pertinentia, 8; Leiden: Brill, 1969).

101"Aramaic," *Current Trends*, 363.

102Ibid., 366.

103In his review of F. Rosenthal, *Die aramaistische Forschung* (1939), *JAOS* 62 (1942) 232.

104See p. 61 above.

105See n. 71 above.

106See *MPAT*.

107"Der Reichsaramäische Einschlag in der ältesten syrischen Literatur," *ZDMG* 116 (1966) 242-54.

108For a handy collection of these texts, see H. J. W. Drijvers, *Old Syriac* (*Edessean* [sic]) *Inscriptions, Edited with an Introduction, Indices and a Glossary* (SSS 3; Leiden: Brill, 1972). See further his articles, "Syrische Inscripties uit de eerste drie eeuwen A.D.," *Phoenix* 15 (1969) 197-205; "Some New Syriac Inscriptions and Archaeological Finds from Edessa and Sumatar Harabesi," *BSOAS* 36 (1973) 1-14 (+ pls. I-XII). Cf. E. Jenni, "Die altsyrischen Inschriften, 1.-3. Jahrhundert nach Christus," *TZ* 21 (1965) 371-85; F. Vattioni, "Appunti sulle iscrizioni siriache antiche," *Augustinianum* 11 (1971) 435-46; 13 (1973) 131-40; "Le iscrizioni siriache antiche," ibid., 279-338; J. B. Segal, *Edessa: 'The Blessed City'* (Oxford: Clarendon, 1970).

109*RB* 74 (1967) 102; see further his review of E. Vogt, *Lexicon linguae aramaicae Veteris Testamenti, RB* 79 (1972) 614-17, esp. p. 617; his review of J. T. Milik, *The Books of Enoch, RB* 83 (1976) 605-18, esp. p. 614. This opinion of Grelot has been blithely cited, and without any scrutiny, by A. Paul, "Bulletin de littérature intertestamentaire," *RSR* 60 (1972) 429-58, esp. p. 440. One would not expect much difference between Official Aramaic and such Qumran texts as 1QapGen, 4QprNab, 4QEnoch, 4QTLevi. As for the differences between this Aramaic of Qumran and that of Daniel, one has only to read E. Y. Kutscher, "The Language of the Genesis Apocryphon" (n. 4 above); cf. H. H. Rowley, "Notes on the Aramaic of the Genesis Apocryphon," *Hebrew and Semitic Studies Presented to Godfrey Rolles Driver* (ed. D. Winton Thomas and W. D. McHardy; Oxford: Clarendon, 1963) 116-29. Grelot (*RQ* 8 [1972-76] 114) bemoans the fact that we do not have a text of Daniel as old as that of 11QtgJob with which to compare the orthography of the two. Perhaps he has forgotten about the Daniel fragments in 1Q*71-72* (DJD, 1. 150-52); see J. C. Trever, "Completion of the Publication of Some Fragments from Qumran Cave I," *RQ* 5 (1964-66) 323-44; "1QDan[a], the Latest of the Qumran Manuscripts," *RQ* 7 (1969-71) 277-86.

[110] *El Targum: Introducción a las traducciones aramaicas de la Biblia* (Barcelona: Consejo superior de investigaciones científicas, 1972) 41-42.

[111] Ibid., 42.

[112] *Neophyti 1: Targum palestinense, MS de la Biblioteca Vaticana: Tomo I, Génesis: Edición príncipe, introducción general y versión castellana* (Madrid / Barcelona: Consejo superior de investigaciones científicas, 1968) 95* (". . . el Neofiti, en su conjunto partinece ya al la época neotestamentaria"); M. Black, *An Aramaic Approach* (p. 21 above, n. 13), 22 ("The language of the Palestinian Pentateuch Targum is, on the other hand, first-century Aramaic.").

[113] *CBQ* 32 (1970) 107-12.

[114] *RevScRel* 47 (1973) 196-231, esp. pp. 179-81; reprinted in *Exégèse biblique et judaïque* (ed. J.-E. Ménard; Strasbourg: Faculté de théologie catholique, 1973 [distributed by E. J. Brill, Leiden]) 15-77, esp. pp. 26-27. The substance of it has been repeated in the introduction to *Neophyti 1, Targum palestinense, MS de la Biblioteca Vaticana: Tomo IV, Números, Edición príncipe, introducción y versión castellana* (Madrid: Consejo superior de investigaciones científicas, 1974) 80*-86*.

[115] See p. 39 above; also *MPAT*, §1-149.

[116] See p. 168 below.

[117] See p. 37 above.

[118] See *MPAT*, App., §A1-A56.

[119] See E. Schwyzer, *Griechische Grammatik* (n. 44 above), 1. 159; T. Nöldeke, *Compendious Syriac Grammar* (n. 39 above), xxxii-xxxiii. Cf. A. Schall, *Studien über griechische Fremdwörter im Syrischen* (Darmstadt: Wissenschaftliche Buchgesellschaft, 1960).

[120] See E. Y. Kutscher, "Aramaic," *Encyclopaedia judaica* (Jerusalem: Keter; New York: Macmillan, 1971), 3. 259-87, esp. col. 271; J. C. Greenfield, Review of M. Black, *Aramaic Approach, JNES* 31 (1972) 58-61.

[121] Indeed, as M. D. Herr notes (*Encyclopaedia judaica* [Jerusalem: Keter; New York: Macmillan, 1971], 7. 399): ". . . *Genesis Rabbah* mentions the last group of Palestinian amoraim who flourished in the second half of the fourth century C.E. . . ." But he thinks that some of the material may have "originated close to the period of the Mishnah" (col. 400). The question, of course, is how much of it originated then or can be traced back to this period.

Chapter 4

The Contribution of Qumran Aramaic to the Study of the New Testament*

Our knowledge of the corpus of extra-biblical and extra-rabbinical Aramaic texts has largely been the acquisition of the last seventy-five to a hundred years. Through numerous discoveries in Egypt, Arabia, Palestine, Syria, Asia Minor, Armenia, Mesopotamia, Persia and the Indus Valley we have come to know what various phases of Aramaic were like from the tenth century B.C. until roughly the eighth century A.D.[1] This knowledge has enabled us to situate the biblical Aramaic of Ezra and Daniel in a matrix similar to that provided by extra-biblical Hebrew texts for biblical Hebrew. And the same can be said for the long-known rabbinical Aramaic texts, the classic targumim and midrashim, not to mention Syriac and related forms of Aramaic.[2] The discoveries of the last two decades, however, have revealed a corpus of Palestinian Aramaic texts, which for all sorts of reasons attract the attention of the biblical commentator.[3] A sizeable bulk of these Palestinian Aramaic texts comes from the first century B.C. or A.D., and a portion of them date from the beginning of the second century A.D. (roughly up to the time of the Second Palestinian Revolt against Rome under Simon ben Kosiba). Many of these texts come from the Qumran caves, and their titles are generally familiar—at least those that are already published. Some of the Qumran Aramaic texts have been studied in great detail, others less so. In some of the detailed studies many scattered items pertinent to the study of the NT have been singled out and commented on; some others are still to be revealed. To describe the contribution of Qumran Aramaic texts to the study of the NT I should like to bring together the more important items in this paper.

But before I turn to the topic proper, I should propose a few preliminary remarks about the general question of the study of Aramaic and the NT. Anyone who begins to be interested in this subject soon realizes in what a morass one finds oneself, for there are all sorts of things that are understood today when one hears the generic expression, "Aramaic and the NT." In a paper on methodology recently delivered at the *Journées Bibliques* of Louvain,[4] I sought to distinguish various aspects of the question—and I readily admit that I am not yet sure that I have them all rightly sorted out. At the moment eight aspects seem to be distinguishable: (1) Aramaic as a language of Jesus, or more broadly, as a language of first-century Palestine; (2) Aramaic words, names and phrases preserved as such in the writings of the NT, Josephus and the early rabbinic tradition (e.g. in the Mishnah, which is otherwise composed in Hebrew); (3) Aramaisms in NT Greek, usually of a lexical or syntactic nature—this is the question of Aramaic interference proper; (4) the problem of mistranslations from an alleged Aramaic substratum; (5) Aramaic literary forms in prose and poetry; (6) Aramaic and variant readings in the NT textual tradition; (7) Jewish literary traditions found in the NT and in known Aramaic literature; (8) Aramaic epistolography. A moment's reflection on these eight aspects of the Aramaic problem suffices to reveal their diversity and the need for a rigorous methodology in approaching them. In each instance one must be, moreover, rigorous in not taking refuge in evidence that is merely "Semitic," for that cannot be invoked as evidence for Aramaic without further ado. Furthermore, the discussion of the entire matter must initially and seriously reckon with all the firm data and admitted advances in the source-critical, form-critical, and redaction-critical study of the Greek NT; it cannot, as it were, go its own way in neglect of these forms of NT study. And consequently, because of such work no conclusion can be drawn from the study of the Aramaic substratum about the authenticity of the sayings of Jesus, John the Baptist, Peter, or any other Gospel figure. If the sayings of such figures prove to be authentic, that will be for reasons other than their mere Aramaic substratum. The discussion of details under each of these aspects has to be left for another occasion; but the mere listing of them here serves to stress the complexity of the problem of Aramaic and the NT.

My purpose now is rather to present some of the more important data which have emerged from Qumran Aramaic texts bearing on the study of the NT. The data cut across the aspects listed above; at a later date it may be possible to sort them out according to such categories, but at the moment my intention is different. I should like to cull from this body of Palestinian Aramaic material some of the things that bear on the study of the NT, even if they do cut across the various aspects just mentioned. The reason is that this form of Palestinian Aramaic—as well as that from other contemporary Palestinian sources—should be recognized for what it is: privileged data that take precedence over the material derived from the classic targumim and midrashim (the dates of which are far from certain and the language of which is suggestive of several centuries later than the NT writings themselves).[5]

What is meant by Qumran Aramaic can be seen from the list of texts provided in chart II—some of which are familiar as already published texts, others are only known to exist and as yet await publication.[6] These works, composed in Palestinian Aramaic, range in date from at least 150 B.C. to A.D. 70.[7] They are known to have been used by the Essene community of Qumran, a community that is often regarded as an esoteric sect in Palestinian Judaism.[8] At least two of the larger Aramaic works in the list, the *Genesis Apocryphon* of Cave I and the targum of Job of Cave XI,[9] display nothing that is clearly an Essene tenet or theologoumenon.[10] Because this is so, the question has been raised whether such texts might have been composed in Aramaic outside the community itself and might have merely been introduced into it for reading and study.[11] If this were so, then the language we find in them might represent a type of Aramaic that was spoken on a wider scale than in the small Essene community at Qumran, where post-biblical Hebrew was used for most of the sectarian writings. At the moment it is not easy to resolve this question with certainty, but J. T. Milik has recently published some fragments of Qumran Cave IV about the Visions of ᶜAmram,[12] in which one finds many of the features of Qumran dualism that have so far been known only from the Hebrew texts of the Manual of Discipline, the War Scroll, etc. Now, however, such expressions as "sons of light" or the the contrast of "light" and "darkness" have turned up in Aramaic, and they suggest that the language was used for active creative writing within the community itself.[13] It gives evidence of an active literary production in Aramaic at a time when it was hitherto unsuspected.[14]

My discussion of the contribution of Qumran Aramaic texts to the study of the NT will highlight what I consider important features of them; it obviously makes no pretence about exhausting the details. The discussion will fall into three sections: (I) lexical matters that supply a first-century Palestinian background to certain NT problems; (II) Jewish Palestinian practices or beliefs that emerge in these texts; and (III) literary parallels that have become known through them.

I. *Lexical Matters Supplying a First-Century Palestinian Background to Certain New Testament Problems*

We shall begin with the Qumran Aramaic material that bears on certain titles of Jesus used in the Greek NT: (ὁ) *κύριος*, *υἱὸς θεοῦ*, *ὁ λόγος*, and (ὁ) *υἱὸς* (*τοῦ*) *ἀνθρώπου*. It is obvious that my remarks will bear largely on the philological aspects of the use of such titles, and what I have to say about the Qumran data and their bearing on the use must presuppose some knowledge of the debates surrounding the titles. It is impossible to recapitulate them all here or to exploit all the aspects of the new material. I shall, therefore, limit myself to essentials.

There has recently come to light the absolute use of מָרֵא, "Lord," as a title for God in the Qumran targum of Job, and no one will fail to realize the pertinence of this evidence to the long-standing debate about the origin of the absolute use of (ὁ) *κύριος* for Jesus in the NT.

At least since the time of G. Dalman it has been repeated that "to speak of 'the Lord' with no suffix is contrary to Palestinian usage."[15] Dalman himself sought the origin of the Greek title for Jesus in Aramaic forms such as *mārī* or *māran*, which he said was the form of address for a teacher or a rabbi.[16] W. Bousset, who rejected this origin of "the specifically religious significance of *κύριος*," repeated that "in Aramaic usage the simple Mara (מרא) without a suffix is quite unusual, and only the form Mari or Maran (my lord, our lord) is found."[17] R. Bultmann proposed it again in his own way: "Judaism, at any rate, never entitled the Messiah 'Lord.' At the very outset the unmodified expression 'the Lord' is unthinkable in Jewish usage. 'Lord' used of God is always given some modifier; we read: 'the Lord of heaven and earth,' 'our Lord' and similar expressions."[18] Both Bousset and Bultmann championed the hellenistic origin of the NT title *κύριος*, regarding it as derived from the use of *κύριος* for earthly rulers or for gods in various hellenistic mystery cults. But scholars such as W. Foerster,[19] O. Cullmann,[20] E. Schweizer[21] and F. Hahn[22] in various ways argued to explain the Greek title as rooted in Palestinian tradition.

Over a decade ago, S. Schulz discussed the Aramaic data that bore on the problem, amassing evidence from the fifth-century Elephantine material onward.[23] He brought forward the Aramaic evidence for the title "Lord" in a construct-chain: e.g., ליהו מרא שמיא, "to Yahu, the Lord of Heaven" (*AP* 30:15); מרא מלכין, "Lord of kings" (Dan 2:47); מרא שמיא, "Lord of heaven" (Dan 5:23);[23a] also for the suffixal form used of God in a form of address: e.g., מרי, "my Lord" (1QapGen 20:12, 14, 15; 22:32).[24] Schulz saw in the use of this title by the Aramaic-speaking Christian community an affirmation of the *königliche Richterautorität* attributed to Jesus as the enthroned Son of Man who was awaited, and not an affirmation of divinity as in the hellenistic Kyrios-Homologie.[25] And this he sought to establish even though the Aramaic evidence that he adduced did not point incontrovertibly to the absolute usage that the Greek (*ὁ*) *κύριος* suggests.[26]

Against the background of such discussions—and I am aware that I have not done justice to the whole background—we should now consider the new Aramaic evidence from the targum of Job of Qumran Cave XI. But before we look at the Aramaic text itself, a comment is necessary about the various names for God in the Hebrew text of Job. In the prologue to the book, in Job's answer to God (42:1-6), and in the epilogue one finds the names of God as יהוה and אלהים; but in the long section of the book known as the dialogue—the debates of Job with his friends, and the speeches of God—the divine names are שדי, אלהים, אלוה, אל,[27] and the name יהוה scarcely appears. Now in the Qumran targum of Job the tetragrammaton in the Hebrew text of Job's answer to God and in the epilogue is translated by אלהא (11QtgJob 37:3 [= Hebr. 42:1]; 38:2bis [= Hebr. 42:9], 3 [Hebr. 42:10], 7 [= Hebr. 42:11]). But in the dialogue, where the tetragrammaton does not normally occur in the Hebrew text, the name שדי is twice rendered by מרא in the absolute state, in one case being partially restored (11QtgJob 24:[5], 7 [= Hebr. 34:10, 12]); it has also been plausibly restored in 26:8 (= Hebr. 35:13). In one instance it significantly stands in parallelism to אלהא.

The Hebrew text of Job 34:12 is part of Elihu's second poetic discourse, in which the just ways of God are extolled. It reads:

Of a truth, God will not act wickedly,	אף אמנם אל לא ירשיע
and the Almighty will not distort justice.	ושדי לא יעות משפט

The Qumran targum (24:6-7), in spite of its fragmentary state, renders this verse thus:

Now will God really do what is deceitful,	הכען צדא אלהא/ישקר
and will the Lord [distort justice]?[28]	ומרא [יעות דינא]

Despite the fact that the name מרא occurs in a broken text here, the parallelism with אלהא assures it of its function in the verse as the name for God. Thus in this Palestinian Jewish document we have an instance of the missing link in the development from the construct and suffixal forms of מרא to the absolute usage of *κύριος* in the NT as a title for both Yahweh and Jesus. It is hard to say how often מרא was used in the whole targum, since only about fifteen percent of the Book of Job is preserved in it. In any case, it is a factor that has to be considered in future discussions of the NT title *κύριος*. Moreover, the parallelism with אלהא would seem to indicate that the meaning of the title is not to be restricted to a judicial, kingly authority, but that it is also suggestive of divine status.

Two further comments on the title מָרֵא must be made before we move on to others. The first is that in none of the Palestinian Aramaic material from the first centuries B.C. or A.D. does the absolute form מָר (*mār*) ever occur. Consequently, the fashion of speaking of a *mār*-christology is clearly dependent on obsolete studies and should be abandoned. To justify this, I shall have to explain the formation of the word and beg the reader's indulgence. Whether the Aramaic word for "lord" is ultimately derived from a *lamedh yodh* or a *lamedh aleph* root can be debated, for, as is well known, these classes of verbs fell together in Aramaic.[29] The absolute state of the word may be the **qāṭal* adjective, **māray*, which became **mārê* (written with a final *aleph* [as in 11QtgJob 24:7] or with a final *he* [as in 1QapGen 20:13, 15] as *matres lectionis*). The suffixal forms, such as מָרְאִי (*mārʾī* ‹ **mārĕʾī* [or **mārĕyī*]) or מָרְאַן (*mārʾan* ‹ *mārĕʾan*), are regularly attested from the eighth century B.C. on, and usually have the *aleph* written.[30] The *aleph*, following a shewa and followed by a full vowel, quiesced in time and produced the form מָרִי, such as we find in the *Genesis Apocryphon*, used not only of men (2:8, 13; 20:25), but also of God (20:12, 14, 15; 22:32), sometimes even in a context of prayer. The forms מָר or מָרָא represent a still later formation, when the original formation was lost sight of, and by the process of back-formation מר (*mār*) was produced from מרי (*mārī*), and the emphatic state was formed accordingly by the addition of final *-ā* (מרא, written with *aleph* as the *mater lectionis*).[31] The forms מָר and מָרָא are well known in Syriac and Palestinian Jewish

Aramaic of later centuries; but they are unattested in first-century Palestinian Aramaic.[32]

Secondly, the absolute usage of מרא may bear on the interpretation of Ps 110:1, as it is used in Mark 12:36 (Matt 22:44; Luke 20:42). The play on *κύριος* in "The Lord said to my lord," is not found in the Hebrew original, נאם יהוה לאדני שב לימני. But it comes across perfectly in the Greek of both the so-called LXX and the NT: Εἶπεν Κύριος τῷ κυρίῳ μου. Leaving aside the question whether the Old Greek translation of the Psalter had already translated the tetragrammaton by *κύριος*,[33] the question is raised about the substitution of other names for it at this period in Palestine. F. Hahn has said, "We should . . . have to assume with Dalman that in Ps 110:1 just as יהוה had been replaced by אֲדֹנָי so אֲדֹנִי had been replaced by מָרִי, but this is an extremely problematic thesis."[34] It has been debated whether the substitution of אדני for יהוה in the reading of Hebrew texts in the synagogues had taken place in pre-Christian times—but there are good reasons for maintaining that it had.[35] Yet the question still remains about the role that the word מרא might have played in an Aramaic form of this verse of Psalm 110. Can one rule out the possibility that the pun in the Greek reflects an Aramaic form such as אֲמַר מָרֵא לְמָרְאִי תִּב לִימִּינִי, "the Lord said to my lord, Sit at my right hand?"[36] I am not so naïve as to wish to conclude from such a possible reconstruction to the authenticity of either the saying or the debate; but others have argued for the authenticity of the saying on other grounds.[37] The consideration that I have been proposing here simply makes arguments of that sort more plausible.

I am aware that I have not produced evidence for מרא as the translation of יהוה with the result that the Aramaic material being discussed is not parallel to the Old Greek translation (in certain manuscripts at least), *κύριος* for יהוה. 11QtgJob has translated שדי by מרא; and that is not exactly the same thing. My point is rather that the title, "the Lord," for God was *not* "unthinkable in Jewish usage" (Bultmann). Once that point is made, we can proceed. For in the Old Greek translations of the Book of Daniel (2:47) מרא is rendered by *κύριος*: מרא מלכין becomes *κύριος τῶν βασιλέων* in both Theodotion and the so-called LXX. Consequently, though one may wonder about the attempted retranslation of Ps 110:1 into Aramaic from the Greek of Mark, the Septuagintal use of *κύριος* as a translation for Aramaic מרא may have to be considered in the future. Admittedly, the evidence from Daniel is not that of the 'absolute usage' of which we spoke earlier; but the evidence, such as it is, cannot be lightly dismissed.[38]

Another Qumran Aramaic text that bears on the titles of Jesus in the NT is a Pseudo-Danielic text from Qumran Cave IV (4QpsDan A^a [=4Q*246*]), in which the title "Son of God" turns up for the first time in a Qumran text. Acquired from Kando, the quondam Syrian cobbler of Bethlehem, on 9 July 1958, it has been in the care of J. T. Milik since that time. Cryptic references have been made to it in a number of writings from time to time,[39] and at length Milik made it public in a lecture at Harvard University in December 1972, at which he passed out a tentative English translation of the text and exposed the Aramaic text.[40] A full discussion of the text is impossible here and must await Milik's own publication of it. But what is known of it can be mentioned here, since it pertains to the topic of this paper.

What is preserved in this document is a two-columned fragment of nine lines, in which the first third of the lines of col. 1 is unfortunately missing (the text having been torn vertically). But it is a striking text, not only because it contains the titles, "Son of God" and "Son of the Most High" but because it has phrases parallel to Luke 1:32 and 35. These are attributed to someone in the text, but because of the torn condition of the fragment the subject of attribution is not clear. And herein the great debate will ensue. In any case, Milik dates the text on palaeographic grounds to the last third of the first century B.C., and in this lies the extreme importance of this text for our purposes.

Before presenting that part of the text which is pertinent, I should like to cull from it the firm data on which the restoration of the missing parts of the lines must depend. The language of the text makes it clear that it is apocalyptic in character. It speaks of distress that will come upon the earth, of the rule of enemies which will be short-lived, and lasting only "until there arises the people of God." But there are also references to a "king of Assyria" and to "Egypt," and one is consequently tempted to see in them allusions to historical figures or places. But are they?

The text begins with a fragmentary narrative sentence: When something happened, someone fell before the throne. The fallen person seems to address the enthroned person, a king, using the second singular independent personal pronoun and pronominal suffixes (-*k*). The enthroned king seems to be described as shaken by the evils that are to come (described in lines 4-6 of col. 1); among them are references to "the king of Assyria" and to "Egypt." This description could continue on to line 7 ("[ ] will be great upon the earth"); but line 7 could also be the beginning of a change that is promised to the enthroned king: "he/it will be great," will be served by all, will be given lofty titles (lines 8-9, and col. 2, line 1). In col. 2, which is completely preserved, the end of line 1 describes the short-lived duration of the enemy's rule (with plural suffix and third plural verbs). Their reign will continue (only) "until there arises the people of God" (line 4). Its/his rule is then extolled: respite from war, everlasting rule, paths of truth and peace with all cities in submission. For the Great God is/has been with it/him, and He will now subject all enemies to it/him.

The problem in interpreting the text is threefold. (*a*) Are the references to the "king of Assyria," to "Egypt," and the plurals being used as allusions to historical figures and situations, or are they of the sort that one finds in col. 1 of the War Scroll (1:2-4)? (*b*) If they are to be taken in an apocalyptic sense rather than a historical sense, to whom do they refer? (*c*) To whom does the third singular masculine refer? Is it "the people of God" (2:4)? Is it an individual person? Or is it a person representing a collectivity (in the manner of the "one like a son of man" in Dan 7:13 (representing the "holy ones of the Most High" in Dan 7:18)?

One further thing should be noted: the speech addressed to the king seems to be largely made up of compound sentences (two short paratactic clauses are connected by the copula *w*- and at times they betray some rhythm—a feature that has to be respected in the restoration of the lacunae of col. 1).

Milik has interpreted the text in a historical sense, identifying the subject of attribution as Alexander Balas, one of the Seleucid rulers of Syria and Palestine (150-145 B.C.), the son of Antiochus IV Epiphanes, successor to Demetrius I Soter, and the one who bestowed the high priesthood on Jonathan (Josephus, *Ant.* 13.1.1-2, §35-45). He explains the titles "Son of God" and "Son of the Most High" as applicable to Alexander Balas, because his coins identify him as *θεοπάτωρ* or *Deo patre natus*; and as an Alexander, he is "named" by the name of the great king (Alexander the Great). But to do this, he has to restore the last line of col. 1 in a most crucial way: וכלא ישמשון / [לה חלפת מלכא ר]בא יתקרא ובשמה יתכנה, ". . . and all of them will serve [him. Successor of the G]reat [King] he will be called and with his name will he name himself." Milik introduces thus the notion of the *Διάδοχοι* and the "Great King."[41]

The text will long be debated because of its fragmentary nature. Because it is broken in the most crucial spot, it is obviously open to another interpretation—at least one other. I prefer to see it throughout as properly apocalyptic. This would suggest that the enthroned king who is addressed in his worries is someone on the Jewish side rather than on the Seleucid side. Since אל רבא, "the Great God," is explicitly mentioned in 2:7, it is not impossible that that expression should be restored in 1:9, and that the subject of the attribution is a "son" or a descendant of the enthroned king who will be supported by the "Great God." In other words, I should prefer to substitute for Milik's "successor" a word for "son." For the crucial lines 7-9 of col. 1 and the beginning of col. 2, I should read:[42]

7 [ו]רב להוה על ארעא
8 [ברך מלכא כלא שלם י]עבדון וכלא ישמשון
9 [לה והוא בר אל ר]בא יתקרא ובשמה יתכנה

1 ברה די אל יתאמר ובר עליון יקרונה כזיקיא
2 די חזותא כן מלכותהן תהוה שני[ן] ימלכון על
3 ארעא וכלא ידשון עם לעם ידוש ומדינה למד[ינ]ה
4 *vacat* עד יקום עם אל וכלא ינוח מן חרב

[But your son] [7]shall be great upon the earth, [8][O King! All (men) shall] make [peace], and all shall serve [9][him. He shall be called the son of] the [G]reat [God], and by his name shall he be named. (Col. 2) [1]He shall be hailed (as) the Son of God, and they shall call him Son of the Most High. As comets (flash) [2]to the sight, so shall be their kingdom. (For some) year[s] they shall rule upon [3]the earth and shall trample everything (under foot); people shall trample upon people, city upon ci[t]y, [4](*vacat*) until there arises the people of God, and everyone rests from the sword.

No matter what interpretation of this text will eventually prove to be acceptable, there is no doubt that the Aramaic titles, בְּרֵה דִי אֵל and בַּר עֶלְיוֹן, as applied to some human being in the apocalyptic setting of this Palestinian text of the last third of the first century B.C., will have to be taken into account for any future discussions of the title used of Jesus in the NT.

At this point I should simply point out four things to be considered. (*a*) These titles are not applied to anyone who is called a messiah or anointed one. If my apocalyptic interpretation proves to be right, then they would be applied to the son of some enthroned king, possibly an heir to the throne of David. What this would mean in the context of Hasmonean rule would have to be further investigated. (*b*) In the first title, ברה די אל, one should note the form of the divine name; it is אל, and not the usual Aramaic form, אלה or אלהא. Though the compound אל עליון turns up in the *Genesis Apocryphon* (12:17; 20:12, 16; 21:2, 20; 22:15, 16 bis, 21), the form אל has not, to my knowledge, been attested in Aramaic of this period heretofore. Even though we still do not have the suffixal form of it (אלי) such as the Greek of Matt 27:46 would call for (ἠλὶ ἠλὶ λεμὰ σαβαχθάνι), this form of the divine name should be recalled in discussions that bear on that verse (it has often been maintained that ἠλί is Hebraic). (*c*) The parallelism of a number of phrases in this text with Luke 1 is tantalizing. Compare:

οὗτος ἔσται μέγας (1:32)	[ו]רב להוה על ארעא (1:7)
υἱὸς ὑψίστου κληθήσεται (1:32)	ובר עליון יקרונה (2:1)
κληθήσεται υἱὸς θεοῦ (1:35)	ברה די אל יתאמר (2:1)
βασιλεύσει . . . εἰς τοὺς αἰῶνας (1:33)	מלכותה מלכות עלם (2:5)
ἐπελεύσεται ἐπὶ σέ (1:35)	[ע]לוהי שרת (1:1)[43]

(*d*) Since this is not the first time that an Aramaic parallel to an expression in the Lucan infancy narrative has turned up in Qumran literature, it raises a further question about the long-standing debate concerning the sources used by Luke in that part of the Third Gospel.[44] Did he compose the infancy narrative in dependence on some Hebrew source, or are the Semitisms in the text merely owing to Luke's imitation of Septuagintal style? In 1957, while working in the scrollery of the Palestine Archaeological Museum, I discovered a phrase in a fragmentary text of Starcky's lot which is related to Luke 2:14, *ἐν ἀνθρώποις εὐδοκίας*, "men of (his) good pleasure": שביעי באנוש רעות[ה וי]קרה "(he [probably Aaron] will be) seventh among men of [his] good will and his [hon]our."[45] In this case the phrase is attested in both

Hebrew and Aramaic.[46] Unfortunately, neither the Aramaic form in that instance nor the new Aramaic parallels in the text just discussed are of a nature to solve the question of Lucan sources in the infancy narrative one way or the other.

Still another title used of Jesus in the Greek NT on which the Qumran Aramaic texts have shed some light is that of מאמר for ὁ Λόγος. As is well known, מאמרא is often used in targumic texts either as a substitute for some anthropomorphism of the Hebrew Scriptures or as an addition to the text when the Hebrew original says that God did, said, commanded, or revealed something. Especially in the latter sense it expresses a certain mediation between Yahweh and the effects of his creative, sustaining or revealing activity and has been regarded as a sort of buffer for his transcendent status.[47] And especially in this sense has it been compared with the Johannine use of λόγος in the prologue of the Fourth Gospel.[48] The so-called Second Targum of Job abounds in instances of מימרא as a buffer. E. Dhorme described the use of it there as attempts "to avoid every kind of anthropomorphism or any expression concerning God that is deemed too realistic."[49] But that targum is clearly of a later date.[50] Now that a targum has been published that clearly dates from pre-Christian times, one naturally wonders whether this feature of the classic targumim is to be found in it. Does מאמר occur in the Qumran targum of Job? The word is used there and the usage has to be scrutinized before we can draw a conclusion about it.

מאמר occurs twice in the Qumran targum of Job, in each case in a suffixal form.[51] The first instance is found in 11QtgJob 28:9, a fragmentary line, which merely reads:

[ ]על מאמרה מ[ ], "at his order" (literally, "his word").

It is part of the Aramaic translation of Job 36:32, which in the Hebrew reads: על כפים כסה אור ויצו עליה במפגיע, 'He covers his hands with the lightning and commands it to strike the mark' (*RSV*). The editors of the Qumran targum think that על מאמרה might correspond to Hebrew על כפים and that the targumist might have sought to avoid the anthropomorphism of God's hands, but they are not sure of it. However, it seems obvious that the targum is not a literal translation of the Hebrew at this point. So one can ask whether על מאמרה is not possibly a paraphrase of Hebrew ויצו. The question would still remain whether the targumist sought to avoid the anthropomorphism of God's hands, especially since the targum does not otherwise eliminate anthropomorphisms. For example, the Hebrew of Job 40:9 reads: ואם זרוע כאל לך ובקול כמהו תרעם, "Have you an arm like God, and can you thunder with a voice like his?" (*RSV*). The Qumran targum renders this verse almost literally: או הא דרע כאלה איתי לך או בקל כותה תרעם, "Or do you have an arm like God, or do you thunder with a voice like his?" (11QtgJob 34:4-5).

The second instance of מאמר in the Qumran targum is better preserved. In fact, it is found in a translation of a verse that has always been problematic in Hebrew and that brings new evidence to support a solution that had been proposed earlier.[52] In Job 39:27 which is part of God's final speech to Job, God says:

"Is it at your command that the eagle mounts up,	אם פיך יגביה נשר
and makes his nest on high?" (*RSV*)	וכי ירים קנו

The Aramaic translation in the targum (11QtgJob 33:8-9) renders it thus:

"Or is it at your word that the eagle mounts up,	או על מאמרך יתגב[ה] נש[רא]
and the black eagle makes his nest on high?"	ועוזא ירים קנ[ה]

(In using עוזא, "the black eagle," the Qumran targum lends its support to the view that כי in the Hebrew text represents the name of a bird, or better is a corrupted form of the name of a bird.)[53] What interests us here is the Hebrew phrase על פיך, "at your command" (*RSV*, but literally "at your mouth[ing]"), which is translated as על מאמרך, "at your word." Here, at first sight, it may seem to be an instance of the substitution of מאמר for Hebrew פה, the substitute for an anthropomorphism. But these are God's words addressed to Job, and the instance is scarcely one of anthropomorphism. Beyond these instances, there is not one example of the buffer usage of מאמרא that is found in the Qumran targum. Since it is precisely the buffer usage which suggests the personification of the Word in the later targumic tradition that has been in question in discussions of the Jewish background of the Johannine λόγος, one still has to ask how early that usage really is in rabbinical writings. While the evidence from the Qumran texts in this matter is really negative, there is always the danger of exaggerating; but, on the other hand, it may suggest a difference between earlier and later targumic traditions. It seems to me that Qumran evidence puts the burden of proof on those who would maintain an early date for the buffer or personified usage of מאמרא in the discussion of the Johannine λόγος. In any case, it is noteworthy that in none of the places where the Second Targum of Job uses מימרא does one find it employed in the Qumran targum, when it has the passage preserved.

Lastly a few words about the Qumran Aramaic data bearing on the title ὁ υἱὸς τοῦ ἀνθρώπου as applied to Jesus in the Greek NT. I shall be discussing this matter elsewhere in some detail,[54] and shall only summarize here the bearing of it on the question of titles with which we are dealing. First of all, בר אנש (or in the slightly Hebraized form בר אנוש) is now clearly attested in Qumran Aramaic as a designation for the individual belonging to the collectivity (mankind), meaning generically "a human being" (so in 11QtgJob 26:3), or as a more indefinite designation, meaning "someone" (or with the negative לא, "no one"; so in 1QapGen 21:13). Secondly, there is no instance of its use either (*a*) as a form of address directed to some person, such as the Hebrew בן אדם used of the prophet Ezekiel; (*b*) as a title for an expected or apocalyptic figure, least of all for a messiah or an anointed one; or (*c*) as a surrogate for "I."[55] Thirdly, just as the fashion of speaking of a *mār*-christology is clearly dependent on obsolete philological studies of that title, so too the fashion of speaking about *bar nāš* or *bar nāšā*. The word for "man" is always written at this period with the initial *aleph*, and this should make us wary about citing evidence for the Aramaic background of the title from passages which have only the tell-tale later forms (either without the initial *aleph* or with the *aleph* but also with the fuller orthography of it, ᵓ*y*-, אינש).[56] Finally, if Milik's latest theory about the second part of Ethiopic Enoch, the so-called Similitudes, proves to be acceptable—that that is a Christian substitution for the Book of the Giants, which is attested in Qumran Aramaic texts[57]—then the whole question of the conflated titles in the second part of *1 Enoch,* including the "Son of Man," must be reworked in the discussions of the material regarding the title as used of Jesus.

Such is the evidence from Qumran Aramaic texts that bears on several titles used of Jesus in the Greek NT. Some of the evidence is positive, some of it is negative; but in all instances it makes its own contribution to the modern discussion and study of those titles. The evidence is such that it bears mainly on the philological aspects of the study; but these are basic, and no theological constructs can be proposed that do not at least reckon with this evidence.

II. *Jewish Practices or Beliefs That Have Emerged from Qumran Aramaic Texts*

I should now like to turn to evidence from the Qumran Aramaic texts that is of a different sort and bears on the interpretation of the NT in other ways, and first of all to Jewish practices and beliefs that have come to light in them. The most obvious example is, first of all, the laying-on of hands to exorcize an unclean spirit or to cure an illness. It is found in the *Genesis Apocryphon,* where Abram is begged by the Pharaoh Zoan and his courtier Hirqanos to lay his hands upon the Pharaoh and pray for him that the evil spirit might be exorcized from him and the plagues and afflictions cease. The passage in 1QapGen 20:21, 28-9 has been discussed by others such as D. Flusser and A. Dupont-Sommer.[58] While the prayer that Abram utters is an imitation of Gen 20:1, the cure is accomplished by the laying on of hands, a rite of healing that is not attested among Jews of the OT period and that is not found in rabbinic literature.[59] Consequently, the pertinence of this Aramaic passage for such NT verses as Mark 5:23; 6:5; 7:32; 8:32-35; 16:18, and especially Luke 4:40-41 (where the laying on of hands and the rebuke both occur); Luke 13:13; Acts 9:12, 17-18; 28:8 is especially obvious. In particular, I may cite 1QapGen 20:28-9:

וצלית על [מר]דפא/הו וסמכת ידי על ראי[שה] ואתפלי מנה מכתשא ואתגערת [מנה רוחא] באישתא וחי, "So I prayed for that [per]secutor, and I laid my hands upon his [he]ad. The plague was removed from him and the evil [spirit] was commanded (to depart) [*or*: was exorcized] [from him], and he was cured." Of importance here is the translation of the verbs סמך and גער in the Greek OT by *ἐπιτιθέναι* (e.g., Exod 29: 10, 15, 19; Lev 1:4, 3:2, 4:4) and *ἐπιτιμᾶν* (Gen 37:10; Ruth 2:16; Zech 3:3), by precisely those used in the pertinent NT passages. Though G. R. Driver was inclined to regard this rite in the *Genesis Apocryphon* as "an echo of a Christian passage,"[60] most commentators see the matter the other way round, even though there is still the further question as to how the rite got into the Palestinian Aramaic text in question and into the Qumran community. Its own background is still open to discussion.[61]

In the same passage two other minor parallels might be pointed out: (*a*) the belief in demon-sickness: when the secondary causality of an affliction is not recognized, a spirit is invoked to explain it; consequently, a cure is considered possible through prayer and a rite (of exorcism); (*b*) prayer for a persecutor (if my reconstruction of the text, as given above, is correct).[62] Possibly, this passage in the *Genesis Apocryphon* fills in the background for Matt 5:44, "Pray for those who persecute you," or Rom 12:17, "Bless those who persecute you."

Another instance of a Qumran tenet that has emerged from an Aramaic text confirms the notion of Melchizedek as a heavenly being. This seems to be the view of him that is presented in 11QMelchizedek, a Hebrew text, and the pertinence of this view to the understanding of the comparison of Christ the high priest with him in Hebrews 7 has been noted elsewhere. [63]But recently J. T. Milik published some fragments of an Aramaic text that presents Melchizedek's counterpart, Malki-reša^{c}, as an evil spirit in the heavenly court.[64] Most of the information about him comes from Hebrew texts, but he is mentioned in a fragment of 4Q^{c}Amram^{b} 2:3′.[65] Aside from the new light that is cast on the dualism in Qumran theology by these two spiritual adversaries, Melchizedek and Malki-reša^{c}, there is now some further Jewish background material for Jude 9 (the archangel Michael contending with the devil over the body of Moses).[66] For in Milik's explanation of the texts Melchizedek is merely another name for Michael.

Such are some of the items that have come to light in Qumran Aramaic texts that reveal Jewish beliefs or practices that have bearing on some NT passages.

III. *Qumran Aramaic Literary Parallels to the New Testament*

To terminate my discussion of the contribution of Qumran Aramaic texts to the study of the NT, I should like to gather together here a number of items that are less easily defined or grouped than those in the two preceding sections.

First of all, with reference to the infancy narratives it is surprising how little the first part of the *Genesis Apocryphon* has been exploited for the type of literature found there. There are certain elements in the story of the birth of Noah that give us clear Palestinian literary parallels to details in the Gospel stories of the childhood of Jesus. For instance, Joseph's doubts about Mary in Matt 1:18-23, and the heavenly reassurance given to him are not without parallel in Lamech's doubts about the conception of Noah (1QapGen 2:1-2). Lamech is not reassured by the angel of the Lord, but his father Methuselah does run to Enoch, whose lot is with the holy ones in paradise; he makes known everything to Methuselah (2:19-23; 5:3-25). The extraordinary character of the child born to Mary is better understood against the background of the doubts about the extraordinary Noah, whose conception Lamech feared might have been caused by the watchers, or the holy ones, or the Nephilim. This Qumran parallel does not solve the problem about the origin of the notion of the virginal conception of Jesus or its *religionsgeschichtliche* background; but it may warn us at least not to search too far afield for parallels about the origins of a child born of something other than human conception. In the broken and fragmentary section of the *Genesis Apocryphon* it is almost certain that Enoch reassures Methuselah that Noah is the child of Lamech (see col. 5), an ordinary human being. Yet the idea of another sort of conception is at least entertained in the *Genesis Apocryphon* itself.

In a similar way perhaps one should relate the dream of Joseph, in which he is warned about the machinations of Herod against the child (Matt 2:13-14) and because of which the child is delivered through the flight to Egypt, to the dream that Abram has on the night of his passing the border of Palestine into Egypt. In it Abram is warned about the covetousness of the Egyptians, especially of the Pharaoh, and he is told how he will be delivered through Sarai herself (1QapGen 19:14-24). The dream of deliverance differs, of course, in each story; and Abram's dream has an allegorical symbolism that none of the heavenly communications in the dreams of the Matthean infancy narrative have. In fact, in its symbolism it is more like the dream-vision in Peter's trance, as narrated in Acts 10:10-16. But the motif of the dream of deliverance is there, and its connection with Egypt is not to be missed.

Finally, literary parallels of another sort may be mentioned. These consist of a number of isolated phrases that are similar to NT expressions and are perhaps significant for the interpretation of the latter. Since they are isolated and somewhat disparate, it is impossible to draw any conclusion from them; but there may be some advantage in gathering them together (without any hope of exhausting the list of them).[67]

Matt 11:25	κύριε τοῦ οὐρανοῦ καὶ τῆς γῆς	מרה שמיא וארעא	1QapGen 22:16
Matt 22:16	ἐν ἀληθείᾳ	בקושט(א)	1QapGen 2:5
Luke 3:4	βίβλῳ λόγων Ἡσαΐου	ל[כתב] מלי חנוך	1QapGen 19:25

Luke 4:25	ἐπ᾽ ἀληθείας	בקושט(א)	1QapGen 2:5
Luke 6:7	ἵνα εὕρωσιν κατηγορεῖν αὐτοῦ	די לא ישכח... לממניה	1QapGen 21:13
Luke 7:21	νόσων καὶ μαστίγων καὶ πνευμάτων πονηρῶν	מכתשיא ונגדיא	1QapGen 20:18
Luke 10:21	κύριε τοῦ οὐρανοῦ καὶ τῆς γῆς	מרה שמיא וארעא	1QapGen 22:16
Luke 13:13	πνεῦμα ἀσθενείας	רוח שחלניא, רוח מכדש	1QapGen 20:26, 16
Luke 16:19	ἐνεδιδύσκετο πορφύραν καὶ βύσσον	לבוש סגי די בוץ וארגואן	1QapGen 20:31
Luke 22:15	ἐπιθυμίᾳ ἐπεθύμησα[68]	ובכית אנה אברם בכי תקיף	1QapGen 20:10-11
Acts 7:2	ὁ θεὸς...ὤφθη τῷ πατρὶ ἡμῶν ᾽Αβραάμ	אתחזי אלהא לאברם בחזוא	1QapGen 22:27
Acts 5:17, etc.	ἀναστάς + verb[69]	קום (asyndetically joined to a verb)	1QapGen 20:5, 29; 21:13
Acts 19:21	τὰ πνεύματα τὰ πονηρά	רוח באישא	1QapGen 20:16-17
Acts 20:3; 15:33; 18:23	ποιήσας τε μῆνας τρεῖς	תרתין עבדתה (understand שנין)	1QapGen 22:28
Gal 1:18	Κηφᾶς	(Hebrew סלע = כפא)	11QtgJob 32:1
2 Thes 2:7	τὸ μυστήριον...τῆς ἀνομίας	רז רשעא	1QapGen 1:3
Jude 9	ὁ δὲ Μιχαὴλ ὁ ἀρχάγγελος, ὅτε τῷ διαβόλῳ διελέγετο περὶ τοῦ Μωϋσέως σώματος	והא תרין דאנין עלי ואמרין	4Q῾Amram[b] 1:10
Matt 7:16; Luke 6:44	(indefinite 3rd pl. = passive verb; cf. BDF §130.2)	יתיבו נה לשרי וינדעוך	1QapGen 20:25 1QapGen 20:15

This list will undoubtedly grow with more study and further publication of the Aramaic texts. In a number of the instances listed above one can find similar phraseology in the OT itself, and hence one may query which was really the source of the NT phrase. For instance, "purple and fine linen" may be derived from Prov 31:22 by both Luke and the author of the *Genesis Apocryphon.* The above listing is intended merely to call attention to parallels, without in this instance moving to the further step of trying to establish literary contacts.[70] The only point being made here is that for some NT expressions literary parallels do exist in Palestinian Aramaic texts of a more or less contemporary period and that these may have to be considered in the last analysis when one is debating the origins of NT traditions.

The data that have emerged from the Qumran Aramaic texts are of diverse nature and they bear on the study of NT problems in various ways. For many students of the NT these items will be of no little interest, as they have been for the present writer.

CHART 1[71]

PALESTINIAN ARAMAIC TEXTS

	Text	*Century*	*Editio princeps or preliminary report*
1	῾Ein Gev Jar Inscription	mid 9th	B. Mazar et al., *IEJ* 14 (1964) 27-29 (+pl. 13B)
2	Tel Dan bowl inscription	9th	N. Avigad, *Yediot* 30 (1966) 209-12; *PEQ* 100 (1968) 42-44 (+pl. XVIII)
3	Deir ῾Alla inscription	mid 8th	H. J. Franken, *VT* 17 (1967) 480-81; cf. J. Naveh, *IEJ* 17 (1967) 256-58
4	Amman inscription	9th-8th	R. D. Barnett, *ADAJ* 1 (1951) 34-36

	Text	Century	Editio princeps or preliminary report
5	Tell Zeror inscription	8th	M. Kochavi, *RB* 72 (1965) 549
6	Inscribed seals	9th on	F. Vattioni, *Augustinianum* 11 (1971) 47-87; cf. *Bib* 50 (1969) 357-87
7	Adon letter	c. 600	A. Dupont-Sommer, *Sem* 1 (1948) 43-68
8	Tell Siran bottle inscription	c. 600	H. O. Thompson and F. Zayadine, *BASOR* 212 (1973) 5-11
9	Elath ostraca	7th-5th	N. Glueck, *BASOR* 80 (1940) 3-10; 82 (1941) 3-11; cf. J. Naveh, *BASOR* 183 (1966) 27-30
10	Heshbon ostraca (?)	525-500	F. M. Cross, *AUSS* 7 (1969) 223-29; 11 (1973) 126-31; cf. J. Naveh, *BASOR* 203 (1971) 27-32
11	Samaria sherds	6th-4th	S. A. Birnbaum, *The Objects from Samaria* (ed. J. W. Crowfoot et al.; London: P.E.F., 1957) 9-34; G. A. Reisner et al., *Harvard Excavations at Samaria 1908-1910* (Cambridge, MA: Harvard, 1924), 1.247-48; 2, pl. 58*a-h*
12	Ashdod ostracon	mid-5th	J. Naveh, *Atiqot* 9-10 (1971) 200-1
13	ʿAraq el-Emir inscription	6th-5th	E. Littmann, *Greek and Latin Inscriptions* (Princeton University Arch. Expedition to Syria 1904-5; Leiden: Brill, 1907) 1-4
14	Lachish incense altar	5th-4th	A. Dupont-Sommer, *Lachish III: The Iron Age* (ed. O. Tufnell; London: Oxford, 1953) 358-59; cf. F. M. Cross, *BASOR* 193 (1969) 21-24
15	Tell Arad ostraca	5th-4th	Y. Aharoni and R. Amiran, *IEJ* 14 (1964) 141-42 (+pl. 38B), 280-83; 17 (1967) 233-49
16	Tell Abu Zeitun jar fragment	Persian P.	J. Kaplan, *Yediot* 22 (1958) 98-99
17	Beersheba ostraca	Persian P.	Y. Aharoni (cf. J. Naveh, *BASOR* 203 [1971] 31)
18	Gibeon jar inscription	Persian P.	J. Naveh, *BASOR* 203 (1971) 31
19	Horvat Dorban jar inscription	Persian P.	Y. Aharoni, *IEJ* 13 (1963) 337
20	Ezra (Aramaic parts)	Persian P.	
21	Wadi ed-Daliyeh papyri	c. 350	F. M. Cross, *BA* 26 (1963) 110-21
22	Yehud jar handles	Persian P.	
23	En-Gedi ostraca	400-350	B. Mazar and I. Dunayevsky, *IEJ* 14 (1964) 123; 15 (1965) 258-59; *Yediot* 27 (1963) pl. 26, fig. 3
24	Nebi Yunis ostracon	350-300	F. M. Cross, *IEJ* 14 (1964) 185-86 (+pl. 41H)
25	Kerak inscription	350-300	J. T. Milik, *SBFLA* 9 (1958-59) 331-41; 10 (1959-60) 147, 154
26	Tell el-Farʿah ostraca	c. 300	A. E. Cowley, *JRAS* (1929) 111-12; E. Macdonald et al., *Beth Pelet II: Prehistoric Fara* (London: British School of Archaeology in Egypt, 1932) 29 (+pl. LXI/3); J. Naveh, *BASOR* 203 (1971) 31
27	Khirbet el-Kom ostraca	277	L. T. Geraty, *BASOR* 220 (1975) 55-61
28	Daniel (Aramaic parts)		
29	Qumran Aramaic texts	150 B.C.-A.D. 70	See chart 2; also my commentary on 1QapGen (2d ed., 1971), p. 20 n. 55

	Text	*Century*	*Editio princeps or preliminary report*
30	Jerusalem ossuaries	100 B.C.-A.D. 100	See my commentary on 1QapGen (2d ed., 1971), pp. 21-22 nn. 58-9; see also pp. 39, 53 above and *MPAT*, ¶68-148
31	Uzziah inscription	1st century B.C./A.D.	E. L. Sukenik, *Tarbiz* 2 (1930-31) 288-92; cf. *CBQ* 32 (1970) 520 n. 68; see p. 53 above
32	Masada ostracon	A.D. 66-73	Y. Yadin, *IEJ* 15 (1965) 111
33	Murabbaʿat Texts	1st-2d centuries A.D.	See my commentary on 1QapGen (2d ed., 1971), p. 28 n. 67; see p. 54 above, n. 76
34	Synagogue inscriptions	3rd-6th centuries A.D.	See p. 54 above, n. 89; *MPAT*, A1-A56
35	Coins		E.g. see F. Vattioni, *Augustinianum* 11 (1971) 47-87; J. Naveh, *IEJ* 18 (1968) 20-25; *AION* 16 (1966) 33-34

CHART 2[72]

QUMRAN ARAMAIC TEXTS

	Siglum	*Brief Description*	*Editio princeps or preliminary report*
1	1QapGen	Book of the Patriarchs	N. Avigad and Y. Yadin, *A Genesis Apocryphon: A Scroll from the Wilderness of Judaea* (Jerusalem: Magnes, 1956)
2	1Q*20*	Part of 1	DJD, 1.86-87
3	1QTLevi	Testament of Levi (= 1Q*21*)	DJD, 1.87-91
4	1Q*23*	Book of the Giants	DJD, 1.97-98; cf. J. T. Milik, "Turfan et Qumran" (see p. above, n. 57), 120-21; *HTR* 64 (1971) 366-72
5	1Q*24*	Book of the Giants (?)	DJD, 1.99; cf. J. T. Milik, *HTR* 64 (1971) 366-72
6	1QNewJerus	New Jerusalem (= 1Q*32*)	DJD, 1.134-35
7	1Q*63-68*	Miscellaneous	DJD, 1.147
8	2QNewJerus	New Jerusalem (= 2Q*24*)	DJD, 3.84-89; M. Baillet, *RB* 62 (1955) 222-45
9	2Q*26*	Book of the Giants	DJD, 3.90-91; cf. J. T. Milik, *HTR* 64 (1971) 366
10	3Q*12*	Fragments	DJD, 3.102
11	3Q*13*	Fragments (Aramaic?)	DJD, 3.102
12	3Q*14*	Fragments	DJD, 3.103
13	4QTLevi^{a,b,c}	Testament of Levi	(MS b) J. T. Milik, *RB* 62 (1955) 398-406; *Ten Years of Discovery in the Wilderness of Judaea* (SBT 26; London: SCM, 1959) 34
14	4QTQahat	Testament of Qahat	J. T. Milik, *RB* 79 (1972) 97
15	4QTBenj	Testament of Benja-min (?)	Starcky's lot
16	4QTestuz	'Precious Tablets'	M. Testuz, *Sem* 5 (1955) 37-38; cf. J. Starcky, *RB* 63 (1956) 66
17	4QṣNab	Prayer of Nabonidus	J. T. Milik, *RB* 63 (1956) 407-11; *Ten Years*, 36-37
18	4QpsDan^{a,b,c}	Pseudo-Daniel Texts	J. T. Milik, *RB* 63 (1956) 411-15
19	4QpsDan A^{a}	Pseudo-Daniel ('Son of God')	J. T. Milik, See pp. 90-94 above
20	4QMess aram	Birth of Noah (end of the Book of Giants)	J. Starcky, *Mémorial du cinquantenaire 1914-1964: Ecole des langues orientales anciennes de l'Institut Catholique de Paris* (Paris: Bloud et Gay, 1964) 51-66; cf. J. T. Milik, *HTR* 64 (1971) 366
	Siglum	*Brief Description*	*Editio princeps or preliminary report*
21	4QTob aram^{a}	Book of Tobit	J. T. Milik, *RB* 63 (1956) 60; *Congress Volume, Strasbourg 1956* (VTSup 4; Leiden: Brill, 1957) 23-24; *RB* 73 (1966) 522-30, esp. p. 522 n. 3
22	4QTob aram^{b,c,d}	Book of Tobit	J. T. Milik, *RB* 63 (1956) 60; 73 (1966) 522 n. 3
23	4QAh A, C	Texts about Aaron	J. T. Milik, *Ten Years*, 36
24	4QBront	Brontologion (Zodiac)	J. T. Milik, *Ten Years*, 42
25	4QDCP	"Devin à la cour perse" (texte pseudo-historique)	J. Starcky, *RB* 63 (1956) 66
26	4Q'Amram^{a}	Visions of Amram^{a}	J. Starcky, *RB* 63 (1956) 66; J. T. Milik, *RB* 79 (1972) 77, 81, 84, 94; *Ten Years*, 36
27	4Q'Amram^{b}	Visions of Amram^{b}	J. T. Milik, *RB* 79 (1972) 78-84
28	4Q'Amram^{c}	Visions of Amram^{c}	J. T. Milik, *RB* 79 (1972) 77
29	4Q'Amram^{d}	Visions of Amram^{d}	J. T. Milik, *RB* 79 (1972) 83-84
30	4Q'Amram^{e}	Visions of Amram^{e}	J. T. Milik, *RB* 79 (1972) 90-92
31	4QḥYa'qob	Vision of Jacob (?)	J. Starcky, *RB* 63 (1956) 66
32	4QNewJerus	New Jerusalem	J. Starcky, *RB* 63 (1956) 66; cf. J. T. Milik, DJD, 3.184-93
33	4QkMika'el	Book of Michael (*Kĕtāb Mîkā'ēl*)	J. Starcky, *RB* 63 (1956) 66
34	4QmNoah	Birth of Noah (*Môlad Nōăh* [part of the Book of Giants?]	J. Starcky, *RB* 63 (1956) 66; J. T. Milik, *Ten Years*, 35; *HTR* 64 (1971) 366

35	4QHenAstr^{a}	Calendar (related to 1 Enoch)	J. T. Milik, *RB* 63 (1956) 60; *HTR* 64 (1971) 336-37; *Ten Years*, 33-34
36	4QHenAstr^{b}	Calendar + 1 Enoch 76:13-82:13	J. T. Milik, *HTR* 64 (1971) 338-39, 342; *RB* 65 (1958) 76
37	4QHenAstr^{c}	Astronomical Part of 1 Enoch 76:3-78:8	J. T. Milik, *RB* 65 (1958) 76; *HTR* 64 (1971) 336-37
38	4QHenAstr^{d}	Astronomical Part following on 1 Enoch 82:20	J. T. Milik, *HTR* 64 (1971) 336-37, 371
39	4QHen^{a}	1 Enoch 1:1-9:3 (with gaps)	J. T. Milik, *HTR* 64 (1971) 336-37, 344-54, 374
40	4QHen^{b}	1 Enoch 5:9-10:12 (with gaps)	J. T. Milik, *HTR* 64 (1971) 336-37, 344-54
41	4QHen^{c}	1 Enoch 1:9-36:4; 84:2-89:37; 104:13-107:2 (with gaps)	J. T. Milik, *HTR* 64 (1971) 336-37, 344-65; *RB* 65 (1958) 70-77
42	4QHen^{d}	1 Enoch 22:13-27:1; 89:11-44 (with gaps)	J. T. Milik, *HTR* 64 (1971) 336-37, 344-54
43	4QHen^{e}	1 Enoch 18:15-34:1; 88:3-89:30 (with gaps)	J. T. Milik, *RB* 65 (1958) 70-77; *HTR* 64 (1971) 336-37, 344-54
44	4QHen^{f}	1 Enoch 86:1-3 (with gaps)	J. T. Milik, *HTR* 64 (1971) 336-37, 354-60
45	4QHen^{g}	1 Enoch 91:10-94:2 (with gaps)	J. T. Milik, *HTR* 64 (1971) 336-37, 360-65, 374
46	4QHenG^{a}	Enoch, "Book of the Giants"	J. T. Milik, "Turfan et Qumran", 125-26; *HTR* 64 (1971) 366-72
47	4QHenG^{b-f}	Enoch, "Book of the Giants"	J. T. Milik, "Turfan et Qumran", 121-25; *HTR* 64 (1971) 366-72
48	4QtgLev	Targum of Leviticus (16:12-15, 18-21)	J. T. Milik, DJD, 6.86-89; R. Le Déaut, *Introduction à la littérature targumique* (Rome: Biblical Institute, 1966) 64-65
49	4QtgJob	Targum of Job (3:4-5; 4:16-5:4)	J. T. Milik, DJD, 6.90
50	5QNewJerus	New Jerusalem (= 5Q*15*)	J. T. Milik, DJD, 3.184-93
51	5Q*24*	Fragment	DJD, 3.196
52	6Q*8*	Book of the Giants	DJD, 3.116-19; cf. J. T. Milik, "Turfan et Qumran", 119-20
53	6Q*14*	"Texte apocalyptique"	DJD, 3.127-28
54	6Q*19*	Genesiac text	DJD, 3.136
55	6Q*23*	Fragments	DJD, 3.138
56	6Q*26*	Fragments	DJD, 3.138-39
57	6Q*31*	Fragments	DJD, 3.141
58	11QtgJob	Targum of Job (= 1/6 of the Hebrew text)	J. P. M. van der Ploeg and A. S. van der Woude, *Le targum de Job de la grotte XI de Qumrân* (Leiden: Brill, 1971)
59	11QNewJerus	New Jerusalem	Cf. J. T. Milik, DJD, 3.184-93

IV. *Addendum: Implications of the 4Q "Son of God" Text*

Since the implications of the use of מרא for Yahweh in Palestinian Judaism of the period contemporary with the NT are spelled out in some detail in the following chapter, it might be well to reflect a little more on the implications of the titles "son of God" and "son of the Most High" which are found, now for the first time, in a Palestinian Aramaic text, discussed briefly above.

The designation of Jesus in the NT as the "Son of God" is widespread, and no other title of his can claim as much significance for later theological development than it. If the title *ὁ υἱὸς τοῦ ἀνθρώπου* outstrips it in enigma, it certainly does not in implication. Whether it is used in the anarthrous form *υἱὸς θεοῦ* or the arthrous form *ὁ υἱὸς τοῦ θεοῦ*, or is uttered by a heavenly voice as *υἱός μου*, or used as a description of Jesus by some NT writer as *υἱὸς αὐτοῦ* or υἱὸς ἑαυτοῦ, its implication is clear: it expresses the distinct relationship that NT writers understood was enjoyed by Jesus of Nazareth to Yahweh, the God of the OT, who is Father.

It is not restricted to the Synoptics (Mark 1:1, 11; 3:11; 5:7; 15:39; Matt 2:15; 3:17; 4:3, 6; 8:29; 14:33; 16:16; 17:5; 26:63; 27:40, 43, 54; Luke 1:32, 35; 3:22; 4:3, 9, 41; 8:28; 9:35; 22:70) and John (1:18, 34, 49; 3:18; 5:25; [9:35]; 10:36; 11:4, 27; 19:7; 20:31); but it is found also in Acts (8:37; 9:20; 13:33), Paul (Rom 1:3-4, 9; 5:10; 8:3, 29, 32; 1 Cor 1:9; 2 Cor 1:19; Gal 1:16; 2:20; 4:4, 6; Eph 4:13; 1 Thes 1:10), Hebrews (1:5; 4:14; 5:5; 6:6; 7:3; 10:29), 1 John (1:3, 7, 8; 3:23; 4:9, 10, 15; 5:5, 9, 10, 11, 12, 13, 20), 2 John (3), Apocalypse (2:18), and 2 Peter (1:17). Moreover, not only is it found in some Pauline passages that are often regarded as kerygmatic fragments (1 Thes 1:10; Rom 1:3-4), but it even develops within the NT itself to the point that it becomes an absolute title, "the Son," on the lips of Jesus himself (Mark 13:32; Matt 24:36), and is so used by Paul (1 Cor 15:28).

This immediately suggests a certain parallelism with the title κύριος, for the absolute (ὁ) κύριος is also found along with modified expressions. On the other hand, interpreters of the NT title ὁ υἱὸς τοῦ Θεοῦ, aware of the various OT uses of the word בן (or υἱός) to designate a relationship of someone to God, have often noted that it is "a long way" from such simple uses in the OT expressions to the solemn and lofty connotation of the title ὁ υἱὸς τοῦ Θεοῦ, as we find it in the NT. W. Bousset posed the question years ago: "May we, without further ado, assume that already the first community of Jesus' disciples had taken the daring step and had creatively formed the title 'the Son of God,' which the Old Testament and the messianic faith of late Judaism did not know, out of Old Testament beginnings (Ps. 2:7) and the tradition about Jesus' baptism and transfiguration? Or did this title ultimately develop first on Greek soil, in the Greek language?"[73]

Though Bousset himself expressed real hesitations about the connection of the NT title with what he called "Jewish messianology"[74] and thought that it came to undisputed dominance in "the area of popular conceptions in the Gentile Christian church and in that of the Pauline-Johannine Christology,"[75] he did not go so far as A. Deissmann had, in seeing its close "connection with the imperial cult and the well-known formula *Divi Filius* (Θεοῦ υἱός...)."[76] Thus, for Bousset, the NT title ὁ υἱὸς τοῦ Θεοῦ was not so clearly of Hellenistic and pagan origin as was κύριος. And yet, as is well known, several writers have sought blatantly to relate this NT title to such an origin; so with varying nuances G. P. Wetter,[77] and W. G. Kümmel.[78]

R. Bultmann hedged somewhat in this matter, for though he asserted that "Hellenistic-Jewish Christians had brought along the *title* "Son of God" embedded in their missionary message, "for the earliest Church had already called Jesus so,"[79] yet he frankly related the connotation of the title as indicative of "divine origin" or of being "filled with divine 'power'" (and not merely messiahship) to a Gentile setting.[80] For him it was a title related to the role of Jesus as θεῖος ἀνήρ[81] (a title that NT writers never gave him), and the real content-element of it was thus of Hellenistic imprint.

Now it would be foolhardy to deny that such Hellenistic notions as "demigods" or "heroes," born of gods or goddesses, or θεῖοι ἄνδρες (to whom the title θεοῦ υἱοί was on occasion given), influenced the early Christian use of it and the connotations that it bore, especially in the Pauline or Johannine writings. But the problem is really to trace that "long way" from the OT data, which many NT interpreters still think were at the root of the title, to the solemn use of the title itself. No little part of this aspect of the problem is the fact that the title "son of God" (in the singular) occurs as such only rarely in late books of the OT in spite of numerous allusions to figures in the OT who are called "son(s)"—scarcely with the connotations that the word or title sometimes has in the NT.

Hence it might be well to review the OT data that bear on the NT title "son of God." The plural expressions in Hebrew בני (ה)אלהים (Gen 6:2, 4; Job 1:6; 2:1; 38:7), בני אלים (Ps 29:1; 89:6), and בני עליון (Ps 82:6),[82] are found in the OT as names of angelic beings in the heavenly court of Yahweh. Again, the plural, either as בני אל חי (Hos 2:1) or simply some form of בנים (Deut 14:1; Isa 1:2; 30:1; Jer 3:22), is used by God of the Israelites. Indeed, on occasion collective Israel is even addressed in the singular as בני, "my son" (Exod 4:22; Hos 11:1). The closest one comes to the singular expression, resembling the NT title, is found not in Hebrew, but in Greek and Aramaic: thus Israel is referred to in the singular as θεοῦ υἱόν (Wis 18:13); and the figure who appears with Shadrach, Meshach, and Abednego walking about unfettered in the fiery furnace is described as דמה לבר אלהין, lit., "resembling a son of (the) god(s)" (Dan 3:25). None of these expressions imply a physical father-son relationship between Yahweh and the person(s) so designated. Hence, it is obvious that neither the descriptive title of the angel(s) nor the collective title for Israel provides an intelligible background to the NT title for Jesus.

On the other hand, the title "son" is given at times to other individuals in the OT tradition. Though he is never called explicitly "son of God," the king who sits on David's throne is three times related to Yahweh as "son": 2 Sam 7:14; Ps 2:7; 89:26-27. Although Ps 2:7 uses of the Davidic king the graphic expressions ילדתיך, "I have begotten you," nevertheless OT commentators are generally loathe to admit that this implies a sort of sacral kingship in the sense of a physical divine sonship of the king, such as could be the connotation of similar expressions in the ancient eastern Mediterranean world.[83] The father-son relationship in the OT rather guarantees divine support and assistance, possibly even divine designation, for the Davidic king, and by implication for his dynasty. This legal legitimation of the dynastic rule is described in poetic language in Ps 89:3-4, 19-37; according to some, it may even have been played out in the concrete in a coronation ritual.[84]

In the deuterocanonical writings of Ben Sira and Wisdom one also finds the name "son" used of the righteous individual Israelite. "Be like a father to the fatherless, help a widow as a husband would; and God will call you son, show you his favor, and save you from the pit" (Sir 4:10).[85] Again, "if the righteous man is God's son, he will help him" (Wis 2:18).[86]

In four instances then we find the singular expression "son of God" used in a titular sense in OT passages: once of an angel, once of collective Israel, and twice of an upright individual Israelite. The connotations vary, but they are all figurative and scarcely approach the nuance of the NT title.

Psalm 2 is the source of the tendency of some biblical interpreters to regard the OT expression as "messianic." Since this adjective properly denotes OT figures who were "anointed" agents of Yahweh in some way or other, the title "son of God" obviously does not express that idea *in se*. And yet, the question, whether the title "son of God" was used of an "anointed" agent—or of a "messiah"—in pre-Christian Judaism is constantly debated. The root of this problem is found in Ps 2:2, where the king on the Davidic throne is called "his [i.e., Yahweh's] anointed" (על יהוה ועל משיחו), whereas v. 7 of the same psalm says, "You are my son, today I have begotten you" (בני אתה אני היום ילדתיך). As has been pointed out many times before, the expression in v. 2 is used of an historical king, not of a future, ideal "David" (such as Jer 30:9 once spoke of: "they shall serve the Lord their God and David their king, whom I will raise up for them"). To cite Psalm 2 as if it were clear evidence in pre-Christian Judaism of a belief in a "messianic" figure (= a future, ideal anointed David) with the title "son of God" is to go beyond the evidence of the psalm (or other related OT passages).[87] The connection between divine sonship and an anointed agent of Yahweh is present in Psalm 2; but it is another question to ask whether the psalm is to be understood "messianically." Moreover, there is no evidence from pre-Christian Palestinian or Diaspora Judaism that Psalm 2 was ever understood or interpreted of a messiah (= a future, ideal anointed Davidic king) nor that the title "son of God" (as such) was applied to a messianic figure, i.e., to an expected "anointed" agent of Yahweh.[88]

It is over against such a background of OT data that we must consider the Qumran text discussed in section I above. In this Aramaic text the titles ברה די אל and בר עליון are applied to some figure or person. Coming from Palestine itself and from the last third of the first century B.C., as is to be judged on palaeographic grounds, it is significant, indeed, since it is the first attestation of such titles in a clearly Aramaic-speaking context. Even if Milik's interpretation of the text were to be correct and the titles were attributed to a Gentile ruler such as Alexander Balas, they were predicated of him by someone who has written in Aramaic but who has apparently borrowed from an OT background. Though Aramaic was also being used in Syria of the period (perhaps in a slightly different dialect), is it likely that it would represent some non-Jewish writing composed in Syria and brought to Qumran? The general thrust of the document and its apocalyptic cast, as well as certain Jewish or OT expressions that it contains (e.g., עם אל; cf. עמי, Jer

6:14, etc.) militate against such an interpretation. The best chances are that the text represents a Jewish composition and that the titles are predicated of some person of Jewish background, possibly historical, but more likely expected. He is not, however, called משיח, an anointed agent of Yahweh.

The implications of this Qumran text and especially of the titles, "son of God" and "son of the Most High," are numerous. First, the titles are clearly related to an *apocalyptic* setting; the trappings or the stage-props (coming distress, flashing comets) serve to enhance the future (eschatological) deliverance, "until there arises the people of God" (2:4).

Second, the *titular* use of the expressions is clear. No matter who the person is to whom the expressions are attributed, they are clearly meant in the titular sense. The verbs יתאמר, "he shall be hailed," and יקרונה, "they shall call him" (in the context of other expressions of naming, יתקרא, יתכנה) leave no doubt about the appellative sense in which the expressions are used. Used presumably of some human being, they raise the question of the precise figurative sense in which they are intended.

Third, unless the figure addressed with these titles was elsewhere called משיחא in the part of the text now lost, there is no indication that he was regarded as an anointed agent of Yahweh. Hence this text supplies no evidence for the alleged *messianic* use of the title "son of God" in pre-Christian Palestinian Judaism. If my thoroughly apocalyptic interpretation of the text were to prove correct, then the titles would be used of a son of some enthroned king, possibly an heir to the Davidic throne. What that would mean, in the context of Hasmonean rule or of opposition to it, would still have to be explored. But, as Bousset and others had maintained earlier, there is still no direct connection between the title "son of God" and "Jewish messianology."[89]

Fourth, if there is no connection of the titles with messianic expectations (in the strict sense) in Palestinian Judaism or even with the messianism of the Qumran community, then there is even less of a connection of the titles with a θεῖος ἀνήρ of a miracle-working setting or an association of them with gnostic redeemer myths.[90] The context of the fragmentary text deals with a political strife, in which the "son of God" figure is hailed as the harbinger of peace and everlasting dominion, as a bearer of those things associated with the restoration of Davidic kingship.

Fifth, the title בר עליון, "son of the Most High," supplies indirectly the Palestinian background for the title used by the demoniac of Gerasa, υἱὲ τοῦ Θεοῦ τοῦ ὑψίστου (Mark 5:7; Luke 8:28). Whereas Ps 82:6 (υἱοὶ ὑψίστου) could be taken as the OT background of Luke 6:35 (υἱοὶ ὑψίστου), where the plural phrase is used, "sons of the Most High," the singular phrase (as used in Mark 5:7) is attested only after a fashion in the OT (in LXX Sir 4:10); and the discovery of the Palestinian usage in this Aramaic text is consequently significant.

Sixth, the Palestinian attestation of the title "son of God" in a pre-

Christian text makes it at least possible that this title was part of the early Christian kerygma that was carried abroad from its Jerusalem matrix to the Hellenistic world, where it encountered the Graeco-Roman use of *divi filius* or Θεοῦ υἱός in the widespread emperor-worship. Whether or not "son of God" was already a kerygmatic title for Jesus will have to be judged on still further grounds, viz., according to the levels of tradition that can be sorted out in the NT passages where it occurs. But at least one cannot rule out the kerygmatic use of the title on the basis that it could only be the product of missionary activity among the Gentiles of the eastern Mediterranean world. Moreover, linked to this question is that about the nature of its traditional character. From the Qumran text it would seem that the titles are associated with someone who will rule, probably the son of a king. This, then, would call in question the suggestion made by W. Grundmann, that "son of God" was the title for the *priestly* messiahship of Jesus.[91]

Lastly, the title "son of God" in the Aramaic text scarcely expresses the divine begetting of the person to whom it is attributed. There is not the slightest hint that the titles are meant in this sense, nor in the sense of an incarnation of God. The connotations with which the NT title for Jesus is fraught and the connections made with it (the implication of pre-existence, adoptionism, miraculous conception, etc.) are left untouched by this Qumran text. But it was scarcely to be expected that a text which would mention a "son of God" in a Palestinian Jewish context would carry with it all the *impedimenta* associated with the NT title itself.

The study of the NT titles for Jesus of Nazareth will continue. The discovery of this Aramaic text with examples of an important title that is attributed to him by NT writers reopens many aspects of the discussion indulged in up to this point. What we have put together here only scratches the surface; and much still remains to be discussed.

NOTES TO CHAPTER 4

*A paper originally read at the Southampton meeting of the S.N.T.S., 31 August 1973, and published in *NTS* 20 (1973-74) 382-407.

[1]For the phases of Aramaic with which one has to deal in these discoveries, see pp. 57–84 above.

[2]For the new discoveries of Old Syriac inscriptions, see p. 83 above, n. 108.

[3]See chart 1 at the end of this chapter for a list of the more important texts from Palestine. "Palestine" is used here in a slightly broad geographical sense to include certain Transjordanian sites that have yielded material which is so similar to finds from Palestine proper that they have to be included in a survey such as this. The pertinence of such finds to the OT commentator is obvious in most cases. In some instances there is hesitation about one text or another because scholars question whether it may be Edomite, Ammonite, Hebrew, or Phoenician, but written in

Aramaic scripts; see p. 77 above, n. 31; cf. J. Naveh, "Hebrew Texts in Aramaic Script in the Persian Period?" *BASOR* 203 (1971) 27-32. It should be noted also that in some instances the text is quite small (e.g., an inscription of a few words on a piece of pottery) and seemingly of little value; this is admitted, but even such small texts attest to the use of the language in Palestine over a long period.

[4]See chap. 1 above.

[5]I have touched upon this problem briefly in a number of places elsewhere: *CBQ* 30 (1968) 420-21; 32 (1970) 110-12, 524-25 (see pp. 40–42 above). Cf. also the statement of J. C. Greenfield, quoted above (p. 8); the review of M. McNamara, *Targum and Testament* (Grand Rapids: Eerdmans, 1972) by B. Z. Wacholder, *JBL* 93 (1974) 133; F. Rosenthal, *Die aramaistische Forschung* (p. 75 above, n. 2), 103-9.

[6]It is readily admitted that none of these texts is complete; all of them are fragmentary, but they do constitute a considerable bulk of material and cannot be dismissed as "miscellaneous 'bits and pieces.'" The list is as complete as I can make it at this time; references are either to the definitive publications or to the provisory and preliminary notices. See further my book, *The Dead Sea Scrolls: Major Publications and Tools for Study* (SBLSBS 8; Missoula: Scholars Press, 1975); cf. C. Burchard, *Bibliographie zu den Handschriften vom Toten Meer II* (BZAW 89; Berlin: Töpelmann, 1965) 321-44; continued in *ZDPV* 83 (1967) 95-101; J. A. Sanders, "Palestinian Manuscripts 1947-1967," *JBL* 86 (1967) 431-40; "Palestinian Manuscripts 1947-1972," *JJS* 23 (1973) 74-83 (also in F. M. Cross and S. Talmon [eds.], *Qumran and the History of the Biblical Text* [Cambridge: Harvard University, 1975] 401-13.

[7]The date of composition of one or other text might well be prior to 150 B.C. By and large, the dates given are based on palaeographical evidence, and one must consult the discussions of the individual texts.

[8]So the community of Qumran is often judged to have been, mainly because of its communal, ascetic, and secret practices. But one should recall that Josephus said of them that they "settled in large numbers in every town" (*JW* 2.8.4 §124). We still do not know how to specify the relation between such groups and those at the "mother-house" of Qumran. This bears on the question of Aramaic as a language used among them and precisely at the Qumran settlement itself. I am presently much taken by the hypothesis proposed by J. Murphy-O'Connor for the origin of the Essenes and the history of their beginnings; see "The Essenes and Their History," *RB* 81 (1974) 215-44.

[9]N. Avigad and Y. Yadin, *A Genesis Apocryphon* (p. 54 above, n. 72); for an extended bibliography on this text, see my commentary (p. 22 above, n. 27), 42-46; a few more recent things can be found in B. Jongeling, C. J. Labuschagne, and A. S. van der Woude (eds.), *Aramaic Texts from Qumran with Translations and Annotations* (SSS 4; Leiden: Brill, 1976) 80-81. J. P. M. van der Ploeg and A. S. van der Woude, *Le targum de Job de la grotte xi de Qumrân* (p. 22 above, n. 32); bibliography on this text is found on pp. 175–76 below.

[10]See further p. 9 above and p. 166 below.

[11]See pp. 8–9 above.

[12]"4Q Visions de ᶜAmram et une citation d'Origène," *RB* 79 (1972) 77-97.

[13]See J. T. Milik, "*Milkî-ṣedeq* et *Milkî-rešaᶜ* dans les anciens écrits juifs et chrétiens," *JJS* 23 (1972) 95-144, esp. pp. 126-29.

[14]Cf. W. F. Albright, *The Archaeology of Palestine* (5th ed.; Baltimore: Penguin, 1960) 201-2. See pp. 38–39 above.

[15]*The Words of Jesus* (p. 23 above, n. 53), 326.

[16]Ibid., 324-40. The reader will want to investigate his connection between Aramaic *mārēʾ* and Hebrew *môreh.* Is there any?

[17]*Kyrios Christos: A History of the Belief in Christ from the Beginnings of Christianity to Irenaeus* (Nashville: Abingdon, 1970) 126-27.

[18]*Theology of the New Testament* (2 vols.; London: SCM, 1956), 1. 51.

[19]*Herr ist Jesus* (Gütersloh: Bertelsmann, 1924); W. Foerster and G. Quell, "Κύριος, etc." *TDNT* 3 (1965) 1046-95.

[20]*The Christology of the New Testament* (London: SCM, 1963) 195-237.

[21]"Discipleship and Belief in Jesus as Lord from Jesus to the Hellenistic Church," *NTS* 2 (1955-56) 87-99.

[22]*The Titles of Jesus in Christology: Their History in Early Christianity* (New York / Cleveland: World, 1969) 68-128.

[23]"Maranatha und Kyrios Jesus," *ZNW* 53 (1962) 125-44. Some of the data amassed there need slight correction today.

[23a]Other instances of the construct-chain usage can be found in Qumran texts: מרה עלמא, "the eternal Lord" (1Q*20* 2:5); מרה עלמיא, "the Lord of the ages" (1QapGen 31:2); במרה רבותא, "by the Great Lord" (lit., "by the Lord of Greatness [or Majesty]", 1QapGen 2:4); מרה שמיא, "the Lord of the heavens" (1QapGen 7:7; 12:17); מרה שמיא וארעא, "the Lord of heaven and earth" (1QapGen 22:16, 21).

[24]See also 4QTLevi 1:10, 18; 2:6. The example of מרי in 1QapGen 20:25, cited by Schulz (*ZNW* 53 [1962] 136) as "Gottesaussage," is actually addressed to the Pharaoh. In 4Q[c] Amram[b] 2:3 one also finds the form, but with the older spelling מראי (see J. T. Milik, *RB* 79 [1972] 79).

[25]*ZNW* 53 (1962) 138.

[26]Lest there be any misunderstanding in the subsequent discussion, it is to be noted that the word "absolute" in the *kyrios*-debate has normally been applied to the use of *the title* (with or without the definite Greek article) *alone*, when it has no possessive adjective (such as "my" or "our") or when it is not modified by a genitive or a prepositional phrase (e.g., *κύριος . . . τοῦ σαββάτου*, Matt 12:8; or *Κύριε τοῦ οὐρανοῦ καὶ τῆς γῆς*, Matt 11:25). This terminology, used of the Greek expression, should not be confused with the absolute *state* of an Aramaic noun. The Aramaic evidence underlying the Greek absolute usage could be in either the absolute state (strictly = "a lord") or the emphatic state ("the lord"). The Greek absolute usage is intended in the sense of *attributlos*. This has been confused by no less a scholar than G. Vermes, *Jesus the Jew: A Historian's Reading of the Gospels* (London: Collins, 1973) 112.

[27]See M. H. Pope, *Job: Introduction, Translation and Notes* (AB 15; 3d ed.; Garden City: Doubleday, 1973) xxiv. Cf., however, Job 12:9 (יד יהוה); but check the *apparatus criticus*.

[28]See J. P. M. van der Ploeg and A. S. van der Woude, *Le targum de Job de la grotte XI de Qumrân* (p. 22 above, n. 32) 58. The top of the *aleph* of מרא is barely visible in the photograph, and the editors have marked it as a probable reading. Even though the lacuna commences immediately after this broken letter, it is unlikely that the word had a suffix, either *ī* or *ān*. One could not, of course, exclude some form of the emphatic state ending (e.g., -*āh*, written with a final *he* instead of the *aleph* because of the preceding *aleph*; the more normative form would be *māryā*ʾ a form now attested in 4QEn[b] 1 iv 5). Indeed, that would make a better parallel with the emphatic אלהא; but it would still mean "the Lord." That the reading מרא is not improbable here can be seen from the support to be had for it in a few other Qumran Aramaic phrases that I had pointed out earlier; one of them is a bit ambiguous, but it can still be cited to support the reading used here. In 1QapGen 20:12-13 Abram prays to God after Sarai has been taken away from him for the Pharaoh: בריך אנתה אל עליון מרי לכול עלמים די אנתה מרה ושליט על כולא "Blessed (are) you, O God Most High, my Lord, for all ages! For you are Lord and Master over all." The form מרה is in the absolute state (as predicate), but it is also *attributlos* (since it is otherwise unattested as construed with the preposition על; the phrase על כולא is dependent on שליט; cf. Dan 2:48 על . . . השלטה). It was the only example of the absolute usage of מרה that I had known in which the title was "close to the Palestinian absolute use" or "Lord" for God, when I wrote my brief sketch of *Pauline Theology* (Englewood Cliffs, NJ: Prentice-Hall, 1967) 36. Whether one hesitates about the coordination here or not, the absolute state is attested and would support the reading in 11QtgJob under discussion. Interestingly, G. Vermes (*Jesus the Jew* [n. 26 above] 112) cites the same instance in 1QapGen 20:12-13, saying that it "comes very close to a titular or absolute use" of "Lord." But he cites a second example, אנתה מרה לכול מלכי ארעא (1QapGen 20:15-16), "you are the Lord of all the kings of the earth." Though מרה occurs here again in the absolute *state*, the following prepositional phrase would preclude its being understood in the absolute sense intended in the discussion of the Greek title, since it is not *attributlos* (see p. 133 below, n. 18).

As for my restoration of line 7, the root עות, used in the Hebrew text, is also known in Aramaic, and so it is retained; the Hebrew noun משפט is translated by דין in 11QtgJob 34:4, and on the basis of that equivalence it is used here. The later targum of Job (see P. de Lagarde, *Hagiographa chaldaice* [Leipzig: Teubner, 1873; reprinted, Osnabrück: Zeller, 1967] 110) translates the verse thus:

ברם בקושטא אלהא לא יחייב ושדי לא יקלקל דינא,

"But truly God will not act in guilty fashion, and the Almighty will not make light of justice." This is a good instance of the difference in the two targums. Save for אלהא and the restored [דינא], the translation in the later targum is quite independent of the Qumran version—as is the case almost everywhere (see pp. 167–74 below).

[29]See F. R. Blake, "Studies in Semitic Grammar, V," *JAOS* 73 (1953) 7-16, esp. pp. 12-14. Cf. G. Widengren, "Aramaica et syriaca," *Hommages à André Dupont-Sommer* (Paris: A. Maisonneuve, 1971) 221-31, esp. pp. 228-31.

[30]*Bar Rākib* 1:5, 6, 9; *Panammu* 19; *AP* 16:8; 37:17; 38:[2]; 39:2; 54:10; 67:7; 68:[9]; 70:1, 2; 77:1; 80:9; *BMAP* 13:1, 9; *AD* 3:3, 5; 4:2; 10:1, 2; *HermWP* 3:1; etc. The form מרי also turns up sporadically before the first century (*Aššur ostracon* 6; *APO* 86:10); but these texts are problematic. In any case, the evidence is not from Palestine.

[31]It should be obvious that מרא cannot be vocalized in the absolute state as *mārāʾ* or *mārāh*. The ending *-āʾ* would make an emphatic state of it; and the ending *-āh* would either be an alternate ending for the masculine emphatic state or the feminine absolute state. Compare G. Vermes, *Jesus the Jew*, 112.

[32]An isolated instance of מר at an earlier date is found on a seal impression from Khorsabad; see M. Sprengling, "An Aramaic Seal Impression from Khorsabad," *AJSL* 49 (1932) 53-55.

[33]Cf. P. E. Kahle, *The Cairo Geniza* (2d ed.; Oxford: Blackwell, 1959) 222; see further below, p. 120.

[34]*The Titles of Jesus* (n. 22 above), 105.

[35]See S. Schulz, "Maranatha und Kyrios," 133; also pp. 126–27 below.

[36]The targum on the Psalms is of no help at this point, since it has preserved two paraphrases of v. 1, and in neither of them is there the play on the words.

אמר יי במימריה לשואה יתי רבון על כל ישראל ברם אמר לי תוב
ואורך לשאול דמן שבטא דבנימן עד דימות ארום לית מלכותא מקרבא
אחברתא ובתר כן אשוי בעלי ,דבבך כביש לרגלך:

"Dixit Dns in verbo suo, se constituturum me dominum totius Israelis, sed dixit mihi denuo, operire vero Saulem, qui est de tribu Benjamin, donec moriatur, quia non convenit regno cum socio, et postea ponam inimicos tuos suppedaneum pedum tuorum." The second targumic paraphrase reads:

אמר יי במימריה למתן לי רבנותא חלף דיתבית לאולפן אוריתא
דימיני אורך עד דאשוי בעל דבבך כביש לרגלך

"Dixit Dns in verbo suo, se daturum mihi dominatione(m), eo quod incubuerim doctrinae Legis dexterae ejus; Expecta donec ponam inimicum tuum suppedaneum pedum tuorum." The text of these targumic paraphrases is taken from B. Walton, *S. S. Biblia polyglotta* (6 vols.; London: Thomas Roycroft, 1957), 3. 266; with slight variations they can be found in P. de Lagarde, *Hagiographa chaldaice*, 67.

[37]See David M. Hay, *Glory at the Right Hand: Psalm 110 in Early Christianity* (SBLMS 18; Nashville: Abingdon, 1973) 158-59.

[38]Further support for this evidence can be found in the remarks of M. Black, "The Christological Use of the Old Testament in the New Testament," *NTS* 18 (1971-72) 1-14, esp. pp. 9-11. For further discussion of the *kyrios*-problem, see pp. 115–42 below.

[39]See A. D. Nock, *Gnomon* 33 (1961) 584; A. J. B. Higgins, *CJT* 6 (1960) 202; J. A. Fitzmyer, *TS* 25 (1964) 429; R. E. Brown, *TS* 33 (1972) 32 n. 86. What is now clear from the text is that the titles used here are not linked with the title "messiah" or "anointed one" (contrast 11Q Melch 18), so that even if the regal figure with whom the text may deal has to be understood in an apocalyptic

sense rather than in a historical sense, this fragmentary text does not yet reveal the explicit conflation of titles such as one finds in the second part of Ethiopic *Enoch.* Hence one should beware of Nock's formulation about Qumran evidence "stating the Messiah's relationship to God in terms of sonship" in this text.

[40]It was reported that Milik was to publish the text shortly in *HTR.* One should recall that he had already published some fragments of a Pseudo-Danielic cycle from Qumran Cave IV; see "'Prière de Nabonide' et autres écrits d'un cycle de Daniel, fragments de Qumrân 4," *RB* 63 (1956) 407-15.

[41]Likewise gratuitous is the introduction of the mention of angels in 1:3. Milik translated אתור as "Syria," rather than as "Assyria" (see 1QM 1:2-4, where it occurs in collocation with מצרים in a Hebrew text of apocalyptic tenor). Again, in 1:4 [ר]ברבין must be masculine, and then it could hardly modify שנין, "years" (as restored by Milik), since this word is feminine. Moreover, in Aramaic רב normally means "great," and not "many" (for which the usual term is שגיא). Lastly, does the feminine form חלפת really mean "successor" in the sense intended?

[42]Details and full discussion of this text will have to await another occasion. For the restoration of 1:8 ("all men shall make peace"), I have simply borrowed an expression that occurs in 2:6 of the text, וכלא יעבד שלם.

[43]Milik supplies רוחה before this phrase, "[and His spirit] rested upon him."

[44]See, for instance, P. Winter, "Some Observations on the Language in the Birth and Infancy Stories of the Third Gospel," *NTS* 1 (1954-55) 111-21; N. Turner, "The Relation of Luke i and ii to Hebraic Sources and to the Rest of Luke-Acts," *NTS* 2 (1955-56) 100-9; P. Benoit, "L'Enfance de Jean-Baptiste selon Luc i," *NTS* 3 (1956-57) 169-94.

[45]"'Peace upon Earth among Men of His Good Will' (Lk 2:14)," *TS* 19 (1958) 225-27; reprinted in *ESBNT,* 101-4.

[46]Ibid., for bibliography on the Hebrew usage.

[47]See M. Ginsburger, "Die Anthropomorphismen in den Thargumim," *Jahrbücher für protestantische Theologie* 17 (1891) 262-80, 430-58; G. F. Moore, "Intermediaries in Jewish Theology: Memra, Shekinah, Metatron," *HTR* 15 (1922) 41-85; V. Hamp, *Der Begriff 'Wort' in den aramäischen Bibelübersetzungen* (Munich: Neuer-Filser-V., 1938).

[48]See, for instance, R. E. Brown, *The Gospel according to John (i-xii)* (AB 29; Garden City: Doubleday, 1966) 523-24. An attempt to remedy the "neglect of targumic evidence" concerning the מאמרא background for John's "choice of Logos as a designation for Christ" has recently been made by M. McNamara (*Targum and Testament: Aramaic Paraphrase of the Hebrew Bible: A Light on the New Testament* [Grand Rapids: Eerdmans, 1972] 102-3). He bases his argument on Tg. Neofiti 1 and its insertion into Exod 12:42 of "a song in honour of four nights" of deliverance in salvation history. He quotes approvingly A. Díez Macho's Aramaic version of John 1:14 (from "El Logos y el Espiritu Santo," *Atlantida* 1 [1963] 389-90), without ever asking himself whether such Aramaic surrogates as מאמרא or שכינתא (in the buffer sense) or such Aramaic words as חמא ("see"), היכמא (conjunction) are otherwise attested at this period in Palestinian Aramaic. See further M. McNamara, "*Logos* of the Fourth Gospel and *Memra* of the Palestinian Targum (Ex 12:42)," *ExpTim* 79 (1967-68) 115-17.

[49]*A Commentary on the Book of Job* (tr. H. Knight; London: Nelson, 1967) ccxviii-ccxix.

[50]This targum is said to be of Palestinian origin and to date from the fourth or fifth century A.D.; see P. Grelot, *RQ* 8 (1972-76) 105; "before the fall of Rome in 476 C.E." (*Encyclopaedia judaica* [Jerusalem: Keter; New York: Macmillan, 1971], 4. 848).

[51]It seems to occur also in 4Q^{c}Amram^b 2:6′ in the sense of "command"; but the text is damaged and little can be concluded from it. See J. T. Milik, "4Q Visions de ^{c}Amram" (n. 12 above), 79.

[52]See J. Reider, "Etymological Studies in Biblical Hebrew," *VT* 4 (1954) 276-95, esp. p. 294; G. R. Driver, "Job 39:27-28: the KY-bird," *PEQ* 104 (1972) 64-66.

[53]See further below, p. 174.

[54]See chap. 6 below.

[55]*Pace* G. Vermes, "Appendix E: The Use of בר נשא / בר נש in Jewish Aramaic," in M. Black, *Aramaic Approach* (3d ed., 1967), 310-28, it is never used as a circumlocution for "I" (p. 320), nor does it "mean 'I'" (p. 323). See the similar criticism levelled against him by J. Jeremias, cited above p. 25, n. 71. Vermes reiterates his position in *Jesus the Jew*, 188–91.

[56]See further *CBQ* 30 (1968) 426-27. To the data given there one should now add the following instances of אנש(א): 11QtgJob 2:8; 9:9; 11:2; 12:[9]; 19:[7]; 21:5; 22:6; 24:4, 5; 25:6; 26:3; 28:[1], 2bis; 31:4.

[57]See "Problèmes de la littérature hénochique à la lumière des fragments de Qumrân," *HTR* 64 (1971) 333–78; "Turfan et Qumran" (p. 24 above, n. 66), 117–27.

[58]D. Flusser, "Healing through the Laying-on of Hands in a Dead Sea Scroll," *IEJ* 7 (1957) 107-8; A. Dupont-Sommer, "Exorcismes et guérisons dans des écrits de Qoumrân," *Congress Volume, Oxford 1959* (VTSup 7; Leiden: Brill, 1960) 246-61; H. C. Kee, "The Terminology of Mark's Exorcism Stories," *NTS* 14 (1967-68) 323-46.

[59]The closest that one comes to it in the OT is 2 Kgs 5:11, there the Syrian Naaman expects that Elisha would "wave his hand over the place" (והניף ידו אל המקום); cf. the LXX. The text is problematic at best; see my comments on it, *CBQ* 22 (1960) 284 n. 27.

[60]*The Judaean Scrolls* (New York: Schocken, 1965) 461. This view, of course, depends on Driver's interpretation of the Qumran Scrolls in general, on which see R. de Vaux, *RB* 73 (1966) 212-35; *NTS* 13 (1966-67) 89-104; *New Blackfriars* 47 (1966) 396-411.

[61]Assyrian or Babylonian? (so A. Dupont-Sommer); Hellenistic? (see O. Weinreich, *Antike Heilungswunder: Untersuchungen zum Wunderglauben der Griechen und Römer* (Religionsgeschichtliche Versuche und Vorarbeiten, 8/1; Giessen: Töpelmann, 1909) 63-66.

[62]Reading [מר]דפא הו in 1QapGen 20:28-29; see my commentary, p. 139. Cf. Giv^{c}at Ha-Mivtar Tomb Inscription, lines 3-4 (*MPAT* § 68). Another possibility would be [מג]דפא הו, "that blasphemer," which really does not suit the context as well.

[63]"Further Light on Melchizedek from Qumran Cave 11," *JBL* 86 (1967) 25-41; reprinted in slightly revised form in *ESBNT*, 245-67.

[64]"Milkî-sedeq et Milkî-reša^{c}" (see n. 13 above).

[65]"4Q Visions de ^{c}Amram" (n. 12 above), 79.

[66]See K. Berger, "Der Streit des guten und des bösen Engels um die Seele: Beobachtungen zu 4Q Amr^{b} und Judas 9," *JSJ* 4 (1973) 1-18.

[67]For a similar list of non-Aramaic parallels, see R. E. Murphy, "The Dead Sea Scrolls and New Testament Comparisons," *CBQ* 18 (1956) 263-72.

[68]Contrast the remarks of G. Dalman, *The Words of Jesus* (p. 23 above, n. 53), 34; *Die Worte Jesu* (2d ed.; Leipzig: Hinrichs, 1930), 27; M. Black, *Aramaic Approach*, 238.

[69]See G. Dalman, *The Words of Jesus*, 23-24; *Die Worte Jesu*, 17-18.

[70]For the distinction between "parallel" and "contact" and its bearing on what S. Sandmel has called "parallelomania," see my remarks, *ESBNT*, 205 n. 1.

[71]The list in this chart is as complete as I can make it at this time. It may be that I have overlooked some texts. I should be grateful to anyone who would inform me of lacunae in it and of the neglected material. When this list first appeared in *NTS* 20 (1973-74) a number of errata were detected at the time of the proofreading of the galleys and were sent in for correction; but, alas, the corrections were not made in the press. We hope that we have remedied the situation here.

[72]Trying to keep track of the published Qumran texts is an arduous task. Aside from the fact that some of the preliminary publications appear in unexpected places, there is the further complication of the change of sigla for some of them. Milik has done this at times with some of the Enoch material. I have tried to sort out the details, and it is to be hoped that I have given them correctly in this chart. Milik has recently published *The Books of Enoch: Aramaic Fragments of Qumran Cave 4* (Oxford: Clarendon, 1976).

[73]*Kyrios Christos* (n. 17 above), 95-96. See further M. Hengel, *Der Sohn Gottes: Die Entstehung der Christologie und die jüdisch-hellenistische Religionsgeschichte* (Tübingen: Mohr [Siebeck], 1975).

[74]Ibid., 207.

[75]Ibid., 97.

[76]Ibid., 207 n. 142. Cf. A. Deissmann, *Bible Studies* (2d ed.; Edinburgh: Clark, 1909) 166-67; *Light from the Ancient East: The New Testament Illustrated by Recently Discovered Texts of the Graeco-Roman World* (New York: G. H. Doran, 1927) 346-47.

[77]*Der Sohn Gottes* (FRLANT 26; Göttingen: Vandenhoeck & Ruprecht, 1916).

[78]*The Theology of the New Testament according to Its Major Witnesses: Jesus—Paul—John* (Nashville: Abingdon, 1973) 76.

[79]*Theology of the New Testament* (n. 18 above), 1. 128.

[80]Ibid., 128.

[81]Ibid., 130.

[82]According to some OT commentators the phrase refers rather to "judges" in this psalm.

[83]See C. J. Gadd, *Ideas of Divine Rule in the Ancient East* (Schweich Lectures of the British Academy, 1945; London: Oxford University, 1948) 45-50.

[84]See G. von Rad, "Das jüdische Krönungsritual," *TLZ* 72 (1947) 211-16; K. H. Rengstorf, "Old and New Testament Traces of a Formula of the Judaean Royal Ritual," *NovT* 5 (1962) 229-44.

[85]The Hebrew text reads: ואל יקראך בן ויחנך ויצילך משחת; the Greek: *καὶ ἔσῃ ὡς υἱὸς ὑψίστου καὶ ἀγαπήσει σε μᾶλλον ἢ μήτηρ σου.*

[86]The Greek text reads: *εἰ γάρ ἐστιν ὁ δίκαιος υἱὸς θεοῦ, ἀντιλήμψεται αὐτοῦ.*

[87]See further my article, "The Son of David Tradition and Mt 22:41-46 and Parallels," *Concilium* (British ed.) 10/2 (1966) 40-46; in slightly revised form, *ESBNT,* 113-26, esp. pp. 115-19.

[88]Indirectly related to this problem is the question raised by one of the Qumran texts about God's begetting of the Messiah. The text concerned is 1QSa 2:11-12 (see D. Barthélemy and J. T. Milik, *Qumran Cave 1* [DJD 1; Oxford: Clarendon, 1955] 108-18; see my comments on it in *ESBNT,* 153).

[89]*Kyrios Christos,* 207. One would now have to modify the way that he phrased the idea on p. 93, where he wrote: "The whole of later Jewish apocalypticism was unacquainted with the messianic title 'Son of God.'" It is now clear that Jewish apocalypticism was not unacquainted with the title "Son of God," but there is no evidence as yet that it associated it with a *messianic* figure, i.e., an anointed agent of Yahweh.

[90]Cf. R. Bultmann, *Theology of the New Testament* (n. 18 above), 1. 130.

[91]See "Sohn Gottes," *ZNW* 47 (1956) 113-33.

Chapter 5

The Semitic Background of the New Testament *Kyrios*-Title*

The title (ὁ) Κύριος is given to Jesus with various nuances by many NT writers, and the use of it has suggested to some commentators that this christological title originated in the kerygma of the early Christian community prior to the writing of the NT books themselves. To others it was not part of the kerygma, but a product of the missionary endeavor of early disciples among the Gentiles. Moreover, the varied use of the title has often been examined, and diverse hypotheses have been proposed to explain the genesis of the title and the development of its use. Part of the debate centers on the background of the title, e.g., whether it was of Palestinian, Hellenistic Jewish, or Hellenistic pagan origin; part of it concerns the original application of the title to a certain phase of Jesus' existence, e.g., whether it was originally predicated of the earthly Jesus, the risen Jesus, the exalted Jesus, the present Jesus, the parousiac Jesus; and part of it concerns the implications of the title, e.g., what did it mean or what does it mean to affirm that "Jesus is Lord." To take up each of these aspects of the *Kyrios*-title in detail would call for a monograph equalling former studies of the topic. But my main purpose is rather to call attention to some new data that bear directly on the background question of this title, and only secondarily to draw some inferences from it about the other subordinate aspects of the problem.[1]

I. *The Background of the* Kyrios-*Title*

Before we look at the new data, however, it might be wise to sketch briefly the four more or less current explanations of the background of the title that are in use.

(1) *A Palestinian Semitic Secular Background,* which sees the title ὁ Κύριος for Jesus as having developed out of the vocative or suffixal forms of either Hebrew אדון or Aramaic מרא, e.g., from אדני, "my lord" (or milord) or מראי, "my lord." Thus F. Hahn, for whom the absolute *(attributlos)* title[2] (ὁ) Κύριος developed from the "secular mode of address" in the course of the earthly life of Jesus and is preserved in the Greek κύριε, "sir" of Mark 7:28;

Matt 15:27; or in "Q" (Matt 8:8; Luke 7:6). This profane usage probably reflects the Aramaic form מראי.[3]

(2) *A Palestinian Semitic Religious Background,* which sees the absolute use of ὁ Κύριος as having originated in the post-Easter Jewish-Christian community of Palestine, in which Jesus would have been hailed as אדון or מרא. This would have been a title derived from one that Palestinian Jews already used for Yahweh. With varying nuances and reasons, this explanation has been proposed by G. Dalman,[4] W. Foerster,[5] O. Cullmann,[6] E. Schweizer,[7] R. H. Fuller,[8] and others. In most instances, these interpreters lean heavily on the Palestinian Jewish evidence of suffixal forms of מרא, such as מראן, "our Lord" or מראי, "my Lord" or on מרא in the construct chain of an Aramaic title for Yahweh such as מרא שמיא (Dan 5:23).

(3) *A Hellenistic Jewish Background,* which sees the absolute title ὁ Κύριος for Jesus as developed by Greek-speaking Jewish-Christians from the Greek equivalents of Semitic suffixal or genitival titles for Yahweh. In some instances, the translation of יהוה by *κύριος* in the so-called LXX has been invoked. In fact, this explanation has often been joined to the preceding one as a more direct explanation of the Greek absolute usage of the NT title. This is often said to represent a transition from the Palestinian Jewish-Christian community to a Hellenistic Jewish-Christian community, by which is meant a non-Palestinian Christian community in the Jewish diaspora. Thus, again with varying nuances, W. Foerster (and G. Quell),[9] O. Cullmann,[10] E. Schweizer,[11] and others can be mentioned.

(4) *A Hellenistic Pagan Background,* which sees the absolute title of Jesus as taken over from the use of *κύριος* as a title for gods or human rulers in the eastern Mediterranean Hellenistic world. This explanation has been proposed, with varying nuances, by W. Bousset,[12] R. Bultmann,[13] P. Vielhauer,[14] H. Conzelmann,[15] and others. Intricately bound up with this explanation is a shift in NT christology itself, influenced not merely by the geographical difference that is implied, but by a development in conception from the primitive Palestinian kerygma to the missionary preaching or evangelization of the Hellenistic world, as the kerygma came into contact with the title used there for gods and human rulers.

These are the four main positions that have been assumed in the present-day debate about the origin of the *Kyrios*-title. My remarks and the data that I should like to present will support the second of these positions. But before I turn to them positively, I should like to comment briefly on two of the other explanations in the light of recent developments.[16] I shall treat the matter then in the following order: (1) A Hellenistic Pagan Background? (2) A Hellenistic Jewish Background? (3) A Palestinian Jewish Religious Background? But by way of transition to the main discussion I should like to make two preliminary remarks.

(a) Attempts have been made to relate the Greek absolute title to the Aramaic form מראן or מראנא reflected in *μαραναθά* (1 Cor 16:22) or to the form of address מרי (attested in 1QapGen 2:9, 13, 24; 20:12, 14, 15, 25; 22:18, 22) or to other titles for Yahweh such as מרא שמיא (Dan 5:23) or מרא עלמיא (1QapGen 21:2). They have usually encountered the objection that such Aramaic forms are either suffixal or in the construct state of the noun and that they do not reflect the absolute usage of the NT Greek title.[17] To be valid evidence in the discussion of the Aramaic background of the Greek title, the form must be: (i) neither suffixal nor in the construct state (or its equivalent);[18] (ii) either in the absolute state or the emphatic state: מרא or מרה (= *mārêʾ / h*), *κύριος*; מראה or מריא (= *mārĕʾāh / mārĕyāʾ*);[19] (iii) *attributlos* (without a modifier).[20]

(b) Sometimes a parallel is drawn between *κύριε / ὁ κύριος*, "lord!"/ "the Lord" and *διδάσκαλε / ὁ διδάσκαλος*, "teacher!"/ "the teacher." It is argued that the shift from a form of address to the absolute usage, from *διδάσκαλε* to *ὁ διδάσκαλος*, is supported by underlying Aramaic usage: behind *διδασκαλε* lies Aramaic רבי. This originally meant "my master, my teacher," but in the course of time it came to be simply a title, "Rabbi." The shift from a vocative or a form of address to the absolute title is thus possible, and one could assume a similar development in the case of *κύριος*.[21] Appeal is further made to the later forms of מר and רב as titles for a human lord or a scribe, both being non-suffixal. What is to be said of this sort of argument? Without getting involved in the questions of the antiquity of the title "Rabbi,"[22] or of the authenticity of the application of it to Jesus in the NT,[23] I should only stress that whereas the titular use of רבי (i.e., the suffixal form meaning simply "Master" or "Teacher" [as an absolute title]) is attested,[24] there is no known instance of the suffixal form מרי which came to be understood simply as "Lord." As far as I know, there is, further, no comparable Greek transliteration of this word in a title like *ῥαββί*. Consequently, for the parallel argument to be valid, one would have to show that מרי, which originally meant "my lord," came in time to mean simply "Lord," just as רבי, which originally meant "my master" came in time to mean "Master" or "Rabbi." Granted, רב did in time come into usage as an absolute form; but at least its suffixal form is attested as a title, which is not the case for מרא.[25]

With these preliminary methodological remarks we may now turn to the various explanations of the origin of the *Kyrios*-title for Jesus.

(1) *Does the Kyrios-title Have a Hellenistic Pagan Background?* Here my remarks will be brief. This solution has in large part been adopted because of the unsatisfactory evidence hitherto adduced for other solutions and because a Pauline passage such as 1 Cor 8:5-6 in the NT itself seemed to reflect it. It is well known that *κύριος* was used absolutely of gods and human rulers in the ancient world of the eastern Mediterranean; the Greek title is attested in this way from *at least* the beginning of the first century B.C. in texts from Egypt, Syria, and Asia Minor.[26] Indeed, it occurs once in the NT itself for Nero (Acts 25:26). So no one who works seriously with the NT title can ignore this

extrabiblical Greek material. However, I should like to call attention to three things.

First, I share the uneasiness of some commentators who do not think that this Greek title *κύριος* was used with a purely political connotation in contrast to the title *θεός*, with which it was sometimes associated for the same person.[27] Even O. Cullmann, who cares little for the Hellenistic origin of the *kyrios*-title for Jesus, has seen that the distinction of *κύριος* as a political title over against *θεός* in Hellenistic pagan usage has little to commend it.[28] Certainly, if it were admitted that the title came from this origin, its application to Jesus in this sense would seem deficient in the light of 1 Cor 8:5-6, where *εἷς κύριος Ἰησοῦς Χριστός* seems to involve precisely a religious connotation, which is not limited to *θεός* alone. The religious connotation of *κύριος* in the NT, when applied to Jesus, must have been *influenced* by this use of the Greek title in the contemporary Hellenistic pagan world.

Second, one must concede that the Hellenistic pagan usage has *influenced* the NT usage. But that still leaves open the question whether that usage is the sole origin or background for the NT use of it for Jesus. Similarly, it leaves open the question whether the missionary endeavors of early Christians in Hellenistic pagan areas were responsible for the adoption of the title and the consequent introduction of a new dimension into early Christian christology. To say that the Hellenistic pagan usage has been the sole origin leaves too many factors unexplained—factors to which I shall be returning below. But at the moment I shall mention only one such here: the pre-Pauline hymn to Christ Jesus in Phil 2:6-11, the background of which is debated.[29] But its climax is found precisely in the bestowal of the title Κύριος on Jesus "to the glory of God the Father." At least since the time of E. Lohmeyer, a strong case has been made for the origin of this passage in a Christian Aramaic setting: that it is not only pre-Pauline, but "wohl ursprünglich griechisch geschrieben ist, aber von einem Dichter, dessen Muttersprache semitisch war." Recently, P. Grelot has proposed a most convincing retroversion of the hymn into contemporary Palestinian Aramaic, which will have to be taken seriously into consideration in any future discussions of this passage.[30] But if there is any validity to his thesis, then it colors radically the contention that the absolute use of the *Kyrios*-title in the NT is drawn solely from the contemporary Hellenistic pagan use of *κύριος*. (I shall return to a detail of Grelot's translation below.)

Third, it might be well to recall that the pagan use of the title "lord" for gods in the period in which we are involved is not exclusively found in Greek material. The title אדן is well attested in Punic inscriptions, and this evidence would have to be classed as Semitic. For instance, it occurs time after time in dedicatory inscriptions from the Punic sanctuary of El-Hofra at Constantine (in modern Algeria).[31] Usually the votive text begins:

לאדן לבעל חמן אש נדר . . . שמע קלא ברכא

"To the Lord, to Baᶜal Ḥammon: (this is) what X son of Y vowed. He heard his voice; he blessed him." The absolute use of אדן in these texts seems unmistakable.[32] Lest it might seem that this is merely a defective spelling for a suffixal form, one can cite a Punic text from the same place written in Greek characters and vocalized:

ΛΑΔΟΥΝ ΛΥ ΒΑΛ ΑΜΟΥΝ ΟΥ
ΛΥ ΡΥΒΑΟΩΝ ΘΙΝΙΘ ΦΑΝΕ ΒΑΛ (read ῥυβαθων)
ΥΣ ΝΑΔΩΡ ΣΩΣΙΠΑΤΙΟΣ ΒΥΝ (read Σωσιπατρος)
ΖΩΠΥΡΟΣ ΣΑΜΩ ΚΟΥΛΩ ΒΑ
ΡΑΧΩ

Au Seigneur, à Ba^{c}al Hammon et
à notre Dame Tinit Phane Baal
ce qu'a voué Sosipatros fils
de Zopyros; il a entendu sa voix,
il l'a béni.[33]

This Punic evidence is certainly not the direct pagan background of the NT *Kyrios*-title, and it does not in any way exclude the more direct influence of the corresponding Hellenistic use of κύριος. But it at least shows that the absolute use of "the Lord" was also known in the *pagan Semitic* world, and that the interplay of Semitic and Hellenistic in that Mediterranean pagan world might also have something to say about the Jewish world of Palestine and its influence on the topic at hand to be discussed below.

(2) *Does the Kyrios-title Have a Hellenistic Jewish Background?* It is not easy to discuss this background of the absolute *kyrios*-title in an isolated fashion. For it is often proposed in conjunction with that of a Palestinian Semitic religious background. Consequently, if it is not a question of the Hellenistic Jewish *origin* of the title, then it is at least a question of the *influence* of Hellenistic Jewish custom at the time that the Greek title was adopted. For the sake of clarity I should like to restrict the discussion of this matter mainly to Palestine and to envisage it as a problem related to Greek-speaking Jewish Christians, not of the diaspora, but of Palestine itself. (I realize that the question about Jews and Jewish-Christians in the diaspora is closely related to it and will in time come into the discussion; but first it is wise to try to deal with the problem in Palestine.) For we must ask whether the absolute title κύριος could owe its origin to a distinction in the early Jewish-Christian community of Palestine between the "Hebrews" and the "Hellenists" (Acts 6:1-6). In other words, were the ^{c}Ἑλληνισταί responsible for translating a suffixal or genitival form of מרא simply by the absolute κύριος? E. Schweizer once wrote: "that an original 'our Lord' becomes in Greek the absolute 'the Lord' under the influence of Hellenistic usage is easily explainable."[34] But is there really a special reason why the shift to the absolute title must be associated with a shift to Hellenistic Greek? Could it not just as easily have taken place in a Semitic context? Moreover, the distinction involves the meaning of the terms

ᶜΕβραῖοι and ᶜΕλληνισταί in the early Palestinian Christian community, and to this I shall return below.

But first one of the arguments associated with the Hellenistic Jewish background of the *kyrios*-title has to be treated, viz., the translation of יהוה by κύριος in the so-called LXX. It has often been assumed that this Greek version of the OT had been in use in first-century Palestine, and it is cited as pre-Christian evidence for the absolute use of the Greek title κύριος for Yahweh. Indeed, this use is said to antedate the pagan use of κύριος for gods and human rulers.[35] But there are serious arguments against this alleged pre-Christian use in the LXX, and H. Conzelmann has succinctly summed them up in his attempt to relate the NT *kyrios*-title to a Hellenistic pagan background. He writes:

> 3. Outside the Septuagint, *Kyrios* is unusual in Judaism as a designation for God.
> 4. It has recently been disputed that the Septuagint in fact renders יהוה by *Kyrios*. *Kyrios* occurs only in Christian manuscripts of the LXX, and not in Jewish ones:
> (a) Papyrus Fouad 266 (second century B.C.): it has יהוה in the quotation from Deut. 31f.: cf. O. Paret, Die Bibel, *Ihre Überlieferung in Druck und Schrift* (1949), p. 75 and table 2.
> (b) 4Q Minor Prophets: also tetragrammaton.
> (c) 4Q fragments of Lev. 2-5 LXX: ΙΑΩ.
> (d) Aquila fragments from Cairo: tetragrammaton.
> (e) Fragments from the second column of the Hexapla; tetragrammaton (cf. Origen and Jerome).
> (f) Examples of ΠΙΠΙ in Hatch and Redpath, *A Concordance to the LXX, Supplement* (1906), p. 126.
> (g) Symmachus: cf. *TWNT* III 1082, lines 12f.
>
> Compare, too, the use of the Old Hebrew scripts in the tetragrammaton in the quotations of the Q *pesharim*: 1QpH; 4QpPs 37; אל: 1QH I 26. II 34. XV 25; 1Q35 I 5.
>
> Thus the Christian use of κύριος cannot be derived from the LXX. The reverse is in fact the case. Once the title began to be used, it was found again in the Bible.[36]

Such arguments may indeed invalidate the claim that early Greek-speaking Christians were influenced by the so-called Septuagintal use of κύριος for Yahweh (either in Palestine or the diaspora). But I am not sure that they close the question, whether Palestinian Jews called or could call Yahweh κύριος. P. Vielhauer, on whom H. Conzelmann largely depends, rapped the knuckles of F. Hahn for not having properly informed himself by consultation of the writings of P. Kahle before writing on LXX problems.[37] Yet it remains to be seen whether Kahle had said the last word on this subject. Moreover, even though the main point of my discussion of the *kyrios*-title does not hinge on the use of κύριος as a title for Yahweh among Greek-speaking Jews, it seems to me that it was a factor in the Palestinian development (among others); and so it must be looked into. Hence I should like to call attention to several points in connection with the possible use of κύριος for Yahweh by Palestinian Jews who spoke Greek.

(a) It is clear that in a number of Greek translations of the OT from pre-Christian or early Christian times, especially in those used by Jews, the Hebrew tetragrammaton was simply preserved,[38] or else it was transcribed as ΙΑΩ,[39] or was written in Greek as ΠΙΠΙ.[40] Moreover, it seems clear that the *widespread use* of *κύριος* in so-called LXX manuscripts dating from Christian times is to be attributed to the habits of Christian scribes.[41] Indeed, the *widespread use* may well have been influenced by the use of *κύριος* for Yahweh in the NT itself.[42] But the question arises, Where did the NT writers get the *kyrios*-title for God (Yahweh)? I have never heard it said that Christian scribes or copyists introduced it as well into NT writings, whereas the writers themselves had actually used some other word for God. For instance, if *κύριος* = יהוה is a device found only in Christian copies of the OT, where did Luke get it when he quoted Deut 6:5 in 10:27, *ἀγαπήσεις κύριον τὸν Θεόν σου*?[43] A facile answer to this question would be, From Christian copies of the Greek OT. But the Lucan verse chosen here as an illustration is found in the oldest copy of Luke, in the Bodmer Papyrus (P^{75}), dating from A.D. ± 200. As far as I know, there is no earlier dated manuscript of the so-called LXX which uses *κύριος* for Yahweh.[44] Hence, as stated above, the widespread use of *κύριος* for יהוה in Christian copies of the so-called LXX may well have been influenced by the use of *κύριος* for Yahweh in the NT, but the question still remains, Where did the NT writers get it?

(b) Though Josephus normally used *δεσπότης* as the Greek equivalent for the tetragrammaton, he does use a form of *κύριος* on two occasions, one of which is significantly in a quotation from the OT. In *Ant.* 20.4.2 §90 he wrote: *εἰ μὴ μάτην, ὦ δέσποτα κύριε, τῆς σῆς ἐγευόμην χρηστότητος, τῶν πάντων δὲ δικαίως μόνον καὶ πρῶτον ἥγημαι κύριον.* This is found in a prayer of King Izates, a convert to Judaism. Again, in *Ant.* 13.3.1 §68 he presents a quotation of Isa 19:9 in a letter from Onias the High Priest. Here Josephus quotes the OT in a form that does not agree with the so-called LXX, and one would have to do some manoeuvring to show that it depends on it. Moreover, Josephus realized that it was not right to make known to foreigners the divine name that God had revealed to Moses,[45] and this undoubtedly influenced his use of *δεσπότης* on various occasions.[46] Whereas it is significant that he did not use *κύριος* more frequently as a name for God, which, in fact, supports the rarity of it in pre-Christian Greek translations of the OT, the fact remains that it does occur at least twice in his writings.[47] One might argue, of course, that it has been introduced into the manuscripts of Josephus in these places in dependence on Christian usage or Christian manuscripts of the LXX. But is that really likely?[48] And why would it be restricted to these places alone? Most discussions of Josephus's use of *κύριος* compare his text with the LXX.[49] But more recent studies of the Greek OT stress the diversity of the versions even in the first century A.D. in Palestine and tend to relate the Greek text of the Scriptures that Josephus used to a Proto-Lucianic revision of the Old Greek made in Palestine itself, a revision of the Old Greek to make it conform to a

Hebrew text then current in Palestine.[50] Is it possible that these stray instances of *κύριος* in Josephus reflect such a revision of the Greek OT in Palestine, even though his composition may have reached its final form outside of that area? This may sound like a speculative question, but the form of the Greek text of the OT in first-century Palestine is an important aspect of the problem that we are discussing. One cannot simply dismiss the use of *κύριος* by an appeal to Christian copies of the so-called LXX. Recent studies of the LXX show us that the issue is much more complex.

Granted that the evidence from Josephus is not much and that he actually wrote in Greek outside of Palestine, the question still remains, How did these isolated examples of *κύριος* get into his Greek text? If they should reflect or be a vestige of an incipient practice among Greek-speaking Jews of Palestine to refer to Yahweh in this way, then that would be important for our discussion.[51]

(c) There is an instance of *κύριος* that is preserved in the Letter of Aristeas to Philocrates, and in this case it is a clear allusion to Deuteronomy, though not an exact quotation of it: "For the chewing of the cud is nothing else than recalling life and its subsistence, since life appears to subsist through taking food. And therefore does he admonish us through Scripture, when he says, 'Thou shalt well remember what great and marvelous things the Lord thy God did in thee'; when clearly understood they do indeed appear 'great and glorious'" (§155). The allusion to Deut 7:18-19 here reads: *μνείᾳ μνησθήσῃ κυρίου τοῦ ποιήσαντος ἐν σοι τὰ μεγάλα καὶ θαυμαστά.*[52] Again, are we to invoke the habits of Christian scribes in a text-tradition such as this? (Similarly, one could here appeal to further pseudepigraphical writings of this period.)

(d) Though the tetragrammaton is normally preserved in the fragments of Aquila's translation of 1 Kgs 20:13-14; 2 Kgs 23:21, 23 (from the Cairo Geniza palimpsest fragments),[53] and in other texts (of the same provenience), such as Ps 91:2, 9; 92:2, 5, 6, 9, 10; 96:7, 8, 9, 10, 13; 97:1, 5, 9, 12; 102:16, 17, 20; 103:2, 6, 8,[54] there is at least one instance (2 Kgs 23:24) where, because of a lack of space at the end of a line, the Hebrew tetragrammaton is replaced by the Greek abbreviation *κ̄ῡ*.[55] Was this a desperate solution to a problem of space borrowed from a Christian practice?[56] Or does it not represent a custom among Jews themselves to translate יהוה on occasion by *κύριος*, a custom that may not yet have become as widespread as it was to become in Christian copies of the so-called LXX? And could this Jewish custom be part at least of the origin of the Christian usage of *κύριος*?

(e) There are manuscripts of the Greek translation of the OT in which ΠΙΠΙ was used for יהוה. Here we may readily grant that the Greek-speaking scribes no longer understood the Jewish problem when they substituted ΠΙΠΙ for יהוה. But what did they say when they read such a text? In any case, I doubt that Jewish readers would normally have said *pee-pee*. What Christian readers made of it is another matter.[57] But here one must distinguish clearly between transcription, translation, and pronunciation. What did a Greek-speaking Jew say when he read his Scriptures and found in it either the tetragrammaton or the letters ΠΙΠΙ?

(f) This evidence for the use of *κύριος* among Jews in pre-Christian times or among Jews contemporary with early Christians in Palestine does not outweigh the evidence for the preservation of the tetragrammaton in most Jewish copies of the Greek OT. But it is evidence that must be considered in the background of the following data that are to be adduced from the Semitic area in the next section of this paper. Before turning to those data, however, there is one last remark to be made. It concerns the distinction between Hebrews and Hellenists in Palestine of the first century A.D., to which I alluded earlier. This is a distinction in the *Jewish Christian* community of Palestine, that we first learn about in Acts 6:1-6. Various explanations of the distinction have been proposed. The only plausible one, in my opinion, is that of C. F. D. Moule, who on the basis of the meagre evidence available proposed that "Hellenists" were "Jews who spoke only Greek," while "Hebrews" were "Jews who, while able to speak Greek, knew a Semitic language *also*."[58] However, this distinction between "Hebrews" and "Hellenists" existed not only within the Jewish Christian community of Palestine, but also among the Jews themselves, as Acts 9:29 intimates.[59] Now if this is so, it too bears on the entire question about the early formulation of the Palestinian Christian kerygma. Was it formulated solely in a Semitic language, as so much of the current argument presupposes? For instance, it has been said that the absolute title *κύριος* used of Jesus "offers a particularly clear reflection of the change from the primitive community to Hellenistic Christianity."[60] And by "Hellenistic Christianity" here is meant that of Greek-speaking communities in a pagan environment (such as Syria, Egypt, or Asia Minor). But can it be excluded that Palestinian Christian Hellenists had part in the formulation of the primitive kerygma? Is it not rather among these Jewish Christian *ᶜΕλληνισταί* that we should seek the emergence of the Greek *kyrios*-title for Jesus—especially if there is some evidence for an absolute usage of its Semitic counterpart for God among the Jewish *ᶜΕβραῖοι* of Palestine itself?

The foregoing consideration of the use of *κύριος* among Greek-speaking Palestinian Jews, meagre as the evidence for it is, is proposed here merely as a backdrop against which the main material now to be presented has to be viewed. The new Aramaic evidence, and the Hebrew evidence, take on a different hue, when seen in this way. Part of the problem with it all—and this is frankly admitted at the outset—is that we are arguing *from Palestinian Jewish* evidence, either Semitic or Greek, *to a Christian* usage. Would that we had some clear Semitic or Greek Palestinian texts used or composed by *Jewish Christian* Hellenists or Hebrews!

(3) *The Kyrios-title Has a Palestinian Jewish Religious Background.* For the Palestinian Semitic religious background of the *Kyrios*-title for Jesus in the

NT one has often invoked the Aramaic phrase μαραναθά, preserved for us in 1 Cor 16:22.[61] 1 Corinthians is the most Hellenistic letter of the Pauline corpus, and the phrase is transmitted to us by one who openly identified himself as ἑβραῖος (2 Cor 11:22; Phil 3:5). But the suffixal form of μαράνα / מראנא has always been seen as the difficulty, because it does not provide the basis for an explanation of the emergence of the absolute usage.[62] At least since the time of G. Dalman it has been repeated that Palestinian Jews did not refer to Yahweh in the absolute sense as "the Lord."[63] R. Bultmann maintained that the "un-modified expression 'the Lord' is unthinkable in Jewish usage."[64] Now it is precisely on this point that the evidence discussed in chap. 4 above has to be brought to bear.

In the recently published targum of Job from Qumran Cave XI we find the absolute usage of Aramaic מרא for God and standing in parallelism with אלהא. The text is fragmentary but clear, and I argue from the form of it that was published by the original editors, who did not suspect the impact of the title being used.[65]

In his poetic discourse, Elihu addresses Job and says to him:

> אף אמנם אל לא ירשיע ושדי לא יעות משפט (34:12)
> Of a truth, God will not do wickedly, and the Almighty will not pervert justice (*RSV*).

The Aramaic version of the targum (24:6-7) reads:

> הכען צדא אלהא / ישקר ומרא [יעות דינא]
> Now will God really prove faithless and [will] the Lord [distort judgment]?

Here God is clearly referred to as מרא, and the Aramaic noun is not only in the absolute state, but it is unmodified; moreover it stands in parallelism with the ordinary word for God, אלהא. See further 11QtgJob 24:[5]; 26:[8]. Two further instances of the absolute state of the title can be found in 1QapGen 20:12-13; 20:15.[66]

But the absolute usage of the title is also attested with the noun in the emphatic state. In the recently published Aramaic fragments of the Books of Enoch I 4QEn^b 1 iv 5 reads:

> [ולגבריאל אמר מ]ריא אז[ל נא על ממזריא],
> [And to Gabriel] the [L]ord [said]: "G[o now to the bastards . . ."]

And the corresponding Greek text of the passage bears the abbreviated form, ὁ $\overline{κς}$.[66a]

What should be noted here is that the *absolute usage* of מרא (and not just the absolute state of the Aramaic noun) is attested in Qumran literature. However, it is not a translation of יהוה in the targum;[67] in 11QtgJob 24:6-7 it rather renders the OT title שדי, which the Old Greek usually translates as *παντοκράτωρ*.[68] Hence, though it is not a case of the tetragrammaton being rendered by מרא, for which we must still await attestation, it is at least scarcely "unthinkable" that the "un-modified expression 'the Lord'" has been in "Jewish usage." Though we do not yet have the equation יהוה = מרא = *κύριος*, we have at least the absolute usage of מרא, "the Lord," for God.

How מרא might have been translated into Greek, I have already discussed above.[69]

Consequently, the absolute use of מרא in 11QtgJob 24:7 becomes one of the missing-links between an OT title for God and the NT use of *κύριος* for God himself, first of all, and then for Jesus.

Here we may return to the hymn to Christ in Phil 2:6-11, which we have mentioned earlier, and especially to the recent retroversion of it into Palestinian Aramaic of the first century attempted by P. Grelot.[70] He translates the last verse of it as follows:

> וכל לשן יודא די מרא ישוע משיחא ליקרה די אלהא אבא
> *καὶ πᾶσα γλῶσσα ἐξομολογήσηται ὅτι κύριος Ἰησοῦς Χριστὸς εἰς δόξαν Θεοῦ πατρός.*
> "and every tongue confess that Jesus Christ is Lord, to the glory of God the Father" (*RSV*).

Interestingly enough, Grelot simply writes מרא, without so much as questioning the existence of such an absolute use of the word.[71] That usage is, of course, now attested in the targum of Job, in the *Genesis Apocryphon*, and in 4Q Enoch, making his suggestion quite valid.

Now if this Aramaic evidence were not enough, there is also some Hebrew evidence from Qumran literature that may support it. This is not the place to discuss the relative position of Hebrew and Aramaic as Semitic languages spoken or used in first-century Palestine, and I may be permitted to refer the reader to chap. 2 above,[72] where the pertinent material is reviewed. But as for the Semitic background of the *kyrios*-title, some Hebrew evidence also has to be considered.

Psalm 151 was known for a long time in Greek, being in the Greek psalter of the so-called LXX. It has turned up in Hebrew in a text from Qumran Cave XI.[73] Significantly enough for the matter under discussion, it contains an example of אדון being used absolutely of Yahweh in the sense of "the Lord," and stands in parallelism to אלוה, "God" (to give us a striking parallel to 11QtgJob 24:6-7). Moreover, it is found in a Hebrew text in which the tetragrammaton is otherwise written in the archaizing paleo-Hebrew script, otherwise known at Qumran. 11QPs[a] 28:7-8 reads:

> ומי ידבר ומי יספר את מעשי אדון הכול ראה אלוה הכול הוא שמע והוא האזין
> "and who can mention and who can recount the deeds of the Lord? Everything has God seen, everything has he heard, and he has heeded."[74]

There is no doubt here that "the Lord" refers to Yahweh, even though his name is otherwise written in paleo-Hebrew script as יהוה. J. A. Sanders, who prepared the scroll for publication, has assigned a date to it "in the first half of the first century A.D."[75] Apparently for those Jews who used or composed the scroll it was not "unthinkable" to refer to Yahweh as "the Lord."

Finally, one should not fail to mention the canonical psalter itself, where in the text of Ps 114:7 we read:

מלפני אדון חולי ארץ מלפני אלוה יעקב

"Tremble, O earth, at the presence of the Lord, at the presence of the God of Jacob" (*RSV*).

One could also compare Mal 3:1; Isa 1:24; 3:1; 10:33; 19:4.

Now when such Aramaic and Hebrew evidence is considered together with the use of *κύριος* in the Greek writings of Josephus, the Letter of Aristeas, and the isolated attestation of it in a text of even Aquila's translation of the OT, one can conclude to at least an incipient custom among Jews of Palestine of referring to Yahweh as "the Lord," a custom that would be supported by such diaspora references as those in Philo's writings and in the NT itself.[76] Granted, what I have presented here is not evidence so widespread for either מרא or אדון as that which was once thought to be available for *κύριος* in the ancient Greek translation of the OT that is now recognized to be preserved in Christian manuscripts. But the evidence does seem to suggest that Palestinian Jews, who were able to refer to God as מרא or אדון, could, on becoming the Ἑβραῖοι of the Palestinian Christian community, transfer the title to Jesus. The evidence also suggests that these Ἑβραῖοι, who also spoke Greek, may well have translated מרא or אדון by *κύριος* in their dealings with the Ἑλληνισταί of the primitive Palestinian community. Thus the absolute usage of "the Lord" as a NT christological title can be traced to the primitive Palestinian Christian community, either as מרא or אדון among the "Hebrews" or as *κύριος* among the "Hellenists" (and the "Hebrews"). A mutual influence of these two language groups in the early Palestinian Christian community was the real matrix of the primitive kerygma which was a-borning.

A final remark about the Palestinian Semitic religious background of the *kyrios*-title is in order. It concerns the reverence for the sacred name יהוה among Palestinian Jews, which is part of the background of the *kyrios*-title. There is not space to discuss this in detail. But if the reason for the substitution of *κύριος* for יהוה in manuscripts of the Greek translation must be recognized as mainly a practice of Christian scribes, the evidence is, nevertheless, abundant that the Jews themselves developed a special reverence for the divine name. In addition to the devices mentioned earlier, we need only recall the various ways of treating the tetragrammaton in Qumran literature: (a) the clear substitution of אדוני for יהוה (and vice versa!) in 1QIsa[a];[77] (b) the writing of the name in archaizing paleo-Hebrew characters,[78] (c) in ordinary square characters,[79] (d) in square characters, but in red ink.[80] Moreover, surrogates for it are found in (a) four dots;[81] (b) the use of אל;[82] (c) the use of אל in paleo-Hebrew script;[83] (d) the use of הואהא.[84] In one instance we even find לאל with the *aleph* written by what looks like an inverted Greek *alpha*.[85] Furthermore, there is the abundant use of אדוני as a title for God in the non-biblical texts of Qumran (such as 1QH 2:20, 31; 3:19, 37; 4:5; 5:5; 7:6, 34; 14:8, 23; etc.).[86] All of this evidence, which comes from roughly 100 B.C. to A.D. 68, provides simply a more generic Palestinian background against which the earlier material has to be judged.

II. *The Original Application of the* Kyrios-*Title to Jesus*

If the evidence available today supports the Palestinian Semitic and Greek religious matrix for the origin of the NT title *κύριος* for Jesus, the next question is, To what phase of Jesus' existence was it originally applied? Was it used as a title for him during his earthly ministry? Was it an expression of faith in him as risen? Was it a title expressive of his exaltation to the Father's right hand? Was it a title meant to convey his actual, ongoing influence exerted on those who put faith in him? Or was it originally a title related to his future coming, his parousia? In other words, was it originally a title for the earthly Jesus, the risen Jesus, the exalted Jesus, the ever-present Jesus, or the parousiac Jesus?

The gospels attest that various persons, disciples or pagans, addressed the earthly Jesus as *κύριε* (e.g., Mark 7:28 [the Syrophoenician woman] = Matt 15:27; Matt 8:6, 8 = Luke 7:6, "Q" [the Roman centurion]; Matt 8:2 = Luke 5:12 [a leper of Palestine]; Luke 5:8 [Peter at the miraculous catch of fish]; Matt 8:25 [disciples in the boat during the tempest]; John 4:11 [the Samaritan woman]; etc.). Three things have to be noted about this usage of *κύριε* in the gospels: (1) The vocative usage in many cases has nothing more than the secular sense, "Sir," which would tell us nothing about the application of the religious title, "Lord," to Jesus during his public ministry. That a pagan or even a disciple might have addressed him as "Sir" has little bearing on the titular sense which we are discussing. (2) In reading the gospels, we must remember that in passages such as Luke 5:8, where Peter exclaims after the miraculous catch of fish, "Depart from me, *κύριε*, for I am a sinful man," or Matt 14:30, where he cries out as he sinks in the waves, "*κύριε*, save me," these instances should rather be translated as "Lord." Here the evangelists have retrojected back into the public ministry narratives that almost certainly stem from post-Eastern appearances of the risen Jesus to Peter. But, the title, "Lord," for the risen Jesus, thus retrojected into the public ministry, tells us little about the use of such a religious title for him during his earthly ministry. (3) The same sort of retrojection of the title is found elsewhere in the gospel tradition, where there is no evidence of appearances of Jesus or of his miraculous powers, e.g., Luke 12:41-42, where Peter asks,

"Lord (κύριε), are you telling this parable for us or for all?" And Luke the evangelist comments, "And the Lord said. . . ." Here we find not only the vocative, but also the absolute title ὁ κύριος. In such cases the evangelist has simply used of the earthly Jesus a title that had already become stereotyped in the early Christian community of his own day and retrojected it into the account of the public ministry. In sum, there is no real evidence pointing to the application of the religious title ὁ κύριος to the earthly Jesus.

That κύριος was applied to the risen Jesus is reflected in various ways in the NT. In the saying of Paul already quoted, "Am I not an apostle? Have I not seen Jesus our Lord?" (1 Cor 9:1), he relates his claim to apostleship to his vision of the risen Jesus. And even though it uses the possessive form, "our Lord," it clearly relates "Lord" to the resurrected phase of Jesus' existence and reflects an affirmation of the post-Easter faith of the Christian community. Elsewhere in 1 Corinthians, Paul insists that "no one can say 'Jesus is Lord' except by the Holy Spirit" (12:3) and thereby clearly shows that the affirmation is one of faith and Spirit-prompted. Thus Paul's use of the title in 1 Cor 9:2 betrays its faith-origin and supports the data of the gospel passages such as we have already considered (Luke 5:8 or Matt 14:30), which imply the application of the title to the risen Jesus.

That the title κύριος was applied even earlier to the exalted Jesus emerges from the pre-Pauline Jewish Christian liturgical hymn in Phil 2:10-11. Paul took over an already existent hymn that climaxes in the confession of Jesus as κύριος. What is remarkable in this hymn is that, for all the phases of Jesus' existence that it details, it bypasses an explicit mention of the resurrection. The structure of the hymn is debated, but some analysts see it proposing six phases: Jesus' pre-existence, his *kenōsis*, his further humiliation in death, his heavenly exaltation, the adoration of him by the universe, and the application to him of the name κύριος. In this hymn κύριος is used of Jesus precisely as the super-exalted one who is worthy of the same adoration as Yahweh himself (as the allusion to Isa 45:23 in v. 10 suggests). This pre-Pauline, cultic usage, applying the absolute title to the exalted Jesus, i.e., to a status posterior to his resurrection as such, is significant.

In a similar way Paul at times uses the title, "the Lord," to express the actual, ever-continuing existence of Jesus on the Christian community or on individual Christians. This usage is found throughout his writings, when he employs the pregnant prepositional phrase, "in the Lord" (ἐν κυρίῳ). This is found especially in greetings, blessings, exhortations (often with imperatives), and in formulations of Paul's own apostolic activity and plans.[87] It denotes for him the influence of the risen or exalted Jesus on the ongoing course of Christian practical life or ethical conduct. These are to be lived out "in the Lord," who is clearly understood as the post-Easter, post-resurrected Jesus.

But there are a few places in his letters which reflect the application of the title to the parousiac Jesus or "the Lord" of future coming. Significantly, this is found in the earliest of Paul's letters, in the eschatological teaching of 1

Thessalonians. Here Paul consoles the young Christians of Thessalonica, concerned about their confrères who have died before the parousia; he assures them that those who have died ἐν Χριστῷ, "in Christ," will rise first, when "the Lord himself will descend from heaven," and "we who are alive, who are left, shall be caught up together with them, . . . and so we shall always be with the Lord (σὺν κυρίῳ, 4:16-17). In this, one of the earliest affirmations of Paul's *kyrios*-faith, he refers to the parousiac Jesus as κύριος four times over (4:15, 16, 17a, b). The destiny of the Christian is to be "with the Lord," with the parousiac Jesus at his coming.

This eschatological application of κύριος is likewise reflected in the Aramaic liturgical acclamation, to which we have referred earlier. By being preserved precisely in Aramaic, μαραναθά (of 1 Cor 16:22) reveals its early, pre-Pauline, and Jewish-Christian provenience. It probably stems from Palestine (though other parts of the early Jewish-Christian world cannot be completely excluded). Though the analysis of the phrase has been debated—does it mean, "Our Lord has come!" or "Our Lord, come!"?—the eschatological or future (imperatival) explanation is preferred today by most commentators, because the Aramaic expression seems to underlie the Greek imperatival acclamation found at the end of the Book of Revelation, ἔρχου, κύριε Ἰησοῦ, "Come, Lord Jesus" (22:20). In this sense, the Christian community applied precisely to the parousiac Jesus the title κύριος, and its early Aramaic form[88] betrays the primitive character of that application.

Moreover, the cultic use of *kyrios*, applied at first to the Jesus of the parousia and later extended to other, earlier phases or events of his existence, seems to be reflected in another passage in Paul, where he speaks of the Eucharist. In 1 Cor 11:23-26 Paul passes on to us a teaching of the early Christian community before him, citing with technical vocabulary the παράδοσις or tradition to which he was himself tributary. For he says that he passed on what he himself had received about the "Lord's supper," and then he quotes from some liturgical formula already in use the words of institution of the Eucharist, ending with the declaration: "For as often as you eat this bread and drink this cup, you proclaim the Lord's death until he comes" (1 Cor 11:26). For Paul the Christian's participation in the Lord's supper is a proclamation of the effects of the Christ-event by the Christian community that ever looks forward to the coming of its "Lord." Paul here speaks of the "death" of the parousiac "Lord," not in the sense that the Jesus of the parousia is expected to die, but that the title for the parousiac Jesus is now applied to the event of his death—again, by retrojection. In this we see the thrust of the process of application at work. At least it gives us the basis for an hypothesis. What evidence there is in the NT itself, and especially in its earliest layers, seems to indicate that the *kyrios*-title was first applied to Jesus of the parousia and that the general extension of it brought about the gradual retrojection of it to other phases or states of his existence, even to that of his earthly mission.

This process of the retrojection of the *kyrios*-title has its parallels in other christological titles. In fact, it can be said to be indicated by the various stages of NT christology in general. For example, there are indications that the title "Messiah" was at one time applied to the parousiac Jesus (see Acts 3:20), and from there it was retrojected to the public ministry. Both John and Paul have a three-staged christology (parousiac, resurrectional, pre-incarnational) which differs from the three-staged christology in Matthew and Luke (resurrectional, public ministry, infancy narrative). This reveals to us a process of the developing awareness in the early church, which accounts for the different uses of *κύριος* that we have been discussing.

If any confirmation of this were needed, it can be found in the late writing of 1 John, where the title *κύριος* is completely avoided. Why this is so we are not sure, but it is probably to be ascribed to the desire to avoid the association of Jesus with the "many 'gods' and many 'lords'" (1 Cor 8:6) of the contemporary Hellenistic-Roman religious world. By the time 1 John was written, it was realized that Jesus as *κύριος* stood on an infinitely higher plane than these empty figures.[89] A similar avoidance of it is noted in the Johannine gospel, where, however, it does occasionally occur (e.g., 4:1; 20:28).

III. *The Implication of the* Kyrios-*Title for Jesus*

Finally, it remains to ask what is implied in calling Jesus *κύριος*. Having asked the questions about the origin of the title and the phase of his existence to which it was originally applied, we should inquire further into its nuances. What did and what does it mean for a Christian to say "Jesus is Lord"?

In a sense, we have already answered this question in part. For if the evidence presented in section I supports the contention that the *kyrios*-title was kerygmatic and was part of the early Palestinian Jewish-Christian proclamation, then it at least implies that early Christians regarded Jesus as sharing in some sense in the transcendence of Yahweh, that he was somehow on a par with him. This, however, is meant in an egalitarian sense, not in an identifying sense, since Jesus was never hailed as אבא. It involved a *Gleichsetzung*, but not an *Identifizierung*.[90] By "transcendence" here is meant that Jesus was somehow regarded as other than a mere human being; but the otherness is not spelled out in the NT with the clarity that would emerge in the Councils of Nicaea or Chalcedon, when the NT data were not only reformulated, but even reconceived in terms of other modes of philosophical thinking. The *Gleichsetzung* can be seen in two ways that involve the title *κύριος*. First of all, the title מרא used of God in the targum of Job, which translated שדי of the Hebrew text, stood in parallelism with אלהא.[91] Even though the nuances of each title may be specifically different, the parallelism in itself is suggestive. The hymn to Christ in Phil 2:6-11 climaxes with the bestowal of the title, which was otherwise used of Yahweh (at least in an incipient way) by Palestinian Jews, on Jesus himself. This suggests that he was somehow regarded as worthy of the same title otherwise employed for Yahweh. Second, if there should be any hesitancy about the first suggestion, it would seem to be confirmed by the adoration that is said to be his in the immediately preceding verse of the hymn. It is widely admitted that Phil 2:10-11 allude to Isa 45:23; in the latter the adoration is directed to Yahweh. Here in Philippians 2 it is accorded to Jesus—and precisely as "Lord."

If this seems to be the implication of the title, it is nevertheless clear that κύριος does not simply mean θεός, "God." If so, we may ask, What is the further nuance connoted by κύριος? As is well known, the NT rarely calls Jesus θεός; and when it does turn up, it is found in the later writings (Heb 1:8; John 1:1; 20:28—to cite only the more or less uncontested occurrences).[92] This usage reflects the time that it took for the early Christian community to come to the realization of faith that the title θεός, otherwise restricted in the NT to Yahweh, could also be given to Jesus. The gradual awareness of him as θεός, as someone on a par with Yahweh, and yet not אבא himself, eventually led to the development of the Christian doctrine of the Trinity. But if in time a Christian writer in the NT period could put on the lips of a Thomas the acclamation addressed to the risen Jesus, "my Lord and my God," that very acclamation suggests a difference in nuance between the two titles.

S. Schulz has investigated the Aramaic background of the suffixal and genitival forms of the title מרא as applied to God in various extrabiblical documents.[93] From the use of it in such texts as Elephantine documents of the fifth century B.C. and literary texts from Qumran he has concluded that the title "lord" connoted the judicial authority of a king *(königliche Richterautorität).* Hence for him, the Aramaic-speaking Christian community, in attributing to Jesus the title "Lord," was not so much affirming his divinity, as might be implied in the use of *kyrios* in the claim that it was a title derived from pagan Hellenistic usage of the eastern Mediterranean, as an assertion of his authority as judge associated with his regal condition. Schulz too was reacting against the exclusive derivation of the title from the pagan Hellenistic background. But his insistence on the judicial aspect of the title is not wholly convincing. Most of his evidence for it, however, comes not from the use of the title itself in the NT but from his association of it with the title "Son of Man." That the latter has judicial nuances in some of the contexts in which it is used (e.g., Mark 8:38 or 13:26 and parallels) goes without saying. But the two titles "Lord" and "Son of Man" should not be confused.[94] Their origins are distinct, their applications are distinct, and their implications should also be kept distinct.

That the *kyrios*-title has regal connotations can be clearly seen in one passage in the Synoptic tradition which depicts Jesus in debate with a temple audience (Mark 12:36), or Pharisees (Matt 22:41), or scribes (Luke 20:39): "How can the scribes say that the Messiah is the son of David? David himself, inspired by the Holy Spirit, declared, 'The Lord said to my Lord, Sit at my right hand, . . .' (Mark 12:36).[95] Here an association is suggested between Jesus as κύριος (or מרא) and a king of the Davidic dynasty; the regal implication of the title is clear.

Moreover, the entire tradition of the royal character of Yahweh in the OT would seem to be associated with the *kyrios*-title.[96]

But there is even more in the NT use of the title for Jesus. This is seen at times in the parallelism between κύριος and δοῦλος, between "lord" and "servant" (or "slave"). Indeed, in the hymn to Christ in Phil 2:6-11, there is an explicit contrast of these two conditions applied to Jesus himself. Despite the fact that he took up "the status of a slave" he was, nevertheless, eventually exalted as "Lord." Moreover, Paul often depicts either himself or the Christian disciple as δοῦλος. For all his proclaiming of the good news of Christian freedom, redemption, and emancipation in Christ Jesus, he insists that in another sense he or the Christian disciple is "the slave of Christ Jesus" (Phil 1:1; Rom 1:1; Gal 1:10; Col 4:12). Indeed, he sums up his entire role thus: "For what we preach is not ourselves, but Jesus Christ as Lord, with ourselves as your servants (*or* slaves) for Jesus' sake" (2 Cor 4:5). In effect, Paul says, "you were bought with a price" (1 Cor 6:20)—you *belong* to Christ, who is your "lord."

Involved in the affirmation that the Christian makes, Jesus is Lord, is the entire concept of Christian faith, as Paul sees it: "If you confess with your lips that Jesus is Lord and believe in your heart that God raised him from the dead, you will be saved" (Rom 10:9). Though that faith begins for Paul as a "hearing" (ἀκοή, "Faith comes from what is heard," Rom 10:17), it does not stop there. It involves the entire personal commitment of a man / woman to Christ Jesus as "Lord." It ends as ὑπακοὴ πίστεως, often mistakenly rendered simply as "the obedience of faith" (*RSV*, Rom 1:5; 16:26). It should rather be understood as "the commitment of faith." The word ὑπακοή implies the "*sub*mission" or total personal response of the believer to the risen Lord.[97]

Finally, it must be remembered that to acknowledge with lips and heart (i.e., with the total self) that "Jesus is Lord" is the essence of Christian faith. It means to acknowledge that one recognizes that "Jesus our Lord, who was put to death for our trespasses and raised for our justification" (Rom 4:25), still exerts an influence over the Christian disciple. The latter belongs to him, is committed to him and his service.[98]

NOTES TO CHAPTER 5

*Originally published as "Der semitische Hintergrund des neutestamentlichen Kyriostitels," *Jesus Christus in Historie und Theologie: Neutestamentliche Festschrift für Hans Conzelmann zum 60. Geburtstag* (ed. G. Strecker; Tübingen: Mohr [Siebeck], 1975) 267-98. This form in English has been somewhat revised and expanded.

[1]This chapter repeats in part some of the Aramaic material presented on pp. 87–90 above, but relates it to other material (Greek, Hebrew, and Punic) which bear on the topic.

[2]On the "absolute" usage of the Greek title, see p. 109 above, n. 26.

[3]*The Titles of Jesus* (p. 109 above, n. 22), 73-89.

[4]*The Words of Jesus* (p. 23 above, n. 53), 324-31.

[5]*Herr ist Jesus* (p. 108 above, n. 19), 201-8.

[6]*Christology* (p. 109 above, n. 20), 195-237.

[7]"Discipleship and Belief," (p. 109 above, n. 21), 87-99. Cf. *Erniedrigung und Erhöhung bei Jesus und seinen Nachfolgern* (ATANT 28; Zürich: Zwingli, 1962) 77-86.

[8]*The Foundations of New Testament Christology* (New York: Scribner, 1965) 50.

[9]"Κύριος, etc.," *TDNT* 3 (1965) 1039-98, esp. p. 1094.

[10]*Christology*, 201-15. "The non-Christian use of the *Kyrios* name in the Hellenistic world, its relation to emperor worship, and above all its use as the name of God in the Septuagint—all this certainly contributed to making *Kyrios* an actual *title* for Christ. But this development would not have been possible had not the original Church already called upon Christ as the Lord" (p. 215).

[11]"Discipleship and Belief," 93.

[12]*Kyrios Christos* (p. 108 above, n. 17), 119-52.

[13]*Theology of the New Testament* (p. 108 above, n. 18), 1. 124. "The Kyrios-cult originated on Hellenistic soil" (1. 51).

[14]"Ein Weg zur neutestamentlichen Christologie? Prüfung der Thesen Ferdinand Hahns," *Aufsätze zum Neuen Testament* (Theologische Bücherei, 31; Munich: C. Kaiser, 1965) 141-98 [leicht verändert vom Original, *EvT* 25 (1965) 24-72].

[15]*An Outline of the Theology of the New Testament* (New York: Harper & Row, 1969) 82-84.

[16]I shall not delay on F. Hahn's attempt (*The Titles of Jesus*, 73-89) to explain the title as a development from a Palestinian Semitic secular usage. The inadequacies of that explanation have already been dealt with by P. Vielhauer ("Ein Weg," 150-57). It amounts to an assertion without proof.

[17]See p. 124 below.

[18]By "its equivalent" I mean some circumlocution for the construct chain, such as the use of Aramaic די/ד with a following noun (absolute or emphatic) or a prepositional phrase.

[19]The various forms of the Aramaic word for "lord" call for some further comment. Throughout the centuries of its attestation the forms of it indicate that it was originally **māray* or **mārî*ᵓ, a *qātal* or a *qātil* noun-type of either a Tertiae Infirmae or a Tertiae Aleph root. The earliest forms in Aramaic turn up with the *aleph*, and early cognates in Canaanite, Ugaritic, and Akkadian also have the *aleph* (see W. F. Albright, "The Early Alphabetic Inscriptions from Sinai and Their Decipherment," *BASOR* 110 [1948] 6-22, esp. p. 21 n. 78; *The Vocalization of the Egyptian Syllabic Orthography* [AOS 5; New Haven: American Oriental Society, 1934] 43, §VIII.A.2; C. H. Gordon, *UT*, 437 §1543; W. von Soden, *Akkadisches Handwörterbuch* [Wiesbaden: Harrassowitz, 1966] 615). It is not certain at what period the mixing of Aramaic verbal forms of Tertiae Aleph and Tertiae Infirmae began, but that they were mixed is certain (see p. 110 above, n. 29). The intervocalic position of the *aleph* or the *yodh* was undoubtedly the reason for the mixing.

The absolute/construct form מָרֵא, in Biblical Aramaic, is perhaps to be explained as a contraction of **māray* (*qātal*-type) › *mārê*, with the final *aleph* (or *he*; cf. 1QapGen 20:13, מרה) being understood as a vowel letter. Cf. בָּנַיִן (Ezra 4:12); F. R. Blake [p. 110 above, n. 29], 13; P. Joüon, *Grammaire de l'hébreu biblique* (Rome: Biblical Institute, 1947) 159 n. 2 (listed as an alternate explanation). Older explanations tended to explain the form as a *qātil*-type: **mārì*ᵓ › *māre*ᵓ › *mārê*. See G. Dalman, *Grammatik des jüdisch-palästinischen Aramäisch—Aramäische Dialektproben* (Darmstadt: Wissenschaftliche Buchgesellschaft, 1960) 152; H. Bauer and P. Leander, *Grammatik des Biblisch-Aramäischen* (Halle/S.: Niemeyer, 1927) §51y´´. Cf. L. F. Hartman, *CBQ* 28 (1966) 497.

In the suffixal form like מָרְאִי the sequence of *shewa/aleph/vowel* led in time to the quiescence of the *aleph* and to the eventual disappearance of it even in the orthography. Thus, מראי (= *mārĕ*ᵓ*ī*, Aššur Ostracon 8; *AP* 16:8) › מרי (*mārī*), both of which forms are attested in Qumran Aramaic texts: 1QapGen 2:9, 13, 24; 4Qᶜ Amramᵇ 2:3 (see J. T. Milik, *RB* 79 [1972] 79).

Once the form מרי developed, the passage to an absolute or construct state in מר (= *mār*) by a back-formation was easy (see p. 89 above). But the form מר is as yet unattested in Palestinian Aramaic of the first century A.D. (*pace* O. Cullmann, *Christology,* 199). It is, however, attested in later Palestinian Jewish Aramaic and in Syriac, along with the further development of an emphatic state in מרא (= *mārāʾ*)—a vocalization that should not be foisted on first-century consonants, *pace* K. G. Kuhn, *TDNT* 4 (1967) 467; G. Vermes, *Jesus the Jew,* 111.

The emphatic state (מריא) is now attested in Palestinian Aramaic (4QEn[b] 1 iv 5); see p. 124 below.

[20]The same must be said, *mutatis mutandis*, of any Hebrew evidence that might be used as part of the Semitic background of the *Kyrios*-title. See p. 125 below.

[21]See, e.g., F. Hahn, *The Titles of Jesus,* 73-81.

[22]See H. Shanks, "Is the Title 'Rabbi' Anachronistic in the Gospels?" *JQR* 53 (1962-63) 337-45; S. Zeitlin, "A Reply," ibid., 345-49. Cf. E. Schürer, *A History of the Jewish People in the Time of Jesus Christ* (Edinburgh: Clark), 2/1 (1890) 315.

It has been argued that an ossuary discovered on Mt. Olivet dating from the period before the destruction of the Temple and bearing on one side the name תדטיון and on the other the title ΔΙΔΑΣΚΑΛΟΥ in the genitive (published by E. L. Sukenik, "מערת קברים יהודית במורד הר הזיתים (ב)," *Tarbiz* 1 [1930] 137-43 [+ pls. א-ח], esp. pp. 139-41; see also *Jüdische Gräber Jerusalems um Christi Geburt* [Jerusalem: (Azriel Printing House), 1931] 17-18; J.-B. Frey, *CII*, 2. §1266; *SEG*, 9. §179) is evidence of the early use of ῥαββί as a title (so W. F. Albright, "Recent Discoveries in Palestine and the Gospel of St. John," *The Background of the New Testament and Its Eschatology: Studies in Honour of Charles Harold Dodd* [ed. W. D. Davies and D. Daube; Cambridge: Cambridge University, 1956] 153-71, esp. pp. 157-58; E. Lohse, "Ῥαββί, ῥαββουνί," *TDNT* 6 [1968] 961-65, esp. p. 963 n. 26). But though the Greek title is thus attested, the alleged extrabiblical evidence for the equivalent of διδάσκαλος and ῥαββί, supposedly supporting John 1:38, is strikingly absent. This ossuary lends no support to the antiquity of the Aramaic title *rabbī*.

[23]See J. Donaldson, "The Title Rabbi in the Gospels—Some Reflections on the Evidence of the Synoptics," *JQR* 63 (1973) 287-91.

[24]See E. Lohse, *TDNT* 6 (1968) 963.

[25]This difficult item also has a remote bearing on an analogous problem that is beginning to emerge in the scholarly debate about the relation of אבי to אבא. The former is attested as a form of address in 1QapGen 2:24, being preceded by an interjection, יא אבי ויא מרי, "O my father and my lord," addressed by Methuselah to Enoch. In three places in the NT we find the Aramaic vocative ἀββά literally translated as ὁ πατήρ (Gal 4:6; Rom 8:15; Mark 14:36); in the Synoptic parallels Matthew has πάτερ μου (26:39), whereas Luke has simply πάτερ (22:42). This matter has often been discussed (see G. Kittel, "ἀββά," *TDNT* 1 [1933] 4-6; G. Schrenk, "πατήρ . . . ," *TDNT* 5 (1967) 977-78, 989-90; J. Jeremias, *Abba: Studien zur neutestamentlichen Theologie und Zeitgeschichte* [Göttingen: Vandenhoeck & Ruprecht, 1966] 15-67). But recently M. McNamara, reviewing the second edition of my commentary on the *Genesis Apocryphon* (*ITQ* 40 [1973] 286), argues that the form אבי is the "earlier and literary Aramaic" vocative, whereas אבא represents the spoken "regular vocative in Palestinian targumic Aramaic," of an equally early period. This may be, but how does he know? Surely, the use of the emphatic state as the vocative is not without attestation in literary texts; I do not refer explicitly to an instance of אבא, but the phenomenon is found in Daniel: מלכא (2:4, 29, 37; 3:4, etc.). Moreover, is it certain that Matthew's πάτερ μου simply reflects Mark's ἀββά, which the Second Evangelist (or his source) literally translated as ὁ πατήρ? After all, πάτερ μου is a strict translation of אבי and could reflect Matthew's change to the other form of address, known perhaps in an independent tradition. On the other hand, Luke's simple πάτερ is a more correct Greek translation of the Marcan ἀββά. I personally would hesitate to say which form, אבי or אבא, was earlier in this instance. Moreover, אבא could be just as "literary" a form as אבי. I would cite precisely its occurrence in targumic Aramaic as the evidence for that. It still has to be shown that targumic Aramaic is nothing more than a "spoken" form of

the language. As far as I am concerned, it is as much a literary form of the language as that of the Qumran texts—but of a different period (see p. 72–73 above).

The reason for mentioning this here, however, is that in it we have an analogous use of a suffixal form and an emphatic state (which when used as a form of address approaches the "absolute usage" of κύριος of which we have been speaking). In this instance, both forms are attested, אבי (in Aramaic) and ἀββά (in Greek, with אבא parallels in later Aramaic texts). Even though the shift from אבי to אבא would not be the same as in רבי, where the shift occurs in different meanings of the same form, it does point up the inadequacey of the parallel argument between κύριε / ὁ κύριος on the one hand, and διδάσκαλε / ὁ διδάσκαλος, on the other.

G. S. Glanzman has called to my attention how complicated this question of suffixal and absolute forms can be, when one compares Hebrew and so-called Septuagintal usage. Compare 2 Kgs 13:14 in the MT (אבי אבי) and the LXX (πάτερ, πάτερ); Gen 22:7 (אבי and πάτερ); Gen 27:18 (אבי and πάτερ μου in cod. A). Similarly, Ps 22:2 (אלי אלי and ὁ θεός, ὁ θεός μου). Other examples could be cited.

There is, moreover, a related problem in the form אדני that is only remotely connected with this issue, but not wholly unrelated. It is usually said that the word originally meant "my lord" and was given the plural vocalization (with pausal lengthening) in "solemn pronunciation" *(Affektbetonung).* Yet H. Bauer and P. Leander (*Historische Grammatik der hebräischen Sprache des Alten Testaments* [Olms Paperbacks, 19; Hildesheim: G. Olms, 1965 (reprint of 1922 edition)] §2*h*, 29*t*, 68*i*) have explained the form as a non-Semitic loanword with an ending *āy*, which was only later taken to be the 1st pers. suffix. If their explanation were correct, and I am not sure that it is, then *ʾădōnāy* would have originally meant only "lord." Cf. O. Eissfeldt, "אדון," *TWAT* 1 (1970) 62-78, esp. pp. 67-68 (which N. Lohfink has called to my attention). Further L. Cerfaux, "Le nom divin 'Kyrios' dans la Bible grecque," *RSPT* 20 (1931) 27-51; "'Adonai' et 'Kyrios,'" *RSPT* 20 (1931) 417-52; J. Lust, "'Mon Seigneur Jahweh' dans le texte hébreu d'Ezéchiel," *ETL* 44 (1968) 482–88; G. H. Dalman, *Studien zur biblischen Theologie: Der Gottesname Adonaj und seine Geschichte* (Berlin: Reuther, 1889) 20-25.

[26]See, e.g., F. Cumont, *Les religions orientales dans le paganisme romain: Conférences faites au Collège de France en 1905* (4th ed.; Paris: P. Geuthner, 1929) 109, 257 n. 56; E. Williger, "Κύριος," *RE* (Pauly-Wissowa) 23 (1924) 176-83; A. Deissmann, *Light from the Ancient East* (2d ed.; London: Hodder & Stoughton, 1927) 348-57; P. Wendland, *Die hellenistisch-römische Kultur in ihren Beziehungen zu Judentum und Christentum* (HNT 1/2-3; 3d ed.; Tübingen: Mohr [Siebeck], 1912) 220-21; H. Lietzmann, *An die Römer* (HNT 8; 4th ed.; Tübingen: Mohr, 1933) 97–101; W. Bousset, *Kyrios Christos* (p. 108 above, n. 17), 138–48; L. Cerfaux and J. Tondriau, *Le culte des souverains dans la civilisation gréco-romaine: Un concurrent du christianisme* (Tournai: Desclée, 1957) with an extensive bibliography, pp. 9-73; W. Fauth, "Kyrios," *Der kleine Pauly* (ed. K. Ziegler and W. Sontheimer; Stuttgart: A. Druckenmüller) 3 (1969) 413-17; W. Foerster, "Κύριος, etc.," *TDNT* 3 (1965) 1046-58; W. W. Baudissin, *Kyrios als Gottesname im Judentum und seine Stelle in der Religionsgeschichte* (4 vols.; Giessen: Töpelmann) 3 (1929) 70-73.

[27]So W. Foerster, *TDNT* 3 (1965) 1056.

[28]*Christology* (p. 109 above, n. 20), 198. Similarly, H. Conzelmann, *Outline of the Theology of the New Testament* (n. 15 above), 84.

[29]See, e.g., E. Lohmeyer, *Kyrios Jesus: Eine Untersuchung zu Phil. 2,5-11* (Sitzungsberichte der Heidelberger Akademie der Wissenschaften, Phil-hist. Kl., 1927-28/4; Heidelberg: C. Winter, 1928; 2d ed., 1961); E. Käsemann, "Kritische Analyse von Phil. 2.5-11," *Exegetische Versuche und Besinnungen* (Göttingen: Vandenhoeck & Ruprecht) 1 (1960) 51-95; F. W. Beare, *A Commentary on the Epistle to the Philippians* (BNTC; London: A. & C. Black, 1956) 76; P. Bonnard, *L'épître de saint Paul aux Philippiens* (CNT 10; Neuchâtel: Delachaux et Niestlé, 1950) 47-48; R. P. Martin, *Carmen Christi: Philippians ii. 5-11 in Recent Interpretation and in the Setting of Early Christian Worship* (SNTSMS 4; Cambridge: Cambridge University, 1967) 38-41; D. Georgi, "Der vorpaulinische Hymnus Phil 2,6-11," *Zeit und Geschichte: Dankesgabe an*

Rudolf Bultmann zum 80. Geburtstag (ed. E. Dinkler; Tübingen: Mohr [Siebeck], 1964) 263-93; J. Jeremias, "Zu Phil 2,7," *NovT* 4 (1963) 182-88; G. Strecker, "Redaktion und Tradition des Christushymnus," *ZNW* 55 (1964) 63-78.

[30]The consideration of the hymn as derived from a Semitic or Aramaic background is derived mainly from E. Lohmeyer (*Kyrios Jesus,* 9). Though he himself never attempted a retroversion of the hymn, it was subsequently done by P. P. Levertoff in W. K. L. Clarke, *New Testament Problems: Essays—Reviews—Interpretations* (London: S.P.C.K.; New York: Macmillan, 1929) 148. Levertoff's translation is reproduced in R. P. Martin, *Carmen Christi,* 40-41. But that Aramaic retroversion is a hodge-podge of forms drawn from Aramaic of various periods and dialects. It has been rightly criticized by P. Grelot ("Deux notes critiques sur Philippiens 2,6-11," *Bib* 54 [1973] 169-86, esp. pp. 176-79). Grelot himself has undertaken a retroversion of the hymn (pp. 180-86). (I should prefer נפשה for גרמה in vv. 7, 8; and I am not happy about שמוע [*šāmōa*ᶜ] for *ὑπήκοος*, but I am unable to suggest a better form at the moment). For the early, pre-Pauline dating of this hymn, see I. H. Marshall, "Palestinian and Hellenistic Christianity: Some Critical Comments," *NTS* 19 (1972-73) 271-87, esp. p. 284 n. 1.

[31]See A. Berthier and R. Charlier, *Le sanctuaire punique d'El-Hofra à Constantine* (Paris: Arts et métiers graphiques, 1955). The earliest dated text is El-Hofra 58, which mentions the 46th year of Masinisan the Prince (= 163/62 B.C.). However, most of the inscriptions are undated. Punic evidence was cited by earlier scholars (see G. H. Dalman, *Studien* [n. 25 above] 13), but it is neglected in many modern discussions.

[32]In Phoenician and Punic texts the suffix of the 1st sg. is *-y* (see *PPG*² §112.1; Z. Harris, *GPL* §15.2). But *-y* is also used at times for the 3d sg. masc. suffix; and in Punic texts -ᵓ (pronounced -*ō*) is used too, as in the examples cited here.

[33]*Le sanctuaire punique d'El-Hofra,* Inscriptions grecques, 1. 167-68. The Punic text that it represents would probably read as follows:

לאדן לבעל חמן ו/לרבתן תנת פן בעל / אש נדר ספפטרס בן / זפרס שמע קלא ב/רכא.

[34]"Discipleship and Belief" (p. 109 above, n. 21), 93.

[35]E.g., O. Cullmann, *Christology* (p. 109 above, n. 20), 201; F. Hahn, *The Titles of Jesus* (p. 109 above, n. 22), 71-73.

[36]*Outline of the Theology of the New Testament* (n. 15 above), 83-84. Less pertinent are Conzelmann's first two arguments: "1. In Paul, the title *Kyrios* in fact serves to distinguish Jesus and his position before God (I Cor. 8.6)." [1 Cor 8:6 would be a valid argument for Conzelmann only against those commentators who conclude from the LXX rendering of יהוה by *κύριος* "that the Christians identified Jesus with Yahweh." But how many NT commentators would conclude to such an *identification*? Suppose one only concludes that the title suggests that Jesus is somehow on a transcendent level with Yahweh? The end of the hymn in Phil 2:6-11 implies this sort of equality, which is not identification.] "2. There is no explanation of the fact that this title is used primarily in acclamations." [True, but so what? These arguments have to do with the use made of the title within the NT rather than with the *origin* of the title. More will be said below about the use of the title.]

[37]"Ein Weg" (n. 14 above), 149.

[38]The name is not preserved in any form in the oldest Greek (Proto-Lucianic!) manuscript, Pap. Ryl. Gk. 458 (from 2d century B.C. (?); see C. H. Roberts, *Two Biblical Papyri in the John Rylands Library, Manchester* [Manchester: Manchester University, 1936]). The most important evidence comes rather from a Palestinian (Proto-Theodotionic) translation of the Minor Prophets published by D. Barthélemy, *Les devanciers d'Aquila: Première publication intégrale du texte des fragments du Dodécaprophéton trouvés dans le Désert de Juda, précédée d'une étude sur les traductions et recensions grecques de la Bible réalisées au premier siècle de notre ère sous l'influence du rabbinat palestinien* (VTSup 10; Leiden: Brill, 1963) 163-78. Barthélemy has dated the fragments, written in two different hands, to "le milieu du premier siècle de notre ère" (p. 168). On this dating, see the opinion of C. H. Roberts and W. Schubart quoted by F. Dunand *Papyrus grecs bibliques (Papyrus F. Inv. 266): Volumina de la Genèse et du Deutéronome* (Recherches

d'archéologie, de philologie et d'histoire, 27; Cairo: L'Institut français d'archéologie orientale, 1966) 31: between 50 B.C. and A.D. 50; cf. P. Kahle, "Problems of the Septuagint," *Studia patristica I* (TU 63; Berlin: Akademie, 1957) 332. This is a modification of the date originally proposed by Barthélemy in *RB* 60 (1953) 19-20. The tetragrammaton, written in archaizing paleo-Hebrew script, is found in the Greek text of Jon 4:2; Mic 1:1, 3; 4:4; 5:3; Hab 2:14, 16, 20; 3:9; Zeph 1:3, 14; Zech 1:3; 3:5, 6, 7; 8:20; 9:1, 4. (On this text, see F. M. Cross, Jr., "The Contribution of the Qumran Discoveries to the Study of the Biblical Text," *IEJ* 16 [1966] 81-95, esp. pp. 84-85; "The History of the Biblical Text in the Light of the Discoveries in the Judean Desert," *HTR* 57 [1964] 282-99, esp. pp. 282-83; S. Jellicoe, *JAOS* 84 [1964] 178-82.)

But the tetragrammaton is also found still earlier in a Greek translation of Deut 32:3, 6, preserved in Papyrus Fuad 266 (of Egyptian provenience in the diaspora, from the 2d / 1st century B.C.). See W. G. Waddell, "The Tetragrammaton in the LXX," *JTS* 45 (1944) 158-61; O. Paret, *Die Bibel: Ihre Überlieferung in Druck und Schrift* (2d ed.; Stuttgart: Privilegierte Würtembergische Bibelanstalt, 1950) 76 and pl. 2. Further fragments of this papyrus were first published in the *New World Translation of the Christian Greek Scriptures* (Brooklyn, NY: Watchtower Bible and Tract Society, 1950) 11-16, esp. pp. 13-14. Cf. A. Vaccari, "Papiro Fuad, Inv. 266: Analisi critica dei frammenti pubblicati in 'New World Translation of the Christian Greek Scriptures,' Brooklyn (N.Y.) 1950, p. 13s.," Appendix to P. Kahle, "Problems of the Septuagint" (see above), pp. 328-41 [יהוה is preserved also in Deut 18:5; 31:27]. Cf. P. Kahle, *Die hebräischen Handschriften aus der Höhle: Franz Delitzsch-Vorlesungen* (Stuttgart: Kohlhammer, 1951) 7-8, 63-64, and pl. 11; *The Cairo Geniza* (2d ed.; Oxford: Blackwell, 1959) 218-28; H. H. Rowley, *The Old Testament and Modern Study* (Oxford: Clarendon, 1951) 249 n. 1; B. J. Roberts, *The Old Testament Texts and Versions* (Cardiff: University of Wales, 1951) 173; M. Noth, *Die Welt des Alten Testaments* (2d ed.; Berlin: Töpelmann, 1953) 254 n. 1; *The Old Testament World* (Philadelphia: Fortress, 1966) 322; E. Würthwein, *The Text of the Old Testament: An Introduction to Kittel-Kahle's Biblia hebraica* (tr. P. R. Ackroyd; New York: Macmillan, 1957) 132-33 (p. 25). Further fragments of this papyrus are now available in F. Dunand, *Papyrus grecs bibliques (Papyrus F. Inv. 266)* (see above), 26, 39-50. Also cf. *Etudes de papyrologie* 9 (1971) 81-150; G. D. Kilpatrick, "The Cairo Papyrus of Genesis and Deuteronomy (P. F. Inv. 266), ibid., 221-26; Z. Aly, "Addenda," ibid., 227-28 (+ pl. I). S. Schulz ("Maranatha und Kyrios Jesus," *ZNW* 53 [1962] 125-44, esp. p. 129) speaks of having had the opportunity to inspect the papyrus and of having counted 31 examples of יהוה in what is now known to be more than 100 fragments of Pap. Fuad 266. It seems that further fragments of this papyrus are still to be published.

The tetragrammaton is regularly preserved also in fragments of Aquila's translation of Kings from the Cairo Geniza (see p. 122 below).

It has likewise been said to be preserved in 3d / 4th century fragments of Symmachus' translation of Ps 69:13, 31, 32 (see C. Wessely, "Un nouveau fragment de la version grecque du Vieux Testament par Aquila," *Mélanges offerts à M. Emile Chatelain (Paris: H. Champion, 1910) 224-29*. But cf. G. Mercati, *"Frammenti di Aquila o di Simmaco?" RB* 8 (1911) 266–72; P. Capelle, "Fragments du psautier d'Aquila?" *Revue bénédictine* 28 (1911) 64-68; D. Barthélemy, "Qui est Symmaque?" *CBQ* 36 (1974) 451-65, esp. p. 455.

Moreover, both Origen and Jerome knew about the practice of writing the name in Hebrew in Greek manuscripts. See Jerome, *Prologus galeatus* (*PL* 28. 594-95): "Nomen Domini tetragrammaton in quibusdam graecis voluminibus usque hodie antiquis expressum litteris invenimus." Again, "(Dei nomen est) tetragrammum, quod *ἀνεκφώνητον*, id est ineffabile, putauerunt et his litteris scribitur: *iod, he, uau, he*. Quod quidam non intellegentes propter elementorum similitudinem, cum in Graecis libris reppererint, ΠΙΠΙ legere consueuerunt" (Ep. 25, *Ad Marcellam*; CSEL 54. 219).

The tetragrammaton is written with two paleo-Hebrew *yodhs* in P. Oxy. 1007 verso 1:4 (= Gen 2:8) and 2:14 (= Gen 2:18), dated by the editor (A. S. Hunt) to "late third century." Compare P. Oxy. 1075 ("third century"), which has $\overline{\mathrm{K\Sigma}}$ on line 12 (= Exod 40:35). A similar abbreviation is partially preserved in P. Oxy. 1166 ("third century"), lines 11 and 24 (= Gen 16:10, 11). Different forms of the abbreviation can also be found in *Papyrus Bodmer IX* ("du début du IVᵉ siècle"), e.g., 1:1, 3, 5, 7 (= Ps 33:2-5), etc.

[39]This form is preserved in 4QLevᵇ as a reading of Lev 4:27 (*τῶν ἐντολῶν* Ἰαώ), and probably also in 3:12; see P. W. Skehan, "The Qumran Manuscripts and Textual Criticism," *Volume du Congrès, Strasbourg 1956* (VTSup 4; Leiden: Brill, 1957) 148-60, esp. p. 157. See also Ezek 1:2 and 11:1 (according to the margin of the 6th century Codex Marchalianus (Vat. gr. 2125): Ἰαώ. Cf. Diodorus Siculus, 1.94: *παρὰ δὲ τοῖς Ἰουδαίοις* Μωυσῆν *τὸν* Ἰαὼ *ἐπικαλούμενον θεόν*; cf. Origen, *In Ps. 2:4* [*PG* 12.1104: Ἰαή]; *Comm. in Ioan.* 2:1 [*GCS* Origen, 4. 53]. See further A. Lukyn Williams, "The Tetragrammaton—Jahweh, Name or Surrogate?" *ZAW* 54 (1936) 262-69, esp. p. 266.

[40]See the end of n. 38 above. Cf. E. Hatch and R. A. Redpath, *A Concordance to the Septuagint and the Other Greek Versions of the Old Testament (Including the Apocryphal Books)* (2 vols. + suppl.; Graz: Akademische Druck- u. Verlagsanstalt, 1954), suppl., p. 126 for examples. Also C. Taylor, *Hebrew-Greek Cairo Genizah Palimpsests from the Taylor-Schechter Collection: Including a Fragment of the Twenty-Second Psalm according to Origen's Hexapla* (Cambridge: Cambridge University, 1900), folio B recto, pl. II (on Ps 22:20).

[41]This is more or less the opinion of P. Kahle (*The Cairo Geniza,* 222; "Problems of the Septuagint," 329); S. Schulz ("Maranatha und Kyrios Jesus," 128-29); P. Vielhauer ("Ein Weg," 149); et al.

[42]Κ*ύριος* as a name for Yahweh in the NT is found, for instance, in Mark 5:19; 13:20; Matt 5:33; Luke 1:6, 9, 28, 46; Rom 4:8; 9:28, 29; 11:34; 2 Thes 3:3; Eph 6:7. See L. Cerfaux, "'Kyrios' dans les citations pauliniennes de l'Ancien Testament," *Recueil Lucien Cerfaux* (BETL 6; Gembloux: Duculot, 1954), 1. 173-88, esp. pp. 174-77.

[43]This issue, of course, is complicated by the transmission of the NT text itself. In the verse cited, Codex Bezae reads *θεός* instead of *κύριος*. But the bulk of the good mss. are against that reading, and it may be there for another reason.

[44]However, Chester Beatty Papyrus VI is dated not "later than the second century" and probably not "after the middle of that century"; see F. G. Kenyon, *Chester Beatty Biblical Papyri . . . Fasciculus V: Numbers and Deuteronomy* (London: E. Walker) Text (1935), Pls. (1958), p. ix. E.g., it has $\overline{κς}$/$\overline{κυ}$ in Num 5:17, 18, 21; Deut 1:25, 27, 30, etc. Cf. Pap. Oxy. 656 ("carefully written in round upright uncials. . . , having in some respects more affinity with types of the second century than of the third"), *The Oxyrhynchus Papyri* (ed. B. P. Grenfell and A. S. Hunt; London: Egypt Exploration Fund) 4 (1904) 29. The editors mention "the absence of the usual contraction for *θεὸς κύριος*, &c." In line 17 "a blank space, sufficient for four letters, was left by the original scribe between *τὰ* and *κατὰ*, and in this *κύριε* was inserted by the second hand" (p. 33). See also lines 122, 166.

But, as R. A. Kraft has pointed out to me, how does one distinguish between Jewish and Christian copies of these Greek texts? Moreover, even P. Kahle ("Problems of the Septuagint," 333) admitted that "the ancient Christians used texts of the Greek Bible which had already been adapted to the Hebrew original by the Jews in pre-Christian times."

A still further question could be asked about the use of *κύριος* in such Greek writings as Judith, Wisdom, Maccabees, the additions to Esther, and 1 Esdras. But here the question is more complicated, because the text of many of these books is contained in the manuscripts of the so-called LXX, and whatever might finally be said about the *kyrios*-problem of the LXX might have to be said about these original Greek compositions as well.

[45]*Ant.* 2.12.4 §276.

[46]*Ant.* 1.3.1 §72; 1.18.6 §272; 2.12.2 §270; 4.3.2 §40, 46; 5.1.13 §41; 5.1.25 §93; 11.3.9 §64; 8.4.3 §111; 11.6.8 §230; *JW* 8.8.6 §323. Josephus also knows of *κύριος* as the Greek equivalent of Hebrew אדון; see *Ant.* 5.2.2 §121.

[47]For an interpretation of this phenomenon, see A. Schlatter, *Die Theologie des Judentums nach dem Bericht des Josefus* (BFCT 2/26; Gütersloh: C. Bertelsmann, 1932) 25-26; *Wie sprach*

Josephus von Gott? (BFCT 14/1; Gütersloh: C. Bertelsmann, 1910) 8-11. Cf. E. Nestle, "Miscellen: 6. Josephus über das Tetragrammaton," *ZAW* 25 (1905) 201-23, esp. p. 206; J. B. Fischer, "The Term ΔΕΣΠΟΤΗΣ in Josephus," *JQR* 49 (1958-59) 132-38. H. St. J. Thackeray, "Note on the Evidence of Josephus," *The Old Testament in Greek, II/1: I and II Samuel* (ed. A. E. Brooke, N. McLean, and H. St. J. Thackeray; Cambridge: Cambridge University, 1927) ix; A. Mez, *Die Bibel des Josephus untersucht für Buch V-VII* (Basel: Jaeger & Kober, 1895); P. Kahle, *The Cairo Geniza* (2d ed.; see p. 110 above, n. 33) 229–35; G. Howard, "*Kaige* Readings in Josephus," *Textus: Annual of the Hebrew University Bible Project* 8 (1973) 45-54.

[48]Even the variant in the margin of ms. A of Josephus' text contains *κύριον*; see LCL, 9. 434.

[49]E.g., by J. B. Fischer, *JQR* 49 (1958-59) 132-38.

[50]See F. M. Cross, Jr., "The Contribution of the Qumran Discoveries" (n. 38 above), 84-85; "The History of the Biblical Text," 281-99; P. W. Skehan, "The Biblical Scrolls from Qumran and the Text of the Old Testament," *BA* 28 (1965) 87-100, esp. pp. 90-95. Compare Kahle's comment in n. 44 above.

[51]One could also ask about Philo's references to Yahweh as *κύριος* in a diaspora situation. Commenting on Exod 3:14 in *De mutatione nominum* (2 §12), he says: "Yet that the human race should not totally lack a title to give to the supreme goodness He allows them to use by licence of language, as though it were His proper name, the title of Lord God of the three natural orders, teaching, perfection, practice, which are symbolized in the records as Abraham, Isaac, and Jacob" (*δίδωσι καταχρῆσθαι ὡς ἂν ὀνόματι κυρίῳ τῷ "κύριος ὁ θεὸς" τῶν τριῶν φύσεων, διδασκαλίας, τελειότητος, ἀσκήσεως, ὧν σύμβολα Ἀβραάμ, Ἰσαάκ, Ἰακὼβ ἀναγράφεται*). Cf. *Quis rerum divinarum heres* 6 §22-29. But Philo also uses the absolute form *κύριος* of God, *ὤφθη κύριος τῷ Ἀβραάμ*, and this precisely in a quotation of Gen 17:1. Where did he get *κύριος*? From Christian manuscripts of the LXX? Or did Christian scribes tamper with his text in its transmission too? It is clear, however, that Philo was aware that his Greek Bible gave Yahweh the title not only of *θεός*, but also of *κύριος*, since he explains the latter as a title betokening sovereignty and kingship (*ἡ γὰρ κύριος πρόσρησις ἀρχῆς καὶ βασιλείας ἐστι*), *De somniis*, 1.63. Cf. *De vita Mosis* 1.14 §75. See H. Wolfson, *Philo: Foundations of Religious Philosophy in Judaism, Christianity, and Islam* (2d ed.; Cambridge: Harvard University, 1948), 2. 120; P. Katz, *Philo's Bible: The Aberrant Text of Bible Quotations in Some Philonic Writings and Its Place in the Textual History of the Greek Bible* (Cambridge: Cambridge University, 1950) 47, 59-60. Cf. G. E. Howard, "The 'Aberrant' Text of Philo's Quotations Reconsidered," *HUCA* 44 (1973) 197-209.

[52]See M. Hadas, *Aristeas to Philocrates (Letter of Aristeas) Edited and Translated* (New York: Harper, 1951) 161; cf. H. St. J. Thackeray, "The Letter of Aristeas," in an appendix to H. B. Swete, *An Introduction to the Old Testament in Greek* (rev. R. R. Ottley; New York: Ktav, 1968) 578 (the *apparatus criticus* gives a variant recorded in Eusebius, which only adds *τοῦ θεοῦ* to *κυρίου*). Cf. E. Bickerman, "Zur Datierung des Pseudo-Aristeas," *Studies in Jewish and Christian History* (AGJU 9; Leiden: Brill, 1976) 109-36.

[53]See F. C. Burkitt, *Fragments of the Books of Kings According to the Translation of Aquila from a MS. Formerly in the Geniza at Cairo* (Cambridge: Cambridge University, 1897) 8, 15-16.

[54]See C. Taylor, *Hebrew-Greek Cairo Geniza Palimpsests* (n. 40 above), 53-65 (+ pls. III-VIII).

[55]See F. C. Burkitt, *Fragments of the Books of Kings* (n. 53 above), 16. Cf. H. B. Swete, *An Introduction* (n. 52 above), 39; F. Dunand, *Papyrus grecs bibliques* (n. 38 above), 51; J. Reider, "Prolegomena to a Greek-Hebrew and Hebrew-Greek Index to Aquila," *JQR* 7 (1916-17) 287-366.

[56]Aquila's concern for literalness in translation and his opposition to the use of the LXX by Christians are well known; see B. J. Roberts, *The Old Testament Texts and Versions* (n. 38 above), 123. Was the scribe who copied Aquila's text a Christian? If so, why was the abbreviation not used throughout (or at least *κύριος*)?

[57]It seems, however, that it was so read at times. See *j. Nedarim* 11:1; also the text of Jerome quoted above in n. 38. Cf. J. Halévy, "L'origine de la transcription du texte hébreu en caractères grecs dans les Hexaples d'Origène," *JA* 9/17 (1901) 335-41; J.-B. Chabot, ibid., 349-50; G.

Mercati, "Il problema della colonna II dell'Esaplo," *Bib* 28 (1947) 173-215, esp. pp. 189-90; "Note bibliche: 1. Sulla scrittura del tetragramma nelle antiche versioni greche del Vecchio Testamento," *Bib* 22 (1941) 339-54 (+ "Post Scriptum," 365-66); J. A. Emerton, "Were Greek Transliterations of the Hebrew Old Testament Used by Jews before the Time of Origen?" *JTS* ns 21 (1970) 17-31, esp. pp. 18-22; N. Fernandez Marcos, "Ἰαΐε, ἐσερεέ, ἀϊά y otros nombres de Dios entre los hebreos," *Sefarad* 35 (1975) 91-106.

One does not have to wonder what the Syriac scribes made of it, when translating or copying from Greek OT manuscripts; they wrote in Syriac *pypy*. See E. Nestle, "Jakob von Edessa über den Schem hammephorasch und andere Gottesnamen: Ein Beitrag zur Geschichte des Tetragrammaton," *ZDMG* 32 (1878) 465-508 (see Severus, *Hom.* 123 [*PO* 29/1.190-207]); "Berichtigungen und Nachträge zu dem Scholion des Jakob von Edessa über den Schem hammerphorasch," *ZDMG* 32 (1878) 735-36; G. Hoffmann, "Zu Nestle's Aufsatz S. 465," *ZDMG* 32 (1878) 736-37. (I am indebted to S. P. Brock of Oxford for some help in this matter.)

[58]See p. 21 above, n. 15.

[59]I do not agree with Moule that the "Hellenists" spoken of in Acts 9:29 were Christians. See E. Haenchen, *The Acts of the Apostles: A Commentary* (Philadelphia: Westminster, 1971) 333; M. Simon, *St Stephen and the Hellenists in the Primitive Church* (London: Longmans, Green and Co., 1958) 14-15.

[60]H. Conzelmann, *Outline of the Theology of the New Testament*, 82. Conzelmann apparently understands the "Hellenists" and the "Hebrews" of Acts 6:1 pretty much as I do. He writes that it is "essential to differentiate between the two types (the primitive community and the Hellenistic community)" (p. 32), although by "the Hellenistic community" he means "the Hellenistic church in the wider sense," which came into being when the Hellenists who regarded "themselves as Jews" were expelled from Jerusalem and began the "mission to the Gentiles (Acts 11.19ff.)" (p. 31). He thus distinguishes between "Hebrews," "Hellenists," and the "Hellenistic community" (in the wider sense). I should only insist that the Jerusalem "Hellenists" were as much a part of the early Christian "primitive community" as were the "Hebrews." And this insistence allows for a conceptualization and a formulation of the primitive kerygma within that community that is both Semitic and Hellenistic in its modes and for a mutual influence of them, especially in the matter of the *kyrios*-title.

[61]On this expression, see K. G. Kuhn, "Μαραναθά," *TDNT* 4 (1967) 466-72; S. Schulz, "Maranatha und Kyrios Jesus" (n. 38 above); C. F. D. Moule, "A Reconsideration of the Context of Maranatha," *NTS* 6 (1959-60) 307-10; J. Betz, "Die Eucharistie in der Didache," *Archiv für Liturgiewissenschaft* 11 (1969) 10-39; W. Dunphy, "Maranatha: Development in Early Christianity," *ITQ* 37 (1970) 294-308; M. Black, "The Maranatha Invocation and Jude 14, 15 (I Enoch 1:9)," *Christ and Spirit in the New Testament: In Honour of Charles Francis Digby Moule* (ed. B. Lindars and S. S. Smalley; Cambridge: Cambridge University, 1973) 189-96. It is not my intention to imply that מראנא played no role in the development of the absolute usage of the Greek title. It certainly had at the same time a great role as an acclamation-form in the cultic setting of early Palestinian Christianity; and that is reflected still in the Greek form (of the vocative) in Rev 22:20, ἔρχου κύριε Ἰησοῦ.

[62]See p. 117 above. The suffixal form has recently turned up as a theophoric element in a proper name; see J. Naveh, "'פחלץ' באוסטרקון ארמי חדש" ['*Pḥlṣ*' in a New Aramaic Ostracon]," *Lěšonénu* 37 (1972-73) 270-74. Line 2 of the fragmentary ostracon reads: [   ]קר בר עבדמראן, "[   ]qar bar ᶜAbedmarᵓan." Naveh thinks that the theophoric element is *Marna(s)*, a deity worshipped in Gaza from the Persian period onwards. Whether this is correct remains to be seen. If it were to refer to Yahweh, then we would have an interesting use of a suffixal form of מרא. Should the first name be restored as [ᵓ*Aḥī*]*qar*? The form מרנא has now turned up in 4QEn[b] 1 iii 14; see J. T. Milik, *The Books of Enoch: Aramaic Fragments of Qumrân Cave 4* (Oxford: Clarendon, 1976) 146-47.

[63]*The Words of Jesus* (p. 23 above, n. 53).

[64]*Theology of the New Testament* (p. 108 above, n. 18), 1. 51. See other opinions cited above, pp. 87-88. Cf. H. Lietzmann, *An die Römer*, 99 "מרא 'der Herr' ist nie so verwendet worden."

[65]See pp. 109 above, n. 28.

[66]Ibid. Cf. one of the passages in Josephus where κύριος is used, *Ant.* 20.4.2 §90, with 1QapGen 20:13.

[66a]See J. T. Milik, *The Books of Enoch,* 175.

[67]On the use of יהוה in the Book of Job, see p. 88 above.

[68]The title שדי is also translated by אלהא in 11QtgJob 6:1 (= Hebr. 22:3); 7:3 (= Hebr. 22:17). Cf. G. Bertram, "Zur Prägung der biblischen Gottesvorstellung in den griechischen Übersetzung des Alten Testaments: Die Wiedergabe von *schaddad* und *schaddaj* im Griechischen," *WO* 2 (1959) 502-13; H. Hommel, "Pantokrator," *Theologia viatorum* 5 (1953-54) 322-78.

[69]See p. 90 above. What is one to make of κύριος in the LXX and Theodotion translation of Dan 2:47? It is not a question of a translation of יהוה. Is this too to be attributed to Christian scribes? Recall that מרא מלכן turns up as a Pharaonic title in the Adon Letter (*KAI* §266); although it is not the same as κύριος βασιλείων of the Rosetta Stone, there is at least some relation here between מרא and κύριος. See my discussion in "The Aramaic Letter of King Adon to the Egyptian Pharaoh," *Bib* 46 (1965) 41-55; reproduced below, pp. 233–35.

[70]"Deux notes critiques," (n. 30 above), 184-86.

[71]Since מרא is the predicate here, it has to be in the absolute *state* in Aramaic; but what is to be noted is that it is used absolutely (as defined on p. 109 above, n. 26), i.e., *attributlos.* For an attempt to retrovert Ps 110:1 into contemporary Aramaic, see p. 90 above. What should be noted is that מרא is now attested as an absolute title for God and the suffixal form מרי is found for a human being in 1QapGen 2:9, 13, 24. The play on the words in Greek (εἶπεν κύριος τῷ κυρίῳ μου, Mark 12:36) can reflect an Aramaic form of Ps 110:1, if we may presume that Hebrew יהוה was translated by מרא.

[72]Pp. 44–46 above.

[73]See J. A. Sanders, *The Psalms Scroll of Qumrân Cave 11* (DJD 4; Oxford: Clarendon, 1965) 49, 55, 57 (28:7-8). See also his *The Dead Sea Psalms Scroll* (Ithaca: Cornell University, 1967) 88-89, 94-103 for further discussions of Psalm 151. Some commentators (I. Rabinowitz, J. Carmignac) have tried to interpret אדון as a construct state with the following הכול. But see P. W. Skehan, "The Apocryphal Psalm 151," *CBQ* 25 (1963) 407-9, for a defense of the absolute usage and the translation, "Who can recount the works of the Lord?" Cf. A. Hurvitz, "The Post-Biblical Epithet אדון הכול," *Tarbiz* 34 (1965) 224-27. The absolute use of אדון is also found in 1QH 10:8, but it is followed there by a prepositional expression (לכול רוח), which is the equivalent of a construct chain; it makes it similar to the use of מרה in 1QapGen 20:15 (see p. 109 above, n. 28). Cf. also Sir 10:7: שנואה לאדון, μισητὴ ἔναντι κυρίου (I am indebted to G. S. Glanzman for calling this instance to my attention). See further P. W. Skehan, *CBQ* 38 (1976) 147.

[74]The Greek version of Ps 151:3, though it twice contains κύριος, is not an exact rendering of the Qumran Hebrew texts: καὶ τίς ἀναγγελεῖ τῷ κυρίῳ μου; αὐτὸς κύριος, αὐτὸς εἰσακούει.

[75]*The Psalms Scroll*, 9; In *The Dead Sea Psalms Scroll*, 6, Sanders sets the date more precisely as "between A.D. 30 and 50."

[76]At this point one should really take time out to look at other Greek writings of the intertestamental period, such as those mentioned toward the end of n. 44 above. Κύριος is found, e.g., in the Greek text of *1 Enoch* 9:4; 10:9; 14:24; 25:3; 106:11, 13.

[77]See 1QIsa[a] 3:20-25 (= Isa 3:15-18). Cf. M. Burrows, "Variant Readings in the Isaiah Manuscript," *BASOR* 113 (1949) 24-32, esp. p. 31; M. Delcor, "Des diverses manières d'écrire le tetragramme sacré dans les anciens documents hébraïques," *RHR* 147 (1955) 145-73; J. P. Siegel, "The Employment of Palaeo-Hebrew Characters for the Divine Names at Qumran in the Light of Tannaitic Sources," *HUCA* 42 (1971) 159-72.

[78]E.g., 1QpHab 6:14 (= Hab 2:2); 10:7, 14 (= Hab 2:13-14); 1QpMic 1-5:1, 2 (= Mic 1:2-3); 11QPs 2:1, 4, 6, 11 (= Ps 146:9, 10; 148:1, 7); etc.

[79]4QFlorilegium (4Q*174*) 1-2 i 3; 1Q*29* 3-4:2.

[80]In fragments as yet unpublished from Qumran Caves IV and XI; see (in part) P. Benoit, "Le travail d'édition des fragments manuscrits de Qumrân," *RB* 63 (1956) 49-67, esp. p. 56.

[81]1QS 8:14 (quoting Isa 40:3); 4QTestimonia (4Q*175*) 1, 19 (quoting Deut 5:28 and 33:11); 4QTanḥumim (4Q*176*) 1-2 i 6, 7, 9; 1-2 ii 3; 8-11:6, 8, 10.

[82] 1QM 15:12 (cf. 1 Sam 18:17).

[83] 1QH 1:26; 2:34; 1Q*27* 1 ii 11; 1QpMic 12:3; 4Q*180* 1:1; 4Q*183* 1 ii 3.

[84] 1QS 8:13.

[85] 4QpPs^{b} 5:4 (= Ps 118:20).

[86] This usage stands in contrast to that of the Mishnah. Cf. S. T. Byington, "יהוה and אדני," *JBL* 76 (1957) 58-59.

[87] See further *Pauline Theology: A Brief Sketch* (p. 109 above, n. 28), 69.

[88] In this case, a suffixal form; see the end of n. 61 above.

[89] See F. C. Grant, *The Gospels: Their Origin and Their Growth* (London: Faber and Faber, 1957) 165; similarly, R. Bultmann, *The Theology of the New Testament* (p. 108 above, n. 18), 2. 36.

[90] H. Conzelmann, (*An Outline of the Theology of the New Testament* [n. 15 above], 83) rightly objects against this sort of terminology. He refers to O. Cullmann in this context. The word "identification" is used in the English translation of Cullmann's *Christology* (p. 109 above, n. 20), 218. But in the original German (*Die Christologie des Neuen Testaments* [Tübingen: Mohr (Siebeck), 1957] 224) Cullmann speaks of *Gleichsetzung*, which, as I understand it, is not the same thing as *Identifizierung*. See n. 36 above.

[91] Compare also the parallelism of אדון and אלוה in Psalm 151 cited above.

[92] See R. E. Brown, "Does the New Testament Call Jesus God?" *TS* 26 (1965) 545-73; reprinted in *Jesus God and Man: Modern Biblical Reflections* (Milwaukee: Bruce, 1967) 1-38.

[93] "Maranatha und Kyrios Jesus," *ZNW* 53 (1962) 125-44.

[94] See further my article, "The Son of David Tradition" (p. 113 above, n. 87).

[95] For a possible retroversion of this saying into Aramaic, see p. 90 above.

[96] See, e.g., L. Cerfaux, "Le titre Kyrios et la dignité royale de Jésus," *RSPT* 11 (1922) 40-71: "un titre du protocole des rois" (p. 42); E. Lipiński, *La royauté de Yahwé dans la poésie et le culte de l'ancien Israël* (Brussels: Paleis der Academiën, 1965).

[97] See further *Pauline Theology: A Brief Sketch* (p. 109 above, n. 28), 64-65.

[98] See further I. H. Marshall, "Palestinian and Hellenistic Christianity: Some Critical Comments," *NTS* 19 (1972-73) 271-87; M. Hengel, "Christologie und neutestamentliche Chronologie: Zu einer Aporie in der Geschichte des Urchristentums," *Neues Testament und Geschichte: Historisches Geschehen und Deutung im Neuen Testament: Oscar Cullmann zum 70. Geburtstag* (ed. H. Baltensweiler and B. Reicke; Zürich: Theologischer Verlag, 1972) 43-67, esp. 60-61. For a further specific interpretation of the implication of the *kyrios*-title in the Matthean Gospel, see J. D. Kingsbury, "The Title 'Kyrios' in Matthew's Gospel," *JBL* 94 (1975) 246-55.

Chapter 6

The New Testament Title "Son of Man" Philologically Considered*

Among the many titles given to Jesus in the NT none has been so contested and continuously debated as that of the "Son of Man." The debate has centered on the origin and background of the title, the occurrence of it on the lips of Jesus and of others in NT writings, and the connotations that it would carry. It is likewise controverted in its application to the various stages of his existence, and the question is raised whether he used it during his earthly ministry either of himself or of another person. These questions reveal that the title has been a complex problem in recent NT interpretation, and the sorting out of the various facets of the problem is not always easy. The philological aspect, being mainly concerned with the origin and background of the title and of the meaning(s) which the phrase might have had in Palestinian Judaism, is more or less propaedeutic to the theological discussion. Yet the latter cannot be seriously engaged in without due regard for the philological question. A disregard of the latter as *belanglos* would be tolerated only in a dialectical interpretation of the NT in which the consideration of new empirical data proves traumatic.

Aspects of the philological consideration of the title have often been rehearsed before this, and if I now address myself to them, it is with the hope that some of these observations may at least query some commonly accepted interpretations and bring some new material to bear upon the problem. Indirectly, my observations will also bear on the theological considerations involved in the title. Moreover, the philological data have to be related to the proper phases of Aramaic; for the disregard of this aspect has been responsible for the introduction of many extraneous and irrelevant notions into the debate.

The literature on the "Son of Man" is vast, and I make no pretense about covering it.[1] But I hope to cope at least with some of the more important recent discussions of the philological aspects of the title.

My remarks will fall under three headings: (1) A brief resume of the NT data and of some recent attempts to translate the phrase; (2) The Semitic data, Hebrew and Aramaic, that bear upon the title; and (3) The connotations of the title in a first-century Palestinian context.

I. *The New Testament Data and Attempts to Translate the Title*

A summary of the NT usage of the title is necessary initially so that a clear view of what is involved may be before us.

The title *ὁ υἱὸς τοῦ ἀνθρώπου* is used of Jesus by other persons in the NT in a few instances: the arthrous form is employed by Stephen in Acts 7:56, whereas the anarthrous form (*υἱὸς ἀνθρώπου*) is used by the author of Revelation (1:13; 14:14, in an allusion to Dan 7:13), and possibly also by the author of the Epistle to the Hebrews (2:6, quoting Ps 8:5).[2] Indirectly, John 12:34a,b implies the application of the arthrous form to him by others. In the passages that allude to or quote the OT, the phrase agrees with the form found in the LXX and Theodotionic versions of the OT books involved.

Within the Synoptic tradition the arthrous phrase is found only on the lips of Jesus. It is applied to him (a) *in his earthly ministry*: in the Marcan source and its parallels (2:10 [= Matt 9:6; Luke 5:24]; 2:28 [= Matt 12:8; Luke 6:51; *10:45 [= Matt 20:28; Luke 22:27 has "I"]; Matt 16:13 [Mark 8:27 and Luke 9:18 have "me"]); from "Q" (*Matt 8:20 = Luke 9:58; *Matt 11:19 = Luke 7:34; Matt 12:32 = Luke 12:10; *Luke 6:22 [Matt 5:11 has "my"]); in Matthew alone (13:37); in Luke alone (19:10; [9:56 in some MSS.]);[3] (b) *in his suffering*: in the Marcan source (8:31 [= Luke 9:22; Matt 16:21 has "he"]; 9:12 [= Matt 17:12]; 9:31 [= Matt 17:22; Luke 9:44]; 10:33 [= Matt 20:18; Luke 18:31]; 14:21bis [= Matt 26:24 bis; Luke 22:22 changes once to "he"]; 14:41 [= Matt 26:45]); in Matthew alone (26:2); in Luke alone (22:48; 24:7); (c) *in his exalted state, sometimes as Judge*: in the Marcan source (†8:38 [= Matt 16:27; Luke 9:26]; 9:9 [= Matt 17:9]; 13:26 [= Matt 24:30b; Luke 21:27]; 14:62 [= Matt 26:64; Luke 22:69]); from "Q" (Matt 12:40 = Luke 11:30; Matt 24:27 = Luke 17:24; Matt 24:37 = Luke 17:26; Matt 24:44 = Luke 12:40; †Luke 12:8 [Matt 10:32 has "I"]); in Matthew alone (10:23; 13:41; 16:28; 19:28; 24:30a; 24:39; 25:31); in Luke alone (17:22, 30; 18:8; 21:26).[4]

Moreover, in the Johannine Gospel the arthrous phrase is found on the lips of Jesus in the majority of instances (11 times in all): in three of them it is applied to his being "lifted up" (3:14; 8:28; 12:34a), and in the others it is used of the exalted "Son of Man" (1:51; 3:13; 6:27, 53, 62; 9:35 [with a *v. l.*]; 12:23; 13:31). The anarthrous phrase, however, is found in the latter sense in 5:27.[5]

Of the two forms of the phrase, the anarthrous *υἱὸς ἀνθρώπου* has proved to be the less objectionable since it can at least be explained as a Semitism, reflecting the construct chain in either Hebrew (בן אדם) or Aramaic (בר אנש). But the arthrous phrase *ὁ υἱὸς τοῦ ἀνθρώπου* has been regarded as a literary monstrosity,[6] and in normal classical or hellenistic Greek it would mean simply "the man's son" or "the son of the man." The tendency of modern biblical translators to render it as "(the) son of man" reflects the Semitic anarthrous phrase and the OT background to which it is judged to be related.

A few years ago J. B. Cortés and F. M. Gatti, in a lengthy discussion of the title, sought to interpret the Greek phrase as "meaning simply the Son of

Adam."[7] Their discussion has proved to be a tour de force. It has apparently made little impression on the modern debate. That Hebrew בן אדם could mean "son of Adam" is undeniable. That this possible meaning of the Hebrew phrase was what was intended by NT writers who used *ὁ υἱὸς τοῦ ἀνθρώπου* is another matter. Since Ἀ*δάμ* is used as a name by NT writers—and, indeed, Luke even traced the genealogy of Jesus back to Ἀ*δάμ* (3:38)—it seems that they would have written *ὁ υἱὸς τοῦ* Ἀ*δάμ*, if they had meant that. Moreover, that "son of Adam" was admitted in late targumic translations of the Hebrew expression seems clear; but that such evidence has anything to do with the NT period is another matter (see p. 151 below).

A further question about the arthrous phrase *ὁ υἱὸς τοῦ ἀνθρώπου* has been raised by C. F. D Moule. He queries whether one should not translate it as "*the* Son of Man" or "*the* human figure," giving almost demonstrative force to the definite article.[8] He would then relate the phrase to Dan 7:13, suggesting that Jesus chose to take that figure of the Book of Daniel as a symbol for his own vocation—"the vocation to *be* God's true people, going to any lengths of suffering in loyalty to do his will, and ultimately to be vindicated in the heavenly court."

Such attempts to translate the peculiar Greek phrase differently have at least pointed up the philological problem. They make it clear that though the phrase functions plainly as a title in the NT, as it now stands, its background and historical usage have to be considered in any attempt to determine its theological overtones and the use that Jesus of Nazareth may have made of it, either in reference to himself or to someone else.

II. *The Semitic Data, Hebrew and Aramaic, That Bear upon the Title*

Because the peculiar Greek arthrous phrase *ὁ υἱὸς τοῦ ἀνθρώπου* is otherwise unattested in non-Christian writings prior to the NT and the Semitic-looking anarthrous phrase *υἱὸς ἀνθρώπου*,[9] is related to it, NT interpreters have looked to a Hebrew or Aramaic background for the expression. A figurative sense of *υἱὸς* is indeed attested in Greek, in the sense of a pupil, a follower, a helper, or an heir (e.g., of guild secrets).[10] But this usage scarcely seems to explain the NT phrase, "Son of Man." Moreover, there are other NT Greek phrases using *υἱὸς* that must be related to Semitic influence, such as *υἱοὶ φωτός* (1 Thes 5:5 [anarthrous]; Luke 16:8 [arthrous]; John 12:36 [anarthrous]),[11] or *υἱοὶ βροντῆς* (Mark 3:17), given as the explanation of the mysterious *βοανηργές*. But even such a consideration of the figurative use of Greek *υἱός* must ultimately yield to the historical attestation of the phrase in the Semitic realm.

In the areas of Hebrew and Aramaic the last thorough survey of the material was presented over twenty years ago by E. Sjöberg, and it need not be repeated here.[12] It will suffice to summarize from it what is pertinent for our purpose and add to it what new material has come to light since Sjöberg wrote. I shall not concern myself with either the singular nouns איש or אנש or the plural expressions בני אנשא or אנשים. Sjöberg also discussed these forms, for they were pertinent to his treatment. But they scarcely bear on the topic that interests us here, viz., the singular phrase that eventually became a title, save in a very indirect way.[13]

In the Hebrew Bible the singular phrase is found in two forms: בן אנוש (Ps 144:3) and בן אדם (93 times in Ezekiel as a form of address or quasi-vocative;[14] and 14 times elsewhere in the OT: Num 23:19; Jer 49:18, 33; 50:40; 51:43; Isa 51:12; 56:2; Ps 8:5; 80:18; 146:3; Job 16:21; 25:6; 35:8; Dan 8:17 [in the last instance like the quasi-vocative in Ezekiel]). As Sjöberg and others have already pointed out, none of these instances reflects ordinary day-to-day usage; they are found only in contexts composed in poetic or solemn diction and style.[15]

The Hebrew expression with the definite article, בן האדם, is unknown either in the OT or the Mishnah. G. Vermes not long ago called attention to the occurrence of it in 1QS 11:20, where the article has been added above the line:[16] "And what is the son of man himself amidst all Thy marvellous works?"[17] But just what nuance בן האדם is to carry here is debatable; when it is compared with לבן אדם of 1QH 4:30, parallel to לאנוש,[18] it is hard to detect any difference. In other words, what precisely is the connotation of the added Hebrew article in this isolated occurrence of it? Vermes may be right in calling it an Aramaism.[19] In any case, this isolated Hebrew instance of the definite expression is hardly likely to be the sort of thing that explains the peculiar Greek arthrous form of the NT expression.

In the postbiblical Hebrew of a still later period we find an isolated instance of בן אדם in rabbinical writings. It is found in the Palestinian Talmud, *Taᶜanit* II.1 (65b), which in its final form was redacted ca. A.D. 425.[20] The instance is found in a saying ascribed to R. Abbahu, of the third generation of Palestinian Amoraim:[21]

א״ר אבהו אם יאמר לך אדם אל אני מכזב הוא, בן אדם אני
סופו לתהות בו, שאני עולה לשמים ההוא אמר ולא יקימינה.

"R. Abbahu said, 'If someone says to you, "I am God," he (is) a liar; "I am the son of Adam (or: a son of Man)," his end will be a regret to him; "I am ascending to heaven," that man has said it (indeed), but he will not substantiate it.'" The passage is usually regarded as an allusion to Num 23:19, the oracle of Balaam in which one finds the sole use of בן אדם in the Pentateuch, and precisely in parallelism with איש: "God is not man, that he should lie, or a son of man, that he should repent. Has he said, and will he not do it? Or has he spoken, and will he not fulfil it?" (*RSV*). It is not easy to determine the thrust of R. Abbahu's statement or the exact meaning of בן אדם in it. The latter may have had titular force at that time, if one were to concede that R. Abbahu, otherwise known for his disputations with Christians,[22] were referring to the Christian use of the phrase for Jesus.[23] This is, however, the surprisingly sole instance of the expression in rabbinical Hebrew writings—

which stands in significant contrast to the frequent attestation of the Aramaic expression.

When one surveys, then, the Hebrew material that might bear on the background of the Greek expression, one sees that it is meagre, indeed, and realizes why the Aramaic material usually commands more attention.

When Sjöberg wrote over twenty years ago, the oldest Aramaic instance of the phrase to which he could point was בר אנש in Dan 7:13,[24] and this instance has been the subject of much debate, as is well known. P. Benoit, in reacting against interpretations of the NT Greek expression that tended to water down its meaning by an appeal to the Aramaic phrase and a claim that it meant no more than "man," once wrote that "Aramaic had other more simple terms to express the latter idea" and that "the formula 'son of man' was rare in Aramaic and was only used in the plural to designate members of the human race (cf. Mark 3:28; Eph 3:5)."[25] Indeed, H. Lietzmann is said to have gone so far as to affirm that "Jesus never applied to Himself the title 'Son of man,' for this term does not exist in Aramaic, and for linguistic reasons is an impossible term."[26] G. Dalman cited this view and labelled it a "grievous error, which careful observation of the biblical Aramaic alone would have rendered impossible."[27] Such assertions sound a little presumptuous today, when newer evidence makes possible a slightly different assessment. However, the instances of בר אנש in pre-Christian Aramaic are still not numerous, when judged against the growing corpus of Aramaic texts and inscriptions that have come to light in the last three quarters of a century.

The earliest occurrence of the phrase is now to be found in one of the treaty stipulations imposed by Bir-Gaᵓyah, king of KTK, on Matiᶜel, son of ᶜAttarsamak, king of Arpad, in the third Sefire inscription (Sf III 16-17):

בכל מה זי ימות בר אנש שקרתם לכ/ל אלהי עדיא זי בספרא זנה

"In whatever way a man shall die,[28] you will have been false to all the gods of the treaty which is in this inscription."[29] Here the phrase בר אנש (absolute) means no more than "someone, anyone," i.e., "a man," a member of the human race (used indefinitely). It differs little from אש (= ᵓîš), which occurs in Sf II B 16 with a prefixed negative in the sense of "no one." The context in which בר אנש occurs in the Sefire inscription is scarcely poetic; engraved on stone as part of several treaty stipulations, it could undoubtedly be regarded as solemn. And yet, the way in which it is used suggests that it reflects the ordinary daily usage of the time.

This instance is isolated in the phase of Old Aramaic. In Official Aramaic there is not one instance of it outside of Dan 7:13. Neither in literary texts like ᵓAḥiqar or the Bar Puneš story nor in the many letters and contracts from Egyptian provenience has an example of the phrase been found.[30] It is difficult to say why this is so. In the sole instance of it in Biblical Aramaic it occurs with a generic meaning in Dan 7:13:

וארו עם־ענני שמיא כבר אנש אתה הוה,

"and lo, with the clouds of heaven one like a human being was coming" (or, more literally, "one like a son of man"). The use of the phrase in Daniel has long been debated, and its contextual sense does not concern us now.[31] What does seem clear, however, is that the generic sense made use of in Daniel scarcely provides the immediate background to the titular use in the Greek phrase of the NT.[32]

The first instance of the expression in extrabiblical Aramaic after Sefire III is to be found in Qumran literature. Here again one finds it in the indefinite sense in the *Genesis Apocryphon* of Qumran Cave I:

ואשגה זרעך כעפר ארעא די לא ישכח כול בר אנוש למניה

"I shall make your descendants as numerous *as the dust of the earth which no man can number"* (1QapGen 21:13, paraphrasing Gen 13:16: ושמתי את־זרעך כעפר הארץ אשר אם־יוכל איש למנות את־עפר הארץ גם־זרעך ימנה).[33] In this instance, the hebraized form בר אנוש translates איש of the Hebrew text of Genesis,[34] and it scarcely means anything more than "no one."

An instance of the generic sense, meaning "a human being" and designating an individual belonging to the collectivity of mankind, can further be found in the Targum of Job from Cave XI:

[לגבר כות]ך חטיך ולבר אנש צדקתך

"Your sin affects a man like yourself, and your righteousness (another) human being" (11QtgJob 26:2-3, translating Job 35:8, לאיש־כמוך רשעך / ולבן־אדם צדקתך).[35] This is said by Elihu, as he asks Job what his sinning against God would really accomplish. Implied is a contrast between "man" and "God." Significantly, בר אנש here translates one of the OT instances of בן אדם.[36] The text of col. 26 is fragmentary, and the editors have restored גבר as the translation of the Hebrew parallel word איש.[37] If the restoration be correct, then בר אנש functions here as a mere synonym for גבר; yet even if one should prefer to restore אנש, the generic sense of the phrase would still be clear. It would be a mere stylistic variant for "man."

Another instance of the generic sense seems to be found in 11QtgJob 9:9 (= Hebr. 25:6); the text is fragmentary and only [ב]ר אנש תולע[תא] is preserved, "[the s]on of man, (who is) a wor[m]." It too is a comparison of man with God in a speech of Bildad the Shuhite, and בר אנש again is a translation of Hebrew בן אדם.[38] From these instances we learn that in at least two of the three passages where the Hebrew of the Book of Job has בן אדם (16:21; 25:6; 35:8) the Qumran targum has rendered it by בר אנש. Since there is no instance of בר אנש being used in the rest of this fragmentary targum, it is hard to say to what extent the expression might have been a translation for other Hebrew words for "man." This must be recalled later, when mention is made of the frequent use of בר נש in later targums, even though we have in the Qumran targum only about one-sixth of the Book of Job preserved.

These few instances in Qumran literature reveal at least that the phrase was in use in the first century B.C. or A.D. in Palestine,[39] and, indeed, both in the indefinite sense of "someone" and the generic sense of "a human being."

Before considering the rabbinic and targumic material of a later period that may bear on this question, I should like to introduce an aspect of the philological argument on which the above judgment is based. I have treated this aspect briefly elsewhere;[40] but since it has been more recently challenged,[41] I should like to reconsider it here with the aid of some new data that affect it.

It is striking that in none of the evidence from the Aramaic texts known to us prior to the Second Revolt do we ever find the form בר נש or בר נשא. Whenever the phrase is found, it is always written with an initial *aleph* on אנש (Sf III 16; 1QapGen 21:13; 11QtgJob 9:9; 26:3). This, moreover, agrees with the numerous instances of the word אנש or אנוש found in various phases of Aramaic prior to the Second Revolt and in various dialects from geographically distinct areas. It is always written with initial *aleph.*[42] On the other hand, the form without *aleph* is well known in Palestinian Jewish and Christian Aramaic of a later date and in Syriac. In the latter dialect it is sometimes retained in the writing, but then fitted with the *linea occultans*, warning the reader not to pronounce it (in carefully pointed texts of the Late Phase). The absence of the initial *aleph* is telltale evidence, therefore, of the later date.[43] Hence, *if* certain senses of the phrase might be attested in expressions using בר נש and going beyond those of an earlier period, one must be careful not to apply the later senses to earlier periods without further ado.

Problematic here is the initial *aleph* with a reduced vowel. It is well known that in Aramaic the whole syllable disappeared eventually with the aphaeresis of the *aleph.* In some instances, in an effort to preserve the syllable the reduced vowel was secondarily given full pronunciation, e.g., in Syriac, *ᵓenā*, "I". The same process explains the full vowel in אִינָשׁ which turns up especially in the Aramaic of the Babylonian Talmud. But this secondary lengthening of the vowel is as much a sign of lateness as the aphaeresis.

Now my argument for the late date of the phrase בר נש from the aphaeresis of the initial *aleph* has been found to be "curious."[44] Objection to it has been raised because the NT form of the Palestinian name *Lazar(us)* is written in Greek without the initial syllable, Λάζαρος (Luke 16:20). Its Semitic counterpart would be אלעזר, a form found in a Murabbaᶜat bill of divorce (Mur 19:29) and on a Jerusalem ossuary, and precisely with the initial *aleph.* Hence it is argued: "Now the form *Lazar* derives from Eleazar by omission of the initial *aleph* in the same way as *nash* is a shortened version of *ᵓenash.* But as is well known, this dropping of the opening guttural is a peculiarity of the Galilean Aramaic dialect, and characteristically the Palestinian—i.e., Galilean—Talmud often truncates the names of Eleazar and Eliezer to read Lazar or Liezer. Similarly, in the Galilean necropolis of Beth Sheᶜarim, Greek-Jewish inscriptions attest the abbreviated form Lazar and even Laze."[45]

Concerning this objection I should like to make several observations: (1) Evidence from proper names is extremely difficult to interpret and to apply to common nouns. It is well known that names develop colloquial abbreviations, nickname-forms, and formal abbreviations (or hypocoristica). Is it certain that Greek *Λάζαρος* or *Λάζαρ* (without the Greek ending), developed simply because of the aphaeresis of initial *aleph* at this period? How do we know that this is not a colloquial or formal abbreviation?[46] (2) In a recently discovered inscription from a tomb in the Givᶜat ha-Mivṭar region of Jerusalem, dated to the first century A.D.[47] or possibly to "the end of the first century B.C. or the first century A.D.,"[48] the very name cited above has turned up and is written in a way that runs counter to the stated objection. For the name is divided, part of it being written at the end of line 1 and part of it at the beginning of line 2. On line 1 the *aleph* alone appears! Here is the text, as I read it:

I, Abba, son of the priest E-	אנה אבה בר כהנה א
leaz‹ar›, son of Aaron the high (priest), I	לעז‹ר› בר אהרן רבה אנ
Abba, the oppressed and the persecuted,	ה אבה מעניה מרד
who was born in Jerusalem,	פה די יליד בירושלם
and went into exile to Babylonia and brought (back to Jerusalem) Mattathi-	וגלא לבבל ואסק למתת
ah, son of Jud(ah); and I buried him in the	י בר יהוד וקברתה במ
cave, which I acquired by the (*or* his?) writ.	ערתה דזבנת בגטה

Now, aside from other interesting features in this inscription, the initial *aleph* of the name אלעז‹ר›[49] is written separately on line 1. To me, it is inconceivable that it would have been so written, if it was not pronounced as a separate syllable. Compare the other divided words in the inscription (lines 2-3, 3-4, 5-6, 6-7). A form of the name is also written fully in 1QapGen 22:34: אליעזר (= ᵓ*Elīᶜēzer*), just as one would expect it at this period. Admittedly, part of the difficulty here is the unvocalized evidence with which we are dealing; but from the standpoint of the consonantal text there is no evidence of the aphaeresis of initial *aleph* at this period, either in the Aramaic / Hebrew forms of proper names or in common nouns. (3) In the Givᶜat ha-Mivṭar tomb inscription I restored the final consonant on the name, אלעז‹ר›, "Eleaz‹ar›." Now it may be that that syllable should not be restored and that it really represents the name *Eleaz*, another shortened form of Eleazar. This form has, in fact, been found in a Greek text from one of the Murabbaᶜat caves (Mur 94 a 7): Ἐλεαζ Βαρη. . .[ ]. The name is found in a list of names and a record of accounts, which P. Benoit, who published the text (DJD 2.224), regards as a "relevé récapitulatif de comptes." It is not dated, but it must have been written shortly before or about the time of the Bar Cochba revolt. What is significant for our discussion is not only the Greek attestation of the form of the name in the Aramaic inscription without the final syllable, but the presence of the first syllable, which supports my contention about the non-aphaeresis of *aleph* with a reduced vowel in such words at this time in Palestine. By the same token, if one consults the list of names in E. Testa, *Il simbolismo dei Giudeo-Cristiani* (Jerusalem: Franciscan Press, 1962) 479, one finds that the forms ליעזר, לזר, לעזר are listed only in inscriptions from the Diaspora, with no reference being given to Murabbaᶜat texts. Seeing that the name Lazarus is found in the canonical gospels—of final redaction in non-Palestinian areas—there may be some significance to this form of the name that is found here. (4) It is rightly asserted that the Palestinian Talmud often truncates the names of Eleazar and Eliezer to read *Lazar* and *Liezer*. But that is exactly what one would expect at the time of the Palestinian Talmud.[50] Implied here, however, is that the evidence of this Talmud is as old as the NT itself—which it is not. (5) The evidence of the Galilean names in the necropolis of Beth Sheᶜarim is scarcely pertinent. Proper account has not been taken of the dating of that necropolis. According to the archaeologists, these burials do not antedate the third century A.D.,[51] and some of the tombs come from even later centuries. Interesting as the inscriptions on these tombs may be, they all belong to the phase of Late Aramaic and are fine examples of Palestinian Jewish Aramaic of the classic, rabbinic period (between the Mishnah and the closing of the Talmud). If one is going to argue on the basis of archaeological material, then one must respect its date and its provenience. For these reasons, I shall continue to consider the forms of the phrase בר נש(א) without the initial *aleph* to be signs of Late Aramaic, until clear evidence from first-century Palestine emerges to the contrary. With this we may turn to the Aramaic evidence from the Late Phase.

In the material of the Late Phase of Aramaic that bears on the problem of the Son of Man, one has to distinguish what is found in the targums from the material in other rabbinical writings. The reason for this is twofold: (a) the translation process, in which some instances of the phrase reflect a Hebrew counterpart and thus give pause about the everyday character of the phrase; (b) the targumic usage may reflect older customs than the talmudic, midrashic, or other material.

In the targumic material, we may first consider those passages in which בן אדם or בן אנוש occur in the Hebrew text of the OT. The only instance of בן אדם in the Pentateuch is found in Num 23:19, in parallelism to איש; both are used in the generic (inclusive) sense of "man" in contrast to God. The verse is expanded in Targum Onqelos: איש is twice rendered by the plural בני אנשא, whereas בן אדם is translated as בני בסרא (literally, "sons of the flesh"). In each case the plural has been used instead of a generic singular. The plural is also found in the Fragmentary Targum of Num 23:19: three instances of בני אנש. Tg. Pseudo-Jonathan, however, used the singular בר נש twice to translate איש, and the plural בני בישרא for Hebrew בן אדם. Neofiti 1 reads בני אנשא three times too. The verse is not found in the fragmentary texts of the Cairo Genizah.

In the Tg. Jonathan of the Prophets one finds בר אנש, in parallelism to אנש, as the translation of בן אדם (in parallelism to איש or אנוש), in Isa 56:2; Jer 49:18, 33; 50:40; 51:43; and in one instance (Isa 51:12), the emphatic form בר אנשא (in parallelism with אנשא).[52] In the late targums on the Writings one usually finds Hebrew בן אדם rendered as בר נש (Ps 8:5; 80:18; 146:3; Job 25:6;

35:8), and Hebrew בן אנוש (Ps 144:3) is likewise so translated. Sometimes בר נש is even introduced as the translation of parallel words such as אנוש (Ps 8:5; Job 25:6) or גבר (Job 16:21). In all of these instances the meaning is generic, "a human being," a stylistic variant of אנש, איש, or גבר. None of these instances differs significantly from the generic usage of 11QtgJob 9:9; 26:2-3.

By contrast, the בן אדם of Ezekiel and Dan 8:17 is consistently rendered as בר אדם, which G. Dalman and others have translated as "son of Adam."[53] In the case of this quasi-vocative usage, this translation seems to be a deliberate shift to avoid the ordinary בר אנש and to insure the solemnity of the phrase.

Beyond the instances in which a form of בר אנש renders Hebrew בן אדם in the targums, there are many instances in which it translates such simple Hebrew words as אדם or האדם (e.g., Gen 1:26 [Neof.], 27 [Neof.]; 2:18 [Neof.]; 8:21 [Neof.]; 9:5 [Neof., Ps.-J.]; Deut 5:21 [Ps.-J.]; 20:19 [Ps.-J.]; Ps 144:4; Job 34:29), or איש (Exod 19:13 [Cairo F]; Deut 34:6 [Cairo F]), or בני אדם (Mic 5:6), or even הנפש ההוא (Num 9:13 [Ps.-J.]). These instances serve merely as stylistic variants of "man" in the generic sense, or of "someone" in the indefinite sense. But this use of a form of בר נש spreads and becomes very frequent in the targums of the Late Phase, where, further, the distinction between the absolute state and the emphatic state is no longer observed.

G. Vermes has collected many examples of the indefinite use of בר נש and of its generic use from the Palestinian Talmud and the midrashim of this period, and there is no need to repeat his material here. Apropos of his treatment of this material in the appendix of the third edition of M. Black's *Aramaic Approach to the Gospels and Acts*, I should like to express the following observations: (1) I cannot agree that the material cited from either the Palestinian Talmud or the *Genesis Rabbah* reflects second century A.D. data;[54] and even if it could be shown at that time to be an older literary tradition, it would not necessarily mean that it was preserved in second-century Aramaic. (2) I cannot agree that the phrase ההוא גברא, which for the sake of the argument *(dato non concesso)* may be a circumlocution for either "I" or "thou,"[55] has anything to do with the alleged circumlocutional use of the phrase בר נש(א). J. Jeremias has already noted the essential difference between the two phrases:

> *Hāhū gabrā*, referring to the person who speaks, means 'I (and no other),' and thus is strictly limited to the speaker; *bar ʾĕnāšā*, on the other hand, keeps its generic or indefinite significance, 'the (or a) man, and therefore also I,' 'the (or a) man like myself,' even where the speaker does include himself. . . .[56]

(3) I grant that the surrogate usage of בר נש for "I" is now found in two parallel targumic translations of Gen 4:14: in Neofiti 1 Cain says, "It is impossible for me to hide" (לית אפשר לי למטמרה), whereas in Cairo Targum B he says, "It is impossible for a man to hide" (לית אפשר לברנש למטמרה).[57] Here at length we are provided with a parallel that is similar to the Synoptic parallels which have

the pronoun in place of ὁ υἱὸς τοῦ ἀνθρώπου. Interesting though this parallel is, it remains to be shown that it represents a first-century Palestinian usage. (4) Many of the examples which are cited by Vermes from the Palestinian Talmud and *Genesis Rabbah* and said to mean "I" or "me" can just as easily be translated "a man" or "man" in an indefinite or generic sense.[58] (5) I could not agree more with Vermes when he states that he has found no evidence in any of the rabbinic material that "*bar nāsh(ā)* was ever employed as a messianic designation."[59] This use is non-existent in both Middle and Late Aramaic texts. The same would have to be said about the "apocalyptic" Son of Man.[60]

III. *The Connotations of the Title in a First-Century Palestinian Context*

From the foregoing survey of the Hebrew and Aramaic material it seems obvious that the Hebrew data have little to offer as an explanation of the NT title. Though the Aramaic phrase בר אנש is attested, at least in the indefinite sense, from the 8th century B.C., and three instances are now known in the extrabiblical Aramaic of Qumran, one in the indefinite sense and two in the generic sense, it is clear that we do not as yet have the abundant and frequent attestation of it such as is found in the rabbinic writings of the Late Period. The phrase is attested in Old Aramaic (Sf III 16), in Official Aramaic (Dan 7:13), in Middle Aramaic (1QapGen 31:13; 11QtgJob 9:9; 26:2-3); thus it is found in inscriptions and literary texts. It is still to be found in what might be called texts representing ordinary, daily usage (letters, contracts, bonds, such as are found in the material from Elephantine, Murrabbaᶜat, etc.). Though it is now no longer as "rare" as it was once thought to be, it is still not as abundantly attested as in the targums and rabbinic writings.

What should above all be noted is that there is no example of any of the following senses in the Aramaic material prior to the composition of the NT—and hence prior to the titular use of ὁ υἱὸς τοῦ ἀνθρώπου: (a) *As a form of address* directed to a person, such as the Hebrew בן אדם, used of Ezekiel or Daniel. Given this biblical use of it, one might expect to find it in the parabiblical literature of the last two pre-Christian centuries. In any case, this quasi-vocative use is scarcely the background for the NT Greek phrase.[61] (b) *As a title for an expected or apocalyptic figure*, least of all for a messiah or an anointed one. The phrase does occur indeed in the apocalyptic chapter of Daniel (7:13), but it is used there in the generic sense, not as a title. It has been regarded as a "messianic" title, mainly because of its association with the title Messiah in Ethiopic Enoch (e.g., 48:2, 10), whereas it in no way suggests an anointed figure *per se*. But if J. T. Milik's latest theory about the second part of the Book of Enoch, the so-called Similitudes, were to prove acceptable, then the entire question of the conflated titles for the mysterious figure in that part of the book would have to be scrutinized again and precisely for the roots of this conflation in pre-Christian Palestinian Judaism. For Milik maintains that the Similitudes represent a Christian substitution. It replaced the Book of the Giants which was part of the Book of Enoch at Qumran and which he has now discovered among some published and unpublished material from Qumran.[62] We cannot go into the problems of that identification now. But it obviously bears on the Palestinian background of the Aramaic phrase בר אנש being used as a title for an individual person. (c) *As a surrogate for "I."*[63] Though this usage can now be documented in the Aramaic translation of Gen 4:14 in the targums Neofiti 1 and Pseudo-Jonathan, it is still problematic for first-century Palestinian usage, unless one is willing to admit such a dating for these targums—which I am not. Indeed, one may well ask whether this usage would ever have been queried or sought for, if it were not for the NT parallels such as Mark 10:45 = Matt 20:28 = Luke 22:27; Mark 8:27 = Matt 16:13 = Luke 9:18; Matt 5:11 = Luke 6:22; Matt 10:32 = Luke 12:8. Even in these NT instances one has to ask whether the phrase "son of Man" has not really been secondarily introduced.[64] If so, is the surrogate usage then a real one for first-century Palestinian Aramaic?

In the Aramaic material from the Late Phase one finds בר נש(א) not only used in the indefinite sense and in the generic sense, as in the earlier phases, but also the surrogate use. But what is significant is the abundant attestation of בר נש(א) as a substitute for the simple words for "man" like איש, גבר, and אנש.

When one views the NT Greek phrase *ὁ υἱὸς τοῦ ἀνθρώπου* over against this background, one sees that the NT usage is special. As it now appears in the Gospels, the arthrous form must be understood as a title for Jesus. Whether it stems from an Aramaic phrase that he himself used, either of himself or of someone else, may be and will continue to be debated, because it is a question to which in the long run only a speculative answer can be given. Certainly, there is nothing in the indefinite or generic Aramaic usage to prove it impossible. That either of these attested uses could be the springboard for the development of the titular usage is not immediately obvious, and the missing-link still has to be found.

It is not at all certain that the Aramaic emphatic state was as moribund in first-century Palestine as it is sometimes supposed to have been. There are clear instances of the emphatic state in Qumran literature.[65] But in any case, the arthrous Greek phrase could be an attempt to translate the emphatic state of the Aramaic; but it may be something more. I suspect that it was deliberately fashioned to carry the nuance of a title.

Aramaic-speaking Christians of later periods certainly understood it in that sense: *ὁ υἱὸς τοῦ ἀνθρώπου* was translated into Syriac and Christian Palestinian Aramaic as *bĕreh dĕ(ᵓ)nāšā* (Pešitta, Mark 2:10) or *ᵓebreh dĕ-gabrā* (CPA, Luke 6:5). Here we are dealing with a stage of the Aramaic language in which there was no longer a difference of meaning between בר נש and בר נשא, and in order to express the determination of the arthrous Greek phrase the prospective pronominal suffix with the following *dĕ*-phrase was employed. For even if they had used ברא דאנשא, it would not necessarily have carried the definite nuance of *ὁ υἱὸς τοῦ ἀνθρώπου*.

These philological considerations of the Semitic background of the NT phrase "Son of Man" are not uncomplicated. They limit in their own way the further discussion of the theological import of the christological title.

For my part, I think that in analyzing the theological or christological use of the title in the gospels, one has to reckon with several factors: (a) the secondary intrusion of the title into passages where it is lacking in parallels; (b) the evidence for the phrase as a *title* for a "supernatural, apocalyptic figure" as quite questionable, since if there is any validity to this sort of extension of the phrase which describes a being resembling a human in Dan 7:13, it is still not clear that this extension predates Jesus himself or even the NT writings; (c) there is no other or more plausible starting-point for the titular use of the phrase for Jesus in the NT than Dan 7:13, even though the phrase is not used in a titular sense there. But the reason for seeing a reference to Daniel in the NT use comes from other phrases and explicit allusions to that passage in some parts of the NT; yet they also seem to suggest a development of the phrase beyond what one finds there. Finally, the NT phrase must be so interpreted as to fit the varied uses made of it in differing situations.

NOTES TO CHAPTER 6

*This essay appears here for the first time. It was originally delivered as one of the Speaker's Lectures at Oxford University, May 1974.

[1]A survey of literature on the title up to 1966 can be found in R. Marlow, "The Son of Man in Recent Journal Literature," *CBQ* 28 (1966) 20-30. More recent surveys can be found in the following discussions: J. Coppens, *De Mensenzoon-Logia in het Markus-Evangelie* (Mededelingen van de koninklijke Academie voor Wetenschappen, Letteren en schone Kunsten van België, Kl. der Letteren, 35/3; Brussels: Paleis der Academiën, 1973); I. H. Marshall, "The Synoptic Son of Man Sayings in Recent Discussion," *NTS* 12 (1966) 327-51; "The Son of Man in Contemporary Debate," *EvQ* 42 (1970) 67-87; R. Maddox, "The Quest for Valid Methods in 'Son of Man' Research," *Australian Biblical Review* 19 (1971) 36-51; C. Colpe, "Der Begriff 'Menschensohn' und die Methode der Erforschung messianischer Prototypen," *Kairos* 11 (1969) 241-63; 12 (1970) 81-112; 13 (1971) 1-17; 14 (1972) 241-57; R. N. Longenecker, "'Son of Man' Imagery: Some Implications for Theology and Discipleship," *Journal of the Evangelical Theological Society* 18 (1975) 3-16; F. J. Moloney, *The Johannine Son of Man* (Biblioteca di scienze religiose, 14; Rome: Libreria ateneo salesiano, 1976); J. Coppens, "Le Fils de l'Homme dans l'évangile johannique," *ETL* 52 (1976) 28-81 (with extensive bibliography in note 3).

[2]It may be debated whether the author intends this phrase of Psalm 8 to refer to Jesus, since the OT quotation is really introduced for another reason.

[3]References with an asterisk (*) indicate passages in which the title expresses service or lowliness; the others, dignity.

[4]References with a dagger (†) may be instances in which Jesus refers to someone other than himself as the coming "Son of Man."

[5]See R. Schnackenburg, "Der Menschensohn im Johannesevangelium," *NTS* 11 (1964-65) 123-37; S. Schulz, *Untersuchungen zur Menschensohn-Christologie im Johannesevangelium* (Göttingen: Vandenhoeck & Ruprecht, 1957); R. E. Brown, *The Gospel According to John (i-xii)* (AB 29; Garden City: Doubleday, 1966) 84; B. Lindars, "The Son of Man in the Johannine Christology," *Christ and Spirit in the New Testament: In Honour of Charles Francis Digby Moule* (ed. B. Lindars and S. S. Smalley; Cambridge: Cambridge University, 1973) 43-60. See also the Moloney entry mentioned in n. 1 above.

[6]G. Dupont, *Le fils d'homme: Essai historique et critique* (Paris: Presses universitaires, 1924) 25: "cet étrange vocable."

[7]"The Son of Man or the Son of Adam," *Bib* 49 (1968) 457-502, esp. p. 486.

[8]"Neglected Features in the Problem of 'the Son of Man,'" *Neues Testament und Kirche: Für Rudolf Schnackenburg* (Freiburg im B.: Herder, 1974) 413-28.

[9]NT grammarians have often so regarded the anarthrous form; see M. Zerwick, *Biblical Greek* (Rome: Biblical Institute, 1963) §183; BDF §259; C. F. D. Moule, *An Idiom Book of New Testament Greek* (2d ed.; Cambridge: Cambridge University, 1959) 177; A. T. Robertson, *A Grammar of the Greek New Testament in the Light of Historical Research* (4th ed.; New York: Hodder and Stoughton, 1914) 651.

[10]See Maximus of Tyre 4.2c; W. Dittenberger, *Sylloge inscriptionum graecarum* (3d ed.; 4 vols.; Leipzig: S. Hirzel, 1915-24), 3. §1169:12. Cf. N. Turner, *Syntax* in J. H. Moulton, *A Grammar of New Testament Greek*, III (Edinburgh: Clark, 1963) 208.

[11]The Semitic counterpart is now well attested in Qumran literature; both in the Hebrew form בני אור (1QS 1:9; 2:16; 3:13, 24, 25; 1QM 1:1, 3, 9, 11, 13) and in an Aramaic form בני נהורא (see J. T. Milik, "4Q Visions de ᶜAmram" [p. 108 above, n. 12], 90). Since this expression occurs neither in the OT nor in rabbinic literature, its use in Qumran literature, along with its counterpart, "sons of darkness," as a designation for two great classes of humanity, is significant for the understanding of the NT phrase. See further *ESBNT*, 208-10; J. Jeremias, *New Testament Theology* (p. 112 above, n. 55), 260.

[12]"בן אדם und בר אנש im Hebräischen und Aramäischen," *AcOr* 21 (1950-53) 57-65, 91-107. Earlier treatments can be found in G. Dalman, *The Words of Jesus* (p. 23 above, n. 53), 234-67; P. Fiebig, *Der Menschensohn: Jesu Selbstbezeichnung mit besonderer Berücksichtigung des aramäischen Sprachgebrauches für "Mensch"* (Tübingen / Leipzig: Mohr, 1901). Cf. C. Colpe, "ὁ υἱὸς τοῦ ἀνθρώπου," *TDNT* 8 (1972) 401-5.

[13]See below pp. 147, 151.

[14]E.g., Ezek 2:1, 3; 3:1, 3, 4, 10. Cf. W. Zimmerli, *Ezechiel* (BKAT 13/1; Neukirchen: Neukirchener Verlag, 1969) 70-71; F. Maass, "אדם," *TWAT* 1 (1970) 81-94, esp. col. 87.

[15]E. Sjöberg, "בן אדם und בר אנש," 57-59.

[16]"The Use of בר נשא / בר נש in Jewish Aramaic," in M. Black, *An Aramaic Approach* (p. 23 above, n. 43), 310-30, esp. p. 327.

[17]A. Dupont-Sommer, *The Essene Writings from Qumran* (tr. G. Vermes; Oxford: Blackwell, 1961) 103. Cf. M. Burrows (ed.), *The Dead Sea Scrolls of St. Mark's Monastery, Volume II, Fascicle 2: Plates and Transcription of the Manual of Discipline* (New Haven: American Schools of Oriental Research, 1951), pl. XI; F. M. Cross et al., *Scrolls from Qumran Cave I: The Great Isaiah Scroll, The Order of the Community, The* Pesher *to Habakkuk, from Photographs by John C. Trever* (Jerusalem: Albright Institute of Archaeological Research and the Shrine of the Book, 1972) 146-47.

[18]Cf. 1QH 10:28 (partly restored).

[19]"The Use of בר נשא/בר נש," 327.

[20]H. L. Strack, *Introduction to the Talmud and Midrash* (Temple Books; New York: Atheneum, 1969) 65 ("at the beginning of the fifth century"). Cf. L. I. Rabinowitz, "Talmud, Jerusalem," *Encyclopaedia judaica* (Jerusalem: Keter; New York: Macmillan, 1971), 15. 773: ". . . many *amoraim* who were active until the middle of the fourth century are quoted in it." Col. 775: "The Jerusalem Talmud was completed about a century before the compilation of the Babylonian Talmud in c. 500."

[21]H. L. Strack, *Introduction to the Talmud and Midrash,* 125.

[22]Ibid.

[23]It is so interpreted by E. Sjöberg, "בן אדם und בר אנש," 59. Cf. C. Colpe, "ὁ υἱὸς τοῦ ἀνθρώπου," *TDNT* 8 (1972) 404 n. 24.

[24]"בן אדם und בר אנש," 60.

[25]"La divinité de Jésus," *Lumière et vie* 9 (1953) 64; reprinted in *Exégèse et théologie* (Paris: Cerf, 1961), 1. 134; cf. "The Divinity of Christ in the Synoptic Gospels," *Son and Saviour: The Divinity of Jesus Christ in the Scriptures* (ed. A. Gelin; Baltimore: Helicon, 1965) 81; reprinted in *Jesus and the Gospel: Volume 1* (tr. B. Weatherhead; New York: Herder and Herder, 1973) 63.

[26]So at least G. Dalman (*The Words of Jesus* [p. 23 above, n. 53], 239) quotes him. Lietzmann actually wrote: "Jesus hat sich selbst nie den Titel 'Menschensohn' beigelegt, weil derselbe im Aramäischen nicht existierte und aus sprachlichen Gründen nicht existieren kann" (*Der Menschensohn: Ein Beitrag zur neutestamentlichen Theologie* [Freiburg im B. / Leipzig: Mohr, 1896], 85). Was Lietzmann referring merely to the titular sense of the phrase?

[27]*The Words of Jesus,* 239.

[28]In the context this verb must refer to death by treachery or assassination. L. A. Bange (*A Study of the Use of Vowel-Letters in Alphabetic Consonantal Writing* [see p. 64 above], 91) prefers to understand *ymwt* as a pual form (*yĕmuwwat,* "is slain" [?]). Cf. R. Degen, *Altaramäische Grammatik* [p. 75 above, n. 16], 28, 75.

[29]See A. Dupont-Sommer and J. Starcky, "Une inscription araméenne de Sfiré," *BMB* 13 (1956 [appeared 1958]) 23-41, esp. pp. 27, 34; cf. my commentary, *The Aramaic Inscriptions of Sefire* (p. 77 above, n. 30), 98, 115. See further G. Garbini, "Nuovo materiale per la grammatica dell'aramaico antico," *RSO* 34 (1959) 41-54, esp. p. 47; F. Vattioni, "La prima menzione aramaica di 'figlio dell'uomo,'" *Biblos-Press* 6/1 (1965) 6-7.

[30]See A. Cowley, *Aramaic Papyri of the Fifth Century B.C. Edited, with Translation and Notes* (Oxford: Clarendon, 1923; reprinted, Osnabrück: Zeller, 1967) 204-48 (= *A*), 179-82 (= *AP* 71). Cf. C.-F. Jean and J. Hoftijzer, *Dictionnaire des inscriptions sémitiques de l'ouest* (Leiden: Brill, 1965) 19; E. Vogt, *Lexicon linguae aramaicae Veteris Testamenti* [p. 23 above, n. 41], 13; I. N. Vinnikov, "Dictionary of the Aramaic Inscriptions," *Palestinkii sbornik* 3 (66, 1958) 205-6, 218.

[31]G. Dalman (*The Words of Jesus,* 237-38) thought that the Danielic phrase was uncongenial to poetry, regarded it as a parallel to עתיק יומיא, and gave it a more solemn, poetic meaning than was necessary. In this he was corrected by P. Fiebig (*Der Menschensohn* [n. 12 above], 53-60), who stressed that the phrase scarcely differed from כאנש in Dan 7:4. For a recent and interesting discussion of the contextual meaning of the phrase, see J. J. Collins, "The Son of Man and the Saints of the Most High in the Book of Daniel," *JBL* 93 (1974) 50-66, esp. pp. 61-62.

[32]Perhaps one should further distinguish the generic sense of this phrase into a collective and an inclusive sense, as is sometimes done elsewhere: the former would be the use of the singular to designate the collectivity, mankind; the latter would be the use of the singular to designate an individual belonging to the collectivity, a human being. In this way 11QtgJob would be an instance of the inclusive sense. It is, however, not always easy to detect this difference, and so I prefer to refer to both of them as the generic sense of the phrase. It is thus a stylistic variant for "man." As such it is clearly to be distinguished from the indefinite usage ("anyone, someone"), the quasi-vocative usage (though this could also be "inclusive" in the sense just defined, but it is used as a form of address), the use for a definite individual, the titular usage (of the NT), and the surrogate usage (on which see below, p. 154).

[33]See N. Avigad and Y. Yadin, *A Genesis Apocryphon* (p. 54 above, n. 72) 45 (+ pl. XXI); on p. לח it is translated into Modern Hebrew as כל איש. See my commentary, *The Genesis Apocryphon of Qumran Cave I* (p. 22 above, n. 27) 68-69, 151. Italics in the translation used above indicate the words that are literally translated into Aramaic from the Hebrew.

[34]It is interesting to compare the translation of Gen 13:16 in the various later targums: Onqelos has

כמא דלית אפשר לגבר דימני ית עפרא דארעא

Pseudo-Jonathan reads

דהיכמא דאית איפשר לגבר למימני ית עפרא דארעא

and Neofiti I has

ארום היך מה דלית אפשר די כל גבר למימני ית עפרא דארעא

The verse is not preserved in the Fragmentary Targum or the targumic texts of the Cairo Genizah.

[35]See *Le targum de Job de la grotte XI de Qumrân* (p. 22 above, n. 32), 62.

[36]The later Targum II translates the Hebrew text thus:

לגבר דרשיעא דיכמך חיובך ולבר נש דכיא צדקתך

"a man of wickedness like yourself your guilt (affects), and an innocent human being, your righteousness." Noteworthy is the orthography of the phrase in this case; see below p. 171.

[37]The Aramaic word גבר is used to translate איש in 11QtgJob 38:7-8 (= Hebr. 42:11), but there it is used in a distributive sense of "each." Elsewhere in the extant passages איש is translated by Aramaic אנש (see 11QtgJob 31:4; 24:5; 21:[5]), save for 11QtgJob 36:2, where it is rendered by אנתה, "woman." The editors were possibly influenced in their restoration by Targum II (see note 36). When גבר occurs elsewhere in the extant parts of the Qumran targum, it usually translates Hebrew גבר (see 24:3; 23:7; 25:10; 30:1; 34:3), save for 15:3, where it renders אשר.

[38]Targum II renders Job 25:6 thus:

אף כל דכן בר נש דהחיוי ריחשא ובר נש דבמותוי מורני

[39]On the dating of the *Genesis Apocryphon,* see my commentary, *The Genesis Apocryphon of Qumran Cave I* (2d ed.) 14-19; on the dating of the Targum of Job, see J. P. M. van der Ploeg and A. S. van der Woude, *Le targum de Job,* 3-4. The editors tend to place the targum between the Book of Daniel and the Genesis Apocryphon. See further S. A. Kaufman, "The Job Targum from Qumran," *JAOS* 93 (1973) 317-27, esp. pp. 325-27; cf. P. Grelot, review of the *editio princeps, RQ* 8 (1972-76) 104-14, esp. pp. 113-14.

[40]See my review of M. Black, *Aramaic Approach* (3d ed.), *CBQ* 30 (1968) 426-27.

[41]By G. Vermes, *Jesus the Jew* (p. 23 above, n. 44), 188-91 ("Excursus II: Debate on the Circumlocutional Use of the Son of Man").

[42]See 1QapGen 20:16, 17, 18, 19; 21:19, 21; 22:15; 1Q*21* 8:2; 5/6Ḥev 14:2 (*Lěšonénu* 25 [1961] 127); 11QtgJob 2:8; 9:9; 11:3; 12:[9]; 19:[7]; 21:5; 22:6; 24:4, 5; 25:6; 26:3; 28:[1], 2bis; 31:4. Cf. I. N. Vinnikov, *Palestinskii sbornik* 3 (66, 1958) 205-6; 11 (74, 1964) 213; C-F. Jean and J. Hoftijzer, *Dictionnaire*, 19, 186-87; J. Cantineau, *Le Nabatéen* (Paris: E. Leroux), 2 (1932) 65; E. Vogt. *Lexicon*, 12-13.

[43]E. Sjöberg, ("בן אדם und בר אנש," p. 102) hints at the same explanation.

[44]G. Vermes, *Jesus the Jew*, 189.

[45]Ibid., 190-91.

[46]G. S. Glanzman has called to my attention the names אחירם (Num 26:38) and חירם (2 Sam 5:11, etc.); the latter is known in a Phoenician inscription as אחרם (*KAI* §1:1), and it turns up in Akkadian as *Ḫi-ru-um-mu*, but in Ugaritic as *aḫrm*. And the short form is almost certainly a hypocoristicon. See F. L. Benz, *Personal Names in the Phoenician and Punic Inscriptions* (Studia Pohl, 8; Rome: Biblical Institute, 1972) 263-64. See C. Taylor's note on the names Laᶜzar and Liᶜezer in *Pirqe Aboth* 2:10 (*Sayings of the Jewish Fathers Comprising Pirqe Aboth in Hebrew and English with Notes and Excursuses* [New York, Ktav, 1969] 33 n. 23; also "Notes on the Text," 143). Cf. R. Travers Herford, *Pirke Aboth: The Ethics of the Talmud: Sayings of the Fathers* (New York: Schocken, 1962) 51.

[47]See E. S. Rosenthal, "The Givᶜat ha-Mivtar Inscription," *IEJ* 23 (1973) 72-91, esp. p. 81 for the date. See *MPAT* §68.

[48]The inscription was also studied by J. Naveh, "An Aramaic Tomb Inscription Written in Paleo-Hebrew Script," *IEJ* 23 (1973) 82-91; see esp. p. 90.

[49]If one would prefer not to restore the final *reš*, אלעז would possibly reflect another nickname-form (similar to those of Beth Sheᶜarim below).

[50]See the date for this writing quoted above in n. 20.

[51]See Moshe Schwabe and Baruch Lifshitz, *Beth Sheᶜarim, Volume Two: The Greek Inscriptions* (Jerusalem: Israel Exploration Society, 1967), §177 (Λαζαρ, p. 73); §93 (Λαζε, p. 34).

However, on p. vii we read: "[Beth Sheᶜarim] était la résidence du patriarche vénéré Rabbi Juda, qui fut inhumé dans cette ville (premier quart du IIIe siècle de l'ère chrétienne). C'est précisément après la mort de Rabbi Juda que Beth Sheᶜarim s'est transformée en une nécropole centrale, parce que les Juifs pieux désiraient être enterrés près de la tombe du patriarche. Nous connaissons la période de la nécropole—la ville a été détruite en 352 par l'armée de Gallus qui a supprimé la révolte juive." Moreover, 1200 coins minted in the first half of the fourth century under Constantine (307-37) and Constantius II (337-62) were found there—and none from the second half of it. Cf. B. Mazar, *Beth Sheᶜarim, Volume One: The Catacombs I-IV* (Jerusalem: Israel Exploration Society, 1957) 21-26.

[52]The emphatic form is also used as the parallel in Isa 56:2.

[53]*The Words of Jesus* (p. 23, n. 53), 237; G. Vermes, "The Use of בר נש / בר נשא," 328.

[54]See H. L. Strack, *Introduction to the Talmud and Midrash*, 65 (for the Palestinian or Jerusalem Talmud). On p. 217 Strack uses the usual date for *Genesis Rabbah*, the first generation of the Amoraim; but this has been contested because it mentions the last group of Palestinian Amoraim of about 150 years later. See M. D. Herr, "Genesis Rabbah," *Encyclopaedia judaica*, 7. 399-400; he dates the final redaction of the work to about "425 C.E."

[55]See P. Haupt, "The Son of Man = hic homo = ego," *JBL* 40 (1921) 183; "Hidalgo and Filius Hominis," ibid., 167-70; C. Colpe, "ὁ υἱὸς τοῦ ἀνθρώπου," *TDNT* 8. 403.

[56]*New Testament Theology* (p. 112 above, n. 55), 261; see also C. Colpe, *TDNT* 8. 403.

[57]See A. Díez Macho, *Neophyti 1: Targum palestinense . . . Génesis* (p. 84 above, n. 112), 25; P. Kahle, *Masoreten des Westens* (BWANT 3/14; Stuttgart: Kohlhammer) 2 (1930) 7. Note the form ברנש, even written here as one word; also the pael infinitive with initial *mem*, which is unknown in first-century Palestinian Aramaic, but characteristic of that of the Late Phase (where it has been levelled through from the peal to all conjugations); compare טמיא (1QapGen 20:15); אסיותה (1QapGen 20:19)—and the haphel infinitives in 11QtgJob, להש[היה] (9:5); להנחתה (31:3); להסבעה (31:4); להנפקה (31:5).

[58]E.g., the instance from *Genesis Rabbah* 7:2 (cited by Vermes on p. 321) could just as easily be translated, "Should a man be scourged who proclaims the word of Scripture?" And even though "you" parallels בר נש in *Numbers Rabbah* 19:3 ("Should a man be scourged who proclaims the word of Scripture?" R. Haggai said, "Yes, because you did not give the right ruling" [cited on p. 321]), the distinction between the question generically put and the answer specifically given may have to be respected. Similarly *j. Ber.* 5c (". . . that a man cannot eat a pound of meat until he has been given a lash!"); *j. Ber.* 5b (cited on p. 323: "A man's disciple is as dear to him as his son"), where the emphatic state in this Late Aramaic is simply indefinite. As for *Genesis Rabbah* 38:13, see the obvious interpretation of it provided by E. Sjöberg, "בן אדם und בר אנש," 94-95.

[59]"The Use of בר נש / בר נשא," 327.

[60]This means that I am fundamentally in agreement with the thesis of R. Leivestad, "Exit the Apocalyptic Son of Man," *NTS* 18 (1971-72) 243-67, although I should want to nuance some of the details in his treatment a little differently. On the other hand, I am not sure that the apocalyptic Son of Man has re-entered; see B. Lindars, "Re-enter the Apocalyptic Son of Man," *NTS* 22 (1975-76) 52-72. The interpretation that Lindars gives is most congenial to me in many respects. But he is too cavalier with philological material and swallows hook-line-and-sinker what G. Vermes says without any personal scrutiny. In this Son-of-Man discussion—perhaps above all others—one simply has to begin with the philological material before one erects theological theories that may prove to be only sand castles.

[61]The quasi-vocative use is apparently reflected in *1 Enoch* 60:10 (addressed to Noah).

[62]See "Problèmes de la littérature hénochique" (p. 112, n. 57), 333-78; "Turfan et Qumran" (see ibid.), 117-27; *The Books of Enoch: Aramaic Fragments of Qumrân Cave 4* (Oxford: Clarendon, 1976) 89-107, 298-317. It, of course, remains to be seen whether Milik's explanation of the presence of the Book of Similitudes in Ethiopic Enoch will be finally accepted. He may be right that the Enoch literature in pre-Christian times was mainly a pentateuch and was so used by the Qumran community. He may also be right in maintaining that the Book of Similitudes was substituted for the Book of Giants in certain circles in the Christian era. But it still remains a

question whether the Book of Similitudes stems from a Christian author. For, though the titles, "anointed One," "righteous One," "elect One," and "Son of Man" are conflated and applied to one individual in the Similitudes, as they are applied to Jesus in the NT, the Similitudes otherwise lack specific "Christian differentia" (to use a phrase of R. H. Fuller [*The Foundations of New Testament Christology* (New York: Scribner, 1965) 38] in a sense a little more widely than he did). Indeed, it still has to be shown that this part of Ethiopic Enoch could not have stemmed from a Jewish author. See further E. Sjöberg, *Der Menschensohn im äthiopischen Henochbuch* (Lund: Gleerup, 1946); J. C. Greenfield, "Prolegomenon," in H. Odeberg, *3 Enoch or The Hebrew Book of Enoch* (New York: Ktav, 1973) xvii-xviii. If, indeed, it could be shown that the Book of Similitudes was an original pre-Christian Jewish writing (that was subsequently substituted for the Books of Giants in the form of the book known from the Ethiopic), then one would have to reckon with an apocalyptic Son of Man in the pre-Christian Jewish tradition, against my skepticism (see n. 60 above). But the evidence for arriving at that origin of the Book of Similitudes is not yet apparent.

[63]See G. Vermes, "The Use of בר נשא / בר נש," 320, 323. He not only calls it a circumlocution for "I" (p. 320), but even says that it "means I" (p. 323). Similarly R. Bultmann, *Theology of the New Testament* (p. 108 above, n. 18), 1. 30: ". . . meant 'man' or 'I.'"

[64]Cf. J. Jeremias, "Die älteste Schicht der Menschensohn-Logien," *ZNW* 58 (1967) 159-72.

[65]See my commentary on the *Genesis Apocryphon of Qumran Cave I* (2d ed., 1971) 221, 217. Despite the attempt of T. Muraoka ("Notes on the Aramaic of the Genesis Apocryphon," *RQ* 8 [1972-76] 7-51, esp. pp. 12-14) to explain all the instances of the emphatic state that I once questioned as definite, I still remain skeptical. I am not at all sure that the waning of the emphatic state is something that can be identified solely with the eastern branch of Aramaic dialects.

Chapter 7

The First-Century Targum of Job from Qumran Cave XI*

Ever since the discovery of Qumran Cave XI in 1956 and the announcement that a targum of Job figured among the texts discovered in that cave,[1] the scholarly world for many reasons patiently awaited the definitive publication of that important Aramaic text.[2] Preliminary reports from the editors, J. P. M. van der Ploeg and A. S. van der Woude, had whetted scholarly appetites in many ways.[3] Since the publication of the *editio princeps* in 1971, reviews and brief articles have commented on the text and pointed out features of it beyond those noted by the editors themselves.[4] It is obvious that the targum of Job from Qumran Cave XI is not only an important text but one that will demand years of study before its secrets are fully divulged. Anyone acquainted with the difficulties of the Hebrew text of Job and of its relationship to extant ancient versions will readily realize what it means to gain access suddenly to another previously unknown ancient version that a priori has the possibility of putting all earlier theories regarding those relationships into a new light. The study of the Qumran targum has only begun, and I should like to record here some preliminary observations about it.

These observations were originally made as a contribution to a volume honoring an American Catholic biblical scholar, Msgr. Patrick W. Skehan, Professor at the Catholic University of America, who has long been noted for his own studies of the problems of the Book of Job. His knowledge of the intricacies of the Hebrew text contributed much to the English translation of that book in the *New American Bible*, and I am sure that it would also have improved many paragraphs among the observations that follow, had he had the opportunity to see them in advance. In any case, they are offered as a token of gratitude, friendship, and esteem.

My observations will be grouped about three points: (1) Job in the Qumran community; (2) the Qumran targum of Job; and (3) the Qumran targum and the Second Targum of Job.

I. *Job in the Qumran Community*

When the word of the Lord came to the prophet Ezekiel about the land that was acting faithlessly toward him, three paragons of righteousness were singled out. But it was made clear to the prophet that not even their righteousness would save such a land: "Even if these three men, Noah, Daniel, and Job, were in it, they would deliver but their own lives by their righteousness" (Ezek 14:14). Though the "Daniel" or "Danʾel" who is mentioned among them was undoubtedly a more ancient figure than the better-known biblical character and was probably even of Canaanite background, the ancient Danʾel and the biblical Daniel were eventually conflated in Jewish tradition of a later date.[5] Similarly, the figure of Job in the Ezekiel passage may refer to a more ancient character who also appears in the substratum of parts of the canonical Book of Job and with whom the poetic dialogues of that book were eventually associated.[6] In any case, the three paragons of righteousness mentioned in Ezekiel eventually took on the shapes of the biblical characters whom we know as Noah, Job, and Daniel.

Now it is not surprising that the three of them turn up as figures who fed the piety of the Qumran community, given its well-known emphasis on the pursuit of righteousness.[7] In one way or another all three of these paragons appear in Qumran literature.

Noah appears in the paraphrase of the biblical story in the *Genesis Apocryphon* of Qumran Cave I;[8] and he figured in this "Book of the Patriarchs," as it undoubtedly should be more properly called,[9] more largely than we can imagine, since much of the story pertaining to him in that scroll has unfortunately been lost. Other as yet unpublished fragments from Qumran Cave IV seem to belong to an Infancy Narrative of Noah.[10] In the *Genesis Apocryphon* itself, one fragmentary sentence, paraphrasing Gen 6:9, makes Noah say, "During all my days I practiced truth" (קושטא, 1QapGen 6:2), a Qumran virtue related to "righteousness."

The esteem for Daniel in Qumran literature is also well attested. He is hailed as a "prophet" in 4Q*174* 1-3 ii 3,[11] and the end of the canonical book ascribed to him has served as the springboard for the introductory columns of the Qumran War Scroll.[12] A cycle of writings, which is only published so far in part, but which is clearly related to that biblical book, exists among the fragments of Qumran Cave IV. J. T. Milik has referred to them as "Pseudo-Danielic," and they seem to include the well-known Prayer of Nabonidus,[13] as well as the Aramaic text that mentions the Son of God and the Son of the Most High in phrases reminiscent of Luke 1:32, 35.[14] Just what the relation of all these fragments actually is to the canonical Book of Daniel will only be made clear when they are all finally published.

Job, the third paragon of righteousness, is now known to us in the targum from Qumran Cave XI, and through it we get a glimpse of the way in which the Qumran community used the biblical book that was ascribed to him. The significance of the targum, however, lies not so much in its recasting of steadfast Job as in the interpretation of the biblical book attributed to him in Palestinian Jewish tradition, as well as in the light that it sheds on targumic origins, and the new evidence that it brings to our understanding of Palestinian Aramaic at the beginning of the Christian era. And yet, we may be sure that one of the reasons why the targum of Job was preserved in Qumran caves was precisely the esteem that the community had for this ancient paragon of righteousness.

Before we turn to the targum itself and the picture of Job that is in it, it might be well to recall that his righteousness was also known outside of Qumran confines. He was singled out from the mass of OT worthies by Ben Sira, as is now clear from the Hebrew text of that book. He has, moreover, recently entered into the English Bible tradition in the *New American Bible*'s version of that book and its "Praise of Famous Men," which makes an explicit reference to Ezekiel's mention of Job: "Ezekiel beheld the vision and described the different creatures of the chariot; he also referred to Job who always persevered in the right path" וגם הזכיר את איוב המכלכל כל דר[כי צ]דק, Sir 49:9.[15] Again, the tradition of Job's righteousness is remembered.

And a Christian writer a few centuries later would sum up Job's career in a way in which he has usually been remembered: *τὴν ὑπομονὴν Ἰὼβ ἠκούσατε, καὶ τὸ τέλος κυρίου εἴδετε, ὅτι πολύσπλαγχνός ἐστιν ὁ κύριος καὶ οἰκτίρμων*, "You have heard of the steadfastness of Job and have seen what the Lord, who is compassionate and merciful, did in the end" (Jas 5:11 *NAB*).[16]

It is against this developing Jewish and Christian picture of the righteous and steadfast Job that we must view the Qumran targum that has come to light. In general, it presents a picture of Job that agrees with that of the Hebrew text. E. W. Tuinstra, who has made a study of the hermeneutical tendencies of the Aramaic version, has pointed out certain shifts of emphasis that appear in the targum. According to him, Job "is not only a righteous sufferer, but also a man upon whom 'knowledge' is bestowed," and he "seems to be a special assignee of God."[17] Tuinstra also thinks that there is in the targum the tendency to depict Job as the Teacher of Righteousness in the Qumran community,[18] a notion to which I shall return later, and that the "tendency to tone down and suppress the defiance-motif, which is a characteristic of the LXX portrayal of Job, is less clear in the targum."[19] If these few distinct traits prove right, then there is a slightly different picture of Job in the targum. But I should hesitate to say with Tuinstra that "the figure of Job in 11QtgJob differs significantly from that of the masoretic text."[20] In any case, the emphasis on Job's wisdom in the targum is interesting, since it fills out in its own way the Wisdom teaching found in other Qumran texts.

II. *The Qumran Targum of Job*

The Aramaic version of Job that has come to light in this targum is unfortunately fragmentary. It contains less than a sixth of the canonical book;

the editors estimate that only about 15 per cent of the text is preserved. Though the fragments range from Job 17:14 to 42:11, it is only from 37:10 on that the text is substantially intact. In the latter section one finds an Aramaic translation of Yahweh's speech following the discourses of Elihu—the section that is often called the "theophany" or "the Voice from the Whirlwind"[21] (38:1–41:34)—then Job's answer (42:1–6), and finally part of the epilogue (42:9-11). The most important part of the book is thus extant in this targum. What is contained in the fragmentary columns that precede this better-preserved portion of the targum is the last part of the second cycle of debates in the dialogue (15:1-21:24, beginning with 17:14), parts of the allegedly disordered third cycle of debates (22:1-31:40), and significantly enough, in the same order as the MT, with even portions of the Hymn to the Inaccessibility of Wisdom (28:1-28). And then considerable parts of the poetic discourses of Elihu (32:1-37:24). Thus this targum of Job gives us an ancient form of the Book of Job that agrees in large part with the structure and build-up of the Hebrew text, as we know it in the MT. There are, of course, verses and parts of verses that are missing in the Aramaic, and this not because of the fragmentary character of the targum, but because of a different recensional activity. Yet such differences do not modify the judgment about the build-up of the book as a whole in this version.

The text ends with Job 42:11 in the middle of a line with a *vacat* following. This indicates the end of a paragraph, as in 11QtgJob 10:6. Conceivably, there could have been a few further lines at the bottom of col. 38, which is now lost. But the space is insufficient for vss. 12-17 of the Hebrew; and the skin on which a following column could have been written is preserved, and it is blank. So the chances are that the targum lacked 42:12-17, verses which are in the present-day Hebrew text of Job, as well as the expanded epilogue of the book found in the LXX.[22]

By and large the targum is a rather literal translation of the Hebrew; at times one finds added phrases or paraphrastic renderings.[23] When the Aramaic does depart from the Hebrew, it is often enough at those spots where the Hebrew text itself has been suspect or scarcely intelligible and where other ancient versions had different renderings.

On the basis of the paleography of the fragments, the editors have suggested a date in the late Herodian period for this copy of the targum.[24] In this they are dependent on the work of W. F. Albright, F. M. Cross, and others, and their suggested date seems to be beyond cavil. That would mean an early first-century A.D. date for the Qumran Cave XI copy.

As for the composition of the targum, the editors have proposed a date somewhere between the final redaction of Daniel and the composition of the *Genesis Apocryphon*, and they list a whole series of details to support their dating.[25] At the moment, I am inclined to go along with their proposal, even though some others have expressed some misgivings about it and the full assessment of the problem will take considerable time yet. This will not be possible until all the linguistic features of the text are completely sorted out and compared with other Qumran Aramaic texts, many of which are still to be published.[26] There is, however, nothing in this material that would militate against a pre-Christian dating of the composition of this targum.

Since the copy from Qumran Cave XI is to be dated early in the first Christian century, and since it is almost certainly not the autograph, and since the language in which it is written could reflect Palestinian usage of at least a century earlier, we are confronted with a targum that for the first time can be truly said to date from a pre-Christian period. Significantly, it is not a version of the Pentateuch, but of one of the books of the *Kĕtûbîm*. Moreover, this targum may even antedate the time when the Book of Job came to be regarded as canonical, though its status as such does not seem to have been much contested.[27]

11QtgJob is not the only targum of Job that is extant from Qumran. Another small fragmentary copy of a targum of this book is reported from Qumran Cave IV, and contains only a few words from Job 3:4-5 and 4:16-5:4.[28] Indeed, it may well be part of the same Aramaic version as that in 11QtgJob. In any case, this situation suggests that the targum of Job existed among the Essenes of Qumran in multiple copies.

Targumic texts at Qumran are represented also by two fragments containing Lev 16:12-15, 18-21, a part of the ritual for the Day of Atonement.[29] This fragmentary text, however, raises a tantalizing problem. Is it part of a full targum of the Pentateuch or a fragment of some other Aramaic work that just happened to quote or use Leviticus 16 for some purpose? The question is not idle, given the interest of the Qumran Essenes in the ritual of the Day of Atonement that is found in other Qumran texts.[30] Milik, who has published these fragments, is convinced that they belong to a full targum; if he is correct, then the existence of a *written pre-Christian targum of the Pentateuch* is also attested. However, if the fragments should only be part of some larger Aramaic text that is really different, then it at least supplies a version of an important pentateuchal passage, either derived from an existing written targum or reduced to writing from some oral version.

All of this material now reveals that written Aramaic translations of OT texts were in use in Palestine of the first century A.D. and undoubtedly also in the first century B.C. as well. This has to be emphasized as the importance of the Qumran discoveries because of the exaggerated claims for the pre-Christian origins of other known targums. Such claims have been legion in recent years and have been more supported by extrapolated conclusions than direct evidence.[31] Milik may well be right in ascribing the paucity of Aramaic translations of biblical books within the Qumran community itself to the "highly educated" character of that community.[32] After all, most of their *sectarian* literature was composed, not in Aramaic, but in Hebrew, and this would seem to indicate that they did not have need of Aramaic translations of biblical books. Indeed, in some instances we even have the Hebrew commentaries *(pěšārîm)* that they had composed on the texts of the prophets and psalms. But was the Hebrew text of Job so difficult even for this community of Jews that it had to have recourse to it in an Aramaic version? Such a question is not easily answered.

It is further complicated by the issue raised by S. Segert, who thinks that the Aramaic texts found at Qumran were really non-Essene compositions, produced elsewhere and brought into the community, in which they were merely read or used by members who otherwise spoke and wrote in Hebrew.[33] If he were correct in this view, then the Qumran Aramaic texts would be witnesses to a form of Aramaic used by Jews in an even wider scope or area than this esoteric community. In my study of the *Genesis Apocryphon*, I came to the conclusion that there was nothing in it that directly or positively betrayed an Essene origin.[34] And I feel the same way about the targum of Job at this point. E. W. Tuinstra, however, is convinced that the Qumran Targum of Job is indeed an Essene composition, as I mentioned earlier.[35] The main reasons which he gives for this view are the remodelling of the figure of Job in the targum after the pattern of the Teacher of Righteousness, and the omission of the mention of Job's "sisters" at the meal that Job finally takes with "his friends, brothers, and acquaintances" (11QtgJob 38:5; contrast Hebr. 42:11)—a reflection of their celibate character. Now such reasons are tantalizing, but the evidence cited in support of them is so slight that it is not convincing. Why the targumist omitted the "sisters" in Job 42:11 is puzzling; it *might* reflect a celibate concern, but that is at best a remote possibility and one that raises the entire question about how celibate the Qumran Essenes really were. In this regard I prefer to remain with the judgment that J. van der Ploeg originally set forth about the targum: nothing, apart from its discovery in Qumran Cave XI, suggests that it had an origin in the Qumran community.[36] It was read there and bears witness to the use of Aramaic in the community, as well as to a literary creativity in Aramaic in Palestine of the first century B.C.

This consideration, however, evokes a further comment. Whereas the targum gives still further evidence of literary activity in Aramaic, that does not necessarily mean that the targum was composed in "the literary Aramaic of the intertestamental period," i.e., "an artificial, literary Aramaic, colored, to be sure, by the local spoken dialect" and "a conscious attempt to imitate a 'classical' language generally similar to Official Aramaic."[37] So to regard the language of the targum is to take refuge in what cannot be substantiated—that the Aramaic of the targum represents an "artificial, literary" type of the language that was clearly different from, albeit influenced by, the spoken form of the language.

Two further aspects of the language of the targum should be considered. First, though it seems to come from a stage between the Book of Daniel and the *Genesis Apocryphon*, and thus otherwise belongs to the phase of Middle Aramaic, it nevertheless contains some Persian words, four—possibly five—of them: פתגם, "word, thing" (9:2; 30:1; 34:3; 29:4; 22:7); דחשת, "desert" (32:5;

15:[7]); נזך, "spear, javelin" (33:5); חרתך, "thorn" (35:5);[38] and possibly דת, "law, religion" (30:8). The appearance of Persian words in Qumran Hebrew or Aramaic texts is not new.[39] The abundance of them in earlier Official (or Imperial) Aramaic is well known,[40] and this undoubtedly accounts for the persistence of them or even the emergence of hitherto unknown forms even in a Qumran targum. Secondly, by way of contrast, the targum is notably lacking in Greek words. To date only one word has been possibly so identified, סיף, "sword" (11QtgJob 33:5), said to be a borrowing of Greek *ξίφος*.[41] Though it appears here for the first time in Qumran Aramaic, it is attested otherwise in earlier Official Aramaic and in Palestinian Aramaic (Strasbourg Ostracon 6; 5/6Ḥev 1 ar: 4).[42] The absence of Greek words in this targum is to be noted in conjunction with the data that I have tried to collect on this question elsewhere.[43] And the absence of them in the Aramaic of the Qumran targum of Job is striking by contrast with the many Greek words that appear in the targums from the period of Late Aramaic, and in Syriac.

So much for the observations on the Qumran targum of Job in itself.

III. *The Qumran Targum and the Second Targum of Job*

It had been known for a long time that versions of the Book of Job in Aramaic were extant in antiquity. The fourth/fifth century MSS of the Greek OT (א,B,A,C) contain an expanded form of the book's epilogue. Whereas the last verse of the Hebrew text reads, "And Job died, an old man, full of days" (42:17), and this is literally rendered in the Old Greek version as *καὶ ἐτελεύτησεν Ἰὼβ πρεσβύτερος καὶ πλήρης ἡμερῶν*, it continues, *γέγραπται δὲ αὐτὸν πάλιν ἀναστήσεσθαι μεθ' ὧν ὁ κύριος ἀνίστησιν· οὗτος ἑρμηνεύεται ἐκ τῆς συριακῆς βίβλου*, "it is written that he will rise again with those whom the Lord raises up; it (or he?) is translated (*or* interpreted?) from the Syrian book" (LXX, 42:17a-b).[44] It further continues with biographical details about Job. The reference to *ἡ συριακὴ βίβλος* has often been understood as an Aramaic version of Job,[45] and it possibly seeks to express some dependence of the Greek version on an Aramaic targum. One might like to argue from this notice to the existence of an Aramaic version of Job that existed prior to the earliest attempt to render Job into Greek; but is that precisely what is meant? The expansion of the epilogue in Greek is problematic in that it is not certain from what period it really dates. Does it come from the same pre-Christian period as the bulk of the Greek translation of Job? Does it further imply that an Aramaic version of Job was known one or two centuries earlier than the Qumran translation that we now have from Cave XI (and Cave IV)?[46] The least one can say is that by the time the Greek epilogue acquired its expansion, an Aramaic version of Job was known, and that possibly the expansion did exist earlier in some Aramaic form. But, in any case, that expansion of the Greek epilogue is neither found in nor derived from 11QtgJob;[47] thus it would seem to refer to some other Aramaic version of Job.

Reference to another Aramaic version of Job is made in rabbinical literature. In the Babylonian Talmud, *Shabbat* 16:1 (fol. 115a), we read:

> Said R. Jose: It once happened that my father Halafta visited R. Gamaliel Berabbi at Tiberias and found him sitting at the table of Johanan b. Nizuf with the Targum of the book of Job in his hand which he was reading. Said he to him: "I remember that R. Gamaliel, your grandfather, was standing on a high eminence of the Temple Mount, when the Book of Job in a Targumic version was brought to him, whereupon he said to the builder, 'Bury it under the bricks.'" He [R. Gamaliel II] too gave orders, and they hid it. R. Jose, son of R. Judah, said: They overturned a tub of mortar upon it. . . .[48]

This rabbinic text thus knows of an Aramaic version of Job that existed toward the end of the first century A.D. (being read by Rabbi Gamaliel II) and of another that had been immured somewhere in the Temple area roughly a half-century earlier (at the order of R. Gamaliel I—who, according to Acts 22:3, was the teacher of Paul of Tarsus in Jerusalem). This text has usually been taken as testimony to the prohibition of written Aramaic versions of the biblical writings.[49] In any case, the question arises whether this rabbinic reference to the targum ordered immured by R. Gamaliel I could be to the targum of Job now known to us from Qumran Cave XI (or from Cave IV). The editors of 11QtgJob are inclined so to regard it.[50] Though there is no certainty about the identification, there is nothing that is against it. E. W. Tuinstra, who, as we have already mentioned, regards the targum as an Essene composition, even goes so far as to say that it was ordered to be immured "because of its heretical, i.e., Essene origin."[51] There is, however, not a shred of evidence for this speculative reason.

Still another Aramaic version of Job has been known for a long time, being found in various polyglot Bibles, and published as part of *Hagiographa chaldaice* by P. de Lagarde.[52] We shall hereafter refer to it as "Targum II." It is said to be of Palestinian origin and to come from the 5th century A.D.[53] The purpose for which it was made is unknown, but it is usually regarded as having had nothing to do with synagogal service, because the Book of Job does not usually figure in synagogal lectionary cycles. The editors of 11QtgJob have already noted that, save for a few common exegetical traditions, the Qumran targum is wholly unrelated to Targum II.[54]

A detailed comparison of 11QtgJob with Targum II is needed for various reasons, not the least to make clear the amount of independence of the latter from the former, but also to highlight the difference in exegetical and translation techniques between a datable early targum and one of clearly later provenience.[55] I have undertaken such a study, and I should like to present a summary of the results. Chart I, which accompanies this paper, reveals that of the 1437 Aramaic words preserved in this Qumran targum,[56] only 295 are identical in Targum II, 133 are the same word but with a later (usually fuller) writing, and 255 words in Targum II are formed of the same root but with either phonological or morphological differences. The total of words that might be said to be *similar* in Targum II is 683 or about 47%, whereas only 428 words or about 30% could be said to be the *same*.[57] While some of the differences might be accounted for by postulating a different Hebrew recension for the Targum II, the significant thing is that the targums are so different. Two things are particularly striking: (a) the choice of entirely different Aramaic synonyms in Targum II to render the Hebrew words; (b) the number of clearly isolable words or phrases that reflect early and late translations. In so many of the latter instances the Qumran Targum has the form or the word that one would expect in the first century B.C. or A.D., whereas the Targum II has forms and words that are easily paralleled in later Jewish Palestinian Aramaic of the classic targumim, midrashim, and the talmud.

As examples of the latter type of differences, the following are to be noted. First of all, in 11QtgJob 25:5 the targumist has preserved the anthropomorphism of the Hebrew text, translating ויסתר פנים ומי ישורנו, "if he hides his face, who then can behold him?" (34:29 *NAB*), by [ויסת]ר אנפוהי מן יתיבנה, "and (if) he hides his face, who will bring him back?" But Targum II translates, ויסלק שכינתא ומן יסכיניה, "and (if) he removes the presence (Shekinah), who will bring him into danger?"[58] This is the only place in Targum II where the surrogate שכינתא is found in a passage corresponding to those extant in 11QtgJob. But the situation is somewhat the same for another such surrogate, מימרא, "the Word."[59] It is never found in the sense of a buffer, a means to safeguard the transcendence of Yahweh, when some creative, sustaining, or revelatory activity of his is described. The difference in treatment between 11QtgJob and Targum II is clearly seen in this regard in the following passage:

MT	*11QtgJob*	*Targum II*
9 וילכו אליפז התימני ובלדד השוחי צפר הנעמתי ויעשו כאשר דבר אליהם יהוה וישא יהוה את פני איוב: 10 ויהוה שב את שבית איוב בהתפללו בעד רעהו ויסף יהוה את כל אשר לאיוב למשנה	]] אלהא ושמע א[ל]הא בקלה די איוב ושבק להון חטאיהון בדילה ותב אלהא לאיוב ברחמין ויהב לה חד תרין בכל די הוא לה	9 ואזלו אליפז דמן תימן ובלדד דמן שוח צופר דמן נעמה ועבדו היך דמליל להום מימרא דיהוה ונסיב מימרא דיהוה ית אפי איוב: 10 ומימרא דיהוה אתיב ית גלוות איוב בצלאותיה מטול דחברוי ואוסיף מימרא דיהוה ית כל די לאיוב בכופלא
(42:9-10)	(38:2-4)	(42:9-10)
Then Eliphaz, the Temanite, and Bildad the Shuhite, and Zophar the Naamathite, went and did as the Lord had commanded them.	[as] God [had commanded them].	Then Eliphaz who was from Tema, and Bildad who was from Shuh, and Zophar who was from Naamah went and did as the Word of Yahweh had spoken to them.
And the Lord accepted the intercession of Job.[60]	And God listened to the voice of Job, and he forgave them their sins because of him.	And the Word of Yahweh accepted the intercession of Job.[60]
Also, the Lord restored the prosperity of Job, after he had prayed for his friends; the Lord even gave to Job twice as much as he had before.	And God returned to Job in mercy and gave him twice as much as all that he had had.	10 And the Word of Yahweh restored the captivity[61] of Job because of his prayer on behalf of his companions; and the Word of Yahweh increased twofold all that belonged to Job.

Though there are other differences in the two targums that might be called to attention, the main item to be noticed here is the absence of מימרא in the Qumran targum and the fourfold use of it in Targum II within two verses. This, of course, raises the real question about the antiquity of such surrogates in the targumic tradition. Admittedly, the evidence from the Qumran targum is negative, but it does have a bearing on the whole question of whether such ideas as שכינתא or מימרא were current among Jews of first-century Palestine and whether they really may be invoked for the explanation of NT passages.[62]

Second, the Qumran targum time after time attests the typically early forms of nouns in contrast to those found in Targum II: for example, ידיכון, "your hands" (11QtgJob 4:4), in contrast to the form with the prosthetic *aleph*, אידא, in Targum II (21:5); or דרע, "arm" (11QtgJob 34:5), in contrast to אדרע (Targum II 40:9);[63] or סגיא, "abundance" (11QtgJob 26:1, 3) in contrast to a form of the same word with *ᶜayin*, סוגעי (Targum II 35:6, 9). Similarly, 11QtgJob consistently has (א)אנש (with initial *aleph*), whereas Targum II has simply נש or בר נש (contrast 11QtgJob 9:9; 22:6; 24:5; 25:6; 26:3; 28:2 with Targum II 25:6; 33:12; 34:11; 34:30; 35:8; 36:25). Again 11QtgJob consistently writes the word for "bad, evil" as באיש (with the medial *aleph*: 19:4; 27:4) in contrast to the form ביש (Targum II 31:29; 36:10).[64]

Third, the verb "to see" in the Qumran targum is consistently a form of חזא (11QtgJob 11:2; 14:2, [5]; 23:4, 7; 28:2bis; 34:7; 37:8). In all the corresponding passages of Targum II one finds instead the verb חמא (27:12; 29:8, 11; 33:26, 28; 36:25; 40:11; 42:5). The use of חזא not only agrees with the biblical Aramaic usage (e.g., Ezra 4:14; Dan 2:41) and that of earlier Aramaic in general,[65] but it is found elsewhere in Qumran Aramaic (e.g., 1QapGen 2:12; 19:14, 23; 20:9, 14, [22]; 21:8, 9bis, 10, 14, 15; 22:27, 29). By contrast, the verb חמא, "see," is never found in the Aramaic of Qumran or earlier. Yet it is often said to be Palestinian.[66] Is it really? Its earliest attestation seems to be in a Palmyrene text, that is still unpublished,[67] and it is used further in the Babylonian Talmud in addition to the so-called Palestinian targums.[68] The instances of חמא in Targum II thus fit in with the evidence of other late texts, where this verb is used abundantly, and stand in contrast to the earlier Palestinian usage.

Fourth, there is the consistent spelling of the third personal pronominal suffix on masculine plural nouns and prepositions, which in 11QtgJob is always written as והי- (with the medial *he*: 5:3; 8:4; 23:4; 25:5; 33:4; 35:3; 36:4), in contrast to the form in Targum II, which is consistently written as וי- (without the medial *he*: 21:21, 24; 24:13; 33:26; 39:23; 40:24; 41:10). There is no instance of וי- in the Aramaic of Qumran, *pace* A. Díez Macho,[69] in the case of the masculine plural nouns of which we are speaking.

Fifth, one can further cite the forms of such a word as איתי, "there is" (11QtgJob 9:5; 23:[1]; 31:5; 34:5, 10), or in the negative form לא איתי (11QtgJob 6:4; 21:3), which agree with the consistent older form of the particle,[70] and stand in contrast to the later form in Targum II, אית, and especially to the contracted negative לית (= *lêt*, 25:3; 33:32; 38:28; negative, 22:5; 32:12). These forms are abundantly attested in Aramaic of the Late Period.

Sixth, whereas the construct chain is still a live feature in 11QtgJob (e.g., צפרי שמיא, "the birds of heaven" [13:12]; [בפ]ום ארמלה, "in a widow's mouth" [14:8]; בגבורת אלהא, "God's power" [29:5]), the substitution of a *dĕ*-clause for it is frequent in Targum II (e.g., in the passages corresponding to those just cited: ומעופא דשמיא, 28:21; ולבא דארמלתא, 29:13; פרישותא דאלהא, 37:14). The construct chain has not wholly disappeared from Targum II, to be sure, but it is not as abundant as it is in 11QtgJob (see further: 5:5; 7:4; 11:1; 13:1, 5; 14:1, 8; 15:3, 5, 7; 20:7; 22:9; 23:3, 4-5; 24:2; 26:1, 7-8; 27:1; 29:1, 3; 30:5, 6; etc.). On the other hand, there is one instance of the genitive expression with די in 11QtgJob 38:2, בקלה די איוב, "to the voice of Job" (= 42:9).[71]

Seventh, the Qumran targum makes use of the conjunction על דברת די, "in order that" (11QtgJob 34:4 [restored too in 1:7]), as a translation of Hebrew למען. This phrase is known in Biblical Aramaic (Dan 2:30; 4:14) and is related to the extrabiblical phrases in Elephantine (*AP* 6:6, 8; 40:3; 45:3; 28:8, 10, 11; 62:5; 71:30; *BMAP* 4:13; 13:2, 6; *A* 202; *RES* 1792A 3), על דברת זי, על דבר דברה, so that there is no doubt about its antiquity. This conjunction, however, is apparently unattested in later Jewish Palestinian Aramaic, and Targum II renders the Hebrew expression as אמטול (in Job 18:4) and as בגלל ד (in Job 40:8). Both of these forms are characteristically late and stand in contrast to על דברת די of the Qumran targum.[72]

Eighth, the Qumran targum uses לעבע, "quickly" (11QtgJob 3:7), which is the same word as לעובע (1QapGen 20:9 [see my commentary, 127]) and an intermediary form between עבק (found in Official Aramaic [*AP* 26:6, 22]) and Late Aramaic אבע. Targum II uses a paraphrase, בעגל.

Lastly, whereas the Qumran targum frequently introduces a question with the prefixed particle -ה(e.g., 33:7; 35:4, 5, 6, 7), Targum II often employs the phrase אפשר ד, lit., "Is it possible that . . . ?" (e.g., 39:26; 40:26, 27, 28, 29).

Still other features could be added to this list.[73] However, these examples suffice to illustrate the difference between an early and a late targum *of the same biblical book*. At the moment, this is important, since this is the only instance in which we can make such a comparison between a clearly pre-Christian targum and one from the Late Period. Now admittedly, the so-called Palestinian targums of the Pentateuch are not in all respects identical with Targum II of Job, and there is always the danger of extrapolating from the evidence given here to pentateuchal targums of the same period. And yet, anyone who has worked with the so-called Palestinian targums of the Pentateuch and with these two targums of Job will easily recognize that the features of Targum II are the ones that one meets mostly in the pentateuchal targums, not those of the Qumran targum. What is presented here is merely the beginning of a comparison that must be carried out on a still greater scale.

Finally, when the fragments of 4QtgLev are published, we shall be in a position to institute a similar comparison of them with the other known targums of the Pentateuch. Unfortunately, in that case the fragments of the Qumran targum are so small and so few that little will be able to be concluded from them.[73a]

CHART 1

11QtgJob COMPARED WITH THE SECOND TARGUM

11QtgJob Column	*Number of Aramaic Words Preserved in 11QtgJob*	*Number of Words Identical in Tg. 11*	*Number of Same Words with Later Orthography*	*Number of Words with Other Forms of Same Root*	*Total Number with Some Similarity*
1(17:14-18:4)	18	3	1	2	6
2(19:11-19)	23	9	3	3	15
3(19:19-20:6)	18	3	2	4	9
4(21:2-10)	24	5	0	3	8
5(21:10-27)	26	9	6	2	17
6(22:3-9)	14	2	1	5	8
7(22:16-22)	13	3	1	0	4
8(24:12-17)	14	3	1	1	5
9(24:24-26:2)	34	10	1	5	16
10(26:10-27:4)	29	4	1	5	10
11(27:11-20)	30	6	2	6	14
12(28:4-13)	8	1	1	0	2
13(28:20-28)	23	7	1	5	13
14(29:7-16)	45	3	2	18	23
15(29:24-30:4)	38	8	4	4	16
16(30:13-20)	33	6	1	4	11
17(30:25-31:1)	10	1	0	1	2
18(31:8-16)	27	9	0	9	18
19(31:26-32)	23	8	4	2	14
20(31:40-32:3)	16	1	3	2	6
21(32:10-17)	38	9	6	4	19
22(33:6-16)	46	11	8	9	28
23(33:24-32)	41	5	5	11	21
24(34:6-17)	45	14	2	6	22
25(34:24-34)	41	8	2	7	17
26(35:6-15)	56	12	9	10	31
27(36:7-16)	51	10	2	11	23
28(36:23-33)	57	9	1	11	21
29(37:10-19)	68	12	2	15	29
30(38:3-13)	69	21	3	13	37
31(38:23-34)	64	18	5	16	39
32(39:1-11)	66	13	6	17	36
33(39:20-29)	63	12	7	5	24
34(40:5-14)	63	9	4	11	24
35(40:23-31)	51	5	11	5	21
36(41:7-17)	52	4	9	9	22
37(41:25-42:6)	47	12	7	5	24
38(42:9-11)	53	10	9	9	28
Totals	1437	295	133	255	683

Given the differences between the two targums of Job that we have pointed out, and still other features—e.g., the greater amount of paraphrasis in Targum II, the occasional introduction into it of a secondary version of certain verses,[74] its use of Greek words in Aramaized forms—it is obvious that only rarely can the version of Targum II be used for the restoration of a lacuna in 11QtgJob. And the editors have normally restrained themselves from this. In attempts to restore the Aramaic text of the lacunae in the Qumran targum the principle should be this: One should look to see whether the Hebrew word to be translated is found elsewhere in the Book of Job and whether that passage is preserved in the extant parts of the Qumran targum; if it is, then the Aramaic counterpart of the Hebrew word found there should be given preference over other possible synonyms such as are often found in Targum II.

There is, of course, at least one other Aramaic translation of Job, with which one should ideally make the same sort of comparison as has been done here with Targum II. That is the version of Job that is found in the Peshitta. It would, of course, be wise to await the critical text of Syriac Job in *Vetus Testamentum syriace*.[75] But that brings up another aspect of the problem to which I have addressed myself above. My use of Targum II has depended solely on the edition of P. de Lagarde, which may not be perfect. It is now time to turn attention to a better edition of Targum II, a critical edition of which is now an obvious desideratum.

My remarks on the Qumran targum have concentrated on the text as an Aramaic version and its relation to another Aramaic rendering of the Book of Job. I noted earlier that the Qumran targum is by and large a literal translation of the Hebrew text, with only rare additions or paraphrastic renderings and no effort made to eliminate the anthropomorphisms of the original. Such a judgment, of course, presupposes a comparison with the present-day Hebrew text—and such comparisons have already been undertaken by others.[76] But it might be well in conclusion to recall that the Hebrew text of the Book of Job at Qumran or elsewhere in contemporary Palestine might not have been in all respects identical with the so-called Masoretic text. The editors of 11QtgJob admit that the targum presupposes a text that "se rapproche de celui des massorètes,"[77] but they also admit that sometimes the targumist seems to have had before him a slightly different Hebrew text. Now a few Hebrew fragments of Job have indeed been found in Qumran caves, and the editors of 11QtgJob have made no allusion to them. There is, for example, a Hebrew fragment of Job 33:28-30, which has been published as 2Q*15*.[78] M. Baillet, who published it, describes it as a fragment that presupposes "un texte du type massorétique."[79] Its tiny text agrees with the MT of Job and is part of Elihu's first poetic discourse. It bears on 11QtgJob 23, which seems, however, to bear witness to a different Hebrew *Vorlage*. Unfortunately, 2Q*15* is so small that it does not help to solve the problem of what might have been the Hebrew text being translated there. Several other fragmentary texts of Hebrew Job are known from Cave IV. Two of them are to be published by F. M. Cross, 4QJob[a, b] and are said to contain part of Job 36.[80] Another fragmentary text is represented by at least three small fragments in paleo-Hebrew script, 4QpaleoJob[c].[81] It is to be published by P. W. Skehan, but it will not affect the study of this targum, since the latter unfortunately lacks chaps. 13-14, which are found in these fragments. Chap. 36, however, has substantial verses preserved in 11QtgJob (cols. 27-28), and so one awaits anxiously Cross' publication of the Hebrew fragments to study this aspect of the targum. An intriguing question, however, is raised by

Skehan's fragments, written in the paleo-Hebrew archaizing script of Qumran: Why should a book such as Job have been copied in such a script? Is it perhaps a further indication of the esteem in which the Book of Job was held in the Qumran community?

My remarks on the Qumran targum of Job have been restricted to only a few aspects of the study of it. Though there is little in it that advances our knowledge of the Aramaic background of the NT, it does make its own contribution to the study of the language of that period in Palestine and thus bears indirectly on this area of investigation as well.[82]

NOTES TO CHAPTER 7

*Originally published as "Some Observations on the Targum of Job from Qumran Cave 11," *CBQ* 36 (1974) 503-24 (in the issue published as the Patrick W. Skehan Festschrift).

[1]See, among others, G. L. Harding, "Recent Discoveries in Jordan," *PEQ* 90 (1958) 7-18, esp. p. 17.

[2]The *editio princeps* was published by J. P. M. van der Ploeg and A. S. van der Woude, *Le targum de Job de la grotte XI de Qumrân* (p. 22 above, n. 32).

[3]See J. van der Ploeg, "Le targum de Job de la grotte 11 de Qumran (11QtgJob), première communication," *Mededelingen der koninklijke nederlandse Akademie van Wetenschappen,* Afd. Letterkunde, Nieuwe Reeks, Deel 25, No. 9 (Amsterdam: N. V. Noord-Hollandsche Uitgevers Maatschappij, 1962) 543-57. Cf. idem, "Een targum van het boek Job: Een nieuwe vondst in de Woestijn van Juda," *Het heilig Land* 15/11 (1962) 145-49; A. S. van der Woude, "Das Hiobtargum aus Qumran Höhle XI," *Congress Volume, Bonn 1962* (VTSup 9; Leiden: Brill, 1963) 322-31; J. P. M. van der Ploeg, "Un targum du livre de Job: Nouvelle découverte dans le désert de Juda," *BVC* 58 (1964) 79-87; A. S. van der Woude, "The Targum of Job from Qumran Cave Eleven," *AJBA* 1 (1969) 19-29 (a translation of VTSup 9 [1963] 322-31).

For secondary literature, based mainly on van der Ploeg's preliminary communication, see G. Fohrer, "4QOrNab, 11QtgJob, und die Hioblegende," *ZAW* 75 (1963) 93-97; A. Dupont-Sommer, "Notes qoumraniennes," *Sem* 15 (1965) 71-78, esp. pp. 71-74; S. Segert, "Sprachliche Bemerkungen zu einigen aramäischen Texten von Qumran," *ArOr* 33 (1965) 190-206, esp. pp. 193, 198; R. Le Déaut, "Le substrat araméen des évangiles: Scolies en marge de l'*Aramaic Approach* de Matthew Black," *Bib* 49 (1968) 388-99, esp. p. 391.

[4]Reviews of the *editio princeps*: B. Z. Wacholder, *JBL* 91 (1972) 414-15; P. Grelot, *RQ* 8 (1972-76) 105-14; D. Lys, *ETR* 47 (1972) 365-66; S. Kaufman, "The Job Targum from Qumran," *JAOS* 93 (1973) 317-27; J. Coppens, *ETL* 48 (1972) 221-22; P. M. Bogaert, *RTL* 3 (1972) 86-90; (G. Fohrer), *ZAW* 84 (1972) 128; M. Dahood, *Bib* 54 (1973) 283-86; G. R. Driver, *Book List 1973* (Durham: SOTS, 1973) 56; E. Cortes, *Estudios franciscanos* 48 (1972) 124–25; S. Medala and Z. J. Kapera, *Folia orientalia* 14 (1972–73) 320–23; C. T. Fritsch, *TToday* 30 (1973–74) 442–43; H. Bardtke, *OLZ* 70 (1975) 468–72.

Other studies based on the *editio princeps*: B. Jongeling, "Een belangrijke Dode-zeerol: Job in het Aramees," *Rondom het Woord* 13 (1971) 282-93; E. 4. Tuinstra, *Hermeneutische Aspecten van de Targum van Job uit Grot XI van Qumrân* (Groningen: Dissertation, 1971 [available from Hendrik Kraemer Instituut, Leidsestraatweg 11 (Postbus 12), Oegstgeest 2407, Holland]); P. Grelot, "Note de critique textuelle sur Job xxxix 27," *VT* 22 (1972) 487-89; J. C. Greenfield and S. Shaked, "Three Iranian Words in the Targum of Job from Qumran," *ZDMG* 122 (1972) 37-45;

M. Dahood, "Is the Emendation of *yādîn* to *yāzîn* Necessary in Job 36,31?" *Bib* 53 (1972) 539-41; H. Bardtke, "Literaturbericht über Qumrān VI. Teil III: Das Hiobtargum aus Höhle XI von Qumrān (11Qtg Job)," *TRu* 37 (1972) 205-19; M. Delcor, "Le targum de Job et l'araméen du temps de Jésus," *Exégèse biblique et judaïsme* (ed. J.-E. Ménard; Strasbourg: Faculté de théologie catholique [distributed by Brill, Leiden], 1973) 78-107; B. Jongeling, "Contributions of the Qumran Job Targum to the Aramaic Vocabulary," *JSS* 17 (1972) 191-97; F. J. Morrow, Jr., "11 Q Targum Job and the Massoretic Text," *RQ* 8 (1972-76) 253-56; A. D. York, "*Zrʿrwmʾh* as an Indication of the Date of 11QtgJob?" *JBL* 93 (1974) 445-46; R. Weiss, "Further Notes on the Qumran Targum to Job," *JSS* 19 (1974) 13–18. See further *MPAT*, pp. 195–97.

A more complete study of the targum has now appeared: M. Sokoloff, *The Targum to Job from Qumran Cave XI* (Bar-Ilan Studies in Near Eastern Languages and Culture; Ramat-Gan, Israel: Bar-Ilan University, 1974). See further B. Jongeling, C. J. Labuschagne, and A. S. van der Woude (eds.), *Aramaic Texts from Qumran* (p. 108 above, n. 9).

[5]See S. Spiegel, "Noah, Danel, and Job," *Louis Ginzberg Jubilee Volume* (New York: Jewish Theological Seminary, 1945) 305-55; M. Noth, "Noah, Daniel und Hiob in Ezechiel XIV," *VT* 1 (1951) 251-60.

[6]See N. M. Sarna, "Epic Substratum in the Prose of Job," *JBL* 76 (1957) 13-25; A. Alt, "Zur Vorgeschichte des Buches Hiob," *ZAW* 55 (1937) 265-68.

[7]See H. Ringgren, *The Faith of Qumran: Theology of the Dead Sea Scrolls* (Philadelphia: Fortress, 1963) 63-67, 108-9; F. Nötscher, *Zur theologischen Terminologie der Qumran-Texte* (BBB 10; Bonn: Hanstein, 1956) 161, 183-87; S. Schulz, "Die Rechtfertigung aus Gnaden in Qumran und bei Paulus," *ZTK* 56 (1959) 155-85; P. Stuhlmacher, *Gerechtigkeit Gottes bei Paulus* (FRLANT 87; Göttingen: Vandenhoeck & Ruprecht, 1965) 148-66; K. Kertelge, *"Rechtfertigung" bei Paulus: Studien zur Struktur und zum Bedeutungsgehalt des paulinischen Rechtfertigungsbegriffs* (NTAbh ns 3; 2d ed.; Münster: Aschendorff, 1967) 28-33; P. Wernberg-Møller, "*Ṣdq, ṣdyq* and *ṣdwq* in the Zadokite Fragments (CDC), the Manual of Discipline (DSD) and the Habakkuk-Commentary (DSH)," *VT* 3 (1953) 310-15.

[8]N. Avigad and Y. Yadin, *A Genesis Apocryphon* (p. 108 above, n. 9), 16–22, 40 (+pl. 11). Cf. my commentary on *The Genesis Apocryphon* (p. 22 above, n. 27), 50–59, 78–104.

[9]Ibid., 5.

[10]See J. T. Milik, *Ten Years* (p. 22 above, n. 31), 35; "'Prière de Nabonide' et autres écrits d'un cycle de Daniel: Fragments araméens de Qumran 4," *RB* 63 (1956) 407-15, esp. p. 412. Cf. C. Burchard, *Bibliographie zu den Handschriften vom Toten Meer II (Nr. 1557-4459)* (BZAW 89; Berlin: Töpelmann, 1965) 333.

[11]See J. M. Allegro (with the collaboration of A. A. Anderson), *Qumrân Cave 4: I (4Q*158-*4Q*186) (DJD 5; Oxford: Clarendon, 1968) 54 *(bspr Dnyʾl hnbyʾ)*. Cf. my article, "David, 'Being Therefore a Prophet . . .' (Acts 2:30)," *CBQ* 34 (1972) 332-39; Josephus, *Ant.* 10.11.7 §266-68; also "Further Light on Melchizedek from Qumran Cave 11," *ESBNT*, 245-67, esp. pp. 248, 250, 265-66.

[12]Cf., e.g., 1QM 1:4-6 and Dan 11:41-44.

[13]"'Prière de Nabonide' et autres écrits d'un cycle de Daniel" (see n. 10 above), 411-15.

[14]See pp. 90–94 above.

[15]*The New American Bible* (Paterson: St. Anthony Guild, 1970) 820. By contrast, the *RSV*, which has a translation of Ben Sira from the Greek (Sirach), reads: "It was Ezekiel who saw the vision of glory which God showed him above the chariot of the cherubim. For God remembered his enemies with storm, and did good to those who directed their ways aright." See F. Vattioni, *Ecclesiastico: Testo ebraico con apparato critico e versioni greca, latina e siriaca* (Pubblicazioni del seminario di semitistica, Testi 1; Naples: Istituto orientale di Napoli, 1968) 266-67; cf. R. Smend, *Die Weisheit des Jesus Sirach hebräisch und deutsch* (Berlin: Reimer, 1906) 57 (Hebr.), 89 (Germ.).

[16]The text of Jas 5:11 has always been problematic. The last six words are an OT allusion (see Exod 34:6; Ps 103:8; 111:4). The problematic phrase is *καὶ τὸ τέλος κυρίου εἴδετε*, which is sometimes translated as above, or (with the *RSV*) as, "you have seen the purpose of the Lord."

The latter meaning of τέλος is explained by BAG (p. 819) as "*the outcome which the Lord brought about* in the case of Job's trials." But the same *Lexicon* offers still another interpretation, "the end = *the death . . . of the* Lord Jesus," which shows how problematic the verse is; cf. A. Bischoff, "Tὸ τέλος κυρίου," *ZNW* 7 (1906) 274-79. However, the *apparatus criticus* in E. Nestle, *Novum Testamentum graece* (24th ed.; Stuttgart: Priv. Württembergische Bibelanstalt, 1960) 252, notes the variant ἔλεος for τέλος in the minuscle ms. 1739* and a few other witnesses. This is interesting, for the allusion in Jas 5:11 is often said to be also to Job 42:10ff. (see the margin in Nestle). In the Aramaic version of Job 42:11, the Qumran targum significantly adds a phrase (38:3): "And God returned to Job *in mercy* (ותב אלהא לאיוב ברחמין) and gave him twice as much as all that he had had." Contrast the *RSV* of the Hebrew text: "And the Lord restored the fortunes of Job, when he had prayed for his friends; and the Lord gave Job twice as much as he had before." Is it possible that Jas 5:11 should preferably be read as τὸ ἔλεος κυρίου εἴδετε, "you have seen the mercy of the Lord"? Or have ms. 1739* and other witnesses possibly been tributary to a Job-tradition represented in 11QtgJob? This is only a question; more evidence would have to be forthcoming before the reading τὸ ἔλεος would prove convincing.

17See *Hermeneutische Aspecten* (n. 4 above), 55-57 (extended discussion); 108 (English summary). Tuinstra contrasts the shift from Job's "speaking" (Hebr. Job 21:3) to his "knowledge" (11QtgJob 4:2) with the reverse in the case of Elihu, whose "knowledge" (Hebr. 32:10, 17) becomes his "words" (11QtgJob 21:1, 9). He also finds Job's qualities stressed (Hebr. 29:25 = 11QtgJob 15:1, 2; Hebr. 29:13 = 11QtgJob 14:1, 6; Hebr. 30:15 = 11QtgJob 16:1, 4; Hebr. 34:31 = 11QtgJob 25:1, 7). Furthermore, the translation of Job 40:10-11 is for him "very striking" because "God's ironic reproach of Job is turned into an assignment for Job to punish the godless. The last words of Job are interpreted in a most remarkable way: instead of repentance there is only a complaint: 'Therefore I am poured out and dissolved and I have become dust and ashes' (42:6; col. XXXVIII, 1.8f; cf. Ps 22:15a)" (p. 108).

18Ibid., 66, 109. Some writers had earlier discussed Job as an "Essene model," basing their remarks on the attitude toward suffering and confidence in God that is displayed in the *Hôdāyôt*. See H. Kosmala, *Hebräer—Essener—Christen: Studien zur Vorgeschichte der frühchristlichen Verkündigung* (Studia post-biblica, 1; Leiden: Brill, 1959) 292; J. Carmignac, "La théologie de la souffrance dans les Hymnes de Qumrân," *RQ* 3 (1961-62) 365-86, esp. p. 386. If there is any validity to these claims, they would rather support the understanding of Job in the Qumran community, as discussed above in this part of the paper.

19*Hermeneutische Aspecten,* 108.

20Ibid.

21See M. Burrows, "The Voice from the Whirlwind," *JBL* 47 (1928) 117-32.

22Cf. L. W. Batten "The Epilogue of the Book of Job," *ATR* 15 (1933) 125-28; A. Alt, "Zur Vorgeschichte" (n. 6 above).

23See *Le targum de Job* (p. 22 above, n. 32), 7. The variants have been discussed in detail by E. W. Tuinstra, *Hermeneutische Aspecten,* chap. 1. Cf. F. J. Morrow, Jr., "11 Q Targum Job and the Massoretic Text," *RQ* 8 (1972-76) 253-56.

24*Le targum de Job*, 2-3.

25Ibid., 3-5. "Appartiendrait-il à la deuxième partie du deuxième siècle av. J.-C.? Ce n'est qu'une suggestion, ou plutôt une question" (p. 4). The editors use as chief criteria the following details: (1) the use of *dī* (never *dĕ*) as the relative or determinative pronoun; (2) the predominance of the haphel as causative (in 1QapGen it is always ᵓaphel); (3) the reflexive in *hit-* (instead of ᵓ*it*); (4) the conditional conjunction as *hen* (never ᵓ*in*); (5) the interrogative *kĕmā*ᵓ (never *kĕmān*); (6) the adverb *tmh* (never *tmn*). See further S. A. Kaufman, "The Job Targum from Qumran" (n. 4 above), 325-27; J. T. Milik in DJD 3. 184-85; P. Grelot, Review of the *editio princeps, RQ* 8 (1972-76) 113; M. Delcor, "Le targum de Job" (n. 4 above), 83-86.

26For a list of Qumran Aramaic texts, see pp. 101–2 above.

27See M. H. Pope, *Job* (AB 15; Garden City: Doubleday, 1965) xxxviii-xxxix; 3d ed. (1973) xlii-xliii.

[28]Private communication from J. Strugnell. Cf. R. Le Déaut, *Introduction à la littérature targumique: Première partie* (Rome: Biblical Institute, 1966) 68. Le Déaut speaks of "two small fragments," which use a final *aleph* or *he* (but in what connection?), *ḥzʾ* ("see") "instead of the Palestinian *ḥamaʾ*" (?), and the suffix *-why*. See now R. de Vaux and J. T. Milik, *Qumrân Grotte 4, II* (DJD 6; Oxford: Clarendon, 1977) 90.

[29]Preliminary notice of this targum has been given by J. T. Milik, *Ten Years* (p. 22 above, n. 31), 31. A. Díez Macho ("La lengua hablada por Jesucristo," *OrAnt* 2 [1963] 96-132, esp. p. 107) records an oral communication made to him by Milik about the text: "two fragments of Leviticus in a literal Aramaic version like that of Onqelos, and in Imperial Aramaic. The fragments come from Qumran Cave IV and seem to be from the 1st century B.C." However, in his article, "Targum" (*Enciclopedia de la Biblia* [Barcelona: Ediciones Garriga, 1965], 6. 867), he speaks of them as "Preonqelos." See further R. Le Déaut, *Introduction,* 64-65. The latter is of the opinion that the literal translation of Leviticus, as well as that of Job in 11QtgJob, indicate that the oldest written targums were actually guides which closely followed the Hebrew text (and which permitted oral improvisation with haggadic embellishments that the translator would draw from a fund of oral tradition; only later on did the more paraphrastic targums come to be written down).

Having seen the fragments of the Leviticus passages in the "scrollery" of the Palestine Archaeological Museum some years ago, I hesitate to characterize the language in them simply as "Imperial Aramaic" (see pp. 71–73 above). It does not differ from that of other Qumran Aramaic texts, which has to be regarded as one of the several developments of Imperial Aramaic between 200 B.C. and A.D. 200. It does not use *kzy*, but rather *kd*[*y*]; the suffix of the 3d plur. masc. is not *-hm*, but *-hwn*. On the other hand, it does not yet have the forms that become frequent in later targums; it has *dm*, "blood," as in 1QapGen 11:17, and not *ʾdmʾ* with the later prosthetic *aleph*; *shwr*, "around" (cf. 1QapGen 21:15-18), instead of *ḥzwr*, which is found in Neofiti 1 and Ps.-Jonathan); the 3d sg. masc. suffix in *-h*, not in *-yh*. See now *Maarav* 1 (1978) 5–23.

[30]See M. R. Lehmann, "'Yom Kippur' in Qumran," *RQ* 3 (1961-62) 117-24. Cf. 11QMelchizedek 7, 25; 1Q*34bis* 2+1:6; 1QpHab 11:7. See further my article, "Further Light on Melchizedek," *ESBNT,* 247, 249, 251, 259.

[31]See M. Black, *Aramaic Approach* (p. 23 above, n. 43), 22; A. Díez Macho, *Neophyti 1, Targum palestinense . . . Génesis* (p. 84 above, n. 112), 95*.

[32]*Ten Years* (p. 22 above, n. 31), 31.

[33]"Sprachliche Bemerkungen zu einigen aramäischen Texten von Qumran," *ArOr* 33 (1965) 190-206, esp. pp. 205-6; "Die Sprachenfragen in der Qumrāngemeinschaft," *Qumran-Probleme* (ed. H. Bardtke; Berlin: Akademie-Verlag, 1963) 313-39, esp. pp. 325-30; and his review of my commentary, *JSS* 13 (1968) 281-82. Similarly, A. G. Lamadrid, *EstBib* 28 (1969) 169.

[34]*The Genesis Apocryphon of Qumran Cave I* (2d ed.) 11-14.

[35]*Hermeneutische Aspecten* (n. 4 above), 65-70, 108-9.

[36]"Première communication" (n. 3 above), 553. See also P. Grelot, *RQ* 8 (1972-76) 113.

[37]S. A. Kaufman, "The Job Targum from Qumran" (n. 4 above), 325.

[38]See now J. C. Greenfield and S. Shaked, "Three Iranian Words in the Targum of Job from Qumran," *ZDMG* 122 (1972) 37-45; J. van der Ploeg, "Première communication," 549.

[39]Recall *rāz*, "secret" (1QapGen 1:2, 3; 1Q*27* 1:2; 1QH 5:36; fr. 50:5; 1QM 14:9; 1QS 3:23; 4:6, 18, etc.); *naḥšîr*, "carnage" (1QM 1:9, 10, 13; 4Q*243* 1:5).

[40]See H. H. Schaeder, *Iranische Beiträge* (see p. 50 above, n. 27), 199–296.

[41]See C. Brockelmann, *Lexicon syriacum* (2d ed.; Halle/S.: Niemeyer, 1928) 472.

[42]The Strasbourg Ostracon is probably of Egyptian provenience; see M. Lidzbarski, *Ephemeris* 3 (1915) 25-26. For 5/6Ḥev 1 ar: 4, see E. Y. Kutscher,"The Languages of the Hebrew and Aramaic Letters of Bar Cocheba and His Contemporaries," *Lěšonénu* 25 (1961) 117-33, esp. p. 119. Neither G. Dalman (*ANHW,* 289) nor M. Jastrow (*A Dictionary of the Targumim, the Talmud Babli and Yerushalmi, and the Midrashic Literature* [New York/Berlin: Choreb, 1926], 978) identify the word as Greek. It is probably nothing more than a **qatl*-type of a hollow root,

swp, "cut off." So it is listed by M. H. Segal, *A Grammar of Mishnaic Hebrew* (Oxford: Clarendon, 1927) 100.

[43]See pp. 40–41 above. Cf. J. C. Greenfield, *JNES* 31 (1972) 59: ". . . The Qumrān Scrolls have very interesting Iranian loan words but one would not use these to date the scrolls in the Persian period."

[44]See A. Rahlfs, *Septuaginta* (2 vols.; Stuttgart: Privil. Württembergische Bibelanstalt, 1949), 2. 344; H. B. Swete, *The Old Testament in Greek according to the Septuagint* (Cambridge: Cambridge University, 1922), 2. 602.

[45]L. Zunz, *Die gottesdienstlichen Vorträge der Juden historisch entwickelt* (rev. ed.; Hildesheim: Olms, 1966) 64, 84; A. Berliner, *Targum Onqelos herausgegeben und erläutert* (2 vols.; Berlin: Gorzelanczyk, 1884), 2. 91.

[46]See A. T. Olmstead, "Could an Aramaic Gospel Be Written?" *JNES* 1 (1942) 41-75, esp. p. 59. Cf. P. Kahle, *The Cairo Geniza: Schweich Lectures, 1941* (London: British Academy, 1947), p. 124; but Kahle omitted this view in the second edition (Oxford: Blackwell, 1959). H. Birkeland (*The Language of Jesus* [p. 22 above, n. 35], 35) argues: "That the Targum of Job was found in Palestine in the time of Rabbi Gamaliel (about 50 A.D.) does not necessarily mean that it was written for Palestinian Jews. Since it seems to be quoted already in the Greek translation of Job (see Kahle, p. 124 [first edition], with reference to Olmstead), it was obviously known in the Hellenized world outside Palestine." But does all that necessarily follow?

The Greek of the expanded epilogue is not easily translated. The version given above is very literal and allows for variant interpretations. It has been translated thus: "This (man) is referred to in the Syriac book as dwelling in Ausis. . . ," or "This man is described in the Syriac book as living in the land of Ausis" (*The Septuagint Version of the Old Testament and Apocrypha with an English Translation* [Grand Rapids: Zondervan, 1972] 698). But this does violence to the verb *ἑρμηνεύεται* and to the preposition *ἐκ*. On the other hand, the "Syrian book" has been understood as a reference to "some Aramaic apocryphal work" by M. McNamara, *Targum and Testament* (p. 26 above, n. 94), 66.

See further P. Winter, "Lc 2 49 and Targum Yerushalmi," *ZNW* 45 (1954) 145-79, esp. pp. 155-58; M. Delcor, "Le Testament de Job, la prière de Nabonide et les traditions targoumiques," *Bibel und Qumran: Beiträge zur Erforschung der Beziehungen zwischen Bibel- und Qumranwissenschaft: Hans Bardtke zum 22. 9. 1966* (Berlin: Evangelische Haupt-Bibelgesellschaft, 1968) 57-74, esp. pp. 68-69; M. H. Pope, *Job* (3d ed.; n. 27 above), 354; G. Gerleman, "Date of the Greek Book of Job," *Studies in the Septuagint: I. Book of Job* (Lunds Universitets Arsskrift, N.F. Avd. 1, Bd. 43, Nr. 2; Lund: Gleerup, 1946) 73-75.

[47]Indeed, the text of Job at this point in the Qumran targum is even shorter than the Hebrew; see above p. 164. F. M. Cross (*The Ancient Library of Qumran and Modern Biblical Studies* [The Haskell Lectures 1956-57; Garden City: Doubleday, 1958) 26 n. 48; rev. ed. [1961] 34 n. 48; *Die antike Bibliothek von Qumran und die moderne biblischen Wissenschaft* [Neukirchen: Neukirchener Verlag, 1967] 48 n. 56) once speculated that the addition at "the end of the Septuagint to Job may be quoted from this Targum," but this has not proved to be the case.

[48]I. Epstein (ed.), *The Babylonian Talmud: Seder Mo*ᶜ*ed* (London: Soncino, 1938) 564-65. The text itself reads:

אמר רבי יוסי: מעשה באבא חלפתא שהלך אצל רבן גמליאל בריבי לטבריא ומצאו שהיה יושב על שלחנו של יוחנן הנזוף ובידו ספר איוב תרגום והוא קורא בו אמר לו זכור אני ברבן גמליאל אבי אביך שהיה עומד על גב מעלה בהר הבית והביאו לפניו ספר איוב תרגום ואמר לבנאי שקעהי תחת הנדבך אף הוא צוה עליו וגנזו רבי יוסי בר יהודה אומר עריבה של טיט כפו עליו.

(L. Goldschmidt, *Der babylonische Talmud* [Berlin: Calvary, 1897], 1. 595).

Slightly different forms of the same story are found in the Jerusalem Talmud, *Shabbat* 16:1 (16a; ed. M. Schwab, *Le Talmud de Jérusalem* [Paris: G.-P. Maisonneuve, 1960], 3. 160-61); the Tosephta, *Shabbat* 13:2 (ed. S.Liebermann [New York: Jewish Theological Seminary, 1962] 57).

[49]R. Le Déaut (*Introduction* [n. 28 above], 70) thinks that such versions were forbidden only in synagogue services. But R. Gamaliel's reaction undoubtedly comes from some other reason. It

probably should rather be explained as part of the general early prohibition of "writing down" what was normally transmitted by oral tradition; see H. L. Strack, *Introduction to the Talmud and Midrash* (New York: Meridian, 1959) 12-13; B. J. Roberts, *The Old Testament Texts and Versions* (p. 137 above, n. 38), 197–98. R. Gamaliel thus probably treated the Aramaic version of Job as comparable to written *haggadah* or *halakah*, i.e., under interdict. The Mishnah (*Yadaim* 4:5) states that "if [Scripture that is in] Hebrew was written in an [Aramaic] translation ᶜ*bryt šktbw trgwm),* or in Hebrew script [i.e., what we often call "paleo-Hebrew" script), it does not render the hands unclean" [i.e., it was not considered *kitbê haqqōdeš*]. See H. Danby, *The Mishnah* (London: Oxford, 1933) 784; G. Lisowsky, *Jadajim* (Die Mischna 6/11; Berlin: Töpelmann, 1956) 71-73. Thus 11QtgJob, 4QtgJob, and even 4QpaleoJob[c] would not have been *kitbê haqqōdeš.*

[50] *Le targum de Job*, 8. See further J. van der Ploeg, "Première communication" (n. 3 above), 552, 556; F. M. Cross, *The Ancient Library of Qumran (1961* [see n. 47 above]*) 34.*

[51] *Hermeneutische Aspecten* (n. 4 above) 109; see also pp. 69–70. Cf. A. Dupont-Sommer, *The Essene Writings from Qumran* (p. 156 above, n. 17), 306.

[52] Leipzig: Teubner, 1973 (reprinted; Osnabrück: Zeller, 1967) 85-118. E. Dhorme (*A Commentary on the Book of Job* [London: Nelson, 1967] ccxviii) says that Targum II was written by the same author as that of the Psalms and before the year A.D. 476. He refers to E. Nestle, "Jüdisch-aramäische Übersetzungen (Targumim)," *Realencyclopädie für protestantische Theologie und Kirche* (3d ed.; Leipzig: Hinrichs, 1897), 3. 103-10. Nestle in turn depends on W. Bacher, "Das Targum zu Hiob," *MGWJ* 20 (1871) 208-23, 283-84. Cf. E. Mangenot, "Targums," *Dictionnaire de la Bible* (Paris: Letouzey et Ané) 5 (1912) 2005-6; A. Weiss, *De libri Jobi paraphrasi chaldaica* (Breslau: H. Lindner, 1873).

[53] P. Grelot (*RQ* 8 [1972-76] 105) would date it to the 4th-5th century, but gives no reason for pushing it back to the fourth century. See W. Bacher, "Das Targum zu Hiob," 216-17. He finds an allusion to the division of the Roman Empire into East and West in the version of 4:10.

[54] *Le targum de Job,* 6.

[55] Cf. A. D. York, "The Dating of Targumic Literature," *JSJ* 5 (1974) 49-62.

[56] I have disregarded in the count the presence or absence of a *waw* as the prefixed conjunction; this varies in the two targums. Similarly, the fluctuation between final *aleph* and *he* on words such as *mā*ʾ or *māh*, a phenomenon that is frequently attested in Middle Aramaic as well as in Late Aramaic. Again, I have not counted separately the prefixed prepositions; in one or other instance, this might make a slight difference, but overall it is so minor as to be negligible. (The only instance that one might query in this regard would be the use of *m-* for *min*; but again, both are attested in the Qumran targum.)

[57] The "same" means here the sum of the figures in cols. 3 and 4 ("Identical" plus "Same").

[58] The Qumran targumist must have taken *yěšûrennû* as a form of *šwb*, confusing the *reš* with a *beth.* On the other hand, the sense of the Aramaic in Targum II is not clear. M. Jastrow (*A Dictionary*, 996) gives as the meaning of *slp*, "twist, pervert," and notes that *wyslp* in Targum II should be read here as *wyslq*, from *sěleq*. The meaning of the verb in the second half of the line is not clear either; it seems to be a deliberate pun, playing on *škynt*ʾ, as G. S. Glanzman has called to my attention.

[59] See pp. 94–95 above.

[60] Lit., "lifted up the countenance of Job."

[61] Targum II seems to have understood *šbyt* of the MT as *šěbît*, whereas *šěbût* is more probably to be understood.

[62] See, e.g., R. E. Brown, *The Gospel according to John (i–xii)* (p. 111 above, n. 48), 33, 523–24. See p. 95 above.

[63] The MT of Ezra 4:23 also has ʾ*edrā*ᶜ, and the question arises when and how that form got into the text. Similarly, in Hebrew (Jer 32:21), ʾ*ezrōa*ᶜ. Even if it were to prove to be from the time of Ezra, the emphasis should rather be put on the frequency with which such forms turn up in Targum II. Obviously, the usage had to begin somewhere, and early isolated examples do not weigh against the otherwise abundant attestation of forms without the prosthetic *aleph.*

[64]The same would have to be said about *byš* as was said about the prosthetic *aleph* in the preceding note. The form without the *aleph* is found in 1Q*20* 1 ii 8; and in the Keseček Köyü inscription from Cilicia (*KAI* §258:3). Here, however, the argument is built on the number of such cases over against isolated early instances.

[65]For references, see E. Vogt, *Lexicon linguae aramaicae Veteris Testamenti* (p. 23 above, n. 41) 61-62.

[66]See R. Le Déaut, quoted in n. 28 above.

[67]See C.-F. Jean and J. Hoftijzer, *Dictionnaire des inscriptions sémitiques de l'ouest* (Leiden: Brill, 1965) 90; J. Cantineau, *Grammaire du Palmyrénien épigraphique* (Publications de l'institut d'études orientales de la faculté des lettres d'Alger, 4; Cairo: Institut français d'archéologie orientale, 1935) 91.

[68]See M. L. Margolis, *A Manual of the Aramaic Language of the Babylonian Talmud* (Clavis linguarum semiticarum, 3; Munich: Beck, 1910) 114*; G. J. Cowling, *Concordance to the Geniza Fragments of the Palestinian Targum* (based on P. Kahle, Masoreten des Westens II, Texts A-F) (London: privately mimeographed, 1969) 23; R. Le Déaut and J. Robert, *Targum des Chroniques* (AnBibl 51; Rome: Biblical Institute, 1971), 2. 180.

[69]See "Le targum palestinien," *Exégèse biblique et judaïsme* (p. 84 above, n. 114) 31. This article is a masterpiece of twisting evidence to fit a preconceived thesis. I shall cite only one instance: the early and later writing of the 3d masc. sg. suffix on a plural noun or a preposition. In Official Aramaic it regularly appears as *-why*. Following the lead of Biblical Aramaic vocalization, most scholars would vocalize it *-ôhī* (for an explanation of the form, see p. 82 above, n. 95). It is well known that in the Aramaic of the Late Period this ending becomes *-wy* in most cases; this is abundantly attested in the classic targumim. The vocalization is undoubtedly *-ôï* (with the loss of the intervocalic *he*). Díez Macho groups all this together and says that "le suffixe pronominal *why/wy-why* est régulier dans l'araméen d'Empire, à Qumrân (4 Qtg Lev, *Apocryphe*, etc.), dans l'Onqelos, dans le Talmud de Babylone, syriaque." Now just where in Imperial Aramaic does one find *-wy* (unless one agrees with Díez Macho that this sort of Aramaic is found beyond 200 B.C.)? The ending *-wy* for this suffix does not occur in Qumran Aramaic texts. Díez Macho cites an example from 1QapGen 21:34, but that is אחוי, which he does read correctly, but vocalizes wrongly (at least by implication). For that is a 3d sg. masc. suffix on a *singular* noun—on a noun, indeed, which has (like a few others) a special formation. "His brother" is in Official Aramaic *ʾăḥūhī* (a dissimilation of **ʾaḥū-hū*); the full writing of the form is found in 1QapGen 22:3, 5, 11 (אחוהי). The form אחוי has, then, nothing to do with the suffix *-why* (= *-ôhī*) for all its consonantal similarity. It does, indeed, represent a similar loss of intervocalic *he*; and this isolated instance is to be expected, because the pronunciation reflected in the later targums, the Talmud, and Syriac had to begin somewhere. The argument, however, is from the abundance of these forms later on. And it still has to be shown that the intervocalic *he*, which is written in the majority of instances in the Aramaic of the Middle Phase, represents historical spelling and nothing more. To take refuge in "contamination" from "spoken Aramaic" is a *petitio principii* at this period.

[70]I do not deny that sporadically one finds *ʾyt* even in Official Aramaic texts (*AP* 46:3[?]; 54:4; 67:7[?]; *BMAP* 7:31 [with lacuna immediately following]; B-M 15). But again it is the frequent incidence of the form *ʾyt* in the targums and the absence of it in the Qumran material. How early is the first attestation of the contracted negative?

[71]This isolated instance is paralleled by a number of instances in 1QapGen (see my commentary [2d ed.], 217). Even A. Díez Macho ("Le targum palestinien," 28) admits the difference of incidence, when he cites 36 examples of the construct chain in *Měgillat Taʿănīt* over against 2 of *d* + the noun there.

[72]On the expression *ʿal dibrat dī*, see F. Rosenthal, *Die aramaistische Forschung* (p. 75 above, n. 2), 51; H. Bauer and P. Leander, *Grammatik des Biblisch-Aramäischen* (Halle / S.: Niemeyer, 1927) §69*z*. I am indebted to G. S. Glanzman for calling this seventh item to my attention.

[73]For the time being, see the list of the items to be considered that A. Díez Macho has drawn up ("Le targum palestinien," 27-31).

[73a]See now my article, "The Targum of Leviticus from Qumran Cave 4," *Maarav* 1 (1978) 5–23.

[74]W. Bacher ("Das Targum zu Hiob" [n. 52 above], 218-19) mentions 46 verses which have "another Targum," a second version of the same Hebrew verse, and in at least four instances a third version (24:19; 28:17; 36:33; 38:25; in the Breslau Codex also 12:5; 13:4). It is usually introduced by תא (= *targūm ʾāḥēr*).

[75]Being published by the Peshiṭta Institute of the University of Leiden (Leiden: Brill). Cf. L. J. Rignell, "Notes on the Peshitta of the Book of Job," *ASTI* 9 (1973) 98-106.

[76]See n. 23 above.

[77]*Le targum de Job*, p. 7.

[78]See M. Baillet, J. T. Milik, and R. de Vaux, *Les 'petites grottes' de Qumrân: Exploration de la falaise, Les grottes 2Q, 3Q, 5Q, 6Q, 7Q à 10Q, Le rouleau de cuivre* (DJD 3; Oxford: Clarendon, 1962) 71.

[79]Ibid.

[80]See C. Burchard, *Bibliographie II* (n. 10 above), 327; cf. "Le travail d'édition des fragments manuscrits de Qumrân," *RB* 63 (1956) 49-67, esp. p. 57; P. Benoit et al., "Editing the Manuscripts Fragments from Qumran," *BA* 19 (1956) 75-96, esp. p. 85 (where Cross then spoke of only "one MS of Job").

[81]See C. Burchard, *Bibliographie II*, 327; "Le travail d'édition," 58; P. Benoit et al., "Editing," 86.

[82]For one important item in 11QtgJob that does affect NT study (the absolute use of מרא as a title for Yahweh and its bearing on the background of the Greek title *κύριος* for Jesus), see pp. 88–90, 124 above.

Chapter 8

Aramaic Epistolography*

Though other areas of Aramaic studies have had a more or less adequate treatment, that of Aramaic epistolograhy has not yet been so blessed. The number of letters and messages preserved in ancient Aramaic is not negligible, but it cannot compare with that in other ancient languages such as Sumerian, Akkadian, Greek, or Latin. Hebrew epistolography is not much better off than Aramaic, and a survey of it might be as useful as this one. In any case, but little interest in this form of Aramaic composition has hitherto been manifested.[1] Even in the present survey the starting-point has been Greek or Hellenistic epistolography, or more specifically NT epistolography; and thus the incentive to look at Aramaic letter-writing has come from an extrinsic concern.[2]

In a sense this inquiry forms but another aspect of the generic problem of the Aramaic background of NT writings, or more properly of Aramaic interference in NT Greek. This may indeed stimulate the comparative study of the two bodies of correspondence; but Aramaic epistolography deserves a full study in and of itself.[3] On the other hand, it should be obvious at the outset that the contribution of Aramaic epistolography to the study of the NT letters cannot be as significant as the Aramaic background of other areas of NT study (e.g., the Aramaic substratum of the sayings of Jesus, or the possible Aramaic sources of various NT writings).[4] For most of the NT letters or epistles come from areas outside of Palestine or Syria, where Aramaic was not spoken. True, we are faced with the anomaly that Paul has preserved for us two clearly Aramaic words, אבא (Gal 4:6) and מראנא תא (1 Cor 16:22), and commentators have discussed at times other possible Aramaisms in his writings or Aramaic sources that he may have used.[5] But the Greek of his letters does not reveal Aramaic interference, or even Semitic interference in general, to the same extent as that of the Gospels and Acts. Furthermore, J. N. Sevenster has raised a question about the Palestinian origin of James and 1 Peter in a new way,[6] and in the light of it one could further ask about the influence of Aramaic epistolography on such letters. It might also be the proper question to ask if one were to consider seriously the proposal that the Captivity Letters in the Pauline corpus were composed in Caesarea Maritima.[7] While there may be initial doubts, therefore, about the validity of the inquiry into the Aramaic background of such NT writings as the epistles, still the inquiry may have a legitimacy, at least in a limited way. But even aside from such considerations there is still the likelihood that the study of the corpus of Aramaic letters and messages would cast some light on the NT epistles, at least from the comparative standpoint, since they represent a form of ancient epistolography from the eastern Mediterranean area.

Obviously a study of Aramaic letter-writing bears also, and more immediately, on certain OT passages, because some examples of ancient Aramaic epistolography have been preserved in the OT itself. Passages in Ezra have often been treated in the light of Aramaic letters discovered only toward the beginning of this century. Save for these biblical examples, an isolated fragment (such as *AP* 77), and letters preserved in rabbinic writings (e.g., of the Gaonic period), the rest of ancient Aramaic letters known today have come to light only since about 1902. About a dozen or so of them have been discovered only in the last quarter of a century.

The earliest phase of the Aramaic language, so-called Old Aramaic, dating roughly from 925 to 700 B.C., is represented entirely by inscriptions; no letters come to us from this period of the language. In the subsequent phase, so-called Official or Imperial Aramaic, dating roughly from 700 to 200 B.C., one finds a considerable number of letters and messages which begin a long list of texts that continues down into the phases of Middle Aramaic, roughly 200 B.C. to A.D. 200, and Late Aramaic, roughly A.D. 200 to 700.[8]

Epistolary correspondence in Aramaic has turned up in texts written on skin, papyrus, and potsherds or ostraca; some of it is also preserved in the Bible and in rabbinic literature. The correspondence which was written on skin or papyrus is, by and large, better known; but the number of messages written on ostraca is not small, and they have their own contributions to make to the study of Aramaic epistolography because of the mundane, everyday character of the messages transmitted in them. Since they were written on ostraca, they are usually brief,[9] and the message is more like a note, often cryptic and difficult to decipher or interpret. Consequently, I shall concentrate for the most part on the letters proper and bring in evidence from the ostraca when it is pertinent for comparison or contrast. My purpose here is to survey in a general way the corpus of Aramaic letters, highlighting those elements that may be of interest to the study of the NT and OT letters; the study of specific details will have to be left to others.[10]

I. *The Types, Provenience, and Contents of Aramaic Letters*

Among the many texts that have been preserved in the corpus of Aramaic epistolography, there is none that could really be called an "epistle" in the sense in which A. Deissmann once defined it: ". . . an artistic literary form, a species of literature, just like the dialogue, the oration, or the drama. It has nothing in common with the letter except its form; apart from that one might venture the paradox that the epistle is the opposite of a real letter. The contents of an epistle are intended for publicity—they aim at interesting 'the public.'"[11] By contrast, Deissmann described a "letter" as "a means of communication between persons who are separated from each other."[12] While there are all sorts of difficulties which modern students of epistolography have with Deissmann's definitions—and especially with the application of them to NT writings[13]—his definitions are being used here merely to indicate that the Aramaic corpus is made up solely of "letters" in Deissmann's broad category. Even though they may deal with official or business matters and be reports sent to or by persons in authority, they can only be described as "letters," for they deal with concrete, *ad hoc* problems, request aid, propose solutions, seek advice, express concern, and so on; and they were hardly intended for publication. The sole departures—and this is problematic—are found in Dan 3:31-33, depending on how one relates that quasi-epistolary introduction to the rest of the story in chap. 4,[14] and Dan 6:25-27, which is a decree in epistolary form. It is, of course, significant that the only possible exceptions are in biblical writings. Aside from these instances there are in the limited Aramaic corpus no examples of epistles or literary letters (either of the philosophical, hortatory, or imaginative types); nor do we know of any spurious or pseudepigraphical letters. Those that have survived are all either private letters or official letters, treating matters either of concern, news, or business.

For the most part the Aramaic letters come from Egypt. The main source of them has been the excavations on the island of Yeb or Elephantine in the Nile opposite the town of Aswan; but a number of them has also come from elsewhere in Egypt, especially from Lower Egypt (Memphis, Saqqarah, and Hermopolis West). The letters preserved in the Book of Ezra, which now have striking parallels in extrabiblical examples, have always been known as instances of Aramaic correspondence between Palestine and the Persian king.[15] A small batch of letters, often referred to as the Arsames correspondence, was found in Egypt but came originally from either Mesopotamia or Persia.[16] A further small group of letters, from either Šimᶜon bar Kosibah or his colleagues, reveals the use of Aramaic for correspondence within Palestine of the early second century A.D.[17] This diverse geographical provenience of the letters merely reflects the status of the language itself, which for a considerable period served as a *lingua franca* in the ancient Near East.

Among the Aramaic letters found in Egypt, some have brought to light interesting international affairs. For instance, one was a papyrus letter, unfortunately not completely preserved, found at Saqqarah in Lower Egypt, that has been dated ca. 604 B.C.[18] Written by ᵓAdon, the ruler of a Philistine(?) town in Palestine(?), and addressed "to the Lord of Kings, the Pharaoh," it informs the Egyptian ruler of the advance of the troops of the Babylonian king and asks for military support against them. Though the date of the letter is not certain, it seems to be related to the advance of Nebuchadrezzar ca. 600 B.C. It is clear testimony to the use of Aramaic for official correspondence on an international level between rulers.

Another example of international correspondence in Aramaic is the letter of the leaders of the Jewish community at Elephantine, Yedaniah and his associates, priests in the fortress Yeb (*AP* 30).[19] It was addressed to Bagohi, the governor of Judah in 408 B.C. (dated precisely: 20 Marḥešwan, 17th year of Darius [II]). It complains about the problems that have faced the Jewish community in Yeb since the departure of Arsames on a visit to the Persian king. Egyptian priests of the god Khnub have plotted with Widarang, the Persian satrap, to bring about the destruction of the sanctuary of Yahu which has been in Yeb and which had been built by the Jews "in the days of the Kings of Egypt," well before "Cambyses entered Egypt." The letter tells how the Jews have sat in sackcloth, prayed, and fasted that Widarang might be requited—which eventually happened. The Jewish leaders recall that they have written previously to Bagohi to enlist his aid, and also to Yoḥanan, the high priest, and his colleagues, the priests in Jerusalem. Now they seek from Bagohi the permission to rebuild the sanctuary in Yeb, in which they promise to offer sacrifice and to pray to Yahu on his behalf. They mention that they have also written about this matter to Delaiah and Shelemiah, sons of Sanballat, the governor of Samaria (probably Sanballat I, known from Neh 2:10, 19; 3:33; 4:1; 6:1, 2, 5, 12, 14; 13:28, grandfather of the Sanballat of the Samaria papyri found in the cave of the Wadi ed-Daliyeh[20]). This is obviously a first-class example of an official letter concerning a matter of moment and importance to the Jews of Elephantine. What is noteworthy about it is that the letter was found at Elephantine itself; it probably represents a copy of the letter that was sent to Bagohi and, what is more, a duplicate of it (*AP* 31) was also found with a version of the letter that is slightly different. Was it an alternate version prepared by a scribe and eventually rejected in favor of the other? Was it a preliminary draft that was emended? Which version was actually sent? Or were both versions slightly different from the letter that Bagohi actually received? We have no way of answering such questions. In any case, it is certain that at least a similar letter was sent, since there is a reply, or better a "memorandum" (זכרן), sent about the matter (*AP* 32), and still further correspondence on the subject (*AP* 27, 33).[21] This gives a brief idea of the most important letters from Elephantine. There are many others that deal with other subjects: the celebration of the Passover (*AP* 21),[22] an appeal to a higher court (*AP* 16), an order to repair a government boat (*AP* 26), etc.

From Egypt, but outside of Elephantine, comes another group of papyri known today as the letters from Hermopolis West.[23] In seven of the eight letters the place of origin seems to have been Memphis, for the addressees are blessed by the sender(s) in the name of the god Ptaḥ, who had a temple in Memphis. They deal with family matters, handle business transactions, or simply express concern for persons who are absent. The place of destination in four of the letters is סון, Syene (modern Aswan), and in three of them אפי,

Luxor. One of the editors of these letters, E. Bresciani, insists on the pagan character of them because of the destination and of the gods whose temples are mentioned in them. Yahu does not appear; the proper names are sometimes Semitic, sometimes Egyptian, sometimes as yet unanalyzed.[24] If their destination was Syene and Luxor, the puzzle is why they were found, folded up, sealed, and for the most part preserved intact in a jar stored in an underground gallery of an Ibieion, dedicated to Thot, at Hermopolis West in the Delta region.

The letters of Bar Cochba from the Cave of Letters in the Wadi Ḫabra (Naḥal Ḥever) are for the most part as yet unpublished. What is presently available is often fragmentary; but the letters reveal the diverse matters of concern to Simon bar Kosibah and his officers at the time of the Second Revolt against Rome (A.D. 132-35). Perhaps the most striking one expresses his concern to have the "palm-branches and citrons," the "myrtle and willow twigs" delivered for the feast of Succoth or Tabernacles.[25] The topic of the letter is of interest because it is the subject not only of an Aramaic letter, but also of a Greek one written about the same time by one who calls himself *Σουμαῖος*. He writes about the same individuals, Yehonathan bar Ba^cyan and Masabbalah (יהונתן בר בעין, מסבלה), to whom the Greek letter is addressed: *Ἰωναθῆι Βαιανοῦ καὶ Μα[σ]άβαλα* (in the dative case).[26] In the Greek letter, instructions are given for the furnishing of *σ[τε]λεοὺς καὶ κίτρια . . . ἰς [κ]ιτρειαβολὴν Ἰουδαίων*, "beams and citrons for the Citron-celebration of the Jews." These two letters come from the same general Palestinian situation, and aside from attesting to the use of the two languages to send messages about rather ordinary affairs and needs, they reveal that Aramaic was not simply a literary language of the period.

Finally, from what has been said it should be obvious that some of the Aramaic correspondence comes from other than Jewish writers. Here one touches on the problem of the identification of the "Jews" and the "Arameans" in the Elephantine texts, a problem that is larger than that of the letters alone.[27] But it is also related to the international character of the language to which we have already alluded.

II. *Some Features of Aramaic Epistolography*

What follows is an attempt to organize briefly under various headings some of the obvious formal elements in Aramaic letters. As I have already indicated, most of the data is drawn from the letters proper, those preserved on skin or papyrus; occasionally formal elements from the ostraca are also used. In a sense, some of these elements may prove to be distinctive of Aramaic epistolography, but a judgment about their distinctive character would imply a comparative study which has not yet been undertaken. Attention is rather being centered here on the features themselves in a descriptive way, without any attempt to compare them or to explain their origin or what might have influenced them. No attempt is being made to analyze all of the features, e.g., the stock phrases that one often finds in letters in other languages expressing rebuke, surprise, etc. My remarks will fall rather under eight headings: (a) the names for the Aramaic letters; (b) the *praescriptio*; (c) the initial greeting; (d) the secondary greetings; (e) the concluding formulae; (f) the mention of a scribe or secretary; (g) the date; and (h) the final or exterior address. Such features, which are found in many of the letters, are easily detected; but it will still remain a question of how many of them actually structure the Aramaic letter. The answer to that question must await a further discussion.

(a) *The Names for the Aramaic Letter*. At least three different terms are found in this type of writing for the "letter": אגרה (אגרתא), ספר (ספרא), and נשתון (נשתונא). The most common term is אגרה, a borrowed Akkadian word, *egertu*, which is also found in biblical Aramaic (Ezra 4:8, 11; 5:6). It is often used with the verb שלח, "send." Thus, e.g.. אגרה חדה בשלמך לא שלחת עלי, "you did not send me a letter about your well-being" (*AP* 41:5). Similarly: *AP* 30:7, 18, 19, 24, 29; 31:6, 17, 18, 28; 38:10; 40:3; *AD* 10:2. Indeed, the frequency of this idiom eventually seems to have given the verb שלח the nuance of "sending a message" (*AD* 12:1; 4:1; 7:5; *Herm WP* 3:6; 5:7; *AP* 16:8; 38:9; etc.), whereas a verb whose meaning was long misunderstood, הושר, became the more normal term for sending other objects (see *BMAP* 13:4; *AD* 13:2, 3), though it too was occasionally used with a message as its object. Other verbs, of course, were used too with אגרה; thus, יהבת, "was delivered" (*AD* 12:1); תמטא, "will arrive" (*AP* 42:6); כתבו, "they wrote" (Ezra 4:8). In one instance, the document itself is explicitly labelled as אגרת שמעון בר כוסבה, "a letter of Simon bar Kosibah" (*5/6Ḥev* 4:1).

The second term is ספר and strictly means a "writing" (often a "book"); but in this type of literature it is used explicitly of the letter. Thus, לשלמכי שלחת ספרא זנה, "I am sending this letter to greet you" (literally, "for your peace [of mind?]"), *Herm WP* 1:12-13; 6:[10]; cf. 2:17; 3:13; 4:12-13; 5:9; 7:4; *Pad* II v 4-5. Cf. *Herm WP* 1:5; 5:4 (with הושר!).

The third term, נשתון, is derived from the Persian **ništavāna*, and probably still carries the nuance of a "written document, decree" (see *AP* 17:3), even in such biblical passages as Ezra 4:18, 23; 5:5.

One further term should be mentioned here, for it is the "label," as it were, given to a document: זכרן, "a memorandum" (*AP* 32:1: זכרן זי בגוהי ודליה), "a memorandum of Bagohi and Delaiah."[28] It is an interesting parallel to Ezra 6:2 (דכרונה).

(b) *The Praescriptio*. The term *praescriptio* is often taken to mean a phrase in a letter like Ἰάκωβος . . . ταῖς δώδεκα φυλαῖς ταῖς ἐν τῇ διασπορᾷ χαίρειν (Jas 1:1), expressing the name of the sender, that of the addressee, and the greeting. But I am limiting the sense of it to indicate solely the names of the sender and the addressee, because the greeting is sometimes absent in the extant Aramaic letters or else is formulated in various elaborate ways that call for a distinct discussion of the initial greeting. However, when the initial greeting is used, it is closely related to the *praescriptio* and this must be recognized, even though they are separated here for the convenience of discussion.

The *praescriptio*, when it is not simply implied,[29] is usually expressed in one of five ways: (i) "To X, your servant / brother / son, (greeting)"; (ii) "To X, from Y, (greeting)"; (iii) "From X, to Y, (greeting)"; (iv) "X to Y, (greeting)"; (v) "To X, (greeting)".

As examples of (i), the following may be singled out: [אל א]חי פרור . . . אחוך בלטר, "[To] my [br]other Pirawur, your brother Beletir . . ." (*AšOst* 1). Similarly (with some form of אח): *AP* 21:1-2; 40:1; 41:[1]; 42:1; Shunnar 1; *Cl-G Ost* 277:1-2; *Bodl Aram Inscr* 3 A 1; *Strasbourg Ost* 1-2; possibly *Pad* III. Or אל מרא מלכן פרעה עבדך אדן מלך [אשקלון], "To the Lord of Kings, the Pharaoh, your servant ᵓAdon, King of [Ashkelon] . . ." (*AdonL* 1).[30] Similarly (with some form of עבד): *AP* 17:1; 30:1; 31:1; 37:1; 38:1-2; 39:1; 70:1; *HermWP* 3:1; *BMAP* 13:1;[31] Ezra 4:11; *ClG Ost* 70 A -2. Or again, אל אמ[י] יה[ו]י[ש]מע ברך שלום בר פטמ[ון], "To [my] mother, Yah[u]yi[sh]maᶜ, your son, Shallum bar Peṭam[on]" (*Pad* II v 1).[32] Similarly (with a form of בר): *Cambr Ost* 131-133:1.

As examples of form (ii) the following may be cited: אל אחתי רעיה מן אחכי מכבנת, "To my sister Raᶜyah, from your brother Makkabanit" (*HermWP* 1:1). Similarly: *HermWP* 2:1; 3:5; 4:1-2; 5:1; 6:1; 7:1; *Pad* I v 1.

As examples of form (iii) we may cite: מן ארשם על וחפרעמחי, "From Arsames, to Waḥpriᶜmaḥi" (*AP* 26:1). In this case no greeting follows. Similarly (with a greeting): *AD* 1:1; 2:1; 3:1; 5:1; (without a greeting): *AD* 4:1; 8:1; 9:1; 10:1; 11:1; 12:1; Letter of R. Judah the Prince; *papMird* A 1-4.[33]

As examples of form (iv) we cite the following: ארתחשסתא מלך מלכיא לעזרא כהנא ספר דתא די אלה שמיא גמיר, "Artaxerxes, the King of Kings, to Ezra the priest, scribe of the religion of the God of Heaven, . . ." (Ezra 7:12).[34] Similarly: Dan 3:31; *5/6Ḥev* 1:1; *5/6Ḥev* 8:1-3; *5/6Ḥev* 10:1; *5/6Ḥev* 11:1; *5/6Ḥev* 14:1-2; *5/6Ḥev* 15:1.

As examples of form (v) the following may be mentioned: לאחנא בני דרומא, "To our brothers, inhabitants of the South, . . . (*Gamaliel*, 1). Similarly: *Bodl Libr Ost* 1 (with אל); *Cairo Ost* 35468a 1 (with על); *Gamaliel* 2 and 3 (both with ל).

Such are the various forms of the *praescriptio* in the Aramaic letters. The difference is at times characteristic of a certain group of letters; thus the form "From X to Y" is preferred in the texts of the so-called Arsames correspondence (letters found in Egypt but written in Mesopotamia or Persia). Yet that form also turns up elsewhere too; and it is not easy to say to what extent local variations or chancery practices are operative.

Three further remarks should be made about the *praescriptio* in an Aramaic letter. First of all, in some of the Hermopolis letters and in one of the Padua papyri there is a peculiar greeting which precedes the *praescriptio*, and it is not to be confused with the "initial greeting," which is also present. It is a greeting addressed to a temple *before* the mention of the sender and the addressee; it begins the letter. Thus, שלם בית נבו, "Greetings to the Temple of Nabu" (*Herm WP* 1:1), or שלם בית בנת בסון, "Greetings to the Temple of Banit in Syene" (*Herm WP* 2:1; 3:1), or ,שלם בית ביתאל ובית מלכת שמין "Greetings to the Temple of Bethel and the Temple of the Queen of Heaven" (*Herm WP* 4:1). The fragmentary text of *Herm WP* 8:1 may have had a similar formula. This greeting, however, is not solely addressed to the temples of pagan gods, for one instance salutes the "Temple of Yahu in Elephantine" (שלם ב[ית יהו ביב], *Pad* I v 1). These letters seem to begin with an invocation of the deity honored in the place where the addressee is found. The greeting is peculiar, and its implications have not yet been fully explored, as far as I know.[35] As far as epistolographic style is concerned, it is a salutation distinct from the initial greeting expressed to the addressee and indicative of the piety of the writer of the letter.

Secondly, one should note the preposition used for "to" in these *praescriptiones.* Though אל was used as an ordinary preposition in Old Aramaic to express motion toward or direction (Sefire I B [29]; II B 13?; III 1ter, [8], 8, 19, 20), it gradually disappeared in Aramaic and was supplanted by על. However, the preposition אל did persist as a stereotype in the *praescriptiones* of letters long after it was supplanted elsewhere. Thus, אל פרעה מרא מלכן, *AdonL* 1; cf. *Herm WP* 1:1; 2:1; 3:5; 4:1; 5:1; 6:1; 7:1; *AP* 17:[1]; 21:[1]; 30:1; 31:1; 37:1; 38:1; 39:1; 40:1; 41:1; 42:[1]; 70:1; Shunnar 1; *Pad* I v 1; *Pad* II v 1; *Pad* III; *Cl-G Ost* 277:1; *Cl-G Ost* 70:1; *BMAP* 13:[1].[36] But the preposition על began to invade the *praescriptio* as well, especially in the Arsames correspondence. Thus, על מראי פסמי, *Herm WP* 3:1; cf. *AP* 26:1; *AD* 1:[1]; 2:1; 3:1; 4:1; 5:1; 6:1; 7:1; 8:1; 9:1; 10:1; 11:1; 12:1; 13:1; Ezra 4:11, 17. Yet even this preposition in time gave way to the simple ל. Thus, לדריוש מלכא, "to Darius, the King" (Ezra 5:7b); cf. Ezra 7:12; Dan 3:31; *5/6Ḥev* 1:1; *5/6Ḥev* 4:1; *5/6Ḥev* 8:2-3; *5/6Ḥev* 10:1; *5/6Ḥev* 11:1; *5/6Ḥev* 14:1-2; *5/6Ḥev* 15:1; *Gamaliel* 1, 2, 3; *R. Judah the Prince; papMird* A 1-3.

Thirdly, note should be made of the titles used in the *praescriptio* to designate the addressee and the sender. The contrast of מרא and עבד causes no problem, since they designate a difference of social rank or persons of varying authority; "servant" and "lord" obviously do not imply slavery, but are used as polite customary expressions among persons of differing rank or status. Among persons of equal rank it seems that the term אח, "brother," was used. That it may sometimes designate a blood-brother is clear; but what is striking is the use of it as a title with a more generic connotation. Thus a father, Osea bar Peṭ[ ], writes to his son, Shelomam, who is away on a caravan, and twice refers to himself as "brother": "To my son, Shelomam; from your 'brother,' Osea." In the exterior address of the letter: "To my 'brother,' Shelomam bar Osea, your 'brother,' Osea bar Peṭ[ ]" (*Pad* I v 1; 1 r 7). In the course of the letter the father refers to אמך, "your mother" (I v 2; I r 5). Such a use of אח was at one time misunderstood, but it is now clear.[37] Moreover, it is confirmed by the related use of אחת, "sister," in what must be a similar polite form of address among men and women of equal standing. In *HermWP* 7:1 the addressee is given as אל אחתי תבי, "to my sister, TBY," but in the exterior address one reads: [ ]אל אמי, "To my mother [ ]." Similarly in *HermWP* 7:1 the letter is addressed: אל אמי עתררמרי, "To my mother, ᶜAttar-RMRY," but the exterior address rather has אל אחתי עתררי, "To my sister, ᶜAttar-RY" (with a different [erroneous?] spelling of the name, *HermWP* 7:5). And to complicate the usage, *HermWP* 3:1, which is addressed, "My lord PSMY, your servant Makkabanit," has the exterior address, "To my father PSMY, from Makkabanit bar PSMY" (*HermWP* 3:14). If further examples of such letters were to be discovered, it is possible that this usage would be further clarified.

On the ostraca one finds, undoubtedly because of the brevity of the messages, an opening that mixes greeting and *praescriptio* (שלם אוריה); we shall comment on this below.

(c) *The Initial Greeting.* Though the initial greeting of an addressee was sometimes omitted in Aramaic letters, especially in those which had an official or quasi-official character (e.g., *AD* 4:2; 7:1; 8:1; 9:1; 10:1; 11:1 [the so-called Arsames correspondence]; *AP* 26:1; Ezra 4:11-12), in the vast majority of instances some expression involving שלם, "peace, well-being," or the verb ברך, "bless," has been used. In a few cases שלם was used alone and probably had only the stereotyped meaning of "greetings," functioning like the Greek *χαίρειν*. Thus, על רחום בעל טעם ושמשי ספרא . . . שלם, "To Rehum, the governor, Shimshai, the scribe, . . . greetings" (Ezra 4:17); see further *AšOst* 1(?); *5/6Ḥev* 1 (spelled סלם!); *5/6Ḥev* 4:1; *5/6Ḥev* 10:2. In Ezra 5:7b one finds שלמא כלא.[38] To this brief, formulaic usage one should probably relate the short greeting, mentioned above, that is often found on ostraca: שלם אוריה, "Greetings, Uriah" (*APE* 76/1:1); see further *AP* 77:1(?); *APE* 78/2:1; *Bodl Aram Inscr* 2:1; *Cl-G Ost* 69 A 1; *Munich* 898 A 1; *Cl-G Ost* 44 A 1; *Cl-G* 70 A 1. Likewise the short formula such as שלם אחי בכל עדן, "Peace (*or* greetings), my brother, at all times" (*Strasbourg Ost* 3).

Such brief formulae, including the name of a person, are undoubtedly stereotyped abridgements of longer greetings. But it is not easy to say from which of the several longer formulae, to be cited below, they would have been abbreviated. In the use of longer formulae one can detect a pattern with variants; I shall list about nine different forms, but one should remember that it may be questionable to regard them as distinct varieties. They fall into two main classes, those using a שלם formula, and those using a ברך formula.

(i) The most commonly attested greeting makes use of this formula: שלם מראי אלהיא כלא [ישאלו] שגיא בכל עדן, "May all the gods be much [concerned] for the well-being of my lord at all times" (*BMAP* 13:1; *AP* 41:1;

Shunnar 1).[39] Sometimes the adjective "all" may be omitted (e.g., *AP* 56:1), and sometimes the deity may be specifically named ("the God of Heaven," *AP* 30:2; 31:2; 38:[1]; 40:[1]; "Yahu Ṣebaoth," *Cl-G Ost* 167:1-2; *Cl-G Ost* 186 A 1; "Bel and Nabu, Shamash and Nergal," *Cl-G Ost* 277:1-2). The mention of the gods seems to characterize this formula as a religious wish; in one form or another it can be found in *AP* 17:1-2; 21:2; 37:1-2; 39:1; 40:1; 41:1; 56:1; *BMAP* 13:1; Shunnar 1.

(ii) An extended form of the preceding formula is found in a few instances: שלם מראן אלה שמיא ישאל שגיא בכל עדן ולרחמן ישימנך קדם דריוהוש מלכא ובני ביתא יתיר מן חד אלף וחין אריכין ינתן לך וחדה ושריר הוי בכל עדן, "May the God of Heaven be much concerned for the well-being of our lord (Bagohi) at all times, and may he show you favor[40] before Darius the King and the princes of the palace a thousand times more than now, and may he grant you a long life, and may you be[41] happy and prosperous at all times" (*AP* 30:1-3). Compare *AP* 31:1-3; *AP* 38:2-3 (expansion: "And may you have favor before the God of Heaven").

(iii) A less pious form of greeting is found in the following formula: שלם וחין שלחת לך, "Peace and life I send you" (*Herm WP* 3:5; 7:1; *Bodl Aram Inscr* 3 A 1-2; *Cambr Ost* 131-133 A 1-2). In one instance this formula is expanded with a ברך formula: שלם וחין שלחת לך ברכתך ליהה ולחנ׳, "Peace and life I send you; I bless you by Yahu and by Khnub" (*Cl-G Ost* 70 A 2-3). Not only is this formula a mixture of the secular and the religious, but it is syncretistic to boot.

(iv) Another form of a secular greeting is found in the following שלם ושררת [שגיא הושרת לך], "[I send you] greetings and prosperity[42] [in abundance]" (*Pad* I v 1). See further *AD* 2:1; 3:1; 5:1; 13:1. In one instance this is expanded by the addition of [אף] שלם תמה קדמיך [יהוי], "[moreover may there be] peace there in your presence" (*AD* 1:1). The fragmentary nature of *AP* 70:1-2 makes it difficult to determine whether the greeting used there belongs in this category or not; possibly it does.

(v) The last form of a שלם greeting is found in biblical and rabbinical texts (in the latter probably in imitation of the biblical formula): שלמכון ישגא, "and may your well-being be increased" (Dan 3:31; 6:26; *Gamaliel* 1; *Gamaliel* 2; *Gamaliel* 3).[43]

In all of these שלם formulae one may wonder whether the word means simply "greetings" or whether it is at times pregnant with further nuances, such as I have tried to bring out in some of the above translations. It is not easy for the twentieth-century reader of these texts to discern accurately the nuance intended in what seem to be stereotyped formulae.

There are two forms of the ברך formula. In the first the verb is used in a finite form: ברכתכי לפתח זי יחזני אפיכי בשלם, "I bless you by Ptaḥ, who may grant me to see your face[44] (again) in peace" (*Herm WP* 2:2). Similarly: *Herm WP* 3:1-2; 4:2; 5:1-2; 6:1-2; 8:1-2. The other form is only found once, in a sort of secondary greeting; but it is related to the first, even though the verb-form is participial: ברך אנת [ליהו אלהא]/[זי יח]וני אנפיך בשלם, "(May) you (be) blessed [by Yahu, the God, who may sh]ow me your face (again) in peace" (*Pad* I v 2-3).[45]

Such are the main features of the initial greetings in the extant Aramaic letters. One last comment should be made about them. The initial greeting is often followed by כענת, וכעת, כעת, וכען, כען, "and now," a word that either introduces the body of the message or is repeated in the course of it as a sort of message divider; it marks logical breaks in the letter and has often been compared to English "stop" in telegrams. The word was often misunderstood in the past, being taken to mean "et cetera,"[46] and was wrongly linked to the preceding greeting (see Ezra 4:10, 11b, 17; 7:12 [following גמיר!]). But now its usage is clear from extrabiblical evidence (see *AP* 30:4; *AD* 4:1; 5:1; 7:1, 3, 5; *Herm WP* 1:6-11).

(d) *The Secondary Greetings.* In some letters after the initial greeting that is closely linked to the *praescriptio* there follows a series of secondary greetings, either of the type, "Say hello to . . . ," or "X sends greetings." In these formulae שלם is again used, but it is found in a cryptic expression which is not always clear; the Aramaic construct chain, which literally means "the peace of X," is used to convey the sense of both "greetings to" and "greetings from." I shall try to sort them out, but opinions may differ about them. Sometimes other words in the phrase or the immediate context help to determine the sense of the construct chain. Thus, שלם בנתסרל וארג ואסרשת ושרדר הרוץ שאל שלמהן וכעת שלם {ל}לחרוץ תנה "Greetings to Banit-SRL and ᵓRG and ᵓSRŠT and Śardur; Ḥorwaṣ asks about their well-being. Now Ḥorwaṣ is well here. . . ." Or, שלם אמי ממה שלם אחי בתי ואנשתה ובנוהי שלם רעיה "Greetings to my mother MMH, greetings to my brother BTY and his wife and children, greetings to Raᶜyah" (*Herm WP* 3:2-3). Similarly: *Herm WP* 4:3, 10-12, 13-14; 7:2, 3-4; *AP* 39:1-3; 40:1; 57:1(?). Two other cases are relatively clear: [אנה ומכ]בנת שאלן שלמכי ושלם תרו[ ], "[I and Makka]banit inquire about your well-being and the well-being of TRW[ ]" (*Herm WP* 6:7-8). וכעת בזנה קדמי שלם אף תמה קדמ[י]ך שלם יהוי, "Now all goes well with me here;[47] and (hopefully) it goes well with you too there" (*AD* 5:1-2).

The problematic greeting is the following: [ ] לך שלם גלגל תנם שלם ינקיה, which I once translated as "To you greetings from Galgul TNM, greetings from the children![ ]."[48] The letters *TNM* should be read as תנה; compare שלם נבושה תנה, "Nabusheh is well here" (*Herm WP* 2:2-3).[49] But then what is to become of לך at the beginning of the line? Moreover, the following phrase also becomes problematic, because שלם must be singular and the following word is plural. Could it mean rather "to you (comes) the greeting of Galgul here, (and) the greeting of the children"? In this case Galgul would be with the writer and would be sending his greetings; hence "greetings from . . ." would be the force of שלם. See further *Pad* I r 5 (שלם אמך וינקיא, "greetings from your mother and the children").

These secondary greetings do not always follow on the heels of the initial greeting; in one instance or other they are found further along in the body of the letter (see *HermWP* 4:10-12, 13-14). In one case the greeting is expressed toward the end of the letter, and one hesitates to include it here because it may rather be part of a concluding formula. There is so far only one example of it and no way of being sure that it is actually formulaic. Hence I include it here: שלם ביתך ובניך עד אלהיא יחוונ[א בהן], "Peace be to your house and your children till the gods let *us* see (our desire) *upon them*" (Cowley's translation, *AP* 34:7).[50]

(e) *The Concluding Formulae.* Only two phrases have appeared so far in a formulaic way that permits them to be described as conclusions to a message. Both of them again make use of שלם, but in different ways. The more common is of this sort: לשלמכי שלחת ספרא זנה, "I have sent this letter for your peace (of mind)" (*HermWP* 1:12-13; 6:[10]). Similarly *HermWP* 2:17; 3:13; 4:12-13; 5:9; 7:4; *Pad* II v 4-5; *Cl-G Ost* 70 B 2. The other formula is shorter and somewhat harder to explain: הוא שלם, "Be (at) peace!" (*5/6Ḥev* 4:5; *5/6Ḥev* 15:5) or in the plural, הוו שלם, "Be (at) peace!" (*5/6Ḥev* 11:3).[51]

(f) *The Mention of a Scribe or Secretary.* Toward the end of a letter one finds at times the mention of a secretary who seems to have drafted the letter and of a scribe who copied it or took the dictation for it. This is found in more or less official letters, usually in the so-called Arsames correspondence. Thus, ענני ספרא בעל [טע]ם נבועקב כתב, "'Anani, the secretary, drafted the order; Nabuᶜaḳab wrote (it)" (*AP* 26:23, Cowley's translation).[52] And on the exterior, just before the date one reads: נבועקב ספרא, "Nabuᶜaqab (was) the scribe."[53] Again, another official is sometimes introduced: בגסרו ידע טעמא זנה אחפפי ספרא, "Bagasraw is cognizant of this order; ᶜAḥpipi (was) the scribe" (*AD* 4:4). Similarly: *AD* 6:6; 7:10; 8:6; 9:3; 10:5. A slightly different formula is found in one of the letters of Simon bar Kosibah: שמעון בר יהודה כתבה, "Šimᶜon bar Yehudah wrote it" (*5/6Ḥev* 8:7).

(g) *The Date.* In a few instances the letter is dated. This is usually done toward the end, but once it follows the initial greeting (*AP* 21:3). In this case the date is more or less part of the message: וכעת שנתא זא שנת 5 דריוהוש מלכא, "Now this year is the 5th year of Darius, the King." Aside from that instance the date normally occurs in a prepositional phrase: ב19 למרחשון שנת 37 ארתחשס[ש], "on the 19th of Marḥešwan, the 37th year of Artaxerxes" (*AP* 17:7).[54] Or again, ב20 למרחשון שנת 17 דריהוש מלכא, "On the 20th of Marḥešwan, the 17th year of Darius, the King" (*AP* 30:30; 31:[29]). Similarly *AP* 26:28. In one instance the name of the month is given with both Egyptian and Babylonian names: ב27 לתעבי ה[ו נים]ן [ש]נת, "On the 27th of Tybi, th[at is Nis]an, [the ?th] year of [ ]" (*AP* 42:14).[55] A fuller form is sometimes used: [ב?] למחיר כתבת אגרתא זא, "[On the ?th] of Meḥir I have written this letter" (*Pad* I r 6).[56]

(h) *The Final or Exterior Address.* When the papyrus or skin letter was completed, it was usually folded up carefully and sealed. On the outside a line was written which indicated the name of the sender and the addressee. In many instances this address was similar to the *praescriptio*, or abbreviated it, or simply repeated it. Two basic forms can be detected: those that begin with the preposition "to" and those that begin with "from."

(i) *The "To" Form.* Usually the same preposition that was employed in the *praescriptio* is found in the exterior address. Thus, [אל] אחי ידניה וכנותה חילא יהודיא אחוכם חנני[ה], '[To] my brothers, Yedaniah and his colleagues, the Jewish garrison, your brother, Hanani[ah]" (*AP* 21:11). In this instance the exterior address is identical with the *praescriptio*. Similarly, to the extent that the address is preserved: *AP* 37:17; 39:5; *Pad* II r 1. Occasionally, the difference is simply a case of the titles (אח, אחת) being omitted in the exterior address (*HermWP* 2:18) or of full names being used in it (*AP* 40:5; 41:[9?]; 42:[15?]; Shunnar 9). But often enough it is a little more complicated. Thus, the titles are changed, as we have noted above (p. 190): *HermWP* 3:15; 6:11; 7:5. Or the titles are omitted, and the full name of the sender alone is given (*HermWP* 4:15). Or the letter is addressed to only one person, though two are named in the *praescriptio*, and the full name of the sender is given (*HermWP* 5:10). Or the titles are changed and full names are used (*Pad* I v 7); or some names and titles used in the *praescriptio* are omitted, but the full name of the sender is given (*AP* 38:12). In one instance the letter is addressed to a different person in the exterior address: אל אבי פסמי בר נבונתן מן מכבנת, "To my father, PSMY bar Nabunathan, from Makkabanit"; but the *praescriptio* reads: אל אחתי רעיה מן אחכי מכבנת, "To my sister, Ra^{c}yah, from your brother, Makkabanit" (*HermWP* 1:1).[57]

In the letters from Hermopolis West a further element appears, a directive for the carrier indicating the destination of the letter, usually given at the end of the line and separated a bit from the address proper. Thus, סון יבל, "(To) be carried (to) Syene" (*HermWP* 1:14; 2:18; 3:14); אפי יבל, "(To) be carried (to) Luxor" (*HermWP* 5:10; 6:11; 7:5); or simply סון, "(To) Syene" (*HermWP* 4:15).[58]

(ii) *The "From" Form.* The exterior address that begins with מן instead of "to" is almost exclusively confined to the so-called Arsames correspondence, and it is not easy to say whether it represents the style of a locality or of an official letter. In many instances there is a little fuller identification of the sender or of the addressee(s), sometimes including the directive, "who are in Egypt." Thus, [מן] אר[שם בר ביתא ע]ל אר[תונת זי במצ]רי[ן], "[From] Ar[sames, the palace prince, t]o Ar[tawont who is in Eg]yp[t]" (*AD* 1).[59] In this case the address adds the identification of Arsames as "the palace prince" and the directive, "who are in Egypt." Similarly: *AD* 2, 3, 5. The simple addition of the directive is found in *AD* 4. In *AD* 7 the address identified the addressee as "the officer who is in Lower Egypt," an addition to the *praescriptio*-formula;

similarly: *AD* 8, 9, 10, 12, 13. Note the form in *AD* 11: מן ורוהי על נחתחור וחנ[ד]סירם ו[כנותה המרכריא זי במצרין], "From Warohi to Neḥtiḥur and the comptroller(?) and his col[leagues, the accountants, who are in Egypt]." Here there are an additional title and an indication of the destination. To this group belongs *AP* 26:27, which is fragmentary.

The Arsames correspondence in *AD* is also distinctive in having a docket written on the outside along with the address; it explains in brief the contents of the letter. For example, על דשנא זי אחחפי פקידא זי [במצ]רין, "Concerning the grant of ᶜAḥḥapi, the officer who is in Egypt" (*AD* 2). This item is often very difficult to read. Traces of it can be found in *AD* 1, 3, 4, 5, 7, 9, 10, 12.

There is one letter in the Arsames correspondence that completely lacks an address, but the nature of the letter explains the reason for the absence of it. It is a sort of passport, a letter to be carried and showed to various subordinate officials along the way to Egypt, who are instructed by it to provide rations and (presumably) lodging for the bearer and his travelling companions (*AD* 6). It is obviously an official letter, addressed to several persons in different places.

III. *Conclusion*

Having come to the end of the enumeration of the items that are formulaic or somewhat stereotyped in Aramaic letters, we may ask now to what extent one can detect a structure in them. This is not easy to answer, but the majority of the letters normally have the following schema: (1) the *praescriptio*, (2) the initial greeting, either religious or secular, (3) secondary greetings, (4) the body of the letter, and (5) a concluding statement. Whether one should include the exterior address is debatable. Many of these features have a similarity with counterparts in other corpora of letters from the ancient eastern Mediterranean world, which a comparative study would illustrate in abundance. As for the biblical letters, those in Ezra supply the closest parallels to the extrabiblical material; those in Daniel less so—and there is a real question whether the latter should even be considered. Certain items in NT epistolography find illustration in some elements of the Aramaic letters discussed above, but a more detailed study of the bearing of Aramaic letters on them remains to be done.

Lastly, it should be noted that because Aramaic was used as a sort of international language over a wide area and for several centuries, some of the different formulae and features may have to be accounted for in this way. There is no certainty that the various features which we have sorted out were all being used simultaneously. At times some of the features were obviously confined to one group of letters or other; hence one has to be careful about extrapolating and predicating such features of Aramaic epistolography as a whole.

CHART 1

ARAMAIC LETTERS ON SKIN OR PAPYRUS

	Name and Provenience	*Museum No.*	*Easy Access*	*Editio Princeps*
1	ʾAdon Letter (Saqqarah)	Cairo 86984	*KAI* 266	A. Dupont-Sommer, *Sem* 1 (1948) 43-68
2	Hermopolis West Papyrus I			E. Bresciani and M. Kamil, *Le lettere aramaiche di Hermopoli* (AdANdL, Memorie VIII/xii/5; Rome: Accademia Nazionale dei Lincei, 1966) 372-82
3	HermWP II			Ibid., 384-90
4	HermWP III			Ibid., 392-96
5	HermWP IV			Ibid., 398-403
6	HermWP V			Ibid., 404-7
7	HermWP VI			Ibid., 408-10
8	HermWP VII			Ibid., 412-15
9	HermWP VIII			Ibid., 416-18
10	Barley(?) Letter (Elephantine, 484 B.C.)	Berlin 13455	*AP* 4	E. Sachau, *Aramäische Papyrus und Ostraka* (Leipzig: Hinrichs, 1911), pl. 36, pap. 41, p. 136
11	Letter to Higher Court (Elephantine, 435 B.C.)	Berlin 13478	*AP* 16	*APO*, pl. 7, pap. 7, pp. 41-43
12	Letter to Arsames (Elephantine, 428 B.C.)	Berlin 13480	*AP* 17	*APO*, pl. 5, pap. 4, pp. 34-35
13	Passover Letter (Elephantine, 419 B.C.)	Berlin 13464	*AP* 21	*APO*, pl. 6, pap. 6, pp. 36-40
14	Letter of Boat Repairs (Elephantine, 412 B.C.)	Berlin 13492	*AP* 26	*APO*, pls. 8-9, pap. 8, pp. 44-49
15	Petition to Satrap (Elephantine, 410 B.C.)	Strasbourg	*AP* 27	J. Euting, *MPAIBL* 11/2 (1903) 297-311
16	Petition to Bagohi (Elephantine, 408 B.C.)	Berlin 13495	*AP* 30	*APO*, pls. 1-2, pap. 1, pp. 3-22
17	Duplicate of §16 (Elephantine, 408 B.C.)	Berlin 13496	*AP* 31	*APO*, pl. 3, pap. 2, pp. 23-26
18	Memo from Bagohi to Jews (Elephantine, 408 B.C.)	Berlin 13497	*AP* 32	*APO*, pl. 4, pap. 3, pp. 28-30
19	Letter to Satrap (Elephantine, 407 B.C.)	Berlin 13472	*AP* 33	*APO*, pl. 4, pap. 5, pp. 31-33
20	Letter to Satrap (Elephantine, 407 B.C.)	Berlin 13471	*AP* 34	*APO*, pl. 15, pap. 15, pp. 63-65
21	Letter from Shewa b. Z. (Elephantine, 399 B.C.)	Brooklyn 47.218.151	*BMAP* 13	E. G. Kraeling, *BMAP*, pp. 281-90
22	Letter to Yedaniah (Elephantine, 5th c.)	Berlin 13468	*AP* 37	*APO*, pl. 11, pap. 10, pp. 51-54
23	Letter to Yedaniah (Elephantine, 5th c.)	Berlin 13494	*AP* 38	*APO*, pl. 12, pap. 11, pp. 55-57
24	Letter to Lady Shelwah (Elephantine, 5/4 c.)	Berlin 13462	*AP* 39	*APO*, pl. 13, pap. 12, pp. 58-59
25	Letter of Hosea to Palṭi (Elephantine, 5/4 c.)	Berlin 13473	*AP* 40	*APO*, pl. 13, pap. 14, pp. 59-60
26	L. to Seḥo, my brother (Elephantine, 5/4 c.)	Berlin 13463	*AP* 41	*APO*, pl. 14, pap. 13, pp. 60-61
27	Business Letter (Elephantine, 5/4 c.)	Berlin 13490	*AP* 42	*APO*, pl. 16, pap. 16, pp. 66-68
28	Fragmentary Letters (Elephantine, 5/4 c.)	Berlin 13457	*AP* 54	*APO*, pl. 36, pap. 39, pp. 133-34
29	Letter Fragment (Elephantine, 5/4 c.)	Berlin 13460	*AP* 55	*APO*, pl. 36, pap. 40, p. 135
30	Letter Fragment (Elephantine, 4th c.)	Berlin 13456	*AP* 56	*APO*, pl. 37, pap. 43, p. 138
31	Letter Fragment (Elephantine, 4th c.)	Berlin 13450	*AP* 57	*APO*, pl. 38, pap. 45, p. 140
32	Address of Letter (Elephantine, 4th c.)	Berlin 13454	*AP* 58	*APO*, pl. 37, pap. 42, pp. 137-38
33	L. to Mithravahisht (Egypt, ?)		*AP* 70	*CIS* 2.144 + pl. XV
34	Garrison Letter (Elephantine, 5/4 c.)		*AP* 80	M. de Vogüé, *CRAIBL* 1902, p. 49
35	Letter Fragments (Elephantine, 5/4 c.)		*RES* 248	M. de Vogüé, *CRAIBL* 1902, 49

	Name and Provenience	*Museum No.*	*Easy Access*	*Editio Princeps*
36	Letter about a Boat (Elephantine, 5/4 c.)	Berlin 23000		Z. Shunnar, in *Geschichte Mittelasiens im Altertum* (eds. F. Altheim and R. Stiehl; Berlin, 1970) 111-17 (+pls. 1-2)
37	Mariette Fragment (Memphis, 4th c.)		*AP* 77	J. Euting, *SPAW* 23 (1887) 670; *CIS* 2. 152, pl. XX
38	Padua Pap. Letter I (Egypt, 5th c.)			E. Bresciani, *RSO* 35 (1960) 11-24 (+pls. 1-5), esp. pp. 18-22
39	Padua Pap. Letter II			Ibid., 22-24
40	Padua Pap. Letter III			Ibid., 24
41	Arsames Letter I (found in Egypt; 5th c.)	Bodleian Library, pellis aramaica VI	*AD* 1	G. R. Driver, *AD*, pp. 10-12
42	Arsames Letter II	Bodl. L. p. a. XII	*AD* 2	Ibid., 12-13
43	Arsames Letter III	Bodl. L. p. a. VII	*AD* 3	Ibid., 13-15
44	Arsames Letter IV	Bodl. L. p. a. II	*AD* 4	Ibid., 16-17
45	Arsames Letter V	Bodl. L. p. a. IV	*AD* 5	Ibid., 17-20
46	Arsames Letter VI	Bodl. L. p. a. VIII	*AD* 6	Ibid., 20-23
47	Arsames Letter VII	Bodl. L. p. a. I	*AD* 7	Ibid., 23-25
48	Arsames Letter VIII	Bodl. L. p. a. XIII	*AD* 8	Ibid., 25-28
49	Arsames Letter IX	Bodl. L. p. a. III	*AD* 9	Ibid., 28-29
50	Arsames Letter X	Bodl. L. p. a. IX	*AD* 10	Ibid., 29-31
51	Warohi Letter (found in Egypt, 5th c.)	Bodl. L. p. a. V	*AD* 11	Ibid., 31-33
52	Warphish Letter (found in Egypt, 5th c.)	Bodl. L. p. a. XIV	*AD* 12	Ibid., 33-35
53	Artahay Letter (found in Egypt, 5th c.)	Bodl. L. p. a. X	*AD* 13	Ibid., 35-36
54	Letter to King Artaxerxes (5th c.)		Ezra 4:11-16	
55	Letter to Rehum and Shimshai (5th c.)		Ezra 4:17-22	
56	Letter to King Darius		Ezra 5:7b-17	
57	Letter(?) to Tattenai		Ezra 6:6-12	
58	Letter to Ezra		Ezra 7:12-26	
59	Nebuchadrezzar's Encyclical(?)		Dan 3:31-33 (98-100)	Cf. LXX 4:37b
60	Darius' Letter to All Peoples		Dan 6:26-28	
61	Letter of Šim'on bar Kosibah I		*5/6Ḥev* 1	E. Y. Kutscher, *Lěš* 25 (1961) 119-21
62	L. of Š. b. Kosibah II		*5/6Ḥev* 2	Ibid., 122
63	L. of Š. b. Kosibah III		*5/6Ḥev* 4	Ibid., 122-24
64	L. of Š. b. Kosibah IV		*5/6Ḥev* 8	Ibid., 124-25
65	L. of Š. b. Kosibah V		*5/6Ḥev* 10	Ibid., 125-26
66	L. of Š. b. Kosibah VI		*5/6Ḥev* 11	Ibid., 126-27
67	L. of Š. b. Kosibah VII		*5/6Ḥev* 14	Ibid., 127-29
68	L. of Š. b. Kosibah VIII		*5/6Ḥev* 15	Ibid., 129
69	Letter of R. Gamaliel I		*ArDial* p. 3	jSanhedrin 18d
70	Letter of R. Gamaliel II		*ArDial* p. 3	jSanhedrin 18d
71	Letter of R. Gamaliel III		*ArDial* p. 3	jSanhedrin 18d
72	L. of R. Judah the Prince to Emperor Antoninus		*AAH* I/1, p. 64	*Běrēšît Rabbāh* 75
73	Christian Palestinian Aramaic Letter (8th-10th c. A.D.)		papMird A	J. T. Milik, *RB* 60 (1953) 533-39; *Bib* 42 (1961) 21-27

CHART 2

ARAMAIC MESSAGES ON OSTRACA

	Name and Provenience	*Museum No.*	*Easy Access*	*Editio Princeps*
1	Asshur Ostracon (650 B.C.)	Berlin 8384	*KAI* 233	M. Lidzbarski, *ZA* 31 (1917-18) 193-202
2	Murabba at Letter(?) (100-50 B.C.)	Ecole Biblique	*Mur* 72	J. T. Milik, *Les grottes de Murabbaʿat* (DJD 2; Oxford: Clarendon, 1961) 172-74
3	Yarḥaw Ostracon (Elephantine, 5/4 c.)	Cl-G Ost 277		A. Dupont-Sommer, *RHR* 128 (1944) 28-39
4	Double Message to Uriah and Ahitab (Elephantine, 5/4 c.)	Berlin 11383	*APE* 76/1	E. Sachau, *APO*, no. 76/1, pl. 63/1, pp. 233-34
5	Ostracon to ḤWNY (Elephantine, 5/4 c.)	Berlin 11364	*APE* 76/2	*APO*, 76/2, pl. 63/2, pp. 234-35
6	Fragmentary Ostracon (Elephantine, 5/4 c.)	Berlin 11369	*APE* 76/3	*APO*, 76/3, pl. 63/3, p. 235
7	Fragmentary Ostracon (Elephantine, 5/4 c.)	Berlin 11384	*APE* 76/4	*APO*, 76/4, pl. 63/4, pp. 235-36
8	Fragmentary Ostracon (Elephantine, 5/4 c.)	Berlin 11377	*APE* 76/5	*APO*, 76/5, pl. 63/5, p. 236
9	Fragmentary Ostracon (Elephantine, 5/4 c.)	Berlin 8763	*RES* 496, 1804	A. Cowley, *PSBA* 25 (1903) 314
10	Passover Ostracon (Elephantine, 5/4 c.)	Berlin 10679	*APE* 77/2	M. Lidzbarski, *Ephemeris*, 2.229-34
11	Hoshaʿyah Ostracon (Elephantine 5/4 c.)	Bodleian Libr. Ost.	*RES* 1793	A. H. Sayce, *PSBA* 33 (1911) 183-84
12	Fragmentary Ostracon (Elephantine, 5/4 c.)	Berlin 11380	*APE* 78/1	*APO*, 78/1, pl. 65/1, pp. 238-39
13	Aḥutab Ostracon (Elephantine, 5/4 c.)	Berlin 10680	*APE* 78/2	M. Lidzbarski, *Ephemeris*, 2.234-36; 3.257, n. 1
14	Dream Ostracon (Elephantine, 5/4 c.)	Berlin 1137	*KAI* 270	A. Dupont-Sommer, *ASAE* 48 (1948) 117-30 (+pl. II)
15	Salt Ostracon (Elephantine, 5/4 c.)	Cl-G Ost 16		A. Dupont-Sommer, *ASAE* 48 (1948) 109-16 (+pl. I)
16	Fragmentary Ostracon (Elephantine, 5/4 c.)	Berlin 11367		*APO*, 80/6, pl. 67/6, p. 242
17	Uriah Ostracon (Elephantine, 5/4 c.)	Ashmolean Mus. (lost)	*APE* 91	A. Cowley, *PSBA* 25 (1903) 259-66
18	Cucumber Ostracon (Elephantine, 5/4 c.)	Bodleian, Aram Inscr 2	*RES* 493, 1801	A. Cowley, *PSBA* 25 (1903) 311-12
19	Fragmentary Ostracon (Elephantine, 5/4 c.)	Bodleian, Aram Inscr 3	*RES* 494, 1802	A. Cowley, *PSBA* 25 (1903) 312
20	Fragmentary Ostracon (Elephantine, 5/4 c.)	British Mus. 14220	*APE* 95	*CIS* 2.139 (+pl. XII)
21	Haggai Ostracon (Elephantine, 5/4 c.)	Cairo Ost 35468a	*RES* 1295	A. H. Sayce, *PSBA* 31 (1909) 154-55
22	Barley Ostracon (Elephantine, 5/4 c.)	Cairo Ost 35468b	*RES* 1296	M. Lidzbarski, *Ephemeris*, 3.121-22; N. Aimé-Giron, *Textes araméens d'Egypte* (Cairo: Institut français, 1931), No. 3
23	Nabudalah Ostracon (Elephantine, 5/4 c.)	Cairo Ost 49635		N. Aimé-Giron, *ASAE* 26 (1926) 23-27
24	Shallu'ah Ostracon (Elephantine, 5/4 c.)	Cairo Ost 48624		N. Aimé-Giron, *ASAE* 26 (1926) 27-29
25	Fragmentary Ostracon (Elephantine, 5/4 c.)	Cairo Ost 49625		N. Aimé-Giron, *ASAE* 26 (1926) 29-31
26	Yirpeyah Ostracon (Elephantine, 5/4 c.)	Munich 898	*RES* 1298	M. Lidzbarski, *Ephemeris*, 3.21-22
27	Fragmentary Ostracon (Elephantine, 5/4 c.)	Munich 899	*RES* 1299	M. Lidzbarski, *Ephemeris*, 3.20-21
28	Yedaniah Ostracon (Elephantine, 5/4 c.)	Cl-G Ost 44		A. Dupont-Sommer, *Hebrew and Semitic Studies: Presented to G. R. Driver* (eds. D. W. Thomas and W. D. McHardy; Oxford: Clarendon, 1963) 53-58
29	Michiah Ostracon (Elephantine, 5/4 c.)	Cl-G Ost 70	*ANET* 491	A. Dupont-Sommer, *RHR* 130 (1945) 17-28

	Name and Provenience	Museum No.	Easy Access	Editio Princeps
30	Yislaḥ Ostracon (Elephantine, 5/4 c.)	Cl-G Ost 152	*AC* 33A	A. Dupont-Sommer, *Sem* 2 (1949) 29-39
31	Yahu-Ṣeba'oth Ostracon (Elephantine, 5/4 c.)	Cl-G Ost 167		A. Dupont-Sommer, *CRAIBL* 1947, pp. 179-81
32	Aḥutab Ostracon (Elephantine, 5/4 c.)	Cl-G Ost 169		A. Dupont-Sommer, *RevEtSém* 1941-45, pp. 65-75
33	Fragmentary Ostracon (Elephantine, 5/4 c.)	Cl-G Ost 186	*AC* 33B	A. Dupont-Sommer, *Scritti in onore di Giuseppe Furlani* (= *RSO* 32 [1957]; Rome: Bardi, 1957) 403-9
34	Parasceve Ostracon (Elephantine, 5/4 c.)	Cl-G Ost 204		A. Dupont-Sommer, *MPAIBL* 15 (1950) 67-88
35	Qawwiliah Ostracon (Elephantine, 5/4 c.)	Cambridge 131-33		A. Cowley, *JRAS* 61 (1929) 107-11
36	Meshullak Ostracon (Elephantine, 5/4 c.)	Berlin 11379		*APO*, 84/7, pl. 71/7, p. 250
37	Yashib Ostracon (bought at Edfu; probably from 2d c. B.C.)	Berlin 10964	*APE* 81/1	*APO*, 81/1, pl. 68/1, p. 243
38	Leptines Ostracon (found in Egypt; Hellenistic period)	Strasbourg Libr.	*RES* 1300	M. Lidzbarski, *Ephemeris*, 3.23-25

NOTES TO CHAPTER 8

*Originally published as "Some Notes on Aramaic Epistolography," *JBL* 93 (1974) 201-25.

1 A cursory treatment of it can be found in G. Beer, "Zur israelitisch-jüdischen Briefliteratur," *Alttestamentliche Studien Rudolf Kittel zum 60. Geburtstag dargebracht* (ed. A. Alt et al.; Leipzig: Hinrichs, 1913) 20-41. See also the article by J. Marty in n. 46 below.

2 This paper grew out of a consultation on ancient letter-writing held at the SBL annual meeting in Chicago, 1973.

3 A study of Aramaic epistolography is being undertaken by John David Whitehead.

4 For instance, the theories of C. C. Torrey about Aramaic Gospels, the Aramaic source(s) of Acts, R. Bultmann's Aramaic Revelatory Discourse source in John, the question of Papias' *logia* underlying Matthew, etc. See my methodological remarks in chap. 1 above (pp. 1–27).

5 See, e.g., the writings of W. C. van Unnik, W. F. Albright and C. S. Mann, and P. Grelot referred to above, p. 21, end of n. 15.

6 *Do You Know Greek? How Much Greek Could the First Jewish Christians Have Known?* (p. 50 above, n. 32).

7 This proposal has been put forth, for instance, for Philippians by H. E. G. Paulus, J. Schmid, E. Lohmeyer, L. Johnson; for Colossians, by M. Goguel, E. Lohmeyer, J. de Zwaan, M. Dibelius, L. Johnson.

8 For further details on these phases of the Aramaic language, see pp. 57–84 above.

9 The notable exception is the Aššur Ostracon, which does not come from Egypt, but was sent (ca. 650 B.C.) from Babylon to Assyria and contains a military report (about fugitive prisoners to be returned) from Beletir, a captain of the Assyrian cavalry, to Pirawur; and another message as well to Nabuzerušabši (whom he tries to appease). The text is written on six fragments of the ostracon, is incomplete, and difficult to interpret. See M. Lidzbarski, *Altaramäische Urkunden aus Assur* (Wissenschaftliche Veröffentlichung der deutschen Orient-Gesellschaft, 38; Leipzig: Hinrichs, 1921) 5-15. See further *Ephemeris* 2. 1-23; *AC* 14; *KAI* §233; also M. Lidzbarski, "Ein aramäischer Brief aus der Zeit Ašurbanipals," *MDOG* 58 (1917) 50-52 [preliminary report]; *ZA*

31 (1917-18) 193-202; D. H. Baneth, "Zu dem aramäischen Brief aus der Zeit Assurbanipals," *OLZ* 22 (1919) 55-58; (Anonymous), "Zeitschriftenschau," *ZAW* 47 (1929) 150-51; R. A. Bowman, "An Interpretation of the Assur Ostracon," *Royal Correspondence of the Assyrian Empire* (ed. L. Waterman; University of Michigan Studies, Humanistic Series, 20; Ann Arbor: University of Michigan) 4 (1936) 273-82; A. Dupont-Sommer, "Séance du 22 octobre," *CRAIBL* 1943, 465-66; "L'ostracon araméen d'Assour," *Syria* 24 (1944-45) 24-61; *Les Araméens* (L'orient ancien illustré; Paris: Maisonneuve, 1949) 85.

[10]As an aid to the reader, two charts listing the known Aramaic letters and ostraca are appended to this article. The author would be grateful to readers who might detect omissions or errors in them and send them on to him; obviously no claim is made for the exhaustive character of these lists. See now D. Pardee, *JBL* 97 (1978) 323 n. 9.

[11]*Light from the Ancient East* (London: Hodder and Stoughton, 1927) 229.

[12]Ibid., 228.

[13]See, e.g., O. Roller, *Das Formular der paulinischen Briefe: Ein Beitrag zur Lehre vom antiken Briefe* (Stuttgart: Kohlhammer, 1933) 23-29 (and Anm. 144-52); J. Sykutris, "Epistolographie," *RE* Suppl. 5 (1931) 187; W. G. Doty, *Letters in Primitive Christianity* (Philadelphia: Fortress, 1973) 24-27; "The Classification of Epistolary Literature," *CBQ* 31 (1969) 183-99.

[14]Engl. 4:1-4. This is the introduction to the story of Nebuchadrezzar's madness. Verse 31 (Engl. 4:1) reads like the *praescriptio* of an ancient Aramaic letter: "King Nebuchadrezzar to all peoples, nations, and languages that dwell in all the earth: Peace be multiplied to you!" The epistolary character of this introduction was recognized in some MSS of the so-called LXX version of Daniel; 3:31(98) reads: *ἀρχὴ τῆς ἐπιστολῆς*. At the end of the story the same version records: *ἔγραψε δὲ ὁ βασιλεὺς* Ναβουχοδόνοσορ *ἐπιστολὴν ἐγκύκλιον πᾶσι τοῖς κατὰ τόπον ἔθνεσι καὶ χώραις καὶ γλώσσαις πάσαις ταῖς οἰκούσαις ἐν πάσαις ταῖς χώραις* . . . (4:37b). But the rest of the introduction (3:32-33 [Engl. 4:2-3]) immediately alerts the reader to a change of literary form, and 4:1 (Engl. 4:4) begins the narrative proper. In the general setting of the stories in Daniel 1-6 one may hesitate about the function of that introduction, and hence about the quasi-epistolary character of this section in Daniel.

[15]The letter of Rehum, the commander, and Shimshai, the scribe, et al., "settled in the cities of Samaria and in the rest of the province Beyond the River," to King Artaxerxes II about the Jews who were rebuilding "that rebellious and wicked city" (Ezra 4:11-16); Artaxerxes' reply to Rehum, Shimshai, and their associates in Jerusalem to stop the rebuilding of the city (Ezra 4:17-22); the letter of Tattenai, governor of the province Beyond the River, and Shethar-bozenai, and their associates to King Darius I about the Jews in the province of Judah who were rebuilding the "house of God which is in Jerusalem" (Ezra 5:7b-17); Darius' reply (lacking a *praescriptio*) to Tattenai, Shethar-bozenai, and their associates, instructing them to "let the work on this house of God alone; let the . . . Jews rebuild this house of God on its site" (Ezra 6:6-12); Letter of Artaxerxes II to Ezra, the priest and scribe, conveying to him the king's decree (permission to go to Jerusalem, to make inquiries about Judah and Jerusalem, to convey the silver and gold which the king and his counsellors offer to the God of Israel), as well as the free-will offerings, money intended for temple sacrifices and other needs, and to take back the temple vessels (Ezra 7:12-26).

[16]See G. R. Driver, *Aramaic Documents* (p. 76 above, n. 21).

[17]Only a few of these letters have seen preliminary publication: see Y. Yadin, "Expedition D," *IEJ* 11 (1961) 36-52; "מחנה ד," *Yediot* 25 (1961) 49-64. Cf. E. Y. Kutscher, "לשונן של האיגרות העבריות והארמיות של בר־כוסבא ובני דורו" [The Languages of the Hebrew and Aramaic Letters of Bar Cocheba and His Contemporaries], *Lĕšonénu* 25 (1961) 117-23; 26 (1962) 7-23; Y. Yadin, "New Discoveries in the Judaean Desert," *BA* 24 (1961) 34-50; "More on the Letters of Bar Cocheba," *BA* 24 (1961) 86-95; "Expedition D—The Cave of Letters," *IEJ* 12 (1962) 227-57; "מחנא ד׳—מערת האיגרות," *Yediot* 26 (1962) 204-36; הממצאים ממי בר־כוכבא במערת האיגרות: *The Finds from the Bar-Kokhba Period in the "Cave of Letters"* (Judean Desert Studies; Jerusalem: Israel Exploration Society and the Bialik Foundation, 1963). Cf. Y. Aharoni, "The Caves of Naḥal Ḥever," *ᶜAtiqot* 3 (1961) 148-62; M. C. Salzmann, "Ricerche in Israele," *BeO* 3 (1961) 23-25.

[18]A. Dupont-Sommer, "Un papyrus araméen d'époque saïte découvert à Saqqarah," *Semitica* 1 (1948) 43–68; see pp. 231–42 below.

[19]This letter was first published by E. Sachau, *Aramäische Papyrus und Ostraka* (see p. 76 above, n. 21), §1, pls. 1-2. The subsequent literature on this letter is vast and cannot be included here.

[20]See F. M. Cross, Jr., "The Discovery of the Samaria Papyri," *BA* 26 (1963) 110-21.

[21]For recent discussions of these texts, see B. Porten, *Archives from Elephantine: The Life of an Ancient Jewish Military Colony* (Berkeley / Los Angeles: University of California, 1968) 105-22; P. Grelot, *Documents araméens d'Egypte* (p. 26 above, n. 89), 386–419.

[22]The so-called Passover Letter (*AP* 21) has been the subject of considerable recent discussion: W. R. Arnold, "The Passover Papyrus from Elephantine," *JBL* 31 (1912) 1-33; J. Barth, "Zu den Papyri von Elephantine (ed. Sachau)," *OLZ* 15 (1912) 10-11; B. Couroyer, "L'origine égyptienne du mot 'Pâque,'" *RB* 62 (1952) 381-96; A. Dupont-Sommer, "La Pâque dans les documents araméens d'Eléphantine," *CRAIBL* 1945, pp. 174-76; "Sur la fête de la Pâque dans les documents arameéns d'Eléphantine," *REJ* 107 (1946–47) 39–51; H. J. Elhorst, "The Passover Papyrus from Elephantine," *JBL* 31 (1912) 147–49; P. Grelot, "Etudes sur le 'Papyrus Pascal' d'Eléphantine," *VT* 4 (1954) 349-84; "Le papyrus pascal d'Eléphantine et le problème du Pentateuque," *VT* 5 (1955) 250-65; "Le papyrus pascal d'Eléphantine: Nouvel examen," *VT* 17 (1967) 114-17; "Le papyrus pascal d'Eléphantine: Essai de restauration," *VT* 17 (1967) 201-7; "Le papyrus pascal d'Eléphantine et les lettres d'Hermopolis," *VT* 17 (1967) 481-83; *Documents araméens d'Egypte,* 373-85; J. Halévy, "La Pâque à Eléphantine," *JA* 19 (1912) 622-23; E. G. Kraeling, *BMAP*, 93 (translation); E. Meyer, "Zu den aramäischen Papyri von Elephantine," *SPAW* 47 (1911) 1026-53; C. Steuernagel, "Die jüdisch-aramäischen Papyri und Ostraka aus Elephantine und ihre Bedeutung für die Kenntnis palästinensischer Verhältnisse," *ZDPV* 35 (1912) 85-105, esp. pp. 101-4; "Zum Passa-Massothfest," *ZAW* 31 (1911) 310; C. C. Torrey, "The Letters Prefixed to Second Maccabees," *JAOS* 60 (1950) 120-50; A. Vincent, *La religion des Judéo-Araméens d'Eléphantine* (Paris: Geuthner, 1937) 237-311; B. Porten, *Archives from Elephantine,* 130-33; S. Talmon, "Divergences in Calendar-Reckoning in Ephraim and Judah," *VT* 8 (1958) 48-74, esp. pp. 72-73. See further my commentary on the *Genesis Apocryphon of Qumran Cave I* (2d ed.) 219.

[23]E. Bresciani and M. Kamil, *Le lettere aramaiche di Hermopoli* (p. 76 above, n. 21), 357–428 (+ pls. I-X). See further M. Dahood, "La regina del cielo in Geremia," *RivB* 8 (1960) 166-68; E. Bresciani, "Nouveaux papyrus araméens d'époque perse provenant d'Hermopolis," *CRAIBL* 1967, pp. 301-2; A. Dupont-Sommer, "Observations sur les papyrus araméens d'époque perse provenant d'Hermopolis," *CRAIBL* 1967, pp. 302-4; P. Grelot, "Le papyrus pascal d'Eléphantine et les lettres d'Hermopolis," *VT* 17 (1967) 481-83; review of the *editio princeps, RB* 74 (1967) 432-37; R. Yaron, "כסף 'זוז' בתעודות יב'," *Lěšonénu* 31 (1967) 287-88; J. T. Milik, "Les papyrus araméens d'Hermoupolis et les cultes syro-phéniciens en Egypte perse," *Bib* 48 (1967) 546-622; B. Porten and J. C. Greenfield, "The Aramaic Papyri from Hermopolis," *ZAW* 80 (1968) 216-31; B. Porten, *Archives from Elephantine,* 164-77; E. Hammershaimb, "Some Remarks on the Aramaic Letters from Hermopolis," *VT* 18 (1968) 265-67; J. P. Hayes and J. Hoftijzer, "Notae hermopolitanae," *VT* 20 (1970) 98-106; R. du Mesnil du Buisson, *Etudes sur les dieux phéniciens hérités par l'empire romain* (Etudes préliminaires aux religions orientales dans l'empire romain, 14; Leiden: Brill, 1970) 81-104; E. Hammershaimb, "De aramaiske papyri frå Hermopolis," *DTT* 34 (1971) 81-104; H. Donner, "Bemerkungen zum Verständnis zweier aramäischer Briefe aus Hermopolis," *Near Eastern Studies in Honor of William Foxwell Albright* (ed. H. Goedicke; London / Baltimore: The Johns Hopkins University, 1971) 75-85; E. Y. Kutscher, "The Hermopolis Papyri," *Israel Oriental Studies* 1 (1971) 103-19; J. Naveh, "The Palaeography of the Hermopolis Papyri," *Israel Oriental Studies* 1 (1971) 120-22; P. Grelot, *Documents araméens d'Egypte,* §25-31; J. C. L. Gibson, *Textbook of Syrian Semitic Inscriptions: Vol. II, Aramaic Inscriptions* (Oxford: Clarendon, 1975) 125-43. The numerous preliminary notices of the discovery of these letters are omitted here.

[24]See P. Grelot, "Les données de l'onomastique," *Documents araméens d'Egypte,* 455-502; "Notes d'onomastique sur les textes araméens d'Egypte," *Sem* 21 (1971) 95-117; M. H. Silverman, "Aramean Name-Types in the Elephantine Documents," *JAOS* 89 (1969) 691-709.

[25]5/6Ḥev 15 aram (see E. Y. Kutscher, *Lĕšonénu* 25 [1961] 129). See my discussion of it, *ESBNT*, 336-38.

[26]The Greek letter apparently comes from the same cave (5/6 Ḥev); see pp. 35–36 above.

[27]See B. Porten, *Archives from Elephantine* (n. 21 above), 3–27.

[28]See further *AP* 32:2; 63:10; cf. Sefire I C 2-3.

[29]As may be the case in Dan 6:26, a literary context that could tolerate the omission of it. Cf. Ezra 6:6.

[30]For an explanation of this translation of the *praescriptio*, see pp. 233–35 below.

[31]Because of the fragmentary nature of this letter, one cannot be certain about the form of the *praescriptio*; it may rather belong to form (ii).

[32]For a discussion of these letters, see pp. 219–30 below.

[33]Possibly one should include here *AP* 54:10 ([מן ע]קבנבו שלם מראי). For a discussion of whether ancient Aramaic letters began with מן or not, see S. Zeitlin, "The Fiction of the Recent Discoveries near the Dead Sea," *JQR* 44 (1953-54) 85-115; S. Yeivin, "Some Notes on the Documents from Wadi Murabbaᶜat Dating from the Days of Bar-Kokhᵓba," *Atiqot* 1 (1955) 95-108.

[34]The translation of גמיר is problematic. H. L. Ginsberg (in *AAH*, 1/2, p. 21) takes it as "et cetera (i.e., 'and the rest of the customary salutation')." E. Vogt (*Lexicon linguae aramaicae Veteris Testamenti* [p. 23 above, n. 41], 35) prefers to supply ‹שלם› before גמיר: "‹salutem› perfectam (precor)."

[35]See E. Bresciani and M. Kamil, *Le lettere aramaiche,* 365-66.

[36]*BMAP* 13:[1] is problematic; Kraeling restores line 1 on the basis of the exterior address, where the *aleph* is far from certain. The preposition also occurs in the final or exterior addresses.

[37]See further *AP* 21:2, 11; 40:1, 5; 41:1, 9; *Cl-G Ost* 227:1-2. Cf. 1QapGen 2:9. See my remarks on this question on p. 221 below.

[38]For further discussion of this phrase, see pp. 210–11 below.

[39]The verb ישאלו is restored with certainty, given the many other instances of its use; literally, "may they seek after."

[40]Literally, "and may he set you for favor before Darius."

[41]Literally, "be happy and prosperous" (הוי is the impv.).

[42]The meaning of שררת is not certain; it is usually translated "prosperity," but it may rather mean "stability" or "security."

[43]This formula probably underlies the greeting in 1 Pet 1:2, which may be influenced, of course, more directly by the Greek of Dan 4:1 (Theodotion).

[44]The verb here is the haphel of חזי, "may he cause me to see." A variant is found in *HermWP* 4:2; 6:2; *Pad* I v 3: יחוני, "may he show me."

[45]"Yahu, the God" is restored on the basis of the temple of Yahu that is greeted in line 1; see pp. 219–22 below.

[46]See J. Marty, "Contribution à l'étude de fragments epistolaires antiques, conservés principalement dans la Bible hébraïque: Les formules de salutation," *Mélanges syriens offerts à Monsieur René Dussaud* (Paris: Geuthner, 1939), 2. 845-55, esp. p. 849.

[47]Literally, "and now in this (place?) before me (there is) peace; moreover there before you may there be peace."

[48]See p. 228 below.

[49]In this case שלם is probably not the noun, but the adjective *šĕlim*; this would fit with Galgul. But how can one construe it with the following ינקיה? Here שלם seems to be a noun in the construct state, as it does also in *Pad* I r 5.

[50]For the restoration and translation of the end of this line, see *AP* 30:16; 31:15.

[51]My translation is literal; the phrase may mean simply something like "goodbye" or "farewell." For the construction, see E. Y. Kutscher, *Lĕšonénu* 25 (1961) 123-24.

[52]Literally, "ᶜAnani, the clerk, (is) the issuer of the order; Nabuᶜaqab, the scribe."

[53]Cowley's translation is wrong at this point.

[54]A peculiar word follows this date, לותהם. It seems to mean "to them," but no adequate explanation of it has yet been proposed.

[55]The double dating, first with an Egyptian name and then with a Babylonian equivalent, is otherwise found in many documents of the Elephantine corpus which are non-epistolary: e.g., *AP* 5:1; 6:1; 8:1; 10:1; *BMAP* 1:1; 3:1; 4:1.

[56]In this case a further note was appended, a sort of postscript.

[57]There is also one instance in which the *praescriptio* is missing so that one cannot tell whether the preserved address conforms to it or not (*AP* 56:4).

[58]The exact construction of this additional element is not clear. There is no difficulty in the lack of a preposition before the place name; this is common in other texts with verbs expressing motion toward a place (see p. 224 below). But how should one explain יבל, since in *HermWP* 7:5 it is written fully as יובל? Is it the 3d sg. masc. impf. causative passive, "Let it (viz., ספרא זנה) be carried"? This seems to be the best explanation.

[59]G. R. Driver chose not to number the addresses in relation to other lines in this correspondence. The address and the docket usually precede the text of the letter in his edition. The restoration of this address is certain, being based on details in other letters of the same group.

Chapter 9

The Syntax of כל, כלא, "All" in Aramaic Texts from Egypt and in Biblical Aramaic*

The new Aramaic documents published by Kraeling and Driver have considerably augmented the *corpus* of Official Aramaic.[1] The number of texts now available permits a more detailed study of the grammar of this dialect of Aramaic than was previously possible. While most of the grammatical analyses of P. Leander[2] have been confirmed by the new texts and hence are still valid, a few additions and minor corrections, however, must be made. In any case, his work still remains an indispensable aid to the study of what he called "Egyptian" Aramaic.

But the syntax of Official Aramaic was never worked out by Leander on the same scale as his treatment of the phonology and morphology. Though scattered syntactical remarks are occasionally found in the morphological section of his grammar, a thorough treatment of the syntax of this phase of Aramaic remains to be done.[3]

Moreover, the value of the Official Aramaic texts for the study of Biblical Aramaic has been remarked upon ever since they were first discovered. The excellent *Grammatik des Biblisch-Aramäischen* of Bauer and Leander frequently illustrates the Biblical Aramaic usage with examples of Official Aramaic.[4] The newly published texts shed further light on the Aramaic of the Bible. Consequently, we are in a position to begin an inductive study of the syntax of Official Aramaic and compare it in detail with that of Biblical Aramaic.

The present essay attempts to present a detailed treatment of an important pronoun used both in the texts found in Egypt and in the Bible. The various forms and uses of כל that occur in the Aramaic texts from Egypt will be classified and discussed, and the corresponding phenomena of Biblical Aramaic will be related to them. Our study of this pronoun will incorporate the partial treatments of Leander (*L* §18e-0) and of Joüon (*J* §48-50).

In the Official Aramaic texts found in Egypt the pronoun כל occurs in three forms, כל, כלא and כלה, aside from the questionably restored form in *A*

166, [כל[ך. The form כל can be either construct or absolute; scholars disagree on the interpretation of כלא, some maintaining it is the emphatic state, others holding it to be an adverbial form of כל; the form כלה is usually interpreted as a suffixal form. In Biblical Aramaic we find כל as construct, כלא (whose function is likewise disputed) and כלהון (once as a *kĕtīb* for כלהין), the suffixal form.

I. כל *in the Absolute State*

Though it may seem at first difficult to decide whether the form כל is absolute or construct in a given case, there are a few instances in the Egyptian documents that offer a clue to the interpretation. Leander (*L* §18g-f) has already distinguished the two uses of the absolute state of כל in these texts. In this respect we follow him with a few slight modifications.

(1) *The Absolute* כל *with Numbers.* כל is used before a number to express a sum or total and is usually found at the end of an enumeration. According to Joüon (*J* §48), "Ils emploient constamment l'indéterminé *kl* devant un nombre (presque toujours écrit en chiffres) indiquant compatibilité." In such a case he translates it, "total x" or "en tout." The latter translation seems to fit the sense better, because the phrase is obviously a *parenthetical addition*, making a technical document more precise. Since it most likely originated in lists, it cannot be accounted for easily within the ordinary syntactical framework of a simple sentence.

והבו פתף לגברן חלכין תרין אמן חד כל תלתה עלימן זילי,
"and give a ration to two Cilicians, one craftsman—in all, three of my servants" (*AD* 6:4).

אנת ואנתתך וברך כל 3,
"you and your wife and your son, in all three" (*AP* 6:4-5).
Similarly: *AP* [2:6];[5] 17:6; 46:15; *Bowm* A6, B7(?).

Special mention should be made here of כל 2, which is often translated "both." Joüon (*J* §48) objects to such a rendering of this phrase. He is probably right, for in all instances where it occurs it can be interpreted simply as the expression of a total after an enumeration.

אמר מחסיה בר נתן 1 ידניה בר נתן 1 כל 2,
"Maḥsiyah, son of Nathan, 1, Yedanyah, son of Nathan, 1, in all 2, said . . ." (*AP* 28:2).[6]
Similarly: *AP* 20:[2], 3, 16, [19], 20; 25:8, 21; 26:8; *BMAP* 3:10; 4:18; 12:3, 11, 33; *NSI* 71:1.[7]

In the foregoing cases כל is followed by a numeral. There are, however, instances in which כל is followed by a noun modified by a number. At first sight, such a phrase might seem to be a construct chain, but its similarity with the foregoing construction is obvious. It is basically the same type of phrase. Hence כל is in the absolute state and means "in all."

כל גברן 5,
"in all, five men" (*AP* 33:5 [at the end of a list of five proper names]).[8]

כל גברן 8,
"in all, 8 men" (*AD* 3:5).
Similarly: *AP* 24:27, [28], [29], [30]; 26:16; 73:17; *AD* 5:5; 12:2; *BMAP* 7:13.

That the form כל in such an expression is absolute and not construct is shown by the following examples:

אמר בגזשת . . . ונשן אובל . . . כל גבר 1 נשן 1,
"Said Bagazust . . . and the woman ᵓUbil . . . , in all, one man, one woman" (*BMAP* 3:3 [in this case כל cannot be construct]).[9]

בכל רעי 10,
"in all, 10 re'i" (*AP* 73:6 [cf. 73:17]).

בכל 5 ת[ ],
"in all, 5 t[. . .]" (*BMAP* 7:19).

The last two examples admittedly come from corrupt texts. Nevertheless, the readings are clear enough and show that כל cannot be taken as the construct.

(2) *Absolute* כל *in Apposition.* There are a few cases where כל follows either a noun in the emphatic state or a definite construct chain and means "all," in the sense of "the entirety of them (it)." In such a case it can only be explained as an absolute form used as an appositive.

אלהיא כל ישאלו שלמכי,
"May the gods all seek your welfare" (Cowley's translation; *AP* 39:1).[10]

כעך עבדיך ידניה וכנותה ויהודיא כל בעלי יב כן אמרין,
"Now your servants Yedanyah and his colleagues and the Jews, all (of them), inhabitants of Yeb, say as follows . . ." (*AP* 30:22).

Cowley has rightly translated this sentence, for the sense does not seem to be: "and the Jews, all the inhabitants of Yeb." That would imply that the Jews were the only inhabitants of Yeb. The sense is rather, "and all the Jews, inhabitants of Yeb."

Were it not for the first example, one might be tempted to label the second case as a "faute de grammaire," as does Joüon (*J* §49). His reason for doing so is that all the other examples of this construction are found in *AP* 30 (lines 14, 17, 22, 27), a document usually judged inferior to the other version found in *AP* 31. In the latter version the corresponding passages read כלא, a form frequently found in apposition. Consequently, Joüon suggests that כל in *AP* 30 be vocalized as *kullāᵓ*, regarding כל as *scriptio defectiva* for the emphatic state. This solution is hardly convincing, especially since Joüon himself, strangely enough, offers a parallel construction found in Syriac, where the absolute state of *kl* is used in apposition to an emphatic plural: *ṭělayê kol* (Matt 2:16S, for *πάντας τοὺς παῖδας* of the Greek).

Neither of these uses of the absolute state of כל is found in Biblical Aramaic.

II. כל *in the Construct State*

As might be expected, the most common use of the pronoun כל is that of its construct state. In this state it means "every" with a singular noun, and "all" with a plural or collective noun. An adequate treatment of the uses of כל in the construct state must account for the various types of words (and their states) that are found with it as *nomina recta.* We shall give, first of all, the uses of כל found in the Aramaic documents from Egypt, indicating whether or not the individual type of construct chain is also found in the Bible. Then we shall list types that are found only in Biblical Aramaic. The headings in the following classification indicate the type of *nomina recta* used with the construct *kl.*

(1) *The Compound Relative* זי.

מפטחיה הי שליטה בביתה . . . וכל זי איתי לה,
"Mipṭaḥiah is entitled to his house . . . and all that he has" (*AP* 15:9).[11]

וכל זי הנעלת בידה תהנפק,
"and all that she brought with her, she shall take away" (*BMAP* 2:8).
Similarly: *AP* 2:[16]; 15:24, 27; 40:3; 43:[10]; 49:4; *A* [132]; *AD* 13:[4]; *BMAP* 2:10; 7:22, 31, 35; *B-M* 9. The same construction (with די) is found in Dan 2:38; 6:8 (כל די יבעא בעו, "everyone who offers a petition"); Ezra 7:21, 23, 26.

(2) *The Absolute Singular.*

מן כל דין,
"from every court-action" (*AP* 6:16; 14:11).
Similarly: *AP* 10:9, 10, 17; 11:6; 37:2b; *A* [96], 97, 98, 127a,b;[12] *Dup* 175 conc 4; *AP* 78:5, 6.

בכל עדן,
"at all times" (*AP* 17:2; 30:2, 3, 26; 31:2, 3; 37:2a; 38:[2]; 39:1; 40:1; 41:[1]; 42:[1]; 56:1; *BMAP* 13:1; *Dup* 186 conc 2.

כל מנדעם זי,
"anything at all which" (*AP* 21:7; 49:3).

The following passages in Biblical Aramaic can be compared with these examples: Dan 2:10(bis), 35; 3:10, 28, 29; 4:6; 5:7; 6:5(bis), 6, 8, 13(bis), 16, 24; Ezra 6:11, 12; 7:16.[13] In Ezra 7:13 the absolute singular is a participle.

(3) *The Emphatic Singular.*

כל כספא,
"all the money" (*AP* 15:13; 42:[4]; 48:2; *BMAP* 2:6).
Similarly: *AP* 2:[13]; 17:2; 24:31; [33]; perhaps also *A* [36].

In Biblical Aramaic this usage is frequent. כל ארעא, "all the earth" (Dan 2:35).

Likewise Dan 2:39; 3:31; 4:8, 9, 17; 6:2, 4, 26; 7:23; Ezra 7:25. With a proper name: Ezra 6:17.

(4) *A Construct Chain.*

כל מאת שנזן,
"all the company of Siniddin" (*AP* 22:19).
Similarly: *AP* 78:5, 6; *BMAP* 7:[15]; 13:6.

This construction is found in Dan 2:12: לכל חכימי בבל, "all the wise men of Babylon" (direct object). Likewise in Dan 2:48(bis); 3:2, 3, 5, 7, 10, 15; 4:3, 15, 32; 5:8; 6:8, 27; Ezra 4:20; 7:16, 25 (participle).

(5) *A Singular Noun with a Suffix.*

כל כספך,
"all your money" (*AP* 11:7). No parallel is found in the Bible.

(6) *A Plural Noun with a Suffix.*

לכל עבדיך,
"for all your servants" (*A* 83).
Similarly: *AP* 45:6.

In Biblical Aramaic: Dan 4:34 (כל מעבדוהי, "all his works"); 5:23; 6:25.

(7) *The Absolute Plural.*

כל שערן וטלפחן,
"all the barley and lentils" (*AP* 2:5; 3:6).

כל נכסן,
"all the goods" (*AP* 14:4; 30:16a; *BMAP* 2:11, 12).
Similarly: *AP* 30:16b; 45:8; 75:[9]; *BMAP* 3:23 (perhaps singular).

The construct כל with an absolute plural *nomen rectum* is not found in the Bible.

(8) *A Participle with a Suffix.*

כל נטחוהי,
"all who meet him" (*A* 167).[14]

This usage is without parallel in Biblical Aramaic.

The preceding eight categories exhaust the usage of the construct of כל in the Aramaic documents of Egypt.[15] A few other combinations are found in the Bible that have not yet appeared in extrabiblical texts from Egypt.

(9) *A Noun in the Emphatic Plural.*

מן כל חייא,
"different from all (other) living beings" (Dan 2:30). Likewise Dan 2:44; 3:7, 31; 5:19; 6:26; 7:7, 14, 23, 27(bis); Ezra 7:21, 24.

(10) *A Demonstrative Pronoun.*

כל אלין תדק,
"it will break all these to pieces" (Dan 2:40). Likewise 5:22; 7:16.

It would be rash to try to draw any conclusion from the foregoing classes regarding the differences between Biblical and non-Biblical Aramaic. The fact that certain constructions appear only in the Bible and others only in the texts from Egypt is almost certainly due to the limited material on which our study is based.

III. *The Emphatic State* כלא

The form כלא has been the subject of some discussion. The dictionary of Gesenius-Buhl listed it as the emphatic state of כל.[16] This was certainly the common interpretation of כלא in Biblical Aramaic until 1923, when James A. Montgomery published an article on "Adverbial *kúlla* in Biblical Aramaic and Hebrew."[17] Instead of accepting the final *aleph* as the emphatic ending *(-āʾ)*, he proposed to regard it as the adverbial ending which is found on a few other words (see *L* §47b; *BLA* §55b). "As an adverb the form is to be explained as a survival of the ancient accusative in *-a,* sc. *kúlla,* not *kullā́.*"[18] Consequently, he suggested that the greeting in Ezra 5:7, שלמא כלא, should be translated, "Peace wholly (be yours)," instead of the usual "all peace." The same interpretation was applied likewise to Dan 2:40, חשל כלא, "smashing wholly," and to 4:25, כלא מטא, "wholly it came upon."

In 1927 Bauer and Leander hesitatingly approved of Montgomery's suggestion.[19] In the following year Leander, discussing כל and כלא in "Egyptian" Aramaic, regarded כל as construct or absolute, but refused to call כלא the emphatic form.[20] In 1932, G. R. Driver, apparently unaware of Montgomery's suggestion, gave the same adverbial interpretation to כלא in *A* 61, a passage already treated by the latter. In his publication, *Aramaic Documents of the Fifth Century, B.C.,* Driver translates כלא as the adverb, "altogether" (*AD* 8:2; 12:6, 7). This interpretation is also accepted by St. Segert in his study of these Aramaic documents.[21]

But P. Joüon objected to this adverbial interpretation of כלא both in Ezra 5:7 and in the Aramaic texts from Egypt (*J* §49). His study has been overlooked at times. Using the texts published by Cowley, he showed that כלא

should be interpreted always as a pronoun in the emphatic state: "est toujours substantif: 'la totalité, le tout'" (*J* §49). Applying this to Ezra 5:7, Joüon translates שלמא כלא, "'le salut, la totalité,' *sous-entendu* 'de lui.'"[22] After examining the texts, both biblical and extrabiblical, I think that Joüon was on the right track. It is necessary, however, to examine the arguments advanced by Montgomery, Driver, and Leander to see how valid they are for the adverbial interpretation of כלא.

Montgomery argued, first of all, that כלא is *milᶜel* in Ezra 5:7, "contrary to the universal rule of the Massora that the emphatic ending *-â* has the tone."[23] Hence, the form must come from *kúlla*, not *kullā̂*. But the greeting is obviously an abbreviated formula,[24] and as such could easily bear a pausal accent.[25] It might be objected that כלא in Dan 4:25 is *milᶜel* and not in pause. True, but then כלא in Dan 4:9, 18 is also *milᶜel* and cannot possibly be an adverb *(ûmāzôn lĕkóllâ˒-bēh).* If it is necessary to justify the Masoretic accent of *kóllâ˒*, the explanation of Bauer and Leander seems sufficient (*BLA* §25h). At any rate, the Masoretic accentuation should not be given preponderance over the syntactical evidence of documents which are fairly contemporaneous with the consonantal text of the Bible.

Secondly, Montgomery suggested that for the meaning, "all peace," we should rather expect כל שלמא or כלה שלמא (like Hebrew *kullô*). Perhaps we should, but as Joüon pointed out, we have extrabiblical evidence for שלמא כלא in the sense, "all peace." From the evidence to be offered below it will be seen that שלמא כלא means the same as the suffixal form would.

Thirdly, Driver remarks, "The use of *kl˒* now with a masc. sing. noun (*DL* 12:6, 7) and now with a fem. plur. noun as here [*AD* 8:2] (s. Cowley, *AP*, 292) shows that the final ˒ is adverbial, being probably the accusative termination. . . ."[26] But if כלא is understood as the emphatic state of the pronoun, it could be used as an appositive or as a resumptive to either a masculine or a feminine noun, singular or plural. Hence we must say that Driver's reason for maintaining that כלא is an adverb is not sufficient or convincing.

Fourthly, Montgomery appealed to the use of כלא in the Elephantine Papyri. When he wrote, he did not have Cowley's excellent edition of them and used only the following 12 examples from Sachau's edition: *AP* 30:11, 12a,b, 29, 30; 31:10, 22, 26, 29; 41:1; *A* 43, 61. Though the adverbial translation, "wholly," might conceivably be suitable in a few cases, it is certainly forced in the majority of the examples that Montgomery used. Moreover, there are now 23 instances of כלא in the Aramaic texts from Egypt on which to base one's judgment.

We shall divide the various occurrences of כלא in the Aramaic texts into five classes, according to the functions it has.

(1) *Independent Usage* (i.e., not as an appositive or resumptive pronoun).

כלא זי עביד לן ארשם לא ידע,

"of all that was done to us Arsames was ignorant" (*AP* 31:29; compare 30:30). The most natural explanation is to take כלא as a pronoun, the antecedent of זי. If כלא followed ידע, then we might have reason to construe it as an adverb; but it does not.

עקי ארז לובר חסין תמים אמן עשרן כלא יהיתה חליפתהם . . . על גנזא,
"planks of cedar, seasoned (?), strong, TMYS, 20 cubits—let relays of them bring it all to the treasury" (*AP* 26:13). This text is very difficult to interpret, since many of the words are not certain. It may be that כלא is a resumptive pronoun following the list of objects that precedes.

In Biblical Aramaic כלא is also used independently in Dan 2:40 ("and smashes everything"); 4:9, 18 ("and there was food for all on it"); 4:25 ("and all [this] befell N.").

(2) *Preceding a Noun.* In one case כלא is found preceding the noun that it qualifies:
אף כלא מליא באגרת חדה שלחן בשמן על דליה ושלמיה,
"We have also sent all the details in a letter in our name to Delaiah and Shelemiah" (*AP* 30:29). Compare Montgomery's translation: "Moreover, wholly we have sent a message in a letter . . ."![27] To take כלא as an adverb here is impossible, for it makes no sense. It qualifies מליא and means the same as כל מליא. Contamination has obviously taken place here, resulting from a confusion of two otherwise frequently used constructions: כל מליא and מליא כלא.[28] The two preceding uses are more or less isolated cases; the more normal constructions with כלא are the following.

(3) *As an Appositive Following a Definite Noun.*

וע]ל עטתה ומלוהי הות אתור כלא],
"and on whose advice and words all Assyria (depended)" (*A* 43).

[ ]ויהודיא כלא בעלי יב כן אמרן,
"and all the Jews, citizens of Yeb, say as follows" (*AP* 31:22). Montgomery did not attempt to translate this sentence, using כלא as an adverb. The fuller context of the sentence can be found in *AP* 30:22. It is difficult to understand how כלא could be an adverb between a noun and its appositive (בעלי יב). Cowley translated the phrase well: "and the Jews, all of them, citizens of Yeb."

ונצ[לה . . .]ויהודיא כלא זי תנה,
"and we shall pr[ay . . .] and all the Jews who are here" (*AP* 31:26; compare 30:26 for the full context).

[שלם אחי אלה]יא כלא ישא[לו]שגי בכ[ל עדן],
"may all the gods seek the welfare of my brother abundantly at all times" (*AP* 41:1). Montgomery used this case as his chief example to illustrate Ezra 5:7; he remarked, "Here again not *klhn* nor *kl ᵓlhyᵓ*; the form is not grammatically related, but is evidently adverbial, 'altogether.'"[29] But what Montgomery

failed to note was the peculiar resumptive character of כלא, which enables it to be used either as an appositive immediately following a noun or a construct chain or as a pronoun separated from the word it qualifies and placed immediately before the verb. The position of the verb in many of the sentences of the Aramaic texts from Egypt is peculiar; it is often found near the end of the sentence. Hence it is not strange that כלא would be used to resume a subject placed at the beginning of the sentence. In *AP* 41:1 we have the verb following the subject and כלא immediately; compare the other examples below.

שלם מראי אלהיא כלא [ישאלו] שגי בכל עדן,
"May all the gods seek the welfare of my lord abundantly at all times" (*BMAP* 13:1).

Appositive כלא has been restored by Cowley in *AP* 6:[5]. In the obscure passage of *AP* 26:17 כלא may be an appositive or it may be a resumptive. From the foregoing examples it should be clear that שלמא כלא of Ezra 5:7 is the same type of construction and means "all peace"—an abbreviated formula similar to those of *AP* 41:1 and *BMAP* 13:1.

שלם אמך וינקיא כלא,
"Greetings from your mother and all the children" (*Pad* I r 5).

(4) *As an Appositive to a Construct Chain or Its Equivalent.*

ועל עטתה ומלוהי חיל [אתו]ר כלא הוו,
"and by his counsel and words all the army of Assyria were (guided)" (*A* 60-61 [Cowley's translation]; cf. *A* [55-56]).[30]

כזי נשי ביתן כלא א[בדו],
"when all the women of our house perished" (*AD* 8:2). G. R. Driver translates: "when the women of our house perished altogether." This translation is, of course, possible in this case; but judged over against the other instances, it loses its plausibility.

חמר לם זי בפפרם ועבור ארקתא כלא נחתחור לקח עבד לנפשה,
"Now the wine which was in Papremis and the grain from the fields Nehtihûr has taken it all (and) made it over to himself" (*AD* 12:6). (Or possibly: "N. has taken the wine that was in P. and all the grain from the fields . . .").

ואגורי אלה[י] מצריא [כ]ל[א מגרו],
"And they overthrew all the temples of the gods of the Egyptians" (*AP* 31:[13]). Cf. *AP* 30:14.

אלך נחש ומטלל אגורא זך כלא[ ],
"those . . . , of bronze, and the roof of the temple, all of it" (*AP* 31:10).

ומטלל עקהן זי ארז כלא עם שירית אשרנא ואחרן זי תמה הוה כלא באשה שרפו,
"and all the roof-beams of cedar which were with the rest of the furnishings and other things which were there, all of it, they burned with fire" (*AP* 30:11-

12). Here the first כלא is an appositive following a זי-clause which is an equivalent of a construct chain. The second כלא really belongs in the following category.

(5) *As a Resumptive Pronoun, Separated from the Phrase It Resumes.*

בזנה זי עביד לן כלא ארשם לא ידע,
"of all this which was done to us Arsames was ignorant" (*AP* 30:30).

ומזרקיא זי זהבא וכספא ומנדעמתא זי הוה באגורא זך כלא לקחו ולפשיהון עבדו,
"and the basons [sic] of gold and silver and everything that was in that temple, all of it, they took and made their own" (*AP* 30:12b [Cowley's translation]).

[ ]בעה באיש לאגורא זך כלא קטילו,
". : . sought to do evil to that temple, all of them, were killed" (*AP* 31:16; cf. *AP* 30:16-17 for the complete context).

כעת חמרא עבורא ומנדע[ם] אחרן זי לקחת כלא התבה,
"now restore all the wine, grain, and anything else that you have taken" (*AD* 12:7).

If Cowley's restoration in *AP* 27:18 is correct, we have another instance of this construction.

From the foregoing examples it can be seen why we prefer to regard כלא as the emphatic state of כל. Moreover, if כל is used in these texts as a construct and an absolute, is it not natural to regard כלא as the emphatic state of the same word, a pronoun?[31]

IV. *The Form* כלה

Aside from *A* 166, where Cowley has restored כל[ך], the only form of כל that occurs with what looks like a suffix in the Aramaic texts from Egypt is כלה. Leander (*L* §18e) and Joüon (*J* §49) regard כלה as the suffixal form. The suffixal form כלה is found in Old Aramaic (Panammu 17, 19) and in Biblical Aramaic (כלהון, Dan 2:38; כלהון [K for כלהין Q], Dan 7:19), not to mention later types of Aramaic. Now in the Aramaic texts from Egypt כלה is found at least four times and is restored in three other places by Cowley. Although the emphatic ending in these texts is normally *aleph*, as noted by Leander and Baumgartner,[32] *he* is also used at times as the emphatic ending. Is it not possible, then, that כלה is just another spelling for כלא? The syntax is the same in both cases. Consequently, it is impossible to state categorically that כלה is not the suffixal form. If כל[ך] in *A* 166 were not a restoration, it could be cited as evidence that the suffixal form is used in these texts. However, כל[א] could be restored just as easily, with the same meaning: "Thou art all thorns to him who touches thee" (Cowley's translation).

In five cases we find אתור כלה in the same sense as אתור כלא, "all Assyria"; but three of them are restorations of the editor (*A* 12, 55, [2], [18], [28]). It would have been just as easy to restore כלא.

Other instances:

מפתחיה הי שליטה בביתה . . . וכל זי איתי לה על אנפי ארעא כלה,
"Miptahiah shall be entitled to his house . . . and all that he possesses on the face of the whole earth" (*AP* 15:20, or perhaps: "on the face of the earth, all of it"—taking כלה as a resumptive pronoun, referring to all that precedes).

אנה ענני גבר אחרן אמי ואבי אח ואחה ואיש אחרן לא ישלט בביתה כלה,
"I, Anani, or another man, my mother or my father, my brother or my sister, or another person, shall not be entitled to this house—any (part) of it" (*BMAP* 4:20). Note also that in this example the emphatic state of בית is written with *he*.[33]

[פ]רסכן זי כלי כלה,
"Your pay which is withheld, all of it"(*Pad* I v 6). Cf. also *Pad* II v 2 and *Pad* I r 5 (p. 224 below).

The foregoing study of the syntax of כל in the Aramaic texts found in Egypt sheds light on the Biblical Aramaic usage of the same word.[34] Further aspects of it in other areas remain to be studied.[35]

NOTES TO CHAPTER 9

*Originally published in *Bib* 38 (1957) 170-84 under the title, "The Syntax of *kl, klʾ* in the Aramaic Texts from Egypt and in Biblical Aramaic."

[1]See p. 75 n. 3 and p. 76 n. 21 above.

[2]*Laut- und Formenlehre des Ägyptisch-Aramäischen* (Hildesheim: G. Olms, 1966); originally published in *Göteborgs högskolas årsskrift* 34/4 (1928) 1-135. Leander's study was based almost wholly on the edition of the Elephantine material published by A. E. Cowley, *Aramaic Papyri of the Fifth Century B.C.* (p. 76 above, n. 21).

[3]The major part of this treatment was undertaken by me in a doctoral dissertation presented to the Johns Hopkins University in 1956. Written under the direction of Profs. W. F. Albright and T. O. Lambdin, it was entitled, *The Syntax of Imperial Aramaic Based on the Documents Found in Egypt* (Baltimore, 1956 [unpublished]). The present essay is an expansion of a small section of chap. 1, "The Syntax of the Pronoun." The syntax of these texts had been treated only in a very skimpy way in earlier publications. Less than one page of Sayce and Cowley's folio publication, *Aramaic Papyri Discovered at Assuan* (p. 76 above, n. 21), was devoted to a few points of syntax. When E. Sachau published *Aramäische Papyrus und Ostraka* (p. 76 above, n. 21) in 1911, he discussed a few syntactical problems in a section of his "Grammatischer Anhang," entitled "Zur Syntax und Wortfolge" (2 pages). Cowley promised a grammatical study of the Aramaic papyri in 1923, but this study has never appeared. Leander brought out his excellent monograph in 1928, but it was devoted exclusively to phonology and morphology. A few syntactical features of the papyri were studied by P. Joüon ("Notes grammaticales, lexicographiques et philologiques sur les papyrus araméens d'Egypte," *MUSJ* 18 [1934] 1-90). As a result, F. Rosenthal was able to point out the lack of a comprehensive study of the syntax of the Aramaic of this period (*Die aramaistische Forschung* [p. 75 above, n. 2] 48) that would compare with that of Bauer and Leander's treatment of the syntax of Biblical Aramaic. My own dissertation sought to remedy

that lack in part at least; it has not been published because it was not conceived along the lines of modern studies in syntax. It followed the method used by Bauer and Leander in their study of Biblical Aramaic. What is really needed is a study of these Official Aramaic texts, conducted along the lines that R. Degen used for his study of the Old Aramaic texts in *Altaramäische Grammatik* (p. 75 above, n. 16). The grammar recently published by S. Segert, *Altaramäische Grammatik* (p. 23 above, n. 53) has an entire section devoted to "Funktion der Wörter im Satz" (pp. 318-445); but it is not a study restricted to Official Aramaic, since Segert understands "Old Aramaic" in the sense that F. Rosenthal used the expression (see p. 58 above). It mixes the syntax, therefore, of texts from the periods that I should call Old, Official, and Middle Aramaic.

[4](Halle/S.: M. Niemeyer, 1927; reprinted, Hildesheim: Olms, 1962). Their remarks on the syntax of "Egyptian" Aramaic can be found in numbers 72b,c, 73b, 81v, 84b, 85d, 87e,f,i, 88j,k,l,m, 91g, 95j,n,o, 96f, 98p, 99o, 100u, 101h, 103g, 104e, 106c, 107j, 108q,t, 109x, 111c.

[5]In this essay the text is cited with the restorations of the editor, but the reference to a text containing a restoration is always bracketed. This policy has been adopted, since some of the restorations are certain and obvious, while others are only probable and vary greatly in degree. Hence each bracketed reference must be judged individually and not simply dismissed as a restored example. The bracket merely indicates that some part of the text is restored; despite the restoration the syntax is often clear.

[6]Joüon (*J* §48) remarks: "Autre exemple avec ce total minimum: 20,2sq. 'Ont dit Menaḥem et ᶜAnaniyah, total 2, fils de Mešullam fils de Selomen à Yadenyah et à Maḥseyah, total 2, fils de Asḥor. . .'. Les sens n'est pas 'both sons of . . .' (Cowley), qui se dirait *kltryn* (26,8)." Though I agree with Joüon's interpretation of *AP* 20:2, it seems far from certain that *kltryn* would have to be used to express the idea of "both."

[7]Leander, after having mentioned that כל is used in the absolute state with numerals (*L* §18f-g), subsequently lists the examples, כל תרין and כל 2, under כל as a construct (with the dual—*L* §18i). This seems illogical. Certainly the sole instance of the number written out in full as one word with כל (*AP* 26:8 כלתרין) does not prove that כל is a construct in this case.

[8]Bauer and Leander (*BLA* §88k, n. 2) cite this instance together with *AP* 30:16 as an example of the construct of כל. But the construction here is not the same as in 30:16, where no numeral is present.

[9]Objection may be made that in *BMAP* 3:3 1 גבר is written above the line as an afterthought, and hence is not valid as evidence. However, it seems quite certain that the addition was made to remedy a scribal omission, when the writer reread the document. No change in thought is the result of the addition; it is clear that 1 גבר should have been written with the rest from the start. For a parallel to the construction discussed in the text in Biblical Hebrew, see Jos 21:39 (*kōl ᶜārîm ʾarbaᶜ*).

[10]In this example כל cannot possibly be the construct, and there is no reason to construe it with שלמכי. One cannot exclude the possibility, however, of a scribal error in this instance; see p. 213 below (III, 3).

[11]For a full treatment of this text, see pp. 243–71 below.

[12]The letters a, b, c in a reference are used to indicate the first, second, and third occurrences of the word in the line.

[13]See the remarks in *BLA* §88k on this particular construction.

[14]On this form, see *BLA* §38b; P. Joüon, *Bib* 22 (1941) 268.

[15]כל also occurs in the following places, too corrupt to permit analysis: *AP* 22:5, 31; 31:15; 73:2.

[16](17th ed.; Berlin: Springer, 1949) 910. See also E. Kautzsch, *Grammatik des Biblisch-Aramäischen* (Leipzig: F. C. W. Vogel, 1884) 150 ("das Heil die Gesamtheit = alles Heil" in Ezra 5:7); H. L. Strack, *Grammatik des Biblisch-Aramäischen* (Munich: C. H. Beck, 1911) 50*; K. Marti, *Kurzgefasste Grammatik der Biblisch-Aramäischen Sprache* (3d ed.; Berlin: Reuther und Reichard, 1925) 74*; L. Palacios, *Grammatica aramaico-biblica* (Rome: Desclée, 1933) 63.

[17]*JAOS* 43 (1923) 391-95.

[18]Ibid., 394.

[19]*BLA* §25h.

[20] *L* §18n.

[21] "Aramäische Studien: I. Die neuen Editionen von Brooklyn Papyri und Aršāms Briefe in ihrer Bedeutung für die Bibelwissenschaft," *ArOr* 24 (1956) 395.

[22] "Notes de grammaire et de lexicographie araméenne," *Bib* 22 (1941) 265.

[23] *JAOS* 43 (1923) 391.

[24] Kraeling (*BMAP*, 296) asks whether the שלמא כלא of Ezra 5:7 could be an abridgement of the "paganizing phraseology" found in the greeting often used in the Aramaic letters. This is hardly likely, even though it may be an abbreviation of a longer formula. See p. 191 above.

[25] So E. Kautzsch, *Grammatik* (n. 16 above), 39.

[26] *AD*, 27.

[27] *JAOS* 43 (1923) 393.

[28] Leander remarks (*L* §18n): "Dass *klᵓ* auch v o r dem Nomen stehen kann (30,29 . . .), spricht für die These Montgomerys, dass es kein St. det., sondern vielmehr ein erstarrter ursem. Akkusativ auf -*ā* ist." Does it really? "Il est même fort douteux que 'totalement' puisse s'exprimer par l'accusatif de *kl.* En arabe, où l'accusatif adverbial est très développé, 'totalement' ne s'exprime pas par *kullā*" (*J* 49 n. 4).

[29] *JAOS* 43 (1923) 392.

[30] Cf. Zenjirli, *Panammu* 17.

[31] Montgomery himself admitted, "In Syriac *klᵓ* is found, apparently, as the emphatic" (*JAOS* 43 [1923] 393).

[32] *L* §15c; W. Baumgartner, "Das Aramäische im Buche Daniel," *ZAW* 45 (1927) 91.

[33] ביתה כלה is also found in Zenjirli, *Panammu* 19.

[34] In the Hermopolis West Papyri the construct state כל occurs three times (1:12; 2:15; 3:7). The form כלה seems to be an appositive in *HermWP* 4:12, but the meaning of the noun to which it is in apposition (סחתה) is unknown. The editors translate the phrase thus: "Saluti a tutto il vicinato(?)" (p. 399). Similarly, the instance of כלה in *HermWP* 4:4.

[35] In 1QapGen the construct state כל is found with a variety of *nomina recta* (nouns and pronouns): 2:4, 7, 16ter; 6:2; 7:1; 10:13; 11:17; 12:10; 16:11; 19:19, 20, 23; 20:3, 4, 5bis, 6bis, 7, 9, 12, 13, 15bis, 16, 17, 18, 19ter, 20bis, 24, 28; 21:1, 3, 5, 9, 10, 11bis, 12bis, 13, 14, 19, 21, 25, 26, 27, 33; 22:1, 3, 10, 11quater, 12, 13, 15, 17, 22bis, 24bis, 25, 29, 30, 33. The form is probably construct in 1Q*20* 1 i 8; 1 ii 4. The emphatic state כולא is used in apposition in 1QapGen 19:10, בארעא דא כולא, "in all this land." The non-appositional use of כולא (= "everything, all") is found in 1QapGen 2:5, [10], 19, 20, 21, 22; 20:13. In a number of instances the suffixal forms of כול emerge in this text; they are used both in apposition and in a non-appositional construction. Thus, in apposition: כולהון (12:10, 13; 20:19-20); כולהא (10:13; 16:13); non-appositional: ולנשי כולנא, "and the wives of all of us" (12:16); ארי הוא רוחא כתש לכולהון, "for the spirit afflicted all of them" (20:20); cf. 20:13; 22:9, 26; לעלא מן כולהן, "high above all of them" (20:7).

In 11QtgJob the construct state כל is found in 2:8; 25:3; 28:2; 29:3; 30:5; 32:7; 34:7b; 37:2; 38:4, 5ter, 6, 7 (and probably in 22:[5], 7a). The emphatic state כלא is used in a non-appositional sense in 37:3, whereas the suffixal form כלכון is found once (11:[2]).

Chapter 10

The Padua Aramaic Papyrus Letters*

The Museo Civico of Padua acquired some time ago fragments of three papyrus letters, which are written in Aramaic and are apparently related to similar Aramaic documents of fifth-century Egypt already known to the scholarly world. Their provenience in Egypt is unfortunately not certain,[1] a fact which complicates the interpretation of the texts. Edda Bresciani has published a study of these letters and has supplied excellent photographs of the papyri.[2] Her study is well done, but there is always room for further comments on the interpretation of such documents. We propose to give an English translation of the texts, suggest some restorations of the lacunae and add several remarks about the language and contents of the letters, thus treating certain points which the original editor has passed over.

The letter, of which the beginning and the end of the lines are unfortunately lost, was written by a father (Osea bar Pet. . .) to his son (Shelomam bar Osea), who had gone off on a caravan. We gather that the son had written to his parents and mentioned something about clothes; the father who resides with the family in Migdol in Lower Egypt writes to inform his son that some salary which is due to him has not been paid and takes up the question of the clothes. If the greeting of the first line of the *verso* is correctly interpreted by the editor, it would seem that the son has gone with the caravan to Upper Egypt, to the vicinity of Elephantine. That seems to be the reason why the father begins the letter with a greeting or blessing invoked in the name of the god of the area where the son is.

Padua Papyrus I (= *Pad* I)

Text[3]

Verso

1 [שלם ב]ית יהו ביב אל ברי שלמם [מ]ן אחוך אושע שלם ושררת [שגיא הושרת לך]
2 [כעת מ]ן יום זי אזלת בארחא זך בר[י] לי טיב אף אמך כעת ברך אנת [ליהו אלהא]
3 [זי יח]וני אנפיך בשלם כעת מן יום [ז]י נפקתם מן מצרין פרס לא י[היב לכן]
4 [וכזי] קבלן לפחותא על פרסכן תנה ב[מ]גדל כן אמיר לן לאמר על זנה[ ]
5 [קבל ל]ספריא ויתיהב לכן כעת כזי תאתון מצרין על[ ]

6 [פ]רסכן זי כלי כלה כעת איך ביתא עביד ואיך נפקת הן יהו[ה]
7 [ש]לם ומחבל לא איתי גבר הוי אל תתאשד עד תאתה [מנפי]

Recto

1 [ ]
2 [כתבת]באגרתא זילך על כתון ולבש כתונך ולבשך עבידן[ ]
3 [ ]לאמך עבדת אל תמלי לבת בזי לא איתית המו מנפי כזי ת[תוב]
4 [תנה איתי] המו קדמתך כעת זבנת לי אנה [כ]תן 1 זי כתן כעת[ ]
5 [ ]דן ולבש עד תאתה שלם אמך וינקיא כלא כעת תנה הוין[ ]
6 [ב ?]למחר כתבת אגרתא זא כע[ת] כן שמיע לן לאמר תתפטרן[ ]

Address

7 [ ] אל אחי שלמם בר [או]שע אחוך אושע בר פטן[ ]

Translation

Verso

[1][Greetings to the temp]le of Yahu in Elephantine! To my son, Shelomam; from your "brother," Osea. [I send you] greetings and prosperity [in abundance!] [2][Sin]ce the day when you went on that caravan, my son, all goes well with me and your mother too. May you be blessed [by Yahu, the God, [3]who may gr]ant me to see your face (again) in peace! Since the day when you left Lower Egypt, the salary has not been gi[ven to you. [4]And when] we lodged a complaint with the governors about your salary here in [Mig]dol, we were told thus: "About this (matter) [5][complain to] the clerks and it will be given to you." When you come (back) to Lower Egypt, about [[6]] your [sa]lary, which has been withheld, all of it. As the house has been made, and as you have departed, so (?) there is [[7] pe]ace, and there is no one who (tries to) seize (it) in pledge (?). Be a man; do not dissipate; until you come (back) [to Memphis]

Recto

[1][ ] [2][You wrote] in your letter about a tunic and clothing. Your tunic and clothing have been made [[3]] for your mother I have done. Do not be angry, because I have not brought them to Memphis. When you [return [4]here, I shall bring] them (there) before you. I have bought for myself a tunic of linen. Now [[5]] . . . and clothing until you come. Greetings from your mother and all the children! Here we have been [[6] On the ? (day)] of Meḥir I have written this letter. We have (just) heard a rumor to the effect that you will be released [ ]

Address

To my "brother" Shelomam bar Osea; your "brother" Osea bar Peṭ[ ].

Notes

Verso

1. [שלם ב[ית יהו ביב: This is Bresciani's restoration, based on similar beginnings of the papyrus letters from Hermopolis (see p. 190 above). The

other Hermopolis letters mention greetings sent to the temples of Nabu, *Bnt* (= Banit, "creatrix"), Bethel, Malkat-šĕmayin. This suggests that letters were begun with a greeting or blessing invoked in the name of the deity of the place in which the addressee was found. The expression בית יהה is found on an ostracon studied by A. Dupont-Sommer, "La maison de Yahvé et vêtements sacrés à Eléphantine," *JA* 235 (1946-47) 79-87, esp. p. 86.

יהו ביב: The veneration of Yahu in Yeb (= Elephantine) is most clearly expressed in *BMAP* 12:2, יהו אלהא שכן יב ברתא, "Yahu, the God, who dwells in Elephantine, the fortress." The simpler formula used here, יהו ביב, occurs in *BMAP* 1:2; 9:2. Cf. יהו אלהא זי ביב ברתא (*BMAP* 2:2; 4:2; 10:2); see further *BMAP* 3:3; 4:10; *AP* 6:4; 25:6; 30:6, 24-26; 31:7, 24-25; 34:8-9.

ברי: This address, which is used again in line 2, indicates the real relationship between the writer and the addressees. It is confirmed by אמך (I v 2; I v 5). See p. 190 above.

אל: The preposition, "to," is used at this period almost exclusively in the addresses of letters; see *AP* 30:1; 31:1; 37:1, 17; 38:1, 12; 39:1, 5; 40:1, 5; 41:1, 9; 63:6(?); 67:8; 70:1; *RES* 3.1300; *Cl-G Ost* 277:1 (*RHR* 128 [1944] 29); *Cl-G Ost* 70: conc. 1 (*CRAIBL,* 1947, 177); *BMAP* 13:[1], 9; *Pad* II v 1, r 1; *Pad* III.1; *RES* §1300. Contrast the addresses in *AD* 1:1; 2:1; 3:1, etc., where the more common preposition of this period, ᶜ*l*, is found; likewise in *RES,* 3.1295.

שלמם: This name occurs in *AP* 49:1 with the same spelling. The full spelling, *šlwmm*, is found elsewhere (*AP* 1:2, 10; 20:2, 6, 12, 13, 17, 19; 46:2, [8], 11, 16. M. Noth, *IPN*, p. 165, regards it as a form of *šālôm* + *-ām*; but he is inclined to separate *šlmm* and *šlwmm* for a reason which is not apparent.

אחוך: See I r 7, where the writer again calls himself אחוך. It may seem that אח is used here merely in the sense of "kinsman." Indeed, in *AP* 40:1, 5 E. Sachau had been confronted with a similar problem and understood אח as "step-brother." But A. E. Cowley corrected this, pointing out that אח was used rather as a polite form of address to an equal, comparing *AP* 21:2, 11. This usage is now confirmed by the clear example in this letter, for it is obvious that it is a father who writes to his son, and uses אח both of himself and of his son in the address. See further *AP* 41:1, 9 and *Cl-G Ost* 277:1-2 (אל אחי חגי אחוך ירחו, which H. L. Ginsberg [*ANET*, p. 491] interprets as a "Greeting from a pagan to a Jew"). Compare also the use of אח in 1QapGen 2:9, where Bit-enosh employs it in addressing her husband, Lamech.

אושע: Osea, shortened form of אושעיה (*AP* 20:18), "Yahu has saved, helped." See M. Noth, *IPN*, p. 176. The shortened form occurs also in *AP* 12:2; 13:14; 22:90, etc. Note that whereas Osea's name is Semitic, his father's name is Egyptian—a phenomenon already well attested in the Elephantine texts.

שלם ושררת [שגיא הושרת לך]: Restored by Bresciani on the basis of *AD* 3:1; 5:1; 13:1; to be read also in *AP* 42:1.

2. [כעת]: Supplied on the basis of further examples which occur regularly at the beginning of sentences; see I v 2, 3, 5, 6; I r 4, 5, 6. It marks the beginning

of a sentence (something like the English "stop"), and meant originally "now." However, for the sake of the smoothness of the English translation we have omitted it.

[מ]ן יום זי: See line 3. The emphatic state of יום might have been expected here, but this and similar uses of the absolute state before a rel. pron. are fairly frequent in Aramaic: . . . ביום זי אלהן (Sf I B 31); ביום זי יעבד כן (Sf I C 20); ביום זי אמות (*Cl-G Ost* 175: conc. 1 [*CRAIBL* 1947, 181]); עד יום זי אשלמנהי (*AP* 11:3, 10); אתר די אנתה יתב (1QapGen 21:9); מן יום די נפקתה (1QapGen 22:28). See also Ezra 7:15; *BLA* §88m.

אזלת: 2d sg. masc. pf. peal. The 2d sg. is used here, as in the suffixal forms (אחוך [I v 1; I r 7]; אמך [I v 2; I r 5]; אנפיך [I v 3]; זילך, כתונך, לבשך [I r 2]; קדמתך [I r 4]); the verbal forms (נפקת [I v 6]; תתאשד [I v 7]; תאתה [I v 7; I r 5]; תמלי [I r 3]); and the independent personal pronoun (אנת [I v 2]). But it is to be noted that the father also addresses his son with the 2d pl. form, apparently without any distinction of meaning. Thus we find נפקתם (I v 3 [which might at first sight seem to refer to the caravan as a whole; cf. line 6]); תאתון (I v 5); תתפטרן (I r 6). There are also plural suffixal forms: פרסכן. As Bresciani rightly points out, כן- is not the 2d pl. fem. suffix, but the masc. with the so-called later spelling.

בארחא זך: "On that caravan." Cf. Hebr. ארחה, "travelling company, caravan" (Gen 37:25; Isa 21:13; Job 6:18-19), a meaning connected with the Hebr. and Aram. word ארח, "road, way."

לי טיב: We have here not the adjective *ṭāb*, but the impersonal use of the 3d sg. masc. pf. peal, as in *BMAP* 1:[4]; 3:6; 12:6, 14, 26; etc. *A* 67 (כנותה ועטתא זא טיבת על) shows that the form is verbal. Cf. *L* §39b.

ברך אנת: Bresciani completes the line with ליהו אלהא, understanding *brk* as defective spelling for *bryk* and comparing the Hebrew expression in 1 Sam for *bryk* and comparing the Hebrew expression in 1 Sam 15:13; 23:21, etc. She admits that קדם יהו אלהא would also be possible, comparing the Carpentras stele (*CIS*, 2. 141; Cooke, *NSI*, §75), line 3. In fact, both *l* and *qdm* are well attested in Aramaic blessing formulas found in graffiti, so that either can be restored here. Bresciani admits that they are equivalent but thinks that the form with *l* "è yahvista ed ebraica, mentre la seconda è tipicamente aramaica" (pp. 20-21). But ל precedes the name חנם (= Khnum) in *Cl-G Ost* 70: conc. 3 (cited by her) and is also found with the names of other Egyptian gods (לחר [*RES* 960, 961]; לאסרי [*RES* 1366]; לוסרי [*RES* 1788]). See further the Ammonite seal published by N. Avigad, חתם מנגאנרת ברך למלכם, "Seal of Mannu-ki-Inurta, blessed by Milkom" (*IEJ* 15 [1965] 222-28). ברך קדם is found also in *RES* 607, 1364, 1368, 1370, 1376, 1377, 1817. In most of these cases the defective spelling *brk* is found, agreeing with the usage here.

3. [זי יח]וני אנפיך בשלם: Lit: "who may make your face known to me in peace." To support this restoration, Bresciani cites similar formulas from the letters of Hermopolis with either the verb חוא or חזא. She points out that this

formula should be read also in *BMAP* 13:3-4. It should preferably be restored also in *AP* 34:7, [עד אלהיא יהוונ]י אנפיך בשלם. Similarly in *AP* 41:8.

נפקתם: 2d pl. masc. pf. peal; see the note on אנלת, line 2.

מצרין: "Lower Egypt," as in Isa 11:11; Jer 1:15; Ezek 30:16, since the context suggests that מגדל and מנפי are in the area, and the greetings in the first line suggest the contrast with Elephantine in Upper Egypt. However, מצרין is often found in the Elephantine texts as the name for Egypt in general (*AP* 30:13, 14, 24; 31:12; 32:2; 38:7; 64:20; 66:6; 71:8, 26; 72:2, 4; cf. *AD* 7:2, 4. See Bresciani's remarks on the identification of מגדל.

פרס: "Salary." The word is found with this meaning in *AP* 11:6; 2:16. Is it a *qatl*-type (like *parsīn*, Dan 5:25) or a *qatāl*-type (like the later Aramaic פְּרָס; cf. G. Dalman, *ANHW*, 350)?

לא י[היב לכן]: "Has not been given to you." Or possibly לא י[הבו לכן], "they (indefinite) have not given (it) to you." I prefer the passive participle because of *AP* 24:42; [י]היב פתף לחיל, "a ration has been given to the army." Bresciani notes the similar use of פרס and פתף in the Elephantine texts, and in *BMAP* 11:5 the פתפא is a ration apparently paid regularly to members of the military דגל stationed in Elephantine; it is doled out from the אוצר מלכא, "the royal storehouse" (11:4), which may be the same as בית פרסא (*BMAP* 9:4, which Kraeling merely transliterates as "beth parsa"). Cf. *AP* 11:6; 2:16. The passive participle of peal is otherwise found in this letter (אמיר [I v 4]; עביד [I v 6; I r 2]; שמיע [I r 6]).

4. קבלן: "We lodged a complaint." This meaning of קבל is well attested in the Elephantine texts. Four formulas are found:

קבל על (object of complaint) קדם (authorities): *AP* 6:5, 16; 10:12, 18; 47:7.
קבל על (object of complaint) ל (authorities): *BMAP* 9:19; 12:28; so here.
קבל על (object of complaint) + direct object (= authorities): *AP* 8:13; *BMAP* 1:5; 1QapGen 20:14.
קבל על (person complained against) בגו (object of complaint): *BMAP* 1:4, 5, 6.

Note that the 1 pl. ending is only *-n*, which is usual for this period; cf. *L* §25a, 12f.

לפחותא: Bresciani has simply transliterated this form, "ai *pḥwt*ʾ," comparing פחה, "governatore," but she is apparently reluctant to use this meaning here. The meaning is clear, however, from *AP* 30:29 (פחת שמרין); 30:1 (פחת יהוד); *B* 18, 38 ([פ]חתא); Dan 3:2, 3, 27 (פחותא). The latter is precisely the form which we have here; it is, furthermore, found there in a list of other rulers like satraps, etc. It is related to the Akkadian *pi/aḫatu*. Hence, the meaning "governor" is to be preferred to that which Bresciani uses in her note, "funzionari (evidentemente collegiali) del 'tesoro'." Moreover, whenever קבל is used in the papyri of lodging a complaint, we find that it is lodged before either דין, סגן, or מרא, names which suggest some person of judicial or executive function in the colony. So too here; the parents lodged the complaint with the "governors," who referred them to the ספריא, the treasury "clerks."—See P. Nober, *VD* 39 (1961) 110-11; E. Y. Kutscher, "פחוא and Its Cognates." *Tarbiẓ* 30 (1960-61) 112-19; G. Garbini, "The Dating of Post-Exilic Stamps," *Excavations at Ramat Raḥel: Seasons 1959 and 1960* (Rome: *Centro di studi semitici*, 1962) 61-68, esp. p. 68 n. 42; *BA* 24 (1961) 110-11.

פרסכן: "Your salary." The suffix is 2d pl. masc., כן- being written with a *nun* instead of the *mem* of the older form, which is otherwise more frequent at this period. Cf. *L* §12m, x, ב. This is apparently the earliest known occurrence of כן- as 2d pl. masc. suffix, but the 3d pl. masc. ending הן- is well attested: להן (*AP* 34:7; 37:4, 14 [to be compared with *BMAP* 4:21]; בהן (*AP* 34:6; 82:11 [to be compared with *AP* 31:6]); ביניהן (*BMAP* 12:19, 21 [to be compared with *BMAP* 3:8, 10; 6:6, 11; *AP* 13:14; 25:7]).

ב[מ]גדל: "In Migdol." Identified with Migdol (Jer 44:1; 46:14) in מצרין (see line 3) by Bresciani. It is located most probably at Tell el-Heir in the east delta about 18 kms. southwest of Pelusium.

לאמר: The stereotyped formula which preserves the old peal inf. without preformative *mem*; see *AP* 2:3; 5:3; 6:4; etc. Contrast *AP* 32:2; 43:2; *A* 115.

5. ספריא: "The clerks" of the treasury, as in *AP* 2:12, 14 (ספרי אוצרא). Cf. *AP* 17:1, 6. Both documents deal with the supplying of grain to a garrison and the ספריא are probably recorders engaged in the work.

לכן: See note on פרסכן in line 4 above. Here, however, the plural may really be meant; but it is not certain, for the father uses the 1 pl. of himself (apparently) in line 4, קבלן.

מצרין: Used with a verb of motion toward it, but without a preposition. Such a construction is found elsewhere in Aramaic: see Sf III 5 (יהכן חלב); *Pad* I r 3 (איתית המו מנפי); *BMAP* 13:3 (יהיתון מנפי); *AP* 42:7 (חת מנפי [contrast 42:11, הן נחת אנת למנפי]); *AP* 83:2 (מטא צחא מנפי); *AD* 6:2, 4, 5. Contrast *AP* 37:11. See further p. 252 below.

6. כלי: "Has been withheld." This specific sense of the verb also occurs in *AP* 37:13, 14, 15.

כלה: Is this the suffixal form of כל or the emph. state written with *he* instead of *aleph*? Cf. *AP* 15:20; *BMAP* 4:20; *A* 12, 55, [2, 18, 28]. So far no clear case of a suffixal form of כל in the Aramaic texts from Egypt has turned up, but there is no reason why it should not. See p. 214 above. Even here the issue is not certain, for the emphatic state with *he* is found in *Pad* II v 2 (ינקיה = ינקיא), II v 5 (ספרה = ספרא). Hence כלה may be merely another spelling of כלא, used as a resumptive pronoun, as in *Pad* I r 5 (שלם אמך וינקיא כלא).

איך ביתא עביד: Bresciani understands this puzzling phrase as a question, "come la casa è fatta e come sei partito?" But this hardly fits the context of a father at home writing to a son on a caravan. It seems better, therefore, to take איך in the sense of "as"; but we cannot be certain because of the broken and fragmentary context. If correct, it would stand for the fuller (זי) איך די; cf. Sf I A 35, 38, 39; Syriac ʾ*ak dě*.

הן: This may well be the conjunction, "if," as interpreted by Bresciani. However, since the context is broken, there is another possibility which must be reckoned with: the emphatic adverb הן, which appears in *AD* 6:2; 12:3; *Cl-G Ost* 152, conc. 3, 7 [*Sem* 2 (1949) 31]. See my discussion of this adverb in Sf I B 36; III 4 (*Aramaic Inscriptions of Sefire* [p. 76 above, n. 29] 70–71). It seems to mean something like "so," a meaning which could correspond to איך.

7. מחבל: Bresciani understands this as a noun, meaning "destruction." This is not impossible, even though no noun forms of the root חבל with preformative *mem* are otherwise attested. The word מחבל in *AP* 27:2, to which she refers, is interpreted by Leander as a pael pass. ptc. (*L* §32d). G. S. Glanzman has suggested to me the possibility that the root may rather be חבל, "to take something as a pledge." The form would then be a pael act. ptc. In the broken context in which a house is mentioned, this is not impossible. The root is well known in Hebr., but found also in the targums in a nominal form, חבולא or חבוליא, "interest." See G. Dalman, *ANHW*, 134.

אל תתאשד: "Do not dissipate," lit., do not pour yourself out. In Syriac the root ᵓšd occurs in a figurative sense; *zabnan ᵓašidā*, "tempus nostrum dissolutum, mollitie diffluens" (*Act. Mart.* i. 166; R. Payne Smith, *Thesaurus syriacus,* 1. 404).

מנפי: Restored according to I r 3; מגדל would also be possible.

Recto

2. כתון: "Tunic," also spelled כתן in line 4. In the same sense the word also occurs in *A* 41 (where it is rent); *AP* 42:8(?), 9, 10, 13; *AD* 13:3; *Cl-G Ost* 16, conv. 2 (*ASAE* 48 [1948] 110); *Cl-G Ost* 49:1 (*JA* 235 [1946-47] 79-87). See G. R. Driver's note on *AD* 13:3.

לבש: Is this the defective spelling for לבוש or was it pronounced *lĕbāš*, as in later Aramaic and Syriac? לבוש is found in Biblical Aramaic (Dan 3:21; 7:9), in Qumran Aramaic (1QapGen 20:31), and also in some of the Elephantine texts themselves (*AP* 14:14; *BMAP* 11:11). Hence, though לבש occurs here and elsewhere (*AP* 15:7, 10; 20:5; *BMAP* 2:4; 7:6, 8, [10], 13, 17, 23; *Cl-G Ost* 70: conc. 4 [*CRAIBL* 1947, 177; *RHR* 130 (1945) 20]), it should be regarded as a defective writing for לבוש, the earlier form.

3. אל תמלי לבת: "Do not be angry," lit., do not be filled with anger. Cf. *AP* 37:11; 41:4; Aššur Ostr. 19-20 (M. Lidzbarski, *Altaramäische Urkunden aus Assur* [Leipzig: Hinrichs, 1921] 8). A. E. Cowley, following D. H. Baneth, related the expression to the Akkadian plural noun *libbātu* and suggested its adoption in Ezek 16:30. This was taken up by G. R. Driver (*JTS* 29 [1927-28] 393; 32 [1930-31] 366); see further my note, "A Note on Ez 16,30," *CBQ* 23 (1961) 460-62. If there were any hesitation about the meaning of the Aramaic phrase before this, because of damaged contexts, we need hesitate no longer, for the sense of the expression is now clear. תמלי is 2d sg. masc. impf. peal. See further *HermWP* 1:6 (זי מלתי לבתי), as recognized also by B. Porten and J. C.

Greenfield, "The Aramaic Papyri from Hermopolis," *ZAW* 80 (1968) 216-31, esp. pp. 226, 228. Contrast J. T. Milik, *Bib* 48 (1967) 581.

בזי: A causal conjunction, as in *AP* 30:23; 37:4, 7.

מנפי: See note above on I v 5 (מצרין).

4. קדמתך: "Before you," preferably to be understood in a temporal sense, since -קדמת usually has this nuance, whereas קדם is used for the local idea. See Dan 6:11; Ezra 5:11; *AP* 30:17; 71:3; *A* 2; *B* 54(?); but in *A* 101 the sense is apparently local.

זי כתן: "Of linen." This meaning for כתן is also found in *AP* 20:5; 26:14, 20; *BMAP* 7:11, 12(?), 13. See note on line 2 above.

5. [ ]דן: Bresciani suggests -רן as also possible. Could it not even be -כן?

שלם אמך וינקיא כלא: "Greetings from your mother and all the children!" The phrase is actually a construct chain, "The peace of your mother and all the children." This has been taken by Bresciani as if it were the equivalent of שלם -ל (like *AP* 57:1?): "Saluti a tua madre e a tutti i bambini." Yet the mother seems to be in Migdol with the father according to I v 2. In *BMAP* 13:6, toward the end of the letter again, we find a broken expression akin to the one here, [ ] שלם ענני בר נריה שלם כל בני. Kraeling (*BMAP*, 289) discussed the possibility of its meaning that greetings were sent from persons with the writer, but rejected it on "the analogy of other letters, notably those from Hermopolis," which suggest that שלם is "a noun and that greetings to people in Elephantine are meant (cf. *AP* 39:2f.)." However, this is not clear. Perhaps even *AP* 39:2-3, as well as 40:1-2, should now be interpreted in the sense of "greetings from. . . ." The evidence is such that שלם is used in these Aramaic texts both in the sense of "greetings to" and "greetings from." Certainly, in the very frequent formula, שלם מראן אלה שמיא שגיא בכל עדן (*AP* 30:2; 31:2; [38:2]; 40:1; 56:1; 18:2; 37:2), the "peace" is the property or quality of the person to whom the greeting is sent. This is even more evident in the case of suffixal forms (*AP* 41:2, 3, 5, 7; 56:1; 39:1; 57:4). However, "peace" can also be sent, as the restored formula in I v 1 shows; see note there for the basis of the restoration. See also *RES* 493:1 (. . . [ש]לם מן). Moreover, *Pad* II v 2, לך שלם גלגל תנה שלם ינקיא, would seem to confirm this interpretation, for לך expresses the person greeted. Hence, when we have a construct chain involving שלם, we must have recourse to the context to determine the sense, whether it means "greetings to" or "greetings from." Cf. *AP* 68:1; 66:9.

6. למחר: "Of Meḥir," the name of an Egyptian month, as rightly interpreted by Bresciani, comparing *BMAP* 13:8 (ב5 לאפף כתיב אגרתי). מחיר appears to be the name of a month in *AP* 24:[34, 35], 44; *RES*, 1801:8(?). See further references in Bresciani's article.

תתפטרן: "You will be released." Cf. *BMAP* 13:7. Could this possibly refer to service in the caravan, a member of which the son is? Is the withholding of the salary somehow connected with this?

Padua Papyrus II (= *Pad* II)

Text

Verso

1 אל אמ[י] יה[ו]י[ש]מע ברך שלום בר פטמ[ון]
2 לך שלם גלגל תנה שלם ינקיה . . . זכ. .[ ]
3 בלא הבה לפחנום בר נבודלה ויעב[ד]
4 יגרוהי והן איתי כסף הבי על פמי ע[ל שלמך]
אמי
5 שלחת ספרה זנה שלם מנחמת שלם[ ]
6 יהוישמע [ ]

Recto

1 [א]ל אמי יה[וי]שמע . . .[ ]

Translation

Verso

[1]To my mother, Yahuyishma^{c}; your son, Shallum bar Peṭam[un.] [2]Greetings to you from Galgul here, greetings from the children! [ ] [3]BLʾ give it to Pakhnum bar Nabudalah and let him d[o] [4]they will prosecute him, and if there is money, give (it) according to my instruction .[For your welfare] [5]I send this note. Greetings from Menaḥemet, my mother (?); greetings [ ] [6]Yahuyishmaʾ.

Recto

(Address) [T]o my mother, Yahuyishmaʾ . . .[ ]

Notes

Verso

1. ברך: If אמי is correctly restored here and in the address (in both places Bresciani puts dots under the letters read without brackets), and if Yahuyishma^{c} is the correct reading, then בר with the suffix *-k* is peculiar, because we would expect ברכי, with a fem. suffix. As a fem. name, יהוישמע occurs frequently in *BMAP* (6:8; 7:3, 4, etc.). The same problem is met in לך (line 2), the impv. הבה (line 3), where we should expect הביה, and the restored לשלמך (line 4). On the other hand, the fem. form of the impv. הבי in line 4 favors the interpretation that the letter is written to a woman. What we have here, then, is simply the use of masc. forms in addressing a woman—a phenomenon which is otherwise attested in the Aramaic texts from Elephantine (e.g., אנת [instead of אנתי], *BMAP* 6:8, 10[?]; 9:14; דילך [instead of דילכי], *BMAP* 9:14; זילך [instead of זילכי], *BMAP* 9:11, 12, 14; לך [instead of לכי], *BMAP* 6:14; 9:12; יגרנך [instead of יגרנכי], *BMAP* 4:16). Note that in *BMAP* 6:3 Anani bar Azariah even calls his daughter, Yahuyishma^{c}, ברי! In this case, however, we may have to regard this as a scribal omission for בר‹ת›י;

cf. 6:8, 17, 19. Note the absence of מן here before the writer's name; cf. *Pad* I v 1.

שלום: Shallum, a name which occurs in *BMAP* 11:13; *AP* 23:6; 25:18; [35:2]; 63:10.

פטמ[ון]: Peṭamun, "the one given by Amon." Cf. *RES* 1364 (פטמון). Bresciani notes that the name occurs also in the Hermopolis letters (4:3); she suggests the possibility also of reading פטמ[ת], as in *AP* 24:1, but that form is by no means a certain reading. See *B-M* 17.

2. לך: See note on ברך, line 1 above.

שלם: See note on *Pad* I r 5.

גלגל תנה: Bresciani reads this all as one word and as the form גלגלתנם. In my original study of this text, I too hesitatingly read the last letter as a *mem*. However, the last three letters are now to be read as תנה, "here." This is certain from *HermWP* 2:2-3 (שלם נבושה תנה); 6:8 (שלם בנתסר תנה); and possibly 8:11 (שלם . . . נ]בושה תנה]). The proper name גלגל (and גלגול) appears in *AP* 49:1; 10:21; *RES* 907; Mur 42:2; 43:2; 44:1; 51:1; 115:4, 5 (vocalized in Greek as Γαλγουλᾶ). M. Noth (*IPN*, 223) related it to the Arabic *juljulun*, "Schelle, Klingel."

ינקיה: Emphatic state written with *he* instead of *aleph*; cf. *sprh* (II v 5).

3. בלא: Owing to the lacuna at the end of line 2 it is impossible to interpret this word with certainty. בלא is found as a proper name in *AP* 28:5, but this hardly fits the context here. Bresciani suggests a connection with the root בלא, "be worn out," used in *AP* 26:1 of a boat. Could it possibly be another spelling of *bĕlô*, "tribute, tax (paid in kind)," which occurs in Ezra 4:13; 7:24?

הבה: Apparently the masc. sg. impv. with a suffix; for *hbyh*, as Bresciani notes.

פחנום: Pakhnum, "the one belonging to Khnum." The name also occurs in *AP* 23:5, spelled פחנם*ᵓ and in BMAP* 11:2, 10, 15.

נבודלה: Nabudalah, "Nabu has drawn up (from the depths, rescued)." Bresciani states that the name is Babylonian; but both H. V. Hilprecht (*The Babylonian Expedition of the University of Pennsylvania* [Philadelphia: University of Pennsylvania, 1898], IX, 64) and K. Tallqvist (*Assyrian Personal Names*, p. 279) regard *Nabû-da-laᵓ* as an Aramaean name. Moreover, Nabu was apparently venerated at Elephantine; see A. Dupont-Sommer, "'Bêl et Nabû, Šamaš et Nergal' sur un ostracon araméen inédit d'Eléphantine," *RHR* 128 (1944) 29-30 (translated by H. L. Ginsberg, *ANET*, 491). Cf. *AD* 6:1 (*Nbwdlᵓ*, but corrected in abridged edition to *Nbwdlny*).

4. יגרוהי: "They will prosecute him." The verb גרא is frequently used in this sense with the suffix in the Elephantine texts; see Kraeling, *BMAP*, 310.

5. שלחת ספרא זנה: Cf. *Cl-G Ost* 70: conv. 2 (לשלמך שלחת ספרא), which supports the restoration of the original editor on line 4.

אמי: This word is written above the line and creates a problem. If it is intended to be an appositive to מנחמת, then it cannot mean the same thing as אמי in line 1; the same is true, if it is the *nomen rectum* and מנחמת is the appositive. In such a case אם would have to be a title of address, similar to אח in *Pad* I v 1. But is אם ever found in that sense? We know of no parallels for it. Is אמי then a vocative? At any rate, it was added later as an afterthought and it seems to upset the sense of the greeting.

מנחמת: Menaḥemet, "the Consoler," a fem. form of Menaḥem. It is also found in *AP* 22:81, [95], 108.

Padua Papyrus III (= *Pad* III)

Text

אל אחתי יהושמע[

]באגורא שלם אושע בר זכ[

Translation

a: To my sister, Yahushema[c] [

b: [ ] in the temple. Greetings from Osea bar Zak[

Notes

a: אחתי: Bresciani understands this word also as a term of address similar to אח. But what is the evidence for this?

יהושמע: Yahushema[c], "Yahu has heard." The name also occurs in *AP* 22:84, 87, 98, 99, 117. Cf. M. Noth, *IPN*, 185.

b: באגורא: "In the temple"; the word (‹ Accad. *ekurru*) is used in the Elephantine texts either of the temple of Yahu (*BMAP* 12:18; *AP* 30:6), or of that of other gods (*AP* 30:14).

[ ]זכר: Possibly Zakkur (*AP* 10:3) or Zekaryah (*AP* 5:5). It is also possible, of course, that the greetings are sent *to* Osea bar Zak. . . .

It is hoped that the above remarks will contribute to the further understanding of these papyrus letters.

NOTES TO CHAPTER 10

*Originally published under the same title in *JNES* 21 (1962) 15-24.

[1]J. C. L. Gibson (*Textbook of Syrian Semitic Inscriptions* [p. 76 above, n. 29], 2. 143–47) regards *Pad* I as coming from Migdol in Egypt. That seems to be the place from which the letter was written; but it is another question as to where it was found.

[2]"Papiri aramaici egiziani di epoca persiana presso il Museo Civico di Padova," *RSO* 35 (1960) 11-24 (+ 5 pls.). For further literature on these texts, see E. Bresciani, "Postilla a RSO, XXV, 11-24," *RSO* 35 (1960) 211; F. Díaz Estaban, "Una formula de cortesia epistolar de Ugarit, repetida en una carta judeo-aramea del siglo V a. C.," *Sefarad* 22 (1962) 101-2; J. Naveh, "Old Aramaic Inscriptions (1960-64)," *AION* 16 (1966) 19-36, esp. pp. 25-29; J. T. Milik, "Les papyrus araméens d'Hermoupolis et les cultes syro-phéniciens en Egypte perse," *Bib* 48 (1967) 546-621, esp. p. 549.

[3]The transcription of the *editio princeps* should be consulted concerning letters which are doubtful in the text. No attempt is made here to mark them or to describe the physical state of the papyri.

Chapter 11

The Aramaic Letter of King Adon to the Egyptian Pharaoh*

The Aramaic letter sent by the king of a small territory in Palestine or Phoenicia, informing the contemporary Egyptian Pharaoh of the advance of the troops of the Babylonian king and asking for the Pharaoh's military support against them, is well known. It was first published in 1948 by A. Dupont-Sommer,[1] and its historical significance has been discussed by several writers since then.[2] It sheds precious light on the period just before the destruction of Jerusalem by Nebuchadrezzar II and the great experience in Israel's history known as the Babylonian Captivity. Though several writers have attempted to bring out further aspects of the letter, either philological or historical, its full message is not yet entirely clear. The main reason is that the letter is fragmentary, since the ends of the nine extant lines are lost. There is no way of telling just how much is lost at the end of the lines. The estimate of one-third, which has been suggested, may be correct, but then it may be that we have only about a half of the lines, since the attempt to fill in the lacunae and establish a plausible coherence between the lines demands a considerable restoration. We are attempting a re-study of the letter, hoping to bring out a few more details and offer some observations on previous interpretations of different phrases which call for some reconsideration.

From the standpoint of the Aramaic language the letter is significant in that a kinglet of Canaanite background writes for aid to his Egyptian overlord in this language. It is a very early example of Official Aramaic, and important in that it is the earliest sample of it to come from Palestine or Phoenicia. Even though the fragment was found at Saqqârah in Egypt, it is important to keep this in mind, as it bears on the interpretation of certain phrases.

The date of the letter is not established with certainty. It is generally agreed—and rightly—that the letter belongs to the period of the contest for power between the 26th (Saite) Dynasty of Egypt and the Neo-Babylonian (Chaldean) Kingdom of Mesopotamia. With the destruction of Nineveh in 612 B.C. and the eventual ejection of the Assyrians from Harran in 610, Egypt and Babylonia strove to dominate Palestine and Syria. The Pharaoh Necho II (609-593) marched to the aid of the Assyrian Asshur-uballiṭ II, hoping to retake Harran from the Babylonians and set up again a center of Assyrian influence. King Josiah of Judah, who tried for some reason to stop Necho, was killed at Megiddo in 609. The Pharaoh was eventually defeated by the Babylonians at Carchemish in 605. But he had already tried to consolidate his holdings in Palestine. After Jehoahaz had reigned for three months as the heir of Josiah, he was summoned to the Pharaoh's headquarters in Riblah (central Syria), deposed, and deported to Egypt (2 Kgs 23:31-35; Jer 22:10-12). Jehoahaz' brother, Eliakim, was put on the throne as an Egyptian vassal, and was given the throne-name of Jehoiakim. The Pharaoh must have attempted to dominate other kings in the area too, for King Adon, who writes this Aramaic letter, seems to have been another such vassal of the Egyptian Pharaoh. The advance of the Babylonians which he mentions in the letter is generally associated—and again rightly—with the campaigns of Nebuchadrezzar II, because it was under the latter that the campaigns against Palestine and Syria took place. It is, however, a matter of dispute as to the year in which the letter was written. D. Winton Thomas' view that it was written in 587 has won scarcely any support, since it is unconvincing. A. Malamat at first preferred to relate the letter to the events of 598, the Babylonian campaign in which Jehoiachin surrendered to the invader and was deported (2 Kgs 24:10-12). Similarly, R. Meyer. However, since the publication of the Chronicles of Nebuchadrezzar, in which the fall of Ashkelon is explicitly mentioned for December 604 B.C.,[3] a date for the writing of this letter has been proposed somewhere in the immediately preceding period, 605-4. In substance, this is the date of W. F. Albright, A. Dupont-Sommer, E. Vogt, A. Malamat, etc.[4]

If the almost contemporary Lachish letters have shed light on such a passage as Jer 34:1-7, esp. 34:7, it is not impossible that the Aramaic letter of King Adon does the same for Jer 36:9-32, the burning of the scroll. This incident has been related to the capture of Ashkelon by Nebuchadrezzar II, as both E. Vogt and A. Malamat have suggested. But more recently (*IEJ* 18 [1968] 142-43) Malamat has preferred "the king of Gaza" as the "most likely" candidate for restoration.

Text

1 אל מרא מלכן פרעה עברך אדן מלך .[שלם מראי עשתרת בעלת]
2 שמיא וארקא ובעלשמין אלה[א רבא ישאלו בבל עדן וישימו כרסא]
3 פרעה כיומי שמין אמין זי[חילא]
4 זי מלך בבל אתו מטאו אפק וש[ראו]
5 [ ] אחזו . ל . . לו . ל[ ]
6 כי מרא מלכן פרעה ידע כי עבד[ך לא יכל למקם קדמוה ירקה מראי]
7 למשלח חיל לחצלתי אל ישבקנ[י מרא מלכן פרעה כי מומאה]
8 וטבתה עבדך נצר ונגדא זנה[ ]
9 פחה במתא וספר שניוי ספ[ ]

Translation

[1]To the Lord of Kings, the Pharaoh, your servant ʾAdon, the king of [May Astarte, the Mistress] [2]of the heavens and the earth, and Baʿalshamayn, [the great] god, [seek the welfare of my lord at all times and make the throne] [3]of Pharaoh (as) enduring as the days of heaven. Since [the troops] [4]of the king of Babylon have come (and) have arrived (at) Aphek, and have enca[mped] [5][. . . .] and have taken .L. .LW .L [ ] [6]for the Lord of Kings, the Pharaoh, knows that [your] servant [cannot withstand him. May my lord be pleased] [7]to send an army to rescue me. May [the Lord of Kings, the Pharaoh], not forsake m[e, for] [8]your servant has kept [his oath] and his good relations. And this commander [has set up] [9] a governor in the land and has recorded his changes (?) [ ]

Notes

1. אל: The preposition ʾ*el* was used in Old Aramaic inscriptions (Sf III 1, 19, 20). Though it was normally replaced by על in Official Aramaic, it was retained in the addresses of letters as here. See the note on *Pad* I 1.

מרא מלכן: "The Lord of Kings." At this period of Aramaic מרא can only be cst. sg.; excluded, therefore, is any such meaning as "the lord, our king," which might be theoretically possible in later Aramaic. The title is the same as that found in Dan 2:47, where it is applied to Yahweh by the Babylonian king Nebuchadrezzar. Dupont-Sommer rightly stressed that the title מרא מלכן is not found in Egyptian documents, and that it should not be confused with the Akkad. *šar šarrāni*, or with the Achaemenid title, "King of Kings," used of Nebuchadrezzar in Ezek 26:7 (מלך מלכים, or the Aram. form, מלך מלכיא, Dan 2:37; Ezra 7:12). For מרא מלכן is rather the equivalent of the Phoen. אדן מלכם (Ešmunʿazor 18), and of the Akkad. *bēl šarrāni* (*ABL* 256.1, 2; 281.3, 16-17, 32; 992.2). The Phoen. expression became more current in the time of the Ptolemies (*NSI* 10:5; 27:1; 28:2; 29:4; cf. also 9:5 [used of Alexander the Great]). Dupont-Sommer compared it to the Greek title *κύριος βασιλέων*, but gave no references to the occurrence of this phrase. H. L. Ginsberg maintained that the title was rather *κύριος βασιλειῶν*. The latter occurs in the Rosetta Stone, line 1 (cf. W. Dittenberger, *OGIS* 1.90,1). This was translated by Ginsberg as "Lord of Kingdoms," and he insisted that מרא מלכן should be translated in the same way (similarly J. Bright, R. Meyer). מלכן would be *molkîn*. He compared Dan 2:47, Arab. *mulk*, and appealed to Phoen. and Ugar. instances of *mlk* equalling *mulk*, "kingdom," "kingship." See C. H. Gordon, *Ugaritic Manual*, 49:V:5; VI:28. —However, even granting that *mlk* in Arab., Phoen. and Ugar. has the meaning "kingdom," it is still not certain that מרא מלכן means anything more than "Lord of Kings." First of all, this Aram. phrase is a reflection of both the Phoen. and Akkad. expressions. In the latter case, *bēl šarrāni* cannot mean anything but "Lord of Kings." Secondly, the connection between מרא מלכן and the Gk. expression is quite tenuous. Ginsberg understood *κύριος βασιλειῶν*, "lord of Kingdoms," to refer to the kingdoms of Upper and Lower Egypt. But this is far from certain, in the Gk. text of the Rosetta stone at least. A spot-check of several translations of that text shows that the meaning normally accepted for *κύριος βασιλείων* is "the Lord of Crowns." So, for instance, E. A. Wallis Budge, *The Rosetta Stone in the British Museum* (London: British Museum, 1929) 51; J. P. Mahaffy, *A History of Egypt Under the Ptolemaic Dynasty* (London: Methuen, 1899) 152; E. Bevan, *A History of Egypt,* vol. 4; London: Methuen, 1927) 263; M. Letronne, "Inscription grecque de Rosette," in C. and T. Müller (ed.), *Fragmenta historicorum graecorum* (Paris: Didot, 1874) App. pp. 1 and 7 [This celebrated translation gives "maître des couronnes," but the commentary admits that one cannot entirely exclude the meaning "royaume"]. In this Gk. expression the reference is to the ten gold crowns of the Ptolemaic king, which were symbolic of power enjoyed (at least at some time) over Egypt, Libya, Syria, Phoenicia, Cyprus, Lycia, Caria, Cyclades, Arabia, Aethiopia (see W. Dittenberger, *OGIS*, 1.90,43). Part of the problem is the uncertainty whether *βασιλείων* is to be taken as the gen. pl. of *βασιλεία* ("kingdom") or of *τὸ βασίλειον* ("diadem, crown"). Given this uncertainty about the meaning of the Gk. expression, one cannot assert apodictically that it shows that Ptolemaic kings were called "Lord of Kingdoms." Further evidence must be adduced to establish the connection between the Aram. מרא מלכן and the Phoen. אדן מלכם, on the one hand, and the Gk. expression *κύριος βασιλείων*, on the other. Does the expression turn up anywhere else in Gk.? We have been unable to discover it. —Moreover, as both Koopmans and Donner-Röllig point out, the normal word for "kingdom" in Aram. is מלכו, which could easily have been used if one wanted to say "Lord of Kingdoms." H. L. Ginsberg objected to Dupont-Sommer's translation, "Au Seigneur des rois," on the grounds that it would demand the emphatic state. This, however, is not the problem that it seems to be at first sight, because it is a title (cf. Dan 2:47). —This note was already written when K. Galling's article arrived, "Eschmunazar und der Herr der Könige," *ZDPV* 79 (1963) 140-51. In it the reader will find further references to Akkad. literature which is contemporary and is probably the source of the Aram. and later Phoen. expression. Galling also explains *βασιλείων* as having nothing to do with *βασιλεία*, which for him is a "Singulare tantum," but as the gen. pl. of *τὸ βασίλειον*. Galling's article is the latest contribution to a discussion on the date of the Ešmunᶜazor inscription, which he carried on earlier with H. L. Ginsberg (see "'King of Kings' and 'Lord of Kingdoms,'" *AJSL* 57 [1940] 71-74; *JBL* 56 [1937] 142-43; K. Galling, "Denkmäler zur Geschichte Syriens und Palästinas unter der Herrschaft der Perser," *PJB* 34 [1938] 59-79, esp. pp. 71-73.) —The upshot of all this is that King Adon, writing to the Egyptian Pharaoh predicates of him an Akkad. or possibly a Phoen. title. There is no evidence so far that it is an Egyptian title, and its relation to the Ptolemaic Greek title is tenuous at best. Cf. J. Friedrich, "Griechisches und römisches in phönizischem und punischem Gewand," *Festschrift Otto Eissfeldt* (Halle/S.: Niemeyer, 1947) 109-24, esp. p. 112.

פרעה: "The Pharaoh." The title, apparently first used in the time of Amenophis IV (ca. 1370 B.C.), became rather common in the Saite dynasty, to which this letter is dated. It is a title meaning, "Great House," and as in many texts in the OT and Akkad. the Pharaoh is not further identified; Sargon II refers in his annals merely to *Pirᵓu*. The Pharaoh in question is almost certainly Necho II (609-593 B.C.), to whom King Adon writes. Cf. 2 Kgs 23:29, 33-35; Jer 46:2; 2 Chr 35:20, 22; 36:4. See S. H. Horn, "Where and When" (n. 2 above), 32.

עבדך: "Your servant," an expression relatively common in letters sent to superiors: *AP* 30:4; 38:2; 54:9; 70:1; *BMAP* 13:9, etc.; Ezra 4:11. See p. 190 above. Cf. also the use of *waradka* in Akkad. texts.

אדן A Canaanite proper name, probably a shortened form of some name like *ᵓAdonîṣedeq* (Jos 10:1, 3), *ᵓAdōnîqām* (Ezra 2:13), *ᵓAdōnîrām* (1 Kgs 4:6), *ᵓdnbᶜl* (*CIS*, 1.138), etc. As a hypocoristicon, it occurs in Akkad. as *A-du-na* (cf. Tallqvist, *APN*, 13), the name of a Phoenician king of ᶜArqa; possibly a genuine Akkad. occurrence is found in [1]*A-du-ni-i* (ND 5447: 12). As a common noun, it means the same as Aram. מרא, "lord." See p. 125 above. But it is a proper name here, as can be seen from the fact that it follows עבדך and precedes מלך. Since this cannot be the name of any king of Judah in this period, it must be the name of a king in one of the Philistine coastal cities (or countries), Gaza, Ashkelon, Ashdod, Ekron, or Gath. —A. Malamat (*IEJ* 18 [1968] 143 n. 11) considers the name *ᵓAdonimelek* a possibility here.

מלך: "King of. . . ." The combination of the name (Adon) and the situation described in the letter call for a restoration of the name of some Philistine or Phoenician town. In Philistia only two are possible, when all is said and done: either Ashkelon or Gaza. W. F. Albright was apparently the first to suggest Ashkelon, and many have found his suggestion plausible. R. Meyer calls it "höchst unsicher," without giving any reasons. What is certain is that Ashkelon had a king about this time, for the mention of "two sons of Agaᵓ, the king of Ashkelon," is found in the Weidner Tablets. See E. F. Weidner, "Jojachin, König von Juda, in babylonischen Keilschrifttexten," *Mélanges syriens offerts à M. René Dussaud* (Paris: Geuthner, 1939) 2. 923-35, esp. p. 928: *2 mārē*^{meš} *šá*[1] *A-ga-ᵓ, šarri ša* ^{māt}*Iš-qil-lu-nu.* It has been suggested that Nebuchadrezzar had deposed Adon after the capture of Ashkelon and set up in his stead Agaᵓ as a Babylonian vassal. Albright sees the two sons of Agaᵓ as hostages; they would have been taken to Babylonia, and the tablets would record rations doled out to them. However, E. Vogt has found some difficulty in this, because the Wiseman Chronicles of Nebuchadrezzar, in recording the capture of Ashkelon, note that he "marched to the city of Ashkelon and captured it in the month of Kislev. He captured its king and plundered it and carried off [spoil from it . . .]. He turned the city into a mound and heaps of ruins, and then in the month of Šebat he marched back to Babylon" (B. M. 21946 obv. 18-20). The destruction of Ashkelon is recorded with the same expressions as that of Nineveh and is quite different from the mention of the appointment of a king "in the city of Judah" (B. M. 21946 rev. 13). Vogt, therefore, concludes that Nebuchadrezzar did not set up a king in Ashkelon and that Agaʾ must have been the last king of Ashkelon—the one whom Nebuchadrezzar besieged and defeated. He and his sons would have been deported; he is not otherwise mentioned in the Weidner Tablets, because he had probably died meanwhile in captivity. Though Vogt's objection is real, it is not serious enough to outweigh the other evidence which points toward Ashkelon as the most likely town over which Adon would have ruled. For one thing, we do not know how long Adon lived after he wrote to the Pharaoh. It is not impossible that Agaʾ had already succeeded Adon before the troops of Nebuchadrezzar arrived at the town. After all, Adon wrote and sent the letter to the Pharaoh in Egypt; there must have been some time which elapsed between the arrival of the Babylonian army at Aphek and its coming to Adon's town; otherwise there would have been little point in writing. —If the objection of E. Vogt is considered a real obstacle to the identification of the town of Adon with Ashkelon, then there remains Gaza, as the Philistine coastal town even closer to Egypt, which would be a possibility. In either case Nebuchadrezzar is presumably advancing from the north (from the area already conquered). Adon's kingdom is to the south of Nebuchadrezzar's position and to the south of Aphek.

But there is no certainty that the city over which Adon ruled was situated in Philistia. H. Donner and W. Röllig consider the possibility of its localization in Phoenicia (*KAI*, 313). J. T. Milik thinks that this is more probable too. Having examined the photograph again, he finds the trace of a letter following מלך, which cannot be an *aleph*. This rules out the possibility of Ashkelon. Nor can it be an ᶜ*ayin*, ruling out the possibility of Gaza. Milik thinks that the only two possibilities are a *daleth* or a *ṣadhe*; he reads either [צ]ידון or preferably [צ]ור, since Tyre was the home of the cult of Melqart, Astarte, and Baᶜalshamayn (*Bib* 48 [1967] 561). Cf. H. Seyrig, "Antiquités syriennes," *Syria* 40 (1963) 19-28.

Since no certainty can be gained in this matter, I have chosen to leave the lacuna blank in this case; but I do think that Milik was right in returning to the suggestion of Dupont-Sommer about the names of the deities to be restored.

[שלם מראי עשתרת בעלת] שמיא וארקא . . . [ישאלו בכל עדן]: "May Astarte, the Mistress of the heavens and the earth . . . seek the welfare of my lord at all times." The greeting is restored according to the usual one found in Aramaic letters from Egypt (*AP* 30:1–2; 21:2; 39:1). See further pp. 191–92 above.

[עשתרת בעלת] שמיא וארקא: "Astarte, the Mistress of the heavens and earth." This was Dupont-Sommer's original restoration, appealing to Akkad. *Ištar bēlit šamē ū irṣitim* (*Hymn to Ishtar*, 27: *ANET*, 383) and comparing Jer 7:18; 44:17–19, 25. Istar and Ba-al-samēmē are also invoked in a treaty between Esarhaddon and Baal, king of Tyre (cf. R. Borger, *Die Inschriften*

Asarhaddons Königs von Assyrien [Beiheft AfO 9; Graz: Private publication, 1956] 69 IV 10 and 18 [p. 109]). This now seems more plausible to me than the suggestion of H. L. Ginsberg to read [מרא], which I originally followed. It would be a reference to the god El (see Sf I A 11; Gen 14:19; 1QapGen 22:16, 21).

2. בעלשמין: "Ba^calshmayn," or more correctly *ba^clšamayn*. He is identical with Hadad, the Syrian storm-god. See Zakir A 3. Cf. O. Eissfeldt, "Ba^calšamēm und Jahwe," *ZAW* 57 (1939) 1-31; M. H. Pope, *El in the Ugaritic Texts* (Leiden: Brill, 1955) 57.

אלה[א רבא]: "The great god." Some epithet seems to have followed the name Ba^calshamayn. We have adopted Ginsberg's suggestion of רבא.

[וישימו כרסא] פרעה כיומי שמין אמין: "May they make the throne of Pharaoh (as) firm as the days of heaven." Or, if there would be space enough, one could add with Dupont-Sommer מרא מלכן at the end of line 2. The restoration is based on Ps 89:30 (שמתי לעד זרעו וכסאו כימי שמים); cf. v. 37; Deut 11:21; Sir 45:15. J. J. Koopmans regards אמין as the pass. ptc. of אמן; it may rather be the normal *qattīl* adjectival type in Aramaic *(^ɔammīn).*

זי: A space precedes this word, and so it is probably to be taken as the beginning of a sentence. It is probably a conjunction. See S. H. Horn, *AUSS* 6 (1968) 31.

4. מלך בבל: "The king of Babylon." This is not the subject of the following verbs, since they are plural. The restoration of חילא is not unlikely; it would have to be understood in a collective sense. Cf. חילא with the plur. adj. אחרנן in *AP* 30:8, with the plur. verb קטלו in B 5, [48]. However, if one were to take a cue from 2 Kgs 24:10 (MT: עבדי נבוכדנאצר מלך בבל), perhaps we should restore עבדיא (= ^c*abdayya*^ɔ), "the servants of the king of Babylon." This would yield a plural with which the verbs would easily agree. —The king is not named. Theoretically, he could be either Nabopolassar or the crown-prince who became king, Nebuchadrezzar II. Since the publication of the Wiseman Chronicles, it is almost certain that Nebuchadrezzar is meant. The title מלך בבל is given to him explicitly in the Louvre Tablet A 6-7 (see J. Starcky, *Syria* 37 [1960] 99-115, esp. p. 100), as well as in Jer 21:2, 7; 2 Kgs 24:1, 7, 11, 12; etc. However, the same title is borne also by Merodach-Baladan (2 Kgs 20:12), Evil-Merodach (2 Kgs 25:27; Jer 52:31), and Artaxerxes I (Neh 13:6). But there can be no question of these three kings here.

אתו: "Have come." See *AP* 30:8.

מטאו: "Have arrived." The two verbs are joined asyndetically. The second verb governs the name of a place directly without a prep., as frequently in earlier and later Aramaic (Sf III 5, *yhkn Ḥlb*; *Pad* I v 5, *t*^ɔ*twn Mṣryn*: I r 3 ^ɔ*ytyt hmw Mnpy*: *BMAP* 13:3; *AP* 42:7; 83:2; *AD* 6.2, 4, 5). Contrast *AP* 37:11; 42:11. —Note the orthography in the two verbs. Both are *tertiae infirmae.* verbs; but in אתו the final *aleph* (already quiescent) is not even written. Hence אתו must = ^ɔ*atô* or possibly ^ɔ*ătô*. But in the case of מטאו the *aleph* is written. Most likely it was no longer pronounced; hence *maṭô* (or even *mĕṭô*). There is as yet no evidence for the reduction of pretonic short vowels in an open syllable at this date.

J. T. Milik (*Bib* 48 [1967] 562) would read instead of מטאו the word מעב[ר]ת and would translate, "[une armée] du roi de Babylone est arrivé à la passe d'Afeq et de Š[. . .]." The last word he understands as *š*[*r*^{c}*yt*], modern *Ser*^{c}*îtā*, on the route from Baalbek to Byblos or Beirut (cf. Aramaic *šĕra*^{c}*tā*^{ᵓ}, "slope").

אפק: "Aphek." The identification of this place is problematic, since there are at least four towns so named in the OT. (1) Aphek, originally a Canaanite town on the plain of Sharon, at Ras el-^{c}Ain, the Antipatris of NT times; cf. Jos 12:18; 1 Sam 4:1; 29:1. It lay E of Jaffa and about 10 mi. N of Lydda, on the upper course of the ^{c}Aujā River. It served as the base of Philistine operations against Israel and was mentioned in the list of Thutmose III (No. 66) as *Ipḳ*. It was also noted in the Annals of Esarhaddon for 671 B.C. as "Apqu which is in the region of Sama[ria?]" (^{uru}*Ap-qu ša pa-ṭi KUR Sa-me-n*[*a?-x*], cf. R. Borger, *Die Inschriften Asarhaddons*, §76: Vs 16 [p. 112]; cf. *ANET*, 292). See W. F. Albright, *BASOR* 11 (1923) 6-7; *JPOS* 3 (1923) 50-53; A. Alt, *PJB* 28 (1932) 19-20; 22 (1926) 69; the results of soundings there are described by A. Eitan, *IEJ* 12 (1962) 151-52; *RB* 69 (1962) 407-8. (2) Aphek in Asher, i.e., Tell Kerdâne in the plain of Akko, at the source of the Na^{c}mên River; cf. Jos 19:30; Judg 1:31. See A. Alt, *PJB* 24 (1928) 59-60; 25 (1929) 41 n. 1. (3) Aphek, to the east of the Lake of Tiberias, i.e., Fiq or Afiq in Jaulan, on the road from Damascus to Beisan; cf. 1 Kgs 20:26, 30; 2 Kgs 13:17. (4) Aphek in Phoenicia, near Byblos, i.e., modern Afqa in the Lebanon Mts. on the upper course of Nahr Ibrāhîm, the Adonis of antiquity; cf. Jos 13:4. —In general, see F.-M. Abel, *Géographie de la Palestine* (2 vols.; Paris: Gabalda, 1933-38), 2. 246-47; R. Dussaud, *Topographie historique de la Syrie antique et mediévale* (Paris: Geuthner, 1927) 13-14; M. du Buit, *Géographie de la terre sainte* (Paris: Cerf, 1958) 182. E. Vogt has discussed the likelihood of these sites in detail; only Aphek in Sharon enjoys any probability as the place named in this letter, if the city of King Adon lay in Philistia. However, if it was situated in Phoenicia, then modern Afqa is the more logical place. But see S. H. Horn, *AUSS* 6 (1968) 34-38, for a fifth possibility in southern Judah, Apheka (Josh 15:53), perhaps Khirbet eḍ-Ḍarrâme, SW of Hebron (so *KAI*, 314).

ושׁ[ראו]: "And have encamped." One cannot entirely exclude the suggestion of Dupont-Sommer that *wš*[is the beginning of another proper name, coordinated with ^{ᵓ}*pq*. Milik follows this suggestion. But it is not impossible that it is a verb, as H. L. Ginsberg suggested. He restored it as the pael *šarrîw*, "they have begun" (cf. Ezra 5:2). It is not, however, impossible that it is the peal form of *šr*^{ᵓ}, "and they have encamped" *(wa-šar*^{ᵓ}*ô < wa-šar*^{ᵓ}*aw)*. See 1QapGen 20:34-21:1.

6. כי: For the use of this conjunction in Aramaic texts, see Sf III 22; Zakir A 13; Aššur Ostracon 8(?); *A* 95, 98, 99.

[עבד[ך: Restored as in line 1. This line expresses the vassal's condition and the reason why he is requesting aid in coping with it.

[לא יכל למקם קדמוהי]: "Cannot withstand him," i.e., the king of Babylon; lit., "is not able to stand before him." Cf. *A* 107 (מן הו זי יקום קדמוהי). It is impossible to decide whether one should write קדמוה (as in the earlier inscriptions and *BMAP* 3:4; *AP* 25:3), or קדמוהי (as in *Aḥiqar*).

[ירקה מראי]: "May my lord be pleased." Some such verb is needed to introduce the inf. in line 7. ירקה is 3 sg. m. peal short impf. (= jussive) of רקה, the early form of רעה (related to Hebr. *rṣh*). The pael of רקה occurs in Sf III 6, 18, 19. The form with the *qoph* is used because of ארקא (line 2).

7. למשלח: "To send" (peal inf.). The peal inf. has the preformative *mem* here, as in Sf I B 34; early infinitives peal often occur without it (Sf I B 32 [שגב]; III 12, 13 [נכה]).

לחצלתי: "To rescue me." Dupont-Sommer reads להצלתי (with *he*), but admits that *ḥeth* is also possible. Ginsberg, Donner-Röllig also read *he*. With Koopmans we prefer to read *ḥeth*, not only because it is the *lectio difficilior*, but because the left shaft is longer than that of *he* in the rest of the letter. Either form is grammatically possible. חצלתי is the pael inf. cst. with a suffix; its root is *ḥlṣ*, "draw off; rescue, deliver." It preserves the same metathesis as in Zakir A 14 (cf. T. Nöldeke, *ZA* 21 [1908] 382). The form with *he* would be the Haph. inf. cst. with a suffix; its root would be נצל, "deliver, set free." —J. J. Koopmans calls the suffix "strange" and expects rather -*ūtánī*. However, this is the form of the suffix on the inf. of derived conjugations in Old Aramaic; cf. Sf III 11, 15 (המתתי, haph. inf. of מות; = *hamītūtī*, "to kill me"). —Cf. Isa 30:3; 31:3.

אל ישבקנ[י]: "Let the Lord of Kings, the Pharaoh, not forsake me." Dupont-Sommer read at first אל שבקנ[י], a negatived impv., which is unlikely, if not impossible. Later he changed it to a 2nd sg. form, תשבקנ[י]. Ginsberg preferred to read the 3d sg., which seems better according to the photo. It is also a polite form, more in keeping with the tone of the rest of the letter. Would the vassal who calls himself עבדך address the Pharaoh so bluntly? —Apparently the help from Egypt was not forthcoming; cf. 2 Kgs 24:7.

[כי מומאה] וטבתה עבדך נצר: "Has kept his oath and his good relations." It is this expression more than any of the others in the letter which makes it clear that King Adon was a vassal of the Egyptian Pharaoh. He uses covenant terminology here and emphasizes that he has been faithful to the Pharaoh, and implies thereby that he deserves to be aided by him. Dupont-Sommer translated טבתה simply as "ses biens (= les biens du Pharaon) ton serviteur a sauve-gardé." But he did not explain what he meant by "biens"; it sounds as though King Adon were protesting that he has watched out for the Pharaoh's possessions in his territory. Given the fragmentary state of the papyrus, one could not really exclude this meaning. But once it is realized that נצר טבתה is a treaty expression, then the last few lines of the letter take on a different nuance. H. L. Ginsberg translated, "Thy servant remembers his kindness," giving נצר another possible meaning, and taking the form not as the pf. but as a ptc. J. Bright simply followed Ginsberg, while Donner-Röllig followed Dupont-Sommer ("und seine Güter hat dein Sklave bewahrt"). But the suffix (apparently 3d sg. m.) on טבתה creates a problem. How can it refer to the Pharaoh when the suffix on the subject (עבדך) is in the 2d sg. m.? True, the Pharaoh is referred to in the 3d sg. in ידע (line 6), as well as in line 7, if the reading ישבקנ[י] be admitted. But with the subject עבדך would not one expect טבתה, if either of the above interpretations were correct? Furthermore, טבתה most likely has the meaning which it has in the Sefîre inscriptions, as has recently been pointed out by W. L. Moran ("A Note on the Treaty Terminology of the Sefîre Stelas," *JNES* 22 [1963] 173-76). He showed that טבתא there means "good relations," or the "friendship" demanded by the pact between the suzerain and the vassal. Cf. Sf II B 2; I C 19-20, 4-5. The likelihood that this meaning is required here is increased by the fact that in certain Akkad. texts the word *ṭabtu* (now shown to have a treaty connotation of "good relations") is used with *naṣāru*, "preserve, guard, keep." Cf. Annals of Asshurbanipal (Rassam Cylinder): *ina a-di-ia iḫ-ṭu-ú ṭabat e-pu-šu-uš lā iṣ-ṣur-ú-ma*, "he has sinned against my treaty; he has not preserved the good relations I made with him" (M. Streck, *Assurbanipal*, Cyl A 7.86 [VAB 7/2.64]). Again, *ina a-di-ia iḫ-ṭu-ú lā iṣ-ṣu-ru ma-mit ilāni rabuti MUN* (= *ṭabat*) *e-pu-us-su-nu-ti im-šū-ma* (Cyl A 1.119 [*VAB* 7/2. 12]). Cf. also Cyl A 9.72-73; Cyl B 7.91-95 [*VAB* 7/2.132]; Asshurbanipal No. CXCI. rs 1-4 (*VAB* 7/1 = Klauber 105 = K 159). The expression also occurs in an Akkadian text of a "brother-king" written to the king of Ugarit (RŠ 10.046: "Now in like manner preserve this friendship for me [*uṣ-ṣú-ur ṭābutta*]," reading the text as C. Virolleaud does in *RA* 38 (1941) 2, and correcting J. Nougayrol, *PRU* 3.10, accordingly. Cf. also D. C. Lyon, *Sargonidentexte,* 4.23. Though the more common expression is to "guard the oaths" and to "be mindful of the treaty," the expressions are often interchanged. Cf. Esarhaddon's Vassal Treaty, col. V. 292-92; *a-de-e an-nu-te uṣ-ra*, "guard this treaty" (Wiseman, p. 51). See also Ps 119:2, 22; 25:10. Such evidence makes our interpretation of the Aram. phrase plausible. Should there be any syntactical difficulty about the word order (Object-Subject-Verb), which is admittedly not usual, one could point to Dan 2:27 and to the common greeting in letters, שלם מראן אלה שמיא ישאל (*AP* 17:1; 30:1-2). —Note that נצר is still written with *ṣ*, and not with the later *ṭ*; cf. Nêrab I. 12-13.—טבתה is probably plur., *ṭābāteh.*[5] (I am indebted to W. L. Moran for help in checking the examples in Akkadian literature and in supplying me with further references. The responsibility for the formulation of the note is mine.)

ונגדא זנה: Dupont-Sommer wrongly read the last word as זכם, and Ginsberg, Donner-Röllig, Koopmans, Malamat repeat it unquestioningly.

But the word is זנה, as F. Rosenthal saw quite independently (*BASOR* 111 [1948] 25 n. 4). R. Meyer calls Rosenthal's reading a "Konjektur" which he regards as unnecessary. But it is not a question of a conjecture. The last letter is quite different from any other clearly written *mem* in the letter (compare מרא [line 1]; למשלח [line 7]). Moreover, there is a vertical shaft on the left side, and the head of the letter slants in the wrong direction for a *mem.* Further, there is a syntactical problem in that זכם, which is an attested demonstrative, normally precedes its noun (cf. *AP* 9:2; 20:4; 65:3; *BMAP* 7:2). Finally, the second last letter is clearly a *nun* (compare מלכן [line 1]). As for the word which precedes *znh*, the reading and meaning of it are anybody's guess. Dupont-Sommer originally read נגדא, which would mean "commander, leader," as in Sf III 10. But to whom does it refer? Could it refer to the vassal king himself? Though this is unlikely, it would explain the use of the proximate demonstrative ("this"). If we may suppose that King Adon has mentioned some official of the Babylonian king's army in the lacuna, then possibly Adon is giving a further report about what he has been doing through the parts of Palestine and Syria already conquered. Dupont-Sommer's other alternative (נגרא), related to Accad. *nāgiru* is less likely. Ginsberg would read נגוא, "this region," i.e., the Philistine coastland; he compares Isa 20:6. There is a difficulty here, in that *nĕgāwātā* in later Aram. is usually fem. Strangely enough, S. H. Horn (*AUSS* 6 [1968] 31) follows Ginsberg in this interpretation despite the masculine demonstrative.

9. פחה: "A governor," see *Panammu* 12; *AP* 30:1, 29; *B* 18, [38]; Dan 3:2, 3, 27; *Pad* I r 4 (see note on p. 223 above).

במתא: "In the land." Though theoretically this word could mean "in / by death," yet the most natural meaning seems to be "in the land," as H. L. Ginsberg suggested. The word is *mātā*, already attested in Aššur Ostracon 2; *A* 36; *CIS* 2. 31; 1QapGen 2:33. Cf. Akkad. *mātu.*

וספר שניוי ספ[ ]: The meaning of this difficult phrase is sheer guesswork. The first word could be a noun: "and an inscription" (cf. Sf I B 8, 28, 33; etc.), or "and a scribe." It could also be a verb, "and he recorded." Could שניוי be related to Hebr. *šinnûy*, later Aram. *šinnûyā,* "change, alteration"? R. Meyer interpreted the words as *waspar šannīwē*, "und die Grenze—verändern wird man sie." Even if ספר could mean "Grenze" and *šannīw* is correctly understood as a verb, how could it have a future meaning? The form would be perfect, and the meaning would be past. This interpretation is quite inadequate. But we are not able to suggest anything more convincing.

It is hoped at least, however, that the above study of the letter of King Adon throws some light on the nature of the letter and the place it had in the treaty relations existing between him and the Egyptian Pharaoh. It is not a military document (*pace* A. Malamat, *JNES* 9 [1950] 222), but rather a political document, in which the Phoenician / Philistine (?) king is using the technical terminology of treaty relations. It is also a letter in which the vassal expresses his plight and reflects the panic that must have seized the Palestinian/Syrian rulers at the news of the advance of Nebuchadrezzar's army. If this line of interpretation is pursued further, perhaps someone will be able to unravel the mysteries of the phrases that still baffle us.

NOTES TO CHAPTER 11

*Originally published in *Bib* 46 (1965) 41-55 under the same title.

[1]"Un papyrus araméen d'époque saïte découvert à Saqqarah," *Sem* 1 (1948) 43-68.

[2]See Zaki Saad Effendi, "Saqqarah: Fouilles royales (1942)," *Chronique d'Egypte* 20 (1945) 80-81; H. L. Ginsberg, "An Aramaic Contemporary of the Lachish Letters," *BASOR* 111 (1948) 24-27; J. Bright, "A New Letter in Aramaic Written to a Pharaoh of Egypt," *BA* 12 (1949) 46-52; A. Dupont-Sommer, *Les Araméens* (Paris: Maisonneuve, 1949) 89; A. Bea, "Epistula aramaica saec. VII exeunte ad Pharaonem scripta," *Bib* 30 (1949) 514–16; A. Malamat, "מכתב ארמי חדש לפרעה מימי ירמיהו," *BJPES* 15 (1949) 34–39; R. Dussaud, *Syria* 26 (1949) 152–53; A. Malamat, "The Last Wars of the Kingdom of Judah," *JNES* 9 (1950) 218–27, esp. pp. 222–23; D. W. Thomas, "The Age of Jeremiah in the Light of Recent Archaeological Discovery," *PEQ* 82 (1950) 1–15, esp. pp. 8–13; R. Meyer, "Ein aramäischer Papyrus aus den ersten Jahren Nebukadnezars II.," *Festschrift für Friedrich Zucker zum 70. Geburtstage* (ed. W. Müller; Berlin: Akademie-Verlag, 1954) 251–62; A. Malamat, "A New Record of Nebuchadrezzar's Palestinian Campaigns," *IEJ* 6 (1956) 246–56, esp. p. 252; E. Vogt, "Die neu-babylonische Chronik über die Schlacht bei Karkemisch und die Einnahme von Jerusalem," *Volume du Congrès, Strasbourg 1956* (VTSup 4; Leiden: Brill, 1957) 67–96, esp. pp. 85–89; J. Bright, *A History of Israel* (Philadelphia: Westminster, 1959) 305; W. D. McHardy, "A Letter from Saqqarah," *Documents of Old Testament Times* (ed. D. W. Thomas; London/New York: Nelson, 1958) 251–55; J. D. Quinn, "Alcaeus 48 (B 16) and the Fall of Ascalon, (604 B.C.)," *BASOR* 16 (1961) 19–20; J. J. Koopmans, *AC* §16; H. Donner and W. Röllig, *KAI* §266; K. Galling, "Eschmunazar und der Herr der Könige," *ZDPV* 79 (1963) 140–51; F. Vattioni, "Il papiro di Saqqarah," *SPap* 5 (1966) 101–17; S. H. Horn, "Where and When Was the Aramaic Saqqara Papyrus Written?" *AUSS* 6 (1968) 29–45; A. Malamat, "The Last Kings of Judah and the Fall of Jerusalem," *IEJ* 18 (1968) 137–56; J. T. Milik, "Les papyrus araméens d'Hermoupolis" (p. 202 above, n. 23), 561–63; A. Malamat, "The Twilight of Judah: In the Egyptian-Babylonian Maelstrom," *Congress Volume, Edinburgh 1974* (VTSup 28; Leiden: Brill, 1975) 123–45.

[3]See D. J. Wiseman, *Chronicles of Chaldaean Kings (626-556 B.C.) in the British Museum* (London: British Museum, 1956) 68 (B.M. 21946 obv. 18-20). Cf. E. Vogt, "Die neu-babylonische Chronik" (n. 2 above), 85-89; A. Malamat, *IEJ* 6 (1956) 246-56; D. N. Freedman, "The Babylonian Chronicle," *BA* 19 (1956) 50-60.

[4]Albright's dating and comments on the text are found in the notes to Ginsberg's article (see n. 2 above), *BASOR* 111 (1948) 24-27. For Malamat's opinion, see *IEJ* 6 (1956) 252; cf. S. H. Horn, *AUSS* 6 (1968) 29-45.

[5]C.-F. Jean and J. Hoftijzer (*DISO*, 99) offer an interpretation which is similar to the one proposed here: "votre serviteur a gardé sa loyauté."

Chapter 12

A Re-Study of an Elephantine Aramaic Marriage Contract (*AP* 15)*

It was to be expected that E. G. Kraeling's publication of the *Brooklyn Museum Aramaic Papyri* would shed new light on some of the problems of older, well-known Elephantine texts. This article is a reconsideration of an Elephantine marriage contract which is often quoted in A. E. Cowley's version, but which needs a new, comprehensive presentation, because data from Kraeling's publication support certain interpretations of details in it that others have proposed, but which were strangely neglected by Cowley and others who treated the text. The foreword of Kraeling's volume acknowledges its indebtedness to Professor William F. Albright, in whose honor the present volume is being published. His interest in things Aramaic has been manifested in many ways during his scholarly career, and it is a privilege to include here a study of this Elephantine text as a tribute to a revered teacher. In it I hope to bring together items from many of the studies and discussions of the text to improve the understanding of the text as a whole. Recent studies of the legal aspects of the Elephantine contracts have also added to our understanding of this document.

The text of the marriage contract was first published by A. H. Sayce and A. E. Cowley in 1906 as papyrus G in the collection, *Aramaic Papyri Discovered at Assuan.*[1] This contract has been difficult to understand, partly because the papyrus is fragmentary and partly because its terminology and phraseology were often ambiguous. When it is studied today against the background of other marriage contracts from Elephantine, especially two in the Kraeling collection, some of the ambiguity can be resolved. In Cowley's publication at least three other texts belong to this genre, although they are rather fragmentary.[2] Among the Brooklyn Museum papyri there are three further contracts that can be used for comparative purposes.[3]

The papyrus in which we are interested contains the contract of a marriage, apparently the third one, of Miphṭaḥiah, the daughter of Maḥsiah, with Esḥor, the son of Ṣeḥo. It sets forth the terms of the marriage agreement: the date (line 1), the identification of the contracting parties (lines 2-3), the formal agreement of marriage (4), the record of the payment of the bride-price (4-6), of the dowry money brought by the bride (6-7), and of the valuable possessions brought with her (7-13). There follows the sum total of the amounts involved in the contract (13-15) and a record of the husband's acknowledgment of all this (15). Then a further list catalogues objects brought by the bride, the value of which is not determined (15-16). Certain stipulations begin in line 17: the bride's right to her husband's property should he die childless (17-20); his inheritance of his wife's property should she die childless (20-22). In case the bride divorces her husband she must pay the divorce fee, but she will be free and have the right to take what is hers (22-26). In case the husband divorces his wife he forfeits the bride-price, and she will be free and have the right to take what she brought to the marriage (26-29). The wife is further protected against a third party who might seek to drive her away from her husband's house and possessions (29-31). The husband is to be fined if he claims that he has another wife or other children (31-34); he is also to be fined if he tries to withdraw his property from his wife (35-36). Witnesses to the contract (37-39).

The Aramaic text of the marriage contract should be read as follows:[4]

1 ב[5]2 [ל]תשרי [הו יום] 6 לירח אפפ [שנת. . .ארתחשס]ש מלכ[א]
2 אמר אסחור בר [צחא] ארדכל זי מלכא למח[סיה א]רמי זי סון לדגל
3 וריזת לאמר אנה [א]תית ביתך למנתן לי [ל]ברתך מפט‹ח›יה לאנתו
4 הי אנתתי ואנה בעלה מן יומא זנה ועד עלם יהבת לך מהר
5 ברתך מפטחיה [כסף] שקלן 5 באבני מלכ[א] על עליך וטב לבבך
6 בגו הנעלת לב[יתי] מפטחיה בידה כס[ף] תכונה כרש 1 שקלן 2 באבני
7 מלכא כסף ר 2 ל10 הנעלת לי בידה לבש 1 זי עמר חדת חטב
8 צבע ידין הוה ארך אמן 8 ב5 [ש]וה כסף כרשן 2 שקלן 8
9 באבני מלכא שביט 1 חדת הוה ארך אמן 8 ב5 שוה
10 כסף שקלן 8 באבני מלכא לבש אחרן זי עמר נשחט הוה
11 ארך אמן 6 ב4 שוה כסף שקלן 7 מחזי 1 זי נחש שוה
12 כסף שקל 1 ר 2 תמ[סא] 1 זי נחש שויה כסף שקל 1 ר 2 כסן זי נחש 2
13 שוין כסף שקלן [2] זלוע 1 זי נחש שוה כסף ר 2 כל כספא
14 ודמי נכסיא כסף כרשן 6 שקל‹ן› 5 חלר[ן] 20 כסף ר 2 ל10 באבני
15 מלכא על עלי [וט]יב לבבי בגו שוי 1 זי גמא בה נעבצן
16 זי אבן 4 פק 1 זי סלק כפן 2 פרכס 1 זי חצן חדת תקם חפנן 5 שנן משאן 1
17 מחר או יום א[חר]ן ימות אסחור ובר דכר ונקבה לא
18 איתי לה מן מפ[טח]יה אנתתה מפטחיה הי שליטה בביתה
19 זי אסחור ונכס[והי] וקנינה וכל זי איתי [ל]ה על אנפי ארעא
20 כלה מחר או יום ‹אחרן› תמות מפטחיה ובר דכר ונקבה לא
21 איתי לה מן אסחור בעלה אסחור הו ירתנה בנכסיה
22 וקנינה מחר [או י]ום אחרן תקום [מפ]טחיה בעדה
23 ותאמר שנאת לאסחור בעלי כסף שנאה בראשה תתב על
24 מוזנא ותתקל ל[אס]חור כסף שקלן 7 ר 2 וכל זי הנעלת
25 בידה תהנפק מן חם עד חוט ותהך [ל]האן זי צבית ולא
26 {י}דין ולא דבב מחר או יום אחרן יקום אסחור בעדה
27 ויאמר שנאת [לאנ]תתי מפטחיה מהרה [י]אבד וכל זי הנעלת

28 בידה תהנפק מן חם עד חוט ביום חד בכף חדה ותהך
29 לה אן זי צבית ולא דין ולא דבב ו[זי] יקום על מפטחיה
30 לתרכותה מן ביתה זי אסחור ונכסוהי וקנינה ינתן לה
31 כסף כרשן 20 ויע[בד] לה דין ספרא זנה ולא אכל אמר
32 איתי לי אנתה אחרה להן מפט‹ח›יה ובנן אחרנן להן בנן זי
33 תלד לי מפטחיה הן אמר איתי לי ב[נן] ואנתה אחר‹נ›ן להן
34 מפטחיה ובניה אנתן למפטחיה כס[ף] כרשן 20 באבני
35 מלכא ולא אכל [אהנ]תר נכסי וקניני מן מפ[טח]יה והן העדת המו
36 מנה {{קבל ס[פר אחר]ן}} אנתן למפטחיה [כסף] כרשן 20 באבני מל[כא]
37 כתב נתן בר ענניה [ספרא זנה כפם אסחור] ושהדיא בגו
38 פנוליה בר יזניה [. . .]יה בר אוריה מנחם בר [ז]כור
39 שהד רעיבל ב[ר]

Translation

[1]On the 2[5th of] Tishri, [that is, the] 6th [day] of the month of Epiph, [the 25th year of Artaxerx]es, [the] king, [2]Esḥor bar [Ṣeḥo], a royal architect, said to Maḥ[siah], an [A]ramean of Syene, of the [3]Varyazāt garrison: I have [co]me (to) your house (to ask you) to give me your daughter Miphṭa‹ḥ›iah in marriage. [4]She is my wife and I am her husband from this day forward. I have given you the bride-price for [5]your daughter Miphṭaḥiah, 5 [silver] shekels by roya[l] weight; you have received it and you are satisfied [6]with it. Miphṭaḥiah has brought into [my] hou[se] with her a dowry su[m] of 1 karsh, 2 shekels by royal [7]weight, (in) silver (of) 2 qu(arters) to the ten-piece. She has (also) brought with her to me: 1 new garment of wool, striped [8]with dye on both edges, measuring 8 cubits by 5, worth (in) cash 2 karshin and 8 shekels [9]by royal weight; 1 new shawl, measuring 8 cubits by 5, [wo]rth [10](in) cash 8 shekels by royal weight; another garment of wool, finely woven, [11]measuring 6 cubits by 4, worth (in) cash 7 shekels; 1 bronze mirror, worth [12](in) cash 1 shekel, 2 qu(arters); 1 bronze bo[wl], worth (in) cash 1 shekel, 2 qu(arters); 2 bronze cups, [13]worth (in) cash [2] shekels; 1 bronze pitcher, worth (in) cash 2 qu(arters). All the money and [14]the value of the possessions are 6 silver karshin, 5 shekel‹s›, 20 hallur[in], (in) silver (of) 2 qu(arters) to the ten-piece by royal [15]weight. I have received it [and] I am [sa]tisfied with it. (Also) 1 reed couch, on which there are [16]4 stone inlays; 1 *pq* of *slq*; 2 ladles; 1 new *prks* of palm-leaves; 5 handfuls of castor oil; 1 (pair of) leather (?) sandals. [17]Should Esḥor die tomorrow or some o[the]r day, having no child, (either) male or female, [18]by his wife Miph[ṭaḥ]iah, Miphṭaḥiah is entitled to the house [19]of Esḥor, [his] possessions and property, and all that he has on the face of the earth, [20]all of it. Should Miphṭaḥiah die tomorrow or ‹some other› day, having no child, (either) male or female, [21]by her husband Esḥor, Esḥor shall inherit her possessions [22]and her property. Should Miphṭaḥiah rise up in an assembly tomorrow [or] some other [da]y [23]and say, "I divorce my husband Esḥor," the divorce fee is on her head; she shall sit by the [24]scale and weigh out

to Esḥor 7 silver shekels, 2 qu(arters); and all that she brought [25]with her, she shall take out, from straw to string, and go [wh]erever she pleases, without [26]suit or process. Should Esḥor rise up in an assembly tomorrow or some other day [27]and say, "I divorce my [wife] Miphṭaḥiah," his bride-price shall go forfeit; and all that she brought [28]with her, she will take out, from straw to string, on one day (and) at one time, and she may go [29]wherever she pleases, without suit or process. [Whoever] rises up against Miphṭaḥiah [30]to drive her out of Esḥor's house or his possessions or his property, shall pay her [31]20 silver karshin and shall carry out in her regard the stipulation of this document. I shall not be able to say, [32]"I have another wife, other than Miphṭa‹ḥ›iah, and other children, other than those that [33]Miphṭaḥiah will bear to me." If I do say, "I have other chi[ldren] and a wife, other than [34]Miphṭaḥiah and her children," I shall pay Miphṭaḥiah 20 sil[ver] karshin by royal [35]weight. Nor shall I be able to [with]draw my possessions and my property from Miph[ṭaḥ]iah. If I do remove them [36]from her (according to [some ot]her doc[ument]), I shall pay Miphṭaḥiah 20 silver karshin by royal weight. [37]Nathan bar ᶜAnaniah wrote [this document at the behest of Esḥor]. The witnesses to it are [38]Penuliah bar Yezaniah, [ ]iah bar Uriah, Menaḥem bar [Z]akkur. [39]Witness: Reᶜibel ba[r].

General Remarks

The text is an example of what the Arameans and Jews at Elephantine in the fifth century B.C. called *sĕpar ᵓintū*, "a document of marriage" (or, more strictly, "of wifehood"); see *AP* 14:4; 35:4-5; *BMAP* 10:7, 9; 12:18. The difference between it and the later *kĕtûbāh* among the Jews has often been noted. How old the custom is that is represented by this text is hard to say. The reference to a written contract in Tob 7:14 seems to be the oldest. In any case, the marriage contracts from Elephantine have a set form that enables one to compare them and use them for interpretation.[5]

When Sayce and Cowley originally published this text they did not correctly understand the verb הנעלת in line 6 and their attempt to explain the total of the objects mentioned in lines 6-13 did not succeed. Though other suggestions were made for the interpretation of these lines,[6] Cowley's subsequent smaller edition repeated the original understanding of the text found in the *editio princeps*, at least on this point.[7] A more recent translation of the text was provided by H. L. Ginsberg, in two slightly differing forms,[8] but he made no attempt to render lines 6-16. Since the identification of some of the objects in the list was problematic—and still is, in fact—he prudently did not try to translate them in such a collection of texts as that for which his version was prepared. However, a notation he gives in the first edition highlights the problem; he writes: "Lines 6-16, Ashor's [or Mahseiah's] gifts to Miphtahiah and—perhaps—hers to him."[9] For the problem was, first, to determine whether the verb הנעלת was a first singular form (referring to Esḥor, who had the contract written), or a second singular masculine form (referring to Maḥsiah, the father of the bride), or a third singular feminine form (referring to Miphṭaḥiah, the bride). Cowley noted the lack of distinction between such forms in the bare consonantal text.

Several writers had seen clearly that הנעלת must be understood as the third singular feminine wherever it occurs in this papyrus,[10] and Kraeling confirmed this, noting that the Brooklyn Museum contracts had the same expression.[11] In *BMAP* 7:5 we read, הנעלת לי יהוישמע אחתך לביתי תכונה זי כסף כרשן ש[קל]ן 2 חלרן 5 "Yahuyishmaᶜ, your sister, has brought to me, into my house, the dowry of 2 silver karshin, 2 shekels, 5 ḥallurin. . . ." Similarly in *BMAP* 2:4, הנעלת לי תמת בידה לבש 1 זי עמר שוה כסף שקלן 7, "Tamut has brought with her to me 1 garment of wool, worth in cash 7 shekels." These texts make it clear that the bride's dowry and possessions are indicated in the contract by the phrase הנעלת לי X לביתי or הנעלת לי X בידה, in which *X* stands for the proper name of the woman. Lidzbarski wanted to restore הנעלת לי [ברתך] in line 6 and הנעלת לי in line 7. Kraeling suggested the restoration of *ly* twice in lines 6 and 7. The restoration is correct for line 7, but a glance at the photo of the papyrus reveals that לי alone is not sufficient in line 6, since the lacuna is too long. Moreover, the head of the letter that follows *lamedh* is not clearly that of a *yodh*, but is possibly that of a *beth*, since this letter is written with different stances in the papyrus. If *yodh* is correct, then one should read לי[לביתי], as in *BMAP* 7:5. But if it is a *beth* that follows *lamedh*, then perhaps one should read simply לב[יתי], "to my house." This would be less crowded. Note too that Cowley read *lb*[.

The same understanding of הנעלת is to be given to the word in lines 24 and 27, "all that she brought with her," as Lidzbarski suggested earlier, but which Cowley did not accept. This suggestion is now confirmed by *BMAP* 7:22, כל זי הנעלת בביתה ינתן לה תכונתה ולבשיה, "all that she brought into his house he shall give to her, her dowry and her garments." Cf. *BMAP* 2:10.

One reason why Cowley did not accept the suggestion of Freund and Jampel, who wanted to understand הנעלת as the second singular masculine, referring to Miphṭaḥiah's father, Maḥsiah, was that for him "the sum total in l. 14 shows that the presents were given by the same person who paid the 5 shekels."[12] But since he did not correctly understand several other expressions in the text, he insisted that Esḥor, not Miphṭaḥiah, was the subject of the verb הנעלת. The five shekels in line 5 represent the מהר, "the bride-price," paid by the groom to the bride's father, Maḥsiah. This is not the "dowry," and though Cowley obviously used this English term for מהר in a loose sense, it is indicative of his basic misunderstanding of the contract as a whole. He understood the difference between "bride-price" and "dowry," as is obvious from his reference to Gen 34:12. However, he misunderstood the term כסף תכונה in line 6, translating it as "the cost of furniture." It is now clear that this is "dowry money," whatever may be the etymological explanation of the phrase. In any case, Cowley was right in saying that the מהר of 5 shekels was included in the sum given in lines 13-14.

To arrive at the sum of 6 karshin, 5 shekels, and 20 ḥallurin, one must total up the dowry (כסף תכונה), the value of the objects brought by Miphṭaḥiah, and the bride-price (מהר) that Esḥor paid. Thus:

Line	Object		Value		
5	Esḥor's	*mhr*		5 shekels	
6	Miphṭaḥiah's	*ksp tkwnh*	1 karsh	2 shekels	
7-8	"	*lbš 1 zy ʿmr*	2 karshin	8 shekels	
9-10	"	*šbyṭ 1*		8 shekels	
10-11	"	*lbš ʾḥrn zy ʿmr*		7 shekels	
11-12	"	*mḥzy 1 zy nḥš*		1 shekel	2 R
12	"	*tmsʾ 1*		1 shekel	2 R
12-13	"	*ksn 2*		2 shekels[13]	
13	"	*zlwʿ 1*			2 R
			3 karshin	34 shekels	6 R

Cowley had shown that a כרש equalled a ten-shekel piece and that ר, probably standing for רבעא, "quarter," i.e., a quarter of a shekel, equalled ten ḥallurin.[14] Hence the above total is easily converted to 6 karshin, 5 shekels, and 20 ḥallurin, the sum formulated in lines 13-14. Cowley was, then, right in maintaining that the bride-price was included in the sum so formulated.

But does it mean that all that is included in the total came from one and the same person? This was Cowley's conclusion and the reason why he insisted that הנעלת was the first singular form, referring to Esḥor's presents. It is, however, clear from *BMAP* 7 that this conclusion is erroneous. Though *BMAP* 7:15 is fragmentary at one point, enough is preserved to show that the dowry and the bride-price were both included in the total, even though these sums come from different persons: [כ]ל [מ]אנ[י . . . נ]חש ותכ[ו]נתא ומהרא כסף כרשן שבעה ה[ו 7 ש]ק[ל]ן תמניה הו 8 חלרן 5 באבני מלכא כסף 2 ר לעשרתא, "all the vessels of [and br]onze, and the dowry, and the bride-price (equal) seven, that is 7, silver karshin, eight, that is 8, shekels, 5 ḥallurin by royal weight, (in) silver of 2 qu(arters) to the ten-piece."[15]

The reason for the inclusion of the מהר in the sum total has been explained in various ways. What seems to be clear is that the מהר was no longer a "bride-price" in the strict sense, i.e., a price paid to the father (or guardian) of the bride. Evidence from Alalakh, Babylonia, and Egypt indicates that the father at least turned it over to the daughter.[16] S. Greengus thinks that it was not paid at all, but represents merely "a penalty which would be forfeited by the divorcing party."[17] H. L. Ginsberg thinks rather that the מהר becomes the divorce fee.[18] The reason for the dispute in the last instance involves *BMAP* 2, where no מהר is mentioned and the sum written on the outside of the papyrus differs considerably from that written within. I shall leave this question aside, since it does not concern the contract now under study. The important thing to realize is that the מהר is included in the sum total and is regarded as something that belongs to the bride.[19]

After these general remarks we may proceed to the analysis of the text of the contract itself.

Notes

1. ב5[2 ל]תשרי: "On the 25th of Tishri." This is the first part of the dating of the contract, which is also done according to the Egyptian calendar in the following phrase. The correspondence of Tishri and Epiph is also found in *BMAP* 4:1 and 7:1. See S. H. Horn and L. H. Wood, "The Fifth Century Jewish Calendar at Elephantine," *JNES* 13 (1954) 1-20. The preposition ב is common in such dates and probably is an abbreviation for ביום; it is usually followed by the cardinal number written in a cipher. In *AP* 26:16 one can find the number written out (and preceded by four hundred). The preposition ל has been restored on the basis of its frequent usage (see *BMAP* 1:1; 3:1; 4:1; 8:1; 9:1; 10:1; 10:1, 10), when the name of the month is not preceded by בירח or לירח. Kraeling omitted it in *BMAP* 6:1, but see plate VI; it is to be restored also in *BMAP* 2:1 (before [תמוז]). It is omitted, however, in *BMAP* 5:1.

[הו יום] 6 לירח אפף: "That is, the 6th day of the month of Epiph." This double dating is found in all the marriage contracts from Elephantine, but not in all other documents. See R. Yaron, "The Schema," p. 34; E. G. Kraeling, *BMAP*, 51-52. The restored form הו, without a final *aleph*, is normal in the Elephantine texts; see I. N. Vinnikov, *Slovar*, p. 194. Judging from the commonly used שנת, which is the construct state, the word יום should also be so regarded. Since the name of the Egyptian month is always written in these texts simply as אפף, I vocalize it as Epiph, not Epiphi. The latter is derived from Greek transcriptions of the name in papyri, but it is not universal in Greek by any means. Alongside of it one finds rather frequently *Epip, Epeip, Epeiph*, and in Coptic also *Epēp* or *Epep*. See F. Preisigke, *Wörterbuch der griechischen Papyrusurkunden*, 3/1 (1929) 86. There is no evidence that the Aramaic form would have been pronounced with a final *i*-vowel. Cf. J. Černý, *ASAE* 43 (1943) 173-81; *BIFAO* 57 (1958) 207.

[שנת] 25 ארתחשסש מלכ[א]: "The 25th year of Artaxerxes, the king." The restoration of the year depends on the usually admitted relation of this contract to *AP* 14, which is clearly dated to this year of Artaxerxes. The latter document is the settlement of a claim connected with the divorce of Miphṭaḥiah from her second husband in 440 B.C. The new third marriage, of which the present text is a record, probably took place a short time afterward. In any case, if it is wrong the date is off only by a year or so. But Horn and Wood (*JNES* 13 [1954] 13) prefer to date this text in 435 B.C. (?), with some hesitation.

The king is almost certainly Artaxerxes I Longimanus (464-24). The name is written in the official Aramaic transcription used in many of these texts, ארתחשסש (*AP* 6:2; 7:1; 10:1; 13:1; *BMAP* 1:1; 3:1; 4:1; etc.). In *BMAP* 2:1 it is written simply as ארתחש, which Kraeling rightly considers to be "a scribal error." In *KAI* 274:1; 275:1 we find the name ארתחשסי מלכא בר זי זריתר,

but is it the same? According to H. H. Schaeder (*Iranische Beiträge I* [Schriften der Königsberger Gelehrten Gesellschaft, Geisteswissenschaftliche Kl., 6/5; Halle: M. Niemeyer, 1930] p. 268) the Aramaic form found in the Elephantine texts represents the Persian *Artaxšassa* (‹ Old Persian *Artaxšathra*), whereas the forms in biblical Aramaic (ᵓ*Artaḥšaśt*ᵓ [Ezra 4:7], ᵓ*Artaḥšaśtā*ᵓ [Ezra 4:7], or ᵓ*Artaḥšastā*ᵓ [Ezra 7:1]) are attempts to come even closer to the Persian form with the final *-a*.

2. [צחא] אסחור בר: "Esḥor bar Ṣeḥo." The groom's father's name is supplied from *AP* 20:3, 20. The groom's name here is Egyptian, equalling *nś-Ḥr*, "Belonging to (the god) Horus," a form of name that is often transcribed into Greek with initial *Es-* or simply *s-* (see H. Ranke, *Die ägyptischen Personennamen* [Glückstadt: Augustin], I [1935] 178, 7). But in three other Elephantine documents the children born of the marriage recorded in this contract are listed thus: "Yedaniah and Maḥsiah, 2 in all, sons of Esḥor bar Ṣeḥo by Miphṭaḥiah, daughter of Maḥsiah" (*AP* 20:3); "Yedaniah bar Nathan and Maḥsiah bar Nathan, his brother, their mother being Mibṭaḥiah, daughter of Maḥsiah bar Yedaniah" (*AP* 25:3); "Maḥsiah bar Nathan 1, Yedaniah bar Nathan I, in all 2, . . . we have divided between us the slaves of Mibṭaḥiah, our mother" (*AP* 28:2-3). There is little doubt that the same children and parents are meant, though this has been contested (see E. Volterra, "*'Yhwdy' e 'ᶜrmy'* nei papiri aramaici del V secolo provenienti dall'Egitto," *ANL*, Rendiconti, Sc. mor. 8/18 [1963] 131-73; cf. R. Yaron, "Who is Who at Elephantine," *Iura* 15 [1964] 167-72; and Volterra's reply, ibid., 173-80). And yet Esḥor's name subsequently appears as Nathan in *AP* 25 and 28. Cowley speculated: Did Esḥor become a proselyte and take a Jewish name, Nathan (*AP*, p. 47)?

The patronymic *bar Ṣeḥo* is given here in its conventional vocalization. The father's name *Ṣḥ*ᵓ is Egyptian and represents *Ḏd-ḥr*, "Horus has spoken," or possibly "The face of X (a god) has spoken," because of the disappearance of final *r*. The name is apparently transcribed into Akkadian as *Ṣi-ḫa-a* and into Greek as *Teōs* or *Tachōs* (see H. Ranke, *Ägyptische Personennamen*, I. 411, 12; G. Fecht, *Wortakzent und Silbenstruktur: Untersuchungen zur Geschichte der ägyptischen Sprache* (ÄF 21; Glückstadt: Augustin, 1960], 84, § 151, n. 254).

ארדכל זי מלכא: "A royal architect," or "a builder to the king" (Ginsberg), i.e., some sort of government-hired builder. The name of the profession is found in *AP* 14:2, spelled ᵓ*rdykl*; it occurs in later Aramaic as ᵓ*ardīkĕlā* or ᵓ*ardēkĕlā*. This is basically an Akkadian word, reflecting the Babylonian *(w)arad ekalli*, "palace slave." The meaning of the word, however, developed within the Mesopotamian area and came to denote not a social class but a profession, specifically a workman in the building trade. See further, A. L. Oppenheim, "AKK. arad ekalli = 'Builder,'" *ArOr* 17 (1949) 227-35. In this sense it is used in these texts.

למח[סיה]: "To Maḥsiah," the father of Miphṭaḥiah. He is the son of Yedaniah (*AP* 25:3) and appears again in *AP* 5:2, 9, 12, 20; 6:3, 22; 8:1, 18, 28, 35; 9:1, 5, 16; 11:14; 13:1, 17bis, 21; 14:2; 25:3, 7; *BMAP* 1:13. The name is undoubtedly Hebrew, *Maḥsi-yāh,* "Yahu is my refuge." It occurs also in Jer 32:12; 51:59; but its Masoretic vocalization is questionable. The root of it is *ḥsy*, and one can understand how the Masoretic pointing *Maḥsēyāh* developed (as a *maqtal*-type); but one may ask whether it is accurate for the fifth century B.C. In any case, the vocalization *Meḥasiah* (S. Greengus, *Aramaic Marriage Contracts*, 122) is wrong.

[א]רמי זי סון: "An Aramean of Syene." This same identification is given to Maḥsiah in *AP* 5:2; 13:2; 14:3. But in *AP* 6:3 he is called יהודי בבירת יב, "a Jew in the fortress of Yeb," and identified in *AP* 8:2 as יהוד[י] מהחסן ביב בירתא, "a Jew owning property in Yeb, the fortress." Again in *AP* 9:2 he seems to be called a י[הודי זי ב]יב, but the text is very fragmentary here. On the problem of one and the same person being called a "Jew" and an "Aramean" in the Elephantine papyri, see E. Volterra, *ANL*, Rendiconti, Sc. mor. 8/18 (1963) 131-73. He seeks to distinguish such persons. But R. Yaron (*Iura* 15 [1964] 167-72) suggests that the terms יהודי and ארמי were used to designate the same persons, but from different points of view. He thinks that יהודי was used "especially in documents in which some non-Jewish factor is involved," and thus serves to identify the persons as such. But the Jews of Elephantine used the term ארמי "amongst themselves." This issue is far from settled, and there seems to be little at present in the text to allow of a solution.

The word ארמי is an appositive to a proper name, and yet occurs in the absolute state (see T. Nöldeke, *ZA* 20 [1907] 142; P. Joüon, "Notes grammaticales, lexicographiques et philologiques sur les papyrus araméens d'Egypte," *MUSJ* 18 [1934] 1-90, esp. pp. 10-11). This is true when the absolute is followed by some determination, as here.

The name סון, Syene, is usually vocalized after the Greek *Syēnē* or the Hebrew *Sĕwēnēh* (Ezek 29:10). Cf. the Coptic *Souan* and Arabic *ʾAswân.*

לדגל וריזת: "Of the Varyazāt garrison." The same identification is given for Maḥsiah in *AP* 5:3; 6:4; 13:2; 14:3; but in *AP* 8:2; 9:2 he seems to be said to belong to the דגל הומדת, "the Hawmadāt garrison." On the Persian names used here, see H. H. Schaeder, *Iranische Beiträge I* (Schriften der Königsberger Gelehrten Gesellschaft, Geisteswissenschaftliche Kl., 6/5; Halle: M. Niemeyer, 1930; reprinted, Darmstadt: Wissenschaftliche Buchgesellschaft, 1972) 269. The exact meaning of דגל is obscure. It is often said that it means basically a "standard" or "banner," but this is far from clear (see Y. Yadin, *The Scroll of the War of the Sons of Light against the Sons of Darkness* [New York: Oxford, 1962] 39). In these texts it seems to denote a military unit or detachment of undetermined size; cf. Num 1:52; 2:2-3, 10, 17-18, 25, 31, 34. To identify it as a military unit is not to deny a social organization that may also be involved in it. The shift from the Varyazāt garrison to the Hawmadāt may represent a real transfer. The proper name of the garrison is not easily explained; it is almost certainly Persian. In *BMAP* 8:11 it occurs as a personal name. Was the name of the garrison derived from the name of some chief or official in it? In any case it is interesting to note that the majority of names of such garrisons at Yeb or Syene are either Persian or Akkadian (e.g., *Hawmadāt, AP* 8:2; 9:2; *Bagapat, TA* 5:7, 9; *ᵓAtroparan, AP* 6:9; *ᵓArtabanu, AP* 6:3; *ᵓIddinnabū, AP* 20:2; *BMAP* 14:2; *Nabūkudurr*[*i*], *AP* 7:3; *ᵓArpaḥu, BMAP* 5:2; *Nmsw, BMAP* 3:2). B. Porten (*Archives from Elephantine*, 30) takes this as evidence that the דגלן were named after their "respective non-Jewish commanders."

3. לאמר: "Saying," a stereotyped, fossilized peal infinitive of אמר, which has persisted in such syntactical contexts, introducing direct statements. It is obviously akin to the Hebrew *lēᵓmōr*; see T. Nöldeke, *ZA* 20 (1907) 137. Peal infinitives without the initial *mem* are found in early Aramaic texts; see above, p. 239. On the other hand, the real Aramaic form, מאמר, is found in *AP* 32:2 and *A* 115.

אנה [א]תית ביתך: "I have come to your house." This seems like a useless detail in the otherwise closely worded contract. It may represent an historical detail that is preserved here, but it may also be stereotyped language. It is peculiar in Aramaic and may involve a scribal error. For though there are many instances of verbs expressing motion toward a place with an object and no preposition (see p. 224 above), this is apparently a lone instance of such an expression with a common noun as object (at least in this period of Aramaic; cf. 1QapGen 10:12). Cf. *BMAP* 14:3 (אנה אתית עליך בבית[ך]); 7:3 (אנה אתית על [בי]תך); 2:3 (אנה אתית עליך). These examples make one suspect that the phrase in this text is a scribal error.

למנתן לי [ל]ברתך: "(To ask you) to give me your daughter." The cumbersome infinitival construction (where the infinitive's subject is different from that of the main verb on which it depends) is perhaps explained by *BMAP* 7:3, אנה אתית על [בי]תך ושאלת מנך לנשן יהוישמע, "I have come to your house and asked of you the woman Yaḥuyishmaᶜ." But the expression found in this text had apparently become stereotyped, since it is also found in *BMAP* 2:3. Cf. *AP* 2:13 (למובל); *HermWP* 2:12-13; Ezra 7:20; Dan 2:24; 4:23.

מפט‹ח›יה: "Miphṭaḥiah." The same scribal omission of *ḥ* occurs in line 32. The name is a dissimilated form of the more original *Mibṭaḥiāh*, "Yahu is my security," *Mibṭaḥī-yāh*, found in *AP* 8:2; 9:3, 7, 10, 12; 14:2, 14; 20:3; 25:3, 7; 28:3, 5, 6. The dissimilation of the voiced bilabial occurs also in *AP* 13:2, 4. The shift from *p* › *b* is found in earlier Aramaic texts: נבש, Sf I A 37; בתן, Sf I A 32; אלב, Hadad 34. But the opposite shift is more rarely attested.

This is apparently Miphṭaḥiah's third marriage. From *AP* 14 (dated ca. 440 B.C.) it seems that her second marriage ended in divorce from an Egyptian named Piᵓ. From *AP* 8:6 it is clear that Miphṭaḥiah was earlier married to Yezan bar Uriah (ca. 460 B.C.). Miphṭaḥiah thus appears to be an adult divorcee, but she is still given in marriage to Esḥor by her father.

לאנתו: "In marriage," or more strictly "for wifehood." This expression occurs again in *AP* 48:3; *BMAP* 2:3; 7:3. It states the purpose of the agreement that is recorded in this contract. Lidzbarski (*Ephemeris,* 3.80) called attention to the use of this phrase in official Jewish marriage contracts of a later date and compared the Mishnah, *Ketuboth*, 4:7ff. He also noted that Targum Onqelos on Gen 16:3 translated the Hebrew phrase *lĕʾiššāh* by *lĕʾintū.* Kraeling (*BMAP*, 146) further compared the expression to the Assyrian *nadānu ana aššūti.*

4. הי אנתתי ואנה בעלה מן יומא זנה ועד עלם: "She is my wife and I am her husband from this day forward," lit., "from this day and forever." The same formula is found in *BMAP* 2:3-4; 7:4 (but with the omission of *w*- before *ᶜd* in the latter text). These words actually record the formal agreement that constitutes the marriage; Esḥor acknowledges his relationship to Miphṭaḥiah. The acknowledgment is formulated solely from the standpoint of the groom. The bride's consent is undoubtedly presupposed, but not recorded, if expressed at all. The omission of this undoubtedly reflects the attitude toward women in the ancient Near East. A few isolated texts record the bride's consent, but they are so isolated as to preclude any generalizations (see Gen 24:8, 58; C. H. Gordon, "The Status of Women in Nuzi Texts," *ZA* 43 [1936] 149). Even in the case of an adult marriage, such as Miphṭaḥiah's third, the consent is not recorded. This raises the question whether בעלה is too weakly translated merely as "her husband."

The last part of the agreement, מן יומא זנה ועד עלם, is also found in documents other than marriage contracts (e.g., *AP* 8:9; 14:6-7; 20:9-10; *BMAP* 4:4-5; 10:8). It in no way guarantees the indissolubility of the marriage, because a provision is made in the contract itself for divorce. Contrast the formula in Mur 20 i 3-4. Cf. S. Loewenstamm, "From This Time and Forevermore," *Tarbiẓ* 32 (1963) 313-16.

In Hos 2:4 one finds the Hebrew counterpart of this agreement negatively expressed, הי לא אשתי ואנכי לא אישה. Though this is scarcely a formal divorce formula, it undoubtedly reflects the ancient marriage formula that we find in this Aramaic text.

יהבת לך מהר ברתך מפטחיה: "I have given you the bride-price for your daughter Miphṭaḥiah." The noun is related to the Hebrew *mōhar* (Gen 34:12; Exod 22:16; 1 Sam 18:25). The construct is to be vocalized *mĕhar*, and the emphatic is either *muhrāʾ* or *mohŏrāʾ*; *pace* R. Yaron, *Introduction*, 45 n. 1, the Aramaic vocalization is not uncertain. No מהר is mentioned in the contract *BMAP* 2, and this has been variously interpreted (see H. L. Ginsberg, *JAOS* 74 [1954] 156; R. Yaron, *Introduction*, 57; S. Greengus, "Aramaic Marriage Contracts," 41-64). The מהר is in reality the same as the Akkad. *terḫatu*; the bride-price was an institution at Ugarit (see *UT* 77:19-20 *watn mhrh labh*) and also in ancient Egypt. But by Saite and Persian times it had lost the implication of a purchase of the bride; though nominally paid to the father or guardian, it apparently became the property of the bride. This usage is reflected in the Elephantine texts too.

5. 5 שקלן [כסף]: "5 silver shekels," or possibly "a sum of 5 shekels." At times—even in this text—כסף seems to be used generically in the sense of "money" or "cash," and it is not easy to tell to what extent it retains the nuance of "silver." My translation shifts back and forth between these two senses, depending on which seems more appropriate. Note the expression in *BMAP* 2:6 ודמי נכסיא כסף כסף שקלן 7, etc. where the double *ksp* may be dittographical; but it may also be an attempt to formulate the two nuances mentioned. The form שקלן is vocalized with the ending *-īn* by T. Nöldeke (*ZA* 20 [1907] 139) and P. Leander (*L* §45a). This vocalization of the masculine plural absolute has been questioned by H. L. Ginsberg, "Aramaic Dialect Problems," *AJSL* 52 (1936) 99-101. He prefers to vocalize it as *-ān* because of the defective spelling.

באבני מלכ[א]: "By royal weight," lit., "by (*or* according to) the stones of the king." This expression occurs again in lines 6-7, 9, 10, 14-15, 34-35, 36, and frequently in other Elephantine texts. The reference is to a standard of silver conforming to governmental stone-weights, which were apparently carried in small pouches and officially used. A similar expression is found in 2 Sam 14:26. Another standard was apparently also used at Elephantine, for in *AP* 11:2 we learn of "stones of Ptaḥ," [בא]בני פתח; cf. *AP* 26:21, תקלת פרס, *prs*, "the Persian weight." See further B. Porten, *Archives from Elephantine*, 63-64.

על עליך וטב לבבך בגו: "You have received it and you are satisfied with it," lit., "it has entered into you and your heart is content therewith." The expression occurs again in line 15. The verb על is the 3d sg. masc. pf. peal of ᶜ*ll*, "enter," and טב, which is sometimes written as טיב (see *AP* 2:9; 15:15; 20:9; *BMAP* 3:6; 12:6, 14, 26; etc.), is to be understood as a stative 3d sg. masc. pf. peal of *ṭyb* (a form like *myt* in *AP* 5:8 or *rim* in Dan 5:20). The adverb בגו is in reality a prepositional phrase, *b* + *gaww* ("interior"), simplified and contracted to *bĕgô*; for similar uses of it, see *AP* 2:9; 8:28; 9:6; *BMAP* 1:4, 10; etc. The implications of this formula in Aramaic business law and its relation to the long recognized analogues in Old Babylonian (*libbašu ṭāb*, "his [the seller's] heart is satisfied") and in Demotic (*dj.k-mtj hꜣtj(.i)*, "you [the buyer] have satisfied my heart") have been extensively investigated in the recent book of Y. Muffs, *Studies in the Aramaic Legal Papyri from Elephantine* (Studia et documenta ad iura orientis antiqui pertinentia, 8; Leiden: Brill, 1969). On pages 53-56 he discusses the implications of the phrase in the clause regarding the מהר.

6. הנעלת לב[יתי] מפטחיה בידה: "Miphṭaḥiah has brought into my house with her," lit., "has caused to enter my house in her (own) hand." See the general remarks above (p. 246) for the reasons for understanding הנעלת as the 3d sg. fem. and for the reading לי [לביתי] or לב[יתי]. The *n* in the form represents the resolution of the secondary doubling of the first radical of the

Double ᶜAyin root *ᶜll.* It is not simply a substitution of nasalization for germination (which is true in this case); but sometimes liquids are used (e.g., *Dammeśeq* ⟩ *Darmeśeq*; *kussĕᵓāᵓ* ⟩ *kuršĕᵓāᵓ*). The phrase used here should be compared with *BMAP* 7:5; 2:4.

כס[ף] תכונה כרש 1 שקלן 2: "A dowry sum of 1 karsh, 2 shekels." The meaning of כסף תכונה has not always been correctly understood; indeed, R. Yaron (*Introduction*, 50) seems to think that its "exact meaning . . . is not clear" at all. Sayce and Cowley translated it hesitatingly, "money for an outfit," and Cowley subsequently used "the cost of furniture." W. Staerk rendered it "als (bar-)wert ihrer Ausstattung" (*Alte und neue aramäische Papyri*, 44). Kraeling (*BMAP*, 209) related it to Nah 2:10 and translated it "substance of silver." The amount designated by כסף תכונה certainly does not include the value of the items subsequently listed, as the list of them and its total reveal (see above, p. 248). It almost certainly represents a sum of money or an amount of silver distinct from the other items and from the *mhr*; it was the dowry sum in the strict sense. The only thing that may be uncertain about it is the etymology, since תכונה seems to be derived from the root *kwn* with a preformative *t*. See P. Leander (*L* §43j''''), who also translated it "Ausstattung." It is the money which has been put up by the bride for the marriage.

The כרש is equal in these texts to ten (heavy) silver shekels, or to the עשרתא, "ten-piece," which is often written in a cipher, as in the following line. The name כרש that is being used in these Aramaic texts from Egypt is undoubtedly derived from the Persian monetary system, but the weight is not exactly the same in Egypt as in Persia. Ten Elephantine shekels weigh 87.6 grams, whereas the karsh-weights found at Persepolis and outside of Egypt weigh between 83.33-83.36 grams. This is roughly 4.3 grams less than the Egyptian ten shekels, or a half shekel less. See further below, on line 7.

The שקל used at Elephantine seems to have weighed 8.76 grams. This calculation is based mainly on *AP* 35:3, כסף ש 2 הו [כס]ף סתתרי 1, "the sum of 2 shekels, that is the sum of one stater," and *BMAP* 12:5, כסף כרש חד הו 1 שקלן תלתה הו 3 כסף יון סתתרי 6 שקל 1 חד, "the sum of one karsh, that is 1, three shekels, that is 3, (in) the money of Greece, 6 staters, one, ‹that is› 1, shekel." See also *BMAP* 12:14. This shows that the Elephantine shekel was equivalent to a half of a stater, or the Athenian tetradrachm, which weighed at this time 17.52 grams. See B. Porten, *Archives from Elephantine*, 64-65.

7. כסף ר2 ל10: "(In) silver (of) 2 qu(arters) to the 10-piece." This expression occurs again in line 14, and in other texts (*BMAP* 7:32). Often the word is written out, עשרתא (*AP* 6:15; 8:14, 21; 9:15; *BMAP* 3:16), but the abbreviation *r* is widespread. Its meaning as רבעא (*ribᶜāᵓ* or *rubᶜāᵓ*), "quarter," is widely admitted today, and almost certainly has nothing to do with the word רעי, found in *AP* 73:6, 13, 15, 17, *pace* S. Greengus, *Aramaic Marriage Contracts*, 51. Other phrases that are similar to this one in these texts make the identification of ר as a quarter shekel almost certain, for

one also finds כסף רז 2 לכרש 1 (*AP* 20:15; 25:15–16; *BMAP* 4:15) and כסף זוז לעשרתא or 10ל (*BMAP* 3:15, 18; 7:17; 8:8), and כסף זוז לכרש 1 (*BAMP* 3:6). In these phrases the *r 2* is equivalent to the *zûz*, or half shekel, indicating that *r 2* is to be understood as *rib*ᶜ*īn 2* or *rub*ᶜ*īn 2*. The "quarter" is the equivalent also of 10 ḥallurin. See R. Yaron, "*Ksp zwz*," *Lešonēnu* 31 (1966-67) 287-88; B. Porten, *Archives from Elephantine*, 62-67, 305-7. The phrase probably does not indicate an alloyed kind of silver, but rather an adjustment of the lighter Persian weight to the standard used in Egypt. This is the plausible explanation well worked out by B. Porten. There is only one slight difficulty in it, and that is to explain the constant appearance of כסף at the beginning of this phrase; perhaps one should rather translate "(with) 2 silver qu(arters) to the tenpiece (*or* karsh)."

לבש 1 זי עמר חדת חטב צבע ידין: "1 new garment of wool, striped with dye on both edges." This phrase begins the list of the items other than money that Miphṭaḥiah brought with her to the marriage; the first is an expensive woolen garment. The word for "wool," עמר, occurs in this text, written ca. 440 B.C., with an initial ᶜ*ayin*. But in a text dated ca. 420 B.C. we find the word written with an initial *qoph* (*BMAP* 7:6, 7, 13). The form עמר also appears in the still earlier text of *BMAP* 2:4 (dated ca. 449 B.C.). The shift from *q* > ᶜ is also attested in Jer 10:11 (both ᵓ*arqā*ᵓ and ᵓ*ar*ᶜ*ā*ᵓ). The *qoph* is certainly older, and its persistence in *BMAP* 7, after the shift to ᶜ*ayin* has taken place, is noteworthy. Cf. *AP* 20:5 (*qmr*, ca. 420 B.C.); 36:3 (*qmr*, undated); 42:9 (*qmr*, undated).

The word חטב is found with the full spelling חטיב in *BMAP* 7:7, confirming the participial explanation proposed by Cowley, who compared it to *ḥṭbwt* in Prov 7:16, "striped cloths."

The form צבע, which also occurs in *BMAP* 7:8; 14a; *AP* 42:9, has been understood by Cowley, Leander (*L* §34a), and Kraeling (*BMAP*, 317), as a participle, "dyed." The latter, however, gives a more plausible explanation in his commentary (*BMAP*, 210), where he takes it as a noun *(ṣb*ᶜᵓ*)*, related to Akkad. *ṣību*, *ṣīpu* (see *CAD*, 16. 205). Hence, "striped with dye." The form צבע has not yet turned up with the full spelling which might support the participial interpretation.

Both Cowley and Kraeling understood *ydyn* to mean "on both sides." G. R. Driver (*PEQ* 87 [1955] 93) sensed the difficulty in this interpretation, maintaining that "no material can be dyed only on one side." He preferred to understand the word to mean "twice dyed," to make the color fast. He compared the biblical phrase עשר ידות (Dan 1:20; Gen 43:34), and called attention to the twice-dyed Tyrian purple garments called *dibapha* (Pliny, *NH* 9.63,137). This is certainly a preferable interpretation, but is there not another possibility? Cannot ידין mean on "two edges"? Cowley had compared the Babylonian use of *idu* for his interpretation, but this would just as well support the idea of "edges" (*CAD*, 7.12). Moreover *BMAP* 7:8, 10 seems to express this idea in a more specific fashion in giving the measurements of the stripes, "1 handbreadth on each border" and "2 fingerbreadths to each border." ידין would in this interpretation be taken adverbially, and as a dual.

8. הוה ארך אמן 8 ב 5: "Measuring 8 cubits by 5," lit., "being (in) length 8 cubits by 5." The same expression occurs again in lines 9, 10-11. The word ארך has the same adverbial function that ידין has in the preceding expression.

[ש]וה כסף כרשן 2 שקלן 8: "Worth (in) cash 2 karshin and 8 shekels," or "worth 2 silver karshin, 8 shekels." It is this sort of phrase that suggests that כסף may no longer have the strict meaning of "silver," and that it is an attempt merely to record the monetary value of the goods. The form שוה is either the peal active participle *(šāwêh)*, "equalling," or (less likely) the passive participle *(šĕwêh)* with active force, "being worth." Cf. the examples of the latter in biblical Aramaic: דחיל (Dan 2:31); מהימן (Dan 2:45). Expressions similar to this phrase occur again in lines 9–10, 11, 11-12, 12, 13(bis). The value of this expensive woolen garment can be realized by comparing it to the price of a piece of property sold in *BMAP* 3:4-6, which is just half of the value given here.

9. שביט 1 חדת: "1 new shawl." The meaning of שביט is not certain. Cowley explained it as "closely-woven" stuff, adding that from its size it could only have been some kind of shawl. Kraeling (*BMAP* 7:9) accepted this meaning too; Staerk used simply "Gewebe" (*Alte und neue aramäische Papyri*, 45). Kutscher (*JAOS* 74 [1954] 236) related the word to Syriac *šbṭ*ᵓ, "a smooth cloth."

10. לבש אחרן זי עמר נשחט: "Another garment of wool, finely woven." The only enigmatic word here is נשחט, which Cowley related to the Hebrew *šāḥûṭ* in Jer 9:7, which is explained by commentators as the equivalent of *nmšk*, "drawn out," and in 2 Chr 9:15, of "gold drawn out," i.e., beaten thin. Lidzbarski (*Ephemeris*, 3. 80) followed him in this and noted that the form may be a niphal, a technical trade-term, possibly borrowed from the Phoenician. Cf. P. Leander, *L*§21b. A related word is said to have been found in a Punic text (see J. Solá-Solé, *Sefarad* 20 [1960] 277-79); but even if it is correctly read there it does not seem to have any pertinence to this text. Another form with the initial *n*- is found in line 15, נעבצן; but its meaning is not fully understood either.

11. מחזי 1 זי נחש: "1 bronze mirror." The word מחזי is normally considered fem. (see P. Leander, *L* §43ś), but it is treated here, perhaps erroneously, as masc., being modified by the masc. ptc. שוה. Cf. the later Aramaic *miḥzîta*ᵓ, and *BMAP* 2:5, מחזי 1 שויה כסף חלרן 7 פלג, in which שויה is fem.

12. כסף שקל 1 ר 2: "(In) cash 1 shekel, 2 qu(arters)." See the comment above on line 7.

תמ[סא] 1 זי נחש: "1 bronze bowl." Cowley had restored the lacuna as תמ[חי], "tray"; Lidzbarski (*Ephemeris*, 3. 131) preferred to read תמ[ני], but he did not attempt to translate it. The word תמסא is now clearly read in *BMAP* 7:13 in a very similar context of dowry items, and Kraeling rightly suggested that it be read here too. The meaning of it, however, is not clear; Kraeling compared it to an Assyr. noun, *nemsētu*, "bowl." This is, of course, possible, but it does not explain all the problems in the word. It is apparently feminine, since שויה follows as a modifier. This would suggest that the final -ᵓ here stands for the fem. sg. abs.; in the rest of the list the item usually stands before the cardinal in the absolute state.

2 כסן זי נחש: "2 bronze cups." A similar expressions occurs in *BMAP* 7:14; cf. *AP* 61:1, 3, 4, 13, 14. Kraeling (*BMAP*, p. 212) quotes Herodotus (2:37), who records that Egyptians drank from bronze cups.

13. זלוע 1 זי נחש: "1 bronze pitcher." The same expression occurs in *BMAP* 7:15; *AP* 36:4; cf. *BMAP* 7:18. The item mentioned here is undoubtedly not a "bowl" (so Cowley and Kraeling understood it), but a spouted jug or pitcher.

כל כספא ודמי נכסיא כסף כרשן 6 שקל‹ן› 5 חלר[ן] 20: "All the money and the value of the possessions are 6 silver karshin, 5 shekels, 20 ḥallurin." Cowley was certainly correct in regarding שקל as a scribal error for שקלן. Lidzbarski's explanation (see *Ephemeris*, 3. 80, 130), which seeks to retain the singular שקל, is too ingenious and strained to be convincing; see the general remarks above, p. 248, n. 13. The sum total given here represents not only the dowry money and the value of the items just enumerated but also includes the bride-price (see above, p. 247). Cf. *BMAP* 7:15 for the justification of this view. It is now clear that this total does not merely represent Esḥor's "own gifts," the value of which is stated because the deed is written in his name and he wants "to make the most of them" (so Cowley). Nor is the lack of a price in the list of items that follows this total due to Esḥor's judgment that it was unnecessary "to state the value of what he receives." All the objects belong to Miphṭaḥiah's dowry. What is not valued must have been considered of little value; but a couch with stone inlays (?) is hard to understand in this category. In any case, the מהר has been included in the sum total, probably for the reason already given above (see p. 247).

חלר[ן] 20: "20 ḥallurin," or a half shekel. The word *ḫalluru* meant in Akkadian a "chickpea" and became the name of a small weight. In the Babylonian scale, it represents one tenth of a shekel. See *CAD*, 6.47-48; A. Ungnad, "Aus den neubabylonischen Privaturkunden," *OLZ* 11 (1908), Beiheft, 26-28. However, according to the scale used in these papyri 40 ḥallurin = 1 shekel, as Cowley rightly established (*AP*, xxxi). Though פלג is used to indicate a half of a ḥallur, it apparently was not used after שקל. On the other hand, זוז could have been used, or else the phrase we have here, 20 ḥallurin. However, Kraeling (*BMAP*, 146) sought to regard the *ḥallur* as a tenth of the shekel, as in the Babylonian system. But this cannot be right. In totals the lower figures are always converted to the next higher weight, when they equal a unit or units of it. There would be no reason to write "20 ḥallurin," if ten of them equalled a shekel; this would have appeared as two shekels more. Moreover, the phrase in *BMAP* 7:14 would be meaningless, 10 ח 1 שקל, "one shekel, 10 ḥ(allurin)."

15. שוי 1 זי גמא: "1 reed couch." The form שוי is probably the same as the later Aramaic word *šiwwāy*, "couch" (see G. H. Dalman, *ANHW*, 417).

גמא: This word must be understood as the Aramaic equivalent of the Hebrew *gōmeᵓ*, "papyrus (nilotica)." It is known in Coptic as *kam* and in later Aramaic as *gamyāᵓ*. For its Egyptian origin, see T. O. Lambdin, "Egyptian Loanwords in the Old Testament," *JAOS* 73 (1953) 144-55, esp. p. 149.

בה נעבצן זי אבן 4: "On which there are 4 stone inlays," lit., "on it (there are) 4 inlays (?) of stone." No relative pronoun occurs in the similar phrase in *BMAP* 7:17. The expression should be compared with the relative clause in Dan 3:1, without a conjunction (see H. Bauer and P. Leander, *GBA* §108a). The meaning of נעבצן is unknown. The following number 4 suggests that the ending *-n* is plural. Sayce and Cowley wondered whether it might denote the stone feet of the reed couch; F. Peiser (*OLZ* 11 [1908] 28) sought an Assyrian cognate in *ḫabāṣu*, "swell up." Kraeling (*BMAP*, 213) related it to the Jewish Aramaic root, *ᶜbṣ*, "grow pale," and to the noun *ᶜbṣᶜ*, "tin," suggesting that it might mean "inlays." Possibly it is another technical trade-expression, a borrowed niphal form; see comment on *nšḥṭ* (line 10 above). The אבן is specified as שש, "alabaster," in *BMAP* 7:18 (see E. Y. Kutscher, *JAOS* 74 [1954] 236; H. L. Ginsberg, ibid., 159). Cf. Amos 6:4.

16. פק 1 זי סלק: "*1 pq* of *slq*." The meaning of this phrase is still unknown. J. N. Epstein (*JJLG* 6 [1908] 366 n. 3 suggested that פק might be another form of בק, related to *baqbūq*, "Krüglein." G. R. Driver compared it with the Akkad. *paqqu*, "bowl," and Scheftelowitz with Old Persian *pāka*, "cooking pot." But all these attempts seem to be difficult because the word has turned up as פיק (*BMAP* 2:6). In the latter passage one might be tempted to think that it is a measure smaller than חפן; but this meaning suits neither this passage nor *BMAP* 7:18. J. Reider (*JQR* 44 [1953-54] 340) translates the phrase as "a bottle of herbs," maintaining that both words occur in the Talmud, though with slightly different meanings; סלקא is a "beet" or "well-boiled vegetable." Is it possible that פיק is related to the Hebrew *pīqāh*, "spindle whorl"? Note that a different phrase using *slq* occurs in *BMAP* 7:18, דמן זי סלק 1, which Kraeling translates as "value of 1 *slq*," concluding that סלק must refer to some metal or coin (p. 147).

כפן 2: "Two ladles," or "2 bowls." In *BMAP* 7:19 the כפן are specified for "the carrying of ointment."

פרכס 1 זי חצן חדת: "1 new *prks* of palm-leaves." The meaning of חצן is now clear, "palm leaves," written חוצן in *AP* 20:6; *BMAP* 7:17. In the former passage the phrase מאני עק וחוצן, "vessels of wood and palm-leaves," would suggest that *prks* is a receptacle of some sort. Jean-Hoftijzer (*DISO*, 235) think that it is a "boite à cosmétiques," and T. Nöldeke (*ZA* 20 [1907] 148) suggested that it might be a tray or a small basket.

5 תקם חפנן: "5 handfuls of castor oil." This phrase and the following one are written above line 16, and it is not certain where one should insert them in the line. It makes little difference in the long run. The meaning of תקם was not understood for a long time. Cowley (*AP*, 49, 308) regarded it as a form of *qwm*, and suggested the meaning "containing," without explaining its morphology. M. Kamil and E. G. Kraeling used the meaning, "jar." But it is now certain that it means "castor oil" (see P. Grelot, "L'huile de ricin à Eléphantine," *Sem* 14 [1964] 63-70; see further H. Farzat, "Encore sur le mot *tqm* dans les documents araméens d'Eléphantine," *Sem* 17 [1967] 77-80; A. Dupont-Sommer, "Note sur le mot *tqm* dans les ostraca araméens d'Eléphantine," *Sem* 14 [1964] 71-72). The word also occurs in *AP* 37:10; *BMAP* 2:6; 7:20; *HermWP* 2:13; 3:12; 4:7; 5:5. The context of the two *BMAP* passages relates *tqm* to other oils or ointments. Grelot related the word to Demotic *tgm* (sometimes spelled *tkm*), and to older Egyptian *dgm*, "castor (oil)." He cited its use in lamps, and B. Porten (*Archives from Elephantine*, 92-93) has pointed out its use in anointing.

Cowley read the phrase as 8 תקם ח, taking *ḥ* as an abbreviation for a measure, as in *AP* 24:38 (and 41). This may be correct in the latter place, but it is to be noted that *ḥ* otherwise occurs as an abbreviation for *ḥlr* (*BMAP* 7:14, 15, 27). Lidzbarski (*Ephemeris*, 3.131) hesitatingly suggested the reading 5 חפנן, which is now almost certain, given its clear full writing in *BMAP* 2:6; 7:20, 21; *HermWP* 2:13; 3:12; *AD* 6:3, 4, 5. The difficulty is that the head of *p* is not clearly made, though the shaft is slightly curved; the two following strokes (for *nn*) are barely distinguishable from the unit strokes in the number that follows.

Aramaic חפנא is the cognate of Hebrew *ḥōpen* and Akkad. *upnu*, "hollow of the hand, handful." Used as a measure of oil it presents a difficult image, but the word was used to designate a commonly used amount, and its original meaning was undoubtedly forgotten. Its amount for this period is unknown. G. R. Driver (*AD*, p. 60) gives an approximation of 500 gr. and cites a third century A.D. inscription of Shapur I where *ḥwpn 5* is given as half a Greek *μόδιος* (see M. Sprengling, "Shahpuhr I, the Great on the Kaabah of Zoroaster (KZ)," *AJSL* 57 [1940] 387, 390).

1 שנן משאן: "1 (pair of) leather sandals." This same expression, the meaning of which is really unknown, occurs in *BMAP* 2:5. משאן probably is the same as the later Aramaic word, "shoe, sandal," see 1QapGen 22:21; cf. J. N. Epstein, *ZAW* 33 [1913] 225. The real difficulty is the meaning of שנן, which seems to be a construct state with משאן. In *BMAP* 7:20 it occurs before זי צל, which almost certainly means "of leather" (compare Jewish Aramaic *ṣallā*; and *AP* 37:10). This again relates the word to an item like sandals. Kutscher (*JAOS* 74 [1954] 234 n. 6) queried whether שאן could reflect the Old Assyrian *šēnān*, "two shoes." J. Reider (*JQR* 44 [1953-54] 339) understands the phrase to refer to a "leather bag." Whatever the meaning of it is, it is almost

certain that שנן is not a measure continuing the preceding phrase, as T. Nöldeke once thought (*ZA* 20 [1907] 147).

This brings us to the end of the dowry items in the contract. From this point on, various stipulations regarding the marriage agreement are recorded.

17. מחר או יום א[חר]ן: "Tomorrow or some other day," a stereotyped phrase that denotes some vague time in the future. It occurs again in lines 20, 22, 26; and in other Elephantine papyrus texts (e.g., *AP* 5:6, 8; 9:8, 13; *BMAP* 2:7, 9, 10, 12, 13; 7:21). J. J. Rabinowitz ("Meaning of the Phrase *mḥr* ᵓ*w ywm* ᵓ*ḥrn* in the Aramaic Papyri," *JNES* 14 [1955] 59-60); *Jewish Law*, 159-63) has compared the phrase to the Hebrew תמול שלשום, "yesterday and the day before yesterday," i.e., "in the past." He would accordingly translate the Aramaic phrase, "tomorrow or the day after (tomorrow)." He further cites kindred expressions from an Akkadian text of Ras Shamra (*urram šēram*, "demain, après-demain" [Thureau-Dangin's translation]), of Boghazkoi, and a Demotic text of the seventh century B.C. Y. Muffs (*Studies*, 206) notes that the Aramaic phrase is merely the last in a long line of idioms which express the idea of "(if), some time in the future," and that no idiom is a literal translation of any other. He cites also Ugar. *šḥr* ᶜ*lmt* and Neo-Assyrian *ina šērtu ina lidiš*. In this he is almost certainly correct, for although Rabinowitz' parallels, especially the one to Hebrew, might suggest that אחרן implies "after" (like ᵓ*ḥr*), it is to be noted that in all other cases where אחרן occurs, it means "other" (= ᵓ*oḥŏrān*). Kraeling (*BMAP*, 147) asked whether יום אחרן means "another day" or "the next day," and compared *b. Baba Mezia* 17a, *lmḥr wlywm*ᵓ ᵓ*ḥr*ᵓ. This is a later expression and may possibly mean "the next day." But it should be noted that it is in the emphatic state, and it is not quite the same thing. For this reason I prefer to remain with the translation given above, basically the same as that used by Cowley. The omission of או in *AP* 1:4 is undoubtedly a scribal error.

ימות אסחור: "Should Esḥor die." The same form of the conditional sentence, with the protasis in the imperfect and without the conjunction *hn*, is also found in lines 20, 22, 26, and in *BMAP* 2:7, 9, 11, 12; 7:21, 34. It is to be contrasted with *BMAP* 7:24 (והן יה[וי]ש[מע] תשנא . . .) and also with *AP* 15:35 (והן העדת המו, "If I do remove them") or *BMAP* 2:14 (והן הנצלתה מנך, "and if I take him away from you"). They are all future conditions. E. Y. Kutscher (*JAOS* 74 [1954] 234) explains the differences between them, by pointing out that הן usually takes the perfect (as in Arabic with ᵓ*in*), but only if the verb follows immediately after הן; the further it is removed from the conjunction the more it tends to occur in the imperfect. Sometimes the imperfect is used when the verb follows immediately, but the converse is not true. It never appears in the perfect if it is removed from הן. Hence in a clause without הן the verb will be in the imperfect. Kutscher's explanation is generally valid; one case, however, may be problematical: in *BMAP* 3:22a one finds ולא כהלן פצלן לה יתה, "and (if) we are not able to recover it for him." It seems to be a conditional use of the perfect without הן. In the preceding sentence הן was used with the perfect, and possibly the *w-* before the verb is to be understood as resuming it.

ובר דכר ונקבה לא איתי לה: "Having no child, male or female," lit., "and there is not to him, a child, male or female." The same expression occurs again in lines 20–21.

18. מפטחיה הי שליטה בביתה זי אסחור: "Miphṭaḥiah is entitled to the house of Esḥor," lit., "has power (*or* authority) over Esḥor's house." The problem in this clause is to determine the sense of *šlyṭ b*, since it undoubtedly expresses a legal situation different from that of Esḥor in the event of Miphṭaḥiah's death. According to line 21 he will inherit her property *(yrtnh)*. The same inheritance is expressed in *BMAP* 7:35. Unfortunately, the papyrus is broken in *BMAP* 7:29 and the phrase that is used of the bride there is not clear (see *BMAP*, 206; cf. J. T. Milik, *RB* 61 [1954] 250; R. Yaron, *JSS* 3 [1958] 8-9 [Yaron is convinced that *yrt* was not used of the woman]). L. Freund (*WZKM* 21 [1907] 177) has pointed out the different legal terms used here and suggests that whereas the husband would inherit his wife's property in the case of her death without children, the wife would be entitled only to the usufruct *(Nutzniessungsrecht)* of Esḥor's house and property, which would revert to her husband's family at her death. Yaron (*JSS* 3 [1958] 9-10), while not rejecting Freund's interpretation, has an alternate explanation. The husband's right was laid down by law and is thus referred to as inheritance *(yrt)*; the provision in the contract concerning him is merely declarative, not constitutive. But Miphṭaḥiah's right is created by the contract. There is really no evidence to support one or other of these interpretations, and so either is plausible. In *BMAP* 2:11, 12 שליט is used of both the husband and the wife; but since this document records the marriage of a slave, there is probably a different legal situation here.

19. וכל זי איתי [ל]ה על אנפי ארעא כלה: "And all that he has on the face of the earth, all of it." The last word כלה is either suffixal or an alternate form of the emphatic state of כל (with a final *he* instead of final *aleph*). If it be suffixal, its vocalization would differ depending on the noun that it resumes: *kulleh*, resuming כל זי, or *kullah*, resuming ארעא. For one could also translate, "and all that he has on the face of the whole earth." On the other hand, if it be emphatic, it could still be resumptive to either of these expressions. See p. 215 above. The resumptive use of כלה after כל זי is also paralleled in 1QapGen 10:13; 12:10; 16:11; see my commentary (p. 22 above, n. 27) 198, §4.

21. אסחור הו ירתנה בנכסיה וקנינה: "Esḥor shall inherit her possessions and her property." For the significance of this clause, see the comment on line 18 above. The use of הו may be emphatic; but it may also be merely influenced by the corresponding feminine in line 18, even though the expression differs. Instances of the emphatic use can be found in *AP* 6:4, 12-13; 10:15; 13:10; 20:9; *A* 24, 84; *BMAP* 3:10; 5:14; 7:35.

22. תקום מפטחיה בעדה ותאמר: "Should Miphṭaḥiah rise up in an assembly and say." The phrase is clear except for the problematic word בעדה. Sayce and Cowley rendered it, "in the congregation," as did Cowley later in his small edition; he was followed by S. Greengus, *Aramaic Marriage Contracts*, 72-73; R. Yaron, *JSS* 3 (1958) 14-16; Y. Muffs, *Studies*, 59. Kraeling (*BMAP*, 147), believing that the preposition בעד occurred in *BMAP* 11:10, sought to translate the word as a preposition here: "on account of her / him," or "on his own (or her) behalf." G. R. Driver (*PEQ* 87 [1955] 92) sought rather to understand בעדה as "behind her," an expression meaning "to find fault with." But neither Kraeling's interpretation nor Driver's have proved acceptable. H. L. Ginsberg (*JNES* 18 [1959] 148-49) disposed of the alleged preposition in *BMAP* 11:10, by showing that the text really reads בערבני "over my security (or pledge)." In his translation of this text he returned to the meaning "congregation," but correctly interpreted it as indefinite, "in a congregation." P. Leander (*L* §55b) and E. Y. Kutscher (*JAOS* 74 [1954] 234) also supported the absolute sense of "congregation," and the latter regarded the noun as a Hebraism, found also in Syriac. He compared Job 30:28, *qamtî baqqāhāl* (an interesting material parallel which has nothing to do formally with marriage or divorce).

The importance of the phrase lies in the need of a public declaration in the case of divorce. The further question about whether this was a court that would examine the reasons for the divorce, or whether *ᶜēdāh* refers to a specific number of persons before whom the declaration had to be made before it was considered valid is one that cannot be resolved on the basis of the data now available. See S. Funk, "Die Papyri von Assuan als älteste Quelle einer Halacha," *JJLG* 7 (1909) 378-79; R. Yaron, *Introduction*, 53-56; B. Porten, *Archives of Elephantine*, 210.

Another more basic consideration that this document manifests is the possibility that a Jewish woman at Elephantine could divorce her husband. In this matter she was the equal of her husband, her *bᶜl*. For the implications of this, see R. Yaron, *Introduction*, 53; and my article, "The Matthean Divorce Texts and Some New Palestinian Evidence," *TS* 37 (1976) 197–226, esp. pp. 204–5.

23. שנאת לאסחור בעלי: "I divorce Esḥor my husband," lit., "I have come to hate (*or* simply) I hate Esḥor." This formula for the declaration of divorce is found again in line 27, and in *BMAP* 2:7, 9; 7:21; for a slightly different formulation, see *BMAP* 7:25. It had already become stereotyped, whereas it undoubtedly expressed originally the motive for the divorce. On the problem of the origin of this term for "divorce," see J. J. Rabinowitz, *Jewish Law*, 40; R. Yaron, *JSS* 3 (1958) 32-34.

כסף שנאה בראשה: "The divorce fee is on her head," i.e., she will be held responsible for the payment of the divorce fee, the amount of which is set forth in the next phrase in the contract. For the idiom בראשה, denoting responsibility, see my note in *TS* 26 (1965) 669 n. 10, apropos of Matt 27:25.

J. J. Rabinowitz ("Demotic Papyri of the Ptolemaic Period and Jewish Sources," *VT* 7 [1957] 398-400) compares a phrase in P. Dem. Leiden 376, lines 28-29, to the Aramaic and NT phrase; but it is not parallel at all, since it lacks the phrase "on the head of."

תתב על מוזנא ותתקל ל[אס]חור כסף שקלן 7 ר2: "She shall sit by the scale and weigh out to Esḥor 7 silver shekels, 2 qu(arters)." This clause is clear, except for the meaning of תתב, which also occurs in *BMAP* 7:26 but is omitted in *BMAP* 2:9-10. Sayce and Cowley understood it as a form of תוב, "she shall return," and in this they were followed by Cowley (*AP*, 46), Leander (*L* §39b), Verger (*Ricerche*, 117, 119). However, T. Nöldeke (*ZA* 20 [1907] 148) interpreted it rather as the impf. peal of יתב, and was followed in this by L. Freund (*WZKM* 21 [1907] 174), E. G. Kraeling (*BMAP*, 207, 215), H. L. Ginsberg (*ANET*², 223). Still another possibility was suggested by S. Jampel (*MGWJ* 51 [1907] 622), seeking to interpret it transitively, as if it were תיתב, "Sie soll als Hauptsumme das Scheidungsgeld auf die Wage legen." Similarly, R. Yaron, *JSS* 3 (1958) 13; *Introduction*, 54 ("she shall put on the scales"); J. J. Rabinowitz (*VT* 7 [1957] 398-400) understood it rather as the aphel of תוב, "she shall pay according to the scales." However, Cowley's peal impf. of תוב would be defectively written and the only other example of such defective spelling in Leander (*L* §39b) is תקם, a form that is now seen to have nothing to do with קום (see comment above on line 16). The defective spelling of the aphel of תוב (Rabinowitz' suggestion) is likewise unparalleled; and the same must be said about Jampel's תיתב. In the long run, then, the best solution is that of Nöldeke, תתב as the 3d sg. fem. peal impf. of יתב, "she shall sit." There are other figurative expressions in this text which would parallel this interpretation.

The כסף שנאה is given here as seven and one-half shekels. While it is one and one-half times the bride-price paid in line 5, as Ginsberg has pointed out (*ANET*², 223), it is to be noted that the divorce fee is always seven and one-half shekels in these texts, when it is explicitly mentioned. See *BMAP* 2:8, 10; 7:26. The penalties, however, for divorce are not always the same; sometimes it involves the payment of the divorce fee, which may have been this fixed sum; sometimes it involves the loss of the bride-price. In this case, the woman divorcing her husband must pay the divorce fee. In *BMAP* 2 the מהר was of the same sum as the divorce fee; but that was probably coincidental.

24. וכל זי הנעלת בידה תהנפק: "And all that she brought with her, she shall take out," lit., "all that she brought in her hand." See the general remarks above, p. 246.

25. מן חם עד חוט: "From straw to string." This is Y. Muff's happy translation of an alliterative phrase, expressing figuratively a totality by the use of extremely small samples. It occurs again in line 28, and in *BMAP* 2:8, 10. The second element in it was always clear, חוט, "a thread." The first was long a problem. Cowley (*AP*, 46) took it as "both shred (?) and thread." G. R.

Driver (*JRAS* [1932] 78) suggested, "both broom and thread," as the humblest symbols of a woman's work in the house. But E. A. Speiser ("A Figurative Equivalent for Totality in Akkadian and West-Semitic," *JAOS* [1934] 200-203; see also p. 299) pointed out a convincing Akkadian parallel and suggested the translation "straw" for *ḥam*. In the treaty between Suppiluliumma and Mattiwaza one finds *ḫāma u ḫuṣāba . . . ul ilqi*, "he did not take away (even) a straw or a splinter" (see *CAD*, 6:259). Though the expression is not the same, several commentators have called attention to Gen 14:23, *miḥūṭ we*ᶜ*ad śerōk-na*ᶜ*al*, "from a thread to a sandal-strap," rendered in Aramaic in 1QapGen 22:21 as מן חוט עד ערקא דמסאן.

ותהך [ל]האן זי צבית: "And she shall go wherever she pleases," lit., "wherever she has pleased." The phrase occurs again in line 28. The form תהך is probably the impf. of הוך; cf. Sf III 5, 6; Sf I A 24; T. Nöldeke, *ZA* 20 (1907) 142. This clause stands in contrast to *BMAP* 7:28, ותהך לבית אבוך, "and she shall go to her father's house." The difference is that Miphṭaḥiah has been married before. See Y. Muffs, *Studies*, 55 n. 5.

ולא {י}דין ולא דבב: "Without suit or process." The expression occurs again in line 29, and often in the Elephantine texts (e.g., *AP* 6:12; *BMAP* 3:12, 13, 14; 9:18, 19—note the defective spelling of דן in *BMAP* 1:5 and the hypercorrection of זין וזבב in *BMAP* 3:17). An Akkadian expression underlies it: *tuāru dīni ū dabābi laššu*, "a re-opening of the case and the litigation is not to be" (see *CAD*, 3.153); compare the Greek formula in later papyrus texts: *ἄνευ δίκης καὶ κρίσεως*. E. Y. Kutscher (*JAOS* 74 [1954] 239-40) notes that the Aramaic formula is undoubtedly the link between the Akkadian and the Greek examples.

27. מהרה [י]אבד: "His bride-price goes forfeit," lit., "he shall lose his bride-price *(muhreh)*," or possibly "he shall lose her bride-price *(muhrah)*," i.e., the bride-price he paid for her. This is one of the most contested phrases in the Elephantine marriage contracts. Whose is it and loses it? Part of the problem is the determination of the meaning of the suffix (*-eh* or *-ah*?); part of it is the meaning of the verb יאבד. It was also complicated for a long time by the misunderstanding I have already mentioned several times about the inclusion of the מהר in the sum total of lines 13-15. It is, however, realized today that the penalties for divorce in these Elephantine contracts are not always the same. The verbal form יאבד could also be intransitive, "his bride-price is lost." No מהר is mentioned in *BMAP* 2, and hence none is lost. In *BMAP* 7:25 the loss of the מהר is included in the woman's penalty for divorce (in addition to the payment of the divorce fee). H. L. Ginsberg (*JAOS* 74 [1954] 159) has discussed the problems of *BMAP* 7 and thinks that the phrase is misplaced there. Whatever the solution to the problem of *BMAP* 7 is—and it is hotly debated—the understanding of *AP* 15 is less problematic. The loss of the מהר is clearly the penalty imposed on Esḥor; hence, either "he shall lose his bride-price" or "his bride-price is lost."

28. ביום חד בכף חדה: "On one day (and) at one time." The phrase seems to mean that there cannot be any partial or temporary withholding of her property. The same expression occurs in *BMAP* 7:28.

29. ו[זי] יקום על מפטחיה: "Whoever rises up against Miphṭaḥiah." Cowley had restored the lacuna with ו[הן], translating, "But if he should rise up." Many commentators followed him; and the clause, thus interpreted of an act of the husband, led to the theory of divorce by illegal expulsion in these texts. There was always a difficulty in this understanding, in that Esḥor was made to speak of himself in the third person (מן ביתה זי אסחור, line 30). In *BMAP* 7:30-32, part of the formula occurs again, but the context is unfortunately broken, the formula, however, is found in *BMAP* 6:16, which is not a marriage contract but a deed recording a gift of a house to a daughter by her father. He makes sure by the formula that she will not be driven out of it by some outsider without legal consequences: זי יקום עליך לתרכתכי מן בתיא, "Who rises up against you to drive you out of the houses. . . ." This sense must be introduced into the marriage contracts. Esḥor is thus making sure that Miphṭaḥiah will have the right to his house and property. The phrase is undoubtedly aimed at relatives of his. See also *AP* 46:8. This interpretation has been confirmed by a similar clause in a Demotic marriage contract from Elephantine, which begins with "Anyone in the world who . . ." (P. Dem. Berlin 13593, dated 198 B.C.; W. Erichsen, *AbhPAW*, Philos.-hist. Kl., 1939, Nr. 8, p. 10). See R. Yaron, "Aramaic Marriage Contracts: Corrigenda and Addenda," *JSS* 5 (1960) 66-70, esp. pp. 66-69. As a result of this interpretation, this clause is not concerned with a form of divorce at all. But compare A. Verger, *Ricerche*, 125-30.

30. לתרכותה מן ביתה זי אסחור ונכסוהי וקנינה: "To drive her out of Esḥor's house and his possessions and his property." Cowley was embarrassed by the phrase ביתה זי אסחור, which contains nothing more than the prospective suffix and means only "Esḥor's house," or "the house of Esḥor." There is no need of the cumbersome translation, "from his, Esḥor's house." Once this is seen, it is possible also to restore *BMAP* 7:30 differently. Instead of simply [י]קום [. . . ע]נניה, one should read, . . . [ומן י]קום ע[ל יהוישמע] לתרכותה, "And whoever rises up against Yahuyishma^{c} to drive her away . . ." Instead of מן, one could also restore זי. The expression *qwm* ^{c}*l*, in the sense of violent or illegal activity against a person, is also found in the Bible; see Deut 28:7; Jdgs 9:18; 20:5. On the nature of this *clausula salvatoria*, see J. J. Rabinowitz, *Jewish Law*, 48-64.

ינתן לה כסף כרשן 20 ויע[בד] לה דין ספרא זנה: "He shall pay her 20 silver karshin and shall carry out in her regard the stipulation of this document." The stipulation is the prescription set forth in lines 29-31, *w*[*zy*] *yqwm* . . . *znh*. The stipulation thus sets a stiff penalty, since the sum of 20 karshin is very high, as can be seen by comparing it with the total dowry sum in lines 13-15; see also the comment on the woolen garment in line 8 (p. 257 above). Sayce and Cowley had restored ויע[מד], translating it, "and (the terms of) this deed shall hold good for her." Cowley later changed the restoration to ויע[די] and translated, "and the provisions of this deed shall be an*nulled*, as far as he is concerned." H. L. Ginsberg (*ANET*², 223) left the lacuna blank: "and the law of this deed shall [ ] for her." The phrase, however, has turned up in *BMAP* 7:32: ויעבד [לה] דין ספרא זנה, whence the reading adopted here. See also *AP* 14:3; *BMAP* 7:40; Ezra 7:26 for related expressions. The penalty כסף כרשן 20, is imposed again in lines 34, 36, and seems to be a fixed penalty in marital offenses.

31. ולא אכל אמר איתי לי אנתה אחרה להן מפטח‹ח›יה: "I shall not be able to say, 'I have another wife, other than Miphṭaḥiah.'" The clause insures the unicity of the marital agreement. The formula used here is slightly different from that in *BMAP* 7:36, where it is stated that "[Anani shall no]t [be able to ta]ke [another] wife," i.e., another wife in the future. It is a protection against future polygamy. Here the formula assures Miphṭaḥiah that Esḥor has no other wife or children who can lay claim to his house or property. For the children born of Miphṭaḥiah and Esḥor, see *AP* 20:3; 25:3. Cf. B. Porten, *Archives of Elephantine*, 254.

33. הן אמר: "If I do say." See the comments on the syntax of the conditional sentence above, on line 17.

איתי לי ב[נן] ואנתה אחר‹נ›ן להן מפטחיה ובניה: "I have other children and a wife, other than Miphṭaḥiah and her children." The clause is not smoothly constructed here, and the form אחרן is undoubtedly a scribal error, as T. Nöldeke suggests (*ZA* 20 [1907] 136).

34. אנתן למפטחיה כס[ף] כרשן 20: "I shall pay Miphṭaḥiah 20 silver karshin." The penalty is the same as in line 31.

35. ולא אכל [אהנ]תר נכסי וקניני: "Nor shall I be able to withdraw my possessions and my property." Sayce and Cowley restored [אהנ]תר, the haphel impf., "take away," admitting that the *resh* was doubtful. The root is attested in Dan 4:11 and occurs possibly in an uncertain Nabatean text, *CIS*, 2. 224. When it occurs later, the causative stem has the nuance of "loose, throw off." The clause prohibits the withdrawal of Esḥor's property from Miphṭaḥiah as long as the marriage persists. As R. Yaron puts it, "the wife had to concur in the alienation of property by her husband. Her dissent could not indeed invalidate the transaction, but the penalty-clause would be a sufficient safeguard" (*JSS* 3 [1958] 25).

והן העדת המו מנה: "And if I do remove them from her." See the comments on line 17 above.

36. קבל ס[פר אחר]ן: "According to some other document." The whole phrase is set in double braces to indicate the scribal erasure of this clause. It is impossible to say what was behind the attempt to erase; it certainly leads one

to suspect that de facto there existed some other document to which Esḥor may have been in some way still obligated.

37. [כתב נתן בר ענניה [ספרא זנה כפם אסחור: "Nathan bar ᶜAnaniah wrote [this document at the behest of Esḥor]." The scribe, Nathan bar ᶜAnaniah, appears also in *AP* 10:20; 13:17; *BMAP* 2:14 in the same capacity. He signs his name as a witness in *AP* 8:32; 9:20, and he was apparently the father of several sons (*AP* 18:3; 22:128; *BMAP* 7:42). The lacuna which occurs here is restored as in *AP* 5:15; 6:17; *BMAP* 7:43. The phrase כפם means literally "according to the mouth of," i.e., at the dictation of (someone). Cf. *AP* 2:18; 11:16 (על פם). The scribe's name is recorded before that of the witnesses to the document, as in many other of these Elephantine texts. This seems to conform to contemporary Egyptian practice; see E. Seidl, *Ägyptische Rechtsgeschichte der Saiten- und Perserzeit* (Ägyptische Forschungen, 20; Glückstadt: Augustin, 1956) 71.

ושהדיא בגו: "The witnesses to it," lit., "thereto," or possibly "within," since בגו clearly functions here as an adverb. Cowley and Kraeling understood בגו in the first sense, "thereto." R. Yaron (*JSS* 2 [1957] 45-46) thinks that the word has a more technical sense, explained in part by a Mishnaic prescription (*Baba Bathra* 10:1: "A plain document has its witnesses within [on the recto]; a tied up document has its witnesses on its back [the verso]"), and in part by a phrase in a Judean deed of sale: כ[ת]בה דנה פשיט וחתמו בגוה (line 14), "this document is simple and they have signed (it) on the inside" (see J. T. Milik, *RB* 61 [1954] 182-90). Yaron is correct in pointing out the striking similarity in phrasing in the last instance. He also notes that the Elephantine practice of signing the contract on the inside differed from the contemporary Egyptian practice. He does not think that the Elephantine practice differed from the Jewish custom, disagreeing with J. J. Rabinowitz (see *BASOR* 136 [1954] 16), who cited Jer 32:10. If the Elephantine expression בגו has the technical meaning that Yaron suggests, then it is very cryptic and stereotyped. On the other hand, the equally stereotyped adverb בגו occurs many times in these texts (see comment on line 5 above). The full formula for the introduction of the names of the witnesses who signed the contract can also be found in many texts (e.g., *AP* 1:8; 2:19; 3:22; 5:15; 8:28; *BMAP* 2:14; 7:43; 8:10; etc.).

38. פנוליה בר יזניה: "Penuliah bar Yezaniah." This witness appears only here in the Elephantine texts, but he may be the father of several children (see *AP* 13:13; 18:5; 22:110; 25:19). The first name, פנוליה, means "Turn to Yahu," as T. Nöldeke (*ZA* 20 [1907] 134) pointed out, comparing the plural element in it to a name like הודויה (*AP* 20:18; Ezra 2:40; 1 Chr 5:24; 9:7). For the sense of it, see Isa 45:22. The other name, יזניה, is not easy to explain. It occurs several times in these texts from Elephantine (*AP* 6:9; 9:2; 19:8; 25:4; 66:10) and is undoubtedly related to ידניה. In the comment on דין ודבב (in line 26) I called attention to the hypercorrection in זין וזבב, found in *BMAP* 3:17. Though one might be tempted to think in terms of this root דין in these names, the form is

unlikely as an impf. of דין. It is probable that יזניה represents an older spelling of ידניה and that we have to do with a root ᵓ*zn*/ᵓ*dn* with the initial *aleph* completely quiesced. The vocalization would then be *Yēzanyāh* (‹ *yi*ᵓ*zan-yāh*), "May Yahu listen." Cf. 2 Kgs 25:23 *(Ya*ᵓ*ăzanyāhû)*. Similarly M. Noth, *IPN*, 198.

[ ]יה בר אוריה: "[ ]iah bar Uriah." There are several possible restorations for the first name: *Re*ᶜ*ūyāh* (*AP* 22:118), *Hôša*ᶜ*yāh* (*AP* 25:2), *Yēzanyāh* (*AP* 6:9; 9:2, etc.).

מנחם בר [ז]כור: "Menaḥem bar Zakkur," who also appears in *BMAP* 2:15 as a witness.

39. [ ]שהד רעיבל ב: "Witness: Reᶜibel ba[r]." One might at first hesitate about the function of *śhd* in such a line-up of witnesses, especially after the introductory formula in line 37. Does it follow the preceding name or precede the following? In some instances elsewhere it is also difficult to tell (*BMAP* 3:23b, 24; 5:17; 8:10), but in others it clearly precedes the name (*AP* 18:4; *BMAP* 10:18-20; 11:13-14; 12:33-34; cf. *BMAP* 2:15; 9:23, 25, 26). This should be taken, then, as the norm and applied even to the cases about which one might hesitate at first. Moreover, it is sometimes clear even from the handwriting. The form שהד is a participle, and may actually have so functioned originally (i.e., So-and-so is witnessing). But it is clearly a stereotyped formula in these texts and has been so understood in my translation.

With the name *Rĕ*ᶜ*ībel* ("Bel is my friend"), compare *Byt*ᵓ*lr*ᶜ*y* (*BMAP* 8:11), "Bethel is my friend," and *R*ᶜ*yh* (*HermWP* 1:1; 2:16; 3:3), "Yahu is my friend."[20]

NOTES TO CHAPTER 12

*Originally published under the same title in *Near Eastern Studies in Honor of William Foxwell Albright* (ed. H. Goedicke; Baltimore / London: The Johns Hopkins University, 1971) 137-68.

[1](London: A. Moring, 1906) 43-44 (with plates); Cairo Museum No. 37110.

[2]See *AP* 18, 36, 48 (Cowley, pp. 54-56, 131-32, 153).

[3]See *BMAP* 2, 7, 14 (Kraeling, pp. 139-50, 199-222, 291-96).

[4]In the transcription of the text, square brackets [ ] denote words or letters that have been editorially restored in a lacuna, angular brackets ‹ › my editorial additions, and braces { } my editorial deletions. In the translation that follows parentheses ( ) are used to spell out an abbreviated word or to indicate English words added for the sake of style, or (in line 36) to indicate an erasure that can still be read.

[5]For the historical questions involved in this matter, see J. J. Rabinowitz, *Jewish Law: Its Influence on the Development of Legal Institutions* (New York: Bloch, 1956) 39-100; R. Yaron, *Introduction to the Law of the Aramaic Papyri* (Oxford: Clarendon, 1961) 44-53; A. Verger, *Ricerche giuridiche sui papiri aramaici di Elefantina* (Studi semitici, 16; Rome: Centro di studi semitici, 1965) 105-30; S. Greengus, "The Aramaic Marriage Contracts in the Light of the Ancient Near East and the Later Jewish Materials" (Master's thesis, University of Chicago, 1959). For the

stereotyped character of the text, see R. Yaron, "The Schema of Aramaic Legal Documents," *JSS* 2 (1957) 33-61.

[6]For instance, L. Freund, "Bemerkungen zu Papyrus G. des Fundes von Assuan.," *WZKM* 21 (1907) 169-77; S. Jampel, "Der Papyrusfund von Assuan," *MGWJ* 51 (1907) 617-34, esp. pp. 621-22; M. Lidzbarski, *Ephemeris,* 3. 129-31.

[7]See *AP*, 46-47. In this he was followed by C. Clermont-Ganneau, Review of *APA, RCHL* 62 (1906) 341-54, esp. p. 349; W. Staerk, *Die jüdisch-aramaeischen Papyri von Assuan* (KIT 22/23; Berlin: de Gruyter, 1907) 28; P. Leander, *L* §41g.

[8]See *ANET*, 222-23; compare the first and second editions (1950, 1955).

[9]Ibid., 223.

[10]For example, W. Staerk, *Alte und neue aramäische Papyri übersetzt und erklärt* (KIT 94; Berlin: de Gruyter, 1912) 44; M. Lidzbarski, *Ephemeris*, 3. 129; B. Cohen, "Dowry in Jewish and Roman Law," *AIPHOS* 13 (1953) 57-85, esp. p. 61.

[11]See *BMAP*, 146. In this he was followed by S. Greengus, "Aramaic Marriage Contracts," 59; R. Yaron, "Aramaic Marriage Contracts from Elephantine," *JSS* 3 (1958) 1-39, esp. p. 6.

[12]See *AP*, 47; also Cowley's note on line 14, p. 48.

[13]There is a lacuna at this point in the papyrus and one stroke of the number following the plural *šqln* remains. In the *editio princeps*, Sayce and Cowley restored the number as [3], without justifying it. But Cowley later restored it more accurately as [2], while still admitting the possibility of [3]. Lidzbarski (*Ephemeris*, 3. 130) also read the number 3. His interpretation of the sum in lines 13-14, however, was erroneous. It was based on his insistence that *šql*, a singular, in line 14 was originally followed only by one stroke, i.e., 6 karshin, 1 shekel, 20 ḥallurin. This represented only Miphṭaḥiah's money and possessions. It did not include the 5 shekels of the *mhr* but did include the extra shekel restored in line 13. Then he suggested that four extra strokes were later added in line 14 to represent the value of the objects listed (without prices) in lines 15-16. It is, however, clear that the latter objects were not included in the sum and there is no evidence of a later addition of four strokes.

[14]Kraeling (*BMAP*, 39, 146) maintains that the *ḥallūr* represents a tenth of the silver shekel. This may be right for the Babylonian scale, but it cannot be correct in these Elephantine texts. See S. Greengus, "Aramaic Marriage Contracts," 44-51; his discussion strangely hesitates in this matter.

[15]A similar detailed list can be constructed for *BMAP* 7 to total up to this sum. However, the text is broken in places and the following list represents only my own way of restoring the individual values:

Line	Object	Value		
5	*mhr*	1 karsh		
5-6	*tkwnh zy ksp*	2 karshin	2 shekels	5 ḥallurin
6-7	*lbš 1 zy qmr*	1 karsh	2 shekels	
7	*gmydh 1 zy qmr*	1 karsh		
8-9	*lbš 1 mʿdr*		7 shekels	
9-10	*šbyṭ 1*		8 shekels	
10	*lbš 1*		[1 shekel	20 ḥallurin]
11	*šnṭʾ 1*		[1 shekel	10 ḥallurin]
11-12	?		[1 shekel]	
12	*? 1 ktn blyh*		1 shekel	
13	*mḥzy 1*		1 shekel	
13-14	*tmsʾ 1*		1 shekel	10 ḥallurin
14	*ks 1*		[1] shekel	
14	*ks 1*			20 ḥallurin
15	*zlwʿ 1*			20 ḥallurin
		5 karshin	26 shekels	85 ḥallurin
	or	7 karshin	8 shekels	5 ḥallurin

[16]See R. Yaron, *Introduction*, 48; "Aramaic Marriage Contracts," 6.

[17]"Aramaic Marriage Contracts," 57; see also idem, *Introduction*, 48; A. Verger, *Ricerche*, 112.

[18]"The Brooklyn Museum Aramaic Papyri," *JAOS* 74 (1954) 153-62, esp. pp. 156, 159.

[19]The issue is further complicated by the occurrence of the forfeiture phrase as a penalty for the bride in *BMAP* 7:24.

[20]See further B. Porten, "The Restoration of Fragmentary Aramaic Marriage Contracts," *Gratz College Anniversary Volume: On the Seventy-fifth Anniversary of the Founding of the College 1895–1970* (ed. I. D. Passow and S. T. Lachs; Philadelphia: Gratz College, 1971) 243–61.

I. INDEX OF SUBJECTS

(The subjects are those of the main text; the reader should check the notes that accompany the passages indicated by the following page numbers.)

II. INDEX OF MODERN SCHOLARS

III. INDEX OF SCRIPTURE REFERENCES

Appendix

In this appendix further comments are made at times on topics discussed in the chapters of *ESBNT* and *WA*. More frequently leads are given to recent discussions of the topics themselves, which may support or disagree with the views proposed here. The first number indicates the page of the original book; the second, the line or the note. An asterisk before the second number means "line from the bottom" (counting a footnote, if present).

ESBNT

8, *4	Read 1 Kgs 21:12.
14, *16	Read 1 Tm 5:18; cf. 1 Sam 25:26.
14, *12	(Add before Again) See also CD 11:20-21; cf. Num 30:7-16.
25, 8	Read rather *spry htwrh hm swkt k’šr ’mr whqymwty ’t swkt hmlk dwd*
44, 11	Read Mt 22:32
58, *1	(Add at end of note 78) F. L. Horton, Jr., "Formulas of Introduction in the Qumran Literature," *RQ* 7 (1969-71) 505-14; J. M. Baumgarten, "A 'Scriptural' Citation in 4Q Fragments of the Damascus Document," *JJS* 43 (1992) 95-98.
100, *1	(Add at end of note 15) B. Mazar, "*hḥpyrwt h’rky’wlwgywt lyd hr-hbyt* (Archaeological Excavations alongside the Temple Mount)," *Zalman Shazar Volume* (Eretz-Israel 10; Jerusalem: Israel Exploration Society, 1971) 1-41 + pl. *kh* (for a seal with *qrbn*).

104, *1 (Add to n. 10) A. Wolters, "*Anthrōpoi eudokias* (Luke 2:14) and *ʾnšy rṣwn* (4Q416)," *JBL* 113 (1994) 291-92.

108, 12 (Add at end of line, after superscript 10) "Mt. Scopus Jewish Family Ossuary 3 *(ʾšwny br šmʿwn br ʾšwny)*" in *Zalman Shazar Volume* (Eretz-Israel 10; Jerusalem: Israel Exploration Society, 1971) 48.

112, *1 (Add as ftn. 17) See W. Kornfeld, "Jüdisch-aramäische Grabinschriften aus Edfu," *Anzeiger der phil.-hist. Kl. der oesterreichischen Akademie der Wissenschaften* 110 (1973) 121-37 (+ pls. 1-9), esp. 130.

118, *7 Read 1 Chr 17:11, 14

147, *3 On the "Three Books," see J. T. Milik, *The Books of Enoch: Aramaic Fragments of Qumrân Cave 4* (Oxford: Clarendon, 1976) 64-67.

160, *1 (Add to ftn. 32) F. García Martínez, "4Q Mes. Aram. y el libro de Noé," *Salmanticensis* 28 (1981) 195-232.

165, *10 Delete: J. Jeremias

184, *1 See now my commentary, *The Gospel according to Luke* (AB 28-28A; Garden City, NY: Doubleday, 1981, 1985) 1094-1111.

204, *1 (Add as ftn. 47) See A. Jaubert, "La voile des femmes (I Cor. xi. 2-16)," *NTS* 18 (1971-72) 419-30; J. Murphy-O'Connor, "The Non-Pauline Character of 1 Corinthians 11:2-16?" *JBL* 95 (1976) 615-21; "Sex and Logic in 1 Corinthians 11:2-16," *CBQ* 42 (1980) 482-500.

210, 16 Instead of 4QIs[d] 13:12 read rather 4QCatena[a] 1:4-8.

217, *1 (Add to ftn. 27) H. D. Betz, "2 Cor. 6:14–7:1: An Anti-Pauline Fragment?" *JBL* 92 (1973) 88-108; G. D. Fee, "II Corinthians vi.14–vii.1 and Food Offered to Idols," *NTS* 23 (1976-77) 140-61; M. E. Thrall, "The Problem of II Cor. vi.14–vii.1 in Some Recent Discussion," *NTS* 24 (1977-78) 132-48; J. Lambrecht, "The Fragment 2 Cor vi 14-vii 1: A Plea for Its Authenticity," *Miscellanea neotestamentica* (NovTSup 47-48; ed. T. Baarda et al.; 2 vols.; Leiden: Brill, 1978), 2.143-61; J. D. M. Derrett, "2 Cor 6,14ff. a Midrash on Dt 22,10," *Bib* 59 (1978) 231-50; D. Rensberger, "2 Corinthians 6:14–7:1: A Fresh Examination," *Studia biblica et theologica* 8 (1978) 25-49; J. Murphy-O'Connor, "Philo and 2 Cor 6:14–7:1," *RB* 95 (1988) 55-69; in *The Diakonia of the Spirit (2 Co 4:7–7:4)* (Monographic Series of 'Benedictina' 10; Rome: St. Paul's Abbey, 1989) 133-60; "Relating 2 Corinthians 6:14–7:1

to its Context," *NTS* 33 (1987) 272-75; W. J. Webb, *Returning Home: New Covenant and Second Exodus as the Context for 2 Corinthians 6.14–7.1* (JSNTSup 85; Sheffield, UK: JSOT, 1993).

226, *3 (Add to the end of ftn. 19) See also J. G. Gammie, "Loci of the Melchizedek Tradition of Genesis 14:18-20," *JBL* 90 (1971) 385-96, esp. 388 n. 23.

239, *10 (Add to ftn. 55) M. Peter, "Wer sprach den Segen nach Genesis xiv 19 über Abraham aus?" *VT* 29 (1979) 114-19.

240, *3 (Add to ftn. 58) Cf. N. C. Habel, "'Yahweh, Maker of Heaven and Earth': A Study in Tradition Criticism," *JBL* 91 (1972) 321-37, esp. 324-26 (he shows that the title is precisely at home in "a blessing context").

259, *5 One should recall that *yôbēl* originally denoted a "leader," and of a flock that would mean a "ram." From this it came to denote the "ram's horn" (see Jos 6:4-5; Lev 25:13 [*šnt hywbl,* "year of the ram," which came to mean "year of the jubilee"]).

260, 8 On the "tenth jubilee," see J. T. Milik, "Problèmes de la littérature hénochique à la lumière des fragments araméens de Qumrân," *HTR* 64 (1971) 333-78, esp. 357.

262, 11 (Add at end of line) Cf. R. B. Salters, "Psalm 82,1 and the Septuagint," *ZAW* 103 (1991) 225-39.

265, 12 (Add at end of line) Cf. Eph 2:17.

267, *1 (Add to ftn. 13) M. Delcor, "Melchizedek from Genesis to the Qumran Texts and the Epistle to the Hebrews," *JSJ* 2 (1971) 115-35; F. L. Horton, *The Melchizedek Tradition* (SNTSMS 30; Cambridge, UK: Cambridge University, 1976); P. J. Kobelski, *Melchizedek and Melchireša'* (CBQMS 10; Washington, DC: Catholic Biblical Association, 1981); A. Rodríguez Carmona, "La figura de Melquisedec en la literatura targúmica: Estudio de las traducciones targúmicas sobre Melquisedec y su relación con el Nuevo Testamento," *EstBíb* 37 (1978) 79-102; G. Henderson, "The Priest Melchizedek," *Biblical Illustrator* 16/3 (1990) 54-57; A. Vivian, "I movimenti che si oppongono al Tempio: Il problema del sacerdozio di Melchisedeq," *Henoch* 14 (1992) 97-112.

287, 9 (Add note at end of line) See H.-J. Klauck, "Gütergemeinschaft in der klassischen Antike, in Qumran und im Neuen Testament," *RQ* 11 (1982-84) 47-79.

313, *8 (Add to ftn. 24) See A. Kloner, "Name of Ancient Israel's Last

	President Discovered on Lead Weight," *BARev* 15/4 [read 14/4] (1988) 12-17.
316, *5	Instead of 58-89, read 59-89.
326, 21	(Add after Hérodium'.) See E. Netzer, "Jewish Rebels Dig Strategic Tunnel System," *BARev* 15/4 [read 14/4] (1988) 18-33.
334, *17	(Add note at end of line) See J. B. Hennessy, "Preliminary Report on Excavations at the Damascus Gate Jerusalem, 1964-6," *Levant* 2 (1970) 22-27. He says, "There can be little doubt that this is the wall started but probably never finished by Agrippa — the commonly argued Third Wall of Jerusalem" (p. 24).
334, *1	(Add to ftn. 82) E. W. Hamrick, "The Third Wall of Agrippa I," *BA* 40 (1977) 18-23.
349, *2	(Add to ftn. 111) D. Ussishkin, "Archaeological Soundings at Betar, Bar-Kochba's Last Stronghold," *Tel Aviv* 20 (1993) 66-97.
354, *1	(Add to ftn. 123) See further S. Applebaum, "*Š'lt hqrqʿ wmrd br-Kwkb'* (The Agrarian Question and the Revolt of Bar-Kokhba)," *E. L. Sukenik Memorial Volume* (Eretz-Israel 8; Jerusalem: Israel Exploration Society, 1967) 283-87; "The Second Jewish Revolt (A.D. 131-35)," *PEQ* 116 (1984) 35-41; A. Oppenheimer, "The Bar Kokhba Revolt," *Immanuel* 14 (1982) 58-76; A. Kloner, "Lead Weights of Bar Kokhba's Administration," *IEJ* 40 (1990) 58-67; P. Schaefer, *Der Bar Kokhba Aufstand: Studien zum zweiten jüdischen Krieg gegen Rom* (Texte und Studien zum antiken Judentum 1; Tübingen: Mohr [Siebeck], 1981); W. J. Fulco, "The Bar Kokhba Rebellion," *BT* 64 (1973) 1041-45; M. Gichon, "New Light into the Bar Kokhba War and a Reappraisal of Dio Cassius 69.12-13," *JQR* 77 (1986) 15-43; L. Mildenberg, "The Bar Kokhba War in the Light of the Coins and Document Finds 1947-1982," *Israel Numismatic Journal* 8 (1984-85) 27-32.
358, 8 and 9	Instead of forty-four, read forty-five.
370, 7	(Add note to end of line) See J. J. Gunther, "The Meaning and Origin of the Name 'Judas Thomas,' " *Muséon* 93 (1980) 113-48.
374, *3	(Add note to end of line) See D. Mueller, "Kingdom of Heaven or Kingdom of God?" *VC* 27 (1973) 266-76.
387, 12	(Add note to end of line) See now J.-E. Ménard, *L'Evangile selon Thomas* (NHS 5; Leiden: Brill, 1975) 87-88.
401, 12	(Add note to end of line) See B. Englezakis, "*Thomas,* Logion 30," *NTS* 25 (1978-79) 262-72; H. W. Attridge, "The Original Text of Gos. Thom., Saying 30," *BASP* 16 (1979) 153-57.

WA

13-14 See now G. Vermes, "The 'Son of Man' Debate," *JSNT* 1 (1978) 19-32 and my reply, "Another View of the 'Son of Man' Debate," *JSNT* 4 (1979) 58-68.

14-15 On the question of alleged mistranslations from an Aramaic substratum in NT Greek, see F. Zimmermann, *The Aramaic Origin of the Four Gospels* (New York: Ktav, 1979), but also the reviews of this book by D. J. Harrington (*CBQ* 42 [1980] 285-87) and myself (*TS* 41 [1980] 193-95).

16, *11 (Add note to the word limited) See now J. C. Greenfield, "Early Aramaic Poetry," *JANESCU* 11 (1979) 45-51; J. C. VanderKam, "The Poetry of 1 Q Ap Gen, xx, 2-8a," *RQ* 10 (1979-81) 57-66.

20, *1 I repeat here a few comments made about this article on the occasion of the 1989 reprint of *Jésus aux origines de la Christologie* (ed. J. Dupont; BETL 40; Louvain: Peeters) 418-19, where it first appeared: Though the ideas on methodology in the study of the Aramaic substratum of Jesus' sayings in the NT that I set forth in the above article have been questioned by G. Vermes in "Jewish Studies and New Testament Exegesis," *JJS* 31 (1980) 1-17; "Jewish Literature and New Testament Exegesis: Reflections on Methodology," *JJS* 33 (1982) 362-76, I still consider them valid. The question of NT Aramaisms must be put today into the larger question of Semitisms in the NT, on which I have also written for the *Dictionary of Biblical Interpretation* (ed. R. Coggins and J. L. Houlden; London: SCM, 1990) 620-21. An attempt must be made to distinguish so-called Semitisms from Septuagintisms, Aramaisms, and Hebraisms in NT Greek. When it comes to the discussion of Aramaisms themselves, I continue to think that the ideas on methodology expressed in the above article are valid. An answer to the criticism of Vermes can be found in "Problems of the Semitic Background of the New Testament," in *The Yahweh/Baal Confrontation and Other Studies in Biblical Literature and Archaeology: Essays in Honour of Emmet Willard Hamrick* . . . [Studies in the Bible and Early Christianity 35; Lewistown, NY: Mellen, 1995] 80-93). Further thoughts on the generic topic are also found in my presidential address to the Society of Biblical Literature, "The Aramaic Language and the Study of the New Testament," *JBL* 99 (1980) 5-21.

See also "Aramaic Evidence Affecting the Interpretation of *Hosanna* in the New Testament," *Tradition and Interpretation in the New Testament: Essays in Honor of E. Earle Ellis . . .* (ed. G. F. Hawthorne and O. Betz; Grand Rapids: Eerdmans, 1987) 110-18; and "The Aramaic Background of Philippians 2:6-11," *CBQ* 50 (1988) 470-83.

23, 12 (Add to n. 41) See also R. Contini, "Problemi dell'aramaico antico," *EVO* 2 (1979) 197-213.

24, n. 59 (Add to note) See B. A. Mastin, "Latin Mam(m)ona and the Semitic Languages: A False Trail and a Suggestion," *Bib* 65 (1984) 87-90.

32, 16 (Add note to end of line) See A. Millard, "Latin in First-Century Palestine," *Solving Riddles and Untying Knots: Biblical, Epigraphic, and Semitic Studies in Honor of Jonas C. Greenfield* (ed. Z. Zevit et al.; Winona Lake, IN: Eisenbrauns, 1995) 451-58.

38, 14 (Add note to end of line) See G. Mussies, "Greek as the Vehicle of Early Christianity," *NTS* 29 (1983) 356-69; D. T. Ariel, "Two Rhodian Amphoras," *IEJ* 35 (1988) 31-35 (+ pls. 7C, 8D); B. Schwank, "Die neuen Grabungen in Sepphoris," *Erbe und Auftrag* 63 (1987) 222-25; *BK* 42 (1987) 75-79.

46, *1 (Add note to end of line) See J. C. Greenfield, "Languages of Palestine, 200 B.C.E.–200 C.E.," *Jewish Languages: Theme and Variations* (ed. H. H. Paper; Cambridge, MA: Association for Jewish Studies, 1978) 143-54; J. Barr, "Hebrew, Aramaic and Greek in the Hellenistic Age," *Cambridge History of Judaism* (2 vols.; ed. W. D. Davies and L. Finkelstein; Cambridge, UK: Cambridge University, 1984, 1989), 2.79-114; J. W. Voelz, "The Language of the New Testament," *ANRW* II/25.2, 893-977; S. Safrai, "Literary Languages in the Time of Jesus," *Jerusalem Perspective* 4 (1991) 3-8.

48, 6 (Add at the end of line) See M. Broshi and G. Barkay, "Excavations in the Chapel of St. Vartan in the Holy Sepulchre," *IEJ* 35 (1985) 108-28, esp. pl. 16 C-D.

48, *15 (Add at end of line) Cf. G. Labbé, "Ponce Pilate et la munificence de Tibère: L'inscription de Césarée," *Revue des études anciennes* 93 (1991) 277-97.

51, *7 Instead of 96-95, read 86-95. Add at end of line: D. Obbink, "Bilingual Literacy and Syrian Greek," *BASP* 28 (1991) 51-57.

52, *1 (Add at end of line) J. M. Ross, "Jesus's Knowledge of Greek,"

	IBS 12 (1990) 41-47; J. A. Fitzmyer, "Did Jesus Speak Greek?" *BARev* 18/5 (1992) 58-63, 76-77; repr. *Approaches to the Bible: The Best of* Bible Review: *Volume I, Composition, Transmission and Language* (2 vols.; ed. H. Minkoff; Washington, DC: Biblical Archaeology Society, 1994), 1.253-62, 343-46; S. E. Porter, "Did Jesus Ever Teach in Greek?" *Tyndale Bulletin* 44 (1993) 199-235.
55, *1	(Add at end of line) J. F. Stenning, *The Targum of Isaiah* (Oxford: Clarendon, 1949) vii: "Aramaic alone held the field."
58, 18	Instead of introducion, read introduction.
71, 16	(Add note at end of line) See A. Vivian, "Dialetti giudaici dell'Aramaico medio e tardo," *OrAn* 15 (1976) 56-60.
72, *17	Instead of Qumram, read Qumran.
74, *10	(Add at end of line) See T. Muraoka, "A Study in Palestinian Jewish Aramaic," *Sefarad* 45 (1985) 3-21.
84, *1	(Add n. 122) See L. H. Feldman, "How Much Hellenism in Jewish Palestine?" *HUCA* 57 (1986) 83-111.
90, *6	On the Son of God text from Qumran Cave 4 (4Q**246**), see now E. Puech, "Fragment d'une apocalypse en araméen (4Q246 = pseudo-Dan^{d}) et le 'royaume de Dieu,'" *RB* 99 (1992) 98-131; J. A. Fitzmyer, "4Q246: The 'Son of God' Document from Qumran," *Bib* 74 (1993) 153-74; "The Aramaic 'Son of God' Text from Qumran Cave 4," *Methods of Investigation of the Dead Sea Scrolls and the Khirbet Qumran Site: Present Realities and Future Prospects* (ed. M. O. Wise et al.; Annals of the New York Academy of Sciences 722; New York: New York Academy of Sciences, 1994) 163-78; E. M. Cook, "4Q246," *BBR* 5 (1995) 43-66. See also J. A. Fitzmyer, "The Palestinian Background of 'Son of God' as a Title for Jesus," *Texts and Contexts: Biblical Texts in Their Textual and Situational Contexts: Essays in Honor of Lars Hartman* (ed. T. Fornberg et al.: Oslo/Stockholm: Scandinavian University Press, 1995) 567-77.
91, 6	Instead of third, read half.
95, 6	Instead of *'m pyk,* read *'m 'l pyk.*
113, *1	Since this article was written, many more Qumran Aramaic texts have been published. The number of them is close to 120, most of them quite fragmentary. I have written an article ("Aramaic") as a survey of them, which is to appear in the forthcoming *Encyclopedia of the Dead Sea Scrolls* (Oxford University Press).
121, *17	Instead of 19:9, read 19:19.

124, *8 Instead of Enoch I 4QEn[b], read Enoch 4QEn[b].

125, *1 (Add at end of line) See P. Auffret, "Structure littéraire et interprétation du Psaume 151 de la grotte 11 de Qumran," *RQ* 9 (1977-78) 163-88; J. Magne, "'Seigneur de l'univers' ou David-Orphée?: Défense de mon interprétation du Psaume 151," ibid., 189-96; A. Hurvitz, "*Lšwnw wzmnw šl mzmwr qn' mqwmr'n* (The Language and Date of Psalm 151 from Qumran)," *E. L. Sukenik Memorial Volume* (Eretz-Israel 8; Jerusalem: Israel Exploration Society, 1967) 82-87, esp. 84.

126, 11 (Add at end of line) Cf. 4Q**403** 1 i 28: *brwk [h]'d[w]n, mlk hkwl* (C. Newsom, *Songs of the Sabbath Sacrifice: A Critical Edition* [HSS 27; Atlanta, GA: Scholars, 1985] 189, 206).

127, 9 (Add at end of line) Cf. G.-W. Nebe, "Psalm 104,11 aus Höhle 4 von Qumran (4QPs[d]) und der Ersatz des Gottesnamens," *ZAW* 93 (1981) 284-90.

133, *22 (Apropos of *aleph*) See M. Heltzer, "An Old-Aramaic Seal-Impression and Some Problems of the History of the Kingdom of Damascus," *Arameans, Aramaic and the Aramaic Literary Tradition* (ed. M. Sokoloff; Ramat-Gan: Bar-Ilan University, 1983) 9-13.

136, n. 33 (At the end) M. Sznycer, "Une inscription punique inédite de Carthage," *Sem* 37 (1987) 63-70.

137, *19 (Add at end of line) F. Vattioni, "Il tetragramma divino nel PFuad inv. 266," *SPap* 18 (1979) 17-29; M. Delcor, "Des diverses manières d'écrire le tetragramme sacré dans les anciens documents hébraïques," *RHR* 147 (1955) 145-73.

141, n. 73 (Add at end) Cf. Pindar, *Isthmian Odes* 5.53: *Zeus ho pantōn kyrios.*

142, *1 (Add at end) P. W. Skehan, "The Divine Name at Qumran, in the Masada Scroll, and in the Septuagint," *BIOSCS* 13 (1980) 14-44; A. Pietersma, "Kyrios or Tetragram: A Renewed Quest for the Original LXX," *De Septuaginta: Studies in Honour of John William Wevers . . .* (ed. A. Pietersma and C. Cox; Mississauga, Ont.: Benben Publications, 1984) 85-101; J. R. Royse, "Philo, *Kyrios,* and the Tetragrammaton," *Heirs of the Septuagint: Philo, Hellenistic Judaism and Early Christianity: Festschrift E. Hilgert* (Studia Philonica Annual: Studies in Hellenistic Judaism III; Brown Judaic Studies 2/30; Atlanta: Scholars, 1991) 167-83.

147, 2 (Add note at end of line) See O. Irsai, "*'mr R. 'bhw: 'm y'mr lk 'dm 'l 'ny mkzb hw'* (Rabbi Abahu Said: If a Man Should Say to You, 'I Am God,' He Is a Liar," *Zion* (Jerusalem) 47 (1982) 173-77.

156 n. 15 (Add at end) See Y. Thorion, "*'dm* und *bn 'dm* in den Qumrantexten," *RQ* 10 (1979-81) 305-8; H. Bietenhard, " 'Der Menschensohn' — *ho huios tou anthrōpou* — Sprachliche, religionsgeschichtliche und exegetische Untersuchungen zu einem Begriff der synoptischen Evangelien: I. Sprachlicher und religionsgeschichtlicher Teil," *ANRW* II/25.1,265-350.

160, *1 (Add to end of note) See further B. McNeil, "The Son of Man and the Messiah: A Footnote," *NTS* 26 (1979-80) 419-21; G. Quispel, "Ezekiel 1:26 in Jewish Mysticism and Gnosis," *VC* 34 (1980) 1-13; R. Kearns, *Vorfragen zur Christologie III: Religionsgeschichtliche und traditionsgeschichtliche Studie zur Vorgeschichte eines christologischen Hoheits-titel* (Tübingen: Mohr [Siebeck], 1982); M. S. Smith, "The 'Son of Man' in Ugaritic," *CBQ* 45 (1983) 59-60; B. Lindars, *Jesus the Son of Man: A Fresh Examination of the Son of Man Sayings in the Gospels in the Light of Recent Research* (London: SPCK, 1983); W. Horbury, "The Messianic Association of 'the Son of Man,' " *JTS* 36 (1985) 34-55; P. M. Casey, "General, Generic and Indefinite: The Use of the Term 'Son of Man' in Aramaic Sources and in the Teaching of Jesus," *JSNT* 29 (1987) 22-56; J. J. Collins, "The Son of Man in First-Century Judaism," *NTS* 38 (1992) 448-66; J. A. Draper, "The Development of 'the Sign of the Son of Man' in the Jesus Tradition," *NTS* 39 (1993) 1-21; D. Burkett, "The Nontitular Son of Man: A History and Critique," *NTS* 40 (1994) 504-21; T. B. Slater, "One Like a Son of Man in First Century CE Judaism," *NTS* 41 (1995) 183-98; C. F. D. Moule, " 'The Son of Man': Some of the Facts," *NTS* 41 (1995) 277-79.

171, *12 (Add note at end of line) See now Deir 'Alla Inscription I.1.16.

180, n. 51 (Add at end) L. Díez Merino, "Manuscritos del targum de Job," *Henoch* 4 (1982) 41-64.

180, n. 52 Instead of 1973, read 1873.

181, n. 65 (Add at end) See H. F. Fuhs, *Sehen und Schauen: Die Wurzel ḥzh* . . . (Forschung zur Bibel 32; Würzburg: Echter-V., 1978).

188, *16 Instead of *spr'*, read *sprh*.

188, *13 Instead of **ništavāna*, read **ništāvana*.

189, 6 Instead of son, (greeting), read son Y, (greeting).

204 *1 (Add at end) See P.-E. Dion, "Les types epistolaires hébréo-

araméens jusqu'au temps de Bar-Kokhbah," *RB* 86 (1979) 544-79; "The Aramaic 'Family Letter' and Related Epistolary Forms in Other Oriental Languages and in Hellenistic Greek," *Studies in Ancient Letter Writing* (Semeia 22; ed. J. L. White; Chico, CA: Scholars, 1982) 59-76; J. A. Fitzmyer, "Aramaic Epistolography," ibid., 25-57; J. M. Lindenberger, *Ancient Aramaic and Hebrew Letters* (SBL Writings from the Ancient World 4; Atlanta: Scholars, 1994); J. L. White, "New Testament Epistolary Literature in the Framework of Ancient Epistolography," *ANRW* II/25.2, 1730-56.

232, *9 Instead of *ʿbrk,* read *ʾbdk.*

Masaki Hayashi Oct. 18 '97
CBD. Peabody MA.